CODE OF FEDERAL REGULATIONS

Title 20
Employees' Benefits

Parts 500 to 656

Revised as of April 1, 2019

Containing a codification of documents
of general applicability and future effect

As of April 1, 2019

Published by the Office of the Federal Register
National Archives and Records Administration
as a Special Edition of the Federal Register

Table of Contents

Cite this Code: CFR

To cite the regulations in this volume use title, part and section number. Thus, 20 CFR 501.1 *refers to title 20, part 501, section 1.*

Explanation

The Code of Federal Regulations is a codification of the general and permanent rules published in the Federal Register by the Executive departments and agencies of the Federal Government. The Code is divided into 50 titles which represent broad areas subject to Federal regulation. Each title is divided into chapters which usually bear the name of the issuing agency. Each chapter is further subdivided into parts covering specific regulatory areas.

Each volume of the Code is revised at least once each calendar year and issued on a quarterly basis approximately as follows:

Title 1 through Title 16 .... as of January 1
Title 17 through Title 27 .... as of April 1
Title 28 through Title 41 .... as of July 1
Title 42 through Title 50 .... as of October 1

The appropriate revision date is printed on the cover of each volume.

LEGAL STATUS

The contents of the Federal Register are required to be judicially noticed (44 U.S.C. 1507). The Code of Federal Regulations is prima facie evidence of the text of the original documents (44 U.S.C. 1510).

HOW TO USE THE CODE OF FEDERAL REGULATIONS

The Code of Federal Regulations is kept up to date by the individual issues of the Federal Register. These two publications must be used together to determine the latest version of any given rule.

To determine whether a Code volume has been amended since its revision date (in this case, April 1, 2019), consult the "List of CFR Sections Affected (LSA)," which is issued monthly, and the "Cumulative List of Parts Affected," which appears in the Reader Aids section of the daily Federal Register. These two lists will identify the Federal Register page number of the latest amendment of any given rule.

EFFECTIVE AND EXPIRATION DATES

Each volume of the Code contains amendments published in the Federal Register since the last revision of that volume of the Code. Source citations for the regulations are referred to by volume number and page number of the Federal Register and date of publication. Publication dates and effective dates are usually not the same and care must be exercised by the user in determining the actual effective date. In instances where the effective date is beyond the cutoff date for the Code a note has been inserted to reflect the future effective date. In those instances where a regulation published in the Federal Register states a date certain for expiration, an appropriate note will be inserted following the text.

OMB CONTROL NUMBERS

The Paperwork Reduction Act of 1980 (Pub. L. 96–511) requires Federal agencies to display an OMB control number with their information collection request.

Many agencies have begun publishing numerous OMB control numbers as amendments to existing regulations in the CFR. These OMB numbers are placed as close as possible to the applicable recordkeeping or reporting requirements.

PAST PROVISIONS OF THE CODE

Provisions of the Code that are no longer in force and effect as of the revision date stated on the cover of each volume are not carried. Code users may find the text of provisions in effect on any given date in the past by using the appropriate List of CFR Sections Affected (LSA). For the convenience of the reader, a "List of CFR Sections Affected" is published at the end of each CFR volume. For changes to the Code prior to the LSA listings at the end of the volume, consult previous annual editions of the LSA. For changes to the Code prior to 2001, consult the List of CFR Sections Affected compilations, published for 1949-1963, 1964-1972, 1973-1985, and 1986-2000.

"[RESERVED]" TERMINOLOGY

The term "[Reserved]" is used as a place holder within the Code of Federal Regulations. An agency may add regulatory information at a "[Reserved]" location at any time. Occasionally "[Reserved]" is used editorially to indicate that a portion of the CFR was left vacant and not accidentally dropped due to a printing or computer error.

INCORPORATION BY REFERENCE

What is incorporation by reference? Incorporation by reference was established by statute and allows Federal agencies to meet the requirement to publish regulations in the Federal Register by referring to materials already published elsewhere. For an incorporation to be valid, the Director of the Federal Register must approve it. The legal effect of incorporation by reference is that the material is treated as if it were published in full in the Federal Register (5 U.S.C. 552(a)). This material, like any other properly issued regulation, has the force of law.

What is a proper incorporation by reference? The Director of the Federal Register will approve an incorporation by reference only when the requirements of 1 CFR part 51 are met. Some of the elements on which approval is based are:

(a) The incorporation will substantially reduce the volume of material published in the Federal Register.

(b) The matter incorporated is in fact available to the extent necessary to afford fairness and uniformity in the administrative process.

(c) The incorporating document is drafted and submitted for publication in accordance with 1 CFR part 51.

What if the material incorporated by reference cannot be found? If you have any problem locating or obtaining a copy of material listed as an approved incorporation by reference, please contact the agency that issued the regulation containing that incorporation. If, after contacting the agency, you find the material is not available, please notify the Director of the Federal Register, National Archives and Records Administration, 8601 Adelphi Road, College Park, MD 20740-6001, or call 202-741-6010.

CFR INDEXES AND TABULAR GUIDES

A subject index to the Code of Federal Regulations is contained in a separate volume, revised annually as of January 1, entitled CFR INDEX AND FINDING AIDS. This volume contains the Parallel Table of Authorities and Rules. A list of CFR titles, chapters, subchapters, and parts and an alphabetical list of agencies publishing in the CFR are also included in this volume.

An index to the text of "Title 3—The President" is carried within that volume.

The Federal Register Index is issued monthly in cumulative form. This index is based on a consolidation of the "Contents" entries in the daily Federal Register.

A List of CFR Sections Affected (LSA) is published monthly, keyed to the revision dates of the 50 CFR titles.

REPUBLICATION OF MATERIAL

There are no restrictions on the republication of material appearing in the Code of Federal Regulations.

INQUIRIES

For a legal interpretation or explanation of any regulation in this volume, contact the issuing agency. The issuing agency's name appears at the top of odd-numbered pages.

For inquiries concerning CFR reference assistance, call 202–741–6000 or write to the Director, Office of the Federal Register, National Archives and Records Administration, 8601 Adelphi Road, College Park, MD 20740-6001 or e-mail *fedreg.info@nara.gov.*

SALES

The Government Publishing Office (GPO) processes all sales and distribution of the CFR. For payment by credit card, call toll-free, 866-512-1800, or DC area, 202-512-1800, M-F 8 a.m. to 4 p.m. e.s.t. or fax your order to 202-512-2104, 24 hours a day. For payment by check, write to: US Government Publishing Office – New Orders, P.O. Box 979050, St. Louis, MO 63197-9000.

ELECTRONIC SERVICES

The full text of the Code of Federal Regulations, the LSA (List of CFR Sections Affected), The United States Government Manual, the Federal Register, Public Laws, Public Papers of the Presidents of the United States, Compilation of Presidential Documents and the Privacy Act Compilation are available in electronic format via *www.govinfo.gov.* For more information, contact the GPO Customer Contact Center, U.S. Government Publishing Office. Phone 202-512-1800, or 866-512-1800 (toll-free). E-mail, *ContactCenter@gpo.gov.*

The Office of the Federal Register also offers a free service on the National Archives and Records Administration's (NARA) World Wide Web site for public law numbers, Federal Register finding aids, and related information. Connect to NARA's web site at *www.archives.gov/federal-register.*

The e-CFR is a regularly updated, unofficial editorial compilation of CFR material and Federal Register amendments, produced by the Office of the Federal Register and the Government Publishing Office. It is available at *www.ecfr.gov.*

OLIVER A. POTTS,
Director,
Office of the Federal Register
April 1, 2019.

THIS TITLE

Title 20—EMPLOYEES' BENEFITS is composed of four volumes. The first volume, containing parts 1–399, includes current regulations issued by the Office of Workers' Compensation Programs, Department of Labor and the Railroad Retirement Board. The second volume, containing parts 400–499, includes all current regulations issued by the Social Security Administration. The third volume, containing parts 500 to 656, includes current regulations issued by the Employees' Compensation Appeals Board, and the Employment and Training Administration. The fourth volume, containing part 657 to End, includes the current regulations issued by the Office of Workers' Compensation Programs, the Benefits Review Board, the Office of the Assistant Secretary for Veterans' Employment and Training Service (all of the Department of Labor) and the Joint Board for the Enrollment of Actuaries. The contents of these volumes represent all current regulations codified under this title of the CFR as of April 1, 2019.

An index to chapter III appears in the second volume.

For this volume, Cheryl E. Sirofchuck was Chief Editor. The Code of Federal Regulations publication program is under the direction of John Hyrum Martinez, assisted by Stephen J. Frattini.

Title 20—Employees' Benefits

(This book contains parts 500 to 656)

CHAPTER IV—EMPLOYEES' COMPENSATION APPEALS BOARD, DEPARTMENT OF LABOR

PART 500 [RESERVED]

PART 501—RULES OF PROCEDURE

AUTHORITY: Federal Employees' Compensation Act (FECA), 5 U.S.C. 8101 *et seq.*

SOURCE: 73 FR 62193, Oct. 20, 2008, unless otherwise noted.

§ 501.1 Definitions.

(a) *FECA* means the Federal Employees' Compensation Act, 5 U.S.C. 8101 *et seq.* and any statutory extension or application thereof.

(b) *The Board* means the Employees' Compensation Appeals Board.

(c) *Chief Judge and Chairman of the Board* means the Chairman of the Employees' Compensation Appeals Board.

(d) *Judge or Alternate Judge* means a member designated and appointed by the Secretary of Labor with authority to hear and make final decisions on appeals taken from determinations and awards by the OWCP in claims arising under the FECA.

(e) *OWCP* means the Office of Workers' Compensation Programs, Employment Standards Administration, U.S. Department of Labor.

(f) *Director* means the Director of the Office of Workers' Compensation Programs or a person delegated authority to perform the functions of the Director. The Director of OWCP is represented before the Board by an attorney designated by the Solicitor of Labor.

(g) *Appellant* means any person adversely affected by a final decision or order of the OWCP who files an appeal to the Board.

(h) *Representative* means an individual properly authorized by an Appellant in writing to act for the Appellant in connection with an appeal before the Board. The Representative may be any individual or an attorney who has been admitted to practice and who is in good standing with any court of competent jurisdiction.

(i) *Decision*, as prescribed by 5 U.S.C. 8149 of the FECA, means the final determinative action made by the Board on appeal of a claim.

(j) *Clerk or Office of the Clerk* means the Clerk of the Office of the Appellate Boards.

§ 501.2 Scope and applicability of rules; composition and jurisdiction of the Board.

(a) The regulations in this part establish the Rules of Practice and Procedure governing the operation of the Employees' Compensation Appeals Board.

(b) The Board consists of three permanent judges, one of whom is designated as Chief Judge and Chairman of the Board, and such alternate judges as are appointed by the Secretary of Labor. The Chief Judge is the administrative officer of the Board. The functions of the Board are quasi-judicial. For organizational purposes, the Board is placed in the Office of the Secretary of Labor and sits in Washington, DC.

(c) The Board has jurisdiction to consider and decide appeals from final decisions of OWCP in any case arising under the FECA. The Board may review all relevant questions of law, fact and exercises of discretion (or failure to exercise discretion) in such cases.

(1) The Board's review of a case is limited to the evidence in the case record that was before OWCP at the time of its final decision. Evidence not before OWCP will not be considered by the Board for the first time on appeal.

(2) There will be no appeal with respect to any interlocutory matter decided (or not decided) by OWCP during the pendency of a case.

(3) The Board and OWCP may not exercise simultaneous jurisdiction over the same issue in a case on appeal. Following the docketing of an appeal before the Board, OWCP does not retain jurisdiction to render a further decision regarding the issue on appeal until after the Board relinquishes jurisdiction.

§ 501.3 Notice of Appeal.

(a) *Who may file.* Any person adversely affected by a final decision of the Director, or his or her authorized Representative, may file for review of such decision by the Board.

(b) *Place of filing.* The notice of appeal shall be filed with the Clerk at 200 Constitution Avenue, NW., Washington, DC 20210.

(c) *Content of notice of appeal.* A notice of appeal shall contain the following information:

(1) Date of Appeal.

(2) Full name, address and telephone number of the Appellant and the full name of any deceased employee on whose behalf an appeal is taken. In addition, the Appellant must provide a signed authorization identifying the full name, address and telephone number of his or her Representative, if applicable.

(3) Employing establishment, and the date, description and place of injury.

(4) Date and Case File Number assigned by OWCP concerning the decision being appealed to the Board.

(5) A statement explaining Appellant's disagreement with OWCP's decision and stating the factual and/or legal argument in favor of the appeal.

(6) *Signature:* An Appellant must sign the notice of appeal.

(d) *Substitution of appellant:* Should the Appellant die after having filed an appeal with the Board, the appeal may proceed to decision provided there is the substitution of a proper Appellant who requests that the appeal proceed to decision by the Board.

(e) *Time limitations for filing.* Any notice of appeal must be filed within 180 days from the date of issuance of a decision of the OWCP. The Board maintains discretion to extend the time period for filing an appeal if an applicant demonstrates compelling circumstances. Compelling circumstances means circumstances beyond the Appellant's control that prevent the timely filing of an appeal and does not include any delay caused by the failure of an individual to exercise due diligence in submitting a notice of appeal.

(f) *Date of filing.* A notice of appeal complying with paragraph (c) of this section is considered to have been filed only if received by the Clerk by the close of business within the period specified under paragraph (e) of this section, except as otherwise provided in this subsection:

(1) If the notice of appeal is sent by United States Mail or commercial carrier and use of the date of delivery as the date of filing would result in a loss of appeal rights, the appeal will be considered to have been filed as of the date of postmark or other carriers' date markings. The date appearing on the U.S. Postal Service postmark or other carriers' date markings (when available and legible) shall be prima facie evidence of the date of mailing. If there is no such postmark or date marking or it is not legible, other evidence, such as, but not limited to, certified mail receipts, certificate of service and affidavits, may be used to establish the mailing date. If a notice of appeal is delivered or sent by means other than United States Mail or commercial carrier, including personal delivery or fax, the notice is deemed to be received when received by the Clerk.

(2) In computing the date of filing, the 180 day time period for filing an appeal begins to run on the day following the date of the OWCP decision. The last day of the period so computed shall be included, unless it is a Saturday, Sunday or Federal holiday, in which event the period runs to the close of the next business day.

(g) *Failure to timely file a notice of appeal.* The failure of an Appellant or Representative to file an appeal with the Board within the period specified under paragraph (e) of this section, including any extensions granted by the Board in its discretion based upon compelling circumstances, will foreclose all right to review. The Board will dismiss any untimely appeal for lack of jurisdiction.

(h) *Incomplete notice of appeal.* Any timely notice of appeal that does not contain the information specified in paragraph (c) of this section will be considered incomplete. On receipt by the Board, the Clerk will inform Appellant of the deficiencies in the notice of appeal and specify a reasonable time to submit the requisite information. Such appeal will be dismissed unless Appellant provides the requisite information in the time specified by the Clerk.

§501.4 Case record; inspection; submission of pleadings and motions.

(a) *Service on OWCP and transmission of OWCP case record.* The Board shall serve upon the Director a copy of each notice of appeal and accompanying documents. Within 60 days from the date of such service, the Director shall provide to the Board the record of the OWCP proceeding to which the notice refers. On application of the Director, the Board may, in its discretion, extend the time period for submittal of the OWCP case record.

(b) *Inspection of record.* The case record on appeal is an official record of the OWCP.

(1) Upon written application to the Clerk, an Appellant may request inspection of the OWCP case record. At the discretion of the Board, the OWCP case record may either be made available in the Office of the Clerk of the Appellate Boards for inspection by the Appellant, or the request may be forwarded to the Director so that OWCP may make a copy of the OWCP case record and forward this copy to the Appellant. Inspection of the papers and documents included in the OWCP case record of any appeal pending before the Board will be permitted or denied in accordance with 5 CFR 10.10 to 10.13. The Chief Judge (or his or her designee) shall serve as the disclosure officer for purposes of Appendix A to 29 CFR Parts 70 and 71.

(2) Copies of the documents generated in the course of the appeal before the Board will be provided to the Appellant and Appellant's Representative by the Clerk. If the Appellant needs additional copies of such documents while the appeal is pending, the Appellant may obtain this information by contacting the Clerk. Pleadings and motions filed during the appeal in proceedings before the Board will be made part of the official case record of the OWCP.

(c) *Pleadings.* The Appellant, the Appellant's Representative and the Director may file pleadings supporting their position and presenting information, including but not limited to briefs, memoranda of law, memoranda of justification, and optional form AB–1. All pleadings filed must contain the docket number and be filed with the Clerk. The Clerk will issue directions specifying the time allowed for any responses and replies.

(1) The Clerk will distribute copies of any pleading received by the Clerk to ensure that the Appellant, his or her Representative and the Director receive all pleadings. Any pleading should be submitted within 60 days of the filing of an appeal. The Board may, in its discretion, extend the time period for the submittal of any pleading.

(2) Proceedings before the Board are informal and there is no requirement that any pleading be filed. Failure to submit a pleading or to timely submit a pleading does not prejudice the rights of either the Appellant or the Director.

(3) Upon receipt of a pleading, the Appellant and the Director will have the opportunity to submit a response to the Board.

(d) *Motions.* Motions are requests for the Board to take specific action in a pending appeal. Motions include, but are not limited to, motions to dismiss, affirm the decision below, remand, request a substitution, request an extension of time, or other such matter as may be brought before the Board. Motions may be filed by the Appellant, the Appellant's Representative and the Director. The motion must be in writing, contain the docket number, state the relief requested and the basis for the relief requested, and be filed with the Clerk. Any motion received will be sent by the Clerk to ensure that the Appellant, his or her Representative and the Director receive all motions. The Clerk will issue directions specifying the timing of any responses and replies. The Board also may act on its own to issue direction in pending appeals, stating the basis for its determination.

(e) *Number of copies.* All filings with the Board, including any notice of appeal, pleading, or motion shall include an original and two (2) legible copies.

§501.5 Oral argument.

(a) *Oral argument.* Oral argument may be held in the discretion of the Board, on its own determination or on application by Appellant or the Director.

(b) *Request.* A request for oral argument must be submitted in writing to the Clerk. The application must specify the issue(s) to be argued and provide a statement supporting the need for oral argument. The request must be made no later than 60 days after the filing of an appeal. Any appeal in which a request for oral argument is not granted by the Board will proceed to a decision based on the case record and any pleadings submitted.

(c) *Notice of argument.* If a request for oral argument is granted, the Clerk will notify the Appellant and the Director at least 30 days before the date set for argument. The notice of oral argument will state the issues that the Board has determined will be heard.

(d) *Time allowed.* Appellant and any Representative for the Director shall be allowed no more than 30 minutes to present oral argument. The Board may, in its discretion, extend the time allowed.

(e) *Appearances.* An Appellant may appear at oral argument before the Board or designate a Representative. Argument shall be presented by the Appellant or a Representative, not both. The Director may be represented by an attorney with the Solicitor of Labor. Argument is limited to the evidence of record on appeal.

(f) *Location.* Oral argument is heard before the Board only in Washington, DC. The Board does not reimburse costs associated with attending oral argument.

(g) *Continuance.* Once oral argument has been scheduled by the Board, a continuance will not be granted except on a showing of good cause. Good cause may include extreme hardship or where attendance by an Appellant or Representative is mandated at a previously scheduled judicial proceeding. Any request for continuance must be received by the Board at least 15 days before the date scheduled for oral argument and be served by the requester upon Appellant and the Director. No request for a second continuance will be entertained by the Board. In such case, the appeal will proceed to a decision based on the case record. The Board may reschedule or cancel oral argument on its own motion at any time.

(h) *Nonappearance.* The absence of an Appellant, his or her Representative, or the Director at the time and place set for oral argument will not delay the Board's resolution of an appeal. In such event, the Board may, in its discretion, reschedule oral argument, or cancel oral argument and treat the case as submitted on the case record.

§ 501.6 Decisions and orders.

(a) *Decisions.* A decision of the Board will contain a written opinion setting forth the reasons for the action taken and an appropriate order. The decision is based on the case record, all pleadings and any oral argument. The decision may consist of an affirmance, reversal or remand for further development of the evidence, or other appropriate action.

(b) *Panels.* A decision of not less than two judges will be the decision of the Board.

(c) *Issuance.* The date of the Board's decision is the date of issuance or such date as determined by the Board. Issuance is not determined by the postmark on any letter containing the decision or the date of actual receipt by Appellant or the Director.

(d) *Finality.* The decisions and orders of the Board are final as to the subject matter appealed, and such decisions and orders are not subject to review, except by the Board. The decisions and orders of the Board will be final upon the expiration of 30 days from the date of issuance unless the Board has fixed a different period of time therein. Following the expiration of that time, the Board no longer retains jurisdiction over the appeal unless a timely petition for reconsideration is submitted and granted.

(e) *Dispositive orders.* The Board may dispose of an appeal on a procedural basis by issuing an appropriate order disposing of part or all of a case prior to reaching the merits of the appeal. The Board may proceed to an order on its own or on the written motion of Appellant or the Director.

(f) *Service.* The Board will send its decisions and orders to the Appellant, his or her Representative and the Director at the time of issuance.

§ 501.7 Petition for reconsideration.

(a) *Time for filing.* The Appellant or the Director may file a petition for reconsideration of a decision or order issued by the Board within 30 days of the date of issuance, unless another time period is specified in the Board's order.

(b) *Where to File.* The petition must be filed with the Clerk. Copies will be sent by the Clerk to the Director, the Appellant and his or her Representative in the time period specified by the Board.

(c) *Content of petition.* The petition must be in writing. The petition must contain the docket number, specify the matters claimed to have been erroneously decided, provide a statement of the facts upon which the petitioner relies, and a discussion of applicable law. New evidence will not be considered by the Board in a petition for reconsideration.

(d) *Panel.* The panel of judges who heard and decided the appeal will rule on the petition for reconsideration. If any member of the original panel is unavailable, the Chief Judge may designate a new panel member. The decision or order of the Board will stand as final unless vacated or modified by the vote of at least two members of the reconsideration panel.

(e) *Answer.* Upon the filing of a petition for reconsideration, Appellant or the Director may file an answer to the petition within such time as fixed by the Board.

(f) *Oral argument and decision on reconsideration.* An oral argument may be allowed at the discretion of the Board upon application of the Appellant or Director or the Board may proceed to address the matter upon the papers filed. The Board shall grant or deny the petition for reconsideration and issue such orders as it deems appropriate.

§501.8 Clerk of the Office of the Appellate Boards; docket of proceedings; records.

(a) *Location and business hours.* The Office of the Clerk of the Appellate Boards is located at 200 Constitution Avenue, NW., Washington, DC 20210. The Office of the Clerk is open during business hours on all days except Saturdays, Sundays and Federal holidays, from 8:30 a.m. to 5 p.m.

(b) *Docket.* The Clerk will maintain a docket containing a record of all proceedings before the Board. Each docketed appeal will be assigned a number in chronological order based upon the date on which the notice of appeal is received. While the Board generally hears appeals in the order docketed, the Board retains discretion to change the order in which a particular appeal will be considered. The Clerk will prepare a calendar of cases submitted or awaiting oral argument and such other records as may be required by the Board.

(c) *Publication of decisions.* Final decisions of the Board will be published in such form as to be readily available for inspection by the general public.

§501.9 Representation; appearances and fees.

(a) *Representation.* In any proceeding before the Board, an Appellant may appear in person or by appointing a duly authorized individual as his or her Representative.

(1) *Counsel.* The designated Representative may be an attorney who has been admitted to practice and who is in good standing with any court of competent jurisdiction.

(2) *Lay representative.* A non-attorney Representative may represent an Appellant before the Board. He or she may be an accredited Representative of an employee organization.

(3) *Former members of the Board and other employees of the Department of Labor.* A former judge of the Board is not allowed to participate as counsel or other Representative before the Board in any proceeding until two years from the termination of his or her status as a judge of the Board. The practice of a former judge or other former employee of the Department of Labor is governed by 29 CFR Part 0, Subpart B.

(b) *Appearance.* No individual may appear as a Representative in a proceeding before the Board without first filing with the Clerk a written authorization signed by the Appellant to be represented. When accepted by the Board, such Representative will continue to be recognized unless the Representative withdraws or abandons such capacity or the Appellant directs otherwise.

(c) *Change of address.* Each Appellant and Representative authorized to appear before the Board must give the

Clerk written notice of any change to the address or telephone number of the Appellant or Representative. Such notice must identify the docket number and name of each pending appeal for that Appellant, or, in the case of a Representative, in which he or she is a Representative before the Board. Absent such notice, the mailing of documents to the address most recently provided to the Board will be fully effective.

(d) *Debarment of Counsel or Representative.* In any proceeding, whenever the Board finds that a person acting as counsel or other Representative for the Appellant or the Director, is guilty of unethical or unprofessional conduct, the Board may order that such person be excluded from further acting as counsel or Representative in such proceeding. Such order may be appealed to the Secretary of Labor or his or her designee, but proceedings before the Board will not be delayed or suspended pending disposition of such appeal. However, the Board may suspend the proceeding of an appeal for a reasonable time for the purpose of enabling Appellant or the Director to obtain different counsel or other Representative. Whenever the Board has issued an order precluding a person from further acting as counsel or Representative in a proceeding, the Board will, within a reasonable time, submit to the Secretary of Labor or his or her designee a report of the facts and circumstances surrounding the issuance of such order. The Board will recommend what action the Secretary of Labor should take in regard to the appearance of such person as counsel or Representative in other proceedings before the Board. Before any action is taken debarring a person as counsel or Representative from other proceedings, he or she will be furnished notice and the opportunity to be heard on the matter.

(e) *Fees for attorney, Representative, or other services.* No claim for a fee for legal or other service performed on appeal before the Board is valid unless approved by the Board. Under 18 U.S.C. 292, collecting a fee without the approval of the Board may constitute a misdemeanor, subject to fine or imprisonment for up to a year or both. No contract for a stipulated fee or on a contingent fee basis will be approved by the Board. No fee for service will be approved except upon written application to the Clerk, supported by a statement of the extent and nature of the necessary work performed before the Board on behalf of the Appellant. The fee application will be served by the Clerk on the Appellant and a time set in which a response may be filed. Except where such fee is *de minimis,* the fee request will be evaluated with consideration of the following factors:

(1) Usefulness of the Representative's services;

(2) The nature and complexity of the appeal;

(3) The capacity in which the Representative has appeared;

(4) The actual time spent in connection with the Board appeal; and

(5) Customary local charges for similar services.

PARTS 502–599 [RESERVED]

CHAPTER V—EMPLOYMENT AND TRAINING ADMINISTRATION, DEPARTMENT OF LABOR

PART 600 [RESERVED]

PART 601—ADMINISTRATIVE PROCEDURE

Subpart A—Approval, Certification and Findings With Respect to State Laws and Plans of Operation for Normal and Additional Tax Credit and Grant Purposes

Subpart B—Grants, Advances and Audits

AUTHORITY: 5 U.S.C. 301; 26 U.S.C. Chapter 23; 29 U.S.C. 49k; 38 U.S.C. Chapters 41 and 42; 39 U.S.C. 3202(a)(1)(E) and 3202 note; 42 U.S.C. 1302; and Secretary of Labor's Order No. 4–75, 40 FR 18515.

SOURCE: 15 FR 5886, Aug. 31, 1950; 23 FR 1267, Mar. 1, 1958, unless otherwise noted.

EDITORIAL NOTE: Nomenclature changes to part 601 appear at 71 FR 35512, June 21, 2006.

Subpart A—Approval, Certification and Findings With Respect to State Laws and Plans of Operation for Normal and Additional Tax Credit and Grant Purposes

§ 601.1 General.

(a) State unemployment compensation laws are approved and certified as provided in section 3304 of the Internal Revenue Code of 1986; findings are made regarding reduced rates permitted by a State law (section 3303(a) of the Internal Revenue Code of 1986) and such laws are certified as provided in section 3303(b) of the Internal Revenue Code of 1986; findings are made regarding the inclusion of specified provisions (section 303(a) of the Social Security Act) in State laws approved under section 3304(a) of the Internal Revenue Code of 1986; findings are made whether the States have accepted the provisions of the Wagner-Peyser Act and whether their plans of operation for public employment offices comply with the provisions of said Act.

(b) Normal and additional tax credit is given to taxpayers against taxes imposed by section 3301 of the Internal Revenue Code of 1986.

(c) Grants of funds are made to States for administration of their employment security laws if their unemployment compensation laws and their plans of operation for public employment offices meet required conditions of Federal law. (Section 303(a) of the Social Security Act; section 3304(a) of the Internal Revenue Code of 1986; sections 6, 7, and 8 of the Wagner-Peyser Act.)

(d) As used throughout this Part, the terms "Secretary" or "Secretary of Labor" shall refer to the Secretary of Labor, U.S. Department of Labor, or his or her designee.

[15 FR 5886, Aug. 31, 1950; 23 FR 1267, Mar. 1, 1958, as amended at 61 FR 19983, May 3, 1996]

§ 601.2 Approval of State unemployment compensation laws.

States may at their option submit their unemployment compensation laws for approval (section 3304(a) of the Internal Revenue Code of 1986).

(a) *Submission.* The States submit to the Employment and Training Administration (ETA), one copy of the State unemployment compensation law properly certified by an authorized State official to be true and complete, together with a written request for approval.

(b) [Reserved]

(c) *Approval.* The Secretary of Labor determines whether the State law contains the provisions required by section 3304(a) of the Internal Revenue Code of 1986. If the State law is approved, the Secretary notifies the Governor of the State within 30 days of the submission of such law.

(d) *Certification.* On October 31 of each taxable year the Secretary of Labor certifies, for the purposes of normal tax credit (section 3302(a)(1) of the Internal Revenue Code of 1986), to the Secretary of the Treasury each State the law of which the Secretary has previously approved. (See also § 601.5.)

(Approved by the Office of Management and Budget under control number 1205–0222)

[15 FR 5886, Aug. 31, 1950; 23 FR 1267, Mar. 1, 1958, as amended at 49 FR 18295, Apr. 30, 1984; 50 FR 51241, Dec. 16, 1985; 71 FR 35513, June 21, 2006]

§ 601.3 Findings with respect to State laws and plans of operation.

For purposes of grants, findings are made regarding the inclusion in State unemployment compensation laws, approved under section 3304(a) of the Internal Revenue Code of 1986, of provisions required by section 303(a) of the Social Security Act (see § 601.2); findings are also made whether a State has accepted the provisions of the Wagner-Peyser Act and whether its plan of operation for public employment offices complies with the provisions of said act. For purposes of additional tax credit, findings are made regarding reduced rates of contributions permitted by the State law (section 3303(a) (1) of the Internal Revenue Code of 1986).

So that the Secretary of Labor may be enabled to determine the status of State laws and plans of operation, all relevant State materials, such as statutes, executive and administrative orders, legal opinions, rules, regulations, interpretations, court decisions, etc., are required to be submitted currently.

(a) *Submission.* The States submit currently to the ETA one copy of relevant State material, properly certified by an authorized State official to be true and complete.

(b) [Reserved]

(c) *Findings.* The Secretary makes findings as provided in the cited sections of the Federal law. In the event that the Secretary is unable to make the findings required for certification for payment or for certification of the law for purposes of additional tax credit, further discussions with State officials are undertaken.

(Approved by the Office of Management and Budget under control number 1205–0222)

[15 FR 5886, Aug. 31, 1950; 23 FR 1267, Mar. 1, 1958, as amended at 49 FR 18295, Apr. 30, 1984; 50 FR 51241, Dec. 16, 1985; 71 FR 35513, June 21, 2006]

§ 601.4 Certification for tax credit.

(a) Within 30 days after submittal of a State unemployment compensation law for such purpose, the Secretary certifies to the State agency, in accordance with the provisions of section 3303(b)(3) of the Internal Revenue Code of 1986, the Secretary's findings regarding reduced rates of contributions allowable under such law. On October 31 of each taxable year the Secretary certifies to the Secretary of the Treasury the law of each State, certified with respect to such year under section 3304 of the Internal Revenue Code of 1986 (see § 601.2), which the Secretary finds allows reduced rates with respect to such taxable year only in accordance with the provisions of section 3303(a) of the Internal Revenue Code of 1986.

(b) With regard to certification for payment, see § 601.6.

[15 FR 5886, Aug. 31, 1950; 23 FR 1267, Mar. 1, 1958, as amended at 71 FR 35513, June 21, 2006]

§ 601.5 Withholding payments and certifications.

(a) *When withheld.* Payment of funds to States or yearend certification of State laws, or both, are withheld when the Secretary finds, after reasonable notice and opportunity for hearing:

(1) That any provision required by section 303(a) of the Social Security Act is no longer included in the State unemployment compensation law; or

(2) That the State unemployment compensation law has been so changed as no longer to meet the conditions required by section 3303(a) of the Internal Revenue Code of 1986 (section 3303(b)(3) of the Internal Revenue Code); or

(3) That the State unemployment compensation law has been so amended as no longer to contain the provisions specified in section 3304(a) or has failed to comply substantially with any such provision and such finding has become effective (section 3304(c) of the Internal Revenue Code of 1986); or

(4) That in the administration of the State unemployment compensation law there has been a failure to comply substantially with required provisions of such law (section 303(b)(2) of the Social Security Act and section 3303(b)(3) of the Internal Revenue Code of 1986); or

(5) That in the administration of the State unemployment compensation law there has been a denial, in a substantial number of cases, of benefits due under such law, except that there may be no such finding until the question of entitlement has been decided by the highest judicial authority given jurisdiction under such State law (section 303(b)(1) of the Social Security Act); or

(6) That a State fails to make its unemployment compensation records available to the Railroad Retirement Board or fails to cooperate with Federal agencies charged with the administration of unemployment compensation laws (section 303(c) of the Social Security Act); or

(7) That a State no longer has a plan of operation for public employment offices complying with the provisions of the Wagner-Peyser Act; or

(8) That a State agency has not properly expended, in accordance with an approved plan of operation, the Federal monies paid it for administration of its public employment service.

(b) *Informal discussion.* Such hearings are generally not called, however, until after every reasonable effort has been made by ETA representatives to resolve the question involved by conference and discussion with State officials. Formal notification of the date and place of a hearing does not foreclose further negotiations with State officials.

(c) *Notice of noncertification.* If, at any time during the taxable year, the Secretary of Labor has reason to believe that a State whose unemployment compensation law he/she has previously approved may not be certified, the Secretary promptly notifies the Governor of the State to that effect (section 3304(d) of the Internal Revenue Code of 1986).

(d) *Notice of hearing.* Notice of hearing is sent by the Secretary of Labor to the State unemployment compensation agency. The notice sets forth the purpose of the hearing, the time, date, and place at which the hearing will be held, and the rules of procedure which will be followed. At a hearing the State is given an opportunity to present arguments and all relevant evidence, written or oral. The Secretary makes the necessary determination or findings, on the basis of the record of such hearings. A notice of the Secretary's determination or finding is sent to the State unemployment compensation agency.

(e) *Civil Rights Act issues.* To the extent that any proposed withholding of funds involves circumstances within the scope of title VI of the Civil Rights Act of 1964 and the regulations promulgated thereunder, the procedure set forth in 29 CFR part 31 shall be applicable.

[30 FR 6942, May 22, 1965, as amended at 43 FR 13828, Mar. 31, 1978; 71 FR 35513, June 21, 2006]

Subpart B—Grants, Advances and Audits

§601.6 Grants for administration of unemployment compensation laws and employment service.

Grants of funds for administration of State unemployment compensation laws and public employment service programs are made to States under section 302(a) of the Social Security Act, the Wagner-Peyser Act, and the Appropriation Acts.

(a) *Requests for funds.* The forms and instructions used by State agencies in requesting funds are available on the ETA Web site (*http://www.ows.doleta.gov/rjm*). The forms and instructions call for detailed information for each budgetary period concerning the specific amounts requested for personal services and other current expenses of State agencies, supported by workload and unit-cost estimates. Supplementary budget requests are processed in the same manner as regular requests. The Administration's representatives in the regional offices furnish assistance to the State agencies in preparing requests for funds.

(b) *Processing of requests.* (1) State agencies send their requests for funds to the Regional Administrator who reviews the requests and forwards them to the ETA National Office with his/her recommendation as to the amounts necessary for proper and efficient administration of the State unemployment compensation law and employment service program.

(2) The ETA National Office appraises the requests and the recommendations

of the regional representatives from a nationwide point of view, examining each State's request in the light of the experience of other States to insure equitable treatment among the States in the allocation of funds made available by Congress for the administration of State unemployment compensation laws and public employment service programs.

(c) *Action by ETA National Office.* If the ETA National Office approves the State's budget request, the State agency is notified; and, provided the conditions precedent to grants continue during the budgetary period, certifications for payment, under the approved budget, stating the amounts, are made by the ETA National Office to the Secretary of the Treasury quarterly. Upon denial of a request, in whole or in part, the State agency is notified and the Regional Administrator is instructed to negotiate with the State with a view to removing the basis for denial.

(Approved by the Office of Management and Budget under control number 1205–0132)

[15 FR 5886, Aug. 31, 1950, as amended at 42 FR 4724, Jan. 25, 1977; 49 FR 18295, Apr. 30, 1984; 71 FR 35513, June 21, 2006]

§ 601.7 [Reserved]

§ 601.8 Agreement with Postmaster General.

The Secretary of Labor and the Postmaster General have been directed by the Congress (title II of the Labor-Federal Security Agency Appropriation Act, 1950) to prescribe a mutually satisfactory procedure whereby official State employment security postal matter will be handled without the prepayment of postage. In lieu of such prepayments, the Secretary periodically certifies to the Secretary of the Treasury for payment to the U.S. Postal Service the amount necessary to cover the cost of State agency mailings. The amount of payment is based on a formula agreed upon by the Secretary of Labor and the U.S. Postal Service.

[15 FR 5886, Aug. 31, 1950, as amended at 42 FR 4724, Jan. 25, 1977]

§ 601.9 Audits.

The Department of Labor's audit regulations at 29 CFR Part 96 and 29 CFR Part 99 shall apply with respect to employment service and unemployment compensation programs.

[46 FR 7766, Jan. 23, 1981, as amended at 71 FR 35513, June 21, 2006]

PART 602—QUALITY CONTROL IN THE FEDERAL-STATE UNEMPLOYMENT INSURANCE SYSTEM

Subpart A—General Provisions

Subpart B—Federal Requirements

Subpart C—State Responsibilities

Subpart D—Federal Responsibilities

Subpart E—Quality Control Grants to States

AUTHORITY: 42 U.S.C. 1302.

SOURCE: 52 FR 33528, Sept. 3, 1987, unless otherwise noted.

EDITORIAL NOTE: Nomenclature changes to part 602 appear at 71 FR 35513, June 21, 2006.

Subpart A—General Provisions

§ 602.1 Purpose.

The purpose of this part is to prescribe a Quality Control (QC) program for the Federal-State unemployment compensation (UC) system, which is applicable to the State UC programs and the Federal unemployment benefit and allowance programs administered by the State unemployment compensation agencies under agreements between the States and the Secretary of

Labor (Secretary). QC will be a major tool to assess the timeliness and accuracy of State administration of the UC program. It is designed to identify errors in claims processes and revenue collections (including payments in lieu of contributions and Extended Unemployment Compensation Account collections), analyze causes, and support the initiation of corrective action.

[52 FR 33528, Sept. 3, 1987, as amended at 71 FR 35513, June 21, 2006]

§602.2 Scope.

This part applies to all State laws approved by the Secretary under the Federal Unemployment Tax Act (section 3304 of the Internal Revenue Code of 1986, 26 U.S.C. section 3304), to the administration of the State laws, and to any Federal unemployment benefit and allowance program administered by the State unemployment compensation agencies under agreements between the States and the Secretary. QC is a requirement for all States, initially being applicable to the largest permanently authorized programs (regular UC including Combined-Wage-Claims) and federally-funded programs (Unemployment Compensation for Ex-Servicemembers and Unemployment Compensation for Federal Employees). Other elements of the QC program (e.g., interstate, extended benefit programs, benefit denials, and revenue collections) will be phased in under a schedule determined by the Department in consultation with State agencies.

[52 FR 33528, Sept. 3, 1987, as amended at 71 FR 35513, June 21, 2006]

Subpart B—Federal Requirements

§602.10 Federal law requirements.

(a) Section 303(a)(1) of the Social Security Act (SSA), 42 U.S.C. 503(a)(1), requires that a State law include provision for:

> Such methods of administration . . . as are found by the Secretary of Labor to be reasonably calculated to insure full payment of unemployment compensation when due.

(b) Section 303(a)(6), SSA, 42 U.S.C. 505(a)(6), requires that a State law include provision for:

> The making of such reports, in such form and containing such information, as the Secretary of Labor may from time to time require, and compliance with such provisions as the Secretary of Labor may from time to time find necessary to assure the correctness and verification of such reports.

(c) Section 303(b), SSA, 42 U.S.C. 503(b), provides in part that:

> Whenever the Secretary of Labor, after reasonable notice and opportunity for hearing to the State agency charged with the administration of the State law, finds that in the administration of the law there is—
>
> * * * * *
>
> (2) a failure to comply substantially with any provision specified in subsection (a);
>
> the Secretary of Labor shall notify such State agency that further payments will not be made to the State until the Secretary of Labor is satisfied that there is no longer any such denial or failure to comply. Until he is so satisfied, he shall make no further certification to the Secretary of the Treasury with respect to such State . . . .

(d) Certification of payment of granted funds to a State is withheld only when the Secretary finds, after reasonable notice and opportunity for hearing to the State agency—

(1) That any provision required by section 303(a) of the Social Security Act is no longer included in the State UC law, or

(2) That in the administration of the State UC law there has been a failure to comply substantially with any required provision of such law.

[52 FR 33528, Sept. 3, 1987, as amended at 71 FR 35513, June 21, 2006]

§602.11 Secretary's interpretation.

(a) The Secretary interprets section 303(a)(1), SSA, to require that a State law provide for such methods of administration as will reasonably ensure the prompt and full payment of unemployment benefits to eligible claimants, and collection and handling of income for the State unemployment fund (particularly taxes and reimbursements), with the greatest accuracy feasible.

(b) The Secretary interprets sections 303(a)(1) and 303(a)(6), SSA, to authorize the Department of Labor to prescribe standard definitions, methods and procedures, and reporting requirements for the QC program and to ensure accuracy and verification of QC findings.

(c) The Secretary interprets section 303(b)(2), SSA to require that, in the administration of a State law, there shall be substantial compliance with the provisions required by sections 303(a) (1) and (6). Further, conformity of the State law with those requirements is required by section 303(a) and § 601.5(a) of this chapter.

(d) To satisfy the requirements of sections 303(a) (1) and (6), a State law must contain a provision requiring, or which is construed to require, the establishment and maintenance of a QC program in accordance with the requirements of this part. The establishment and maintenance of such a QC program in accordance with this part shall not require any change in State law concerning authority to undertake redeterminations of claims or liabilities or the finality of any determination, redetermination or decision.

Subpart C—State Responsibilities

§ 602.20 Organization.

Each State shall establish a QC unit independent of, and not accountable to, any unit performing functions subject to evaluation by the QC unit. The organizational location of this unit shall be positioned to maximize its objectivity, to facilitate its access to information necessary to carry out its responsibilities, and to minimize organizational conflict of interest.

§ 602.21 Standard methods and procedures.

Each State shall:

(a) Perform the requirements of this section in accordance with instructions issued by the Department, pursuant to § 602.30(a) of this part, to ensure standardization of methods and procedures in a manner consistent with this part;

(b) Select representative samples for QC study of at least a minimum size specified by the Department to ensure statistical validity (for benefit payments, a minimum of 400 cases of weeks paid per State per year);

(c) Complete prompt and in-depth case investigations to determine the degree of accuracy and timeliness in the administration of the State UC law and Federal programs with respect to benefit determinations, benefit payments, and revenue collections; and conduct other measurements and studies necessary or appropriate for carrying out the purposes of this part; and in conducting investigations each State shall:

(1) Inform claimants in writing that the information obtained from a QC investigation may affect their eligibility for benefits and inform employers in writing that the information obtained from a QC investigation of revenue may affect their tax liability,

(2) Use a questionnaire, prescribed by the Department, which is designed to obtain such data as the Department deems necessary for the operation of the QC program; require completion of the questionnaire by claimants in accordance with the eligibility and reporting authority under State law,

(3) Collect data identified by the Department as necessary for the operation of the QC program; however, the collection of demographic data will be limited to those data which relate to an individual's eligibility for UC benefits and necessary to conduct proportions tests to validate the selection of representative samples (the demographic data elements necessary to conduct proportions tests are claimants' date of birth, sex, and ethnic classification); and

(4) Conclude all findings of inaccuracy as detected through QC investigations with appropriate official actions, in accordance with the applicable State and Federal laws; make any determinations with respect to individual benefit claims in accordance with the Secretary's "Standard for Claim Determinations—Separation Information" in the *Employment Security Manual*, part V, sections 6010–6015 (appendix A of this part);

(d) Classify benefit case findings resulting from QC investigations as:

(1) Proper payments, underpayments, or overpayments in benefit payment cases, or

(2) Proper denials or underpayments in benefit denial cases;

(e) Make and maintain records pertaining to the QC program, and make all such records available in a timely manner for inspection, examination, and audit by such Federal officials as the Secretary may designate or as may be required or authorized by law;

(f) Furnish information and reports to the Department, including weekly transmissions of case data entered into the automated QC system and annual reports, without, in any manner, identifying individuals to whom such data pertain; and

(g) Release the results of the QC program at the same time each year, providing calendar year results using a standardized format to present the data as prescribed by the Department; States will have the opportunity to release this information prior to any release by the Department.

(Approved by the Office of Management and Budget under Control Number 1205–0245)

§ 602.22 Exceptions.

If the Department determines that the QC program, or any constituent part of the QC program, is not necessary for the proper and efficient administration of a State law or in the Department's view is not cost effective, the Department shall use established procedures to advise the State that it is partially or totally excepted from the specified requirements of this part. Any determination under this section shall be made only after consultations with the State agency.

Subpart D—Federal Responsibilities

§ 602.30 Management.

(a) The Department shall establish required methods and procedures (as specified in § 602.21 of this part); and provide technical assistance as needed on the QC process.

(b) The Department shall consider and explore alternatives to the prescribed sampling, study, recordkeeping, and reporting methodologies. This shall include, but not be limited to, testing the obtaining of information needed for QC by telephone and mail rather than in face-to-face interviews.

(c) The Department shall maintain a computerized data base of QC case data which is transmitted to the Department under § 602.21, which will be combined with other data for statistical and other analysis such as assessing the impact of economic cycles, funding levels, and workload levels on program accuracy and timeliness.

§ 602.31 Oversight.

The Department shall review QC operational procedures and samples, and validate QC methodology to ensure uniformity in the administration of the QC program and to ensure compliance with the requirements of this part. The Department shall, for purposes of determining eligibility for grants described in § 602.40, annually review the adequacy of the administration of a State's QC program.

Subpart E—Quality Control Grants to States

§ 602.40 Funding.

(a) The Department shall use established procedures to notify States of the availability of funds for the operation of QC programs in accordance with this part.

(b) The Department may allocate additional resources, if available, to States for analysis of data generated by the QC program, to increase the number of claims sampled in areas where more information is needed, for pilot studies for the purpose of expanding the QC program, and for corrective action.

[52 FR 33528, Sept. 3, 1987, as amended at 71 FR 35513, June 21, 2006]

§ 602.41 Proper expenditure of Quality Control granted funds.

The Secretary may, after reasonable notice and opportunity for hearing to the State agency, take exception to and require repayment of an expenditure for the operation of a QC program if it is found by the Secretary that such expenditure is not necessary for the proper and efficient administration of the QC program in the State. See sections 303(a)(8), 303(a)(9) and 303(b)(2), SSA, and 20 CFR 601.5. For purposes of this section, an expenditure will be found not necessary for proper and efficient administration if such expenditure fails to comply with the requirements of subpart C of this part.

[52 FR 33528, Sept. 3, 1987, as amended at 52 FR 34343, Sept. 10, 1987]

§ 602.42 Effect of failure to implement Quality Control program.

Any State which the Secretary finds, after reasonable notice and opportunity for hearing, has not implemented or maintained a QC program in accordance with this part will not be eligible for any grants under title III of the Social Security Act until such time as the Secretary is satisfied that there is no longer any failure to conform or to comply substantially with any provision specified in this part. See sections 303(a)(1), 303(a)(6), and 303(b)(2), SSA, and 20 CFR 601.5.

§ 602.43 No incentives or sanctions based on specific error rates.

Neither sanctions nor funding incentives shall be used by the Department to influence the achievement of specified error rates in State UC programs.

APPENDIX A TO PART 602—STANDARD FOR CLAIM DETERMINATIONS—SEPARATION INFORMATION

EMPLOYMENT SECURITY MANUAL (PART V, SECTIONS 6010–6015)

6010 *Federal Law Requirements.* Section 303(a)(1) of the Social Security Act requires that a State law include provision for:

"Such methods of administration . . . as are found by the Secretary to be reasonably calculated to insure full payment of unemployment compensation when due."

Section 303(a)(3) of the Social Security Act requires that a State law include provision for:

"Opportunity for a fair hearing before an impartial tribunal, for all individuals whose claims for unemployment compensation are denied."

Section 3304(a)(4) of the Federal Unemployment Tax Act and section 303(a)(5) of the Social Security Act require that a State law include provision for:

"Expenditure of all money withdrawn from an unemployment fund of such State, in the payment of unemployment compensation. . . ."

Section 3306(h) of the Federal Unemployment Tax Act defines "compensation" as "cash benefits payable to individuals with respect to their unemployment."

6011 *Secretary's Interpretation of Federal Law Requirements.* The Secretary interprets the above sections to require that a State law include provisions which will insure that:

A. Individuals who may be entitled to unemployment compensation are furnished such information as will reasonably afford them an opportunity to know, establish, and protect their rights under the unemployment compensation law of such State, and

B. The State agency obtains and records in time for the prompt determination and review of benefit claims such information as will reasonably insure the payment of benefits to individuals to whom benefits are due.

6012 *Criteria for Review of State Law Conformity with Federal Requirements:*

In determining the conformity of a State law with the above requirements of the Federal Unemployment Tax Act and the Social Security Act as interpreted by the Secretary, the following criteria will be applied:

A. Is it required that individuals who may be entitled to unemployment compensation be furnished such information of their potential rights to benefits, including the manner and places of filing claims, the reasons for determinations, and their rights of appeal, as will insure them a reasonable opportunity to know, establish, and protect their rights under the law of the State?

B. Is the State agency required to obtain, in time for prompt determination of rights to benefits such information as will reasonably insure the payment of benefits to individuals to whom benefits are due?

C. Is the State agency required to keep records of the facts considered in reaching determinations of rights to benefits?

6013 *Claim Determinations Requirements Designed To Meet Department of Labor Criteria:*

A. *Investigation of claims.* The State agency is required to obtain promptly and prior to a determination of an individual's right to benefits, such facts pertaining thereto as will be sufficient reasonably to insure the payment of benefits when due.

This requirement embraces five separate elements:

1. It is the responsibility of the agency to take the initiative in the discovery of information. This responsibility may not be passed on to the claimant or the employer. In addition to the agency's own records, this information may be obtained from the worker, the employer, or other sources. If the information obtained in the first instance discloses no essential disagreement and provides a sufficient basis for a fair determination, no further investigation is necessary. If the information obtained from other sources differs essentially from that furnished by the

claimant, the agency, in order to meet its responsibility, is required to inform the claimant of such information from other sources and to afford the claimant an opportunity to furnish any further facts he may have.

2. Evidentiary facts must be obtained as distinguished from ultimate facts or conclusions. That a worker was discharged for misconduct is an ultimate fact or conclusion; that he destroyed a machine upon which he was working is a primary or evidentiary fact, and the sort of fact that the requirement refers to.

3. The information obtained must be sufficient reasonably to insure the payment of benefits when due. In general, the investigation made by the agency must be complete enough to provide information upon which the agency may act with reasonable assurance that its decision is consistent with the unemployment compensation law. On the other hand, the investigation should not be so exhaustive and time-consuming as unduly to delay the payment of benefits and to result in excessive costs.

4. Information must be obtained promptly so that the payment of benefits is not unduly delayed.

5. If the State agency requires any particular evidence from the worker, it must give him a reasonable opportunity to obtain such evidence.

B. *Recording of facts.* The agency must keep a written record of the facts considered in reaching its determinations.

C. *Determination notices.*

1. The agency must give each claimant a written notice of:

a. Any monetary determination with respect to his benefit year;

b. Any determination with respect to purging a disqualification if, under the State law, a condition or qualification must be satisfied with respect to each week of disqualification; but in lieu of giving written notice of each determination for each week in which it is determined that the claimant has met the requirements for purging, the agency may inform the claimant that he has purged the disqualification for a week by notation of his applicant identification card or otherwise in writing.

c. Any other determination which adversely affects[1] his rights to benefits, except that written notice of determination need not be given with respect to:

(1) A week in a benefit year for which the claimant's weekly benefit amount is reduced in whole or in part by earnings if, the first time in the benefit year that there is such a reduction, he is required to be furnished a booklet or leaflet containing the information set forth below in paragraph 2f(1). However, a written notice of determination is required if: (a) there is a dispute concerning the reduction with respect to any week (e.g., as to the amount computed as the appropriate reduction, etc.); or (b) there is a change in the State law (or in the application thereof) affecting the reduction; or

(2) Any week in a benefit year subsequent to the first week in such benefit year in which benefits were denied, or reduced in whole or in part for reasons other than earnings, if denial or reduction for such subsequent week is based on the same reason and the same facts as for the first week, and if written notice of determination is required to be given to the claimant with respect to such first week, and with such notice of determination, he is required to be given a booklet or pamphlet containing the information set forth below in paragraphs 2f(2) and 2h. However, a written notice of determination is required if: (a) there is a dispute concerning the denial or reduction of benefits with respect to such week; or (b) there is a change in the State law (or in the application thereof) affecting the denial or reduction; or (c) there is a change in the amount of the reduction except as to the balance covered by the last reduction in a series of reductions.

NOTE: This procedure may be applied to determinations made with respect to any subsequent weeks for the same reason and on the basis of the same facts: (a) that claimant is unable to work, unavailable for work, or is disqualified under the labor dispute provision; and (b) reducing claimant's weekly benefit amount because of income other than earnings or offset by reason of overpayment.

2. The agency must include in written notices of determinations furnished to claimants sufficient information to enable them to understand the determinations, the reasons therefor, and their rights to protest, request reconsideration, or appeal.

[1] A determination "adversely affects" claimant's right to benefits if it (1) results in a denial to him of benefits (including a cancellation of benefits or wage credits or any reduction in whole or in part below the weekly or maximum amount established by his monetary determination) for any week or other period; or (2) denies credit for a waiting week; or (3) applies any disqualification or penalty; or (4) determines that he has not satisfied a condition of eligibility, requalification for benefits, or purging a disqualification; or (5) determines that an overpayment has been made or orders repayment or recoupment of any sum paid to him; or (6) applies a previously determined overpayment, penalty, or order for repayment or recoupment; or (7) in any other way denies claimant a right to benefits under the State law.

The written notice of monetary determination must contain the information specified in the following items (except h) unless an item is specifically not applicable. A written notice of any other determination must contain the information specified in as many of the following items as are necessary to enable the claimant to understand the determination and to inform him of his appeal rights. Information specifically applicable to the individual claimant must be contained in the written notice of determination. Information of general application such as (but not limited to) the explanation of benefits for partial unemployment, information as to deductions, seasonality factors, and information as to the manner and place of taking an appeal, extension of the appeal period, and where to obtain information and assistance may be contained in a booklet or leaflet which is given the claimant with his monetary determination.

a. *Base period wages.* The statement concerning base-period wages must be in sufficient detail to show the basis of computation of eligibility and weekly and maximum benefit amounts. (If maximum benefits are allowed, it may not be necessary to show details of earnings.)

b. *Employer name.* The name of the employer who reported the wages is necessary so that the worker may check the wage transcript and know whether it is correct. If the worker is given only the employer number, he may not be able to check the accuracy of the wage transcript.

c. *Explanation of benefit formula—weekly and maximum benefit amounts.* Sufficient information must be given the worker so that he will understand how his weekly benefit amount, including allowances for dependents, and his maximum benefit amount were figured. If benefits are computed by means of a table contained in the law, the table must be furnished with the notice of determination whether benefits are granted or denied.

The written notice of determination must show clearly the weekly benefit amount and the maximum potential benefits to which the claimant is entitled.

The notice to a claimant found ineligible by reason of insufficient earnings in the base period must inform him clearly of the reason for ineligibility. An explanation of the benefit formula contained in a booklet or pamphlet should be given to each claimant at or prior to the time he receives written notice of a monetary determination.

d. *Benefit year.* An explanation of what is meant by the benefit year and identification of the claimant's benefit year must be included in the notice of determination.

e. *Information as to benefits for partial unemployment.* There must be included either in the written notice of determination or in a booklet or pamphlet accompanying the notice an explanation of the claimant's rights to partial benefits for any week with respect to which he is working less than his normal customary full-time workweek because of lack of work and for which he earns less than his weekly benefit amount or weekly benefit amount plus earnings, whichever is provided by the State law. If the explanation is contained in the notice of determination, reference to the item in the notice in which his weekly benefit amount is entered should be made.

f. *Deductions from weekly benefits.*

(1) *Earnings.* Although written notice of determinations deducting earnings from a claimant's weekly benefit amount is generally not required (see paragraph 1 c (1) above), where written notice of determination is required (or given) it shall set forth the amount of earnings, the method of computing the deduction in sufficient detail to enable the claimant to verify the accuracy of the deduction, and his right to protest, request redetermination, and appeal. Where a written notice of determination is given to the claimant because there has been a change in the State law or in the application of the law, an explanation of the change shall be included.

Where claimant is not required to receive a written notice of determination, he must be given a booklet or pamphlet the first time in his benefit year that there is a deduction for earnings which shall include the following information:

(a) The method of computing deductions for earnings in sufficient detail to enable the claimant to verify the accuracy of the deduction;

(b) That he will not automatically be given a written notice of determination for a week with respect to which there is a deduction for earnings (unless there is a dispute concerning the reduction with respect to a week or there has been a change in the State law or in the application of the law affecting the deduction) but that he may obtain such a written notice upon request; and

(c) A clear statement of his right to protest, request a redetermination, and appeal from any determination deducting earnings from his weekly benefit amount even though he does not automatically receive a written notice of determination; and if the State law requires written notice of determination in order to effectuate a protest, redetermination, or appeal, he must be so advised and advised also that he must request a written notice of determination before he takes any such action.

(2) *Other deductions.*

(a) A written notice of determination is required with respect to the first week in claimant's benefit year in which there is a reduction from his benefits for a reason other than earnings. This notice must describe the deduction made from claimant's weekly benefit amount, the reason for the deduction, the method of computing it in sufficient detail to enable him to verify the accuracy of such deduction, and his right to protest, request redetermination, or appeal.

(b) A written notice of determination is not required for subsequent weeks that a deduction is made for the same reason and on the basis of the same facts, if the notice of determination pursuant to (2)(a), or a booklet or pamphlet given him with such notice explains (i) the several kinds of deductions which may be made under the State law (e.g., retirement pensions, vacation pay, and overpayments); (ii) the method of computing each kind of deduction in sufficient detail that claimant will be able to verify the accuracy of deductions made from his weekly benefit payments; (iii) any limitation on the amount of any deduction or the time in which any deduction may be made; (iv) that he will not automatically be given a written notice of determination for subsequent weeks with respect to which there is a deduction for the same reason and on the basis of the same facts, but that he may obtain a written notice of determination upon request; (v) his right to protest, request redetermination, or appeal with respect to subsequent weeks for which there is a reduction from his benefits for the same reason, and on the basis of the same facts even though he does not automatically receive a written notice of determination; and (vi) that if the State law requires written notice of determination in order to effectuate a protest, redetermination, or appeal, he must be so advised and advised also that he must request a written notice of determination before he takes any such action.

g. *Seasonality factors*. If the individual's determination is affected by seasonality factors under the State law, an adequate explanation must be made. General explanation of seasonality factors which may affect determinations for subsequent weeks may be included in a booklet or pamphlet given claimant with his notice of monetary determination.

h. *Disqualification or ineligibility*. If a disqualification is imposed, or if the claimant is declared ineligible for one or more weeks, he must be given not only a statement of the period of disqualification or ineligibility and the amount of wage-credit reductions, if any, but also an explanation of the reason for the ineligibility or disqualification. This explanation must be sufficiently detailed so that he will understand why he is ineligible or why he has been disqualified, and what he must do in order to requalify for benefits or purge the disqualification. The statement must be individualized to indicate the facts upon which the determination was based, e.g., state, "It is found that you left your work with Blank Company because you were tired of working; the separation was voluntary, and the reason does not constitute good cause," rather than merely the phrase "voluntary quit." Checking a box as to the reason for the disqualification is not a sufficiently detailed explanation. However, this statement of the reason for the disqualification need not be a restatement of all facts considered in arriving at the determination.

i. *Appeal rights*. The claimant must be given information with respect to his appeal rights.

(1) The following information shall be included in the notice of determination:

(a) A statement that he may appeal or, if the State law requires or permits a protest or redetermination before an appeal, that he may protest or request a redetermination.

(b) The period within which an appeal, protest, or request for redetermination must be filed. The number of days provided by statute must be shown as well as either the beginning date or ending date of the period. (It is recommended that the ending date of the appeal period be shown, as this is the more understandable of the alternatives.)

(2) The following information must be included either in the notice of determination or in separate informational material referred to in the notice:

(a) The manner in which the appeal, protest, or request for redetermination must be filed, e.g., by signed letter, written statement, or on a prescribed form, and the place or places to which the appeal, protest, or request for redetermination may be mailed or hand-delivered.

(b) An explanation of any circumstances (such as nonworkdays, good cause, etc.) which will extend the period for the appeal, protest, or request for redetermination beyond the date stated or identified in the notice of determination.

(c) That any further information claimant may need or desire can be obtained together with assistance in filing his appeal, protest, or request for redetermination from the local office.

If the information is given in separate material, the notice of determination would adequately refer to such material if it said, for example, "For other information about your (appeal), (protest), (redetermination) rights, see pages ____ to ____ of the _______ (name of pamphlet or booklet) heretofore furnished to you."

6014 *Separation Information Requirements Designed To Meet Department of Labor Criteria:*

A. *Information to agency*. Where workers are separated, employers are required to furnish the agency promptly, either upon agency request or upon such separation, a notice describing the reasons for and the circumstances of the separation and any additional information which might affect a claimant's right to benefits. Where workers are working less than full time, employers are required to furnish the agency promptly, upon agency request, information concerning a claimant's hours of work and his wages during the claim periods involved, and other facts which might affect a claimant's eligibility for benefits during such periods.

When workers are separated and the notices are obtained on a request basis, or when workers are working less than full time and the agency requests information, it is essential to the prompt processing of claims that the request be sent out promptly after the claim is filed and the employer be given a specific period within which to return the notice, preferably within 2 working days.

When workers are separated and notices are obtained upon separation, it is essential that the employer be required to send the notice to the agency with sufficient promptness to insure that, if a claim is filed, it may be processed promptly. Normally, it is desirable that such a notice be sent to the central office of the agency, since the employer may not know in which local office the workers will file his claim. The usual procedure is for the employer to give the worker a copy of the notice sent by the employer to the agency.

B. *Information to worker.*

1. *Information required to be given.* Employers are required to give their employees information and instructions concerning the employees' potential rights to benefits and concerning registration for work and filing claims for benefits.

The information furnished to employees under such a requirement need not be elaborate; it need only be adequate to insure that the worker who is separated or who is working less than full time knows he is potentially eligible for benefits and is informed as to what he is to do or where he is to go to file his claim and register for work. When he files his claim, he can obtain more detailed information.

In States that do not require employers to furnish periodically to the State agency detailed reports of the wages paid to their employees, each employer is required to furnish to his employees information as to (a) the name under which he is registered by the State agency, (b) the address where he maintains his payroll records, and (c) the workers' need for this information if and when they file claims for benefits.

2. *Methods for giving information.* The information and instructions required above may be given in any of the following ways:

a. *Posters prominently displayed in the employer's establishment.* The State agency should supply employers with a sufficient number of posters for distribution throughout their places of business and should see that the posters are conspicuously displayed at all times.

b. *Leaflets.* Leaflets distributed either periodically or at the time of separation or reduction of hours. The State agency should supply employers with a sufficient number of leaflets.

c. *Individual notices.* Individual notices given to each employee at the time of separation or reduction in hours.

It is recommended that the State agency's publicity program be used to supplement the employer-information requirements. Such a program should stress the availability and location of claim-filing offices and the importance of visiting those offices whenever the worker is unemployed, wishes to apply for benefits, and to seek a job.

6015 *Evaluation of Alternative State Provisions with Respect to Claim Determinations and Separation Information.* If the State law provisions do not conform to the suggested requirements set forth in sections 6013 and 6014, but the State law contains alternative provisions, the Bureau of Employment Security, in collaboration with the State agency, will study the actual or anticipated effects of the alternative provisions. If the Administrator of the Bureau concludes that the alternative provisions satisfy the criteria in section 6012, he will so notify the State agency. If the Administrator of the Bureau does not so conclude, he will submit the matter to the Secretary. If the Secretary concludes that the alternative provisions satisfy the criteria in section 6012, the State agency will be so notified. If the Secretary concludes that there is a question as to whether the alternative provisions satisfy the criteria, the State agency will be advised that unless the State law provisions are appropriately revised, a notice of hearing will be issued as required by the Code of Federal Regulations, title 20, section 601.5.

PART 603—FEDERAL-STATE UNEMPLOYMENT COMPENSATION (UC) PROGRAM; CONFIDENTIALITY AND DISCLOSURE OF STATE UC INFORMATION

Subpart A—In General

Sec.

Subpart B—Confidentiality and Disclosure Requirements

AUTHORITY: Secs. 116, 189, 503, Pub. L. 113–128, 128 Stat. 1425 (Jul. 22, 2014); 20 U.S.C 1232g.

SOURCE: 71 FR 56842, Sept. 27, 2006, unless otherwise noted.

Subpart A—In General

§ 603.1 What are the purpose and scope of this part?

The purpose of this part is to implement the requirements of Federal UC law concerning confidentiality and disclosure of UC information. This part applies to States and State UC agencies, as defined in § 603.2(f) and (g).

§ 603.2 What definitions apply to this part?

For the purposes of this part:

(a)(1) *Claim information* means information about:

(i) Whether an individual is receiving, has received, or has applied for UC;

(ii) The amount of compensation the individual is receiving or is entitled to receive; and

(iii) The individual's current (or most recent) home address.

(2) For purposes of subpart C (IEVS), claim information also includes:

(i) Whether the individual has refused an offer of work and, if so, a description of the job offered including the terms, conditions, and rate of pay; and

(ii) Any other information contained in the records of the State UC agency that is needed by the requesting agency to verify eligibility for, and the amount of, benefits.

(b) *Confidential UC information* and *confidential information* mean any UC information, as defined in paragraph (j) of this section, required to be kept confidential under § 603.4.

(c) *Public domain information* means—

(1) Information about the organization of the State and the State UC agency and appellate authorities, including the names and positions of officials and employees thereof;

(2) Information about the State UC law (and applicable Federal law) provisions, rules, regulations, and interpretations thereof, including statements of general policy and interpretations of general applicability; and

(3) Any agreement of whatever kind or nature, including interstate arrangements and reciprocal agreements and any agreement with the Department of Labor or the Secretary, relating to the administration of the State UC law.

(d) *Public official* means:

(1) An official, agency, or public entity within the executive branch of Federal, State, or local government who (or which) has responsibility for administering or enforcing a law, or an elected official in the Federal, State, or local government.

(2) Public postsecondary educational institutions established and governed under the laws of the State. These include the following:

(i) Institutions that are part of the State's executive branch. This means the head of the institution must derive his or her authority from the Governor, either directly or through a State WDB, commission, or similar entity established in the executive branch under the laws of the State.

(ii) Institutions which are independent of the executive branch. This means the head of the institution derives his or her authority from the State's chief executive officer for the State education authority or agency when such officer is elected or appointed independently of the Governor.

(iii) Publicly governed, publicly funded community and technical colleges.

(3) Performance accountability and customer information agencies designated by the Governor of a State to be responsible for coordinating the assessment of State and local education or workforce training program performance and/or evaluating education or workforce training provider performance.

(4) The chief elected official of a local area as defined in WIOA sec. 3(9).

(5) A State educational authority, agency, or institution as those terms are used in the Family Educational Rights and Privacy Act, to the extent they are public entities.

(e) *Secretary* and *Secretary of Labor* mean the cabinet officer heading the United States Department of Labor, or his or her designee.

(f) *State* means a State of the United States of America, the District of Columbia, the Commonwealth of Puerto Rico, and the United States Virgin Islands.

(g) *State UC agency* means an agency charged with the administration of the State UC law.

(h) *State UC law* means the law of a State approved under Section 3304(a) of the Internal Revenue Code of 1986 (26 U.S.C. 3304(a)).

(i) *Unemployment compensation* (UC) means cash benefits payable to individuals with respect to their unemployment.

(j) *UC information* and *State UC information* means information in the records of a State or State UC agency that pertains to the administration of the State UC law. This term includes those State wage reports collected under the IEVS (Section 1137 of the Social Security Act (SSA)) that are obtained by the State UC agency for determining UC monetary eligibility or are downloaded to the State UC agency's files as a result of a crossmatch but does not otherwise include those wage reports. It does not include information in a State's Directory of New Hires, but does include any such information that has been disclosed to the State UC agency for use in the UC program. It also does not include the personnel or fiscal information of a State UC agency.

(k) *Wage information* means information in the records of a State UC agency (and, for purposes of § 603.23 (IEVS)), information reported under provisions of State law which fulfill the requirements of Section 1137, SSA) about the—

(1) Wages paid to an individual,

(2) Social security account number (or numbers, if more than one) of such individual, and

(3) Name, address, State, and the Federal employer identification number of the employer who paid such wages to such individual.

[71 FR 56842, Sept. 27, 2006, as amended at 81 FR 56333, Aug. 19, 2016]

Subpart B—Confidentiality and Disclosure Requirements

§ 603.3 What is the purpose and scope of this subpart?

This subpart implements the basic confidentiality requirement derived from Section 303(a)(1), SSA, and the disclosure requirements of Sections 303(a)(7), (c)(1), (d), (e), (h), and (i), SSA, and Section 3304(a)(16), Federal Unemployment Tax Act (FUTA). This subpart also establishes uniform minimum requirements for the payment of costs, safeguards, and data-sharing agreements when UC information is disclosed, and for conformity and substantial compliance with this proposed rule. This subpart applies to States and State UC agencies, as defined in § 603.2(f) and (g), respectively.

§ 603.4 What is the confidentiality requirement of Federal UC law?

(a) *Statute*. Section 303(a)(1) of the SSA (42 U.S.C. 503(a)(1)) provides that, for the purposes of certification of payment of granted funds to a State under Section 302(a) (42 U.S.C. 502(a)), State law must include provision for such methods of administration as are found by the Secretary of Labor to be reasonably calculated to insure full payment of unemployment compensation when due.

(b) *Interpretation*. The Department of Labor interprets Section 303(a)(1), SSA, to mean that "methods of administration" that are reasonably calculated to insure the full payment of UC when due must include provision for maintaining the confidentiality of any UC information which reveals the name or any identifying particular about any individual or any past or present employer or employing unit, or which could foreseeably be combined with other publicly available information to reveal any such particulars, and must include provision for barring the disclosure of any such information, except as provided in this part.

(c) *Application.* Each State law must contain provisions that are interpreted and applied consistently with the interpretation in paragraph (b) of this section and with this subpart, and must provide penalties for any disclosure of confidential UC information that is inconsistent with any provision of this subpart.

§ 603.5 What are the exceptions to the confidentiality requirement?

The following are exceptions to the confidentiality requirement. Disclosure of confidential UC information is permissible under the exceptions in paragraphs (a) through (g) of this section only if authorized by State law and if such disclosure does not interfere with the efficient administration of the State UC law. Disclosure of confidential UC information is permissible under the exceptions in paragraphs (h) and (i) of this section without such restrictions.

(a) *Public domain information.* The confidentiality requirement of § 603.4 does not apply to public domain information, as defined at § 603.2(c).

(b) *UC appeals records.* Disclosure of appeals records and decisions, and precedential determinations on coverage of employers, employment, and wages, is permissible provided all social security account numbers have been removed and such disclosure is otherwise consistent with Federal and State law.

(c) *Individual or employer.* Disclosure for non-UC purposes, of confidential UC information about an individual to that individual, or of confidential UC information about an employer to that employer, is permissible.

(d) *Informed consent.* Disclosure of confidential UC information on the basis of informed consent is permissible in the following circumstances—

(1) *Agent*—to one who acts for or in the place of an individual or an employer by the authority of that individual or employer if—

(i) In general—

(A) The agent presents a written release (which may include an electronically submitted release that the State determines is authentic) from the individual or employer being represented;

(B) When a written release is impossible or impracticable to obtain, the agent presents such other form of consent as is permitted by the State UC agency in accordance with State law;

(ii) In the case of an elected official performing constituent services, the official presents reasonable evidence (such as a letter from the individual or employer requesting assistance or a written record of a telephone request from the individual or employer) that the individual or employer has authorized such disclosure; or

(iii) In the case of an attorney retained for purposes related to the State's UC law, the attorney asserts that he or she is representing the individual or employer.

(2) *Third party (other than an agent) or disclosure made on an ongoing basis*—to a third party that is not acting as an agent or that receives confidential information following an informed consent disclosure on an ongoing basis (even if such entity is an agent), but only if that entity obtains a written release from the individual or employer to whom the information pertains.

(i) The release must be signed and must include a statement—

(A) Specifically identifying the information that is to be disclosed;

(B) That State government files will be accessed to obtain that information;

(C) Of the specific purpose or purposes for which the information is sought and a statement that information obtained under the release will only be used for that purpose or purposes; and

(D) Indicating all the parties who may receive the information disclosed.

(ii) The purpose specified in the release must be limited to—

(A) Providing a service or benefit to the individual signing the release that such individual expects to receive as a result of signing the release; or

(B) Carrying out administration or evaluation of a public program to which the release pertains.

NOTE TO PARAGRAPH (d): The Electronic Signatures in Global and National Commerce Act of 2000 (E-Sign), Pub. L. 106–229, may apply where a party wishes to effectuate electronically an informed consent release (§ 603.5(d)(2)) or a disclosure agreement (§ 603.10(a)) with an entity that uses informed consent releases. E-Sign, among other things, sets forth the circumstances under which electronic signatures, contracts, and other records relating to such transactions (in lieu of paper documents) are legally binding. Thus, an electronic communication may suffice under E-Sign to establish a legally binding contract. The States will need to consider E-Sign's application to these informed consent releases and disclosure agreements. In particular, a State must, to conform and substantially comply with this regulation, assure that these informed consent releases and disclosure agreements are legally enforceable. If an informed consent release or disclosure agreement is to be effectuated electronically, the State must determine whether E-Sign applies to that transaction, and, if so, make certain that the transaction satisfies the conditions imposed by E-Sign. The State must also make certain that the electronic transaction complies with every other condition necessary to make it legally enforceable.

(e) *Public official.* Disclosure of confidential UC information to a public official for use in the performance of his or her official duties is permissible.

(1) "Performance of official duties" means administration or enforcement of law or the execution of the official responsibilities of a Federal, State, or local elected official. Administration of law includes research related to the law administered by the public official. Execution of official responsibilities does not include solicitation of contributions or expenditures to or on behalf of a candidate for public or political office or a political party.

(2) For purposes of § 603.2(d)(2) through (5), "performance of official duties" includes, in addition to the activities set out in paragraph (e)(1) of this section, use of the confidential UC information for the following limited purposes:

(i) State and local performance accountability under WIOA sec. 116, including eligible training provider performance accountability under WIOA secs. 116(d) and 122;

(ii) The requirements of discretionary Federal grants awarded under WIOA; or

(iii) As otherwise required for education or workforce training program performance accountability and reporting under Federal or State law.

(f) *Agent or contractor of public official.* Disclosure of confidential UC information to an agent or contractor of a public official to whom disclosure is permissible under paragraph (e) of this section.

(g) *Bureau of Labor Statistics.* The confidentiality requirement does not apply to information collected exclusively for statistical purposes under a cooperative agreement with the Bureau of Labor Statistics (BLS). Further, this part does not restrict or impose any condition on the transfer of any other information to the BLS under an agreement, or the BLS's disclosure or use of such information.

(h) *Court order; official with subpoena authority.* Disclosure of confidential UC information in response to a court order or to an official with subpoena authority is permissible as specified in § 603.7(b).

(i) *UC Program Oversight and Audits.* The confidentiality requirement does not apply to any disclosure to a Federal official for purposes of UC program oversight and audits, including disclosures under 20 CFR part 601 and 29 CFR parts 96 and 97.

[71 FR 56842, Sept. 27, 2006, as amended at 81 FR 56333, Aug. 19, 2016]

§ 603.6 What disclosures are required by this subpart?

(a) The confidentiality requirement of 303(a)(1), SSA, and § 603.4 are not applicable to this paragraph (a) and the Department of Labor interprets Section 303(a)(1), SSA, as requiring disclosure of all information necessary for the proper administration of the UC program. This includes disclosures to claimants, employers, the Internal Revenue Service (for purposes of UC tax administration), and the U.S. Citizenship and Immigration Services (for purposes of verifying a claimant's immigration status).

(b) In addition to Section 303(f), SSA (concerning an IEVS), which is addressed in subpart C, the following provisions of Federal UC law also specifically require disclosure of State UC information and State-held information pertaining to the Federal UC and benefit programs of Unemployment Compensation for Federal Employees (UCFE), Unemployment Compensation for Ex-Servicemembers (UCX), Trade Adjustment Assistance (TAA) (except for confidential business information collected by States), Disaster Unemployment Assistance (DUA), and any Federal UC benefit extension program:

(1) Section 303(a)(7), SSA, requires State law to provide for making available, upon request, to any agency of the United States charged with the administration of public works or assistance through public employment, disclosure of the following information with respect to each recipient of UC—

(i) Name;

(ii) Address;

(iii) Ordinary occupation;

(iv) Employment status; and

(v) A statement of such recipient's rights to further compensation under the State law.

(2) Section 303(c)(1), SSA, requires each State to make its UC records available to the Railroad Retirement Board, and to furnish such copies of its UC records to the Railroad Retirement Board as the Board deems necessary for its purposes.

(3) Section 303(d)(1), SSA, requires each State UC agency, for purposes of determining an individual's eligibility benefits, or the amount of benefits, under a food stamp program established under the Food Stamp Act of 1977, to disclose, upon request, to officers and employees of the Department of Agriculture, and to officers or employees of any State food stamp agency, any of the following information contained in the records of the State UC agency—

(i) Wage information,

(ii) Whether an individual is receiving, has received, or has made application for, UC, and the amount of any such compensation being received, or to be received, by such individual,

(iii) The current (or most recent) home address of such individual, and

(iv) Whether an individual has refused an offer of employment and, if so, a description of the employment so offered and the terms, conditions, and rate of pay therefore.

(4) Section 303(e)(1), SSA, requires each State UC agency to disclose, upon request, directly to officers or employees of any State or local child support enforcement agency, any wage information contained in the records of the State UC agency for purposes of establishing and collecting child support obligations (not to include custodial parent support obligations) from, and locating, individuals owing such obligations.

(5) Section 303(h), SSA, requires each State UC agency to disclose quarterly, to the Secretary of Health and Human Services (HHS), wage information and claim information as required under Section 453(i)(1) of the SSA (establishing the National Directory of New Hires), contained in the records of such agency, for purposes of Subsections (i)(1), (i)(3), and (j) of Section 453, SSA (establishing the National Directory of New Hires and its uses for purposes of child support enforcement, Temporary Assistance to Needy Families (TANF), TANF research, administration of the earned income tax credit, and use by the Social Security Administration).

(6) Section 303(i), SSA, requires each State UC agency to disclose, upon request, to officers or employees of the Department of Housing and Urban Development (HUD) and to representatives of a public housing agency, for purposes of determining an individual's eligibility for benefits, or the amount of benefits, under a housing assistance program of HUD, any of the following information contained in the records of such State agency about any individual applying for or participating in any housing assistance program administered by HUD who has signed a consent form approved by the Secretary of HUD—

(i) Wage information, and

(ii) Whether the individual is receiving, has received, or has made application for, UC, and the amount of any such compensation being received (or to be received) by such individual.

(7) Section 3304(a)(16), FUTA requires each State UC agency—

(i) To disclose, upon request, to any State or political subdivision thereof administering a Temporary Assistance to Needy Families Agency (TANF) program funded under part A of Title IV of the SSA, wage information contained in the records of the State UC agency which is necessary (as determined by the Secretary of HHS in regulations) for purposes of determining an individual's eligibility for TANF assistance or the amount of TANF assistance; and

(ii) To furnish to the Secretary of HHS, in accordance with that Secretary's regulations at 45 CFR 303.108, wage information (as defined at 45 CFR 303.108(a)(2)) and UC information (as defined at 45 CFR 303.108(a)(3)) contained in the records of such agency for the purposes of the National Directory of New Hires established under Section 453(i) of the SSA.

(8) To comply with WIOA sec. 116(e)(4), States must, to the extent practicable, cooperate in the conduct of evaluations (including related research projects) provided for by the Secretary of Labor or the Secretary of Education under the provisions of Federal law identified in WIOA sec. 116(e)(1); WIOA secs. 169 and 242(c)(2)(D); sec. 12(a)(5), 14, and 107 of the Rehabilitation Act of 1973 (29 U.S.C. 709(a)(5), 711, 727) (applied with respect to programs carried out under title I of that Act (29 U.S.C. 720 *et seq.*)); and the investigations provided for by the Secretary of Labor under sec. 10(b) of the Wagner-Peyser Act (29 U.S.C. 49i(b)). For purposes of this part, States must disclose confidential UC information to a Federal official (or an agent or contractor of a Federal official) requesting such information in the course of such evaluations. This disclosure must be done in accordance with appropriate privacy and confidentiality protections established in this part. This disclosure must be made to the "extent practicable", which means that the disclosure would not interfere with the efficient administration of the State UC law, as required by § 603.5.

(c) Each State law must contain provisions that are interpreted and applied consistently with the requirements listed in this section.

[71 FR 56842, Sept. 27, 2006, as amended at 81 FR 56333, Aug. 19, 2016]

§ 603.7 What requirements apply to subpoenas, other compulsory processes, and disclosure to officials with subpoena authority?

(a) *In general.* Except as provided in paragraph (b) of this section, when a subpoena or other compulsory process is served upon a State UC agency or the State, any official or employee thereof, or any recipient of confidential UC information, which requires the production of confidential UC information or appearance for testimony upon any matter concerning such information, the State or State UC agency or recipient must file and diligently pursue a motion to quash the subpoena or other compulsory process if other means of avoiding the disclosure of confidential UC information are not successful or if the court has not already ruled on the disclosure. Only if such motion is denied by the court or other forum may the requested confidential UC information be disclosed, and only upon such terms as the court or forum may order, such as that the recipient protect the disclosed information and pay the State's or State UC agency's costs of disclosure.

(b) *Exceptions.* The requirement of paragraph (a) of this section to move to quash subpoenas shall not be applicable, so that disclosure is permissible, where—

(1) *Court Decision*—a subpoena or other compulsory legal process has been served and a court has previously issued a binding precedential decision that requires disclosures of this type, or a well-established pattern of prior court decisions have required disclosures of this type, or

(2) *Official with subpoena authority*—Confidential UC information has been subpoenaed, by a local, State or Federal governmental official, other than a clerk of court on behalf of a litigant, with authority to obtain such information by subpoena under State or Federal law. The State or State UC agency may choose to disclose such confidential UC information to these officials without the actual issuance of a subpoena.

§ 603.8 What are the requirements for payment of costs and program income?

(a) *In general.* Except as provided in paragraph (b) of this section, grant funds must not be used to pay any of the costs of making any disclosure of UC information. Grant funds may not be used to pay any of the costs of making any disclosures under § 603.5(d)(2) (third party (other than an agent) or disclosure made on an ongoing basis), § 603.5(e) (optional disclosure to a public official), § 603.5(f) (optional disclosure to an agent or contractor of a public official), and § 603.5(g) (optional disclosure to BLS), § 603.6(b) (mandatory disclosures for non-UC purposes), or § 603.22 (mandatory disclosure for purposes of an IEVS).

(b) *Use of grant funds permitted.* Grant funds paid to a State under Section 302(a), SSA, may be used to pay the costs of only those disclosures necessary for proper administration of the UC program. (This may include some disclosures under § 603.5(a) (concerning public domain information), § 603.5(c) (to an individual or employer), and § 603.5(d)(1) (to an agent).) In addition, grant funds may be used to pay costs of disclosures under § 603.5(i) (for UC Program Oversight and Audits) and § 603.6(a) (for the proper administration of the UC program). Grant funds may also be used to pay costs associated with disclosures under § 603.7(b)(1) (concerning court-ordered compliance with subpoenas) if a court has denied recovery of costs, or to pay costs associated with disclosures under § 603.7(b)(2) (to officials with subpoena authority) if the State UC agency has attempted but not been successful in obtaining reimbursement of costs. Finally, grant funds may be used to pay costs associated with any disclosure of UC information if not more than an incidental amount of staff time and no more than nominal processing costs are involved in making the disclosure.

(c) *Calculation of costs.* The costs to a State or State UC agency of processing and handling a request for disclosure of information must be calculated in accordance with the cost principles and administrative requirements of 29 CFR part 97 and Office of Management and Budget Circular No. A–87 (Revised). For the purpose of calculating such costs, any initial start-up costs incurred by the State UC agency in preparation for making the requested disclosure(s), such as computer reprogramming necessary to respond to the request, and the costs of implementing safeguards and agreements required by §§ 603.9 and 603.10, must be charged to and paid by the recipient. (Start-up costs do not include the costs to the State UC agency of obtaining, compiling, or maintaining information for its own purposes.) Postage or other delivery costs incurred in making any disclosure are part of the costs of making the disclosure. Penalty mail, as defined in 39 U.S.C. 3201(1), must not be used to transmit information being disclosed, except information disclosed for purposes of administration of State UC law. As provided in Sections 453(e)(2) and 453(g) of the SSA, the Secretary of HHS has the authority to determine what constitutes a reasonable amount for the reimbursement for disclosures under Section 303(h), SSA, and Section 3304(a)(16)(B), FUTA.

(d) *Payment of costs.* The costs to a State or State UC agency of making a disclosure of UC information, calculated in accordance with paragraph (c) of this section, must be paid by the recipient of the information or another source paying on behalf of the recipient, either in advance or by way of reimbursement. If the recipient is not a public official, such costs, except for good reason must be paid in advance. For the purposes of this paragraph (d), payment in advance means full payment of all costs before or at the time the disclosed information is given in hand or sent to the recipient. The requirement of payment of costs in this paragraph is met when a State UC agency has in place a reciprocal cost agreement or arrangement with the recipient. As used in this section, *reciprocal* means that the relative benefits received by each are approximately equal. Payment or reimbursement of costs must include any initial start-up costs associated with making the disclosure.

(e) *Program income.* Costs paid as required by this section, and any funds generated by the disclosure of UC information under this part, are program income and may be used only as permitted by 29 CFR 97.25(g) (on program income). Such income may not be used to benefit a State's general fund or other program.

§ 603.9 What safeguards and security requirements apply to disclosed information?

(a) *In general.* For disclosures of confidential UC information under § 603.5(d)(2) (to a third party (other than an agent) or disclosures made on an ongoing basis); § 603.5(e) (to a public official), except as provided in paragraph (d) of this section; § 603.5(f) (to an agent or contractor of a public official); § 603.6(b)(1) through (4), (6), and (7)(i) (as required by Federal UC law); and § 603.22 (to a requesting agency for purposes of an IEVS), a State or State UC agency must require the recipient to safeguard the information disclosed against unauthorized access or redisclosure, as provided in paragraphs (b) and (c) of this section, and must subject the recipient to penalties provided by the State law for unauthorized disclosure of confidential UC information.

(b) *Safeguards to be required of recipients.* (1) The State or State UC agency must:

(i) Require the recipient to use the disclosed information only for purposes authorized by law and consistent with an agreement that meets the requirements of § 603.10;

(ii) Require the recipient to store the disclosed information in a place physically secure from access by unauthorized persons;

(iii) Require the recipient to store and process disclosed information maintained in electronic format, such as magnetic tapes or discs, in such a way that unauthorized persons cannot obtain the information by any means;

(iv) Require the recipient to undertake precautions to ensure that only authorized personnel are given access to disclosed information stored in computer systems;

(v) Require each recipient agency or entity to:

(A) Instruct all personnel having access to the disclosed information about confidentiality requirements, the requirements of this subpart B, and the sanctions specified in the State law for unauthorized disclosure of information, and

(B) Sign an acknowledgment that all personnel having access to the disclosed information have been instructed in accordance with paragraph (b)(1)(v)(A) of this section and will adhere to the State's or State UC agency's confidentiality requirements and procedures which are consistent with this subpart B and the agreement required by § 603.10, and agreeing to report any infraction of these rules to the State UC agency fully and promptly,

(vi) Require the recipient to dispose of information disclosed or obtained, and any copies thereof made by the recipient agency, entity, or contractor, after the purpose for which the information is disclosed is served, except for disclosed information possessed by any court. Disposal means return of the information to the disclosing State or State UC agency or destruction of the information, as directed by the State or State UC agency. Disposal includes deletion of personal identifiers by the State or State UC agency in lieu of destruction. In any case, the information disclosed must not be retained with personal identifiers for longer than such period of time as the State or State UC agency deems appropriate on a case-by-case basis; and

(vii) Maintain a system sufficient to allow an audit of compliance with the requirements of this part.

(2) In the case of disclosures made under § 603.5(d)(2) (to a third party (other than an agent) or disclosures made on an ongoing basis), the State or State UC agency must also—

(i) Periodically audit a sample of transactions accessing information disclosed under that section to assure that the entity receiving disclosed information has on file a written release authorizing each access. The audit must ensure that the information is not being used for any unauthorized purpose;

(ii) Ensure that all employees of entities receiving access to information disclosed under § 603.5(d)(2) are subject to the same confidentiality requirements, and State criminal penalties for violation of those requirements, as are employees of the State UC agency.

(c) *Redisclosure of confidential UC information.* (1) A State or State UC agency may authorize any recipient of confidential UC information under paragraph (a) of this section to redisclose information only as follows:

(i) To the individual or employer who is the subject of the information;

(ii) To an attorney or other duly authorized agent representing the individual or employer;

(iii) In any civil or criminal proceedings for or on behalf of a recipient agency or entity;

(iv) In response to a subpoena only as provided in §603.7;

(v) To an agent or contractor of a public official only if the person redisclosing is a public official, if the redisclosure is authorized by the State law, and if the public official retains responsibility for the uses of the confidential UC information by the agent or contractor;

(vi) From one public official to another if the redisclosure is authorized by the State law;

(vii) When so authorized by Section 303(e)(5), SSA, (redisclosure of wage information by a State or local child support enforcement agency to an agent under contract with such agency for purposes of carrying out child support enforcement) and by State law; or

(viii) When specifically authorized by a written release that meets the requirements of §603.5(d) (to a third party with informed consent).

(2) Information redisclosed under paragraphs (c)(1)(v) and (vi) of this section must be subject to the safeguards in paragraph (b) of this section.

(d) The requirements of this section do not apply to disclosures of UC information to a Federal agency which the Department has determined, by notice published in the FEDERAL REGISTER, to have in place safeguards adequate to satisfy the confidentiality requirement of Section 303(a)(1), SSA.

§603.10 What are the requirements for agreements?

(a) *Requirements.* (1) For disclosures of confidential UC information under §603.5(d)(2) (to a third party (other than an agent) or disclosures made on an ongoing basis); §603.5(e) (to a public official), except as provided in paragraph (d) of this section; §603.5(f) (to an agent or contractor of a public official); §603.6(b)(1) through (4), (6), and (7)(i) (as required by Federal UC law); and §603.22 (to a requesting agency for purposes of an IEVS), a State or State UC agency must enter into a written, enforceable agreement with any agency or entity requesting disclosure(s) of such information. The agreement must be terminable if the State or State UC agency determines that the safeguards in the agreement are not adhered to.

(2) For disclosures referred to in §603.5(f) (to an agent or contractor of a public official), the State or State UC agency must enter into a written, enforceable agreement with the public official on whose behalf the agent or contractor will obtain information. The agreement must hold the public official responsible for ensuring that the agent or contractor complies with the safeguards of §603.9. The agreement must be terminable if the State or State UC agency determines that the safeguards in the agreement are not adhered to.

(b) *Contents of agreement*—(1) *In general.* Any agreement required by paragraph (a) of this section must include, but need not be limited to, the following terms and conditions:

(i) A description of the specific information to be furnished and the purposes for which the information is sought;

(ii) A statement that those who request or receive information under the agreement will be limited to those with a need to access it for purposes listed in the agreement;

(iii) The methods and timing of requests for information and responses to those requests, including the format to be used;

(iv) Provision for paying the State or State UC agency for any costs of furnishing information, as required by §603.8 (on costs);

(v) Provision for safeguarding the information disclosed, as required by §603.9 (on safeguards); and

(vi) Provision for on-site inspections of the agency, entity, or contractor, to assure that the requirements of the

State's law and the agreement or contract required by this section are being met.

(2) In the case of disclosures under § 603.5(d)(2) (to a third party (other than an agent) or disclosures made on an ongoing basis), the agreement required by paragraph (a) of this section must assure that the information will be accessed by only those entities with authorization under the individual's or employer's release, and that it may be used only for the specific purposes authorized in that release.

(c) *Breach of agreement*—(1) *In general.* If an agency, entity, or contractor, or any official, employee, or agent thereof, fails to comply with any provision of an agreement required by this section, including timely payment of the State's or State UC agency's costs billed to the agency, entity, or contractor, the agreement must be suspended, and further disclosure of information (including any disclosure being processed) to such agency, entity, or contractor is prohibited, until the State or State UC agency is satisfied that corrective action has been taken and there will be no further breach. In the absence of prompt and satisfactory corrective action, the agreement must be canceled, and the agency, entity, or contractor must be required to surrender to the State or State UC agency all confidential UC information (and copies thereof) obtained under the agreement which has not previously been returned to the State or State UC agency, and any other information relevant to the agreement.

(2) *Enforcement.* In addition to the actions required to be taken by paragraph (c)(1) of this section, the State or State UC agency must undertake any other action under the agreement, or under any law of the State or of the United States, to enforce the agreement and secure satisfactory corrective action or surrender of the information, and must take other remedial actions permitted under State or Federal law to effect adherence to the requirements of this subpart B, including seeking damages, penalties, and restitution as permitted under such law for any charges to granted funds and all costs incurred by the State or the State UC agency in pursuing the breach of the agreement and enforcement as required by this paragraph (c).

(d) The requirements of this section do not apply to disclosures of UC information to a Federal agency which the Department has determined, by notice published in the FEDERAL REGISTER, to have in place safeguards adequate to satisfy the confidentiality requirement of Section 303(a)(1), SSA, and an appropriate method of paying or reimbursing the State UC agency (which may involve a reciprocal cost arrangement) for costs involved in such disclosures. These determinations will be published in the FEDERAL REGISTER.

§ 603.11 How do States notify claimants and employers about the uses of their information?

(a) *Claimants.* Every claimant for compensation must be notified, at the time of application, and periodically thereafter, that confidential UC information pertaining to the claimant may be requested and utilized for other governmental purposes, including, but not limited to, verification of eligibility under other government programs. Notice on or attached to subsequent additional claims will satisfy the requirement for periodic notice thereafter.

(b) *Employers.* Every employer subject to a State's law must be notified that wage information and other confidential UC information may be requested and utilized for other governmental purposes, including, but not limited to, verification of an individual's eligibility for other government programs.

§ 603.12 How are the requirements of this part enforced?

(a) *Resolving conformity and compliance issues.* For the purposes of resolving issues of conformity and substantial compliance with the requirements set forth in subparts B and C, the provisions of 20 CFR 601.5(b) (informal discussions with the Department of Labor to resolve conformity and substantial compliance issues), and 20 CFR 601.5(d) (Secretary of Labor's hearing and decision on conformity and substantial compliance) apply.

(b) *Conformity and substantial compliance.* Whenever the Secretary of Labor, after reasonable notice and opportunity for a hearing to the State UC agency of a State, finds that the State law fails to conform, or that the State or State UC agency fails to comply substantially, with:

(1) The requirements of Title III, SSA, implemented in subparts B and C of this part, the Secretary of Labor shall notify the Governor of the State and such State UC agency that further payments for the administration of the State UC law will not be made to the State until the Secretary of Labor is satisfied that there is no longer any such failure. Until the Secretary of Labor is so satisfied, the Department of Labor shall make no further payments to such State.

(2) The FUTA requirements implemented in this subpart B, the Secretary of Labor shall make no certification under that section to the Secretary of the Treasury for such State as of October 31 of the 12-month period for which such finding is made.

Subpart C—Mandatory Disclosure for Income and Eligibility Verification System (IEVS)

§ 603.20 What is the purpose and scope of this subpart?

(a) *Purpose.* Subpart C implements Section 303(f), SSA. Section 303(f) requires States to have in effect an income and eligibility verification system, which meets the requirements of Section 1137, SSA, under which information is requested and exchanged for the purpose of verifying eligibility for, and the amount of, benefits available under several federally assisted programs, including the Federal-State UC program.

(b) *Scope.* This subpart C applies only to a State UC agency.

NOTE TO PARAGRAPH (b): Although not implemented in this part 603, Section 1137(a)(1), SSA, provides that each State must require claimants for compensation to furnish to the State UC agency their social security account numbers, as a condition of eligibility for compensation, and further requires States to utilize such account numbers in the administration of the State UC laws. Section 1137(a)(3), SSA, further provides that employers must make quarterly wage reports to a State UC agency, or an alternative agency, for use in verifying eligibility for, and the amount of, benefits. Section 1137(d)(1), SSA, provides that each State must require claimants for compensation, as a condition of eligibility, to declare in writing, under penalty of perjury, whether the individual is a citizen or national of the United States, and, if not, that the individual is in a satisfactory immigration status. Other provisions of Section 1137(d), SSA, not implemented in this regulation require the States to obtain, and individuals to furnish, information which shows immigration status, and require the States to verify immigration status with the Bureau of Citizenship and Immigration Services.

§ 603.21 What is a requesting agency?

For the purposes of this subpart C, *requesting agency* means:

(a) *Temporary Assistance to Needy Families Agency*—Any State or local agency charged with the responsibility of administering a program funded under part A of Title IV of the SSA.

(b) *Medicaid Agency*—Any State or local agency charged with the responsibility of administering the provisions of the Medicaid program under a State plan approved under Title XIX of the SSA.

(c) *Food Stamp Agency*—Any State or local agency charged with the responsibility of administering the provisions of the Food Stamp Program under the Food Stamp Act of 1977.

(d) *Other SSA Programs Agency*—Any State or local agency charged with the responsibility of administering a program under a State plan approved under Title I, X, XIV, or XVI (Supplemental Security Income for the Aged, Blind, and Disabled) of the SSA.

(e) *Child Support Enforcement Agency*—Any State or local child support enforcement agency charged with the responsibility of enforcing child support obligations under a plan approved under part D of Title IV of the SSA.

(f) *Social Security Administration*—Commissioner of the Social Security Administration in establishing or verifying eligibility or benefit amounts under Titles II (Old-Age, Survivors, and Disability Insurance Benefits) and XVI (Supplemental Security Income for the Aged, Blind, and Disabled) of the SSA.

§ 603.22 What information must State UC agencies disclose for purposes of an IEVS?

(a) *Disclosure of information.* Each State UC agency must disclose, upon request, to any requesting agency, as defined in § 603.21, that has entered into an agreement required by § 603.10, wage information (as defined at § 603.2(k)) and claim information (as defined at § 603.2(a)) contained in the records of such State UC agency.

(b) *Format.* The State UC agency must adhere to standardized formats established by the Secretary of HHS (in consultation with the Secretary of Agriculture) and set forth in 42 CFR 435.960 (concerning standardized formats for furnishing and obtaining information to verify income and eligibility).

§ 603.23 What information must State UC agencies obtain from other agencies, and crossmatch with wage information, for purposes of an IEVS?

(a) *Crossmatch with information from requesting agencies.* Each State UC agency must obtain such information from the Social Security Administration and any requesting agency as may be needed in verifying eligibility for, and the amount of, compensation payable under the State UC law.

(b) *Crossmatch of wage and benefit information.* The State UC agency must crossmatch quarterly wage information with UC payment information to the extent that such information is likely, as determined by the Secretary of Labor, to be productive in identifying ineligibility for benefits and preventing or discovering incorrect payments.

PART 604—REGULATIONS FOR ELIGIBILITY FOR UNEMPLOYMENT COMPENSATION

Sec.

AUTHORITY: 42 U.S.C. 1302(a); 42 U.S.C. 503(a)(2) and (5); 26 U.S.C. 3304(a)(1) and (4); 26 U.S.C. 3306(h); 42 U.S.C. 1320b–7(d); Secretary's Order No. 4–75 (40 FR 18515); and Secretary's Order No. 14–75 (November 12, 1975).

SOURCE: 72 FR 1893, Jan. 16, 2007, unless otherwise noted.

§ 604.1 Purpose and scope.

The purpose of this Part is to implement the requirements of Federal UC law that limit a State's payment of UC to individuals who are able to work and available for work. This regulation applies to all State UC laws and programs.

§ 604.2 Definitions.

(a) *Department* means the United States Department of Labor.

(b) *FUTA* means the Federal Unemployment Tax Act, 26 U.S.C. 3301 *et seq.*

(c) *Social Security Act* means the Social Security Act, 42 U.S.C. 501 *et seq.*

(d) *State* means a State of the United States of America, the District of Columbia, the Commonwealth of Puerto Rico, and the United States Virgin Islands.

(e) *State UC agency* means the agency of the State charged with the administration of the State's UC law.

(f) *State UC law* means the law of a State approved under Section 3304(a), FUTA (26 U.S.C. 3304(a)).

(g) *Unemployment Compensation (UC)* means cash benefits payable to individuals with respect to their unemployment.

(h) *Week of unemployment* means a week of total, part-total or partial unemployment as defined in the State's UC law.

§ 604.3 Able and available requirement—general principles.

(a) A State may pay UC only to an individual who is able to work and available for work for the week for which UC is claimed.

(b) Whether an individual is able to work and available for work under paragraph (a) of this section must be tested by determining whether the individual is offering services for which a labor market exists. This requirement does not mean that job vacancies must exist, only that, at a minimum, the type of services the individual is able and available to perform is generally performed in the labor market. The State must determine the geographical scope of the labor market for an individual under its UC law.

(c) The requirement that an individual be able to work and available for work applies only to the week of unemployment for which UC is claimed. It does not apply to the reasons for the individual's separation from employment, although the separation may indicate the individual was not able to work or available for work during the week the separation occurred. This Part does not address the authority of States to impose disqualifications with respect to separations. This Part does not limit the States' ability to impose additional able and available requirements that are consistent with applicable Federal laws.

§ 604.4 Application—ability to work.

(a) A State may consider an individual to be able to work during the week of unemployment claimed if the individual is able to work for all or a portion of the week claimed, provided any limitation on his or her ability to work does not constitute a withdrawal from the labor market.

(b) If an individual has previously demonstrated his or her ability to work and availability for work following the most recent separation from employment, the State may consider the individual able to work during the week of unemployment claimed despite the individual's illness or injury, unless the individual has refused an offer of suitable work due to such illness or injury.

§ 604.5 Application—availability for work.

(a) *General application.* A State may consider an individual to be available for work during the week of unemployment claimed under any of the following circumstances:

(1) The individual is available for any work for all or a portion of the week claimed, provided that any limitation placed by the individual on his or her availability does not constitute a withdrawal from the labor market.

(2) The individual limits his or her availability to work which is suitable for such individual as determined under the State UC law, provided the State law definition of suitable work does not permit the individual to limit his or her availability in such a way that the individual has withdrawn from the labor market. In determining whether the work is suitable, States may, among other factors, take into consideration the education and training of the individual, the commuting distance from the individual's home to the job, the previous work history of the individual (including salary and fringe benefits), and how long the individual has been unemployed.

(3) The individual is on temporary lay-off and is available to work only for the employer that has temporarily laid-off the individual.

(b) *Jury service.* If an individual has previously demonstrated his or her availability for work following the most recent separation from employment and is appearing for duty before any court under a lawfully issued summons during the week of unemployment claimed, a State may consider the individual to be available for work. For such an individual, attendance at jury duty may be taken as evidence of continued availability for work. However, if the individual does not appear as required by the summons, the State must determine if the reason for non-attendance indicates that the individual is not able to work or is not available for work.

(c) *Approved training.* A State must not deny UC to an individual for failure to be available for work during a week if, during such week, the individual is in training with the approval of the State agency. However, if the individual fails to attend or otherwise participate in such training, the State must determine if the reason for non-attendance or non-participation indicates that the individual is not able to work or is not available for work.

(d) *Self-employment assistance.* A State must not deny UC to an individual for failure to be available for work during a week if, during such week, the individual is participating in a self-employment assistance program and meets all the eligibility requirements of such self-employment assistance program.

(e) *Short-time compensation.* A State must not deny UC to an individual participating in a short-time compensation (also known as worksharing) program under State UC law for failure to be available for work during a week, but such individual will be required to be available for his or her normal workweek.

(f) *Alien status.* To be considered available for work in the United States for a week, the alien must be legally authorized to work that week in the United States by the appropriate agency of the United States government. In determining whether an alien is legally authorized to work in the United States, the State must follow the requirements of section 1137(d) of the SSA (42 U.S.C. 1320b-7(d)), which relate to verification of and determination of an alien's status.

(g) *Relation to ability to work requirement.* A State may consider an individual available for work if the State finds the individual able to work under § 604.4(b) despite illness or injury.

(h) *Work search.* The requirement that an individual be available for work does not require an active work search on the part of the individual. States may, however, require an individual to be actively seeking work to be considered available for work, or States may impose a separate requirement that the individual must actively seek work.

§ 604.6 Conformity and substantial compliance.

(a) *In general.* A State's UC law must conform with, and the administration of its law must substantially comply with, the requirements of this regulation for purposes of certification under:

(1) Section 3304(c) of the FUTA (26 U.S.C. 3304(c)), with respect to whether employers are eligible to receive credit against the Federal unemployment tax established by section 3301 of the FUTA (26 U.S.C. 3301), and

(2) Section 302 of the SSA (42 U.S.C. 502), with respect to whether a State is eligible to receive Federal grants for the administration of its UC program.

(b) *Resolving Issues of Conformity and Substantial Compliance.* For the purposes of resolving issues of conformity and substantial compliance with the requirements of this regulation, the following provisions of 20 CFR 601.5 apply:

(1) Paragraph (b) of this section, pertaining to informal discussions with the Department of Labor to resolve conformity and substantial compliance issues, and

(2) Paragraph (d) of this section, pertaining to the Secretary of Labor's hearing and decision on conformity and substantial compliance.

(c) *Result of failure to conform or substantially comply*—(1) *FUTA requirements.* Whenever the Secretary of Labor, after reasonable notice and opportunity for a hearing to the State UC agency, finds that the State UC law fails to conform, or that the State or State UC agency fails to comply substantially, with the requirements of the FUTA, as implemented in this regulation, then the Secretary of Labor shall make no certification under such act to the Secretary of the Treasury for such State as of October 31 of the 12-month period for which such finding is made. Further, the Secretary of Labor must notify the Governor of the State and such State UC agency that further payments for the administration of the State UC law will not be made to the State.

(2) *SSA requirements.* Whenever the Secretary of Labor, after reasonable notice and opportunity for a hearing to the State UC agency, finds that the State UC law fails to conform, or that the State or State UC agency fails to comply substantially, with the requirements of title III, SSA (42 U.S.C. 501–504), as implemented in this regulation, then the Secretary of Labor must notify the Governor of the State and such State UC agency that further payments for the administration of the State UC law will not be made to the State until the Secretary of Labor is satisfied that there is no longer any such failure. Until the Secretary of Labor is so satisfied, the Department of Labor will not make further payments to such State.

PART 606—TAX CREDITS UNDER THE FEDERAL UNEMPLOYMENT TAX ACT; ADVANCES UNDER TITLE XII OF THE SOCIAL SECURITY ACT

Subpart A—General

Sec.

Subpart B—Tax Credit Reduction [Reserved]

Subpart C—Relief From Tax Credit Reduction

Subpart D—Interest on Advances

Subpart E—Relief from Interest Payment

AUTHORITY: 42 U.S.C. 1102; 42 U.S.C. 1322(b)(2)(C); 26 U.S.C. 7805(a); Secretary's Order No. 3–2007, April 3, 2007 (72 FR 15907).

SOURCE: 53 FR 37429, Sept. 26, 1988, unless otherwise noted.

EDITORIAL NOTE: Nomenclature changes to part 606 appear at 71 FR 35513, June 21, 2006.

Subpart A—General

§ 606.1 Purpose and scope.

(a) *In general.* The regulations in this part 606 are issued to implement the tax credit provisions of the Federal Unemployment Tax Act, and the loan provisions of title XII of the Social Security Act. The regulations on tax credits cover all of the subjects of 3302 of the Federal Unemployment Tax Act (FUTA), except subsections (c)(3) and (e). The regulations on loans cover all of the subjects in title XII of the Social Security Act.

(b) *Scope.* This part 606 covers general matters relating to this part in this subpart A, and in the following subparts includes specific subjects described in general terms as follows:

(1) Subpart B describes the tax credit reductions under the Federal Unemployment Tax Act, which relate to outstanding balances of advances made under title XII of the Social Security Act.

(2) Subpart C describes the various forms of relief from tax credit reductions, and the criteria and standards for grant of such relief in the form of—

(i) A cap on tax credit reduction,

(ii) Avoidance of tax credit reduction, and

(iii) Waiver of and substitution for additional tax credit reduction.

(3) Subpart D describes the interest rates on advances made under title XII of the Social Security Act, dues dates for payment of interest, and other related matters.

(4) Subpart E describes the various forms of relief from payment of interest, and the criteria and standards for grant of such relief in the form of—

(i) May/September delay of interest payments,

(ii) High unemployment deferral of interest payments,

(iii) High unemployment delay of interest payments, and

(iv) Maintenance of solvency effort required to retain a deferral previously granted.

§ 606.2 Total credits allowable.

The total credits allowed to an employer subject to the tax imposed by section 3301 of the Federal Unemployment Tax Act shall not exceed 5.4 percent with respect to taxable years beginning after December 31, 1984.

§ 606.3 Definitions.

For the purposes of the Acts cited and this part—

Act means as appropriate the Federal Unemployment Tax Act (26 U.S.C. 3301–3311), or title XII of the Social Security Act (42 U.S.C. 1321–1324).

Advance means a transfer of funds to a State unemployment fund, for the purpose of paying unemployment compensation, from the Federal unemployment account in the Unemployment

Trust Fund, pursuant to section 1202 of the Social Security Act.

Average High Cost Multiple (AHCM) for a State as of December 31 of a calendar year is calculated by dividing the State's reserve ratio, as defined in § 606.3, by the State's average high cost rate (AHCR), as defined in § 606.3, for the same year. Final calculations are rounded to the nearest multiple of 0.01.

Average High Cost Rate (AHCR) for a State is calculated as follows:

(1) Determine the time period over which calculations are to be made by selecting the longer of:

(i) The 20-calendar year period that ends with the year for which the AHCR calculation is made; or

(ii) The number of years beginning with the calendar year in which the first of the last three completed national recessions began, as determined by the National Bureau of Economic Research, and ending with the calendar year for which the AHCR is being calculated.

(2) For each calendar year during the selected time period, calculate the benefit-cost ratio, as defined in § 606.3; and

(3) Average the three highest calendar year benefit cost ratios for the selected time period from paragraph (2) of this definition. Final calculations are rounded to the nearest multiple of 0.01 percent.

Benefit-cost ratio for a calendar year is the percentage obtained by dividing—

(1) The total dollar sum of—

(i) All compensation actually paid under the State law during such calendar year, including in such total sum all regular, additional, and extended compensation, as defined in section 205 of the Federal-State Extended Unemployment Compensation Act of 1970, and excluding from such total sum—

(A) Any such compensation paid for which the State is entitled to reimbursement or was reimbursed under the provisions of any Federal Law, and

(B) Any such compensation paid which is attributable to services performed for a reimbursing employer, and which is not included in the total dollar amount reported under paragraph (c)(1)(i)(A) of this section, and

(ii) Any interest paid during such calendar year on any advance, by

(2) The total wages (as defined in § 606.3) with respect to such calendar year.

(3) For cap purposes, if any percentage determined by this computation for a calendar year is not a multiple of 0.1 percent, such percentage shall be reduced to the nearest multiple of 0.1 percent. For funding goal purposes, if any percentage determined by this computation for a calendar year is not a multiple of 0.01 percent, such percentage is rounded to the nearest multiple of 0.01 percent.

Contributions means payments required by a State law to be made into an unemployment fund by any person on account of having individuals in his employ, to the extent that such payments are made by him without being deducted or deductible from the remuneration of individuals in his employ.

Federal unemployment tax means the excise tax imposed under section 3301 of the Federal Unemployment Tax Act on employers with respect to having individuals in their employ.

Fiscal year means the Federal fiscal year which begins on October 1 of a year and ends on September 30, of the next succeeding year.

FUTA refers to the Federal Unemployment Tax Act.

Reserve ratio is calculated by dividing the balance in the State's account in the unemployment trust fund (UTF) as of December 31 of such year by the total wages paid workers covered by the unemployment compensation (UC) program during the 12 months ending on December 31 of such year. Final calculations are rounded to the nearest multiple of 0.01 percent.

State unemployment fund or *unemployment fund* means a special fund established under a State law for the payment of unemployment compensation to unemployed individuals, and which is an "unemployment fund" as defined in section 3306(f) of the Federal Unemployment Tax Act.

Taxable year means the calendar year.

Unemployment tax rate means, for any taxable year and with respect to any

State, the percentage obtained by dividing the total amount of contributions paid into the State unemployment fund with respect to such taxable year by total wages as defined in § 606.3.

Wages, taxable means the total sum of remuneration which is subject to contributions under a State law.

Wages, total means the total sum of all remuneration covered by a State law, disregarding any dollar limitation on the amount of remuneration which is subject to contributions under the State law.

[53 FR 37429, Sept. 26, 1988, as amended at 71 FR 35513, June 21, 2006; 75 FR 57156, Sept. 17, 2010]

§ 606.4 Redelegation of authority.

(a) *Redelegation to OWS Administrator.* The Administrator, Office of Workforce Security (hereinafter "OWS Administrator"), is redelegated authority to make the determinations required under this part. This redelegation is contained in Employment and Training Order No. 1–84, published in the FEDERAL REGISTER on November 14, 1983 (48 FR 51870).

(b) *Delegation by Governor.* The Governor of a State, as used in this part, refers to the highest executive official of a State. Wherever in this part an action is required by or of the Governor of a State, such action may be taken by the Governor or may be taken by a delegatee of the Governor if the Department is furnished appropriate proof of an authoritative delegation of authority.

[53 FR 37429, Sept. 26, 1988, as amended at 71 FR 35514, June 21, 2006]

§ 606.5 Verification of estimates and review of determinations.

The Department of Labor (hereinafter "Department") shall verify all information and data provided by a State under this part, and the State shall comply with such provisions as the Department considers necessary to assure the correctness and verification of such information and data. The State agency of a State affected by a determination made by the OWS Administrator under this part may seek review of such determination by a higher level official of the Employment and Training Administration.

§ 606.6 Information, reports, and studies.

A State shall furnish to the Secretary of Labor such information and reports and conduct such studies as the Secretary determines are necessary or appropriate for carrying out the purposes of this part, including any additional information or data the OWS Administrator may require for the purposes of making determinations under subparts C and E of this part.

[53 FR 37429, Sept. 26, 1988, as amended at 71 FR 35514, June 21, 2006]

Subpart B—Tax Credit Reduction [Reserved]

Subpart C—Relief From Tax Credit Reduction

§ 606.20 Cap on tax credit reduction.

(a) *Applicability.* Subsection (f) of section 3302 of FUTA authorizes a limitation (cap) on the reduction of tax credits by reason of an outstanding balance of advances, if the OWS Administrator determines with respect to a State, on or before November 10 of a taxable year, that—

(1) No action was taken by the State during the 12-month period ending on September 30 of such taxable year which has resulted, or will result, in a reduction in the State's unemployment tax effort, as defined in § 606.21(a);

(2) No action was taken by the State during the 12-month period ending on September 30 of such taxable year which has resulted, or will result, in a net decrease in the solvency of the State unemployment compensation system, as defined in § 606.21(b);

(3) The State unemployment tax rate (as defined in § 606.3) for the taxable year equals or exceeds the average benefit-cost ratio (as defined in § 606.3) for the calendar years in the five-calendar year period ending with the calendar year immediately preceding the taxable year for which the cap is requested, under the rules specified in § 606.21 (c) and (d); and

(4) The outstanding balance of advances to the State on September 30 of the taxable year was not greater than the outstanding balance of advances to

the State on September 30 of the third preceding taxable year.

(b) *Maximum tax credit reduction.* If a State qualifies for a cap, the maximum tax credit reduction for the taxable year shall not exceed 0.6 percent, or, if higher, the tax credit reduction that was in effect for the taxable year preceding the taxable year for which the cap is requested.

(c) *Year not taken into account.* If a State qualifies for a cap for any year, the year and January 1 of the year to which the cap applies will not be taken into account for purposes of determining reduction of tax credit for subsequent taxable years.

(d) *Partial caps.* Partial caps obtained under subsection (f)(8) are no longer available. Nevertheless, for the purposes of applying section 3302(c)(2) to subsequent taxable years, partial cap credits earned will be taken into account for purposes of determining reduction of tax credits. Also, the taxable year to which the partial cap applied (and January 1 thereof) will be taken into account for purposes of determining reduction of tax credits for subsequent taxable years.

[53 FR 37429, Sept. 26, 1988, as amended at 75 FR 57156, Sept. 17, 2010]

§ 606.21 Criteria for cap.

(a) *Reduction in unemployment tax effort.* (1) For purposes of paragraph (a)(1) of § 606.20, a reduction in a State's unemployment tax effort will have occurred with respect to a taxable year if any action is or was taken (legislative, judicial, or administrative,) that is effective during the 12-month period ending on September 30 of such taxable year, which has resulted in or will result in a reduction of the amount of contributions paid or payable or the amounts that were or would have been paid or payable but for such action.

(2) Actions that will result in a reduction in tax effort include, but are not limited to, a reduction in the taxable wage base, the tax rate schedule, tax rates, or taxes payable (including surtaxes) that would not have gone into effect but for the legislative, judicial, or administrative action taken. Notwithstanding the foregoing criterion, a reduction in unemployment tax effort resulting from any provision of the State law enacted prior to August 13, 1981, will not be taken into account as a reduction in the State's unemployment tax effort for the purposes of this section.

(b) *Net decrease in solvency.* For purposes of paragraph (a)(2) of § 606.20, a net decrease in the solvency of the State's unemployment compensation system will have occurred with respect to a taxable year if any action is or was taken (legislative, judicial, or administrative), that is effective during the 12-month period ending on September 30 of such taxable year, which has resulted in or will result in an increase in benefits without at least an equal increase in taxes, or a decrease in taxes without at least an equal decrease in benefits. Notwithstanding the foregoing criterion, a decrease in solvency resulting from any provision of the State law enacted prior to August 13, 1981, will not be taken into account as a reduction in solvency of the State's unemployment compensation system for the purposes of this section.

(c) *State unemployment tax rate.* For purposes of paragraph (a)(3) of § 606.20, the State unemployment tax rate is defined in § 606.3. If such percentage is not a multiple of 0.1 percent, the percentage shall remain unrounded.

(d) *State five-year average benefit cost ratio.* The average benefit-cost ratio for the 5 preceding calendar years is the percentage determined by dividing the sum of the benefit-cost ratios for the 5 years by five. If such percentage is not a multiple of 0.1 percent, the percentage shall remain unrounded.

[53 FR 37429, Sept. 26, 1988, as amended at 75 FR 57156, Sept. 17, 2010]

§ 606.22 Application for cap.

(a) *Application.* (1) The Governor of the State shall make application, addressed to the Secretary of Labor, no later than July 1 of a taxable year with respect to which a State requests a cap on tax credit reduction. The Governor is required to notify the Department on or before October 15 of such taxable year of any action occurring after the date of the initial application and effective prior to October 1 of such year that would impact upon the State's application.

(2) The OWS Administrator will make a determination on the application on or before November 10 of such taxable year, will notify the applicant and the Secretary of the Treasury of such determination, and will cause notice of such determination to be published in the FEDERAL REGISTER.

(b) *Anticipated impact statement.* In support of the application by the Governor, there shall be submitted with the application (on or before October 15), for the purposes of the criteria described in §§ 606.20(a) (1) and (2) and 606.21 (a) and (b), a description of all statutory provisions enacted or amended, regulations adopted or revised, administrative policies and procedures adopted or revised, and judicial decisions given effect, which are effective during the 12-month period ending on September 30 of the taxable year for which a cap on tax credit reduction is requested, and an anticipated impact statement (AIS) for each such program action in the following respect—

(1) The estimated dollar effect on each program action upon expenditures for compensation from the State unemployment fund and for the amounts of contributions paid or payable in such 12-month period, including the effect of interaction among program actions, and with respect to program actions for which dollar impact cannot be estimated or is minor or negligible, indicate whether the impact is positive or negative;

(2) If a program action has no such dollar effect, an explanation of why there is or will be no such effect;

(3) A description of assumptions and methodology used and the basis for the financial estimate of the impact of each program action described in paragraphs (b)(1) and (b)(2) of this section; and

(4) A comparision of the program actions described in paragraphs (b)(1) and (b)(2) of this section with the program actions prior to the Federal fiscal year (as defined in § 606.3) which ends on such September 30.

(c) *Unemployment tax rate.* With respect to the unemployment tax rate criterion described in §§ 606.20(a)(3) and 606.21(c), the application shall include an estimate for the taxable year with respect to which a cap on tax credit reduction is requested and actual data for the prior two years as follows:

(1) The amount of taxable wages as defined in § 606.3;

(2) The amount of total wages as defined in § 606.3; and

(3) The estimated distribution of taxable wages, as defined in § 606.3, by tax rate under the State law.

(d) *Benefit cost ratio.* With respect to the benefit cost ratio criterion described in §§ 606.20(a)(3) and 606.21(d), the application shall include for each of the five calendar years prior to the taxable year for which a cap on tax credit reduction is requested, the following data:

(1) The total dollar sum of compensation actually paid under the State law during the calendar year, including in such total sum all regular, additional, and extended compensation as defined in section 205 of the Federal-State Extended Unemployment Compensation Act of 1970, but excluding from such total sum—

(i) The total dollar amount of such compensation paid for which the State is entitled to reimbursement or was reimbursed under the provisions of any Federal law;

(ii) The total dollar amount of such compensation paid which is attributable to services performed for a reimbursing employer, and which is not included in the total amount reported under paragraph (d)(1)(i) of this section;

(2) The total dollar amount of interest paid during the calendar year on any advance; and

(3) The total dollar amount of wages (as defined in § 606.3) with respect to such calendar year.

(e) *Documentation required.* Copies of the sources of or authority for each program action described in paragraph (b) of this section shall be submitted with each application for a cap on tax credit reduction. In addition, a notation shall be made on each AIS of where all figures referred to are contained in reports required by the Department or in other data sources.

(f) *State contact person.* The Department may request additional information or clarification of information submitted bearing upon an application for a cap on tax credit reduction. To expedite requests for such information, the name and telephone number of an appropriate State official shall be included in the application by the Governor.

[53 FR 37429, Sept. 26, 1988, as amended at 75 FR 57156, Sept. 17, 2010]

§ 606.23 Avoidance of tax credit reduction.

(a) *Applicability.* Subsection (g) of section 3302 of FUTA authorizes a State to avoid a tax credit reduction for a taxable year by meeting the three requirements of subsection (g). These requirements are met if the OWS Administrator determines that:

(1) Advances were repaid by the State during the one-year period ending on November 9 of the taxable year in an amount not less than the sum of—

(i) The potential additional taxes (as estimated by the OWS Administrator) that would be payable by the State's employers if paragraph (2) of section 3302(c) of FUTA were applied for such taxable year (as estimated with regard to the cap on tax credit reduction for which the State qualifies under §§ 606.20 to 606.22 with respect to such taxable year), and

(ii) Any advances made to such State during such one-year period under title XII of the Social Security Act;

(2) There will be adequate funds in the State unemployment fund (as estimated by the OWS Administrator) sufficient to pay all benefits when due and payable under the State law during the three-month period beginning on November 1 of such taxable year without receiving any advance under title XII of the Social Security Act; and

(3) There is a net increase (as estimated by the OWS Administrator) in the solvency of the State unemployment compensation system for the taxable year and such net increase equals or exceeds the potential additional taxes for such taxable year as estimated under paragraph (a)(1)(i) of this section.

(b) *Net increase in solvency.* (1) The net increase in solvency for a taxable year, as determined for the purposes of paragraph (a)(3) of this section, must be attributable to legislative changes made in the State law after the later of—

(i) September 3, 1982, or

(ii) The date on which the first advance is taken into account in determining the amount of the potential additional taxes.

(2) The OWS Administrator shall determine the net increase in solvency by first estimating the difference between revenue receipts and benefit outlays under the law in effect for the year for which avoidance is requested, as if the relevant changes in State law referred to in paragraph (b)(1) of this section were not in effect for such year. The OWS Administrator shall then estimate the difference between revenue receipts and benefit outlays under the law in effect for the year for which the avoidance is requested, taking into account the relevant changes in State law referred to in paragraph (b)(1) of this section. The amount (if any) by which the second estimated difference exceeds the first estimated difference shall constitute the net increase in solvency for the purposes of this section.

(c) *Year taken into account.* If a State qualifies for avoidance for any year, that year and January 1 of that year to which the avoidance applies will be taken into account for purposes of determining reduction of tax credits for subsequent taxable years.

§ 606.24 Application for avoidance.

(a) *Application.* (1) The Governor of the State shall make application, addressed to the Secretary of Labor, no later than July 1 of a taxable year with respect to which a State requests avoidance of tax credit reduction. The Governor is required to notify the Department on or before October 15 of such taxable year of any action impacting upon the State's application occurring subsequent to the date of the initial application and on or before November 10.

(2) The OWS Administrator will make a determination on the application as of November 10 of such taxable year, will notify the applicant and the Secretary of the Treasury of such determination, and will cause notice of such determination to be published in the FEDERAL REGISTER.

(b) *Information.* (1) The application shall include a statement of the amount of advances repaid and to be repaid during the one-year period ending on November 9 of the taxable year for which avoidance is requested. If the amount repaid as of the date of the application is less than the amount required to satisfy the provisions of § 606.23(a)(1), the Governor shall provide a report later of the additional repayments that have been made in the remainder of the one-year period ending on November 9 of the taxable year, for the purposes of meeting the provisions of § 606.23(a)(1).

(2) The application also shall include estimates of revenue receipts, benefit outlays, and end-of-month fund balance for each month in the period beginning with September of the taxable year for which avoidance is requested through the subsequent January. Actual data for the comparable period of the preceding year also shall be included in the application in order to determine the reasonableness of such estimates.

(3) The application also shall include a description of State law changes, effective for the taxable year for which the avoidance is requested, which resulted in a net increase in the solvency of the State unemployment compensation system, and documentation which supports the State's estimate of the net increase in solvency for such taxable year.

§ 606.25 Waiver of and substitution for additional tax credit reduction.

A provision of subsection (c)(2) of section 3302 of FUTA provides that, for a State that qualifies, the additional tax credit reduction applicable under subparagraph (C), beginning in the fifth consecutive year of a balance of outstanding advances, shall be waived and the additional tax credit reduction applicable under subparagraph (B) shall be substituted. The waiver and substitution are granted if the OWS Administrator determines that the State has taken no action, effective during the 12-month period ending on September 30 of the year for which the waiver and substitution are requested, which has resulted or will result in a net decrease in the solvency of the State unemployment compensation system as determined for the purposes of §§ 606.20(a)(2) and 606.21(b).

§ 606.26 Application for waiver and substitution.

(a) *Application.* The Governor of the State shall make application addressed to the Secretary of Labor, no later than July 1 of a taxable year with respect to which a State requests waiver and substitution. Any such application shall contain the supportive data and information required by § 606.22(b) for the purposes of §§ 606.20(a)(2) and 606.21(b). The Governor is required to notify the Department on or before October 15 of such taxable year of action occurring after the date of the initial application and effective prior to October 1 of such year that would impact upon the State's application.

(b) *Notification of determination.* The OWS Administrator will make a determination on the application as of November 10 of the taxable year, will notify the applicant and the Secretary of the Treasury of the resulting tax credit reduction to be applied, and will cause notice of such determination to be published in the FEDERAL REGISTER.

Subpart D—Interest on Advances

§ 606.30 Interest rates on advances.

Advances made to States pursuant to title XII of the Social Security Act shall be subject to interest payable on the due dates specified in § 606.31.[1] The interest rate for each calendar year will be 10 percent or, if less, the rate determined by the Secretary of the Treasury and announced to the States by the Department.

[53 FR 37429, Sept. 26, 1988, as amended at 71 FR 35514, June 21, 2006]

§ 606.31 Due dates for payment of interest. [Reserved]

§ 606.32 Types of advances subject to interest.

(a) *Payment of interest.* Except as otherwise provided in paragraph (b) of this section each State shall pay interest on any advance made to such State under title XII of the Social Security Act.

(b) *Cash flow loans*—(1) *Availability of interest-free advances.* Advances are

[1] (EDITORIAL NOTE: This section will be added at a later date.)

deemed cash flow loans and shall be free of interest provided that:

(i) The advances are repaid in full prior to October 1 of the calendar year in which the advances are made;

(ii) The State does not receive an additional advance after September 30 of the same calendar year in which the advance is made. If the State receives an additional advance after September 30 of the same calendar year in which earlier advances were made, interest on the fully repaid earlier advance(s) is due and payable not later than the day following the date of the first such additional advance. The administrator of the State agency must notify the Secretary of Labor no later than September 10 of the same calendar year of those loans deemed to be cash flow loans and not subject to interest. This notification must include the date and amount of each loan made beginning January 01 through September 30 of the same calendar year, and a copy of documentation sent to the Secretary of the Treasury requesting loan repayment transfer(s) from the State's account in the UTF to the Federal unemployment account in the UTF; and

(iii) The State has met the funding goals described in paragraph (b)(2) or (b)(3) of this section.

(2) *Funding goals.* This paragraph (b)(2) is applicable to all States as of January 1, 2019. A State has met the funding goals requirement if:

(i) The State, as of December 31 of any of the 5 consecutive calendar years preceding the calendar year in which such advances are made, had an AHCM of at least 1.00, as determined under § 606.3; and

(ii) The State maintained tax effort as determined under paragraph (b)(4) of this section.

(3) *Phasing in funding goals.* This paragraph (b)(3) applies for calendar years 2014 through 2018. A State has met the funding goals requirement if it has satisfied the solvency criterion in paragraph (i), and the maintenance of tax effort criteria in paragraph (ii), of this § 606.32(b)(3).

(i) A State has met the solvency criterion if:

(A) For calendar year 2014, as of December 31 of any of the 5 consecutively preceding calendar years, the State had an AHCM of at least 0.50, as determined under § 606.3;

(B) For calendar year 2015, as of December 31 of any of the 5 consecutively preceding calendar years, the State had an AHCM of at least 0.60, as determined under § 606.3;

(C) For calendar year 2016, as of December 31 of any of the 5 consecutively preceding calendar years, the State had an AHCM of at least 0.70, as determined under § 606.3;

(D) For calendar year 2017, as of December 31 of any of the 5 consecutively preceding calendar years, the State had an AHCM of at least 0.80, as determined under § 606.3;

(E) For calendar year 2018, as of December 31 of any of the 5 consecutively preceding calendar years, the State had an AHCM of at least 0.90, as determined under § 606.3;

(ii) A State has met the maintenance of tax effort criteria if it maintained tax effort as determined under paragraph (b)(4) of this section.

(4) *Maintenance of tax effort criteria.* A State has maintained tax effort if, for every year between the last calendar year in which it met the solvency criterion in paragraph (b)(2)(i) or (b)(3)(i) of this section and the calendar year in which an interest-free advance is taken, the State's unemployment tax rate as defined in § 606.3 for the calendar year is at least—

(i) 80 percent of the prior year's unemployment tax rate; and

(ii) 75 percent of the State 5-year average benefit-cost ratio, as determined under § 606.21(d).

[53 FR 37429, Sept. 26, 1988, as amended at 75 FR 57156, Sept. 17, 2010]

§ 606.33 No payment of interest from unemployment fund. [Reserved]

§ 606.34 Reports of interest payable. [Reserved]

§ 606.35 Order of application for repayments. [Reserved]

Subpart E—Relief from Interest Payment

§ 606.40 May/September delay.

Subsection (b)(3)(B) of section 1202 of the Social Security Act permits a

State to delay payment of interest accrued on advances made during the last five months of the Federal fiscal year (May, June, July, August, and September) to no later than December 31 of the next succeeding calendar year. If the payment is delayed, interest on the delayed payment will accrue from the normal due date (*i.e.*, September 30) and in the same manner as if the interest due on the advance(s) was an advance made on such due date. The Governor of a State which has decided to delay such interest payment shall notify the Secretary of Labor no later than September 1 of the year with respect to which the delay is applicable.

§ 606.41 High unemployment deferral.

(a) *Applicability*. Subsection (b)(3)(C) of section 1202 of the Social Security Act permits a State to defer payment of, and extend the payment for, 75 percent of interest charges otherwise due prior to October 1 of a year if the OWS Administrator determines that high unemployment conditions existed in the State.

(b) *High unemployment defined*. For purposes of this section, high unemployment conditions existed in the State if the State's rate of insured unemployment (as determined for purposes of 20 CFR 615.12) under the State law with respect to the period consisting of the first six months of the preceding calendar year equalled or exceeded 7.5 percent; this means that in weeks 1 (that week which includes January 1 of the year) through 26 of such preceding calendar year, the rate of insured unemployment reported by the State and accepted by the Department under 20 CFR part 615 must have averaged a percentage equalling or exceeding 7.5 percent.

(c) *Schedule of deferred payments*. The State must pay prior to October 1 one-fourth of the interest due, and must pay a minimum of one-third of the deferred amount prior to October 1 in each of the three years following the year in which deferral was granted; at the State's option payment of deferred interest may be accelerated.

(d) *Related criteria*. Timely payment of one-fourth of the interest due prior to October 1 is a precondition to obtaining deferral of payment of 75 percent of the interest due. No interest shall accrue on such deferred interest.

(e) *Application for deferral and determination*. (1) The Governor of a State which has decided to request such deferral of interest payment shall apply to the Secretary of Labor no later than July 1 of the taxable year for which the deferral is requested.

(2) The OWS Administrator will determine whether deferral is or is not granted on the basis of the Department's records of reports of the rates of insured unemployment and information obtained from the Department of the Treasury as to the timely and full payment of one-fourth of the interest due.

§ 606.42 High unemployment delay.

(a) *Applicability*. Paragraph (9) of section 1202 (b) of the Social Security Act permits a State to delay for a period not exceeding nine months the interest payment due prior to October 1 if, for the most recent 12-month period prior to such October 1 for which data are available, the State had an average total unemployment rate of 13.5 percent or greater.

(b) *Delayed due date*. An interest payment delayed under paragraph (9) must be paid in full not later than the last official Federal business day prior to the following July 1; at the State's option payment of delayed interest may be accelerated. No interest shall accrue on such delayed payment.

(c) *Application for delay in payment and determination*. (1) The Governor of a State which has decided to request delay in payment of interest under paragraph (9) shall apply to the Secretary of Labor no later than July 1 of the taxable year for which the delay is requested.

(2) The OWS Administrator will determine whether delay is or is not granted on the basis of seasonally unadjusted civilian total unemployment rate data published by the Department's Bureau of Labor Statistics.

§ 606.44 Notification of determinations.

The OWS Administrator will make determinations under §§ 606.41, 606.42, and 606.43 on or before September 10 of the taxable year, will promptly notify the applicants and the Secretary of the

Treasury of such determinations, and will cause notice of such determinations to be published in the FEDERAL REGISTER. The OWS Administrator also will inform the Secretary of the Treasury and cause notice to be published in the FEDERAL REGISTER of information with respect to delayed payment of interest as provided in §606.40.

PART 609—UNEMPLOYMENT COMPENSATION FOR FEDERAL CIVILIAN EMPLOYEES

Subpart A—General Provisions

Subpart B—Administration of UCFE Program

Subpart C—Responsibilities of Federal Agencies

AUTHORITY: 5 U.S.C. 8508; Secretary's Order No. 4–75, 40 FR 18515; (5 U.S.C. 301). Interpret and apply secs. 8501–8508 of title 5, United States Code.

SOURCE: 47 FR 54687, Dec. 3, 1982, unless otherwise noted.

Subpart A—General Provisions

§609.1 Purpose and application.

(a) *Purpose.* Subchapter I of chapter 85, title 5 of the United States Code, as amended by Pub. L. 94–566, 90 Stat. 2667, 5 U.S.C. 8501–8508, provides for a permanent program of unemployment compensation for unemployed Federal civilian employees. The unemployment compensation provided for in subchapter I is hereinafter referred to as unemployment compensation for Federal employees, or UCFE. The regulations in this part are issued to implement the UCFE Program.

(b) *First rule of construction.* The Act and the implementing regulations in this part shall be construed liberally so as to carry out the purposes of the Act.

(c) *Second rule of construction.* The Act and the implementing regulations in this part shall be construed so as to assure insofar as possible the uniform interpretation and application of the Act throughout the United States.

(d) *Effectuating purpose and rules of construction.* (1) In order to effectuate the provisions of this section, each State agency shall forward to the United States Department of Labor (hereafter Department), not later than 10 days after issuance, a copy of each judicial or administrative decision ruling on an individual's entitlement to payment of UCFE or to credit for a waiting period. On request of the Department, a State agency shall forward to the Department a copy of any determination or redetermination ruling on an individual's entitlement to UCFE or waiting period credit.

(2) If the Department believes that a determination, redetermination, or decision is inconsistent with the Department's interpretation of the Act or this part, the Department may at any time notify the State agency of the Department's view. Thereafter the State agency shall issue a redetermination or appeal if possible, and shall not follow such determination, redetermination, or decision as a precedent; and, in any subsequent proceedings which involve such determination, redetermination, or decision, or wherein such determination, redetermination, or decision is cited as precedent or otherwise relied upon, the State agency shall inform

the claims deputy or hearing officer or court of the Department's view and shall make all reasonable efforts, including appeal or other proceedings in an appropriate forum, to obtain modification, limitation, or overruling of the determination, redetermination, or decision.

(3) If the Department believes that a determination, redetermination, or decision is patently and flagrantly violative of the Act or this part, the Department may at any time notify the State agency of the Department's view. If the determination, redetermination, or decision in question denies UCFE to a claimant, the steps outlined in paragraph (d)(2) of this section shall be followed by the State agency. If the determination, redetermination, or decision in question awards UCFE to a claimant, the benefits are "due" within the meaning of section 303(a)(1) of the Social Security Act, 42 U.S.C. 503(a)(1), and therefore must be paid promptly to the claimant. However, the State agency shall take the steps outlined in paragraph (d)(2) of this section, and payments to the claimant may be temporarily delayed if redetermination or appeal action is taken not more than one business day following the day on which the first payment otherwise would be issued to the claimant; and the redetermination action is taken or appeal is filed to obtain a reversal of the award of UCFE and a ruling consistent with the Department's view; and the redetermination action or appeal seeks an expedited redetermination or appeal within not more than two weeks after the redetermination action is taken or the appeal is filed. If redetermination action is not taken or appeal is not filed within the above time limit, or a redetermination or decision is not obtained within the two-week limit, or any redetermination or decision or order is issued which affirms the determination, redetermination, or decision awarding UCFE or allows it to stand in whole or in part, the benefits awarded must be paid promptly to the claimant.

(4)(i) If any determination, redetermination, or decision, referred to in paragraph (d)(2) or paragraph (d)(3) of this section, is treated as a precedent for any future UCFE claim or claim under the UCX Program (part 614 of this chapter), the Secretary will decide whether the Agreement with the State entered into under the Act shall be terminated.

(ii) In the case of any determination, redetermination, or decision that is not legally warranted under the Act or this part, including any determination, redetermination, or decision referred to in paragraph (d)(3) of this section, the Secretary will decide whether the State shall be required to restore the funds of the United States for any sums paid under such a determination, redetermination, or decision, and whether, in the absence of such restoration, the Agreement with the State shall be terminated and whether other action shall be taken to recover such sums for the United States.

(5) A State agency may request reconsideration of a notice issued pursuant to paragraph (d)(2) of paragraph (d)(3) of this section, and shall be given an opportunity to present views and arguments if desired.

(6) Concurrence of the Department in a determination, redetermination, or decision shall not be presumed from the absence of a notice issued pursuant to this section.

§ 609.2 Definitions of terms.

For the purposes of the Act and this part:

(a) *Act* means subchapter I of chapter 85, title 5, United States Code, 5 U.S.C. 8501–8508.

(b) *Agreement* means the agreement entered into pursuant to the Act between a State and the Secretary under which the State agency of the State agrees to make payments of unemployment compensation in accordance with the Act and the regulations and procedures thereunder prescribed by the Department.

(c) *Based period* means the base period as defined by the applicable State law for the benefit year.

(d) *Benefit year* means the benefit year as defined by the applicable State law, and if not so defined the term means the period prescribed in the agreement with the State or, in the absence of an Agreement, the period prescribed by the Department.

(e) *Federal agency* means any department, agency, or governmental body of the United States, including any instrumentality wholly or partially owned by the United States, in any branch of the Government of the United States, which employs any individual in Federal civilian service.

(f) *Federal civilian service* means service performed in the employ of any Federal agency, except service performed—

(1) By an elective official in the executive or legislative branches of the Government of the United States;

(2) As a member of the Armed Forces or the Commissioned Corps of the National Oceanic and Atmospheric Administration;

(3) By Foreign Service personnel for whom special separation allowances are provided under chapter 14 of title 22 of the United States Code;

(4) Outside the 50 States, the Commonwealth of Puerto Rico, the Virgin Islands, and the District of Columbia, by an individual who is not a citizen of the United States;

(5) By an individual excluded by regulations of the Office of Personnel Management from civil service retirement coverage provided by subchapter III of chapter 83 of title 5 of the United States Code because the individual is paid on a contract or fee basis;

(6) By an individual receiving nominal pay and allowances of $12 or less a year;

(7) In a hospital, home, or other institution of the United States by a patient or inmate thereof;

(8) By a student-employee as defined by 5 U.S.C. 5351; that is: (i) A student nurse, medical or dental intern, resident-in-training, student dietitian, student physical therapist, or student occupational therapist, assigned or attached to a hospital, clinic, or medical or dental laboratory operated by an agency as defined in section 5351; or

(ii) Any other student-employee, assigned or attached primarily for training purposes to such a hospital, clinic, or medical or dental laboratory operated by such an agency, who is designated by the head of the agency with the approval of the Office of Personnel Management;

(9) By an individual serving on a temporary basis in case of fire, storm, earthquake, flood, or other similar emergency;

(10) By an individual employed under a Federal relief program to relieve the individual from unemployment;

(11) As a member of a State, county, or community committee under the Agricultural Stabilization and Conservation Service or of any other board, council, committee, or other similar body, unless such body is composed exclusively of individuals otherwise in the full-time employ of the United States;

(12) By an officer or member of the crew on or in connection with an American vessel which is:

(i) Owned by or bareboat chartered to the United States, and

(ii) The business of which is conducted by a general agent of the Secretary of Commerce; and

(iii) If contributions on account of such service are required under section 3305(g) of the Internal Revenue Code of 1986 (26 U.S.C. 3305(g)) to be made to an unemployment fund under a State law;

(13) By an individual excluded by any other Federal law from coverage under the UCFE Program; or

(14) By an individual whose service is covered by the UCX Program to which part 614 of this chapter applies.

(g) *Federal employee* means an individual who has performed Federal civilian service.

(h) *Federal findings* means the facts reported by a Federal agency pertaining to an individual as to: (1) Whether or not the individual has performed Federal civilian service for such an agency;

(2) The period or periods of such Federal civilian service;

(3) The individual's Federal wages; and

(4) The reasons for termination of the individual's Federal civilian service.

(i) *Federal wages* means all pay and allowances, in cash and in kind, for Federal civilian service.

(j) *First claim* means an initial claim for unemployment compensation under the UCFE Program, the UCX Program (part 614 of this chapter), a State law, or some combination thereof, whereby a benefit year is established under an applicable State law.

(k) *Official station* means the State (or country, if outside the United States) designated on a Federal employee's notification of personnel action terminating the individual's Federal civilian service (Standard Form 50 or its equivalent) as the individual's "duty station." If the form of notification does not specify the Federal employee's "duty station", the individual's official station shall be the State or country designated under "name and location of employing office" on such form or designated as the individual's place of employment on an equivalent form.

(l) *Secretary* means the Secretary of Labor of the United States.

(m) *State* means the 50 States, the District of Columbia, the Commonwealth of Puerto Rico, and the Virgin Islands.

(n) *State agency* means the agency of the State which administers the applicable State law and is administering the UCFE Program in the State pursuant to an Agreement with the Secretary.

(o)(1) *State law* means the unemployment compensation law of a State approved by the Secretary under section 3304 of the Internal Revenue Code of 1986, 26 U.S.C. 3304, if the State is certified under section 3304(c) of the Internal Revenue Code of 1986, 26 U.S.C. 3304(c).

(2) *Applicable State law* means the State law made applicable to a UCFE claimant by § 609.8.

(p)(1) *Unemployment compensation* means cash benefits (including dependents' allowances) payable to individuals with respect to their unemployment, and includes regular, additional, emergency, and extended compensation.

(2) *Regular compensation* means unemployment compensation payable to an individual under any State law, but not including additional compensation or extended compensation.

(3) *Additional compensation* means unemployment compensation totally financed by a State and payable under a State law by reason of conditions of high unemployment or by reason of other special factors.

(4) *Emergency compensation* means supplementary unemployment compensation payable under a temporary Federal law after exhaustion of regular and extended compensation.

(5) *Extended compensation* means unemployment compensation payable to an individual for weeks of unemployment in an extended benefit period, under those provisions of a State law which satisfy the requirements of the Federal-State Extended Unemployment Compensation Act of 1970, as amended, 26 U.S.C. 3304 note, and part 615 of this chapter, with respect to the payment of extended compensation.

(q) *Week* means, for purposes of eligibility for and payment of UCFE, a week as defined in the applicable State law.

(r) *Week of unemployment* means a week of total, part-total, or partial unemployment as defined in the applicable State law, which shall be applied in the same manner and to the same extent to all employment and earnings, and in the same manner and to the same extent for the purposes of the UCFE Program, as if the individual filing for UCFE were filing a claim for State unemployment compensation.

[47 FR 54687, Dec. 3, 1982, as amended at 71 FR 35514, June 21, 2006]

Subpart B—Administration of UCFE Program

§ 609.3 Eligibility requirements for UCFE.

An individual shall be eligible to receive a payment of UCFE or to waiting period credit with respect to a week of unemployment if:

(a) The individual has Federal civilian service and Federal wages in the base period under the applicable State law;

(b) The individual meets the qualifying employment and wage requirements of the applicable State law, either on the basis of Federal civilian service and Federal wages alone or in combination with service and wages covered under a State law or under the UCX Program (part 614 of this chapter);

(c) The individual has filed an initial claim for UCFE and, as appropriate, has filed a timely claim for waiting period credit or a payment of UCFE with respect to that week of unemployment; and

(d) The individual is totally, part-totally, or partially unemployed, and is able to work, available for work, and seeking work within the meaning of or as required by the applicable State law, and is not subject to disqualification under this part or the applicable State law, with respect to that week of unemployment.

§ 609.4 Weekly and maximum benefit amounts.

(a) *Total unemployment.* The weekly amount of UCFE payable to an eligible individual for a week of total unemployment shall be the amount that would be payable to the individual as unemployment compensation for a week of total unemployment as determined under the applicable State law.

(b) *Partial and part-total unemployment.* The weekly amount of UCFE payable for a week of partial or part-total unemployment shall be the amount that would be payable to the individual as unemployment compensation for a week of partial or part-total unemployment as determined under the applicable State law.

(c) *Maximum amount.* The maximum amount of UCFE which shall be payable to an eligible individual during and subsequent to the individual's benefit year shall be the maximum amount of all unemployment compensation that would be payable to the individual as determined under the applicable State law.

(d) *Computation rules.* (1) The weekly and maximum amounts of UCFE payable to an individual under the UCFE Program shall be determined under the applicable State law to be in the same amount, on the same terms, and subject to the same conditions as the State unemployment compensation which would be payable to the individual under the applicable State law if the individual's Federal civilian service and Federal wages assigned or transferred under this part to the State had been included as employment and wages covered by that State law.

(2) All Federal civilian service and Federal wages for all Federal agencies shall be considered employment with a single employer for purposes of the UCFE Program.

§ 609.5 Claims for UCFE.

(a) *First claims.* A first claim for UCFE shall be filed by an individual in any State agency of any State (or Canada) according to the applicable State law, and on a form prescribed by the Department which shall be furnished to the individual by the State agency where the claim is filed.

(b) *Weekly claims.* Claims for waiting week credit and payments of UCFE for weeks of unemployment shall be filed in any State agency (or Canada) at the times and in the manner as claims for State unemployment compensation are filed under the applicable State law, and on forms prescribed by the Department which shall be furnished to the individual by the State agency where the claim is filed.

(c) *Secretary's standard.* The procedure for reporting and filing claims for UCFE and waiting period credit shall be consistent with this part 609 and the Secretary's "Standard for Claim Filing, Claimant Reporting, Job Finding and Employment Services" (*Employment Security Manual*, part V, sections 5000 *et seq.*).

§ 609.6 Determinations of entitlement; notices to individual.

(a) *Determination of first claim.* The State agency whose State law applies to an individual under § 609.8 shall, promptly upon the filing of a first claim for UCFE, determine whether the individual is eligible and whether a disqualification applies, and, if the individual is found to be eligible, the individual's benefit year and the weekly and maximum amounts of UCFE payable to the individual.

(b) *Determinations of weekly claims.* The State agency promptly shall, upon the filing of a claim for payment of UCFE or waiting period credit with respect to a week, determine whether the individual is entitled to a payment of UCFE or waiting period credit with respect to such week, and, if entitled, the amount of UCFE or waiting period credit to which the individual is entitled.

(c) *Redetermination.* The provisions of the applicable State law concerning the right to request, or authority to undertake, reconsideration of a determination pertaining to State unemployment compensation under the applicable State law shall apply to determinations pertaining to UCFE.

(d) *Notices to individual.* The State agency promptly shall give notice in writing to the individual of any determination or redetermination of a first claim, and, except as may be authorized under paragraph (g) of this section, of any determination or redetermination of any weekly claim which denies UCFE or waiting period credit or reduces the weekly amount or maximum amount initially determined to be payable. Each notice of determination or redetermination shall include such information regarding the determination or redetermination and notice of right to reconsideration or appeal, or both, as is furnished with written notices of determinations and redeterminations with respect to claims for State unemployment compensation; and where information furnished by a Federal agency was considered in making the determination, or redetermination, the notice thereof shall include an explanation of the right of the individual to seek additional information pursuant to § 609.23 and/or a reconsideration of Federal findings pursuant to § 609.24.

(e) *Obtaining information for claim determinations.* (1) Information required for the determination of claims for UCFE shall be obtained by the State agency from claimants, employers, and others, in the same manner as information is obtained for claim purposes under the applicable State law, but information (including additional and reconsidered Federal findings) shall be obtained from the Federal agency that employed the UCFE claimant as prescribed in §§ 609.21 through 609.25. On request by a UCFE claimant, the State agency shall seek additional information pursuant to § 609.23 and reconsideration of Federal findings pursuant to § 609.24.

(2) If Federal findings have not been received from a Federal agency within 12 days after the request for information was submitted to the Federal agency, the State agency shall determine the individual's entitlement to UCFE on the basis of an affidavit completed by the individual on a form prescribed by the Department. In addition, the individual shall submit for examination by the State agency any documents issued by the Federal agency (for example, Standard Form 50 or W–2) verifying that the individual performed services for and received wages from such Federal agency.

(3) If Federal findings received by a State agency after a determination has been made under this section contain information which would result in a change in the individual's eligibility for or entitlement to UCFE, the State agency promptly shall make a redetermination and notify the individual, as provided in this section. All payments of UCFE made prior to or after such redetermination shall be adjusted in accordance therewith.

(f) *Promptness.* Full payment of UCFE when due shall be consistent with this part 609 and shall be made with the greatest promptness that is administratively feasible, but the provisions of part 640 of this chapter (relating to promptness of benefit payments) shall not be applicable to the UCFE Program.

(g) *Secretary's standard.* The procedures for making determinations and redeterminations, and furnishing written notices of determinations, redeterminations, and rights of appeal to individuals applying for UCFE, shall be consistent with this part 609 and with the Secretary's "Standard for Claim Determinations—Separation Information" (*Employment Security Manual,* part V, sections 6010 *et seq.*).

[47 FR 54687, Dec. 3, 1982, as amended at 71 FR 35514, June 21, 2006]

§ 609.7 Appeal and review.

(a) *Applicable State law.* The provisions of the applicable State law concerning the right of appeal and fair hearing from a determination or redetermination of entitlement to State unemployment compensation shall apply to determinations and redeterminations of eligibility for or entitlement to UCFE and waiting period credit. Any such determination or redetermination shall be subject to appeal and review only in the manner and to the extent provided in the applicable State law with respect to determinations and redeterminations of entitlement to State unemployment compensation.

(b) *Rights of appeal and fair hearing.* The provisions on right to appeal and opportunity for a fair hearing with respect to claims for UCFE shall be consistent with this part and with sections 303(a)(1) and 303(a)(3) of the Social Security Act, 42 U.S.C. 503(a)(1) and 503(a)(3).

(c) *Promptness on appeals.* (1) Decisions on appeals under the UCFE Program shall accord with the Secretary's "Standard for Appeals Promptness—Unemployment Compensation" in part 650 of this chapter, and with § 609.1(d).

(2) Any provision of an applicable State law for advancement or priority of unemployment compensation cases on judicial calendars, or otherwise intended to provide for the prompt payment of unemployment compensation when due, shall apply to proceedings involving claims for UCFE.

(d) *Appeal and review by Federal agency.* If a Federal agency believes that a State agency's determination or redetermination of an individual's eligibility for or entitlement to UCFE is incorrect, the Federal agency may seek appeal and review of such determination or redetermination in the same manner as an interested employer may seek appeal and review under the applicable State law.

[47 FR 54687, Dec. 3, 1982, as amended at 71 FR 35514, June 21, 2006]

§ 609.8 The applicable State for an individual.

(a) *The applicable State.* The applicable State for an individual shall be the State to which the individual's Federal civilian service and Federal wages are assigned or transferred under this section. The applicable State law for the individual shall be the State law of such State.

(b) *Assignment of service and wages.* (1) An individual's Federal civilian service and Federal wages shall be assigned to the State in which the individual had his or her last official station prior to filing a first claim unless:

(i) At the time a first claim is filed the individual resides in another State in which, after separation from Federal civilian service, the individual performed service covered under the State law, in which case all of the individual's Federal civilian service and wages shall be assigned to the latter State; or

(ii) Prior to filing a first claim an individual's last official station was outside the States, in which case all of the individual's Federal civilian service and Federal wages shall be assigned to the State in which the individual resides at the time the individual files a first claim, provided the individual is personally present in a State when the individual files the first claim.

(2) Federal civilian service and wages assigned to a State in error shall be reassigned for use by the proper State agency. An appropriate record of a reassignment shall be made by the State agency which makes the reassignment.

(3) Federal civilian service and Federal wages assigned to a State shall be transferred to another State where such transfer is necessary for the purposes of a combined-wage claim filed by an individual.

(c) *Assignment deemed complete.* All of an individual's Federal civilian service and Federal wages shall be deemed to have been assigned to a State upon the filing of a first claim. Federal civilian service and Federal wages shall be assigned to a State only in accordance with paragraph (b) of this section.

(d) *Use of assigned service and wages.* All assigned Federal civilian service and Federal wages shall be used only by the State to which assigned or transferred in accordance with paragraph (b) of this section.

§ 609.9 Provisions of State law applicable to UCFE claims.

(a) *Particular provisions applicable.* Except where the result would be inconsistent with the provisions of the Act or this part or the procedures thereunder prescribed by the Department, the terms and conditions of the applicable State law which apply to claims for, and the payment of, State unemployment compensation shall apply to claims for, and the payment of, UCFE and claims for waiting period credit. The provisions of the applicable State law which shall apply include, but are not limited to:

(1) Claim filing and reporting;

(2) Information to individuals, as appropriate;

(3) Notices to individuals and Federal agencies, as appropriate, including notice to each individual of each determination and redetermination of eligibility for or entitlement to UCFE;

(4) Determinations and redeterminations;

(5) Ability to work, availability for work, and search for work; and

(6) Disqualifications.

(b) *IBPP.* The *Interstate Benefit Payment Plan* shall apply, where appropriate, to individuals filing claims for UCFE.

(c) *Wage combining.* The State's provisions complying with the *Interstate Arrangement for Combining Employment and Wages* (part 616 of this chapter) shall apply, where appropriate, to individuals filing claims for UCFE.

(d) *Procedural requirements.* The provisions of the applicable State law which apply hereunder to claims for and the payment of UCFE shall be applied consistently with the requirements of title III of the Social Security Act and the Federal Unemployment Tax Act which are pertinent in the case of State unemployment compensation, including but not limited to those standards and requirements specifically referred to in the provisions of this part, except as provided in paragraph (f) of § 609.6.

§ 609.10 Restrictions on entitlement.

(a) *Disqualification.* If the week of unemployment for which an individual claims UCFE is a week to which a disqualification for State unemployment compensation applies under the applicable State law, or would apply but for the fact that the individual has no right to such compensation, the individual shall not be entitled to a payment of UCFE for that week.

(b) *Allocation of terminal annual leave payments.* Lump-sum terminal annual leave payments shall not be allocated by a Federal agency and shall be allocated by a State agency in the same manner as similar payments to individuals employed by private employers are allocated under the applicable State law. In a State in which a private employer has an option as to the period to which such payments shall be allocated, such payments shall be allocated to the date of separation from employment.

§ 609.11 Overpayments; penalties for fraud.

(a) *False statements and representations.* Section 8507(a) of the Act provides that if a State agency, the Department, or a court of competent jurisdiction finds that an individual—

(1) Knowingly has made, or caused to be made by another, a false statement or representation of a material fact, or knowingly has failed, or caused another to fail, to disclose a material fact; and

(2) As a result of that action has received an amount as UCFE to which the individual was not entitled; the individual shall repay the amount to the State agency or the Department. Instead of requiring repayments, the State agency or the Department may recover the amount by deductions from UCFE payable to the individual during the 2-year period after the date of the finding. A finding by a State agency or the Department may be made only after an opportunity for a fair hearing, subject to such further review as may be appropriate under § 609.7.

(b) *Prosecution for fraud.* Section 1919 of title 18, United States Code, provides that whoever makes a false statement or representation of a material fact knowing it to be false, or knowingly fails to disclose a material fact, to obtain or increase for himself or for any other individual any payment authorized to be paid under chapter 85 of title 5, United States Code, or under an agreement thereunder, shall be fined not more than $1,000 or imprisoned not more than one year, or both.

(c) *Absence of fraud.* If a State agency or court of competent jurisdiction finds that an individual has received a payment of UCFE to which the individual was not entitled under the Act and this part, which was not due to a false statement or representation as provided in paragraph (a) or (b) of this section, the individual shall be liable to repay to the applicable State the total sum of the payment to which the individual was not entitled, and the State agency shall take all reasonable measures authorized under any State law or Federal law to recover for the account of the United States the total sum of the payment to which the individual was not entitled.

(d) *Recovery by offset.* (1) The State agency shall recover, insofar as is possible, the amount of any overpayment which is not repaid by the individual, by deductions from any UCFE payable to the individual under the Act and this part, or from any unemployment compensation payable to the individual under any Federal unemployment compensation law administered by the State agency, or from any assistance or allowance payable to the individual with respect to unemployment under any other Federal law administered by the State agency.

(2) A State agency shall also recover, insofar as is possible, the amount of any overpayment of UCFE made to the individual by another State, by deductions from any UCFE payable by the State agency to the individual under the Act and this part, or from any unemployment compensation payable to the individual under any Federal unemployment compensation law administered by the State agency, or from any assistance or allowance payable to the individual with respect to unemployment under any other Federal law administered by the State agency.

(3) Recoupment of fraudulent overpayments referred to in paragraph (a) of this section shall be limited to the 2-year period stated in that paragraph. Recoupment of fraudulent overpayments referred to in paragraph (b) of this section, and nonfraudulent overpayments referred to in paragraph (c) of this section shall be subject to any time limitation on recoupment provided for in the State law that applies to the case.

(e) *Debts due the United States.* UCFE payable to an individual shall be applied by the State agency for the recovery by offset of any debt due to the United States from the individual, but shall not be applied or used by the State agency in any manner for the payment of any debt of the individual to any State or any other entity or person except pursuant to a court order for child support or alimony in accordance with the law of the State and section 459 of the Social Security Act, 42 U.S.C. 659.

(f) *Application of State law.* (1) Except as indicated in paragraph (a) of this section, any provision of State law that may be applied for the recovery of overpayments or prosecution for fraud, and any provision of State law authorizing waiver of recovery of overpayments of unemployment compensation, shall be applicable to UCFE.

(2) In the case of any finding of false statement or representation under the Act and paragraph (a) of this section, or prosecution for fraud under 18 U.S.C. 1919 or pursuant to paragraph (f)(1) of this section, the individual shall be disqualified or penalized in accordance with the provisions of the applicable State law relating to fraud in connection with a claim for State unemployment compensation.

(g) *Final decision.* Recovery of any overpayment of UCFE shall not be enforced by the State agency until the determination or redetermination establishing the overpayment has become final, or if appeal is taken from the determination or redetermination, until the decision after opportunity for a fair hearing has become final.

(h) *Procedural requirements.* (1) The provisions of paragraphs (c), (d), and (g) of § 609.6 shall apply to determinations and redeterminations made pursuant to this section.

(2) The provisions of § 609.7 shall apply to determinations and redeterminations made pursuant to this section.

(i) *Fraud detection and prevention.* Provisions in the procedures of each State with respect to detection and prevention of fraudulent overpayments of UCFE shall be, as a minimum, commensurate with the procedures adopted by the State with respect to State unemployment compensation and consistent with the Secretary's "Standard for Fraud and Overpayment Detection" (*Employment Security Manual,* part V, section 7510 *et seq.*).

(j) *Recovered overpayments.* An amount repaid or recouped under this section shall be—

(1) Deposited in the fund from which payment was made, if the repayment was to a State agency; or

(2) Returned to the Treasury of the United States and credited to the current applicable appropriation, fund, or

account from which payment was made, if the repayment was to the Department.

§609.12 Inviolate rights to UCFE.

Except as specifically provided in this part, the rights of individuals to UCFE shall be protected in the same manner and to the same extent as the rights of persons to State unemployment compensation are protected under the applicable State law. Such measures shall include protection of applicants for UCFE from waiver, release, assignment, pledge, encumbrance, levy, execution, attachment, and garnishment of their rights to UCFE, except as provided in §609.11. In the same manner and to the same extent, individuals shall be protected from discrimination and obstruction in regard to seeking, applying for, and receiving any right to UCFE.

§609.13 Recordkeeping; disclosure of information.

(a) *Recordkeeping.* Each State agency will make and maintain records pertaining to the administration of the UCFE Program as the Department requires, and will make all such records available for inspection, examination, and audit by such Federal officials or employees as the Department may designate or as may be required by law.

(b) *Disclosure of Information.* Information in records maintained by a State agency in administering the UCFE Program shall be kept confidential, and information in such records may be disclosed only in the same manner and to the same extent as information with respect to State unemployment compensation and the entitlement of individuals thereto may be disclosed under the applicable State law. This provision on the confidentiality of information maintained in the administration of the UCFE Program shall not apply, however, to the Department or for the purposes of §§609.11 or 609.13, or in the case of information, reports and studies required pursuant to §§609.17 or 609.25, or where the result would be inconsistent with the Freedom of Information Act (5 U.S.C. 552), the Privacy Act of 1974, as amended (5 U.S.C. 552a), or regulations of the Department promulgated thereunder.

[47 FR 54687, Dec. 3, 1982, as amended at 71 FR 35514, June 21, 2006]

§609.14 Payments to States.

(a) *State entitlement.* Each State is entitled to be paid by the United States with respect to each individual whose base period wages included Federal wages, an amount bearing the same ratio to the total amount of compensation paid to such individual as the amount of the individual's Federal wages in the individual's base period bears to the total amount of the individual's base period wages.

(b) *Payment.* Each State shall be paid, either in advance or by way of reimbursement, as may be determined by the Department, the sum that the Department estimates the State is entitled to receive under the Act and this part for each calendar month. The sum shall be reduced or increased by the amount which the Department finds that its estimate for an earlier calendar month was greater or less than the sum which should have been paid to the State. An estimate may be made on the basis of a statistical, sampling, or other method agreed on by the Department and the State agency.

(c) *Certification by the Department.* The Department, from time to time, shall certify to the Secretary of the Treasury the sum payable to each State under this section. The Secretary of the Treasury, before audit or settlement by the General Accounting Office, shall pay the State in accordance with the certification from the funds for carrying out the purposes of the Act and this part.

(d) *Use of money.* Money paid a State under the Act and this part may be used solely for the purposes for which it is paid. Money so paid which is not used solely for these purposes shall be returned, at the time specified by the Agreement, to the Treasury of the United States and credited to the current applicable appropriation, fund, or account from which payments to states under the Act and this part may be made.

§ 609.15 Public access to Agreements.

The State agency of a State will make available to any individual or organization a true copy of the Agreement with the State for inspection and copying. Copies of an Agreement may be furnished on request to any individual or organization upon payment of the same charges, if any, as apply to the furnishing of copies of other records of the State agency.

§ 609.16 Administration in absence of an Agreement.

(a) *Administering Program.* The Department shall administer the UCFE Program through personnel of the Department or through other arrangements under procedures prescribed by the Department, in the case of any State which does not have an Agreement with the Secretary as provided for in 5 U.S.C. 8502. The procedures prescribed by the Department under this section shall be consistent with the Act and this part.

(b) *Applicable State law.* On the filing by an individual of a claim for UCFE in accordance with arrangements under this section, UCFE shall be paid to the individual, if eligible, in the same amount, on the same terms, and subject to the same conditions as would be paid to the individual under the applicable State law if the individual's Federal civilian service and Federal wages had been included as employment and wages under the State law. Any such claim shall include the individual's Federal civilian service and Federal wages, combined with any service and wages covered by State law. However, if the individual, without regard to his or her Federal civilian service and Federal wages, has employment or wages sufficient to qualify for compensation during the benefit year under that State law, then payments of UCFE under this section may be made only on the basis of the individual's Federal civilian service and Federal wages.

(c) *Fair hearing.* An individual whose claim for UCFE is denied under this section is entitled to a fair hearing under rules of procedure prescribed by the Department. A final determination by the Department with respect to entitlement to UCFE under this section is subject to review by the courts in the same manner and to the same extent as is provided by section 205(g) of the Social Security Act, 42 U.S.C. 405(g).

§ 609.17 Information, reports, and studies.

State agencies shall furnish to the Department such information and reports and conduct such studies as the Department determines are necessary or appropriate for carrying out the purposes of the UCFE Program.

Subpart C—Responsibilities of Federal Agencies

§ 609.20 Information to Federal civilian employees.

Each Federal agency shall:

(a) Furnish information to its employees as to their rights and responsibilities under the UCFE Program and 18 U.S.C. 1919; and

(b) Furnish a completed copy of a form approved by the Department, "Notice to Federal Employee About Unemployment Compensation," in accordance with instructions thereon, to each employee at the time of separation from Federal civilian service, when transferred from one payroll office to another, or when the office responsible for distribution of the form is advised that an individual is in nonpay status for seven consecutive days or more.

§ 609.21 Findings of Federal agency.

(a) *Answering request.* Within four workdays after receipt from a State agency of a request for Federal findings on a form furnished by the State agency, and prescribed by the Department, a Federal agency shall make such Federal findings, complete all copies of the form, and transmit the completed copies to the State agency. If documents necessary for completion of the form have been assigned to an agency records center or the Federal Records Center in St. Louis, the Federal agency shall obtain the necessary information from the records center. Any records center shall give priority to such a request.

(b) *Failure to meet time limit.* If a completed form containing the Federal agency's findings cannot be returned within four workdays of receipt, the Federal agency immediately shall inform the State agency, and shall include an estimated date by which the completed form will be returned.

(c) *Administrative control.* Each Federal agency shall maintain a control of all requests for Federal findings received by it, and the Federal agency's response to each request. The records shall be maintained so as to enable the Federal agency to ascertain at any time the number of such forms that have not been returned to State agencies, and the dates of the Federal agency's receipt of such unreturned forms.

§ 609.22 Correcting Federal findings.

If a Federal agency ascertains at any time within one year after it has returned a completed form reporting its findings, that any of its findings were erroneous, it shall promptly correct its error and forward its corrected findings to the State agency.

§ 609.23 Furnishing additional information.

On receipt of a request for additional information from a State agency, a Federal agency shall consider the information it supplied initially in connection with such request and shall review its findings. The Federal agency promptly shall forward to the State agency such additional findings as will respond to the request. The Federal agency shall, if possible, respond within four workdays after the receipt of a request under this section.

§ 609.24 Reconsideration of Federal findings.

On receipt of a request for reconsideration of Federal findings from a State agency, the Federal agency shall consider the initial information supplied in connection with such request and shall review its findings. The Federal agency shall correct any errors or omissions in its findings and shall affirm, modify, or reverse any or all of its findings in writing. The Federal agency promptly shall forward its reconsidered findings to the requesting authority. The Federal agency shall, if possible, respond within four workdays after the receipt of a request under this section.

§ 609.25 Furnishing other information.

(a) *Additional Information.* In addition to the information required by §§ 609.21, 609.22, 609.23, and 609.24, a Federal agency shall furnish to a State agency or the Department, within the time requested, any information which it is not otherwise prohibited from releasing by law, which the Department determines is necessary for the administration of the UCFE Program.

(b) *Reports.* Federal agencies shall furnish to the Department or State agencies such reports containing such information as the Department determines are necessary or appropriate for carrying out the purposes of the UCFE Program.

§ 609.26 Liaison with Department.

To facilitate the Department's administration of the UCFE Program, each Federal agency shall designate one or more of its officials to be the liaison with the Department. Each Federal agency will inform the Department of its designation(s) and of any change in a designation.

PART 614—UNEMPLOYMENT COMPENSATION FOR EX-SERVICEMEMBERS

Subpart A—General Provisions

Sec.

Subpart B—Administration of UCX Program

Subpart C—Responsibilities of Federal Military Agencies and State Agencies

AUTHORITY: 5 U.S.C. 8508; Secretary's Order No. 4–75 (40 FR 18515).

SOURCE: 47 FR 54697, Dec. 3, 1982, unless otherwise noted.

Subpart A—General Provisions

§ 614.1 Purpose and application.

(a) *Purpose.* Subchapter II of chapter 85, title 5 of the United States Code (5 U.S.C. 8521-8525) provides for a permanent program of unemployment compensation for unemployed individuals separated from the Armed Forces. The unemployment compensation provided for in subchapter II is hereinafter referred to as Unemployment Compensation for Ex-servicemembers, or UCX. The regulations in this part are issued to implement the UCX Program.

(b) *First rule of construction.* The Act and the implementing regulations in this part shall be construed liberally so as to carry out the purposes of the Act.

(c) *Second rule of construction.* The Act and the implementing regulations in this part shall be construed so as to assure insofar as possible the uniform interpretation and application of the Act throughout the United States.

(d) *Effectuating purpose and rules of construction.* (1) In order to effectuate the provisions of this section, each State agency shall forward to the United States Department of Labor (hereafter Department), not later than 10 days after issuance, a copy of each judicial or administrative decision ruling on an individual's entitlement to payment of UCX or to credit for a waiting period. On request of the Department, a State agency shall forward to the Department a copy of any determination or redetermination ruling on an individual's entitlement to UCX or waiting period credit.

(2)(i) If the Department believes that a determination, redetermination, or decision is inconsistent with the Department's interpretation of the Act or this part, the Department may at any time notify the State agency of the Department's view. Thereafter, the State agency shall issue a redetermination or appeal if possible, and shall not follow such determination, redetermination, or decision as a precedent; and, in any subsequent proceedings which involve such determination, redetermination, or decision, or wherein such determination, redetermination, or decision is cited as precedent or otherwise relied upon, the State agency shall inform the claims deputy or hearing officer or court of the Department's view and shall make all reasonable efforts, including appeal or other proceedings in an appropriate forum, to obtain modification, limitation, or overruling of the determination, redetermination, or decision.

(ii) If the Department believes that a State agency has failed to use, or use in a timely manner, the crossmatch mechanism at the claims control center designated by the Department, the Department may at any time notify the State of the Department's view. Thereafter, the State agency shall take action to ensure that operable procedures for the effective utilization of the claims control center are in place and adhered to. In any case of any determination, redetermination, or decision that is not legally warranted under the Act or this part had the State used, or used in a timely manner, the crossmatch mechanism at the claims control center designated by the Department, State agency shall take the steps outlined in paragraph (d)(2)(i) of this section.

(3) If the Department believes that a determination, redetermination, or decision is patently and flagrantly violative of the Act or this part, the Department may at any time notify the State agency of the Department's view. If the determination, redetermination, or decision in question denies UCX to a

claimant, the steps outlined in paragraph (2) above shall be followed by the State agency. If the determination, redetermination, or decision in question awards UCX to a claimant, the benefits are "due" within the meaning of section 303(a)(1) of the Social Security Act, 42 U.S.C. 503(a)(1), and therefore must be paid promptly to the claimant. However, the State agency shall take the steps outlined in paragraph (d)(2) of this section, and payments to the claimant may be temporarily delayed if redetermination or appeal action is taken not more than one business day following the day on which the first payment otherwise would be issued to the claimant; and the redetermination action is taken or appeal is filed to obtain a reversal of the award of UCX and a ruling consistent with the Department's view; and the redetermination action or appeal seeks an expedited redetermination or appeal within not more than two weeks after the redetermination action is taken or the appeal is filed. If redetermination action is not taken or appeal is not filed within the above time limit, or a redetermination or decision is not obtained within the two-week limit, or any redetermination or decision or order is issued which affirms the determination, redetermination, or decision awarding UCX or allows it to stand in whole or in part, the benefits awarded must be paid promptly to the claimant.

(4)(i) If any determination, redetermination, or decision, referred to in paragraph (d)(2) or paragraph (d)(3) of this section, is treated as a precedent for any future UCX claim or claim under the UCFE Program (part 609 of this chapter), the Secretary will decide whether the Agreement with the State entered into under the Act shall be terminated.

(ii) In the case of any determination, redetermination, or decision that is not legally warranted under the Act or this part, including any determination, redetermination, or decision referred to in paragraph (d)(2) or in paragraph (d)(3) of this section, the Secretary will decide whether the State shall be required to restore the funds of the United States for any sums paid under such a determination, redetermination, or decision, and whether, in absence of such restoration, the Agreement with the State shall be terminated and whether other action shall be taken to recover such sums for the United States.

(5) A State agency may request reconsideration of a notice issued pursuant to paragraph (d)(2) or paragraph (d)(3) of this section, and shall be given an opportunity to present views and arguments if desired.

(6) Concurrence of the Department in a determination, redetermination, or decision shall not be presumed from the absence of a notice issued pursuant to this section.

(Approved by the Office of Management and Budget under control number 1205–0163)

[47 FR 54697, Dec. 3, 1982, as amended at 53 FR 40553, Oct. 17, 1988; 53 FR 43799, Oct. 26, 1988; 57 FR 59799, Dec. 15, 1992]

§ 614.2 Definitions of terms.

For purposes of the Act and this part:

(a) *Act* means subchapter II of chapter 85 of title 5 of the United States Code, 5 U.S.C. 8521–8525.

(b) *Agreement* means the Agreement entered into pursuant to 5 U.S.C. 8502 between a State and the Secretary under which the State agency of the State agrees to make payments of unemployment compensation in accordance with the Act and the regulations and procedures thereunder prescribed by the Department.

(c) *Base period* means the base period as defined by the applicable State law for the benefit year.

(d) *Benefit year* means the benefit year as defined by the applicable State law, and if not so defined the term means the period prescribed in the Agreement with the State or, in the absence of an Agreement, the period prescribed by the Department.

(e) *Ex-servicemember* means an individual who has performed Federal military service.

(f) *Federal military agency* means any of the Armed Forces of the United States, including the Army, Air Force, Navy, Marine Corps, and Coast Guard, and the National Oceanic and Atmospheric Administration (Department of Commerce).

(g) *Federal military service* means active service (not including active duty in a reserve status unless for a continuous period of 90 days or more) in the Armed Forces or the Commissioned Corps of the National Oceanic and Atmospheric Administration if with respect to that service—

(1) The individual was discharged or released under honorable conditions (and, if an officer, did not resign for the good of the service); and

(2)(i) The individual was discharged or released after completing his/her first full term of active service which the individual initially agreed to serve, or

(ii) The individual was discharged or released before completing such term of active service—

(A) For the convenience of the Government under an early release program,

(B) Because of medical disqualification, pregnancy, parenthood, or any service-incurred injury or disability,

(C) Because of hardship, or

(D) Because of personality disorders or inaptitude but only if the service was continuous for 365 days or more.

(h) *Federal military wages* means all pay and allowances in cash and in kind for Federal military service, computed on the basis of the pay and allowances for the pay grade of the individual at the time of his or her latest discharge or release from Federal/military service, as determined in accordance with the Schedule of Remuneration applicable at the time the individual files his or her first claim for compensation for a benefit year.

(i) *First claim* means an initial claim for unemployment compensation under the UCX Program, the UCFE Program (part 609 of this chapter), or a State law, or some combination thereof, first filed by an individual after the individual's latest discharge or release from Federal military service, whereby a benefit year is established under an applicable State law.

(j) *Military document* means an official document or documents issued to an individual by a Federal military agency relating to the individual's Federal military service and discharge or release from such service.

(k) *Period of active service* means a period of continuous active duty (including active duty for training purposes) in a Federal military agency or agencies, beginning with the date of entry upon active duty and ending on the effective date of the first discharge or release thereafter which is not qualified or conditional.

(l) *Schedule of Remuneration* means the schedule issued by the Department from time to time under 5 U.S.C. 8521(a)(2) and this part, which specifies for purposes of the UCX Program, the pay and allowances for each pay grade of servicemember.

(m) *Secretary* means the Secretary of Labor of the United States.

(n) *State* means the 50 States, the District of Columbia, the Commonwealth of Puerto Rico, and the Virgin Islands.

(o) *State agency* means the agency of the State which administers the applicable State unemployment compensation law and is administering the UCX Program in the State pursuant to an Agreement with the Secretary.

(p)(1) *State law* means the unemployment compensation law of a State approved by the Secretary under section 3304 of the Internal Revenue Code of 1986, 26 U.S.C. 3304, if the State is certified under section 3304(c) of the Internal Revenue Code of 1986, 26 U.S.C. 3304(c).

(2) *Applicable State law* means the State law made applicable to a UCX claimant by § 614.8.

(q)(1) *Unemployment compensation* means cash benefits (including dependents' allowances) payable to individuals with respect to their unemployment, and includes regular, additional, emergency, and extended compensation.

(2) *Regular compensation* means unemployment compensation payable to an individual under any State law, but not including additional compensation or extended compensation.

(3) *Additional compensation* means unemployment compensation totally financed by a State and payable under a State law by reason of conditions of high unemployment or by reason of other special factors.

(4) *Emergency compensation* means supplementary unemployment compensation payable under a temporary Federal law after exhaustion of regular and extended compensation.

(5) *Extended compensation* means unemployment compensation payable to an individual for weeks of unemployment in an extended benefit period, under those provisions of a State law which satisfy the requirements of the Federal-State Extended Unemployment Compensation Act of 1970, as amended, 26 U.S.C. 3304 note, and part 615 of this chapter, with respect to the payment of extended compensation.

(r) *Unemployment Compensation for Ex-Servicemember* means the unemployment compensation payable under the Act to claimants eligible for the payments, and is referred to as UCX.

(s) *Week* means, for purposes of eligibility for and payment of UCX, a week as defined in the applicable State law.

(t) *Week of unemployment* means a week of total, part-total, or partial unemployment as defined in the applicable State law, which shall be applied in the same manner and to the same extent to all employment and earnings, and in the same manner and to the same extent for the purposes of the UCX Program, as if the individual filing for UCX were filing a claim for State unemployment compensation.

[47 FR 54697, Dec. 3, 1982, as amended at 53 FR 40554, Oct. 17, 1988; 53 FR 43799, Oct. 26, 1988; 57 FR 59799, Dec. 15, 1992]

Subpart B—Administration of UCX Program

§614.3 Eligibility requirements for UCX.

An individual shall be eligible to receive a payment of UCX or waiting period credit with respect to a week of unemployment if:

(a) The individual has Federal military service and Federal military wages in the base period under the applicable State law;

(b) The individual meets the qualifying employment and wage requirements of the applicable State law, either on the basis of Federal military service and Federal military wages alone or in combination with service and wages covered under a State law or under the UCFE Program (part 609 of this chapter);

(c) The individual has filed an initial claim for UCX and, as appropriate, has filed a timely claim for waiting period credit or payment of UCX with respect to that week of unemployment; and

(d) The individual is totally, part-totally, or partially unemployed, and is able to work, available for work, and seeking work within the meaning of or as required by the applicable State law, and is not subject to disqualification under this part or the applicable State law, with respect to that week of unemployment.

[47 FR 54697, Dec. 3, 1982, as amended at 53 FR 40554, Oct. 17, 1988; 57 FR 59799, Dec. 15, 1992]

§614.4 Weekly and maximum benefit amounts.

(a) *Total unemployment.* The weekly amount of UCX payable to an eligible individual for a week of total unemployment shall be the amount that would be payable to the individual as unemployment compensation for a week of total unemployment as determined under the applicable State law.

(b) *Partial and part-total unemployment.* The weekly amount of UCX payable for a week of partial or part-total unemployment shall be the amount that would be payable to the individual as unemployment compensation for a week of partial or part-total unemployment as determined under the applicable State law.

(c) *Maximum amount.* The maximum amount of UCX which shall be payable to an eligible individual during and subsequent to the individual's benefit year shall be the maximum amount of all unemployment compensation that would be payable to the individual as determined under the applicable State law.

(d) *Computation rules.* The weekly and maximum amounts of UCX payable to an individual under the UCX Program shall be determined under the applicable State law to be in the same amount, on the same terms, and subject to the same conditions as the State unemployment compensation which would be payable to the individual under the applicable State law if the individual's Federal military service and Federal military wages assigned or transferred under this part to the State had been included as employment and wages covered by that State law, subject to the use of the applicable Schedule of Remuneration.

[47 FR 54697, Dec. 3, 1982, as amended at 53 FR 40554, Oct. 17, 1988; 57 FR 59800, Dec. 15, 1992]

§ 614.5 Claims for UCX.

(a) *First claims.* A first claim for UCX shall be filed by an individual in any State agency of any State according to the applicable State law, and on a form prescribed by the Department which shall be furnished to the individual by the State agency where the claim is filed.

(b) *Weekly claims.* Claims for waiting week credit and payments of UCX for weeks of unemployment shall be filed in any State agency (or Canada) at the times and in the manner as claims for State unemployment compensation are filed under the applicable State law, and on forms prescribed by the Department which shall be furnished to the individual by the State agency where the claim is filed.

(c) *Secretary's standard.* The procedures for reporting and filing claims for UCX and waiting period credit shall be consistent with this part 614 and the Secretary's "Standard for Claim Filing, Claimant Reporting, Job Finding and Employment Services" in the *Employment Security Manual,* part V, sections 5000–5004 (appendix A of this part).

[47 FR 54697, Dec. 3, 1982, as amended at 53 FR 40554, Oct. 17, 1988]

§ 614.6 Determinations of entitlement; notices to individual and Federal military agency.

(a) *Determinations of first claim.* Except for findings of a Federal military agency and the applicable Schedule of Remuneration which are final and conclusive under § 614.23, the State agency whose State law applies to an individual under § 614.8 shall, promptly upon the filing of a first claim for UCX, determine whether the individual is otherwise eligible, and, if the individual is found to be eligible, the individual's benefit year and the weekly and maximum amounts of UCX payable to the individual.

(b) *Determinations of weekly claims.* The State agency promptly shall, upon the filing of a claim for a payment of UCX or waiting period credit with respect to a week, determine whether the individual is entitled to a payment of UCX or waiting period credit respect to such week, and, if entitled, the amount of UCX or waiting period credit to which the individual is entitled.

(c) *Redetermination.* The provisions of the applicable State law concerning the right to request, or authority to undertake, reconsideration of a determination pertaining to State unemployment compensation under the applicable State law shall apply to determinations pertaining to UCX.

(d) *Notices to individual and Federal military agency.* (1) The State agency promptly shall give notice in writing to the individual of any determination or redetermination of a first claim, and, except as may be authorized under paragraph (g) of this section, of any determination or redetermination of any weekly claim which denies UCX or waiting period credit or reduces the weekly amount or maximum amount initially determined to be payable. Each notice of determination or redetermination shall include such information regarding the determination or redetermination and notice of right to reconsideration or appeal, or both, as is furnished with written notices of determinations and redeterminations with respect to claims for State unemployment compensation. Such notice shall include the findings of any Federal military agency utilized in making the determination or redetermination, and shall inform the individual of the finality of Federal findings and the individual's right to request correction of such findings as is provided in § 614.22.

(2) A notice of claim filing and subsequent notices of monetary and nonmonetary determinations on a UCX claim shall be sent to each Federal military agency for which the individual performed Federal military service during the appropriate base period, together with notice of appeal rights of the Federal military agency to the same extent that chargeable employers are given such notices under State law and practice unless an alternate mechanism is established by the Department of Labor in lieu of such notices.

(e) *Obtaining information for claim determinations.* (1) Information required for the determination of claims for UCX shall be obtained by the State agency from claimants, employers, and others, in the same manner as information is obtained for claim purposes under the applicable State law, but Federal military findings shall be obtained from military documents, the applicable Schedule of Remuneration, and from Federal military agencies as prescribed in §§614.21 through 614.24.

(f) *Promptness.* Full payment of UCX when due shall be consistent with this part and shall be made with the greatest promptness that is administratively feasible, but the provisions of part 640 of this chapter (relating to promptness of benefit payments) shall not be applicable to the UCX Program.

(g) *Secretary's standard.* The procedures for making determinations and redeterminations, and furnishing written notices of determinations, redeterminations, and rights of appeal to individuals applying for UCX and to appropriate Federal military agencies shall be consistent with this part 614 and the Secretary's "Standard for Claim Determinations-Separation Information" in the *Employment Security Manual,* part V, sections 6010–6015 (Appendix B of this part).

[47 FR 54697, Dec. 3, 1982, as amended at 53 FR 40554, Oct. 17, 1988; 71 FR 35514, June 21, 2006]

§614.7 Appeal and review.

(a) *Applicable State Law.* The provisions of the applicable State law concerning the right of appeal and fair hearing from a determination or redetermination of entitlement to State unemployment compensation (exclusive of findings which are final and conclusive under §614.25) shall apply to determinations and redeterminations of eligibility for or entitlement to UCX and waiting period credit. Any such determination or redetermination shall be subject to appeal and review only in the manner and to the extent provided in the applicable State law with respect to determinations and redeterminations of entitlement to State unemployment compensation.

(Section 614.24 governs appeals of findings of the Veterans Administration)

(b) *Rights of appeal and fair hearing.* The provisions on right of appeal and opportunity for a fair hearing with respect to claims for UCX shall be consistent with this part and with sections 303(a)(1) and 303(a)(3) of the Social Security Act, 42 U.S.C. 503(a)(1) and 503(a)(3).

(c) *Promptness on appeals.* (1) Decisions on appeals under the UCX Program shall accord with the Secretary's "Standard for Appeals Promptness—Unemployment Compensation" in part 650 of this chapter, and with §614.1(d).

(2) Any provision of an applicable State law for advancement or priority of unemployment compensation cases on judicial calendars, or otherwise intended to provide for the prompt payment of unemployment compensation when due, shall apply to proceedings involving claims for UCX.

(d) *Appeal and review by Federal military agency.* If a Federal military agency believes that a State agency's determination or redetermination of an individual's eligibility for or entitlement to UCX is incorrect, the Federal military agency may seek appeal and review of such determination or redetermination in the same manner as an interested employer may seek appeal and review under the applicable State law.

§614.8 The applicable State for an individual.

(a) *The applicable State.* The applicable State for an individual shall be the State to which the individual's Federal military service and Federal military wages are assigned or transferred under this section. The applicable State law for the individual shall be the State law of such State.

(b) *Assignment of service and wages.* (1) When an individual files a first claim, all of the individual's Federal military service and Federal military wages shall be deemed to be assigned to the State in which such claim is filed, which shall be the "Paying State" in the case of a combined-wage claim. (§616.6(e) of this chapter.)

(2) Federal military service and Federal military wages assigned to a State in error shall be reassigned for use by the proper State agency. An appropriate record of the reassignment shall

be made by the State agency which makes the reassignment.

(c) *Assignment deemed complete.* All of an individual's Federal military service and Federal military wages shall be deemed to have been assigned to a State upon the filing of a first claim. Federal military service and Federal military wages shall be assigned to a State only in accordance with paragraph (b) of this section.

(d) *Use of assigned service and wages.* All assigned Federal military service and Federal military wages shall be used only by the State to which assigned in accordance with paragraph (b) of this section, except that any Federal military service and Federal military wages which are not within the base period of the State to which they were assigned shall be subject to transfer in accordance with part 616 of this chapter for the purposes of any subsequent Combined-Wage Claim filed by the individual.

§ 614.9 Provisions of State law applicable to UCX claims.

(a) *Particular provisions applicable.* Except where the result would be inconsistent with the provisions of the Act or this part or the procedures thereunder prescribed by the Department, the terms and conditions of the applicable State law which apply to claims for, and the payment of, State unemployment compensation shall apply to claims for, and the payment of, UCX and claims for waiting period credit. The provisions of the applicable State law which shall apply include, but are not limited to:

(1) Claim filing and reporting;

(2) Information to individuals, as appropriate;

(3) Notices to individuals, as appropriate, including notice to each individual of each determination and redetermination of eligibility for or entitlement to UCX;

(4) Determinations and redeterminations;

(5) Ability to work, availability for work, and search for work; and

(6) Disqualifications, except in regard to separation from any Federal military agency.

(b) *IBPP.* The *Interstate Benefit Payment Plan* shall apply, where appropriate, to individuals filing claims for UCX.

(c) *Wage combining.* The State's provisions complying with the *Interstate Arrangement for Combining Employment and Wages* (part 616 of this chapter) shall apply, where appropriate, to individuals filing claims for UCX.

(d) *Procedural requirements.* The provisions of the applicable State law which apply hereunder to claims for and the payment of UCX shall be applied consistently with the requirements of title III of the Social Security Act and the Federal Unemployment Tax Act which are pertinent in the case of State unemployment compensation, including but not limited to those standards and requirements specifically referred to in the provisions of this part, except as provided in paragraph (f) of § 614.6.

§ 614.10 Restrictions on entitlement.

(a) *Disqualification.* If the week of unemployment for which an individual claims UCX is a week to which a disqualification for State unemployment compensation applies under the applicable State law, the individual shall not be entitled to a payment of UCX for that week. As provided in § 614.9(a), no disqualification shall apply in regard to separation from any Federal military agency.

(b) *Effect of "days lost".* The continuity of a period of an individual's Federal military service shall not be deemed to be interrupted by reason of any "days lost" in such period, but "days lost" shall not be counted for purposes of determining:

(1) Whether an individual has performed Federal military service;

(2) Whether an individual meets the wage and employment requirements of a State law; or

(3) The amount of an individual's Federal military wages.

(c) *Allocation of military accrued leave.* A State agency shall allocate the number of days of unused military leave specified in an ex-servicemember's military document, for which a lump-sum payment has been made, in the same manner as similar payments by private employers to their employees are allocated under the applicable State law, except that the applicable Schedule of Remuneration instead of the lump-sum payment shall be used to determine the amount of the claimant's Federal military wages. In a State in which a private employer has an option as to the period to which such payments shall be allocated, such payments shall be allocated to the date of the individual's latest discharge or release from Federal military service. An allocation under this paragraph shall be disregarded in determining whether an individual has had a period of active service constituting Federal military service.

(d) *Education and training allowances.* An individual is not entitled to UCX under the Act or this part for a period with respect to which the individual receives:

(1) A subsistence allowance for vocational rehabilitation training under chapter 31 of title 38 of the United States Code, 38 U.S.C. 1501 *et seq.*, or under part VIII of Veterans Regulation Numbered 1(a); or

(2) An educational assistance allowance or special training allowance under chapter 35 of title 38 of the United States Code, 38 U.S.C. 1700 *et seq.*

§614.11 Overpayments; penalties for fraud.

(a) *False statements and representations.* Section 8507(a) of the Act provides that if a State agency, the Department, or a court of competent jurisdiction finds that an individual—

(1) Knowingly has made, or caused to be made by another, a false statement or representation of a material fact, or knowingly has failed, or caused another to fail, to disclose a material fact; and

(2) As a result of that action has received an amount as UCX to which the individual was not entitled; the individual shall repay the amount to the State agency or the Department. Instead of requiring repayment, the State agency or the Department may recover the amount by deductions from UCX payable to the individual during the 2-year period after the date of the finding. A finding by a State agency or the Department may be made only after an opportunity for a fair hearing, subject to such further review as may be appropriate under §614.7.

(b) *Prosecution for fraud.* Section 1919 of title 18, United States Code, provides that whoever makes a false statement or representation of a material fact knowing it to be false, or knowingly fails to disclose a material fact, to obtain or increase for himself or for any other individual any payment authorized to be paid under chapter 85 of title 5, United States Code, or under an agreement thereunder, shall be fined not more than $1,000 or imprisoned not more than one year, or both.

(c) *Absence of fraud.* If a State agency or court of competent jurisdiction finds that an individual has received a payment of UCX to which the individual was not entitled under the Act and this part, which was not due to a false statement or representation as provided in paragraph (a) or (b) of this section, the individual shall be liable to repay to the applicable State the total sum of the payment to which the individual was not entitled, and the State agency shall take all reasonable measures authorized under any State law or Federal law to recover for the account of the United States the total sum of the payment to which the individual was not entitled.

(d) *Recovery by offset.* (1) The State agency shall recover, insofar as is possible, the amount of any overpayment which is not repaid by the individual, by deductions from any UCX payable to the individual under the Act and this part, or from any unemployment compensation payable to the individual under any Federal unemployment compensation law administered by the State agency, or from any assistance or allowance payable to the individual with respect to unemployment under any other Federal law administered by the State agency.

(2) A State agency shall also recover, insofar as is possible, the amount of any overpayment of UCX made to the individual by another State by deductions from any UCX payable by the State agency to the individual under the Act and this part, or from any unemployment compensation payable to the individual under any Federal unemployment compensation law administered by the State agency, or from any assistance or allowance payable to

the individual with respect to unemployment under any other Federal law administered by the State agency.

(3) Recoupment of fraudulent overpayments referred to in paragraph (a) of this section shall be limited to the 2-year period stated in that paragraph. Recoupment of fraudulent overpayments referred to in paragraph (b) of this section, and nonfraudulent overpayments referred to in paragraph (c) of this section shall be subject to any time limitation on recoupment provided for in the State law that applies to the case.

(e) *Debts due the United States.* UCX payable to an individual shall be applied by the State agency for the recovery by offset of any debt due to the United States from the individual, but shall not be applied or used by the State agency in any manner for the payment of any debt of the individual to any State or any other entity or person except pursuant to a court order for child support or alimony in accordance with the law of the State and section 459 of the Social Security Act, 42 U.S.C. 659.

(f) *Application of State law.* (1) Except as indicated in paragraph (a) of this section, any provision of State law that may be applied for the recovery of overpayments or prosecution for fraud, and any provision of State law authorizing waiver of recovery of overpayments of unemployment compensation, shall be applicable to UCX.

(2) In the case of any finding of false statement of representation under the Act and paragraph (a) of this section, or prosecution for fraud under 18 U.S.C. 1919 or pursuant to paragraph (f)(1) of this section, the individual shall be disqualified or penalized in accordance with the provision of the applicable State law relating to fraud in connection with a claim for State unemployment compensation.

(g) *Final decision.* Recovery of any overpayment of UCX shall not be enforced by the State agency until the determination or redetermination establishing the overpayment has become final, or if appeal is taken from the determination or redetermination, until the decision after opportunity for a fair hearing has become final.

(h) *Procedural requirements.* (1) The provisions of paragraphs (c), (d), and (g) of § 614.6 shall apply to determinations and redeterminations made pursuant to this section.

(2) The provisions of § 614.7 shall apply to determinations and redeterminations made pursuant to this section.

(i) *Fraud detection and prevention.* Provisions in the procedures of each State with respect to detection and prevention of fraudulent overpayments of UCX shall be, as a minimum, commensurate with the procedures adopted by the State with respect to State unemployment compensation and consistent with this part 614 and the Secretary's "Standard for Fraud and Overpayment Detection" in the *Employment Security Manual,* part V, sections 7510–7515 (Appendix C of this part), and provide for timely use of any crossmatch mechanism established by the Department.

(j) *Recovered overpayments.* An amount repaid or recouped under this section shall be—

(1) Deposited in the fund from which payment was made, if the repayment was to a State agency; or

(2) Returned to the Treasury of the United States and credited to the current applicable appropriation, fund, or account from which payment was made, if the repayment was to the Department.

[47 FR 54697, Dec. 3, 1982, as amended at 53 FR 40555, Oct. 17, 1988]

§ 614.12 Schedules of remuneration.

(a) *Authority.* Section 8521(a)(2) of chapter 85, title 5 of the United States Code, 5 U.S.C. 8521(a)(2), requires the Secretary of Labor to issue from time to time, after consultation with the Secretary of Defense, a Schedule of Remuneration specifying the pay and allowances for each pay grade of members of the Armed Forces.

(b) *Elements of schedule.* A schedule reflects representative amounts for appropriate elements of the pay and allowances, whether in cash or kind, for each pay grade of members of the Armed Forces, with a statement of the effective date of the schedule. Benefit amounts for the UCX Program are computed on the basis of the Federal military wages for the pay grade of the individual at the time of the individual's latest discharge or release from Federal military service, as specified in the schedule applicable at the time the individual files his or her first claim for compensation for the benefit year.

(c) *Effective date.* Any new Schedule of Remuneration shall take effect beginning with the first week of the calendar quarter following the calendar quarter in which such schedule is issued, and shall remain applicable until a subsequent schedule becomes effective. Prior schedules shall continue to remain applicable for the periods they were in effect.

(d) *Publication.* Any new Schedule of Remuneration shall be issued by the Secretary of Labor to the State agencies and the Federal military agencies. Promptly after the issuance of a new Schedule of Remuneration it shall be published as a notice in the FEDERAL REGISTER.

§614.13 Inviolate rights to UCX.

Except as specifically provided in this part, the rights of individuals to UCX shall be protected in the same manner and to the same extent as the rights of persons to State unemployment compensation are protected under the applicable State law. Such measures shall include protection of applicants for UCX from waiver, release, assignment, pledge, encumbrance, levy, execution, attachment, and garnishment of their rights to UCX, except as provided in §614.11. In the same manner and to the same extent, individuals shall be protected from discrimination and obstruction in regard to seeking, applying for, and receiving any right to UCX.

§614.14 Recordkeeping; disclosure of information.

(a) *Recordkeeping.* Each State agency will make and maintain records pertaining to the administration of the UCX Program as the Department requires, and will make all such records available for inspection, examination, and audit by such Federal officials or employees as the Department may designate or as may be required by law.

(b) *Disclosure of information.* Information in records maintained by a State agency in administering the UCX Program shall be kept confidential, and information in such records may be disclosed only in the same manner and to the same extent as information with respect to State unemployment compensation and the entitlement of individuals thereto may be disclosed under the applicable State law. This provision on the confidentiality of information maintained in the administration of the UCX Program shall not apply, however, to the Department or for the purposes of §§614.11 or 614.14, or in the case of information, reports and studies required pursuant to §§614.18 or 614.26, or where the result would be inconsistent with the Freedom of Information Act, 5 U.S.C. 552, the Privacy Act of 1974, 5 U.S.C. 552a, or regulations of the Department promulgated thereunder.

§614.15 Payments to States.

(a) *State entitlement.* Each State is entitled to be paid by the United States with respect to each individual whose base period wages included Federal military wages, an amount bearing the same ratio to the total amount of compensation paid to such individual as the amount of the individual's Federal military wages in the individual's base period bears to the total amount of the individual's base period wages.

(b) *Payment.* Each State shall be paid, either in advance or by way of reimbursement, as may be determined by the Department, the sum that the Department estimates the State is entitled to receive under the Act and this part for each calendar month. The sum shall be reduced or increased by the amount which the Department finds that its estimate for an earlier calendar month was greater or less than the sum which should have been paid to the State. An estimate may be made on the basis of a statistical, sampling, or other method agreed on by the Department and the State agency.

(c) *Certification by the Department.* The Department, from time to time, shall certify to the Secretary of the Treasury the sum payable to each State under this section. The Secretary of the Treasury, before audit or settlement by the General Accounting Office, shall pay the State in accordance with the certification from the funds for carrying out the purposes of the Act and this part.

(d) *Use of money.* Money paid a State under the Act and this part may be used solely for the purposes for which it is paid. Money so paid which is not used solely for these purposes shall be returned, at the time specified by the Agreement, to the Treasury of the United States and credited to the current applicable appropriation, fund, or account from which payments to States under the Act and this part may be made.

§ 614.16 Public access to Agreements.

The State agency of a State will make available to any individual or organization a true copy of the Agreement with the State for inspection and copying. Copies of an Agreement may be furnished on request to any individual or organization upon payment of the same charges, if any, as apply to the furnishing of copies of other records of the State agency.

§ 614.17 Administration in absence of an Agreement.

(a) *Administering program.* The Department shall administer the UCX Program through personnel of the Department or through other arrangements under procedures prescribed by the Department, in the case of any State which does not have an Agreement with the Secretary as provided for in 5 U.S.C. 8502. The procedures prescribed by the Department under this section shall be consistent with the Act and this part.

(b) *Applicable State law.* On the filing by an individual of a claim for UCX in accordance with arrangements under this section, UCX shall be paid to the individual, if eligible, in the same amount, on the same terms, and subject to the same conditions as would be paid to the individual under the applicable State law if the individual's Federal military service and Federal military wages had been included as employment and wages under the State law. Any such claims shall include the individual's Federal military service and Federal military wages, combined with any service and wages covered by State law. However, if the individual, without regard to his or her Federal military service and Federal military wages, has employment or wages sufficient to qualify for compensation during the benefit year under that State law, then payments of UCX under this section may be made only on the basis of the individual's Federal military service and Federal military wages.

(c) *Fair hearing.* An individual whose claim for UCX is denied under this section is entitled to a fair hearing under rules of procedures prescribed by the Department. A final determination by the Department with respect to entitlement to UCX under this section is subject to review by the courts in the same manner and to the same extent as is provided by section 205(g) of the Social Security Act, 42 U.S.C. 405(g).

§ 614.18 Information, reports, and studies.

State agencies shall furnish to the Department such information and reports and conduct such studies as the Department determines are necessary or appropriate for carrying out the purposes of the UCX Program.

Subpart C—Responsibilities of Federal Military Agencies and State Agencies

§ 614.20 Information to ex-servicemembers.

At the time of discharge or release from Federal military service, each Federal military agency shall furnish to each ex-servicemember information explaining rights and responsibilities under the UCX Program and 18 U.S.C. 1919, and military documents necessary for filing claims for UCX.

§ 614.21 Findings of Federal military agency.

(a) *Findings in military documents.* Information contained in a military document furnished to an ex-servicemember shall constitute findings to which § 614.23 applies as to:

(1) Whether the individual has performed active service in the Armed Forces or the Commissioned Corps of the National Oceanic and Atmospheric Administration;

(2) The beginning and ending dates of the period of active service and "days lost" during such period;

(3) The type of discharge or release terminating the period of active service;

(4) The individuals' pay grade at the time of discharge or release from active service; and

(5) The narrative reason or other reason for separation from active service.

(b) *Discharges not under honorable conditions.* A military document which shows that an individual's discharge or release was under other than honorable conditions shall also be a finding to which §614.23 applies.

[53 FR 40555, Oct. 17, 1988]

§614.22 Correcting Federal findings.

(a) *Request for correction.* (1) If an individual believes that a finding specified in §614.21 is incorrect or that information as to any finding has been omitted from a military document, the individual may request the issuing Federal military agency to correct the military document. A request for correction may be made through the State agency, which shall forward such request and any supporting information submitted by the individual to the Federal military agency.

(2) The Federal military agency shall promptly forward to the individual or State agency making the request the corrected military document. Information contained in a corrected military document issued pursuant to such a request shall constitute the findings of the Federal military agency under §614.21.

(3) If a determination or redetermination based on a finding as to which correction is sought has been issued by a State agency before a request for correction under this paragraph is made, the individual who requested such correction shall file a request for redetermination or appeal from such determination or redetermination with the State agency, and shall inform the State agency of the request for correction.

(4) An individual who files a request for correction of findings under this paragraph shall promptly notify the State agency of the action of the Federal military agency on such request.

(b) *State agency procedure when request made.* (1) If a determination of entitlement has not been made when an individual notifies a State agency of a request for correction under paragraph (a) of this section, the State agency may postpone such determination until the individual has notified the State agency of the action of the Federal military agency on the request.

(2) If a determination of entitlement has been made when an individual notifies a State agency that a request for correction of Federal findings has been made, or if an individual notifies a State agency prior to a determination of entitlement that a request has been made but such determination is not postponed by the State agency, the individual may file a request for redetermination or appeal in accordance with the applicable State law.

(3) Except as provided in paragraph (c) of this section, no redetermination shall be made or hearing scheduled on an appeal until the individual has notified the State agency of the action of the Federal military agency on a request for correction under paragraph (a) of this section.

(c) *State agency procedure when request answered.* On receipt of notice of the action of a Federal military agency on a request for correction of its findings, a State agency shall:

(1) Make a timely determination or redetermination of the individual's entitlement, or

(2) Promptly schedule a hearing on the individual's appeal.

If such notice is not received by a State agency within one year of the date on which an individual first filed a claim, or such notice is not given promptly by an individual, a State agency without further postponement may make such determination or redetermination or schedule such hearing.

(d) *Findings corrected without request.* Information as to any finding specified in §614.21 contained in a corrected military document issued by a Federal military agency on its own motion shall constitute the findings of such agency under §614.21, if notice thereof is received by a State agency before the period for redetermination or appeal has expired under the State law. On timely receipt of such notice a

State agency shall take appropriate action under the applicable State law to give effect to the corrected findings.

§ 614.23 Finality of findings.

The findings of a Federal military agency referred to in §§ 614.21 and 614.22, and the Schedules of Remuneration issued by the Department pursuant to the Act and § 614.12, shall be final and conclusive for all purposes of the UCX Program, including appeal and review pursuant to § 614.7 or § 614.17.

[53 FR 40555, Oct. 17, 1988]

§ 614.24 Furnishing other information.

(a) *Additional information.* In addition to the information required by §§ 614.21 and 614.22, a Federal military agency shall furnish to a State agency or the Department, within the time requested, any information which it is not otherwise prohibited from releasing by law, which the Department determines is necessary for the administration of the UCX Program.

(b) *Reports.* Federal military agencies shall furnish to the Department or State agencies such reports containing such information as the Department determines are necessary or appropriate for carrying out the purposes of the UCX Program.

[47 FR 54697, Dec. 3, 1982, as amended at 53 FR 40555, Oct. 17, 1988]

§ 614.25 Liaison with Department

To facilitate the Department's administration of the UCX program, each Federal military agency shall designate one or more of its officials to be the liaison with the Department. Each Federal military agency will inform the Department of its designation(s) and of any change in a designation.

[53 FR 40555, Oct. 17, 1988]

APPENDIX A TO PART 614—STANDARD FOR CLAIM FILING, CLAIMANT REPORTING, JOB FINDING, AND EMPLOYMENT SERVICES

EMPLOYMENT SECURITY MANUAL (PART V, SECTIONS 5000–5004) *

5000–5099 *Claims Filing*

5000 *Standards for Claim Filing, Claimant Reporting, Job Finding, and Employment Services*

A. *Federal law requirements.* Section 3304(a)(1) of the Federal Unemployment Tax Act and section 303(a)(2) of the Social Security Act require that a State law provide for:

"Payment of unemployment compensation solely through public employment offices or such other agencies as the Secretary may approve."

Section 3304(a)(4) of the Federal Unemployment Tax Act and section 303(a)(5) of the Social Security Act require that a State law provide for:

"Expenditure of all money withdrawn from an unemployment fund of such State, in the payment of unemployment compensation. * * *"

Section 303(a)(1) of the Social Security Act requires that the State law provide for:

"Such methods of administration * * * as are found by the Secretary to be reasonably calculated to insure full payment of unemployment compensation when due."

B. *Secretary's interpretation of Federal law requirements.*

1. The Secretary interprets section 3304(a)(1) of the Federal Unemployment Tax Act and section 303(a)(2) of the Social Security Act to require that a State law provide for payment of unemployment compensation solely through public employment offices or claims offices administered by the State employment security agency if such agency provides for such coordination in the operations of its public employment offices and claims offices as will insure: (a) The payment of benefits only to individuals who are unemployed and who are able to work and available for work, and (b) that individuals claiming unemployment compensation (claimants) are afforded such placement and other employment services as are necessary and appropriate to return them to suitable work as soon as possible.

2. The Secretary interprets all the above sections to require that a State law provide for:

a. Such contact by claimants with public employment offices or claims offices or both, (1) as will reasonably insure the payment of unemployment compensation only to individuals who are unemployed and who are able to work and available for work, and (2)

* Revises subgrouping 5000–5004.

that claimants are afforded such placement and other employment services as are necessary and appropriate to facilitate their return to suitable work as soon as possible; and

b. Methods of administration which do not unreasonably limit the opportunity of individuals to establish their right to unemployment compensation due under such State law.

5001 *Claim Filing and Claimant Reporting Requirements Designed to Satisfy Secretary's Interpretation*

A. *Claim filing—total or part-total unemployment.*

1. Individuals claiming unemployment compensation for total or part-total unemployment are required to file a claim weekly or biweekly, in person or by mail, at a public employment office or a claims office (these terms include offices at itinerant points) as set forth below.

2. Except as provided in paragraph 3, a claimant is required to file in person:

a. His new claim with respect to a benefit year, or his continued claim for a waiting week or for his first compensable week of unemployment in such year; and

b. Any other claim, when requested to do so by the claims personnel at the office at which he files his claim(s) because questions about his right to benefits are raised by circumstances such as the following:

(1) The conditions or circumstances of his separation from employment;

(2) The claimant's answers to questions on mail claim(s) indicate that he may be unable to work or that there may be undue restrictions on his availability for work or that his search for work may be inadequate or that he may be disqualified;

(3) The claimant's answers to questions on mail claims create uncertainty about his credibility or indicate a lack of understanding of the applicable requirement; or

(4) The claimant's record shows that he has previously filed a fraudulent claim.

In such circumstances, the claimant is required to continue to file claims in person each week (or biweekly) until the State agency determines that filing claims in person is no longer required for the resolution of such questions.

3. A claimant must be permitted to file a claim by mail in any of the following circumstances:

a. He is located in an area requiring the expenditure of an unreasonable amount of time or money in traveling to the nearest facility established by the State agency for filing claims in person;

b. Conditions make it impracticable for the agency to take claims in person;

c. He has returned to full-time work on or before the scheduled date for his filing a claim, unless the agency makes provision for in-person filing at a time and place that does not interfere with his employment;

d. The agency finds that he has good cause for failing to file a claim in person.

4. A claimant who has been receiving benefits for partial unemployment may continue to file claims as if he were a partially unemployed worker for the first four consecutive weeks of total or part-total unemployment immediately following his period of partial unemployment so long as he remains attached to his regular employer.

B. *Claim filing—partial unemployment.* Each individual claiming unemployment compensation for a week (or other claim period) during which, because of lack of work, he is working less than his normal customary full-time hours for his regular employer and is earning less than the earnings limit provided in the State law, shall not be required to file a claim for such week or other claim period earlier than 2 weeks from the date that wages are paid for such claim period or, if a low earnings report is required by the State law, from the date the employer furnished such report to the individual. State agencies may permit claims for partial unemployment to be filed either in person or by mail, except that in the circumstances set forth in section A 3, filing by mail must be permitted, and in the circumstances set forth in section A 2 b, filing in person may be required.

5002 *Requirement for Job Finding, Placement, and other Employment Services Designed to Satisfy Secretary's Interpretation*

A. Claims personnel are required to assure that each claimant is doing what a reasonable individual in his circumstances would do to obtain suitable work.

B. In the discretion of the State agency:

1. The claims personnel are required to give each claimant such necessary and appropriate assistance as they reasonably can in finding suitable work and at their discretion determine when more complete placement and employment services are necessary and appropriate for a claimant; and if they determine more complete services are necessary and appropriate, the claims personnel are to refer him to employment service personnel in the public employment office in which he has been filing claim(s), or, if he has been filing in a claims office, in the public employment office most accessible to him; *or*

2. All placement and employment services are required to be afforded to each claimant by employment service personnel in the public employment office most accessible to him, in which case the claims personnel in the office in which the claimant files his claim are to refer him to the employment service personnel when placement or other employment services are necessary and appropriate for him.

C. The personnel to whom the State agency assigns the responsibilities outlined in paragraph B above are required to give claimants such job-finding assistance, placement, and other employment services as are necessary and appropriate to facilitate their return to suitable work as soon as possible.

In some circumstances, no such services or only limited services may be required. For example, if a claimant is on a short-term temporary layoff with a fixed return date, the only service necessary and appropriate to be given to him during the period of the layoff is a referral to suitable temporary work if such work is being performed in the labor market area.

Similarly, claimants whose unemployment is caused by a labor dispute presumably will return to work with their employer as soon as the labor dispute is settled. They generally do not need services, nor do individuals in occupations where placement customarily is made by other nonfee charging placement facilities such as unions and professional associations.

Claimants who fall within the classes which ordinarily would require limited services or no services shall, if they request placement and employment services, be afforded such services as are necessary and appropriate for them to obtain suitable work or to achieve their reasonable employment goals.

On the other hand, a claimant who is permanently separated from his job is likely to require some services. He may need only some direction in how to get a job; he may need placement services if he is in an occupation for which there is some demand in the labor market area; if his occupation is outdated, he may require counseling and referral to a suitable training course. The extent and character of the services to be given any particular claimant may change with the length of his unemployment and depend not only on his own circumstances and conditions, but also on the condition of the labor market in the area.

D. Claimants are required to report to employment service personnel, as directed, but such personnel and the claims personnel are required to so arrange and coordinate the contacts required of a claimant as not to place an unreasonable burden on him or unreasonably limit his opportunity to establish his rights to compensation. As a general rule, a claimant is not required to contact in person claims personnel or employment service personnel more frequently than once a week, unless he is directed to report more frequently for a specific service such as referral to a job or a training course or counseling which cannot be completed in one visit.

E. Employment service personnel are required to report promptly to claims personnel in the office in which the claimant files his claim(s): (1) His failure to apply for or accept work to which he was referred by such personnel or when known, by any other nonfee-charging placement facility such as a union or a professional association; and (2) any information which becomes available to it that may have a bearing on the claimant's ability to work or availability for work, or on the suitability of work to which he was referred or which was offered to him.

5004 *Evaluation of Alternative State Provisions.* If the State law provisions do not conform to the "suggested State law requirements" set forth in sections 5001 and 5002, but the State law contains alternative provisions, the Manpower Administrator, in collaboration with the State agency, will study the actual or anticipated effect of the alternative provisions. If the Manpower Administrator concludes that the alternative provisions satisfy the requirements of the Federal law as construed by the Secretary (see section 5000 B) he will so notify the State agency. If he does not so conclude, he will submit the matter to the Secretary. If the Secretary concludes that the alternative provisions satisfy such requirements, the State agency will be so notified. If the Secretary concludes that there is a question as to whether the alternative provisions satisfy such requirements, the State agency will be advised that unless the State law provisions are appropriately revised, a notice of hearing will be issued as required by the Code of Federal Regulations, title 20, section 601.3.

[53 FR 40555, Oct. 17, 1988; 53 FR 43799, Oct. 26, 1988]

Appendix B to Part 614—Standard for Claim Determination—Separation Information

Employment Security Manual (Part V, Sections 6010–6015)

6010–6019 *Standard for Claim Determinations—Separation Information**

6010 *Federal Law Requirements.* Section 303(a)(1) of the Social Security Act requires that a State law include provision for:

"Such methods of administration . . . as are found by the Secretary to be reasonably calculated to insure full payment of unemployment compensation when due."

Section 303(a)(3) of the Social Security Act requires that a State law include provision for:

"Opportunity for a fair hearing before an impartial tribunal, for all individuals whose claims for unemployment compensation are denied."

*Revises subgrouping 6010–6019

Section 3304(a)(4) of the Federal Unemployment Tax Act and section 303(a)(5) of the Social Security Act require that a State law include provision for:

"Expenditure of all money withdrawn from an unemployment fund of such State, in the payment of unemployment compensation * * *.

Section 3306(h) of the Federal Unemployment Tax Act defines "compensation" as "cash benefits payable to individuals with respect to their unemployment."

6011 *Secretary's Interpretation of Federal Law Requirements.* The Secretary interprets the above sections to require that a State law include provisions which will insure that:

A. Individuals who may be entitled to unemployment compensation are furnished such information as will reasonably afford them an opportunity to know, establish, and protect their rights under the unemployment compensation law of such State, and

B. The State agency obtains and records in time for the prompt determination and review of benefit claims such information as will reasonably insure the payment of benefits to individuals to whom benefits are due.

6012 *Criteria for Review of State Law Conformity with Federal Requirements*

In determining the conformity of a State law with the above requirements of the Federal Unemployment Tax Act and the Social Security Act as interpreted by the Secretary, the following criteria will be applied:

A. Is it required that individuals who may be entitled to unemployment compensation be furnished such information of their potential rights to benefits, including the manner and places of filing claims, the reasons for determinations, and their rights of appeal, as will insure them a reasonable opportunity to know, establish, and protect their rights under the law of the State?

B. Is the State agency required to obtain, in time for prompt determination of rights to benefits such information as will reasonably insure the payment of benefits to individuals to whom benefits are due?

C. Is the State agency required to keep records of the facts considered in reaching determinations of rights to benefits?

6013 *Claim Determinations Requirements Designed To Meet Department of Labor Criteria*

A. *Investigation of claims.* The State agency is required to obtain promptly and prior to a determination of an individual's right to benefits, such facts pertaining thereto as will be sufficient reasonably to insure the payment of benefits when due.

This requirement embraces five separate elements:

1. It is the responsibility of the agency to take the initiative in the discovery of information. This responsibility may not be passed on the claimant or the employer. In addition to the agency's own records, this information may be obtained from the worker, the employer, or other sources. If the information obtained in the first instance discloses no essential disagreement and provides a sufficient basis for a fair determination, no further investigation is necessary. If the information obtained from other sources differs essentially from that furnished by the claimant, the agency, in order to meet its responsibility, is required to inform the claimant of such information from other sources and to afford the claimant an opportunity to furnish any further facts he may have.

2. Evidentiary facts must be obtained as distinguished from ultimate facts or conclusions. That a worker was discharged for misconduct is an ultimate fact or conclusion; that he destroyed a machine upon which he was working is a primary or evidentiary fact, and the sort of fact that the requirement refers to.

3. The information obtained must be sufficient reasonably to insure the payment of benefits when due. In general, the investigation made by the agency must be complete enough to provide information upon which the agency may act with reasonable assurance that its decision is consistent with the unemployment compensation law. On the other hand, the investigation should not be so exhaustive and time-consuming as unduly to delay the payment of benefits and to result in excessive costs.

4. Information must be obtained promptly so that the payment of benefits is not unduly delayed.

5. If the State agency requires any particular evidence from the worker, it must give him a reasonable opportunity to obtain such evidence.

B. *Recording of facts.* The agency must keep a written record of the facts considered in reaching its determinations.

C. *Determination notices*

1. The agency must give each claimant a written notice of:

a. Any monetary determination with respect to his benefit year;

b. Any determination with respect to purging a disqualification if, under the State law, a condition or qualification must be satisfied with respect to each week of disqualification; but in lieu of giving written notice of each determination for each week in which it is determined that the claimant has met the requirements for purging the agency may inform the claimant that he has purged the disqualification for a week by notation on his applicant identification card or otherwise in writing.

c. Any other determination which adversely affects[1] his rights to benefits, except that written notice of determination need not be given with respect to:

(1) A week in a benefit year for which the claimant's weekly benefit amount is reduced in whole or in part by earnings if, the first time in the benefit year that there is such a reduction, he is required to be furnished a booklet or leaflet containing the information set forth below in paragraph 2f(1). However, a written notice of determination is required if: (a) There is a dispute concerning the reduction with respect to any week (e.g., as to the amount computed as the appropriate reduction, etc.); or (b) there is a change in the State law (or in the application thereof) affecting the reduction; or

(2) Any week in a benefit year subsequent to the first week in such benefit year in which benefits were denied, or reduced in whole or in part for reasons other than earnings, if denial or reduction for such subsequent week is based on the same reason and the same facts as for the first week, and if written notice of determination is required to be given to the claimant with respect to such first week, and with such notice of determination, he is required to be given a booklet or pamphlet containing the information set forth below in paragraphs 2f(2) and 2h. However, a written notice of determination is required if: (a) There is a dispute concerning the denial or reduction of benefits with respect to such week; or (b) there is a change in the State law (or in the application thereof) affecting the denial or reduction; or (c) there is a change in the amount of the reduction except as to the balance covered by the last reduction in a series of reductions.

NOTE: This procedure may be applied to determinations made with respect to any subsequent weeks for the same reason and on the basis of the same facts: (a) That claimant is unable to work, unavailable for work, or is disqualified under the labor dispute provision; and (b) reducing claimant's weekly benefit amount because of income other than earnings or offset by reason of overpayment.

2. The agency must include in written notices of determinations furnished to claimants sufficient information to enable them to understand the determinations, the reasons therefor, and their rights to protest, request reconsideration, or appeal.

The written notice of monetary determination must contain the information specified in the following items (except h) unless an item is specifically not applicable. A written notice of any other determination must contain the information specified in as many of the following items as are necessary to enable the claimant to understand the determination and to inform him of his appeal rights. Information specifically applicable to the individual claimant must be contained in the written notice of determination. Information of general application such as (but not limited to) the explanation of benefits for partial unemployment, information as to deductions, seasonality factors, and information as to the manner and place of taking an appeal, extension of the appeal period, and where to obtain information and assistance may be contained in a booklet or leaflet which is given the claimant with his monetary determination.

a. *Base period wages.* The statement concerning base-period wages must be in sufficient detail to show the basis of computation of eligibility and weekly and maximum benefit amounts. (If maximum benefits are allowed, it may not be necessary to show details of earnings.)

b. *Employer name.* The name of the employer who reported the wages is necessary so that the worker may check the wage transcript and know whether it is correct. If the worker is given only the employer number, he may not be able to check the accuracy of the wage transcript.

c. *Explanation of benefit formula—weekly and maximum benefit amounts.* Sufficient information must be given the worker so that he will understand how his weekly benefit amount, including allowances for dependents, and his maximum benefit amount were figured. If benefits are computed by means of a table contained in the law, the table must be furnished with the notice of determination whether benefits are granted or denied.

The written notice of determination must show clearly the weekly benefit amount and the maximum potential benefits to which the claimant is entitled.

The notice to a claimant found ineligible by reason of insufficient earnings in the base period must inform him clearly of the reason for ineligibility. An explanation of the benefit formula contained in a booklet or pamphlet should be given to each claimant at or

[1] A determination "adversely affects" claimant's right to benefits if it: (1) Results in a denial to him of benefits (including a cancellation of benefits or wage credits or any reduction in whole or in part below the weekly or maximum amount established by his monetary determination) for any week or other period; or (2) denies credit for a waiting week; or (3) applies any disqualification or penalty; or (4) determines that he has not satisfied a condition of eligibility, requalification for benefits, or purging a disqualification; or (5) determines that an overpayment has been made or orders repayment or recoupment of any sum paid to him; or (6) applies a previously determined overpayment, penalty, or order for repayment or recoupment; or (7) in any other way denies claimant a right to benefits under the State law.

prior to the time he receives written notice of a monetary determination.

d. *Benefit year*. An explanation of what is meant by the benefit year and identification of the claimant's benefit year must be included in the notice of determination.

e. *Information as to benefits for partial unemployment*. There must be included either in the written notice of determination or in a booklet or pamphlet accompanying the notice an explanation of the claimant's rights to partial benefits for any week with respect to which he is working less than his normal customary full-time workweek because of lack of work and for which he earns less than his weekly benefit amount or weekly amount plus earnings, whichever is provided by the State law. If the explanation is contained in the notice of determination, reference to the item in the notice in which his weekly benefit amount is entered should be made.

f. *Deductions from weekly benefits*.

(1) *Earnings*. Although written notice of determinations deducting earnings from a claimant's weekly benefit amount is generally not required (see paragraph 1c (1) above), where written notice of determination is required (or given) it shall set forth the amount of earnings, the method of computing the deduction in sufficient detail to enable the claimant to verify the accuracy of the deduction, and his right to protest, request redetermination, and appeal. Where a written notice of determination is given to the claimant because there has been a change in the State law or in the application of the law, an explanation of the change shall be included.

Where claimant is not required to receive a written notice of determination, he must be given a booklet or pamphlet the first time in his benefit year that there is a deduction for earnings which shall include the following information:

(a) The method of computing deductions for earnings in sufficient detail to enable the claimant to verify the accuracy of the deduction;

(b) That he will not automatically be given a written notice of determination for a week with respect to which there is a deduction for earnings (unless there is a dispute concerning the reduction with respect to a week or there has been a change in the State law or in the application of the law affecting the deduction) but that he may obtain such a written notice upon request; and

(c) A clear statement of his right to protest, request a redetermination, and appeal from any determination deducting earnings from his weekly benefit amount even though he does not automatically receive a written notice of determination; and if the State law requires written notice of determination in order to effectuate a protest, redetermination, or appeal, he must be so advised and advised also that he must request a written notice of determination before he takes any such action.

(2) *Other deductions*.

(a) A written notice of determination is required with respect to the first week in claimant's benefit year in which there is a reduction from his benefits for a reason other than earnings. This notice must describe the deduction made from claimant's weekly benefit amount, the reason for the deduction, the method of computing it in sufficient detail to enable him to verify the accuracy of such deduction, and his right to protest, request redetermination, or appeal.

(b) A written notice of determination is not required for subsequent weeks that a deduction is made for the same reason and on the basis of the same facts, if the notice of determination pursuant to (2)(a), or a booklet or pamphlet given him with such notice explains: (i) The several kinds of deductions which may be made under the State law (e.g., retirement pensions, vacation pay, and overpayments); (ii) the method of computing each kind of deduction in sufficient detail that claimant will be able to verify the accuracy of deductions made from his weekly benefit payments; (iii) any limitation on the amount of any deduction or the time in which any deduction may be made; (iv) that he will not automatically be given a written notice of determination for subsequent weeks with respect to which there is a deduction for the same reason and on the basis of the same facts, but that he may obtain a written notice of determination upon request; (v) his right to protest, request redetermination, or appeal with respect to subsequent weeks for which there is a reduction from his benefits for the same reason, and on the basis of the same facts even though he does not automatically receive a written notice of determination; and (vi) that if the State law requires written notice of determination in order to effectuate a protest, redetermination, or appeal, he must be so advised and advised also that he must request a written notice of determination before he takes any such action.

g. *Seasonality factors*. If the individual's determination is affected by seasonality factors under the State law, an adequate explanation must be made. General explanations of seasonality factors which may affect determinations for subsequent weeks may be included in a booklet or pamphlet given with his notice of monetary determination.

h. *Disqualification or ineligibility*. If a disqualification is imposed, or if the claimant is declared ineligible for one or more weeks, he must be given not only a statement of the period of disqualification or ineligibility and the amount of wage-credit reductions, if any, but also an explanation of the reason for the ineligibility or disqualification. This explanation must be sufficiently detailed so that he will understand why he is ineligible or why he has been disqualified, and what he must do in order to requalify for benefits or purge the disqualification. The statement must be individualized to indicate the facts upon which the determination was based, e.g., state, "It is found that you left your work with Blank Company because you were tired of working; the separation was voluntary, and the reason does not constitute good cause," rather than merely the phrase "voluntary quit." Checking a box as to the reason for the disqualification is not a sufficiently detailed explanation. However, this statement of the reason for the disqualification need not be a restatement of all facts considered in arriving at the determination.

i. *Appeal rights.* The claimant must be given information with respect to his appeal rights.

(1) The following information shall be included in the notice of determination:

(a) A statement that he may appeal or, if the State law requires or permits a protest or redetermination before an appeal, that he may protest or request a redetermination.

(b) The period within which an appeal, protest, or request for redetermination must be filed. The number of days provided by statute must be shown as well as either the beginning date or ending date of the period. (It is recommended that the ending date of the appeal period be shown, as this is the more understandable of the alternatives.)

(2) The following information must be included either in the notice of determination or in separate informational material referred to in the notice:

(a) The manner in which the appeal, protest, or request for redetermination must be filed, e.g., by signed letter, written statement, or on a prescribed form, and the place or places to which the appeal, protest, or request for redetermination may be mailed or hand-delivered.

(b) An explanation of any circumstances (such as nonworkdays, good cause, etc.) which will extend the period for the appeal, protest, or request for redetermination beyond the date stated or identified in the notice of determination.

(c) That any further information claimant may need or desire can be obtained together with assistance in filing his appeal, protest, or request for redetermination from the local office.

If the information is given in separate material, the notice of determination would adequately refer to such material if it said, for example, "For other information about your (appeal), (protest), (redetermination) rights, see pages ____ to ____ of the ____________________ (name of pamphlet or booklet) heretofore furnished to you."

6014 *Separation Information Requirements Designed To Meet Department of Labor Criteria*

A. *Information to agency.* Where workers are separated, employers are required to furnish the agency promptly, either upon agency request or upon such separation, a notice describing the reasons for and the circumstances of the separation and any additional information which might affect a claimant's right to benefits. Where workers are working less than full time, employers are required to furnish the agency promptly, upon agency request, information concerning a claimant's hours of work and his wages during the claim periods invovled, and other facts which might affect a claimant's eligibility for benefits during such periods.

When workers are separated and the notices are obtained on a request basis, or when workers are working less than full time and the agency requests information, it is essential to the prompt processing of claims that the request be sent out promptly after the claim is filed and the employer be given a specific period within which to return the notice, preferably within 2 working days.

When workers are separated and notices are obtained upon separation, it is essential that the empolyer be required to send the notice to the agency with sufficient promptness to insure that, if a claim is filed, it may be processed promptly. Normally, it is desirable that such a notice be sent to the central office of the agency, since the employer may not know in which local office the worker will file his claim. The usual procedure is for the employer to give the worker a copy of the notice sent by the employer to the agency.

B. *Information to worker.*

1. *Information required to be given.* Employees are required to give their employers information and instructions concerning the employees' potential rights to benefits and concerning registration for work and filing claims for benefits.

The information furnished to employees under such a requirement need not be elaborate; it need only be adequate to insure that the worker who is separated or who is working less than full time knows he is potentially eligible for benefits and is informed as to what he is to do or where he is to go to file his claim and register for work. When he files his claim, he can obtain more detailed information.

In States that do not require employers to furnish periodically to the State agency detailed reports of the wages paid to their employees, each employer is required to furnish to his employees information as to: (a) The name under which he is registered by the State agency, (b) the address where he maintains his payroll records, and (c) the workers' need for this information if and when they file claims for benefits.

2. *Methods for giving information.* The information and instructions required above may be given in any of the following ways:

a. *Posters prominently displayed in the employer's establishment.* The State agency should supply employers with a sufficient number of posters for distribution throughout their places of business and should see that the posters are conspicuously displayed at all times.

b. *Leaflets.* Leaflets distributed either periodically or at the time of separation or reduction of hours. The State agency should supply employers with a sufficient number of leaflets.

c. *Individual notices.* Individual notices given to each employee at the time of separation or reduction in hours.

It is recommended that the State agency's publicity program be used to supplement the employer-information requirements. Such a program should stress the availability and location of claim-filing offices and the importance of visiting those offices whenever the worker is unemployed, wishes to apply for benefits, and to seek a job.

6015 *Evaluation of Alternative State Provisions with Respect to Claim Determinations and Separation Information.* If the State law provisions do not conform to the suggested requirements set forth in sections 6013 and 6014, but the State law contains alternative provisions, the Bureau of Employment Security, in collaboration with the State agency, will study the actual or anticipated effects of the alternative provisions. If the Administrator of the Bureau concludes that the alternative provisions satisfy the criteria in section 6012, he will so notify the State agency. If the Administrator of the Bureau does not so conclude, he will submit the matter to the Secretary. If the Secretary concludes that the alternative provisions satisfy the criteria in section 6012, the State agency will be so notified. If the Secretary concludes that there is a question as to whether the alternative provisions satisfy the criteria, the State agency will be advised that unless the State law provisions are appropriately revised, a notice of hearing will be issued as required by the Code of Federal Regulations, title 20, §601.5.

[53 FR 40557, Oct. 17, 1988; 53 FR 43799, Oct. 26, 1988]

APPENDIX C TO PART 614—STANDARD FOR FRAUD AND OVERPAYMENT DETECTION

EMPLOYMENT SECURITY MANUAL (PART V, SECTIONS 7510–7515)

7510–7519 *Standard for Fraud and Overpayment Detection*

7510 *Federal Law Requirements.* Section 303(a)(1) of the Social Security Act requires that a State law include provision for:

"Such methods of administration * * * as are found by the Secretary to be reasonably calculated to insure full payment of unemployment compensation when due."

Section 1603(a)(4) of the Internal Revenue Code and section 3030(a)(5) of the Social Security Act require that a State law include provision for:

"Expenditure for all money withdrawn from an unemployment fund of such State, in the payment of unemployment compensation * * *"

Section 1607(h) of the Internal Revenue Code defines "compensation" as "cash benefits payable to individuals with respect to their unemployment."

7511 *The Secretary's Interpretation of Federal Law Requirements.* The Secretary of Labor interprets the above sections to require that a State law include provision for such methods of administration as are, within reason, calculated (1) to detect benefits paid through error by the agency or through willful misrepresentation or error by the claimant or others, and (2) to deter claimants from obtaining benefits through willful misrepresentation.

7513 *Criteria for Review of State Conformity With Federal Requirements.* In detemining State conformity with the above requirements of the Internal Revenue Code and the Social Security Act, as interpreted by the Secretary of Labor, the following criteria will be applied:

A. *Are investigations required to be made after the payment of benefits, (or, in the case of interstate claims, are investigations made by the agent State after the processing of claims) as to claimants' entitlement to benefits paid to them in a sufficient proportion of cases to test the effectiveness of the agency's procedures for the prevention of payments which are not due? To carry out investigations, has the agency assigned to some individual or unit, as a basic function, the responsibility of making or functionally directing such investigations?*

Explantaion: It is not feasible to prescribe the extent to which the above activities are required; however, they should always be carried on to such an extent that they will show whether or not error or willful misrepresentation is increasing or decreasing, and will reveal problem areas. The extent and nature of the above activities should be varied according to the seriousness of the problem in the State. The responsible individual or unit should:

1. Check paid claims for overpayment and investigate for willful misrepresentation or, alternatively, advise and assist the operating units in the performance of such functions, or both;

2. Perform consultative services with respect to methods and procedures for the prevention and detection of fraud; and

3. Perform other services which are closely related to the above.

Although a State agency is expected to make a full-time assignment of responsibility to a unit or individual to carry on the functions described above, a small State agency might make these functions a part-time responsibility of one individual. In connection with the detection of overpayments, such a unit or individual might, for example:

(a) Investigate information on suspected benefit fraud received from any agency personnel, and from sources outside the agency, including anonymous complaints;

(b) Investigate information secured from comparisons of benefit payments with employment records to detect cases of concurrent working (whether in covered or noncovered work) and claiming of benefits (including benefit payments in which the agency acted as agent for another State).

The benefit fraud referred to herein may involve employers, agency employees, and witnesses, as well as claimants.

Comparisons of benefit payments with employment records are commonly made either by post-audit or by industry surveys. The so-called "post-audit" is a matching of central office wage-record files against benefit payments for the same period. "Industry surveys" or "mass audits" are done in some States by going directly to employers for pay-roll information to be checked against concurrent benefit lists. A plan

A. of investigation based on a sample post-audit will be considered as partial fulfillment of the investigation program; it would need to be supplemented by other methods capable of detecting overpayments to persons who have moved into noncovered occupations or are claiming interstate benefits.

B. *Are adequate records maintained by which the results of investigations may be evaluated?**

Explanation. To meet this criterion, the State agency will be expected to maintain records of all its activities in the detection of overpayments, showing whether attributable to error or willful misrepresentation, measuring the results obtained through various methods, and noting the remedial action taken in each case. The adequacy and effectiveness of various methods of checking for willful misrepresentation can be evaluated only if records are kept of the results obtained. Internal reports on fraudulent and erroneous overpayments are needed by State agencies for self-evaluation. Detailed records should be maintained in order that the State agency may determine, for example, which of several methods of checking currently used are the most productive. Such records also will provide the basis for drawing a clear distinction between fraud and error.

*Revises section 7513 as issued 5/5/50.

C. *Does the agency take adequate action with respect to publicity concerning willful misrepresentation and its legal consequences to deter fraud by claimants?**

Explanation. To meet this criterion, the State agency must issue adequate material on claimant eligibility requirements and must take necessary action to obtain publicity on the legal consequences of willful misrepresentation or willful nondisclosure of facts.

Public announcements on convictions and resulting penalties for fraud are generally considered necessary as a deterrent to other persons, and to inform the public that the agency is carrying on an effective program to prevent fraud. This alone is not considered adequate publicity. It is important that information be circulated which will explain clearly and understandably the claimant's rights, and the obligations which he must fulfill to be eligible for benefits. Leaflets for distribution and posters placed in local offices are appropriate media for such information.

7515 *Evalauation of Alternative State Provisions with Respect to Erroneous and Illegal Payments.* If the methods of administration provided for by the State law do not conform to the suggested methods of meeting the requirements set forth in section 7511, but a State law does provide for alternative methods of administration designed to accomplish the same results, the Bureau of Employment Security, in collaboration with the State agency, will study the actual or anticipated effect of the alternative methods of administration. If the Bureau concludes that the alternative methods satisfy the criteria in section 7513, it will so notify the State agency. If the Bureau does not so conclude, it will submit to the Secretary the results of the study for his determination of whether the State's alternative methods of administration meet the criteria.*

PART 615—EXTENDED BENEFITS IN THE FEDERAL-STATE UNEMPLOYMENT COMPENSATION PROGRAM

Sec.

*Revises section 7513 as issued 5/5/50.

AUTHORITY: 26 U.S.C. 7805; 26 U.S.C. 1102; Secretary's Order No. 6–10.

SOURCE: 53 FR 27937, July 25, 1988, unless otherwise noted.

EDITORIAL NOTE: Nomenclature changes to part 615 appear at 81 FR 57778, Aug. 24, 2016.

§ 615.1 Purpose.

This part implements the "Federal-State Extended Unemployment Compensation Act of 1970" (EUCA). Under the Federal Unemployment Tax Act, 26 U.S.C. 3304(a)(11), an approved State law must provide for the payment of extended compensation to eligible individuals who have exhausted all rights to regular compensation during specified periods of unemployment, as prescribed in EUCA and this part.

[81 FR 57778, Aug. 24, 2016]

§ 615.2 Definitions.

For the purposes of the EUCA and this part—

Additional compensation means compensation totally financed by a State and payable under a State law by reason of conditions of high unemployment or by reason of other special factors and, when so payable, includes compensation payable pursuant to 5 U.S.C. chapter 85.

And, as used in section 202(a)(3)(D)(ii), shall be interpreted to mean "or".

Applicable benefit year means, with respect to an individual, the current benefit year if, at the time an initial claim for extended compensation is filed, the individual has an unexpired benefit year only in the State in which such claim is filed, or, in any other case, the individual's most recent benefit year. For this purpose, the most recent benefit year for an individual who has unexpired benefit years in more than one State when an initial claim for extended compensation is filed, is the benefit year with the latest ending date or, if such benefit years have the same ending date, the benefit year in which the latest continued claim for regular compensation was filed. The individual's most recent benefit year which expires in an extended benefit period, when either extended compensation or high unemployment extended compensation is payable, is the applicable benefit year if the individual cannot establish a second benefit year or is precluded from receiving regular compensation in a second benefit year solely by reason of a State law provision which meets the requirement of section 3304(a)(7) of the Internal Revenue Code of 1986 (26 U.S.C. 3304(a)(7)).

Applicable State means, with respect to an individual, the State with respect to which the individual is an "exhaustee" as defined in § 615.5, and in the case of a combined wage claim for regular compensation, the term means the "paying State" as defined in § 616.6(e) of this chapter.

Applicable State law means the law of the State which is the applicable State for an individual.

Average weekly benefit amount, for the purposes of section 202(a)(3)(D)(i), means the weekly benefit amount (including dependents' allowances payable for a week of total unemployment and before any reduction because of earnings, pensions or other requirements) applicable to the week in which the individual failed to take an action which results in a disqualification as required by section 202(a)(3)(B) of the EUCA.

Base period means, with respect to an individual, the base period as determined under the applicable State law for the individual's applicable benefit year.

Benefit structure as used in section 204(a)(2)(D), for the requirement to round down to the "nearest lower full dollar amount" for Federal reimbursement of sharable regular and sharable extended compensation means all of the following:

(1) Amounts of regular weekly benefit payments,

(2) Amounts of additional and extended weekly benefit payments,

(3) The State maximum or minimum weekly benefit,

(4) Partial and part-total benefit payments,

(5) Amounts payable after deduction for pensions, and

(6) Amounts payable after any other deduction required by State law.

Benefit year means, with respect to an individual, the benefit year as defined in the applicable State law.

Claim filed in any State under the interstate benefit payment plan, as used in section 202(c), means:

(1) Any interstate claim for a week of unemployment filed pursuant to the Interstate Benefit Payment Plan, but does not include—

(i) A claim filed in Canada,

(ii) A visiting claim filed by an individual who has received permission from his/her regular reporting office to report temporarily to a local office in another State and who has been furnished intrastate claim forms on which to file claims, or

(iii) A transient claim filed by an individual who is moving from place to place searching for work, or an intrastate claim for Extended Benefits filed by an individual who does not reside in a State that is in an Extended Benefit Period,

(2) *The first 2 weeks*, as used in section 202(c), means the first 2 weeks for which the individual files compensable claims for Extended Benefits under the Interstate Benefit Payment Plan in an agent State in which an Extended Benefit Period is not in effect during such weeks.

Compensation and *unemployment compensation* means cash benefits (including dependents' allowances) payable to individuals with respect to their unemployment, and includes regular compensation, additional compensation and extended compensation as defined in this section.

Date of a disqualification, as used in section 202(a)(4), means the date the disqualification begins, as determined under the applicable State law.

Department means the United States Department of Labor, and shall include the Employment and Training Administration, the agency of the United States Department of Labor headed by the Assistant Secretary of Labor for Employment and Training to whom has been delegated the Secretary's authority under the EUCA in Secretary's Order No. 6–2010 (75 FR 66268) or any subsequent order.

Eligibility period means, for an individual, the period consisting of—

(1) The weeks in the individual's applicable benefit year which begin in an extended benefit period or high unemployment period, or for a single benefit year, the weeks in the benefit year which begin in more than one extended benefit period or high unemployment period, and

(2) If the applicable benefit year ends within an extended benefit period or high unemployment period, any weeks thereafter which begin in such extended benefit period or high unemployment period,

(3) An individual may not have more than one eligibility period for any one exhaustion of regular benefits, or carry over from one eligibility period to another any entitlement to extended compensation.

Employed, for the purposes of section 202(a)(3)(B)(ii) of the EUCA, and *employment*, for the purposes of section 202(a)(4) of the EUCA, mean service performed in an employer-employee relationship as defined in the State law; and that law also shall govern whether that service must be covered by it, must consist of consecutive weeks, and must consist of more weeks of work than are required under section 202(a)(3)(B) of the EUCA.

EUCA means the Federal-State Extended Unemployment Compensation Act of 1970, title II of Public Law 91–373, 84 Stat. 695, 708 (codified in note to 26 U.S.C. 3304), as amended.

Extended benefit period means the weeks during which extended compensation is payable in a State in accordance with § 615.11.

Extended Benefits Program or *EB Program* means the entire program under which monetary payments are made to workers who have exhausted their regular compensation during periods of high unemployment.

Extended compensation or *extended benefits* means the funds payable to an individual for weeks of unemployment which begin in a regular EB period or high unemployment period (HUP), under those provisions of a State law which satisfy the requirements of

EUCA and this part with respect to the payment of extended unemployment compensation, and, when so payable, includes compensation payable under 5 U.S.C. chapter 85, but does not include regular compensation or additional compensation.

Extended compensation account is the account established for each individual claimant for the payment of regular extended compensation or high unemployment extended compensation.

Extended unemployment compensation means:

(1) Regular extended compensation paid to an eligible individual under those provisions of a State law which are consistent with EUCA and this part, and that does not exceed the smallest of the following:

(i) 50 percent of the total amount of regular compensation payable to the individual during the applicable benefit year; or

(ii) 13 times the individual's weekly amount of extended compensation payable for a week of total unemployment, as determined under §615.6(a); or

(iii) 39 times the individual's weekly benefit amount, referred to in paragraph (1)(ii) of this definition, reduced by the regular compensation paid (or deemed paid) to the individual during the applicable benefit year; or

(2) High unemployment extended compensation paid to an eligible individual under an optional TUR indicator enacted under State law when the State is in a high unemployment period, in accordance with §615.11(e) of this part, and that does not exceed the smallest of the following:

(i) 80 percent of the total amount of regular compensation payable to the individual during the applicable benefit year; or

(ii) 20 times the individual's weekly amount of extended compensation payable for a week of total unemployment, as determined under §615.6(a); or

(iii) 46 times the individual's weekly benefit amount, referred to in paragraph (1)(ii) of this definition, reduced by the regular compensation paid (or deemed paid) to the individual during the applicable benefit year.

Gross average weekly remuneration, for the purposes of section 202(a)(3)(D)(i), means the remuneration offered for a week of work before any deductions for taxes or other purposes and, in case the offered pay may vary from week to week, it shall be determined on the basis of recent experience of workers performing work similar to the offered work for the employer who offered the work.

High unemployment extended compensation means the benefits payable to an individual for weeks of unemployment which begin in a high unemployment period, under those provisions of a State law which satisfy the requirements of EUCA and this part for the payment of high unemployment extended compensation. When so payable, high unemployment extended compensation includes compensation payable under 5 U.S.C. chapter 85, but does not include regular compensation or additional compensation. Regular extended unemployment compensation, along with high unemployment extended compensation, are part of the program referred to in this part as Extended Benefits.

High unemployment period (or HUP) means a period where the Department determines that the Trigger Value in a State, which has enacted the alternative Total Unemployment Rate indicator in law, for the most recent 3 months for which data for all States is published, equals or exceeds 8 percent and such Trigger Value equals or exceeds 110 percent of such Trigger Value for either or both of the corresponding 3-month periods ending in the 2 preceding calendar years.

Hospitalized for treatment of an emergency or life-threatening condition, as used in section 202(a)(3)(A)(ii), has the following meaning: "Hospitalized for treatment" means an individual was admitted to a hospital as an inpatient for medical treatment. Treatment is for an "emergency or life threatening condition" if determined to be such by the hospital officials or attending physician that provide the treatment for a medical condition existing upon or arising after hospitalization. For purposes of this definition, the term "medical treatment" refers to the application of any remedies which have the objective of effecting a cure of the emergency or life-threatening condition. Once an "emergency condition" or a "life-threatening condition" has been determined to exist by the hospital officials or attending physician, the status of the individual as so determined shall remain unchanged until release from the hospital.

Individual's capabilities, for the purposes of section 202(a)(3)(C), means work which the individual has the physical and mental capacity to perform and which meets the minimum requirements of section 202(a)(3)(D).

Insured Unemployment Rate means the percentage derived by dividing the average weekly number of individuals filing claims for regular compensation in a State for weeks of unemployment in the most recent 13-consecutive-week period as determined by the State on the basis of State reports to the United States Secretary of Labor by the average monthly employment covered under State law for the first 4 of the most recent 6 completed calendar quarters before the end of such 13-week period.

Jury duty, for purposes of section 202(a)(3)(A)(ii), means the performance of service as a juror, during all periods of time an individual is engaged in such service, in any court of a State or the United States pursuant to the law of the State or the United States and the rules of the court in which the individual is engaged in the performance of such service.

Provisions of the applicable State law, as used in section 202(a)(3)(D)(iii) of EUCA, means that State law provisions must not be inconsistent with sections 202(a)(3)(C) and 202(a)(3)(E). Therefore, decisions based on State law provisions must not require an individual to take a job which requires traveling an unreasonable distance to work, or which involves an unreasonable risk to the individual's health, safety or morals. Such State law provisions must also include labor standards and training provisions required under sections 3304(a)(5) and 3304(a)(8) of the Internal Revenue Code of 1986 and section 236(d) of the Trade Act of 1974.

Reasonably short period, for the purposes of section 202(a)(3)(C), means the number of weeks provided by the applicable State law.

Regular compensation means compensation payable to an individual under a State law, and, when so payable, includes compensation payable pursuant to 5 U.S.C. chapter 85, but does not include extended compensation or additional compensation.

Regular extended compensation means the benefits payable to an individual for weeks of unemployment which begin in an extended benefit period, under those provisions of a State law which satisfy the requirements of EUCA and this part for the payment of extended unemployment compensation, and, when so payable, includes compensation payable under 5 U.S.C. chapter 85, but does not include regular compensation or additional compensation. Regular extended compensation, along with high unemployment extended compensation, are part of the program referred to in this part as Extended Benefits.

Regular EB period means a period in which a state is "on" the EB Program because either the mandatory or optional IUR indicator satisfies the criteria to be "on" and the state is not in a 13-week mandatory "off" period; or the State is "on" the EB Program because the TUR indicator's Trigger Value is at least 6.5 percent and it is at least 110 percent of the Trigger Value for the comparable 3 months in either of the prior 2 years.

Secretary means the Secretary of Labor of the United States.

Sharable compensation means:

(1) Extended compensation paid to an eligible individual under those provisions of a State law which are consistent with EUCA and this part, and that does not exceed the smallest of the following:

(i) 50 percent of the total amount of regular compensation payable to the individual during the applicable benefit year; or

(ii) 13 times the individual's weekly amount of extended compensation payable for a week of total unemployment, as determined under § 615.6(a); or

(iii) 39 times the individual's weekly benefit amount, referred to in paragraph (1)(ii) of this definition, reduced by the regular compensation paid (or deemed paid) to the individual during the applicable benefit year.

(2) Extended compensation paid to an eligible individual under an optional

TUR indicator enacted under State law when the State is in a high unemployment period, in accordance with §615.12(f) of this part, and that does not exceed the smallest of the following:

(i) 80 percent of the total amount of regular compensation payable to the individual during the applicable benefit year; or

(ii) 20 times the individual's weekly amount of extended compensation payable for a week of total unemployment, as determined under §615.6(a); or

(iii) 46 times the individual's weekly benefit amount, referred to in paragraph (1)(ii) of this definition, reduced by the regular compensation paid (or deemed paid) to the individual during the applicable benefit year.

(3) Regular compensation paid to an eligible individual for weeks of unemployment in the individual's eligibility period, but only to the extent that the sum of such compensation, plus the regular compensation paid (or deemed paid) to the individual for prior weeks of unemployment in the applicable benefit year, exceeds 26 times and does not exceed 39 times the average weekly benefit amount (including allowances for dependents) for weeks of total unemployment payable to the individual under the State law in such benefit year: Provided, that such regular compensation is paid under provisions of a State law which are consistent with EUCA and this part.

(4) Notwithstanding the preceding provisions of this paragraph, sharable compensation does not include any regular or extended compensation for which a State is not entitled to a payment under section 202(a)(6) or 204 of EUCA or §615.14 of this part.

State means the States of the United States, the District of Columbia, the Commonwealth of Puerto Rico, and the U. S. Virgin Islands.

State agency means the State unemployment compensation agency of a State which administers the State law.

State law means the unemployment compensation law of a State, approved by the Secretary under section 3304(a) of the Internal Revenue Code of 1986 (26 U.S.C. 3304(a)).

A *systematic and sustained effort*, for the purposes of section 202(a)(3)(E), means—

(i) A high level of job search activity throughout the given week, compatible with the number of employers and employment opportunities in the labor market reasonably applicable to the individual,

(ii) A plan of search for work involving independent efforts on the part of each individual which results in contacts with persons who have the authority to hire or which follows whatever hiring procedure is required by a prospective employer in addition to any search offered by organized public and private agencies such as the State employment service or union or private placement offices or hiring halls,

(iii) Actions by the individual comparable to those actions by which jobs are being found by people in the community and labor market, but not restricted to a single manner of search for work such as registering with and reporting to the State employment service and union or private placement offices or hiring halls, in the same manner that such work is found by people in the community,

(iv) A search not limited to classes of work or rates of pay to which the individual is accustomed or which represent the individual's higher skills, and which includes all types of work within the individual's physical and mental capabilities, except that the individual, while classified by the State agency as provided in §615.8(d) as having "good" job prospects, shall search for work that is suitable work under State law provisions which apply to claimants for regular compensation (which is not sharable),

(v) A search by every claimant, without exception for individuals or classes of individuals other than those in approved training, as required under section 3304(a)(8) of the Internal Revenue Code of 1986 or section 236(e) of the Trade Act of 1974,

(vi) A search suspended only when severe weather conditions or other calamity forces suspension of such activities by most members of the community, except that

(vii) The individual, while classified by the State agency as provided in §615.8(d) as having "good" job prospects, if such individual normally obtains customary work through a hiring hall, shall search for work that is suitable work under State law provisions which apply to claimants for regular compensation (which is not sharable).

Tangible evidence of an active search for work, for the purposes of section 202(a)(3)(E), means a written record which can be verified, and which includes the actions taken, methods of applying for work, types of work sought, dates and places where work was sought, the name of the employer or person who was contacted and the outcome of the contact.

Total Unemployment Rate means the number of unemployed individuals in a State (seasonally adjusted) divided by the civilian labor force (seasonally adjusted) in the State for the same period.

Trigger Value or *average rate of total unemployment* means the ratio computed using 3 months of the level of seasonally adjusted unemployment in a State in the numerator and 3 months of the level of the seasonally adjusted civilian labor force in the State in the denominator. This rate is used for triggering States "on" and "off" the optional Total Unemployment Rate indicator as described in § 615.12(e).

Week means:

(1) For purposes of eligibility for and payment of extended compensation, a week as defined in the applicable State law.

(2) For purposes of computation of extended compensation "on" and "off" and "no change" indicators and insured unemployment rates and the beginning and ending of an EB Period or a HUP, a calendar week.

Week of unemployment means:

(1) A week of total, part-total, or partial unemployment as defined in the applicable State law, which shall be applied in the same manner and to the same extent to the Extended Benefit Program as if the individual filing a claim for Extended Benefits were filing a claim for regular compensation, except as provided in paragraph (2) of this definition.

(2) *Week of unemployment* in section 202(a)(3)(A) of the EUCA means a week of unemployment, as defined in paragraph (1) of this definition, for which the individual claims Extended Benefits or sharable regular benefits.

[81 FR 57778, Aug. 24, 2016]

§ 615.3 Effective period of the program.

An Extended Benefit Program conforming with EUCA and this part shall be a requirement for a State law effective on and after January 1, 1972, pursuant to section 3304(a)(11) of the Internal Revenue Code of 1986, (26 U.S.C. 3304(a)(11)). Continuation of the program by a State in conformity and substantial compliance with EUCA and this part, throughout any 12-month period ending on October 31 of a year subsequent to 1972, shall be a condition of the certification of the State with respect to such 12-month period under section 3304(c) of the Internal Revenue Code of 1986 (26 U.S.C. 3304(c)). Conformity with EUCA and this part in the payment of regular compensation, regular extended compensation, and high unemployment extended compensation (if State law so provides) to any individual is a continuing requirement, applicable to every week as a condition of a State's entitlement to payment for any compensation as provided in EUCA and this part.

[53 FR 27937, July 25, 1988, as amended at 81 FR 57781, Aug. 24, 2016]

§ 615.4 Eligibility requirements for Extended Benefits.

(a) *General.* An individual is entitled to Extended Benefits for a week of unemployment which begins in the individual's eligibility period if, with respect to such week, the individual is an exhaustee as defined in § 615.5, files a timely claim for Extended Benefits, and satisfies the pertinent requirements of the applicable State law which are consistent with EUCA and this part.

(b) *Qualifying for Extended Benefits.* The State law shall specify whether an individual qualifies for Extended Benefits by earnings and employment in the base period for the individual's applicable benefit year as required by section 202(a)(5) of EUCA, (and if it does not also apply this requirement to the payment of sharable regular benefits, the

State will not be entitled to a payment under §615.14), as follows:

(1) One and one-half times the high quarter wages; or

(2) Forty times the most recent weekly benefit amount, and if this alternative is adopted, it shall use the weekly benefit amount (including dependents' allowances) payable for a week of total unemployment (before any reduction because of earnings, pensions or other requirements) which applied to the most recent week of regular benefits; or

(3) Twenty weeks of full-time insured employment, and if this alternative is adopted, the term "full-time" shall have the meaning provided by the State law.

§615.5 Definition of "exhaustee."

(a)(1) "Exhaustee" means an individual who, with respect to any week of unemployment in the individual's eligibility period:

(i) Has received, prior to such week, all of the regular compensation that was payable under the applicable State law or any other State law (including regular compensation payable to Federal civilian employees and Ex-Servicemembers under 5 U.S.C. chapter 85) for the applicable benefit year that includes such week; or

(ii) Has received, prior to such week, all of the regular compensation that was available under the applicable State law or any other State law (including regular compensation available to Federal civilian employees and Ex-Servicemembers under 5 U.S.C. chapter 85) in the benefit year that includes such week, after the cancellation of some or all of the individual's wage credits or the total or partial reduction of the individual's right to regular compensation; or

(iii) The applicable benefit year having expired prior to such week and the individual is precluded from establishing a second (new) benefit year, or the individual established a second benefit year but is suspended indefinitely from receiving regular compensation, solely by reason of a State law provision which meets the requirement of section 3304(a)(7) of the Internal Revenue Code of 1986 (26 U.S.C. 3304(a)(7)): *Provided*, that, an individual shall not be entitled to Extended Benefits based on regular compensation in a second benefit year during which the individual is precluded from receiving regular compensation solely by reason of a State law provision which meets the requirement of section 3304(a)(7) of the Internal Revenue Code of 1986 (26 U.S.C. 3304(a)(7)); or

(iv) The applicable benefit year having expired prior to such week, the individual has insufficient wages or employment, or both, on the basis of which a new benefit year could be established in any State that would include such week; and

(v) Has no right to unemployment compensation for such week under the Railroad Unemployment Insurance Act or such other Federal laws as are specified by the Department pursuant to this paragraph; and

(vi) Has not received and is not seeking for such week unemployment compensation under the unemployment compensation law of Canada, unless the Canadian agency finally determines that the individual is not entitled to unemployment compensation under the Canadian law for such week.

(2) An individual who becomes an exhaustee as defined above shall cease to be an exhaustee commencing with the first week that the individual becomes eligible for regular compensation under any State law or 5 U.S.C. chapter 85, or has any right to unemployment compensation as provided in paragraph (a)(1)(v) of this section, or has received or is seeking unemployment compensation as provided in paragraph (a)(1)(vi) of this section. The individual's Extended Benefit Account shall be terminated upon the occurrence of any such week, and the individual shall have no further right to any balance in that Extended Benefit Account.

(b) *Special Rules*. For the purposes of paragraphs (a)(1)(i) and (a)(1)(ii) of this section, an individual shall be deemed to have received in the applicable benefit year all of the regular compensation payable according to the monetary determination, or available to the individual, as the case may be, even though—

(1) As a result of a pending appeal with respect to wages or employment

or both that were not included in the original monetary determination with respect to such benefit year, the individual may subsequently be determined to be entitled to more or less regular compensation, or

(2) By reason of a provision in the State law that establishes the weeks of the year in which regular compensation may be paid to the individual on the basis of wages in seasonal employment—

(i) The individual may be entitled to regular compensation with respect to future weeks of unemployment in the next season or off season, as the case may be, but such compensation is not payable with respect to the week of unemployment for which Extended Benefits are claimed, and

(ii) The individual is otherwise an exhaustee within the meaning of this section with respect to rights to regular compensation during the season or off season in which that week of unemployment occurs, or

(3) Having established a benefit year, no regular compensation is payable during such year because wage credits were cancelled or the right to regular compensation was totally reduced as the result of the application of a disqualification.

(c) *Adjustment of week.* If it is subsequently determined as the result of a redetermination or appeal that an individual is an exhaustee as of a different week than was previously determined, the individual's rights to Extended Benefits shall be adjusted so as to accord with such redetermination or decision.

[53 FR 27937, July 25, 1988, as amended at 71 FR 35514, June 21, 2006]

§615.6 Extended Benefits; weekly amount.

(a) *Total unemployment.* (1) The weekly amount of Extended Benefits payable to an individual for a week of total unemployment in the individual's eligibility period shall be the amount of regular compensation payable to the individual for a week of total unemployment during the applicable benefit year. If the individual had more than one weekly amount of regular compensation for total unemployment during such benefit year, the weekly amount of extended compensation for total unemployment shall be one of the following which applies as specified in the applicable State law:

(i) The average of such weekly amounts of regular compensation,

(ii) The last weekly benefit amount of regular compensation in such benefit year, or

(iii) An amount that is reasonably representative of the weekly amounts of regular compensation payable during such benefit year.

(2) If the method in paragraph (a)(1)(iii) of this section is adopted by a State, the State law shall specify how such amount is to be computed. If the method in paragraph (a)(1)(i) of this section is adopted by a State, and the amount computed is not an even dollar amount, the amount shall be raised or lowered to an even dollar amount as provided by the applicable State law for regular compensation.

(b) *Partial and part-total unemployment.* The weekly amount of Extended Benefits payable for a week of partial or part-total unemployment shall be determined under the provisions of the applicable State law which apply to regular compensation, computed on the basis of the weekly amount of Extended Benefits payable for a week of total unemployment as determined pursuant to paragraph (a) of this section.

§615.7 Extended Benefits; maximum amount.

(a) *Individual account.* An Extended Benefit Account shall be established for each individual determined to be eligible for Extended Benefits, in the sum of the maximum amount potentially payable to the individual as computed in accordance with paragraph (b) of this section.

(b) *Computation of amount in individual account.* (1) The amount established in the Extended Benefit Account of an individual, as the maximum amount potentially payable to the individual during the individual's eligibility period, shall be equal to the lesser of—

(i) 50 percent of the total amount of regular compensation (including dependents' allowances) payable to the individual during the individual's applicable benefit year; or

(ii) 13 times the individual's weekly amount of Extended Benefits payable for a week of total unemployment, as determined pursuant to §615.6(a); or

(iii) 39 times the individual's weekly benefit amount referred to in (ii), reduced by the regular compensation paid (or deemed paid) to the individual during the individual's applicable benefit year.

(2) If the State law so provides, the amount in the individual's Extended Benefit Account shall be reduced by the aggregate amount of additional compensation paid (or deemed paid) to the individual under such law for prior weeks of unemployment in such benefit year which did not begin in an Extended Benefit Period.

(3) If State law provides, in accordance with §615.12(e), for a high unemployment period for weeks of unemployment beginning after March 6, 1993, the provisions of paragraph (b)(1) of this section are applied by substituting:

(i) 80 percent for 50 percent in (b)(1)(i),

(ii) 20 for 13 in (b)(1)(ii), and

(iii) 46 for 39 in (b)(1)(iii).

NOTE TO PARAGRAPH (b)(3). *Provided*, that if an individual's extended compensation account is determined in accordance with the provisions of paragraphs (b)(3)(i) through (b)(3)(iii) (for a "high unemployment period" as defined in §615.2) during the individual's eligibility period, upon termination of the high unemployment period, such individual's account must be reduced by the amount in the account that is more than the maximum amount of extended compensation or high extended compensation payable to the individual. *Provided further*, if the account balance is equal to or less than the maximum amount of extended compensation or high unemployment extended compensation payable, there will be no reduction in the account balance upon termination of a high unemployment period. In no case will the individual receive more regular extended compensation or high unemployment extended compensation than the amount determined in accordance with paragraphs (b)(1)(i) through (iii) of this section, nor more extended compensation or high unemployment extended compensation than as provided in paragraphs (b)(2)(i) through (iii) of this section.

(c) *Changes in accounts.* (1) If an individual is entitled to more or less Extended Benefits as a result of a redetermination or an appeal which awarded more or less regular compensation or Extended Benefits, an appropriate change shall be made in the individual's Extended Benefit Account pursuant to an amended determination of the individual's entitlement to Extended Benefits.

(2) If an individual who has received Extended Benefits for a week of unemployment is determined to be entitled to more regular compensation with respect to such week as the result of a redetermination or an appeal, the Extended Benefits paid shall be treated as if they were regular compensation up to the greater amount to which the individual has been determined to be entitled, and the State agency shall make appropriate adjustments between the regular and extended accounts. If the individual is entitled to more Extended Benefits as a result of being entitled to more regular compensation, an amended determination shall be made of the individual's entitlement to Extended Benefits. If the greater amount of regular compensation results in an increased duration of regular compensation, the individual's status as an exhaustee shall be redetermined as of the new date of exhaustion of regular compensation.

(3) If an individual who has received Extended Benefits for a week of unemployment is determined to be entitled to less regular compensation as the result of a redetermination or an appeal, and as a consequence is entitled to less Extended Benefits, any Extended Benefits paid in excess of the amount to which the individual is determined to be entitled after the redetermination or decision on appeal shall be considered an overpayment which the individual shall have to repay on the same basis and in the same manner that excess payments of regular compensation are required to be repaid under the applicable State law. If such decision reduces the duration of regular compensation payable to the individual, the claim for Extended Benefits shall

be backdated to the earliest date, subsequent to the date when the redetermined regular compensation was exhausted and within the individual's eligibility period, that the individual was eligible to file a claim for Extended Benefits. Any such changes shall be made pursuant to an amended determination of the individual's entitlement to Extended Benefits.

(d) *Reduction because of trade readjustment allowances.* Section 233(c) of the Trade Act of 1974 (and section 204(a)(2)(C) of EUCA), requiring a reduction of extended compensation because of the receipt of trade readjustment allowances, must be applied as follows:

(1) The reduction of Extended Benefits shall apply only to an individual who has not exhausted his/her Extended Benefits at the end of the benefit year;

(2) The amount to be deducted is the product of the weekly benefit amount for Extended Benefits multiplied by the number of weeks for which trade readjustment allowances were paid (regardless of the amount paid for any such week) up to the close of the last week that begins in the benefit year; and

(3) The amount to be deducted shall be deducted from the balance of Extended Benefits not used as of the close of the last week which begins in the benefit year.

[53 FR 27937, July 25, 1988, as amended at 81 FR 57781, Aug. 24, 2016]

§ 615.8 Provisions of State law applicable to claims.

(a) *Particular provisions applicable.* Except where the result would be inconsistent with the provisions of EUCA or this part, the terms and conditions of the applicable State law which apply to claims for, and the payment of, regular compensation shall apply to claims for, and the payment of, Extended Benefits. The provisions of the applicable State law which shall apply to claims for, and the payment of, Extended Benefits include, but are not limited to:

(1) Claim filing and reporting;

(2) Information to individuals, as appropriate;

(3) Notices to individuals and employers, as appropriate;

(4) Determinations, redeterminations, and appeal and review;

(5) Ability to work and availability for work, except as provided otherwise in this section;

(6) Disqualifications, including disqualifying income provisions, except as provided by paragraph (c) of this section;

(7) Overpayments, and the recovery thereof;

(8) Administrative and criminal penalties;

(9) The Interstate Benefit Payment Plan;

(10) The Interstate Arrangement for Combining Employment and Wages, in accordance with part 616 of this chapter.

(b) *Provisions not to be applicable.* The State law and regulations shall specify those of its terms and conditions which shall not be applicable to claims for, or payment of, Extended Benefits. Among such terms and conditions shall be at least those relating to—

(1) Any waiting period;

(2) Monetary or other qualifying requirements, except as provided in § 615.4(b); and

(3) Computation of weekly and total regular compensation.

(c) *Terminating disqualifications.* A disqualification in a State law, as to any individual who voluntarily left work, was suspended or discharged for misconduct, gross misconduct or the commission or conviction of a crime, or refused an offer of or a referral to work, as provided in sections 202(a) (4) and (6) of EUCA—

(1) As applied to regular benefits which are not sharable, is not subject to any limitation in sections 202(a) (4) and (6);

(2) As applied to eligibility for Extended Benefits, shall require that the individual be employed again subsequent to the date of the disqualification before it may be terminated, even though it may have been terminated on other grounds for regular benefits which are not sharable; and if the State law does not also apply this provision to the payment of what would otherwise be sharable regular benefits, the State will not be entitled to a payment under EUCA and § 615.14 in regard to such regular compensation; and

(3) Will not apply in regard to eligibility for Extended Benefits in a subsequent eligibility period.

(d) *Classification and determination of job prospects.* (1) As to each individual who files an initial claim for Extended Benefits (or sharable regular compensation), the State agency shall classify the individual's prospects for obtaining work in his/her customary occupation within a reasonably short period, as "good" or "not good," and shall promptly (not later than the end of the week in which the initial claim is filed) notify the individual in writing of such classification and of the requirements applicable to the individual under the provisions of the applicable State law corresponding to section 202(a)(3) of EUCA and this part. Such requirements shall be applicable beginning with the week following the week in which the individual is furnished such written notice.

(2) If an individual is thus classified as having good prospects, but those prospects are not realized by the close of the period the State law specifies as a reasonably short period, the individual's prospects will be automatically reclassified as "not good" or classified as "good" or "not good" depending on the individual's job prospects as of that date.

(3) Whenever, as part of a determination of an individual's eligibility for benefits, an issue arises concerning the individual's failure to apply for or accept an offer of work (sections 202(a)(3)(A)(i) and (F) of EUCA and paragraphs (e) and (f) of this section), or to actively engage in seeking work (sections 202(a)(3)(A)(ii) and (E) of EUCA and paragraph (g) of this section), a written appealable determination shall be made which includes a finding as to the individual's job prospects at the time the issue arose. The reasons for allowing or denying benefits in the written notice of determination shall explain how the individual's job prospects relate to the decision to allow or deny benefits.

(4) If an individual's job prospects are determined in accordance with the preceding paragraph (3) to be "good," the suitability of work will be determined under the standard State law provisions applicable to claimants for regular compensation which is not sharable; and if determined to be "not good," the suitability of work will be determined under the definition of suitable work in the State law provisions corresponding to sections 202(a)(3) (C) and (D) of EUCA and this part. Any determination or classification of an individual's job prospects is mutually exclusive, and only one suitable work definition shall be applied to a claimant as to any failure to accept or apply for work or seek work with respect to any week.

(e) *Requirement of referral to work.* (1) The State law shall provide, as required by section 202(a)(3)(F) of EUCA and this part, that the State Workforce Agency shall refer every claimant for Extended Benefits to work which is "suitable work" as provided in paragraph (d)(4) of this section, beginning with the week following the week in which the individual is furnished a written notice of classification of job prospects as required by paragraphs (d)(1) and (h) of this section.

(2) To make such referrals, the State Workforce Agency shall assure that each Extended Benefit claimant is registered for work and continues to be considered for referral to job openings as long as he/she continues to claim benefits.

(3) In referring claimants to available job openings, the State Workforce Agency shall apply to Extended Benefit claimants the same priorities, policies, and judgments as it does to other applicants, except that it shall not restrict referrals only to work at higher skill levels, prior rates of pay, customary work, or preferences as to work or pay for individuals whose prospects of obtaining work in their customary occupations have been classified as or determined to be "not good."

(4) For referral purposes, any work which does not exceed the individual's capabilities shall be considered suitable work for an Extended Benefit claimant whose job prospects have been classified as or determined to be "not good", except as modified by this paragraph (e).

(5) For Extended Benefit claimants whose prospects of obtaining work in their customary occupations have been classified as or determined to be "not

good'', work shall not be suitable, and referral to a job shall not be made, if—

(i) The gross average weekly remuneration for the work for any week does not exceed the sum of the individual's weekly benefit amount plus any supplemental unemployment benefits (SUB) (as defined in section 501(c)(17)(D) of the Internal Revenue Code of 1986) payable to the individual,

(ii) The work is not offered in writing or is not listed with the State employment service,

(iii) The work pays less than the higher of the minimum wage set in section 6(a)(1) of the Fair Labor Standards Act of 1938, or any applicable State or local minimum wage, without regard to any exemption elsewhere in those laws, or

(iv) Failure to accept or apply for the work would not result in a denial of compensation under the provisions of the applicable State law as defined in § 615.2(o)(7).

(6) In addition, if the State Workforce Agency classifies or determines that an individual's prospects for obtaining work in his/her customary occupation within a reasonably short period are "good," referral shall not be made to a job if such referral would not be made under the State law provisions applicable to claimants for regular benefits which are not sharable, and such referrals shall be limited to work which the individual is required to make a "systematic and sustained effort" to search for as defined in § 615.2(o)(8).

(7) For the purposes of the foregoing paragraphs of this paragraph (e), State law applies regarding whether members of labor organizations shall be referred to nonunion work in their customary occupations.

(8) If the State law does not also apply this paragraph (e) to individuals who claim what would otherwise be sharable regular compensation, the State will not be entitled to payment under EUCA and § 615.14 in regard to such regular compensation.

(f) *Refusal of work.* (1) The State law shall provide, as required by section 202(a)(3)(A)(i) of EUCA and this part, that if an individual who claims Extended Benefits fails to accept an offer of work or fails to apply for work to which he/she was referred by the State Workforce Agency—

(i) If the individual's prospects for obtaining work in his/her customary occupation within a reasonably short period are determined to be "good," the State agency shall determine whether the work is suitable under the standard State law provisions which apply to claimants for regular compensation which is not sharable, and if determined to be suitable the individual shall be ineligible for Extended Benefits for the week in which the individual fails to apply for or accept an offer of suitable work and thereafter until the individual is employed in at least four weeks with wages from such employment totalling not less than four times the individual's weekly benefit amount, as provided by the applicable State law; or

(ii) If the individual's prospects for obtaining work in his/her customary occupation are determined to be "not good," the State agency shall determine whether the work is suitable under the applicable State law provisions corresponding to sections 202(a)(3) (C) and (D) of EUCA and paragraphs (e)(5) and (f)(2) of this section, and if determined to be suitable the individual shall be ineligible for Extended Benefits for the week in which the individual fails to apply for or accept an offer of suitable work and thereafter until the individual is employed in at least four weeks with wages from such employment totalling not less than four times the individual's weekly benefit amount, as provided by the applicable State law.

(2) For an individual whose prospects of obtaining work in his/her customary occupation within the period specified by State law are classified or determined to be "not good," the term "suitable work" shall mean any work which is within the individual's capabilities, except that work shall not be suitable if—

(i) The gross average weekly remuneration for the work for any week does not exceed the sum of the individual's weekly benefit amount plus any supplemental unemployment compensation benefits (as defined in section 501(c)(17)(D) of the Internal Revenue Code of 1986) payable to the individual,

(ii) The work is not offered in writing or is not listed with the State employment service,

(iii) The work pays less than the higher of the minimum wage set in section 6(a)(1) of the Fair Labor Standards Act of 1938, or any applicable State or local minimum wage, without regard to any exemption elsewhere in those laws, or

(iv) Failure to accept or apply for the work would not result in a denial of compensation under the provisions of the applicable State law as defined in §615.2(o)(7).

(3) For the purposes of the foregoing paragraphs of this paragraph (f), State law applies regarding whether members of labor organizations shall be referred to nonunion work in their customary occupations.

(4) If the State law does not also apply this paragraph (f) to individuals who claim what would otherwise be sharable regular compensation, the State will not be entitled to payment under EUCA and §615.14 in regard to such regular compensation.

(g) *Actively seeking work.* (1) The State law shall provide, as required by sections 202(a)(3) (A)(ii) and (E) of EUCA and this part, that an individual who claims Extended Benefits shall be required to make a systematic and sustained effort (as defined in §615.2(o)(8)) to search for work which is "suitable work" as provided in paragraph (d)(4) of this section, throughout each week beginning with the week following the week in which the individual is furnished a written notice of classification of job prospects as required by paragraphs (d)(1) and (h) of this section, and to furnish to the State agency with each claim tangible evidence of such efforts.

(2) If the individual fails to thus search for work, or to furnish tangible evidence of such efforts, he/she shall be ineligible for Extended Benefits for the week in which the failure occurred and thereafter until the individual is employed in at least four weeks with wages from such employment totalling not less than four times the individual's weekly benefit amount, as provided by the applicable State law.

(3)(i) A State law may provide that eligibility for Extended Benefits be determined under the applicable provisions of State law for regular compensation which is not sharable, without regard to the active search provisions otherwise applicable in paragraph (g)(1) of this section, for any individual who fails to engage in a systematic and sustained search for work throughout any week because such individual is—

(A) Serving on jury duty, or

(B) Hospitalized for treatment of an emergency or life-threatening condition.

(ii) The conditions in (i) (A) and (B) must be applied to individuals filing claims for Extended Benefits in the same manner as applied to individuals filing claims for regular compensation which is not sharable compensation.

(4) For the purposes of the foregoing paragraphs of this paragraph (g), State law applies regarding whether members of labor organizations shall be required to seek nonunion work in their customary occupations.

(5) If the State law does not also apply this paragraph (g) to individuals who claim what would otherwise be sharable regular compensation, the State will not be entitled to payment under EUCA and §615.14 in regard to such regular compensation.

(h) *Information to claimants.* The State agency or State Workforce Agency, as applicable, shall assure that each Extended Benefit claimant (and claimant for sharable regular compensation) is informed in writing—

(1) Of the State agency's classification of his/her prospects for finding work in his/her customary occupation within the time set out in paragraph (d) as "good" or "not good,"

(2) What kind of jobs he/she may be referred to, depending on the classification of his/her job prospects,

(3) What kind of jobs he/she must be actively engaged in seeking each week depending on the classification of his/her job prospects, and what tangible evidence of such search must be furnished to the State agency with each claim for benefits. In addition, the State must inform the claimant that

he/she is required to apply for and accept suitable work, and

(4) The resulting disqualification if he/she fails to apply for work to which referred, or fails to accept work offered, or fails to actively engage in seeking work or to furnish tangible evidence of such search for each week for which extended compensation or sharable regular benefits is claimed, beginning with the week following the week in which such information shall be furnished in writing to the individual.

[53 FR 27937, July 25, 1988, as amended at 71 FR 35514, June 21, 2006; 81 FR 57781, Aug. 24, 2016]

§ 615.9 Restrictions on entitlement.

(a) *Disqualifications.* If the week of unemployment for which an individual claims Extended Benefits is a week to which a disqualification for regular compensation applies, including a reduction because of the receipt of disqualifying income, or would apply but for the fact that the individual has exhausted all rights to such compensation, the individual shall be disqualified in the same degree from receipt of Extended Benefits for that week.

(b) *Additional compensation.* No individual shall be paid additional compensation and Extended Benefits with respect to the same week. If both are payable by a State with respect to the same week, the State law may provide for the payment of Extended Benefits instead of additional compensation with respect to the week. If Extended Benefits are payable to an individual by one State and additional compensation is payable to the individual for the same week by another State, the individual may elect which of the two types of compensation to claim.

(c) *Interstate claims.* An individual who files claims for Extended Benefits under the Interstate Benefit Payment Plan, in a State which is not in an Extended Benefit Period for the week(s) for which Extended Benefits are claimed, shall not be paid more than the first two weeks for which he/she files such claims.

(d) *Other restrictions.* The restrictions on entitlement specified in this section are in addition to other restrictions in EUCA and this part on eligibility for and entitlement to Extended Benefits.

§ 615.10 Special provisions for employers.

(a) *Charging contributing employers.* (1) Section 3303(a)(1) of the Internal Revenue Code of 1986 (26 U.S.C. 3303(a)(1)) does not require that Extended Benefits paid to an individual be charged to the experience rating accounts of employers.

(2) A State law may, however, consistently with section 3303(a)(1), require the charging of Extended Benefits paid to an individual; and if it does, it may provide for charging all or any portion of such compensation paid.

(3) Sharable regular compensation must be charged as all other regular compensation is charged under the State law.

(b) *Payments by reimbursing employers.* If an employer is reimbursing the State unemployment fund in lieu of paying contributions pursuant to the requirements of State law conforming with sections 3304(a)(6)(B) and 3309(a)(2) of the Internal Revenue Code of 1986 (26 U.S.C. 3304(a)(6)(B) and 3309(a)(2)), the State law shall require the employer to reimburse the State unemployment fund for not less than 50 percent of any sharable compensation that is attributable under the State law to service with such employer; and as to any compensation which is not sharable compensation under § 615.14, the State law shall require the employer to reimburse the State unemployment fund for 100 percent, instead of 50 percent, of any such compensation paid.

§ 615.11 Extended Benefit Periods.

(a) *Beginning date.* Except as provided in paragraph (d) of this section, an extended benefit period or high unemployment period begins in a State on the first day of the third calendar week after a week for which there is a State "on" indicator in that State under either § 615.12(a) or (b).

(b) *Ending date.* Except as provided in paragraphs (c) and (e) of this section, an extended benefit period or high unemployment period in a State ends on the last day of the third week after the first week for which there is a State "off" indicator in that State, unless another indicator is in "on" status.

(c) *Duration.* When an extended benefit period and/or high unemployment period becomes effective in any State, or triggers "off," the attained status must continue in effect for not less than 13 consecutive weeks.

(d) *Limitation.* No extended benefit period or high unemployment period may begin or end in any State before the most recent week for which data used to trigger the State "on" or "off" or "no change" indicator has been published.

(e) *Specific applications of the 13-week rule.* (1) If a State concludes a 13-week mandatory "on" period by virtue of the IUR indicator which, at the end of the 13-week period no longer satisfies the requirements for a State to be "on," the extended benefit period continues if the TUR indicator is "on" during the 11th week of the 13-week mandatory "on" period.

(2) If a State concludes a 13-week mandatory "on" period by virtue of the TUR indicator which, at the end of the 13-week period no longer satisfies the requirements for a State to be "on," the extended benefit period continues if the IUR indicator is "on" during the 11th week of the 13-week mandatory "on" period.

(f) *Determining if a State remains "off" as a result of a total unemployment rate indicator after the 13-week mandatory "off" period ends.* (1) The State remains "off" if there is not an IUR "on" indicator the 11th week of the 13-week mandatory "off" period, and there is a TUR "off" indicator for the third week before the last week of the 13-week mandatory "off" period.

[81 FR 57781, Aug. 24, 2016]

§615.12 Determination of "on" and "off" indicators.

(a) *Standard State indicators.* (1) There is a State "on" indicator in a State for a week if the head of the State agency determines, in accordance with this section, that, for the period consisting of that week and the immediately preceding 12 weeks, the rate of insured unemployment (not seasonally adjusted) under the State law—

(i) Equalled or exceeded 120 percent of the average of such rates for the corresponding 13-week periods ending in each of the preceding two calendar years, and

(ii) Equalled or exceeded 5.0 percent.

(2) There is a State "off" indicator in a State for a week if the head of the State agency determines, in accordance with this section, that, for the period consisting of that week and the immediately preceding 12 weeks, the rate of insured unemployment (not seasonally adjusted) under the State law—

(i) Was less than 120 percent of the average of such rates for the corresponding 13 week periods ending in each of the preceding two calendar years, or

(ii) Was less than 5.0 percent.

(3) The standard State indicators in this paragraph (a) shall apply to weeks beginning after September 25, 1982.

(b) *Optional State indicators.* (1)(i) A State may, in addition to the State indicators in paragraph (a) of this section, provide by its law that there shall be a State "on" indicator in the State for a week if the head of the State agency determines, in accordance with this section, that, for the period consisting of that week and the immediately preceding 12 weeks, the rate of insured unemployment (not seasonally adjusted) under the State law equalled or exceeded 6.0 percent even though it did not meet the 120 percent factor required under paragraph (a).

(ii) A State which adopts the optional State indicator must also provide that, when it is in an Extended Benefit Period, there will not be an "off" indicator until (A) the State rate of insured unemployment is less than 6.0 percent, and (B) either its rate of insured unemployment is less than 5.0 percent or is less than 120 percent of the average of such rates for the corresponding 13-week periods ending in each of the preceding two calendar years.

(2) The optional State indicators in this paragraph (b) shall apply to weeks beginning after September 25, 1982.

(c) *Computation of rate of insured unemployment*—(1) *Equation.* Each week the State agency head shall calculate the rate of insured unemployment under the State law (not seasonally adjusted) for purposes of determining the State "on" and "off" and "no change" indicators. In making such calculations the State agency head shall use a fraction, the numerator of which shall be the weekly average number of weeks claimed in claims filed (not seasonally adjusted) in the State in the 13-week period ending with the week for which the determination is made, and the denominator of which shall be the average monthly employment covered by the State law for the first four of the last six calendar quarters ending before the close of the 13-week period. The quotient obtained is to be computed to four decimal places, and is not otherwise rounded, and is to be expressed as a percentage by multiplying the resultant decimal fraction by 100.

(2) *Counting weeks claimed.* To determine the average number of weeks claimed in claims filed to serve as the numerator under paragraph (c)(1), the State agency shall include claims for all weeks for regular compensation, including claims taken as agent State under the Interstate Benefit Payment Plan. It shall exclude claims—

(i) For Extended Benefits under any State law,

(ii) For additional compensation under any State law, and

(iii) Under any Federal law except joint claims which combine regular compensation and compensation payable under 5 U.S.C. chapter 85.

(3) *Method of computing the State 120 percent factor.* The rate of insured unemployment for a current 13-week period shall be divided by the average of the rates of insured unemployment for the corresponding 13-week periods in each of the two preceding calendar years to determine whether the rate is equal to 120 percent of the average rate for the two years. The quotient obtained shall be computed to four decimal places and not otherwise rounded, and shall be expressed as a percentage by multiplying the resultant decimal fraction by 100. The average of the rates for the corresponding 13-week periods in each of the two preceding calendar years shall be one-half the sum of such rates computed to four decimal places and not otherwise rounded. To determine which are the corresponding weeks in the preceding years—

(i) The weeks shall be numbered starting with week number 1 as the first week ending in each calendar year.

(ii) The 13-week period ending with any numbered week in the current year shall correspond to the period ending with that same numbered week in each preceding year.

(iii) When that period in the current year ends with week number 53, the corresponding period in preceding years shall end with week number 52 if there is no week number 53.

(d) *Amendment of State indicator rates.* (1) Any determination by the head of a State agency of an "on" or "off" or "no change" IUR indicator may not be corrected more than three weeks after the close of the week to which it applies. If any figure used in the computation of a rate of insured unemployment is later found to be wrong, the correct figure must be used to redetermine the rate of insured unemployment and the 120 percent factor for that week and all later weeks, but no determination of previous "on" or "off" or "no change" indicator shall be affected unless the redetermination is made within the time the indicator may be corrected under the first sentence of this paragraph (d)(1). Any change is subject to the concurrence of the Department as provided in paragraph (e) of this section.

(2) The initial release of the TUR by the Bureau of Labor Statistics (BLS) is subject to revision. However, once a State's TUR indicator is determined using the initial release of the TUR data, it is not subject to revision even if the BLS TUR for that period of time is revised.

(3) The "on" period under a State's optional IUR or TUR indicator may not begin before the later of the date of the State's adoption of the optional insured unemployment rate or total unemployment rate indicator, or the effective date of that enactment. The "off" period under a State's optional insured unemployment rate or total unemployment rate indicator may not occur until after the effective date of the repeal of the optional insured unemployment rate or total unemployment rate indicator from State law.

(e) *Other optional indicators.* (1) A State may, as an option, in addition to the State indicators in paragraphs (a) and (b) of this section, provide by its law that there is a State "on" or "off" indicator in the State for a week if we determine that—

(i) The Trigger Value in such State computed using the most recent 3 months for which data for all States are published before the close of such week equals or exceeds 6.5 percent; and

(ii) The Trigger Value computed using data from the 3-month period referred to in paragraph (e)(1)(i) of this section equals or exceeds 110 percent of the Trigger Value for either (or both) of the corresponding 3-month periods ending in the 2 preceding calendar years. This "look-back" is computed by dividing the Trigger Value by the same measure for the corresponding 3 months in each of the applicable prior years, and the resulting decimal fraction is rounded to the hundredths place, multiplied by 100 and reported as an integer and compared to the statutory threshold to help determine the State's EB Program status; and

(iii) There is a State "off" indicator for a week if either the requirements of paragraph (e)(1)(i) or (ii) of this section are not satisfied.

(2) Where a State adopts the optional indicator under paragraph (e)(1) of this section, there is a State "on" indicator for a high unemployment period (as defined in § 615.2) under State law if—

(i) The Trigger Value in the State computed using the most recent 3 months for which data for all States are published before the close of such week equals or exceeds 8.0 percent, and

(ii) The Trigger Value in the State computed using data from the 3-month period referred to in paragraph (e)(2)(i) of this section equals or exceeds 110 percent of the Trigger Value for either (or both) of the corresponding 3-month periods ending in the 2 preceding calendar years. This "look-back" is computed by dividing the Trigger Value by the same measure for the corresponding 3 months in each of the applicable prior years, and the resulting decimal fraction is rounded to the hundredths place, multiplied by 100 and reported as an integer and compared to the statutory threshold to help determine the State's EB Program status; and

(iii) There is a State "off" indicator for high unemployment period for a week if either the requirements of paragraph (e)(2)(i) or (ii) of this section are not satisfied.

(3) *Method of computing the average rate of total unemployment.* The average rate of total unemployment is computed by dividing the average of 3 months of the level of seasonally adjusted unemployment in the State by the average of 3 months of the level of seasonally adjusted unemployment and employment in the State. The resulting rate is multiplied by 100 to convert it to a percentage basis and then rounded to the tenths place (the first digit to the right of the decimal place).

(4) *Method of computing the State "look-back."* The average rate of total unemployment, ending with a given month, is divided by the same measure for the corresponding 3 months in each of the applicable prior years. The resultant decimal fraction is then rounded to the hundredths place (the second digit to the right of the decimal place). The resulting number is then multiplied by 100 and reported as an integer (no decimal places) and compared to the statutory threshold to help determine the State's EB Program status.

(f) *Notice to Secretary.* Within 10 calendar days after the end of any week for which the head of a State agency has determined that there is an "on," or "off," or "no change" IUR indicator in the State, the head of the State agency must notify the Secretary of the determination. The notice must state clearly the State agency head's determination of the specific week for which there is a State "on" or "off" or "no change" indicator. The notice must include also the State agency head's findings supporting the determination, with a certification that the findings are made in accordance with the requirements of § 615.15. The Secretary may provide additional instructions for the contents of the notice to assure the correctness and verification of notices given under this paragraph. The Secretary will accept determinations and findings made in accordance with the provisions of this paragraph and of any instructions issued under this paragraph. A notice does not become final for purposes of EUCA and this part until the Secretary accepts the notice.

[53 FR 27937, July 25, 1988, as amended at 81 FR 57782, Aug. 24, 2016]

§615.13 Announcement of the beginning and ending of Extended Benefit Periods or High Unemployment Periods.

(a) *State indicators*—(1) *Extended benefit period.* Upon receipt of a notice required by §615.12(f) which the Department determines is acceptable, the Department will publish in the FEDERAL REGISTER a notice of the State agency head's determination that there is an "on" or an "off" indicator in the State, as the case may be, the name of the State and the beginning or ending of the extended benefit period, or high unemployment period, whichever is appropriate. If an "on" or "off" EB period is determined by the Department to be based on a State's TUR Trigger Value, the Department publishes that information in the FEDERAL REGISTER as well.

(2) *Notification.* The Department also notifies the heads of all other State agencies, and the Regional Administrators of the Employment and Training Administration of the State agency head's determination of the State "on" or "off" indicator for an extended benefit period, or high unemployment period (based on the insured unemployment rate in the State), or of the Department's determination of an "on" or "off" indicator (based on the total unemployment rate in a State) for an extended benefit period or high unemployment period and of the indicator's effect.

(b) *Publicity by State.* (1) Whenever a State agency head determines that there is an "on" indicator in the State by reason of which an extended benefit period (based on the insured unemployment rate in the State) will begin in the State, or an "off" indicator by reason of which an extended benefit period in the State (based on the insured unemployment rate) will end, the head of the State agency must promptly announce the determination through appropriate news media in the State after the Department accepts notice from the agency head in accordance the 615.12(f).

(2) Whenever the head of a State agency receives notification from the Department in accordance with §615.12(f) that there is an "on" indicator by reason of which an extended benefit period or high unemployment period (based on the total unemployment rate in the State) will begin in the State, or an "off" indicator by reason of which a regular extended benefit period or high unemployment period (based on the total unemployment rate) will end, the head of the State agency must promptly announce the determination through the appropriate news media in the State.

(3) Announcements made in accordance with paragraphs (b)(1) or (b)(2) of this section must include the beginning or ending date of the extended benefit period or high unemployment period, whichever is appropriate. In the case of a regular EB period or high unemployment period that is about to begin, the announcement must describe clearly the unemployed individuals who may be eligible for extended compensation or high extended compensation during the period, and in the case of a regular EB period or high unemployment period that is about to end, the announcement must also describe clearly the individuals whose entitlement to extended compensation or high extended compensation will be terminated. If a high unemployment period is ending, but an extended benefit period will remain "on," the announcement must clearly state that fact and the effect on entitlement to extended compensation.

(c) *Notice to individuals.* (1) Whenever there has been a determination that a regular extended benefit period or high unemployment period will begin in a State, the State agency must provide prompt written notice of potential entitlement to Extended Benefits to each individual who has established a benefit year in the State that will not end before the beginning of the regular extended benefit period or high unemployment period, and who exhausted all rights under the State law to regular compensation before the beginning of the regular extended benefit period or high unemployment period.

(2) The State agency must provide the notice promptly to each individual

who begins to claim sharable regular benefits or who exhausts all rights under the State law to regular compensation during a regular extended benefit period or high unemployment period, including exhaustion by reason of the expiration of the individual's benefit year.

(3) The notices required by paragraphs (c)(1) and (2) of this section must describe the actions required of claimants for sharable regular compensation and extended compensation and those disqualifications which apply to the benefits which are different from those applicable to other claimants for regular compensation which is not sharable.

(4) Whenever there is a determination that a regular extended benefit period or high unemployment period will end in a State, the State agency must provide prompt written notice to each individual who is currently filing claims for extended compensation of the forthcoming end of the regular extended benefit period or high unemployment period and its effect on the individual's right to extended compensation.

[81 FR 57783, Aug. 24, 2016]

§615.14 Payments to States.

(a) *Sharable compensation.* (1) The Department shall promptly upon receipt of a State's report of its expenditures for a calendar month reimburse the State in the amount of the sharable compensation the State is entitled to receive under EUCA and this part.

(2) The Department may instead advance to a State for any period not greater than one day the amount the Department estimates the State will be entitled to be paid under EUCA and this part for that period.

(3) Any payment to a State under this section shall be based upon the Department's determination of the amount the State is entitled to be paid under EUCA and this part, and such amount shall be reduced or increased, as the case may be, by any amount by which the Department finds that a previous payment was greater or less than the amount that should have been paid to the State.

(4) Any payment to a State pursuant to this paragraph (a) shall be made by a transfer from the extended unemployment compensation account in the Unemployment Trust Fund to the account of the State in such Fund, in accordance with section 204(e) of EUCA.

(b) *Payments not to be made to States.* Because a State law must contain provisions fully consistent with sections 202 and 203 of EUCA, the Department shall make no payment under paragraph (a) of this section, whether or not the State is certified under section 3304(c) of the Internal Revenue Code of 1986—

(1) In respect of any regular or extended compensation paid to any individual for any week if the State does not apply—

(i) The provisions of the State law required by section 202(a)(3) and this part, relating to failure to accept work offered or to apply for work or to actively engage in seeking work or the provisions of State law required by section 202(a)(4) and this part, relating to terminating a disqualification;

(ii) The provisions of the State law required by section 202(a)(5) and this part, relating to qualifying employment; or

(2) In respect of any regular or extended compensation paid to any individual for any week which was not payable by reason of the provision of the State law required by section 202(c) and this part as determined by the Department with regard to each State.

(c) *Payments not to be reimbursed.* The Department shall make no payment under paragraph (a) of this section, whether or not the State is certified under section 3304(c) of the Internal Revenue Code of 1986, in respect of any regular or extended compensation paid under a State law—

(1) As provided in section 204(a)(1) of EUCA and this part, if the payment made was not sharable extended compensation or sharable regular compensation;

(2) As provided in section 204(a)(2)(A) of EUCA, if the State is entitled to reimbursement for the payment under the provisions of any Federal law other than EUCA;

(3) As provided in section 204(a)(2)(B) of EUCA, if for the first week in an individual's eligibility period with respect to which Extended Benefits or sharable regular benefits are paid to

the individual and the State law provides for the payment (at any time or under any circumstances) of regular compensation to any individual for the first week of unemployment in any such individual's benefit year; except that—

(i) In the case of a State law which is changed so that regular compensation is not paid at any time or under any circumstances with respect to the first week of unemployment in any individual's benefit year, this paragraph (c)(3) shall not apply to any week which begins after the effective date of such change in the State law; and

(ii) In the case of a State law which is changed so that regular compensation is paid at any time or under any circumstances with respect to the first week of unemployment in any individual's benefit year, this paragraph (c)(3) shall apply to all weeks which begin after the effective date of such change in the State law;

(4) As provided in section 204(a)(2)(C) of EUCA, for any week in which extended compensation is not payable because of the payment of trade readjustment allowances, as provided in section 233(c) of the Trade Act of 1974, and §615.7(d).

(5) As provided in section 204(a)(2)(D) of EUCA and this part, if the State does not provide for a benefit structure under which benefits are rounded down to the next lower dollar amount, for the 50 percent Federal share of the amount by which sharable regular or Extended Benefits paid to any individual exceeds the nearest lower full dollar amount.

(6) As provided in section 204(a)(3) of EUCA, to the extent that such compensation is based upon employment and wages in service performed for governmental entities or instrumentalities to which section 3306(c)(7) of the Internal Revenue Code of 1986 (26 U.S.C. 3306(c)(7)) applies, in the proportion that wages for such service in the base period bear to the total base period wages;

(7) If the payment made was not sharable extended compensation or sharable regular compensation because the payment was not consistent with the requirements of—

(i) Section 202(a)(3) of EUCA, and §615.8 (e), (f), or (g);

(ii) Section 202(a)(4) of EUCA, and §615.8(c); or

(iii) Section 202(a)(5) of EUCA, and §615.4(b);

(8) If the payment made was not sharable extended compensation or sharable regular compensation because there was not in effect in the State an Extended Benefit Period in accord with the Act and this part; or

(9) For any week with respect to which the claimant was either ineligible for or not entitled to the payment.

(d) *Effectuating authorization for reimbursement.* (1) If the Department believes that reimbursement should not be authorized with respect to any payments made by a State that are claimed to be sharable compensation paid by the State, because the State law does not contain provisions required by EUCA and this part, or because such law is not interpreted or applied in rules, regulations, determinations or decisions in a manner that is consistent with those requirements, the Department may at any time notify the State agency in writing of the Department's view. The State agency shall be given an opportunity to present its views and arguments if desired.

(2) The Department shall thereupon decide whether the State law fails to include the required provisions or is not interpreted and applied so as to satisfy the requirements of EUCA and this part. If the Department finds that such requirements are not met, the Department shall notify the State agency of its decision and the effect thereof on the State's entitlement to reimbursement under this section and the provisions of section 204 of EUCA.

(3) Thereafter, the Department shall not authorize any payment under paragraph (a) of this section in respect of any sharable regular or extended compensation if the State law does not contain all of the provisions required by sections 202 and 203 of EUCA and this part, or if the State law, rules, regulations, determinations or decisions are not consistent with such requirements, or which would not have been payable if the State law contained

the provisions required by EUCA and this part or if the State law, rules, regulations, determinations or decisions had been consistent with such requirements. Loss of reimbursement for such compensation shall begin with the date the State law was required to contain such provisions, and shall continue until such time as the Department finds that such law, rules and regulations have been revised or the interpretations followed pursuant to such determinations and decisions have been overruled and payments are made or denied so as to accord with the Federal law requirements of EUCA and this part, but no reimbursement shall be authorized with respect to any payment that did not fully accord with EUCA and this part.

(4) A State agency may request reconsideration of a decision issued pursuant to paragraph (d)(2) above, within 10 calendar days of the date of such decision, and shall be given an opportunity to present views and arguments if desired.

(5) Concurrence of the Department in any State law provision, rule, regulation, determination or decision shall not be presumed from the absence of notice issued pursuant to this section or from a certification of the State issued pursuant to section 3304(c) of the Internal Revenue Code of 1986.

(6) Upon finding that a State has made payments for which it claims reimbursement that are not consistent with EUCA or this part, such claim shall be denied; and if the State has already been paid such claim in advance or by reimbursement, it shall be required to repay the full amount to the Department. Such repayment may be made by transfer of funds from the State's account in the Unemployment Trust Fund to the Extended Unemployment Compensation Account in the Fund, or by offset against any current advances or reimbursements to which the State is otherwise entitled, or the amount repayable may be recovered for the Extended Unemployment Compensation Account by other means and from any other sources that may be available to the United States or the Department.

(e) *Compensation under Federal unemployment compensation programs.* The Department shall promptly reimburse each State which has paid sharable compensation based on service covered by the UCFE and UCX Programs (parts 609 and 614 of this chapter, respectively) pursuant to 5 U.S.C. chapter 85, an amount which represents the full amount of such sharable compensation paid under the State law, or may make advances to the State. Such amounts shall be paid from the Federal Employees Compensation Account established for those programs, rather than from the Extended Unemployment Compensation Account.

(f) *Combined-wage claims.* If an individual was paid benefits under the Interstate Arrangement for Combining Employment and Wages (part 616 of this chapter) any payment required by paragraph (a) of this section shall be made to the States which contributed the wage credits.

(g) *Interstate claims.* Where sharable compensation is paid to an individual under the provisions of the Interstate Benefit Payment Plan, any payment required by paragraph (a) of this section shall be made only to the liable State.

[53 FR 27937, July 25, 1988, as amended at 71 FR 35514, June 21, 2006; 81 FR 57783, Aug. 24, 2016]

§ 615.15 Records and reports.

(a) *General.* State agencies must furnish to the Secretary such information and reports and make such studies as the Secretary decides are necessary or appropriate for carrying out the purposes of this part.

(b) *Recordkeeping.* Each State agency must make and maintain records pertaining to the administration of the Extended Benefit Program as the Department requires, and must make all such records available for inspection, examination and audit by such Federal officials or employees as the Department may designate or as may be required by law.

[81 FR 57783, Aug. 24, 2016]

PART 616—INTERSTATE ARRANGEMENT FOR COMBINING EMPLOYMENT AND WAGES

AUTHORITY: 26 U.S.C. 3304(a)(9)(B); Secretary's Order No. 3–2007, Apr. 3, 2007 (72 FR 15907).

SOURCE: 36 FR 24992, Dec. 28, 1971, unless otherwise noted.

§ 616.1 Purpose of arrangement.

This arrangement is approved by the Secretary under the provisions of section 3304(a)(9)(B) of the Federal Unemployment Tax Act to establish a system whereby an unemployed worker with covered employment or wages in more than one State may combine all such employment and wages in one State, in order to qualify for benefits or to receive more benefits.

§ 616.2 Consultation with the State agencies.

As required by section 3304(a)(9)(B), this arrangement has been developed in consultation with the State unemployment compensation agencies. For purposes of such consultation in its formulation and any future amendment the Secretary recognizes, as agents of the State agencies, the duly designated representatives of the National Association of State Workforce Agencies (NASWA).

[36 FR 24992, Dec. 28, 1971, as amended at 71 FR 35514, June 21, 2006]

§ 616.3 Interstate cooperation.

Each State agency will cooperate with every other State agency by implementing such rules, regulations, and procedures as may be prescribed for the operation of this arrangement. Each State agency shall identify the paying and the transferring State with respect to Combined-Wage Claims filed in its State.

§ 616.4 Rules, regulations, procedures, forms—resolution of disagreements.

All State agencies shall operate in accordance with such rules, regulations, and procedures, and shall use such forms, as shall be prescribed by the Secretary in consultation with the State unemployment compensation agencies. All rules, regulations, and standards prescribed by the Secretary with respect to intrastate claims will apply to claims filed under this arrangement unless they are clearly inconsistent with the arrangement. The Secretary shall resolve any disagreement between State agencies concerning the operation of the arrangement, with the advice of the duly designated representatives of the State agencies.

§ 616.6 Definitions.

These definitions apply for the purpose of this arrangement and the procedures issued to effectuate it.

(a) *State.* "State" includes the States of the United States of America, the District of Columbia, the Commonwealth of Puerto Rico, and the Virgin Islands.

(b) *State agency.* The agency which administers the unemployment compensation law of a State.

(c) *Combined-Wage Claim.* A claim filed under this arrangement.

(d) *Combined-Wage Claimant.* A claimant who has covered wages under the unemployment compensation law of more than one State and who has filed a claim under this arrangement.

(e) *Paying State.* A single State against which the claimant files a Combined-Wage Claim, if the claimant has wages and employment in that State's base period(s) and the claimant qualifies for unemployment benefits under the unemployment compensation law of that State using combined wages and employment.

(f) *Transferring State.* A State in which a Combined-Wage Claimant had covered employment and wages in the base period of a paying State, and which transfers such employment and wages to the paying State for its use in determining the benefit rights of such claimant under its law.

(g) *Employment and wages.* "Employment" refers to all services which are covered under the unemployment compensation law of a State, whether expressed in terms of weeks of work or otherwise. "Wages" refers to all remuneration for such employment.

(h) *Secretary.* The Secretary of Labor of the United States.

(i) *Base period and benefit year.* The base period and benefit year applicable under the unemployment compensation law of the paying State.

[36 FR 24992, Dec. 28, 1971, as amended at 39 FR 45215, Dec. 31, 1974; 43 FR 2625, Jan. 17, 1978; 71 FR 35514, June 21, 2006; 73 FR 63072, Oct. 23, 2008]

§ 616.7 Election to file a Combined-Wage Claim.

(a) Any unemployed individual who has had employment covered under the unemployment compensation law of two or more States, whether or not the individual is monetarily qualified under one or more of them, may elect to file a Combined-Wage Claim. The individual may not so elect, however, if the individual has established a benefit year under any State or Federal unemployment compensation law and:

(1) The benefit year has not ended, and

(2) The individual still has unused benefit rights based on such benefit year. [1]

(b) For the purposes of this arrangement, a claimant will not be considered to have unused benefit rights based on a benefit year which the claimant has established under a State or Federal unemployment compensation law if:

(1) The claimant has exhausted his/her rights to all benefits based on such benefit year; or

(2) The claimant's rights to such benefits have been postponed for an indefinite period or for the entire period in which benefits would otherwise be payable; or

(3) Benefits are affected by the application of a seasonal restriction.

(c) If an individual elects to file a Combined-Wage Claim, all employment and wages in all States in which the individual worked during the base period of the paying State must be included in such combining, except employment and wages which are not transferrable under the provisions of § 616.9(b).

(d) A Combined-Wage Claimant may withdraw his/her Combined-Wage Claim within the period prescribed by the law of the paying State for filing an appeal, protest, or request for redetermination (as the case may be) from the monetary determination of the Combined-Wage Claim, provided the claimant either:

(1) Repays in full any benefits paid to him thereunder, or

(2) Authorizes the State(s) against which the claimant files a substitute claim(s) for benefits to withhold and forward to the paying State a sum sufficient to repay such benefits.

(e) If the Combined-Wage Claimant files his/her claim in a State other than the paying State, the claimant shall do so pursuant to the Interstate Benefit Payment Plan.

(f) If a State denies a Combined-Wage Claim, it must inform the claimant of the option to file in another State in which the claimant has wages and employment during that State's base period(s).

[36 FR 24992, Dec. 28, 1971, as amended at 71 FR 35514, 35515, June 21, 2006; 73 FR 63072, Oct. 23, 2008]

§ 616.8 Responsibilities of the paying State.

(a) *Transfer of employment and wages—payment of benefits.* The paying State shall request the transfer of a Combined-Wage Claimant's employment and wages in all States during its base period, and shall determine the claimant's entitlement to benefits (including additional benefits, extended benefits

[1] The Federal-State Extended Unemployment Compensation Act of 1970, title II, Public Law 91–373, section 202(a)(1), limits the payment of extended benefits with respect to any week to individuals who have no rights to regular compensation with respect to such week under any State unemployment compensation law or to compensation under any other Federal law and in certain other instances. This provision precludes any individual from receiving any Federal-State extended benefits with respect to any week for which the individual is eligible to receive regular benefits based on a Combined Wage Claim. (See section 5752, part V of the Employment Security Manual.)

and dependents' allowances when applicable) under the provisions of its law based on employment and wages in the paying State, and all such employment and wages transferred to it hereunder. The paying State shall apply all the provisions of its law to each determination made hereunder, except that the paying State may not determine an issue which has previously been adjudicated by a transferring State. Such exception shall not apply, however, if the transferring State's determination of the issue resulted in making the Combined-Wage Claim possible under §616.7(b)(2). If the paying State fails to establish a benefit year for the Combined-Wage Claimant, or if the claimant withdraws his/her claim as provided herein, it shall return to each transferring State all employment and wages thus unused.

(b) *Notices of determination.* The paying State shall give to the claimant a notice of each of its determinations on his/her Combined-Wage Claim that he/she is required to receive under the Secretary's Claim Determinations Standard and the contents of such notice shall meet such Standard. When the claimant is filing his/her Combined-Wage Claims in a State other than the paying State, the paying State shall send a copy of each such notice to the local office in which the claimant filed such claims.

(c) *Redeterminations.* (1) Redeterminations may be made by the paying State in accordance with its law based on additional or corrected information received from any source, including a transferring State, except that such information shall not be used as a basis for changing the paying State if benefits have been paid under the Combined-Wage Claim.

(2) When a determination is made, as provided in paragraph (a) of this section, which suspends the use of wages earned in employment with an educational institution during a prescribed period between successive academic years or terms or other periods as prescribed in the law of the paying State in accordance with section 3304(a)(6)(A)(i)–(iv) of the Internal Revenue Code of 1986, the paying State shall furnish each transferring State involved in the combined-Wage Claim an adjusted determination used to recompute each State's proportionate share of any charges that may accumulate for benefits paid during the period of suspended use of school wages. Wages which are suspended shall be retained by the paying State for possible future reinstatement to the Combined-Wage Claim and shall not be returned to the transferring State.

(d) *Appeals.* (1) Except as provided in paragraph (d)(3) of this section, where the claimant files his/her Combined-Wage Claim in the paying State, any protest, request for redetermination or appeal shall be in accordance with the law of such State.

(2) Where the claimant files his/her Combined-Wage Claim in a State other than the paying State, or under the circumstances described in paragraph (d)(3) of this section, any protest, request for redetermination or appeal shall be in accordance with the Interstate Benefit Payment Plan.

(3) To the extent that any protest, request for redetermination or appeal involves a dispute as to the coverage of the employing unit or services in a transferring State, or otherwise involves the amount of employment and wages subject to transfer, the protest, request for redetermination or appeal shall be decided by the transferring State in accordance with its law.

(e) *Recovery of prior overpayments.* If there is an overpayment outstanding in a transferring State and such transferring State so requests, the overpayment shall be deducted from any benefits the paying State would otherwise pay to the claimant on his/her Combined-Wage Claim except to the extent prohibited by the law of the paying State. The paying State shall transmit the amount deducted to the transferring State or credit the deduction against the transferring State's required reimbursement under this arrangement. This paragraph shall apply to overpayments only if the transferring State certifies to the paying State that the determination of overpayment was made within 3 years before the Combined-Wage Claim was filed and that repayment by the claimant is legally required and enforceable against him/her under the law of the transferring State.

(f) *Statement of benefit charges.* (1) At the close of each calendar quarter, the paying State shall send each transferring State a statement of benefits charged during such quarter to such State as to each Combined-Wage Claimant.

(2) Except as provided in paragraphs (c)(2), (f)(3), and (f)(5) of this section, each such charge shall bear the same ratio to the total benefits paid to the Combined-Wage Claimant by the paying State as the claimant's wages transferred by the transferring State bear to the total wages used in such determination. Each such ratio shall be computed as a percentage, to three or more decimal places.

(3) Charges to the transferring State shall not include the costs of any benefits paid which are funded or reimbursed from the Federal Unemployment Benefits and Allowances account in the U.S. Department of Labor appropriation, including:

(i) Benefits paid pursuant to 5 U.S.C. 8501–8525; and

(ii) Benefits which are reimbursable under part B of title II of the Emergency Jobs and Unemployment Assistance Act of 1974 (Pub. L. 93–567).

(4) Except as provided in paragraphs (f)(3) and (f)(5) of this section, all transferring States will be charged by the paying State for Extended Benefits in the same manner as for regular benefits.

(5) The United States shall be charged directly by the paying State, in the same manner as is provided in paragraphs (f)(1) and (f)(2) of this section, in regard to Federal civilian service and wages and Federal military service and wages assigned or transferred to the paying State and included in Combined-Wage Claims in accordance with this part and parts 609 and 614 of this chapter.

(26 U.S.C. 3304(a)(9)(B); Secretary's Order No. 4–75, (40 FR 18515))

[36 FR 24992, Dec. 28, 1971, as amended at 43 FR 2625, Jan. 17, 1978; 45 FR 47109, July 11, 1980; 71 FR 35515, June 21, 2006; 73 FR 63072, Oct. 23, 2008]

§ 616.9 Responsibilities of transferring States.

(a) *Transfer of employment and wages.* Each transferring State shall promptly transfer to the Paying State the employment and wages the Combined-Wage Claimant had in covered employment during the base period of the paying State. Any employment and wages so transferred shall be transferred without restriction as to their use for determination and benefit payments under the provisions of the paying State's law.

(b) *Employment and wages not transferable.* Employment and wages transferred to the paying State by a transferring State shall not include:

(1) Any employment and wages which have been transferred to any other paying State and not returned unused, or which have been used in the transferring State as the basis of a monetary determination which established a benefit year.

(2) Any employment and wages which have been canceled or are otherwise unavailable to the claimant as a result of a determination by the transferring State made prior to its receipt of the request for transfer, if such determination has become final or is in the process of appeal but is still pending. If the appeal is finally decided in favor of the Combined-Wage Claimant, any employment and wages involved in the appeal shall forthwith be transferred to the paying State and any necessary redetermination shall be made by such paying State.

(c) *Reimbursement of paying State.* Each transferring State shall, as soon as practicable after receipt of a quarterly statement of charges described herein, reimburse the paying State accordingly.

(26 U.S.C. 3304(a)(9)(B); Secretary's Order No. 4–75, (40 FR 18515))

[36 FR 24992, Dec. 28, 1971, as amended at 45 FR 47109, July 11, 1980]

§ 616.10 Reuse of employment and wages.

Employment and wages which have been used under this arrangement for a determination of benefits which establishes a benefit year shall not thereafter be used by any State as the basis for another monetary determination of benefits.

§ 616.11 Amendment of arrangement.

Periodically the Secretary shall review the operation of this arrangement, and shall propose such amendments to the arrangement as the Secretary believes are necessary or appropriate. Any State unemployment compensation agency or NASWA may propose amendments to the arrangement. Any proposal shall constitute an amendment to the arrangement upon approval by the Secretary in consultation with the State unemployment compensation agencies. Any such amendment shall specify when the change shall take effect, and to which claims it shall apply.

[36 FR 24992, Dec. 28, 1971, as amended at 71 FR 35515, June 21, 2006]

PART 617—TRADE ADJUSTMENT ASSISTANCE FOR WORKERS UNDER THE TRADE ACT OF 1974

AUTHORITY: 19 U.S.C. 2320; Secretary's Order No. 3–81, 46 FR 31117.

SOURCE: 51 FR 45848, Dec. 22, 1986, unless otherwise noted.

Subpart A—General

§617.1 Scope.

The regulations in this part 617 pertain to:

(a) Adjustment assistance, such as counseling, testing, training, placement, and other supportive services for workers adversely affected under the terms of chapter 2 of title II of the Trade Act of 1974, as amended (hereafter referred to as the Act);

(b) Trade readjustment allowances (hereafter referred to as TRA) and other allowances such as allowances while in training, job search and relocation allowances; and

(c) Administrative requirements applicable to State agencies to which such individuals may apply.

§617.2 Purpose.

The Act created a program of trade adjustment assistance (hereafter referred to as TAA) to assist individuals, who became unemployed as a result of increased imports, return to suitable employment. The TAA program provides for reemployment services and allowances for eligible individuals. The regulations in this part 617 are issued to implement the Act.

§617.3 Definitions.

For the purposes of the Act and this part 617:

(a) *Act* means chapter 2 of title II of the Trade Act of 1974, Pub. L. 93–618, 88 Stat. 1978, 2019–2030 (19 U.S.C. 2271–2322), as amended.

(b) *Adversely affected employment* means employment in a firm or appropriate subdivision of a firm, including workers in any agricultural firm or subdivision of an agricultural firm, if workers of such firm or appropriate subdivision are certified under the Act as eligible to apply for TAA.

(c) *Adversely affected worker* means an individual who, because of lack of work in adversely affected employment:

(1) Has been totally or partially separated from such employment; or

(2) Has been totally separated from employment with the firm in a subdivision of which such adversely affected employment exists.

(d) *Appropriate week* means the week in which the individual's first separation occurred.

(e) *Average weekly hours* means a figure obtained by dividing:

(1) Total hours worked (excluding overtime) by a partially separated individual in adversely affected employment in the 52 weeks (excluding weeks in such period during which the individual was sick or on vacation) preceding the individual's first qualifying separation, by

(2) The number of weeks in such 52 weeks (excluding weeks in such period during which the individual was sick or on vacation) in which the individual actually worked in such employment.

(f) *Average weekly wage* means one-thirteenth of the total wages paid to an individual in the individual's high quarter. The high quarter for an individual is the quarter in which the total wages paid to the individual were highest among the first four of the last five completed calendar quarters preceding the individual's appropriate week.

(g) *Average weekly wage in adversely affected employment* means a figure obtained by dividing:

(1) Total wages earned by a partially separated individual in adversely affected employment in the 52 weeks (excluding the weeks in that period the individual was sick or on vacation) preceding the individual's first qualifying separation, by

(2) The number of weeks in such 52 weeks (excluding the weeks in that period the individual was sick or on vacation) the individual actually worked in such employment.

(h) *Benefit period* means, with respect to an individual:

(1) The benefit year and any ensuing period, as determined under the applicable State law, during which the individual is eligible for regular compensation, additional compensation, extended compensation, or federal supplemental compensation, as these terms are defined by paragraph (oo) of this section; or

(2) The equivalent to such a benefit year or ensuing period provided for under the Federal unemployment insurance law.

(i) *Bona fide application for training* means an individual's signed and dated application for training filed with the State agency administering the TAA training program, on a form necessarily containing the individual's name, petition number, local office number, and specific occupational training. This form shall be signed and dated by a State agency representative upon receipt.

(j)(1) *Certification* means a certification of eligibility to apply for TAA issued under section 223 of the Act with respect to a specified group of workers of a firm or appropriate subdivision of a firm.

(2) *Certification period* means the period of time during which total and partial separations from adversely affected employment within a firm or appropriate subdivision of a firm are covered by the certification.

(k) *Commuting area* means the area in which an individual would be expected to travel to and from work on a daily basis as determined under the applicable State law.

(l) *Date of separation* means:

(1) With respect to a total separation—

(i) For an individual in employment status, the last day worked; and

(ii) For an individual on employer-authorized leave, the last day the individual would have worked had the individual been working; and

(2) With respect to a partial separation, the last day of the week in which the partial separation occurred.

(m) *Eligibility period* means the period of consecutive calendar weeks during which basic or additional TRA is payable to an otherwise eligible individual, and for an individual such eligibility period is—

(1) *Basic TRA.* With respect to a total qualifying separation (as defined in paragraph (t)(3)(i) of this section) the 104-week period beginning with the first week following the week in which such total qualifying separation occurred; provided, that an individual who has a second or subsequent total qualifying separation within the certification period of the same certification shall be determined to have a new 104-week eligibility period based upon the most recent such total qualifying separation.

(2) *Additional TRA.* With respect to additional weeks of TRA, and any individual determined under this part 617 to be entitled to additional TRA, the consecutive calendar weeks that occur in the 26-week period that—

(i) Immediately follows the last week of entitlement to basic TRA otherwise payable to the individual, or

(ii) Begins with the first week of training approved under this part 617, if such training begins after the last week described in paragraph (m)(2)(i) of this section, or

(iii) Begins with the first week in which such training is approved under this part 617, if such training is so approved after the training has commenced; but approval of training under this part 617 after the training has commenced shall not imply or justify approval of a payment of basic or additional TRA with respect to any week which ended before the week in which such training was approved, nor approval of payment of any costs of training or any costs or expenses associated with such training (such as travel or subsistence) which were incurred prior to the date of the approval of such training under this part 617.

(n) *Employer* means any individual or type of organization, including the Federal government, a State government, a political subdivision, or an instrumentality of one or more governmental entities, with one or more individuals performing service in employment for it within the United States.

(o) *Employment* means any service performed for an employer by an officer of a corporation or an individual for wages.

(p) *Exhaustion of UI* means exhaustion of all rights to UI in a benefit period by reason of:

(1) Having received all UI to which an individual was entitled under the applicable State law or Federal unemployment compensation law with respect to such benefit period; or

(2) The expiration of such benefit period.

(q) *Family* means the following members of an individual's household whose principal place of abode is with the individual in a home the individual maintains or would maintain but for unemployment:

(1) A spouse;

(2) An unmarried child, including a stepchild, adopted child, or foster child, under age 21 or of any age if incapable of self-support because of mental or physical incapacity; and

(3) Any other person whom the individual would be entitled to claim as a dependent for income tax purposes under the Internal Revenue Code of 1986.

(r) *First benefit period* means the benefit period established after the individual's first qualifying separation or in which such separation occurs.

(s) *First exhaustion of UI* means the first time in an individual's first benefit period that the individual exhausts all rights to UI; first exhaustion shall be deemed to be complete at the end of the week the exhaustion occurs.

(t)(1) *First separation* means, for an individual to qualify as an adversely affected worker for the purposes of TAA program benefits (without regard to whether the individual also qualifies for TRA), the individual's first total or partial separation within the certification period of a certification, irrespective of whether such first separation also is a qualifying separation as defined in paragraph (t)(2) of this section;

(2) *Qualifying separation* means for an individual to qualify as an adversely affected worker and for basic TRA, any total separation of the individual within the certification period of a certification with respect to which the individual meets all of the requirements in § 617.11(a)(2)(i) through (iv), and which qualifies as a total qualifying separation as defined in paragraph (B) of (t)(3)(i) of this section.

(3) *First qualifying separation* means—

(i) For the purposes of determining an individual's eligibility period for basic TRA, the first total separation of the individual within the certification period of a certification, with respect to which the individual meets all of the requirements in § 617.11(a)(2)(i) through (iv).

(ii) For the purposes of determining the weekly and maximum amounts of basic TRA payable to an individual, with respect to a separation that occurs before, on, or after August 23, 1988, the individual's first (total or partial) separation within the certification period of a certification if, with respect to such separation, the individual meets the requirements of § 617.11(a)(1) (i), (ii) and (iv) or § 617.11(a)(2) (i), (ii) and (iv).

(u) *Head of family* means an individual who maintains a home for a family. An individual maintains a home if over half the cost of maintenance is furnished by the individual or would be furnished but for unemployment.

(v) *Impact date* means the date stated in a certification issued under the Act on which total or partial separations began or threatened to begin in a firm or a subdivision of a firm.

(w) *Job search program* means a job search workshop or job finding club.

(x) *Job search workshop* means a short (1 to 3 days) seminar designed to provide participants with knowledge that will enable the participants to find jobs. Subjects should include, but not be limited to, labor market information, resume writing, interviewing techniques, and techniques for finding job openings.

(y) *Job finding club* means a job search workshop which includes a period of 1 to 2 weeks of structured, supervised activity in which participants attempt to obtain jobs.

(z) *Layoff* means a suspension of or separation from employment by a firm for lack of work, initiated by the employer, and expected to be for a definite or indefinite period of not less than seven consecutive days.

(aa) *Liable State* and *Agent State* are defined as follows:

(1) *Liable State* means, with respect to any individual, the State whose State law is the applicable State law as determined under § 617.16 for all purposes of this Part 617.

(2) *Agent State* means, with respect to any individual, any State other than the State which is the liable State for such individual.

(bb) *On-the-job training* means training provided by an employer to an individual who is employed by the employer.

(cc) *Partial separation* means that during a week ending on or after the impact date specified in the certification under which an adversely affected worker is covered, the individual had:

(1) Hours of work reduced to 80 percent or less of the individual's average weekly hours in adversely affected employment; and

(2) Wages reduced to 80 percent or less of the individual's average weekly wage in such adversely affected employment.

(dd) *Regional Administrator* means the appropriate Regional Administrator of the Employment and Training Administration, United States Department of Labor (hereafter Department).

(ee) *Remuneration* means remuneration as defined in the applicable State law.

(ff) *Secretary* means the Secretary of Labor, U.S. Department of Labor, or his or her designee.

(gg) *Separate maintenance* means maintaining another (second) residence, in addition to the individual's regular place of residence, while attending a training facility outside the individual's commuting area.

(hh) *State* means the States of the United States, the District of Columbia, and the Commonwealth of Puerto Rico, and the term "United States" when used in a geographical sense includes such Commonwealth.

(ii) *State agency* means the State Workforce Agency; the employment service of the State; any State agency carrying out title I, Subchapter B of the Workforce Investment Act; or any other State or local agency administering job training or related programs with which the Secretary has an agreement to carry out any of the provisions of the Act.

(jj) *State law* means the unemployment compensation law of a State approved by the Secretary under section 3304 of the Internal Revenue Code of 1986 (26 U.S.C. 3304).

(kk) *Suitable work* means, with respect to an individual:

(1) Suitable work as defined in the applicable State law for claimants for regular compensation (as defined in paragraph (oo)(1) of this section); or

(2) Suitable work as defined in applicable State law provisions consistent with section 202(a)(3) of the Federal-State Extended Unemployment Compensation Act of 1970;

whichever is applicable, but does not in any case include self-employment or employment as an independent contractor.

(ll) *Total separation* means a layoff or severance of an individual from employment with a firm in which, or in a subdivision of which, adversely affected employment exists.

(mm) *Trade adjustment assistance (TAA)* means the services and allowances provided for achieving reemployment of adversely affected workers, including TRA, training and other reemployment services, and job search allowances and relocation allowances.

(nn) *Trade readjustment allowance (TRA)* means a weekly allowance payable to an adversely affected worker with respect to such worker's unemployment under subpart B of this part 617.

(oo) *Unemployment insurance (UI)* means the unemployment compensation payable to an individual under any State law or Federal unemployment compensation law, including chapter 85, title 5 of the United States Code, and the Railroad Unemployment Insurance Act. "UI" includes "regular compensation," "additional compensation," "extended compensation," and "federal supplemental compensation," defined as follows:

(1) *Regular compensation* means unemployment compensation payable to an individual under any State law, and, when so payable, includes unemployment compensation payable pursuant to chapter 85, title 5 of the United States Code, but does not include extended compensation, additional compensation, or federal supplemental compensation;

(2) *Additional compensation* means unemployment compensation totally financed by a State and payable under a State law by reason of conditions of high unemployment or by reason of other special factors and, when so payable, includes unemployment compensation payable pursuant to chapter 85, title 5 of the United States Code; and

(3) *Extended compensation* means the extended unemployment compensation payable to an individual for weeks of

unemployment which begin in an Extended Benefit Period, under those provisions of a State law which satisfy the requirements of the Federal-State Extended Unemployment Compensation Act of 1970 and regulations governing the payment of extended unemployment compensation, and, when so payable, includes unemployment compensation payable pursuant to chapter 85, title 5 of the United States Code, but does not include regular compensation, additional compensation, or federal supplemental compensation. Extended compensation is also referred to in this part 617 as Extended Benefits or EB.

(4) *Federal supplemental compensation* means the supplemental unemployment compensation payable to individuals who have exhausted their rights to regular and extended compensation, and which is payable under the Federal Supplemental Compensation Act of 1982 or any similar Federal law enacted before or after the 1982 Act.

(pp) *Wages* means all compensation for employment for an employer, including commissions, bonuses, and the cash value of all compensation in a medium other than cash.

(qq) *Week* means a week as defined in the applicable State law.

(rr) *Week of unemployment* means a week of total, part total, or partial unemployment as determined under the applicable State law or Federal unemployment compensation law.

[51 FR 45848, Dec. 22, 1986, as amended at 53 FR 32348, Aug. 24, 1988; 59 FR 926, 927, Jan. 6, 1994; 61 FR 19983, May 3, 1996; 71 FR 35515, June 21, 2006]

§617.4 Benefit information to workers.

(a) *Providing information to workers.* State agencies shall provide full information to workers about the benefit allowances, training, and other employment services available under subparts B through E of this part 617 and about the petition and application procedures, and the appropriate filing dates, for such allowances, training and services.

(b) *Providing assistance to workers.* State agencies shall provide whatever assistance is necessary to enable groups of workers, including unorganized workers, to prepare petitions or applications for program benefits.

(c) *Providing information to State vocational education agencies and others.* State agencies shall inform the State Board for Vocational Education or equivalent agency and other public or private agencies, institutions, and employers, as appropriate, of each certification issued under section 223 of the Act and of projections, if available, of the needs for training under section 236 of the Act as a result of such certification.

(d) *Written and newspaper notices*—(1) *Written notices to workers.* (i) Upon receipt of a certification issued by the Department of Labor, the State agency shall provide a written notice through the mail of the benefits available under subparts B through E of this part 617 to each worker covered by a certification issued under section 223 of the Act when the worker is partially or totally separated or as soon as possible after the certification is issued if such workers are already partially or totally separated from adversely affected employment.

(ii) The State agency will satisfy this requirement by obtaining from the firm, or other reliable source, the names and addresses of all workers who were partially or totally separated from adversely affected employment before the certification was received by the agency, and workers who are thereafter partially or totally separated within the certification period. The State agency shall mail a written notice to each such worker of the benefits available under the TAA Program. The notice must include the following information:

(A) Worker group(s) covered by the certification, and the article(s) produced as specified in the copy of the certification furnished to the State agency.

(B) Name and the address or location of workers' firm.

(C) Impact, certification, and expiration dates in the certification document.

(D) Benefits and reemployment services available to eligible workers.

(E) Explanation of how workers apply for TAA benefits and services.

(F) Whom to call to get additional information on the certification.

(G) When and where the workers should come to apply for benefits and services.

(2) *Newspaper notices.* (i) Upon receipt of a copy of a certification issued by the Department affecting workers in a State, the State agency shall publish a notice of such certification in a newspaper of general circulation in areas in which such workers reside. Such a newspaper notice shall not be required to be published, however, in the case of a certification with respect to which the State agency can substantiate, and enters in its records evidence substantiating, that all workers covered by the certification have received written notice required by paragraph (d)(1) of this section.

(ii) A published notice must include the following kinds of information:

(A) Worker group(s) covered by the certification, and the article(s) produced as specified in the copy of the certification furnished to the State agency.

(B) Name and the address or location of workers' firm.

(C) Impact, certification, and expiration dates in the certification document.

(D) Benefits and reemployment services available to eligible workers.

(E) Explanation of how and where workers should apply for TAA benefits and services.

(e) *Advice and assistance to workers.* In addition to the information and assistance to workers as required under paragraphs (a) and (b) of this section, State agencies shall—

(1) Advise each worker who applies for unemployment insurance under the State law of the benefits available under subparts B through E of this part and the procedures and deadlines for applying for such benefits.

(2) Facilitate the early filing of petitions under section 221 of the Act and §617.4(b) for any workers that the agency considers are likely to be eligible for benefits. State agencies shall utilize information received by the State's dislocated worker unit to facilitate the early filing of petitions under section 221 of the Act by workers potentially adversely affected by imports.

(3) Advise each adversely affected worker to apply for training under §617.22(a) before, or at the same time as, the worker applies for trade readjustment allowances under subpart B of this part.

(4) Interview each adversely affected worker, as soon as practicable, regarding suitable training opportunities available to the worker under §617.22(a) and review such opportunities with the worker.

[51 FR 45848, Dec. 22, 1986, as amended at 59 FR 927, Jan. 6, 1994]

Subpart B—Trade Readjustment Allowances (TRA)

§617.10 Applications for TRA.

(a) *Before and after certification.* An individual covered under a certification or a petition for certification may apply to a State agency for TRA. A determination shall be made at any time to the extent necessary to establish or protect an individual's entitlement to TRA or other TAA, but no payment of TRA or other TAA may be made by a State agency until a certification is made and the State agency determines that the individual is covered thereunder.

(b) *Timing of applications.* An initial application for TRA, and applications for TRA for weeks of unemployment beginning before the initial application for TRA is filed, may be filed within a reasonable period of time after publication of the determination certifying the appropriate group of workers under section 223 of the Act. However, an application for TRA for a week of unemployment beginning after the initial application is filed shall be filed within the time limit applicable to claims for regular compensation under the applicable State law. For purposes of this paragraph (b), a reasonable period of time means such period of time as the individual had good cause for not filing earlier, which shall include, but not be limited to, the individual's lack of knowledge of the certification or misinformation supplied the individual by the State agency.

(c) *Applicable procedures.* Applications shall be filed in accordance with this subpart B and on forms which shall be furnished to individuals by the State agency. The procedures for reporting and filing applications for TRA shall be consistent with this part 617 and the Secretary's "Standard for Claim Filing, Claimant Reporting, Job Finding and Employment Services", *Employment Security Manual,* part V, sections 5000 *et seq.* (Appendix A of this part).

(d) *Advising workers to apply for training.* State agencies shall advise each worker of the qualifying requirements for entitlement to TRA and other TAA benefits at the time the worker files an initial claim for State UI, and shall advise each adversely affected worker to apply for training under subpart C of this part before, or at the same time, the worker applies for TRA, as required by §617.4(e)(1) and (3).

[51 FR 45848, Dec. 22, 1986, as amended at 59 FR 928, 943, Jan. 6, 1994]

§617.11 Qualifying requirements for TRA.

(a) *Basic qualifying requirements for entitlement*—(1) [Reserved]

(2) To qualify for TRA for any week of unemployment an individual must meet each of the following requirements of paragraphs (a)(2) (i) through (vii) of this section:

(i) *Certification.* The individual must be an adversely affected worker covered under a certification.

(ii) *Separation.* The individual's first qualifying separation (as defined in paragraph (t)(3)(i) of §617.3) before application for TRA must occur:

(A) On or after the impact date of such certification; and

(B) Before the expiration of the two-year period beginning on the date of such certification, or, if earlier, before the termination date, if any, of such certification.

(iii) *Wages and employment.* (A) In the 52-week period (*i.e.,* 52 consecutive calendar weeks) ending with the week of the individual's first qualifying separation, or any subsequent total qualifying separation under the same certification, the individual must have had at least 26 weeks of employment at wages of $30 or more a week in adversely affected employment with a single firm or subdivision of a firm. Evidence that an individual meets this requirement shall be obtained as provided in §617.12. Employment and wages covered under more than one certification may not be combined to qualify for TRA.

(B)(*1*) For the purposes of paragraph (a)(2)(iii) of this section, any week in which such individual—

(*i*) Is on employer-authorized leave from such adversely affected employment for purposes of vacation, sickness, injury, maternity, or inactive duty or active duty military service for training, or

(*ii*) Does not work in such adversely affected employment because of a disability compensable under a workers' compensation law or plan of a State or the United States, or

(*iii*) Had adversely affected employment interrupted to serve as a full-time representative of a labor organization in such firm or subdivision, or

(*iv*) Is on call-up for the purpose of active duty in a reserve status in the Armed Forces of the United States (if such week began after August 1, 1990), provided such active duty is "Federal service" as defined in part 614 of this chapter,

shall be treated as a week of employment at wages of $30 or more;

(*2*) *Provided,* that—

(*i*) Not more than 7 weeks in the case of weeks described in paragraph (a)(2)(iii)(B)(*1*) (*i*) or (*iii*) of this section, or both, and

(*ii*) Not more than 26 weeks described in paragraph (a)(2)(iii)(B)(*1*) (*ii*) or (*iv*) of this section,

may be treated as weeks of employment for purposes of paragraph (a)(2)(iii) of this section.

(C) Wages and employment creditable under paragraph (a)(2)(iii) of this section shall not include employment or wages earned or paid for employment which is contrary to or prohibited by any Federal law.

(iv) *Entitlement to UI.* The individual must have been entitled to (or would have been entitled to if the individual had applied therefor) UI for a week within the benefit period—

(A) in which the individual's first qualifying separation occurred, or

(B) which began (or would have begun) by reason of the filing of a claim for UI by the individual after such first qualifying separation.

(v) *Exhaustion of UI.* The individual must:

(A) Have exhausted all rights to any UI to which the individual was entitled (or would have been entitled if the individual had applied therefor); and

(B) Not have an unexpired waiting period applicable to the individual for any such UI.

(vi) *Extended Benefit work test.* (A) The individual must—

(*1*) Accept any offer of suitable work, as defined in §617.3(kk), and actually apply for any suitable work the individual is referred to by the State agency, and

(*2*) Actively engage in seeking work and furnish the State agency tangible evidence of such efforts each week, and

(*3*) Register for work and be referred by the State agency to suitable work,

in accordance with those provisions of the applicable State law which apply to claimants for Extended Benefits and which are consistent with part 615 of this chapter.

(B) The Extended Benefit work test shall not apply to an individual with respect to claims for TRA for weeks of unemployment beginning prior to the filing of an initial claim for TRA, nor for any week which begins before the individual is notified that the individual is covered by a certification issued under the Act and is fully informed of the Extended Benefit work test requirements of paragraph (a)(2)(vi) of this section and §617.17. Prior to such notification and advice, the individual shall not be subject to the Extended Benefit work test requirements, nor to any State timely filing requirement, but shall be required to be unemployed and able to work and available for work with respect to any such week except as provided in §617.17(b)(2) for workers enrolled in, or participating in, a training program approved under §617.22(a).

(vii) *Participation in training.* (A) The individual must—

(*1*) Be enrolled in or participating in a training program approved pursuant to §617.22(a), or

(*2*) Have completed a training program approved under §617.22(a), after a total or partial separation from adversely affected employment within the certification period of a certification issued under the Act, or

(*3*) Have received from the State agency a written statement under §617.19 waiving the participation in training requirement for the individual.

(B) The participation in training requirement of paragraph (a)(2)(vii) of this section shall not apply to an individual with respect to claims for TRA for weeks of unemployment beginning prior to the filing of an initial claim for TRA, nor for any week which begins before the individual is notified that the individual is covered by a certification issued under the Act and is fully informed of the participation in training requirement of paragraph (a)(2)(vii) of this section and §617.19.

(C) The participation in training requirement of paragraph (a)(2)(vii) of this section shall apply, as a qualifying requirement for TRA, to an individual with respect to claims for TRA for weeks of unemployment commencing on or after November 21, 1988, and beginning with the first week following the week in which a certification covering the individual is issued under the Act, unless the State agency has issued a written statement to the individual under §617.19 waiving the participation in training requirement for the individual.

(D) For purposes of paragraph (a)(2)(vii) of this section, the following definitions shall apply:

(*1*) *Enrolled in training.* A worker shall be considered to be enrolled in training when the worker's application for training is approved by the State agency and the training institution has furnished written notice to the State agency that the worker has been accepted in the approved training program which is to begin within 30 calendar days of the date of such approval. (A waiver under §617.19 shall not be required for an individual who is enrolled in training as defined herein.)

(*2*) *Completed training.* A worker shall be considered to have completed a training program if the training program was approved, or was approvable and is approved, pursuant to §617.22, and the training was completed subsequent to the individual's total or partial separation from adversely affected employment within the certification period of a certification issued under the Act, and the training provider has certified that all the conditions for completion of the training program have been satisfied.

(3)–(4) [Reserved]

(b) *First week of entitlement.* The first week any individual may be entitled to a payment of basic TRA shall be the later of:

(1) The first week beginning more than 60 days after the date of the filing of the petition which resulted in the certification under which the individual is covered; or

(2) The first week beginning after the individual's exhaustion of all rights to UI including waiting period credit, as determined under §617.11(a)(2).

[59 FR 928, Jan. 6, 1994, as amended at 71 FR 35515, June 21, 2006]

§617.12 Evidence of qualification.

(a) *State agency action.* When an individual applies for TRA, the State agency having jurisdiction under §617.50(a) shall obtain information necessary to establish:

(1) Whether the individual meets the qualifying requirements in §617.11;

(2) The individual's average weekly wage; and

(3) For an individual claiming to be partially separated, the average weekly hours and average weekly wage in adversely affected employment.

(b) *Insufficient data.* If information specified in paragraph (a) of this section is not available from State agency records or from any employer, the State agency shall require the individual to submit a signed statement setting forth such information as may be required for the State agency to make the determinations required by paragraph (a) of this section.

(c) *Verification.* A statement made under paragraph (b) of this section shall be certified by the individual to be true to the best of the individual's knowledge and belief and shall be supported by evidence such as Forms W–2, paycheck stubs, union records, income tax returns, or statements of fellow workers, and shall be verified by the employer.

(d) *Determinations.* The State agency shall make the necessary determinations on the basis of information obtained pursuant to this section, except that if, after reviewing information obtained under paragraph (b) of this section against other available data, including agency records, it concludes that such information is not reasonably accurate, it shall make appropriate adjustments and shall make the determination on the basis of the adjusted data.

§617.13 Weekly amounts of TRA.

(a) *Regular allowance.* The amount of TRA payable for a week of total unemployment (including a week of training approved under subpart C of this part 617 or under the provisions of the applicable State law) shall be an amount equal to the most recent weekly benefit amount of UI (including dependents' allowances) payable to the individual for a week of total unemployment preceding the individual's first exhaustion of UI following the individual's first qualifying separation: *Provided,* that in a State in which weeks of UI are paid in varying amounts related to wages with separate employers, the weekly amount of TRA shall be calculated as it would be to pay extended compensation: *Provided, further,* that where a State calculates a base amount of UI and calculates dependents' allowances on a weekly supplemental basis. TRA weekly benefit amounts shall be calculated in the same manner and under the same terms and conditions as apply to claimants for UI, except that the base amount shall not change.

(b) *Increased allowance.* An individual in training approved under subpart C of this part 617 who is thereby entitled for any week to TRA and a training allowance under any other Federal law for the training of workers shall be paid in the amount computed under paragraph (a) of this section or, if greater, the amount to which the individual would be entitled under such other Federal law if the individual applied for such allowance, as provided in section 232(b) of the Act. A payment under this paragraph (b) shall be in lieu of any training allowance to which the individual is entitled under such other Federal law.

(c) *Reduction of amount.* An amount of TRA payable under paragraph (a) or (b) of this section for any week shall be reduced (but not below zero) by:

(1) Income that is deductible from UI under the disqualifying income provisions of the applicable State law or Federal unemployment compensation law;

(2) The amount of a training allowance (other than a training allowance referred to in paragraph (b) of this section) under any Federal law that the individual receives for such week, as provided in section 232(c) of the Act. This paragraph (c) shall apply to Veterans Educational Assistance, Pell Grants, Supplemental Educational Opportunity Grants, and other training allowances under any Federal law other than for the training of workers; and

(3) Any amount that would be deductible from UI for days of absence from training under the provisions of the applicable State law which apply to individuals in approved training.

[51 FR 45848, Dec. 22, 1986, as amended at 53 FR 32349, Aug. 24, 1988]

§617.14 Maximum amount of TRA.

(a) *General rule.* Except as provided under paragraph (b) of this section, the maximum amount of TRA payable to an individual under a certification shall be the amount determined by:

(1) Multiplying by 52 the weekly amount of TRA payable to such individual for a week of total unemployment, as determined under §617.13(a); and

(2) Subtracting from the product derived under paragraph (a)(1) of this section, the total sum of UI to which the individual was entitled (or would have been entitled if the individual had applied therefor) in the individual's first benefit period described in §617.11(a)(1)(iv) or, as appropriate, §617.11(a)(2)(iv). The individual's full entitlement shall be subtracted under this paragraph, without regard to the amount, if any, that was actually paid to the individual with respect to such benefit period.

(b) *Exceptions.* The maximum amount of TRA determined under paragraph (a) of this section will not include:

(1) The amount of dependents' allowances paid as a supplement to the base weekly amount determined under §617.13(a);

(2) The amount of the difference between the individual's weekly increased allowances determined under §617.13(b) and the individual's weekly amount determined under §617.13(a); and

(3) The amounts paid for additional weeks determined under §617.15(b);

but nothing in this paragraph (b) shall affect an individual's eligibility for such supplemental, increased or additional allowances.

(c) *Reduction for Federal training allowance.* (1) If a training allowance referred to in §617.13(c)(2) is paid to an individual for any week of unemployment with respect to which the individual would be entitled (determined without regard to any disqualification under §617.18(b)(2)) to TRA, if the individual applied for TRA for such week, each week shall be deducted from the total number of weeks of TRA otherwise payable to the individual.

(2) If the training allowance referred to in paragraph (c)(1) of this section is less than the amount of TRA otherwise payable to the individual for such week, the individual shall, when the individual applies for TRA for such week, be paid TRA in an amount not to exceed the amount equal to the difference between the individual's regular weekly TRA amount, as determined under §617.13(a), and the amount of the training allowance paid to the individual for such week, as provided in section 232(c) of the Act.

[51 FR 45848, Dec. 22, 1986, as amended at 53 FR 32349, Aug. 24, 1988; 54 FR 22277, May 23, 1989; 59 FR 931, Jan. 6, 1994]

§617.15 Duration of TRA.

(a) *Basic weeks.* An individual shall not be paid basic TRA for any week beginning after the close of the 104-week eligibility period (as defined in §617.3(m)(1)), which is applicable to the individual as determined under §§617.3 (m)(1), 617.3(t), and 617.67(e).

(b) *Additional weeks.* (1) To assist an individual to complete training approved under subpart C of this part, payments may be made as TRA for up to 26 additional weeks in the 26-week eligibility period (as defined in §617.3(m)(2)) which is applicable to the individual as determined under §§617.3(m)(2) and 617.67(f).

(2) To be eligible for TRA for additional weeks, an individual must make a bona fide application for such training—

(i) within 210 days after the date of the first certification under which the individual is covered, or

(ii) if later, within 210 days after the date of the individual's most recent partial or total separation (as defined in §§617.3(cc) and 617.3(ll)) under such certification.

(3) Except as provided in paragraph (d) of this section, payments of TRA for additional weeks may be made only for those weeks in the 26-week eligibility period during which the individual is actually participating fully in training approved under §617.22(a).

(c) *Limit.* The maximum TRA payable to any individual on the basis of a single certification is limited to the maximum amount of basic TRA as determined under §617.14 plus additional TRA for up to 26 weeks as provided in paragraph (b) of this section.

(d) *Scheduled breaks in training.* (1) An individual who is otherwise eligible will continue to be eligible for basic and additional weeks of TRA during scheduled breaks in training, but only if a scheduled break is not longer than 14 days, and the following additional conditions are met:

(i) The individual was participating in the training approved under §617.22(a) immediately before the beginning of the break; and

(ii) The break is provided for in the published schedule or the previously established schedule of training issued by the training provider or is indicated in the training program approved for the worker; and, further

(iii) The individual resumes participation in the training immediately after the break ends.

(2) A scheduled break in training shall include all periods within or between courses, terms, quarters, semesters and academic years of the approved training program.

(3) No basic or additional TRA will be paid to an individual for any week which begins and ends within a scheduled break that is 15 days or more.

(4) The days within a break in a training program that shall be counted in determining the number of days of the break for the purposes of paragraph (d) of this section shall include all calendar days beginning with the first day of the break and ending with the last day of the break, as provided for in the schedule of the training provider, except that any Saturday, Sunday, or official State or National holiday occurring during the scheduled break in training, on which training would not normally be scheduled in the training program if there were no break in training, shall not be counted in determining the number of days of the break for the purposes of paragraph (d) of this section.

(5) When the worker is drawing basic TRA, the maximum amount of TRA payable is not affected by the weeks the worker does not receive TRA while in a break period, but the weeks will count against the 104-week eligibility period.

(6) When the worker is drawing additional weeks of TRA to complete training, any weeks for which TRA is not paid will count against the continuous 26-week eligibility period and the number of weeks payable.

[59 FR 931, Jan. 6, 1994]

§617.16 Applicable State law.

(a) *What law governs.* The applicable State law for any individual, for all of the purposes of this part 617, is the State law of the State—

(1) In which the individual is entitled to UI (whether or not the individual has filed a claim therefor) immediately following the individual's first separation (as defined in paragraph (t)(1) of §617.3), or

(2) If the individual is not so entitled to UI under the State law of any State immediately following such first separation, or is entitled to UI under the Railroad Unemployment Insurance Act (RRUI), the State law of the State in which such first separation occurred.

(b) *Change of law.* The State law determined under paragraph (a) of this section to be the applicable State law for an individual shall remain the applicable State law for the individual until the individual becomes entitled to UI under the State law of another State (whether or not the individual files a claim therefor).

(c) *UI entitlement.* (1) An individual shall be deemed to be entitled to UI under a State law if the individual satisfies the base period employment and wage qualifying requirements of such State law.

(2) In the case of a combined-wage claim (Part 616 of this chapter), UI entitlement shall be determined under the law of the paying State.

(3) In case of a Federal UI claim, or a joint State and Federal UI claim (Parts 609 and 614 of this Chapter), UI entitlement shall be determined under the law of the State which is the applicable State for such claims.

(d) *RRUI claimants.* If an individual is entitled to UI under the Railroad Unemployment Insurance Act, the applicable State law for purposes of paragraphs (a) and (b) of this section is the law of the State in which the individual's first qualifying separation occurs.

(e) *Liable State.* The State whose State law is determined under this section to be the applicable State law for any individual shall be the liable State for the individual for all purposes of this part 617. Any State other than the liable State shall be an agent State.

[59 FR 932, Jan. 6, 1994]

§617.17 Availability and active search for work.

(a) *Extended Benefit work test applicable.* Except as provided in paragraph (b) of this section, an individual shall, as a basic condition of entitlement to basic TRA for a week of unemployment—

(1) be unemployed, as defined in the applicable State law for UI claimants, and

(2) be able to work and available for work, as defined in the applicable State law for UI claimants, and

(3) satisfy the Extended Benefit work test in each week for which TRA is claimed, as set forth in §§617.11(a)(1)(vi) and 617.11(a)(2)(vi).

(b) *Exceptions*—(1) *Prior to November 21, 1988.* The conditions stated in paragraphs (a) and (b) of this section shall not be applicable to an individual actually participating in training approved under the applicable State law or under §617.22(a), or during a scheduled break in the training program if (as determined for the purposes of §617.15 (d)) the individual participated in the training immediately before the beginning of the break and resumes participation in the training immediately after the break ends, unless the individual is ineligible or subject to disqualification under the applicable State law or §617.18 (b)(2).

(2) *On and after November 21, 1988.* The conditions stated in paragraphs (a)(2) and (a)(3) of this section shall not be applicable to an individual who is enrolled in or participating in a training program approved under §617.22 (a), or during a break in the training program if (as determined for the purposes of §617.15(d)) the individual participated in the training immediately before the beginning of the break and resumes participation in the training immediately after the break ends.

[59 FR 932, Jan. 6, 1994]

§617.18 Disqualifications.

(a) *State law applies.* Except as stated in paragraph (b) of this section and §617.55(b), an individual shall not be paid TRA for any week of unemployment the individual is or would be disqualified to receive UI under the disqualification provisions of the applicable State law, including the provisions of the applicable State law which apply to EB claimants and which are consistent with section 202(a)(3) of the Federal-State Extended Unemployment Compensation Act of 1970.

(b) *Disqualification of trainees*—(1) *State law inapplicable.* A State law shall not be applied to disqualify an individual from receiving either UI or TRA because the individual:

(i) Is enrolled in or is participating in a training program approved under §617.22(a); or

(ii) Refuses work to which the individual has been referred by the State agency, if such work would require the individual to discontinue training, or if added to hours of training would occupy the individual more than 8 hours a day or 40 hours a week, except that paragraph (b)(1)(ii) of this section shall not apply to an individual who is ineligible under paragraph (b)(2) of this section; or

(iii) Quits work, if the individual was employed in work which was not suitable (as defined in §617.22(a)(1)), and it was reasonable and necessary for the individual to quit work to begin or continue training approved for the individual under §617.22(a).

(2) *Trainees ineligible.* (i) An individual who, without justifiable cause, fails to begin participation in a training program which is approved under §617.22(a), or ceases to participate in such training, or for whom a waiver is revoked pursuant to §617.19(c), shall not be eligible for basic TRA, or any other payment under this part 617, for the week in which such failure, cessation, or revocation occurred, or any succeeding week thereafter until the week in which the individual begins or resumes participation in a training program that is approved under §617.22(a).

(ii) For purposes of this section and other provisions of this Part 617, the following definitions shall be used:

(A) *Failed to begin participation.* A worker shall be determined to have failed to begin participation in a training program when the worker fails to attend all scheduled training classes and other training activities in the first week of the training program, without justifiable cause.

(B) *Ceased participation.* A worker shall be determined to have ceased participation in a training program when the worker fails to attend all scheduled training classes and other training activities scheduled by the training institution in any week of the training program, without justifiable cause.

(C) *Justifiable cause.* For the purposes of paragraph (b)(2) of this section, the term "justifiable cause" means such reasons as would justify an individual's conduct when measured by conduct expected of a reasonable individual in like circumstances, including but not limited to reasons beyond the individual's control and reasons related to the individual's capability to participate in or complete an approved training program.

(c) *Disqualification while in OJT.* In no case may an individual receive TRA for any week with respect to which the worker is engaged in on-the-job training.

[51 FR 45848, Dec. 22, 1986, as amended at 53 FR 32350, Aug. 24, 1988; 59 FR 932, Jan. 6, 1994]

§617.19 Requirement for participation in training.

(a) *In general*—(1) *Basic requirement.* (i) All individuals otherwise entitled to basic TRA, for each week, must either be enrolled in or participating in a training program approved under §617.22(a), or have completed a training program approved under §617.22(a), as provided in §617.11(a)(2)(vii), in order to be entitled to basic TRA payments for any such week (except for continuation of payments during scheduled breaks in training of 14 days or less under the conditions stated in §617.15(d)). The training requirement of paragraph (a)(1)(i) of this section shall be waived in writing on an individual basis, solely in regard to entitlement to basic TRA, if approval of training for the individual is not feasible or is not appropriate, as determined in accordance with paragraph (a)(2) of this section.

(ii) As a principal condition of entitlement to additional TRA payments, all individuals must actually be participating in a training program approved under §617.22(a) for each week, and for all weeks beginning on and after November 21, 1988 (except for continuation of payments during breaks in training under the conditions stated in §617.15(d)). Paragraph (a)(2) of this section is not applicable in regard to additional TRA, and the participation in training requirement of paragraph (a)(1)(ii) of this section may not be waived under any circumstances.

(2) *Waiver of participation requirement.* When it is determined, in accordance with paragraph (a)(2) of this section, that it is not feasible or is not appropriate (as such terms are defined in paragraph (b) of this section) to approve a training program for an individual otherwise entitled to basic TRA, the individual shall be furnished a formal written notice of waiver, with an explanation of the reason(s) for the

waiver and a statement of why training is not feasible or is not appropriate in the case of such individual. At a minimum, the written statement furnished to the individual shall contain information required by § 617.50(e) as well as the following information:

(i) Name and social security number of the individual;

(ii) Petition number under which the worker was certified;

(iii) A statement why the agency has determined that it is not feasible or is not appropriate to approve training for the individual at that time, and the reason(s) for the finding;

(iv) A statement that the waiver will be revoked at any time that feasible and appropriate training becomes available;

(v) Any other advice or information the State agency deems appropriate in informing the individual;

(vi) Signature block (with signature) for the appropriate State official; and

(vii) Signature block (with signature) for the worker's acknowledgement of receipt.

(3) *Denial of a waiver.* In any case in which a determination is made to deny to any individual a waiver of the participation requirement, the individual shall be furnished a formal written notice of denial of waiver, which shall contain all of the information required of formal written notices under paragraph (a)(2) of this section.

(4) *Procedure.* Any determination under paragraph (a)(2) or paragraph (a)(3) of this section shall be a determination to which §§ 617.50 and 617.51 apply, including the requirement that any written notice furnished to an individual shall include notice of the individual's appeal rights as is provided in § 617.50(e).

(b) *Reasons for issuing a waiver.* (1) For the purposes of paragraphs (a)(2) and (a)(3) of this section, a waiver of the participation in training requirement shall be issued to an individual only upon a supported finding that approval of a § 617.22(a) training program for that individual is not feasible or is not appropriate at that time.

(i) *Feasible and appropriate.* For the purposes of this section:

(A) *Feasible.* The term *feasible* means:

(*1*) Training is available at that time which meets all the criteria of § 617.22(a);

(*2*) The individual is so situated as to be able to take full advantage of the training opportunity and complete the training; and

(*3*) Funding is available to pay the full costs of the training and any transportation and subsistence expenses which are compensable. The funding referred to in paragraph (b)(1)(i)(A)(*3*) of this section includes not only TAA program funds but also all other funds available under any of the provisions of the Title I, Subchapter B of the Workforce Investment Act or any other Federal, State or private source that may be utilized for training approvable under § 617.22(a). Further, the individual's situation in respect to undertaking training (as referred to in paragraph (b)(1)(i)(A)(*2*) of this section) shall include taking into account personal circumstances that preclude the individual from being able to participate in and complete the training program, such as the availability of transportation, the ability to make arrangements for necessary child care, and adequate financial resources if the weeks of training exceeds the duration of UI and TRA payments.

(B) *Appropriate.* The term *appropriate* means being suitable or compatible, fitting, or proper. Appropriate, therefore, refers to suitability of the training for the worker (including whether there is a reasonable prospect which is reasonably foreseeable that the individual will be reemployed by the firm from which separated), and compatibility of the training for the purposes of the TAA Program. In these respects, suitability of training for the individual is encompassed within the several criteria in § 617.22 (a), and compatibility with the program is covered by the various provisions of subpart C of this part which describe the types of training approvable under § 617.22(a) and the limitations thereon.

(ii) *Basis for application.* Whether training is feasible or appropriate at any given time is determined by finding whether, at that time, training suitable for the worker is available, the training is approvable under subpart C of this part including the criteria in

§617.22(a), the worker is so situated as to be able to take full advantage of the training and satisfactorily complete the training, full funding for the training is available from one or more sources in accordance with §§617.24 and 617.25, the worker has the financial resources to complete the training when the duration of the training program exceeds the worker's eligibility for TRA, and the training will commence within 30 days of approval.

(2) *Particular applications.* The reasons for any determination that training is not feasible or is not appropriate shall be in accord with the following:

(i) *Not feasible* because—

(A) The beginning date of approved training is beyond 30 days, as required by the definition for "Enrolled in training" in §617.11(a)(2)(vii)(D),

(B) Training is not reasonably available to the individual,

(C) Training is not available at a reasonable cost,

(D) Funds are not available to pay the total costs of training, or

(E) Personal circumstances such as health or financial resources, preclude participation in training or satisfactory completion of training,

(F) Other (explain).

(ii) *Not appropriate* because—

(A)(*1*) The firm from which the individual was separated plans to recall the individual within the reasonably foreseeable future (State agencies must verify planned recalls with the employer),

(*2*) *Planned recall.* For the purpose of determining whether the recall or reemployment of an individual is reasonably foreseeable (for the purposes of this section and §617.22), either a specific or general type of recall (as set out) shall be deemed to be sufficient.

(*i*) *Specific recall.* A specific recall is where an individual or group of individuals who was separated from employment is identified and notified by the employer to return to work within a specified time period.

(*ii*) *General recall.* A general recall is where the employer announces an intention to recall an individual or group of individuals, or by other action reasonably signals an intent to recall, without specifying any certain date or specific time period.

(*iii*) *Reasonably foreseeable.* For purposes of determining whether training should be denied and a training waiver granted, because of a planned recall that is reasonably foreseeable, such a planned recall includes a specific recall and also includes a general recall (as defined in paragraph (b)(2)(ii)(A)(*2*) of this section) if the general recall in each individual's case is reasonably expected to occur before the individual exhausts eligibility for any regular UI payments for which the individual is or may become entitled. A general recall, in which the timing of the recall is reasonably expected to occur after the individual's exhaustion of any regular UI to which the individual is or may become entitled, shall not be treated as precluding approval of training, but shall be treated as any other worker separation for these purposes.

(B) The duration of training suitable for the individual exceeds the individual's maximum entitlement to basic and additional TRA payments and the individual cannot assure financial responsibility for completing the training program,

(C) The individual possesses skills for "suitable employment" and there is a reasonable expectation of employment in the foreseeable future, or

(D) Other (explain).

(3) *Waivers and able and available.* An individual who has been furnished a written notice of waiver under paragraph (a)(2) of this section (or denial of waiver under paragraph (a)(3) of this section) shall be subject to all of the requirements of §617.17(a), which shall continue until the individual is enrolled in a training program as required by paragraph (a)(2)(vii) of §617.11.

(c) *Waiver review and revocations.* (1) State agencies must have a procedure for reviewing regularly (*i.e.*, every 30 days or less) all waivers issued under this section to individuals, to ascertain that the conditions upon which the waivers were granted continue to exist. In any case in which the conditions have changed—*i.e.*, training has become feasible and appropriate—then the waiver must be revoked, and a written notice of revocation shall be furnished to the individual involved.

(2) In addition to the periodic reviews required by paragraph (c)(1) of this section, State agencies must have a procedure for revoking waivers in individual cases promptly whenever a change in circumstances occurs. For example, a written notice of revocation shall be issued to the individual concurrent with the approval of the training in which the individual has enrolled (if such training is scheduled to commence within 30 days), and shall not be issued prior to such approval.

(3) State agencies may incorporate a revocation section in the waiver form or on a separate revocation form. Any determination under paragraph (c) of this section shall be a determination to which §§ 617.50 and 617.51 apply. The information included in a written notice of revocation issued under this paragraph (c) shall include all of the information required for written notices issued under paragraph (a)(2) of this section.

(d) *Recordkeeping and reporting.* (1) State agencies must develop procedures for compiling and reporting on the number of waivers issued and revoked, by reason, as specified in paragraphs (b) and (c) of this section, and report such data to the Department of Labor as requested by the Department.

(2) State agencies are not required to forward copies of individual waiver and revocation notices to the Department of Labor, unless specifically requested by the Department. However, each State agency shall retain a copy of every individual waiver and revocation notice issued by the State, for such period of time as the Department requires.

(Approved by the Office of Management and Budget under control number 1205–0016)

[59 FR 932, Jan. 6, 1994, as amended at 71 FR 35515, June 21, 2006]

Subpart C—Reemployment Services

§ 617.20 Responsibilities for the delivery of reemployment services.

(a) *State agency referral.* Cooperating State agencies shall be responsible for:

(1) Advising each adversely affected worker to apply for training with the State agency responsible for reemployment services, while the worker is receiving UI payments, and at the time the individual files an initial claim for TRA; and

(2) Referring each adversely affected worker to the State agency responsible for training and other reemployment services in a timely manner.

(b) *State agency responsibilities.* The responsibilities of cooperating State agencies under subpart C of this part include, but are not limited to:

(1) Interviewing each adversely affected worker regarding suitable training opportunities reasonably available to each individual under subpart C of this part, reviewing such opportunities with each individual, informing each individual of the requirement for participation in training as a condition for receiving TRA, and accepting each individual's application for training. Such training may be approved for any adversely affected worker at any time after a certification is issued and the worker is determined to be covered without regard to whether the worker has exhausted all rights to unemployment insurance;

(2) Registering adversely affected workers for work;

(3) Informing adversely affected workers of the reemployment services and allowances available under the Act and this Part 617, the application procedures, the filing date requirements for such reemployment services and the training requirement for receiving TRA;

(4) Determining whether suitable employment, as defined in § 617.22(a)(1), is available;

(5) Providing counseling, testing, placement, and supportive services;

(6) Providing or procuring self-directed job search training, when necessary;

(7) Providing training, job search and relocation assistance;

(8) Developing a training plan with the individual;

(9) Determining which training institutions offer training programs at a reasonable cost and with a reasonable expectation of employment following the completion of such training, and procuring such training;

(10) Documenting the standards and procedures used to select occupations

and training institutions in which training is approved;

(11) Making referrals and approving training programs;

(12) Monitoring the progress of workers in approved training programs;

(13) Developing, and periodically reviewing and updating reemployment plans for adversely affected workers;

(14) Developing and implementing a procedure for reviewing training waivers and revocations at least every 30 days to determine whether the conditions under which they are issued have changed; and

(15) Coordinating the administration and delivery of employment services, benefits, training, and supplemental assistance for adversely affected workers with programs under the Act and under Title I, Subchapter B of the Workforce Investment Act.

[59 FR 934, Jan. 6, 1994, as amended at 71 FR 35515, June 21, 2006]

§617.21 Reemployment services and allowances.

Reemployment services and allowances shall include, as appropriate, the services and allowances as set forth in this section, provided that those services included within the scope of paragraphs (a) through (e) of this section shall be provided for under any other Federal law other than the Act.

(a) *Employment registration.* To ensure, so far as practical, that individuals are placed in jobs which utilize their highest skills and that applicants qualified for job openings are appropriately referred, applications for registration shall be taken on adversely affected workers who apply for reemployment services.

(b) *Employment counseling.* When local job opportunities are not readily available, counseling shall be used to assist individuals to gain a better understanding of themselves in relation to the labor market so that they can more realistically choose or change an occupation or make a suitable job adjustment.

(c) *Vocational testing.* Testing shall be used to determine which individual skills or potentials can be developed by appropriate training.

(d) *Job development.* A State agency shall develop jobs for individuals by soliciting job interviews from public or private employers and shall work with potential employers to customize or restructure particular jobs to meet individual needs.

(e) *Supportive services.* Supportive services shall be provided so individuals can obtain or retain employment or participate in employment and training programs leading to eventual placement in permanent employment. Such services may include work orientation, basic education, communication skills, child care, and any other services necessary to prepare an individual for full employment in accordance with the individual's capabilities and employment opportunities.

(f) *On-the-job training (OJT).* OJT is training, in the public or private sector, and may be provided to an individual who meets the conditions for approval of training, as provided in §617.22(a), and who has been hired by the employer, while the individual is engaged in productive work which provides knowledge or skills essential to the full and adequate performance of the job.

(g) *Classroom training.* This training activity is any training of the type normally conducted in a classroom setting, including vocational education, and may be provided to individuals when the conditions for approval of training are met, as provided in §617.22(a), to impart technical skills and information required to perform a specific job or group of jobs. Training designed to enhance the employability of individuals by upgrading basic skills, through the provision of courses such as remedial education or English-as-a-second-language, shall be considered as remedial education approvable under §617.22(a) if the criteria for approval of training under §617.22(a) are met.

(h) *Self-directed job search.* Self-directed job search programs shall be initiated to assist individuals in developing skills and techniques for finding a job. Such programs vary in design and operation and call for a carefully structured approach to individual needs. There are basic elements or activities common to all approaches. These include:

(1) *Job search workshop.* A short (1–3 days) seminar designed to provide participants with knowledge on how to find jobs, including labor market information, applicant resume writing, interviewing techniques, and finding job openings.

(2) *Job finding club.* Encompasses all elements of the Job Search Workshop plus a period (1–2 weeks) of structured, supervised application where participants actually seek employment.

(i) *Job search allowances.* The individual, if eligible, shall be provided job search allowances under subpart D of this part 617 to defray the cost of seeking employment outside of the commuting area.

(j) *Relocation allowances.* The individual, if eligible, shall be provided relocation allowances under subpart E of this part 617 to defray the cost of moving to a new job outside of the commuting area.

[51 FR 45848, Dec. 22, 1986, as amended at 59 FR 934, Jan. 6, 1994]

§ 617.22 Approval of training.

(a) *Conditions for approval.* Training shall be approved for an adversely affected worker if the State agency determines that:

(1) *There is no suitable employment (which may include technical and professional employment) available for an adversely affected worker.*

(i) This means that for the worker for whom approval of training is being considered under this section, no suitable employment is available at that time for that worker, either in the commuting area, as defined in § 617.3(k), or outside the commuting area in an area in which the worker desires to relocate with the assistance of a relocation allowance under subpart E of this part, and there is no reasonable prospect of such suitable employment becoming available for the worker in the foreseeable future. For the purposes of paragraph (a)(1) of this section only, the term "suitable employment" means, with respect to a worker, work of a substantially equal or higher skill level than the worker's past adversely affected employment, and wages for such work at not less that 80 percent of the worker's average weekly wage.

(2) *The worker would benefit from appropriate training.* (i) This means that there is a direct relationship between the needs of the worker for skills training or remedial education and what would be provided by the training program under consideration for the worker, and that the worker has the mental and physical capabilities to undertake, make satisfactory progress in, and complete the training. This includes the further criterion that the individual will be job ready on completion of the training program.

(3) *There is a reasonable expectation of employment following completion of such training.* (i) This means that, for that worker, given the job market conditions expected to exist at the time of the completion of the training program, there is, fairly and objectively considered, a reasonable expectation that the worker will find a job, using the skills and education acquired while in training, after completion of the training. Any determination under this criterion must take into account that "a reasonable expectation of employment" does not require that employment opportunities for the worker be available, or offered, immediately upon the completion of the approved training. This emphasizes, rather than negates, the point that there must be a fair and objective projection of job market conditions expected to exist at the time of completion of the training.

(4) *Training approved by the Secretary is reasonably available to the worker from either governmental agencies or private sources (which may include area vocational technical education schools, as defined in Carl D. Perkins Vocational and Applied Technology Education Act, and employers).* (i) This means that training is reasonably accessible to the worker within the worker's commuting area at any governmental or private training (or education) provider, particularly including on-the-job training with an employer, and it means training that is suitable for the worker and meets the other criteria in paragraph (a) of this section. It also means that emphasis must be given to finding accessible training for the worker, although not precluding training outside the commuting area if none is available at the time within the worker's commuting

area. Whether the training is within or outside the commuting area, the training must be available at a reasonable cost as prescribed in paragraph (a)(6) of this section.

(ii) In determining whether or not training is reasonably available, first consideration shall be given to training opportunities available within the worker's normal commuting area. Training at facilities outside the worker's normal commuting area should be approved only if such training is not available in the area or the training to be provided outside the normal commuting area will involve less charges to TAA funds.

(5) *The worker is qualified to undertake and complete such training.* (i) This emphasizes the worker's personal qualifications to undertake and complete approved training. Evaluation of the worker's personal qualifications must include the worker's physical and mental capabilities, educational background, work experience and financial resources, as adequate to undertake and complete the specific training program being considered.

(ii) Evaluation of the worker's financial ability shall include an analysis of the worker's remaining weeks of UI and TRA payments in relation to the duration of the training program. If the worker's UI and TRA payments will be exhausted before the end of the training program, it shall be ascertained whether personal or family resources will be available to the worker to complete the training. It must be noted on the worker's record that financial resources were discussed with the worker before the training was approved.

(iii) When adequate financial resources will not be available to the worker to complete a training program which exceeds the duration of UI and TRA payments, the training shall not be approved and consideration shall be given to other training opportunities available to the worker.

(6) *Such training is suitable for the worker and available at a reasonable cost.* (i) Such training means the training being considered for the worker. Suitable for the worker means that paragraph (a)(5) of this section is met and that the training is appropriate for the worker given the worker's capabilities, background and experience.

(ii) Available at a reasonable cost means that training may not be approved at one provider when, all costs being considered, training substantially similar in quality, content and results can be obtained from another provider at a lower total cost within a similar time frame. It also means that training may not be approved when the costs of the training are unreasonably high in comparison with the average costs of training other workers in similar occupations at other providers. This criterion also requires taking into consideration the funding of training costs from sources other than TAA funds, and the least cost to TAA funding of providing suitable training opportunities to the worker. Greater emphasis will need to be given to these elements in determining the reasonable costs of training, particularly in view of the requirements in §617.11(a)(2) and (3) that TRA claimants be enrolled in and participate in training.

(iii) For the purpose of determining reasonable costs of training, the following elements shall be considered:

(A) Costs of a training program shall include tuition and related expenses (books, tools, and academic fees), travel or transportation expenses, and subsistence expenses;

(B) In determining whether the costs of a particular training program are reasonable, first consideration must be given to the lowest cost training which is available within the commuting area. When training, substantially similar in quality, content and results, is offered at more than one training provider, the lowest cost training shall be approved; and

(C) Training at facilities outside the worker's normal commuting area that involves transportation or subsistence costs which add substantially to the total costs shall not be approved if other appropriate training is available.

(b) *Allowable amounts for training.* In approving a worker's application for training, the conditions for approval in paragraph (a) of this section must be found to be satisfied, including assurance that the training is suitable for the worker, is at the lowest reasonable cost, and will enable the worker to obtain employment within a reasonable period of time. An application for training shall be denied if it is for training in an occupational area which requires an extraordinarily high skill level and for which the total costs of the training are substantially higher than the costs of other training which is suitable for the worker.

(c) *Previous approval of training under State law.* Training previously approved for a worker under State law or other authority is not training approved under paragraph (a) of this section. Any such training may be approved under paragraph (a) of this section, if all of the requirements and limitations of paragraph (a) of this section and other provisions of Subpart C of this part are met, but such approval shall not be retroactive for any of the purposes of this Part 617, including payment of the costs of the training and payment of TRA to the worker participating in the training. However, in the case of a redetermination or decision reversing a determination denying approval of training, for the purposes of this Part 617 such redetermination or decision shall be given effect retroactive to the issuance of the determination that was reversed by such redetermination or decision; but no costs of training may be paid unless such costs actually were incurred for training in which the individual participated, and no additional TRA may be paid with respect to any week the individual was not actually participating in the training.

(d) *Applications.* Applications for, selection for, approval of, or referral to training shall be filed in accordance with this subpart C and on forms which shall be furnished to individuals by the State agency.

(e) *Determinations.* Selection for, approval of, or referral of an individual to training under this subpart C, or a decision with respect to any specific training or non-selection, non-approval, or non-referral for any reason shall be a determination to which §§ 617.50 and 617.51 apply.

(f) *Length of training and hours of attendance.* The State agency shall determine the appropriateness of the length of training and the hours of attendance as follows:

(1) The training shall be of suitable duration to achieve the desired skill level in the shortest possible time;

(2) *Length of training.* The maximum duration for any approvable training program is 104 weeks (during which training is conducted) and no individual shall be entitled to more than one training program under a single certification.

(3) *Training program.* (i) For purposes of this Part 617, a training program may consist of a single course or group of courses which is designed and approved by the State agency for an individual to meet a specific occupational goal.

(ii) When an approved training program involves more than one course and involves breaks in training (within or between courses, or within or between terms, quarters, semesters and academic years), all such breaks in training are subject to the "14-day break in training" provision in § 617.15(d), for purposes of receiving TRA payments. An individual's approved training program may be amended by the State agency to add a course designed to satisfy unforeseen needs of the individual, such as remedial education or specific occupational skills, as long as the length of the amended training program does not exceed the 104-week training limitation in paragraph (f)(2) of this section.

(4) *Full-time training.* Individuals in TAA approved training shall attend training full time, and when other training is combined with OJT attendance at both shall be not less than full-time. The hours in a day and days in a week of attendance in training shall be full-time in accordance with established hours and days of training of the training provider.

(g) *Training of reemployed workers.* Adversely affected workers who obtain new employment which is not suitable employment, as described in § 617.22(a)(1), and have been approved for training may elect to:

(1) Terminate their jobs, or

(2) Continue in full- or part-time employment, to undertake such training, and shall not be subject to ineligibility or disqualification for UI or TRA as a

result of such termination or reduction in employment.

(h) *Fees prohibited.* In no case shall an individual be approved for training under this subpart C for which the individual is required to pay a fee or tuition.

(i) *Training outside the United States.* In no case shall an individual be approved for training under this subpart C which is conducted totally or partially at a location outside the United States.

[51 FR 45848, Dec. 22, 1986, as amended at 53 FR 32350, Aug. 24, 1988; 59 FR 935, Jan. 6, 1994; 71 FR 35515, June 21, 2006]

§617.23 Selection of training methods and programs.

(a) *State agency responsibilities.* If suitable employment as described in §617.22(a)(1), is not otherwise available to an individual or group of individuals, it is the responsibility of the State agency to explore, identify, develop and secure training opportunities and to establish linkages with other public and private agencies, Workforce Investment Boards (WIBs), employers, and Workforce Investment Act (WIA) service delivery area (SDA) grant recipients, as appropriate, which return adversely affected workers to employment as soon as possible.

(b) *Firm-specific retraining program.* To the extent practicable before referring an adversely affected worker to approved training, the State agency shall consult with the individual's adversely affected firm and certified or recognized union, or other authorized representative, to develop a retraining program that meets the firm's staffing needs and preserves or restores the employment relationship between the individual and the firm. The fact that there is no need by other employers in the area for individuals in a specific occupation for which training is undertaken shall not preclude the development of an individual retraining program for such occupation with the adversely affected firm.

(c) *Methods of training.* Adversely affected workers may be provided either one or a combination of the following methods of training:

(1) Insofar as possible, priority will be given to on-the-job training, which includes related education necessary to acquire skills needed for a position within a particular occupation, in the firm or elsewhere pursuant to §§617.24, 617.25, and 617.26, including training for which the firm pays the costs. This ensures that on-the-job training provides the skills necessary for the individual to obtain employment in an occupation rather than a particular job at a specific site; and

(2) Institutional training, with priority given to providing the training in public area vocational education schools if it is determined that such schools are at least as effective and efficient as other institutional alternatives, pursuant to §§617.24, 617.25, and 617.26.

(d) *Standards and procedures.* The State agency shall document the standards and procedures used to select occupations and training institutions in which training is approved. Such occupations and training shall offer a reasonable expectation (not necessarily a prior guarantee) of employment following such training.

(1) *Standards.* The State agency shall approve training in occupations for which an identifiable demand exists either in the local labor market or in other labor markets for which relocation planning has been implemented. If practicable, placement rates and employer reviews of curriculum shall be used as guides in the selection of training institutions.

(2) *Procedures.* In determining the types of training to be provided, the State agency shall consult with local employers, appropriate labor organizations, WIBs and other WIA One-Stop partners, WIBs, local educational organizations, local apprenticeship programs, local advisory councils established under the Carl D. Perkins Vocational Education Act, and post-secondary institutions.

(3) *Exclusions.* In determining suitable training the State agency shall exclude certain occupations, where:

(i) Lack of employment opportunities exist as substantiated by job orders and other pertinent labor market data; or

(ii) The occupation provides no reasonable expectation of permanent employment.

[51 FR 45848, Dec. 22, 1986, as amended at 71 FR 35515, June 21, 2006]

§ 617.24 Preferred training.

Training programs that may be approved under § 617.22(a) include, but are not limited to—

(a) On-the-job training,

(b) Any training program provided by a State pursuant to Title I, subchapter B of the Workforce Investment Act,

(c) Any training program approved by a Workforce Investment Board established under the Workforce Investment Act,

(d) Any program of remedial education,

(e) Any training program (other than a training program described in paragraph (c) of § 617.25) for which all, or any portion, of the costs of training the worker are paid—

(1) Under any other Federal or State program other than this subpart C, or

(2) From any other source other than this section, but not including sources personal to the individual, such as self, relatives, or friends, and

(f) Any other training program approved by the Department.

[59 FR 936, Jan. 6, 1994, as amended at 71 FR 35515, June 21, 2006]

§ 617.25 Limitations on training under Subpart C of this part.

The second sentence of amended section 236(a)(1) of the Act provides that an adversely affected worker shall be entitled to have payment of the costs of training approved under the Act paid on the worker's behalf, subject, however, "to the limitations imposed by" section 236. The limitations in section 236 which are implemented in this section concern the restrictions on approval of training which are related directly or indirectly to the conditions on training which are approvable or on the funding of training costs.

(a) *On-the-job training.* The costs of on-the-job training approved subpart C of this part for a worker, which are paid from TAA funds, shall be paid in equal monthly installments. Such costs may be paid from TAA funds, and such training may be approved under subpart C of this part, however, only if the State agency determines that:

(1) No currently employed individual is displaced by such eligible worker, including partial displacement such as a reduction in the hours of non-overtime work, wages, or employment benefits;

(2) Such training does not impair existing contracts for services or collective bargaining agreements;

(3) In the case of training which would be inconsistent with the terms of a collective bargaining agreement, written concurrence has been obtained from the concerned labor organization;

(4) No other individual is on layoff from the same or any substantially equivalent job for which such eligible worker is being trained;

(5) The employer has not terminated the employment of any regular employee or otherwise reduced the work force with the intention of filling the vacancy so created by hiring the eligible worker;

(6) The job for which the eligible worker is being trained is not being created in a promotional line that will infringe in any way upon the promotional opportunities of currently employed individuals;

(7) Such training is not for the same occupation from which the worker was separated and with respect to which such worker's group was certified pursuant to section 222 of the Act;

(8) The employer certifies to the State agency that the employer will continue to employ the eligible worker for at least 26 weeks after completing the training if the worker desires to continue such employment and the employer does not have due cause to terminate such employment;

(9) The employer has not received payment under this subpart C or under any other Federal law for any other on-the-job training provided by such employer which failed to meet the requirements of paragraphs (a)(1) through (a)(6) of this section or such other Federal law; and

(10) The employer has not taken, at any time, any action which violated the terms of any certification described in paragraph (a)(8) of this section made by the employer with respect to any other on-the-job training provided by the employer for which the

employer has received a payment under subpart C of this part (or the prior provisions of subpart C of this part).

(b) *Other authority and restrictions on funding*—

(1) *In general.* Section 236(a) contains several provisions which allow the costs of a training program approved under the Act to be paid—

(i) Solely from TAA funds,

(ii) Solely from other public or private funds, or

(iii) Partly from TAA funds and partly from other public or private funds,

but also precludes the use of TAA funds or funds under another Federal law where such use of funds would result in duplication of payment of training costs. Those authorities and restrictions are spelled out in paragraph (b) of this section: *Provided*, that, private funds may not include funds from sources personal to the individual, such as self, relatives, or friends.

(2) *Section 236(a)(5)(E) of the Act.* (i) *In general.* Paragraph (5)(E) of section 236(a) of the Act specifies one of the types of training programs approvable under the Act, as including a program (other than a training program described in section 236(a)(7) (paragraph (b)(5) of this section)) for which all, or any portion, of the costs of the training program are paid—

(A) Under any Federal or State program other than the Act, or

(B) From any source other than TAA funds.

(ii) *Application.* Paragraph (E) of section 236(a)(5) of the Act thus authorizes prearrangements between cooperating State agencies administering the TAA program and the authorities administering any other Federal, State, or private funding source, to agree upon any mix of TAA funds and other funds for paying the costs of a training program approved under subpart C of this part. Any such prearrangement must contain specific commitments from the other authorities to pay the costs they agree to assume.

(3) *Section 236(a)(6) of the Act.* (i) *In general.* Paragraph (6) of section 236(a) of the Act is related to section 236(a)(5)(E) in providing that the costs of a training program approved under the Act are not required to be paid from TAA funds to the extent that such costs are paid under any Federal or State program other than the Act or from any source other than the Act.

(ii) *Application.* (A) Although paragraph (6) of section 236(a) of the Act is expressed in terms of the costs not being *required* to be paid from TAA funds, it authorizes the mixing of TAA funds and funds from any other Federal, State or private source. Therefore, sharing the future costs of training is authorized where prior costs were paid from another Federal, State or private source, but this does not authorize reimbursement from TAA funds of any training costs which were incurred and for which payment became due prior to the approval of the training program under subpart C of this part. In utilizing the authority under paragraph (b)(3) of this section for sharing training costs, prearrangements shall be entered into as required under paragraph (b)(2) of this section before any TAA funds are obligated.

(B) Paragraph (6) of section 236(a) contains a special restriction on the authority derived thereunder to use TAA funds in sharing training costs. Therefore, before approving any training program under subpart C of this part, which may involve sharing of the training costs under the authority of paragraph (b)(3) of this section, the cooperating State agencies for the TAA program shall require the worker to enter into a written agreement with the State under which TAA funds will not be applied for or used to pay any portion of the costs of the training the worker has reason to believe will be paid by any other governmental or private source.

(4) *Section 236(a)(4) of the Act.* (i) *In general.* (A) Paragraph (4) of section 236(a) of the Act (paragraph (3) of section 236(a) before August 23, 1988) continues to provide, as it did before the addition of paragraphs (5)(E), (6), and (7) to section 236(a), that:

(*1*) When the costs of training are paid from TAA funds under subpart C of this part, no other payment for such costs of training may be made under any other Federal law; and

(*2*) When the payment of the costs of training has already been made under any other Federal law, or the costs are reimbursable under any other Federal law and a portion of the costs has already been paid under such other Federal law, payment of such training costs may not be made from TAA funds.

(B) Paragraph (4) of section 236(a) also requires that: The provisions of paragraphs (b)(4)(i) (A)(*1*) and (A)(*2*) of this section shall not apply to, or take into account, any funds provided under any other provision of Federal law which are used for any purpose other than the direct payment of the identical costs incurred in training the adversely affected worker under the TAA Program, even if such other use has the effect of indirectly paying or reducing any portion of the costs involved in training the adversely affected worker.

(ii) *Application.* (A) Although the prohibition on duplicate payments in the first part of section 236(a)(4) remains fully implemented in this section, the second part of section 236(a)(4) on the sharing of costs from TAA funds and other Federal fund sources is modified by the explicit provisions of paragraphs (5)(E) and (6) of section 236(a), as set forth in paragraphs (b)(2) and (b)(3) of this section.

(B) When the direct costs of a training program approvable under subpart C of this part are payable from TAA funds and are also wholly or partially payable under another Federal law, or under any State law or from private, nongovernmental sources, the TAA Program agencies shall establish procedures which ensure that TAA funds shall not be utilized to duplicate funds available from another source, but this preclusion of duplication does not prohibit and shall not discourage sharing of costs under prearrangements authorized under paragraphs (b)(2) and (b)(3) of this section.

(C)(*1*) Therefore, pursuant to paragraph (4) of section 236(a), paragraph (b)(4) of this section continues to prohibit duplicate payment of training costs, which is consistent with the general prohibition expressed in subpart C of this part, against any use of TAA funds to duplicate payment of training costs in any circumstances. Paragraph (b)(4) of this section also continues to prohibit taking into account, in determining whether training costs are payable from TAA funds, any payments to the worker under any other Federal law which may have the effect of indirectly paying all or a portion of the training costs. Such indirect payments include Veterans Educational Assistance, Pell Grants, and Supplemental Educational Opportunity Grants, which are paid to the individual. However, any payments to the individual under these programs are deductible from TRA payable to the individual under § 617.13(c)(2).

(*2*) When payments of Veterans Educational Assistance, Pell Grants, and Supplemental Educational Opportunity Grants are made to the training provider, instead of the individual, and are used for training costs, such payments shall be taken into account as direct payment of the training costs under other Federal law for the purposes of this section.

(5) *Section 236(a)(7) of the Act.* (i) *In general.* Paragraph (7) of section 236(a) of the Act provides that a training program shall not be approved under the Act if—

(A) all or a portion of the costs of such training program are paid under any nongovernmental plan or program,

(B) the adversely affected worker has a right to obtain training or funds for training under such plan or program, and

(C) such plan or program requires the worker to reimburse the plan or program from funds provided under the Act, or from wages paid under such training program, for any portion of the costs of such training program paid under the plan or program.

(ii) *Application.* Paragraph (7) of section 236(a), which is implemented in paragraph (b)(5) of this section, reinforces the prohibition in § 617.22(h) against approval of a training program under subpart C of this part if the worker is required to pay a fee or tuition. The provisions of paragraph (b) and paragraph (h) of this section shall be given effect as prohibiting the approval under subpart C of this part of any training program if the worker would be requested or required, at any time or under any circumstances, to pay any of the costs of a training program, however small, from any TAA funds given to the worker or from any other funds belonging to the worker from any source whatever. Aside from this stringent limitation, however, paragraph (7) of section 236(a) of the Act implicitly authorizes training approved under this subpart C to be wholly or partly funded from nongovernmental (*i.e.*, employer, union or other private) sources.

[59 FR 936, Jan. 6, 1994]

§617.26 Liable and agent State responsibilities.

(a) *Liable State.* The liable State means, for any individual, the State which administers the applicable State law (as determined under §617.16). The liable State is responsible for making all determinations, redeterminations, and decisions on appeals on all claims for program benefits under this part 617, including waivers and revocations of waivers pursuant to §617.19, subsistence payments pursuant to §617.27, and transportation payments pursuant to §617.28. Upon receiving a copy of a certification issued by the Department, with respect to an affected firm in the State, the liable State also is responsible for publishing newspaper notices as provided in §617.4(d), furnishing information and assistance to workers as provided in §617.4, furnishing reemployment services under subparts C, D, and E of this part to all eligible workers covered by such certification, and carrying out other activities and functions required by the State's Agreement with the Secretary entered into pursuant to §617.59. All determinations pertaining to any individual's eligibility for or entitlement to any program benefit under this part 617 shall be subject to the provisions of §§617.50 and 617.51.

(b) *Agent State.* Agent State means, for any individual, any State other than the liable State for the individual. Agent States shall be responsible for cooperating fully with the liable State and assisting the liable State in carrying out its activities and functions. These agent State responsibilities shall be part of the activities and functions undertaken by the agent States under their Agreements entered into pursuant to §617.59. Agent State responsibilities include cooperating with liable States in taking applications and claims for TAA, providing reemployment services to certified workers in accordance with subparts B, C, D and E of this part, providing interstate claimants with TAA program information and assistance, assisting applicants or claimants to file claims for TAA program benefits and services, cooperating with the liable State by providing information needed to issue determinations, redeterminations, and decisions on appeals, and procuring and paying the cost of any approved training, including subsistence and transportation costs, according to determinations issued by the liable State.

[59 FR 938, Jan. 6, 1994]

§617.27 Subsistence payments.

(a) *Eligibility.* A trainee under this subpart C shall be afforded supplemental assistance necessary to pay costs of separate maintenance when the training facility is located outside the commuting area, but may not receive such supplemental assistance for any period for which the trainee receives such a payment under the Workforce Investment Act, or any other law, or for any day referred to under §617.28(c)(3) pursuant to which a transportation allowance is payable to the individual, or to the extent the individual is entitled to be paid or reimbursed for such expenses from any other source.

(b) *Amount.* Subsistence payments shall not exceed the lesser of:

(1) The individual's actual per diem expenses for subsistence; or

(2) 50 percent of the prevailing per diem rate authorized under the Federal travel regulations (*see* 41 CFR part 101–7) for the locale of the training.

(c) *Applications.* Applications for subsistence payments shall be filed in accordance with this subpart C and on forms which shall be furnished to trainees by the State agency. Such payments shall be made on completion of a week of training, except that at the beginning of a training project a State agency may advance a payment for a week if it determines that such advance is necessary to enable a trainee to accept training. An adjustment shall be made if the amount of an advance is less or more than the amount to which the trainee is entitled under paragraph (b) of this section. A determination as to an application made under this section shall be subject to §§ 617.50 and 617.51.

(d) *Unexcused absences.* No subsistence payment shall be made to an individual for any day of unexcused absence as certified by the responsible training facility.

[51 FR 45848, Dec. 22, 1986, as amended at 71 FR 35516, June 21, 2006]

§ 617.28 Transportation payments.

(a) *Eligibility.* A trainee under this subpart C shall be afforded supplemental assistance necessary to pay transportation expenses if the training is outside the commuting area, but may not receive such assistance if transportation is arranged for the trainee as part of a group and paid for by the State agency or to the extent the trainee receives a payment of transportation expenses under another Federal law, or to the extent the individual is entitled to be paid or reimbursed for such expenses from any other source.

(b) *Amount.* A transportation allowance shall not exceed the lesser of:

(1) The actual cost for travel by the least expensive means of transportation reasonably available between the trainee's home and the training facility; or

(2) The cost per mile at the prevailing mileage rate authorized under the Federal travel regulations. *See* 41 CFR part 101–7.

(c) *Travel included.* Travel for which a transportation allowance shall be paid includes travel:

(1) At the beginning and end of the training program;

(2) When the trainee fails for good cause, as described in § 617.18(b)(2), to complete the training program; and

(3) For daily commuting, in lieu of subsistence, but not exceeding the amount otherwise payable as subsistence for each day of commuting.

(d) *Applications.* Applications for transportation payments shall be filed in accordance with this subpart C and on forms which shall be furnished to trainees by the State agency. Payments may be made in advance. An adjustment shall be made if the amount of an advance is less or more than the amount to which the trainee is entitled under paragraph (b) of this section. A determination as to an application made under this section shall be subject to §§ 617.50 and 617.51.

§ 617.29 Application of EB work test.

(a) *Registration for employment.* Adversely affected workers who have exhausted all rights to UI and who otherwise qualify for TRA under § 617.11, shall, except as provided in paragraph (b) of this section:

(1) Register for work and be referred to work by the State agency in the same manner as required for EB claimants under the applicable State law provisions which are consistent with section 202(a)(3) of the Federal-State Extended Unemployment Compensation Act of 1970; and

(2) Be subject to the work test requirements for EB claimants under the applicable State law provisions which are consistent with section 202(a)(3) of the Federal-State Extended Unemployment Compensation Act of 1970.

(b) *Exceptions.* Paragraph (a) of this section shall not apply to any week an individual is undergoing training approved under this subpart C.

Subpart D—Job Search Allowances

§ 617.30 General.

A job search allowance shall be granted an adversely affected worker to assist the individual in securing a job within the United States as provided in this subpart D.

§ 617.31 Applications.

(a) *Forms.* Applications for job search allowances shall be filed in accordance with this subpart D and on forms which shall be furnished to individuals by the State agency.

(b) *Submittal.* An application may be submitted to a State agency at any time by an individual who has been totally or partially separated whether or not a certification covering the individual has been made. However, an application must be submitted to a State agency before the job search begins for the job search allowance to be granted, and the job search may not be approved until after the individual is covered under a certification.

(c) *Time limits.* Notwithstanding paragraph (b) of this section, a job search allowance application may be approved only if submitted before:

(1) The 365th day after the date of the certification under which the individual is covered, or the 365th day after the date of the individual's last total separation, whichever is later; or

(2) The 182d day after the concluding date of training approved under subpart C of this part 617, or approved under the regulations superseded by this part 617.

§617.32 Eligibility.

(a) *Conditions.* Job search allowance eligibility requires:

(1) A timely filed application;

(2) Total separation from adversely affected employment at the time the job search commences;

(3) Registration with the State agency which shall furnish the individual such reemployment services as are appropriate under subpart C of this part 617.

(4) A determination by the State agency that the individual has no reasonable expectation of securing suitable employment in the commuting area, and has a reasonable expectation of obtaining suitable employment of long-term duration outside the commuting area and in the area where the job search will be conducted. For the purposes of this section, the term "suitable employment" means suitable work as defined in §617.3(kk) (1) or (2), whichever is applicable to the individual; and

(5) Completion of the job search within a reasonable period not exceeding 30 days after the day on which the job search began.

(b) *Completion of job search.* A job search is deemed completed when the individual either secures employment or has contacted each employer to whom referred by the State agency in connection with a job search.

(c) *Verification of employer contacts.* The State agency shall verify contacts with employers certified by the individual.

[51 FR 45848, Dec. 22, 1986, as amended at 59 FR 938, Jan. 6, 1994]

§617.33 Findings required.

(a) *Findings by liable State.* Before final payment of a job search allowance may be approved, the following findings shall be made by the liable State:

(1) The individual meets the eligibility requirements for a job search allowance specified in §617.32(a) (1) through (4);

(2) The application for a job search allowance was submitted by the individual within the time limits specified in §617.31(c); and

(3) The individual completed the job search within the time limits stated in §617.32(a)(5), and the requirements of paragraphs (b) and (c) of §617.32 have been met.

(b) *Agent State.* (1) When an individual files an application for a job search allowance with respect to a job search conducted in a State other than the liable State, the State agency of the State in which the individual conducts the job search shall serve as the agent State and be responsible for assisting the individual in conducting the job search and in filing an application for a job search allowance with the liable State, and for assisting the liable State by furnishing to it any information required for the liable State's determination of the claim.

(2) The agent State shall cooperate fully with the liable State in carrying out its activities and functions with regard to such applications.

[59 FR 938, Jan. 6, 1994]

§617.34 Amount.

(a) *Computation.* The amount of a job search allowance shall be 90 percent of the total costs of each of the following allowable transportation and subsistence items:

(1) *Travel.* The more cost effective mode of travel reasonably available shall be approved by using:

(i) The actual cost of round trip travel by the most economical public transportation the individual reasonably can be expected to take from the individual's residence to the area of job search; or

(ii) The cost per mile at the prevailing mileage rate authorized under the Federal travel regulations (*see* 41

CFR part 101–7) for such roundtrip travel by the usual route from the individual's residence to the area of job search.

(2) *Lodging and meals*. The cost allowable for lodging and meals shall not exceed the lesser of:

(i) The actual cost to the individual of lodging and meals while engaged in the job search; or

(ii) 50 percent of the prevailing per diem allowance rate authorized under the Federal travel regulations (*see* 41 CFR part 101–7) for the locality where the job search is conducted.

(b) *Limit*. The total job search allowances paid to an individual under a certification may not exceed $800, regardless of the number of job searches undertaken by the individual. The amounts otherwise payable under paragraph (a) of this section shall be reduced by any amounts the individual is entitled to be paid or reimbursed for such expenses from any other source.

[51 FR 45848, Dec. 22, 1986, as amended at 51 FR 45869, Dec. 22, 1986; 53 FR 32351, Aug. 24, 1988; 59 FR 939, Jan. 6, 1994]

§ 617.35 Time and method of payment.

(a) *Determinations*. A State agency shall promptly make and record determinations necessary to assure entitlement of an individual to a job search allowance at any time, before or after a certification covering the individual is made. No job search allowance may be paid or advanced to an individual until the State agency determines that the individual is covered under a certification. A State agency shall make payment as promptly as possible upon determining that the individual is covered under a certification and is otherwise eligible.

(b) *Payment*. Unless paragraph (a) of this section applies, a job search allowance shall be paid promptly after an individual completes a job search and complies with paragraph (d) of this section.

(c) *Advances*. A State agency may advance an individual (except an individual not yet covered under a certification) 60 percent of the estimated amount of the job search allowance payable on completion of the job search, but not exceeding $360, within 5 days prior to commencement of a job search. Such advance shall be deducted from any payment under paragraph (b) of this section.

(d) *Worker evidence*. On completion of a job search, the individual shall certify on forms furnished by the State agency as to employer contacts made and amounts expended daily for lodging and meals. Receipts shall be required for all lodging and purchased transportation expenses incurred by the individual pursuant to the job search. An adjustment shall be made if the amount of an advance is less or more than the amount to which the individual is entitled under § 617.34.

Subpart E—Relocation Allowances

§ 617.40 General.

A relocation allowance shall be granted an adversely affected worker to assist the individual and the individual's family, if any, to relocate within the United States as stated in this subpart E. A relocation allowance may be granted an individual only once under a certification. A relocation allowance shall not be granted to more than one member of a family with respect to the same relocation. If applications for a relocation allowance are made by more than one member of a family as to the same relocation, the allowance shall be paid to the head of the family if otherwise eligible.

§ 617.41 Applications.

(a) *Forms*. Applications for a relocation allowance shall be filed in accordance with this subpart E and on forms which shall be furnished by the State agency.

(b) *Submittal*. An application may be submitted to the State agency at any time by an individual who has been totally or partially separated regardless of whether a certification covering the individual has been made. However, an application must be submitted to a State agency before the relocation begins for the relocation allowance to be granted, and the relocation may not be approved until after the individual is covered under a certification.

(c) *Time limits*. Notwithstanding paragraph (b) of this section, an application for a relocation allowance may not be approved unless submitted before:

(1) The 425th day after the date of the certification under which the individual is covered, or the 425th day after the date of the individual's last total separation, whichever is later; or

(2) The 182d day after the concluding date of training approved under subpart C of this part 617, or approved under the regulations superseded by this part 617.

§617.42 Eligibility.

(a) *Conditions.* Eligibility for a relocation allowance requires:

(1) A timely filed application;

(2) Total separation from adversely affected employment at the time relocation commences;

(3) No prior receipt of a relocation allowance under the same certification;

(4) Relocation within the United States and outside the individual's present commuting area;

(5) Registration with the State agency which shall furnish the individual such reemployment services as are appropriate under subpart C of this part 617;

(6) A determination by the State agency that the individual has no reasonable expectation of securing suitable employment in the commuting area, and has obtained suitable employment affording a reasonable expectation of employment of long-term duration, or a bona fide offer of such suitable employment, outside the commuting area and in the area of intended relocation. For the purposes of this section, the term "suitable employment" means suitable work as defined in §617.3(kk) (1) and (2), whichever is applicable to the individual; and

(7) Relocation beginning within a reasonable period, as determined under §617.43(b), and completion of such relocation within a reasonable period of time as determined in accordance with Federal travel regulations and §617.43(a).

(b) *Job search.* Applications for a relocation allowance and a job search allowance may not be approved concurrently, but the prior payment of a job search allowance shall not otherwise preclude the payment of a relocation allowance.

[51 FR 45848, Dec. 22, 1986, as amended at 59 FR 939, Jan. 6, 1994]

§617.43 Time of relocation.

(a) *Applicable considerations.* In determining whether an individual's relocation is completed in a reasonable period of time, a State agency, among other factors, shall consider whether:

(1) Suitable housing is available in the area of relocation;

(2) The individual can dispose of the individual's residence;

(3) The individual or a family member is ill; and

(4) A member of the individual's family is attending school and when the member can best be transferred to a school in the area of relocation.

(b) *Time limits.* The reasonable period for actually beginning a relocation move shall expire 182 days after the date of application for a relocation allowance, or 182 days after the conclusion of training approved under subpart C of this part 617, or approved under the regulations in former 29 CFR part 91, in effect prior to its redesignation as this 20 CFR part 617 and its concurrent revision.

§617.44 Findings required.

(a) *Findings by liable State.* Before final payment of a relocation allowance may be approved, the following findings shall be made by the liable State:

(1) The individual meets the eligibility requirements for a relocation allowance specified in §617.42(a) (1) to (6) and §617.42(b).

(2) The application for a relocation allowance was submitted by the individual within the time limits specified in §617.41(c);

(3) The individual began and completed the relocation within the limitations specified in §617.42(a)(7) and §617.43; and

(4) The liable State has verified (directly or through the agent State) with the employer, and finds, that the individual has obtained suitable employment affording a reasonable expectation of long-term duration, or a bona fide offer of such suitable employment, in the area of intended relocation, in accordance with §617.42(a)(6).

(b) *Agent State.* (1) When an individual relocates in a State other than the liable State, the State agency of the

State in which the individual relocates shall serve as the agent State and be responsible for:

(i) Assisting the individual in relocating to the State, and in filing an application for a relocation allowance with the liable State, and

(ii) Assisting the liable State by furnishing to it any information required for the liable State's determination on the claim.

(2) The agent State shall cooperate with the liable State in carrying out its activities and functions with regard to such applications. When requested by the liable State, the agent State shall verify with the employer and report to the liable State whether the individual has obtained suitable employment affording a reasonable expectation of employment of long-term duration, or a bona fide offer of such suitable employment.

[59 FR 939, Jan. 6, 1994]

§ 617.45 Amount.

(a) *Items allowable.* The amount payable as a relocation allowance shall include the following items:

(1) 90 percent of the travel expenses for the individual and family, if any, from the individual's place of residence to the area of relocation, as determined under § 617.46;

(2) 90 percent of the expenses of moving household goods and personal effects of the individual and family, if any, not to exceed the maximum number of pounds net weight authorized under the Federal travel regulations (*see* 41 CFR part 101-7), between such locations, as determined under § 617.47; and

(3) A lump sum payment, equal to 3 times the individual's average weekly wage, not to exceed $800.

(b) *Reduction.* The amount otherwise payable under paragraphs (a)(1) and (a)(2) of this section shall be reduced by any amount the individual is entitled to be paid or reimbursed for such expenses from any other source.

[51 FR 45848, Dec. 22, 1986, as amended at 51 FR 45869, Dec. 22, 1986]

§ 617.46 Travel allowance.

(a) *Computation.* The amount of travel allowance (including lodging and meals) payable under § 617.45(a)(1) shall be 90 percent of the total costs of each of the following allowable transportation and subsistence items:

(1) *Transportation.* The more cost effective mode of transportation reasonably available shall be approved by using:

(i) The actual cost of transportation for the individual and family, if any, by the most economical public transportation the individual and family reasonably can be expected to take from the individual's old residence to the individual's new residence in the area of relocation; or

(ii) The cost per mile at the prevailing mileage rate authorized under the Federal travel regulations (*see* 41 CFR part 101-7) for the usually traveled route from the individual's old residence to the individual's new residence in the area of relocation. No additional mileage shall be payable for family members traveling on the same trip in the same vehicle.

(2) *Lodging and meals.* The cost allowable for lodging and meals for an individual or each member of the individual's family shall not exceed the lesser of:

(i) The actual cost to the individual for lodging and meals while in travel status; or

(ii) 50 percent of the prevailing per diem allowance rate authorized under the Federal travel regulations (*see* 41 CFR part 101-7) for the locality to which the relocation is made.

(b) *Separate travel.* If, for good cause, a member or members of an individual's family must travel separately to the individual's new residence, 90 percent of the total costs of such separate travel, computed in accordance with paragraph (a) of this section, shall be included in calculating the total amount the individual is entitled to be paid under this subpart E. For purposes of this paragraph (b), good cause means such reasons as would justify the family member's inability to relocate with the other members of the individual's family, including but not limited to reasons related to the family member's health, schooling or economic circumstances.

(c) *Limitation.* In no case may the individual be paid a travel allowance for the individual or a member of the individual's family more than once in connection with a single relocation.

[51 FR 45848, Dec. 22, 1986, as amended at 53 FR 32351, Aug. 24, 1988]

§617.47 Moving allowance.

(a) *Computation.* The amount of a moving allowance payable under §617.45(a)(2) shall be 90 percent of the total of the allowable costs under either (1), (2), or (3) of this paragraph, and 90 percent of the total allowable costs under (4) of this paragraph:

(1) *Commercial carrier.* Allowable costs for moving household goods and personal effects of an individual and family, if any, shall not exceed the maximum number of pounds net weight authorized under the Federal travel regulations (*see* 41 CFR part 101-7) by commercial carrier from the individual's old residence to the individual's new residence in the area of relocation, including reasonable and necessary accessorial charges, by the most economical commercial carrier the individual reasonably can be expected to use. Before undertaking such move, the individual must submit to the State agency an estimate from a commercial carrier as to the cost thereof. Accessorial charges shall include the cost of insuring such goods and effects for their actual value or $10,000, whichever is least, against loss or damage in transit, if a bid from a licensed insurer is obtained by the individual and approved by the State agency before departure. If a State agency finds it is more economical to pay a carrier an extra charge to assume the responsibility of a common carrier for such goods and effects, 90 percent of such extra charge, but not exceeding $50, shall be paid in lieu of the cost of insurance.

(2) *Trailer or rental truck*—(i) *Trailer.* If household goods and personal effects are moved by trailer, the allowable costs shall be:

(A) If the trailer is hauled by private vehicle, the cost per mile for the use of the private vehicle at the prevailing mileage rate authorized under the Federal travel regulations (*see* 41 CFR part 101-7) for the usually traveled route from the individual's old residence to the individual's new residence in the area of relocation; and

(B) If the trailer is rented, and of the type customarily used for moving household goods and personal effects, the rental fee for each day reasonably required to complete the move; or

(C) The actual charge if hauling is by commercial carrier,

(ii) *Rental truck.* If household goods and personal effects are moved by rental truck of the type customarily used for moving household goods and personal effects, the allowable costs shall be:

(A) The rental fee for each day reasonably required to complete the move; and

(B) The necessary fuel for such rental truck paid by the individual.

(3) *House trailer.* If a house trailer or mobile home was used as the individual's place of residence in the old area and will be so used in the new area, the allowable costs of moving such house trailer or mobile home shall be:

(i) The commercial carrier's charges for moving the house trailer or mobile home;

(ii) Charges for unblocking and reblocking;

(iii) Ferry charges, bridge, road, and tunnel tolls, taxes, fees fixed by a State or local authority for permits to transport the unit in or through its jurisdiction, and retention of necessary flagmen; and

(iv) The cost of insuring the house trailer or mobile home, and the personal effects of the individual and family, against loss or damage in transit, in accordance with the provisions in paragraph (a)(1) of this section.

(4) *Temporary storage.* If temporary storage of household goods and personal effects is necessary, the cost of such temporary storage for a period not to exceed 60 days.

(b) *Travel.* Payments under this section shall be in addition to payments for travel expenses for the individual and family, if any, under §617.45(a)(1), except that the allowable cost for a private vehicle used to haul a trailer may not be paid under this section if any cost with respect to such private vehicle is payable under any other provisions of this subpart E.

§ 617.48 Time and method of payment.

(a) *Determinations.* A State agency shall promptly make and record determinations necessary to assure an individual's entitlement to a relocation allowance at any time, before or after a certification covering the individual is made. No relocation allowance may be paid or advanced to an individual until the State agency determines that the individual is covered under a certification. A State agency shall make payment as promptly as possible upon determining that the individual is covered under a certification and is otherwise eligible.

(b) *Travel and moving allowances.* Allowances computed under §§ 617.46 and 617.47 shall be paid as follows:

(1) *Travel*—(i) *Transportation and subsistence.* The amounts estimated under § 617.46 at 90 percent of the lowest allowable costs shall be paid in advance at the time an individual departs from the individual's residence to begin relocation or within 10 days prior thereto. An amount payable for a family member approved for separate travel shall be paid to the individual at the time of such family member's departure or within 10 days prior thereto.

(ii) *Worker evidence.* On completion of a relocation, the individual shall certify on forms furnished by the State agency as to the amount expended daily for lodging and meals. Receipts shall be required for all lodging and purchased transportation expenses incurred by the individual and family, if any, pursuant to the relocation. An adjustment shall be made if the amount of an advance is less or more than the amount to which the individual is entitled under § 617.46.

(2) *Moving.* The amount estimated under § 617.47 at 90 percent of the lowest allowable costs shall be paid:

(i) *Commercial carrier.* (A) If household goods and personal effects are moved by commercial carrier, 90 percent of the amount of the estimate submitted by the individual under § 617.47(a)(1) and approved by the State agency for covering the cost of such move, and 90 percent of the other charges approved by the State agency under § 617.47(a)(1) shall be advanced by check or checks payable to the carrier and insurer, and delivered to the individual at the time of the scheduled shipment or within 10 days prior thereto. On completion of the move, the individual shall promptly submit to the State agency a copy of the bill of lading prepared by the carrier, including a receipt evidencing payment of moving costs. The individual shall with such submittal reimburse the State agency the amount, if any, by which the advance made under this paragraph (b)(2)(i) exceeds 90 percent of the actual moving costs approved by the State agency. The individual shall be paid the difference if the amount advanced was less than 90 percent of the actual moving costs approved by the State agency.

(B) If more economical, a State agency may make direct arrangements for moving and insuring an individual's household goods and personal effects with a carrier and insurer selected by the individual and may make payment of 90 percent of moving and insurance costs directly to the carrier and insurer. No such arrangement shall release a carrier from liability otherwise provided by law or contract for loss or damage to the individual's goods and effects. The United States shall not be or become liable to either party for personal injury or property loss damage under any circumstances.

(ii) *Trailer or rental truck*—(A) *Private vehicle with trailer.* If the move is by private vehicle and trailer, the allowable cost for the use of the private vehicle shall be made at the time payment is made under paragraph (b)(1) of this section.

(B) *Rental trailer or rental truck.* If the move is by rental trailer or rental truck:

(*1*) The individual shall submit an estimate of the rental cost from the rental agency; and

(*2*) 90 percent of such estimated rental cost may be advanced by check payable to the order of the individual and the rental agency at the time payment is made under paragraph (b)(1) of this section; and

(*3*) On completion of the move the individual shall submit promptly to the State agency a receipted bill itemizing and evidencing payment of the rental charges for the trailer or truck and fuel costs, and shall reimburse the State agency for the amount, if any, by which the advance made for the trailer or truck exceeds 90 percent of the rental charges approved by the State agency. If the amount of the advance was less than 90 percent of the rental charges, the individual shall be paid the difference.

(iii) *House trailer.* If a house trailer or mobile home is moved by commercial carrier, the individual shall submit to the State agency an estimate of the cost of the move by the commercial carrier. A check for 90 percent of the amount of the estimate, if approved, payable to the individual and the carrier, may be delivered to the individual at the time of the scheduled move or within 10 days prior thereto.

(c) *Lump sum allowance.* The lump sum allowance provided in § 617.45(a)(3) shall be paid when arrangements are completed for relocation of the individual and family, if any, but not more than 10 days before the earlier of the individual's anticipated departure from the individual's residence to begin relocation or the anticipated date of shipment of the individual's household goods and personal effects.

(d) *Relocation completed.* A relocation is completed when an individual and family, if any, and their household goods and personal effects arrive at the individual's residence in the area of relocation. If no household goods and personal effects are moved, a relocation is completed when the individual and family, if any, arrive in the area of relocation and establish a residence in the new area. The later arrival of a family member approved for separate travel shall not alter the date a relocation was completed.

Subpart F—Job Search Program

§ 617.49 Job Search Program.

(a) *Program requirements.* (1) A worker, after being separated from adversely affected employment, must participate in an approved job search program (JSP), or have completed a JSP, as a condition for receiving TRA, except where the State agency determines that an acceptable JSP is not reasonably available.

(2) A TRA claimant is subject to participation in a JSP as a condition for receiving TRA for weeks of unemployment which begin after the date the claimant is notified of the requirement and has filed an initial claim for TRA. The claimant is not subject to the JSP as a condition for receiving TRA for weeks which begin prior to that date.

(3) When the State agency determines that the worker has failed to begin participation in an approved JSP, or ceased to participate in such a JSP before completion, and there is no justifiable cause for such failure or cessation, no TRA may be paid to the worker for weeks beginning with the week that failure or cessation occurred when it is determined that such failure or cessation was without justifiable cause. TRA may be paid thereafter to an otherwise eligible worker only for weeks beginning with the week the worker begins or resumes participation in an approved JSP or complete the JSP. For purposes of this paragraph (a)(3), justifiable cause means such reasons as would justify an individual's conduct when measured by conduct expected of a reasonable individual in like circumstances, including but not limited to reasons beyond the individual's control and reasons related to the individual's capability to enroll in an approved JSP or complete the JSP.

(4) A worker in training approved under §§ 617.22 through 617.26, or approved by the State agency under State law, is excepted from the JSP qualifying requirement while the worker is attending and making satisfactory progress in the training. This exception applies whether training begins before or after entitlement to basic TRA commences, and also applies after training begins for a worker who is attending a JSP program. Exceptions to the JSP qualifying requirement must be documented in the worker's claim file by the State agency.

(b) *Approved JSPs.* A job search program may be approved if:

(1) The JSP is provided through the Workforce Investment Act, the public employment service, or any other Federal or State funded program, and complies with paragraphs (w), (x), and (y) of § 617.3.

(2) The JSP is sponsored by a company or firm from which the worker has been separated, and complies with paragraphs (w), (x), and (y) of § 617.3.

(c) *Determination of reasonably available.* (1) Reasonably available means an existing approved JSP that is located in the worker's normal commuting area, as defined in § 617.3, and has sufficient capacity to accommodate the worker.

(2) When the State determines that a JSP is not reasonably available for a worker, the requirement is not a condition of qualifying for TRA for the weeks involved. When a determination is made with respect to a worker, the State agency must document its determination, and the weeks involved, in the worker's claim file, prior to making TRA payments to the worker.

(3) The State agency may issue a blanket waiver of the JSP qualifying requirement for TRA for groups of workers, where deemed appropriate, when it is determined that there is no functioning JSP.

(4) All determinations that a JSP is not reasonably available should extend only for that period of time that a JSP is not reasonably available, and the exception for workers in approved training should extend until the completion of training. If the State determines that a JSP is reasonably available at a later date, then the JSP qualifying requirement must be met for entitlement to basic TRA for weeks of unemployment beginning with the week in which JSP becomes reasonably available.

(d) *JSP allowances.* Subsistence and transportation costs shall be approved for workers participating in JSPs when deemed appropriate and within available State funding levels. Costs incurred may not exceed those allowable for training under §§ 617.27 and 617.28, if, and when, the State refers a worker to a JSP outside the normal commuting area.

(e) *Termination of requirement.* The job search program requirement set out in this section shall not be a condition of entitlement to TRA for any week.

[53 FR 32351, Aug. 24, 1988, as amended at 54 FR 22277, May 23, 1989; 59 FR 939, Jan. 6, 1994; 71 FR 35516, June 21, 2006]

Subpart G—Administration by Applicable State Agencies

§ 617.50 Determinations of entitlement; notices to individuals.

(a) *Determinations of initial applications for TRA or other TAA.* The State Agency whose State law is the applicable State law under § 617.16 shall upon the filing of an initial application for TRA or other TAA promptly determine the individual's entitlement to such TRA or other TAA under this part 617, and may accept for such purposes information and findings supplied by another State agency under this part 617.

(b) *Determinations of subsequent applications for TRA or other TAA.* The State agency shall, upon the filing of an application for payment of TRA, or subsistence and transportation under §§ 617.27 and 617.28, with respect to a week, promptly determine whether the individual is eligible for a payment of TRA, or subsistence and transportation, with respect to such week, and, if eligible, the amount of TRA, or subsistence and transportation, for which the individual is eligible. In addition, the State agency promptly shall, upon the filing of a subsequent application for job search allowances (where the total of previous job search allowances paid the individual was less than $600), determine whether the individual is eligible for job search allowances, and, if eligible, the amount of job search allowances for which the individual is eligible.

(c) *Redeterminations.* The provisions of the applicable State law concerning the right to request, or authority to undertake, reconsideration of a determination pertaining to a claim for UI under the applicable State law shall apply to determinations pertaining to all forms of TAA under this part 617.

(d) *Use of State law.* In making determinations or redeterminations under this section, or in reviewing such determinations or redeterminations under § 617.51, a State agency shall apply the regulations in this part 617. As to matters committed by this part 617 to the applicable State law, a State agency, a hearing officer, or a State court shall apply the applicable State law and regulations thereunder, including procedural requirements of such

State law or regulations, except so far as such State law or regulations are inconsistent with this part 617 or the purpose of this part 617: *Provided*, that, no provision of State law or regulations on good cause for waiver of any time limit, or for late filing of any claim, shall apply to any time limitation referred to or specified in this part 617, unless such State law or regulation is made applicable by a specific provision of this part 617.

(e) *Notices to individual.* The State agency shall notify the individual in writing of any determination or redetermination as to entitlement to TAA. Each determination or redetermination shall inform the individual of the reason for the determination or redetermination and of the right to reconsideration or appeal in the same manner as determinations of entitlement to UI are subject to redetermination or appeal under the applicable State law.

(f) *Promptness.* Full payment of TAA when due shall be made with the greatest promptness that is administratively feasible.

(g) *Procedure.* Except where otherwise required by the Act or this part 617, the procedures for making and furnishing determinations and written notices of determinations to individuals, shall be consistent with the Secretary's "Standard for Claim Determinations—Separation Information," *Employment Security Manual*, part V, sections 6010–6015 (appendix B of this part).

[51 FR 45848, Dec. 22, 1986, as amended at 59 FR 939, 943, Jan. 6, 1994]

§617.51 Appeals and hearings.

(a) *Applicable State law.* A determination or redetermination under this part 617 shall be subject to review in the same manner and to the same extent as determinations and redeterminations under the applicable State law, and only in that manner and to that extent. Proceedings for review of a determination or redetermination may be consolidated or joined with proceedings for review of a determination or redetermination under the State law where convenient or necessary. Procedures as to the right of appeal and opportunity for fair hearing shall be consistent with sections 303(a) (1) and (3) of the Social Security Act (42 U.S.C. 503(a) (1) and (3)).

(b) *Appeals promptness.* Appeals under paragraph (a) of this section shall be decided with a degree of promptness meeting the Secretary's "Standard on Appeals Promptness—Unemployment Compensation" (part 650 of this chapter). Any provisions of the applicable State law for advancement or priority of UI cases on judicial calendars, or otherwise intended to provide for prompt payment of UI when due, shall apply to proceedings involving entitlement to TAA under this part 617.

§617.52 Uniform interpretation and application.

(a) *First rule of construction.* The Act and the implementing regulations in this part 617 shall be construed liberally so as to carry out the purpose of the Act.

(b) *Second rule of construction.* The Act and the implementing regulations in this part 617 shall be construed so as to assure insofar as possible the uniform interpretation and application of the Act and this part 617 throughout the United States.

(c) *Effectuating purpose and rules of construction.* (1) To effectuate the purpose of the Act and this part 617 and to assure uniform interpretation and application of the Act and this part 617 throughout the United States, a State agency shall forward, not later than 10 days after issuance, to the Department a copy of any judicial or administrative decision ruling on an individual's entitlement to TAA under this part 617. On request of the Department, a State agency shall forward to the Department a copy of any determination or redetermination ruling on an individual's entitlement to TAA under this part 617.

(2) If the Department believes that a determination, redetermination, or decision is inconsistent with the Department's interpretation of the Act or this part 617, the Department may at any time notify the State agency of the Department's view. Thereafter, the State agency shall issue a redetermination or appeal if possible, and shall not follow such determination, redetermination, or decision as a precedent; and, in any subsequent proceedings which involve

such determination, redetermination, or decision, or wherein such determination, redetermination, or decision is cited as precedent or otherwise relied upon, the State agency shall inform the claims deputy or hearing officer or court of the Department's view and shall make all reasonable efforts, including appeal or other proceedings in an appropriate forum, to obtain modification, limitation, or overruling of the determination, redetermination, or decision.

(3) If the Department believes that a determination, redetermination, or decision is patently and flagrantly violative of the Act or this part 617, the Department may at any time notify the State agency of the Department's view. If the determination, redetermination, or decision in question denies TAA to an individual, the steps outlined in paragraph (c)(2) of this section shall be followed by the State agency. If the determination, redetermination, or decision in question awards TAA to an individual, the benefits are "due" within the meaning of section 303(a)(1) of the Social Security Act (42 U.S.C. 503(a)(1)), and therefore must be paid promptly to the individual. However, the State agency, shall take the steps outlined in paragraph (c)(2) of this section, and payments to the individual may be temporarily delayed if redetermination or appeal action is taken not more than one business day following the day on which the first payment otherwise would be issued to the individual; and the redetermination action is taken or appeal is filed to obtain a reversal of the award of TAA and a ruling consistent with the Department's view; and the redetermination action or appeal seeks an expedited redetermination or appeal within not more than two weeks after the redetermination action is taken or the appeal is filed. If redetermination action is not taken or appeal is not filed within the above time limit, or a redetermination or decision is not obtained within the two-week limit, or any redetermination or decision or order is issued which affirms the determination, redetermination, or decision awarding TAA or allows it to stand in whole or in part, the benefits awarded must be paid promptly to the individual.

(4)(i) If any determination, redetermination, or decision, referred to in paragraph (c)(2) or paragraph (c)(3) of this section, is treated as a precedent for any future application for TAA, the Secretary will decide whether the Agreement with the State entered into under the Act and this part 617 shall be terminated and § 617.59(f) applied.

(ii) In the case of any determination, redetermination, or decision that is not legally warranted under the Act or this part 617, including any determination, redetermination, or decision referred to in paragraph (c)(2) or paragraph (c)(3) of this section, the Secretary will decide whether the State shall be required to restore the funds of the United States for any sums paid under such a determination, redetermination, or decision, and whether, in the absence of such restoration, the Agreement with the State shall be terminated and § 617.59(f) applied and whether other action shall be taken to recover such sums for the United States.

(5) A State agency may request reconsideration of a notice issued pursuant to paragraph (c)(2) or paragraph (c)(3) of this section, and shall be given an opportunity to present views and arguments if desired. Such request shall be made to the Secretary and may include views and arguments on the matters to be decided by the Secretary under paragraph (c)(4) of this section.

(6) Concurrence of the Department in a determination, redetermination, or decision shall not be presumed from the absence of a notice issued pursuant to this section.

(Approved by the Office of Management and Budget under control number 1205–0222)

§ 617.53 Subpoenas.

A State agency may issue subpoenas for attendance of witnesses and production of records on the same terms and conditions as under the State law. Compliance may be enforced on the same terms and conditions as under the State law, or, if a State court declines to enforce a subpoena issued under this section, the State agency may petition for an order requiring compliance with such subpoena to the United States District Court within the jurisdiction of which the relevant proceeding under this part 617 is conducted.

§617.54 State agency rulemaking.

A State agency may establish supplemental procedures not inconsistent with the Act or this part 617 or procedures prescribed by the Department to further effective administration of this part 617. The exact text of such supplemental procedure or procedures, certified as accurate by a responsible official, employee, or counsel of the State agency, shall be submitted to the Department, on a form supplied by the Department. No supplemental procedure shall be effective unless and until approved by the Department. Approval may be granted on a temporary basis, not to exceed 90 days, in cases of administrative necessity. On reasonable notice to a State agency, approval of a supplemental procedure may be withdrawn at any time. If public notice and opportunity for hearing would be required under a State law for adoption of a similar or analogous procedure involving UI, such public notice and opportunity for hearing shall be afforded by the State agency as to the supplemental procedure.

(Approved by the Office of Management and Budget under control number 1205–0222)

§617.55 Overpayments; penalties for fraud.

(a) *Determination and repayment.* (1) If a State agency or a court of competent jurisdiction determines that any person or individual has received any payment under this part 617 to which the person or individual was not entitled, including a payment referred to in paragraph (b) or paragraph (c) of this section, such person or individual shall be liable to repay such amount to the State agency, and the State agency shall recover any such overpayment in accordance with the provisions of this part 617; except that the State agency may waive the recovery of any such overpayment if the State agency determines, in accordance with the guidelines prescribed in paragraph (a)(2) of this section, that:

(i) The payment was made without fault on the part of such person or individual; and

(ii) Requiring such repayment would be contrary to equity and good conscience.

(2)(i)(A) In determining whether fault exists for purposes of paragraph (a)(1)(i) of this section, the following factors shall be considered:

(*1*) Whether a material statement or representation was made by the person or individual in connection with the application for TAA that resulted in the overpayment, and whether the person or individual knew or should have known that the statement or representation was inaccurate.

(*2*) Whether the person or individual failed or caused another to fail to disclose a material fact, in connection with an application for TAA that resulted in the overpayment, and whether the person or individual knew or should have known that the fact was material.

(*3*) Whether the person or individual knew or could have been expected to know, that the person or individual was not entitled to the TAA payment.

(*4*) Whether, for any other reason, the overpayment resulted directly or indirectly, and partially or totally, from any act or omission of the person or individual or of which the person or individual had knowledge, and which was erroneous or inaccurate or otherwise wrong.

(*5*) Whether there has been a determination of fraud under paragraph (b) of this section or section 243 of the Act.

(B) An affirmative finding on any one of the factors in paragraphs (a)(2)(i)(A) of this section precludes waiver of overpayment recovery.

(ii)(A) In determining whether equity and good conscience exists for purposes of paragraph (a)(1)(ii) of this section, the following factors shall be considered:

(*1*) Whether the overpayment was the result of a decision on appeal, whether the State agency had given notice to the person or individual that the case has been appealed and that the person or individual may be required to repay the overpayment in the event of a reversal on appeal, and whether recovery of the overpayment will not cause extraordinary and lasting financial hardship to the person or individual.

(*2*) Whether recovery of the overpayment will not cause extraordinary financial hardship to the person or individual, and there has been no affirmative finding under paragraph (a)(2)(ii)(A) of this section with respect to such person or individual and such overpayment.

(B) An affirmative finding on either of the foregoing factors in paragraphs (a)(2)(ii)(A) of this section precludes waiver of overpayment recovery.

(C)(*1*) For the purpose of paragraph (a)(2)(ii) of this section, an extraordinary financial hardship shall exist if recovery of the overpayment would result directly in the person's or individual's loss of or inability to obtain minimal necessities of food, medicine, and shelter for a substantial period of time; and an extraordinary and lasting financial hardship shall be extraordinary as described above and may be expected to endure for the foreseeable future.

(*2*) In applying this test in the case of attempted recovery by repayment, a substantial period of time shall be 30 days, and the foreseeable future shall be at least three months. In applying this test in the case of proposed recoupment from other benefits, a substantial period of time and the foreseeable future shall be the longest potential period of benefit entitlement as seen at the time of the request for a waiver determination. In making these determinations, the State agency shall take into account all potential income of the person or individual and the person's or individual's firm, organization, or family and all cash resources available or potentially available to the person or individual and the person's or individual's firm, organization, or family in the time period being considered.

(*3*) Determinations granting or denying waivers of overpayments shall be made only on request for a waiver determination. Such request shall be made on a form which shall be furnished to the person or individual by the State agency. Notices of determination of overpayments shall include an accurate description of the waiver provisions of paragraph (a) of this section, if the State agency has elected to allow waivers of TAA overpayments.

(*4*) Each State shall have the option to establish a policy as to whether the waiver provisions of this section shall be applied to TAA overpayments. A State's decision on its policy shall not be controlled by whether it waives UI overpayments, but the State's decision shall be published for the information of the public and the Department.

(*5*)(i) Unless an overpayment is otherwise recovered, or is waived under paragraph (a) of this section, the State agency shall recover the overpayment by deduction from any sums payable to such person or individual under:

(A) This part 617;

(B) Any Federal unemployment compensation law administered by the State agency; or

(C) Any other Federal law administered by the State agency which provides for the payment of unemployment assistance or an allowance with respect to unemployment.

(ii) In addition, a State agency may recover the overpayment from unemployment insurance payable to such person or individual under the State law.

(b) *Fraud.* If a State agency or a court of competent jurisdiction finds that any person or individual:

(1) Knowingly has made, or caused another to make, a false statement or representation of a material fact; or

(2) Knowingly has failed, or caused another to fail, to disclose a material fact; and as a result of such false statement or representation, or of such nondisclosure, such individual has received any payment under this part 617 to which the person or individual was not entitled, such person or individual shall, in addition to any other penalty provided by law, be ineligible for any further payments under this part 617.

(c) *Training, job search and relocation allowances.* (1) If an individual fails, with good cause, to complete training, a job search, or a relocation, any payment or portion of a payment made under this part 617 to such individual or any person that is not properly and necessarily expended in attempting to complete such training, job search, or relocation, shall constitute an overpayment.

(2) If an individual fails, without good cause, to complete training, a job

search, or a relocation, any payment made under this part 617 to such individual or any person shall constitute an overpayment.

(3) Such overpayment shall be recovered or waived as provided in paragraph (a) of this section.

(d) *Final determination.* Except for overpayments determined by a court of competent jurisdiction, no repayment may be required, and no deduction may be made, under this section until a determination under paragraph (a) of this section by the State agency has been made, notice of the determination and an opportunity for a fair hearing thereon has been given to the person or individual concerned, and the determination has become final.

(e) *Deposit.* Any amount recovered by a State agency under this section shall be deposited into the Federal fund or account from which payment was made.

(f) *Procedural requirements.* (1) The provisions of paragraphs (c), (e), and (g) of §617.50 shall apply to determinations and redeterminations made pursuant to this section.

(2) The provisions of §617.51 shall apply to determinations and redeterminations made pursuant to this section.

(g) *Fraud detection and prevention.* State procedures for the detection and prevention of fraudulent overpayments of TAA shall be, as a minimum, commensurate with the procedures adopted by the State with respect to State unemployment compensation and consistent with the Secretary's "Standard for Fraud and Overpayment Detection," Employment Security Manual, Part V, sections 7510–7515 (Appendix C of this part).

(h) *Debts due the United States or Others.* (1) Notwithstanding any provision of this part 617, TAA payable to a person or an individual under this part 617 shall be applied by the State agency for the recovery by offset of any debt due the United States from the person or individual.

(2) TAA shall not be applied or used by the State agency in any manner for the payment of any debt of any person or individual to any State or any other entity or person, except that TRA payable to an individual shall be payable to someone other than the individual if required by State law and Federal law to satisfy the individual's obligation for child support or alimony.

(i) *Definition of person.* For purposes of this section, a person includes any employer or other entity or organization as well as the officers and officials thereof who may bear individual responsibility.

[59 FR 939, Jan. 6, 1994, as amended at 59 FR 943, Jan. 6, 1994]

§617.56 Inviolate rights to TAA.

Except as specifically provided in this part 617, the rights of individuals to TAA shall be protected in the same manner and to the same extent as the rights of persons to UI are protected under the applicable State law. Such measures shall include protection of applicants for TAA from waiver, release, assignment, pledge, encumbrance, levy, execution, attachment, and garnishment of their rights to TAA, except as provided in §617.55. In the same manner and to the same extent, individuals shall be protected from discrimination and obstruction in regard to seeking, applying for, and receiving any right to TAA.

§617.57 Recordkeeping; disclosure of information.

(a) *Recordkeeping.* Each State agency will make and maintain records pertaining to the administration of the Act as the Secretary requires and will make all such records available for inspection, examination and audit by such Federal officials as the Secretary may designate or as may be required by law. Such recordkeeping will be adequate to support the reporting of TAA activity on reporting form ETA 563 approved under OMB control number 1205–0016.

(b) *Disclosure of information.* Information in records maintained by a State agency in administering the Act shall be kept confidential, and information in such records may be disclosed only in the same manner and to the same extent as information with respect to UI and the entitlement of individuals thereto may be disclosed under the applicable State law. Such information shall not, however, be disclosed to an employer or any other person except to the extent necessary to obtain information from the employer or other person for the purposes of this part 617. This provision on the confidentiality of information maintained in the administration of the Act shall not apply, however, to the Department or for the purposes of §617.55 or paragraph (a) of this section, or in the case of information, reports and studies required pursuant to §617.61, or where the result would be inconsistent with the Freedom of Information Act (5 U.S.C. 552), the Privacy Act of 1974 (5 U.S.C. 552a), or regulations of the Department promulgated thereunder (*see* 29 CFR parts 70 and 70a).

§617.58 Unemployment insurance.

Unemployment insurance payable to an adversely affected worker shall not be denied or reduced for any week by reason of any right to a payment of TAA under the Act and this part 617.

§617.59 Agreements with State agencies.

(a) *Authority.* Before performing any function or exercising any jurisdiction under the Act and this part 617, a State or State agency (as defined in §617.3(ii)) shall execute an Agreement with the Secretary meeting the requirements of the Act.

(b) *Execution.* An Agreement under paragraph (a) of this section shall be signed on behalf of a State or State agency by an authorized official of the State or such State agency, and the signature shall be dated. The authority of the State or State agency official shall be certified by the Attorney General of the State or counsel for the State agency, unless the Agreement is signed by the Governor of the State. An agreement will be executed on behalf of the United States by the Secretary.

(c) *Public access to Agreements.* The State agency will make available to any individual or organization an accurate copy of the Agreement with the Agency for inspection and copying. Copies of an Agreement may be furnished on request to any individual or organization upon payment of the same charges, if any, as apply to the furnishing of copies of other records of the State agency.

(d) *Amended Agreement.* A State or State agency shall execute an amended Agreement with the Secretary prior to administering any amendments to the TAA provisions of the Trade Act of 1974.

(e) *Agent of United States.* In making determinations, redeterminations, and in connection with proceedings for review thereof, a State or State agency which has executed an Agreement as provided in this section shall be an agent of the United States and shall carry out fully the purposes of the Act and this part 617.

(f) *Breach.* If the Secretary finds that a State or State agency has not fulfilled its commitments under its Agreement under this section, section 3302(c)(3) of the Internal Revenue Code of 1986 shall apply. A State or State agency shall receive reasonable notice and opportunity for hearing before a finding is made under section 3302(c)(3) whether there has been a failure to fulfill the commitments under the Agreement.

(g) *Secretary's review of State agency compliance.* The appropriate Regional Administrator shall be initially responsible for the periodic monitoring and reviewing of State and State agency compliance with the Agreement entered into under this section.

(h) *Program coordination.* State agencies providing employment services, training and supplemental assistance under Subpart C of this part shall, in accordance with their Agreements under this section, coordinate such services and payments with programs and services provided by the Workforce Investment Act and with the State agency administering the State law.

(i) *Administration absent State Agreement.* In any State in which no Agreement under this section is in force, the Secretary shall administer the Act and this part 617 and pay TAA hereunder through appropriate arrangements made by the Department, and for this purpose the Secretary or the Department shall be substituted for the State or cooperating State agency wherever appropriate in this part 617. Such arrangements shall include the requirement that TAA be administered in accordance with this part 617, and the provisions of the applicable State law except to the extent that such State law is inconsistent with any provision of this part 617 or section 303 of the Social Security Act (42 U.S.C. 503) or section 3304(a) of the Internal Revenue Code of 1986 (26 U.S.C. 3304(a)), and shall also include provision for a fair hearing for any individual whose application for TAA is denied. A final determination under paragraph (i) of this section as to entitlement to TAA shall be subject to review by the courts in the same manner and to the same extent as is provided by section 205(g) of the Social Security Act (42 U.S.C. 405(g)).

[51 FR 45848, Dec. 22, 1986, as amended at 53 FR 32351, Aug. 24, 1988; 59 FR 941, Jan. 6, 1994; 71 FR 35516, June 21, 2006]

§ 617.60 Administration requirements. [Reserved]

§ 617.61 Information, reports, and studies.

A State agency shall furnish to the Secretary such information and reports and conduct such studies as the Secretary determines are necessary or appropriate for carrying out the purposes of the Act and this part 617.

§ 617.64 Termination of TAA program benefits.

The following rules are applicable to the termination of TAA benefits under the Act:

(a) No application for TRA, or transportation or subsistence payment while in training approved under subpart C of this part 617, shall be approved, and no payment of TRA or payment for transportation or subsistence occurring on or before the termination date shall be made after the termination date specified in the Act, unless the claim for TRA or an invoice for transportation and subsistence is presented to the State agency and a final determination is made on the amount payable on or before the termination date in the Act.

(b) No payment of job search or relocation allowances shall be made after the termination date specified in the Act, unless an application for such allowances was approved, such job search or relocation was completed, and a final determination made on the amount payable for such benefits by the State agency on or before the termination date in the Act.

(c) No training under subpart C of this part shall be approved unless a determination regarding the approval of such training was made on or before the termination date in the Act, and such training commenced on or before such termination date. Consistent with the requirements of section 236(a)(1) of the Act, and the termination provisions of paragraph (c) of this section, a final determination must be made on the invoice for the training costs by the State agency on or before the termination date specified in the Act to cover tuition related expenses. Determinations on tuition bills shall be limited to the training term, quarter, semester or other period beginning on or before the termination date in the Act. The training period should be in accord with normal billing practices of the training provider and/or State agency approval practices.

[59 FR 941, Jan. 6, 1994]

Appendix A to Part 617—Standard for Claim Filing, Claimant Reporting, Job Finding, and Employment Services

Employment Security Manual (Part V, Sections 5000–5004)

5000–5099 *Claims Filing*

5000 *Standard for Claim Filing, Claimant Reporting, Job Finding, and Employment Services*

A. *Federal law requirements.* Section 3304(a)(1) of the Federal Unemployment Tax Act and section 303(a)(2) of the Social Security Act require that a State law provide for:

"Payment of unemployment compensation solely through public employment offices or such other agencies as the Secretary may approve."

Section 3304(a)(4) of the Federal Unemployment Tax and section 303(a)(5) of the Social Security Act require that a State law provide for:

"Expenditure of all money withdrawn from an unemployment fund of such State, in the payment of unemployment compensation * * *"

Section 303(a)(1) of the Social Security Act requires that the State law provide for:

"Such methods of administration * * * as are found by the Secretary to be reasonably calculated to insure full payment of unemployment compensation when due."

B. *Secretary's interpretation of federal law requirements.*

1. The Secretary interprets section 3304(a)(1) of the Federal Unemployment Tax Act and section 303(a)(2) of the Social Security Act to require that a State law provide for payment of unemployment compensation solely through public employment offices or claims offices administered by the State employment security agency if such agency provides for such coordination in the operations of its public employment offices and claims offices as will insure (a) the payment of benefits only to individuals who are unemployed and who are able to work and available for work, and (b) that individuals claiming unemployment compensation (claimants) are afforded such placement and other employment services as are necessary and appropriate to return them to suitable work as soon as possible.

2. The Secretary interprets all the above sections to require that a State law provide for:

a. Such contact by claimants with public employment offices or claims offices or both, (1) as will reasonably insure the payment of unemployment compensation only to individuals who are unemployed and who are able to work and available for work, and (2) that claimants are afforded such placement and other employment services as are necessary and appropriate to facilitate their return to suitable work as soon as possible; and

b. Methods of administration which do not unreasonably limit the opportunity of individuals to establish their right to unemployment compensation due under such States law.

5001 *Claim Filing and Claimant Reporting Requirements Designed To Satisfy Secretary's Interpretation*

A. *Claim filing—total or part-total unemployment*

1. Individuals claiming unemployment compensation for total or part-total unemployment are required to file a claim weekly or biweekly, in person or by mail, at a public employment office or a claims office (these terms include offices at itinerant points) as set forth below.

2. Except as provided in paragraph 3, a claimant is required to file in person.

a. His new claim with respect to a benefit year, or his continued claim for a waiting week or for his first compensable week of unemployment in such year; and

b. Any other claim, when requested to do so by the claims personnel at the office at which he files his claim(s) because questions about his right to benefits are raised by circumstances such as the following:

(1) The conditions or circumstances of his separation from employment;

(2) The claimant's answers to questions on mail claim(s) indicate that he may be unable to work or that there may be undue restrictions on his availability for work or that his search for work may be inadequate or that he may be disqualified;

(3) The claimant's answers to questions on mail claims create uncertainty about his credibility or indicate a lack of understanding of the applicable requirements; or

(4) The claimant's record shows that he has previously filed a fraudulent claim.

In such circumstances, the claimant is required to continue to file claims in person each week (or biweekly) until the State agency determines that filing claims in person is no longer required for the resolution of such questions.

3. A claimant must be permitted to file a claim by mail in any of the following circumstances:

a. He is located in an area requiring the expenditure of an unreasonable amount of time or money in traveling to the nearest facility established by the State agency for filing claims in person;

b. Conditions make it impracticable for the agency to take claims in person;

c. He has returned to full-time work on or before the scheduled date for his filing a claim, unless the agency makes provision for in-person filing at a time and place that does not interfere with his employment;

d. The agency finds that he has good cause for failing to file a claim in person.

4. A claimant who has been receiving benefits for partial unemployment may continue to file claims as if he were a partially unemployed worker for the first four consecutive weeks of total or part-total unemployment immediately following his period of partial unemployment so long as he remains attached to his regular employer.

B. *Claim filing—partial unemployment.* Each individual claiming unemployment compensation for a week (or other claim period) during which, because of lack of work, he is working less than his normal customary full-time hours for his regular employer and is earning less than the earnings limit provided in the State law, shall not be required to file a claim for such week or other claim period earlier than 2 weeks from the date that wages are paid for such claim period or, if a low earnings report is required by the State law, from the date the employer furnished such report to the individual. State agencies may permit claims for partial unemployment to be filed either in person or by mail, except that in the circumstances set forth in section A 3, filing by mail must be permitted, and in the circumstances set forth in section A 2 b, filing in person may be required.

5002 *Requirement for Job Finding, Placement, and Other Employment Services Designed To Satisfy Secretary's Interpretation*

A. Claims personnel are required to assure that each claimant is doing what a reasonable individual in his circumstances would do to obtain suitable work.

B. In the discretion of the State agency:

1. The claims personnel are required to give each claimant such necessary and appropriate assistance as they reasonably can in finding suitable work and at their discretion determine when more complete placement and employment services are necessary and appropriate for a claimant; and if they determine more complete services are necessary and appropriate, the claims personnel are to refer him to employment service personnel in the public employment office in which he has been filing claim(s), or, if he has been filing in a claims office, in the public employment office most accessible to him; *or*

2. All placement and employment services are required to be afforded to each claimant by employment service personnel in the public employment office most accessible to him in which case the claims personnel in the office in which the claimant files his claim are to refer him to the employment service personnel when placement or other employment services are necessary and appropriate for him.

C. The personnel to whom the State agency assigns the responsibilities outlined in paragraph B above are required to give claimants such job-finding assistance, placement, and other employment services as are necessary and appropriate to facilitate their return to suitable work as soon as possible.

In some circumstances, no such services or only limited services may be required. For example, if a claimant is on a short-term temporary layoff with a fixed return date, the only service necessary and appropriate to be given to him during the period of the layoff is a referral to suitable temporary work if such work is being performed in the labor market area.

Similarly, claimants whose unemployment is caused by a labor dispute presumably will return to work with their employer as soon as the labor dispute is settled. They generally do not need services, nor do individuals in occupations where placement customarily is made by other nonfee charging placement facilities such as unions and professional associations.

Claimants who fall within the classes which ordinarily would require limited services or no services shall, if they request placement and employment services, be afforded such services as are necessary and appropriate for them to obtain suitable work or to achieve their reasonable employment goals.

On the other hand, a claimant who is permanently separated from his job is likely to require some services. He may need only some direction in how to get a job; he may need placement services if he is in an occupation for which there is some demand in the labor market area; if his occupation is outdated, he may require counseling and referral to a suitable training course. The extent and character of the services to be given any particular claimant may change with the length of his unemployment and depend not only on his own circumstances and conditions, but also on the condition of the labor market in the area.

D. Claimants are required to report to employment service personnel, as directed, but such personnel and the claims personnel required to so arrange and coordinate the contacts required of a claimant as not to place an unreasonable burden on him or unreasonably limit his opportunity to establish his rights to compensation. As a general rule, a claimant is not required to contact in person claims personnel or employment service personnel more frequently than once a week, unless he is directed to report more frequently for a specific service such as referral to a job or a training course or counseling which cannot be completed in one visit.

E. Employment service personnel are required to report promptly to claims personnel in the office in which the claimant files his claim(s): (1) his failure to apply for or accept work to which he was referred by such personnel or when known, by any other nonfee-charging placement facility such as a union or a professional association; and (2) any information which becomes available to it that may have a bearing on the claimant's ability to work or availability for work, or on the suitability of work to which he was referred or which was offered to him.

5004 *Evaluation of Alternative State Provisions*

If the State law provisions do not conform to the "suggested State law requirements" set forth in sections 5001 and 5002, but the State law contains alternative provisions, the Manpower Administrator, in collaboration with the State agency, will study the actual or anticipated affect of the alternative provisions. If the Manpower Administrator concludes that the alternative provisions satisfy the requirements of the Federal law as construed by the Secretary (see section 5000 B) he will so notify the State agency. If he does not so conclude, he will submit the matter to the Secretary. If the Secretary concludes that the alternative provisions satisfy such requirements, the State agency will be so notified. If the Secretary concludes that there is a question as to whether the alternative provisions satisfy such requirements, the State agency will be advised that unless the State law provisions are appropriately revised, a notice of hearing will be issued as required by the Code of Federal Regulations, title 20, section 601.3.

[59 FR 943, Jan. 6, 1994]

APPENDIX B TO PART 617—STANDARD FOR CLAIM DETERMINATIONS—SEPARATION INFORMATION

6010 *Federal Law Requirements.* Section 303(a)(1) of the Social Security Act requires that a State law include provision for:

"Such methods of administration . . . as are found by the Secretary to be reasonably calculated to insure full payment of unemployment compensation when due."

Section 303(a)(3) of the Social Security Act requires that a State law include provision for:

"Opportunity for a fair hearing before an impartial tribunal, for all individuals whose claims for unemployment compensation are denied."

Section 3304(a)(4) of the Federal Unemployment Tax Act and section 303(a)(5) of the Social Security Act require that a State law include provision for:

"Expenditure of all money withdrawn from an unemployment fund of such State, in the payment of unemployment compensation. . . .

Section 3306(h) of the Federal Unemployment Tax Act defines "compensation" as "cash benefits payable to individuals with respect to their unemployment."

6011 *Secretary's Interpretation of Federal Law Requirements.* The Secretary interprets the above sections to require that a State law include provisions which will insure that:

A. Individuals who may be entitled to unemployment compensation are furnished such information as will reasonably afford them an opportunity to know, establish, and protect their rights under the unemployment compensation law of such State, and

B. The State agency obtains and records in time for the prompt determination and review of benefit claims such information as will reasonably insure the payment of benefits to individuals to whom benefits are due.

6012 *Criteria for Review of State Law Conformity with Federal Requirements:*

In determining the conformity of a State law with the above requirements of the Federal Unemployment Tax Act and the Social Security Act as interpreted by the Secretary, the following criteria will be applied:

A. Is it required that individuals who may be entitled to unemployment compensation be furnished such information of their potential rights to benefits, including the manner and places of filing claims, the reasons for determinations, and their rights of appeal, as will insure them a reasonable opportunity to know, establish, and protect their rights under the law of the State?

B. Is the State agency required to obtain, in time for prompt determination of rights to benefits such information as will reasonably insure the payment of benefits to individuals to whom benefits are due?

C. Is the State agency required to keep records of the facts considered in reaching determinations of rights to benefits?

6013 *Claim Determinations Requirements Designed To Meet Department of Labor Criteria:*

A. *Investigation of claims.* The State agency is required to obtain promptly and prior to a determination of an individual's right to benefits, such facts pertaining thereto as will be sufficient reasonably to insure the payment of benefits when due.

This requirement embraces five separate elements:

1. It is the responsibility of the agency to take the initiative in the discovery of information. This responsibility may not be passed on to the claimant or the employer. In addition to the agency's own records, this information may be obtained from the worker, the employer, or other sources. If the information obtained in the first instance discloses no essential disagreement and provides a sufficient basis for a fair determination, no further investigation is necessary. If the information obtained from other sources differs essentially from that furnished by the claimant, the agency, in order to meet its responsibility, is required to inform the claimant of such information from other sources and to afford the claimant an opportunity to furnish any further facts he may have.

2. Evidentiary facts must be obtained as distinguished from ultimate facts or conclusions. That a worker was discharged for misconduct is an ultimate fact or conclusion; that he destroyed a machine upon which he was working is a primary or evidentiary fact, and the sort of fact that the requirement refers to.

3. The information obtained must be sufficient reasonably to insure the payment of benefits when due. In general, the investigation made by the agency must be complete enough to provide information upon which the agency may act with reasonable assurance that its decision is consistent with the unemployment compensation law. On the other hand, the investigation should not be so exhaustive and time-consuming as unduly to delay the payment of benefits and to result in excessive costs.

4. Information must be obtained promptly so that the payment of benefits is not unduly delayed.

5. If the State agency requires any particular evidence from the worker, it must give him a reasonable opportunity to obtain such evidence.

B. *Recording of facts.* The agency must keep a written record of the facts considered in reaching its determinations.

C. *Determination notices:*

1. The agency must give each claimant a written notice of:

a. Any monetary determination with respect to his benefit year;

b. Any determination with respect to purging a disqualification if, under the State law, a condition or qualification must be satisfied with respect to each week of disqualification; but in lieu of giving written notice of each determination for each week in which it is determined that the claimant has met the requirements for purging, the agency may inform the claimant that he has purged the disqualification for a week by notation on his applicant identification card or otherwise in writing.

c. Any other determination which adversely affects his rights to benefits, except that written notice of determination need not be given with respect to:

(1) A week in a benefit year for which the claimant's weekly benefit amount is reduced in whole or in part by earnings if, the first time in the benefit year that there is such a reduction, he is required to be furnished a booklet or leaflet containing the information set forth below in paragraph 2f(1). However, a written notice of determination is required if: (a) there is a dispute concerning the reduction with respect to any week (e.g., as to the amount computed as the appropriate reduction, etc.); or (b) there is a change in the State law (or in the application thereof) affecting the reduction; or

(2) Any week in a benefit year subsequent to the first week in such benefit year in which benefits were denied, or reduced in whole or in part for reasons other than earnings, if denial or reduction for such subsequent week is based on the same reason and the same facts as for the first week, and if written notice of determination is required to be given to the claimant with respect to such first week, and with such notice of determination, he is required to be given a booklet or pamphlet containing the information set forth below in paragraph 2f(2) and 2h. However, a written notice of determination is required if: (a) there is a dispute concerning the denial or reduction of benefits with respect to such week; or (b) there is a change in the State law (or in the application thereof) affecting the denial or reduction; or (c) there is a change in the amount of the reduction except as to the balance covered by the last reduction in a series of reductions.

NOTE: This procedure may be applied to determinations made with respect to any subsequent weeks for the same reason and on the basis of the same facts: (a) that claimant is unable to work, unavailable for work, or is disqualified under the labor dispute provision; and (b) reducing claimant's weekly benefit amount because of income other than earnings or offset by reason of overpayment.

2. The agency must include in written notices of determinations furnished to claimants sufficient information to enable them to understand the determinations, the reasons therefor, and their rights to protest, request reconsideration, or appeal.

The written notice of monetary determination must contain the information specified in the following items (except h) unless an item is specifically not applicable. A written notice of any other determination must contain the information specified in as many of the following items as are necessary to enable the claimant to understand the determination and to inform him of his appeal rights. Information specifically applicable to the individual claimant must be contained in the written notice of determination. Information of general application such as (but not limited to) the explanation of benefits for partial unemployment, information as to deductions, seasonality factors, and information as to the manner and place of taking an appeal, extension of the appeal period, and where to obtain information and assistance may be contained in a booklet or leaflet which is given the claimant with his monetary determination.

a. *Base period wages.* The statement concerning base-period wages must be in sufficient detail to show the basis of computation of eligibility and weekly and maximum benefit amounts. (If maximum benefits are allowed, it may not be necessary to show details of earnings.)

b. *Employer name.* The name of the employer who reported the wage is necessary so that the worker may check the wage transcript and know whether it is correct. If the worker is given only the employer number, he may not be able to check the accuracy of the wage transcript.

c. *Explanation of benefit formula—weekly and maximum benefit amounts.* Sufficient information must be given the worker so that he will understand how his weekly benefit amount, including allowances for dependents, and his maximum benefit amount were figured. If benefits are computed by means of a table contained in the law, the table must be furnished with the notice of determination whether benefits are granted or denied.

The written notice of determination must show clearly the weekly benefit amount and the maximum potential benefits to which the claimant is entitled.

The notice to a claimant found ineligible by reason of insufficient earnings in the base period must inform him clearly of the reason for ineligibility. An explanation of the benefit formula contained in a booklet or pamphlet should be given to each claimant at or prior to the time he receives written notice of a monetary determination.

d. *Benefit year*. An explanation of what is meant by the benefit year and identification of the claimant's benefit year must be included in the notice of determination.

e. *Information as to benefits for partial unemployment*. There must be included either in the written notice of determination or in a booklet or pamphlet accompanying the notice an explanation of the claimant's rights to partial benefits for any week with respect to which he is working less than his normal customary full-time workweek because of lack of work and for which he earns less than his weekly benefit amount or weekly benefit amount plus earnings, whichever is provided by the State law. If the explanation is contained in the notice of determination, reference to the item in the notice in which his weekly benefit amount is entered should be made.

f. *Deductions from weekly benefits:*

(1) *Earnings*. Although written notice of determinations deducting earnings from a claimant's weekly benefit amount is generally not required (see paragraph 1 c (1) above), where written notice of determination is required (or given) it shall set forth the amount of earnings, the method of computing the deduction in sufficient detail to enable the claimant to verify the accuracy of the deduction, and his right to protest, request redetermination, and appeal. Where a written notice of determination is given to the claimant because there has been a change in the State law or in the application of the law, an explanation of the change shall be included.

When claimant is not required to receive a written notice of determination, he must be given a booklet or pamphlet the first time in his benefit year that there is a deduction for earnings which shall include the following information:

(a) The method of computing deductions for earnings in sufficient detail to enable the claimant to verify the accuracy of the deduction;

(b) That he will not automatically be given a written notice of determination for a week with respect to which there is a deduction for earnings (unless there is a dispute concerning the reduction with respect to a week or there has been a change in the State law or in the application of the law affecting the deduction) but that he may obtain such a written notice upon request; and

(c) A clear statement of his right to protest, request a redetermination, and appeal from any determination deducting earnings from his weekly benefit amount even though he does not automatically receive a written notice of determination; and if the State law requires written notice of determination in order to effectuate a protest, redetermination, or appeal, he must be so advised and advised also that he must request a written notice of determination before he takes any such action.

(2) *Other deductions:*

(a) A written notice of determination is required with respect to the first week in claimant's benefit year in which there is a reduction from his benefits for a reason other than earnings. This notice must describe the deduction made from claimant's weekly benefit amount, the reason for the deduction, the method of computing it in sufficient detail to enable him to verify the accuracy of such deduction, and his right to protest, request redetermination, or appeal.

(b) A written notice of determination is not required for subsequent weeks that a deduction is made for the same reason and on the basis of the same facts, if the notice of determination pursuant to (2) (a), or a booklet or pamphlet given him with such notice explains (i) the several kinds of deductions which may be made under the State law (e.g., retirement pensions, vacation pay, and overpayments); (ii) the method of computing each kind of deduction in sufficient detail that claimant will be able to verify the accuracy of deductions made from his weekly benefit payments; (iii) any limitation on the amount of any deduction or the time in which any deduction may be made; (iv) that he will not automatically be given a written notice of determination for subsequent weeks with respect to which there is a deduction for the same reason and on the basis of the same facts, but that he may obtain a written notice of determination upon request; (v) his right to protest, request redetermination, or appeal with respect to subsequent weeks for which there is a reduction from his benefits for the same reason, and on the basis of the same facts even though he does not automatically receive a written notice of determination; and (vi) that if the State law requires written notice of determination in order to effectuate a protest, redetermination, or appeal, he must be so advised and advised also that he must request a written notice of determination before he takes any such action.

g. *Seasonality factors*. If the individual's determination is affected by seasonality factors under the State law, an adequate explanation must be made. General explanations of seasonality factors which may affect determinations for subsequent weeks may be included in a booklet or pamphlet given claimant with his notice of monetary determinations.

h. *Disqualification or ineligibility*. If a disqualification is imposed, or if the claimant is declared ineligible for one or more weeks, he must be given not only a statement of the period of disqualification or ineligibility and the amount of wage-credit reductions, if any, but also an explanation of the reason for the ineligibility or disqualification. This explanation must be sufficiently detailed so that he will understand why he is ineligible or why he has been disqualified, and what he must do in order to requalify for benefits or purge the disqualification. The statement must be individualized to indicate the facts upon which the determination was based, e.g., state, "It is found that you left your work with Blank Company because you were tired of working; the separation was voluntary, and the reason does not constitute good cause," rather than merely the phrase "voluntary quit." Checking a box as to the reason for the disqualification is not a sufficiently detailed explanation. However, this statement of the reason for the disqualification need not be a restatement of all facts considered in arriving at the determination.

i. *Appeal rights.* The claimant must be given information with respect to his appeal rights.

(1) The following information shall be included in the notice of determination:

(a) A statement that he may appeal or, if the State law requires or permits a protest or redetermination before an appeal, that he may protest or request a redetermination.

(b) The period within which an appeal, protest, or request for redetermination must be filed. The number of days provided by statute must be shown as well as either the beginning date or ending date of the period. (It is recommended that the ending date of the appeal period be shown, as this is the more understandable of the alternatives.)

(2) The following information must be included either in the notice of determination or in separate informational material referred to in the notice:

(a) The manner in which the appeal, protest, or request for redetermination must be filed, e.g., by signed letter, written statement, or on a prescribed form, and the place or places to which the appeal, protest, or request for redetermination may be mailed or hand-delivered.

(b) An explanation of any circumstances (such as nonworkdays, good cause, etc.) which will extend the period for the appeal, protest, or request for redetermination beyond the date stated or identified in the notice of determination.

(c) That any further information claimant may need or desire can be obtained together with assistance in filing his appeal, protest, or request for redetermination from the local office.

If the information is given in separate material, the notice of determination would adequately refer to such material if it said, for example, "For other information about your (appeal), (protest), (redetermination) rights, see pages ____ to ____ of the ____ (name of pamphlet or booklet) heretofore furnished to you."

6014 *Separation Information Requirements Designed To Meet Department of Labor Criteria:*

A. *Information to agency.* Where workers are separated, employers are required to furnish the agency promptly, either upon agency request or upon such separation, a notice describing the reasons for and the circumstances of the separation and any additional information which might affect a claimant's right to benefits. Where workers are working less than full time, employers are required to furnish the agency promptly, upon agency request, information concerning a claimant's hours of work and his wages during the claim periods involved, and other facts which might affect a claimant's eligibility for benefits during such periods.

When workers are separated and the notices are obtained on a request basis, or when workers are working less than full time and the agency requests information, it is essential to the prompt processing of claims that the request be sent out promptly after the claim is filed and the employer be given a specific period within which to return the notice, preferably within 2 working days.

When workers are separated and notices are obtained upon separation, it is essential that the employer be required to send the notice to the agency with sufficient promptness to insure that, if a claim is filed, it may be processed promptly. Normally, it is desirable that such a notice be sent to the central office of the agency, since the employer may not know in which local office the worker will file his claim. The usual procedure is for the employer to give the worker a copy of the notice sent by the employer to the agency.

B. *Information to worker:*

1. *Information required to be given.* Employers are required to give their employees information and instructions concerning the employees' potential rights to benefits and concerning registration for work and filing claims for benefits.

The information furnished to employees under such a requirement need not be elaborate; it need only be adequate to insure that the worker who is separated or who is working less than full time knows he is potentially eligible for benefits and is informed as to what he is to do or where he is to go to file his claim and register for work. When he files his claim, he can obtain more detailed information.

In States that do not require employers to furnish periodically to the State agency detailed reports of the wages paid to their employees, each employer is required to furnish to his employees information as to (a) the name under which he is registered by the State agency, (b) the address where he maintains his payroll records, and (c) the workers' need for this information if and when they file claims for benefits.

2. *Methods for giving information.* The information and instructions required above may be given in any of the following ways:

a. *Posters prominently displayed in the employer's establishment.* The State agency should supply employers with a sufficient number of posters for distribution throughout their places of business and should see that the posters are conspicuously displayed at all times.

b. *Leaflets.* Leaflets distributed either periodically or at the time of separation or reduction of hours. The State agency should supply employers with a sufficient number of leaflets.

c. *Individual notices.* Individual notices given to each employee at the time of separation or reduction in hours.

It is recommended that the State agency's publicity program be used to supplement the employer-information requirements. Such a program should stress the availability and location of claim-filing offices and the importance of visiting those offices whenever the worker is unemployed, wishes to apply for benefits, and to seek a job.

6015 *Evaluation of Alternative State Provisions with Respect to Claim Determinations and Separation Information.* If the State law provisions do not conform to the suggested requirements set forth in sections 6013 and 6014, but the State law contains alternative provisions, the Bureau of Employment Security, in collaboration with the State agency, will study the actual or anticipated effects of the alternative provisions. If the Administrator of the Bureau concludes that the alternative provisions satisfy the criteria in section 6012, he will so notify the State agency. If the Administrator of the Bureau does not so conclude, he will submit the matter to the Secretary. If the Secretary concludes that the alternative provisions satisfy the criteria in section 6012, the State agency will be so notified. If the Secretary concludes that there is a question as to whether the alternative provisions satisfy the criteria, the State agency will be advised that unless the State law provisions are appropriately revised, a notice of hearing will be issued as required by the Code of Federal Regulations, title 20, § 601.5.

[51 FR 45848, Dec. 22, 1986. Redesignated at 59 FR 943, Jan. 6, 1994]

Appendix C to Part 617—Standard for Fraud and Overpayment Detection

7510 *Federal Law Requirements.* Section 303(a)(1) of the Social Security Act requires that a State law include provision for:

"Such methods of administration . . . as are found by the Secretary to be reasonably calculated to insure full payment of unemployment compensation when due."

Section 1603(a)(4) of the Internal Revenue Code and section 3030(a)(5) of the Social Security Act require that a State law include provision for:

"Expenditure of all money withdrawn from an unemployment fund of such State, in the payment of unemployment compensation . . ."

Section 1607(h) of the Internal Revenue Code defines "compensation" as "cash benefits payable to individuals with respect to their unemployment."

7511 *The Secretary's Interpretation of Federal Law Requirements.* The Secretary of Labor interprets the above sections to require that a State law include provision for such methods of administration as are, within reason, calculated (1) to detect benefits paid through error by the agency or through willful misrepresentation or error by the claimant or others, and (2) to deter claimants from obtaining benefits through willful misrepresentation.

7513 *Criteria for Review of State Conformity With Federal Requirements.* In determining State conformity with the above requirements of the Internal Revenue Code and the Social Security Act, as interpreted by the Secretary of Labor, the following criteria will be applied:

A. *Are investigations required to be made after the payment of benefits, (or, in the case of interstate claims, are investigations made by the agent State after the processing of claims) as to claimants' entitlement to benefits paid to them in a sufficient proportion of cases to test the effectiveness of the agency's procedures for the prevention of payments which are not due? To carry out investigations, has the agency assigned to some individual or unit, as a basic function, the responsibility of making or functionally directing such investigations?*

Explanation: It is not feasible to prescribe the extent to which the above activities are required; however, they should always be carried on to such an extent that they will show whether or not error or willful misrepresentation is increasing or decreasing, and will reveal problem areas. The extent and nature of the above activities should be varied according to the seriousness of the problem in the State. The responsible individual or unit should:

1. Check paid claims for overpayment and investigate for willful misrepresentation or, alternatively, advise and assist the operating units in the performance of such functions, or both;

2. Perform consultative services with respect to methods and procedures for the prevention and detection of fraud; and

3. Perform other services which are closely related to the above.

Although a State agency is expected to make a full-time assignment of responsibility to a unit or individual to carry on the functions described above, a small State agency might make these functions a part-time responsibility of one individual. In connection with the detection of overpayments, such a unit or individual might, for example:

(a) Investigate information on suspected benefit fraud received from any agency personnel, and from sources outside the agency, including anonymous complaints;

(b) Investigate information secured from comparisons of benefit payments with employment records to detect cases of concurrent working (whether in covered or noncovered work) and claiming of benefits (including benefit payments in which the agency acted as agent for another State).

The benefit fraud referred to herein may involve employers, agency employees, and witnesses, as well as claimants.

Comparisons of benefit payments with employment records are comonly made either by post-audit or by industry surveys. The so-called "post-audit" is a matching of central office wage-record files against benefit payments for the same period. "Industry surveys" or "mass audits" are done in some States by going directly to employers for pay-roll information to be checked against concurrent benefit lists. A plan of investigation based on a sample post-audit will be considered as partial fulfillment of the investigation program; it would need to be supplemented by other methods capable of detecting overpayments to persons who have moved into noncovered occupations or are claiming interstate benefits.

B. *Are adequate records maintained by which the results of investigations may be evaluated?*

Explanation. To meet this criterion, the State agency will be expected to maintain records of all its activities in the detection of overpayments, showing whether attributable to error or willful misrepresentation, measuring the results obtained through various methods, and noting the remedial action taken in each case. The adequacy and effectiveness of various methods of checking for willful misrepresentation can be evaluated only if records are kept of the results obtained. Internal reports on fraudulent and erroneous overpayments are needed by State agencies for self-evaluation. Detailed records should be maintained in order that the State agency may determine, for example, which of several methods of checking currently used are the most productive. Such records also will provide the basis for drawing a clear distinction between fraud and error.

C. *Does the agency take adequate action with respect to publicity concerning willful misrepresentation and its legal consequences to deter fraud by claimants?*

Explanation. To meet this criterion, the State agency must issue adequate material of claimant eligibility requirements and must take necessary action to obtain publicity on the legal consequences of willful misrepresentation or willful nondisclosure of facts.

Public announcements on convictions and resulting penalties for fraud are generally considered necessary as a deterrent to other persons, and to inform the public that the agency is carrying on an effective program to prevent fraud. This alone is not considered adequate publicity. It is important that information be circulated which will explain clearly and understandably the claimant's rights, and the obligations which he must fulfill to be eligible for benefits. Leaflets for distribution and posters placed in local offices are appropriate media for such information.

*7515 *Evaluation of Alternative State Provisions with Respect to Erroneous and Illegal Payments.* If the methods of administration provided for by the State law do not conform to the suggested methods of meeting the requirements set forth in section 7511, but a State law does provide for alternative methods of administration designed to accomplish the same results, the Bureau of Employment Security, in collaboration with the State agency, will study the actual or anticipated effect of the alternative methods of administration. If the Bureau concludes that the alternative methods satisfy the criteria in section 7513, it will so notify the State agency. If the Bureau does not so conclude, it will submit to the Secretary the results of the study for his determination of whether the State's alternative methods of administration meet the criteria.

[51 FR 45848, Dec. 22, 1986. Redesignated at 59 FR 943, Jan. 6, 1994]

PART 618—TRADE ADJUSTMENT ASSISTANCE UNDER THE TRADE ACT OF 1974, AS AMENDED

Subparts A–G [Reserved]

Subpart H—Administration by Applicable State Agencies

Sec.

Subpart I—Allocation of Training Funds to States

SOURCE: 75 FR 17000, Apr. 2, 2010, unless otherwise noted.

Subparts A–G [Reserved]

Subpart H—Administration by Applicable State Agencies

AUTHORITY: 19 U.S.C. 2320; Secretary's Order No. 03–2009, 74 FR 2279, Jan. 14, 2009.

§ 618.890 Merit staffing.

(a) *Merit-based State personnel.* The State must, subject to the transition period in paragraph (b) of this section, engage only State government personnel to perform Trade Adjustment Assistance (TAA)-funded functions undertaken to carry out the worker adjustment assistance provisions of the Trade Act of 1974, as amended, and must apply to such personnel the standards for a merit system of personnel administration applicable to personnel covered under 5 CFR part 900, subpart F.

(b) *Transition period.* A State not already in compliance with the merit system requirement of paragraph (a) of this section must comply by December 15, 2010.

(c) *Exemptions for States with employment service operation exemptions.* A State whose employment service received an exemption from merit staffing requirements from the Secretary of Labor (Secretary) under the Wagner-Peyser Act will retain an exemption from the requirements of paragraph (a) of this section. The exemption does not apply to the State's administration of trade readjustment allowances which remain subject to the requirements of paragraph (a) of this section. To the extent that a State with an authorized ES exemption provides TAA-funded services using staff not funded under the Wagner-Peyser Act, the exemption in this paragraph does not apply, and they remain subject to the requirements of paragraph (a) of this section.

(d) *Exceptions for non-inherently governmental functions.* The requirements of paragraph (a) of this section do not prohibit a State from outsourcing functions that are not inherently governmental, as defined in Office of Management and Budget (OMB) Circular No. A–76 (Revised), in any supplemental OMB guidance or superseding authority, and in DOL guidance.

Subpart I—Allocation of Training Funds to States

AUTHORITY: 19 U.S.C. 2320; 19 U.S.C. 2296(g); Secretary's Order No. 03–2009, 74 FR 2279, Jan. 14, 2009.

§ 618.900 Annual training cap.

The total amount of payments that may be made for the costs of training will not exceed the cap established under section 236(a)(2)(A) of the Trade Act.

(a) For each of the fiscal years 2009 and 2010, this cap is $575,000,000; and

(b) For the period beginning October 1, 2010, and ending December 31, 2010, this cap is $143,750,000.

§ 618.910 Distribution of initial allocation of training funds.

(a) *Initial allocation.* The initial allocation for a fiscal year will total 65 percent of the training funds available for that fiscal year. The Department of Labor (Department) will announce the amount of each State's initial allocation of funds in accordance with the requirements of this section at the beginning of each fiscal year. The Department will determine this initial allocation on the basis of the full amount of the training cap for that year, even if the full amount has not been appropriated to the Department at that time.

(b) *Timing of the distribution of the initial allocation.* The Department will, as soon as practical after the beginning of each fiscal year, distribute the initial allocation announced under paragraph (a) of this section. However, the Department will not distribute the full amount of the initial allocation until it receives the entire fiscal year's appropriation of training funds. If the full year's appropriated amount of training funds is less than the training cap, then the Department will distribute 65 percent of the amount appropriated.

(c) *Hold harmless provision.* Except as provided in paragraph (d) of this section, in no case will the amount of the initial allocation to a State in a fiscal year be less than 25 percent of the initial allocation to that State in the preceding fiscal year.

(d) *Minimum initial allocation.* If a State has an adjusted initial allocation of less than $100,000, as calculated in accordance with paragraph (e)(2) of this section, that State will not receive any initial allocation, and the funds that otherwise would have been allocated to that State instead will be allocated among the other States in accordance with this section. A State that does not receive an initial distribution may apply under §618.920(b) for reserve funds to obtain the training funding that it requires.

(e) *Process of determining initial allocation.* (1) The Department will first apply the factors described in paragraph (f) of this section to determine an unadjusted initial allocation for each State.

(2) The Department will then apply the hold harmless provision of paragraph (c) of this section to the unadjusted initial allocation, as follows:

(i) A State whose unadjusted initial allocation is less than its hold harmless amount but is $100,000 or more, will have its initial allocation adjusted up to its hold harmless amount. If a State's unadjusted allocation is less than $100,000, the State will receive no initial allocation, in accordance with paragraph (d) of this section. Those funds will be shared among other States as provided in paragraph (e)(3) of this section.

(ii) A State whose unadjusted initial allocation is no less than its hold harmless threshold will receive its hold harmless amount and will also receive an adjustment equal to the State's share of the remaining initial allocation funds, as provided in paragraph (e)(3) of this section.

(3) The initial allocation funds remaining after the adjusted initial allocations are made to those States receiving only their hold harmless amounts, as described in paragraph (e)(2)(i) of this section, will be distributed among the States with unadjusted initial allocations that were no less than their hold harmless amounts, as described in paragraph (e)(2)(ii) of this section (the remaining States). The distribution of the remaining initial allocation funds among the remaining States will be made by reapplying the calculation in paragraph (f) of this section. This recalculation will disregard States receiving only their hold harmless amount under paragraph (e)(2)(i) of this section, so that the combined percentages of the remaining States total 100 percent.

(f) *Initial allocation factors.* (1) In determining how to make the initial allocation of training funds, the Department will apply, as provided in paragraph (f)(3) of this section, the following factors with respect to each State:

(i) The trend in the number of workers covered by certifications of eligibility during the most recent four consecutive calendar quarters for which data are available. The trend will be established by assigning a greater weight to the most recent quarters, giving those quarters a larger share of the factor;

(ii) The trend in the number of workers participating in training during the most recent four consecutive calendar quarters for which data are available. The trend will be established by assigning a greater weight to the most recent quarters, giving those quarters a larger share of the factor;

(iii) The number of workers estimated to be participating in training during the fiscal year. The estimate will be calculated by dividing the weighted average number of training participants for the State determined in paragraph (f)(1)(ii) of this section by the sum of the weighted averages for all States and multiplying the resulting ratio by the projected national average of training participants for the fiscal year, using the estimates underlying the Department's most recent budget submission or update; and

(iv) The amount of funding estimated to be necessary to provide approved training to such workers during the fiscal year. The estimate will be calculated by multiplying the estimated number of participants in paragraph (f)(1)(iii) of this section by the average training cost for the State. The average training cost will be calculated by dividing total training expenditures for the most recent four quarters by the average number of training participants for the same time period.

(2) The Department may use such other factors that it considers appropriate.

(3) The Department will assign each of the factors listed in paragraphs (f)(1)(i) through (f)(1)(iv) of this section an equal weight. For each of these weighted factors, the Department will determine the national total and each State's percentage of the national total. Based on a State's percentage of each of these weighted factors, the Department will determine the percentage that the State will receive of the amount available for initial allocations. The percentages of initial allocation amounts calculated for all States combined will total 100 percent of initial allocation funds.

(4) The Department may, by administrative guidance published for comment, change the weights provided in paragraphs (f)(1) and (f)(3) of this section, or add additional factors. No such changes or additions will take effect before December 31, 2010.

§ 618.920 Reserve fund distributions.

(a) The remaining 35 percent of the training funds for a fiscal year will be held by the Department as a reserve. Reserve funds will be used, as needed, for additional distributions during the remainder of the fiscal year and for those States that do not receive an initial distribution. States may not receive reserve funds for TAA administration or employment and case management services without a request for training funds.

(b) A State requesting reserve funds must demonstrate that at least 50 percent of its training funds have been expended, or that it needs more funds to meet unusual and unexpected events. A State requesting reserve funds also must provide a documented estimate of expected funding needs through the end of the fiscal year. That estimate must be based on an analysis that includes at least the following:

(1) The average cost of training in the State;

(2) The expected number of participants in training through the end of the fiscal year; and

(3) The remaining funds the State has available for training.

§ 618.930 Second distribution.

The Department will distribute at least 90 percent of the total training funds for a fiscal year to the States no later than July 15 of that fiscal year. The Department will first fund all acceptable requests for reserve funds filed before June 1. If there are any funds remaining to be distributed after these reserve fund requests are satisfied, those funds will be distributed to those States that received an initial allocation in an amount greater than their hold harmless amount, using the methodology described in § 618.910.

§ 618.940 Insufficient funds.

If, during a fiscal year, the Department estimates that the amount of funds necessary to pay the costs of approved training will exceed the training cap under § 618.900, the Department will decide how the amount of available training funds that have not been distributed at the time of the estimate will be allocated among the States for the remainder of the fiscal year. That decision will be communicated through administrative notice.

PART 619—UNEMPLOYMENT COMPENSATION DATA EXCHANGE STANDARDIZATION FOR IMPROVED INTEROPERABILITY

Sec.

AUTHORITY: 42 U.S.C. 1111; Section 2104(b) of Pub. L. 112–96; 42 U.S.C. 1302(a).

SOURCE: 79 FR 9411, Feb. 19, 2014, unless otherwise noted.

§ 619.1 Definitions.

As used in this part—

Administrator of the Office of Unemployment Insurance means the Department's Employment and Training Administration's chief administrative officer directly responsible for the operation of the Unemployment Insurance (UI) program and oversight of the Unemployment Compensation (UC) program and UC laws.

Department means the United States Department of Labor.

eXtensible Markup Language or *XML* means a markup language that defines a set of rules for encoding documents in a format designed to structure, store and transport data between applications or systems over the Internet. This term includes any future upgrades, iterations, or releases of XML-based language.

Federal funds or *Federally-funded* means funds that include, but are not limited to:

(1) Supplemental budget funds that are designated by the Department for State IT modernization efforts;

(2) General State UI administration funding for State program operations (an administrative grant issued by the Department at the beginning of each fiscal year); and

(3) Special UI funding distributions.

Interstate Connection Network or *ICON* means a secure multi-purpose telecommunications network that supports the transfer of data among the SWAs.

Interstate Wages and Benefits Inquiries/Responses means the ICON application which supports online transmission of interstate wages and benefits inquiries and responses between SWAs.

Major IT Modernization Project means conversion, re-engineering, rewriting, or transferring of an existing system to a modernized framework such as transferring a process from mainframe operations to Web-based operations, converting to modern computer programming languages, or upgrading software libraries, protocols, or hardware platform and infrastructure. These are projects to upgrade UI Benefits and Tax Systems by SWAs using Federal funds.

State or *States* refers to, individually or collectively, the 50 States of the United States of America, the District of Columbia, the Commonwealth of Puerto Rico, and the United States Virgin Islands.

State Identification Inquiry means the ICON application which allows SWAs to inquire about wages reported to other SWAs by Social Security Number.

State Information Data Exchange System or *SIDES* means an automated response system used by SWAs to collect claim-related information from employers and third-party administrators.

State unemployment compensation law or *UC law* means the law of a State approved under Section 3304(a) of the Internal Revenue Code of 1986 (26 U.S.C. 3304(a)).

State Workforce Agency or *SWA* means the agency of the State charged with the administration of the State's Unemployment Compensation (UC) law.

Unemployment Compensation or *UC* means cash benefits payable to individuals with respect to their unemployment, as defined in 26 U.S.C. 3306(h).

Unemployment Insurance or *UI* means the Federal-State system and operations administering and implementing UC law.

Withdrawn/Invalid Claims means the ICON application which allows for the posting and viewing of withdrawn or invalid claim information for SWAs.

§619.2 Data exchange standardization for ICON.

(a) XML is the data exchange standard for the real-time ICON applications. These applications are: Interstate Wages and Benefits Inquiries/Responses; Withdrawn/Invalid Claims; and State Identification Inquiry.

(b) All SWAs using real-time ICON applications must comply with this XML data exchange standard no later than September 30, 2018. A SWA may request an extension of this deadline if it demonstrates that resources are not available to meet this requirement. These requests must be submitted in writing to the Administrator of the Office of Unemployment Insurance no later than 6 months before the deadline; requests will be approved or denied within 30 days.

§619.3 Data exchange standardization for SIDES.

(a) XML is the data exchange standard for SIDES.

(b) This standard applies to any Federally-funded SIDES consortium, and any future agents of the Department providing vendor services for the development, maintenance, support, and operations of the SIDES, and for any State that adopts SIDES. A SIDES consortium involves a group of two or more States jointly establishing a project team to oversee the design, development, and implementation of a new SIDES data exchange module. As States implement SIDES or new data exchange modules of SIDES, they must conform to this data exchange standard by application design.

(c) XML is designated as the data exchange standard to govern the reporting of information through SIDES data exchange modules. The regulation applies to current SIDES data exchange modules and any future SIDES data exchange modules developed with Federal funds.

(d) The standard designated in paragraphs (a), (b), and (c) of this section is effective March 21, 2014.

§619.4 Data exchange standardization for the UI Benefits and Tax Systems.

(a) XML is the data exchange standard for the real time ICON applications set out in §619.2 and for the SIDES exchanges set out in §619.3 associated with major IT modernization projects, to upgrade UI Benefits and Tax Systems by SWAs using Federal funds.

(b) The standard designated in paragraph (a) of this section is effective March 21, 2014.

PART 621 [RESERVED]

PART 625—DISASTER UNEMPLOYMENT ASSISTANCE

Sec.

AUTHORITY: 42 U.S.C. 1302; 42 U.S.C. 5164; 42 U.S.C. 5189a(c); 42 U.S.C. 5201(a); Executive Order 12673 of March 23, 1989 (54 FR 12571); delegation of authority from the Director of the Federal Emergency Management Agency to the Secretary of Labor, effective December 1, 1985 (51 FR 4988); Secretary's Order No. 4–75 (40 FR 18515).

SOURCE: 42 FR 46712, Sept. 16, 1977, unless otherwise noted.

§625.1 Purpose; rules of construction.

(a) *Purpose.* Section 410 of "The Robert T. Stafford Disaster Relief and Emergency Assistance Act" amended the program for the payment of unemployment assistance to unemployed individuals whose unemployment is caused by a major disaster, and to provide reemployment assistance services to those individuals. The unemployment assistance provided for in section 410 of the Act is hereinafter referred to as Disaster Unemployment Assistance, or DUA. The regulations in this part are issued to implement sections 410 and 423 of the Act.

(b) *First rule of construction.* Sections 410 and 423 of the Act and the implementing regulations in this part shall be construed liberally so as to carry out the purposes of the Act.

(c) *Second rule of construction.* Sections 410 and 423 of the Act and the implementing regulations in this part shall be construed so as to assure insofar as possible the uniform interpretation and application of the Act throughout the United States.

(d) *Effectuating purpose and rules of construction.* (1) In order to effectuate the provisions of this section, each State agency shall forward to the United States Department of Labor, on receipt of a request from the Department, a copy of any determination or redetermination ruling on an individual's entitlement to DUA.

(2) If the Department believes a determination or redetermination is inconsistent with the Secretary's interpretation of the Act, the Department may at any time notify the State agency of the department's view. Thereafter, the State agency shall appeal if possible, and shall not follow such determination or redetermination as a precedent; and in any subsequent proceedings which involve such determination or redetermination, or wherein such determination or redetermination is cited as precedent or otherwise relied upon, the State agency shall inform the hearing officer of the Department's view and shall make all reasonable efforts to obtain modification, limitation, or overruling of the determination or redetermination.

(3) A State agency may request reconsideration of a notice that a determination or redetermination is inconsistent with the Act, and shall be given an opportunity to present views and arguments if desired. If a determination or redetermination setting a precedent becomes final, which the Department believes to be inconsistent with the Act, the Secretary will decide whether the Agreement with the State shall be terminated.

(4) Concurrence of the Department in a determination or redetermination shall not be presumed from the absence of a notice issued pursuant to this paragraph.

[42 FR 46712, Sept. 16, 1977, as amended at 55 FR 554, Jan. 5, 1990]

§ 625.2 Definitions.

For the purposes of the Act and this part:

(a) *Act* means sections 410 and 423 of *The Robert T. Stafford Disaster Relief and Emergency Assistance Act* (formerly section 407 of the "Disaster Relief Act of 1974", Pub. L. 93–288, 88 Stat. 143, 156, approved May 22, 1974), 42 U.S.C. 5177, 5189a, as amended by The Disaster Relief and Emergency Assistance Amendments of 1988, Pub. L. 100–707, 102 Stat. 4689, 4704, 4705, approved November 23, 1988.

(b) *Agreement* means the Agreement entered into pursuant to the Act, between a State and the Secretary of Labor of the United States, under which the State agency of the State agrees to make payments of Disaster Unemployment Assistance in accordance with the Act and the regulations and procedures thereunder prescribed by the Secretary.

(c) *Announcement date* means the first day on which the State agency publicly announces the availability of Disaster Unemployment Assistance in the State, pursuant to § 625.17.

(d) *Compensation* means unemployment compensation as defined in section 85(b) of the Internal Revenue Code of 1986, and shall include any assistance or allowance payable to an individual with respect to such individual's unemployment under any State law or Federal unemployment compensation law unless such governmental unemployment compensation program payments are not considered "compensation" by ruling of the Internal Revenue Service or specific provision of Federal and/or State law because such payments are based on employee contributions which are not deductible from Federal income tax liability until the total nondeductible contributions paid by the employee to such program has been paid or are not "compensation" as defined under paragraph (d)(5) of this section. Governmental unemployment compensation programs include (but are not limited to) programs established under: a State law approved by the Secretary of Labor pursuant to section 3304 of the Internal Revenue Code, chapter 85 of title 5 of the United States Code, the Railroad Unemployment Insurance Act (45 U.S.C. 351 *et seq.*), any Federal supplementary compensation law, and trade readjustment allowances payable under chapter 2 of title II of the Trade Act of 1974 (19 U.S.C. 2271 *et seq.*). "Compensation" also includes "regular compensation", "additional compensation", "extended compensation", "Federal supplementary compensation", and "disability payments" defined as follows:

(1) *Regular compensation* means compensation payable to an individual

under any State law or the unemployment compensation plan of a political subdivision of a State and, when so payable, includes compensation payable pursuant to 5 U.S.C. chapter 85 (parts 609 and 614 of this chapter), but not including extended compensation or additional compensation.

(2) *Additional compensation* means compensation totally financed by a State and payable under a State law by reason of conditions of high unemployment or by reason of other special factors, and, when so payable, includes compensation payable pursuant to 5 U.S.C. chapter 85.

(3) *Extended compensation* means compensation payable to an individual for weeks of unemployment in an extended benefit period, under those provisions of a State law which satisfy the requirements of the Federal-State Extended Unemployment Compensation Act of 1970 (title II, Pub. L. 91–373; 84 Stat. 695, 708; part 615 of this chapter), as amended with respect to the payment of extended compensation, and, when so payable, includes additional compensation and compensation payable pursuant to 5 U.S.C. chapter 85.

(4) *Federal supplementary compensation* means supplemental compensation payable under a temporary Federal law after exhaustion of regular and extended compensation.

(5) *Disability payments* means cash disability payments made pursuant to a governmental program as a substitute for cash unemployment payments to an individual who is ineligible for such payments solely because of the disability, except for payments made under workmen's compensation acts for personal injuries or sickness.

(e) *Date the major disaster began* means the date a major disaster first occurred, as specified in the understanding between the Federal Emergency Management Agency and the Governor of the State in which the major disaster occurred.

(f) *Disaster Assistance Period* means the period beginning with the first week following the date the major disaster began, and ending with the 26th week subsequent to the date the major disaster was declared.

(g) *Disaster Unemployment Assistance* means the assistance payable to an individual eligible for the assistance under the Act and this part, and which is referred to as DUA.

(h) *Federal Coordinating Officer* means the official appointed pursuant to section 302 of The Robert T. Stafford Disaster Relief and Emergency Assistance Act, to operate in the affected major disaster area.

(i) *Governor* means the chief executive of a State.

(j) *Initial application* means the first application for DUA filed by an individual, on the basis of which the individual's eligibility for DUA is determined.

(k) *Major disaster* means a major disaster as declared by the President pursuant to section 401 of The Robert T. Stafford Disaster Relief and Emergency Assistance Act.

(l) *Major disaster area* means the area identified as eligible for Federal assistance by the Federal Emergency Management Agency, pursuant to a Presidential declaration of a major disaster.

(m) *Secretary* means the Secretary of Labor of the United States.

(n) *Self-employed individual* means an individual whose primary reliance for income is on the performance of services in the individual's own business, or on the individual's own farm.

(o) *Self-employment* means services performed as a self-employed individual.

(p) *State* means any State of the United States, the District of Columbia, the Commonwealth of Puerto Rico, the United States Virgin Islands, the Territory of Guam, American Samoa, Commonwealth of the Northern Mariana Islands, Federated States of Micronesia, Republic of the Marshall Islands, and the Trust Territory of the Pacific Islands.

(q) *State agency* means—

(1) In all States except the Territory of Guam, American Samoa, Commonwealth of the Northern Mariana Islands, Federated States of Micronesia, Republic of the Marshall Islands and the Trust Territory of the Pacific Islands, the agency administering the State law; and

(2) In the Territory of Guam, American Samoa, Commonwealth of the Northern Mariana Islands, Federated States of Micronesia, Republic of the

Marshall Islands and the Trust Territory of the Pacific Islands, the agency designated in the Agreement entered into by the State.

(r)(1) *State law* means, with respect to—

(i) The States of the United States, the District of Columbia, the Commonwealth of Puerto Rico, and the Virgin Islands, the unemployment compensation law of the State which has been approved under section 3304(a) of the Internal Revenue Code of 1986 (26 U.S.C. 3304(a)); and

(ii) The Territory of Guam, American Samoa, Commonwealth of the Northern Mariana Islands, Federated States of Micronesia, Republic of the Marshall Islands and the Trust Territory of the Pacific Islands, the Hawaii Employment Security Law.

(2) *Applicable State law* means, for an individual, the State law of the applicable State for an individual as provided in § 625.12.

(s) *Unemployed worker* means an individual who was employed in or was to commence employment in the major disaster area at the time the major disaster began, and whose principal source of income and livelihood is dependent upon the individual's employment for wages, and whose unemployment is caused by a major disaster as provided in § 625.5(a).

(t) *Unemployed self-employed individual* means an individual who was self-employed in or was to commence self-employment in the major disaster area at the time the major disaster began, and whose principal source of income and livelihood is dependent upon the individual's performance of service in self-employment, and whose unemployment is caused by a major disaster as provided in § 625.5(b).

(u) *Wages* means remuneration for services performed for another, and, with respect to a self-employed individual, net income from services performed in self-employment.

(v) *Week* means a week as defined in the applicable State law.

(w) *Week of unemployment* means—

(1) For an unemployed worker, any week during which the individual is totally, part-totally, or partially unemployed. A week of total unemployment is a week during which the individual performs no work and earns no wages, or has less than full-time work and earns wages not exceeding the minimum earnings allowance prescribed in the applicable State law. A week of part-total unemployment is a week of otherwise total unemployment during which the individual has odd jobs or subsidiary work and earns wages not exceeding the maximum earnings allowance prescribed in the applicable State law. A week of partial unemployment is a week during which the individual works less than regular, full-time hours for the individual's regular employer, as a direct result of the major disaster, and earns wages not exceeding the maximum earnings allowance prescribed by the applicable State law.

(2) For an unemployed self-employed individual, any week during which the individual is totally, part-totally, or partially unemployed. A week of total unemployment is a week during which the individual performs no services in self-employment or in an employer-employee relationship, or performs services less than full-time and earns wages not exceeding the minimum earnings allowance prescribed in the applicable State law. A week of part-total unemployment is a week of otherwise total unemployment during which the individual has odd jobs or subsidiary work and earns wages not exceeding the maximum earnings allowance prescribed in the applicable State law. A week of partial unemployment is a week during which the individual performs less than the customary full-time services in self-employment, as a direct result of the major disaster, and earns wages not exceeding the maximum earnings allowance prescribed by the applicable State law, or during which the only activities or services performed are for the sole purpose of enabling the individual to resume self-employment.

(3) If the week of unemployment for which an individual claims DUA is a week with respect to which the individual is reemployed in a suitable position or has commenced services in self-employment, that week shall be treated as a week of partial unemployment

if the week qualifies as a week of partial unemployment as defined in this paragraph.

[42 FR 46712, Sept. 16, 1977, as amended at 55 FR 554, Jan. 5, 1990; 56 FR 22805, May 16, 1991]

§ 625.3 Reemployment assistance.

(a) *State assistance.* Except as provided in paragraph (b) of this section, the applicable State shall provide, without reimbursement from any funds provided under the Act, reemployment assistance services under any other law administered by the State to individuals applying for DUA and all other individuals who are unemployed because of a major disaster. Such services shall include, but are not limited to, counseling, referrals to suitable work opportunities, and suitable training, to assist the individuals in obtaining reemployment in suitable positions as soon as possible.

(b) *Federal assistance.* In the case of American Samoa, Commonwealth of the Northern Mariana Islands, Federated States of Micronesia, Republic of the Marshall Islands, and the Trust Territory of the Pacific Islands, the Department of Labor, in consultation with the Federal Emergency Management Agency, will determine what reemployment services are needed by DUA applicants, and if any available Federal programs of reemployment assistance services can be implemented in that jurisdiction.

[55 FR 554, Jan. 5, 1990, as amended at 56 FR 22806, May 16, 1991]

§ 625.4 Eligibility requirements for Disaster Unemployment Assistance.

An individual shall be eligible to receive a payment of DUA with respect to a week of unemployment, in accordance with the provisions of the Act and this part if:

(a) That week begins during a Disaster Assistance Period;

(b) The applicable State for the individual has entered into an Agreement which is in effect with respect to that week;

(c) The individual is an unemployed worker or an unemployed self-employed individual;

(d) The individual's unemployment with respect to that week is caused by a major disaster, as provided in § 625.5;

(e) The individual has filed a timely initial application for DUA and, as appropriate, a timely application for a payment of DUA with respect to that week;

(f) That week is a week of unemployment for the individual;

(g) The individual is able to work and available for work within the meaning of the applicable State law: *Provided,* That an individual shall be deemed to meet this requirement if any injury caused by the major disaster is the reason for inability to work or engage in self-employment; or, in the case of an unemployed self-employed individual, the individual performs service or activities which are solely for the purpose of enabling the individual to resume self-employment;

(h) The individual has not refused a bona fide offer of employment in a suitable position, or refused without good cause to resume or commence suitable self-employment, if the employment or self-employment could have been undertaken in that week or in any prior week in the Disaster Assistance Period; and

(i) The individual is not eligible for compensation (as defined in § 625.2(d)) or for waiting period credit for such week under any other Federal or State law, except that an individual determined ineligible because of the receipt of disqualifying income shall be considered eligible for such compensation or waiting period credit. An individual shall be considered ineligible for compensation or waiting period credit (and thus potentially eligible for DUA) if the individual is under a disqualification for a cause that occurred prior to the individual's unemployment due to the disaster, or for any other reason is ineligible for compensation or waiting period credit as a direct result of the major disaster.

[42 FR 46712, Sept. 16, 1977, as amended at 55 FR 555, Jan. 5, 1990]

§ 625.5 Unemployment caused by a major disaster.

(a) *Unemployed worker.* The unemployment of an unemployed worker is caused by a major disaster if—

(1) The individual has a "week of unemployment" as defined in § 625.2(w)(1) following the "date the major disaster began" as defined in § 625.2(e), and such unemployment is a direct result of the major disaster; or

(2) The individual is unable to reach the place of employment as a direct result of the major disaster; or

(3) The individual was to commence employment and does not have a job or is unable to reach the job as a direct result of the major disaster; or

(4) The individual has become the breadwinner or major support for a household because the head of the household has died as a direct result of the major disaster; or

(5) The individual cannot work because of an injury caused as a direct result of the major disaster.

(b) *Unemployed self-employed individual.* The unemployment of an unemployed self-employed individual is caused by a major disaster if—

(1) The individual has a "week of unemployment" as defined in § 625.2(w)(2) following the "date the major disaster began" as defined in § 625.2(e), and such unemployment is a direct result of the major disaster; or

(2) The individual is unable to reach the place where services as a self-employed individual are performed, as a direct result of the major disaster; or

(3) The individual was to commence regular services as a self-employed individual, but does not have a place or is unable to reach the place where the services as a self-employed individual were to be performed, as a direct result of the major disaster; or

(4) The individual cannot perform services as a self-employed individual because of an injury caused as a direct result of the major disaster.

(c) *Unemployment is a direct result of the major disaster.* For the purposes of paragraphs (a)(1) and (b)(1) of this section, a worker's or self-employed individual's unemployment is a direct result of the major disaster where the unemployment is an immediate result of the major disaster itself, and not the result of a longer chain of events precipitated or exacerbated by the disaster. Such an individual's unemployment is a direct result of the major disaster if the unemployment resulted from:

(1) The physical damage or destruction of the place of employment;

(2) The physical inaccessibility of the place of employment in the major disaster area due to its closure by or at the request of the federal, state or local government, in immediate response to the disaster; or

(3) Lack of work, or loss of revenues, provided that, prior to the disaster, the employer, or the business in the case of a self-employed individual, received at least a majority of its revenue or income from an entity in the major disaster area that was either damaged or destroyed in the disaster, or an entity in the major disaster area closed by the federal, state or local government in immediate response to the disaster.

[42 FR 46712, Sept. 16, 1977, as amended at 55 FR 555, Jan. 5, 1990; 56 FR 22806, May 16, 1991; 66 FR 56962, Nov. 13, 2001; 68 FR 10937, Mar. 6, 2003]

§ 625.6 Weekly amount; jurisdictions; reductions.

(a) In all States, except as provided in paragraphs (c) and (d) of this section, the amount of DUA payable to an unemployed worker or unemployed self-employed individual for a week of total unemployment shall be the weekly amount of compensation the individual would have been paid as regular compensation, as computed under the provisions of the applicable State law for a week of total unemployment. In no event shall such amount be in excess of the maximum amount of regular compensation authorized under the applicable State law for that week.

(1) Except as provided in paragraph (a)(2) or (b) of this section, in computing an individual's weekly amount of DUA, qualifying employment and wage requirements and benefit formula of the applicable State law shall be applied; and for purposes of this section, employment, wages, and self-employment which are not covered by the applicable State law shall be treated in the same manner and with the same effect as covered employment and wages, but shall not include employment or self-employment, or wages earned or

paid for employment or self-employment, which is contrary to or prohibited by any Federal law, such as, but not limited to, section 3304(a)(14)(A) of the Federal Unemployment Tax Act (26 U.S.C. 3304(a)(14)(A)).

(2) For purposes of paragraph (a)(1) of this section, the base period to be utilized in computing the DUA weekly amount shall be the most recent tax year that has ended for the individual (whether an employee or self-employed) prior to the individual's unemployment that was a direct result of the major disaster. The self-employment income to be treated as wages for purposes of computing the weekly amount under this paragraph (a) shall be the net income reported on the tax return of the individual as income from all self-employment that was dependent upon the performance of services by the individual. If an individual has not filed a tax return for the most recent tax year that has ended at the time of such individual's initial application for DUA, such individual shall have a weekly amount determined in accordance with paragraph (e)(3) of this section.

(3) As of the date of filing an initial application for DUA, family members over the age of majority, as defined under the statutes of the applicable State, who were customarily or routinely employed or self-employed as a family unit or in the same self-employment business prior to the individuals' unemployment that was a direct result of the major disaster, shall have the wages from such employment or net income from the self-employment allocated equally among such adult family members for purposes of computing a weekly amount under this paragraph (a), unless the documentation to substantiate employment or self-employment and wages earned or paid for such employment or self-employment submitted as required by paragraph (e) of this section supports a different allocation. Family members under the age of majority as of the date of filing an initial application for DUA shall have a weekly amount computed under this paragraph (a) based on the actual wages earned or paid for employment or self-employment rather than an equal allocation.

(b) If the weekly amount computed under paragraph (a) of this section is less than 50 percent of the average weekly payment of regular compensation in the State, as provided quarterly by the Department, or, if the individual has insufficient wages from employment or insufficient or no net income from self-employment (which includes individuals falling within paragraphs (a)(3) and (b)(3) of § 625.5) in the applicable base period to compute a weekly amount under paragraph (a) of this section, the individual shall be determined entitled to a weekly amount equal to 50 percent of the average weekly payment of regular compensation in the State.

(1) If an individual was customarily or routinely employed or self-employed less than full-time prior to the individual's unemployment as a direct result of the major disaster, such individual's weekly amount under this paragraph (b)(1) shall be determined by calculating the percent of time the individual was employed or self-employed compared to the customary and usual hours per week that would constitute the average per week hours for year-round full-time employment or self-employment for the occupation, then applying the percentage to the determined 50 percent of the average weekly amount of regular compensation paid in the State. The State agency shall utilize information furnished by the applicant at the time of filing an initial application for DUA and any labor market or occupational information available within the State agency to determine the average per week hours for full-time employment or self-employment for the occupation. If the weekly amount computed for an individual under this paragraph (b)(1) is less than the weekly amount computed under paragraph (a) of this section for the individual, the individual shall be entitled to the higher weekly amount.

(2) The weekly amount so determined under paragraph (b)(1) of this section, if not an even dollar amount, shall be rounded in accordance with the applicable State law.

(c) In the Territory of Guam and the Commonwealth of the Northern Mariana Islands, the amount of DUA payable to an unemployed worker or unemployed self-employed individual for a week of total unemployment shall be the average of the payments of regular compensation made under all State laws referred to in §625.2(r)(1)(i) for weeks of total unemployment in the first four of the last five completed calendar quarters immediately preceding the quarter in which the major disaster began. The weekly amount so determined, if not an even dollar amount, shall be rounded to the next higher dollar.

(d) In American Samoa, Federated States of Micronesia, Republic of the Marshall Islands and the Trust Territory of the Pacific Islands, the amount of DUA payable to an unemployed worker or unemployed self-employed individual for a week of total unemployment shall be the amount agreed upon by the Regional Administrator, Employment and Training Administration, for Region VI (San Francisco), and the Federal Coordinating Officer, which shall approximate 50 percent of the area-wide average of the weekly wages paid to individuals in the major disaster area in the quarter immediately preceding the quarter in which the major disaster began. The weekly amount so determined, if not an even dollar amount, shall be rounded to the next higher dollar.

(e) The State agency shall immediately determine, upon the filing of an initial application for DUA, a weekly amount under the provisions of paragraphs (a) through (d) of this section, as the case may be, based on the individual's statement of employment or self-employment preceding the individual's unemployment that was a direct result of the major disaster, and wages earned or paid for such employment or self-employment. An immediate determination of a weekly amount shall also be made where, in conjunction with the filing of an initial application for DUA, the individual submits documentation substantiating employment or self-employment and wages earned or paid for such employment or self-employment, or, in the absence of documentation, where any State agency records of employment or self-employment and wages earned or paid for such employment or self-employment, justify the determination of a weekly amount. An immediate determination shall also be made based on the individual's statement or in conjunction with the submittal of documentation in those cases where the individual was to commence employment or self-employment on or after the date the major disaster began but was prevented from doing so as a direct result of the disaster.

(1) In the case of a weekly amount determined in accordance with paragraph (e) of this section, based only on the individual's statement of earnings, the individual shall furnish documentation to substantiate the employment or self-employment or wages earned from or paid for such employment or self-employment or documentation to support that the individual was to commence employment or self-employment on or after the date the major disaster began. In either case, documentation shall be submitted within 21 calendar days of the filing of the initial application for DUA.

(2) Any individual who fails to submit documentation to substantiate employment or self-employment or the planned commencement of employment or self-employment in accordance with paragraph (e)(1) of this section, shall be determined ineligible for the payment of DUA for any week of unemployment due to the disaster. Any weeks for which DUA was already paid on the application prior to the date of the determination of ineligibility under this paragraph (e)(2) are overpaid and a determination shall be issued in accordance with §625.14(a). In addition, the State agency shall consider whether the individual is subject to a disqualification for fraud in accordance with the provisions set forth in §625.14(i).

(3) For purposes of a computation of a weekly amount under paragraph (a) of this section, if an individual submits documentation to substantiate employment or self-employment in accordance with paragraph (e)(1), but not documentation of wages earned or paid during the base period set forth in paragraph (a)(2) of this section, including those cases where the individual has

not filed a tax return for the most recent tax year that has ended, the State agency shall immediately redetermine the weekly amount of DUA payable to the individual in accordance with paragraph (b) of this section.

(4) Any individual determined eligible for a weekly amount of DUA under the provisions of paragraph (e)(3) of this section may submit necessary documentation to substantiate wages earned or paid during the base period set forth in paragraph (a)(2) of this section, including those cases where the individual has not filed a tax return for the most recent tax year that has ended, at any time prior to the end of the disaster assistance period. A redetermination of the weekly amount payable, as previously determined under paragraph (b) of this section, shall immediately be made if the wages earned or paid for services performed in employment or self-employment reflected in such documentation is sufficient to permit a computation under paragraph (a) of this section of a weekly amount higher than was determined under paragraph (b) of this section. Any higher amount so determined shall be applicable to all weeks during the disaster assistance period for which the individual was eligible for the payment of DUA.

(f)(1) The weekly amount of DUA payable to an unemployed worker or unemployed self-employed individual for a week of partial or part-total unemployment shall be the weekly amount determined under paragraph (a), (b), (c) or (d) of this section, as the case may be, reduced (but not below zero) by the amount of wages that the individual earned in that week as determined by applying to such wages the earnings allowance for partial or part-total employment prescribed by the applicable State law.

(2) The weekly amount of DUA payable to an unemployed self-employed individual for a week of unemployment shall be the weekly amount determined under paragraph (a), (b), (c) or (d) of this section, as the case may be, reduced (but not below zero) by the full amount of any income received during the week for the performance of services in self-employment, regardless of whether or not any services were performed during the week, by applying the earnings allowance as set forth in paragraph (f)(1) of this section. Notwithstanding the definition of "wages" for a self-employed individual under § 625.2(u), the term "any income" for purposes of this paragraph (f)(2) means gross income.

[60 FR 25568, May 11, 1995, as amended at 71 FR 35516, June 21, 2006]

§ 625.7 Disaster Unemployment Assistance: Duration.

DUA shall be payable to an eligible unemployed worker or eligible unemployed self-employed individual for all weeks of unemployment which begin during a Disaster Assistance Period.

§ 625.8 Applications for Disaster Unemployment Assistance.

(a) *Initial application.* An initial application for DUA shall be filed by an individual with the State agency of the applicable State within 30 days after the announcement date of the major disaster as the result of which the individual became unemployed, and on a form prescribed by the Secretary which shall be furnished to the individual by the State agency. An initial application filed later than 30 days after the announcement date of the major disaster shall be accepted as timely by the State agency if the applicant had good cause for the late filing, but in no event shall an initial application be accepted by the State agency if it is filed after the expiration of the Disaster Assistance Period. If the 30th day falls on a Saturday, Sunday, or a legal holiday in the major disaster area, the 30-day time limit shall be extended to the next business day.

(b) *Weekly applications.* Applications for DUA for weeks of unemployment shall be filed with respect to the individual's applicable State at the times and in the manner as claims for regular compensation are filed under the applicable State law, and on forms prescribed by the Secretary which shall be furnished to the individual by the State agency.

(c) *Filing in person.* (1) Except as provided in paragraph (c)(2) of this section, all applications for DUA, including initial applications, shall be filed in person.

(2) Whenever an individual has good cause for not filing any application for DUA in person, the application shall be filed at such time, in such place, and in such a manner as directed by the State agency and in accordance with this part and procedures prescribed by the Secretary.

(d) *IBPP.* The "Interstate Benefit Payment Plan" shall apply, where appropriate, to an individual filing applications for DUA.

(e) *Wage combining.* The "Interstate Arrangement for Combining Employment and Wages" (part 616 of this chapter) shall apply, where appropriate, to an individual filing applications for DUA: *Provided,* That the "Paying State" shall be the applicable State for the individual as prescribed in § 625.12.

(f) *Procedural requirements.* (1) The procedures for reporting and filing applications for DUA shall be consistent with this part, and with the Secretary's "Standard for Claim Filing, Claimant Reporting, Job Finding and Employment Services," *Employment Security Manual.* Part V, sections 5000 *et seq.* (appendix A of this part), insofar as such standard is not inconsistent with this part.

(2) The provisions of the applicable State law which apply hereunder to applications for and the payment of DUA shall be applied consistent with the requirements of title III of the Social Security Act and the Federal Unemployment Tax Act which are pertinent in the case of regular compensation, including but not limited to those standards and requirements specifically referred to in the provisions of this part.

(Approved by the Office of Management and Budget under control number 1205–0051)

(Pub. L. No. 96–511)

[42 FR 46712, Sept. 16, 1977, as amended at 49 FR 18295, Apr. 30, 1984; 55 FR 555, Jan. 5, 1990]

§ 625.9 Determinations of entitlement; notices to individual.

(a) *Determination of initial application.* (1) The State agency shall promptly, upon the filing of an initial application for DUA, determine whether the individual is eligible, and if the individual is found to be eligible, the weekly amount of DUA payable to the individual and the period during which DUA is payable.

(2) An individual's eligibility for DUA shall be determined, where a reliable record of employment, self-employment and wages is not obtainable, on the basis of an affidavit submitted to the State agency by the individual, and on a form prescribed by the Secretary which shall be furnished to the individual by the State agency.

(b) *Determinations of weekly applications.* The State agency shall promptly, upon the filing of an application for a payment of DUA with respect to a week of unemployment, determine whether the individual is entitled to a payment of DUA with respect to that week, and, if entitled, the amount of DUA to which the individual is entitled.

(c) *Redetermination.* The provisions of the applicable State law concerning the right to request, or authority to undertake, reconsideration of a determination pertaining to regular compensation under the applicable State law shall apply to determinations pertaining to DUA.

(d) *Notices to individual.* The State agency shall give notice in writing to the individual, by the most expeditious method, of any determination or redetermination of an initial application, and of any determination of an application for DUA with respect to a week of unemployment which denies DUA or reduces the weekly amount initially determined to be payable, and of any redetermination of an application for DUA with respect to a week of unemployment. Each notice of determination or redetermination shall include such information regarding the determination or redetermination and notice of right to reconsideration or appeal, or both, as is furnished with written notices of determination and written notices of redeterminations with respect to claims for regular compensation.

(e) *Promptness.* Full payment of DUA when due shall be made with the greatest promptness that is administratively feasible.

(f) *Secretary's Standard.* The procedures for making determinations and redeterminations, and furnishing written notices of determinations, redeterminations, and rights of appeal to individuals applying for DUA, shall be consistent with this part and with the Secretary's "Standard for Claim Determinations—Separation Information," *Employment Security Manual*. Part V, sections 6010 *et seq*. (Appendix B of this part).

(Approved by the Office of Management and Budget under control number 1205–0051)

(Pub. L. No. 96–511)

[42 FR 46712, Sept. 16, 1977, as amended at 49 FR 18295, Apr. 30, 1984; 55 FR 555, Jan. 5, 1990]

§ 625.10 Appeal and review.

(a) *States of the United States*. (1) Any determination or redetermination made pursuant to § 625.9, by the State agency of a State (other than the State agency of the Territory of Guam, American Samoa, Commonwealth of the Northern Mariana Islands, Federated States of Micronesia, Republic of the Marshall Islands, or the Trust Territory of the Pacific Islands) may be appealed by the applicant in accordance with the applicable State law to the first-stage administrative appellate authority in the same manner and to the same extent as a determination or redetermination of a right to regular compensation may be appealed under the applicable State law, except that the period for appealing shall be 60 days from the date the determination or redetermination is issued or mailed instead of the appeal period provided for in the applicable State law. Any decision on a DUA first-stage appeal must be made and issued within 30 days after receipt of the appeal by the State.

(2) Notice of the decision on appeal, and the reasons therefor, shall be given to the individual by delivering the notice to such individual personally or by mailing it to the individual's last known address, whichever is most expeditious. The decision shall contain information as to the individual's right to review of the decision by the appropriate Regional Administrator, Employment and Training Administration, if requested within 15 days after the decision was mailed or delivered in person to the individual. The notice will include the manner of requesting such review, and the complete address of the Regional Administrator. Notice of the decision on appeal shall be given also to the State agency (with the same notice of right to review) and to the appropriate Regional Administrator.

(b) *Guam, American Samoa, and the Trust Territory of the Pacific Islands*. (1) In the case of an appeal by an individual from a determination or redetermination by the State agency of the Territory of Guam, American Samoa, Commonwealth of the Northern Mariana Islands, Federated States of Micronesia, Republic of the Marshall Islands, or the Trust Territory of the Pacific Islands, the individual shall be entitled to a hearing and decision in accordance with § 625.30 of this part.

(2) Notice of the referee's decision, and the reasons therefor, shall be given to the individual by delivering the notice to the individual personally or by mailing it to the individual's last known address, whichever is most expeditious. The notice of decision shall contain information as to the individual's right to review of the decision by the Regional Administrator, Employment and Training Administration, for Region VI (San Francisco), and the manner of obtaining such review, including the address of the Regional Administrator. Notice of the decision on appeal shall be given also to the State agency and to the Regional Administrator.

(c) *Review by Regional Administrator*. (1) The appropriate Regional Administrator, Employment and Training Administration, upon request for review by an applicant or the State agency shall, or upon the Regional Administrator's own motion may, review a decision on appeal issued pursuant to paragraph (a) or (b) of this section.

(2) Any request for review by an applicant or a State agency shall be filed, and any review on the Regional Administrator's own motion shall be undertaken, within 15 days after notice of the decision on appeal was delivered or mailed to the individual.

(3)(i) A request for review by an individual may be filed with the appropriate State agency, which shall forward the request to the appropriate Regional Administrator, Employment and

Training Administration, or may be filed directly with the appropriate Regional Administrator.

(ii) A request for review by a State agency shall be filed with the appropriate Regional Administrator, and a copy shall be served on the individual by delivery to the individual personally or by mail to the individual's last known address.

(iii) When a Regional Administrator undertakes a review of a decision on the Regional Administrator's own motion, notice thereof shall be served promptly on the individual and the State agency.

(iv) Whenever review by a Regional Administrator is undertaken pursuant to an appeal or on the Regional Administrator's own motion, the State agency shall promptly forward to the Regional Administrator the entire record of the case.

(v) Where service on the individual is required by paragraph (c)(3)(ii) of this section, adequate proof of service shall be furnished for the record before the Regional Administrator, and be a condition of the Regional Administrator undertaking review pursuant to this paragraph.

(4) The decision of the Regional Administrator on review shall be rendered promptly, and not later than the earlier of—

(i) 45 days after the appeal is received or is undertaken by the Regional Administrator, or

(ii) 90 days from the date the individual's appeal from the determination or redetermination was received by the State agency.

(5) Notice of the Regional Administrator's decision shall be mailed promptly to the last known address of the individual, to the State agency of the applicable State, and to the Administrator, Office of Workforce Security. The decision of the Regional Administrator shall be the final decision under the Act and this part, unless there is further review by the Assistant Secretary as provided in paragraph (d) of this section.

(d) *Further review by the Assistant Secretary.* (1) The Assistant Secretary for Employment and Training on his or her own motion may review any decision by a Regional Administrator issued pursuant to paragraph (c) of this section.

(2) Notice of a motion for review by the Assistant Secretary shall be given to the applicant, the State agency of the applicable State, the appropriate Regional Administrator, and the Administrator, Office of Workforce Security.

(3) When the Regional Administrator and the State agency are notified of the Assistant Secretary's motion for review, they shall forward all records in the case to the Assistant Secretary.

(4) Review by the Assistant Secretary shall be solely on the record in the case, any other written contentions or evidence requested by the Assistant Secretary, and any further evidence or arguments offered by the individual, the State agency, the Regional Administrator, or the Administrator, Office of Workforce Security, which are mailed to the Assistant Secretary within 15 days after mailing the notice of motion for review.

(5) Upon review of a case under this paragraph, the Assistant Secretary may affirm, modify, or reverse the decision of the Regional Administrator, and may remand the case for further proceedings and decision in accordance with the Assistant Secretary's decision.

(6) The decision of the Assistant Secretary shall be made promptly, and notice thereof shall be sent to the applicant, the State agency, the Regional Administrator, and the Administrator, Office of Workforce Security.

(7) The decision of the Assistant Secretary shall be final and conclusive, and binding on all interested parties, and shall be a precedent applicable throughout the States.

(e) *Procedural requirements.* (1) All decisions on first-stage appeals from determinations or redeterminations by the State agencies must be made within 30 days of the appeal; therefore, the Secretary's "Standard for Appeals Promptness-Unemployment Compensation" in part 650 of this chapter shall not apply to the DUA program.

(2) The provisions on right of appeal and opportunity for hearing and review with respect to applications for DUA shall be consistent with this part and with sections 303(a)(1) and 303(a)(3) of

the Social Security Act, 42 U.S.C. 503(a)(1) and 503(a)(3).

(3) Any petition or other matter required to be filed within a time limit under this section shall be deemed to be filed at the time it is delivered to an appropriate office, or at the time of the postmark if it is mailed via the United States Postal Service to an appropriate office.

(4) If any limited time period specified in this section ends on a Saturday, Sunday, or a legal holiday in the major disaster area, the time limit shall be extended to the next business day.

[42 FR 46712, Sept. 16, 1977, as amended at 55 FR 555, Jan. 5, 1990; 56 FR 22805, May 16, 1991; 71 FR 35516, June 21, 2006]

§ 625.11 Provisions of State law applicable.

The terms and conditions of the State law of the applicable State for an individual, which apply to claims for, and the payment of regular compensation, shall apply to applications for, and the payment of, DUA to each such individual, only as specifically set forth in the provisions of this part.

§ 625.12 The applicable State for an individual.

(a) *Applicable State*. The applicable State for an individual shall be that State in which the individual's unemployment is the result of a major disaster.

(b) *Limitation*. DUA is payable to an individual only by an applicable State as determined pursuant to paragraph (a) of this section, and—

(1) Only pursuant to an Agreement entered into pursuant to the Act and this part, and with respect to weeks in which the Agreement is in effect; and

(2) Only with respect to weeks of unemployment that begin during a Disaster Assistance Period.

[42 FR 46712, Sept. 16, 1977, as amended at 55 FR 556, Jan. 5, 1990; 71 FR 35516, June 21, 2006]

§ 625.13 Restrictions on entitlement; disqualification.

(a) *Income reductions*. The amount of DUA payable to an individual for a week of unemployment, as computed pursuant to § 625.6, shall be reduced by the amount of any of the following that an individual has received for the week or would receive for the week if the individual filed a claim or application therefor and took all procedural steps necessary under the appropriate law, contract, or policy to receive such payment:

(1) Any benefits or insurance proceed from any source not defined as "compensation" under § 625.2(d) for loss of wages due to illness or disability;

(2) A supplemental unemployment benefit pursuant to a collective bargaining agreement.

(3) Private income protection insurance;

(4) Any workers' compensation by virtue of the death of the head of the household as the result of the major disaster in the major disaster area, prorated by weeks, if the individual has become the head of the household and is seeking suitable work because the head of the household died as the result of the major disaster in the major disaster area; and

(5) The prorated amount of a retirement pension or annuity under a public or private retirement plan or system, prorated, where necessary, by weeks, but only if, and to the extent that, such amount would be deducted from regular compensation payable under the applicable State law.

(6) The prorated amount of primary benefits under title II of the Social Security Act, but only to the extent that such benefits would be deduced from regular compensation if payable to the individual under the applicable State law.

(b) *Disqualification*. (1) An individual shall not be entitled to DUA for any week after the week in which the individual is reemployed in a suitable position.

(2) An individual who refuses without good cause to accept a bona fide offer of reemployment in a position suitable to the individual, or to investigate or accept a referral to a position which is suitable to and available to the individual, shall not be entitled to DUA with respect to the week in which such refusal occurs or in any subsequent week in the Disaster Assistance Period. For the purposes of this paragraph, a position shall not be deemed to be suitable for an individual if the circumstances present any unusual risk

to the health, safety, or morals of the individual, if it is impracticable for the individual to accept the position, or if acceptance for the position would, as to the individual, be inconsistent with any labor standard in section 3304(a)(5) of the Federal Unemployment Tax Act, 26 U.S.C. 3304(a)(5), or the comparable provisions of the applicable State law.

[42 FR 46712, Sept. 16, 1977, as amended at 55 FR 556, Jan. 5, 1990]

§625.14 Overpayments; disqualification for fraud.

(a) *Finding and repayment.* If the State agency of the applicable State finds that an individual has received a payment of DUA to which the individual was not entitled under the Act and this part, whether or not the payment was due to the individual's fault or misrepresentation, the individual shall be liable to repay to the applicable State the total sum of the payment to which the individual was not entitled, and the State agency shall take all reasonable measures authorized under any State law or Federal law to recover for the account of the United States the total sum of the payment to which the individual was not entitled.

(b) *Recovery by offset.* (1) The State agency shall recover, insofar as is possible, the amount of any outstanding overpayment of DUA made to the individual by the State, by deductions from any DUA payable to the individual under the Act and this part, or from any compensation payable to the individual under any Federal unemployment compensation law administered by the State agency, or from any assistance or allowance payable to the individual with respect to unemployment under any other Federal law administered by the State agency.

(2) The State agency shall also recover, insofar as possible, the amount of any outstanding overpayment of DUA made to the individual by another State, by deductions from any DUA payable by the State agency to the individual under the Act and this part, or from any compensation payable to the individual under any Federal unemployment compensation law administered by the State agency, or from any assistance or allowance payable to the individual with respect to unemployment under any other Federal law administered by the State agency.

(3) If the State has in effect an agreement to implement the cross-program offset provisions of section 303(g)(2) of the Social Security Act (42 U.S.C. 503(g)(2)), the State shall apply the provisions of such agreement to the recovery of outstanding DUA overpayments.

(c) *Debts due the United States.* DUA payable to an individual shall be applied by the State agency for the recovery by offset of any debt due to the United States from the individual, but shall not be applied or used by the State agency in any manner for the payment of any debt of the individual to any State or any other entity or person.

(d) *Recovered overpayments.* Overpayments recovered in any manner shall be credited or returned, as the case may be, to the appropriate account of the United States.

(e) *Application of State law.* Any provision of State law authorizing waiver of recovery of overpayments of compensation shall not be applicable to DUA.

(f) *Final decision.* Recovery of any overpayment of DUA shall not be enforced by the State agency until the determination establishing the overpayment has become final, or if appeal is taken from the determination, until the decision after opportunity for a fair hearing has become final.

(g) *Procedural requirements.* (1) The provisions of paragraphs (c), (d), and (f) of §625.9 shall apply to determinations and redeterminations made pursuant to this section.

(2) The provisions of §625.10 shall apply to determinations and redeterminations made pursuant to this section.

(h) *Fraud detection and prevention.* Provisions in the procedures of each State with respect to detection and prevention of fraudulent overpayments of DUA shall be, as a minimum, commensurate with the procedures adopted by the State with respect to regular compensation and consistent with the Secretary's "Standard for Fraud and Overpayment Detection," *Employment Security Manual*, part V, sections 7510 *et seq.* (Appendix C of this part).

(i) *Disqualification for fraud.* Any individual who, with respect to a major disaster, makes or causes another to make a false statement or misrepresentation of a material fact, knowing it to be false, or knowingly fails or causes another to fail to disclose a material fact, in order to obtain for the individual or any other person a payment of DUA to which the individual or any other person is not entitled, shall be disqualified as follows:

(1) If the false statement, misrepresentation, or nondisclosure pertains to an initial application for DUA—

(i) The individual making the false statement, misrepresentation, or nondisclosure shall be disqualified from the receipt of any DUA with respect to that major disaster; and

(ii) If the false statement, misrepresentation, or nondisclosure was made on behalf of another individual, and was known to such other individual to be a false statement, misrepresentation, or nondisclosure, such other individual shall be disqualified from the receipt of any DUA with respect to that major disaster; and

(2) If the false statement, misrepresentation, or nondisclosure pertains to a week for which application for a payment of DUA is made—

(i) The individual making the false statement, misrepresentation, or nondisclosure shall be disqualified from the receipt of DUA for that week and the first two compensable weeks in the Disaster Assistance Period that immediately follow that week, with respect to which the individual is otherwise entitled to a payment of DUA; and

(ii) If the false statement, misrepresentation, or nondisclosure was made on behalf of another individual, and was known to such other individual to be a false statement, misrepresentation, or nondisclosure, such other individual shall be disqualified from the receipt of DUA for that week and the first two compensable weeks in the Disaster Assistance Period that immediately follow that week, with respect to which the individual is otherwise entitled to a payment of DUA.

(j) *Criminal penalties.* The provisions of this section on recovery of overpayments and disqualification for fraudulently claiming or receiving any DUA to which an individual was not entitled under the Act and this part shall be in addition to and shall not preclude any applicable criminal prosecution and penalties under State or Federal law.

[42 FR 46712, Sept. 16, 1977, as amended at 55 FR 556, Jan. 5, 1990; 71 FR 35516, June 21, 2006]

§ 625.15 Inviolate rights to DUA.

Except as specifically provided in this part, the right of individuals to DUA shall be protected in the same manner and to the same extent as the rights of persons to regular unemployment compensation are protected under the applicable State law. Such measures shall include protection of applicants for DUA from waiver, release, assignment, pledge, encumbrance, levy, execution, attachment, and garnishment, of their rights to DUA. In the same manner and to the same extent, individuals shall be protected from discrimination and obstruction in regard to seeking, applying for and receiving any right to DUA.

§ 625.16 Recordkeeping; disclosure of information.

(a) *Recordkeeping.* Each State agency will make and maintain records pertaining to the administration of the Act as the Secretary requires, and will make all such records available for inspection, examination, and audit by such Federal officials or employees as the Secretary may designate or as may be required by law.

(b) *Disclosure of information.* Information in records made and maintained by a State agency in administering the Act shall be kept confidential, and information in such records may be disclosed only in the same manner and to the same extent as information with respect to regular compensation and the entitlement of individuals thereto may be disclosed under the applicable State law, and consistently with section 303(a)(1) of the Social Security Act, 42 U.S.C. 503(a)(1). This provision on the confidentiality of information obtained in the administration of the Act shall not apply, however, to the United States Department of Labor, or in the case of information, reports and studies requested pursuant to § 625.19, or where the result would be inconsistent with the Freedom of Information Act (5 U.S.C. 552), the Privacy Act of 1974 (5 U.S.C. 552a), or regulations of the United States Department of Labor promulgated thereunder.

§ 625.17 Announcement of the beginning of a Disaster Assistance Period.

Whenever a major disaster is declared in a State, the State agency shall promptly announce throughout the major disaster area by all appropriate news media that individuals who are unemployed as the result of the major disaster may be entitled to DUA; that they should file initial applications for DUA as soon as possible, but not later than the 30th day after the announcement date; the beginning date of the Disaster Assistance Period; and where individuals may obtain further information and file applications for DUA.

§ 625.18 Public access to Agreements.

The State agency of a State will make available to any individual or organization a true copy of the Agreement with the State for inspection and copying. Copies of an Agreement may be furnished on request to any individual or organization upon payment of the same charges, if any, as apply to the furnishing of copies of other records of the State agency.

§ 625.19 Information, reports and studies.

(a) *Routine responses.* State agencies shall furnish to the Secretary such information and reports and make such studies as the Secretary decides are necessary or appropriate for carrying out the purposes of the Act and this part.

(b) *Final report.* In addition to such other reports as may be required by the Secretary, within 60 days after all payments of Disaster Unemployment Assistance as the result of a major disaster in the State have been made, the State agency shall submit a final report to the Secretary. A final report shall contain a narrative summary, a chronological list of significant events, pertinent statistics about the Disaster Unemployment Assistance provided to disaster victims, brief statements of major problems encountered, discussion of lessons learned, and suggestions for improvement of the program during future major disasters.

(Approved by the Office of Management and Budget under control number 1205–0051)

(Pub. L. No. 96–511)

[15 FR 5886, Aug. 31, 1950; 23 FR 1267, Mar. 1, 1958, as amended at 49 FR 18295, Apr. 30, 1984]

§ 625.20 [Reserved]

§ 625.30 Appeal Procedures for Guam, American Samoa, Commonwealth of the Northern Mariana Islands, Federated States of Micronesia, Republic of the Marshall Islands, and the Trust Territory of the Pacific Islands.

(a) *Designation of referee.* The Director of the Unemployment Insurance Service shall designate a referee of a State agency to hear and decide appeals under this section from determinations and redeterminations by the State agencies of the Territory of Guam, American Samoa, Commonwealth of the Northern Mariana Islands, Federated States of Micronesia, Republic of the Marshall Islands, and the Trust Territory of the Pacific Islands.

(b) *Appeals to referee.* (1) A DUA applicant may appeal from a determination or redetermination issued by the State agency of the Territory of Guam, American Samoa, Commonwealth of the Northern Mariana Islands, Federated States of Micronesia, Republic of the Marshall Islands, or the Trust Territory of the Pacific Islands within 60 days after the mailing of notice and a copy of such determination or redetermination to such applicant's last known address, or in the absence of mailing within 60 days after delivery in person thereof to such applicant. The appeal shall be in writing and may be filed with any office of the State agency.

(2) Notice that an appeal has been filed may be given or mailed, in the discretion of the referee, to any person who has offered or is believed to have evidence with respect to the claim.

(3) An appeal shall be promptly scheduled and heard, in order that a decision on the appeal can be issued within 30 days after receipt of the appeal by the State agency. Written notice of hearing, specifying the time and place

thereof and those questions known to be in dispute, shall be given or mailed to the applicant, the State agency, and any person who has offered or is believed to have evidence with respect to the claim 7 days or more before the hearing, except that a shorter notice period may be used with the consent of the applicant.

(c) *Conduct of hearings.* Hearings before the referee shall be informal, fair, and impartial, and shall be conducted in such manner as may be best suited to determine the DUA applicants' right to compensation. Hearings shall be open to the public unless sufficient cause for a closed hearing is shown. The referee shall open a hearing by ascertaining and summarizing the issue or issues involved in the appeal. The applicant may examine and cross-examine witnesses, inspect documents, and explain or rebut any evidence. An opportunity to present argument shall be afforded such applicant, and such argument shall be made part of the record. The referee shall give such applicant, if not represented by counsel or other representative, every assistance that does not interfere with the impartial discharge of the referee's duties. The referee may examine such applicant and other witnesses to such extent as the referee deems necessary. Any issue involved in the claim shall be considered and passed upon even though such issue was not set forth as a ground of appeal.

(d) *Evidence.* Oral or written evidence of any nature, whether or not conforming to the legal rules of evidence, may be accepted. Any official record of the State agency, including reports submitted in connection with administration of the DUA program, may be included in the record if the applicant is given an opportunity to examine and rebut the same. A written statement under oath or affirmation may be accepted when it appears impossible or unduly burdensome to require the attendance of a witness, but a DUA applicant adversely affected by such a statement must be given the opportunity to examine such statement, to comment on or rebut any or all portions thereof, and whenever possible to cross-examine a witness whose testimony has been introduced in written form by submitting written questions to be answered in writing.

(e) *Record.* All oral testimony before the referee shall be taken under oath or affirmation and a transcript thereof shall be made and kept. Such transcript together with all exhibits, papers, and requests filed in the proceeding shall constitute the record for decision.

(f) *Withdrawal of appeal.* A DUA applicant who has filed an appeal may withdraw such appeal with the approval of the referee.

(g) *Nonappearance of DUA applicant.* Failure of a DUA applicant to appear at a hearing shall not result in a decision being automatically rendered against such applicant. The referee shall render a decision on the basis of whatever evidence is properly before him/her unless there appears to be a good reason for continuing the hearing. An applicant who fails to appear at a hearing with respect to his/her appeal may within seven days thereafter petition for a reopening of the hearing. Such petition shall be granted if it appears to the referee that such applicant has shown good cause for his/her failure to attend.

(h) *Notice of referee's decision and further review*—(1) *Decision.* A copy of the referee's decision, which shall include findings and conclusions, shall promptly be given or mailed to the applicant, the State agency, and to the Regional Administrator, Employment and Training Administration, for Region VI (San Francisco). The decision of the referee shall be accompanied by an explanation of the right of such applicant or State agency to request review by the Regional Administrator and the time and manner in which such review may be instituted, as provided in paragraph (a)(2) of § 625.10.

(2) *Time limit for decision.* A decision on an appeal to a referee under this section shall be made and issued by the referee not later than 30 days after receipt of the appeal by the State agency.

(3) *Further review.* Further review by the Regional Administrator or the Assistant Secretary with respect to an appeal under this section shall be in accordance with paragraphs (c) and (d) of § 625.10.

(i) *Consolidation of appeals.* The referee may consolidate appeals and conduct joint hearings thereon where the same or substantially similar evidence is relevant and material to the matters in issue. Reasonable notice of consolidation and the time and place of hearing shall be given or mailed to the applicants or their representatives, the State agency, and to persons who have offered or are believed to have evidence with respect to the DUA claims.

(j) *Representation.* A DUA applicant may be represented by counsel or other representative in any proceedings before the referee or the Regional Administrator. Any such representative may appear at any hearing or take any other action which such applicant may take under this part. The referee, for cause, may bar any person from representing an applicant, in which event such action shall be set forth in the record. No representative shall charge an applicant more than an amount fixed by the referee for representing the applicant in any proceeding under this section.

(k) *Postponement, continuance, and adjournment of hearings.* A hearing before the referee shall be postponed, continued, or adjourned when such action is necessary to afford a DUA applicant reasonable opportunity for a fair hearing. In such case notice of the subsequent hearing shall be given to any person who received notice of the prior hearing.

(l) *Information from agency records.* Information shall be available to a DUA applicant, either from the records of the State agency or as obtained in any proceeding herein provided for, to the extent necessary for proper presentation of his/her case. All requests for information shall state the nature of the information desired as clearly as possible and shall be in writing unless made at a hearing.

(m) *Filing of decisions.* Copies of all decisions of the referee shall be kept on file at his/her office or agency for at least 3 years.

[55 FR 557, Jan. 5, 1990, as amended at 56 FR 22805, May 16, 1991; 71 FR 35516, June 21, 2006]

APPENDIX A TO PART 625—STANDARD FOR CLAIM FILING, CLAIMANT REPORTING, JOB FINDING, AND EMPLOYMENT SERVICES

EMPLOYMENT SECURITY MANUAL (PART V, SECTIONS 5000–5004)

5000 *Standard for Claim Filing, Claimant Reporting, Job Finding, and Employment Services*

A. *Federal law requirements.* Section 3304(a)(1) of the Federal Unemployment Tax Act and section 303(a)(2) of the Social Security Act require that a State law provide for: "Payment of unemployment compensation solely through public employment offices or such other agencies as the Secretary may approve."

Section 3304(a)(4) of the Federal Unemployment Tax Act and section 303(a)(5) of the Social Security Act require that a State law provide for: "Expenditure of all money withdrawn from an unemployment fund of such State, in the payment of unemployment compensation * * *"

Section 303(a)(1) of the Social Security Act requires that the State law provide for: "Such methods of administration . . . as are found by the Secretary to be reasonably calculated to insure full payment of unemployment compensation when due."

B. *Secretary's interpretation of federal law requirements:* 1. The Secretary interprets section 3304(a)(1) of the Federal Unemployment Tax Act and section 303(a)(2) of the Social Security Act to require that a State law provide for payment of unemployment compensation solely through public employment offices or claims offices administered by the State employment security agency if such agency provides for such coordination in the operations of its public employment offices and claims offices as will insure (a) the payment of benefits only to individuals who are unemployed and who are able to work and available for work, and (b) that individuals claiming unemployment compensation (claimants) are afforded such placement and other employment services as are necessary and appropriate to return them to suitable work as soon as possible.

2. The Secretary interprets all the above sections to require that a State law provide for: a. Such contact by claimants with public employment offices or claims offices or both, (1) as will reasonably insure the payment of unemployment compensation only to individuals who are unemployed and who are able to work and available for work, and (2) that claimants are afforded such placement and other employment services as are necessary and appropriate to facilitate their return to suitable work as soon as possible; and b. Methods of administration which do not unreasonably limit the opportunity of

individuals to establish their right to unemployment compensation due under such State law.

5001 *Claim Filing and Claimant Reporting Requirements Designed To Satisfy Secretary's Interpretation*

A. *Claim filing—total or part-total unemployment:* 1. Individuals claiming unemployment compensation for total or part-total unemployment are required to file a claim weekly or biweekly, in person or by mail, at a public employment office or a claims office (these terms include offices at itinerant points) as set forth below.

2. Except as provided in paragraph 3, a claimant is required to file in person: a. His new claim with respect to a benefit year, or his continued claim for a waiting week or for his first compensable week of unemployment in such year; and b. Any other claim, when requested to do so by the claims personnel at the office at which he files his claim(s) because questions about his right to benefits are raised by circumstances such as the following:

(1) The conditions or circumstances of his separation from employment;

(2) The claimant's answers to questions on mail claim(s) indicate that he may be unable to work or that there may be undue restrictions on his availability for work or that his search for work may be inadequate or that he may be disqualified;

(3) The claimant's answers to questions on mail claims create uncertainty about his credibility or indicate a lack of understanding of the applicable requirements; or

(4) The claimant's record shows that he has previously filed a fraudulent claim.

In such circumstances, the claimant is required to continue to file claims in person each week (or biweekly) until the State agency determines that filing claims in person is no longer required for the resolution of such questions.

3. A claimant must be permitted to file a claim by mail in any of the following circumstances: a. He is located in an area requiring the expenditure of an unreasonable amount of time or money in traveling to the nearest facility established by the State agency for filing claims in person; b. Conditions make it impracticable for the agency to take claims in person; c. He has returned to full-time work on or before the scheduled date for his filing a claim, unless the agency makes provision for in-person filing at a time and place that does not interfere with his employment; d. The agency finds that he has good cause for failing to file a claim in person.

4. A claimant who has been receiving benefits for partial unemployment may continue to file claims as if he were a partially unemployed worker for the first four consecutive weeks of total or part-total unemployment immediately following his period of partial unemployment so long as he remains attached to his regular employer.

B. *Claim filing—partial unemployment.* Each individual claiming unemployment compensation for a week (or other claim period) during which, because of lack of work, he is working less than his normal customary full-time hours for his regular employer and is earning less than the earnings limit provided in the State law, shall not be required to file a claim for such week or other claim period earlier than 2 weeks from the date that wages are paid for such claim period or, if a low earnings report is required by the State law, from the date the employer furnished such report to the individual. State agencies may permit claims for partial unemployment to be filed either in person or by mail, except that in the circumstances set forth in section A 3, filing by mail must be permitted, and in the circumstances set forth in section A 2 b, filing in person may be required.

5002 *Requirement for Job Finding, Placement, and other Employment Services Designed To Satisfy Secretary's Interpretation*

A. Claims personnel are required to assure that each claimant is doing what a reasonable individual in his circumstances would do to obtain suitable work.

B. In the discretion of the State agency: 1. The claims personnel are required to give each claimant such necessary and appropriate assistance as they reasonably can in finding suitable work and at their discretion determine when more complete placement and employment services are necessary and appropriate for a claimant; and if they determine more complete services are necessary and appropriate, the claims personnel are to refer him to employment service personnel in the public employment office in which he has been filing claim(s), or, if he has been filing in a claims office, in the public employment office most accessible to him; *or*

2. All placement and employment services are required to be afforded to each claimant by employment service personnel in the public employment office most accessible to him in which case the claims personnel in the office in which the claimant files his claim are to refer him to the employment service personnel when placement or other employment services are necessary and appropriate for him.

C. The personnel to whom the State agency assigns the responsibilities outlined in paragraph B above are required to give claimants such job-finding assistance, placement, and other employment services as are necessary and appropriate to facilitate their return to suitable work as soon as possible.

In some circumstances, no such services or only limited services may be required. For example, if a claimant is on a short-term temporary layoff with a fixed return date, the only service necessary and appropriate to be given to him during the period of the layoff is a referral to suitable temporary work if such work is being performed in the labor market area.

Similarly, claimants whose unemployment is caused by a labor dispute presumably will return to work with their employer as soon as the labor dispute is settled. They generally do not need services, nor do individuals in occupations where placement customarily is made by other nonfee charging placement facilities such as unions and professional associations.

Claimants who fall within the classes which ordinarily would require limited services or no services shall, if they request placement and employment services, be afforded such services as are necessary and appropriate for them to obtain suitable work or to achieve their reasonable employment goals.

On the other hand, a claimant who is permanently separated from his job is likely to require some services. He may need only some direction in how to get a job; he may need placement services if he is in an occupation for which there is some demand in the labor market area; if his occupation is outdated, he may require counseling and referral to a suitable training course. The extent and character of the services to be given any particular claimant may change with the length of his unemployment and depend not only on his own circumstances and conditions, but also on the condition of the labor market in the area.

D. Claimants are required to report to employment service personnel, as directed, but such personnel and the claims personnel are required to so arrange and coordinate the contracts required of a claimant as not to place an unreasonable burden on him or unreasonably limit his opportunity to establish his rights to compensation. As a general rule, a claimant is not required to contact in person claims personnel or employment service personnel more frequently than once a week, unless he is directed to report more frequently for a specific service such as referral to a job or a training course or counseling which cannot be completed in one visit.

E. Employment service personnel are required to report promptly to claims personnel in the office in which the claimant files his claim(s): (1) his failure to apply for or accept work to which he was referred by such personnel or when known, by any other nonfee-charging placement facility such as a union or a professional association; and (2) any information which becomes available to it that may have a bearing on the claimant's ability to work or availability for work, or on the suitability of work to which he was referred or which was offered to him.

5004 *Evaluation of Alternative State Provisions*

If the State law provisions do not conform to the "suggested State law requirements" set forth in sections 5001 and 5002, but the State law contains alternative provisions, the Manpower Administrator, in collaboration with the State agency, will study the actual or anticipated affect of the alternative provisions. If the Manpower Administrator concludes that the alternative provisions satisfy the requirements of the Federal law as construed by the Secretary (see section 5000 B) he will so notify the State agency. If he does not so conclude, he will submit the matter to the Secretary. If the Secretary concludes that the alternative provisions satisfy such requirements, the State agency will be so notified. If the Secretary concludes that there is a question as to whether the alternative provisions satisfy such requirements, the State agency will be advised that unless the State law provisions are appropriately revised, a notice of hearing will be issued as required by the Code of Federal Regulations, title 20, section 601.5.

[55 FR 558, Jan. 5, 1990]

APPENDIX B TO PART 625—STANDARD FOR CLAIM DETERMINATIONS—SEPARATION INFORMATION

EMPLOYMENT SECURITY MANUAL (PART V, SECTIONS 6010–6015)

6010–6019 *Standard for Claim Determinations—Separation Information*

6010 *Federal Law Requirements.* Section 303(a)(1) of the Social Security Act requires that a State law include provision for: "Such methods of administration . . . as are found by the Secretary to be reasonably calculated to insure full payment of unemployment compensation when due."

Section 303(a)(3) of the Social Security Act requires that a State law include provision for: "Opportunity for a fair hearing before an impartial tribunal, for all individuals whose claims for unemployment compensation are denied."

Section 3304(a)(4) of the Federal Unemployment Tax Act and section 303(a)(5) of the Social Security Act require that a State law include provision for: "Expenditure of all money withdrawn from an unemployment fund of such State, in the payment of unemployment compensation . . . ."

Section 3306(h) of the Federal Unemployment Tax Act defines "compensation" as "cash benefits payable to individuals with respect to their unemployment."

6011 *Secretary's Interpretation of Federal Law Requirements.* The Secretary interprets the above sections to require that a State law include provisions which will insure that: A. Individuals who may be entitled to unemployment compensation are furnished such information as will reasonably afford them an opportunity to know, establish, and protect their rights under the unemployment compensation law of such State, and

B. The State agency obtains and records in time for the prompt determination and review of benefit claims such information as will reasonably insure the payment of benefits to individuals to whom benefits are due.

6012 *Criteria for Review of State Law Conformity with Federal Requirements.* In determining the conformity of a State law with the above requirements of the Federal Unemployment Tax Act and the Social Security Act as interpreted by the Secretary, the following criteria will be applied:

A. Is it required that individuals who may be entitled to unemployment compensation be furnished such information of their potential rights to benefits, including the manner and places of filing claims, the reasons for determinations, and their rights of appeal, as will insure them a reasonable opportunity to know, establish, and protect their rights under the law of the State?

B. Is the State agency required to obtain, in time for prompt determination of rights to benefits such information as will reasonably insure the payment of benefits to individuals to whom benefits are due?

C. Is the State agency required to keep records of the facts considered in reaching determinations of rights to benefits?

6013 *Claim Determinations Requirements Designed To Meet Department of Labor Criteria.*

A. *Investigation of claims.* The State agency is required to obtain promptly and prior to a determination of an individual's right to benefits, such facts pertaining thereto as will be sufficient reasonably to insure the payment of benefits when due.

This requirement embraces five separate elements:

1. It is the responsibility of the agency to take the initiative in the discovery of information. This responsibility may not be passed on to the claimant or the employer. In addition to the agency's own records, this information may be obtained from the worker, the employer, or other sources. If the information obtained in the first instance discloses no essential disagreement and provides a sufficient basis for a fair determination, no further investigation is necessary. If the information obtained from other sources differs essentially from that furnished by the claimant, the agency, in order to meet its responsibility, is required to inform the claimant of such information from other sources and to afford the claimant an opportunity to furnish any further facts he may have.

2. Evidentiary facts must be obtained as distinguished from ultimate facts or conclusions. That a worker was discharged for misconduct is an ultimate fact or conclusion; that he destroyed a machine upon which he was working is a primary or evidentiary fact, and the sort of fact that the requirement refers to.

3. The information obtained must be sufficient reasonably to insure the payment of benefits when due. In general, the investigation made by the agency must be complete enough to provide information upon which the agency may act with reasonable assurance that its decision is consistent with the unemployment compensation law. On the other hand, the investigation should not be so exhaustive and time-consuming as unduly to delay the payment of benefits and to result in excessive costs.

4. Information must be obtained promptly so that the payment of benefits is not unduly delayed.

5. If the State agency requires any particular evidence from the worker, it must give him a reasonable opportunity to obtain such evidence.

B. *Recording of facts.* The agency must keep a written record of the facts considered in reaching its determinations.

C. *Determination notices*

1. The agency must give each claimant a written notice of:

a. Any monetary determination with respect to his benefit year;

b. Any determination with respect to purging a disqualification if, under the State law, a condition or qualification must be satisfied with respect to each week of disqualification; but in lieu of giving written notice of each determination for each week in which it is determined that the claimant has met the requirements for purging, the agency may inform the claimant that he has purged the disqualification for a week by notation on his application identification card or otherwise in writing.

c. Any other determination which adversely affects[1] his rights to benefits, except

[1] A determination "adversely affects" claimant's right to benefits if it (1) results in a denial to him of benefits (including a cancellation of benefits or wage credits or any reduction in whole or in part below the weekly or maximum amount established by his monetary determination) for any week or other period; or (2) denies credit for a waiting week; or (3) applies any disqualification or penalty; or (4) determines that he has not satisfied a condition of eligibility, requalification for benefits, or purging a disqualification; or (5) determines that an overpayment has been made or orders repayment or recoupment of any sum paid to him; or (6) applies a previously determined overpayment, penalty, or order for repayment or recoupment; or (7) in any other way denies claimant a right to benefits under the State law.

that written notice of determination need not be given with respect to:

(1) A week in a benefit year for which the claimant's weekly benefit amount is reduced in whole or in part by earnings if, the first time in the benefit year that there is such a reduction, he is required to be furnished a booklet or leaflet containing the information set forth below in paragraph 2 f (1). However, a written notice of determination is required if: (a) there is a dispute concerning the reduction with respect to any week (e.g., as to the amount computed as the appropriate reduction, etc.); or (b) there is a change in the State law (or in the application thereof) affecting the reduction; or

(2) Any week in a benefit year subsequent to the first week in such benefit year in which benefits were denied, or reduced in whole or in part for reasons other than earnings, if denial or reduction for such subsequent week is based on the same reason and the same facts as for the first week, and if written notice of determination is required to be given to the claimant with respect to such first week, and with such notice of determination, he is required to be given a booklet or pamphlet containing the information set forth below in paragraphs 2 f (2) and 2 h. However, a written notice of determination is required if: (a) there is a dispute concerning the denial or reduction of benefits with respect to such week; or (b) there is a change in the State law (or in the application thereof) affecting the denial or reduction; or (c) there is a change in the amount of the reduction except as to the balance covered by the last reduction in a series of reductions.

NOTE: This procedure may be applied to determinations made with respect to any subsequent weeks for the same reason and on the basis of the same facts: (a) that claimant is unable to work, unavailable for work, or is disqualified under the labor dispute provision; and (b) reducing claimant's weekly benefit amount because of income other than earnings or offset by reason of overpayment.

2. The agency must include in written notices of determinations furnished to claimants sufficient information to enable them to understand the determinations, the reasons therefor, and their rights to protest, request reconsideration, or appeal.

The written notice of monetary determination must contain the information specified in the following items (except h) unless an item is specifically not applicable. A written notice of any other determination must contain the information specified in as many of the following items as are necessary to enable the claimant to understand the determination and to inform him of his appeal rights. Information specifically applicable to the individual claimant must be contained in the written notice of determination. Information of general application such as (but not limited to) the explanation of benefits for partial unemployment, information as to deductions, seasonality factors, and information as to the manner and place of taking an appeal, extension of the appeal period, and where to obtain information and assistance may be contained in a booklet or leaflet which is given the claimant with his monetary determination.

a. *Base period wages.* The statement concerning base-period wages must be in sufficient detail to show the basis of computation of eligibility and weekly and maximum benefit amounts. (If maximum benefits are allowed, it may not be necessary to show details of earnings.)

b. *Employer name.* The name of the employer who reported the wages is necessary so that the worker may check the wage transcript and know whether it is correct. If the worker is given only the employer number, he may not be able to check the accuracy of the wage transcript.

c. *Explanation of benefit formula—weekly and maximum benefit amounts.* Sufficient information must be given the worker so that he will understand how his weekly benefit amount, including allowances for dependents, and his maximum benefit amount were figured. If benefits are computed by means of a table contained in the law, the table must be furnished with the notice of determination whether benefits are granted or denied.

The written notice of determination must show clearly the weekly benefit amount and the maximum potential benefits to which the claimant is entitled.

The notice to a claimant found ineligible by reason of insufficient earnings in the base period must inform him clearly of the reason for ineligibility. An explanation of the benefit formula contained in a booklet or pamphlet should be given to each claimant at or prior to the time he receives written notice of a monetary determination.

d. *Benefit year.* An explanation of what is meant by the benefit year and identification of the claimant's benefit year must be included in the notice of determination.

e. *Information as to benefits for partial unemployment.* There must be included either in the written notice of determination or in a booklet or pamphlet accompanying the notice an explanation of the claimant's rights to partial benefits for any week with respect to which he is working less than his normal customary full-time workweek because of lack of work and for which he earns less than his weekly benefit amount or weekly benefit amount plus earnings, whichever is provided by the State law. If the explanation is contained in the notice of determination, reference to the item in the notice in which his weekly benefit amount is entered should be made.

f. *Deductions from weekly benefits*

(1) *Earnings.* Although written notice of determinations deducting earnings from a claimant's weekly benefit amount is generally not required (see paragraph 1 c(1) above), where written notice of determination is required (or given) it shall set forth the amount of earnings, the method of computing the deduction in sufficient detail to enable the claimant to verify the accuracy of the deduction, and his right to protest, request redetermination, and appeal. Where a written notice of determination is given to the claimant because there has been a change in the State law or in the application of the law, an explanation of the change shall be included.

Where claimant is not required to receive a written notice of determination, he must be given a booklet or pamphlet the first time in his benefit year that there is a deduction for earnings which shall include the following information:

(a) The method of computing deductions for earnings in sufficient detail to enable the claimant to verify the accuracy of the deduction;

(b) That he will not automatically be given a written notice of determination for a week with respect to which there is a deduction for earnings (unless there is a dispute concerning the reduction with respect to a week or there has been a change in the State law or in the application of the law affecting the deduction) but that he may obtain such a written notice upon request; and

(c) A clear statement of his right to protest, request a redetermination, and appeal from any determination deducting earnings from his weekly benefit amount even though he does not automatically receive a written notice of determination; and if the State law requires written notice of determination in order to effectuate a protest, redetermination, or appeal, he must be so advised and advised also that he must request a written notice of determination before he takes any such action.

(2) *Other deductions*

(a) A written notice of determination is required with respect to the first week in claimant's benefit year in which there is a reduction from his benefits for a reason other than earnings. This notice must describe the deduction made from claimaint's weekly benefit amount, the reason for the deduction, the method of computing it in sufficient detail to enable him to verify the accuracy of such deduction, and his right to protest, request redetermination, or appeal.

(b) A written notice of determination is not required for subsequent weeks that a deduction is made for the same reason and on the basis of the same facts, if the notice of determination pursuant to (2)(a), or a booklet or pamphlet given him with such notice explains (i) the several kinds of deductions which may be made under the State law (e.g., retirement pensions, vacation pay, and overpayments); (ii) the method of computing each kind of deduction in sufficient detail that claimant will be able to verify the accuracy of deductions made from his weekly benefit payments; (iii) any limitation on the amount of any deduction or the time in which any deduction may be made; (iv) that he will not automatically be given a written notice of determination for subsequent weeks with respect to which there is a deduction for the same reason and on the basis of the same facts, but that he may obtain a written notice of determination upon request; (v) his right to protest, request redetermination, or appeal with respect to subsequent weeks for which there is a reduction from his benefits for the same reason, and on the basis of the same facts even though he does not automatically receive a written notice of determination; and (vi) that if the State law requires written notice of determination in order to effectuate a protest, redetermination, or appeal, he must be so advised and advised also that he must request a written notice of determination before he takes any such action.

g. *Seasonality factors.* If the individual's determination is affected by seasonality factors under the State law, an adequate explanation must be made. General explanations of seasonality factors which may affect determinations for subsequent weeks may be included in a booklet or pamphlet given claimant with his notice of monetary determination.

h. *Disqualification or ineligibility.* If a disqualification is imposed, or if the claimant is declared ineligible for one or more weeks, he must be given not only a statement of the period of disqualification or ineligibility and the amount of wage-credit reductions, if any, but also an explanation of the reason for the ineligibility or disqualification. This explanation must be sufficiently detailed so that he will understand why he is ineligible or why he has been disqualified, and what he must do in order to requalify for benefits or purge the disqualification. The statement must be individualized to indicate the facts upon which the determination was based, e.g., state, "It is found that you left your work with Blank Company because you were tired of working; the separation was voluntary, and the reason does not constitute good cause," rather than merely the phrase "voluntary quit." Checking a box as to the reason for the disqualification is not a sufficiently detailed explanation. However, this statement of the reason for the disqualification need not be a restatement of all facts considered in arriving at the determination.

1. *Appeal rights.* The claimant must be given information with respect to his appeal rights.

(1) The following information shall be included in the notice of determination:

(a) A statement that he may appeal or, if the State law requires or permits a protest or redetermination before an appeal, that he may protest or request a redetermination.

(b) The period within which an appeal, protest, or request for redetermination must be filed. The number of days provided by statute must be shown as well as either the beginning date or ending date of the period. (It is recommended that the ending date of the appeal period be shown, as this is the more understandable of the alternatives.)

(2) The following information must be included either in the notice of determination or in separate informational material referred to in the notice:

(a) The manner in which the appeal, protest, or request for redetermination must be filed, e.g., by signed letter, written statement, or on a prescribed form, and the place or places to which the appeal, protest, or request for redetermination may be mailed or hand-delivered.

(b) An explanation of any circumstances (such as nonworkdays, good cause, etc.) which will extend the period for the appeal, protest, or request for redetermination beyond the date stated or identified in the notice of determination.

(c) That any further information claimant may need or desire can be obtained together with assistance in filing his appeal, protest, or request for redetermination from the local office.

If the information is given in separate material, the notice of determination would adequately refer to such material if it said, for example, "For other information about your (appeal), (protest), (redetermination) rights, see pages ____ to ____ of the ______________ (name of pamphlet or booklet) heretofore furnished to you."

6014 *Separation Information Requirements Designed To Meet Department of Labor Criteria*

A. *Information to agency*. Where workers are separated, employers are required to furnish the agency promptly, either upon agency request or upon such separation, a notice describing the reasons for and the circumstances of the separation and any additional information which might affect a claimant's right to benefits. Where workers are working less than full time, employers are required to furnish the agency promptly, upon agency request, information concerning a claimant's hours of work and his wages during the claim periods involved, and other facts which might affect a claimant's eligibility for benefits during such periods.

When workers are separated and the notices are obtained on a request basis, or when workers are working less than full time and the agency requests information, it is essential to the prompt processing of claims that the request be sent out promptly after the claim is filed and the employer be given a specific period within which to return the notice, preferably within 2 working days.

When workers are separated and notices are obtained upon separation, it is essential that the employer be required to send the notice to the agency with sufficient promptness to insure that, if a claim is filed, it may be processed promptly. Normally, it is desirable that such a notice be sent to the central office of the agency, since the employer may not know in which local office the worker will file his claim. The usual procedure is for the employer to give the worker a copy of the notice sent by the employer to the agency.

B. *Information of worker*. 1. *Information required to be given*. Employers are required to give their employees information and instructions concerning the employees' potential rights to benefits and concerning registration for work and filing claims for benefits.

The information furnished to employees under such a requirement need not be elaborate; it need only be adequate to insure that the worker who is separated or who is working less than full time knows he is potentially eligible for benefits and is informed as to what he is to do or where he is to go to file his claim and register for work. When he files his claim, he can obtain more detailed information.

In States that do not require employers to furnish periodically to the State agency detailed reports of the wages paid to their employees, each employer is required to furnish to his employees information as to (a) the name under which he is registered by the State agency, (b) the address where he maintains his payroll records, and (c) the workers' need for this information if and when they file claims for benefits.

2. *Methods for giving information*. The information and instructions required above may be given in any of the following ways:

a. *Posters prominently displayed in the employer's establishment*. The State agency should supply employers with a sufficient number of posters for distribution throughout their places of business and should see that the posters are conspicuously displayed at all times.

b. *Leaflets*. Leaflets distributed either periodically or at the time of separation or reduction of hours. The State agency should supply employers with a sufficient number of leaflets.

c. *Individual notices*. Individual notices given to each employee at the time of separation or reduction in hours.

It is recommended that the State agency's publicity program be used to supplement the employer-information requirements. Such a program should stress the availability and location of claim-filing offices and the importance of visiting those offices whenever the worker is unemployed, wishes to apply for benefits, and to seek a job.

6015 *Evaluation of Alternative State Provisions with Respect to Claim Determinations and Separation Information.* If the State law provisions do not conform to the suggested requirements set forth in sections 6013 and 6014, but the State law contains alternative provisions, the Bureau of Employment Security, in collaboration with the State agency, will study the actual or anticipated effects of the alternative provisions. If the Administrator of the Bureau concludes that the alternative provisions satisfy the criteria in section 6012, he will so notify the State agency. If the Administrator of the Bureau does not so conclude, he will submit the matter to the Secretary. If the Secretary concludes that the alternative provisions satisfy the criteria in section 6012, the State agency will be so notified. If the Secretary concludes that there is a question as to whether the alternative provisions satisfy the criteria, the State agency will be advised that unless the State law provisions are appropriately revised, a notice of hearing will be issued as required by the Code of Federal Regulations, title 20, section 601.5.

[55 FR 559, Jan. 5, 1990]

Appendix C to Part 625—Standard for Fraud and Overpayment Detection

Employment Security Manual (Part V, Sections 7510–7515)

7510–7519 *Standard for Fraud and Overpayment Detection*

7510 *Federal Law Requirements.* Section 303(a)(1) of the Social Security Act requires that a State law include provision for:

"Such methods of administration * * * as are found by the Secretary to be reasonably calculated to insure full payment of unemployment compensation when due."

Section 1603(a)(4) of the Internal Revenue Code and section 3030(a)(5) of the Social Security Act require that a State law include provision for:

"Expenditure of all money withdrawn from an unemployment fund of such State, in the payment of unemployment compensation * * *"

Section 1607(h) of the Internal Revenue Code defines "compensation" as "cash benefits payable to individuals with respect to their unemployment."

7511 *The Secretary's Interpretation of Federal Law Requirements.* The Secretary of Labor interprets the above sections to require that a State law include provision for such methods of administration as are, within reason, calculated (1) to detect benefits paid through error by the agency or through willful misrepresentation or error by the claimant or others, and (2) to deter claimants from obtaining benefits through willful misrepresentation.

7513 *Criteria for Review of State Conformity With Federal Requirements.* In determining State conformity with the above requirements of the Internal Revenue Code and the Social Security Act, as interpreted by the Secretary of Labor, the following criteria will be applied:

A. *Are investigations required to be made after the payment of benefits, (or, in the case of interstate claims, are investigations made by the agent State after the processing of claims) as to claimants' entitlement to benefits paid to them in a sufficient proportion of cases to test the effectiveness of the agency's procedures for the prevention of payments which are not due? To carry out investigations, has the agency assigned to some individual or unit, as a basic function, the responsibility of making or functionally directing such investigations?*

Explanation: It is not feasible to prescribe the extent to which the above activities are required; however, they should always be carried on to such an extent that they will show whether or not error or willful misrepresentation is increasing or decreasing, and will reveal problem areas. The extent and nature of the above activities should be varied according to the seriousness of the problem in the State. The responsible individual or unit should:

1. Check paid claims for overpayment and investigate for willful misrepresentation or, alternatively, advise and assist the operating units in the performance of such functions, or both;
2. Perform consultative services with respect to methods and procedures for the prevention and detection of fraud; and
3. Perform other services which are closely related to the above.

Although a State agency is expected to make a full-time assignment of responsibility to a unit or individual to carry on the functions described above, a small State agency might make these functions a part-time responsibility of one individual. In connection with the detection of overpayments, such a unit or individual might, for example:

(a) Investigate information on suspected benefit fraud received from any agency personnel, and from sources outside the agency, including anonymous complaints;

(b) Investigate information secured from comparisons of benefit payments with employment records to detect cases of concurrent working (whether in covered or non-covered work) and claiming of benefits (including benefit payments in which the agency acted as agency for another State).

The benefit fraud referred to herein may involve employers, agency employees, and witnesses, as well as claimants.

Comparisons of benefit payments with employment records are commonly made either by post-audit or by industry surveys. The so-called "post-audit" is a matching of central office wage-record files against benefit payments for the same period. "Industry surveys" or "mass audits" are done in some States by going directly to employers for pay-roll information to be checked against concurrent benefit lists. A plan

A. of investigation based on a sample post-audit will be considered as partial fulfillment of the investigation program; it would need to be supplemented by other methods capable of detecting overpayments to persons who have moved into noncovered occupations or are claiming interstate benefits.

B. *Are adequate records maintained by which the results of investigations may be evaluated?*

Explanation: To meet this criterion, the State agency will be expected to maintain records of all its activities in the detection of overpayments, showing whether attributable to error or willful misrepresentation, measuring the results obtained through various methods, and noting the remedial action taken in each case. The adequacy and effectiveness of various methods of checking for willful misrepresentation can be evaluated only if records are kept of the results obtained. Internal reports on fraudulent and erroneous overpayments are needed by State agencies for self-evaluation. Detailed records should be maintained in order that the State agency may determine, for example, which of several methods of checking currently used are the most productive. Such records also will provide the basis for drawing a clear distinction between fraud and error.

C. *Does the agency take adequate action with respect to publicity concerning willful misrepresentation and its legal consequences to deter fraud by claimants?*

Explanation: To meet this criterion, the State agency must issue adequate material on claimant eligibility requirements and must take necessary action to obtain publicity on the legal consequences of willful misrepresentation or willful nondisclosure of facts.

Public announcements on convictions and resulting penalties for fraud are generally considered necessary as a deterrent to other persons, and to inform the public that the agency is carrying on an effective program to prevent fraud. This alone is not considered adequate publicity. It is important that information be circulated which will explain clearly and understandably the claimant's rights, and the obligations which he must fulfill to be eligible for benefits. Leaflets for distribution and posters placed in local offices are appropriate media for such information.

7515 *Evaluation of Alternative State Provisions with Respect to Erroneous and Illegal Payments.* If the methods of administration provided for by the State law do not conform to the suggested methods of meeting the requirements set forth in section 7511, but a State law does provide for alternative methods of administration designed to accomplish the same results, the Bureau of Employment Security, in collaboration with the State agency, will study the actual or anticipated effect of the alternative methods of administration. If the Bureau concludes that the alternative methods satisfy the criteria in section 7513, it will so notify the State agency. If the Bureau does not so conclude, it will submit to the Secretary the results of the study for his determination of whether the State's alternative methods of administration meet the criteria.

[55 FR 562, Jan. 5, 1990]

PARTS 626–634 [RESERVED]

PARTS 636–638 [RESERVED]

PART 639—WORKER ADJUSTMENT AND RETRAINING NOTIFICATION

Sec.

AUTHORITY: 29 U.S.C. 2107(a).

SOURCE: 54 FR 16064, Apr. 20, 1989, unless otherwise noted.

§ 639.1 Purpose and scope.

(a) *Purpose of WARN.* The Worker Adjustment and Retraining Notification Act (WARN or the Act) provides protection to workers, their families and communities by requiring employers to provide notification 60 calendar days in advance of plant closings and mass layoffs. Advance notice provides workers and their families some transition time to adjust to the prospective loss of employment, to seek and obtain alternative jobs and, if necessary, to enter skill training or retraining that will allow these workers to successfully compete in the job market. WARN also provides for notice to State dislocated worker units so that dislocated worker assistance can be promptly provided.

(b) *Scope of these regulations.* These regulations establish basic definitions and rules for giving notice, implementing the provisions of WARN. The Department's objective is to establish clear principles and broad guidelines which can be applied in specific circumstances. However, the Department recognizes that Federal rulemaking cannot address the multitude of industry and company-specific situations in which advance notice will be given.

(c) *Notice encouraged where not required.* Section 7 of the Act states:

It is the sense of Congress that an employer who is not required to comply with the notice requirements of section 3 should, to the extent possible, provide notice to its employees about a proposal to close a plant or permanently reduce its workforce.

(d) *WARN enforcement.* Enforcement of WARN will be through the courts, as provided in section 5 of the statute. Employees, their representatives and units of local government may initiate civil actions against employers believed to be in violation of §3 of the Act. The Department of Labor has no legal standing in any enforcement action and, therefore, will not be in a position to issue advisory opinions of specific cases. The Department will provide assistance in understanding these regulations and may revise them from time to time as may be necessary.

(e) *Notice in ambiguous situations.* It is civically desirable and it would appear to be good business practice for an employer to provide advance notice to its workers or unions, local government and the State when terminating a significant number of employees. In practical terms, there are some questions and ambiguities of interpretation inherent in the application of WARN to business practices in the market economy that cannot be addressed in these regulations. It is therefore prudent for employers to weigh the desirability of advance notice against the possibility of expensive and time-consuming litigation to resolve disputes where notice has not been given. The Department encourages employers to give notice in all circumstances.

(f) *Coordination with job placement and retraining programs.* The Department, through these regulations and through the Trade Adjustment Assistance Program (TAA) and Economic Dislocation and Worker Adjustment Assistance Act (EDWAA) regulations, encourages maximum coordination of the actions and activities of these programs to assure that the negative impact of dislocation on workers is lessened to the extent possible. By providing for notice to the State dislocated worker unit, WARN notice begins the process of assisting workers who will be dislocated.

(g) *WARN not to supersede other laws and contracts.* The provisions of WARN do not supersede any laws or collective bargaining agreements that provide for additional notice or additional rights and remedies. If such law or agreement provides for a longer notice period, WARN notice shall run concurrently with that additional notice period. Collective bargaining agreements may be used to clarify or amplify the terms and conditions of WARN, but may not reduce WARN rights.

§ 639.2 What does WARN require?

WARN requires employers who are planning a plant closing or a mass layoff to give affected employees at least 60 days' notice of such an employment action. While the 60-day period is the minimum for advance notice, this provision is not intended to discourage employers from voluntarily providing longer periods of advance notice. Not all plant closings and layoffs are subject to the Act, and certain employment thresholds must be reached before the Act applies. WARN sets out specific exemptions, and provides for a reduction in the notification period in particular circumstances. Damages and civil penalties can be assessed against employers who violate the Act.

§ 639.3 Definitions.

(a) *Employer.* (1) The term "employer" means any business enterprise that employs—

(i) 100 or more employees, excluding part-time employees; or

(ii) 100 or more employees, including part-time employees, who in the aggregate work at least 4,000 hours per week, exclusive of hours of overtime.

Workers on temporary layoff or on leave who have a reasonable expectation of recall are counted as employees. An employee has a "reasonable expectation of recall" when he/she understands, through notification or through industry practice, that his/her employment with the employer has been temporarily interrupted and that he/she will be recalled to the same or to a similar job. The term "employer" includes non-profit organizations of the requisite size. Regular Federal, State, local and federally recognized Indian tribal governments are not covered. However, the term "employer" includes public and quasi-public entities which engage in business (*i.e.*, take part in a commercial or industrial enterprise, supply a service or good on a mercantile basis, or provide independent management of public assets, raising revenue and making desired investments), and which are separately organized from the regular government, which have their own governing bodies and which have independent authority to manage their personnel and assets.

(2) Under existing legal rules, independent contractors and subsidiaries which are wholly or partially owned by a parent company are treated as separate employers or as a part of the parent or contracting company depending upon the degree of their independence from the parent. Some of the factors to be considered in making this determination are (i) common ownership, (ii) common directors and/or officers, (iii) de facto exercise of control, (iv) unity of personnel policies emanating from a common source, and (v) the dependency of operations.

(3) Workers, other than part-time workers, who are exempt from notice under section 4 of WARN are nonetheless counted as employees for purposes of determining coverage as an employer.

(4) An employer may have one or more sites of employment under common ownership or control. An example would be a major auto maker which has dozens of automobile plants throughout the country. Each plant would be considered a site of employment, but there is only one "employer", the auto maker.

(b) *Plant closing.* The term "plant closing" means the permanent or temporary shutdown of a "single site of employment", or one or more "facilities or operating units" within a single site of employment, if the shutdown results in an "employment loss" during *any 30-day period* at the single site of employment for *50 or more* employees, excluding any part-time employees. An employment action that results in the effective cessation of production or the work performed by a unit, even if a few employees remain, is a shutdown. A "temporary shutdown" triggers the notice requirement only if there are a sufficient number of terminations, layoffs exceeding 6 months, or reductions in hours of work as specified under the definition of "employment loss."

(c) *Mass layoff.* (1) The term "mass layoff" means a reduction in force which first, is not the result of a plant closing, and second, results in an employment loss at the single site of employment during *any 30-day period* for:

(i) *At least 33 percent* of the active employees, excluding part-time employees, and

(ii) *At least 50 employees,* excluding part-time employees.

Where 500 or more employees (excluding part-time employees) are affected, the 33% requirement does not apply, and notice is required if the other criteria are met. Plant closings involve employment loss which results from the shutdown of one or more distinct units within a single site or the entire site. A mass layoff involves employment loss, regardless of whether one or more units are shut down at the site.

(2) Workers, other than part-time workers, who are exempt from notice under section 4 of WARN are nonetheless counted as employees for purposes of determining coverage as a plant closing or mass layoff. For example, if an employer closes a temporary project on which 10 permanent and 40 temporary workers are employed, a covered plant closing has occurred although only 10 workers are entitled to notice.

(d) *Representative.* The term "representative" means an exclusive representative of employees within the meaning of section 9(a) or 8(f) of the

National Labor Relations Act or section 2 of the Railway Labor Act.

(e) *Affected employees.* The term "affected employees" means employees who may reasonably be expected to experience an employment loss as a consequence of a proposed plant closing or mass layoff by their employer. This includes individually identifiable employees who will likely lose their jobs because of bumping rights or other factors, to the extent that such individual workers reasonably can be identified at the time notice is required to be given. The term "affected employees" includes managerial and supervisory employees, but does not include business partners. Consultant or contract employees who have a separate employment relationship with another employer and are paid by that other employer, or who are self-employed, are not "affected employees" of the business to which they are assigned. In addition, for purposes of determining whether coverage thresholds are met, either incumbent workers in jobs being eliminated or, if known 60 days in advance, the actual employees who suffer an employment loss may be counted.

(f) *Employment loss.* (1) The term "employment loss" means (i) an employment termination, other than a discharge for cause, voluntary departure, or retirement, (ii) a layoff exceeding 6 months, or (iii) a reduction in hours of work of individual employees of more than 50% during each month of any 6-month period.

(2) Where a termination or a layoff (see paragraphs (f)(1)(i) and (ii) of this section) is involved, an employment loss does not occur when an employee is reassigned or transferred to employer-sponsored programs, such as retraining or job search activities, as long as the reassignment does not constitute a constructive discharge or other involuntary termination.

(3) An employee is not considered to have experienced an employment loss if the closing or layoff is the result of the relocation or consolidation of part or all of the employer's business and, prior to the closing or layoff—

(i) The employer offers to transfer the employee to a different site of employment within a reasonable commuting distance with no more than a 6-month break in employment, or

(ii) The employer offers to transfer the employee to any other site of employment regardless of distance with no more than a 6-month break in employment, and the employee accepts within 30 days of the offer or of the closing or layoff, whichever is later.

(4) A "relocation or consolidation" of part or all of an employer's business, for purposes of paragraph § 639.3(h)(4), means that some definable business, whether customer orders, product lines, or operations, is transferred to a different site of employment and that transfer results in a plant closing or mass layoff.

(g) *Unit of local government.* The term "unit of local government" means any general purpose political subdivision of a State, which has the power to levy taxes and spend funds and which also has general corporate and police powers. When a covered employment site is located in more than one unit of local government, the employer must give notice to the unit to which it determines it directly paid the highest taxes for the year preceding the year for which the determination is made. All local taxes directly paid to the local government should be aggregated for this purpose.

(h) *Part-time employee.* The term "part-time" employee means an employee who is employed for an average of fewer than 20 hours per week or who has been employed for fewer than 6 of the 12 months preceding the date on which notice is required, including workers who work full-time. This term may include workers who would traditionally be understood as "seasonal" employees. The period to be used for calculating whether a worker has worked "an average of fewer than 20 hours per week" is the shorter of the actual time the worker has been employed or the most recent 90 days.

(i) *Single site of employment.* (1) A single site of employment can refer to either a single location or a group of contiguous locations. Groups of structures which form a campus or industrial park, or separate facilities across the street from one another, may be considered a single site of employment.

(2) There may be several single sites of employment within a single building, such as an office building, if separate employers conduct activities within such a building. For example, an office building housing 50 different businesses will contain 50 single sites of employment. The offices of each employer will be its single site of employment.

(3) Separate buildings or areas which are not directly connected or in immediate proximity may be considered a single site of employment if they are in reasonable geographic proximity, used for the same purpose, and share the same staff and equipment. An example is an employer who manages a number of warehouses in an area but who regularly shifts or rotates the same employees from one building to another.

(4) Non-contiguous sites in the same geographic area which do not share the same staff or operational purpose should not be considered a single site. For example, assembly plants which are located on opposite sides of a town and which are managed by a single employer are separate sites if they employ different workers.

(5) Contiguous buildings owned by the same employer which have separate management, produce different products, and have separate workforces are considered separate single sites of employment.

(6) For workers whose primary duties require travel from point to point, who are outstationed, or whose primary duties involve work outside any of the employer's regular employment sites (e.g., railroad workers, bus drivers, salespersons), the single site of employment to which they are assigned as their home base, from which their work is assigned, or to which they report will be the single site in which they are covered for WARN purposes.

(7) Foreign sites of employment are not covered under WARN. U.S. workers at such sites are counted to determine whether an employer is covered as an employer under § 639.3(a).

(8) The term "single site of employment" may also apply to truly unusual organizational situations where the above criteria do not reasonably apply. The application of this definition with the intent to evade the purpose of the Act to provide notice is not acceptable.

(j) *Facility or operating unit.* The term "facility" refers to a building or buildings. The term "operating unit" refers to an organizationally or operationally distinct product, operation, or specific work function within or across facilities at the single site.

(k) *State dislocated worker unit.* The term "State dislocated worker unit" means a unit designated or created in each State by the Governor under title III of the Job Training Partnership Act, as amended by EDWAA.

(l) *State.* For the purpose of WARN, the term "State" includes the 50 States, the District of Columbia, the Commonwealth of Puerto Rico, and the U.S. Virgin Islands.

§ 639.4 Who must give notice?

Section 3(a) of WARN states that "an employer shall not order a plant closing or mass layoff until the end of a 60-day period after the employer serves written notice of such an order * * *." Therefore, an employer who is anticipating carrying out a plant closing or mass layoff is required to give notice to affected employees or their representative(s), the State dislocated worker unit and the chief elected official of a unit of local government. (See definitions in § 639.3 of this part.)

(a) It is the responsibility of the employer to decide the most appropriate person within the employer's organization to prepare and deliver the notice to affected employees or their representative(s), the State dislocated worker unit and the chief elected official of a unit of local government. In most instances, this may be the local site plant manager, the local personnel director or a labor relations officer.

(b) An employer who has previously announced and carried out a short-term layoff (6 months or less) which is being extended beyond 6 months due to business circumstances (including unforeseeable changes in price or cost) not reasonably foreseeable at the time of the initial layoff is required to give notice when it becomes reasonably foreseeable that the extension is required. A layoff extending beyond 6 months from the date the layoff commenced for any other reason shall be treated as an employment loss from the date of its commencement.

(c) In the case of the sale of part or all of a business, section 2(b)(1) of WARN defines who the "employer" is. The seller is responsible for providing notice of any plant closing or mass layoff which takes place up to and including the effective date (time) of the sale, and the buyer is responsible for providing notice of any plant closing or mass layoff that takes place thereafter. Affected employees are always entitled to notice; at all times the employer is responsible for providing notice.

(1) If the seller is made aware of any definite plans on the part of the buyer to carry out a plant closing or mass layoff within 60 days of purchase, the seller may give notice to affected employees as an agent of the buyer, if so empowered. If the seller does not give notice, the buyer is, nevertheless, responsible to give notice. If the seller gives notice as the buyer's agent, the responsibility for notice still remains with the buyer.

(2) It may be prudent for the buyer and seller to determine the impacts of the sale on workers, and to arrange between them for advance notice to be given to affected employees or their representative(s), if a mass layoff or plant closing is planned.

§ 639.5 When must notice be given?

(a) *General rule.* (1) With certain exceptions discussed in paragraphs (b), (c) and (d) of this section and in § 639.9 of this part, notice must be given at least 60 calendar days prior to any planned plant closing or mass layoff, as defined in these regulations. When all employees are not terminated on the same date, the date of the first individual termination within the statutory 30-day or 90-day period triggers the 60-day notice requirement. A worker's last day of employment is considered the date of that worker's layoff. The first and each subsequent group of terminees are entitled to a full 60 days' notice. In order for an employer to decide whether issuing notice is required, the employer should—

(i) Look ahead 30 days and behind 30 days to determine whether employment actions both taken and planned will, in the aggregate for any 30-day period, reach the minimum numbers for a plant closing or a mass layoff and thus trigger the notice requirement; and

(ii) Look ahead 90 days and behind 90 days to determine whether employment actions both taken and planned each of which separately is not of sufficient size to trigger WARN coverage will, in the aggregate for any 90-day period, reach the minimum numbers for a plant closing or a mass layoff and thus trigger the notice requirement. An employer is not, however, required under section 3(d) to give notice if the employer demonstrates that the separate employment losses are the result of separate and distinct actions and causes, and are not an attempt to evade the requirements of WARN.

(2) The point in time at which the number of employees is to be measured for the purpose of determining coverage is the date the first notice is required to be given. If this "snapshot" of the number of employees employed on that date is clearly unrepresentative of the ordinary or average employment level, then a more representative number can be used to determine coverage. Examples of unrepresentative employment levels include cases when the level is near the peak or trough of an employment cycle or when large upward or downward shifts in the number of employees occur around the time notice is to be given. A more representative number may be an average number of employees over a recent period of time or the number of employees on an alternative date which is more representative of normal employment levels. Alternative methods cannot be used to evade the purpose of WARN, and should only be used in unusual circumstances.

(b) *Transfers.* (1) Notice is not required in certain cases involving transfers, as described under the definition of "employment loss" at § 639.3(f) of this part.

(2) An offer of reassignment to a different site of employment should not be deemed to be a "transfer" if the new job constitutes a constructive discharge.

(3) The meaning of the term "reasonable commuting distance" will vary with local and industry conditions. In determining what is a "reasonable

commuting distance", consideration should be given to the following factors: geographic accessibility of the place of work, the quality of the roads, customarily available transportation, and the usual travel time.

(4) In cases where the transfer is beyond reasonable commuting distance, the employer may become liable for failure to give notice if an offer to transfer is not accepted within 30 days of the offer or of the closing or layoff (whichever is later). Depending upon when the offer of transfer was made by the employer, the normal 60-day notice period may have expired and the plant closing or mass layoff may have occurred. An employer is, therefore, well advised to provide 60-day advance notice as part of the transfer offer.

(c) *Temporary employment.* (1) No notice is required if the closing is of a temporary facility, or if the closing or layoff is the result of the completion of a particular project or undertaking, and the affected employees were hired with the understanding that their employment was limited to the duration of the facility or the project or undertaking.

(2) Employees must clearly understand at the time of hire that their employment is temporary. When such understandings exist will be determined by reference to employment contracts, collective bargaining agreements, or employment practices of an industry or a locality, but the burden of proof will lie with the employer to show that the temporary nature of the project or facility was clearly communicated should questions arise regarding the temporary employment understandings.

(3) Employers in agriculture and construction frequently hire workers for harvesting, processing, or for work on a particular building or project. Such work may be seasonal but recurring. Such work falls under this exemption if the workers understood at the time they were hired that their work was temporary. In uncertain situations, it may be prudent for employers to clarify temporary work understandings in writing when workers are hired. The same employers may also have permanent employees who work on a variety of jobs and tasks continuously through most of the calendar year. Such employees are not included under this exemption. Giving written notice that a project is temporary will not convert permanent employment into temporary work, making jobs exempt from WARN.

(4) Certain jobs may be related to a specific contract or order. Whether such jobs are temporary depends on whether the contract or order is part of a long-term relationship. For example, an aircraft manufacturer hires workers to produce a standard airplane for the U.S. fleet under a contract with the U.S. Air Force with the expectation that its contract will continue to be renewed during the foreseeable future. The employees of this manufacturer would not be considered temporary.

(d) *Strikes or lockouts.* The statute provides an exemption for strikes and lockouts which are not intended to evade the requirements of the Act. A lockout occurs when, for tactical or defensive reasons during the course of collective bargaining or during a labor dispute, an employer lawfully refuses to utilize some or all of its employees for the performance of available work. A lockout not related to collective bargaining which is intended as a subterfuge to evade the Act does not qualify for this exemption. A plant closing or mass layoff at a site of employment where a strike or lockout is taking place, which occurs for reasons unrelated to a strike or lockout, is not covered by this exemption. An employer need not give notice when permanently replacing a person who is deemed to be an economic striker under the National Labor Relations Act. Non-striking employees at the same single site of employment who experience a covered employment loss as a result of a strike are entitled to notice; however, situations in which a strike or lockout affects non-striking employees at the same plant may constitute an unforeseeable business circumstance, as discussed in § 639.9, and reduced notice may apply. Similarly, the "faltering company" exception, also discussed in § 639.9 may apply in strike situations. Where a union which is on strike represents more than one bargaining unit at the single site, non-strikers includes the non-striking bargaining unit(s).

Notice also is due to those workers who are not a part of the bargaining unit(s) which is involved in the labor negotiations that led to the lockout. Employees at other plants which have not been struck, but at which covered plant closings or mass layoffs occur as a direct or indirect result of a strike or lockout are not covered by the strike/lockout exemption. The unforeseeable business circumstances exception to 60 days' notice also may apply to these closings or layoffs at other plants.

§ 639.6 Who must receive notice?

Section 3(a) of WARN provides for notice to each representative of the affected employees as of the time notice is required to be given or, if there is no such representative at that time, to each affected employee. Notice also must be served on the State dislocated worker unit and the chief elected official of the unit of local government within which a closing or layoff is to occur. Section 2(b)(1) of the Act states that "any person who is an employee of the seller (other than a parttime employee) as of the effective date [time] of the sale shall be considered an employee of the purchaser immediately after the effective date [time] of the sale." This provision preserves the notice rights of the employees of a business that has been sold, but creates no other employment rights. Although a technical termination of the seller's employees may be deemed to have occurred when a sale becomes effective, WARN notice is only required where the employees, in fact, experience a covered employment loss.

(a) *Representative(s) of affected employees.* Written notice is to be served upon the chief elected officer of the exclusive representative(s) or bargaining agent(s) of affected employees at the time of the notice. If this person is not the same as the officer of the local union(s) representing affected employees, it is recommended that a copy also be given to the local union official(s).

(b) *Affected employees.* Notice is required to be given to employees who may reasonably be expected to experience an employment loss. This includes employees who will likely lose their jobs because of bumping rights or other factors, to the extent that such workers can be identified at the time notice is required to be given. If, at the time notice is required to be given, the employer cannot identify the employee who may reasonably be expected to experience an employment loss due to the elimination of a particular position, the employer must provide notice to the incumbent in that position. While part-time employees are not counted in determining whether plant closing or mass layoff thresholds are reached, such workers are due notice.

(c) *State dislocated worker unit.* Notice is to be served upon the State dislocated worker unit. Since the States are restructuring to implement training under EDWAA, service of notice upon the State Governor constitutes service upon the State dislocated worker unit until such time as the Governor makes public State procedures for serving notice to this unit.

(d) *Chief elected official of the unit of local government.* The identity of the chief elected official will vary according to the local government structure. In the case of elected boards, the notice is to be served upon the board's chairperson.

§ 639.7 What must the notice contain?

(a) *Notice must be specific.* (1) All notice must be specific.

(2) Where voluntary notice has been given more than 60 days in advance, but does not contain all of the required elements set out in this section, the employer must ensure that all of the information required by this section is provided in writing to the parties listed in § 639.6 at least 60 days in advance of a covered employment action.

(3) Notice may be given conditional upon the occurrence or nonoccurrence of an event, such as the renewal of a major contract, only when the event is definite and the consequences of its occurrence or nonoccurrence will necessarily, in the normal course of business, lead to a covered plant closing or mass layoff less than 60 days after the event. For example, if the non-renewal of a major contract will lead to the closing of the plant that produces the articles supplied under the contract 30 days after the contract expires, the employer may give notice at least 60 days in advance of the projected closing

date which states that if the contract is not renewed, the plant closing will occur on the projected date. The notice must contain each of the elements set out in this section.

(4) The information provided in the notice shall be based on the best information available to the employer at the time the notice is served. It is not the intent of the regulations, that errors in the information provided in a notice that occur because events subsequently change or that are minor, inadvertent errors are to be the basis for finding a violation of WARN.

(b) As used in this section, the term "date" refers to a specific date or to a 14-day period during which a separation or separations are expected to occur. If separations are planned according to a schedule, the schedule should indicate the specific dates on which or the beginning date of each 14-day period during which any separations are expected to occur. Where a 14-day period is used, notice must be given at least 60 days in advance of the first day of the period.

(c) Notice to each representative of affected employees is to contain:

(1) The name and address of the employment site where the plant closing or mass layoff will occur, and the name and telephone number of a company official to contact for further information;

(2) A statement as to whether the planned action is expected to be permanent or temporary and, if the entire plant is to be closed, a statement to that effect;

(3) The expected date of the first separation and the anticipated schedule for making separations;

(4) The job titles of positions to be affected and the names of the workers currently holding affected jobs.

The notice may include additional information useful to the employees such as information on available dislocated worker assistance, and, if the planned action is expected to be temporary, the estimated duration, if known.

(d) Notice to each affected employee who does not have a representative is to be written in language understandable to the employees and is to contain:

(1) A statement as to whether the planned action is expected to be permanent or temporary and, if the entire plant is to be closed, a statement to that effect;

(2) The expected date when the plant closing or mass layoff will commence and the expected date when the individual employee will be separated;

(3) An indication whether or not bumping rights exist;

(4) The name and telephone number of a company official to contact for further information.

The notice may include additional information useful to the employees such as information on available dislocated worker assistance, and, if the planned action is expected to be temporary, the estimated duration, if known.

(e) The notices separately provided to the State dislocated worker unit and to the chief elected official of the unit of local government are to contain:

(1) The name and address of the employment site where the plant closing or mass layoff will occur, and the name and telephone number of a company official to contact for further information;

(2) A statement as to whether the planned action is expected to be permanent or temporary and, if the entire plant is to be closed, a statement to that effect;

(3) The expected date of the first separation, and the anticipated schedule for making separations;

(4) The job titles of positions to be affected, and the number of affected employees in each job classification;

(5) An indication as to whether or not bumping rights exist;

(6) The name of each union representing affected employees, and the name and address of the chief elected officer of each union.

The notice may include additional information useful to the employees such as a statement of whether the planned action is expected to be temporary and, if so, its expected duration.

(f) As an alternative to the notices outlined in paragraph (e) above, an employer may give notice to the State dislocated worker unit and to the unit of local government by providing them with a written notice stating the name of address of the employment site where the plant closing or mass layoff will occur; the name and telephone number of a company official to contact for further information; the expected date of the first separation; and the number of affected employees. The employer is required to maintain the other information listed in § 639.7(e) on site and readily accessible to the State disclocated worker unit and to the unit of general local government. Should this information not be available when requested, it will be deemed a failure to give required notice.

§ 639.8 How is the notice served?

Any reasonable method of delivery to the parties listed under § 639.6 of this part which is designed to ensure receipt of notice of least 60 days before separation is acceptable (e.g., first class mail, personal delivery with optional signed receipt). In the case of notification directly to affected employees, insertion of notice into pay envelopes is another viable option. A ticketed notice, *i.e.*, preprinted notice regularly included in each employee's pay check or pay envelope, does not meet the requirements of WARN.

§ 639.9 When may notice be given less than 60 days in advance?

Section 3(b) of WARN sets forth three conditions under which the notification period may be reduced to less than 60 days. The employer bears the burden of proof that conditions for the exceptions have been met. If one of the exceptions is applicable, the employer must give as much notice as is practicable to the union, non-represented employees, the State dislocated worker unit, and the unit of local government and this may, in some circumstances, be notice after the fact. The employer must, at the time notice actually is given, provide a brief statement of the reason for reducing the notice period, in addition to the other elements set out in § 639.7.

(a) The exception under section 3(b)(1) of WARN, termed "faltering company", applies to plant closings but not to mass layoffs and should be narrowly construed. To qualify for reduced notice under this exception:

(1) An employer must have been actively seeking capital or business at the time that 60-day notice would have been required. That is, the employer must have been seeking financing or refinancing through the arrangement of loans, the issuance of stocks, bonds, or other methods of internally generated financing; or the employer must have been seeking additional money, credit, or business through any other commercially reasonable method. The employer must be able to identify specific actions taken to obtain capital or business.

(2) There must have been a realistic opportunity to obtain the financing or business sought.

(3) The financing or business sought must have been sufficient, if obtained, to have enabled the employer to avoid or postpone the shutdown. The employer must be able to objectively demonstrate that the amount of capital or the volume of new business sought would have enabled the employer to keep the facility, operating unit, or site open for a reasonable period of time.

(4) The employer reasonably and in good faith must have believed that giving the required notice would have precluded the employer from obtaining the needed capital or business. The employer must be able to objectively demonstrate that it reasonably thought that a potential customer or source of financing would have been unwilling to provide the new business or capital if notice were given, that is, if the employees, customers, or the public were aware that the facility, operating unit, or site might have to close. This condition may be satisfied if the employer can show that the financing or business source would not choose to do business with a troubled company or with a company whose workforce would be looking for other jobs. The actions of an employer relying on the "faltering company" exception will be viewed in a company-wide context. Thus, a company with access to capital markets or with cash reserves may not avail itself of this exception by looking solely at the financial condition of the facility, operating unit, or site to be closed.

(b) The "unforeseeable business circumstances" exception under section 3(b)(2)(A) of WARN applies to plant closings and mass layoffs caused by business circumstances that were not reasonably foreseeable at the time that 60-day notice would have been required.

(1) An important indicator of a business circumstance that is not reasonably foreseeable is that the circumstance is caused by some sudden, dramatic, and unexpected action or condition outside the employer's control. A principal client's sudden and unexpected termination of a major contract with the employer, a strike at a major supplier of the employer, and an unanticipated and dramatic major economic downturn might each be considered a business circumstance that is not reasonably foreseeable. A government ordered closing of an employment site that occurs without prior notice also may be an unforeseeable business circumstance.

(2) The test for determining when business circumstances are not reasonably foreseeable focuses on an employer's business judgment. The employer must exercise such commercially reasonable business judgment as would a similarly situated employer in predicting the demands of its particular market. The employer is not required, however, to accurately predict general economic conditions that also may affect demand for its products or services.

(c) The "natural disaster" exception in section 3(b)(2)(B) of WARN applies to plant closings and mass layoffs due to any form of a natural disaster.

(1) Floods, earthquakes, droughts, storms, tidal waves or tsunamis and similar effects of nature are natural disasters under this provision.

(2) To qualify for this exception, an employer must be able to demonstrate that its plant closing or mass layoff is a direct result of a natural disaster.

(3) While a disaster may preclude full or any advance notice, such notice as is practicable, containing as much of the information required in § 639.7 as is available in the circumstances of the disaster still must be given, whether in advance or after the fact of an employment loss caused by a natural disaster.

(4) Where a plant closing or mass layoff occurs as an indirect result of a natural disaster, the exception does not apply but the "unforeseeable business circumstance" exception described in paragraph (b) of this section may be applicable.

§ 639.10 When may notice be extended?

Additional notice is required when the date or schedule of dates of a planned plant closing or mass layoff is extended beyond the date or the ending date of any 14-day period announced in the original notice as follows:

(a) If the postponement is for less than 60 days, the additional notice should be given as soon as possible to the parties identified in § 639.6 and should include reference to the earlier notice, the date (or 14-day period) to which the planned action is postponed, and the reasons for the postponement. The notice should be given in a manner which will provide the information to all affected employees.

(b) If the postponement is for 60 days or more, the additional notice should be treated as new notice subject to the provisions of §§ 639.5, 639.6 and 639.7 of this part. Rolling notice, in the sense of routine periodic notice, given whether or not a plant closing or mass layoff is impending, and with the intent to evade the purpose of the Act rather than give specific notice as required by WARN, is not acceptable.

PART 640—STANDARD FOR BENEFIT PAYMENT PROMPTNESS—UNEMPLOYMENT COMPENSATION

Sec.

AUTHORITY: Sec. 1102, Social Security Act (42 U.S.C. 1302); Secretary's order No. 4–75, dated April 16, 1975 (40 FR 18515) (5 U.S.C. 553). Interpret and apply secs. 303(a)(1) and 303(b)(2) of the Social Security Act (42 U.S.C. 503(a)(1), 503(b)(2)).

SOURCE: 43 FR 33225, July 28, 1978, unless otherwise noted.

§ 640.1 Purpose and scope.

(a) *Purpose.* (1) Section 303(a)(1) of the Social Security Act requires, for the purposes of title III of that Act, that a State unemployment compensation law include provision for methods of administration of the law that are reasonably calculated to insure the full payment of unemployment compensation when determined under the State law to be due to claimants. The standard in this part is issued to implement section 303(a)(1) in regard to promptness in the payment of unemployment benefits to eligible claimants.

(2) Although the standard applies to the promptness of all benefit payments and the criteria apply directly to the promptness of first benefit payments, it is recognized that adequate performance is contingent upon the prompt determination of eligibility by the State as a condition for the payment or denial of benefits. Accordingly, implicit in prompt performance with respect to benefit payments is the corresponding need for promptness by the State in making determinations of eligibility. However, applicable Federal laws provide no authority for the Secretary of Labor to determine the eligibility of individuals under a State law.

(b) *Scope.* (1) The standard in this part applies to all State laws approved by the Secretary of Labor under the Federal Unemployment Tax Act (section 3304 of the Internal Revenue Code of 1986, 26 U.S.C. 3304), and to the administration of the State laws.

(2) The standard specified in § 640.4 applies to all claims for unemployment compensation. The criteria for State compliance in § 640.5 apply to first payments of unemployment compensation under the State law to eligible claimants following the filing of initial claims and first compensable claims.

[43 FR 33225, July 28, 1978, as amended at 71 FR 35516, June 21, 2006]

§ 640.2 Federal law requirements.

(a) *Conformity.* Section 303(a)(1) of the Social Security Act, 42 U.S.C. 503(a)(1), requires that a State law include provision for:

> Such methods of administration * * * as are found by the Secretary of Labor to be reasonably calculated to insure full payment of unemployment compensation when due.

(b) *Compliance.* Section 303(b)(2) of the Social Security Act, 42 U.S.C. 503(b)(2), provides in part that:

> Whenever the Secretary of Labor, after reasonable notice and opportunity for hearing to the State agency charged with the administration of the State law, finds that in the administration of the law there is:
> (1) * * *
> (2) a failure to comply substantially with any provision specified in subsection (a) of this section;
> the Secretary of Labor shall notify such State agency that further payments will not be made to the State until the Secretary of Labor is satisfied that there is no longer any such * * * failure to comply.
>
> Until he is so satisfied, he shall make no further certification to the Secretary of the Treasury with respect to such State * * *.

§ 640.3 Interpretation of Federal law requirements.

(a) *Section 303(a)(1).* The Secretary interprets section 303(a)(1) of the Social Security Act to require that a State law include provision for such methods of administration as will reasonable insure the full payment of unemployment benefits to eligible claimants with the greatest promptness that is administratively feasible.

(b) *Section 303(b)(2).* (1) The Secretary interprets section 303(b)(2) of the Social Security Act to require that, in the administration of a State law, there shall be substantial compliance with the provision required by section 303(a)(1).

(2) The greatest promptness that is administratively feasible will depend upon the circumstances in each State that impacts upon its performance in paying benefits. Factors reasonably beyond a State's control may cause its performance to drop below the level of adequacy expressed in the table below as criteria for substantial compliance applicable to all States. Where it is demonstrated that failure to meet the criteria of adequacy is attributable to factors reasonably beyond the State's control and, in light of those factors, the State has performed at the highest level administratively feasible, it will be considered that the State is in substantial compliance with the Standard for conformity. Whether or not the State is in substantial compliance, the remedial provisions of §§ 640.7 and 640.8

will be applicable when the pertinent criteria are not met.

§ 640.4 Standard for conformity.

A State law will satisfy the requirement of section 303(a)(1), if it contains a provision requiring, or which is construed to require, such methods of administration as will reasonably insure the full payment of unemployment benefits to eligible claimants with the greatest promptness that is administratively feasible.

§ 640.5 Criteria for compliance.

The criteria in the schedule below shall apply in determining whether, in the administration of a State law, there has been substantial compliance with the provision required by section 303(a)(1) in the issuance of benefit payments to eligible claimants for the first compensable weeks of unemployment in their benefit years:

	Percentage of first payments issued—days following end of first compensable week		
	14 days, waiting week States	21 days, non-waiting week States [1]	35 days, all States
Intrastate Claims			
Performance to be achieved for the 12-mo. period ending on March 31 of each year	87	87	93
Interstate Claims			
Performance to be achieved for the 12-mo. period ending on March 31 of each year	70	70	78

[1] A nonwaiting week State is any State whose law does not require that a non-compensable period of unemployment be served before the payment of benefits commences.

A State will be deemed to comply substantially, as set out in §§ 640.2(b) and 640.3(b), if its average performance, for the period of review, meets or exceeds the applicable criteria set forth above.

[43 FR 33225, July 28, 1978, as amended at 71 FR 35516, June 21, 2006]

§ 640.6 Review of State compliance.

(a) *Annual reviews.* The administration of each State law shall be reviewed annually for compliance, as set out in §§ 640.2(b) and 640.3(b). Annual reviews shall be for the 12-month period ending on March 31 of each year. An annual review with respect to any State shall be based upon the monthly reports of performance submitted to the Department by the State agency, any special reports of performance submitted to the Department by the State agency, any benefit payment performance plan applicable to the period being reviewed, any study or anylysis of performance relevant to the period being reviewed, and any other audit, study, or analysis as directed by the Department of Labor.

(b) *Periodic review.* The administration of any State law may be reviewed at any other time, when there is reason to believe that there may be failure of compliance as set out in §§ 640.2(b) and 640.3(b). Such a review shall be based upon the same elements as may be required for an annual review.

§ 640.7 Benefit payment performance plans.

(a) *Annual plan.* An annual benefit payment performance plan shall be submitted by a State agency to the Department of Labor when average performance over a 12-month period ending on March 31 of any year does not meet the criteria specified in § 640.5. An annual plan shall be submitted by July 31 following the applicable March 31, and shall be a plan for the fiscal year that begins on the succeeding October 1. An annual plan shall be subject to continuing appraisal during the period it is in effect, and shall be subject to modification from time to time as may be directed by the Department of Labor after consultation with the State agency.

(b) *Periodic plan.* A periodic benefit payment performance plan shall be submitted by a State agency when directed by the Department of Labor. A periodic plan may be in addition to, or a modification of an annual plan and may be required even though an annual plan covering the same period is not required. A periodic plan shall be subject to continuing appraisal during the period it is in effect, and shall be subject to modification from time to time as may be directed by the Department of Labor.

(c) *Content of plan.* An annual plan or periodic plan shall set forth such corrective actions, performance and evaluation plans, and other matters as the Department of Labor directs, after consultation with the State agency.

(Approved by the Office of Management and Budget under control number 1205–0132)

(Pub. L. No. 96–511)

[43 FR 33225, July 28, 1978, as amended at 49 FR 18295, Apr. 30, 1984]

§ 640.8 Enforcement of the standard.

(a) *Action by the Department of Labor.* When a State agency fails, for an extended period, to meet the standard set forth in § 640.4 or the criteria specified in § 640.5, or fails to show satisfactory improvement after having submitted a benefit payment performance plan of action, the Department of Labor shall pursue any of the following remedial steps that it deems necessary before considering application of the provisions of § 640.2:

(1) Initiate informal discussion with State agency officials pursuant to § 601.5(b) of this chapter.

(2) Conduct an evaluation of the State's benefit payment processes and analyze the reasons for the State's failure to meet the standard.

(3) Recommend specific actions for the State to take to improve its benefit payment performance.

(4) Request the State to submit a plan for complying with the standard by a prescribed date.

(5) Initiate special reporting requirements for a specified period of time.

(6) Consult with the Governor of the State regarding the consequences of the State's noncompliance with the standard.

(7) Propose to the Governor of the State and on an agreed upon basis arrange for the use of expert Federal staff to furnish technical assistance to the State agency with respect to its payment operations.

(b) *Action by the Assistant Secretary.* If, after all remedial steps have been exhausted, a State fails to take appropriate action, or otherwise fails to meet the standard specified in § 640.4, the Assistant Secretary for Employment and Training shall, after taking all factors into consideration, recommend to the Secretary of Labor that appropriate notice be sent to the State agency and that an opportunity for a hearing be extended in accordance with section 303(b) of the Social Security Act.

§ 640.9 Information, reports and studies.

A State shall furnish to the Secretary of Labor such information and reports and make such studies as the Secretary decides are necessary or appropriate to carry out this part.

PART 641—PROVISIONS GOVERNING THE SENIOR COMMUNITY SERVICE EMPLOYMENT PROGRAM

Subpart A—Purpose and Definitions

Sec.

Subpart B—Coordination With the Workforce Innovation and Opportunity Act

Subpart C—The State Plan

Subpart D—Grant Application and Responsibility Review Requirements for State and National SCSEP Grants

Subpart E—Services to Participants

Subpart F—Pilot, Demonstration, and Evaluation Projects

AUTHORITY: 42 U.S.C. 3056 *et seq.;* Pub. L. 114–144, 130 Stat. 334 (Apr. 19, 2016).

SOURCE: 75 FR 53812, Sept. 1, 2010, unless otherwise noted.

Subpart A—Purpose and Definitions

§ 641.100 What does this part cover?

Part 641 contains the Department of Labor's regulations for the Senior Community Service Employment Program (SCSEP), authorized under title V of the Older Americans Act (OAA), 42 U.S.C. 3056 *et seq.*, as amended by the Older Americans Act Reauthorization Act of 2016, Public Law 114–144 (Apr. 19, 2016). This part and other pertinent regulations set forth the regulations applicable to the SCSEP.

(a) Subpart A of this part contains introductory provisions and definitions that apply to this part.

(b) Subpart B of this part describes the required relationship between the OAA and the Workforce Innovation and Opportunity Act (WIOA), Public Law 113–128 (July 22, 2014). These provisions discuss the coordinated efforts to provide services through the integration of the SCSEP within the One-Stop delivery system.

(c) Subpart C of this part sets forth the requirements for the State Plan, such as the four-year strategy, required coordination efforts, public comments, and equitable distribution.

(d) Subpart D of this part establishes grant planning and application requirements, including grantee eligibility and responsibility review provisions that apply to the Department's award of SCSEP funds for State and national grants.

(e) Subpart E of this part details SCSEP participant services.

(f) Subpart F of this part provides the rules for pilot, demonstration, and evaluation projects.

(g) Subpart G of this part outlines the performance accountability requirements. This subpart establishes requirements for performance measures, defines such measures, and establishes corrective actions for failure to meet core performance measures.

(h) Subpart H of this part sets forth the administrative requirements for SCSEP funds.

(i) Subpart I of this part describes the grievance and appeals processes and requirements.

[75 FR 53812, Sept. 1, 2010, as amended at 82 FR 56880, Dec. 1, 2017]

§ 641.110 What is the SCSEP?

The Senior Community Service Employment Program (SCSEP) is a program administered by the Department of Labor that serves unemployed low-income persons who are 55 years of age and older and who have poor employment prospects by training them in part-time community service assignments and by assisting them in developing skills and experience to facilitate their transition to unsubsidized employment.

§ 641.120 What are the purposes of the SCSEP?

The purposes of the SCSEP are to foster individual economic self-sufficiency and promote useful part-time opportunities in community service assignments for unemployed low-income persons who are 55 years of age or older, particularly persons who have poor employment prospects, and to increase the number of older persons who may enjoy the benefits of unsubsidized employment in both the public and private sectors. (OAA § 502(a)(1)).

§ 641.130 What is the scope of this part?

The regulations in this part address the requirements that apply to the SCSEP. More detailed policies and procedures are contained in administrative guidelines issued by the Department. Throughout this part, phrases such as, "according to instructions (procedures) issued by the Department" or "additional guidance will be provided through administrative issuance" refer to the documents issued under the Secretary's authority to administer the SCSEP, such as Training and Employment Guidance Letters (TEGLs), Training and Employment Notices (TENs), previously issued SCSEP Older Worker Bulletins that are still in effect, technical assistance guides, and other SCSEP guidance.

§ 641.140 What definitions apply to this part?

The following definitions apply to this part:

At risk for homelessness means an individual is likely to become homeless and the individual lacks the resources and support networks needed to obtain housing.

Authorized position level means the number of SCSEP enrollment opportunities that can be supported for a 12-month period based on the average national unit cost. The authorized position level is derived by dividing the total amount of funds appropriated for a Program Year by the national average unit cost per participant for that Program Year as determined by the Department. The national average unit cost includes all costs of administration, other participant costs, and participant wage and benefit costs as defined in § 506(g) of the OAA.

Career services means those services described in sec. 134(c)(2) of WIOA.

Co-enrollment applies to any individual who meets the qualifications for SCSEP participation and is also enrolled as a participant in WIOA or another employment and training program, as provided in the Individual Employment Plan (IEP).

Community service means:

(1) Social, health, welfare, and educational services (including literacy tutoring), legal and other counseling services and assistance, including tax counseling and assistance and financial counseling, and library, recreational, and other similar services;

(2) Conservation, maintenance, or restoration of natural resources;

(3) Community betterment or beautification;

(4) Antipollution and environmental quality efforts;

(5) Weatherization activities;

(6) Economic development; and

(7) Other such services essential and necessary to the community as the Secretary determines by rule to be appropriate. (OAA § 518(a)(1)).

Community service assignment means part-time, temporary employment paid with grant funds in projects at host agencies through which eligible individuals are engaged in community service and receive work experience and job skills that can lead to unsubsidized employment. (OAA § 518(a)(2)).

Community Service Employment means part-time, temporary employment paid with grant funds in projects at host agencies through which eligible individuals are engaged in community service and receive work experience and job skills that can lead to unsubsidized employment. (OAA sec. 518(a)(2).) The term community service assignment is used interchangeably with community service employment.

Core measures means hours (in the aggregate) of community service employment; the percentage of project participants who are in unsubsidized employment during the second quarter after exit from the project; the percentage of project participants who are in unsubsidized employment during the fourth quarter after exit from the project; the median earnings of project participants who are in unsubsidized employment during the second quarter after exit from the project; indicators of effectiveness in serving employers, host agencies, and project participants; the number of eligible individuals served; and most-in-need (the number of individuals described in sec. 518(a)(3)(B)(ii) or (b)(2) of the OAA). (OAA sec. 513(b)(1).)

Department or DOL means the United States Department of Labor, including its agencies and organizational units.

Disability means a disability attributable to a mental or physical impairment, or a combination of mental and physical impairments, that results in substantial functional limitations in one or more of the following areas of major life activity:

(1) Self-care;

(2) Receptive and expressive language;

(3) Learning;

(4) Mobility;

(5) Self-direction;

(6) Capacity for independent living;

(7) Economic self-sufficiency;

(8) Cognitive functioning; and

(9) Emotional adjustment. (42 U.S.C. 3002(13)).

Equitable distribution report means a report based on the latest available Census or other reliable data, which lists the optimum number of participant positions in each designated area in the State, and the number of authorized participant positions each grantee serves in that area, taking into account the needs of underserved counties and incorporated cities as necessary. This report provides a basis for improving the distribution of SCSEP positions.

Frail means an individual 55 years of age or older who is determined to be functionally impaired because the individual—

(1)(i) Is unable to perform at least two activities of daily living without substantial human assistance, including verbal reminding, physical cueing, or supervision; or

(ii) At the option of the State, is unable to perform at least three such activities without such assistance; or

(2) Due to a cognitive or other mental impairment, requires substantial supervision because the individual behaves in a manner that poses a serious health or safety hazard to the individual or to another individual. (42 U.S.C. 3002(22)).

Grant period means the time period between the effective date of the grant award and the ending date of the award, which includes any modifications extending the period of performance, whether by the Department's exercise of options contained in the grant agreement or otherwise. This is also referred to as "project period" or "award period."

Grantee means an entity receiving financial assistance directly from the Department to carry out SCSEP activities. The grantee is the legal entity that receives the award and is legally responsible for carrying out the SCSEP, even if only a particular component of the entity is designated in the grant award document. Grantees include public and nonprofit private agencies and organizations, agencies of a State, tribal organizations, and Territories, that receive SCSEP grants from the Department. (OAA §§502(b)(1), 506(a)(2)). As used here, "grantee" includes "grantee" as defined in 29 CFR 97.3 and "recipient" as defined in 29 CFR 95.2(gg).

Greatest economic need means the need resulting from an income level at or below the poverty guidelines established by the Department of Health and Human Services and approved by the Office of Management and Budget (OMB). (42 U.S.C. 3002(23)).

Greatest social need means the need caused by non-economic factors, which include: Physical and mental disabilities; language barriers; and cultural, social, or geographical isolation, including isolation caused by racial or ethnic status, which restricts the ability of an individual to perform normal daily tasks or threatens the capacity of the individual to live independently. (42 U.S.C. 3002(24)).

Homeless includes:

(1) An individual who lacks a fixed, regular, and adequate nighttime residence; and

(2) An individual who has a primary nighttime residence that is:

(i) A supervised publicly or privately operated shelter designed to provide temporary living accommodations (including welfare hotels, congregate shelters, and transitional housing for the mentally ill);

(ii) An institution that provides a temporary residence for individuals intended to be institutionalized; or

(iii) A public or private place not designed for, or ordinarily used as, regular sleeping accommodations for human beings. (42 U.S.C. 11302(a)).

Host agency means a public agency or a private nonprofit organization exempt from taxation under §501(c)(3) of the Internal Revenue Code of 1986 which provides a training work site and supervision for one or more participants. Political parties cannot be host agencies. A host agency may be a religious organization as long as the projects in which participants are being trained do not involve the construction, operation, or maintenance of any facility used or to be used as a place for sectarian religious instruction or worship. (OAA §502(b)(1)(D)).

Indian means a person who is a member of an Indian tribe. (42 U.S.C. 3002(26)).

Indian tribe means any tribe, band, nation, or other organized group or community of Indians (including Alaska Native village or regional or village corporation as defined in or established pursuant to the Alaska Native Claims Settlement Act, 43 U.S.C. 1601 *et seq.*) which: (1) Is recognized as eligible for the special programs and services provided by the United States to Indians because of their status as Indians; or (2) is located on, or in proximity to, a Federal or State reservation or Rancheria. (42 U.S.C. 3002(27)).

Individual employment plan (IEP) means a plan for a participant that is based on an assessment of that participant conducted by the grantee or subrecipient, or a recent assessment or plan developed by another employment and training program, and a related service strategy. The IEP must include an appropriate employment goal (except that after the first IEP, subsequent IEPs need not contain an employment goal if such a goal is not feasible), objectives that lead to the goal, a timeline for the achievement of the objectives; and be jointly agreed upon with the participant. (OAA § 502(b)(1)(N)).

Jobs for Veterans Act means Public Law 107–288 (2002). Section 2(a) of the Jobs for Veterans Act, codified at 38 U.S.C. 4215(a), provides a priority of service for Department of Labor employment and training programs for veterans, and certain spouses of veterans, who otherwise meet the eligibility requirements for participation. Priority is extended to veterans. Priority is also extended to the spouse of a veteran who died of a service-connected disability; the spouse of a member of the Armed Forces on active duty who has been listed for a total of more than 90 days as missing in action, captured in the line of duty by a hostile force, or forcibly detained by a foreign government or power; the spouse of any veteran who has a total disability resulting from a service-connected disability; and the spouse of any veteran who died while a disability so evaluated was in existence. (See § 641.520(b)).

Job ready refers to individuals who do not require further education or training to perform work that is available in their labor market.

Limited English proficiency means individuals who do not speak English as their primary language and who have a limited ability to read, speak, write, or understand English.

Local Board means a Local Workforce Development Board established under sec. 107 of the Workforce Innovation and Opportunity Act.

Local Workforce Development Area or *local area* means an area designated by the Governor of a State under sec. 106 of the Workforce Innovation and Opportunity Act.

Low employment prospects means the likelihood that an individual will not obtain employment without the assistance of the SCSEP or another workforce development program. Persons with low employment prospects have a significant barrier to employment. Significant barriers to employment may include but are not limited to: Lacking a substantial employment history, basic skills, and/or English-language proficiency; lacking a high school diploma or the equivalent; having a disability; being homeless; or residing in socially and economically isolated rural or urban areas where employment opportunities are limited.

Low literacy skills means the individual computes or solves problems, reads, writes, or speaks at or below the 8th grade level or is unable to compute or solve problems, read, write, or speak at a level necessary to function on the job, in the individual's family, or in society.

Most-in-need means participants with one or more of the following characteristics: Have a severe disability; are frail; are age 75 or older; are age-eligible but not receiving benefits under title II of the Social Security Act; reside in an area with persistent unemployment and have severely limited employment prospects; have limited English proficiency; have low literacy skills; have a disability; reside in a rural area; are veterans; have low employment prospects; have failed to find employment after using services provided under title I of the Workforce Innovation and Opportunity Act; or are homeless or at risk for homelessness. (OAA sec. 513(b)(1)(F).)

National grantee means a public or non-profit private agency or organization, or Tribal organization, that receives a grant under title V of the OAA (42 U.S.C. 3056 *et seq.*) to administer a SCSEP project. (*See* OAA § 506(g)(5)).

OAA means the Older Americans Act, 42 U.S.C. 3001 *et seq.*, as amended.

One-Stop Center means the One-Stop Center system in a WIOA local area, which must include a comprehensive One-Stop Center through which One-Stop partners provide applicable career services and which provides access to other programs and services carried out by the One-Stop partners. (*See* WIOA sec. 121(e)(2).)

One-Stop delivery system means a system under which employment and training programs, services, and activities are available through a network of eligible One-Stop partners, which assures that information about and access to career services are available regardless of where the individuals initially enter the workforce development system. (*See* WIOA sec. 121(e)(2).)

One-Stop partner means an entity described in sec. 121(b)(1) of the Workforce Innovation and Opportunity Act, *i.e.*, required partners, or an entity described in sec. 121(b)(2) of the Workforce Innovation and Opportunity Act, *i.e.*, additional partners.

Other participant (enrollee) costs means the costs of participant training, including the payment of reasonable costs to instructors, classroom rental, training supplies, materials, equipment, and tuition, and which may be provided before or during a community service assignment, in a classroom setting, or under other appropriate arrangements; job placement assistance, including job development and job search assistance; participant supportive services to enable a participant to successfully participate in a project, including the payment of reasonable costs of transportation, health care and medical services, special job-related or personal counseling, incidentals (such as work shoes, badges, uniforms, eyeglasses, and tools), child and adult care, temporary shelter, and follow-up services; and outreach, recruitment and selection, intake orientation, and assessments. (OAA § 502(c)(6)(A)(ii)–(v)).

Pacific Island and Asian Americans means Americans having origins in any of the original peoples of the Far East, Southeast Asia, the Indian Subcontinent, or the Pacific Islands. (OAA sec. 518(a)(6).)

Participant means an individual who is determined to be eligible for the SCSEP, is given a community service assignment, and is receiving any service funded by the program as described in subpart E.

Persistent unemployment means that the annual average unemployment rate for a county or city is more than 20 percent higher than the national average for two out of the last three years.

Poor employment prospects means the significant likelihood that an individual will not obtain employment without the assistance of the SCSEP or another workforce development program. Persons with poor employment prospects have a significant barrier to employment; significant barriers to employment include but are not limited to: lacking a substantial employment history, basic skills, and/or English-language proficiency; lacking a high school diploma or the equivalent; having a disability; being homeless; or residing in socially and economically isolated rural or urban areas where employment opportunities are limited.

Program operator means a grantee or sub-recipient that receives SCSEP funds from a SCSEP grantee or a higher-tier SCSEP sub-recipient and performs the following activities for all its participants: Eligibility determination, participant assessment, and development of and placement into community service assignments.

Program Year means the one-year period beginning on July 1 and ending on June 30.

Project means an undertaking by a grantee or sub-recipient in accordance with a grant or contract agreement that provides service to communities and training and employment opportunities to eligible individuals.

Recipient means grantee. As used here, "recipient" includes "recipient" as defined in 29 CFR 95.2(gg) and "grantee" as defined in 29 CFR 97.3.

Residence means an individual's declared dwelling place or address as demonstrated by appropriate documentation.

Rural means an area not designated as a metropolitan statistical area by the Census Bureau; segments within metropolitan counties identified by codes 4 through 10 in the Rural Urban Commuting Area (RUCA) system; and RUCA codes 2 and 3 for census tracts that are larger than 400 square miles and have population density of less than 30 people per square mile.

SCSEP means the Senior Community Service Employment Program authorized under title V of the OAA.

Secretary means the Secretary of the U.S. Department of Labor.

Service area means the geographic area served by a local SCSEP project in accordance with a grant agreement.

Severe disability means a severe, chronic disability attributable to mental or physical impairment, or a combination of mental and physical impairments, that—

(1) Is likely to continue indefinitely; and

(2) Results in substantial functional limitation in 3 or more of the following areas of major life activity:

(i) Self-care;

(ii) Receptive and expressive language;

(iii) Learning;

(iv) Mobility;

(v) Self-direction;

(vi) Capacity for independent living;

(vii) Economic self-sufficiency. (42 U.S.C. 3002(48)).

Severely limited employment prospects means the substantial likelihood that an individual will not obtain employment without the assistance of the SCSEP or another workforce development program. Persons with severely limited employment prospects have more than one significant barrier to employment; significant barriers to employment may include but are not limited to: Lacking a substantial employment history, basic skills, and/or English-language proficiency; lacking a high school diploma or the equivalent; having a disability; being homeless; or residing in socially and economically isolated rural or urban areas where employment opportunities are limited.

State Board means a State Workforce Development Board established under WIOA sec. 101.

State grantee means the entity designated by the Governor, or the highest government official, to enter into a grant with the Department to administer a State or Territory SCSEP project under the OAA. Except as applied to funding distributions under § 506 of the OAA, this definition applies to the 50 States, Puerto Rico, the District of Columbia and the following Territories: Guam, American Samoa, U.S. Virgin Islands, and the Commonwealth of the Northern Mariana Islands.

State Plan means a plan that the Governor, or the highest government official, of a State must submit to the Secretary that outlines a four-year strategy, and describes the planning and implementation process, for the statewide provision of community service employment and other authorized activities for eligible individuals under SCSEP. (*See* § 641.300).

Sub-recipient means the legal entity to which a sub-award of financial assistance is made by the grantee (or by a higher-tier sub-recipient), and that is accountable to the grantee for the use of the funds provided. As used here, "sub-recipient" includes "sub-grantee" as defined in 29 CFR 97.3 and "sub-recipient" as defined in 29 CFR 95.2(kk).

Supportive services means services, such as transportation, health and medical services, special job-related or personal counseling, incidentals (such as work shoes, badges, uniforms, eyeglasses, and tools), child and adult care, housing, including temporary shelter, follow-up services, and needs-related payments, which are necessary to enable an individual to participate in activities authorized under the SCSEP. (OAA secs. 502(c)(6)(A)(iv) and 518(a)(8).)

Title V of the OAA means 42 U.S.C. 3056 *et seq.*, as amended.

Training services means those services authorized by WIOA sec. 134(c)(3).

Tribal organization means the recognized governing body of any Indian tribe, or any legally established organization of Indians which is controlled, sanctioned, or chartered by such governing body. (42 U.S.C. 3002(54)).

Unemployed means an individual who is without a job and who wants and is available for work, including an individual who may have occasional employment that does not result in a constant source of income. (OAA sec. 518(a)(9).)

Veteran means an individual who is a "covered person" for purposes of the Jobs for Veterans Act, 38 U.S.C. 4215(a)(1).

Workforce Innovation and Opportunity Act (WIOA) means the Workforce Innovation and Opportunity Act, Public Law 113–128 (July 22, 2014), as amended.

Workforce Innovation and Opportunity Act (WIOA) regulations means the regulations in parts 675 through 688 of this chapter, the Wagner-Peyser Act regulations in parts 651 through 654 and part 658 of this chapter, and the regulations implementing WIOA sec. 188 in 29 CFR part 38.

[75 FR 53812, Sept. 1, 2010, as amended at 77 FR 4661, Jan. 31, 2012; 82 FR 56880, Dec. 1, 2017]

Subpart B—Coordination With the Workforce Innovation and Opportunity Act

SOURCE: 82 FR 56881, Dec. 1, 2017, unless otherwise noted.

§ 641.200 What is the relationship between the SCSEP and the Workforce Innovation and Opportunity Act?

The SCSEP is a required partner under the Workforce Innovation and Opportunity Act. As such, it is a part of the One-Stop delivery system. When acting in their capacity as WIOA partners, SCSEP grantees and sub-recipients are required to follow all applicable rules under WIOA and its regulations. *See* WIOA sec. 121(b)(1)(B)(v) and 20 CFR 678.400 through 678.440.

§ 641.210 What services, in addition to the applicable career services, must SCSEP grantees and sub-recipients provide through the One-Stop delivery system?

In addition to providing career services, as defined at 20 CFR 678.430, SCSEP grantees and sub-recipients must make arrangements through the One-Stop delivery system to provide eligible and ineligible individuals with referrals to WIOA career and training services and access to other activities and programs carried out by other One-Stop partners.

§ 641.220 Does title I of WIOA require the SCSEP to use OAA funds for individuals who are not eligible for SCSEP services or for services that are not authorized under the OAA?

No, SCSEP requirements continue to apply. OAA title V resources may not be used to serve individuals who are not SCSEP-eligible. The Workforce Innovation and Opportunity Act creates a seamless service delivery system for individuals seeking workforce development services by linking the One-Stop partners in the One-Stop delivery system. Although the overall effect is to provide universal access to career services, SCSEP resources may only be used to provide services that are authorized and provided under the SCSEP to eligible individuals. Note, however, that one allowable SCSEP cost is a SCSEP project's proportionate share of One-Stop costs. *See* § 641.850(d). Title V funds can be used to pay wages to SCSEP participants receiving career and training services under title I of WIOA provided that the SCSEP participants have each received a community service assignment. All other individuals who are in need of the services provided under the SCSEP, but who do not meet the eligibility criteria to enroll in the SCSEP, should be referred to or enrolled in WIOA or other appropriate partner programs. WIOA sec. 121(b)(1). These arrangements should be negotiated in the Memorandum of Understanding (MOU), which is an agreement developed and executed between the Local Workforce Development Board, with the agreement of the chief local elected official, and the One-Stop partners relating to the operation of the One-Stop delivery system in the local area. The MOU is further described in the WIOA regulations at 20 CFR 678.500 through 678.510.

§ 641.230 Must the individual assessment conducted by the SCSEP grantee or sub-recipient and the assessment performed by the One-Stop delivery system be accepted for use by either entity to determine the individual's need for services in the SCSEP and adult programs under title I, subtitle B of WIOA?

Yes, sec. 502(b)(3) of the OAA provides that an assessment or IEP completed by the SCSEP satisfies any condition for an assessment, service strategy, or IEP completed at the One-Stop and vice-versa. (OAA sec. 502(b)(3).) These reciprocal arrangements and the contents of the SCSEP IEP and WIOA IEP should be negotiated in the MOU.

§ 641.240 Are SCSEP participants eligible for career and training services under title I of WIOA?

(a) Although SCSEP participants are not automatically eligible for career and training services under title I of WIOA, local boards may deem SCSEP participants, either individually or as a group, as satisfying the requirements for receiving adult career and training services under title I of WIOA.

(b) SCSEP participants who have been assessed and for whom an IEP has been developed have received a career service under 20 CFR 680.220(a) of the WIOA regulations. In order to enhance skill development related to the IEP, it may be necessary to provide training beyond the community service assignment to enable participants to meet their unsubsidized employment objectives. The SCSEP grantee or sub-recipient, the host agency, the WIOA program, or another One-Stop partner may provide training as appropriate and as negotiated in the MOU. (See § 641.540 for a further discussion of training for SCSEP participants.)

Subpart C—The State Plan

§ 641.300 What is the State Plan?

The State Plan is a plan, submitted by the Governor, or the highest government official, in each State, as an independent document or as part of the WIOA Combined State Plan, that outlines a 4-year strategy for the statewide provision of community service employment and other authorized activities for eligible individuals under the SCSEP as described in § 641.302. The State Plan also describes the planning and implementation process for SCSEP services in the State, taking into account the relative distribution of eligible individuals and employment opportunities within the State. The State Plan is intended to foster coordination among the various SCSEP grantees and sub-recipients operating within the State and to facilitate the efforts of stakeholders, including State and local boards under WIOA, to work collaboratively through a participatory process to accomplish the SCSEP's goals. (OAA sec. 503(a)(1).) The State Plan provisions are listed in § 641.325.

[82 FR 56882, Dec. 1, 2017]

§ 641.302 What is a four-year strategy?

The State Plan must outline a four-year strategy for the statewide provision of community service employment and other authorized activities for eligible individuals under the SCSEP program. (OAA § 503(a)(1)). The four-year strategy must specifically address the following:

(a) The State's long-term strategy for achieving an equitable distribution of SCSEP positions within the State that:

(1) Moves positions from over-served to underserved locations within the State, under § 641.365;

(2) Equitably serves rural and urban areas; and

(3) Serves individuals afforded priority for service, pursuant to § 641.520;

(b) The State's long-term strategy for avoiding disruptions to the program when new Census or other reliable data become available, or when there is over-enrollment for any other reason;

(c) The State's long-term strategy for serving minority older individuals under SCSEP;

(d) Long-term projections for job growth in industries and occupations in the State that may provide employment opportunities for older workers, and how those relate to the types of unsubsidized jobs for which SCSEP participants will be trained, and the types of skill training to be provided;

(e) The State's long-term strategy for engaging employers to develop and promote opportunities for the placement of SCSEP participants in unsubsidized employment;

(f) The State's strategy for continuous improvement in the level of performance for entry into unsubsidized employment;

(g) Planned actions to coordinate activities of SCSEP grantees with the activities being carried out in the State under title I of WIOA, including plans for using the WIOA One-Stop delivery system and its partners to serve individuals aged 55 and older;

(h) Planned actions to coordinate activities of SCSEP grantees with the activities being carried out in the State under other titles of the OAA;

(i) Planned actions to coordinate the SCSEP with other public and private entities and programs that provide services to older Americans, such as community and faith-based organizations, transportation programs, and programs for those with special needs or disabilities;

(j) Planned actions to coordinate the SCSEP with other labor market and job training initiatives; and

(k) The State's long-term strategy to improve SCSEP services, including planned longer-term changes to the design of the program within the State, and planned changes in the use of SCSEP grantees and program operators to better achieve the goals of the program; this may include recommendations to the Department, as appropriate.

[75 FR 53812, Sept. 1, 2010, as amended at 82 FR 56882, Dec. 1, 2017]

§ 641.305 Who is responsible for developing and submitting the State Plan?

The Governor, or the highest governmental official, of each State is responsible for developing and submitting the State Plan to the Department.

§ 641.310 May the Governor, or the highest government official, delegate responsibility for developing and submitting the State Plan?

(a) Yes, the Governor, or the highest governmental official of each State, may delegate responsibility for developing and submitting the State Plan, provided that any such delegation is consistent with State law and regulations.

(b) To delegate responsibility, the Governor, or the highest government official, must submit to the Department a signed statement indicating the individual and/or organization that will be submitting the State Plan on his or her behalf.

§ 641.315 Who participates in developing the State Plan?

(a) In developing the State Plan the Governor, or the highest government official, must seek the advice and recommendations of representatives from:

(1) The State and area agencies on aging;

(2) State and local boards under WIOA;

(3) Public and private nonprofit agencies and organizations providing employment services, including each grantee operating a SCSEP project within the State, except as provided in § 641.320(b);

(4) Social service organizations providing services to older individuals;

(5) Grantees under title III of the OAA;

(6) Affected communities;

(7) Unemployed older individuals;

(8) Community-based organizations serving older individuals;

(9) Business organizations; and

(10) Labor organizations.

(b) The Governor, or the highest government official, may also obtain the advice and recommendations of other interested organizations and individuals, including SCSEP program participants, in developing the State Plan. (OAA § 503(a)(2)).

[75 FR 53812, Sept. 1, 2010, as amended at 82 FR 56882, Dec. 1, 2017]

§ 641.320 Must all national grantees operating within a State participate in the State planning process?

(a) The eligibility provision at OAA § 514(c)(6) requires national grantees to coordinate activities with other organizations at the State and local levels. Therefore, except as provided in paragraph (b) of this section, any national grantee that does not participate in the State planning process may be deemed ineligible to receive SCSEP funds in the following Program Year.

(b) National grantees serving older American Indians, or Pacific Island and Asian Americans, with funds reserved under OAA sec. 506(a)(3), are exempted from the requirement to participate in the State planning processes under sec. 503(a)(9) of the OAA. Although these national grantees may choose not to participate in the State planning process, the Department encourages their participation. Only those grantees using reserved funds are exempt; if a grantee is awarded one grant with reserved funds and another grant with non-reserved funds, the grantee is required under paragraph (a) of this section to participate in the State planning process for purposes of the non-reserved funds grant.

[75 FR 53812, Sept. 1, 2010, as amended at 82 FR 56882, Dec. 1, 2017]

§ 641.325 What information must be provided in the State Plan?

The Department issues instructions detailing the information that must be provided in the State Plan. At a minimum, the State Plan must include the State's four-year strategy, as described in § 641.302, and information on the following:

(a) The ratio of eligible individuals in each service area to the total eligible population in the State;

(b) The relative distribution of:

(1) Eligible individuals residing in urban and rural areas within the State;

(2) Eligible individuals who have the greatest economic need;

(3) Eligible individuals who are minorities;

(4) Eligible individuals who are limited English proficient; and

(5) Eligible individuals who have the greatest social need;

(c) The current and projected employment opportunities in the State (such as by providing information available under sec. 15 of the Wagner-Peyser Act (29 U.S.C. 491–2) by occupation), and the types of skills possessed by eligible individuals;

(d) The localities and populations for which projects of the type authorized by OAA title V are most needed;

(e) Actions taken and/or planned to coordinate activities of SCSEP grantees in the State with activities carried out in the State under title I of WIOA;

(f) A description of the process used to obtain advice and recommendations on the State Plan from representatives of organizations and individuals listed in § 641.315, and advice and recommendations on steps to coordinate SCSEP services with activities funded under title I of WIOA from representatives of organizations listed in § 641.335;

(g) A description of the State's procedures and time line for ensuring an open and inclusive planning process that provides meaningful opportunity for public comment as required by § 641.350;

(h) Public comments received, and a summary of the comments;

(i) A description of the steps taken to avoid disruptions to the greatest extent possible as provided in § 641.365; and

(j) Such other information as the Department may require in the State Plan instructions. (OAA § 503(a)).

[75 FR 53812, Sept. 1, 2010, as amended at 82 FR 56882, Dec. 1, 2017]

§ 641.330 How should the State Plan reflect community service needs?

The Governor, or the highest government official, must ensure that the State Plan identifies the types of community services that are needed and the places where these services are most needed. The State Plan should specifically identify the needs and locations of those individuals most in need of community services and the groups working to meet their needs. (OAA § 503(a)(4)(E)).

§ 641.335 How should the Governor, or the highest government official, address the coordination of SCSEP services with activities funded under title I of WIOA?

The Governor, or the highest government official, must seek the advice and recommendations from representatives of the State and local area agencies on aging in the State and the State and local boards established under title I of WIOA. (OAA sec. 503(a)(2).) The State Plan must describe the steps that are being taken to coordinate SCSEP activities within the State with activities being carried out under title I of WIOA. (OAA sec. 503(a)(4)(F).) The State Plan must describe the steps being taken to ensure that the SCSEP is an active partner in each One-Stop delivery system and the steps that will be taken to encourage and improve coordination with the One-Stop delivery system.

[82 FR 56882, Dec. 1, 2017]

§ 641.340 How often must the Governor, or the highest government official, update the State Plan?

(a) Under instructions issued by the Department, the Governor, or the highest government official, must review the State Plan and submit an update to the State Plan to the Secretary for consideration and approval not less often than every two years. OAA § 503(a)(1). States are encouraged to review their State Plan more frequently than every two years, however, and make modifications as circumstances warrant, under § 641.345.

(b) Before development of the update to the State Plan, the Governor, or the highest government official, must seek the advice and recommendations of the individuals and organizations identified in § 641.315 about what, if any, changes are needed, and must publish the State Plan, showing the changes, for public comment. OAA §section 503(a)(2), 503(a)(3).

§641.345 What are the requirements for modifying the State Plan?

(a) Modifications may be submitted anytime circumstances warrant.

(b) Modifications to the State Plan are required when:

(1) There are changes in Federal or State law or policy that substantially change the assumptions upon which the State Plan is based;

(2) There are significant changes in the State's vision, four-year strategy, policies, performance indicators, or organizational responsibilities; or

(3) There is a change in a grantee or grantees.

(c) Modifications to the State Plan are subject to the same public comment requirements that apply to the development of the State Plan under §641.350.

(d) States are not required to seek the advice and recommendations of the individuals and organizations identified in §641.315 when modifying the State Plan, except that States must seek the advice and recommendations of any national grantees operating in the State. While not required, states are strongly encouraged to seek the advice and recommendation of the relevant entities listed in §641.315 when or if modifying the State Plan becomes necessary.

(e) The Department will issue additional instructions for the procedures that must be followed when requesting modifications to the State Plan.

§641.350 How should public comments be solicited and collected?

The Governor, or the highest government official, should follow established State procedures to solicit and collect public comments. The State Plan must include a description of the State's procedures and schedule for ensuring an open and inclusive planning process that provides meaningful opportunity for public comment.

§641.355 Who may comment on the State Plan?

Any individual or organization may comment on the Plan.

§641.360 How does the State Plan relate to the equitable distribution report?

The two documents address some of the same areas, but are prepared at different points in time. The equitable distribution report is prepared by State grantees at the beginning of each fiscal year and provides a "snapshot" of the actual distribution of all of the authorized positions within the State, grantee-by-grantee, and the optimum number of participant positions in each designated area based on the latest available Census or other reliable data. The State Plan is prepared by the Governor, or the highest government official, and covers many areas in addition to equitable distribution, as discussed in §641.325, and sets forth a proposed plan for distribution of authorized positions in the State. Any distribution or redistribution of positions made as a result of a State Plan proposal will be reflected in the next equitable distribution report, which then forms the basis for the proposed distribution in the next State Plan update. This process is iterative in that it moves the authorized positions from overserved areas to underserved areas over a period of time.

§641.365 How must the equitable distribution provisions be reconciled with the provision that disruptions to current participants should be avoided?

(a) Governors, or highest government officials, must describe in the State Plan the steps that are being taken to comply with the statutory requirement to avoid disruptions in the provision of services for participants. (OAA sec. 503(a)(7).)

(b) When there is new Census or other reliable data indicating that there has been a shift in the location of the eligible population or when there is over-enrollment for any other reason, the Department recommends a gradual shift in positions as they become vacant to areas where there has been an increase in the eligible population.

(c) The Department does not define disruptions to mean that participants are entitled to remain in a subsidized community service assignment indefinitely. As discussed in §641.570, there is a time limit on SCSEP participation, thus permitting positions to be transferred over time.

(d) Grantees and sub-recipients must not transfer positions from one geographic area to another without first notifying the State agency responsible for preparing the State Plan and equitable distribution report.

(e) Grantees must submit, in writing, any proposed changes in distribution that occur after submission of the equitable distribution report to the Department for approval.

(f) All grantees are required to coordinate any proposed changes in position distribution with the other grantees in the State, including the State project director, before submitting the proposed changes to the Department for approval. The request for the Department's approval must include the comments of the State project director, which the Department will consider in making its decision.

[75 FR 53812, Sept. 1, 2010, as amended at 82 FR 56882, Dec. 1, 2017]

§ 641.370 May a State incorporate its 4-year plan for SCSEP into a Combined State Plan under WIOA?

Yes. A State may include its 4-year plan for SCSEP in its WIOA Combined State Plan according to the requirements in 20 CFR 676.140 through 676.145. For a State that obtains approval of that Combined State Plan under 20 CFR 676.143, the requirements of sec. 103 of WIOA and 20 CFR part 676 will apply in lieu of sec. 503(a) of the OAA and this subpart, and any reference in this part to a "State Plan" will be considered to be a reference to that Combined State Plan.

[82 FR 56883, Dec. 1, 2017]

Subpart D—Grant Application and Responsibility Review Requirements for State and National SCSEP Grants

§ 641.400 What entities are eligible to apply to the Department for funds to administer SCSEP projects?

(a) *National grants.* Entities eligible to apply for national grants include nonprofit organizations, Federal public agencies, and tribal organizations. These entities must provide information to establish that they are capable of administering a multi-State program, as required by the Secretary. State and local agencies may not apply for these funds.

(b) *State grants.* (1) Section 506(e) of the OAA requires the Department to award each State a grant to provide SCSEP services. Governors, or highest government officials, designate an individual State agency as the organization to administer SCSEP funds.

(2) If the State fails to meet its expected levels of performance for the core indicators for three consecutive years, it is not eligible to designate an agency to administer SCSEP funds in the following year. Instead, the State must conduct a competition to select an organization as the grantee of the funds allotted to the State under § 506(e). Public and nonprofit private agencies and organizations, State agencies other than the previously designated, failed agency, and tribal organizations, are eligible to be selected as a grantee for the funds. Other States may not be selected as a grantee for this funding.

§ 641.410 How does an eligible entity apply?

(a) *General.* An eligible entity must follow the application guidelines issued by the Department. The Department will issue application guidelines announcing the availability of national funds and State funds, whether they are awarded on a competitive or non-competitive basis. The guidelines will contain application due dates, application instructions, evaluation criteria, and other necessary information.

(b) *National grant applicants.* All applicants for SCSEP national grant funds, except for applications for grants proposing to serve older Indians and Pacific Island and Asian Americans with funds reserved under OAA § 506(a)(3), must submit their applications to the Governor, or the highest government official, of each State in which projects are proposed so that he or she has a reasonable opportunity to make the recommendations described in § 641.480, before submitting the application to the Department. (OAA § 503(a)(5)).

(c) *State applicants*. A State that submits a Combined State Plan under sec. 103 of WIOA may include the State's SCSEP grant application in its Combined State Plan. Any State that submits a SCSEP grant application as part of its WIOA Combined State Plan must address all of the application requirements as published in the Department's instructions. Sections 641.300 through 641.370 address State Plans and modifications.

[75 FR 53812, Sept. 1, 2010, as amended at 82 FR 56883, Dec. 1, 2017]

§641.420 What are the eligibility criteria that each applicant must meet?

To be eligible to receive SCSEP funds, each applicant must demonstrate:

(a) An ability to administer a program that serves the greatest number of eligible participants, giving particular consideration to individuals with greatest economic need, individuals with greatest social need, and individuals described in §641.570(b) or §641.520(a)(2) through (a)(8).

(b) An ability to administer a program that provides employment in community service assignments for eligible individuals in communities in which they reside, or in nearby communities, that will contribute to the general welfare of the community;

(c) An ability to administer a program that moves eligible participants into unsubsidized employment;

(d) Where the applicant has previously received a SCSEP grant, the applicant's prior performance in meeting SCSEP core measures of performance and addressing SCSEP additional measures of performance; and where the applicant has not received a SCSEP grant, the applicant's prior performance under other Federal or State programs; relevant past performance will also be used for scoring criterion and will be set forth more fully in the Solicitation for Grant Applications (see §641.460);

(e) An ability to move participants with multiple barriers to employment, including individuals described in §641.570(b) or §641.520(a)(2) through (a)(8), into unsubsidized employment;

(f) An ability to coordinate activities with other organizations at the State and local levels, including the One-Stop delivery system;

(g) An ability to properly manage the program, as reflected in its plan for fiscal management of the SCSEP;

(h) An ability to administer a project that provides community service;

(i) An ability to minimize program disruption for current participants and in community services provided if there is a change in project sponsor and/or location, and its plan for minimizing disruptions;

(j) Any additional criteria that the Department deems appropriate to minimize disruptions for current participants. (OAA §514(c)).

§641.430 What are the responsibility conditions that an applicant must meet?

Subject to §641.440, each applicant must meet the listed responsibility "tests" by not having committed the following acts:

(a) The Department has been unable to recover a debt from the applicant, whether incurred by the applicant or by one of its sub-recipients, or the applicant has failed to comply with a debt repayment plan to which it agreed. In this context, a debt is established by final agency action, followed by three demand letters to the applicant, without payment in full by the applicant.

(b) Established fraud or criminal activity of a significant nature within the applicant's organization.

(c) Serious administrative deficiencies identified by the Department, such as failure to maintain a financial management system as required by Federal regulations.

(d) Willful obstruction of the auditing or monitoring process.

(e) Failure to provide services to applicants as agreed to in a current or recent grant or to meet applicable core performance measures or address other applicable indicators of performance.

(f) Failure to correct deficiencies brought to the grantee's attention in writing as a result of monitoring activities, reviews, assessments, or other activities.

(g) Failure to return a grant closeout package or outstanding advances within 90 days after the grant expiration date or receipt of closeout package, whichever is later, unless an extension has been requested and granted.

(h) Failure to submit required reports.

(i) Failure to properly report and dispose of Government property as instructed by the Department.

(j) Failure to have maintained effective cash management or cost controls resulting in excess cash on hand.

(k) Failure to ensure that a sub-recipient complies with applicable audit requirements, including OMB Circular A–133 and the audit requirements specified at § 641.821.

(l) Failure to audit a sub-recipient within the period required under § 641.821.

(m) Final disallowed costs in excess of five percent of the grant or contract award if, in the judgment of the Grant Officer, the disallowances are egregious findings.

(n) Failure to establish a mechanism to resolve a sub-recipient's audit in a timely fashion. (OAA § 514(d)(4)).

§ 641.440 Are there responsibility conditions that alone will disqualify an applicant?

(a) Yes, an applicant may be disqualified if

(1) Either of the first two responsibility tests, a or b, listed in § 641.430 is not met, or

(2) The applicant substantially, or persistently for two or more consecutive years, fails one of the other responsibility tests listed in § 641.430.

(b) The second responsibility test addresses "fraud or criminal activity of a significant nature." The Department will determine the existence of significant fraud or criminal activity which typically will include willful or grossly negligent disregard for the use or handling of, or other fiduciary duties concerning, Federal funding, where the grantee has no effective systems, checks, or safeguards to detect or prevent fraud or criminal activity. Additionally, significant fraud or criminal activity will typically include coordinated patterns or behaviors that pervade a grantee's administration or are committed by the higher levels of a grantee's management or authority. The Department will determine whether "fraud or criminal activity of a significant nature" has occurred on a case-by-case basis, regardless of what party identifies the alleged fraud or criminal activity.

§ 641.450 How will the Department examine the responsibility of eligible entities?

The Department will review available records to assess each applicant's overall fiscal and administrative ability to manage Federal funds. The Department's responsibility review may consider all relevant information, including the organization's history of managing other grants awarded by the Department or by other Federal agencies. (OAA § 514(d)(1) and (d)(2)).

§ 641.460 What factors will the Department consider in selecting national grantees?

The Department will select national grantees from among applicants that are able to meet the eligibility and responsibility review criteria at § 514 of the OAA. (Section 641.420 contains the eligibility criteria and §§ 641.430 and 641.440 contain the responsibility criteria.) The Department also will take the rating criteria described in the Solicitation for Grant Applications or other instrument into consideration. These rating criteria will include relevant past performance.

§ 641.465 Under what circumstances may the Department reject an application?

(a) The Department may question any proposed project component of an application if it believes that the component will not serve the purposes of the SCSEP. The Department may reject the application if the applicant does not submit or negotiate an acceptable alternative.

(b) The Department may reject any application that the Grant Officer determines unacceptable based on the content of the application, rating score, past performance, fiscal management, or any other factor the Grant Officer believes serves the best interest of the program, including the application's comparative rating in a competition.

§ 641.470 What happens if an applicant's application is rejected?

(a) Any entity whose application is rejected in whole or in part will be informed that it has not been selected. The non-selected entity may request an explanation of the Department's basis for its rejection. If requested, the Department will provide the entity with feedback on its proposal. The non-selected entity may follow the procedures in § 641.900.

(b) Incumbent grantees will not have an opportunity to obtain technical assistance provided by the Department under OAA § 513(d)(2)(B)(i) to cure, in an open competition, any deficiency in a proposal because that will create inequity in favor of incumbents. Nor, during an open competition, will the Department provide assistance to any applicant to improve its application.

(c) If the Administrative Law Judge (ALJ) rules, under § 641.900, that the organization should have been selected, in whole or in part, the matter must be remanded to the Grant Officer. The Grant Officer must, within 10 working days, determine whether the organization continues to meet the requirements of this part, and whether the positions which are the subject of the ALJ's decision will be awarded, in whole or in part, to the organization and the timing of the award. In making this determination, the Grant Officer must take into account disruption to participants, disruption to grantees, and the operational needs of the SCSEP.

(d) In the event that the Grant Officer determines that it is not feasible to award any positions to the appealing applicant, the applicant will be awarded its bid preparation costs, or a pro rata share of those costs if the Grant Officer's finding applies to only a portion of the funds that would be awarded. If positions are awarded to the appealing applicant, that applicant is not entitled to the full grant amount but will only receive the funds remaining in the grant that have not been expended by the current grantee through its operation of the grant and its subsequent closeout. The available remedy in a SCSEP non-selection appeal is neither retroactive nor immediately effective selection; rather it is the potential to be selected as a SCSEP grantee as quickly as administratively feasible in the future, for the remainder of the grant cycle.

(e) In the event that any party notifies the Grant Officer that it is not satisfied with the Grant Officer's decision, the Grant Officer must return the decision to the ALJ for review.

(f) Any organization selected and/or funded as a SCSEP grantee is subject to having its positions reduced or to being removed as a SCSEP grantee if an ALJ decision so orders. The Grant Officer provides instructions on transition and closeout to both the newly designated grantee and to the grantee whose positions are affected or which is being removed. All parties must agree to the provisions of this paragraph as a condition of being a SCSEP grantee.

§ 641.480 May the Governor, or the highest government official, make recommendations to the Department on national grant applications?

(a) Yes, in accordance with § 641.410(b), each Governor, or highest government official, will have a reasonable opportunity to make comments on any application to operate a SCSEP project located in the Governor's, or the highest government official's, State before the Department makes a final decision on a grant award. The Governor's, or the highest government official's, comments should be directed to the Department and may include the anticipated effect of the proposal on the overall distribution of program positions within the State; recommendations for redistribution of positions to underserved areas as vacancies occur in previously encumbered positions in other areas; and recommendations for distributing any new positions that may become available as a result of an increase in funding for the State. The Governor's, or the highest government official's, recommendations should be consistent with the State Plan. (OAA § 503(a)(5)).

(b) The Governor, or the highest government official, has the option of making the authorized recommendations on all applications or only on those applications proposed for award following the rating process. It is incumbent on each Governor, or the highest government official, to inform the Department of his or her intent to review the applications before or after the rating process.

§ 641.490 When will the Department compete SCSEP grant awards?

(a)(1) The Department will hold a full and open competition for national grants every four years. (OAA § 514(a)(1)).

(2) If a national grantee meets the expected level of performance for each of the core indicators for each of the four years, the Department may provide an additional one-year grant to the national grantee. (OAA § 514(a)(2)).

§ 641.495 When must a State compete its SCSEP award?

If a State grantee fails to meet its expected levels of performance for three consecutive Program Years, the State must hold a full and open competition, under such conditions as the Secretary may provide, for the State SCSEP funds for the full Program Year following the determination of consecutive failure. (OAA § 513(d)(3)(B)(iii)). The incumbent (failed) grantee is not eligible to compete. Other states are also not eligible to compete for these funds. § 641.400(b)(2).

Subpart E—Services to Participants

§ 641.500 Who is eligible to participate in the SCSEP?

Anyone who is at least 55 years old, unemployed (as defined in § 641.140), and who is a member of a family with an income that is not more than 125 percent of the family income levels prepared by the Department of Health and Human Services and approved by OMB (Federal poverty guidelines) is eligible to participate in the SCSEP. (OAA sec. 518(a)(3), (9).) A person with a disability may be treated as a "family of one" for income eligibility determination purposes at the option of the applicant.

[82 FR 56883, Dec. 17, 2017]

§ 641.505 When is eligibility determined?

Initial eligibility is determined at the time individuals apply to participate in the SCSEP. Once individuals become SCSEP participants, the grantee or sub-recipient is responsible for verifying their continued eligibility at least once every 12 months. Grantees and sub-recipients may also verify an individual's eligibility as circumstances require, including instances when enrollment is delayed.

§ 641.507 How is applicant income computed?

An applicant's income is computed by calculating the includable income received by the applicant during the 12-month period ending on the date an individual submits an application to participate in the SCSEP, or the annualized income for the 6-month period ending on the application date. The Department requires grantees to use whichever method is more favorable to the individual. (OAA § 518(a)(4)).

§ 641.510 What types of income are included and excluded for participant eligibility determinations?

(a) With certain exceptions, the Department will use the definition of income from the U.S. Census Bureau's Current Population Survey (CPS) as the standard for determining SCSEP applicant income eligibility.

(b) Any income that is unemployment compensation, a benefit received under title XVI of the Social Security Act (42 U.S.C. 1381 *et seq.*), a payment made to or on behalf of veterans or former members of the Armed Forces under the laws administered by the Secretary of Veterans Affairs, or 25 percent of a benefit received under title II of the Social Security Act (42 U.S.C. 401 *et seq.*), must be excluded from SCSEP income eligibility determinations. (OAA § 518(a)(3)(A)).

(c) The Department has issued administrative guidance on income inclusions and exclusions and procedures for determining SCSEP income eligibility. This guidance may be updated periodically.

§ 641.512 May grantees and sub-recipients enroll otherwise eligible job ready individuals and place them directly into unsubsidized employment?

No, grantees and sub-recipients may not enroll as SCSEP participants job-ready individuals who can be directly placed into unsubsidized employment. Such individuals should be referred to an employment provider, such as the One-Stop Center for job placement assistance under WIOA or another employment program.

[82 FR 56883, Dec. 1, 2017]

§ 641.515 How must grantees and sub-recipients recruit and select eligible individuals for participation in the SCSEP?

(a) Grantees and sub-recipients must develop methods of recruitment and selection that assure that the maximum number of eligible individuals have an opportunity to participate in the program. To the extent feasible, grantees and sub-recipients should seek to enroll minority and Indian eligible individuals, eligible individuals with limited English proficiency, and eligible individuals with greatest economic need, at least in proportion to their numbers in the area, taking into consideration their rates of poverty and unemployment. (OAA § 502(b)(1)(M)).

(b) Grantees and sub-recipients must use the One-Stop delivery system as one method in the recruitment and selection of eligible individuals to ensure that the maximum number of eligible individuals have an opportunity to participate in the project. (OAA § 502(b)(1)(H)).

(c) States may enter into agreements among themselves to permit cross-border enrollment of eligible participants. Such agreements should cover both State and national grantee positions and must be submitted to the Department for approval in the grant application or a modification of the grant.

§ 641.520 Are there any priorities that grantees and sub-recipients must use in selecting eligible individuals for participation in the SCSEP?

(a) Yes, in selecting eligible individuals for participation in the SCSEP, priority must be given to individuals who have one or more of the following characteristics:

(1) Are 65 years of age or older;

(2) Have a disability;

(3) Have limited English proficiency or low literacy skills;

(4) Reside in a rural area;

(5) Are veterans (or, in some cases, spouses of veterans) for purposes of § 2(a) of the Jobs for Veterans Act, 38 U.S.C. 4215(a) as set forth in paragraph (b) of this section;

(6) Have low employment prospects;

(7) Have failed to find employment after using services provided through the One-Stop delivery system; or

(8) Are homeless or are at risk for homelessness. (OAA § 518(b)).

(b) Section 2(a) of the Jobs for Veterans Act creates a priority for service for veterans (and, in some cases, spouses of veterans) who otherwise meet the program eligibility criteria for the SCSEP. 38 U.S.C. 4215(a). Priority is extended to veterans. Priority is also extended to the spouse of a veteran who died of a service-connected disability; the spouse of a member of the Armed Forces on active duty who has been listed for a total of more than 90 days as missing in action, captured in the line of duty by a hostile force, or forcibly detained by a foreign government or power; the spouse of any veteran who has a total disability resulting from a service-connected disability; and the spouse of any veteran who died while a disability so evaluated was in existence.

(c) Grantees and sub-recipients must apply these priorities in the following order:

(1) Persons who qualify as a veteran or qualified spouse under § 2(a) of the Jobs for Veterans Act, 38 U.S.C. 4215(a), and who possess at least one of the other priority characteristics;

(2) Persons who qualify as a veteran or qualified spouse under § 2(a) of the Jobs for Veterans Act, 38 U.S.C. 4215(a), who do not possess any other of the priority characteristics;

(3) Persons who do not qualify as a veteran or qualified spouse under § 2(a) of the Jobs for Veterans Act (non-veterans), and who possess at least one of the other priority characteristics.

§ 641.535 What services must grantees and sub-recipients provide to participants?

(a) When individuals are selected for participation in the SCSEP, the grantee or sub-recipient is responsible for:

(1) Providing orientation to the SCSEP, including information on project goals and objectives, community service assignments, training opportunities, available supportive services, the availability of a free physical examination, participant rights and responsibilities, and permitted and prohibited political activities;

(2)(i) Assessing participants' work history, skills and interests, talents, physical capabilities, aptitudes, needs for supportive services, occupational preferences, training needs, potential for performing community service assignments, and potential for transition to unsubsidized employment;

(ii) Performing an initial assessment upon program entry, unless an assessment has already been performed under title I of WIOA as provided in § 641.230. Subsequent assessments may be made as necessary, but must be made no less frequently than two times during a 12-month period (including the initial assessment);

(3)(i) Using the information gathered during the initial assessment to develop an IEP that includes an appropriate employment goal for each participant, except that if an assessment has already been performed and an IEP developed under title I of WIOA, the WIOA assessment and IEP will satisfy the requirement for a SCSEP assessment and IEP as provided in § 641.230;

(ii) Updating the IEP as necessary to reflect information gathered during the subsequent participant assessments (OAA § 502(b)(1)(N));

(iii) The initial IEP should include an appropriate employment goal for each participant. Thereafter, if the grantee determines that the participant is not likely to obtain unsubsidized employment, the IEP must reflect other approaches to help the participant achieve self-sufficiency, including the transition to other services or programs.

(4) Placing participants in appropriate community service assignments in the community in which they reside, or in a nearby community (OAA § 502(b)(1)(B));

(5) Providing or arranging for training identified in participants' IEPs and consistent with the SCSEP's goal of unsubsidized employment (OAA § 502(a)(1), 502(b)(1)(B), 502(b)(1)(I), 502(b)(1)(N)(ii));

(6) Assisting participants in obtaining needed supportive services identified in their IEPs (OAA § 502(b)(1)(N));

(7) Providing appropriate services for participants, or referring participants to appropriate services, through the One-Stop delivery system established under WIOA (OAA sec. 502(b)(1)(O));

(8) Providing counseling on participants' progress in meeting the goals and objectives identified in their IEPs, and in meeting their supportive service needs (OAA § 502(b)(1)(N)(iii));

(9) Providing participants with wages and benefits for time spent in the community service assignment, orientation, and training (OAA § 502(b)(1)(I), 502(b)(1)(J), 502(c)(6)(A)(i)) (see also §§ 641.565 and 641.540(f), addressing wages and benefits);

(10) Ensuring that participants have safe and healthy working conditions at their community service employment worksites (OAA § 502(b)(1)(J));

(11) Assisting participants in obtaining unsubsidized employment, including providing or arranging for employment counseling in support of their IEPs;

(b) The Department may issue administrative guidance that clarifies the requirements of paragraph (a).

(c) Grantees may not use SCSEP funds for job ready individuals who only need job search assistance or job referral services. Grantees may provide job search assistance and job club activities to participants who are enrolled in the SCSEP and are assigned to community service assignments. (See also § 641.512).

[75 FR 53812, Sept. 1, 2010, as amended at 82 FR 56883, Dec. 1, 2017]

§ 641.540 What types of training may grantees and sub-recipients provide to SCSEP participants in addition to the training received at a community service assignment?

(a) In addition to the training provided in a community service assignment, grantees and sub-recipients may arrange skill training provided that it:

(1) Is realistic and consistent with the participants' IEP;

(2) Makes the most effective use of the participant's skills and talents; and

(3) Prepares the participant for unsubsidized employment.

(b) Training may be provided before or during a community service assignment.

(c) Training may be in the form of lectures, seminars, classroom instruction, individual instruction, online instruction, and on-the-job experiences. Training may be provided by the grantee or through other arrangements, including but not limited to, arrangements with other workforce development programs such as WIOA. (OAA sec. 502(c)(6)(A)(ii).)

(d) Grantees and sub-recipients are encouraged to obtain training through locally available resources, including host agencies, at no cost or reduced cost to the SCSEP.

(e) Grantees and sub-recipients may pay for participant training, including the payment of reasonable costs of instructors, classroom rental, training supplies, materials, equipment, and tuition. (OAA § 502(c)(6)(A)(ii)).

(f) Participants must be paid wages while in training, as described in § 641.565(a). (OAA § 502(b)(1)(I)).

(g) As provided in § 641.545, grantees and sub-recipients may pay for costs associated with supportive services, such as transportation, necessary to participate in training. (OAA § 502(b)(1)(L)).

(h) Nothing in this section prevents or limits participants from engaging in self-development training available through other sources, at their own expense, during hours when not performing their community service assignments.

[75 FR 53812, Sept. 1, 2010, as amended at 82 FR 56883, Dec. 1, 2017]

§ 641.545 What supportive services may grantees and sub-recipients provide to participants?

(a) Grantees and sub-recipients are required to assess all participants' need for supportive services and to make every effort to assist participants in obtaining needed supportive services. Grantees and sub-recipients may provide directly or arrange for supportive services that are necessary to enable an individual to successfully participate in a SCSEP project, including but not limited to payment of reasonable costs of transportation; health and medical services; special job-related or personal counseling; incidentals such as work shoes, badges, uniforms, eyeglasses, and tools; dependent care; housing, including temporary shelter; needs-related payments; and follow-up services. (OAA secs. 502(c)(6)(A)(iv), 518(a)(8).)

(b) To the extent practicable, the grantee or sub-recipient should arrange for the payment of these expenses from other resources.

(c) Grantees and sub-recipients are encouraged to contact placed participants throughout the first 12 months following placement to determine if they have the necessary supportive services to remain in the job and to provide or arrange to provide such services if feasible.

[75 FR 53812, Sept. 1, 2010, as amended at 82 FR 56883, Dec. 1, 2017]

§ 641.550 What responsibility do grantees and sub-recipients have to place participants in unsubsidized employment?

For those participants whose IEPs include a goal of unsubsidized employment, grantees and sub-recipients are responsible for working with participants to ensure that the participants are receiving services and taking actions designed to help them achieve this goal. Grantees and sub-recipients must contact private and public employers directly or through the One-Stop delivery system to develop or identify suitable unsubsidized employment opportunities. They must also encourage host agencies to assist participants in their transition to unsubsidized employment, including unsubsidized employment with the host agency.

§ 641.565 What policies govern the provision of wages and benefits to participants?

(a) *Wages.* (1)(i) Grantees and sub-recipients must pay participants the highest applicable required wage for time spent in orientation, training, and community service assignments.

(ii) SCSEP participants may be paid the highest applicable required wage while receiving WIOA career services.

(2) The highest applicable required wage is either the minimum wage applicable under the Fair Labor Standards Act of 1938; the State or local minimum wage for the most nearly comparable covered employment; or the prevailing rate of pay for persons employed in similar public occupations by the same employer.

(3) Grantees and sub-recipients must make any adjustments to minimum wage rates payable to participants as may be required by Federal, State, or local statute during the grant term.

(b) *Benefits*—(1) *Required benefits.* Except as provided in paragraph (b)(2) of this section, grantees and sub-recipients must ensure that participants receive such benefits as are required by law.

(i) Grantees and sub-recipients must provide benefits uniformly to all participants within a project or subproject, unless the Department agrees to waive this provision due to a determination that such a waiver is in the best interests of applicants, participants, and project administration.

(ii) Grantees and sub-recipients must offer participants the opportunity to receive physical examinations annually.

(A) Physical examinations are a benefit, and not an eligibility criterion. The examining physician must provide, to the participant only, a written report of the results of the examination.

(B) Participants may choose not to accept the physical examination. In that case, the grantee or sub-recipient must document this refusal, through a signed statement, within 60 workdays after commencement of the community service assignment. Each year thereafter, grantees and sub-recipients must offer the physical examination and document the offer and any participant's refusal.

(C) Grantees and sub-recipients may use SCSEP funds to pay the costs of physical examinations.

(iii) When participants are not covered by the State workers' compensation law, the grantee or sub-recipient must provide participants with workers' compensation benefits equal to those provided by law for covered employment. OAA § 504(b).

(iv) If required by State law, grantees/sub-recipients must provide unemployment compensation coverage for participants.

(v) Grantees and sub-recipients must provide compensation for scheduled work hours during which a host agency's business is closed for a Federal holiday, which may be paid or in the form of rescheduled work time.

(vi) Grantees and sub-recipients must provide necessary sick leave that is not part of an accumulated sick leave program, which may be paid or in the form of rescheduled work time.

(2) *Prohibited wage and benefits costs.* (i) Participants may not carry over allowable benefits from one Program Year to the next;

(ii) Grantees and sub-recipients may not provide payment or otherwise compensate participants for unused benefits such as sick leave or holidays;

(iii) Grantees and sub-recipients may not use SCSEP funds to cover costs associated with the following participant benefits:

(A) Retirement. Grantees and sub-recipients may not use SCSEP funds to provide contributions into a retirement system or plan, or to pay the cost of pension benefits for program participants.

(B) Annual leave.

(C) Accumulated sick leave.

(D) Bonuses. (OAA § 502(c)(6)(A)(i)).

[75 FR 53812, Sept. 1, 2010, as amended at 82 FR 56883, Dec. 1, 2017]

§ 641.570 Is there a time limit for participation in the program?

(a) *Individual time limit.* (1) Eligible individuals may participate in the program for a maximum duration of 48 months in the aggregate (whether or not consecutive), from the later of July 1, 2007, or the date of the individual's enrollment in the program.

(2) At the time of enrollment, the grantee or sub-recipient must inform the participant of this time limit and the possible extension available under paragraph (b) of this section, and the grantee or sub-recipient must provide for a system to transition participants to unsubsidized employment or other assistance before the maximum enrollment duration has expired. Provisions for transition must be reflected in the participant's IEP.

(3) If requested by a grantee or sub-recipient, the Department will authorize an extension for individuals who meet the criteria in paragraph (b) of this section. Notwithstanding any individual extensions granted, grantees and sub-recipients must ensure that projects do not exceed the overall average participation cap for all participants, as described in paragraph (c) of this section.

(b) *Increased periods of individual participation.* If requested by a grantee, the Department will authorize increased periods of participation for individuals who:

(1) Have a severe disability;

(2) Are frail or are age 75 or older;

(3) Meet the eligibility requirements related to age for, but do not receive, benefits under title II of the Social Security Act (42 U.S.C. 401 *et seq.*);

(4) Live in an area with persistent unemployment and are individuals with severely limited employment prospects; or

(5) Have limited English proficiency or low literacy skills.

(c) *Average grantee participation cap.* (1) Notwithstanding any individual extension authorized under paragraph (b) of this section, each grantee must manage its SCSEP project in such a way that the grantee does not exceed an average participation cap for all participants of 27 months (in the aggregate).

(2) A grantee may request, and the Department may authorize, an extended average participation period of up to 36 months (in the aggregate) for a particular project area in a given Program Year if the Department determines that extenuating circumstances exist to justify an extension, due to one more of the following factors:

(i) High rates of unemployment or of poverty or of participation in the program of block grants to States for temporary assistance for needy families established under part A of title IV of the Social Security Act, in the areas served by a grantee, relative to other areas of the State involved or the Nation;

(ii) Significant downturns in the economy of an area served by the grantee or in the national economy;

(iii) Significant numbers or proportions of participants with one or more barriers to employment, including "most-in-need" individuals described in § 641.710(a)(6), served by a grantee relative to such numbers or proportions for grantees serving other areas of the State or Nation;

(iv) Changes in Federal, State, or local minimum wage requirements; or

(v) Limited economies of scale for the provision of community service employment and other authorized activities in the areas served by the grantee.

(3) For purposes of the average participation cap, each grantee will be considered to be one project.

(d) *Authorized break in participation.* On occasion a participant takes an authorized break in participation from the program, such as a formal leave of absence necessitated by personal circumstances or a break caused because a suitable community service assignment is not available. Such an authorized break, if taken under a formal grantee policy allowing such breaks and formally entered into the SCSEP Performance and Results Quarterly Performance Reporting (SPARQ) system, will not count toward the individual time limit described in paragraph (a) or the average participation cap described in paragraph (c) of this section.

(e) *Administrative guidance.* The Department will issue administrative guidance detailing the process by which a grantee may request increased periods of individual participation, and the process by which a grantee may request an extension of the average participation cap. The process will require that the determination of individual participant extension requests is made in a fair and equitable manner.

(f) *Grantee authority.* Grantees may limit the time of participation for individuals to less than the 48 months described in paragraph (a) of this section, if the grantee uniformly applies the lower participation limit, and if the grantee submits a description of the lower participation limit policy in its grant application or modification of the grant and the Department approves the policy. (OAA §§ 502(b)(1)(C), 518(a)(3)(B)).

§ 641.575 May a grantee or sub-recipient establish a limit on the amount of time its participants may spend at a host agency?

Yes, grantees and sub-recipients may establish limits on the amount of time that participants spend at a particular host agency, and are encouraged to rotate participants among different host agencies, or to different assignments within the same host agency, as such rotations may increase participants' skills development and employment opportunities. Such limits must be established in the grant agreement or modification of the grant, and approved by the Department. The Department will not approve any limit that does not require an individualized determination that rotation is in the best interest of the participant and will further the acquisition of skills listed in the IEP. Host agency rotations have no effect on either the individual participation limit or the average participation cap.

§ 641.577 Is there a limit on community service assignment hours?

While there is no specific limit on the number of hours that may be worked in a community service assignment, a community service assignment must be a part-time position. However, the Department strongly encourages grantees to use 1,300 hours as a benchmark and good practice for monitoring community service hours.

§ 641.580 Under what circumstances may a grantee or sub-recipient terminate a participant?

(a) If, at any time, a grantee or sub-recipient determines that a participant was incorrectly declared eligible as a result of false information knowingly given by that individual, the grantee or sub-recipient must give the participant immediate written notice explaining the reason(s) for termination and may terminate the participant 30 days after it has provided the participant with written notice.

(b) If, during eligibility verification under § 641.505, a grantee or sub-recipient finds a participant to be no longer eligible for enrollment, the grantee or sub-recipient must give the participant written notice explaining the reason(s) for termination and may terminate the participant 30 days after it has provided the participant with written notice.

(c) If, at any time, the grantee or sub-recipient determines that it incorrectly determined a participant to be eligible for the program through no fault of the participant, the grantee or sub-recipient must give the participant immediate written notice explaining the reason(s) for termination and may terminate the participant 30 days after it has provided the participant with written notice.

(d) A grantee or sub-recipient may terminate a participant for cause. Grantees must include their policies concerning for-cause terminations in the grant application and obtain the Department's approval. The grantee or sub-recipient must give the participant written notice explaining the reason(s) for termination and may terminate the participant 30 days after it has provided the participant with written notice.

(e) A grantee or sub-recipient may terminate a participant if the participant refuses to accept a reasonable number of job offers or referrals to unsubsidized employment consistent with the IEP and there are no extenuating circumstances that would hinder the participant from moving to unsubsidized employment. The grantee or sub-recipient must give the participant written notice explaining the reason(s) for termination and may terminate the participant 30 days after it has provided the participant with written notice.

(f) When a grantee or sub-recipient makes an unfavorable determination of enrollment eligibility under paragraph (b) or (c) of this section, it should refer the individual to other potential sources of assistance, such as the One-Stop delivery system. When a grantee or sub-recipient terminates a participant under paragraph (d) or (e) of this section, it may refer the individual to other potential sources of assistance, such as the One-Stop delivery system.

(g) Grantees and sub-recipients must provide each participant at the time of enrollment with a written copy of its policies for terminating a participant for cause or otherwise, and must verbally review those policies with each participant.

(h) Any termination, as described in paragraphs (a) through (e) of this section, must be consistent with administrative guidelines issued by the Department and the termination notice must inform the participant of the grantee's grievance procedure, and the termination must be subject to the applicable grievance procedures described in § 641.910.

(i) Participants may not be terminated from the program solely on the basis of their age. Grantees and sub-recipients may not impose an upper age limit for participation in the SCSEP.

§ 641.585 What is the employment status of SCSEP participants?

(a) Participants are not considered Federal employees solely as a result of their participation in the SCSEP. (OAA § 504(a)).

(b) Grantees must determine whether or not a participant qualifies as an employee of the grantee, sub-recipient, local project, or host agency, under applicable law. Responsibility for this determination rests with the grantee even when a Federal agency is a grantee or host agency.

Subpart F—Pilot, Demonstration, and Evaluation Projects

§ 641.600 What is the purpose of the pilot, demonstration, and evaluation projects authorized under § 502(e) of the OAA?

The purpose of the pilot, demonstration, and evaluation projects authorized under § 502(e) of the OAA is to develop and implement techniques and approaches, and to demonstrate the effectiveness of these techniques and approaches, in addressing the employment and training needs of individuals eligible for SCSEP.

§ 641.610 How are pilot, demonstration, and evaluation projects administered?

The Department may enter into agreements with States, public agencies, nonprofit private organizations, or private business concerns, as may be necessary, to conduct pilot, demonstration, and evaluation projects.

§ 641.620 How may an organization apply for pilot, demonstration, and evaluation project funding?

Organizations applying for pilot, demonstration, and evaluation project funding must follow the instructions issued by the Department. Instructions for these unique funding opportunities are published in TEGLs available at *http://www.doleta.gov/Seniors*.

§ 641.630 What pilot, demonstration, and evaluation project activities are allowable under the Older Americans Act?

Allowable pilot, demonstration and evaluation projects include:

(a) Activities linking businesses and eligible individuals, including activities providing assistance to participants transitioning from subsidized activities to private sector employment;

(b) Demonstration projects and pilot projects designed to:

(1) Attract more eligible individuals into the labor force;

(2) Improve the provision of services to eligible individuals under One-Stop delivery systems established under title I of WIOA;

(3) Enhance the technological skills of eligible individuals; and

(4) Provide incentives to SCSEP grantees for exemplary performance and incentives to businesses to promote their participation in the SCSEP;

(c) Demonstration projects and pilot projects, as described in paragraph (b) of this section, for workers who are older individuals (but targeted to eligible individuals) only if such demonstration projects and pilot projects are designed to assist in developing and implementing techniques and approaches in addressing the employment and training needs of eligible individuals;

(d) Provision of training and technical assistance to support a SCSEP project;

(e) Dissemination of best practices relating to employment of eligible individuals; and

(f) Evaluation of SCSEP activities.

[75 FR 53812, Sept. 1, 2010, as amended at 82 FR 56884, Dec. 1, 2017]

§ 641.640 Should pilot, demonstration, and evaluation project entities coordinate with SCSEP grantees and sub-recipients, including area agencies on aging?

(a) To the extent practicable, the Department will provide an opportunity, before the development of a demonstration or pilot project, for the appropriate area agency on aging and SCSEP grantees and sub-grantees to submit comments on the project in order to ensure coordination of SCSEP activities with activities carried out under this subpart.

(b) To the extent practicable, entities carrying out pilot, demonstration, and evaluation projects must consult with appropriate area agencies on aging, SCSEP grantees and sub-grantees, and other appropriate agencies and entities to promote coordination of SCSEP and pilot, demonstration, and evaluation activities. (OAA § 502(e)).

Subpart G—Performance Accountability

SOURCE: 82 FR 56884, Dec. 1, 2017, unless otherwise noted.

§ 641.700 What performance measures apply to Senior Community Service Employment Program grantees?

(a) *Measures of performance.* There are seven core performance measures. Core measures (defined in § 641.710) are subject to goal-setting and corrective action (described in § 641.720); that is, performance level goals for each core measure must be agreed upon between the Department and each grantee as described in § 641.720, and if a grantee fails to meet the performance level goals for the core measures, that grantee is subject to corrective action.

(b) *Core measures.* Section 513(b)(1) of the OAA establishes the following core measures of performance:

(1) Hours (in the aggregate) of community service employment;

(2) The percentage of project participants who are in unsubsidized employment during the second quarter after exit from the project;

(3) The percentage of project participants who are in unsubsidized employment during the fourth quarter after exit from the project;

(4) The median earnings of project participants who are in unsubsidized employment during the second quarter after exit from the project;

(5) Indicators of effectiveness in serving employers, host agencies, and project participants;

(6) The number of eligible individuals served; and

(7) The number of most-in-need individuals served (the number of participating individuals described in OAA sec. 518(a)(3)(B)(ii) or (b)(2)).

(c) *Affected entities.* The core measures of performance are applicable to each grantee without regard to whether such grantee operates the program directly or through sub-contracts, sub-grants, or agreements with other entities. Grantees must assure that their sub-grantees and lower-tier sub-grantees are collecting and reporting program data.

(d) *Required evaluation and reporting.* An agreement to be evaluated on the core measures of performance is a requirement for application for, and is a condition of, all SCSEP grants.

§ 641.710 How are the performance measures defined?

The core measures are defined as follows:

(a) "Hours of community service employment" is defined as the total number of hours of community service provided by SCSEP participants divided by the number of hours of community service funded by the grantee's grant, after adjusting for differences in minimum wage among the States and areas. Paid training hours are excluded from this measure.

(b) "The percentage of project participants who are in unsubsidized employment during the second quarter after exit from the project" is defined by the formula: The number of participants who exited during the reporting period who are employed in unsubsidized employment during the second quarter after the exit quarter divided by the number of participants who exited during the reporting period multiplied by 100.

(c) "The percentage of project participants who are in unsubsidized employment during the fourth quarter after exit from the project" is defined by the formula: The number of participants who exited during the reporting period who are employed in unsubsidized employment during the fourth quarter after the exit quarter divided by the number of participants who exited during the reporting period multiplied by 100.

(d) "The median earnings of project participants who are in unsubsidized employment during the second quarter after exit from the project" is defined by the formula: For all participants who exited and are in unsubsidized employment during the second quarter after the exit quarter: The wage that is at the midpoint (of all the wages) between the highest and lowest wage earned in the second quarter after the exit quarter.

(e) "Indicators of effectiveness in serving employers, host agencies, and project participants" is defined as the combined results of customer assessments of the services received by each of these three customer groups.

(f) "The number of eligible individuals served" is defined as the total number of participants served divided by a grantee's authorized number of positions, after adjusting for differences in minimum wage among the States and areas.

(g) "Most-in-need" or the number of participating individuals described in OAA sec. 518(a)(3)(B)(ii) or (b)(2) is defined by counting the total number of the following characteristics for all participants and dividing by the number of participants served. Participants are characterized as most-in-need if they:

(1) Have a severe disability;

(2) Are frail;

(3) Are age 75 or older;

(4) Meet the eligibility requirements related to age for, but do not receive, benefits under title II of the Social Security Act (42 U.S.C. 401 *et seq.*);

(5) Live in an area with persistent unemployment and are individuals with severely limited employment prospects;

(6) Have limited English proficiency;

(7) Have low literacy skills;

(8) Have a disability;

(9) Reside in a rural area;

(10) Are veterans;

(11) Have low employment prospects;

(12) Have failed to find employment after utilizing services provided under title I of the Workforce Innovation and Opportunity Act; or

(13) Are homeless or at risk for homelessness.

§ 641.720 How will the Department and grantees initially determine and then adjust expected levels of the core performance measures?

(a) *First 2 years.* Before the beginning of the first program year of the grant, each grantee must reach agreement with the Department on levels of performance for each measure listed in § 641.700 for each of the first 2 program years covered by the grant agreement. In reaching the agreement, the grantee and the Department must take into account the expected levels of performance proposed by the grantee and the factors described in paragraph (c) of this section.

The levels agreed to will be considered the expected levels of performance for the grantee for such program years. Funds may not be awarded under the grant until such agreement is reached.

At the conclusion of negotiations concerning the performance levels with all grantees, the Department will make available for public review the final negotiated expected levels of performance for each grantee, including any comments submitted by the grantee regarding the grantee's satisfaction with the negotiated levels.

(b) *Third and fourth year.* Each grantee must reach agreement with the Department prior to the third program year covered by the grant agreement, on levels of performance for each measure listed in § 641.700, for each of the third and fourth program years so covered. In reaching the agreement, the grantee and the Department must take into account the expected levels of performance proposed by the grantee and the factors described in paragraph (c) of this section. The levels agreed to will be considered to be the expected levels of performance for the grantee for such program years. Funds may not be awarded under the grant until such agreement is reached. At the conclusion of negotiations concerning the performance levels with all grantees, the Department will make available for public review the final negotiated expected levels of performance for each grantee, including any comments submitted by the grantee regarding the grantee's satisfaction with the negotiated levels.

(c) *Factors.* In reaching the agreements described in paragraphs (a) and (b) of this section, each grantee and the Department must:

(1) Take into account how the levels involved compare with the expected levels of performance established for other grantees;

(2) Ensure that the levels involved are adjusted, using an objective statistical model based on the model established by the Secretary of Labor with the Secretary of Education in accordance with sec. 116(b)(3)(A)(viii) of the Workforce Innovation and Opportunity Act (29 U.S.C. 3141(b)(3)(A)(viii)); and

(3) Take into account the extent to which the levels involved promote continuous improvement in performance accountability on the core measures and ensure optimal return on the investment of Federal funds.

(d) *Adjustments based on economic conditions and individuals served during the program year.* The Department will, in accordance with the objective statistical model developed pursuant to paragraph (c)(2) of this section, adjust the expected levels of performance for a program year for grantees to reflect the actual economic conditions and characteristics of participants in the corresponding projects during such program year.

§ 641.730 How will the Department assist grantees in the transition to the new core performance measures?

As soon as practicable after January 2, 2018, the Department will determine if a SCSEP grantee's performance under the measures in effect prior to January 2, 2018 would have met the expected levels of performance for the Program Year 2018. If the Department determines that the grantee would have failed to meet the Program Year 2018 expected levels of performance, the Department will provide technical assistance to help the grantee to transition to eventually meet the expected levels of performance under the measures in § 641.700.

§ 641.740 How will the Department determine whether a grantee fails, meets, or exceeds the expected levels of performance and what will be the consequences of failing to meet expected levels of performance?

(a) *Aggregate calculation of performance.* Not later than 120 days after the end of each program year, the Department will determine if a grantee has met the expected levels of performance including any adjustments to such levels made in accordance with § 641.720(d) by aggregating the grantee's core measures. The aggregate is calculated by combining the percentage of goal achieved on each of the individual core measures to obtain an average score. A grantee will fail to meet its performance measures when it is does not meet 80 percent of the agreed-upon level of performance for the aggregate of all the core measures. Performance in the range of 80 to 100 percent constitutes meeting the level for the core performance measures. Performance in excess of 100 percent constitutes exceeding the level for the core performance measures.

(b) *Consequences*—(1) *National grantees*. (i) If the Department determines that a national grantee fails to meet the expected levels of performance in a program year, as described in paragraph (a) of this section, the Department, after each year of such failure, will provide technical assistance and will require such grantee to submit a corrective action plan not later than 160 days after the end of the program year.

(ii) The corrective action plan must detail the steps the grantee will take to meet the expected levels of performance in the next program year.

(iii) Any national grantee that has failed to meet the expected levels of performance for 4 consecutive years will not be allowed to compete in the subsequent grant competition, but may compete in the next grant competition after that subsequent competition.

(2) *State grantees*. (i) If the Department determines that a State fails to meet the expected levels of performance, as described in paragraph (a) of this section, the Department, after each year of such failure, will provide technical assistance and will require the State to submit a corrective action plan not later than 160 days after the end of the program year.

(ii) The corrective action plan must detail the steps the State will take to meet the expected levels of performance in the next program year.

(iii) If the Department determines that the State fails to meet the expected levels of performance for 3 consecutive program years the Department will require the State to conduct a competition to award the funds allotted to the State under sec. 506(e) of the OAA for the first full program year following the Department's determination. The new grantee will be responsible for administering the SCSEP in the State and will be subject to the same requirements and responsibilities as had been the State grantee.

(c) *Evaluation*. The Department will annually evaluate, publish and make available for public review, information on the actual performance of each grantee with respect to the levels achieved for each of the core measures of performance, compared to the expected levels of performance established under § 641.720 (including any adjustments to such levels made in accordance with § 641.720(d)). The results of the Department's annual evaluation will be reported to Congress.

§ 641.750 Will there be performance-related incentives?

The Department is authorized by OAA secs. 502(e)(2)(B)(iv) and 517(c)(1) to use recaptured SCSEP funds to provide incentive awards. The Department will exercise this authority at its discretion.

Subpart H—Administrative Requirements

§ 641.800 What uniform administrative requirements apply to the use of SCSEP funds?

(a) SCSEP recipients and sub-recipients must follow the uniform administrative requirements and allowable cost requirements that apply to their type of organization. (OAA § 503(f)(2)).

(b) Governments, State, local, and Indian tribal organizations that receive SCSEP funds under grants or cooperative agreements must follow the common rule implementing OMB Circular A–102, "Grants and Cooperative Agreements with State and Local Governments" (10/07/1994) (further amended 08/29/1997), codified at 29 CFR part 97.

(c) Nonprofit and commercial organizations, institutions of higher education, hospitals, other nonprofit organizations, and commercial organizations that receive SCSEP funds under grants or cooperative agreements must follow the common rule implementing OMB Circular A–110, codified at 29 CFR part 95.

§ 641.803 What is program income?

Program income, as described in 29 CFR 97.25 (State and local governments) and 29 CFR 95.2(bb) (non-profit and commercial organizations), is income earned by the recipient or sub-recipient during the grant period that is directly generated by an allowable activity supported by grant funds or earned as a result of the award of grant funds. Program income includes income earned from license fees and royalties for copyrighted material, patents, patent applications, trademarks, and inventions produced under an award. (*See* 29 CFR 95.24(e) (non-profit and commercial organizations) and 29 CFR 97.25(e) (State and local governments)). Costs of generating SCSEP program income may be deducted from gross income received by SCSEP recipients and sub-recipients to determine SCSEP program income earned or generated provided these costs have not been charged to the SCSEP.

§ 641.806 How must SCSEP program income be used?

(a) SCSEP recipients that earn or generate program income during the grant period must add the program income to the Federal and non-Federal funds committed to the SCSEP and must use it to further the purposes of the program and in accordance with the terms and conditions of the grant award. Program income may only be spent during the grant period in which it was earned (except as provided for in paragraph (b)), as provided in 29 CFR 95.24(a) (non-profit and commercial organizations) or 29 CFR 97.25(g) (2) (State and local governments), as applicable.

(b)(1) Except as provided for in paragraph (b)(2), recipients that continue to receive a SCSEP grant from the Department must spend program income earned from SCSEP-funded activities in the Program Year in which the earned income was received.

(2) Any program income remaining at the end of the Program Year in which it was earned will remain available for expenditure in the subsequent Program Year only. Any program income remaining after the second Program Year must be remitted to the Department.

(c) Recipients that do not continue to receive a SCSEP grant from the Department must remit unexpended program income earned during the grant period from SCSEP funded activities to the Department at the end of the grant period. These recipients have no obligation to the Department for program income earned after the end of the grant period.

§ 641.809 What non-Federal share (matching) requirements apply to the use of SCSEP funds?

(a) The Department will pay no more than 90 percent of the total cost of activities carried out under a SCSEP grant. (OAA sec. 502(c)(1)).

(b) All SCSEP recipients, including Federal agencies if there is no statutory exemption, must provide or ensure that at least 10 percent of the total cost of activities carried out under a SCSEP grant (non-Federal share of costs) consists of allowable costs paid for with non-Federal funds, except as provided in paragraphs (e) and (f) of this section.

(c) Recipients must determine the non-Federal share of costs in accordance with 29 CFR 97.24 for governmental units, or 29 CFR 95.23 for non-profit and commercial organizations.

(d) The non-Federal share of costs may be provided in cash, or in-kind, or a combination of the two. (OAA § 502(c)(2)).

(e) A recipient may not require a sub-recipient or host agency to provide non-Federal resources for the use of the SCSEP project as a condition of entering into a sub-recipient or host agency relationship. This does not preclude a sub-recipient or host agency from voluntarily contributing non-Federal resources for the use of the SCSEP project.

(f) The Department may pay all of the costs of activities in an emergency or disaster project or a project in an economically distressed area. (OAA § 502(c)(1)(B)).

§ 641.812 What is the period of availability of SCSEP funds?

(a) Except as provided in § 641.815, recipients must expend SCSEP funds during the Program Year for which they are awarded (July 1–June 30). (OAA § 517(b)).

(b) SCSEP recipients must ensure that no sub-agreement provides for the expenditure of any SCSEP funds before the start of the grant year, or after the end of the grant period, except as provided in § 641.815.

§641.815 May the period of availability be extended?

SCSEP recipients may request in writing, and the Department may grant, an extension of the period during which SCSEP funds may be obligated or expended. SCSEP recipients requesting an extension must justify that an extension is necessary. (OAA §517(b)). The Department will notify recipients in writing of the approval or disapproval of any such requests.

§641.821 What audit requirements apply to the use of SCSEP funds?

(a) Recipients and sub-recipients receiving Federal awards of SCSEP funds must follow the audit requirements in paragraphs (b) and (c) of this section that apply to their type of organization. As used here, Federal awards of SCSEP funds include Federal financial assistance and Federal cost-reimbursement contracts received directly from the Department or indirectly under awards by SCSEP recipients or higher-tier sub-recipients. (OAA §503(f)(2)).

(b) All governmental and nonprofit organizations that are recipients or sub-recipients must follow the audit requirements of OMB Circular A–133. These requirements are codified at 29 CFR parts 96 and 99 and referenced in 29 CFR 97.26 for governmental organizations and in 29 CFR 95.26 for institutions of higher education, hospitals, and other nonprofit organizations.

(c)(1) The Department is responsible for audits of SCSEP recipients that are commercial organizations.

(2) Commercial organizations that are sub-recipients under the SCSEP and that expend more than the minimum level specified in OMB Circular A–133 ($500,000, for fiscal years ending after December 31, 2003) must have either an organization-wide audit or a program-specific financial and compliance audit conducted in accordance with OMB Circular A–133.

§641.824 What lobbying requirements apply to the use of SCSEP funds?

SCSEP recipients and sub-recipients must comply with the restrictions on lobbying codified in the Department's regulations at 29 CFR part 93. (Also refer to §641.850(c), "Lobbying costs.")

§641.827 What general nondiscrimination requirements apply to the use of SCSEP funds?

(a) SCSEP recipients, sub-recipients, and host agencies are required to comply with the nondiscrimination provisions codified in the Department's regulations at 29 CFR parts 31 and 32 and the provisions on the equal treatment of religious organizations at 29 CFR part 2 subpart D.

(b) Recipients and sub-recipients of SCSEP funds are required to comply with the nondiscrimination provisions codified in the Department's regulations at 29 CFR part 38 if:

(1) The recipient:

(i) Is a One-Stop partner listed in sec. 121(b) of WIOA, and

(ii) Operates programs and activities that are part of the One-Stop delivery system established under WIOA; or

(2) The recipient otherwise satisfies the definition of "recipient" in 29 CFR 38.4.

(c) Recipients must ensure that participants are provided informational materials relating to age discrimination and/or their rights under the Age Discrimination in Employment Act of 1975 that are distributed to recipients by the Department as required by §503(b)(3) of the OAA.

(d) Questions about or complaints alleging a violation of the nondiscrimination requirements cited in this section may be directed or mailed to the Director, Civil Rights Center, U.S. Department of Labor, Room N–4123, 200 Constitution Avenue, NW., Washington, DC, 20210, for processing. (See §641.910(d)).

(e) The specification of any right or protection against discrimination in paragraphs (a) through (d) of this section must not be interpreted to exclude or diminish any other right or protection against discrimination in connection with a SCSEP project that may be available to any participant, applicant for participation, or other individual under any applicable Federal, State, or local laws prohibiting discrimination, or their implementing regulations.

[75 FR 53812, Sept. 1, 2010, as amended at 82 FR 56886, Dec. 1, 2017]

§ 641.833 What policies govern political patronage?

(a) A recipient or sub-recipient must not select, reject, promote, or terminate an individual based on political services provided by the individual or on the individual's political affiliations or beliefs. In addition, as provided in § 641.827(b), certain recipients and sub-recipients of SCSEP funds are required to comply with WIOA nondiscrimination regulations in 29 CFR part 38. These regulations prohibit discrimination on the basis of political affiliation or belief.

(b) A recipient or sub-recipient must not provide, or refuse to provide, funds to any sub-recipient, host agency, or other entity based on political affiliation.

(c) SCSEP recipients must ensure that every entity that receives SCSEP funds through the recipient is applying the policies stated in paragraphs (a) and (b) of this section.

[75 FR 53812, Sept. 1, 2010, as amended at 82 FR 56886, Dec. 1, 2017]

§ 641.836 What policies govern political activities?

(a) No project under title V of the OAA may involve political activities. SCSEP recipients must ensure compliance with the requirements and prohibitions involving political activities described in paragraphs (b) and (c) of this section.

(b) State and local employees involved in the administration of SCSEP activities may not engage in political activities prohibited under the Hatch Act (5 U.S.C. chapter 15), including:

(1) Seeking partisan elective office;

(2) Using official authority or influence for the purpose of affecting elections, nominations for office, or fundraising for political purposes. (5 U.S.C. 1502).

(c) SCSEP recipients must provide all persons associated with SCSEP activities with a written explanation of allowable and unallowable political activities under the Hatch Act. A notice explaining these allowable and unallowable political activities must be posted in every workplace in which SCSEP activities are conducted. The Department will provide the form and content of the notice and explanatory material by administrative issuance. (OAA § 502(b)(1)(P)).

(d) SCSEP recipients must ensure that:

(1) No SCSEP participants or staff persons engage in partisan or nonpartisan political activities during hours for which they are being paid with SCSEP funds.

(2) No participants or staff persons engage in partisan political activities in which such participants or staff persons represent themselves as spokespersons for the SCSEP.

(3) No participants are employed or out-stationed in the offices of a Member of Congress, a State or local legislator, or on the staff of any legislative committee.

(4) No participants are employed or out-stationed in the immediate offices of any elected chief executive officer of a State or unit of general government, except that:

(i) Units of local government may serve as host agencies for participants, provided that their assignments are non-political; and

(ii) While assignments may place participants in such offices, such assignments actually must be concerned with program and service activities and not in any way involved in political functions.

(5) No participants are assigned to perform political activities in the offices of other elected officials. Placement of participants in such offices in non-political assignments is permissible, however, provided that:

(i) SCSEP recipients develop safeguards to ensure that participants placed in these assignments are not involved in political activities; and

(ii) These safeguards are described in the grant agreement and are approved by the Department and are subject to review and monitoring by the SCSEP recipient and by the Department.

§ 641.839 What policies govern union organizing activities?

Recipients must ensure that SCSEP funds are not used in any way to assist, promote, or deter union organizing.

§641.841 What policies govern nepotism?

(a) SCSEP recipients must ensure that no recipient or sub-recipient hires, and no host agency serves as a worksite for, a person who works in a SCSEP community service assignment if a member of that person's immediate family is engaged in a decision-making capacity (whether compensated or not) for that project, subproject, recipient, sub-recipient, or host agency. The Department may exempt worksites on Native American reservations and in rural areas from this requirement provided that adequate justification can be documented, such as that no other persons are eligible and available for participation in the program.

(b) To the extent that an applicable State or local legal nepotism requirement is more restrictive than this provision, SCSEP recipients must ensure that the more restrictive requirement is followed.

(c) For purposes of this section, "immediate family" means wife, husband, son, daughter, mother, father, brother, sister, son-in-law, daughter-in-law, mother- in-law, father-in-law, brother-in-law, sister-in-law, aunt, uncle, niece, nephew, stepparent, stepchild, grandparent, or grandchild.

§641.844 What maintenance of effort requirements apply to the use of SCSEP funds?

(a) A community service assignment for a participant under title V of the OAA is permissible only when specific maintenance of effort requirements are met.

(b) Each project funded under title V:

(1) Must not reduce the number of employment opportunities or vacancies that would otherwise be available to individuals not participating in the program;

(2) Must not displace currently employed workers (including partial displacement, such as a reduction in the hours of non-overtime work, wages, or employment benefits);

(3) Must not impair existing contracts or result in the substitution of Federal funds for other funds in connection with work that would otherwise be performed; and

(4) Must not employ or continue to employ any eligible individual to perform the same work or substantially the same work as that performed by any other individual who is on layoff. (OAA §502(b)(1)(G)).

§641.847 What uniform allowable cost requirements apply to the use of SCSEP funds?

(a) *General.* Unless specified otherwise in this part or the grant agreement, recipients and sub-recipients must follow the uniform allowable cost requirements that apply to their type of organization. For example, a local government sub-recipient receiving SCSEP funds from a nonprofit organization must use the allowable cost requirements for governmental organizations in OMB Circular A–87. The Department's regulations at 29 CFR 95.27 (non-profit and commercial organizations) and 29 CFR 97.22 (State and local governments) identify the Federal principles for determining allowable costs that each kind of organization must follow. The applicable Federal principles for each kind of organization are described in paragraphs (b)(1) through (b)(5) of this section. (OAA §503(f)(2)).

(b) *Allowable costs/cost principles.* (1) Allowable costs for State, local, and Indian tribal government organizations must be determined under OMB Circular A–87, "Cost Principles for State, Local and Indian Tribal Governments."

(2) Allowable costs for nonprofit organizations must be determined under OMB Circular A–122, "Cost Principles for Non-Profit Organizations."

(3) Allowable costs for institutions of higher education must be determined under OMB Circular A–21, "Cost Principles for Educational Institutions."

(4) Allowable costs for hospitals must be determined in accordance with appendix E of 45 CFR part 74, "Principles for Determining Costs Applicable to Research and Development Under Grants and Contracts with Hospitals."

(5) Allowable costs for commercial organizations and those nonprofit organizations listed in Attachment C to OMB Circular A–122 must be determined under the provisions of the Federal Acquisition Regulation (FAR), at 48 CFR part 31.

§ 641.850 Are there other specific allowable and unallowable cost requirements for the SCSEP?

(a) Yes, in addition to the generally applicable cost principles in § 641.847(b), the cost principles in paragraphs (b) through (g) of this section apply to SCSEP grants.

(b) *Claims against the Government.* For all types of entities, legal expenses for the prosecution of claims against the Federal Government, including appeals to an Administrative Law Judge, are unallowable.

(c) *Lobbying costs.* In addition to the prohibition contained in 29 CFR part 93, SCSEP funds must not be used to pay any salaries or expenses related to any activity designed to influence legislation or appropriations pending before the Congress of the United States or any State legislature. (See § 641.824).

(d) *One-Stop costs.* Costs of participating as a required partner in the One-Stop delivery system established in accordance with sec. 121(e) of WIOA are allowable, provided that SCSEP services and funding are provided in accordance with the MOU required by WIOA and OAA sec. 502(b)(1)(O), and costs are determined in accordance with the applicable cost principles. The costs of services provided by the SCSEP, including those provided by participants/enrollees, may comprise a portion or the total of a SCSEP project's proportionate share of One-Stop costs.

(e) *Building repairs and acquisition costs.* Except as provided in this paragraph and as an exception to the allowable cost principles in § 641.847(b), no SCSEP funds may be used for the purchase, construction, or renovation of any building except for the labor involved in:

(1) Minor remodeling of a public building necessary to make it suitable for use for project purposes;

(2) Minor repair and rehabilitation of publicly used facilities for the general benefit of the community; and

(3) Repair and rehabilitation by participants of housing occupied by persons with low incomes who are declared eligible for such services by authorized local agencies.

(f) *Accessibility and reasonable accommodation.* Recipients and sub-recipients may use SCSEP funds to meet their obligations under § 504 of the Rehabilitation Act of 1973, as amended, and the Americans with Disabilities Act of 1990, as amended, and any other applicable Federal disability nondiscrimination laws, to provide physical and programmatic accessibility and reasonable accommodation/modifications for, and effective communications with, individuals with disabilities. (29 U.S.C. 794).

(g) *Participants' benefit costs.* Recipients and sub-recipients may use SCSEP funds for participant benefit costs only under the conditions set forth in § 641.565.

[75 FR 53812, Sept. 1, 2010, as amended at 82 FR 56886, Dec. 1, 2017]

§ 641.853 How are costs classified?

(a) All costs must be classified as "administrative costs" or "programmatic activity costs." (OAA § 502(c)(6)).

(b) Recipients and sub-recipients must assign participants' wage and benefit costs and other participant (enrollee) costs such as supportive services to the programmatic activity cost category. (See § 641.864). When a participant's community service assignment involves functions whose costs are normally classified as administrative costs, compensation provided to the participants must be charged as programmatic activity costs instead of administrative costs, since participant wage and benefit costs are always charged to the programmatic activity cost category.

§ 641.856 What functions and activities constitute administrative costs?

(a) Administrative costs are that allocable portion of necessary and reasonable allowable costs of recipients and program operators that are associated with those specific functions identified in paragraph (b) of this section and that are not related to the direct provision of programmatic activities specified in § 641.864. These costs may be both personnel and non-personnel and both direct and indirect costs.

(b) Administrative costs are the costs associated with:

(1) Performing general administrative and coordination functions, including:

(i) Accounting, budgeting, financial, and cash management functions;

(ii) Procurement and purchasing functions;

(iii) Property management functions;

(iv) Personnel management functions;

(v) Payroll functions;

(vi) Coordinating the resolution of findings arising from audits, reviews, investigations, and incident reports;

(vii) Audit functions;

(viii) General legal services functions;

(ix) Developing systems and procedures, including information systems, required for these administrative functions;

(x) Preparing administrative reports; and

(xi) Other activities necessary for general administration of government funds and associated programs.

(2) Oversight and monitoring responsibilities related to administrative functions;

(3) Costs of goods and services used for administrative functions of the program, including goods and services such as rental or purchase of equipment, utilities, office supplies, postage, and rental and maintenance of office space;

(4) Travel costs incurred for official business in carrying out administrative activities or the overall management of the program;

(5) Costs of information systems related to administrative functions (for example, personnel, procurement, purchasing, property management, accounting, and payroll systems) including the purchase, systems development, and operating costs of such systems and;

(6) Costs of technical assistance, professional organization membership dues, and evaluating results obtained by the project involved against stated objectives. (OAA § 502(c)(4)).

§ 641.859 What other special rules govern the classification of costs as administrative costs or programmatic activity costs?

(a) Recipients and sub-recipients must comply with the special rules for classifying costs as administrative costs or programmatic activity costs set forth in paragraphs (b) through (e) of this section.

(b)(1) Costs of awards by recipients and program operators that are solely for the performance of their own administrative functions are classified as administrative costs.

(2) Costs incurred by recipients and program operators for administrative functions listed in § 641.856(b) are classified as administrative costs.

(3) Costs incurred by vendors and sub-recipients performing the administrative functions of recipients and program operators are classified as administrative costs. (See 29 CFR 99.210 for a discussion of factors differentiating sub-recipients from vendors.)

(4) Except as provided in paragraph (b)(3) of this section, all costs incurred by all vendors, and only those sub-recipients below program operators, are classified as programmatic activity costs. (*See* 29 CFR 99.210 for a discussion of factors differentiating sub-recipients from vendors.)

(c) Personnel and related non-personnel costs of staff who perform both administrative functions specified in § 641.856(b) and programmatic services or activities must be allocated as administrative or programmatic activity costs to the benefiting cost objectives/categories based on documented distributions of actual time worked or other equitable cost allocation methods.

(d) The allocable share of indirect or overhead costs charged to the SCSEP grant are to be allocated to the administrative and programmatic activity cost categories in the same proportion as the costs in the overhead or indirect cost pool are classified as programmatic activity or administrative costs.

(e) Costs of the following information systems including the purchase, systems development and operating (e.g., data entry) costs are charged to the programmatic activity cost category:

(1) Tracking or monitoring of participant and performance information;

(2) Employment statistics information, including job listing information, job skills information, and demand occupation information; and

(3) Local area performance information.

§ 641.861 Must SCSEP recipients provide funding for the administrative costs of sub-recipients?

(a) Recipients and sub-recipients must obtain funding for administrative costs to the extent practicable from non-Federal sources. (OAA § 502(c)(5)).

(b) SCSEP recipients must ensure that sufficient funding is provided for the administrative activities of sub-recipients that receive SCSEP funding through the recipient. Each SCSEP recipient must describe in its grant application the methodology used to ensure that sub-recipients receive sufficient funding for their administrative activities. (OAA § 502(b)(1)(R)).

§ 641.864 What functions and activities constitute programmatic activity costs?

Programmatic activity costs include, but are not limited to, the costs of the following functions:

(a) Participant wages, such benefits as are required by law (such as workers' compensation or unemployment compensation), the costs of physical examinations, compensation for scheduled work hours during which a host agency is closed for a Federal holiday, and necessary sick leave that is not part of an accumulated sick leave program, except that no amounts provided under the grant may be used to pay the cost of pension benefits, annual leave, accumulated sick leave, or bonuses, as described in § 641.565;

(b) Outreach, recruitment and selection, intake, orientation, assessment, and preparation and updating of IEPs;

(c) Participant training, as described in § 641.540, which may be provided before commencing or during a community service assignment, and which may be provided at a host agency, in a classroom setting, or using other appropriate arrangements, which may include reasonable costs of instructors' salaries, classroom space, training supplies, materials, equipment, and tuition;

(d) Subject to the restrictions in § 641.535(c), job placement assistance, including job development and job search assistance, job fairs, job clubs, and job referrals; and

(e) Participant supportive services, to enable an individual to successfully participate in a SCSEP project, as described in § 641.545. (OAA § 502(c)(6)(A)).

§ 641.867 What are the limitations on the amount of SCSEP administrative costs?

(a) Except as provided in paragraph (b), no more than 13.5 percent of the SCSEP funds received for a Program Year may be used for administrative costs.

(b) The Department may increase the amount available for administrative costs to not more than 15 percent, in accordance with § 641.870. (OAA § 502(c)(3)).

§ 641.870 Under what circumstances may the administrative cost limitation be increased?

(a) SCSEP recipients may request that the Department increase the amount available for administrative costs. The Department may honor the request if:

(1) The Department determines that it is necessary to carry out the project; and

(2) The recipient demonstrates that:

(i) Major administrative cost increases are being incurred in necessary program components, such as liability insurance, payments for workers' compensation for staff, costs associated with achieving unsubsidized placement goals, and other operation requirements imposed by the Department;

(ii) The number of community service assignment positions in the project or the number of minority eligible individuals participating in the project will decline if the amount available for paying the cost of administration is not increased; or

(iii) The size of the project is so small that the amount of administrative costs incurred to carry out the project necessarily exceeds 13.5 percent of the grant amount. (OAA § 502(c)(3)).

(b) A request by a recipient or prospective recipient for an increase in the amount available for administrative costs may be submitted as part of the grant application or as a separate submission at any time after the grant award.

§641.873 What minimum expenditure levels are required for participant wages and benefits?

(a) Except as provided in §641.874 or in paragraph (c) of this section, not less than 75 percent of the SCSEP funds provided under a grant from the Department must be used to pay for wages and benefits of participants as described in §641.864(a). (OAA §502(c)(6)(B)).

(b) A SCSEP recipient is in compliance with this provision if at least 75 percent of the total expenditure of SCSEP funds provided to the recipient was for wages and benefits, even if one or more sub-recipients did not expend at least 75 percent of their SCSEP sub-recipient award for wages and benefits.

(c) A SCSEP grantee may submit to the Department a request for approval to use not less than 65 percent of the grant funds to pay wages and benefits under §641.874.

§641.874 What conditions apply to a SCSEP grantee request to use additional funds for training and supportive service costs?

(a) A grantee may submit to the Department a request for approval—

(1) To use not less than 65 percent of the grant funds to pay the wages and benefits described in §641.864(a);

(2) To use the percentage of grant funds specified in §641.867 to pay for administrative costs as described in §641.856;

(3) To use the 10 percent of grant funds that would otherwise be devoted to wages and benefits under §641.873 to provide participant training (as described in §641.540(e)) and participant supportive services to enable participants to successfully participate in a SCSEP project (as described in §641.545), in which case the grantee must provide (from the funds described in this paragraph) the wages for those individual participants who are receiving training from the funds described in this paragraph, but may not use the funds described in this paragraph to pay for any administrative costs; and

(4) To use the remaining grant funds to provide participant training, job placement assistance, participant supportive services, and outreach, recruitment and selection, intake, orientation and assessment.

(b) In submitting the request the grantee must include in the request—

(1) A description of the activities for which the grantee will spend the grant funds described in paragraphs (a)(3) and (a)(4) of this section;

(2) An explanation documenting how the provision of such activities will improve the effectiveness of the project, including an explanation of whether any displacement of eligible individuals or elimination of positions for such individuals will occur, information on the number of such individuals to be displaced and of such positions to be eliminated, and an explanation of how the activities will improve employment outcomes for the individuals served, based on the assessment conducted under §641.535(a)(2); and

(3) A proposed budget and work plan for the activities, including a detailed description of how the funds will be spent on the activities described in paragraphs (a)(3) and (a)(4) of this section.

(c)(1) If a grantee wishes to amend an existing grant agreement to use additional funds for training and supportive service costs, the grantee must submit such a request not later than 90 days before the proposed date of implementation contained in the request. Not later than 30 days before the proposed date of implementation, the Department will approve, approve as modified, or reject the request, on the basis of the information included in the request.

(2) If a grantee submits a request to use additional funds for training and supportive service costs in the grant application, the request will be accepted and processed as a part of the grant review process.

(d) Grantees may apply this provision to individual sub-recipients but need not provide this opportunity to all their sub-recipients.

§641.876 How will compliance with cost limitations and minimum expenditure levels be determined?

The Department will determine compliance by examining expenditures of SCSEP funds. The cost limitations and minimum expenditure level requirements must be met at the time all such funds have been expended or the period of availability of such funds has expired, whichever comes first.

§ 641.879 What are the financial and performance reporting requirements for recipients?

(a) In accordance with 29 CFR 97.41 (State and local governments) or 29 CFR 95.52 (non-profit and commercial organizations), each SCSEP recipient must submit a SCSEP Financial Status Report (FSR, ETA Form 9130) in electronic format to the Department via the Internet within 45 days after the ending of each quarter of the Program Year. Each SCSEP recipient must also submit a final closeout FSR to the Department via the Internet within 90 days after the end of the grant period. The Department will provide instructions for the preparation of this report. (OAA § 503(f)(3)).

(1) Financial data must be reported on an accrual basis, and cumulatively by funding year of appropriation. Financial data may also be required on specific program activities as required by the Department.

(2) If the SCSEP recipient's accounting records are not normally kept on the accrual basis of accounting, the SCSEP recipient must develop accrual information through an analysis of the documentation on hand.

(b) In accordance with 29 CFR 97.40 (State and local governments) or 29 CFR 95.51 (non-profit and commercial organizations), each SCSEP recipient must submit updated data on participants (including data on demographic characteristics and data regarding the performance measures), host agencies, and employers in an electronic format specified by the Department via the Internet within 30 days after the end of each of the first three quarters of the Program Year, on the last day of the fourth quarter of the Program Year, and within 90 days after the last day of the Program Year. Recipients wishing to correct data errors or omissions for their final Program Year report must do so within 90 days after the end of the Program Year. The Department will generate SCSEP Quarterly Progress Reports (QPRs), as well as the final QPR, as soon as possible after receipt of the data. (OAA § 503(f)(3)).

(c) Each State agency receiving title V funds must annually submit an equitable distribution report of SCSEP positions by all recipients in the State. The Department will provide instructions for the preparation of this report. (OAA § 508).

(d) In addition to the data required to be submitted under paragraph (b) of this section, each SCSEP recipient may be required to collect data and submit reports on the performance measures. See subpart G. The Department will provide instructions detailing these measures and how recipients must prepare this report.

(e) In addition to the data required to be submitted under paragraph (b) of this section, each SCSEP recipient may be required to collect data and submit reports about the demographic characteristics of program participants. The Department will provide instructions detailing these measures and how recipients must prepare these reports.

(f) Federal agencies that receive and use SCSEP funds under interagency agreements must submit project financial and progress reports in accordance with this section. Federal recipients must maintain the necessary records that support required reports according to instructions provided by the Department. (OAA § 503(f)(3)).

(g) Recipients may be required to maintain records that contain any other information that the Department determines to be appropriate in support of any other reports that the Department may require. (OAA § 503(f)(3)).

(h) Grantees submitting reports that cannot be validated or verified as accurately counting and reporting activities in accordance with the reporting instructions may be treated as failing to submit reports, which may result in failing one of the responsibility tests outlined in § 641.430 and OAA § 514(d).

§ 641.881 What are the SCSEP recipient's responsibilities relating to awards to sub-recipients?

(a) Recipients are responsible for ensuring that all awards to sub-recipients are conducted in a manner to provide, to the maximum extent practicable, full and open competition in accordance with the procurement procedures in 29 CFR 95.43 (non-profit and commercial organizations) and 29 CFR 97.36 (State and local governments).

(b) The SCSEP recipient is responsible for all grant activities, including the performance of SCSEP activities by sub-recipients, and ensuring that sub-recipients comply with the OAA and this part. (See also OAA §514(d) and §641.430 of this part on responsibility tests).

(c) Recipients must follow their own procedures for allocating funds to other entities. The Department will not grant funds to another entity on the recipient's behalf.

(d)(1) National grantees that receive grants to provide services in an area where a substantial population of individuals with barriers to employment exists must, in selecting sub-recipients, give special consideration to organizations (including former national grant recipients) with demonstrated expertise in serving such individuals. (OAA §514(e)(2)).

(2) For purposes of this section, the term "individuals with barriers to employment" means minority individuals, Indian individuals, individuals with greatest economic need, and most-in-need individuals. (OAA §514(e)(1)).

§641.884 What are the grant closeout procedures?

SCSEP recipients must follow the grant closeout procedures at 29 CFR 97.50 (State and local governments) or 29 CFR 95.71 (non-profit and government organizations), as appropriate. The Department will issue supplementary closeout instructions to OAA title V recipients as necessary.

Subpart I—Grievance Procedures and Appeals Process

§641.900 What appeal process is available to an applicant that does not receive a grant?

(a) An applicant for financial assistance under title V of the OAA that is dissatisfied because it was not awarded financial assistance in whole or in part may request that the Grant Officer provide an explanation for not awarding financial assistance to that applicant. The request must be filed within 10 days of the date of notification indicating that financial assistance would not be awarded. The Grant Officer must provide the protesting applicant with feedback concerning its proposal within 21 days of the protest. Applicants may appeal to the U.S. Department of Labor, Office of Administrative Law Judges (OALJ), within 21 days of the date of the Grant Officer's feedback on the proposal, or within 21 days of the Grant Officer's notification that financial assistance would not be awarded if the applicant does not request feedback on its proposal. The appeal may be for a part or the whole of the denied funding. This appeal will not in any way interfere with the Department's decisions to fund other organizations to provide services during the appeal period.

(b) Failure to file an appeal within the 21 days provided in paragraph (a) of this section constitutes a waiver of the right to a hearing.

(c) A request for a hearing under this section must state specifically those issues in the Grant Officer's notification upon which review is requested. Those provisions of the Grant Officer's notification not specified for review are considered resolved and not subject to further review.

(d) A request for a hearing must be transmitted by certified mail, return receipt requested, to the Chief Administrative Law Judge, U.S. Department of Labor, Suite 400 North, 800 K Street, NW., Washington, DC 20001, with one copy to the Departmental official who issued the determination.

(e) The decision of the ALJ constitutes final agency action unless, within 21 days of the decision, a party dissatisfied with the ALJ's decision, in whole or in part, has filed a petition for review with the Administrative Review Board (ARB) (established under Secretary's Order No. 2–96, published at 61 FR 19978, May 3, 1996), specifically identifying the procedure, fact, law, or policy to which exception is taken. The mailing address for the ARB is 200 Constitution Ave., NW., Room N5404, Washington, DC 20210. The Department will deem any exception not specifically urged to have been waived. A copy of the petition for review must be sent to the grant officer at that time. If, within 30 days of the filing of the petition for review, the ARB does not notify the parties that the case has been accepted for review, then the decision of the ALJ constitutes final agency action. Any case accepted by the ARB must be decided within 180 days of acceptance. If not so decided, the decision of the ALJ constitutes final agency action.

(f) The Rules of Practice and Procedures for Administrative Hearings Before the Office of Administrative Law Judges, at 29 CFR part 18, govern the conduct of hearings under this section, except that:

(1) The appeal is not considered a complaint; and

(2) Technical rules of evidence, such as the Federal Rules of Evidence and subpart B of 29 CFR part 18, will not apply to any hearing conducted under this section. However, rules designed to assure production of the most credible evidence available and to subject testimony to test by cross-examination will be applied when the ALJ conducting the hearing considers them reasonably necessary. The certified copy of the administrative file transmitted to the ALJ by the official issuing the notification not to award financial assistance must be part of the evidentiary record of the case and need not be moved into evidence.

(g) The ALJ should render a written decision no later than 90 days after the closing of the record.

(h) The remedies available are provided in §641.470.

§641.910 What grievance procedures must grantees make available to applicants, employees, and participants?

(a) Each grantee must establish, and describe in the grant agreement, grievance procedures for resolving complaints, other than those described by paragraph (d) of this section, arising between the grantee, employees of the grantee, sub-recipients, and applicants or participants.

(b) The Department will not review final determinations made under paragraph (a) of this section, except to determine whether the grantee's grievance procedures were followed, and according to paragraph (c) of this section.

(c) Allegations of violations of Federal law, other than those described in paragraph (d) of this section, which are not resolved within 60 days under the grantee's procedures, may be filed with the Chief, Division of Adult Services, Employment and Training Administration, U.S. Department of Labor, 200 Constitution Avenue, NW., Washington, DC 20210. Allegations determined to be substantial and credible will be investigated and addressed.

(d) Questions about, or complaints alleging a violation of, the nondiscrimination requirements of title VI of the Civil Rights Act of 1964, sec. 504 of the Rehabilitation Act of 1973, sec. 188 of the Workforce Innovation and Opportunity Act (WIOA), or their implementing regulations, may be directed or mailed to the Director, Civil Rights Center, U.S. Department of Labor, Room N–4123, 200 Constitution Avenue NW., Washington, DC 20210. In the alternative, complaints alleging violations of WIOA sec. 188 may be filed initially at the grantee level. See 29 CFR 38.69, 38.72. In such cases, the grantee must use complaint processing procedures meeting the requirements of 29 CFR 38.69 through 38.76 to resolve the complaint.

[75 FR 53812, Sept. 1, 2010, as amended at 82 FR 56886, Dec. 1, 2017]

§641.920 What actions of the Department may a grantee appeal and what procedures apply to those appeals?

(a) Appeals from a final disallowance of costs as a result of an audit must be made under 29 CFR 96.63.

(b) Appeals of suspension or termination actions taken on the grounds of discrimination are processed under 29 CFR part 31 or 29 CFR part 38, as appropriate.

(c) Protests and appeals of decisions not to award a grant, in whole or in part, will be handled under §641.900.

(d) Upon a grantee's receipt of the Department's final determination relating to costs (except final disallowance of costs as a result of an audit, as described in paragraph (a) of this section), payment, suspension or termination, or the imposition of sanctions, the grantee may appeal the final determination to the Department's Office of Administrative Law Judges, as follows:

(1) Within 21 days of receipt of the Department's final determination, the grantee may transmit by certified mail, return receipt requested, a request for a hearing to the Chief Administrative Law Judge, United States Department of Labor, Suite 400 North, 800 K Street, NW., Washington, DC 20001 with a copy to the Department official who signed the final determination.

(2) The request for hearing must be accompanied by a copy of the final determination, and must state specifically those issues of the determination upon which review is requested. Those provisions of the determination not specified for review, or the entire determination when no hearing has been requested within the 21 days, are considered resolved and not subject to further review.

(3) The Rules of Practice and Procedures for Administrative Hearings Before the Office of Administrative Law Judges, at 29 CFR part 18, govern the conduct of hearings under this section, except that:

(i) The appeal is not considered as a complaint; and

(ii) Technical rules of evidence, such as the Federal Rules of Evidence and subpart B of 29 CFR part 18, will not apply to any hearing conducted under this section. However, rules designed to assure production of the most credible evidence available and to subject testimony to test by cross-examination will be applied when the Administrative Law Judge conducting the hearing considers them reasonably necessary. The certified copy of the administrative file transmitted to the Administrative Law Judge by the official issuing the final determination must be part of the evidentiary record of the case and need not be moved into evidence.

(4) The Administrative Law Judge should render a written decision no later than 90 days after the closing of the record. In ordering relief, the ALJ may exercise the full authority of the Secretary under the OAA.

(5) The decision of the ALJ constitutes final agency action unless, within 21 days of the decision, a party dissatisfied with the ALJ's decision, in whole or in part, has filed a petition for review with the ARB (established under Secretary's Order No. 2–96), specifically identifying the procedure, fact, law, or policy to which exception is taken. The mailing address for the ARB is 200 Constitution Ave., NW., Room N5404, Washington, DC 20210. The Department will deem any exception not specifically argued to have been waived. A copy of the petition for review must be sent to the grant officer at that time. If, within 30 days of the filing of the petition for review, the ARB does not notify the parties that the case has been accepted for review, then the decision of the ALJ constitutes final agency action. Any case accepted by the ARB must be decided within 180 days of acceptance. If not so decided, the decision of the ALJ constitutes final agency action.

[75 FR 53812, Sept. 1, 2010, as amended at 82 FR 56886, Dec. 1, 2017]

§ 641.930 Is there an alternative dispute resolution process that may be used in place of an OALJ hearing?

(a) Parties to a complaint that has been filed according to the requirements of § 641.920 (a), (c), and (d) may choose to waive their rights to an administrative hearing before the OALJ. Instead, they may choose to transfer the settlement of their dispute to an individual acceptable to all parties who will conduct an informal review of the stipulated facts and render a decision in accordance with applicable law. A written decision must be issued within 60 days after submission of the matter for informal review.

(b) Unless the parties agree in writing to extend the period, the waiver of the right to request a hearing before the OALJ will automatically be revoked if a settlement has not been reached or a decision has not been issued within the 60 days provided in paragraph (a) of this section.

(c) The decision rendered under this informal review process will be treated as the final agency decision.

PART 645—PROVISIONS GOVERNING WELFARE-TO-WORK GRANTS

Subpart A—Scope and Purpose

Subpart B—General Program and Administrative Requirements

Subpart C—Additional Formula Grant Administrative Requirements and Procedures

Subpart D—State Formula Grant Administration

Subpart E—Welfare-to-Work Competitive Grants

Subpart F—Administrative Appeal Process

AUTHORITY: 42 U.S.C. 603 (a)(5)(C)(viii).

SOURCE: 66 FR 2711, Jan. 11, 2001, unless otherwise noted.

Subpart A—Scope and Purpose

§ 645.100 What does this part cover?

(a) Subpart A establishes regulatory provisions that apply to the Welfare-to-Work (WtW) programs conducted at the State and at the local area levels.

(b) Subpart B provides general program requirements applicable to all WtW formula and competitive funds. The provisions of this subpart govern how WtW funds must be spent, who is eligible to participate in the program, allowable activities and their relationship to TANF, Governor's projects for long-term recipients, administrative and fiscal provisions, and program oversight requirements. This subpart also addresses worker protections and the establishment of a State grievance system.

(c) Subpart C sets forth additional administrative standards and procedures for WtW Formula Grants, such as matching requirements and reallotment procedures.

(d) Subpart D sets forth the conditions under which the Governor may request a waiver to designate an alternate administering agency, sets forth the formula elements that must be included in the within-State distribution formula, the submission of a State annual plan, the factors for measuring State performance, and the roles and responsibilities of the States and the local boards or alternate administering agencies.

(e) Subpart E outlines general conditions and requirements for the WtW Competitive Grants.

(f) Subpart F sets forth the administrative appeals process.

(g) Regulatory provisions applicable to the Indian and Native American Welfare-to-Work Program (INA WtW) are found at 20 CFR part 646.

§ 645.110 What are the purposes of the Welfare-to-Work Program?

The purposes of the WtW program are:

(a) To facilitate the placement of hard-to-employ welfare recipients and certain noncustodial parents into transitional employment opportunities which will lead to lasting unsubsidized employment and self-sufficiency;

(b) To provide a variety of activities, grounded in TANF's "work first" philosophy, to prepare individuals for, and to place them in, lasting unsubsidized employment;

(c) To provide for a variety of post-employment and job retention services which will assist the hard-to-employ welfare recipient and certain noncustodial parents to secure lasting unsubsidized employment;

(d) To provide targeted WtW funds to high poverty areas with large numbers of hard-to-employ welfare recipients.

§ 645.120 What definitions apply to this part?

The following definitions apply under this part:

Act means Title IV, Part A of the Social Security Act, 42 U.S.C. 601–619.

Adult means an individual who is not a minor child.

Chief Elected Official(s) (CEOs) means:

(1) The chief elected official of the sole unit of general local government in the service delivery area,

(2) The individual or individuals selected by the chief elected officials of all units of general local government in such area as their authorized representative, or

(3) In the case of a service delivery area designated under section 101(a)(4)(A)(iii) of JTPA, the representative of the chief elected official for such area (as defined in section 4(4)(C) of JTPA) or as defined in section 101 of the Workforce Investment Act of 1988.

Competitive grants means those grants in which WtW funds have been awarded by the Department under a competitive application process to local governments, PICs, and private entities (such as community development corporations, community-based and faith-based organizations, disability community organizations, and community action agencies) who apply in conjunction with a PIC or local government.

Department or *DOL* means the U.S. Department of Labor.

Employment activities means the activities enumerated at § 645.220(b).

ETA means the Employment and Training Administration of the U.S. Department of Labor.

Fiscal year (FY) means any 12-month period ending on September 30 of a calendar year.

Formula grants means those grants in which WtW funds have been allotted to each Welfare-to-Work State, based on a formula prescribed by the Act, which equally considers States' shares of the national number of poor individuals and of adult recipients of assistance under TANF. The State is required to distribute not less than 85 percent of the allotted formula grant funds to service delivery areas in the State; and the State may retain not more than 15 percent for projects to help long-term recipients of assistance enter unsubsidized employment. Unless otherwise specified, the term "formula grant" refers to the 85 percent and 15 percent funds.

Governor means the Chief Executive Officer of a State.

IV-D Agency (Child Support Enforcement) means the organizational unit in the State that has the responsibility for administering or supervising the administration of the State plan under title IV-D of the Act (SSA).

Job Training Partnership Act or *JTPA* means Public Law (Pub. L.) 97–300, as amended, 29 U.S.C. 1501, *et seq*.

Local area means a local workforce investment area designated under section 116 of the Workforce investment Act of 1998, or a service delivery area designated under section 101 of the Job Training partnership Act, as appropriate.

Local workforce investment board (local board) means a local board established under section 117 of the Workforce Investment Act, or a *Private Industry Council* established under section 102 of the Job Training Partnership Act (JTPA), which performs the functions authorized at section 103 of the JTPA, or an alternate administering agency designated under section 405(a)(5)(A)(vii)(II) of the Act and § 645.400 of this part.

Minor child means an individual who has not attained 18 years of age, or has not attained 19 years of age and is a full-time student in a secondary school (or in the equivalent level of vocational or technical training).

MOE means maintenance of effort. Under TANF, States are required to maintain a certain level of spending on welfare based on "historic" FY 1994 expenditure levels (Section 409(a)(7) of the Act).

PIC means a Private Industry Council established under Section 102 of the Job Training Partnership Act, which performs the functions authorized at Section 103 of the JTPA.

Political subdivision of a State means a unit of general purpose local government, as provided for in State laws and/or Constitution, which has the power to levy taxes and spend funds and which also has general corporate and police powers.

Private entity means any organization, public or private, which is not a local board, PIC or alternate administering agency or a political subdivision of a State.

PRWORA means the Personal Responsibility and Work Opportunity Reconciliation Act of 1996, Public Law (Pub. L.) 104–193, which established the TANF program.

SDA means a service delivery area designated under section 101 of the Job Training Partnership Act or a local area designated under section 116 of the Workforce Investment Act of 1998, as appropriate.

Secretary means the Secretary of Labor.

Separate State program means a program operated outside of TANF in which the expenditures of State funds may count for TANF MOE purposes.

State means the 50 States of the United States, the District of Columbia, the Commonwealth of Puerto Rico, the US Virgin Islands, Guam, and American Samoa, unless otherwise specified.

State TANF Program means those funds expended under the State Family Assistance Grant (SFAG), the basic block grant allocated to the States under Section 403(a)(1) of the Act.

TANF means Temporary Assistance for Needy Families Program established under PRWORA.

TANF MOE means the expenditure of State funds that must be made in order to meet the Temporary Assistance for Needy Families Maintenance of Effort requirement.

Unemployed means the individual is without a job and wants and is available for work.

WIA means the Workforce Investment Act of 1998 (Pub. L. 105–220)(29 U.S.C. 2801 *et seq.*).

WtW means Welfare-to-Work.

WtW State means those States that the Secretary of Labor determines have met the five conditions established at Section 403(a)(5)(A)(ii) of the Act. Only States that are determined to be WtW States can receive WtW grant funds.

WtW statute means those provisions of the Balanced Budget Act of 1997 containing certain amendments to PRWORA and establishing the new Welfare-to-Work program, amending Title IV of the Social Security Act, (codified at 42 U.S.C. 601–619).

§645.125 What are the roles of the local and State governmental partners in the governance of the WtW program?

(a) Local boards or alternate administering agencies, in coordination with CEO's should establish policies, interpretations, guidelines and definitions to implement provisions of the WtW statute to the extent that such policies, interpretations, guidelines and definitions are not inconsistent with the WtW statute or regulations or with State policies.

(b) States should establish policies, interpretations, guidelines and definitions to implement provisions of the WtW statute to the extent that such policies, interpretations, guidelines and definitions are not inconsistent with the WtW statute or regulations.

(c) The Secretary, in consultation with other Federal Agencies, as appropriate, may publish guidance on interpretations of statutory and regulatory provisions. State and local policies, interpretations, guidelines and definitions that are consistent with interpretations contained in such guidance will be considered to be consistent with the WtW statute for purposes of this section.

§645.130 What are the effective dates for the Welfare-to-Work 1999 Amendments?

The legislative changes made by the 1999 amendments:

(a) Are effective on November 29, 1999, except as provided in paragraphs (b) and (c) of this section;

(b) Provisions relating to the eligibility of participants for WtW competitive grants are effective on January 1, 2000;

(c)(1) Provisions relating to the eligibility of participants for WtW formula grants are effective on July 1, 2000, except that expenditures from allotments to the States, as discussed in §645.135 of this subpart, must not have been made before October 1, 2000, for individuals who would not have been eligible under the criteria in effect before the changes made by the 1999 Amendments;

(2) Provisions authorizing pre-placement vocational educational training and job training for WtW formula grants, at §645.220(b) of this part, are effective on July 1, 2000, except that expenditures from allotments to the States, as discussed in §645.135 of this subpart, must not have been made before October 1, 2000.

§645.135 What is the effective date for spending Federal Welfare-to-Work formula funds on newly eligible participants and newly authorized services?

States and local areas may expend matching funds beginning July 1, 2000. States and local areas may incur unpaid obligations within the normal course of business, beginning July 1, 2000, provided that the timing of those transactions ensures that drawdown of federal Welfare-to-Work formula funds to liquidate the obligations did not occur until October 1, 2000.

Subpart B—General Program and Administrative Requirements

§ 645.200 What does this subpart cover?

This subpart provides general program and administrative requirements for WtW formula funds, including Governors' funds for long-term recipients of assistance, and for competitive grant funding (section 403(a)(5)).

§ 645.210 What is meant by the terms "entity" and "project" in the statutory phrase "an entity that operates a project" with Welfare-to-Work funds?

The terms "entity" and "project", in the statutory phrase "an entity that operates a project", means:

(a) For WtW substate formula funds:

(1) "Entity" means the PIC, local board (or the alternate administering agency designated by the Governor and approved by the Secretary pursuant to § 645.400 of this part) which administers the WtW substate formula funds in a local area(s). This entity is referred to in §§ 645.211 through 645.225 of this part as the "operating entity."

(2) "Project" means all activities, administrative and programmatic, supported by the total amount of the WtW substate formula funds allotted to the entity described in section (a)(1) of this paragraph.

(b) For WtW Governors' funds for long-term recipients of assistance:

(1) "Entity" means the agency, group, or organization to which the Governor has distributed any of the funds for long-term recipients of assistance, as described in § 645.410 (b) and (c) of this part. This entity is referred to in §§ 645.211 through 645.225 of this part as the "operating entity."

(2) "Project" means all activities, administrative and programmatic, supported by the total amount of one discrete award of WtW Governors' funds for long-term recipients of assistance awarded to the entity described in section (b)(1) of this paragraph.

(c) For competitive WtW funds:

(1) "Entity" means an eligible applicant, as described in § 645.500 of this part, which is awarded a competitive WtW grant. This entity is referred to in §§ 645.211 through 645.225 of this part as the "operating entity."

(2) "Project" means all of the activities, administrative and programmatic, supported by the total amount of one discrete WtW competitive grant awarded to the entity described in section (c)(1) of this paragraph (section 403(a)(5)(C)).

§ 645.211 How must Welfare-to-Work funds be spent by the operating entity?

An operating entity, as described in § 645.210 of this subpart, may spend not more than 30 percent of the WtW funds allotted to or awarded to the operating entity to assist individuals who meet the "other eligibles" eligibility requirements under § 645.213 of this subpart. The remaining funds allotted to or awarded to the operating entity are to be spent to benefit individuals who meet the "general eligibility" and/or "noncustodial parents" eligibility requirements, under § 645.212 of this subpart. (section 403(a)(5)(C) of the Act).

§ 645.212 Who may be served under the general eligibility and noncustodial parent eligibility (primary eligibility) provision?

An individual may be served under this provision if:

(a)(1) (S)he is currently receiving TANF assistance under a State TANF program, and/or its predecessor program, for at least 30 months, although the months do not have to be consecutive; or

(2) (S)he will become ineligible for assistance within 12 months due to either Federal or State-imposed time limits on the receipt of TANF assistance. This criterion includes individuals (as well as children of noncustodial parents) exempted from the time limits due to hardship under section 408(a)(7)(C) of the Act or due to a waiver because of domestic violence under section 402(a)(7) of the Act, who would become ineligible for assistance within 12 months without the exemption or waiver;

(b) (S)he is no longer receiving TANF assistance because (s)he has reached either the Federal five-year limit or a State-imposed time limit on receipt of TANF assistance (section 403(a)(5)(C) of the Act); or

(c) (S)he is a noncustodial parent of a minor child if:

(1) The noncustodial parent is:

(i) "Unemployed," as defined in § 645.120 of this part,

(ii) "Underemployed," as defined by the State in consultation with local boards and WtW competitive grantees, or

(iii) "Having difficulty paying child support obligations," as defined by the State in consultation with local boards and WtW competitive grantees and the State Child Support Enforcement (IV-D) Agency, and

(2) At least one of the following applies:

(i) The minor child, or the custodial parent of the minor child, meets the long-term recipient of TANF requirements of paragraph (a) of this section;

(ii) The minor child is receiving or is eligible for TANF benefits and services;

(iii) The minor child received TANF benefits and services during the preceding year; or

(iv) The minor child is receiving or eligible for assistance under the Food Stamp program, the Supplemental Security Income program, Medicaid, or the Children's Health Insurance Program; and

(3) The noncustodial parent is in compliance with the terms of a written or oral personal responsibility contract meeting the requirements of § 645.215 of this subpart.

(d) For purposes of determining whether an individual is receiving TANF assistance in paragraphs (a)(1) of this section and § 645.213(a), TANF assistance means any TANF benefits and services for the financially needy according to the appropriate income and resource criteria (if applicable) specified in the State TANF plan.

§ 645.213 Who may be served as an individual in the "other eligibles" (30 percent) provision?

Any individual may be served under this provision if (s)he:

(a) Is currently receiving TANF assistance (as described in § 645.212(d)) and either:

(1) Has characteristics associated with, or predictive of, long-term welfare dependence, such as having dropped out of school, teenage pregnancy, or having a poor work history. States, in consultation with the operating entity, may designate additional characteristics associated with, or predictive, of long term-welfare dependence; or

(2) Has significant barriers to self-sufficiency, under criteria established by the local board or alternate administering agency.

(b) Was in foster care under the responsibility of the State before s(he) attained 18 years of age and is at least 18 but not 25 years of age or older at the time of application for WtW. Eligible individuals include those who were recipients of foster care maintenance payments as defined in section 475(4) under part E of the Social Security Act, or

(c)(1) Is a custodial parent with income below 100 percent of the poverty line, determined in accordance with the most recent HHS Poverty Guidelines established under section 673(2) of the Omnibus Budget Reconciliation Act of 1981 (Pub. L. 97–35), including any revisions required by such section, applicable to a family of the size involved.

(2) For purposes of paragraph (c)(1) of this section, income is defined as total family income for the last six months, exclusive of unemployment compensation, child support payments, and old-age and survivors benefits received under section 202 of the Social Security Act (42 U.S.C. 402).

(3) A custodial parent with a disability whose own income meets the requirements of a program described in paragraph (c)(1) or (c)(3)(i) but who is a member of a family whose income does not meet such requirements is considered to have met the requirements of paragraph (c)(1) of this section.

§ 645.214 How will Welfare-to-Work participant eligibility be determined?

(a) The operating entity, as described in § 645.210(a)(1), (b)(1), and (c)(1) of this subpart, is accountable for ensuring that WtW funds are spent only on individuals eligible for WtW projects.

(b) The operating entity must ensure that there are mechanisms in place to determine WtW eligibility for individuals who are receiving TANF assistance. These mechanisms:

(1) Must include arrangements with the TANF agency to ensure that a WtW eligibility determination is based on information, current at the time of the WtW eligibility determination, about whether an individual is receiving TANF assistance, the length of receipt of TANF assistance, and when an individual may become ineligible for assistance, pursuant to §§ 645.212 and 645.213 of this part (section 403(a)(5)(I)(A)(ii)(dd)).

(2) May include a determination of WtW eligibility for characteristics of long-term welfare dependence and for significant barriers to self-sufficiency under § 645.213(a) of this subpart, based on information collected by the operating entity and/or the TANF agency up to six months prior to the WtW eligibility determination.

(c) The operating entity must ensure that there are mechanisms in place to determine WtW eligibility for individuals who have reached the time limit on receipt of TANF, under § 645.212(b) of this subpart; individuals who are not receiving TANF assistance (*i.e.*, noncustodial parents under § 645.212(c) of this subpart; individuals who are former foster care recipients under § 645.213(b) of this subpart, and low-income custodial parents under § 645.213(c) of this subpart). The mechanisms for establishing noncustodial parent eligibility must include a process for applying the preference required under § 645.215(a) of this subpart, and may include an objective standard to be used as a presumptive determination for establishing the eligibility of the minor child for the programs specified in § 645.212(c)(2)(iv) of this subpart.

§ 645.215 What must a WtW operating entity that serves noncustodial parent participants do?

(a) In programs that serve noncustodial parents, the operating entity must give preference to those noncustodial parents who qualify under § 645.212(c)(2)(i) of this subpart over other noncustodial parents. The preference for admission into the program applies only to noncustodial parents and not to any other group eligible under the "general eligibility" provisions of § 645.212(a) or (b) or the "other eligibles" provisions of § 645.213. The preference does not require that the category of noncustodial parents eligible under § 645.212(c)(2)(i) must be exhausted before any other category of eligible noncustodial parents may be served. The operating entity may establish a process that gives preference to noncustodial parents eligible under § 645.212(c)(2)(i) and that also provides WtW services to noncustodial parents eligible under the other provisions of § 645.212(c)(2).

(b) In order to protect custodial parents and children who may be at risk of domestic violence, the operating entity must consult with domestic violence prevention and intervention organizations in the development of its WtW project serving noncustodial parents; and must not require the cooperation of the custodial parent as a condition of participation in the WtW program for either parent; and

(c) The operating entity must ensure that personal responsibility contracts:

(1) Take into account the employment and child support status of the noncustodial parent;

(2) Include all of the following parties:

(i) The noncustodial parent,

(ii) The operating entity, and

(iii) The agency responsible for administering the State Child Support Enforcement program as described under Title IV-D of the Act, unless the operating entity demonstrates to the Secretary of Labor with written documentation that it is not able to coordinate with the State IV-D agency;

(3) Include the following elements:

(i) A commitment by the noncustodial parent to cooperate:

(A) In the establishment of paternity (if the participant is male) of the minor child at the earliest opportunity, through voluntary acknowledgment or other procedures, and

(B) In the establishment of a child support order;

(ii) A commitment by the noncustodial parent to cooperate in the payment of child support for the minor child. This commitment may include a modification of an existing support order to take into account:

(A) The ability of the noncustodial parent to pay such support; and

(B) The participation of the noncustodial parent in the WtW program, and

(iii) A commitment by the noncustodial parent to participate in employment or related activities that will enable the noncustodial parent to make regular child support payments. For noncustodial parents who have not reached 20 years of age, such activities may include:

(A) Completion of high school,

(B) Earning a general equivalency degree, or

(C) Participating in other education directly related to employment;

(iv) A description of the services to be provided to the noncustodial parent under the WtW program;

(4) Contain a commitment by the noncustodial parent to participate in the services that are described in the personal responsibility contract under paragraph (c)(3)(iv) of this section; and

(5) Be entered into no later than thirty (30) days after the individual is enrolled in and is receiving services through a WtW project funded under this part, unless the operating entity has determined that good cause exists to extend this period. This extension may not extend to a date more than ninety (90) days after the individual is enrolled in and receiving services through a WtW project funded under this part.

§ 645.220 What activities are allowable under this part?

Entities operating WtW projects may use WtW funds for the following:

(a) Job readiness activities, subject to the requirements of § 645.221 of this subpart.

(b) Vocational educational training or job training. A participant is limited to six calendar months of such training if (s)he is not also employed or participating in an employment activity, as described in paragraph (c) of this section.

(c) Employment activities which consist of any of the following:

(1) Community service programs;

(2) Work experience programs;

(3) Job creation through public or private sector employment wage subsidies; and

(4) On-the-job training.

(d) Job placement services subject to the requirements of § 645.221 of this subpart.

(e) Post-employment services which are provided after an individual is placed in one of the employment activities listed in paragraph (c) of this section, or in any other subsidized or unsubsidized job, subject to the requirements of § 645.221 of this subpart. Post-employment services include such services as:

(1) Basic educational skills training;

(2) Occupational skills training;

(3) English as a second language training; and

(4) Mentoring.

(f) Job retention services and support services that are provided after an individual is placed in a job readiness activity, as specified in paragraph (a) of this section; in vocational education or job training, as specified in paragraph (b) of this section; in one of the employment activities, as specified in paragraph (c) of this section, or in any other subsidized or unsubsidized job. WtW participants who are enrolled in Workforce Investment Act (WIA) or JTPA activities, such as occupational skills training, may also receive job retention and support services funded with WtW monies while they are participating in WIA activities. Job retention and support services can be provided with WtW funds only if they are not otherwise available to the participant. Job retention and support services include such services as:

(1) Transportation assistance;

(2) Substance abuse treatment (except that WtW funds may not be used to provide medical treatment);

(3) Child care assistance;

(4) Emergency or short term housing assistance; and

(5) Other supportive services.

(g) Individual development accounts which are established in accordance with the Act.

(h) Outreach, recruitment, intake, assessment, eligibility determination, development of an individualized service strategy, and case management may be incorporated in the design of any of the allowable activities listed in paragraphs (a) through (g) of this section (section 403(a)(5)(C) of the Act).

§ 645.221 For what activities and services must local boards use contracts or vouchers?

(a) Local boards and PIC's must provide the following activities and services through vouchers or contracts with public or private providers: the job readiness activities described in § 645.220(a) of this subpart, the job placement services described in § 645.220(d) of this subpart, and the post-employment services described in § 645.220(e) of this subpart. Job placement services provided with contracts or vouchers are subject to the payment requirements at § 645.230(a)(3) of this subpart. If an operating entity is not a local board or a PIC, it may provide such services directly.

(b) Local boards and PIC's which are directly providing job readiness activities or job placement and/or post-employment services must conform to the requirement in paragraph (a) of this section, to provide such services through contract or voucher, by February 12, 2001.

§ 645.225 How do Welfare-to-Work activities relate to activities provided through TANF and other related programs?

(a) Activities provided through WtW must be coordinated effectively at the State and local levels with activities being provided through TANF (section 403(a)(5)(A)(vii)(II)).

(b) The operating entity must ensure that there is an assessment of skills, prior work experience, employability, and other relevant information in place for each WtW participant. Where appropriate, the assessment performed by the TANF agency or JTPA should be used for this purpose.

(c) The operating entity must ensure that there is an individualized strategy for transition to unsubsidized employment in place for each participant which takes into account participant assessments, including the TANF assessment and any JTPA assessment. Where appropriate, the TANF individual responsibility plan (IRP), a WIA individual employment plan, or a JTPA individual service strategy should be used for this purpose.

(d) Coordination of resources should include not only those available through WtW and TANF grant funds, and the Child Care and Development Block Grant, but also those available through other related activities and programs such as the WIA or JTPA programs (One-Stop systems), the State employment service, private sector employers, labor organizations, business and trade associations, education agencies, housing agencies, community development corporations, transportation agencies, community-based and faith-based organizations, disability community organizations, community action agencies, and colleges and universities which provide some of the assistance needed by the targeted population (section 402(a)(5)(A)).

§ 645.230 What general fiscal and administrative rules apply to the use of Federal funds?

(a) *Uniform fiscal and administrative requirements.* (1) State, local, and Indian tribal government organizations are required to follow the common rule "Uniform Administrative Requirements for Grants and Cooperative Agreements to State and Local Governments" which is codified in the DOL regulations at 29 CFR part 97.

(2) Institutions of higher education, hospitals, and other non-profit organizations and other commercial organizations are required to follow OMB Circular A–110 which is codified in the DOL regulations at 29 CFR part 95.

(3) In addition to the requirements at 29 CFR 95.48 and 29 CFR 97.36(i), contracts or vouchers for job placement services supported by funds provided for this program must include a provision to require that at least one-half (½) of the payment occur after an eligible individual placed into the workforce has been in the workforce for six (6) months. This provision applies only to placement in unsubsidized jobs (section 403(a)(5)(C)(i)).

(4) In addition to the requirements at 29 CFR 95.42 and 29 CFR 97.36(b)(3) which address codes of conduct and conflict of interest issues related to employees, it is also required that:

(i) A local board or alternate administering agency member shall neither cast a vote on, nor participate in, any decision making capacity on the provision of services by such member (or any organization which that member directly represents), nor on any matter which would provide any direct financial benefit to that member or a member of his immediate family; and

(ii) Neither membership on the local board or alternate administering agency nor the receipt of WtW funds to provide training and related services shall be construed, by itself, to violate these conflict of interest provisions.

(5) The addition method, described at 29 CFR 97.25(g)(2), is required for the use of all program income earned under WtW grants. When the cost of generating program income has been charged to the program, the gross amount earned must be added to the WtW program. However, the cost of generating program income must be subtracted from the amount earned to establish the net amount of program income available for use under the grants when these costs have not been charged to the WtW program.

(6) Any excess revenue over costs incurred for services provided by a governmental or non-profit entity must be included in program income earned.

(b) *Audit requirements*. All recipients and subrecipients of Department of Labor WtW awards must comply with the audit requirements codified at 29 CFR part 96.

(1) All governmental and non-profit organizations must follow the audit requirements of OMB Circular A–133 which is codified at 29 CFR part 99. This requirement is imposed at 29 CFR 97.26 for governmental organizations and at 29 CFR 95.26 for institutions of higher education, hospitals, and other non-profit organizations.

(2) The Department is responsible for audits of commercial organizations which are direct recipients of WtW grants.

(3) Commercial organizations which are WtW subrecipients and which expend more than the minimum level specified in OMB Circular A–133 ($300,000 as of April 15, 1999) must have either an organization-wide audit conducted in accordance with 29 CFR part 99 or a program specific financial and compliance audit.

(c) *Allowable costs/cost principles*. The DOL regulations at 29 CFR 95.27 and 29 CFR 97.22 identify the Federal principles for determining allowable costs which each kind of recipient and subrecipient must follow. For those selected items of cost requiring prior approval, the authority to grant or deny approval is delegated to the Governor.

(1) State, local, and Indian tribal government organizations must determine allowability of costs in accordance with the provisions of OMB Circular A–87, "Cost Principles for State and Local Governments."

(2) Non-profit organizations must determine allowability of costs in accordance with OMB Circular A–122, "Cost Principles for Non-Profit Organizations."

(3) Institutions of higher education must determine allowability of costs in accordance with OMB Circular A–21, "Cost Principles for Education Institutions."

(4) Hospitals must determine allowability of costs in accordance with the provisions of Appendix E of 45 CFR Part 74, "Principles for Determining Costs Applicable to Research and Development Under Grants and Contracts with Hospitals."

(5) Commercial organizations and those non-profit organizations listed in Attachment C to OMB Circular A–122 must determine allowability of costs in accordance with the provisions of the Federal Acquisition Regulation (FAR) at 48 CFR Part 31.

(d) *Information technology costs*. In addition to the allowable cost provisions identified in § 645.235 of this subpart, the costs of information technology—computer hardware and software—will only be allowable under WtW grants when such computer technology is "Year 2000 compliant." To meet this requirement, information technology must be able to accurately process date/time data (including, but not limited to, calculating, comparing and sequencing) from, into and between the twentieth and twenty-first centuries, and the years 1999 and 2000. The information technology must also be able to make leap year calculations. Furthermore, "Year 2000 compliant" information technology when used in combination with other technology shall accurately process date/time data if the other information technology properly exchanges date/time data with it.

(e) *Prohibition on construction or purchase of facilities.* WtW federal funds may not be used to pay for the construction or purchase of facilities or buildings.

(f) *Prohibition on business start-up costs.* WtW federal funds may not be used to cover the costs of business start-up and/or capital ventures.

(g) *Government-wide debarment and suspension, and government-wide drug-free workplace requirements.* All WtW grant recipients and subrecipients are required to comply with:

(1) Government-wide requirements for debarment and suspension which are codified at 29 CFR part 98, subparts A through E; and

(2) The government-wide requirements for a drug-free workplace. Recipients and subrecipients are required to comply with 29 CFR part 98, subpart F, except that the definition of "grantee" shall be read to include recipients and subrecipients.

(h) *Restrictions on lobbying.* All WtW grant recipients and subrecipients are required to comply with the restrictions on lobbying which are codified in the DOL regulations at 29 CFR Part 93.

(i) *Nondiscrimination.* All WtW grant recipients and subrecipients are required to comply with the nondiscrimination provisions codified in the DOL regulations at 29 CFR parts 31 and 32. In addition, 29 CFR part 37 applies to recipients of WtW financial assistance who are also WIA recipients and applies to recipients of WtW financial assistance who operate programs that are part of the One-Stop system established under the Workforce Investment Act, to the extent that the WtW programs and activities are being conducted as part of the One-Stop delivery system. Furthermore, WtW programs that are part of larger State agencies that are recipients of WIA title I financial assistance must also comply with the provisions of 29 CFR part 37. For purposes of this paragraph, the term "recipient" has the same meaning as the term is defined in 29 CFR part 37. That part also contains participant rights related to nondiscrimination.

(j) *Nepotism.* (1) No individual may be placed in a WtW employment activity if a member of that person's immediate family is engaged in an administrative capacity for the employing agency.

(2) To the extent that an applicable State or local legal requirement regarding nepotism is more restrictive than this provision, such State or local requirement shall be followed.

§ 645.233 What are the time limitations on the expenditure of Welfare-to-Work grant funds?

(a) *Formula grant funds:* The maximum time limit for the expenditure of a given fiscal year allotment is three years from the effective date of the Federal grant award to the State. The maximum time limit will be allowed and will be specified in the Department's formula grant document for each fiscal year of funds provided to the State. Any remaining funds that have not been expended at the end of the expenditure period must be returned to the Department in accordance with the applicable closeout procedures for formula grants.

(b) *Competitive grant funds:* The maximum time limit for the expenditure of these funds is three years from the effective date of award, but will, in all cases, be determined by the grant period and the terms and conditions specified in the Federal grant award agreement (including any applicable grant modification documents). Any remaining funds that have not been expended at the end of the approved grant period must be returned to the Department in accordance with the applicable closeout procedures for competitive grants (section 503(a)(5)(C)(vii)).

§ 645.235 What types of activities are subject to the administrative cost limit on Welfare-to-Work grants?

(a) *Administrative cost limitation (section 404(b)(1))*—(1) *Formula grants to states.* Expenditures for administrative purposes under WtW formula grants to States are limited to fifteen percent (15%) of the grant award.

(2) *Competitive grants.* The limitation on expenditures for administrative purposes under WtW competitive grants will be specified in the grant agreement but in no case shall the limitation be more than fifteen percent (15%) of the grant award.

(3) Although administrative in nature, costs of information technology—computer hardware and software—needed for tracking and monitoring of WtW program, participant, or performance requirements, are excluded from the administrative cost limit calculation.

(b) The costs of administration are that allocable portion of necessary and allowable costs associated with those specific functions identified in paragraph (c) of this section for the administration of the WtW program and which are not related to the direct provision of services to participants. These costs can be both personnel and non-personnel and both direct and indirect.

(c) The costs of administration are the costs associated with performing the following functions:

(1) Performing overall general administrative functions and coordination of those functions under WtW including:

(i) Accounting, budgeting, financial and cash management functions;

(ii) Procurement and purchasing functions;

(iii) Property management functions;

(iv) Personnel management functions;

(v) Payroll functions;

(vi) Coordinating the resolution of findings arising from audits, reviews, investigations and incident reports;

(vii) Audit functions;

(viii) General legal services functions; and

(ix) Developing systems and procedures, including information systems, required for these administrative functions;

(2) Performing oversight and monitoring responsibilities related to WtW administrative functions,

(3) Costs of goods and services required for administrative functions of the program, including goods and services such as rental or purchase of equipment, utilities, office supplies, postage, and rental and maintenance of office space;

(4) Travel costs incurred for official business in carrying out administrative activities or the overall management of the WtW system; and

(5) Costs of information systems related to administrative functions (for example, personnel, procurement, purchasing, property management, accounting and payroll systems) including the purchase, systems development and operating costs of such systems.

(d)(1) Only that portion of the costs of WtW grantees that are associated with the performance of the administrative functions described in paragraph (c) of this section and awards to subrecipients or vendors that are solely for the performance of these administrative functions are classified as administrative costs. All other costs are considered to be for the direct provision of WtW activities and are classified as program costs.

(2) Personnel and related non-personnel costs of staff who perform both administrative functions specified in paragraph (c) of this section and programmatic services or activities are to be allocated as administrative or program costs to the benefitting cost objectives/categories based on documented distributions of actual time worked or other equitable cost allocation methods.

(3) Specific costs charged to an overhead or indirect cost pool that can be identified directly as a program cost may be charged as a program cost. Documentation of such charges must be maintained.

(4) Except as provided at paragraph (d)(1) of this section, all costs incurred for functions and activities of subrecipients and vendors are program costs.

(5) Costs of the following information systems including the purchase, systems development and operating (e.g., data entry) costs are charged to the program category.

(i) Tracking or monitoring of participant and performance information;

(ii) Employment statistics information, including job listing information, job skills information, and demand occupation information; and

(iii) Local area performance information.

§ 645.240 What are the reporting requirements for Welfare-to-Work programs?

(a) *General.* State formula and other direct competitive grant recipients must report financial and participant data in accordance with revised instructions that will be issued by the Department after consultation with the Secretary of Health and Human Services, States, and organizations that represent State or local governments. Reports must be submitted to the Department quarterly. Existing WtW financial reporting instructions and formats are available on the WtW web site at *http://wtw.doleta.gov/linkpages/tegltein.htm.* The Internet reporting system for WtW grantees is accessible at *http://www.etareports.doleta.gov.*

(b) *Subrecipient reporting.* A State formula or other direct competitive grant recipient may impose different forms or formats, shorter due dates, and more frequent reporting requirements on subrecipients. However, the recipient is required to meet the reporting requirements imposed by the Department.

(c) *Financial reports.* Each grant recipient must submit financial reports to the Department. Reported expenditures and program income must be on the accrual basis of accounting and cumulative by fiscal year of appropriation. If the recipient's accounting records are not normally kept on the accrual basis of accounting, the recipient must develop accrual information through an analysis of the documentation on hand.

(d) *Participant reports.* Each grant recipient must submit participant reports to the Department. Participant data must be aggregate data, and, for most data elements, must be cumulative by fiscal year of appropriation.

(e) *Due dates.* Financial and participant reports are due no later than 45 days after the end of each quarter. A final financial and participant report is required 90 days after the expiration of a funding period or the termination of grant support.

§ 645.245 Who is responsible for oversight and monitoring of Welfare-to-Work grants?

(a) The Secretary may monitor all recipients and subrecipients of all grants awarded and funds expended under WtW. Federal oversight will be conducted primarily at the State level for formula grants and at the recipient level for competitive grants.

(b) The Governor must monitor local boards (or other approved administrative entities) funded under the State's formula allocated grants on a periodic basis for compliance with applicable laws and regulations. The Governor must develop and make available for review a State monitoring plan.

§ 645.250 What procedures apply to the resolution of findings arising from audits, investigations, monitoring and oversight reviews?

(a) Resolution of subrecipient level findings.

(1) The WtW grantee is responsible for the resolution of findings that arise from its monitoring reviews, investigations and audits (including OMB Circular A–133 audits) of subrecipients.

(2) A State or competitive grantee, as appropriate, must use the audit resolution, debt collection and appeal procedures that it uses for other Federal grant programs.

(3) If a State or competitive grantee, as appropriate, does not have such procedures, it must prescribe standards and procedures for the WtW grant program.

(b) Resolution of State level findings.

(1) The Secretary is responsible for the resolution of findings that arise from Federal audits, monitoring reviews, investigations, incident reports, and recipient level OMB Circular A–133 audits.

(2) The Secretary will use the DOL audit resolution process, consistent with the Single Audit Act of 1996 and OMB Circular A–133.

(3) A final determination issued by a grant officer pursuant to this process may be appealed to the DOL Office of Administrative Law Judges under the procedures at § 645.800.

(c) Resolution of nondiscrimination findings. Findings arising from investigations or reviews conducted under nondiscrimination laws shall be resolved in accordance with those laws and the applicable implementing regulations.

§645.255 What nondiscrimination protections apply to participants in Welfare-to-Work programs?

(a) All participants in WtW programs under this part shall have such rights as are available under all applicable Federal, State and local laws prohibiting discrimination, and their implementing regulations, including:

(1) The Age Discrimination Act of 1975 (42 U.S.C. 6101 *et seq.*);

(2) Section 504 of the Rehabilitation Act of 1973 (29 U.S.C. 794);

(3) The Americans with Disabilities Act of 1990 (42 U.S.C. 12101 *et seq.*); and

(4) Title VI of the Civil Rights Act of 1964 (42 U.S.C. 2000d *et seq.*).

(b) Participants in work activities, as defined in section 407(a) of the Social Security Act, operated with WtW funds, shall not be discriminated against because of gender. Participants alleging gender discrimination may file a complaint using the State's grievance system procedures as described in §645.270 of this subpart (section 403(a)(5)(J)(iii)) of the Act). Participants alleging gender discrimination in WtW programs conducted by One-Stop partners as part of the One-Stop delivery system may file a complaint using the complaint processing procedures developed and published by the State in accordance with the requirements of 29 CFR 37.70–37.80.

(c) Complaints alleging discrimination in violation of any applicable Federal, State or local law, such as Title VII of the Civil Rights Act of 1964 (42 U.S.C. 2000e *et seq.*), Title IX of the Education Amendments of 1972 (20 U.S.C. 1681 *et seq.*), the Pregnancy Discrimination Act (42 U.S.C. 2000e (paragraph k)), or Section 188 of the Workforce Investment Act of 1998 (29 U.S.C. 2938), as well as those listed in paragraph (a) of this section, shall be processed in accordance with those laws and the implementing regulations.

(d) Questions about or complaints alleging a violation of the nondiscrimination laws in paragraph (a) of this section may be directed or mailed to the Director, Civil Rights Center, U.S. Department of Labor, Room N–4123, 200 Constitution Avenue, NW, Washington, D.C. 20210 for processing.

§645.260 What health and safety provisions apply to participants in Welfare-to-Work programs?

(a) Participants in an employment activity operated with WtW funds, as defined in §645.220 of this part, are subject to the same health and safety standards established under State and Federal law which are applicable to similarly employed employees, of the same employer, who are not participants in programs under WtW.

(b) Participants alleging a violation of these health and safety standards may file a complaint pursuant to the procedures contained in §645.270 of this part (section 403(a)(5)(J)(ii)).

§645.265 What safeguards are there to ensure that participants in Welfare-to-Work employment activities do not displace other employees?

(a) An adult participating in an employment activity operated with WtW funds, as described in §645.220 (b) and (c) of this subpart, may fill an established position vacancy subject to the limitations in paragraph (c) of this section.

(b) An employment activity operated with WtW funds, as described in §645.220(c) of this subpart, must not violate existing contracts for services or collective bargaining agreements. Where such an employment activity would violate a collective bargaining agreement, the appropriate labor organization and employer must provide written concurrence before the employment activity is undertaken.

(c) An adult participating in an employment activity operated with WtW funds, as described in §645.220(c) of this subpart, must not be employed or assigned:

(1) When any other individual is on layoff from the same or any substantially equivalent job within the same organizational unit;

(2) If the employer has terminated the employment of any regular, unsubsidized employee or otherwise caused an involuntary reduction in its workforce with the intention of filling the vacancy so created with the WtW participant; and,

(3) If the employer has caused an involuntary reduction to less than full time in hours of any employee in the same or substantially equivalent job within the same organizational unit.

(d) Regular employees and program participants alleging displacement may file a complaint pursuant to § 645.270 of this part (section 403(a)(5)(J)(i)).

§ 645.270 What procedures are there to ensure that currently employed workers may file grievances regarding displacement and that Welfare-to-Work participants in employment activities may file grievances regarding displacement, health and safety standards and gender discrimination?

(a) The State shall establish and maintain a grievance procedure for resolving complaints from:

(1) Regular employees that the placement of a participant in an employment activity operated with WtW funds, as described in § 645.220 of this part, violates any of the prohibitions described in § 645.265 of this part; and

(2) Program participants in an employment activity operated with WtW funds, as described in § 645.220 of this part, that any employment activity violates any of the prohibitions described in §§ 645.255(d), 645.260, or 645.265 of this part.

(b) Such grievance procedure should include an opportunity for informal resolution.

(c) If no informal resolution can be reached within the specified time as established by the State as part of its grievance procedure, such procedure shall provide an opportunity for the dissatisfied party to receive a hearing upon request.

(d) The State shall specify the time period and format for the hearing portion of the grievance procedure, as well as the time period by which the complainant will be provided the written decision by the State.

(e) A decision by the State under paragraph (d) of this section may be appealed by any dissatisfied party within 30 days of the receipt of the State's written decision, according to the time period and format for the appeals portion of the grievance procedure as specified by the State.

(f) The State shall designate the State agency which will be responsible for hearing appeals. This agency shall be independent of the State or local agency which is administering, or supervising the administration of the State TANF and WtW programs.

(g) No later than 120 days of receipt of an individual's original grievance, the State agency, as designated in paragraph (f) of this section, shall provide a written final determination of the individual's appeal.

(h) The grievance procedure shall include remedies for violations of §§ 645.255(d), 645.260, and 645.265 of this part which may continue during the grievance process and which may include:

(1) Suspension or termination of payments from funds provided under this part;

(2) Prohibition of placement of a WtW participant with an employer that has violated §§ 645.255(b), 645.260, and 645.265 of this part;

(3) Where applicable, reinstatement of an employee, payment of lost wages and benefits, and reestablishment of other relevant terms, conditions, and privileges of employment; and,

(4) Where appropriate, other equitable relief (section 403(a)(5)(J)(iv)).

(i) Participants alleging gender discrimination by WtW programs that are not part of the One-Stop system may file a complaint using the grievance system procedures described above. Participants alleging gender discrimination by WtW programs that are part of the One-Stop system may file a complaint using the procedures developed by the State under the WIA non-discrimination regulations at 29 CFR 37.70–37.80.

Subpart C—Additional Formula Grant Administrative Standards and Procedures

§ 645.300 What constitutes an allowable match?

(a) A State is entitled to receive two (2) dollars of Federal funds for every one (1) dollar of State match expenditures, up to the amount available for allotment to the State based on the State's percentage for WtW formula grant for the fiscal year. The State is not required to provide a level of match necessary to support the total amount available to it based on the State's percentage for WtW formula grant. However, if the proposed match is less than the amount required to support the full level of Federal funds, the grant amount will be reduced accordingly (section 403(a)(5)(A)(i)(I)).

(b) States shall follow the match or cost-sharing requirements of the "Common Rule" *Uniform Administrative Requirements for Grants and Cooperative Agreements to State and Local Governments* (codified for DOL at 29 CFR 97.24). Paragraphs (b)(1)(i) and (ii), (b)(3), and (b)(4) and (c)(1) of this section are in addition to the common rule requirements. Also, paragraphs included in the common rule which relate to the use of donated buildings and other real property as match have been excluded from this provision.

(1) Only costs that would be allowable if paid for with WtW grant funds will be accepted as match.

(i) Because the use of Federal funds is prohibited for construction or purchase of facilities or buildings except where there is explicit statutory authority permitting it, costs incurred for the construction or purchase of facilities or buildings shall not be acceptable as match for a WtW grant.

(ii) Because the costs of construction or purchase of facilities or buildings are unallowable as match, the donation of a building or property as a third party in-kind contribution is also unallowable as a match for a WtW grant.

(2) A match or cost-sharing requirement may be satisfied by either or both of the following:

(i) Allowable costs incurred by the grantee, subgrantee or a cost type contractor under the assistance agreement. This includes allowable cost borne by non-Federal grants or by others and cash donations from non-Federal third parties.

(ii) The value of third party in-kind contributions applicable to the FY period to which the cost-sharing or matching requirement applies.

(3) No more than seventy-five percent (75%) of the total match expenditures may be in the form of third party in-kind contributions.

(4) Match expenditures must be recorded in the books of account of the entity that incurred the cost or received the contribution. These amounts may be rolled up and reported as aggregate State level match.

(c) Qualifications and exceptions—

(1) The matching requirements may not be met by the use of an employer's share of participant wage payments (e.g., employer share of OJT wages).

(2) *Costs borne by other Federal grant agreements.* A cost-sharing or matching requirement may not be met by costs borne by another Federal grant. This prohibition does not apply to income earned by a grantee or subgrantee from a contract awarded under another Federal grant.

(3) *General revenue sharing.* For the purpose of this section, general revenue sharing funds distributed under 31 U.S.C. 6702 are not considered Federal grant funds.

(4) *Cost or contributions counted towards other Federal cost-sharing requirements.* Neither costs nor the values of third party in-kind contributions may count towards satisfying a cost-sharing or matching requirement of a grant agreement if they have been or will be counted towards satisfying a cost-sharing or matching requirement of another Federal grant agreement, a Federal procurement contract, or any other award of Federal funds.

(5) *Costs financed by program income.* Costs financed by program income, as defined in 29 CFR 97.25, shall not count towards satisfying a cost-sharing or matching requirement unless they are expressly permitted in the terms of the assistance agreement. (This use of general program income is described in 29 CFR 97.25(g)).

(6) *Services or property financed by income earned by contractors.* Contractors under a grant may earn income from the activities carried out under the contract in addition to the amounts earned from the party awarding the contract. No costs of services or property supported by this income may count toward satisfying a cost-sharing or matching requirement unless other provisions of the grant agreement expressly permit this kind of income to be used to meet the requirement.

(7) *Records.* Costs and third party in-kind contributions counting towards satisfying a cost-sharing or matching requirement must be verifiable from the records of grantees and subgrantee or cost-type contractors. These records must show how the value placed on third party in-kind contributions was derived. To the extent feasible, volunteer services will be supported by the same methods that the organization uses to support the allocability of regular personnel costs.

(8) *Special standards for third party in-kind contributions.* (i) Third party in-kind contributions count towards satisfying a cost-sharing or matching requirement only where, if the party receiving the contributions were to pay for them, the payments would be allowable costs.

(ii) Some third party in-kind contributions are goods and services that, if the grantee, subgrantee, or contractor receiving the contribution had to pay for them, the payments would have been an indirect costs. Cost sharing or matching credit for such contributions shall be given only if the grantee, subgrantee, or contractor has established, along with its regular indirect cost rate, a special rate for allocating to individual projects or programs the value of the contributions.

(iii) A third party in-kind contribution to a fixed-price contract may count towards satisfying a cost-sharing or matching requirement only if it results in:

(A) An increase in the services or property provided under the contract (without additional cost to the grantee or subgrantee) or

(B) A cost savings to the grantee or subgrantee.

(iv) The values placed on third party in-kind contributions for cost-sharing or matching purposes must conform to the rules in the succeeding sections of this part. If a third party in-kind contribution is a type not treated in those sections, the value placed upon it must be fair and reasonable.

(d) *Valuation of donated services*—(1) *Volunteer services.* Unpaid services provided to a grantee or subgrantee by individuals must be valued at rates consistent with those ordinarily paid for similar work in the grantee's or subgrantee's organization. If the grantee or subgrantee does not have employees performing similar work, the rates must be consistent with those ordinarily paid by other employers for similar work in the same labor market. In either case, a reasonable amount for fringe benefits may be included in the valuation.

(2) *Employees of other organizations.* When an employer other than a grantee, subgrantee, or cost-type contractor furnishes free of charge the services of an employee in the employee's normal line of work, the services must be valued at the employee's regular rate of pay exclusive of the employee's fringe benefits and overhead costs. If the services are in a different line of work, paragraph (d)(1) of this section applies.

(e) *Valuation of third party donated supplies and loaned equipment or space.* (1) If a third party donates supplies, the contribution must be valued at the market value of the supplies at the time of donation.

(2) If a third party donates the use of equipment or space in a building but retains title, the contribution must be valued at:

(i) the fair rental rate of the equipment or space for property donated by non-governmental entities, or

(ii) a depreciation or use-allowance based on the property's market value at the time it was donated for property donated by governmental entities.

§ 645.310 What assurance must a State provide that it will make the required matching expenditures?

In its State plan, a State must provide a written estimate of planned matching expenditures and describe the process by which the funds will be tracked and reported to ensure that the State meets its projected match (section 403(a)(5)(A)(i)(I)).

§ 645.315 What actions are to be taken if a State fails to make the required matching expenditures?

(a) If State match expenditures do not satisfy the requirements of the FY grant award by the end of the three year fund availability period, the grant award amount will be reduced by the appropriate corresponding amount (*i.e.*, the grant will be reduced by two (2) dollars for each one (1) dollar shortfall in State matching funds) when the grant is closed out.

(b) Compliance with the fifteen percent (15%) administrative cost limit will be recalculated based on the FY formula grant award amount, as reduced under paragraph (a) of this section.

Subpart D—State Formula Grants Administration

§ 645.400 Under what conditions may the Governor request a waiver to designate an alternate local administering agency?

(a)(1) The Governor may include in the State's WtW Plan a waiver request to select an agency other than the local board or PIC to administer the program for one or more local areas or SDA's in a State; or

(2) When the Governor determines the local board or alternate administering agency has not coordinated its expenditures with the expenditure of funds provided to the State under TANF, pursuant to section 403(a)(5)(A)(vii)(II) of the Act, the Governor must request a waiver.

(b) The Governor shall bear the burden of proving that the designated alternate administering agency, rather than the local board or other alternate administering agency, would improve the effectiveness or efficiency of the administration of WtW funds in the SDA. The Governor's waiver request shall include information to meet that burden. The Governor shall provide a copy of the waiver request and any supporting information submitted to the Secretary to the local board and CEO of the local area for which an alternative administering agency is requested.

(c) The local board and CEO shall have fifteen (15) days in which to submit his or her written response to the Department. The local board and CEO shall provide a copy of such response to the Governor.

(d) The Secretary will assess the waiver information submitted by the Governor, including input from the local board and CEO in reaching the decision whether to permit the use of an alternate administering agency.

(e) The Secretary shall approve a waiver request if she determines that the Governor has established that the designated alternate administering agency, rather than the local board or other administering agency, will improve the effectiveness or efficiency of the administration of WtW funds provided for the benefit of the local area.

(f) Where an alternate administering agency is approved by the Secretary, such administrative entity shall coordinate with the CEO for the applicable local area(s) regarding the expenditure of WtW grant funds in the local area(s).

(g) The decision of the Secretary to approve or deny a waiver request will be issued promptly and shall constitute final agency action.

§ 645.410 What elements will the State use in distributing funds within the State?

(a) Of the WtW funds allotted to the State, not less than 85 percent of the State allotment must be distributed to the local areas or SDA's in the State.

(1) The State shall prescribe a formula for determining the amount of funds to be distributed to each local area or SDA in the State using no factors other than the three factors described in paragraphs (2) and (3) of this paragraph;

(2) The formula prescribed by the Governor must include as one of the formula factors for distributing funds the provision at section 403(a)(5)(A)(vi)(I)(aa) of the Act. The Governor is to distribute funds to a local area or SDA based on the number by which the population of the area with an income that is less than the poverty line exceeds 7.5 percent of the total population of the area, compared to all such numbers in all such areas in the State. The Governor must assign a weight of not less than 50 percent to this factor;

(3) The Governor shall distribute the remaining funds, if any, to the local area or SDA's utilizing only one or both of the following factors:

(i) the local area or SDA's share of the number of adults receiving assistance under TANF or the predecessor program in the local area or SDA for 30 months or more (whether consecutive or not), relative to the number of such adults residing in the State;

(ii) the local area or SDA's share of the number of unemployed individuals residing in the local area or SDA, relative to the number of such individuals residing in the State.

(4) If the amount to be distributed to a local area or SDA by the Governor's formula is less than $100,000, the funds shall be available to be used by the Governor to fund projects described at paragraph (b) of this section.

(5) States shall use the guidance provided at section 403(a)(5)(D) of the Act in determining the number of individuals with an income that is less than the poverty line.

(6) Local Boards (or alternate administering agency) shall determine, pursuant to section 403(a)(5)(A)(vii)(I) of the Act, on which individual(s) and on which allowable activities to expend its WtW fund allocation.

(7) The State must distribute the local boards' or SDAs' allocations in a timely manner, but not longer than 30 days from receipt of the State's fund allotment.

(b) Of the funds allocated to the State, up to 15 percent of the funds may be retained at the State level to fund projects that appear likely to help long-term recipients of assistance enter unsubsidized employment. Any additional funds available as a result of the process described at paragraph (a)(4) of this section, shall also be available to be used to fund projects to help long-term recipients of assistance enter unsubsidized jobs.

(c) The Governors may distribute the funds retained pursuant to paragraph (b) of this section to a variety of workforce organizations, in addition to local boards or alternate administering agencies, and other entities such as One-Stop systems, private sector employers, labor organizations, business and trade associations, education agencies, housing agencies, community development corporations, transportation agencies, community-based and faith-based organizations, disability community organizations, community action agencies, and colleges and universities which provide some of the assistance needed by the targeted population.

§ 645.415 What planning information must a State submit in order to receive a formula grant?

(a) Each State seeking financial assistance under the formula grant portion of the WtW legislation must submit an annual plan meeting the requirements prescribed by the Secretary. This plan shall be in the form of an addendum to the TANF State plan and shall be submitted to the Secretaries of Labor and Health and Human Services.

(b) The Secretary shall review the State plan for compliance with the statutory and regulatory provisions of the WtW program. The Secretary's decision whether to accept a State plan as in compliance with the Act shall constitute final agency action.

(c) If the Governor has requested a waiver to permit the selection of an alternate administering agency in the State plan, the provisions of § 645.400 of this part shall apply (section 403(a)(5)(A)(ii)).

§ 645.420 What factors will be used in measuring State performance?

(a) The Department will use the following factors to measure State performance:

(1) Job entry rate as measured by the proportion of WtW participants who enter either subsidized employment or unsubsidized employment,

(2) Substantive job entry rate as measured by the proportion of WtW participants who are placed in or who have moved into subsidized or unsubsidized employment of 30 hours or more per week,

(3) Retention as measured by the proportion of WtW participants who remain in unsubsidized employment six months in the second subsequent quarter after the quarter in which placement occurred after initial placement, and

(4) Measured earnings gains of WtW participants who remain in unsubsidized employment six months after initial placement.

(b) The formula for calculating the performance bonus is weighted as follows:

(1) 30 percent on job entry rate,

(2) 30 percent on substantive job entry rate,

(3) 20 percent on retention in unsubsidized employment,

(4) 20 percent on earnings gains in unsubsidized employment.

The formula will reflect general economic conditions on a State-by-State basis.

(c) The formula shall serve as the basis for the award of FY 2000 bonus grants based on successful performance to be made in FY 2001 (section 403(a)(5)(E)).

§ 645.425 What are the roles and responsibilities of the State(s) and local boards or alternate administering agencies?

(a) State roles and responsibilities. A State:

(1) Designates State WtW administering agency;

(2) Provides overall administration of WtW funds, consistent with the WtW statute, WtW regulations and the State's WtW Plan;

(3) Develops the State WtW Plan in consultation and coordination with appropriate entities in substate areas, such as One-Stop systems, private sector employers, labor organizations, business and trade associations, education agencies, housing agencies, community development corporations, transportation agencies, community-based and faith-based organizations, disability community organizations, community action agencies, and colleges and universities which provide some of the assistance needed by the targeted population (section 403(a)(5)(A)(ii)(I)(cc));

(4) Distributes funds to SDAs, consistent with the provisions described at § 645.410(a) (section 403(a)(5)(A)(ii)(I)(bb));

(5) Conducts oversight and monitoring of WtW activities and fund expenditures at the State and local levels for compliance with applicable laws and regulations, consistent with the provisions at § 645.245 and provides technical assistance as appropriate;

(6) Ensures coordination of local board or alternate administering agency fund expenditures with the State TANF expenditures and other programs (section 403(a)(5)(A)(ii)(I)(dd));

(7) Determines whether to request waivers to select an alternate administering agency consistent with the provisions described at § 645.400 of this part (sections 403(a)(5)(A)(ii)(I)(ee) and 403(a)(5)(A)(vii)(III));

(8) Manages and distributes State level WtW funds (15 percent), consistent with the provisions at § 645.410(b) and (c) (section 403(a)(5)(A)(vi)(III));

(9) Ensures that the 15 percent administration limitation and the match requirement are met;

(10) Ensures that worker protections provisions are observed and establishes an appropriate grievance process, consistent with §§ 645.255 through 645.270 of this part (section 403(a)(5)(J));

(11) Provides comments on Competitive Grant Application(s) from eligible entities within the State, consistent with § 645.510 of this part (section 403(a)(5)(B)(ii));

(12) Cooperates with the Department of Health and Human Services on the evaluation of WtW programs (section 403(a)(5)(A)(ii)(III));

(13) Provides technical assistance to PIC's, local boards or alternate administering agencies; and

(14) Establishes internal reporting requirements to ensure Federal reports are accurate, complete and are submitted on a timely basis, consistent with § 645.240 of this part.

(b) Local Boards (or alternate administering agency) roles and responsibilities. A local board:

(1) Has sole authority, in coordination with CEOs, to expend formula funds (section 403(a)(5)(A)(vii)(I));

(2) Has authority to determine the individuals to be served in the local area (section 403(a)(5)(A)(vii)(I));

(3) Has authority to determine the services to be provided in the local area (section 403(a)(5)(A)(vii)(I));

(4) Ensures funds are expended on eligible recipients and on allowable activities, consistent with § 645.410(a)(5) of this part;

(5) Coordinates WtW fund expenditures with State TANF expenditures and other programs (section 403(a)(5)(A)(ii)(dd));

(6) Ensures that there is an assessment and an individual service strategy in place for each WtW participant, consistent with § 645.225(a) and (b) of this part;

(7) Conducts oversight and monitoring of subrecipients, consistent with the provisions at § 645.245 of this part;

(8) Ensures worker protection provisions and grievance process are observed, consistent with State guidelines (section 403(a)(5)(J)); and

(9) Consults with and provides comments on private entity Competitive Grant Application(s), consistent with the provisions at § 645.500(b)(1)(i) of this part.

§ 645.430 How does the Welfare-to-Work program relate to the One-Stop system and Workforce Investment Act (WIA) programs?

(a) As provided in the Workforce Investment Act regulations at 20 CFR 663.620, the local WtW formula grant program operator is a required partner in the One-Stop system. 20 CFR part 662 describes the roles of such partners in the One-Stop system and applies to the WtW formula grant program operators. A Memorandum of Understanding must be developed between the Local Workforce Investment Board and the WtW program that meets the requirements of 20 CFR 662.300, such as containing provisions relating to the services to be provided through the One-Stop system and methods for referring individuals between the One-Stop operator and the partner WtW program.

(b) WtW participants may also be served by the WIA programs and, through appropriate linkages and referrals, these individuals will have access to a broader range of activities and services through the cooperation of the WtW and WIA programs in the One-Stop system. For example, WtW participants, who are also determined eligible for WIA, and who need occupational skills training, may be referred through the One-Stop system to receive WIA training. These participants are also eligible to receive services available under WtW, such as transportation and child care while participating in the WIA activity.

(c) WIA participants, who are determined to be eligible for WtW, may also be served by the WtW programs through cooperation with the WIA programs in the One-Stop system. For example, WIA participants, who are also determined eligible for WtW, may be referred to the WtW program for job placement and other WtW assistance.

(d) 29 CFR part 37 applies to recipients of WtW financial assistance who operate programs that are part of the One-Stop system established under WIA to the extent that the WtW programs and activities are being conducted as part of the One-Stop delivery system.

Subpart E—Welfare-To-Work Competitive Grants

§ 645.500 Who are eligible applicants for competitive grants?

(a) Eligible applicants for competitive grants are:

(1) Local boards or alternate administering agencies

(2) Political subdivisions of a State; and

(3) Private entities, as defined in § 645.120 of this part, including nonprofit organizations such as community development corporations, community-based and faith-based organizations, disability community organizations, community action agencies, and public and private colleges and universities, and other qualified private organizations.

(b) Entities other than a local board or alternate administering agency or a political subdivision of the State must submit an application for competitive grant funds in conjunction with the applicable local board or alternate administering agency or political subdivision.

(1) The term "in conjunction with" shall mean that the application submitted by such an entity must include a signed certification by both the applicant and either the applicable local board or alternate administering agency or political subdivision that:

(i) The applicant has consulted with the applicable local board or alternate administering agency or political subdivision during the development of the application; and

(ii) The activities proposed in the application are consistent with, and will be coordinated with, WtW efforts of the local board or alternate administering agency or political subdivision.

(2) If the applicant is unable to include such a certification in its application, the applicant will be required to certify, and provide information indicating that efforts were undertaken to consult with the local board or alternate administering agency or political subdivision and that the local board or alternate administering agency or political subdivision was provided a sufficient opportunity to cooperate in the development of the project plan and to review and comment on the application prior to its submission to the Secretary. "Sufficient opportunity for local Board or alternate administering agency or political subdivision review and comment" shall mean at least 30 calendar days.

(3) The certification described in paragraph (b)(1) of this section, or the evidence of efforts to consult described in paragraph (b)(2), must be with each local board or alternate administering agency or political subdivision included in the geographic area in which the project proposed in the application is to operate (section 403(a)(5)(B)(ii)).

§ 645.510 What is the required consultation with the Governor?

(a) All applicants for competitive grants, including local boards or alternate administering agencies and political subdivisions, must consult with the Governor by submitting their application to the Governor or the designated State administrative entity for the WtW program for review and comment prior to submission of the application to the Secretary. The application submitted to the Secretary must include:

(1) Comments on the application from the State; or

(2) Information indicating that the State was provided a sufficient opportunity for review and comment prior to submission to the Secretary. "Sufficient opportunity for State review and comment" shall mean at least 15 calendar days.

(b) For private entity applicants, the submission of the application for State review and comment must follow the 30 day period provided for local board or alternate administering agency/political subdivision review. Evidence of local board or alternate administering agency or political subdivision review should be included in the submission to the State (section 403(a)(5)(B)(ii)).

§ 645.515 What are the program and administrative requirements that apply to both the formula grants and competitive grants?

(a) All of the general program requirements and administrative standards set by 29 CFR Part 645 Subpart B apply (section 403(a)(5)(C) and section 404(b)).

(b) In addition, competitive grants will be subject to:

(1) Supplemental reporting requirements; and

(2) Additional monitoring and oversight requirements based on the negotiated scope-of-work of individual grant awards (section 403(a)(5)(B)(iii) and (v)).

§ 645.520 What are the application procedures and timeframes for competitive grant funds?

(a) The Secretary shall establish appropriate application procedures, selection criteria and an approval process to ensure that grant awards accomplish the purpose of the competitive grant funds and that available funds are used in an effective manner.

(b) The Secretary shall publish such procedures in the FEDERAL REGISTER and establish submission timeframes in a manner that allows eligible applicants sufficient time to develop and submit quality project plans (section 403(a)(5)(B)(i) and (iii)).

§ 645.525 What special consideration will be given to rural areas and cities with large concentrations of poverty?

(a) Competitive grant awards will be targeted to geographic areas of significant need. In developing application procedures, special consideration will be given to rural areas and cities with large concentrations of residents living in poverty.

(b) Grant application guidelines will clarify specific requirements for documenting need in the local area (section 403(a)(5)(B)(iv)).

Subpart F—Administrative Appeal Process

§ 645.800 What administrative remedies are available under this Part?

(a) Within 21 days of receipt of a final determination that has directly imposed a sanction or corrective action pursuant to § 645.250(b) of this part, a recipient, subrecipient, or a vendor directly against which the Grant Officer has imposed a sanction or corrective action, may request a hearing before the Department of Labor Office of Administrative Law Judges, pursuant to the provisions of 29 CFR part 96 subpart 96.6.

(b) In accordance with 29 CFR 96.603(b)(2), the rules of practice and procedure published at 29 CFR part 18 shall govern the conduct of hearings under this section, except that a request for hearing under this section shall not be considered a complaint to which the filing of an answer by DOL or a DOL agency is required. Technical rules of evidence shall not apply to a hearing conducted pursuant to this part; however, rules or principles designed to assure production of the most credible evidence available and to subject testimony to cross-examination shall apply.

(c) The decision of the Administrative Law Judge (ALJ) shall constitute final agency action unless, within 20 days of the decision, a party dissatisfied with the decision of the ALJ has filed a petition for review with the Administrative Review Board (ARB) (established pursuant to the provisions of Secretary's Order No. 2–96, published at 61 FR 19977 (May 3, 1996)), specifically identifying the procedure, fact, law or policy to which exception is taken. Any exception not specifically urged shall be deemed to have been waived. A copy of the petition for review must be sent to the opposing party at that time. Thereafter, the decision of the ALJ shall constitute final agency action unless the ARB, within 30 days of the filing of the petition for review, has notified the parties that the case has been accepted for review. Any case accepted by the ARB shall be decided within 120 days of such acceptance. If not so decided, the decision of the ALJ shall constitute final agency action.

PART 646 [RESERVED]

PART 650—STANDARD FOR APPEALS PROMPTNESS—UNEMPLOYMENT COMPENSATION

Sec.

AUTHORITY: Sec. 1102 of the Social Security Act, 42 U.S.C. 1302; Secretary's Order No. 4–75, dated April 16, 1975. Interpret and apply secs. 303(a)(1), 303(a)(3), and 303(b)(2) of the Social Security Act (42 U.S.C. 503(a)(1), 503(a)(3), 503(b)(2)).

SOURCE: 37 FR 16173, Aug. 11, 1972, unless otherwise noted.

§ 650.1 Nature and purpose of the standard.

(a) This standard is responsive to the overriding concern of the U.S. Supreme Court in California Department of Human Resources v. Java, 402 U.S. 121 (1971), and that of other courts with delay in payment of unemployment compensation to eligible individuals, including delays caused specifically by the adjudication process. The standard seeks to assure that all administrative appeals affecting benefit rights are heard and decided with the greatest promptness that is administratively feasible.

(b) Sections 303(a) (1) and (3) of the Social Security Act require, as a condition for the receipt of granted funds, that State laws include provisions for methods of administration reasonably calculated to insure full payment of unemployment compensation when due, and opportunity for a fair hearing for all individuals whose claims for unemployment compensation are denied. The Secretary has construed these provisions to require, as a condition for receipt of granted funds, that State laws include provisions for hearing and deciding appeals for all unemployment insurance claimants who are parties to an administrative benefit appeal with the greatest promptness that is administratively feasible. What is the greatest promptness that is administratively feasible in an individual case depends on the facts and circumstances of that case. For example, the greatest promptness that is administratively feasible will be longer in cases that involve interstate appeals, complex issues of fact or law, reasonable requests by parties for continuances or rescheduling of hearings or other unforeseen and uncontrollable factors than it will be for other cases.

(c) In addition, the Secretary has construed section 303(b)(2) of the Social Security Act as requiring States to comply substantially with the required provisions of State law. The Secretary considers as substantial compliance the issuance of minimum percentages of first level benefit appeal decisions within the periods of time specified in § 650.4.

(d) Although the interpretation of Federal law requirements in § 650.3 below applies to both first and second level administrative benefit appeals, the criteria for review of State compliance in § 650.3(b) apply only to first level benefit appeals.

§ 650.2 Federal law requirements.

(a) Section 303(a)(1) of the Social Security Act requires that a State law include provision for:

Such methods of administration * * * as are found by the Secretary of Labor to be reasonably calculated to insure full payment of unemployment compensation when due.

(b) Section 303(a)(3) of the Social Security Act requires that a State law include provision for:

Opportunity for a fair hearing, before an impartial tribunal, for all individuals whose claims for unemployment compensation are denied.

(c) Section 303(b)(2) of the Social Security Act provides that:

Whenever the Secretary of Labor, after reasonable notice and opportunity for hearing to the State agency charged with the administration of the State law, finds that in the administration of the law there is—

(1) * * *

(2) A failure to comply substantially with any provision specified in subsection (a) [303(a)]; the Secretary of Labor shall notify such State agency that further payments will not be made to the State until he is satisfied that there is no longer any such denial or failure to comply. Until the Secretary of Labor is so satisfied, he shall make no further certification to the Secretary of the Treasury with respect to such State * * *

§ 650.3 Secretary's interpretation of Federal law requirements.

(a) The Secretary interprets sections 303(a)(1) and 303(a)(3) above to require that a State law include provision for—

(1) Hearing and decision for claimants who are parties to an appeal from a benefit determination to an administrative tribunal with the greatest promptness that is administratively feasible, and

(2) Such methods of administration of the appeals process as will reasonably assure hearing and decision with the greatest promptness that is administratively feasible.

(b) The Secretary interprets section 303(b)(2) above to require a State to comply substantially with provisions specified in paragraph (a) of this section.

§ 650.4 Review of State law and criteria for review of State compliance.

(a) A State law will satisfy the requirements of § 650.3(a) if it contains a provision requiring, or is construed to require, hearing and decision for claimants who are parties to an administrative appeal affecting benefit rights with the greatest promptness that is administratively feasible.

(b) A State will be deemed to comply substantially with the State law requirements set forth in § 650.3(a) with respect to first level appeals, the State has issued at least 60 percent of all first level benefit appeal decisions within 30 days of the date of appeal, and at least 80 percent of all first level benefit appeal decisions within 45 days. These computations will be derived from the State's regular reports required pursuant to the Unemployment

Compensation Manual, part III, sections 4400–4450.[1]

[37 FR 16173, Aug. 11, 1972, as amended at 41 FR 6757, Feb. 13, 1976; 71 FR 35517, June 21, 2006]

§ 650.5 Annual appeals performance plan.

No later than December 15 of each year, each State shall submit an appeals performance plan showing how it will operate during the following calendar year so as to achieve or maintain the issuance of at least 60 percent of all first level benefit appeals decisions within 30 days of the date of appeal, and 80 percent within 45 days.

(Approved by the Office of Management and Budget under control number 1205–0132)

(Pub. L. No. 96–511)

[41 FR 6757, Feb. 13, 1976, as amended at 49 FR 18295, Apr. 30, 1984; 71 FR 35517, June 21, 2006]

PART 651—GENERAL PROVISIONS GOVERNING THE WAGNER-PEYSER ACT EMPLOYMENT SERVICE

AUTHORITY: 29 U.S.C. 49a; 38 U.S.C. part III, 4101, 4211; Secs. 503, 3, 189, Pub. L. 113–128, 128 Stat. 1425 (Jul. 22, 2014).

§ 651.10 Definitions of terms used in this part and parts 652, 653, 654, and 658 of this chapter.

In addition to the definitions set forth in sec. 3 of WIOA, the following definitions apply to the regulations in parts 652, 653, 654, and 658 of this chapter:

Act means the Wagner-Peyser Act (codified at 29 U.S.C. 49 *et seq.*).

Administrator, Office of Workforce Investment (OWI Administrator) means the chief official of the Office of Workforce Investment (OWI) or the Administrator's designee.

Affirmative action means positive, result-oriented action imposed on or assumed by an employer pursuant to legislation, court order, consent decree, directive of a fair employment practice authority, government contract, grant or loan, or voluntary affirmative action plan adopted pursuant to the affirmative action guidelines of the Equal Employment Opportunity Commission (see 29 CFR part 1608) to provide equal employment opportunities for members of a specified group which for reasons of past custom, historical practice, or other non-occupationally valid purposes has been discouraged from entering certain occupational fields.

Agricultural employer means any employer as defined in this part who owns or operates a farm, ranch, processing establishment, cannery, gin, packing shed or nursery, or who produces or conditions seed, and who either recruits, solicits, hires, employs, furnishes, or transports any migrant or seasonal farmworker or any agricultural employer as described in 29 U.S.C. 1802(2).

Agricultural worker see *Farmworker.*

Applicant holding office means a Wagner-Peyser Act Employment Service (ES) office that is in receipt of a clearance order and has access to U.S. workers who may be willing and available to perform farmwork on a less than year-round basis.

Applicant Holding State means a State Workforce Agency that is in receipt of a clearance order from another State and potentially has U.S. workers who may be willing and available to perform farmwork on a less than year-round basis.

Bona fide occupational qualification (BFOQ) means that an employment decision or request based on age, sex, national origin or religion is based on a finding that such characteristic is necessary to the individual's ability to perform the job in question. Since a BFOQ is an exception to the general prohibition against discrimination on the basis of age, sex, national origin, or religion, it must be interpreted narrowly in accordance with the Equal Employment Opportunity Commission regulations set forth at 29 CFR parts 1604, 1605, and 1627.

Career services means the services described in sec. 134(c)(2) of the Workforce Innovation and Opportunity Act (WIOA) and § 678.430 of this chapter.

[1] The Unemployment Compensation Manual is available at each regional office of the Department of Labor and at the headquarters' office of each State unemployment compensation agency.

Clearance order means a job order that is processed through the clearance system under the Agricultural Recruitment System (ARS).

Clearance system means the orderly movement of U.S. job seekers as they are referred through the employment placement process by an ES office. This includes joint action of local ES offices in different labor market areas and/or States.

Complainant means the individual, employer, organization, association, or other entity filing a complaint.

Complaint means a representation made or referred to a State or ES office of an alleged violation of the ES regulations and/or other Federal laws enforced by the Department's Wage and Hour Division (WHD) or Occupational Safety and Health Administration (OSHA), as well as other Federal, State, or local agencies enforcing employment-related law.

Decertification means the rescission by the Secretary of the year-end certification made under sec. 7 of the Wagner-Peyser Act to the Secretary of the Treasury that the State agency may receive funds authorized by the Wagner-Peyser Act.

Department means the United States Department of Labor, including its agencies and organizational units.

Employer means a person, firm, corporation, or other association or organization which currently has a location within the United States to which U.S. workers may be referred for employment, and which proposes to employ a worker at a place within the United States and which has an employer relationship with respect to employees under this subpart as indicated by the fact that it hires, pays, fires, supervises, and otherwise controls the work of such employees. An association of employers is considered an employer if it has all of the indicia of an employer set forth in this definition. Such an association, however, is considered as a joint employer with the employer member if either shares in exercising one or more of the definitional indicia.

Employment and Training Administration (ETA) means the component of the Department of Labor that administers Federal government job training and worker dislocation programs, Federal grants to States for public ES programs, and unemployment insurance benefits. These services are provided primarily through State and local workforce development systems.

Employment-related laws means those laws that relate to the employment relationship, such as those enforced by the Department's WHD, OSHA, or by other Federal, State, or local agencies.

Employment Service (ES) office means a site in a local WDB where staff of the State Workforce Agency, consistent with the requirements of §652.215 of this chapter, provide Wagner-Peyser Act services as a one-stop partner program. A site must be colocated with a one-stop center consistent with the requirements of §§678.305 through 678.315 of this chapter.

Employment Service (ES) regulations means the Federal regulations at this part and parts 652, 653, 654, 658 of this chapter, and 29 CFR part 75.

Establishment means a public or private economic employing unit generally at a single physical location which produces and/or sells goods or services, for example, a mine, factory, store, farm, orchard or ranch. It is usually engaged in one, or predominantly one, type of commercial or governmental activity. Each branch or subsidiary unit of a large employer in a geographical area or community must be considered an individual establishment, except that all such units in the same physical location is considered a single establishment. A component of an establishment which may not be located in the same physical structure (such as the warehouse of a department store) also must be considered as part of the parent establishment. For the purpose of the "seasonal farmworker" definition, farm labor contractors and crew leaders are not considered establishments; it is the organizations to which they supply the workers that are the establishments.

Farmwork means the cultivation and tillage of the soil, dairying, the production, cultivation, growing, and harvesting of any agricultural or horticultural commodities. This includes the raising of livestock, bees, fur-bearing animals, or poultry, the farming of fish, and any practices (including any forestry or lumbering operations) performed by a farmer or on a farm as an incident to or in conjunction with such farming operations, including preparation for market, delivery to storage or to market or to carriers for transportation to market. It also includes the handling, planting, drying, packing, packaging, processing, freezing, or grading prior to delivery for storage of any agricultural or horticultural commodity in its unmanufactured state. For the purposes of this definition, agricultural commodities means all commodities produced on a farm including crude gum (oleoresin) from a living tree products processed by the original producer of the crude gum (oleoresin) from which they are derived, including gum spirits of turpentine and gum rosin. *Farmwork* also means any service or activity covered under § 655.103(c) of this chapter and/or 29 CFR 500.20(e) and any service or activity so identified through official Department guidance such as a Training and Employment Guidance Letter.

Farmworker means an individual employed in farmwork, as defined in this section.

Field checks means random, unannounced appearances by State Workforce Agency personnel at agricultural worksites to which ES placements have been made through the intrastate or interstate clearance system to ensure that conditions are as stated on the job order and that the employer is not violating an employment-related law.

Field visits means appearances by Monitor Advocates or State Workforce Agency outreach personnel to the working and living areas of migrant and seasonal farmworkers (MSFWs), to discuss employment services and other employment-related programs with MSFWs, crew leaders, and employers. Monitor Advocates or outreach personnel must keep records of each such visit.

Governor means the chief executive of a State or an outlying area.

Hearing Officer means a Department of Labor Administrative Law Judge, designated to preside at Department administrative hearings.

Individual with a disability means an individual with a disability as defined in sec. 3 of the Americans with Disabilities Act of 1990 (42 U.S.C. 12102).

Interstate clearance order means an agricultural job order for temporary employment (employment on a less than year-round basis) describing one or more hard-to-fill job openings, which an ES office uses to request recruitment assistance from other ES offices in a different State.

Intrastate clearance order means an agricultural job order for temporary employment (employment on a less than year-round basis) describing one or more hard-to-fill job openings, which an ES office uses to request recruitment assistance from other ES offices within the State.

Job development means the process of securing a job interview with a public or private employer for a specific participant for whom the ES office has no suitable opening on file.

Job information means information derived from data compiled in the normal course of ES activities from reports, job orders, applications, and the like.

Job opening means a single job opportunity for which the ES office has on file a request to select and refer participants.

Job order means the document containing the material terms and conditions of employment relating to wages, hours, working conditions, worksite and other benefits, submitted by an employer.

Job referral means:

(1) The act of bringing to the attention of an employer a participant or group of participants who are available for specific job openings or for a potential job; and

(2) The record of such referral. "Job referral" means the same as "referral to a job."

Labor market area means an economically integrated geographic area within which individuals can reside and find employment within a reasonable distance or can readily change employment without changing their place of residence. Such an area must be identified in accordance with criteria used by the Department's Bureau of Labor Statistics in defining such areas or similar criteria established by a Governor.

Local Office Manager means the official in charge of all ES activities in a one-stop center.

Local Workforce Development Board or *Local WDB* means a Local Workforce Development Board established under sec. 107 of WIOA.

Migrant farmworker means a seasonal farmworker (as defined in this section) who travels to the job site so that the farmworker is not reasonably able to return to his/her permanent residence within the same day. Full-time students traveling in organized groups rather than with their families are excluded.

Migrant food processing worker see *Migrant Farmworker.*

MSFW means a migrant farmworker or a seasonal farmworker.

*Occupational Information Network (O*NET)* system means the online reference database which contains detailed descriptions of U.S. occupations, distinguishing characteristics, classification codes, and information on tasks, knowledge, skills, abilities, and work activities as well as information on interests, work styles, and work values.

One-stop center means a physical center within the one-stop delivery system, as described in sec. 121(e)(2)(A) of WIOA.

One-stop delivery system means a one-stop delivery system described in sec. 121(e) of WIOA.

One-stop partner means an entity described in sec. 121(b) of WIOA and §678.400 of this chapter that is participating in the operation of a one-stop delivery system.

*O*NET–SOC* means the occupational codes and titles used in the O*NET system, based on and grounded in the Standard Occupational Classification (SOC), which are the titles and codes utilized by Federal statistical agencies to classify workers into occupational categories for the purpose of collecting, calculating, and disseminating data. The SOC system is issued by the Office of Management and Budget and the Department of Labor is authorized to develop additional detailed O*NET occupations within existing SOC categories. The Department uses O*NET–SOC titles and codes for the purposes of collecting descriptive occupational information and for State reporting of data on training, credential attainment, and placement in employment by occupation.

Onsite review means an appearance by the State Monitor Advocate and/or Federal staff at an ES office to monitor the delivery of services and protections afforded by ES regulations to MSFWs by the State Workforce Agency and local ES offices.

Order holding office means an ES office that has accepted a clearance order from an employer seeking U.S. workers to perform farmwork on a less than year-round basis through the Agricultural Recruitment System.

Outreach contact means each MSFW that receives the presentation of information, offering of assistance, or follow-up activity from an outreach worker.

Participant means a reportable individual who has received services other than the services described in §677.150(a)(3) of this chapter, after satisfying all applicable programmatic requirements for the provision of services, such as eligibility determination. (*See* §677.150(a) of this chapter.)

(1) The following individuals are not Participants, subject to §677.150(a)(3)(ii) and(iii) of this chapter:

(i) Individuals who only use the self-service system; and

(ii) Individuals who receive information-only services or activities.

(2) Wagner-Peyser Act participants must be included in the program's performance calculations

Placement means the hiring by a public or private employer of an individual referred by the ES office for a job or an interview, provided that the employment office completed all of the following steps:

(1) Prepared a job order form prior to referral, except in the case of a job development contact on behalf of a specific participant;

(2) Made prior arrangements with the employer for the referral of an individual or individuals;

(3) Referred an individual who had not been specifically designated by the employer, except for referrals on agricultural job orders for a specific crew leader or worker;

(4) Verified from a reliable source, preferably the employer, that the individual had entered on a job; and

(5) Appropriately recorded the placement.

Public housing means housing operated by or on behalf of any public agency.

Regional Administrator (RA) means the chief Department of Labor Employment and Training Administration (ETA) official in each Department regional office.

Reportable individual means an individual who has taken action that demonstrates an intent to use Wagner-Peyser Act services and who meets specific reporting criteria of the Wagner-Peyser Act (*see* §677.150(b) of this chapter), including:

(1) Individuals who provide identifying information;

(2) Individuals who only use the self-service system; or

(3) Individuals who only receive information-only services or activities.

Respondent means the employer, individual, or State agency (including a State agency official) who is alleged to have committed the violation described in a complaint.

Seasonal farmworker means an individual who is employed, or was employed in the past 12 months, in farmwork (as defined in this section) of a seasonal or other temporary nature and is not required to be absent overnight from his/her permanent place of residence. Non-migrant individuals who are full-time students are excluded. Labor is performed on a seasonal basis where, ordinarily, the employment pertains to or is of the kind exclusively performed at certain seasons or periods of the year and which, from its nature, may not be continuous or carried on throughout the year. A worker who moves from one seasonal activity to another, while employed in farmwork, is employed on a seasonal basis even though he/she may continue to be employed during a major portion of the year. A worker is employed on other temporary basis where he/she is employed for a limited time only or his/her performance is contemplated for a particular piece of work, usually of short duration. Generally, employment which is contemplated to continue indefinitely is not temporary.

Secretary means the Secretary of the U.S. Department of Labor or the Secretary's designee.

Significant MSFW one-stop centers are those designated annually by the Department and include those ES offices where MSFWs account for 10 percent or more of annual participants in employment services and those local ES offices which the administrator determines must be included due to special circumstances such as an estimated large number of MSFWs in the service area. In no event may the number of significant MSFW one-stop centers be less than 100 centers on a nationwide basis.

Significant MSFW States are those States designated annually by the Department and must include the 20 States with the highest number of MSFW participants.

Significant multilingual MSFW one-stop centers are those designated annually by the Department and include those significant MSFW ES offices where 10 percent or more of MSFW participants are estimated to require service provisions in a language(s) other than English unless the administrator determines other one-stop centers also must be included due to special circumstances.

Solicitor means the chief legal officer of the U.S. Department of Labor or the Solicitor's designee.

Standard Metropolitan Statistical Area (SMSA) means a metropolitan area designated by the Bureau of Census which contains:

(1) At least 1city of 50,000 inhabitants or more; or

(2) Twin cities with a combined population of at least 50,000.

State means any of the 50 States, the District of Columbia, Guam, Puerto Rico, and the Virgin Islands.

State Administrator means the chief official of the SWA.

State agency or *State Workforce Agency (SWA)* means the State ES agency designated under sec. 4 of the Wagner-Peyser Act.

State hearing official means a State official designated to preside at State administrative hearings convened to resolve complaints involving ES regulations pursuant to subpart E of part 658 of this chapter.

State Workforce Development Board or *State WDB* means the entity within a State appointed by the Governor under sec. 101 of WIOA.

Supply State(s) means a State that potentially has U.S. workers who may be recruited for referral through the Agricultural Recruitment System to the area of intended employment in a different State.

Supportive services means services that are necessary to enable an individual to participate in activities authorized under WIOA or the Wagner-Peyser Act. These services may include, but are not limited to, the following:

(1) Linkages to community services;

(2) Assistance with transportation;

(3) Assistance with child care and dependent care;

(4) Assistance with housing;

(5) Needs-related payments;

(6) Assistance with educational testing;

(7) Reasonable accommodations for individuals with disabilities;

(8) Referrals to health care;

(9) Assistance with uniforms or other appropriate work attire and work-related tools, including such items as eyeglasses and protective eye gear;

(10) Assistance with books, fees, school supplies, and other necessary items for students enrolled in postsecondary education classes; and

(11) Payments and fees for employment and training-related applications, tests, and certifications.

Tests means a standardized method of measuring an individual's possession of, interest in, or ability to acquire, job skills and knowledge. Use of tests by one-stop staff must be in accordance with the provisions of:

(1) Title 41 CFR part 60–3, Uniform Guidelines on Employee Selection Procedures;

(2) Title 29 CFR part 1627, Records To Be Made or Kept Relating to Age; Notices To Be Posted; Administrative Exemptions; and

(3) The Department of Labor's regulations on Nondiscrimination on the Basis of Handicap in Programs and Activities Receiving or Benefiting from Federal Financial Assistance, which have been published as 29 CFR part 32.

Training services means services described in sec. 134(c)(3) of WIOA.

Unemployment insurance claimant means a person who files a claim for benefits under any State or Federal unemployment compensation law.

Veteran means a person who served in the active military, naval, or air service, and who was discharged or released therefrom under conditions other than dishonorable, as defined under 38 U.S.C. 101 and sec. 3(63)(A) of WIOA.

Wagner-Peyser Act Employment Service (ES) also known as Employment Service (ES) means the national system of public ES offices described under the Wagner-Peyser Act. Employment services are delivered through a nationwide system of one-stop centers, and are managed by State Workforce Agencies and the various local offices of the State Workforce Agencies, and funded by the United States Department of Labor.

WIOA means the Workforce Innovation and Opportunity Act (codified at 29 U.S.C. 3101 *et seq.*).

Workforce and Labor Market Information (WLMI) means the body of knowledge that describes the relationship between labor demand and supply. This includes identification and analysis of the socio-economic factors that influence employment, training, and business decisions, such as worker preparation, educational program offerings and related policy decisions within national, State, Substate, and local labor market areas. WLMI includes, but is not limited to:

(1) Employment numbers by occupation and industry;

(2) Unemployment numbers and rates;

(3) Short- and long-term industry and occupational employment projections;

(4) Information on business employment dynamics, including the number and nature of business establishments, and share and location of industrial production;

(5) Local employment dynamics, including business turnover rates; new hires, job separations, net job losses;

(6) Job vacancy counts;

(7) Job seeker and job posting data from the public labor exchange system;

(8) Identification of high growth and high demand industries, occupations, and jobs;

(9) Information on employment and earnings for wage and salary workers and for the self-employed;

(10) Information on work hours, benefits, unionization, trade disputes, conditions of employment, and retirement;

(11) Information on occupation-specific requirements regarding education, training, skills, knowledge, and experience;

WLMI also may include, as either source data or as outputs of analysis of source data:

(12) Population and workforce growth and decline, classified by age, sex, race, and other demographic characteristics;

(13) Identification of emerging occupations and evolving skill demands;

(14) Business skill and hiring requirements;

(15) Workforce characteristics, which may include skills, experience, education, credential attainment, competencies, etc.;

(16) Workforce available in geographic areas;

(17) Information on regional and local economic development activity, including job creation through business start-ups and expansions;

(18) Enrollments in and completers from educational programs, training and registered apprenticeship;

(19) Trends in industrial and occupational restructuring;

(20) Shifts in consumer demands;

(21) Data contained in governmental or administrative reporting including wage records as identified in §652.301 of this chapter;

(22) Labor market intelligence gained from interaction with businesses, industry or trade associations, education agencies, government entities, and the public; and

(23) Other economic factors.

Workforce and Labor Market Information System (WLMIS) means the system that collects, analyzes, interprets, and disseminates workforce characteristics and employment-related data, statistics, and information at national, State, and local labor market areas and makes that information available to the public, workforce development system, one-stop partner programs, and the education and economic development communities.

Workforce development activity means an activity carried out through a workforce development program as defined in sec. 3 of WIOA.

Working days or *business days* means those days that the order-holding ES office is open for public business, for purposes of the Agricultural Recruitment System.

Work test means activities designed to ensure that an individual whom a State determines to be eligible for unemployment insurance benefits is able to work, available for work, and actively seeking work in accordance with the State's unemployment compensation law.

[81 FR 56333, Aug. 19, 2016]

PART 652—ESTABLISHMENT AND FUNCTIONING OF STATE EMPLOYMENT SERVICE

Subpart A—Employment Service Operations

Sec.

Subpart B—Services for Veterans

Subpart C—Wagner-Peyser Act Services in a One-Stop Delivery System Environment

Subpart D—Workforce and Labor Market Information

AUTHORITY: 29 U.S.C. 491–2; Secs. 189 and 503, Public Law 113–128, 128 Stat. 1425 (Jul. 22, 2014).

SOURCE: 81 FR 56337, Aug. 19, 2016, unless otherwise noted.

Subpart A—Employment Service Operations

§ 652.1 Introduction.

These regulations implement the provisions of the Wagner-Peyser Act, known hereafter as the Wagner-Peyser Act, as amended by title III of the Workforce Innovation and Opportunity Act (WIOA), Public Law 113–128. The Wagner-Peyser Act Employment Service (ES) is a core program under the WIOA, and an integral component of the one-stop delivery system. Congress intended that the States exercise broad authority in implementing provisions of the Wagner-Peyser Act.

§ 652.2 Scope and purpose of the Wagner-Peyser Act Employment Service.

The basic purpose of the ES is to improve the functioning of the nation's labor markets by bringing together individuals who are seeking employment and employers who are seeking workers.

§ 652.3 Public labor exchange services system.

At a minimum, each State must administer a labor exchange system which has the capacity, to:

(a) Assist job seekers in finding employment, including promoting their familiarity with the Department's electronic tools;

(b) Assist employers in filling jobs;

(c) Facilitate the match between job seekers and employers;

(d) Participate in a system for clearing labor among the States, including the use of standardized classification systems issued by the Secretary, under sec. 15 of the Wagner-Peyser Act;

(e) Meet the work test requirements of the State unemployment compensation system; and

(f) Provide labor exchange services as identified in § 678.430(a) of this chapter, sec. 7(a) of the Wagner-Peyser Act, and sec. 134(c)(2)(A)(iv) of WIOA.

§ 652.4 Allotment of funds and grant agreement.

(a) *Allotments*. The Secretary must provide planning estimates in accordance with sec. 6(b)(5) of the Wagner-Peyser Act. Within 30 days of receipt of planning estimates from the Secretary, the State must make public the sub-State resource distributions, and describe the process and schedule under which these resources will be issued, planned, and committed. This notification must include a description of the procedures by which the public may review and comment on the sub-State distributions, including a process by which the State will resolve any complaints.

(b) *Grant agreement.* To establish a continuing relationship under the Wagner-Peyser Act, the Governor and the Secretary must sign a grant agreement, including a statement assuring that the State must comply with the Wagner-Peyser Act and all applicable rules and regulations. Consistent with this agreement and sec. 6 of the Wagner-Peyser Act, State allotments will be obligated through a notification of obligation.

§ 652.5 Services authorized.

The funds allotted to each State under sec. 6 of the Wagner-Peyser Act must be expended consistent with an approved plan under §§ 676.100 through 676.145 of this chapter and § 652.211. At a minimum, each State must provide the minimum labor exchange elements listed at § 652.3.

§§ 652.6–652.7 [Reserved]

§ 652.8 Administrative provisions.

(a) *Administrative requirements.* The Employment Security Manual is not applicable to funds appropriated under the Wagner-Peyser Act. Except as provided for in paragraph (f) of this section, administrative requirements and cost principles applicable to grants under this part are as specified in 2 CFR parts 200 and 2900 which govern the Uniform Guidelines, cost principles, and audit requirements for Federal awards.

(b) *Management systems, reporting, and recordkeeping.* (1) The State must ensure that a financial system provides fiscal control and accounting procedures sufficient to permit preparation of required reports, and the tracing of funds to a level of expenditure adequate to establish that funds have not been expended in violation of the restrictions on the use of such funds. (sec. 10(a) of the Wagner-Peyser Act)

(2) The financial management system and the program information system must provide Federally-required records and reports that are uniform in definition, accessible to authorized Federal and State staff, and verifiable for monitoring, reporting, audit and evaluation purposes. (sec. 10(c) of the Wagner-Peyser Act)

(c) *Reports required.* (1) Each State must make reports pursuant to instructions issued by the Secretary and in such format as the Secretary prescribes.

(2) The Secretary is authorized to monitor and investigate pursuant to sec. 10 of the Wagner-Peyser Act.

(d) *Special administrative and cost provisions.* (1) Neither the Department nor the State is a guarantor of the accuracy or truthfulness of information obtained from employers or applicants in the process of operating a labor exchange activity.

(2) Prior approval authority—as described in various sections of 29 CFR part 97, Uniform Administrative Requirements for Grants and Cooperative Agreements to State and Local Governments, and Office of Management and Budget Circular A–87 (Revised)—is delegated to the State except that the Secretary reserves the right to require transfer of title on nonexpendable Automated Data Processing Equipment (ADPE), in accordance with provisions contained in 2 CFR parts 200 and 2900. The Secretary reserves the right to exercise prior approval authority in other areas, after providing advance notice to the State.

(3) Application for financial assistance and modification requirements must be as specified under this part.

(4) Cost of promotional and informational activities consistent with the provisions of the Wagner-Peyser Act, describing services offered by employment security agencies, job openings, labor market information, and similar items are allowable.

(5) Each State must retain basic documents for the minimum period specified below, consistent with 2 CFR parts 200 and 2900:

(i) Work application: 3 years.

(ii) Job order: 3 years.

(6) Payments from the State's Wagner-Peyser Act allotment made into a State's account in the Unemployment Trust Fund for the purpose of reducing charges against Reed Act funds (sec. 903(c) of the Social Security Act, as

amended (42 U.S.C. 1103(c)) are allowable costs, provided that:

(i) The charges against Reed Act funds were for amounts appropriated, obligated, and expended for the acquisition of automatic data processing installations or for the acquisition or major renovation of State-owned office building; and

(ii) With respect to each acquisition of improvement of property pursuant to paragraph (d)(6)(i) of this section, the payments are accounted for in the State's records as credits against equivalent amounts of Reed Act funds used for administrative expenditures.

(e) *Disclosure of information.* (1) The State must assure the proper disclosure of information pursuant to sec. 3(b) of the Wagner-Peyser Act.

(2) The information specified in sec. 3(b) and other sections of the Wagner-Peyser Act, also must be provided to officers or any employee of the Federal government or of a State government lawfully charged with administration of unemployment compensation laws, ES activities under the Wagner-Peyser Act or other related legislation, but only for purposes reasonably necessary for the proper administration of such laws.

(f) *Audits.* (1) The State must follow the audit requirements found at § 683.210 of this chapter, except that funds expended pursuant to sec. 7(b) of the Wagner-Peyser Act must be audited annually.

(2) The Comptroller General and the Inspector General of the Department have the authority to conduct audits, evaluations or investigations necessary to meet their responsibilities under sec. 9(b)(1) and 9(b)(2), respectively, of the Wagner-Peyser Act.

(3) The audit, conducted pursuant to paragraph (f)(1) or (2) of this section, must be submitted to the Secretary who will follow the resolution process specified in §§ 683.420 through 683.440 of this chapter.

(g) *Sanctions for violation of the Wagner-Peyser Act.* (1) The Secretary may impose appropriate sanctions and corrective actions for violation of the Wagner-Peyser Act, regulations, or State Plan, including the following:

(i) Requiring repayment, for debts owed the government under the grant, from non-Federal funds;

(ii) Offsetting debts arising from the misexpenditure of grant funds, against amounts to which the State is or may be entitled under the Wagner-Peyser Act, provided that debts arising from gross negligence or willful misuse of funds may not be offset against future grants. When the Secretary reduces amounts allotted to the State by the amount of the misexpenditure, the debt must be fully satisfied;

(iii) Determining the amount of Federal cash maintained by the State or a subrecipient in excess of reasonable grant needs, establishing a debt for the amount of such excessive cash, and charging interest on that debt; and

(iv) Imposing other appropriate sanctions or corrective actions, except where specifically prohibited by the Wagner-Peyser Act or regulations.

(2) To impose a sanction or corrective action, the Secretary must utilize the initial and final determination procedures outlined in paragraph (f)(3) of this section and specified in the administrative provisions at §§ 683.420 through 683.440 of this chapter.

(h) *Other violations.* Violations or alleged violations of the Wagner-Peyser Act, regulations, or grant terms and conditions except those pertaining to audits or discrimination must be determined and handled in accordance with part 658, subpart H, of this chapter.

(i) *Fraud and abuse.* Any persons having knowledge of fraud, criminal activity or other abuse must report such information directly and immediately to the Secretary, including all complaints involving such matters.

(j) *Nondiscrimination and affirmative action requirements.* States must:

(1) Assure that no individual be excluded from participation in, denied the benefits of, subjected to discrimination under, or denied employment in the administration or in connection with any services or activities authorized under the Wagner-Peyser Act in violation of any applicable nondiscrimination law. All complaints alleging discrimination must be filed and processed according to the procedures in the applicable Department of Labor nondiscrimination regulations.

(2) Assure that discriminatory job orders will not be accepted, except where the stated requirement is a bona fide occupational qualification (BFOQ). See, generally, 42 U.S.C. 2000(e)–2(e), 29 CFR parts 1604, 1606, and 1625.

(3) Assure that employers' valid affirmative action requests will be accepted and a significant number of qualified applicants from the target group(s) will be included to enable the employer to meet its affirmative action obligations.

(4) Assure that employment testing programs will comply with 41 CFR part 60–3 and 29 CFR part 32 and 29 CFR 1627.3(b)(1)(iv).

(5) Nondiscrimination and equal opportunity requirements and procedures, including complaint processing and compliance reviews, will be governed by the applicable Department of Labor nondiscrimination regulations.

§652.9 Labor disputes.

(a) State agencies may not make a job referral on job orders which will aid directly or indirectly in the filling of a job opening which is vacant because the former occupant is on strike, or is being locked out in the course of a labor dispute, or the filling of which is otherwise an issue in a labor dispute involving a work stoppage.

(b) Written notification must be provided to all applicants referred to jobs not at issue in the labor dispute that a labor dispute exists in the employing establishment and that the job to which the applicant is being referred is not at issue in the dispute.

(c) When a job order is received from an employer reportedly involved in a labor dispute involving a work stoppage, State agencies must:

(1) Verify the existence of the labor dispute and determine its significance with respect to each vacancy involved in the job order; and

(2) Notify all potentially affected staff concerning the labor dispute.

(d) State agencies must resume full referral services when they have been notified of, and verified with the employer and workers' representative(s), that the labor dispute has been terminated.

(e) State agencies must notify the regional office in writing of the existence of labor disputes which:

(1) Result in a work stoppage at an establishment involving a significant number of workers; or

(2) Involve multi-establishment employers with other establishments outside the reporting State.

Subpart B—Services for Veterans

§652.100 Services for veterans.

Veterans receive priority of service for all Department-funded employment and training programs as described in 20 CFR part 1010. The Department's Veterans' Employment and Training Service (VETS) administers the Jobs for Veterans State Grants (JVSG) program under chapter 41 of title 38 of the U.S. Code and other activities and training programs which provide services to specific populations of eligible veterans. VETS' general regulations are located in parts 1001, 1002, and 1010 of this title.

Subpart C—Wagner-Peyser Act Services in a One-Stop Delivery System Environment

§652.200 What is the purpose of this subpart?

(a) This subpart provides guidance to States to implement the services provided under the Wagner-Peyser Act, as amended by WIOA, in a one-stop delivery system environment.

(b) Except as otherwise provided, the definitions contained in part 651 of this chapter and sec. 2 of the Wagner-Peyser Act apply to this subpart.

§652.201 What is the role of the State Workforce Agency in the one-stop delivery system?

(a) The role of the State Workforce Agency (SWA) in the one-stop delivery system is to ensure the delivery of services authorized under sec. 7(a) of the Wagner-Peyser Act. The SWA is a required one-stop partner in each local one-stop delivery system and is subject to the provisions relating to such partners that are described at part 678 of this chapter.

(b) Consistent with those provisions, the State agency must:

(1) Participate in the one-stop delivery system in accordance with sec. 7(e) of the Wagner-Peyser Act;

(2) Be represented on the Workforce Development Boards (WDBs) that oversee the local and State one-stop delivery system and be a party to the Memorandum of Understanding, described at § 678.500 of this chapter, addressing the operation of the one-stop delivery system; and

(3) Provide these services as part of the one-stop delivery system.

§ 652.202 May local Employment Service offices exist outside of the one-stop delivery system?

No. Local ES offices may not exist outside of the one-stop service delivery system. A State must colocate ES, as provided in §§ 678.310 through 678.315 of this chapter.

§ 652.203 Who is responsible for funds authorized under the Wagner-Peyser Act in the workforce development system?

The SWA retains responsibility for all funds authorized under the Wagner-Peyser Act, including those funds authorized under sec. 7(a) required for providing the services and activities delivered as part of the one-stop delivery system.

§ 652.204 Must funds authorized under the Wagner-Peyser Act (the Governor's Reserve) flow through the one-stop delivery system?

No, sec. 7(b) of the Wagner-Peyser Act provides that 10 percent of the State's allotment under the Wagner-Peyser Act is reserved for use by the Governor for performance incentives, supporting exemplary models of service delivery, professional development and career advancement of SWA staff, and services for groups with special needs. However, these funds may flow through the one-stop delivery system.

§ 652.205 May funds authorized under the Wagner-Peyser Act be used to supplement funding for labor exchange programs authorized under separate legislation?

(a) Section 7(c) of the Wagner-Peyser Act enables States to use funds authorized under sec. 7(a) or 7(b) of the Wagner-Peyser Act to supplement funding of any workforce activity carried out under WIOA.

(b) Funds authorized under the Wagner-Peyser Act may be used under sec. 7(c) to provide additional funding to other activities authorized under WIOA if:

(1) The activity meets the requirements of the Wagner-Peyser Act, and its own requirements;

(2) The activity serves the same individuals as are served under the Wagner-Peyser Act;

(3) The activity provides services that are coordinated with services under the Wagner-Peyser Act; and

(4) The funds supplement, rather than supplant, funds provided from non-Federal sources.

§ 652.206 May a State use funds authorized under the Wagner-Peyser Act to provide applicable "career services," as defined in the Workforce Innovation and Opportunity Act?

Yes, funds authorized under sec. 7(a) of the Wagner-Peyser Act must be used to provide basic career services as identified in § 678.430(a) of this chapter and secs. 134(c)(2)(A)(i)–(xi) of WIOA, and may be used to provide individualized career services as identified in § 678.430(b) of this chapter and sec. 134(c)(2)(A)(xii) of WIOA. Funds authorized under sec. 7(b) of the Wagner-Peyser Act may be used to provide career services. Career services must be provided consistent with the requirements of the Wagner-Peyser Act.

§ 652.207 How does a State meet the requirement for universal access to services provided under the Wagner-Peyser Act?

(a) A State has discretion in how it meets the requirement for universal access to services provided under the Wagner-Peyser Act. In exercising this discretion, a State must meet the Wagner-Peyser Act's requirements.

(b) These requirements are:

(1) Labor exchange services must be available to all employers and job seekers, including unemployment insurance (UI) claimants, veterans, migrant and seasonal farmworkers, and individuals with disabilities;

(2) The State must have the capacity to deliver labor exchange services to

employers and job seekers, as described in the Wagner-Peyser Act, on a statewide basis through:

(i) Self-service, including virtual services;

(ii) Facilitated self-help service; and

(iii) Staff-assisted service;

(3) In each local area, in at least one comprehensive physical center, staff funded under the Wagner-Peyser Act must provide labor exchange services (including staff-assisted labor exchange services) and career services as described in § 652.206; and

(4) Those labor exchange services provided under the Wagner-Peyser Act in a local area must be described in the Memorandum of Understanding (MOU) described in § 678.500 of this chapter.

§ 652.208 How are applicable career services related to the methods of service delivery described in in this part?

Career services may be delivered through any of the applicable three methods of service delivery described in § 652.207(b)(2). These methods are:

(a) Self-service, including virtual services;

(b) Facilitated self-help service; and

(c) Staff-assisted service.

§ 652.209 What are the requirements under the Wagner-Peyser Act for providing reemployment services and other activities to referred unemployment insurance claimants?

(a) In accordance with sec. 3(c)(3) of the Wagner-Peyser Act, the SWA, as part of the one-stop delivery system, must provide reemployment services to UI claimants for whom such services are required as a condition for receipt of UI benefits. Services must be appropriate to the needs of UI claimants who are referred to reemployment services under any Federal or State UI law.

(b) The SWA also must provide other activities, including:

(1) Coordination of labor exchange services with the provision of UI eligibility services as required by sec. 5(b)(2) of the Wagner-Peyser Act;

(2) Administration of the work test, conducting eligibility assessments, and registering UI claimants for employment services in accordance with a State's unemployment compensation law, and provision of job finding and placement services as required by sec. 3(c)(3) and described in sec. 7(a)(3)(F) of the Wagner-Peyser Act; and

(3) Referring UI claimants to, and providing application assistance for, training and education resources and programs, including Federal Pell grants and other student assistance under title IV of the Higher Education Act, the Montgomery GI Bill, Post–9/11 GI Bill, and other Veterans Educational Assistance, training provided for youth, and adult and dislocated workers, as well as other employment training programs under WIOA, and for Vocational Rehabilitation Services under title I of the Rehabilitation Act of 1973.

§ 652.210 What are the Wagner-Peyser Act's requirements for administration of the work test, including eligibility assessments, as appropriate, and assistance to unemployment insurance claimants?

(a) State UI law or rules establish the requirements under which UI claimants must register and search for work in order to fulfill the UI work test requirements.

(b) Staff funded under the Wagner-Peyser Act must assure that:

(1) UI claimants receive the full range of labor exchange services available under the Wagner-Peyser Act that are necessary and appropriate to facilitate their earliest return to work, including career services specified in § 652.206 and listed in sec. 134(c)(2)A) of WIOA;

(2) UI claimants requiring assistance in seeking work receive the necessary guidance and counseling to ensure they make a meaningful and realistic work search; and

(3) ES staff will provide UI program staff with information about UI claimants' ability or availability for work, or the suitability of work offered to them.

§ 652.211 What are State planning requirements under the Wagner-Peyser Act?

The ES is a core program identified in WIOA and must be included as part of each State's Unified or Combined State Plans. See §§ 676.105 through 676.125 of this chapter for planning requirements for the core programs.

§ 652.215 Do any provisions in the Workforce Innovation and Opportunity Act change the requirement that State merit staff employees must deliver services provided under the Wagner-Peyser Act?

No, the Secretary requires that labor exchange services provided under the authority of the Wagner-Peyser Act, including services to veterans, be provided by State merit-staff employees. This interpretation is authorized by and consistent with the provisions in secs. 3(a) and 5(b) of the Wagner-Peyser Act and the Intergovernmental Personnel Act (42 U.S.C 4701 *et seq.*). The Secretary has and has exercised the legal authority under sec. 3(a) of the Wagner-Peyser Act to set additional staffing standards and requirements and to conduct demonstrations to ensure the effective delivery of services provided under the Wagner-Peyser Act. No additional exemptions, other than the ones previously authorized under the Wagner-Peyser Act as amended by WIA, will be authorized.

§ 652.216 May the one-stop operator provide guidance to State merit staff employees in accordance with the Wagner-Peyser Act?

Yes, the one-stop delivery system envisions a partnership in which Wagner-Peyser Act labor exchange services are coordinated with other activities provided by other partners in a one-stop setting. As part of the local Memorandum of Understanding described in § 678.500 of this chapter, the SWA, as a one-stop partner, may agree to have staff receive guidance from the one-stop operator regarding the provision of labor exchange services. Personnel matters, including compensation, personnel actions, terms and conditions of employment, performance appraisals, and accountability of State merit staff employees funded under the Wagner-Peyser Act, remain under the authority of the SWA. The guidance given to employees must be consistent with the provisions of the Wagner-Peyser Act, the local Memorandum of Understanding, and applicable collective bargaining agreements.

Subpart D—Workforce and Labor Market Information

§ 652.300 What role does the Secretary of Labor have concerning the Workforce and Labor Market Information System?

(a) The Secretary of Labor must oversee the development, maintenance, and continuous improvement of the workforce and labor market information system defined in Wagner-Peyser Act sec. 15 and § 651.10 of this chapter. The Department also will identify parameters of continuous improvement. The Secretary will consult with the Workforce Information Advisory Council on these matters and consider the council's recommendations.

(b) With respect to data collection, analysis, and dissemination of workforce and labor market information as defined in Wagner-Peyser Act sec. 15 and § 651.10 of this chapter, the Secretary must:

(1) Assign responsibilities within the Department of Labor for elements of the workforce and labor market information system described in sec. 15(a) of the Wagner-Peyser Act to ensure that the statistical and administrative data collected are consistent with appropriate Bureau of Labor Statistics standards and definitions, and that the information is accessible and understandable to users of such data;

(2) Actively seek the cooperation of heads of other Federal agencies to establish and maintain mechanisms for ensuring complementarity and non-duplication in the development and operation of statistical and administrative data collection activities;

(3) Solicit, receive, and evaluate the recommendations of the Workforce Information Advisory Council established by Wagner-Peyser Act sec. 15(d);

(4) Eliminate gaps and duplication in statistical undertakings;

(5) Through the Bureau of Labor Statistics and the Employment and Training Administration, and in collaboration with States, develop and maintain the elements of the workforce and labor market information system, including the development of consistent procedures and definitions for use by States in collecting and reporting the

workforce and labor market information data described in Wagner-Peyser Act sec. 15 and defined in § 651.10 of this chapter;

(6) Establish procedures for the system to ensure that the data and information are timely, and paperwork and reporting for the system are reduced to a minimum; and

(7) Prepare a 2-year plan for the workforce and labor market information system, as described in the Wagner-Peyser Act sec. 15(c), as amended by WIOA sec. 308(d).

§ 652.301 What are wage records for purposes of the Wagner-Peyser Act?

Wage records, for purposes of the Wagner-Peyser Act, are records that contain "wage information" as defined in § 603.2(k) of this chapter. In this part, "State wage records" refers to wage records produced or maintained by a State.

§ 652.302 How do the Secretary of Labor's responsibilities described in this part apply to State wage records?

(a) A significant portion of the workforce and labor market information—defined in § 651.10 of this chapter—are developed using State wage records.

(b) Based on the Secretary of Labor's responsibilities described in Wagner-Peyser Act sec. 15 and § 652.300, the Secretary of Labor will, in consultation with Federal agencies, and States, and considering recommendations from the Workforce Information Advisory Council described in Wagner-Peyser Act sec. 15(d), develop:

(1) Standardized definitions for the data elements comprising "wage records" as defined in § 652.301; and

(2) Improved processes and systems for the collection and reporting of wage records.

(c) In carrying out these activities, the Secretary also may consult with other stakeholders, such as employers.

§ 652.303 How do the requirements of part 603 of this chapter apply to wage records?

All information collected by the State in wage records referred to in § 652.302 is subject to the confidentiality regulations at part 603 of this chapter.

PART 653—SERVICES OF THE WAGNER-PEYSER ACT EMPLOYMENT SERVICE SYSTEM

AUTHORITY: Secs. 167, 189, 503, Public Law 113–128, 128 Stat. 1425 (Jul. 22, 2014); 29 U.S.C. chapter 4B; 38 U.S.C. part III, chapters 41 and 42.

SOURCE: 81 FR 56341, Aug. 19, 2016, unless otherwise noted.

Subpart A [Reserved]

Subpart B—Services for Migrant and Seasonal Farmworkers (MSFWs)

§ 653.100 Purpose and scope of subpart.

(a) This subpart sets forth the principal regulations of the Wagner-Peyser Act Employment Service (ES) concerning the provision of services for MSFWs consistent with the requirement that all services of the workforce development system be available to all job seekers in an equitable fashion.

This includes ensuring MSFWs have access to these services in a way that meets their unique needs. MSFWs must receive services on a basis which is qualitatively equivalent and quantitatively proportionate to services provided to non-MSFWs.

(b) This subpart contains requirements that State Workforce Agencies (SWAs) establish a system to monitor their own compliance with ES regulations governing services to MSFWs.

(c) Established under this subpart are special services to ensure MSFWs receive the full range of career services as defined in WIOA sec. 134(c)(2).

§ 653.101 Provision of services to migrant and seasonal farmworkers.

Each one-stop center must offer MSFWs the full range of career and supportive services, benefits and protections, and job and training referral services as are provided to non-MSFWs. In providing such services, the one-stop centers must consider and be sensitive to the preferences, needs, and skills of individual MSFWs and the availability of job and training opportunities.

§ 653.102 Job information.

All SWAs must make job order information conspicuous and available to MSFWs by all reasonable means. Such information must, at minimum, be available through internet labor exchange systems and through the one-stop centers. One-stop centers must provide adequate staff assistance to MSFWs to access job order information easily and efficiently. In designated significant MSFW multilingual offices, such assistance must be provided to MSFWs in their native language, whenever requested or necessary.

§ 653.103 Process for migrant and seasonal farmworkers to participate in workforce development activities.

(a) Each one-stop center must determine whether participants are MSFWs as defined at § 651.10 of this chapter.

(b) All SWAs will ensure that MSFWs who are English Language Learners (ELLs) receive, free of charge, the language assistance necessary to afford them meaningful access to the programs, services, and information offered by the one-stop centers.

(c) One-stop center staff must provide MSFWs a list of available career and supportive services in their native language.

(d) One-stop center staff must refer and/or register MSFWs for services, as appropriate, if the MSFW is interested in obtaining such services.

§§ 653.104–653.106 [Reserved]

§ 653.107 Outreach and Agricultural Outreach Plan.

(a) *State Workforce Agency (SWA) outreach responsibilities.* (1) Each SWA must employ an adequate number of outreach workers to conduct MSFW outreach in their service areas. SWA Administrators must ensure State Monitor Advocates and outreach workers coordinate their outreach efforts with WIOA title I sec. 167 grantees as well as with public and private community service agencies and MSFW groups.

(2) As part of their outreach, SWAs must:

(i) Communicate the full range of workforce development services to MSFWs.

(ii) Conduct thorough outreach efforts with extensive follow-up activities in supply States.

(3) For purposes of hiring and assigning staff to conduct outreach duties, and to maintain compliance with SWAs' Affirmative Action programs, SWAs must seek, through merit system procedures, qualified candidates who:

(i) Are from MSFW backgrounds;

(ii) Speak a language common among MSFWs in the State; or

(iii) Are racially or ethnically representative of the MSFWs in the service area.

(4) The 20 States with the highest estimated year-round MSFW activity, as identified in guidance issued by the Secretary, must assign, in accordance with State merit staff requirements, full-time, year-round staff to conduct outreach duties. The remainder of the States must hire year-round part-time outreach staff and, during periods of the highest MSFW activity must hire full-time outreach staff. All outreach staff must be multilingual if warranted by the characteristics of the MSFW

population in the State, and must spend a majority of their time in the field.

(5) The SWA must publicize the availability of employment services through such means as newspaper and electronic media publicity. Contacts with public and private community agencies, employers and/or employer organizations, and MSFW groups also must be utilized to facilitate the widest possible distribution of information concerning employment services.

(b) *Outreach worker's responsibilities.* Outreach workers must locate and contact MSFWs who are not being reached by the normal intake activities conducted by the ES offices. Outreach workers' responsibilities include:

(1) Explaining to MSFWs at their working, living, or gathering areas (including day-haul sites), by means of written and oral presentations either spontaneous or recorded, in a language readily understood by them, the following:

(i) The services available at the local one-stop center (which includes the availability of referrals to training, supportive services, and career services, as well as specific employment opportunities), and other related services;

(ii) Information on the Employment Service and Employment-related Law Complaint System;

(iii) Information on the other organizations serving MSFWs in the area; and

(iv) A basic summary of farmworker rights, including farmworker rights with respect to the terms and conditions of employment.

(2) Outreach workers must not enter work areas to perform outreach duties described in this section on an employer's property without permission of the employer unless otherwise authorized to enter by law; must not enter workers' living areas without the permission of the workers; and must comply with appropriate State laws regarding access.

(3) After making the presentation, outreach workers must urge the MSFWs to go to the local one-stop center to obtain the full range of employment and training services.

(4) If an MSFW cannot or does not wish to visit the local one-stop center, the outreach worker must offer to provide on-site the following:

(i) Assistance in the preparation of applications for employment services;

(ii) Assistance in obtaining referral(s) to current and future employment opportunities;

(iii) Assistance in the preparation of either ES or employment-related law complaints;

(iv) Referral of complaints to the ES office Complaint Specialist or ES office manager;

(v) Referral to supportive services and/or career services in which the individual or a family member may be interested; and

(vi) As needed, assistance in making appointments and arranging transportation for individual MSFW(s) or members of his/her family to and from local one-stop centers or other appropriate agencies.

(5) Outreach workers must make follow-up contacts as necessary and appropriate to provide the assistance specified in paragraphs (b)(1) through (4) of this section.

(6) Outreach workers must be alert to observe the working and living conditions of MSFWs and, upon observation or upon receipt of information regarding a suspected violation of Federal or State employment-related law, document and refer information to the ES office manager for processing in accordance with § 658.411 of this chapter. Additionally, if an outreach worker observes or receives information about apparent violations (as described in § 658.419 of this chapter), the outreach worker must document and refer the information to the appropriate ES office manager.

(7) Outreach workers must be trained in local office procedures and in the services, benefits, and protections afforded MSFWs by the ES, including training on protecting farmworkers against sexual harassment. While sexual harassment is the primary requirement, training also may include similar issues such as sexual coercion, assault, and human trafficking. Such trainings are intended to help outreach workers identify when such issues may be occurring in the fields and how to document and refer the cases to the appropriate enforcement agencies. They

also must be trained in the procedure for informal resolution of complaints. The program for such training must be formulated by the State Administrator, pursuant to uniform guidelines developed by the Employment and Training Administration (ETA). The SMA must be given an opportunity to review and comment on the State's program.

(8) Outreach workers must maintain complete records of their contacts with MSFWs and the services they perform. These records must include a daily log, a copy of which must be sent monthly to the ES office manager and maintained on file for at least 2 years. These records must include the number of contacts, the names of contacts (if available), and the services provided (e.g., whether a complaint was received, whether a request for career services was received, and whether a referral was made). Outreach workers also must maintain records of each possible violation or complaint of which they have knowledge, and their actions in ascertaining the facts and referring the matters as provided herein. These records must include a description of the circumstances and names of any employers who have refused outreach workers access to MSFWs pursuant to paragraph (b)(2) of this section.

(9) Outreach workers must not engage in political, unionization, or anti-unionization activities during the performance of their duties.

(10) Outreach workers must be provided with, carry and display, upon request, identification cards or other material identifying them as employees of the SWA.

(11) Outreach workers in significant MSFW local offices must conduct especially vigorous outreach in their service areas.

(c) *ES office outreach responsibilities.* Each ES office manager must file with the SMA a monthly summary report of outreach efforts. These reports must summarize information collected, pursuant to paragraph (b)(8) of this section. The ES office manager and/or other appropriate State office staff must assess the performance of outreach workers by examining the overall quality and productivity of their work, including the services provided and the methods and tools used to offer services. Performance must not be judged solely by the number of contacts made by the outreach worker. The monthly reports and daily outreach logs must be made available to the SMA and Federal on-site review teams.

(d) *State Agricultural Outreach Plan (AOP).* (1) Each SWA must develop an AOP every 4 years as part of the Unified or Combined State Plans required under sec. 102 or 103 of WIOA.

(2) The AOP must:

(i) Provide an assessment of the unique needs of MSFWs in the area based on past and projected agricultural and MSFW activity in the State;

(ii) Provide an assessment of available resources for outreach;

(iii) Describe the SWA's proposed outreach activities including strategies on how to contact MSFWs who are not being reached by the normal intake activities conducted by the one-stop center;

(iv) Describe the activities planned for providing the full range of employment and training services to the agricultural community, including both MSFWs and agricultural employers, through the one-stop centers; and

(v) Provide an assurance that the SWA is complying with the requirements under §653.111 if the State has significant MSFW one-stop centers.

(3) In developing the AOP, the SWA must solicit information and suggestions from WIOA sec. 167 National Farmworker Jobs Program (NFJP) grantees, other appropriate MSFW groups, public agencies, agricultural employer organizations, and other interested organizations. In addition, at least 45 calendar days before submitting its final AOP to the Department, the SWA must provide the proposed AOP to NFJP grantees, public agencies, agricultural employer organizations, and other organizations expressing an interest and allow at least 30 calendar days for review and comment. The SWA must:

(i) Consider any comments received in formulating its final proposed AOP.

(ii) Inform all commenting parties in writing whether their comments have been incorporated and, if not, the reasons therefore.

(iii) Transmit the comments and recommendations received and its responses to the Department with the submission of the AOP. (If the comments are received after the submission of the AOP, they may be sent separately to the Department.)

(4) The AOP must be submitted in accordance with paragraph (d) of this section and planning guidance issued by the Department.

(5) The Annual Summaries required at § 653.108(s) must update the Department on the SWA's progress toward meetings its goals set forth in the AOP.

§ 653.108 State Workforce Agency and State Monitor Advocate responsibilities.

(a) State Administrators must ensure their SWAs monitor their own compliance with ES regulations in serving MSFWs on an ongoing basis. The State Administrator has overall responsibility for SWA self-monitoring.

(b) The State Administrator must appoint a State Monitor Advocate. The State Administrator must inform farmworker organizations and other organizations with expertise concerning MSFWs of the opening and encourage them to refer qualified applicants to apply through the State merit system prior to appointing a State Monitor Advocate. Among qualified candidates determined through State merit system procedures, the SWAs must seek persons:

(1) Who are from MSFW backgrounds; or

(2) Who speak Spanish or other languages of a significant proportion of the State MSFW population; or

(3) Who have substantial work experience in farmworker activities.

(c) The SMA must have direct, personal access, when necessary, to the State Administrator. The SMA must have status and compensation as approved by the civil service classification system and be comparable to other State positions assigned similar levels of tasks, complexity, and responsibility.

(d) The SMA must be assigned staff necessary to fulfill effectively all of the duties set forth in this subpart. The number of staff positions must be determined by reference to the number of MSFWs in the State, as measured at the time of the peak MSFW population, and the need for monitoring activity in the State. The SMA must devote full-time to Monitor Advocate functions. Any State that proposes less than full-time dedication must demonstrate to its Regional Administrator that the SMA function can be effectively performed with part-time staffing.

(e) All SMAs and their staff must attend, within the first 3 months of their tenure, a training session conducted by the Regional Monitor Advocate. They also must attend whatever additional training sessions are required by the Regional or National Monitor Advocate.

(f) The SMA must provide any relevant documentation requested from the SWA by the Regional Monitor Advocate or the National Monitor Advocate.

(g) The SMA must:

(1) Conduct an ongoing review of the delivery of services and protections afforded by the ES regulations to MSFWs by the SWA and ES offices (including progress made in achieving affirmative action staffing goals). The SMA, without delay, must advise the SWA and local offices of problems, deficiencies, or improper practices in the delivery of services and protections afforded by these regulations and may request a corrective action plan to address these deficiencies. The SMA must advise the SWA on means to improve the delivery of services.

(2) Participate in on-site reviews on a regular basis, using the following procedures:

(i) Before beginning an onsite review, the SMA or review staff must study:

(A) Program performance data;

(B) Reports of previous reviews;

(C) Corrective action plans developed as a result of previous reviews;

(D) Complaint logs; and

(E) Complaints elevated from the office or concerning the office.

(ii) Ensure that the onsite review format, developed by ETA, is used as a guideline for onsite reviews.

(iii) Upon completion of an onsite monitoring review, the SMA must hold one or more wrap-up sessions with the ES office manager and staff to discuss any findings and offer initial recommendations and appropriate technical assistance.

(iv) After each review the SMA must conduct an in-depth analysis of the review data. The conclusions and recommendations of the SMA must be put in writing and must be sent to the State Administrator, to the official of the SWA with authority over the ES office, and other appropriate SWA officials.

(v) If the review results in any findings of noncompliance with the regulations under this chapter, the ES office manager must develop and propose a written corrective action plan. The plan must be approved or revised by appropriate superior officials and the SMA. The plan must include actions required to correct or to take major steps to correct any compliance issues within 30 business days, and if the plan allows for more than 30 business days for full compliance, the length of, and the reasons for, the extended period must be specifically stated. SWAs are responsible for assuring and documenting that the ES office is in compliance within the time period designated in the plan.

(vi) SWAs must submit to the appropriate ETA regional office copies of the onsite review reports and corrective action plans for ES offices.

(vii) The SMA may recommend that the review described in paragraph (g)(2) of this section be delegated to a responsible, professional member of the administrative staff of the SWA, if and when the State Administrator finds such delegation necessary. In such event, the SMA is responsible for and must approve the written report of the review.

(3) Ensure all significant MSFW one-stop centers not reviewed onsite by Federal staff, are reviewed at least once per year by State staff, and that, if necessary, those ES offices in which significant problems are revealed by required reports, management information, the Complaint System, or other means are reviewed as soon as possible.

(4) Review and approve the SWA's Agricultural Outreach Plan (AOP).

(5) On a random basis, review outreach workers' daily logs and other reports including those showing or reflecting the workers' activities.

(6) Write and submit annual summaries to the State Administrator with a copy to the Regional Administrator as described in paragraph (s) of this section.

(h) The SMA must participate in Federal reviews conducted pursuant to part 658, subpart G, of this chapter.

(i) At the discretion of the State Administrator, the SMA may be assigned the responsibility as the Complaint Specialist. The SMA must participate in and monitor the performance of the Complaint System, as set forth at §§ 658.400 and 658.401 of this chapter. The SMA must review the ES office's informal resolution of complaints relating to MSFWs and must ensure that the ES office manager transmits copies of the Complaint System logs pursuant to part 658, subpart E, of this chapter to the SWA.

(j) The SMA must serve as an advocate to improve services for MSFWs.

(k) The SMA must establish an ongoing liaison with WIOA sec. 167 National Farmworker Jobs Program (NFJP) grantees and other organizations serving farmworkers, employers, and employer organizations in the State.

(l) The SMA must meet (either in person or by alternative means), at minimum, quarterly, with representatives of the organizations pursuant to paragraph (k) of this section, to receive complaints, assist in referrals of alleged violations to enforcement agencies, receive input on improving coordination with ES offices or improving the coordination of services to MSFWs. To foster such collaboration, the SMAs must establish Memorandums of Understanding (MOUs) with the NFJP grantees and may establish MOUs with other organizations serving farm workers as appropriate.

(m) The SMA must conduct frequent field visits to the working, living, and gathering areas of MSFWs, and must discuss employment services and other employment-related programs with MSFWs, crew leaders, and employers. Records must be kept of each such field visit.

(n) The SMA must participate in the appropriate regional public meeting(s) held by the Department of Labor Regional Farm Labor Coordinated Enforcement Committee, other Occupational Safety and Health Administration and Wage and Hour Division task forces, and other committees as appropriate.

(o) The SMA must ensure that outreach efforts in all significant MSFW ES offices are reviewed at least yearly. This review will include accompanying at least one outreach worker from each significant MSFW ES office on field visits to MSFWs' working, living, and/or gathering areas. The SMA must review findings from these reviews with the ES office managers.

(p) The SMA must review on at least a quarterly basis all statistical and other MSFW-related data reported by ES offices in order:

(1) To determine the extent to which the SWA has complied with the ES regulations; and

(2) To identify the areas of non-compliance.

(q) The SMA must have full access to all statistical and other MSFW-related information gathered by SWAs and ES offices, and may interview SWA and ES office staff with respect to reporting methods. Subsequent to each review, the SMA must consult, as necessary, with the SWA and ES offices and provide technical assistance to ensure accurate reporting.

(r) The SMA must review and comment on proposed State ES directives, manuals, and operating instructions relating to MSFWs and must ensure:

(1) That they accurately reflect the requirements of the regulations; and

(2) That they are clear and workable. The SMA also must explain and make available at the requestor's cost, pertinent directives and procedures to employers, employer organizations, farmworkers, farmworker organizations, and other parties expressing an interest in a readily identifiable directive or procedure issued and receive suggestions on how these documents can be improved.

(s) The SMA must prepare for the State Administrator, the Regional Monitor Advocate, and the National Monitor Advocate an Annual Summary describing how the State provided employment services to MSFWs within the State based on statistical data, reviews, and other activities as required in this chapter. The summary must include:

(1) A description of the activities undertaken during the program year by the SMA pertaining to his/her responsibilities set forth in this section and other applicable regulations in this chapter.

(2) An assurance that the SMA has direct, personal access, whenever he/she finds it necessary, to the State Administrator and that the SMA has status and compensation approved by the civil service classification system, and is comparable to other State positions assigned similar levels of tasks, complexity, and responsibility.

(3) An assurance the SMA devotes all of his/her time to monitor advocate functions. Or, if the SWA proposed the SMA conducts his/her functions on a part-time basis, an explanation of how the SMA functions are effectively performed with part-time staffing.

(4) A summary of the monitoring reviews conducted by the SMA, including:

(i) A description of any problems, deficiencies, or improper practices the SMA identified in the delivery of services;

(ii) A summary of the actions taken by the SWA to resolve the problems, deficiencies, or improper practices described in its service delivery; and

(iii) A summary of any technical assistance the SMA provided for the SWA and the ES offices.

(5) A summary of the outreach efforts undertaken by all significant and non-significant MSFW ES offices.

(6) A summary of the State's actions taken under the Complaint System described in part 658, subpart E, of this chapter, identifying any challenges, complaint trends, findings from reviews of the Complaint System, trainings offered throughout the year, and steps taken to inform MSFWs and employers, and farmworker advocacy groups about the Complaint System.

(7) A summary of how the SMA is working with WIOA sec. 167 NFJP

grantees and other organizations serving farmworkers, employers and employer organizations, in the State, and an assurance that the SMA is meeting at least quarterly with representatives of these organizations.

(8) A summary of the statistical and other MSFW-related data and reports gathered by SWAs and ES offices for the year, including an overview of the SMA's involvement in the SWA's reporting systems.

(9) A summary of the training conducted for SWA personnel, including ES office personnel, on techniques for accurately reporting data.

(10) A summary of activities related to the AOP and an explanation of how those activities helped the State reach the goals and objectives described in the AOP. At the end of the 4-year AOP cycle, the summary must include a synopsis of the SWA's achievements over the previous 4 years to accomplish the goals set forth in the AOP, and a description of the goals which were not achieved and the steps the SWA will take to address those deficiencies.

(11) For significant MSFW ES offices, a summary of the functioning of the State's affirmative action staffing program under § 653.111.

§ 653.109 Data collection and performance accountability measures.

SWAs must:

(a) Collect career service indicator data for the career services specified in WIOA sec. 134(c)(2)(A)(xii).

(b) Collect data, in accordance with applicable ETA Reports and Guidance, on:

(1) The number of MSFWs contacted through outreach activities;

(2) The number of MSFWs and non-MSFWs registered for career services;

(3) The number of MSFWs referred to and placed in agricultural jobs;

(4) The number of MSFWs referred to and placed in non-agricultural jobs;

(5) The percentage of MSFW program participants who are in unsubsidized employment during the second quarter after exit from the program;

(6) The median earnings of MSFW program participants who are in unsubsidized employment during the second quarter after exit from the program;

(7) The percentage of MSFW program participants who are in unsubsidized employment during the fourth quarter after exit from the program;

(8) The number of MSFWs served who identified themselves as male, female, Hispanic or Latino, Black or African-American, American Indian or Alaska Native, Asian, Native Hawaiian or Pacific Islander, or White;

(9) Agricultural clearance orders (including field checks), MSFW complaints and apparent violations, and monitoring activities; and

(10) Any other data required by the Department.

(c) Provide necessary training to SWA personnel, including ES office personnel, on techniques for accurately reporting data.

(d) Collect and submit data on MSFWs required by the Unified or Combined State Plan, as directed by the Department.

(e) Periodically verify data required to be collected under this section, take necessary steps to ensure its validity, and submit the data for verification to the Department, as directed by the Department.

(f) Submit additional reports to the Department as directed.

(g) Meet equity indicators that address ES controllable services and include, at a minimum, individuals referred to a job, receiving job development, and referred to supportive or career services.

(h) Meet minimum levels of service in significant MSFW States. That is, only significant MSFW SWAs will be required to meet minimum levels of service to MSFWs. Minimum level of service indicators must include, at a minimum, individuals placed in a job, individuals placed long-term (150 days or more) in a non-agricultural job, a review of significant MSFW ES offices, field checks conducted, outreach contacts per week, and processing of complaints. The determination of the minimum service levels required of significant MSFW States for each year must be based on the following:

(1) Past SWA performance in serving MSFWs, as reflected in on-site reviews and data collected under paragraph (b) of this section.

(2) The need for services to MSFWs in the upcoming year, comparing prior and projected levels of MSFW activity.

§ 653.110 Disclosure of data.

(a) SWAs must disclose to the public, on written request, in conformance with applicable State and Federal law, the data collected by SWAs and ES offices pursuant to § 653.109, if possible within 10 business days after receipt of the request.

(b) If a request for data held by a SWA is made to the ETA national or regional office, the ETA must forward the request to the SWA for response.

(c) If the SWA cannot supply the requested data within 10 business days after receipt of the request, the SWA must respond to the requestor in writing, giving the reason for the delay and specifying the date by which it expects to be able to comply.

(d) SWA intra-agency memoranda and reports (or parts thereof) and memoranda and reports (or parts thereof) between the SWA and the ETA, to the extent that they contain statements of opinion rather than facts, may be withheld from public disclosure provided the reason for withholding is given to the requestor in writing. Similarly, documents or parts thereof, which, if disclosed, would constitute an unwarranted invasion of personal or employer privacy, also may be withheld provided the reason is given to the requestor in writing.

§ 653.111 State Workforce Agency staffing requirements.

(a) The SWA must implement and maintain an affirmative action program for staffing in significant MSFW one-stop centers, and must employ ES staff in a manner facilitating the delivery of employment services tailored to the special needs of MSFWs, including:

(1) The positioning of multilingual staff in offices serving a significant number of Spanish-speaking or ELL participants; and

(2) The hiring of staff members from the MSFW community or members of community-based migrant programs.

(b) The SWA must hire sufficient numbers of qualified, permanent minority staff in significant MSFW ES offices. SWAs will determine whether a "sufficient number" of staff have been hired by conducting a comparison between the characteristics of the staff and the workforce and determining if the composition of the local office staff(s) is representative of the racial and ethnic characteristics of the workforce in the ES office service area(s). SWAs with significant MSFW ES offices, must undertake special efforts to recruit MSFWs and persons from MSFW backgrounds for its staff.

(1) Where qualified minority applicants are not available to be hired as permanent staff, qualified minority part-time, provisional, or temporary staff must be hired in accordance with State merit system procedures, where applicable.

(2) If an ES office does not have a sufficient number of qualified minority staff, the SWA must establish a goal to achieve sufficient staffing at the ES office. The SWA also must establish a reasonable timetable for achieving the staffing goal by hiring or promoting available, qualified staff in the underrepresented categories. In establishing timetables, the SWA must consider the vacancies anticipated through expansion, contraction, and turnover in the office(s) and available funds. All affirmative action programs must establish timetables that are designed to achieve the staffing goal no later than 1year after the submission of the Unified or Combined State Plan or Annual Summary, whichever is sooner. Once such goals have been achieved, the SWA must submit a State Plan modification request to the Department with the assurance that the requirements of paragraph (b) of this section have been achieved.

(3) The SMA, Regional Monitor Advocate, or the National Monitor Advocate, as part of his/her regular reviews of SWA compliance with these regulations, must monitor the extent to which the SWA has complied with its affirmative action program.

Subparts C–E [Reserved]

Subpart F—Agricultural Recruitment System for U.S. Workers (ARS)

§ 653.500 Purpose and scope of subpart.

This subpart includes the requirements for the acceptance of intrastate and interstate job clearance orders which seek U.S. workers to perform farmwork on a temporary, less than year-round basis. Orders seeking workers to perform farmwork on a year-round basis are not subject to the requirements of this subpart. This subpart affects all job orders for workers who are recruited through the ES intrastate and interstate clearance systems for less than year-round farmwork, including both MSFWs and non-MSFW job seekers.

§ 653.501 Requirements for processing clearance orders.

(a) *Assessment of need.* No ES office or SWA may place a job order seeking workers to perform farmwork into intrastate or interstate clearance unless:

(1) The ES office and employer have attempted and have not been able to obtain sufficient workers within the local labor market area; or

(2) The ES office anticipates a shortage of local workers.

(b) *ES office responsibilities.* (1) Each ES office must ensure the agricultural clearance form prescribed by the Department (ETA Form 790 or its subsequently issued form), and its attachments are complete when placing intrastate or interstate clearance orders seeking workers.

(2) All clearance orders must be posted in accordance with applicable ETA guidance. If the job order for the ES office incorporates offices beyond the local office commuting area, the ES office must suppress the employer information in order to facilitate the orderly movement of workers within the ES.

(3) ES staff must determine, through a preoccupancy housing inspection performed by ES staff or an appropriate public agency, that the housing assured by the employer is either available and meets the applicable housing standards or has been approved for conditional access to the clearance system as set forth in § 653.502; except that mobile range housing for sheepherders and goatherders must meet existing Departmental guidelines and/or applicable regulations.

(c) *SWA responsibilities.* (1) SWAs must ensure intrastate and interstate clearance orders:

(i) Include the following language: "In view of the statutorily established basic function of the ES as a no-fee labor exchange, that is, as a forum for bringing together employers and job seekers, neither the ETA nor the SWAs are guarantors of the accuracy or truthfulness of information contained on job orders submitted by employers. Nor does any job order accepted or recruited upon by the ES constitute a contractual job offer to which the ETA or a SWA is in any way a party;"

(ii) Do not contain an unlawful discriminatory specification including, for beneficiaries (as defined in 29 CFR 38.4) only, on the basis of citizenship status or participant status;

(iii) Are signed by the employer; and

(iv) State all the material terms and conditions of the employment, including:

(A) The crop;

(B) The nature of the work;

(C) The anticipated period and hours of employment;

(D) The anticipated starting and ending date of employment and the anticipated number of days and hours per week for which work will be available;

(E) The hourly wage rate or the piece rate estimated in hourly wage rate equivalents for each activity and unit size;

(F) Any deductions to be made from wages;

(G) A specification of any non-monetary benefits to be provided by the employer;

(H) Any hours, days, or weeks for which work is guaranteed, and, for each guaranteed week of work except as provided in paragraph (c)(3)(i) of this section, the exclusive manner in which the guarantee may be abated due to weather conditions or other acts of God beyond the employer's control; and

(I) Any bonus or work incentive payments or other expenses which will be paid by the employer in addition to the basic wage rate, including the anticipated time period(s) within which such payments will be made.

(2) SWAs must ensure:

(i) The wages and working conditions offered are not less than the prevailing wages and working conditions among similarly employed farmworkers in the area of intended employment or the applicable Federal or State minimum wage, whichever is higher. If the wages offered are expressed as piece rates or as base rates and bonuses, the employer must make the method of calculating the wage and supporting materials available to ES staff who must check if the employer's calculation of the estimated hourly wage rate is reasonably accurate and is not less than the prevailing wage rate or applicable Federal or State minimum wage, whichever is higher; and

(ii) The employer has agreed to provide or pay for the transportation of the workers and their families at or before the end of the period of employment specified in the job order on at least the same terms as transportation is commonly provided by employers in the area of intended employment to farmworkers and their families recruited from the same area of supply. Under no circumstances may the payment or provision of transportation occur later than the departure time needed to return home to begin the school year, in the case of any worker with children 18 years old or younger, or be conditioned on the farmworker performing work after the period of employment specified in the job order.

(3) SWAs must ensure the clearance order includes the following assurances:

(i) The employer will provide to workers referred through the clearance system the number of hours of work cited in paragraph (c)(1)(iv)(D) of this section for the week beginning with the anticipated date of need, unless the employer has amended the date of need at least 10 business days prior to the original date of need (pursuant to paragraph (c)(3)(iv) of this section) by so notifying the order-holding office in writing (email notification may be acceptable). The SWA must make a record of this notification and must attempt to inform referred workers of the change expeditiously.

(ii) No extension of employment beyond the period of employment specified in the clearance order may relieve the employer from paying the wages already earned, or if specified in the clearance order as a term of employment, providing transportation or paying transportation expenses to the worker's home.

(iii) The working conditions comply with applicable Federal and State minimum wage, child labor, social security, health and safety, farm labor contractor registration and other employment-related laws.

(iv) The employer will expeditiously notify the order-holding office or SWA by emailing and telephoning immediately upon learning that a crop is maturing earlier or later, or that weather conditions, over-recruitment or other factors have changed the terms and conditions of employment.

(v) The employer, if acting as a farm labor contractor ("FLC") or farm labor contractor employee ("FLCE") on the order, has a valid Federal FLC certificate or Federal FLCE identification card and when appropriate, any required State farm labor contractor certificate.

(vi) The availability of no cost or public housing which meets the Federal standards and which is sufficient to house the specified number of workers requested through the clearance system. This assurance must cover the availability of housing for only those workers, and when applicable, family members who are not reasonably able to return to their residence in the same day.

(vii) Outreach workers must have reasonable access to the workers in the conduct of outreach activities pursuant to § 653.107.

(viii) The job order contains all the material terms and conditions of the job. The employer must assure this by signing the following statement in the clearance order: "This clearance order describes the actual terms and conditions of the employment being offered by me and contains all the material terms and conditions of the job."

(4) If a SWA discovers that an employer's clearance order contains a material misrepresentation, the SWA may initiate the Discontinuation of Services as set forth in part 658, subpart F of this chapter.

(5) If there is a change to the anticipated date of need and the employer fails to notify the order-holding office at least 10 business days prior to the original date of need the employer must pay eligible (pursuant to paragraph (d)(4) of this section) workers referred through the clearance system the specified hourly rate of pay, or if the pay is piece-rate, the higher of the Federal or State minimum wage for the first week starting with the originally anticipated date of need or provide alternative work if such alternative work is stated on the clearance order. If an employer fails to comply under this section the order holding office may notify the Department's Wage and Hour Division for possible enforcement.

(d) *Processing clearance orders.* (1) The order-holding office must transmit an electronic copy of the approved clearance order to its SWA. The SWA must distribute additional electronic copies of the form with all attachments (except that the SWA may, at its discretion, delegate this distribution to the local office) as follows:

(i) At least one copy of the clearance order must be sent to each of the SWAs selected for recruitment (areas of supply);

(ii) At least one copy of the clearance order must be sent to each applicant-holding ETA regional office;

(iii) At least one copy of the clearance order must be sent to the order-holding ETA regional office; and

(iv) At least one copy of the clearance order must be sent to the Regional Farm Labor Coordinated Enforcement Committee and/or other Occupational Safety and Health Administration and Wage and Hour Division regional agricultural coordinators, and/or other committees as appropriate in the area of employment.

(2) The ES office may place an intrastate or interstate order seeking workers to perform farmwork for a specific farm labor contractor or for a worker preferred by an employer provided the order meets ES nondiscrimination criteria. The order would not meet such criteria, for example, if it requested a "white male crew leader" or "any white male crew leader."

(3) The approval process described in paragraph (d)(3) of this section does not apply to clearance orders that are attached to applications for foreign temporary agricultural workers pursuant to part 655, subpart B, of this chapter; such clearance orders must be sent to the processing center as directed by ETA in guidance. For non-criteria clearance orders (orders that are not attached to applications under part 655, subpart B, of this chapter), the ETA regional office must review and approve the order within 10 business days of its receipt of the order, and the Regional Administrator or his/her designee must approve the areas of supply to which the order will be extended. Any denial by the Regional Administrator or his/her designee must be in writing and state the reasons for the denial.

(4) The applicant holding office must notify all referred farmworkers, farm labor contractors on behalf of farmworkers, or family heads on behalf of farmworker family members, to contact an ES office, preferably the order-holding office, to verify the date of need cited in the clearance order between 9 and 5 business days prior to the original date of need cited in the clearance order; and that failure to do so will disqualify the referred farmworker from the first weeks' pay as described in paragraph (c)(3)(i) of this section. The SWA must make a record of this notification.

(5) If the worker referred through the clearance system contacts an ES office (in any State) other than the order holding office, that ES office must assist the referred worker in contacting the order holding office on a timely basis. Such assistance must include, if necessary, contacting the order holding office by telephone or other timely means on behalf of the worker referred through the clearance system.

(6) ES office staff must assist all farmworkers, upon request in their native language, to understand the terms and conditions of employment set forth in intrastate and interstate clearance orders and must provide such workers

with checklists in their native language showing wage payment schedules, working conditions, and other material specifications of the clearance order.

(7) If an order holding office learns that a crop is maturing earlier than expected or that other material factors, including weather conditions and recruitment levels have changed since the date the clearance order was accepted, the SWA must contact immediately the applicant holding office which must inform immediately crews and families scheduled to report to the job site of the changed circumstances and must adjust arrangements on behalf of such crews and families.

(8) When there is a delay in the date of need, SWAs must document notifications by employers and contacts by individual farmworkers or crew leaders on behalf of farmworkers or family heads on behalf of farmworker family members to verify the date of need.

(9) If weather conditions, over-recruitment, or other conditions have eliminated the scheduled job opportunities, the SWAs involved must make every effort to place the workers in alternate job opportunities as soon as possible, especially if the worker(s) is/(are) already en-route or at the job site. ES office staff must keep records of actions under this section.

(10) Applicant-holding offices must provide workers referred on clearance orders with a checklist summarizing wages, working conditions and other material specifications in the clearance order. Such checklists, where necessary, must be in the workers' native language. The checklist must include language notifying the worker that a copy of the original clearance order is available upon request. SWAs must use a standard checklist format provided by the Department (such as in Form WH516 or a successor form).

(11) The applicant-holding office must give each referred worker a copy of the list of worker's rights described in the Department's ARS Handbook.

(12) If the labor supply SWA accepts a clearance order, the SWA must actively recruit workers for referral. In the event a potential labor supply SWA rejects a clearance order, the reasons for rejection must be documented and submitted to the Regional Administrator having jurisdiction over the SWA. The Regional Administrator will examine the reasons for rejection, and, if the Regional Administrator agrees, will inform the Regional Administrator with jurisdiction over the order-holding SWA of the rejection and the reasons. If the Regional Administrator who receives the notification of rejection does not concur with the reasons for rejection, that Regional Administrator will inform the National Monitor Advocate, who, in consultation with the appropriate ETA higher authority, will make a final determination on the acceptance or rejection of the order.

§ 653.502 Conditional access to the Agricultural Recruitment System.

(a) *Filing requests for conditional access*—(1) *"Noncriteria" employers.* Except as provided in paragraph (a)(2) of this section, an employer whose housing does not meet applicable standards may file with the ES office serving the area in which its housing is located, a written request for its clearance orders to be conditionally allowed into the intrastate or interstate clearance system, provided that the employer's request assures its housing will be in full compliance with the requirements of the applicable housing standards at least 20 calendar days (giving the specific date) before the housing is to be occupied.

(2) *"Criteria" employers.* If the request for conditional access described in paragraph (a)(1) of this section is from an employer filing a clearance order pursuant to an application for temporary alien agricultural labor certification for H–2A workers under subpart B of part 655 of this chapter, the request must be filed with the Certifying Officer (CO) at the processing center designated by ETA in guidance to make determinations on applications for temporary employment certification under the H–2A program.

(3) *Assurance.* The employer's request pursuant to paragraph (a)(1) or (2) of this section must contain an assurance that the housing will be in full compliance with the applicable housing standards at least 20 calendar days (stating

the specific date) before the housing is to be occupied.

(b) *Processing requests*—(1) *SWA processing.* Upon receipt of a written request for conditional access to the intrastate or interstate clearance system under paragraph (a)(1) of this section, the ES office must send the request to the SWA, which, in turn, must forward it to the Regional Administrator.

(2) *Regional office processing and determination.* Upon receipt of a request for conditional access pursuant to paragraph (b)(1) of this section, the Regional Administrator must review the matter and, as appropriate, must either grant or deny the request.

(c) *Authorization.* The authorization for conditional access to the intrastate or interstate clearance system must be in writing, and must state that although the housing does not comply with the applicable standards, the employer's job order may be placed into intrastate or interstate clearance until a specified date. The Regional Administrator must send the authorization to the employer and must send copies (hard copy or electronic) to the appropriate SWA and ES office. The employer must submit and the ES office must attach copies of the authorization to each of the employer's clearance orders which is placed into intrastate or interstate clearance.

(d) *Notice of denial.* If the Regional Administrator denies the request for conditional access to the intrastate or interstate clearance system he/she must provide written notice to the employer, the appropriate SWA, and the ES office, stating the reasons for the denial.

(e) *Inspection.* The ES office serving the area containing the housing of any employer granted conditional access to the intrastate or interstate clearance system must assure that the housing is inspected no later than the date by which the employer has promised to have its housing in compliance with the applicable housing standards. An employer however, may request an earlier preliminary inspection. If, on the date set forth in the authorization, the housing is not in full compliance with the applicable housing standards as assured in the request for conditional access, the ES office must afford the employer 5 calendar days to bring the housing into full compliance. After the 5-calendar-day period, if the housing is not in full compliance with the applicable housing standards as assured in the request for conditional access, the ES office must immediately:

(1) Notify the RA or the NPC designated by the Regional Administrator;

(2) Remove the employer's clearance orders from intrastate and interstate clearance; and

(3) If workers have been recruited against these orders, in cooperation with the ES agencies in other States, make every reasonable attempt to locate and notify the appropriate crew leaders or workers, and to find alternative and comparable employment for the workers.

§ 653.503 Field checks.

(a) If a worker is placed on a clearance order, the SWA must notify the employer in writing that the SWA, through its ES offices, and/or Federal staff, must conduct random, unannounced field checks to determine and document whether wages, hours, and working and housing conditions are being provided as specified in the clearance order.

(b) Where the SWA has made placements on 10 or more agricultural clearance orders (pursuant to this subpart) during the quarter, the SWA must conduct field checks on at least 25 percent of the total of such orders. Where the SWA has made placements on nine or fewer job orders during the quarter (but at least one job order), the SWA must conduct field checks on 100 percent of all such orders. This requirement must be met on a quarterly basis.

(c) Field checks must include visit(s) to the worksite at a time when workers are present. When conducting field checks, ES staff must consult both the employees and the employer to ensure compliance with the full terms and conditions of employment.

(d) If SWA or Federal personnel observe or receive information, or otherwise have reason to believe that conditions are not as stated in the clearance order or that an employer is violating an employment-related law, the SWA must document the finding and attempt informal resolution where appropriate (for example, informal resolution must not be attempted in certain cases, such as E.O. related issues and others identified by the Department through guidance.) If the matter has not been resolved within 5 business days, the SWA must initiate the Discontinuation of Services as set forth at part 658, subpart F, of this chapter and must refer apparent violations of employment-related laws to appropriate enforcement agencies in writing.

(e) SWAs may enter into formal or informal arrangements with appropriate State and Federal enforcement agencies where the enforcement agency staff may conduct field checks instead of and on behalf of SWA personnel. The agreement may include the sharing of information and any actions taken regarding violations of the terms and conditions of the employment as stated in the clearance order and any other violations of employment-related laws. An enforcement agency field check must satisfy the requirement for SWA field checks where all aspects of wages, hours, working and housing conditions have been reviewed by the enforcement agency. The SWA must supplement enforcement agency efforts with field checks focusing on areas not addressed by enforcement agencies.

(f) ES staff must keep records of all field checks.

PART 654—SPECIAL RESPONSIBILITIES OF THE EMPLOYMENT SERVICE SYSTEM

Subpart A—Responsibilities Under Executive Order 12073

Sec.

Subpart B—Responsibilities Under Executive Order 10582

Subparts C–D [Reserved]

Subpart E—Housing for Farmworkers

PURPOSE AND APPLICABILITY

HOUSING STANDARDS

AUTHORITY: 29 U.S.C. 49k; 8 U.S.C. 1188(c)(4); 41 Op.A.G. 406 (1959).

SOURCE: 44 FR 1689, Jan. 5, 1979, unless otherwise noted.

Subpart A—Responsibilities Under Executive Order 12073

AUTHORITY: 41 U.S.C. 10a *et seq;* 29 U.S.C. 49 *et seq;* 15 U.S.C. 644(n); E.O. 12073; 10582, as amended by E.O. 11051 and 12148.

§ 654.1 Purpose of subpart.

This subpart implements the responsibilities of the Secretary of Labor in classifying labor surplus areas in accordance with Executive Order 12073 (Federal Procurement in Labor Surplus Areas). The Secretary of Labor has delegated responsibilities to the Assistant Secretary, Employment and Training Administration.

[44 FR 1689, Jan. 5, 1979, as amended at 48 FR 15616, Apr. 12, 1983]

§ 654.3 Description of Executive Order 12073.

Executive Order 12073 requires executive agencies to emphasize procurement set-asides in labor surplus areas. The Secretary of Labor is responsible under this order for classifying and designating labor surplus areas.

[44 FR 1689, Jan. 5, 1979, as amended at 48 FR 15616, Apr. 12, 1983]

§ 654.4 Definitions.

(a) *Assistant Secretary* shall mean Assistant Secretary for Employment and Training, U.S. Department of Labor.

(b) *Civil jurisdiction* shall mean:

(1) Cities of 25,000 or more population on the basis of the most recently available Bureau of the Census estimates; or

(2) Towns and townships in the States of New Jersey, New York, Michigan, and Pennsylvania of 25,000 or more population and which possess powers and functions similar to cities; or

(3) All counties, except those counties which contain any of the types of political jurisdictions defined in paragraphs (b) (1) and (2) of this section; or

(4) All other counties are defined as "balance of county" (*i.e.*, total county less component cities and townships identified in paragraphs (b) (1) and (2) of this section); or

(5) County equivalents which are towns in the States of Massachusetts, Rhode Island and Connecticut.

(c) *Labor surplus area* shall mean a civil jurisdiction that, in accordance with the criteria specified in § 654.5, has been classified as a labor surplus area.

(d) *Reference period* shall mean the two year period ending December 31 of the year prior to the October 1 annual date of eligibility determination.

[44 FR 1689, Jan. 5, 1979, as amended at 44 FR 26071, May 5, 1979; 48 FR 15616, Apr. 12, 1983; 53 FR 23347, June 21, 1988]

§ 654.5 Classification of labor surplus areas.

(a) *Basic criteria*. The Assistant Secretary shall classify a civil jurisdiction as a labor surplus area whenever, as determined by the Bureau of Labor Statistics, the average unemployment rate for all civilian workers in the civil jurisdiction for the reference period is (1) 120 percent of the national average unemployment rate for civilian workers or higher for the reference period as determined by the Bureau of Labor Statistics, or (2) 10 percent or higher. No civil jurisdiction shall be classified as a labor surplus area if the average unemployment rate for all civilian workers for the reference period is less than 6.0 percent.

(b) *Criteria for exceptional circumstances*. The Assistant Secretary, upon petition submitted by the appropriate State Workforce Agency, may classify a civil jurisdiction, a Metropolitan Statistical Area, or a Primary Metropolitan Statistical Area as a labor surplus area whenever such an area meets or is expected to meet the unemployment tests established under § 654.5(a) as a result of exceptional circumstances. For purposes of this paragraph "exceptional circumstances" shall mean catastrophic events, such as natural disasters, plant closings, and contract cancellations expected to have a long-term impact on labor market area conditions, discounting temporary or seasonal factors. For purposes of this paragraph, "Metropolitan Statistical Area" and "Primary Metropolitan Statistical Area" shall mean the areas officially defined and designated as such by the Office of Management and Budget.

(Approved by OMB under control number 1205–0207)

[48 FR 15616, Apr. 12, 1983, as amended at 53 FR 23347, June 21, 1988; 71 FR 35518, June 21, 2006]

§ 654.6 Termination of classification.

(a) *Basic procedure*. The Assistant Secretary shall terminate the classification of a civil jurisdiction as a labor surplus area after any year in which the Assistant Secretary determines that the criteria established under § 654.5 (a) are no longer met.

(b) *Procedure for exceptional circumstances*. The Assistant Secretary shall terminate the classification of a civil jurisdiction classified as a labor surplus area pursuant to the provisions of § 654.5(b) after any year in which the Assistant Secretary determines that the exceptional circumstances criteria of that paragraph are no longer met.

[44 FR 1689, Jan. 5, 1979, as amended at 48 FR 15616, Apr. 12, 1983]

§ 654.7 Publication of area classifications.

The Assistant Secretary shall publish annually a list of labor surplus areas together with geographic descriptions thereof. The Assistant Secretary periodically may cause these lists to be published in the FEDERAL REGISTER.

[44 FR 1689, Jan. 5, 1979, as amended at 48 FR 15616, Apr. 12, 1983]

§ 654.8 Services to firms and individuals in labor surplus areas.

To carry out the purposes and policy objectives of Executive Order 12073 and Executive Order 10582, the Assistant Secretary shall cooperate with and assist the State Workforce Agencies and the Secretary of Commerce, as appropriate, to:

(a) Provide relevant labor market data and related economic information to assist in the initiation of industrial expansion programs in labor surplus areas;

(b) Identify upon request the skills and numbers of unemployed persons available for work in labor surplus areas, providing such information to firms interested in establishing new plants and facilities or expanding existing plants and facilities in such areas;

(c) Identify the occupational composition and skill requirements of industries contemplating locating in labor surplus areas and make such information available to training and apprenticeship agencies and resources in the community for purposes of appropriate training and skill development;

(d) Identify unemployed individuals in need of, and having the potential for, training in occupations and skills required by new or expanding industries and refer such individuals to appropriate training opportunities;

(e) Receive job openings on a voluntary basis and/or under the mandatory listing program provided by 38 U.S.C. 2012 and Executive Order 11701 and refer qualified unemployed workers to such openings, making appropriate efforts to refer to such openings qualified individuals who reside in the labor surplus area.

[44 FR 1689, Jan. 5, 1979, as amended at 48 FR 15616, Apr. 12, 1983; 71 FR 35518, June 21, 2006]

§ 654.9 Filing of complaints.

Complaints alleging that the Department of Labor has violated the labor surplus area regulations should be mailed to the Assistant Secretary for Employment and Training, U.S. Department of Labor, Washington, DC 20210. Such complaints should include: (a) The allegations of wrongdoing; (b) the date of the incident; and (c) any other relevant information available to the complainant. The Assistant Secretary shall make a determination and respond to the complainant after investigation of the incident. If the complaint is not resolved following this investigation, the Assistant Secretary, at his discretion, may offer, in writing by certified mail, the complainant a hearing before a Department of Labor Administrative Law Judge, provided that the complainant requests such a hearing from the Assistant Secretary within 20 working days of the certified date of receipt of the Assistant Secretary's offer of a hearing.

[48 FR 15616, Apr. 12, 1983]

§ 654.10 Transition provisions.

The annual list of labor surplus areas for the period June 1, 1982, through May 31, 1983, shall be extended through September 30, 1983.

[48 FR 15616, Apr. 12, 1983]

Subpart B—Responsibilities Under Executive Order 10582

AUTHORITY: 41 U.S.C. 10a *et seq.*; 29 U.S.C. 49 *et seq.*; 15 U.S.C. 644(n); E.O. 12073, E.O. 10582 as amended by E.O. 11051 and 12148.

§ 654.11 Purpose of subpart.

This subpart implements the responsibilities of the Secretary of Labor in determining areas of substantial unemployment in accordance with Executive Order 10582 issued pursuant to the Buy American Act, 41 U.S.C. 10a *et seq.*

§ 654.12 Description of Executive Order 10582.

(a) Under the Buy American Act, heads of executive agencies are required to determine, as a condition precedent to the purchase by their agencies of materials of foreign origin for public use within the United States, (1) that the price of like materials of domestic origin is unreasonable, or (2) that the purchase of like materials of domestic origin is inconsistent with the public interest.

(b) Section 3(c) of Executive Order 10582 issued pursuant to the Buy American Act permits executive agencies to reject a bid or offer to furnish materials of foreign origin in any situation in which the domestic supplier, offering the lowest price for furnishing the desired materials, undertakes to produce substantially all of the materials in areas of substantial unemployment, as determined by the Secretary of Labor.

§ 654.13 Determination of areas of substantial unemployment.

An area of substantial unemployment, for purposes of Executive Order 10582, shall be any area classified as a labor surplus area at § 654.5 of this part pursuant to the procedures set forth at subpart A of this part.

§ 654.14 Filing of complaints.

Complaints arising under subpart B of this part alleging that the Department of Labor has violated the labor surplus area regulations shall be made pursuant to the procedures set forth at § 654.9 of this part.

[48 FR 15616, Apr. 12, 1983]

Subparts C–D [Reserved]

Subpart E—Housing for Farmworkers

SOURCE: 81 FR 56349, Aug. 19, 2016, unless otherwise noted.

PURPOSE AND APPLICABILITY

§ 654.400 Scope and purpose.

(a) This subpart sets forth the Department's Employment and Training Administration (ETA) standards for agricultural housing and variances. Local Wagner-Peyser Act Employment Service (ES) offices, as part of the State ES agencies and in cooperation with the ES program, assist employers in recruiting farmworkers from places outside the area of intended employment. The experiences of the ES agencies indicate that employees so referred have on many occasions been provided with inadequate, unsafe, and unsanitary housing conditions. To discourage this practice, it is the policy of the Federal-State ES system to deny its intrastate and interstate recruitment services to employers until the State ES agency has ascertained that the employer's housing meets certain standards.

(b) To implement this policy, § 653.501 of this chapter provides that recruitment services must be denied unless the employer has signed an assurance that if the workers are to be housed, a preoccupancy inspection has been conducted, and the ES staff has ascertained that, with respect to intrastate or interstate clearance orders, the employer's housing meets the full set of standards set forth at 29 CFR 1910.142 or this subpart, except that mobile range housing for sheepherders or goatherders must meet existing Departmental guidelines and/or applicable regulations.

§ 654.401 Applicability.

(a) Employers whose housing was completed or under construction prior to April 3, 1980, or was under a signed contract for construction prior to March 4, 1980, may continue to follow the full set of the Department's ETA standards set forth in this subpart.

(b) The Department will consider agricultural housing which complies with ETA transitional standards set forth in this subpart also to comply with the Occupational Safety and Health Administration (OSHA) temporary labor camp standards at 29 CFR 1910.142.

§ 654.402 Variances.

(a) An employer may apply for a structural variance from a specific standard(s) in this subpart by filing a written application for such a variance with the local ES office serving the area in which the housing is located. This application must:

(1) Clearly specify the standard(s) from which the variance is desired;

(2) Adequately justify that the variance is necessary to obtain a beneficial use of an existing facility, and to prevent a practical difficulty or unnecessary hardship; and

(3) Clearly set forth the specific alternative measures which the employer has taken to protect the health and safety of workers and adequately show

that such alternative measures have achieved the same result as the standard(s) from which the employer desires the variance.

(b) Upon receipt of a written request for a variance under paragraph (a) of this section, the local ES office must send the request to the State office which, in turn, must forward it to the ETA Regional Administrator (RA). The RA must review the matter and, after consultation with OSHA, must either grant or deny the request for a variance.

(c) The variance granted by the RA must be in writing, must state the particular standard(s) involved, and must state as conditions of the variance the specific alternative measures which have been taken to protect the health and safety of the workers. The RA must send the approved variance to the employer and must send copies to OSHA's Regional Administrator, the Regional Administrator of the Wage and Hour Division (WHD), and the appropriate State Workforce Agency (SWA) and the local ES office. The employer must submit and the local ES office must attach copies of the approved variance to each of the employer's job orders which is placed into intrastate or interstate clearance.

(d) If the RA denies the request for a variance, the RA must provide written notice stating the reasons for the denial to the employer, the appropriate SWA, and the local ES office. The notice also must offer the employer an opportunity to request a hearing before a Department of Labor Hearing Officer, provided the employer requests such a hearing from the RA within 30 calendar days of the date of the notice. The request for a hearing must be handled in accordance with the complaint procedures set forth at §§ 658.424 and 658.425 of this chapter.

(e) The procedures of paragraphs (a) through (d) of this section only apply to an employer who has chosen, as evidenced by its written request for a variance, to comply with the ETA housing standards at §§ 654.404 through 654.417.

§ 654.403 [Reserved]

HOUSING STANDARDS

§ 654.404 Housing site.

(a) Housing sites must be well drained and free from depressions in which water may stagnate. They must be located where the disposal of sewage is provided in a manner which neither creates nor is likely to create a nuisance, or a hazard to health.

(b) Housing must not be subject to, or in proximity to, conditions that create or are likely to create offensive odors, flies, noise, traffic, or any similar hazards.

(c) Grounds within the housing site must be free from debris, noxious plants (poison ivy, etc.) and uncontrolled weeds or brush.

(d) The housing site must provide a space for recreation reasonably related to the size of the facility and the type of occupancy.

§ 654.405 Water supply.

(a) An adequate and convenient supply of water that meets the standards of the State health authority must be provided.

(b) A cold water tap must be available within 100 feet of each individual living unit when water is not provided in the unit. Adequate drainage facilities must be provided for overflow and spillage.

(c) Common drinking cups are not permitted.

§ 654.406 Excreta and liquid waste disposal.

(a) Facilities must be provided and maintained for effective disposal of excreta and liquid waste. Raw or treated liquid waste may not be discharged or allowed to accumulate on the ground surface.

(b) Where public sewer systems are available, all facilities for disposal of excreta and liquid wastes must be connected thereto.

(c) Where public sewers are not available, a subsurface septic tank-seepage system or other type of liquid waste treatment and disposal system, privies or portable toilets must be provided. Any requirements of the State health authority must be complied with.

§ 654.407 Housing.

(a) Housing must be structurally sound, in good repair, in a sanitary condition and must provide protection to the occupants against the elements.

(b) Housing must have flooring constructed of rigid materials, smooth finished, readily cleanable, and so located as to prevent the entrance of ground and surface water.

(c) The following space requirements must be provided:

(1) For sleeping purposes only in family units and in dormitory accommodations using single beds, not less than 50 square feet of floor space per occupant;

(2) For sleeping purposes in dormitory accommodations using double bunk beds only, not less than 40 square feet per occupant; and

(3) For combined cooking, eating, and sleeping purposes not less than 60 square feet of floor space per occupant.

(d) Housing used for families with one or more children over 6 years of age must have a room or partitioned sleeping area for the husband and wife. The partition must be of rigid materials and installed so as to provide reasonable privacy.

(e) Separate sleeping accommodations must be provided for each sex or each family.

(f) Adequate and separate arrangements for hanging clothing and storing personal effects for each person or family must be provided.

(g) At least one-half of the floor area in each living unit must have a minimum ceiling height of 7 feet. No floor space may be counted toward minimum requirements where the ceiling height is less than 5 feet.

(h) Each habitable room (not including partitioned areas) must have at least one window or skylight opening directly to the out-of-doors. The minimum total window or skylight area, including windows in doors, must equal at least 10 percent of the usable floor area. The total openable area must equal at least 45 percent of the minimum window or skylight area required, except where comparably adequate ventilation is supplied by mechanical or some other method.

§ 654.408 Screening.

(a) All outside openings must be protected with screening of not less than 16 mesh.

(b) All screen doors must be tight fitting, in good repair, and equipped with self-closing devices.

§ 654.409 Heating.

(a) All living quarters and service rooms must be provided with properly installed, operable heating equipment capable of maintaining a temperature of at least 68 degrees Fahrenheit (°F) if during the period of normal occupancy the temperature in such quarters falls below 68 °F.

(b) Any stoves or other sources of heat utilizing combustible fuel must be installed and vented in such a manner as to prevent fire hazards and a dangerous concentration of gases. No portable heaters other than those operated by electricity may be provided. If a solid or liquid fuel stove is used in a room with wooden or other combustible flooring, there must be a concrete slab, insulated metal sheet, or other fireproof material on the floor under each stove, extending at least 18 inches beyond the perimeter of the base of the stove.

(c) Any wall or ceiling within 18 inches of a solid or liquid fuel stove or a stovepipe must be of fireproof material. A vented metal collar must be installed around a stovepipe, or vent passing through a wall, ceiling, floor, or roof.

(d) When a heating system has automatic controls, the controls must be of the type which cut off the fuel supply upon the failure or interruption of the flame or ignition, or whenever a predetermined safe temperature or pressure is exceeded.

§ 654.410 Electricity and lighting.

(a) All housing sites must be provided with electric service.

(b) Each habitable room and all common use rooms, and areas such as: laundry rooms, toilets, privies, hallways, stairways, etc., must contain adequate ceiling or wall-type light fixtures. At least one wall-type electrical convenience outlet must be provided in each individual living room.

(c) Adequate lighting must be provided for the yard area, and pathways to common use facilities.

(d) All wiring and lighting fixtures must be installed and maintained in a safe condition.

§ 654.411 Toilets.

(a) Toilets must be constructed, located, and maintained so as to prevent any nuisance or public health hazard.

(b) Water closets or privy seats for each sex must be in the ratio of not less than one such unit for each 15 occupants, with a minimum of one unit for each sex in common use facilities.

(c) Urinals, constructed of nonabsorbent materials, may be substituted for men's toilet seats on the basis of one urinal or 24 inches of trough-type urinal for one toilet seat up to a maximum of one-third of the required toilet seats.

(d) Except in individual family units, separate toilet accommodations for men and women must be provided. If toilet facilities for men and women are in the same building, they must be separated by a solid wall from floor to roof or ceiling. Toilets must be distinctly marked "men" and "women" in English and in the native language of the persons expected to occupy the housing.

(e) Where common use toilet facilities are provided, an adequate and accessible supply of toilet tissue, with holders, must be furnished.

(f) Common use toilets and privies must be well lighted and ventilated and must be clean and sanitary.

(g) Toilet facilities must be located within 200 feet of each living unit.

(h) Privies may not be located closer than 50 feet from any living unit or any facility where food is prepared or served.

(i) Privy structures and pits must be fly-tight. Privy pits must have adequate capacity for the required seats.

§ 654.412 Bathing, laundry, and hand washing.

(a) Bathing and hand washing facilities, supplied with hot and cold water under pressure, must be provided for the use of all occupants. These facilities must be clean and sanitary and located within 200 feet of each living unit.

(b) There must be a minimum of 1 showerhead per 15 persons. Showerheads must be spaced at least 3 feet apart, with a minimum of 9 square feet of floor space per unit. Adequate, dry dressing space must be provided in common use facilities. Shower floors must be constructed of nonabsorbent nonskid materials and sloped to properly constructed floor drains. Except in individual family units, separate shower facilities must be provided each sex. When common use shower facilities for both sexes are in the same building they must be separated by a solid nonabsorbent wall extending from the floor to ceiling, or roof, and must be plainly designated "men" or "women" in English and in the native language of the persons expected to occupy the housing.

(c) Lavatories or equivalent units must be provided in a ratio of 1 per 15 persons.

(d) Laundry facilities, supplied with hot and cold water under pressure, must be provided for the use of all occupants. Laundry trays or tubs must be provided in the ratio of 1 per 25 persons. Mechanical washers may be provided in the ratio of 1 per 50 persons in lieu of laundry trays, although a minimum of 1 laundry tray per 100 persons must be provided in addition to the mechanical washers.

§ 654.413 Cooking and eating facilities.

(a) When workers or their families are permitted or required to cook in their individual unit, a space must be provided and equipped for cooking and eating. Such space must be provided with:

(1) A cookstove or hot plate with a minimum of two burners;

(2) Adequate food storage shelves and a counter for food preparation;

(3) Provisions for mechanical refrigeration of food at a temperature of not more than 45 °F;

(4) A table and chairs or equivalent seating and eating arrangements, all commensurate with the capacity of the unit; and

(5) Adequate lighting and ventilation.

(b) When workers or their families are permitted or required to cook and eat in a common facility, a room or building separate from the sleeping facilities must be provided for cooking and eating. Such room or building must be provided with:

(1) Stoves or hot plates, with a minimum equivalent of 2 burners, in a ratio of 1 stove or hot plate to 10 persons, or 1 stove or hot plate to 2 families;

(2) Adequate food storage shelves and a counter for food preparation;

(3) Mechanical refrigeration for food at a temperature of not more than 45 °F;

(4) Tables and chairs or equivalent seating adequate for the intended use of the facility;

(5) Adequate sinks with hot and cold water under pressure;

(6) Adequate lighting and ventilation; and

(7) Floors must be of nonabsorbent, easily cleaned materials.

(c) When central mess facilities are provided, the kitchen and mess hall must be in proper proportion to the capacity of the housing and must be separate from the sleeping quarters. The physical facilities, equipment, and operation must be in accordance with provisions of applicable State codes.

(d) Wall surface adjacent to all food preparation and cooking areas must be of nonabsorbent, easily cleaned material. In addition, the wall surface adjacent to cooking areas must be of fire-resistant material.

§ 654.414 Garbage and other refuse.

(a) Durable, fly-tight, clean containers in good condition of a minimum capacity of 20 gallons, must be provided adjacent to each housing unit for the storage of garbage and other refuse. Such containers must be provided in a minimum ratio of 1 per 15 persons.

(b) Provisions must be made for collection of refuse at least twice a week, or more often if necessary. The disposal of refuse, which includes garbage, must be in accordance with State and local law.

§ 654.415 Insect and rodent control.

Housing and facilities must be free of insects, rodents, and other vermin.

§ 654.416 Sleeping facilities.

(a) Sleeping facilities must be provided for each person. Such facilities must consist of comfortable beds, cots, or bunks, provided with clean mattresses.

(b) Any bedding provided by the housing operator must be clean and sanitary.

(c) Triple deck bunks may not be provided.

(d) The clear space above the top of the lower mattress of a double deck bunk and the bottom of the upper bunk must be a minimum of 27 inches. The distance from the top of the upper mattress to the ceiling must be a minimum of 36 inches.

(e) Beds used for double occupancy may be provided only in family accommodations.

§ 654.417 Fire, safety, and first aid.

(a) All buildings in which people sleep or eat must be constructed and maintained in accordance with applicable State or local fire and safety laws.

(b) In family housing and housing units for less than 10 persons, of one story construction, two means of escape must be provided. One of the two required means of escape may be a readily accessible window with an openable space of not less than 24 × 24 inches.

(c) All sleeping quarters intended for use by 10 or more persons, central dining facilities, and common assembly rooms must have at least two doors remotely separated so as to provide alternate means of escape to the outside or to an interior hall.

(d) Sleeping quarters and common assembly rooms on the second story must have a stairway, and a permanent, affixed exterior ladder or a second stairway.

(e) Sleeping and common assembly rooms located above the second story must comply with the State and local fire and building codes relative to multiple story dwellings.

(f) Fire extinguishing equipment must be provided in a readily accessible place located not more than 100 feet from each housing unit. Such equipment must provide protection equal to a 2½ gallon stored pressure or 5-gallon pump-type water extinguisher.

(g) First aid facilities must be provided and readily accessible for use at all time. Such facilities must be equivalent to the 16 unit first aid kit recommended by the American Red Cross, and provided in a ratio of 1 per 50 persons.

(h) No flammable or volatile liquids or materials must be stored in or adjacent to rooms used for living purposes, except for those needed for current household use.

(i) Agricultural pesticides and toxic chemicals may not be stored in the housing area.

PART 655—TEMPORARY EMPLOYMENT OF FOREIGN WORKERS IN THE UNITED STATES

Subpart B—Labor Certification Process for Temporary Agricultural Employment in the United States (H–2A Workers)

PREFILING PROCEDURES

APPLICATION FOR TEMPORARY EMPLOYMENT CERTIFICATION FILING PROCEDURES

PROCESSING OF APPLICATION FOR TEMPORARY EMPLOYMENT CERTIFICATION

POST-ACCEPTANCE REQUIREMENTS

LABOR CERTIFICATION DETERMINATIONS

POST CERTIFICATION

INTEGRITY MEASURES

LABOR CERTIFICATION PROCESS FOR TEMPORARY AGRICULTURAL EMPLOYMENT IN RANGE SHEEP HERDING, GOAT HERDING, AND PRODUCTION OF LIVESTOCK OCCUPATIONS

Subparts C–D [Reserved]

Subpart E—Labor Certification Process for Temporary Employment in the Commonwealth of the Northern Marianas Islands (CW–1 Workers)

PREFILING PROCEDURES

Subpart H—Labor Condition Applications and Requirements for Employers Seeking To Employ Nonimmigrants on H–1b Visas in Specialty Occupations and as Fashion Models, and Requirements for Employers Seeking To Employ Nonimmigrants on H–1b1 and E–3 Visas in Specialty Occupations

Subpart I—Enforcement of H–1B Labor Condition Applications and H–1B1 and E–3 Labor Attestations

Subparts J–K [Reserved]

Subpart L—What requirements must a facility meet to employ H–1C nonimmigrant workers as registered nurses?

Subpart M—What are the Department's enforcement obligations with respect to H–1C Attestations?

Subpart N—Labor Certification Process for Temporary Agricultural Employment in the United States (H–2A Workers)

AUTHORITY: Section 655.0 issued under 8 U.S.C. 1101(a)(15)(E)(iii), 1101(a)(15)(H)(i) and (ii), 8 U.S.C. 1103(a)(6), 1182(m), (n) and (t), 1184(c), (g), and (j), 1188, and 1288(c) and (d); sec. 3(c)(1), Pub. L. 101–238, 103 Stat. 2099, 2102 (8 U.S.C. 1182 note); sec. 221(a), Pub. L. 101–649, 104 Stat. 4978, 5027 (8 U.S.C. 1184 note); sec. 303(a)(8), Pub. L. 102–232, 105 Stat. 1733, 1748 (8 U.S.C. 1101 note); sec. 323(c), Pub. L. 103–206, 107 Stat. 2428; sec. 412(e), Pub. L. 105–277, 112 Stat. 2681 (8 U.S.C. 1182 note); sec.

2(d), Pub. L. 106–95, 113 Stat. 1312, 1316 (8 U.S.C. 1182 note); 29 U.S.C. 49k; Pub. L. 107–296, 116 Stat. 2135, as amended; Pub. L. 109–423, 120 Stat. 2900; 8 CFR 214.2(h)(4)(i); and 8 CFR 214.2(h)(6)(iii).

Subpart A issued under 8 CFR 214.2(h).

Subpart B issued under 8 U.S.C. 1101(a)(15)(H)(ii)(a), 1184(c), and 1188; and 8 CFR 214.2(h).

Subparts F and G issued under 8 U.S.C. 1288(c) and (d); sec. 323(c), Pub. L. 103–206, 107 Stat. 2428; and 28 U.S.C. 2461 note, Pub. L. 114–74 at section 701.

Subparts H and I issued under 8 U.S.C. 1101(a)(15)(H)(i)(b) and (b)(1), 1182(n) and (t), and 1184(g) and (j); sec. 303(a)(8), Pub. L. 102–232, 105 Stat. 1733, 1748 (8 U.S.C. 1101 note); sec. 412(e), Pub. L. 105–277, 112 Stat. 2681; 8 CFR 214.2(h); and 28 U.S.C. 2461 note, Pub. L. 114–74 at section 701.

Subparts L and M issued under 8 U.S.C. 1101(a)(15)(H)(i)(c) and 1182(m); sec. 2(d), Pub. L. 106–95, 113 Stat. 1312, 1316 (8 U.S.C. 1182 note); Pub. L. 109–423, 120 Stat. 2900; and 8 CFR 214.2(h).

EFFECTIVE DATE NOTE: At 84 FR 12431, Apr. 1, 2019, the authority citation for part 655 was revised, effective Apr. 4, 2019. For the convenience of the user, the revised text is set forth as follows:

AUTHORITY: Section 655.0 issued under 8 U.S.C. 1101(a)(15)(E)(iii), 1101(a)(15)(H)(i) and (ii), 8 U.S.C. 1103(a)(6), 1182(m), (n), and (t), 1184(c), (g), and (j), 1188, and 1288(c) and (d); sec. 3(c)(1), Pub. L. 101–238, 103 Stat. 2099, 2102 (8 U.S.C. 1182 note); sec. 221(a), Pub. L. 101–649, 104 Stat. 4978, 5027 (8 U.S.C. 1184 note); sec. 303(a)(8), Pub. L. 102–232, 105 Stat. 1733, 1748 (8 U.S.C. 1101 note); sec. 323(c), Pub. L. 103–206, 107 Stat. 2428; sec. 412(e), Pub. L. 105–277, 112 Stat. 2681 (8 U.S.C. 1182 note); sec. 2(d), Pub. L. 106–95, 113 Stat. 1312, 1316 (8 U.S.C. 1182 note); 29 U.S.C. 49k; Pub. L. 107–296, 116 Stat. 2135, as amended; Pub. L. 109–423, 120 Stat. 2900; 8 CFR 214.2(h)(4)(i); 8 CFR 214.2(h)(6)(iii); and sec. 6, Pub. L. 115–218, 132 Stat. 1547 (48 U.S.C. 1806).

Subpart A issued under 8 CFR 214.2(h).

Subpart B issued under 8 U.S.C. 1101(a)(15)(H)(ii)(a), 1184(c), and 1188; and 8 CFR 214.2(h).

Subpart E issued under 48 U.S.C. 1806.

Subparts F and G issued under 8 U.S.C. 1288(c) and (d); sec. 323(c), Pub. L. 103–206, 107 Stat. 2428; and 28 U.S.C. 2461 note, Pub. L. 114–74 at section 701.

Subparts H and I issued under 8 U.S.C. 1101(a)(15)(H)(i)(b) and (b)(1), 1182(n) and (t), and 1184(g) and (j); sec. 303(a)(8), Pub. L. 102–232, 105 Stat. 1733, 1748 (8 U.S.C. 1101 note); sec. 412(e), Pub. L. 105–277, 112 Stat. 2681; 8 CFR 214.2(h); and 28 U.S.C. 2461 note, Pub. L. 114–74 at section 701.

Subparts L and M issued under 8 U.S.C. 1101(a)(15)(H)(i)(c) and 1182(m); sec. 2(d), Pub. L. 106–95, 113 Stat. 1312, 1316 (8 U.S.C. 1182 note); Pub. L. 109–423, 120 Stat. 2900; and 8 CFR 214.2(h).

SOURCE: 42 FR 45899, Sept. 13, 1977, unless otherwise noted.

EDITORIAL NOTE: Nomenclature changes to part 655 appear at 71 FR 35521, 35522, June 21, 2006.

§655.0 Scope and purpose of part.

(a) *Subparts A, B, and C*—(1) *General.* Subparts A, B, and C of this part set out the procedures adopted by the Secretary to secure information sufficient to make factual determinations of: (i) Whether U.S. workers are available to perform temporary employment in the United States, for which an employer desires to employ nonimmigrant foreign workers, and (ii) whether the employment of aliens for such temporary work will adversely affect the wages or working conditions of similarly employed U.S. workers. These factual determinations (or a determination that there are not sufficient facts to make one or both of these determinations) are required to carry out the policies of the Immigration and Nationality Act (INA), that a nonimmigrant alien worker not be admitted to fill a particular temporary job opportunity unless no qualifed U.S. worker is available to fill the job opportunity, and unless the employment of the foreign worker in the job opportunity will not adversely affect the wages or working conditions of similarly employed U.S. workers.

(2) *The Secretary's determinations.* Before any factual determination can be made concerning the availability of U.S. workers to perform particular job opportunities, two steps must be taken. First, the minimum level of wages, terms, benefits, and conditions for the particular job opportunities, below which similarly employed U.S. workers would be adversely affected, must be established. (The regulations in this part establish such minimum levels for wages, terms, benefits, and conditions of employment.) Second, the wages, terms, benefits, and conditions offered and afforded to the aliens must be compared to the established minimum levels. If it is concluded that adverse effect would result, the ultimate determination of availability within the meaning of the INA cannot

be made since U.S. workers cannot be expected to accept employment under conditions below the established minimum levels. *Florida Sugar Cane League, Inc.* v. *Usery*, 531 F. 2d 299 (5th Cir. 1976).

Once a determination of no adverse effect has been made, the availability of U.S. workers can be tested only if U.S. workers are actively recruited through the offer of wages, terms, benefits, and conditions at least at the minimum level or the level offered to the aliens, whichever is higher. The regulations in this part set forth requirements for recruiting U.S. workers in accordance with this principle.

(3) *Construction.* This part and its subparts shall be construed to effectuate the purpose of the INA that U.S. workers rather than aliens be employed wherever possible. *Elton Orchards, Inc.* v. *Brennan*, 508 F. 2d 493, 500 (1st Cir. 1974), *Flecha* v. *Quiros*, 567 F. 2d 1154 (1st Cir. 1977). Where temporary alien workers are admitted, the terms and conditions of their employment must not result in a lowering of the terms and conditions of domestic workers similarly employed, *Williams* v. *Usery*, 531 F. 2d 305 (5th Cir. 1976); *Florida Sugar Cane League, Inc.* v. *Usery*, 531 F. 2d 299 (5th Cir. 1976), and the job benefits extended to any U.S. workers shall be at least those extended to the alien workers.

(b) *Subparts D and E.* Subparts D and E of this part set forth the process by which health care facilities can file attestations with the Department of Labor for the purpose of employing or otherwise using nonimmigrant registered nurses under H–1A visas.

(c) *Subparts F and G.* Subparts F and G of this part set forth the process by which employers can file attestations with the Department of Labor for the purpose of employing alien crewmembers in longshore work under D-visas and enforcement provisions relating thereto.

(d) *Subparts H and I of this part.* Subpart H of this part sets forth the process by which employers can file labor condition applications (LCAs) with, and the requirements for obtaining approval from, the Department of Labor to temporarily employ the following three categories of nonimmigrants in the United States: (1) H–1B visas for temporary employment in specialty occupations or as fashion models of distinguished merit and ability; (2) H–1B1 visas for temporary employment in specialty occupations of nonimmigrant professionals from countries with which the United States has entered into certain agreements identified in section 214(g)(8)(A) of the INA; and (3) E–3 visas for nationals of the Commonwealth of Australia for temporary employment in specialty occupations. Subpart I of this part establishes the enforcement provisions that apply to the H–1B, H–1B1, and E–3 visa programs.

(e) *Subparts J and K of this part.* Subparts J and K of this part set forth the process by which employers can file attestations with the Department of Labor for the purpose of employing nonimmigrant alien students on F-visas in off-campus employment and enforcement provisions relating thereto.

[43 FR 10312, Mar. 10, 1978, as amended at 52 FR 20507, June 1, 1987; 55 FR 50510, Dec. 6, 1990; 56 FR 24667, May 30, 1991; 56 FR 54738, Oct. 22, 1991; 56 FR 56875, Nov. 6, 1991; 57 FR 1337, Jan. 13, 1992; 57 FR 40989, Sept. 8, 1992; 69 FR 68226, Nov. 23, 2004; 73 FR 19947, Apr. 11, 2008]

§ 655.00 Authority of the Office of Foreign Labor Certification (OFLC) Administrator under subparts A, B, and C.

Pursuant to the regulations under this part, temporary labor certification determinations under subparts A, B, and C of this part are ordinarily made by the Office of Foreign Labor Certification (OFLC) Administrator (OFLC Administrator) of the Employment and Training Administration. The OFLC Administrator will informally advise the employer or agent of the name of the official who will make determinations with respect to the application.

[71 FR 35518, June 21, 2006]

Subpart A—Labor Certification Process for Temporary Non-Agricultural Employment in the United States (H–2B Workers)

SOURCE: 80 FR 24108, Apr. 29, 2015, unless otherwise noted.

§ 655.1 Scope and purpose of this subpart.

Section 214(c)(1) of the Immigration and Nationality Act (INA), 8 U.S.C. 1184(c)(1), requires the Secretary of Homeland Security to consult with appropriate agencies before authorizing the classification of aliens as H–2B workers. Department of Homeland Security (DHS) regulations at 8 CFR 214.2(h)(6)(iii)(D) designate the Secretary of Labor as an appropriate authority with whom DHS consults regarding the H–2B program, and specifies that the Secretary of Labor, in carrying out this consultative function, shall issue regulations regarding the issuance of temporary labor certifications. DHS regulations at 8 CFR 214.2(h)(6)(iv) further provide that an employer's petition to employ H–2B nonimmigrant workers for temporary non-agricultural employment in the United States (U.S.), except for Guam, must be accompanied by an approved temporary labor certification from the Secretary of Labor (Secretary).

(a) *Purpose*. The temporary labor certification reflects a determination by the Secretary that:

(1) There are not sufficient U.S. workers who are qualified and who will be available to perform the temporary services or labor for which an employer desires to hire foreign workers, and that

(2) The employment of the H–2B worker(s) will not adversely affect the wages and working conditions of U.S. workers similarly employed.

(b) *Scope*. This subpart sets forth the procedures governing the labor certification process for the temporary employment of nonimmigrant foreign workers in the H–2B nonimmigrant classification, as defined in 8 U.S.C. 1101(a)(15)(H)(ii)(b), section 101(a)(15)(H)(ii)(b) of the INA. It also establishes obligations with respect to the terms and conditions of the temporary labor certification with which H–2B employers must comply, as well as their obligations to H–2B workers and workers in corresponding employment. Additionally, this subpart sets forth integrity measures for ensuring employers' continued compliance with the terms and conditions of the temporary labor certification.

§ 655.2 Authority of the agencies, offices, and divisions in the Department of Labor.

(a) *Authority and role of the Office of Foreign Labor Certification (OFLC)*. The Secretary has delegated authority to make determinations under this subpart, pursuant to 8 CFR 214.2(h)(6)(iii)(D) and (h)(6)(iv), to the Assistant Secretary for the Employment and Training Administration (ETA), who in turn has delegated that authority to OFLC. Determinations on an *Application for Temporary Employment Certification* in the H–2B program are made by the Administrator, OFLC who, in turn, may delegate this responsibility to designated staff members, e.g., a Certifying Officer (CO).

(b) *Authority of the Wage and Hour Division (WHD)*. Pursuant to its authority under section 214(c)(14)(B) of the INA, 8 U.S.C. 1184(c)(14)(B), DHS has delegated to the Secretary certain investigatory and enforcement functions with respect to terms and conditions of employment in the H–2B program. The Secretary has, in turn, delegated that authority to WHD. The regulations governing WHD investigation and enforcement functions, including those related to the enforcement of temporary labor certifications, issued under this subpart, may be found in 29 CFR part 503.

(c) *Concurrent authority*. OFLC and WHD have concurrent authority to impose a debarment remedy under § 655.73 or under 29 CFR 503.24.

§ 655.3 Territory of Guam.

This subpart does not apply to temporary employment in the Territory of Guam, except that an employer who applies for a temporary labor certification for a job opportunity on Guam will need to obtain a prevailing wage from the U.S. Department of Labor

(DOL) in accordance with § 655.10, subject to the transfer of authority to set the prevailing wage for a job opportunity on Guam to DOL in title 8 of the Code of Federal Regulations. DOL does not certify to DHS the temporary employment of H–2B nonimmigrant foreign workers, or enforce compliance with the provisions of the H–2B visa program, in the Territory of Guam.

§ 655.4 Transition procedures.

(a) The NPWC shall continue to process an *Application for Prevailing Wage Determination* submitted prior to April 29, 2015, in accordance with the prevailing wage methodology at 20 CFR part 655, subpart A, revised as of April 1, 2009, except for § 655.10(b)(2), see 20 CFR part 655, subpart A, revised as of April 1, 2014. Employers with a pending *Application for Prevailing Wage Determination* who seek a prevailing wage based on an alternate wage source must submit a new *Application for Prevailing Wage Determination*.

(b) The NPWC shall process an *Application for a Prevailing Wage Determination* submitted on or after April 29, 2015, in accordance with the wage methodology established in § 655.10 of the final prevailing wage rule.

(c) The NPC shall continue to process an *Application for Temporary Employment Certification* submitted prior to April 29, 2015, in accordance with 20 CFR part 655, subpart A, revised as of April 1, 2009.

(d) The NPC shall process an *Application for Temporary Employment Certification* submitted on or after April 29, 2015, and that has a start date of need prior to October 1, 2015, as follows:

(1) Employers will be permitted to file an *Application for Temporary Employment Certification* job order with the NPC using the emergency situations provision at § 655.17. The *Application for Temporary Employment Certification* must include a signed and dated copy of the new Appendix B associated with the ETA Form 9142B containing the requisite program assurances and obligations under this rule. In the case of a job contractor filing as a joint employer with its employer-client, the NPC must receive a separate attachment containing the employer-client's business and contact information (*i.e.*, sections C and D of the ETA Form 9142B) as well as a separate signed and dated copy of the Appendix B for its employer-client, as required by § 655.19.

(2) The NPC will waive the regulatory filing timeframe under § 655.15 and process the *Application for Temporary Employment Certification* and job order in a manner consistent with the handling of applications under § 655.17 for emergency situations, including the recruitment of U.S. workers on an expedited basis, and make a determination as required by § 655.50. The recruitment of U.S. workers on an expedited basis will consist of placing a new job order with the SWA serving the area of intended employment that contains the job assurances and contents set forth in § 655.18 for a period of not less than 10 calendar days. In addition, employers who have not placed any newspaper advertisements under the rule published at 20 CFR part 655, subpart A, revised as of April 1, 2009. must place one newspaper advertisement, which may be published on any day of the week, meeting the advertising requirements of § 655.41, during the period of time the SWA is actively circulating the job order for intrastate clearance.

(3) If the Chicago NPC grants a temporary labor certification, the employer will receive an original certified ETA Form 9142B and a Final Determination letter. Upon receipt of the original certified ETA Form 9142B, the employer or its agent or attorney, if applicable, must complete the footer on the original Appendix B of the *Application for Temporary Employment Certification*, retain the original Appendix B, and submit a signed copy of Appendix B, together with the original certified ETA Form 9142B directly to USCIS. Under the document retention requirements in § 655.56, the employer must retain a copy of the temporary labor certification and the original signed Appendix B.

(4) An employer who did not submit an *Application for a Prevailing Wage Determination* prior to April 29, 2015, but who has a start date of need prior to October 1, 2015 may submit a completed

Application for a Prevailing Wage Determination to the NPC with its emergency *Application for Temporary Employment Certification* requesting a prevailing wage determination for the job opportunity. Upon receipt, the NPC will transmit, on behalf of the employer, a copy of the *Application for a Prevailing Wage Determination* to the NPWC for processing and issuance of a prevailing wage determination using the wage methodology established in § 655.10.

(e) The NPC shall process an *Application for Temporary Employment Certification* submitted on or after April 29, 2015, and that has a start date of need after October 1, 2015, in accordance with all application filing requirements under this rule, and the employer must obtain a valid prevailing wage determination under the wage methodology established in § 655.10 prior to filing the job order with the SWA under § 655.16.

(f) Employers with a prevailing wage determination issued by the NPWC, or who have a pending or granted *Application for Temporary Employment Certification* on April 29, 2015, may seek a supplemental prevailing wage determination (SPWD) in order to obtain a prevailing wage based on an alternate wage source under this rule.

(1) The SPWD will apply during the validity period of the certification, except that such SPWD will be applicable only to those H–2B workers who are not yet employed in the certified position on the date of the issuance of the SPWD. The SPWD will not be applicable to H–2B workers who are already employed in the certified position at the time of the issuance of the SPWD, and it will not apply to U.S. workers recruited and hired under the original job order. For seafood employers whose workers' entry into the U.S. may be staggered under § 655.15(f), an SPWD issued under this provision will apply only to those H–2B workers who have not yet entered the U.S. and are therefore not yet employed in the certified position at the time of the issuance of the SPWD.

(2) In order to receive an SPWD under this provision, the employer must submit a new ETA Form 9141 to the NPWC that contains in Section E.a.5 Job Duties the original PWD tracking number (starting with P–400), the H–2B temporary employment certification application number (starting with H–400), and the words "Request for a Supplemental Prevailing Wage Determination." Electronic submission through the iCERT Visa Portal System is preferred. Upon receipt of the request, the NPWC will issue to the employer, or if applicable, the employer's attorney or agent, an SPWD in an expedited manner and provide a copy to the Chicago NPC.

§ 655.5 Definition of terms.

For purposes of this subpart:

Act means the Immigration and Nationality Act or INA, as amended, 8 U.S.C. 1101 *et seq.*

Administrative Law Judge (ALJ) means a person within the Department's Office of Administrative Law Judges appointed under 5 U.S.C. 3105.

Administrator, Office of Foreign Labor Certification (OFLC) means the primary official of the Office of Foreign Labor Certification, ETA, or the Administrator's designee.

Administrator, Wage and Hour Division (WHD) means the primary official of the WHD, or the Administrator's designee.

Agent means:

(1) A legal entity or person who:

(i) Is authorized to act on behalf of an employer for temporary nonagricultural labor certification purposes;

(ii) Is not itself an employer, or a joint employer, as defined in this part with respect to a specific application; and

(iii) Is not an association or other organization of employers.

(2) No agent who is under suspension, debarment, expulsion, disbarment, or otherwise restricted from practice before any court, the Department of Labor, the Executive Office for Immigration Review under 8 CFR 1003.101, or DHS under 8 CFR 292.3 may represent an employer under this part.

Agricultural labor or services means those duties and occupations defined in subpart B of this part.

Applicant means a U.S. worker who is applying for a job opportunity for which an employer has filed an *Application for Temporary Employment Certification* (ETA Form 9142B and the appropriate appendices).

Application for Temporary Employment Certification means the Office of Management and Budget (OMB)-approved ETA Form 9142B and the appropriate appendices, a valid wage determination, as required by § 655.10, and a subsequently-filed U.S. worker recruitment report, submitted by an employer to secure a temporary labor certification determination from DOL.

Area of intended employment means the geographic area within normal commuting distance of the place (worksite address) of the job opportunity for which the certification is sought. There is no rigid measure of distance that constitutes a normal commuting distance or normal commuting area, because there may be widely varying factual circumstances among different areas (e.g., average commuting times, barriers to reaching the worksite, or quality of the regional transportation network). If the place of intended employment is within a Metropolitan Statistical Area (MSA), including a multistate MSA, any place within the MSA is deemed to be within normal commuting distance of the place of intended employment. The borders of MSAs are not controlling in the identification of the normal commuting area; a location outside of an MSA may be within normal commuting distance of a location that is inside (e.g., near the border of) the MSA.

Area of substantial unemployment means a contiguous area with a population of at least 10,000 in which there is an average unemployment rate equal to or exceeding 6.5 percent for the 12 months preceding the determination of such areas made by the ETA.

Attorney means any person who is a member in good standing of the bar of the highest court of any State, possession, territory, or commonwealth of the U.S., or the District of Columbia. No attorney who is under suspension, debarment, expulsion, disbarment, or otherwise restricted from practice before any court, the Department of Labor, the Executive Office for Immigration Review under 8 CFR 1003.101, or DHS under 8 CFR 292.3 may represent an employer under this subpart.

Board of Alien Labor Certification Appeals (BALCA or Board) means the permanent Board established by part 656 of this chapter, chaired by the Chief Administrative Law Judge (Chief ALJ), and consisting of ALJs assigned to the Department of Labor and designated by the Chief ALJ to be members of BALCA.

Certifying Officer (CO) means an OFLC official designated by the Administrator, OFLC to make determinations on applications under the H–2B program. The Administrator, OFLC is the National CO. Other COs may also be designated by the Administrator, OFLC to make the determinations required under this subpart.

Chief Administrative Law Judge (Chief ALJ) means the chief official of the Department's Office of Administrative Law Judges or the Chief Administrative Law Judge's designee.

Corresponding employment means:

(1) The employment of workers who are not H–2B workers by an employer that has a certified H–2B *Application for Temporary Employment Certification* when those workers are performing either substantially the same work included in the job order or substantially the same work performed by the H–2B workers, except that workers in the following two categories are not included in corresponding employment:

(i) Incumbent employees continuously employed by the H–2B employer to perform substantially the same work included in the job order or substantially the same work performed by the H–2B workers during the 52 weeks prior to the period of employment certified on the *Application for Temporary Employment Certification* and who have worked or been paid for at least 35 hours in at least 48 of the prior 52 workweeks, and who have worked or been paid for an average of at least 35 hours per week over the prior 52 weeks, as demonstrated on the employer's payroll records, provided that the terms and working conditions of their employment are not substantially reduced during the period of employment covered by the job order. In determining whether this standard was met, the employer may take credit for any hours that were reduced by the employee voluntarily choosing not to work due to personal reasons such as illness or vacation; or

(ii) Incumbent employees covered by a collective bargaining agreement or an individual employment contract that guarantees both an offer of at least 35 hours of work each workweek and continued employment with the H–2B employer at least through the period of employment covered by the job order, except that the employee may be dismissed for cause.

(2) To qualify as corresponding employment, the work must be performed during the period of the job order, including any approved extension thereof.

Date of need means the first date the employer requires services of the H–2B workers as listed on the *Application for Temporary Employment Certification.*

Department of Homeland Security (DHS) means the Federal Department having jurisdiction over certain immigration-related functions, acting through its component agencies, including USCIS.

Employee means a person who is engaged to perform work for an employer, as defined under the general common law. Some of the factors relevant to the determination of employee status include: The hiring party's right to control the manner and means by which the work is accomplished; the skill required to perform the work; the source of the instrumentalities and tools for accomplishing the work; the location of the work; the hiring party's discretion over when and how long to work; and whether the work is part of the regular business of the hiring party. Other applicable factors may be considered and no one factor is dispositive. The terms employee and worker are used interchangeably in this subpart.

Employer means a person (including any individual, partnership, association, corporation, cooperative, firm, joint stock company, trust, or other organization with legal rights and duties) that:

(1) Has a place of business (physical location) in the U.S. and a means by which it may be contacted for employment;

(2) Has an employer relationship (such as the ability to hire, pay, fire, supervise or otherwise control the work of employees) with respect to an H–2B worker or a worker in corresponding employment; and

(3) Possesses, for purposes of filing an *Application for Temporary Employment Certification,* a valid Federal Employer Identification Number (FEIN).

Employer-client means an employer that has entered into an agreement with a job contractor and that is not an affiliate, branch or subsidiary of the job contractor, under which the job contractor provides services or labor to the employer on a temporary basis and will not exercise substantial, direct day-to-day supervision and control in the performance of the services or labor to be performed other than hiring, paying and firing the workers.

Employment and Training Administration (ETA) means the agency within the Department of Labor that includes OFLC and has been delegated authority by the Secretary to fulfill the Secretary's mandate under the DHS regulations for the administration and adjudication of an *Application for Temporary Employment Certification* and related functions.

Federal holiday means a legal public holiday as defined at 5 U.S.C. 6103.

Full-time means 35 or more hours of work per week.

H–2B Petition means the DHS Form I–129 *Petition for a Nonimmigrant Worker,* with H Supplement or successor form or supplement, and accompanying documentation required by DHS for employers seeking to employ foreign persons as H–2B nonimmigrant workers

H–2B Registration means the OMB-approved ETA Form 9155, submitted by an employer to register its intent to hire H–2B workers and to file an *Application for Temporary Employment Certification.*

H–2B worker means any temporary foreign worker who is lawfully present in the U.S. and authorized by DHS to perform nonagricultural labor or services of a temporary or seasonal nature under 8 U.S.C. 1101(a)(15)(H)(ii)(b), INA section 101(a)(15)(H)(ii)(b).

Job contractor means a person, association, firm, or a corporation that meets the definition of an employer and that contracts services or labor on a temporary basis to one or more employers, which is not an affiliate, branch or subsidiary of the job contractor and where the job contractor will not exercise substantial, direct day-to-day supervision and control in the performance of the services or labor to be performed other than hiring, paying and firing the workers.

Job offer means the offer made by an employer or potential employer of H–2B workers to both U.S. and H–2B workers describing all the material terms and conditions of employment, including those relating to wages, working conditions, and other benefits.

Job opportunity means one or more openings for full-time employment with the petitioning employer within a specified area(s) of intended employment for which the petitioning employer is seeking workers.

Job order means the document containing the material terms and conditions of employment relating to wages, hours, working conditions, worksite and other benefits, including obligations and assurances under 29 CFR part 503 and this subpart that is posted between and among the State Workforce Agencies (SWAs) on their job clearance systems.

Joint employment means that where two or more employers each have sufficient definitional indicia of being an employer to be considered the employer of a worker, those employers will be considered to jointly employ that worker. Each employer in a joint employment relationship to a worker is considered a joint employer of that worker.

Layoff means any involuntary separation of one or more U.S. employees without cause.

Metropolitan Statistical Area (MSA) means a geographic entity defined by OMB for use by Federal statistical agencies in collecting, tabulating, and publishing Federal statistics. A metro area contains a core urban area of 50,000 or more population, and a micro area contains an urban core of at least 10,000 (but fewer than 50,000) population. Each metro or micro area consists of one or more counties and includes the counties containing the core urban area, as well as any adjacent counties that have a high degree of social and economic integration (as measured by commuting to work) with the urban core.

National Prevailing Wage Center (NPWC) means that office within OFLC from which employers, agents, or attorneys who wish to file an *Application for Temporary Employment Certification* receive a prevailing wage determination (PWD).

NPWC Director means the OFLC official to whom the Administrator, OFLC has delegated authority to carry out certain NPWC operations and functions.

National Processing Center (NPC) means the office within OFLC which is charged with the adjudication of an *Application for Temporary Employment Certification* or other applications. For purposes of this subpart, the NPC receiving a request for an *H–2B Registration* and an *Application for Temporary Employment Certification* is the Chicago NPC whose address is published in the FEDERAL REGISTER.

NPC Director means the OFLC official to whom the Administrator, OFLC has delegated authority for purposes of certain Chicago NPC operations and functions.

Non-agricultural labor and services means any labor or services not considered to be agricultural labor or services as defined in subpart B of this part. It does not include the provision of services as members of the medical profession by graduates of medical schools.

Occupational employment statistics (OES) survey means the program under the jurisdiction of the Bureau of Labor Statistics (BLS) that provides annual wage estimates for occupations at the State and MSA levels.

Offered wage means the wage offered by an employer in an H–2B job order. The offered wage must equal or exceed the highest of the prevailing wage or Federal, State or local minimum wage.

Office of Foreign Labor Certification (OFLC) means the organizational component of the ETA that provides national leadership and policy guidance and develops regulations to carry out the Secretary's responsibilities, including determinations related to an employer's request for *H–2B Registration*,

Application for Prevailing Wage Determination, or *Application for Temporary Employment Certification*.

Prevailing wage determination (PWD) means the prevailing wage for the position, as described in § 655.10, that is the subject of the *Application for Temporary Employment Certification*. The PWD is made on ETA Form 9141, *Application for Prevailing Wage Determination*.

Professional athlete means an individual who is employed as an athlete by:

(1) A team that is a member of an association of six or more professional sports teams whose total combined revenues exceed $10,000,000 per year, if the association governs the conduct of its members and regulates the contests and exhibitions in which its member teams regularly engage; or

(2) Any minor league team that is affiliated with such an association.

Seafood is defined as fresh or saltwater finfish, crustaceans, other forms of aquatic animal life, including, but not limited to, alligator, frog, aquatic turtle, jellyfish, sea cucumber, and sea urchin and the roe of such animals, and all mollusks.

Secretary means the Secretary of Labor, the chief official of the U.S. Department of Labor, or the Secretary's designee.

Secretary of Homeland Security means the chief official of the U.S. Department of Homeland Security (DHS) or the Secretary of Homeland Security's designee.

Secretary of State means the chief official of the U.S. Department of State or the Secretary of State's designee.

State Workforce Agency (SWA) means a State government agency that receives funds under the Wagner-Peyser Act (29 U.S.C. 49 *et seq.*) to administer the State's public labor exchange activities.

Strike means a concerted stoppage of work by employees as a result of a labor dispute, or any concerted slowdown or other concerted interruption of operation (including stoppage by reason of the expiration of a collective bargaining agreement).

Successor in interest means:

(1) Where an employer has violated 29 CFR part 503, or this subpart, and has ceased doing business or cannot be located for purposes of enforcement, a successor in interest to that employer may be held liable for the duties and obligations of the violating employer in certain circumstances. The following factors, as used under Title VII of the Civil Rights Act and the Vietnam Era Veterans' Readjustment Assistance Act, may be considered in determining whether an employer is a successor in interest; no one factor is dispositive, but all of the circumstances will be considered as a whole:

(i) Substantial continuity of the same business operations;

(ii) Use of the same facilities;

(iii) Continuity of the work force;

(iv) Similarity of jobs and working conditions;

(v) Similarity of supervisory personnel;

(vi) Whether the former management or owner retains a direct or indirect interest in the new enterprise;

(vii) Similarity in machinery, equipment, and production methods;

(viii) Similarity of products and services; and

(ix) The ability of the predecessor to provide relief.

(2) For purposes of debarment only, the primary consideration will be the personal involvement of the firm's ownership, management, supervisors, and others associated with the firm in the violation(s) at issue.

United States (U.S.) means the continental United States, Alaska, Hawaii, the Commonwealth of Puerto Rico, Guam, the U.S. Virgin Islands, and the Commonwealth of the Northern Mariana Islands (CNMI).

U.S. Citizenship and Immigration Services (USCIS) means the Federal agency within DHS that makes the determination under the INA whether to grant petitions filed by employers seeking H-2B workers to perform temporary nonagricultural work in the U.S.

United States worker (U.S. worker) means a worker who is:

(1) A citizen or national of the U.S.;

(2) An alien who is lawfully admitted for permanent residence in the U.S., is admitted as a refugee under 8 U.S.C. 1157, section 207 of the INA, is granted asylum under 8 U.S.C. 1158, section 208

of the INA, or is an alien otherwise authorized under the immigration laws to be employed in the U.S.; or

(3) An individual who is not an unauthorized alien (as defined in 8 U.S.C. 1324a(h)(3), section 274a(h)(3) of the INA) with respect to the employment in which the worker is engaging.

Wage and Hour Division (WHD) means the agency within the Department of Labor with investigatory and law enforcement authority, as delegated from DHS, to carry out the provisions under 8 U.S.C. 1184(c), section 214(c) of the INA.

Wages mean all forms of cash remuneration to a worker by an employer in payment for personal services.

§ 655.6 Temporary need.

(a) An employer seeking certification under this subpart must establish that its need for non-agricultural services or labor is temporary, regardless of whether the underlying job is permanent or temporary.

(b) The employer's need is considered temporary if justified to the CO as one of the following: A one-time occurrence; a seasonal need; a peakload need; or an intermittent need, as defined by DHS regulations. Except where the employer's need is based on a one-time occurrence, the CO will deny a request for an *H–2B Registration* or an *Application for Temporary Employment Certification* where the employer has a need lasting more than 9 months.

(c) A job contractor will only be permitted to seek certification if it can demonstrate through documentation its own temporary need, not that of its employer-client(s). A job contractor will only be permitted to file applications based on a seasonal need or a one-time occurrence.

(d) Nothing in this paragraph (d) is intended to limit the authority of the Secretary of Homeland Security, in the course of adjudicating an H–2B petition, to make the final determination as to whether a prospective H–2B employer's need is temporary in nature.

§ 655.7 Persons and entities authorized to file.

(a) *Persons authorized to file.* In addition to the employer applicant, a request for an *H–2B Registration* or an *Application for Temporary Employment Certification* may be filed by an attorney or agent, as defined in § 655.5.

(b) *Employer's signature required.* Regardless of whether the employer is represented by an attorney or agent, the employer is required to sign the *H–2B Registration* and *Application for Temporary Employment Certification* and all documentation submitted to the Department of Labor.

§ 655.8 Requirements for agents.

An agent filing an *Application for Temporary Employment Certification* on behalf of an employer must provide:

(a) A copy of the agent agreement or other document demonstrating the agent's authority to represent the employer; and

(b) A copy of the Migrant and Seasonal Agricultural Worker Protection Act (MSPA) Farm Labor Contractor Certificate of Registration, if the agent is required under MSPA, at 29 U.S.C. 1801 *et seq.*, to have such a certificate, identifying the specific farm labor contracting activities the agent is authorized to perform.

§ 655.9 Disclosure of foreign worker recruitment.

(a) The employer, and its attorney or agent, as applicable, must provide a copy of all agreements with any agent or recruiter whom it engages or plans to engage in the recruitment of H–2B workers under this *Application for Temporary Employment Certification*. These agreements must contain the contractual prohibition against charging fees as set forth in § 655.20(p).

(b) The employer, and its attorney or agent, as applicable, must also provide the identity and location of all persons and entities hired by or working for the recruiter or agent referenced in paragraph (a) of this section, and any of the agents or employees of those persons and entities, to recruit prospective foreign workers for the H–2B job opportunities offered by the employer.

(c) The Department of Labor will maintain a publicly available list of agents and recruiters who are party to the agreements referenced in paragraph (a) of this section, as well as the persons and entities referenced in paragraph (b) of this section and the locations in which they are operating.

PREFILING PROCEDURES

§655.10 Determination of prevailing wage for temporary labor certification purposes.

(a) *Offered wage.* The employer must advertise the position to all potential workers at a wage at least equal to the prevailing wage obtained from the NPWC, or the Federal, State or local minimum wage, whichever is highest. The employer must offer and pay this wage (or higher) to both its H–2B workers and its workers in corresponding employment. The issuance of a PWD under this section does not permit an employer to pay a wage lower than the highest wage required by any applicable Federal, State or local law.

(b) *Determinations.* Prevailing wages shall be determined as follows:

(1) Except as provided in paragraph (i) of this section, if the job opportunity is covered by a collective bargaining agreement (CBA) that was negotiated at arms' length between the union and the employer, the wage rate set forth in the CBA is considered as not adversely affecting the wages of U.S. workers, that is, it is considered the "prevailing wage" for labor certification purposes.

(2) If the job opportunity is not covered by a CBA, the prevailing wage for labor certification purposes shall be the arithmetic mean of the wages of workers similarly employed in the area of intended employment using the wage component of the BLS Occupational Employment Statistics Survey (OES), unless the employer provides a survey acceptable to OFLC under paragraph (f) of this section.

(c) *Request for PWD.* (1) An employer must request and receive a PWD from the NPWC before filing the job order with the SWA.

(2) The PWD must be valid on the date the job order is posted.

(d) *Multiple worksites.* If the job opportunity involves multiple worksites within an area of intended employment and different prevailing wage rates exist for the opportunity within the area of intended employment, the prevailing wage is the highest applicable wage among all the worksites.

(e) *NPWC action.* The NPWC will provide the PWD, indicate the source, and return the Application for Prevailing Wage Determination (ETA Form 9141) with its endorsement to the employer.

(f) *Employer-provided survey.* (1) If the job opportunity is not covered by a CBA, or by a professional sports league's rules or regulations, the NPWC will consider a survey provided by the employer in making a Prevailing Wage Determination only if the employer submission demonstrates that the survey falls into one of the following categories:

(i) The survey was independently conducted and issued by a state, including any state agency, state college, or state university;

(ii) The survey is submitted for a geographic area where the OES does not collect data, or in a geographic area where the OES provides an arithmetic mean only at a national level for workers employed in the SOC;

(iii)(A) The job opportunity is not included within an occupational classification of the SOC system; or

(B) The job opportunity is within an occupational classification of the SOC system designated as an "all other" classification.

(2) The survey must provide the arithmetic mean of the wages of all workers similarly employed in the area of intended employment, except that if the survey provides a median but does not provide an arithmetic mean, the prevailing wage applicable to the employer's job opportunity shall be the median of the wages of workers similarly employed in the area of intended employment.

(3) Notwithstanding paragraph (f)(2) of this section, the geographic area surveyed may be expanded beyond the area of intended employment, but only as necessary to meet the requirements of paragraph (f)(4)(ii) of this section. Any geographic expansion beyond the area of intended employment must include only those geographic areas that are contiguous to the area of intended employment.

(4) In each case where the employer submits a survey under paragraph (f)(1)

of this section, the employer must submit, concurrently with the ETA Form 9141, a completed Form ETA–9165 containing specific information about the survey methodology, including such items as sample size and source, sample selection procedures, and survey job descriptions, to allow a determination of the adequacy of the data provided and validity of the statistical methodology used in conducting the survey. In addition, the information provided by the employer must include the attestation that:

(i) The surveyor either made a reasonable, good faith attempt to contact all employers employing workers in the occupation and geographic area surveyed or conducted a randomized sampling of such employers;

(ii) The survey includes wage data from at least 30 workers and three employers;

(iii) If the survey is submitted under paragraph (f)(1)(ii) or (iii) of this section, the collection was administered by a bona fide third party. The following are not bona fide third parties under this rule: Any H–2B employer or any H–2B employer's agent, representative, or attorney;

(iv) The survey was conducted across industries that employ workers in the occupation; and

(v) The wage reported in the survey includes all types of pay, consistent with Form ETA–9165.

(5) The survey must be based upon recently collected data: The survey must be the most current edition of the survey and must be based on wages paid not more than 24 months before the date the survey is submitted for consideration.

(g) *Review of employer-provided surveys.* (1) If the NPWC finds an employer-provided survey not to be acceptable, the NPWC shall inform the employer in writing of the reasons the survey was not accepted.

(2) The employer, after receiving notification that the survey it provided for consideration is not acceptable, may request review under § 655.13.

(h) *Validity period.* The NPWC must specify the validity period of the prevailing wage, which in no event may be more than 365 days and no less than 90 days from the date that the determination is issued.

(i) *Professional athletes.* In computing the prevailing wage for a professional athlete when the job opportunity is covered by professional sports league rules or regulations, the wage set forth in those rules or regulations is considered the prevailing wage.

(j) *Retention of documentation.* The employer must retain the PWD for 3 years from the date of issuance or the date of a final determination on the *Application for Temporary Employment Certification,* whichever is later, and submit it to a CO if requested by a Notice of Deficiency, described in § 655.31, or audit, as described in § 655.70, or to a WHD representative during a WHD investigation.

(k) *Guam.* The requirements of this section apply to any request filed for an H–2B job opportunity on Guam, subject to the transfer of authority to set the prevailing wage for a job opportunity on Guam to DOL in Title 8 of the Code of Federal Regulations.

[80 FR 24108, Apr. 29, 2015, as amended at 80 FR 24184, Apr. 29, 2015]

§ 655.11 Registration of H–2B employers.

All employers, including job contractors, that desire to hire H–2B workers must establish their need for services or labor is temporary by filing an *H–2B Registration* with the Chicago NPC.

(a) *Registration filing.* An employer must file an *H–2B Registration.* The *H–2B Registration* must be accompanied by documentation evidencing:

(1) The number of positions that will be sought in the first year of registration;

(2) The time period of need for the workers requested;

(3) That the nature of the employer's need for the services or labor to be performed is non-agricultural and temporary, and is justified as either a one-time occurrence, a seasonal need, a peakload need, or an intermittent need, as defined by DHS regulations and § 655.6 (or in the case of job contractors, a seasonal need or one-time occurrence); and

(4) For job contractors, the job contractor's own seasonal need or one-

time occurrence, such as through the provision of payroll records.

(b) *Original signature.* The *H–2B Registration* must bear the original signature of the employer (and that of the employer's attorney or agent if applicable). If and when the *H–2B Registration* is permitted to be filed electronically, the employer will satisfy this requirement by signing the *H–2B Registration* as directed by the CO.

(c) *Timeliness of registration filing.* A completed request for an *H–2B Registration* must be received by no less than 120 calendar days and no more than 150 calendar days before the employer's date of need, except where the employer submits the *H–2B Registration* in support of an emergency filing under §655.17.

(d) *Temporary need.* (1) The employer must establish that its need for non-agricultural services or labor is temporary, regardless of whether the underlying job is permanent or temporary, consistent with DHS regulations. A job contractor must also demonstrate through documentation its own seasonal need or one-time occurrence.

(2) The employer's need will be assessed in accordance with the definitions provided by the Secretary of Homeland Security and as further defined in §655.6.

(e) *NPC review.* The CO will review the *H–2B Registration* and its accompanying documentation for completeness and make a determination based on the following factors:

(1) The job classification and duties qualify as non-agricultural;

(2) The employer's need for the services or labor to be performed is temporary in nature, and for job contractors, demonstration of the job contractor's own seasonal need or one-time occurrence;

(3) The number of worker positions and period of need are justified; and

(4) The request represents a bona fide job opportunity.

(f) *Mailing and postmark requirements.* Any notice or request pertaining to an *H–2B Registration* sent by the CO to an employer requiring a response will be mailed to the address provided on the *H–2B Registration* using methods to assure next day delivery, including electronic mail. The employer's response to the notice or request must be mailed using methods to assure next day delivery, including electronic mail, and be sent by the due date specified by the CO or by the next business day if the due date falls on a Saturday, Sunday or Federal holiday.

(g) *Request for information (RFI).* If the CO determines the *H–2B Registration* cannot be approved, the CO will issue an RFI. The RFI will be issued within 7 business days of the CO's receipt of the *H–2B Registration.* The RFI will:

(1) State the reason(s) why the *H–2B Registration* cannot be approved and what supplemental information or documentation is needed to correct the deficiencies;

(2) Specify a date, no later than 7 business days from the date the RFI is issued, by which the supplemental information or documentation must be sent by the employer;

(3) State that, upon receipt of a response to the RFI, the CO will review the *H–2B Registration* as well as any supplemental information and documentation and issue a Notice of Decision on the *H–2B Registration.* The CO may, at his or her discretion, issue one or more additional RFIs before issuing a Notice of Decision on the *H–2B Registration;* and

(4) State that failure to comply with an RFI, including not responding in a timely manner or not providing all required documentation within the specified timeframe, will result in a denial of the *H–2B Registration.*

(h) *Notice of Decision.* The CO will notify the employer in writing of the final decision on the *H–2B Registration.*

(1) Approved *H–2B Registration.* If the *H–2B Registration* is approved, the CO will send a Notice of Decision to the employer, and a copy to the employer's attorney or agent, if applicable. The Notice of Decision will notify the employer that it is eligible to seek H–2B workers in the occupational classification for the anticipated number of positions and period of need stated on the approved *H–2B Registration.* The CO may approve the *H–2B Registration* for a period of up to 3 consecutive years.

(2) Denied *H–2B Registration.* If the *H–2B Registration* is denied, the CO will

send a Notice of Decision to the employer, and a copy to the employer's attorney or agent, if applicable. The Notice of Decision will:

(i) State the reason(s) why the *H–2B Registration* is denied;

(ii) Offer the employer an opportunity to request administrative review under § 655.61 within 10 business days from the date the Notice of Decision is issued and state that if the employer does not request administrative review within that period the denial is final.

(i) *Retention of documents.* All employers filing an *H–2B Registration* are required to retain any documents and records not otherwise submitted proving compliance with this subpart. Such records and documents must be retained for a period of 3 years from the date of certification of the last *Application for Temporary Employment Certification* supported by the *H–2B Registration*, if approved, or 3 years from the date the decision is issued if the *H–2B Registration* is denied or 3 years from the day the Department of Labor receives written notification from the employer withdrawing its pending *H–2B Registration.*

(j) *Transition period.* In order to allow OFLC to make the necessary changes to its program operations to accommodate the new registration process, OFLC will announce in the FEDERAL REGISTER a separate transition period for the registration process, and until that time, will continue to adjudicate temporary need during the processing of applications.

§ 655.12 Use of registration of H–2B employers.

(a) Upon approval of the *H–2B Registration*, the employer is authorized for the specified period of up to 3 consecutive years from the date the *H–2B Registration* is approved to file an *Application for Temporary Employment Certification*, unless:

(1) The number of workers to be employed has increased by more than 20 percent (or 50 percent for employers requesting fewer than 10 workers) from the initial year;

(2) The dates of need for the job opportunity have changed by more than a total of 30 calendar days from the initial year for the entire period of need;

(3) The nature of the job classification and/or duties has materially changed; or

(4) The temporary nature of the employer's need for services or labor to be performed has materially changed.

(b) If any of the changes in paragraphs (a)(1) through (4) of this section apply, the employer must file a new *H–2B Registration* in accordance with § 655.11.

(c) The *H–2B Registration* may not be transferred from one employer to another unless the employer to which it is transferred is a successor in interest to the employer to which it was issued.

§ 655.13 Review of PWDs.

(a) *Request for review of PWDs.* Any employer desiring review of a PWD must make a written request for such review to the NPWC Director within 7 business days from the date the PWD is issued. The request for review must clearly identify the PWD for which review is sought; set forth the particular grounds for the request; and include any materials submitted to the NPWC for purposes of securing the PWD.

(b) *NPWC review.* Upon the receipt of the written request for review, the NPWC Director will review the employer's request and accompanying documentation, including any supplementary material submitted by the employer, and after review shall issue a Final Determination letter; that letter may:

(1) Affirm the PWD issued by the NPWC; or

(2) Modify the PWD.

(c) *Request for review by BALCA.* Any employer desiring review of the NPWC Director's decision on a PWD must make a written request for review of the determination by BALCA within 10 business days from the date the Final Determination letter is issued.

(1) The request for BALCA review must be in writing and addressed to the NPWC Director who made the final determinations. Upon receipt of a request for BALCA review, the NPWC will prepare an appeal file and submit it to BALCA.

(2) The request for review, statements, briefs, and other submissions of

the parties must contain only legal arguments and may refer to only the evidence that was within the record upon which the decision on the PWD was based.

(3) BALCA will handle appeals in accordance with § 655.61.

§ 655.14 [Reserved]

APPLICATION FOR TEMPORARY EMPLOYMENT CERTIFICATION FILING PROCEDURES

§ 655.15 Application filing requirements.

All registered employers that desire to hire H–2B workers must file an *Application for Temporary Employment Certification* with the NPC designated by the Administrator, OFLC. Except for employers that qualify for emergency procedures at § 655.17, employers that fail to register under the procedures in § 655.11 and/or that fail to submit a PWD obtained under § 655.10 will not be eligible to file an *Application for Temporary Employment Certification* and their applications will be returned without review.

(a) *What to file.* A registered employer seeking H–2B workers must file a completed *Application for Temporary Employment Certification* (ETA Form 9142B and the appropriate appendices and valid PWD), a copy of the job order being submitted concurrently to the SWA serving the area of intended employment, as set forth in § 655.16, and copies of all contracts and agreements with any agent and/or recruiter, executed in connection with the job opportunities and all information required, as specified in §§ 655.8 and 655.9.

(b) *Timeliness.* A completed *Application for Temporary Employment Certification* must be filed no more than 90 calendar days and no less than 75 calendar days before the employer's date of need.

(c) *Location and method of filing.* The employer must submit the *Application for Temporary Employment Certification* and all required supporting documentation to the NPC either electronically or by mail.

(d) *Original signature.* The *Application for Temporary Employment Certification* must bear the original signature of the employer (and that of the employer's authorized attorney or agent if the employer is so represented). If the *Application for Temporary Employment Certification* is filed electronically, the employer must satisfy this requirement by signing the *Application for Temporary Employment Certification* as directed by the CO.

(e) *Requests for multiple positions.* Certification of more than one position may be requested on the *Application for Temporary Employment Certification* as long as all H–2B workers will perform the same services or labor under the same terms and conditions, in the same occupation, in the same area of intended employment, and during the same period of employment.

(f) *Separate applications.* Except as otherwise permitted by this paragraph (f), only one *Application for Temporary Employment Certification* may be filed for worksite(s) within one area of intended employment for each job opportunity with an employer for each period of employment. Except where otherwise permitted under § 655.4, an association or other organization of employers is not permitted to file master applications on behalf of its employer-members under the H–2B program.

(1) Subject to paragraph (f)(2) of this section, if a petition for H–2B nonimmigrants filed by an employer in the seafood industry is granted, the employer may bring the nonimmigrants described in the petition into the United States at any time during the 120-day period beginning on the start date for which the employer is seeking the services of the nonimmigrants without filing another petition.

(2) An employer in the seafood industry may not bring H–2B nonimmigrants into the United States after the date that is 90 days after the start date for which the employer is seeking the services of the nonimmigrants unless the employer conducts new recruitment, that begins at least 45 days after, and ends before the 90th day after, the certified start date of need as follows:

(i) Completes a new assessment of the local labor market by—

(A) Listing the job orders in local newspapers on 2 separate Sundays; and

(B) Placing new job orders for the job opportunity with the State Workforce Agency serving the area of intended employment and posting the job opportunity at the place of employment for at least 10 days; and

(C) Offering the job to an equally or better qualified United States worker who—

(*1*) Applies for the job; and

(*2*) Will be available at the time and place of need.

(3) In order to comply with this provision, employers in the seafood industry must—

(*1*) Sign and date an attestation form stating the employer's compliance with this subparagraph. The attestation form is available at *http://www.foreignlaborcert.doleta.gov/form.cfm;*

(*2*) Provide each H–2B nonimmigrant worker seeking admission to the United States a copy of the signed and dated attestation, with instructions that the worker must present the documentation upon request to the Department of State's consular officers when they apply for a visa and/or the Department of Homeland Security's U.S Customs and Border Protection officers when seeking admission to the United States. Without this attestation, an H–2B nonimmigrant may be denied a visa or admission to the United States if seeking to enter at any time other than the start date stated in the petition. (The attestation is not necessary when filing an amended petition based on a worker who is being substituted in accordance with DHS regulations.) The attestation presented by an H–2B nonimmigrant worker must be the official attestation downloaded from OFLC's Web site and may not be altered or revised in any manner; and

(*3*) Retain the additional recruitment documentation, together with their prefiling recruitment documentation, for a period of 3 years from the date of certification, consistent with the document retention requirements under § 655.56. Seafood industry employers who conduct the required additional recruitment should not submit proof of the additional recruitment to the Office of Foreign Labor Certification.

(g) *One-time occurrence.* Where a one-time occurrence lasts longer than 1 year, the CO will instruct the employer on any additional recruitment requirements with respect to the continuing validity of the labor market test or offered wage obligation.

(h) *Information dissemination.* Information received in the course of processing a request for an *H–2B Registration*, an *Application for Temporary Employment Certification* or program integrity measures such as audits may be forwarded from OFLC to WHD, or any other Federal agency as appropriate, for investigative and/or enforcement purposes.

§ 655.16 Filing of the job order at the SWA.

(a) *Submission of the job order.* (1) The employer must submit the job order to the SWA serving the area of intended employment at the same time it submits the *Application for Temporary Employment Certification* and a copy of the job order to the NPC in accordance with § 655.15. If the job opportunity is located in more than one State within the same area of intended employment, the employer may submit the job order to any one of the SWAs having jurisdiction over the anticipated worksites, but must identify the receiving SWA on the copy of the job order submitted to the NPC with its *Application for Temporary Employment Certification.* The employer must inform the SWA that the job order is being placed in connection with a concurrently submitted *Application for Temporary Employment Certification* for H–2B workers.

(2) In addition to complying with State-specific requirements governing job orders, the job order submitted to the SWA must satisfy the requirements set forth in § 655.18.

(b) *SWA review of the job order.* The SWA must review the job order and ensure that it complies with criteria set forth in § 655.18. If the SWA determines that the job order does not comply with the applicable criteria, the SWA must inform the CO at the NPC of the noted deficiencies within 6 business days of receipt of the job order.

(c) *Intrastate and interstate clearance.* Upon receipt of the Notice of Acceptance, as described in § 655.33, the SWA must promptly place the job order in intrastate clearance, and in interstate clearance by providing a copy of the job order to other states as directed by the CO.

(d) *Duration of job order posting and SWA referral of U.S. workers.* Upon receipt of the Notice of Acceptance, any SWA in receipt of the employer's job order must keep the job order on its active file until the end of the recruitment period, as set forth in §655.40(c), and must refer to the employer in a manner consistent with §655.47 all qualified U.S. workers who apply for the job opportunity or on whose behalf a job application is made.

(e) *Amendments to a job order.* The employer may amend the job order at any time before the CO makes a final determination, in accordance with procedures set forth in §655.35.

§655.17 Emergency situations.

(a) *Waiver of time period.* The CO may waive the time period(s) for filing an *H–2B Registration* and/or an *Application for Temporary Employment Certification* for employers that have good and substantial cause, provided that the CO has sufficient time to thoroughly test the domestic labor market on an expedited basis and to make a final determination as required by §655.50.

(b) *Employer requirements.* The employer requesting a waiver of the required time period(s) must submit to the NPC a request for a waiver of the time period requirement, a completed *Application for Temporary Employment Certification* and the proposed job order identifying the SWA serving the area of intended employment, and must otherwise meet the requirements of §655.15. If the employer did not previously apply for an *H–2B Registration*, the employer must also submit a completed *H–2B Registration* with all supporting documentation, as required by §655.11. If the employer did not previously apply for a PWD, the employer must also submit a completed PWD request. The employer's waiver request must include detailed information describing the good and substantial cause that has necessitated the waiver request. Good and substantial cause may include, but is not limited to, the substantial loss of U.S. workers due to Acts of God, or a similar unforeseeable man-made catastrophic event (such as an oil spill or controlled flooding) that is wholly outside of the employer's control, unforeseeable changes in market conditions, or pandemic health issues. A denial of a previously submitted *H–2B Registration* in accordance with the procedures set forth in §655.11 does not constitute good and substantial cause necessitating a waiver under this section.

(c) *Processing of emergency applications.* The CO will process the emergency *H–2B Registration* and/or *Application for Temporary Employment Certification* and job order in a manner consistent with the provisions of this subpart and make a determination on the *Application for Temporary Employment Certification* in accordance with §655.50. If the CO grants the waiver request, the CO will forward a Notice of Acceptance and the approved job order to the SWA serving the area of intended employment identified by the employer in the job order. If the CO determines that the certification cannot be granted because, under paragraph (a) of this section, the request for emergency filing is not justified and/or there is not sufficient time to make a determination of temporary need or ensure compliance with the criteria for certification contained in §655.51, the CO will send a Final Determination letter to the employer in accordance with §655.53.

§655.18 Job order assurances and contents.

(a) *General.* Each job order placed in connection with an *Application for Temporary Employment Certification* must at a minimum include the information contained in paragraph (b) of this section. In addition, by submitting the *Application for Temporary Employment Certification,* an employer agrees to comply with the following assurances with respect to each job order:

(1) *Prohibition against preferential treatment.* The employer's job order must offer to U.S. workers no less than the same benefits, wages, and working conditions that the employer is offering, intends to offer, or will provide to H–2B workers. Job offers may not impose on U.S. workers any restrictions or obligations that will not be imposed on the employer's H–2B workers. This does not relieve the employer from providing to H–2B workers at least the minimum benefits, wages, and working

conditions which must be offered to U.S. workers consistent with this section.

(2) *Bona fide job requirements.* Each job qualification and requirement must be listed in the job order and must be bona fide and consistent with the normal and accepted qualifications and requirements imposed by non-H–2B employers in the same occupation and area of intended employment.

(b) *Contents.* In addition to complying with the assurances in paragraph (a) of this section, the employer's job order must meet the following requirements:

(1) State the employer's name and contact information;

(2) Indicate that the job opportunity is a temporary, full-time position, including the total number of job openings the employer intends to fill;

(3) Describe the job opportunity for which certification is sought with sufficient information to apprise U.S. workers of the services or labor to be performed, including the duties, the minimum education and experience requirements, the work hours and days, and the anticipated start and end dates of the job opportunity;

(4) Indicate the geographic area of intended employment with enough specificity to apprise applicants of any travel requirements and where applicants will likely have to reside to perform the services or labor;

(5) Specify the wage that the employer is offering, intends to offer, or will provide to H–2B workers, or, in the event that there are multiple wage offers, the range of wage offers, and ensure that the wage offer equals or exceeds the highest of the prevailing wage or the Federal, State, or local minimum wage;

(6) If applicable, specify that overtime will be available to the worker and the wage offer(s) for working any overtime hours;

(7) If applicable, state that on-the-job training will be provided to the worker;

(8) State that the employer will use a single workweek as its standard for computing wages due;

(9) Specify the frequency with which the worker will be paid, which must be at least every 2 weeks or according to the prevailing practice in the area of intended employment, whichever is more frequent;

(10) If the employer provides the worker with the option of board, lodging, or other facilities, including fringe benefits, or intends to assist workers to secure such lodging, disclose the provision and cost of the board, lodging, or other facilities, including fringe benefits or assistance to be provided;

(11) State that the employer will make all deductions from the worker's paycheck required by law. Specify any deductions the employer intends to make from the worker's paycheck which are not required by law, including, if applicable, any deductions for the reasonable cost of board, lodging, or other facilities;

(12) Detail how the worker will be provided with or reimbursed for transportation and subsistence from the place from which the worker has come to work for the employer, whether in the U.S. or abroad, to the place of employment, if the worker completes 50 percent of the period of employment covered by the job order, consistent with § 655.20(j)(1)(i);

(13) State that the employer will provide or pay for the worker's cost of return transportation and daily subsistence from the place of employment to the place from which the worker, disregarding intervening employment, departed to work for the employer, if the worker completes the certified period of employment or is dismissed from employment for any reason by the employer before the end of the period, consistent with § 655.20(j)(1)(ii);

(14) If applicable, state that the employer will provide daily transportation to and from the worksite;

(15) State that the employer will reimburse the H–2B worker in the first workweek for all visa, visa processing, border crossing, and other related fees, including those mandated by the government, incurred by the H–2B worker (but need not include passport expenses or other charges primarily for the benefit of the worker);

(16) State that the employer will provide to the worker, without charge or deposit charge, all tools, supplies, and equipment required to perform the duties assigned, in accordance with § 655.20(k);

(17) State the applicability of the three-fourths guarantee, offering the worker employment for a total number of work hours equal to at least three-fourths of the workdays of each 12-week period, if the period of employment covered by the job order is 120 or more days, or each 6-week period, if the period of employment covered by the job order is less than 120 days, in accordance with §655.20(f); and

(18) Instruct applicants to inquire about the job opportunity or send applications, indications of availability, and/or resumes directly to the nearest office of the SWA in the State in which the advertisement appeared and include the SWA contact information.

§655.19 Job contractor filing requirements.

(a) Provided that a job contractor and any employer-client are joint employers, a job contractor may submit an *Application for Temporary Employment Certification* on behalf of itself and that employer-client.

(b) A job contractor must have separate contracts with each different employer-client. Each contract or agreement may support only one *Application for Temporary Employment Certification* for each employer-client job opportunity within a single area of intended employment.

(c) Either the job contractor or its employer-client may submit an ETA Form 9141, *Application for Prevailing Wage Determination,* describing the job opportunity to the NPWC. However, each of the joint employers is separately responsible for ensuring that the wage offer listed on the *Application for Temporary Employment Certification,* ETA Form 9142B, and related recruitment at least equals the prevailing wage rate determined by the NPWC and that all other wage obligations are met.

(d)(1) A job contractor that is filing as a joint employer with its employer-client must submit to the NPC a completed *Application for Temporary Employment Certification,* ETA Form 9142, that clearly identifies the joint employers (the job contractor and its employer-client) and the employment relationship (including the actual worksite), in accordance with the instructions provided by the Department of Labor. The *Application for Temporary Employment Certification* must bear the original signature of the job contractor and the employer-client and be accompanied by the contract or agreement establishing the employers' relationship related to the workers sought.

(2) By signing the *Application for Temporary Employment Certification,* each employer independently attests to the conditions of employment required of an employer participating in the H–2B program and assumes full responsibility for the accuracy of the representations made in the application and for all of the responsibilities of an employer in the H–2B program.

(e)(1) Either the job contractor or its employer-client may place the required job order and conduct recruitment as described in §655.16 and §§655.42 through 655.46. Also, either one of the joint employers may assume responsibility for interviewing applicants. However, both of the joint employers must sign the recruitment report that is submitted to the NPC with the *Application for Temporary Employment Certification,* ETA Form 9142B.

(2) The job order and all recruitment conducted by joint employers must satisfy the content requirements identified in §§655.18 and 655.41. Additionally, in order to fully apprise applicants of the job opportunity and avoid potential confusion inherent in a job opportunity involving two employers, joint employer recruitment must clearly identify both employers (the job contractor and its employer-client) by name and must clearly identify the worksite location(s) where workers will perform labor or services.

(3)(i) Provided that all of the employer-clients' job opportunities are in the same occupation and area of intended employment and have the same requirements and terms and conditions of employment, including dates of employment, a job contractor may combine more than one of its joint employer employer-clients' job opportunities in a single advertisement. Each advertisement must fully apprise potential workers of the job opportunity available with each employer-client and otherwise satisfy the advertising content requirements required for all

H–2B-related advertisements, as identified in § 655.41. Such a shared advertisement must clearly identify the job contractor by name, the joint employment relationship, and the number of workers sought for each job opportunity, identified by employer-client name and location (e.g., 5 openings with Employer-Client 1 (worksite location), 3 openings with Employer-Client 2 (worksite location)).

(ii) In addition, the advertisement must contain the following statement: "Applicants may apply for any or all of the jobs listed. When applying, please identify the job(s) (by company and work location) you are applying to for the entire period of employment specified." If an applicant fails to identify one or more specific work location(s), that applicant is presumed to have applied to all work locations listed in the advertisement.

(f) If an application for joint employers is approved, the NPC will issue one certification and send it to the job contractor. In order to ensure notice to both employers, a courtesy copy of the certification cover letter will be sent to the employer-client. (g) When submitting a certified *Application for Temporary Employment Certification* to USCIS, the job contractor should submit the complete ETA Form 9142B containing the original signatures of both the job contractor and employer-client.

ASSURANCES AND OBLIGATIONS

§ 655.20 Assurances and obligations of H–2B employers.

An employer employing H–2B workers and/or workers in corresponding employment under an *Application for Temporary Employment Certification* has agreed as part of the *Application for Temporary Employment Certification* that it will abide by the following conditions with respect to its H–2B workers and any workers in corresponding employment:

(a) *Rate of pay.* (1) The offered wage in the job order equals or exceeds the highest of the prevailing wage or Federal minimum wage, State minimum wage, or local minimum wage. The employer must pay at least the offered wage, free and clear, during the entire period of the *Application for Temporary Employment Certification* granted by OFLC.

(2) The offered wage is not based on commissions, bonuses, or other incentives, including paying on a piece-rate basis, unless the employer guarantees a wage earned every workweek that equals or exceeds the offered wage.

(3) If the employer requires one or more minimum productivity standards of workers as a condition of job retention, the standards must be specified in the job order and the employer must demonstrate that they are normal and usual for non-H–2B employers for the same occupation in the area of intended employment.

(4) An employer that pays on a piece-rate basis must demonstrate that the piece rate is no less than the normal rate paid by non-H–2B employers to workers performing the same activity in the area of intended employment. The average hourly piece rate earnings must result in an amount at least equal to the offered wage. If the worker is paid on a piece rate basis and at the end of the workweek the piece rate does not result in average hourly piece rate earnings during the workweek at least equal to the amount the worker would have earned had the worker been paid at the offered hourly wage, then the employer must supplement the worker's pay at that time so that the worker's earnings are at least as much as the worker would have earned during the workweek if the worker had instead been paid at the offered hourly wage for each hour worked.

(b) *Wages free and clear.* The payment requirements for wages in this section will be satisfied by the timely payment of such wages to the worker either in cash or negotiable instrument payable at par. The payment must be made finally and unconditionally and "free and clear." The principles applied in determining whether deductions are reasonable and payments are received free and clear and the permissibility of deductions for payments to third persons are explained in more detail in 29 CFR part 531.

(c) *Deductions.* The employer must make all deductions from the worker's paycheck required by law. The job order must specify all deductions not required by law which the employer will make from the worker's pay; any such deductions not disclosed in the job order are prohibited. The wage payment requirements of paragraph (b) of this section are not met where unauthorized deductions, rebates, or refunds reduce the wage payment made to the worker below the minimum amounts required by the offered wage or where the worker fails to receive such amounts free and clear because the worker "kicks back" directly or indirectly to the employer or to another person for the employer's benefit the whole or part of the wages delivered to the worker. Authorized deductions are limited to: Those required by law, such as taxes payable by workers that are required to be withheld by the employer and amounts due workers which the employer is required by court order to pay to another; deductions for the reasonable cost or fair value of board, lodging, and facilities furnished; and deductions of amounts which are authorized to be paid to third persons for the worker's account and benefit through his or her voluntary assignment or order or which are authorized by a collective bargaining agreement with bona fide representatives of workers which covers the employer. Deductions for amounts paid to third persons for the worker's account and benefit which are not so authorized or are contrary to law or from which the employer, agent or recruiter including any agents or employees of these entities, or any affiliated person derives any payment, rebate, commission, profit, or benefit directly or indirectly, may not be made if they reduce the actual wage paid to the worker below the offered wage indicated on the *Application for Temporary Employment Certification*.

(d) *Job opportunity is full-time*. The job opportunity is a full-time temporary position, consistent with § 655.5, and the employer must use a single workweek as its standard for computing wages due. An employee's workweek must be a fixed and regularly recurring period of 168 hours—seven consecutive 24-hour periods. It need not coincide with the calendar week but may begin on any day and at any hour of the day.

(e) *Job qualifications and requirements*. Each job qualification and requirement must be listed in the job order and must be bona fide and consistent with the normal and accepted qualifications and requirements imposed by non-H–2B employers in the same occupation and area of intended employment. The employer's job qualifications and requirements imposed on U.S. workers must not be less favorable than the qualifications and requirements that the employer is imposing or will impose on H–2B workers. A qualification means a characteristic that is necessary to the individual's ability to perform the job in question. A requirement means a term or condition of employment which a worker is required to accept in order to obtain the job opportunity. The CO may require the employer to submit documentation to substantiate the appropriateness of any job qualification and/or requirement specified in the job order.

(f) *Three-fourths guarantee*. (1) The employer must guarantee to offer the worker employment for a total number of work hours equal to at least three-fourths of the workdays in each 12-week period (each 6-week period if the period of employment covered by the job order is less than 120 days) beginning with the first workday after the arrival of the worker at the place of employment or the advertised first date of need, whichever is later, and ending on the expiration date specified in the job order or in its extensions, if any. See the exception in paragraph (y) of this section.

(2) For purposes of this paragraph (f) a workday means the number of hours in a workday as stated in the job order. The employer must offer a total number of hours of work to ensure the provision of sufficient work to reach the three-fourths guarantee in each 12-week period (each 6-week period if the period of employment covered by the job order is less than 120 days) during the work period specified in the job order, or during any modified job order period to which the worker and employer have mutually agreed and that has been approved by the CO.

(3) In the event the worker begins working later than the specified beginning date the guarantee period begins with the first workday after the arrival

of the worker at the place of employment, and continues until the last day during which the job order and all extensions thereof are in effect.

(4) The 12-week periods (6-week periods if the period of employment covered by the job order is less than 120 days) to which the guarantee applies are based upon the workweek used by the employer for pay purposes. The first 12-week period (or 6-week period, as appropriate) also includes any partial workweek, if the first workday after the worker's arrival at the place of employment is not the beginning of the employer's workweek, with the guaranteed number of hours increased on a pro rata basis (thus, the first period may include up to 12 weeks and 6 days (or 6 weeks and 6 days, as appropriate)). The final 12-week period (or 6-week period, as appropriate) includes any time remaining after the last full 12-week period (or 6-week period) ends, and thus may be as short as 1 day, with the guaranteed number of hours decreased on a pro rata basis.

(5) Therefore, if, for example, a job order is for a 32-week period (a period greater than 120 days), during which the normal workdays and work hours for the workweek are specified as 5 days a week, 7 hours per day, the worker would have to be guaranteed employment for at least 315 hours in the first 12-week period (12 weeks × 35 hours/week = 420 hours × 75 percent = 315), at least 315 hours in the second 12-week period, and at least 210 hours (8 weeks × 35 hours/week = 280 hours × 75 percent = 210) in the final partial period. If the job order is for a 16-week period (less than 120 days), during which the normal workdays and work hours for the workweek are specified as 5 days a week, 7 hours per day, the worker would have to be guaranteed employment for at least 157.5 hours (6 weeks × 35 hours/week = 210 hours × 75 percent = 157.5) in the first 6-week period, at least 157.5 hours in the second 6-week period, and at least 105 hours (4 weeks × 35 hours/week = 140 hours × 75 percent = 105) in the final partial period.

(6) If the worker is paid on a piece rate basis, the employer must use the worker's average hourly piece rate earnings or the offered wage, whichever is higher, to calculate the amount due under the guarantee.

(7) A worker may be offered more than the specified hours of work on a single workday. For purposes of meeting the guarantee, however, the worker will not be required to work for more than the number of hours specified in the job order for a workday. The employer, however, may count all hours actually worked in calculating whether the guarantee has been met. If during any 12-week period (6-week period if the period of employment covered by the job order is less than 120 days) during the period of the job order the employer affords the U.S. or H–2B worker less employment than that required under paragraph (f)(1) of this section, the employer must pay such worker the amount the worker would have earned had the worker, in fact, worked for the guaranteed number of days. An employer has not met the work guarantee if the employer has merely offered work on three-fourths of the workdays in an 12-week period (or 6-week period, as appropriate) if each workday did not consist of a full number of hours of work time as specified in the job order.

(8) Any hours the worker fails to work, up to a maximum of the number of hours specified in the job order for a workday, when the worker has been offered an opportunity to work in accordance with paragraph (f)(1) of this section, and all hours of work actually performed (including voluntary work over 8 hours in a workday), may be counted by the employer in calculating whether each 12-week period (or 6-week period, as appropriate) of guaranteed employment has been met. An employer seeking to calculate whether the guaranteed number of hours has been met must maintain the payroll records in accordance with this part.

(g) *Impossibility of fulfillment.* If, before the expiration date specified in the job order, the services of the worker are no longer required for reasons beyond the control of the employer due to fire, weather, or other Act of God, or similar unforeseeable man-made catastrophic event (such as an oil spill or controlled flooding) that is wholly outside the employer's control that makes the fulfillment of the job order impossible, the employer may terminate the job order with the approval of the CO. In the event of such termination of a job order, the employer must fulfill a three-fourths guarantee, as described in paragraph (f) of this section, for the time that has elapsed from the start date listed in the job order or the first workday after the arrival of the worker at the place of employment, whichever is later, to the time of its termination. The employer must make efforts to transfer the H–2B worker or worker in corresponding employment to other comparable employment acceptable to the worker and consistent with the INA, as applicable. If a transfer is not effected, the employer must return the worker, at the employer's expense, to the place from which the worker (disregarding intervening employment) came to work for the employer, or transport the worker to the worker's next certified H–2B employer, whichever the worker prefers.

(h) *Frequency of pay.* The employer must state in the job order the frequency with which the worker will be paid, which must be at least every 2 weeks or according to the prevailing practice in the area of intended employment, whichever is more frequent. Employers must pay wages when due.

(i) *Earnings statements.* (1) The employer must keep accurate and adequate records with respect to the workers' earnings, including but not limited to: Records showing the nature, amount and location(s) of the work performed; the number of hours of work offered each day by the employer (broken out by hours offered both in accordance with and over and above the three-fourths guarantee in paragraph (f) of this section); the hours actually worked each day by the worker; if the number of hours worked by the worker is less than the number of hours offered, the reason(s) the worker did not work; the time the worker began and ended each workday; the rate of pay (both piece rate and hourly, if applicable); the worker's earnings per pay period; the worker's home address; and the amount of and reasons for any and all deductions taken from or additions made to the worker's wages.

(2) The employer must furnish to the worker on or before each payday in one or more written statements the following information:

(i) The worker's total earnings for each workweek in the pay period;

(ii) The worker's hourly rate and/or piece rate of pay;

(iii) For each workweek in the pay period the hours of employment offered to the worker (showing offers in accordance with the three-fourths guarantee as determined in paragraph (f) of this section, separate from any hours offered over and above the guarantee);

(iv) For each workweek in the pay period the hours actually worked by the worker;

(v) An itemization of all deductions made from or additions made to the worker's wages;

(vi) If piece rates are used, the units produced daily;

(vii) The beginning and ending dates of the pay period; and

(viii) The employer's name, address and FEIN.

(j) *Transportation and visa fees.* (1)(i) *Transportation to the place of employment.* The employer must provide or reimburse the worker for transportation and subsistence from the place from which the worker has come to work for the employer, whether in the U.S. or abroad, to the place of employment if the worker completes 50 percent of the period of employment covered by the job order (not counting any extensions). The employer may arrange and pay for the transportation and subsistence directly, advance at a minimum the most economical and reasonable common carrier cost of the transportation and subsistence to the worker before the worker's departure, or pay the worker for the reasonable costs incurred by the worker. When it is the prevailing practice of non-H–2B employers in the occupation in the area to do so or when the employer extends such benefits to similarly situated H–2B workers, the employer must advance the required transportation and subsistence costs (or otherwise provide them) to workers in corresponding employment who are traveling to the employer's worksite. The amount of the transportation payment must be no less (and is not required to be more) than the most economical and reasonable common carrier transportation charges for the distances involved. The amount of the daily subsistence must be at least the amount permitted in § 655.173. Where the employer will reimburse the reasonable costs incurred by the worker, it must keep accurate and adequate records of: The costs of transportation and subsistence incurred by the worker; the amount reimbursed; and the date(s) of reimbursement. Note that the FLSA applies independently of the H–2B requirements and imposes obligations on employers regarding payment of wages.

(ii) *Transportation from the place of employment.* If the worker completes the period of employment covered by the job order (not counting any extensions), or if the worker is dismissed from employment for any reason by the employer before the end of the period, and the worker has no immediate subsequent H–2B employment, the employer must provide or pay at the time of departure for the worker's cost of return transportation and daily subsistence from the place of employment to the place from which the worker, disregarding intervening employment, departed to work for the employer. If the worker has contracted with a subsequent employer that has not agreed in the job order to provide or pay for the worker's transportation from the employer's worksite to such subsequent employer's worksite, the employer must provide or pay for that transportation and subsistence. If the worker has contracted with a subsequent employer that has agreed in the job order to provide or pay for the worker's transportation from the employer's worksite to such subsequent employer's worksite, the subsequent employer must provide or pay for such expenses.

(iii) *Employer-provided transportation.* All employer-provided transportation must comply with all applicable Federal, State, and local laws and regulations and must provide, at a minimum, the same vehicle safety standards, driver licensure requirements, and vehicle insurance as required under 49 CFR parts 390, 393, and 396.

(iv) *Disclosure.* All transportation and subsistence costs that the employer will pay must be disclosed in the job order.

(2) The employer must pay or reimburse the worker in the first workweek for all visa, visa processing, border crossing, and other related fees (including those mandated by the government) incurred by the H–2B worker, but not for passport expenses or other charges primarily for the benefit of the worker.

(k) *Employer-provided items.* The employer must provide to the worker, without charge or deposit charge, all tools, supplies, and equipment required to perform the duties assigned.

(l) *Disclosure of job order.* The employer must provide to an H–2B worker outside of the U.S. no later than the time at which the worker applies for the visa, or to a worker in corresponding employment no later than on the day work commences, a copy of the job order including any subsequent approved modifications. For an H–2B worker changing employment from an H–2B employer to a subsequent H–2B employer, the copy must be provided no later than the time an offer of employment is made by the subsequent H–2B employer. The disclosure of all documents required by this paragraph (l) must be provided in a language understood by the worker, as necessary or reasonable.

(m) *Notice of worker rights.* The employer must post and maintain in a conspicuous location at the place of employment a poster provided by the Department of Labor that sets out the rights and protections for H–2B workers and workers in corresponding employment. The employer must post the poster in English. To the extent necessary, the employer must request and post additional posters, as made available by the Department of Labor, in any language common to a significant portion of the workers if they are not fluent in English.

(n) *No unfair treatment.* The employer has not and will not intimidate, threaten, restrain, coerce, blacklist, discharge or in any manner discriminate against, and has not and will not cause any person to intimidate, threaten, restrain, coerce, blacklist, discharge, or in any manner discriminate against, any person who has:

(1) Filed a complaint under or related to 8 U.S.C. 1184(c), section 214(c) of the INA, 29 CFR part 503, or this subpart, or any other regulation promulgated thereunder;

(2) Instituted or caused to be instituted any proceeding under or related to 8 U.S.C. 1184(c), section 214(c) of the INA, 29 CFR part 503, or this subpart or any other regulation promulgated thereunder;

(3) Testified or is about to testify in any proceeding under or related to 8 U.S.C. 1184(c), section 214(c) of the INA, 29 CFR part 503, or this subpart or any other regulation promulgated thereunder;

(4) Consulted with a workers' center, community organization, labor union, legal assistance program, or an attorney on matters related to 8 U.S.C. 1184(c), section 214(c) of the INA, 29 CFR part 503, or this subpart or any other regulation promulgated thereunder; or

(5) Exercised or asserted on behalf of himself/herself or others any right or protection afforded by 8 U.S.C. 1184(c), section 214(c) of the INA, 29 CFR part 503, or this subpart or any other regulation promulgated thereunder.

(o) *Comply with the prohibitions against employees paying fees.* The employer and its attorney, agents, or employees have not sought or received payment of any kind from the worker for any activity related to obtaining H–2B labor certification or employment, including payment of the employer's attorney or agent fees, application and *H–2B Petition* fees, recruitment costs, or any fees attributed to obtaining the approved *Application for Temporary Employment Certification.* For purposes of this paragraph (o), payment includes, but is not limited to, monetary payments, wage concessions (including deductions from wages, salary, or benefits), kickbacks, bribes, tributes, in-kind payments, and free labor. All wages must be paid free and clear. This provision does not prohibit employers or their agents from receiving reimbursement for costs that are the responsibility and primarily for the benefit of the worker, such as government-required passport fees.

(p) *Contracts with third parties to comply with prohibitions.* The employer must contractually prohibit in writing any agent or recruiter (or any agent or employee of such agent or recruiter) whom the employer engages, either directly or indirectly, in recruitment of H–2B workers to seek or receive payments or other compensation from prospective workers. The contract must include the following statement: "Under this agreement, [name of agent, recruiter] and any agent of or employee of [name of agent or recruiter] are prohibited from seeking or receiving payments from any prospective employee of [employer name] at any time, including before or after the worker obtains employment. Payments include but are not limited to, any direct or indirect fees paid by such employees for recruitment, job placement, processing, maintenance, attorneys' fees, agent fees, application fees, or petition fees."

(q) *Prohibition against preferential treatment of foreign workers.* The employer's job offer must offer to U.S. workers no less than the same benefits, wages, and working conditions that the employer is offering, intends to offer, or will provide to H–2B workers. Job offers may not impose on U.S. workers any restrictions or obligations that will not be imposed on the employer's H–2B workers. This does not relieve the employer from providing to H–2B workers at least the minimum benefits, wages, and working conditions which must be offered to U.S. workers consistent with this section.

(r) *Non-discriminatory hiring practices.* The job opportunity is, and through the period set forth in paragraph (t) of this section must continue to be, open to any qualified U.S. worker regardless of race, color, national origin, age, sex, religion, disability, or citizenship. Rejections of any U.S. workers who applied or apply for the job must only be for lawful, job-related reasons, and those not rejected on this basis have been or will be hired. In addition, the employer has and will continue to retain records of all hired workers and rejected applicants as required by § 655.56.

(s) *Recruitment requirements.* The employer must conduct all required recruitment activities, including any additional employer-conducted recruitment activities as directed by the CO, and as specified in §§ 655.40 through 655.46.

(t) *Continuing requirement to hire U.S. workers.* The employer has and will continue to cooperate with the SWA by accepting referrals of all qualified U.S. workers who apply (or on whose behalf a job application is made) for the job opportunity, and must provide employment to any qualified U.S. worker who applies to the employer for the job opportunity, until 21 days before the date of need.

(u) *No strike or lockout.* There is no strike or lockout at any of the employer's worksites within the area of intended employment for which the employer is requesting H–2B certification at the time the *Application for Temporary Employment Certification* is filed.

(v) *No recent or future layoffs.* The employer has not laid off and will not lay off any similarly employed U.S. worker in the occupation that is the subject of the *Application for Temporary Employment Certification* in the area of intended employment within the period beginning 120 calendar days before the date of need through the end of the period of certification. A layoff for lawful, job-related reasons such as lack of work or the end of a season is permissible if all H–2B workers are laid off before any U.S. worker in corresponding employment.

(w) *Contact with former U.S. employees.* The employer will contact (by mail or other effective means) its former U.S. workers, including those who have been laid off within 120 calendar days before the date of need (except those who were dismissed for cause or who abandoned the worksite), employed by the employer in the occupation at the place of employment during the previous year, disclose the terms of the job order, and solicit their return to the job.

(x) *Area of intended employment and job opportunity.* The employer must not place any H–2B workers employed under the approved *Application for Temporary Employment Certification* outside the area of intended employment or in a job opportunity not listed on the approved *Application for Temporary Employment Certification* unless the employer has obtained a new approved *Application for Temporary Employment Certification.*

(y) *Abandonment/termination of employment.* Upon the separation from employment of worker(s) employed under the *Application for Temporary Employment Certification* or workers in corresponding employment, if such separation occurs before the end date of the employment specified in the *Application for Temporary Employment Certification,* the employer must notify OFLC in writing of the separation from employment not later than 2 work days after such separation is discovered by the employer. In addition, the employer must notify DHS in writing (or any other method specified by the Department of Labor or DHS in the FEDERAL REGISTER or the Code of Federal Regulations) of such separation of an H–2B worker. An abandonment or abscondment is deemed to begin after a worker fails to report for work at the regularly scheduled time for 5 consecutive working days without the consent of the employer. If the separation is due to the voluntary abandonment of employment by the H–2B worker or worker in corresponding employment, and the employer provides appropriate notification specified under this paragraph (y), the employer will not be responsible for providing or paying for the subsequent transportation and subsistence expenses of that worker under this section, and that worker is not entitled to the three-fourths guarantee described in paragraph (f) of this section. The employer's obligation to guarantee three-fourths of the work described in paragraph (f) ends with the last full 12-week period (or 6-week period, as appropriate) preceding the worker's voluntary abandonment or termination for cause.

(z) *Compliance with applicable laws.* During the period of employment specified on the *Application for Temporary Employment Certification,* the employer must comply with all applicable Federal, State and local employment-related laws and regulations, including health and safety laws. This includes compliance with 18 U.S.C. 1592(a), with respect to prohibitions against employers, the employer's agents or their attorneys knowingly holding, destroying or confiscating workers' passports, visas, or other immigration documents.

(aa) *Disclosure of foreign worker recruitment.* The employer, and its attorney or agent, as applicable, must comply with § 655.9 by providing a copy of all agreements with any agent or recruiter whom it engages or plans to engage in the recruitment of H–2B workers, and the identity and location of the persons or entities hired by or working for the agent or recruiter and any of the agents or employees of those persons and entities, to recruit foreign workers. Pursuant to § 655.15(a), the agreements and information must be filed with the *Application for Temporary Employment Certification.*

(bb) *Cooperation with investigators.* The employer must cooperate with any employee of the Secretary who is exercising or attempting to exercise the Department's authority pursuant to 8 U.S.C. 1184(c)(14)(B), section 214(c)(14)(B) of the INA.

§§ 655.21–655.29 [Reserved]

PROCESSING OF AN APPLICATION FOR TEMPORARY EMPLOYMENT CERTIFICATION

§ 655.30 Processing of an application and job order.

(a) *NPC review.* The CO will review the *Application for Temporary Employment Certification* and job order for compliance with all applicable program requirements.

(b) *Mailing and postmark requirements.* Any notice or request sent by the CO to an employer requiring a response will be mailed to the address provided in the *Application for Temporary Employment Certification* using methods to assure next day delivery, including electronic mail. The employer's response to such a notice or request must be mailed using methods to assure next day delivery, including electronic mail, and be sent by the due date or the next business day if the due date falls on a Saturday, Sunday or Federal holiday.

(c) *Information dissemination.* OFLC may forward information received in the course of processing an *Application for Temporary Employment Certification* and program integrity measures to WHD, or any other Federal agency, as appropriate, for investigation and/or enforcement purposes.

§ 655.31 Notice of deficiency.

(a) *Notification timeline.* If the CO determines the *Application for Temporary Employment Certification* and/or job order is incomplete, contains errors or inaccuracies, or does not meet the requirements set forth in this subpart, the CO will notify the employer within 7 business days from the CO's receipt of the *Application for Temporary Employment Certification.* If applicable, the Notice of Deficiency will include job order deficiencies identified by the SWA under § 655.16. The CO will send a copy of the Notice of Deficiency to the SWA serving the area of intended employment identified by the employer on its job order, and if applicable, to the employer's attorney or agent.

(b) *Notice content.* The Notice of Deficiency will:

(1) State the reason(s) why the *Application for Temporary Employment Certification* or job order fails to meet the criteria for acceptance and state the modification needed for the CO to issue a Notice of Acceptance;

(2) Offer the employer an opportunity to submit a modified *Application for Temporary Employment Certification* or job order within 10 business days from the date of the Notice of Deficiency. The Notice will state the modification needed for the CO to issue a Notice of Acceptance;

(3) Offer the employer an opportunity to request administrative review of the Notice of Deficiency before an ALJ under provisions set forth in § 655.61. The Notice will inform the employer that it must submit a written request for review to the Chief ALJ of DOL within 10 business days from the date the Notice of Deficiency is issued by facsimile or other means normally assuring next day delivery, and that the employer must simultaneously serve a copy on the CO. The Notice will also state that the employer may submit any legal arguments that the employer believes will rebut the basis of the CO's action; and

(4) State that if the employer does not comply with the requirements of

this section by either submitting a modified application within 10 business days or requesting administrative review before an ALJ under § 655.61, the CO will deny the *Application for Temporary Employment Certification*. The Notice will inform the employer that the denial of the *Application for Temporary Employment Certification* is final, and cannot be appealed. The Department of Labor will not further consider that *Application for Temporary Employment Certification*.

§ 655.32 Submission of a modified application or job order.

(a) *Review of a modified Application for Temporary Employment Certification or job order*. Upon receipt of a response to a Notice of Deficiency, including any modifications, the CO will review the response. The CO may issue one or more additional Notices of Deficiency before issuing a decision. The employer's failure to comply with a Notice of Deficiency, including not responding in a timely manner or not providing all required documentation, will result in a denial of the *Application for Temporary Employment Certification*.

(b) *Acceptance of a modified Application for Temporary Employment Certification or job order*. If the CO accepts the modification(s) to the *Application for Temporary Employment Certification* and/or job order, the CO will issue a Notice of Acceptance to the employer. The CO will send a copy of the Notice of Acceptance to the SWA instructing it to make any necessary modifications to the not yet posted job order and, if applicable, to the employer's attorney or agent, and follow the procedure set forth in § 655.33.

(c) *Denial of a modified Application for Temporary Employment Certification or job order*. If the CO finds the response to Notice of Deficiency unacceptable, the CO will deny the *Application for Temporary Employment Certification* in accordance with the labor certification determination provisions in § 655.51.

(d) *Appeal from denial of a modified Application for Temporary Employment Certification or job order*. The procedures for appealing a denial of a modified *Application for Temporary Employment Certification* and/or job order are the same as for appealing the denial of a non-modified *Application for Temporary Employment Certification* outlined in § 655.61.

(e) *Post acceptance modifications*. Irrespective of the decision to accept the *Application for Temporary Employment Certification*, the CO may require modifications to the job order at any time before the final determination to grant or deny the *Application for Temporary Employment Certification* if the CO determines that the offer of employment does not contain all the minimum benefits, wages, and working condition provisions as set forth in § 655.18. The employer must make such modification, or certification will be denied under § 655.53. The employer must provide all workers recruited in connection with the job opportunity in the *Application for Temporary Employment Certification* with a copy of the modified job order no later than the date work commences, as approved by the CO.

§ 655.33 Notice of acceptance.

(a) *Notification timeline*. If the CO determines the *Application for Temporary Employment Certification* and job order are complete and meet the requirements of this subpart, the CO will notify the employer in writing within 7 business days from the date the CO received the *Application for Temporary Employment Certification* and job order or modification thereof. A copy of the Notice of Acceptance will be sent to the SWA serving the area of intended employment identified by the employer on its job order and, if applicable, to the employer's attorney or agent.

(b) *Notice content*. The notice will:

(1) Direct the employer to engage in recruitment of U.S. workers as provided in §§ 655.40 through 655.46, including any additional recruitment ordered by the CO under § 655.46;

(2) State that such employer-conducted recruitment is in addition to the job order being circulated by the SWA(s) and that the employer must conduct recruitment within 14 calendar days from the date the Notice of Acceptance is issued, consistent with § 655.40;

(3) Direct the SWA to place the job order into intra- and interstate clearance as set forth in §655.16 and to commence such clearance by:

(i) Sending a copy of the job order to other States listed as anticipated worksites in the *Application for Temporary Employment Certification* and job order, if applicable; and

(ii) Sending a copy of the job order to the SWAs for all States designated by the CO for interstate clearance;

(4) Instruct the SWA to keep the approved job order on its active file until the end of the recruitment period as defined in §655.40(c), and to transmit the same instruction to other SWAs to which it circulates the job order in the course of interstate clearance;

(5) Where the occupation or industry is traditionally or customarily unionized, direct the SWA to circulate a copy of the job order to the following labor organizations:

(i) The central office of the State Federation of Labor in the State(s) in which work will be performed; and

(ii) The office(s) of local union(s) representing employees in the same or substantially equivalent job classification in the area(s) in which work will be performed;

(6) Advise the employer, as appropriate, that it must contact the appropriate designated community-based organization(s) with notice of the job opportunity; and

(7) Require the employer to submit a report of its recruitment efforts as specified in §655.48.

§655.34 Electronic job registry.

(a) *Location of and placement in the electronic job registry.* Upon acceptance of the *Application for Temporary Employment Certification* under §655.33, the CO will place for public examination a copy of the job order posted by the SWA on the Department's electronic job registry, including any amendments or required modifications approved by the CO.

(b) *Length of posting on electronic job registry.* The Department of Labor will keep the job order posted on the electronic job registry until the end of the recruitment period, as set forth in §655.40(c).

(c) *Conclusion of active posting.* Once the recruitment period has concluded the job order will be placed in inactive status on the electronic job registry.

§655.35 Amendments to an application or job order.

(a) *Increases in number of workers.* The employer may request to increase the number of workers noted in the *H–2B Registration* by no more than 20 percent (50 percent for employers requesting fewer than 10 workers). All requests for increasing the number of workers must be made in writing and will not be effective until approved by the CO. In considering whether to approve the request, the CO will determine whether the proposed amendment(s) are sufficiently justified and must take into account the effect of the changes on the underlying labor market test for the job opportunity. Upon acceptance of an amendment, the CO will submit to the SWA any necessary changes to the job order and update the electronic job registry. The employer must promptly provide copies of any approved amendments to all U.S. workers hired under the original job order.

(b) *Minor changes to the period of employment.* The employer may request minor changes to the total period of employment listed on its *Application for Temporary Employment Certification* and job order, for a period of up to 14 days, but the period of employment may not exceed a total of 9 months, except in the event of a one-time occurrence. All requests for minor changes to the total period of employment must be made in writing and will not be effective until approved by the CO. In considering whether to approve the request, the CO will determine whether the proposed amendment(s) are sufficiently justified and must take into account the effect of the changes on the underlying labor market test for the job opportunity. Upon acceptance of an amendment, the CO will submit to the SWA any necessary changes to the job order and update the electronic job registry. The employer must promptly provide copies of any approved amendments to all U.S. workers hired under the original job order

(c) *Other amendments to the Application for Temporary Employment Certification and job order.* The employer may request other amendments to the *Application for Temporary Employment Certification* and job order. All such requests must be made in writing and will not be effective until approved by the CO. In considering whether to approve the request, the CO will determine whether the proposed amendment(s) are sufficiently justified and must take into account the effect of the changes on the underlying labor market test for the job opportunity. Upon acceptance of an amendment, the CO will submit to the SWA any necessary changes to the job order and update the electronic job registry.

(d) *Amendments after certification are not permitted.* The employer must promptly provide copies of any approved amendments to all U.S. workers hired under the original job order.

§§ 655.36–655.39 [Reserved]

POST-ACCEPTANCE REQUIREMENTS

§ 655.40 Employer-conducted recruitment.

(a) *Employer obligations.* Employers must conduct recruitment of U.S. workers to ensure that there are not qualified U.S. workers who will be available for the positions listed in the *Application for Temporary Employment Certification.* U.S. Applicants can be rejected only for lawful job-related reasons.

(b) *Employer-conducted recruitment period.* Unless otherwise instructed by the CO, the employer must conduct the recruitment described in §§ 655.42 through 655.46 within 14 calendar days from the date the Notice of Acceptance is issued. All employer-conducted recruitment must be completed before the employer submits the recruitment report as required in § 655.48.

(c) *U.S. workers.* Employers must continue to accept referrals and applications of all U.S. applicants interested in the position until 21 days before the date of need.

(d) *Interviewing U.S. workers.* Employers that wish to require interviews must conduct those interviews by phone or provide a procedure for the interviews to be conducted in the location where the worker is being recruited so that the worker incurs little or no cost. Employers cannot provide potential H–2B workers with more favorable treatment with respect to the requirement for, and conduct of, interviews.

(e) *Qualified and available U.S. workers.* The employer must consider all U.S. applicants for the job opportunity. The employer must accept and hire any applicants who are qualified and who will be available.

(f) *Recruitment report.* The employer must prepare a recruitment report meeting the requirements of § 655.48.

§ 655.41 Advertising requirements.

(a) All recruitment conducted under §§ 655.42 through 655.46 must contain terms and conditions of employment that are not less favorable than those offered to the H–2B workers and, at a minimum, must comply with the assurances applicable to job orders as set forth in § 655.18(a).

(b) All advertising must contain the following information:

(1) The employer's name and contact information;

(2) The geographic area of intended employment with enough specificity to apprise applicants of any travel requirements and where applicants will likely have to reside to perform the services or labor;

(3) A description of the job opportunity for which certification is sought with sufficient information to apprise U.S. workers of the services or labor to be performed, including the duties, the minimum education and experience requirements, the work hours and days, and the anticipated start and end dates of the job opportunity;

(4) A statement that the job opportunity is a temporary, full-time position including the total number of job openings the employer intends to fill;

(5) If applicable, a statement that overtime will be available to the worker and the wage offer(s) for working any overtime hours;

(6) If applicable, a statement indicating that on-the-job training will be provided to the worker;

(7) The wage that the employer is offering, intends to offer or will provide to the H–2B workers or, in the event

that there are multiple wage offers, the range of applicable wage offers, each of which must equal or exceed the highest of the prevailing wage or the Federal, State, or local minimum wage;

(8) If applicable, any board, lodging, or other facilities the employer will offer to workers or intends to assist workers in securing;

(9) All deductions not required by law that the employer will make from the worker's paycheck, including, if applicable, reasonable deduction for board, lodging, and other facilities offered to the workers;

(10) A statement that transportation and subsistence from the place where the worker has come to work for the employer to the place of employment and return transportation and subsistence will be provided, as required by § 655.20(j)(1);

(11) If applicable, a statement that work tools, supplies, and equipment will be provided to the worker without charge;

(12) If applicable, a statement that daily transportation to and from the worksite will be provided by the employer;

(13) A statement summarizing the three-fourths guarantee as required by § 655.20(f); and

(14) A statement directing applicants to apply for the job opportunity at the nearest office of the SWA in the State in which the advertisement appeared, the SWA contact information, and, if applicable, the job order number.

§ 655.42 Newspaper advertisements.

(a) The employer must place an advertisement (which must be in a language other than English, where the CO determines appropriate) on 2 separate days, which may be consecutive, one of which must be a Sunday (except as provided in paragraph (b) of this section), in a newspaper of general circulation serving the area of intended employment and appropriate to the occupation and the workers likely to apply for the job opportunity.

(b) If the job opportunity is located in a rural area that does not have a newspaper with a Sunday edition, the CO may direct the employer, in place of a Sunday edition, to advertise in the regularly published daily edition with the widest circulation in the area of intended employment.

(c) The newspaper advertisements must satisfy the requirements in § 655.41.

(d) The employer must maintain copies of newspaper pages (with date of publication and full copy of the advertisement), or tear sheets of the pages of the publication in which the advertisements appeared, or other proof of publication furnished by the newspaper containing the text of the printed advertisements and the dates of publication, consistent with the document retention requirements in § 655.56. If the advertisement was required to be placed in a language other than English, the employer must maintain a translation and retain it in accordance with § 655.56.

§ 655.43 Contact with former U.S. employees.

The employer must contact (by mail or other effective means) its former U.S. workers, including those who have been laid off within 120 calendar days before the date of need, employed by the employer in the occupation at the place of employment during the previous year (except those who were dismissed for cause or who abandoned the worksite), disclose the terms of the job order, and solicit their return to the job. The employer must maintain documentation sufficient to prove such contact in accordance with § 655.56.

§ 655.44 [Reserved]

§ 655.45 Contact with bargaining representative, posting and other contact requirements.

(a) If there is a bargaining representative for any of the employer's employees in the occupation and area of intended employment, the employer must provide written notice of the job opportunity, by providing a copy of the *Application for Temporary Employment Certification* and the job order, and maintain documentation that it was sent to the bargaining representative(s). An employer governed by this paragraph (a) must include information in its recruitment report that confirms that the bargaining representative(s) was contacted and notified of the position openings and whether the organization referred qualified U.S. worker(s), including the number of referrals, or was non-responsive to the employer's requests.

(b) If there is no bargaining representative, the employer must post the availability of the job opportunity in at least 2 conspicuous locations at the place(s) of anticipated employment or in some other manner that provides reasonable notification to all employees in the job classification and area in which the work will be performed by the H–2B workers. Electronic posting, such as displaying the notice prominently on any internal or external Web site that is maintained by the employer and customarily used for notices to employees about terms and conditions of employment, is sufficient to meet this posting requirement as long as it otherwise meets the requirements of this section. The notice must meet the requirements under § 655.41 and be posted for at least 15 consecutive business days. The employer must maintain a copy of the posted notice and identify where and when it was posted in accordance with § 655.56.

(c) If appropriate to the occupation and area of intended employment, as indicated by the CO in the Notice of Acceptance, the employer must provide written notice of the job opportunity to a community-based organization, and maintain documentation that it was sent to any designated community-based organization. An employer governed by this paragraph (c) must include information in its recruitment report that confirms that the community-based organization was contacted and notified of the position openings and whether the organization referred qualified U.S. worker(s), including the number of referrals, or was non-responsive to the employer's requests.

§ 655.46 Additional employer-conducted recruitment.

(a) *Requirement to conduct additional recruitment.* The employer may be instructed by the CO to conduct additional reasonable recruitment. Such recruitment may be required at the discretion of the CO where the CO has determined that there is a likelihood that U.S. workers who are qualified and will be available for the work, including but not limited to where the job opportunity is located in an Area of Substantial Unemployment.

(b) *Nature of the additional employer-conducted recruitment.* The CO will describe the precise number and nature of the additional recruitment efforts. Additional recruitment may include, but is not limited to, posting on the employer's Web site or another Web site, contact with additional community-based organizations, additional contact with State One-Stop Career Centers, and other print advertising, such as using a professional, trade or ethnic publication where such a publication is appropriate for the occupation and the workers likely to apply for the job opportunity. When assessing the appropriateness of a particular recruitment method, the CO will consider the cost of the additional recruitment and the likelihood that the additional recruitment method(s) will identify qualified and available U.S. workers.

(c) *Proof of the additional employer-conducted recruitment.* The CO will specify the documentation or other supporting evidence that must be maintained by the employer as proof that the additional recruitment requirements were met. Documentation must be maintained as required in § 655.56.

§ 655.47 Referrals of U.S. workers.

SWAs may only refer for employment individuals who have been apprised of all the material terms and conditions of employment and who are qualified and will be available for employment.

§ 655.48 Recruitment report.

(a) *Requirements of the recruitment report.* The employer must prepare, sign, and date a recruitment report. Where recruitment was conducted by a job contractor or its employer-client, both joint employers must sign the recruitment report in accordance with § 655.19(e). The recruitment report must be submitted by a date specified by the CO in the Notice of Acceptance and contain the following information:

(1) The name of each recruitment activity or source (e.g., job order and the name of the newspaper);

(2) The name and contact information of each U.S. worker who applied or was referred to the job opportunity up to the date of the preparation of the recruitment report, and the disposition of each worker's application. The employer must clearly indicate whether the job opportunity was offered to the U.S. worker and whether the U.S. worker accepted or declined;

(3) Confirmation that former U.S. employees were contacted, if applicable, and by what means;

(4) Confirmation that the bargaining representative was contacted, if applicable, and by what means, or that the employer posted the availability of the job opportunity to all employees in the job classification and area in which the work will be performed by the H–2B workers;

(5) Confirmation that the community-based organization designated by the CO was contacted, if applicable;

(6) If applicable, confirmation that additional recruitment was conducted as directed by the CO; and

(7) If applicable, for each U.S. worker who applied for the position but was not hired, the lawful job-related reason(s) for not hiring the U.S. worker.

(b) *Duty to update recruitment report.* The employer must continue to update the recruitment report throughout the recruitment period. In a joint employment situation, either the job contractor or the employer-client may update the recruitment report. The updated report must be signed, dated and need not be submitted to the Department of Labor, but must be made available in the event of a post-certification audit or upon request by DOL.

§ 655.49 [Reserved]

LABOR CERTIFICATION DETERMINATIONS

§ 655.50 Determinations.

(a) *Certifying Officers (COs).* The Administrator, OFLC is the Department's National CO. The Administrator, OFLC and the CO(s), by virtue of delegation from the Administrator, OFLC, have the authority to certify or deny *Applications for Temporary Employment Certification* under the H–2B nonimmigrant classification. If the Administrator, OFLC directs that certain types of temporary labor certification applications or a specific *Application for Temporary Employment Certification* under the H–2B nonimmigrant classification be handled by the OFLC's National Office, the Director of the NPC will refer such applications to the Administrator, OFLC.

(b) *Determination.* Except as otherwise provided in this paragraph (b), the CO will make a determination either to certify or deny the *Application for Temporary Employment Certification.* The CO will certify the application only if the employer has met all the requirements of this subpart, including the criteria for certification in §655.51, thus demonstrating that there is an insufficient number of U.S. workers who are qualified and who will be available for the job opportunity for which certification is sought and that the employment of the H–2B workers will not adversely affect the wages and working conditions of similarly employed U.S. workers.

§ 655.51 Criteria for certification.

(a) The criteria for certification include whether the employer has a valid *H–2B Registration* to participate in the H–2B program and has complied with all of the requirements necessary to grant the labor certification.

(b) In making a determination whether there are insufficient U.S. workers to fill the employer's job opportunity, the CO will count as available any U.S. worker referred by the SWA or any U.S. worker who applied (or on whose behalf an application is made) directly to the employer, but who was rejected by the employer for other than a lawful job-related reason.

(c) A certification will not be granted to an employer that has failed to comply with one or more sanctions or remedies imposed by final agency actions under the H–2B program.

§ 655.52 Approved certification.

If a temporary labor certification is granted, the CO will send the approved *Application for Temporary Employment Certification* and a Final Determination letter to the employer by means normally assuring next day delivery, including electronic mail, and a copy, if applicable, to the employer's attorney or agent. If the *Application for Temporary Employment Certification* is electronically filed, the employer must sign the certified *Application for Temporary Employment Certification* as directed by the CO. The employer must retain a signed copy of the *Application for Temporary Employment Certification* and the original signed Appendix B of the Application, as required by § 655.56.

§ 655.53 Denied certification.

If a temporary labor certification is denied, the CO will send the Final Determination letter to the employer by means normally assuring next day delivery, including electronic mail, and a copy, if applicable, to the employer's attorney or agent. The Final Determination letter will:

(a) State the reason(s) certification is denied, citing the relevant regulatory standards;

(b) Offer the employer an opportunity to request administrative review of the denial under § 655.61; and

(c) State that if the employer does not request administrative review in accordance with § 655.61, the denial is final and the Department of Labor will not accept any appeal on that *Application for Temporary Employment Certification.*

§ 655.54 Partial certification.

The CO may issue a partial certification, reducing either the period of need or the number of H–2B workers or both for certification, based upon information the CO receives during the course of processing the *Application for Temporary Employment Certification.* The number of workers certified will be reduced by one for each U.S. worker who is qualified and who will be available at the time and place needed to perform the services or labor and who has not been rejected for lawful job-related reasons. If a partial labor certification is issued, the CO will amend the *Application for Temporary Employment Certification* and then return it to the employer with a Final Determination letter, with a copy to the employer's attorney or agent, if applicable. The Final Determination letter will:

(a) State the reason(s) why either the period of need and/or the number of H–2B workers requested has been reduced, citing the relevant regulatory standards;

(b) If applicable, address the availability of U.S. workers in the occupation;

(c) Offer the employer an opportunity to request administrative review of the partial certification under § 655.61; and

(d) State that if the employer does not request administrative review in accordance with § 655.61, the partial certification is final and the Department of Labor will not accept any appeal on that *Application for Temporary Employment Certification.*

§ 655.55 Validity of temporary labor certification.

(a) *Validity period.* A temporary labor certification is valid only for the period as approved on the *Application for Temporary Employment Certification.* The certification expires on the last day of authorized employment.

(b) *Scope of validity.* A temporary labor certification is valid only for the number of H–2B positions, the area of intended employment, the job classification and specific services or labor to be performed, and the employer specified on the approved *Application for Temporary Employment Certification,* including any approved modifications. The temporary labor certification may not be transferred from one employer to another unless the employer to which it is transferred is a successor in interest to the employer to which it was issued.

§ 655.56 Document retention requirements of H–2B employers.

(a) *Entities required to retain documents.* All employers filing an *Application for Temporary Employment Certification* requesting H–2B workers are required to retain the documents and records proving compliance with 29 CFR part 503 and this subpart, including but not limited to those specified in paragraph (c) of this section.

(b) *Period of required retention.* The employer must retain records and documents for 3 years from the date of certification of the *Application for Temporary Employment Certification,* or from the date of adjudication if the *Application for Temporary Employment Certification* is denied, or 3 years from the day the Department of Labor receives the letter of withdrawal provided in accordance with § 655.62. For the purposes of this section, records and documents required to be retained in connection with an *H–2B Registration* must be retained in connection with all of the *Applications for Temporary Employment Certification* that are supported by it.

(c) *Documents and records to be retained by all employer applicants.* All employers filing an *H–2B Registration* and an *Application for Temporary Employment Certification* must retain the following documents and records and must provide the documents and records to the Department of Labor and other Federal agencies in the event of an audit or investigation:

(1) Documents and records not previously submitted during the registration process that substantiate temporary need;

(2) Proof of recruitment efforts, as applicable, including:

(i) Job order placement as specified in § 655.16;

(ii) Advertising as specified in §§ 655.41 and 655.42;

(iii) Contact with former U.S. workers as specified in § 655.43;

(iv) Contact with bargaining representative(s), or a copy of the posting of the job opportunity, if applicable, as specified in § 655.45(a) or (b); and

(v) Additional employer-conducted recruitment efforts as specified in § 655.46;

(3) Substantiation of the information submitted in the recruitment report prepared in accordance with § 655.48, such as evidence of nonapplicability of contact with former workers as specified in § 655.43;

(4) The final recruitment report and any supporting resumes and contact information as specified in § 655.48;

(5) Records of each worker's earnings, hours offered and worked, location(s) of work performed, and other information as specified in § 655.20(i);

(6) If appropriate, records of reimbursement of transportation and subsistence costs incurred by the workers, as specified in § 655.20(j).

(7) Evidence of contact with U.S. workers who applied for the job opportunity in the *Application for Temporary Employment Certification*, including documents demonstrating that any rejections of U.S. workers were for lawful, job-related reasons, as specified in § 655.20(r);

(8) Evidence of contact with any former U.S. worker in the occupation at the place of employment in the *Application for Temporary Employment Certification*, including documents demonstrating that the U.S. worker had been offered the job opportunity in the *Application for Temporary Employment Certification*, as specified in § 655.20(w), and that the U.S. worker either refused the job opportunity or was rejected only for lawful, job-related reasons, as specified in § 655.20(r);

(9) The written contracts with agents or recruiters as specified in §§ 655.8 and 655.9, and the list of the identities and locations of persons hired by or working for the agent or recruiter and these entities' agents or employees, as specified in § 655.9;

(10) Written notice provided to and informing OFLC that an H–2B worker or worker in corresponding employment has separated from employment before the end date of employment specified in the *Application for Temporary Employment Certification*, as specified in § 655.20(y);

(11) The *H–2B Registration*, job order and a copy of the *Application for Temporary Employment Certification* and the original signed Appendix B of the Application. If the *Application for Temporary Employment Certification* and *H–2B Registration* is electronically filed, a printed copy of each adjudicated *Application for Temporary Employment Certification*, including any modifications, amendments or extensions must be signed by the employer as directed by the CO and retained;

(12) The *H–2B Petition*, including all accompanying documents; and

(13) Any collective bargaining agreement(s), individual employment contract(s), or payroll records from the previous year necessary to substantiate any claim that certain incumbent workers are not included in corresponding employment, as specified in § 655.5.

(d) *Availability of documents for enforcement purposes.* An employer must make available to the Administrator,

WHD within 72 hours following a request by the WHD the documents and records required under 29 CFR part 503 and this section so that the Administrator, WHD may copy, transcribe, or inspect them.

§ 655.57 Request for determination based on nonavailability of U.S. workers.

(a) *Standards for requests.* If a temporary labor certification has been partially granted or denied, based on the CO's determination that qualified U.S. workers are available, and, on or after 21 calendar days before the date of need, some or all of those qualified U.S. workers are, in fact no longer available, the employer may request a new temporary labor certification determination from the CO. Prior to making a new determination the CO will promptly ascertain (which may be through the SWA or other sources of information on U.S. worker availability) whether specific qualified replacement U.S. workers are available or can be reasonably expected to be present at the employer's establishment within 72 hours from the date the employer's request was received. The CO will expeditiously, but in no case later than 72 hours after the time a complete request (including the signed statement included in paragraph (b) of this section) is received, make a determination on the request. An employer may appeal a denial of such a determination in accordance with procedures contained in § 655.61.

(b) *Unavailability of U.S. workers.* The employer's request for a new determination must be made directly to the CO by electronic mail or other appropriate means and must be accompanied by a signed statement confirming the employer's assertion. In addition, unless the employer has provided to the CO notification of abandonment or termination of employment as required by § 655.20(y), the employer's signed statement must include the name and contact information of each U.S. worker who became unavailable and must supply the reason why the worker has become unavailable.

(c) *Notification of determination.* If the CO determines that U.S. workers have become unavailable and cannot identify sufficient available U.S. workers who are qualified or who are likely to become available, the CO will grant the employer's request for a new determination. However, this does not preclude an employer from submitting subsequent requests for new determinations, if warranted, based on subsequent facts concerning purported nonavailability of U.S. workers or referred workers not being qualified because of lawful job-related reasons.

§§ 655.58–655.59 [Reserved]

POST CERTIFICATION ACTIVITIES

§ 655.60 Extensions.

An employer may apply for extensions of the period of employment in the following circumstances. A request for extension must be related to weather conditions or other factors beyond the control of the employer (which may include unforeseeable changes in market conditions), and must be supported in writing, with documentation showing why the extension is needed and that the need could not have been reasonably foreseen by the employer. The CO will notify the employer of the decision in writing. Except in extraordinary circumstances, the CO will not grant an extension where the total work period under that *Application for Temporary Employment Certification* and the authorized extension would exceed 9 months for employers whose temporary need is seasonal, peakload, or intermittent, or 3 years for employers that have a one-time occurrence of temporary need. The employer may appeal a denial of a request for an extension by following the procedures in § 655.61. The H–2B employer's assurances and obligations under the temporary labor certification will continue to apply during the extended period of employment. The employer must immediately provide to its workers a copy of any approved extension.

§ 655.61 Administrative review.

(a) *Request for review.* Where authorized in this subpart, employers may request an administrative review before the BALCA of a determination by the CO. In such cases, the request for review:

(1) Must be sent to the BALCA, with a copy simultaneously sent to the CO who issued the determination, within 10 business days from the date of determination;

(2) Must clearly identify the particular determination for which review is sought;

(3) Must set forth the particular grounds for the request;

(4) Must include a copy of the CO's determination; and

(5) May contain only legal argument and such evidence as was actually submitted to the CO before the date the CO's determination was issued.

(b) *Appeal file.* Upon the receipt of a request for review, the CO will, within 7 business days, assemble and submit the Appeal File using means to ensure same day or next day delivery, to the BALCA, the employer, and the Associate Solicitor for Employment and Training Legal Services, Office of the Solicitor, U.S. Department of Labor.

(c) *Briefing schedule.* Within 7 business days of receipt of the Appeal File, the counsel for the CO may submit, using means to ensure same day or next day delivery, a brief in support of the CO's decision.

(d) *Assignment.* The Chief ALJ may designate a single member or a three member panel of the BALCA to consider a particular case.

(e) *Review.* The BALCA must review the CO's determination only on the basis of the Appeal File, the request for review, and any legal briefs submitted and must:

(1) Affirm the CO's determination; or

(2) Reverse or modify the CO's determination; or

(3) Remand to the CO for further action.

(f) *Decision.* The BALCA should notify the employer, the CO, and counsel for the CO of its decision within 7 business days of the submission of the CO's brief or 10 business days after receipt of the Appeal File, whichever is later, using means to ensure same day or next day delivery.

§655.62 Withdrawal of an Application for Temporary Employment Certification.

Employers may withdraw an *Application for Temporary Employment Certification* after it has been accepted and before it is adjudicated. The employer must request such withdrawal in writing.

§655.63 Public disclosure.

The Department of Labor will maintain an electronic file accessible to the public with information on all employers applying for temporary non-agricultural labor certifications. The database will include such information as the number of workers requested, the date filed, the date decided, and the final disposition.

§655.65 Special Document Retention Provisions for Fiscal Years 2017 through 2020 under the Consolidated Appropriations Act.

(a) An employer that files a petition with USCIS to employ H–2B workers in fiscal year 2017 under authority of the temporary increase in the numerical limitation under Public Law 115–31 must maintain for a period of 3 years from the date of certification, consistent with 20 CFR 655.56 and 29 CFR 503.17, the following:

(1) A copy of the attestation filed pursuant to regulations governing that temporary increase;

(2) Evidence establishing that employer's business is likely to suffer irreparable harm (that is, permanent and severe financial loss), if it cannot employ H–2B nonimmigrant workers in fiscal year 2017;

(3) If applicable, evidence of additional recruitment and a recruitment report that meets the requirements set forth in 20 CFR 655.48(a)(1), (2), and (7).

DOL or DHS may inspect these documents upon request.

(b) This section expires on October 1, 2020.

EFFECTIVE DATE NOTE: At 82 FR 32999, July 19, 2017, §655.65 was added, effective July 19, 2017, through Sept. 30, 2020.

§655.66 Special document retention provisions for Fiscal Years 2018 through 2021 under the Consolidated Appropriations Act, 2018, Public Law 115–141.

(a) An employer that files a petition with USCIS to employ H–2B workers in fiscal year 2018 under authority of the temporary increase in the numerical limitation under section 205 of Division M, Public Law 115–141 must maintain for a period of 3 years from the date of certification, consistent with 20 CFR 655.56 and 29 CFR 503.17, the following:

(1) A copy of the attestation filed pursuant to regulations governing that temporary increase;

(2) Evidence establishing that employer's business is likely to suffer irreparable harm (that is, permanent and severe financial loss), if it cannot employ H–2B nonimmigrant workers in fiscal year 2018; and

(3) If applicable, evidence of additional recruitment and a recruitment report that meets the requirements set forth in 20 CFR 655.48(a)(1), (2), and (7).

DOL or DHS may inspect these documents upon request.

(b) This section expires on October 1, 2021.

EFFECTIVE DATE NOTE: At 83 FR 24918, May 31, 2018, § 655.66 was added, effective May 31, 2018 through Sept. 30, 2021.

§ 655.67–655.69 [Reserved]

INTEGRITY MEASURES

§ 655.70 Audits.

The CO may conduct audits of adjudicated temporary employment certification applications.

(a) *Discretion.* The CO has the sole discretion to choose the applications selected for audit.

(b) *Audit letter.* Where an application is selected for audit, the CO will send an audit letter to the employer and a copy, if appropriate, to the employer's attorney or agent. The audit letter will:

(1) Specify the documentation that must be submitted by the employer;

(2) Specify a date, no more than 30 calendar days from the date the audit letter is issued, by which the required documentation must be sent to the CO; and

(3) Advise that failure to fully comply with the audit process may result:

(i) In the requirement that the employer undergo the assisted recruitment procedures in § 655.71 in future filings of H–2B temporary employment certification applications for a period of up to 2 years, or

(ii) In a revocation of the certification and/or debarment from the H–2B program and any other foreign labor certification program administered by the Department Labor.

(c) *Supplemental information request.* During the course of the audit examination, the CO may request supplemental information and/or documentation from the employer in order to complete the audit. If circumstances warrant, the CO can issue one or more requests for supplemental information.

(d) *Potential referrals.* In addition to measures in this subpart, the CO may decide to provide the audit findings and underlying documentation to DHS, WHD, or other appropriate enforcement agencies. The CO may refer any findings that an employer discouraged a qualified U.S. worker from applying, or failed to hire, discharged, or otherwise discriminated against a qualified U.S. worker to the Department of Justice, Civil Rights Division, Office of Special Counsel for Unfair Immigration Related Employment Practices.

§ 655.71 CO-ordered assisted recruitment.

(a) *Requirement of assisted recruitment.* If, as a result of audit or otherwise, the CO determines that a violation has occurred that does not warrant debarment, the CO may require the employer to engage in assisted recruitment for a defined period of time for any future *Application for Temporary Employment Certification.*

(b) *Notification of assisted recruitment.* The CO will notify the employer (and its attorney or agent, if applicable) in writing of the assisted recruitment that will be required of the employer for a period of up to 2 years from the date the notice is issued. The notification will state the reasons for the imposition of the additional requirements, state that the employer's agreement to accept the conditions will constitute their inclusion as bona fide conditions and terms of an application for temporary employment certification, and offer the employer an opportunity to request an administrative review. If administrative review is requested, the procedures in § 655.61 apply.

(c) *Assisted recruitment.* The assisted recruitment process will be in addition to any recruitment required of the employer by §§ 655.41 through 655.46 and may consist of, but is not limited to, one or more of the following:

(1) Requiring the employer to submit a draft advertisement to the CO for review and approval at the time of filing the *Application for Temporary Employment Certification;*

(2) Designating the sources where the employer must recruit for U.S. workers, including newspapers and other publications, and directing the employer to place the advertisement(s) in such sources;

(3) Extending the length of the placement of the advertisement and/or job order;

(4) Requiring the employer to notify the CO and the SWA in writing when the advertisement(s) are placed;

(5) Requiring an employer to perform any additional assisted recruitment directed by the CO;

(6) Requiring the employer to provide proof of the publication of all advertisements as directed by the CO, in addition to providing a copy of the job order;

(7) Requiring the employer to provide proof of all SWA referrals made in response to the job order;

(8) Requiring the employer to submit any proof of contact with all referrals and past U.S. workers; and/or

(9) Requiring the employer to provide any additional documentation verifying it conducted the assisted recruitment as directed by the CO.

(d) *Failure to comply.* If an employer materially fails to comply with requirements ordered by the CO under this section, the certification will be denied and the employer and/or its attorney or agent may be debarred under § 655.73.

§ 655.72 Revocation.

(a) *Basis for DOL revocation.* The Administrator, OFLC may revoke a temporary labor certification approved under this subpart, if the Administrator, OFLC finds:

(1) The issuance of the temporary labor certification was not justified due to fraud or willful misrepresentation of a material fact in the application process, as defined in § 655.73(d);

(2) The employer substantially failed to comply with any of the terms or conditions of the approved temporary labor certification. A substantial failure is a willful failure to comply that constitutes a significant deviation from the terms and conditions of the approved certification and is further defined in § 655.73(d) and (e);

(3) The employer failed to cooperate with a DOL investigation or with a DOL official performing an investigation, inspection, audit (under § 655.73), or law enforcement function under 29 CFR part 503 or this subpart; or

(4) The employer failed to comply with one or more sanctions or remedies imposed by WHD, or with one or more decisions or orders of the Secretary with the respect to the H–2B program.

(b) *DOL procedures for revocation*—(1) *Notice of Revocation.* If the Administrator, OFLC makes a determination to revoke an employer's temporary labor certification, the Administrator, OFLC will send to the employer (and its attorney or agent, if applicable) a Notice of Revocation. The notice will contain a detailed statement of the grounds for the revocation and inform the employer of its right to submit rebuttal evidence or to appeal. If the employer does not file rebuttal evidence or an appeal within 10 business days from the date the Notice of Revocation is issued, the notice is the final agency action and will take effect immediately at the end of the 10-day period.

(2) *Rebuttal.* If the employer timely submits rebuttal evidence, the Administrator, OFLC will inform the employer of the final determination on the revocation within 10 business days of receiving the rebuttal evidence. If the Administrator, OFLC determines that the certification should be revoked, the Administrator, OFLC will inform the employer of its right to appeal according to the procedures of § 655.61. If the employer does not appeal the final determination, it will become the final agency action.

(3) *Appeal.* An employer may appeal a Notice of Revocation, or a final determination of the Administrator, OFLC after the review of rebuttal evidence, according to the appeal procedures of § 655.61. The ALJ's decision is the final agency action.

(4) *Stay.* The timely filing of rebuttal evidence or an administrative appeal will stay the revocation pending the outcome of those proceedings.

(5) *Decision.* If the temporary labor certification is revoked, the Administrator, OFLC will send a copy of the final agency action to DHS and the Department of State.

(c) *Employer's obligations in the event of revocation.* If an employer's temporary labor certification is revoked, the employer is responsible for:

(1) Reimbursement of actual inbound transportation and other expenses;

(2) The workers' outbound transportation expenses;

(3) Payment to the workers of the amount due under the three-fourths guarantee; and

(4) Any other wages, benefits, and working conditions due or owing to the workers under this subpart.

§ 655.73 Debarment.

(a) *Debarment of an employer.* The Administrator, OFLC may not issue future labor certifications under this subpart to an employer or any successor in interest to that employer, subject to the time limits set forth in paragraph (c) of this section, if the Administrator, OFLC finds that the employer committed the following violations:

(1) Willful misrepresentation of a material fact in its *H–2B Registration, Application for Prevailing Wage Determination, Application for Temporary Employment Certification,* or *H–2B Petition;*

(2) Substantial failure to meet any of the terms and conditions of its *H–2B Registration, Application for Prevailing Wage Determination, Application for Temporary Employment Certification,* or *H–2B Petition.* A substantial failure is a willful failure to comply that constitutes a significant deviation from the terms and conditions of such documents; or

(3) Willful misrepresentation of a material fact to the DOS during the visa application process.

(b) *Debarment of an agent or attorney.* If the Administrator, OFLC finds, under this section, that an attorney or agent committed a violation as described in paragraphs (a)(1) through (3) of this section or participated in an employer's violation, the Administrator, OFLC may not issue future labor certifications to an employer represented by such agent or attorney, subject to the time limits set forth in paragraph (c) of this section.

(c) *Period of debarment.* Debarment under this subpart may not be for less than 1 year or more than 5 years from the date of the final agency decision.

(d) *Determining whether a violation is willful.* A willful misrepresentation of a material fact or a willful failure to meet the required terms and conditions occurs when the employer, attorney, or agent knows a statement is false or that the conduct is in violation, or shows reckless disregard for the truthfulness of its representation or for whether its conduct satisfies the required conditions.

(e) *Determining whether a violation is significant.* In determining whether a violation is a significant deviation from the terms and conditions of the *H–2B Registration, Application for Prevailing Wage Determination, Application for Temporary Employment Certification,* or *H–2B Petition,* the factors that the Administrator, OFLC may consider include, but are not limited to, the following:

(1) Previous history of violation(s) under the H–2B program;

(2) The number of H–2B workers, workers in corresponding employment, or improperly rejected U.S. applicants who were and/or are affected by the violation(s);

(3) The gravity of the violation(s);

(4) The extent to which the violator achieved a financial gain due to the violation(s), or the potential financial loss or potential injury to the worker(s); and

(5) Whether U.S. workers have been harmed by the violation.

(f) *Violations.* Where the standards set forth in paragraphs (d) and (e) in this section are met, debarrable violations would include but would not be limited to one or more acts of commission or omission which involve:

(1) Failure to pay or provide the required wages, benefits or working conditions to the employer's H–2B workers and/or workers in corresponding employment;

(2) Failure, except for lawful, job-related reasons, to offer employment to qualified U.S. workers who applied for the job opportunity for which certification was sought;

(3) Failure to comply with the employer's obligations to recruit U.S. workers;

(4) Improper layoff or displacement of U.S. workers or workers in corresponding employment;

(5) Failure to comply with one or more sanctions or remedies imposed by the Administrator, WHD for violation(s) of obligations under the job order or other H–2B obligations, or with one or more decisions or orders of the Secretary or a court under this subpart or 29 CFR part 503;

(6) Failure to comply with the Notice of Deficiency process under this subpart;

(7) Failure to comply with the assisted recruitment process under this subpart;

(8) Impeding an investigation of an employer under 29 CFR part 503 or an audit under this subpart;

(9) Employing an H–2B worker outside the area of intended employment, in an activity/activities not listed in the job order, or outside the validity period of employment of the job order, including any approved extension thereof;

(10) A violation of the requirements of § 655.20(o) or (p);

(11) A violation of any of the provisions listed in § 655.20(r);

(12) Any other act showing such flagrant disregard for the law that future compliance with program requirements cannot reasonably be expected;

(13) Fraud involving the *H–2B Registration*, *Application for Prevailing Wage Determination*, *Application for Temporary Employment Certification*, or the *H–2B Petition;* or

(14) A material misrepresentation of fact during the registration or application process.

(g) *Debarment procedure*—(1) *Notice of Debarment.* If the Administrator, OFLC makes a determination to debar an employer, attorney, or agent, the Administrator, OFLC will send the party a Notice of Debarment. The Notice will state the reason for the debarment finding, including a detailed explanation of the grounds for and the duration of the debarment and inform the party subject to the notice of its right to submit rebuttal evidence or to request a debarment hearing. If the party does not file rebuttal evidence or request a hearing within 30 calendar days of the date of the Notice of Debarment, the notice is the final agency action and the debarment will take effect at the end of the 30-day period. The timely filing of an rebuttal evidence or a request for a hearing stays the debarment pending the outcome of the appeal as provided in paragraphs (g)(2) through (6) of this section.

(2) *Rebuttal.* The party who received the Notice of Debarment may choose to submit evidence to rebut the grounds stated in the notice within 30 calendar days of the date the notice is issued. If rebuttal evidence is timely filed, the Administrator, OFLC will issue a final determination on the debarment within 30 calendar days of receiving the rebuttal evidence. If the Administrator, OFLC determines that the party should be debarred, the Administrator, OFLC will inform the party of its right to request a debarment hearing according to the procedures in this section. The party must request a hearing within 30 calendar days after the date of the Administrator, OFLC's final determination, or the Administrator OFLC's determination will be the final agency order and the debarment will take effect at the end of the 30-day period.

(3) *Hearing.* The recipient of a Notice of Debarment seeking to challenge the debarment must request a debarment hearing within 30 calendar days of the date of a Notice of Debarment or the date of a final determination of the Administrator, OFLC after review of rebuttal evidence submitted under paragraph (g)(2) of this section. To obtain a debarment hearing, the recipient must, within 30 days of the date of the Notice or the final determination, file a written request with the Chief ALJ, United States Department of Labor, 800 K Street NW., Suite 400–N, Washington, DC 20001–8002, and simultaneously serve a copy on the Administrator, OFLC. The debarment will take effect

30 calendar days from the date the Notice of Debarment or final determination is issued, unless a request for review is timely filed. Within 10 business days of receipt of the request for a hearing, the Administrator, OFLC will send a certified copy of the ETA case file to the Chief ALJ by means normally assuring next day delivery. The Chief ALJ will immediately assign an ALJ to conduct the hearing. The procedures in 29 CFR part 18 apply to such hearings, except that the request for a hearing will not be considered to be a complaint to which an answer is required.

(4) *Decision.* After the hearing, the ALJ must affirm, reverse, or modify the Administrator, OFLC's determination. The ALJ will prepare the decision within 60 calendar days after completion of the hearing and closing of the record. The ALJ's decision will be provided to the parties to the debarment hearing by means normally assuring next day delivery. The ALJ's decision is the final agency action, unless either party, within 30 calendar days of the ALJ's decision, seeks review of the decision with the Administrative Review Board (ARB).

(5) *Review by the ARB.* (i) Any party wishing review of the decision of an ALJ must, within 30 calendar days of the decision of the ALJ, petition the ARB to review the decision. Copies of the petition must be served on all parties and on the ALJ. The ARB will decide whether to accept the petition within 30 calendar days of receipt. If the ARB declines to accept the petition, or if the ARB does not issue a notice accepting a petition within 30 calendar days after the receipt of a timely filing of the petition, the decision of the ALJ is the final agency action. If a petition for review is accepted, the decision of the ALJ will be stayed unless and until the ARB issues an order affirming the decision. The ARB must serve notice of its decision to accept or not to accept the petition upon the ALJ and upon all parties to the proceeding.

(ii) Upon receipt of the ARB's notice to accept the petition, the Office of Administrative Law Judges will promptly forward a copy of the complete hearing record to the ARB.

(iii) Where the ARB has determined to review the decision and order, the ARB will notify each party of the issue(s) raised, the form in which submissions must be made (e.g., briefs or oral argument), and the time within which the presentation must be submitted.

(6) *ARB Decision.* The ARB's final decision must be issued within 90 calendar days from the notice granting the petition and served upon all parties and the ALJ.

(h) *Concurrent debarment jurisdiction.* OFLC and the WHD have concurrent jurisdiction to debar under this section or under 29 CFR 503.24. When considering debarment, OFLC and the WHD will coordinate their activities. A specific violation for which debarment is imposed will be cited in a single debarment proceeding. Copies of final debarment decisions will be forwarded to DHS and DOS promptly.

(i) *Debarment from other foreign labor programs.* Upon debarment under this subpart or 29 CFR 503.24, the debarred party will be disqualified from filing any labor certification applications or labor condition applications with the Department of Labor by, or on behalf of, the debarred party for the same period of time set forth in the final debarment decision.

§§ 655.74–655.76 [Reserved]

§§ 655.80–655.99 [Reserved]

Subpart B—Labor Certification Process for Temporary Agricultural Employment in the United States (H–2A Workers)

SOURCE: 75 FR 6959, Feb. 12, 2010, unless otherwise noted.

§ 655.100 Scope and purpose of subpart B.

This subpart sets out the procedures established by the Secretary of the United States Department of Labor (the Secretary) under the authority given in 8 U.S.C. 1188 to acquire information sufficient to make factual determinations of:

(a) Whether there are sufficient able, willing, and qualified United States (U.S.) workers available to perform the temporary and seasonal agricultural employment for which an employer desires to import nonimmigrant foreign workers (H–2A workers); and

(b) Whether the employment of H–2A workers will adversely affect the wages and working conditions of workers in the U.S. similarly employed.

§655.101 Authority of the Office of Foreign Labor Certification (OFLC) Administrator.

The Secretary has delegated her authority to make determinations under 8 U.S.C. 1188 to the Assistant Secretary for the Employment and Training Administration (ETA), who in turn has delegated that authority to the Office of Foreign Labor Certification (OFLC). The determinations are made by the OFLC Administrator who, in turn, may delegate this responsibility to designated staff members; e.g., a Certifying Officer (CO).

§655.102 Special procedures.

To provide for a limited degree of flexibility in carrying out the Secretary's responsibilities under the Immigration and Nationality Act (INA), while not deviating from statutory requirements, the OFLC Administrator has the authority to establish, continue, revise, or revoke special procedures for processing certain H–2A applications. Employers must demonstrate upon written application to the OFLC Administrator that special procedures are necessary. These include special procedures currently in effect for the handling of applications for sheepherders in the Western States (and adaptation of such procedures to occupations in the range production of other livestock), and for custom combine harvesting crews. Similarly, for work in occupations characterized by other than a reasonably regular workday or workweek, such as the range production of sheep or other livestock, the OFLC Administrator has the authority to establish monthly, weekly, or semi-monthly adverse effect wage rates (AEWR) for those occupations for a statewide or other geographical area. Prior to making determinations under this section, the OFLC Administrator may consult with affected employer and worker representatives. Special Procedures in place on the effective date of this regulation will remain in force until modified by the Administrator.

§655.103 Overview of this subpart and definition of terms.

(a) *Overview.* In order to bring nonimmigrant workers to the U.S. to perform agricultural work, an employer must first demonstrate to the Secretary that there are not sufficient U.S. workers able, willing, and qualified to perform the work in the area of intended employment at the time needed and that the employment of foreign workers will not adversely affect the wages and working conditions of U.S. workers similarly employed. This rule describes a process by which the Department of Labor (Department or DOL) makes such a determination and certifies its determination to the Department of Homeland Security (DHS).

(b) *Definitions.* For the purposes of this subpart:

Administrative Law Judge (ALJ). A person within the Department's Office of Administrative Law Judges appointed pursuant to 5 U.S.C. 3105.

Adverse effect wage rate (AEWR). The annual weighted average hourly wage for field and livestock workers (combined) in the States or regions as published annually by the U.S. Department of Agriculture (USDA) based on its quarterly wage survey.

Agent. A legal entity or person, such as an association of agricultural employers, or an attorney for an association, that:

(1) Is authorized to act on behalf of the employer for temporary agricultural labor certification purposes;

(2) Is not itself an employer, or a joint employer, as defined in this subpart with respect to a specific application; and

(3) Is not under suspension, debarment, expulsion, or disbarment from practice before any court, the Department, the Executive Office for Immigration Review, or DHS under 8 CFR 292.3 or 1003.101.

Agricultural association. Any nonprofit or cooperative association of farmers, growers, or ranchers (including but not limited to processing establishments, canneries, gins, packing sheds, nurseries, or other similar fixed-site agricultural employers), incorporated or qualified under applicable State law, that recruits, solicits, hires, employs, furnishes, houses, or transports any worker that is subject to 8 U.S.C. 1188. An agricultural association may act as the agent of an employer, or may act as the sole or joint employer of any worker subject to 8 U.S.C. 1188.

Area of intended employment. The geographic area within normal commuting distance of the place of the job opportunity for which the certification is sought. There is no rigid measure of distance that constitutes a normal commuting distance or normal commuting area, because there may be widely varying factual circumstances among different areas (e.g., average commuting times, barriers to reaching the worksite, or quality of the regional transportation network). If the place of intended employment is within a Metropolitan Statistical Area (MSA), including a multistate MSA, any place within the MSA is deemed to be within normal commuting distance of the place of intended employment. The borders of MSAs are not controlling in the identification of the normal commuting area; a location outside of an MSA may be within normal commuting distance of a location that is inside (e.g., near the border of) the MSA.

Attorney. Any person who is a member in good standing of the bar of the highest court of any State, possession, territory, or commonwealth of the U.S., or the District of Columbia. Such a person is also permitted to act as an agent under this subpart. No attorney who is under suspension, debarment, expulsion, or disbarment from practice before any court, the Department, the Executive Office for Immigration Review under 8 CFR 1003.101, or DHS under 8 CFR 292.3 may represent an employer under this subpart.

Certifying Officer (CO). The person who makes determination on an *Application for Temporary Employment Certification* filed under the H–2A program. The OFLC Administrator is the national CO. Other COs may be designated by the OFLC Administrator to also make the determinations required under this subpart.

Corresponding employment. The employment of workers who are not H–2A workers by an employer who has an approved H–2A *Application for Temporary Employment Certification* in any work included in the job order, or in any agricultural work performed by the H–2A workers. To qualify as corresponding employment the work must be performed during the validity period of the job order, including any approved extension thereof.

Date of need. The first date the employer requires the services of H–2A workers as indicated in the *Application for Temporary Employment Certification.*

Employee. A person who is engaged to perform work for an employer, as defined under the general common law of agency. Some of the factors relevant to the determination of employee status include: The hiring party's right to control the manner and means by which the work is accomplished; the skill required to perform the work; the source of the instrumentalities and tools for accomplishing the work; the location of the work; the hiring party's discretion over when and how long to work; and whether the work is part of the regular business of the hiring party. Other applicable factors may be considered and no one factor is dispositive.

Employer. A person (including any individual, partnership, association, corporation, cooperative, firm, joint stock company, trust, or other organization with legal rights and duties) that:

(1) Has a place of business (physical location) in the U.S. and a means by which it may be contacted for employment;

(2) Has an employer relationship (such as the ability to hire, pay, fire, supervise or otherwise control the work of employee) with respect to an H–2A worker or a worker in corresponding employment; and

(3) Possesses, for purposes of filing an *Application for Temporary Employment Certification,* a valid Federal Employer Identification Number (FEIN).

Federal holiday. Legal public holiday as defined at 5 U.S.C. 6103.

Fixed-site employer. Any person engaged in agriculture who meets the definition of an employer, as those terms are defined in this subpart, who owns or operates a farm, ranch, processing establishment, cannery, gin, packing shed, nursery, or other similar fixed-site location where agricultural activities are performed and who recruits, solicits, hires, employs, houses, or transports any worker subject to 8 U.S.C. 1188, 29 CFR part 501, or this subpart as incident to or in conjunction with the owner's or operator's own agricultural operation.

H–2A Labor Contractor (H–2ALC). Any person who meets the definition of employer under this subpart and is not a fixed-site employer, an agricultural association, or an employee of a fixed-site employer or agricultural association, as those terms are used in this part, who recruits, solicits, hires, employs, furnishes, houses, or transports any worker subject to 8 U.S.C. 1188, 29 CFR part 501, or this subpart.

H–2A worker. Any temporary foreign worker who is lawfully present in the U.S. and authorized by DHS to perform agricultural labor or services of a temporary or seasonal nature pursuant to 8 U.S.C. 1101(a)(15)(H)(ii)(a), as amended.

Job offer. The offer made by an employer or potential employer of H–2A workers to both U.S. and H–2A workers describing all the material terms and conditions of employment, including those relating to wages, working conditions, and other benefits.

Job opportunity. Full-time employment at a place in the U.S. to which U.S. workers can be referred.

Job Order. The document containing the material terms and conditions of employment that is posted by the State Workforce Agency (SWA) on its inter- and intra-state job clearance systems based on the employer's *Agricultural and Food Processing Clearance Order* (Form ETA–790), as submitted to the SWA.

Joint employment. Where two or more employers each have sufficient definitional indicia of being an employer to be considered the employer of a worker, those employers will be considered to jointly employ that worker. Each employer in a joint employment relationship to a worker is considered a joint employer of that worker.

Master application. An *Application for Temporary Employment Certification* filed by an association of agricultural producers as a joint employer with its employer-members. A master application must cover the same occupations or comparable agricultural employment; the same start date of need for all employer-members listed on the *Application for Temporary Employment Certification;* and may cover multiple areas of intended employment within a single State but no more than two contiguous States.

National Processing Center (NPC). The office within OFLC in which the COs operate and which are charged with the adjudication of *Applications for Temporary Employment Certification.*

Office of Foreign Labor Certification (OFLC). OFLC means the organizational component of the ETA that provides national leadership and policy guidance and develops regulations and procedures to carry out the responsibilities of the Secretary under the INA concerning the admission of foreign workers to the U.S. to perform work described in 8 U.S.C. 1101(a)(15)(H)(ii)(a).

OFLC Administrator. The primary official of the Office of Foreign Labor Certification (OFLC), or the OFLC Administrator's designee.

Positive recruitment. The active participation of an employer or its authorized hiring agent, performed under the auspices and direction of the OFLC, in recruiting and interviewing individuals in the area where the employer's job opportunity is located and any other State designated by the Secretary as an area of traditional or expected labor supply with respect to the area where the employer's job opportunity is located, in an effort to fill specific job openings with U.S. workers.

Prevailing practice. A practice engaged in by employers, that:

(1) Fifty percent or more of employers in an area and for an occupation engage in the practice or offer the benefit; and

(2) This 50 percent or more of employers also employs 50 percent or more of U.S. workers in the occupation and area (including H–2A and non-H–2A employers) for purposes of determinations concerning the provision of family housing, and frequency of wage payments, but non-H–2A employers only

for determinations concerning the provision of advance transportation and the utilization of labor contractors.

Prevailing wage. Wage established pursuant to 20 CFR 653.501(d)(4).

State Workforce Agency (SWA). State government agency that receives funds pursuant to the Wagner-Peyser Act (29 U.S.C. 49 *et seq.*) to administer the State's public labor exchange activities.

Strike. A concerted stoppage of work by employees as a result of a labor dispute, or any concerted slowdown or other concerted interruption of operation (including stoppage by reason of the expiration of a collective bargaining agreement).

Successor in interest. (1) Where an employer has violated 8 U.S.C. 1188, 29 CFR part 501, or these regulations, and has ceased doing business or cannot be located for purposes of enforcement, a successor in interest to that employer may be held liable for the duties and obligations of the violating employer in certain circumstances. The following factors, as used under Title VII of the Civil Rights Act and the Vietnam Era Veterans' Readjustment Assistance Act, may be considered in determining whether an employer is a successor in interest; no one factor is dispositive, but all of the circumstances will be considered as a whole:

(i) Substantial continuity of the same business operations;

(ii) Use of the same facilities;

(iii) Continuity of the work force;

(iv) Similarity of jobs and working conditions;

(v) Similarity of supervisory personnel;

(vi) Whether the former management or owner retains a direct or indirect interest in the new enterprise;

(vii) Similarity in machinery, equipment, and production methods;

(viii) Similarity of products and services; and

(ix) The ability of the predecessor to provide relief.

(2) For purposes of debarment only, the primary consideration will be the personal involvement of the firm's ownership, management, supervisors, and others associated with the firm in the violation(s) at issue.

Temporary agricultural labor certification. Certification made by the OFLC Administrator with respect to an employer seeking to file with DHS a visa petition to employ one or more foreign nationals as an H–2A worker, pursuant to 8 U.S.C. 1101(a)(15)(H)(ii)(a), 1184(a) and (c), and 1188.

United States (U.S.). The continental U.S., Alaska, Hawaii, the Commonwealth of Puerto Rico, and the territories of Guam, the U.S. Virgin Islands, and the Commonwealth of the Northern Mariana Islands (CNMI).

United States worker (U.S. worker). A worker who is:

(1) A citizen or national of the U.S.; or

(2) An alien who is lawfully admitted for permanent residence in the U.S., is admitted as a refugee under 8 U.S.C. 1157, is granted asylum under 8 U.S.C. 1158, or is an immigrant otherwise authorized (by the INA or by DHS) to be employed in the U.S.; or

(3) An individual who is not an unauthorized alien (as defined in 8 U.S.C. 1324a(h)(3)) with respect to the employment in which the worker is engaging.

Wages. All forms of cash remuneration to a worker by an employer in payment for personal services.

Work contract. All the material terms and conditions of employment relating to wages, hours, working conditions, and other benefits, including those required by 8 U.S.C. 1188, 29 CFR part 501, or this subpart. The contract between the employer and the worker may be in the form of a separate written document. In the absence of a separate written work contract incorporating the required terms and conditions of employment, agreed to by both the employer and the worker, the work contract at a minimum will be the terms of the job order and any obligations required under 8 U.S.C. 1188, 28 CFR part 501, or this subpart.

(c) *Definition of agricultural labor or services.* For the purposes of this subpart, agricultural labor or services, pursuant to 8 U.S.C. 1101(a)(15)(H)(ii)(a), is defined as: agricultural labor as defined and applied in sec. 3121(g) of the Internal Revenue Code of 1986 at 26 U.S.C. 3121(g); agriculture as defined and applied in sec. 3(f) of the Fair Labor Standards Act of

1938 (FLSA) at 29 U.S.C. 203(f); the pressing of apples for cider on a farm; or logging employment. An occupation included in either statutory definition is agricultural labor or services, notwithstanding the exclusion of that occupation from the other statutory definition. For informational purposes, the statutory provisions are listed below.

(1)(i) *Agricultural labor* for the purpose of paragraph (c) of this section means all service performed:

(A) On a farm, in the employ of any person, in connection with cultivating the soil, or in connection with raising or harvesting any agricultural or horticultural commodity, including the raising, shearing, feeding, caring for, training, and management of livestock, bees, poultry, and fur-bearing animals and wildlife;

(B) In the employ of the owner or tenant or other operator of a farm, in connection with the operation, management, conservation, improvement, or maintenance of such farm and its tools and equipment, or in salvaging timber or clearing land of brush and other debris left by a hurricane, if the major part of such service is performed on a farm;

(C) In connection with the production or harvesting of any commodity defined as an agricultural commodity in section 15(g) of the Agricultural Marketing Act, as amended (12 U.S.C. 1141j), or in connection with the ginning of cotton, or in connection with the operation or maintenance of ditches, canals, reservoirs, or waterways, not owned or operated for profit, used exclusively for supplying and storing water for farming purposes;

(D) In the employ of the operator of a farm in handling, planting, drying, packing, packaging, processing, freezing, grading, storing, or delivering to storage or to market or to a carrier for transportation to market, in its unmanufactured state, any agricultural or horticultural commodity; but only if such operator produced more than one-half of the commodity with respect to which such service is performed;

(E) In the employ of a group of operators of farms (other than a cooperative organization) in the performance of service described in paragraph (c)(1)(iv) of this section but only if such operators produced all of the commodity with respect to which such service is performed. For purposes of this paragraph, any unincorporated group of operators shall be deemed a cooperative organization if the number of operators comprising such group is more than 20 at any time during the calendar year in which such service is performed;

(F) The provisions of paragraphs (c)(1)(iv) and (c)(1)(v) of this section shall not be deemed to be applicable with respect to service performed in connection with commercial canning or commercial freezing or in connection with any agricultural or horticultural commodity after its delivery to a terminal market for distribution for consumption; or

(G) On a farm operated for profit if such service is not in the course of the employer's trade or business or is domestic service in a private home of the employer.

(ii) As used in this section, the term farm includes stock, dairy, poultry, fruit, fur-bearing animal, and truck farms, plantations, ranches, nurseries, ranges, greenhouses or other similar structures used primarily for the raising of agricultural or horticultural commodities, and orchards.

(2) *Agriculture*. For purposes of paragraph (c) of this section, agriculture means farming in all its branches and among other things includes the cultivation and tillage of the soil, dairying, the production, cultivation, growing, and harvesting of any agricultural or horticultural commodities (including commodities defined as agricultural commodities in 1141j(g) of title 12, the raising of livestock, bees, fur-bearing animals, or poultry, and any practices (including any forestry or lumbering operations) performed by a farmer or on a farm as an incident to or in conjunction with such farming operations, including preparation for market, delivery to storage or to market or to carriers for transportation to market. See sec. 29 U.S.C. 203(f), as amended (sec. 3(f) of the FLSA, as codified). Under 12 U.S.C. 1141j(g) agricultural commodities include, in addition to other agricultural commodities, crude gum (oleoresin) from a living tree, and the following products as processed by the original producer of

the crude gum (oleoresin) from which derived: gum spirits of turpentine and gum rosin. In addition as defined in 7 U.S.C. 92, gum spirits of turpentine means spirits of turpentine made from gum (oleoresin) from a living tree and gum rosin means rosin remaining after the distillation of gum spirits of turpentine.

(3) *Apple pressing for cider.* The pressing of apples for cider on a farm, as the term farm is defined and applied in sec. 3121(g) of the Internal Revenue Code at 26 U.S.C. 3121(g) or as applied in sec. 3(f) of the FLSA at 29 U.S.C. 203(f), pursuant to 29 CFR part 780.

(4) *Logging employment.* Operations associated with felling and moving trees and logs from the stump to the point of delivery, such as, but not limited to, marking danger trees and trees/logs to be cut to length, felling, limbing, bucking, debarking, chipping, yarding, loading, unloading, storing, and transporting machines, equipment and personnel to, from and between logging sites.

(d) *Definition of a temporary or seasonal nature.* For the purposes of this subpart, employment is of a seasonal nature where it is tied to a certain time of year by an event or pattern, such as a short annual growing cycle or a specific aspect of a longer cycle, and requires labor levels far above those necessary for ongoing operations. Employment is of a temporary nature where the employer's need to fill the position with a temporary worker will, except in extraordinary circumstances, last no longer than 1 year.

PREFILING PROCEDURES

§655.120 Offered wage rate.

(a) To comply with its obligation under §655.122(l), an employer must offer, advertise in its recruitment, and pay a wage that is the highest of the AEWR, the prevailing hourly wage or piece rate, the agreed-upon collective bargaining wage, or the Federal or State minimum wage, except where a special procedure is approved for an occupation or specific class of agricultural employment.

(b) If the prevailing hourly wage rate or piece rate is adjusted during a work contract, and is higher than the highest of the AEWR, the prevailing wage, the agreed-upon collective bargaining wage, or the Federal or State minimum wage, in effect at the time the work is performed, the employer must pay that higher prevailing wage or piece rate, upon notice to the employer by the Department.

(c) The OFLC Administrator will publish, at least once in each calendar year, on a date to be determined by the OFLC Administrator, the AEWRs for each State as a notice in the FEDERAL REGISTER.

§655.121 Job orders.

(a) *Area of intended employment.* (1) Prior to filing an *Application for Temporary Employment Certification*, the employer must submit a job order, Form ETA–790, to the SWA serving the area of intended employment for intrastate clearance, identifying it as a job order to be placed in connection with a future *Application for Temporary Employment Certification* for H–2A workers. The employer must submit this job order no more than 75 calendar days and no fewer than 60 calendar days before the date of need. If the job opportunity is located in more than one State within the same area of intended employment, the employer may submit a job order to any one of the SWAs having jurisdiction over the anticipated worksites.

(2) Where the job order is being placed in connection with a future master application to be filed by an association of agricultural employers as a joint employer, the association may submit a single job order to be placed in the name of the association on behalf of all employers that will be duly named on the *Application for Temporary Employment Certification.*

(3) The job order submitted to the SWA must satisfy the requirements for agricultural clearance orders in 20 CFR part 653, subpart F and the requirements set forth in §655.122.

(b) *SWA review.* (1) The SWA will review the contents of the job order for compliance with the requirements specified in 20 CFR part 653, subpart F and this subpart, and will work with the employer to address any noted deficiencies. The SWA must notify the employer in writing of any deficiencies in its job order no later than 7 calendar days after it has been submitted. The SWA notification will direct the employer to respond to the noted deficiencies. The employer must respond to the deficiencies noted by the SWA within 5 calendar days after receipt of the SWA notification. The SWA must respond to the employer's response within 3 calendar days.

(2) If, after providing responses to the deficiencies noted by the SWA, the employer is not able to resolve the deficiencies with the SWA, the employer may file an *Application for Temporary Employment Certification* pursuant to the emergency filing procedures contained in §655.134, with a statement describing the nature of the dispute and demonstrating compliance with its requirements under this section. In the event the SWA does not respond within the stated timelines, the employer may use the emergency filing procedures noted above. If upon review of the *Application for Temporary Employment Certification* and the job order and all other relevant information, the CO concludes that the job order is acceptable, the CO will direct the SWA to place the job order into intrastate and interstate clearance and otherwise process the Application in accordance with the procedures contained in §655.134(c). If the CO determines the job order is not acceptable, the CO will issue a Notice of Deficiency to the employer under §655.143 of this subpart directing the employer to modify the job order pursuant to paragraph (e) of this section The Notice of Deficiency will offer the employer the right to appeal.

(c) *Intrastate clearance.* Upon its clearance of the job order, the SWA must promptly place the job order in intrastate clearance and commence recruitment of U.S. workers. Where the employer's job order references an area of intended employment which falls within the jurisdiction of more than one SWA, the originating SWA will also forward a copy of the approved job order to the other SWAs serving the area of intended employment.

(d) *Duration of job order posting.* The SWA must keep the job order on its active file until the end of the recruitment period, as set forth in §655.135(d), and must refer each U.S. worker who applies (or on whose behalf an *Application for Temporary Employment Certification* is made) for the job opportunity.

(e) *Modifications to the job order.* (1) Prior to the issuance of the final determination, the CO may require modifications to the job order when the CO determines that the offer of employment does not contain all the minimum benefits, wages, and working condition provisions. Such modifications must be made or certification will be denied pursuant to §655.164 of this subpart.

(2) The employer may request a modification of the job order, Form ETA–790, prior to the submission of an *Application for Temporary Employment Certification.* However, the employer may not reject referrals against the job order based upon a failure on the part of the applicant to meet the amended criteria, if such referral was made prior to the amendment of the job order. The employer may not amend the job order on or after the date of filing an *Application for Temporary Employment Certification.*

(3) The employer must provide all workers recruited in connection with the *Application for Temporary Employment Certification* with a copy of the modified job order or work contract which reflects the amended terms and conditions, on the first day of employment, in accordance with §655.122(q), or as soon as practicable, whichever comes first.

§655.122 Contents of job offers.

(a) *Prohibition against preferential treatment of aliens.* The employer's job offer must offer to U.S. workers no less than the same benefits, wages, and working conditions that the employer is offering, intends to offer, or will provide to H–2A workers. Job offers may not impose on U.S. workers any restrictions or obligations that will not be imposed on the employer's H–2A workers. This does not relieve the employer from providing to H–2A workers at least the same level of minimum benefits, wages, and working conditions which must be offered to U.S. workers consistent with this section.

(b) *Job qualifications and requirements.* Each job qualification and requirement listed in the job offer must be bona fide and consistent with the normal and accepted qualifications required by employers that do not use H–2A workers in the same or comparable occupations and crops. Either the CO or the SWA may require the employer to submit documentation to substantiate the appropriateness of any job qualification specified in the job offer.

(c) *Minimum benefits, wages, and working conditions.* Every job order accompanying an *Application for Temporary Employment Certification* must include each of the minimum benefit, wage, and working condition provisions listed in paragraphs (d) through (q) of this section.

(d) *Housing.* (1) Obligation to provide housing. The employer must provide housing at no cost to the H–2A workers and those workers in corresponding employment who are not reasonably able to return to their residence within the same day. Housing must be provided through one of the following means:

(i) *Employer-provided housing.* Employer-provided housing must meet the full set of DOL Occupational Safety and Health Administration (OSHA) standards set forth at 29 CFR 1910.142, or the full set of standards at §§ 654.404 through 654.417 of this chapter, whichever are applicable under § 654.401 of this chapter. Requests by employers whose housing does not meet the applicable standards for conditional access to the interstate clearance system, will be processed under the procedures set forth at § 654.403 of this chapter; or

(ii) *Rental and/or public accommodations.* Rental or public accommodations or other substantially similar class of habitation must meet local standards for such housing. In the absence of applicable local standards, State standards will apply. In the absence of applicable local or State standards, DOL OSHA standards at 29 CFR 1910.142 will apply. Any charges for rental housing must be paid directly by the employer to the owner or operator of the housing. The employer must document to the satisfaction of the CO that the housing complies with the local, State, or Federal housing standards.

(2) *Standards for range housing.* Housing for workers principally engaged in the range production of livestock must meet standards of DOL OSHA for such housing. In the absence of such standards, range housing for sheepherders and other workers engaged in the range production of livestock must meet guidelines issued by OFLC.

(3) *Deposit charges.* Charges in the form of deposits for bedding or other similar incidentals related to housing must not be levied upon workers. However, employers may require workers to reimburse them for damage caused to housing by the individual worker(s) found to have been responsible for damage which is not the result of normal wear and tear related to habitation.

(4) *Charges for public housing.* If public housing provided for migrant agricultural workers under the auspices of a local, county, or State government is secured by the employer, the employer must pay any charges normally required for use of the public housing units directly to the housing's management.

(5) *Family housing.* When it is the prevailing practice in the area of intended employment and the occupation to provide family housing, it must be provided to workers with families who request it.

(6) *Certified housing that becomes unavailable.* If after a request to certify housing, such housing becomes unavailable for reasons outside the employer's control, the employer may substitute other rental or public accommodation housing that is in compliance with the local, State, or Federal housing standards applicable under this section. The employer must promptly notify the SWA in writing of the change in accommodations and the reason(s) for such change and provide the SWA evidence of compliance with the applicable local, State or Federal safety and health standards, in accordance with the requirements of this section. If, upon inspection, the SWA determines the substituted housing does not meet the applicable housing standards, the SWA must promptly provide written notification to the employer to cure the deficiencies with a copy to the CO. An employer's failure to provide housing that complies with the applicable standards will result in either a

denial of a pending *Application for Temporary Employment Certification* or revocation of the temporary labor certification granted under this subpart.

(e) *Workers' compensation.* (1) The employer must provide workers' compensation insurance coverage in compliance with State law covering injury and disease arising out of and in the course of the worker's employment. If the type of employment for which the certification is sought is not covered by or is exempt from the State's workers' compensation law, the employer must provide, at no cost to the worker, insurance covering injury and disease arising out of and in the course of the worker's employment that will provide benefits at least equal to those provided under the State workers' compensation law for other comparable employment.

(2) Prior to issuance of the temporary labor certification, the employer must provide the CO with proof of workers' compensation insurance coverage meeting the requirements of this paragraph, including the name of the insurance carrier, the insurance policy number, and proof of insurance for the dates of need, or, if appropriate, proof of State law coverage.

(f) *Employer-provided items.* The employer must provide to the worker, without charge or deposit charge, all tools, supplies, and equipment required to perform the duties assigned.

(g) *Meals.* The employer either must provide each worker with three meals a day or must furnish free and convenient cooking and kitchen facilities to the workers that will enable the workers to prepare their own meals. Where the employer provides the meals, the job offer must state the charge, if any, to the worker for such meals. The amount of meal charges is governed by § 655.173.

(h) *Transportation; daily subsistence*—(1) *Transportation to place of employment.* If the employer has not previously advanced such transportation and subsistence costs to the worker or otherwise provided such transportation or subsistence directly to the worker by other means and if the worker completes 50 percent of the work contract period, the employer must pay the worker for reasonable costs incurred by the worker for transportation and daily subsistence from the place from which the worker has come to work for the employer, whether in the U.S. or abroad to the place of employment. When it is the prevailing practice of non-H–2A agricultural employers in the occupation in the area to do so, or when the employer extends such benefits to similarly situated H–2A workers, the employer must advance the required transportation and subsistence costs (or otherwise provide them) to workers in corresponding employment who are traveling to the employer's worksite. The amount of the transportation payment must be no less (and is not required to be more) than the most economical and reasonable common carrier transportation charges for the distances involved. The amount of the daily subsistence payment must be at least as much as the employer would charge the worker for providing the worker with three meals a day during employment (if applicable), but in no event less than the amount permitted under § 655.173(a). Note that the FLSA applies independently of the H–2A requirements and imposes obligations on employers regarding payment of wages.

(2) *Transportation from place of employment.* If the worker completes the work contract period, or if the employee is terminated without cause, and the worker has no immediate subsequent H–2A employment, the employer must provide or pay for the worker's transportation and daily subsistence from the place of employment to the place from which the worker, disregarding intervening employment, departed to work for the employer. If the worker has contracted with a subsequent employer who has not agreed in such work contract to provide or pay for the worker's transportation and daily subsistence expenses from the employer's worksite to such subsequent employer's worksite, the employer must provide or pay for such expenses. If the worker has contracted with a subsequent employer who has agreed in such work contract to provide or pay for the worker's transportation and daily subsistence expenses from the employer's worksite to such subsequent employer's worksite, the subsequent employer must provide or

pay for such expenses. The employer is not relieved of its obligation to provide or pay for return transportation and subsistence if an H–2A worker is displaced as a result of the employer's compliance with the 50 percent rule as described in §655.135(d) of this subpart with respect to the referrals made after the employer's date of need.

(3) *Transportation between living quarters and worksite.* The employer must provide transportation between housing provided or secured by the employer and the employer's worksite at no cost to the worker.

(4) *Employer-provided transportation.* All employer-provided transportation must comply with all applicable Federal, State or local laws and regulations, and must provide, at a minimum, the same transportation safety standards, driver licensure, and vehicle insurance as required under 29 U.S.C. 1841 and 29 CFR 500.105 and 29 CFR 500.120 to 500.128. If workers' compensation is used to cover transportation, in lieu of vehicle insurance, the employer must either ensure that the workers' compensation covers all travel or that vehicle insurance exists to provide coverage for travel not covered by workers' compensation and they must have property damage insurance.

(i) *Three-fourths guarantee*—(1) *Offer to worker.* The employer must guarantee to offer the worker employment for a total number of work hours equal to at least three-fourths of the workdays of the total period beginning with the first workday after the arrival of the worker at the place of employment or the advertised contractual first date of need, whichever is later, and ending on the expiration date specified in the work contract or in its extensions, if any.

(i) For purposes of this paragraph a workday means the number of hours in a workday as stated in the job order and excludes the worker's Sabbath and Federal holidays. The employer must offer a total number of hours to ensure the provision of sufficient work to reach the three-fourths guarantee. The work hours must be offered during the work period specified in the work contract, or during any modified work contract period to which the worker and employer have mutually agreed and that has been approved by the CO.

(ii) The work contract period can be shortened by agreement of the parties only with the approval of the CO. In the event the worker begins working later than the specified beginning date of the contract, the guarantee period begins with the first workday after the arrival of the worker at the place of employment, and continues until the last day during which the work contract and all extensions thereof are in effect.

(iii) Therefore, if, for example, a work contract is for a 10-week period, during which a normal workweek is specified as 6 days a week, 8 hours per day, the worker would have to be guaranteed employment for at least 360 hours (10 weeks × 48 hours/week = 480 hours × 75 percent = 360). If a Federal holiday occurred during the 10-week span, the 8 hours would be deducted from the total hours for the work contract, before the guarantee is calculated. Continuing with the above example, the worker would have to be guaranteed employment for 354 hours (10 weeks × 48 hours/week = 480 hours − 8 hours (Federal holiday) × 75 percent = 354 hours).

(iv) A worker may be offered more than the specified hours of work on a single workday. For purposes of meeting the guarantee, however, the worker will not be required to work for more than the number of hours specified in the job order for a workday, or on the worker's Sabbath or Federal holidays. However, all hours of work actually performed may be counted by the employer in calculating whether the period of guaranteed employment has been met. If during the total work contract period the employer affords the U.S. or H–2A worker less employment than that required under this paragraph, the employer must pay such worker the amount the worker would have earned had the worker, in fact, worked for the guaranteed number of days. An employer will not be considered to have met the work guarantee if the employer has merely offered work on three-fourths of the workdays if each workday did not consist of a full number of hours of work time as specified in the job order.

(2) *Guarantee for piece rate paid worker.* If the worker is paid on a piece rate basis, the employer must use the worker's average hourly piece rate earnings or the required hourly wage rate, whichever is higher, to calculate the amount due under the guarantee.

(3) *Failure to work.* Any hours the worker fails to work, up to a maximum of the number of hours specified in the job order for a workday, when the worker has been offered an opportunity to work in accordance with paragraph (i)(1) of this section, and all hours of work actually performed (including voluntary work over 8 hours in a workday or on the worker's Sabbath or Federal holidays), may be counted by the employer in calculating whether the period of guaranteed employment has been met. An employer seeking to calculate whether the number of hours has been met must maintain the payroll records in accordance with this subpart.

(4) *Displaced H–2A worker.* The employer is not liable for payment of the three-fourths guarantee to an H–2A worker whom the CO certifies is displaced because of the employer's compliance with the 50 percent rule described in § 655.135(d) with respect to referrals made during that period.

(5) *Obligation to provide housing and meals.* Notwithstanding the three-fourths guarantee contained in this section, employers are obligated to provide housing and meals in accordance with paragraphs (d) and (g) of this section for each day of the contract period up until the day the workers depart for other H–2A employment, depart to the place outside of the U.S. from which the worker came, or, if the worker voluntarily abandons employment or is terminated for cause, the day of such abandonment or termination.

(j) *Earnings records.* (1) The employer must keep accurate and adequate records with respect to the workers' earnings, including but not limited to field tally records, supporting summary payroll records, and records showing the nature and amount of the work performed; the number of hours of work offered each day by the employer (broken out by hours offered both in accordance with and over and above the three-fourths guarantee at paragraph (i)(3) of this section); the hours actually worked each day by the worker; the time the worker began and ended each workday; the rate of pay (both piece rate and hourly, if applicable); the worker's earnings per pay period; the worker's home address; and the amount of and reasons for any and all deductions taken from the worker's wages.

(2) Each employer must keep the records required by this part, including field tally records and supporting summary payroll records, safe and accessible at the place or places of employment, or at one or more established central recordkeeping offices where such records are customarily maintained. All records must be available for inspection and transcription by the Secretary or a duly authorized and designated representative, and by the worker and representatives designated by the worker as evidenced by appropriate documentation (an Entry of Appearance as Attorney or Representative, Form G–28, signed by the worker, or an affidavit signed by the worker confirming such representation). Where the records are maintained at a central recordkeeping office, other than in the place or places of employment, such records must be made available for inspection and copying within 72 hours following notice from the Secretary, or a duly authorized and designated representative, and by the worker and designated representatives as described in this paragraph.

(3) To assist in determining whether the three-fourths guarantee in paragraph (i) of this section has been met, if the number of hours worked by the worker on a day during the work contract period is less than the number of hours offered, as specified in the job offer, the records must state the reason or reasons therefore.

(4) The employer must retain the records for not less than 3 years after the date of the certification.

(k) *Hours and earnings statements.* The employer must furnish to the worker on or before each payday in one or more written statements the following information:

(1) The worker's total earnings for the pay period;

(2) The worker's hourly rate and/or piece rate of pay;

(3) The hours of employment offered to the worker (showing offers in accordance with the three-fourths guarantee as determined in paragraph (i) of this section, separate from any hours offered over and above the guarantee);

(4) The hours actually worked by the worker;

(5) An itemization of all deductions made from the worker's wages;

(6) If piece rates are used, the units produced daily;

(7) Beginning and ending dates of the pay period; and

(8) The employer's name, address and FEIN.

(l) *Rates of pay.* If the worker is paid by the hour, the employer must pay the worker at least the AEWR, the prevailing hourly wage rate, the prevailing piece rate, the agreed-upon collective bargaining rate, or the Federal or State minimum wage rate, in effect at the time work is performed, whichever is highest, for every hour or portion thereof worked during a pay period.

(1) The offered wage may not be based on commission, bonuses, or other incentives, unless the employer guarantees a wage paid on a weekly, semimonthly, or monthly basis that equals or exceeds the AEWR, prevailing hourly wage or piece rate, the legal Federal or State minimum wage, or any agreed-upon collective bargaining rate, whichever is highest; or

(2) If the worker is paid on a piece rate basis and at the end of the pay period the piece rate does not result in average hourly piece rate earnings during the pay period at least equal to the amount the worker would have earned had the worker been paid at the appropriate hourly rate:

(i) The worker's pay must be supplemented at that time so that the worker's earnings are at least as much as the worker would have earned during the pay period if the worker had instead been paid at the appropriate hourly wage rate for each hour worked;

(ii) The piece rate must be no less than the piece rate prevailing for the activity in the area of intended employment; and

(iii) If the employer who pays by the piece rate requires one or more minimum productivity standards of workers as a condition of job retention, such standards must be specified in the job offer and be no more than those required by the employer in 1977, unless the OFLC Administrator approves a higher minimum, or, if the employer first applied for H–2A temporary labor certification after 1977, such standards must be no more than those normally required (at the time of the first *Application for Temporary Employment Certification*) by other employers for the activity in the area of intended employment.

(m) *Frequency of pay.* The employer must state in the job offer the frequency with which the worker will be paid, which must be at least twice monthly or according to the prevailing practice in the area of intended employment, whichever is more frequent. Employers must pay wages when due.

(n) *Abandonment of employment or termination for cause.* If the worker voluntarily abandons employment before the end of the contract period, or is terminated for cause, and the employer notifies the NPC, and DHS in the case of an H–2A worker, in writing or by any other method specified by the Department or DHS in a manner specified in a notice published in the FEDERAL REGISTER not later than 2 working days after such abandonment occurs, the employer will not be responsible for providing or paying for the subsequent transportation and subsistence expenses of that worker under this section, and that worker is not entitled to the three-fourths guarantee described in paragraph (i) of this section. Abandonment will be deemed to begin after a worker fails to report for work at the regularly scheduled time for 5 consecutive working days without the consent of the employer.

(o) *Contract impossibility.* If, before the expiration date specified in the work contract, the services of the worker are no longer required for reasons beyond the control of the employer due to fire, weather, or other Act of God that makes the fulfillment of the contract impossible, the employer may terminate the work contract. Whether such an event constitutes a contract impossibility will be determined by the CO. In the event of such termination of a contract, the employer must fulfill a three-fourths guarantee for the time that has elapsed from the start of the work contract to the time of its termination, as described in paragraph (i)(1) of this section. The employer must make efforts to transfer the worker to other comparable employment acceptable to the worker, consistent with existing immigration law, as applicable. If such transfer is not affected, the employer must:

(1) Return the worker, at the employer's expense, to the place from which the worker (disregarding intervening employment) came to work for the employer, or transport the worker to the worker's next certified H-2A employer, whichever the worker prefers;

(2) Reimburse the worker the full amount of any deductions made from the worker's pay by the employer for transportation and subsistence expenses to the place of employment; and

(3) Pay the worker for any costs incurred by the worker for transportation and daily subsistence to that employer's place of employment. Daily subsistence must be computed as set forth in paragraph (h) of this section. The amount of the transportation payment must not be less (and is not required to be more) than the most economical and reasonable common carrier transportation charges for the distances involved.

(p) *Deductions.* (1) The employer must make all deductions from the worker's paycheck required by law. The job offer must specify all deductions not required by law which the employer will make from the worker's paycheck. All deductions must be reasonable. The employer may deduct the cost of the worker's transportation and daily subsistence expenses to the place of employment which were borne directly by the employer. In such circumstances, the job offer must state that the worker will be reimbursed the full amount of such deduction upon the worker's completion of 50 percent of the work contract period. However, an employer subject to the FLSA may not make deductions that would violate the FLSA.

(2) A deduction is not reasonable if it includes a profit to the employer or to any affiliated person. A deduction that is primarily for the benefit or convenience of the employer will not be recognized as reasonable and therefore the cost of such an item may not be included in computing wages. The wage requirements of § 655.120 will not be met where undisclosed or unauthorized deductions, rebates, or refunds reduce the wage payment made to the employee below the minimum amounts required under this subpart, or where the employee fails to receive such amounts free and clear because the employee kicks back directly or indirectly to the employer or to another person for the employer's benefit the whole or part of the wage delivered to the employee. The principles applied in determining whether deductions are reasonable and payments are received free and clear, and the permissibility of deductions for payments to third persons are explained in more detail in 29 CFR part 531.

(q) *Disclosure of work contract.* The employer must provide to an H-2A worker no later than the time at which the worker applies for the visa, or to a worker in corresponding employment no later than on the day work commences, a copy of the work contract between the employer and the worker in a language understood by the worker as necessary or reasonable. For an H-2A worker going from an H-2A employer to a subsequent H-2A employer, the copy must be provided no later than the time an offer of employment is made by the subsequent H-2A employer. At a minimum, the work contract must contain all of the provisions required by this section. In the absence of a separate, written work contract entered into between the employer and the worker, the required terms of the job order and the certified *Application for Temporary Employment Certification* will be the work contract.

APPLICATION FOR TEMPORARY EMPLOYMENT CERTIFICATION FILING PROCEDURES

§ 655.130 Application filing requirements.

All agricultural employers who desire to hire H–2A foreign agricultural workers must apply for a certification from the Secretary by filing an *Application for Temporary Employment Certification* with the NPC designated by the OFLC Administrator. The following section provides the procedures employers must follow when filing.

(a) *What to file.* An employer, whether individual, association, or an H–2ALC, that desires to apply for temporary employment certification of one or more nonimmigrant foreign workers must file a completed *Application for Temporary Employment Certification* form and, unless a specific exemption applies, a copy of Form ETA–790, submitted to the SWA serving the area of intended employment, as set forth in § 655.121(a).

(b) *Timeliness.* A completed *Application for Temporary Employment Certification* must be filed no less than 45 calendar days before the employer's date of need.

(c) *Location and method of filing.* The employer may send the *Application for Temporary Employment Certification* and all required supporting documentation by U.S. Mail or private mail courier to the NPC. The Department will publish a Notice in the FEDERAL REGISTER identifying the address(es), and any future address changes, to which *Applications for Temporary Employment Certification* must be mailed, and will also post these addresses on the OFLC Internet Web site at *http://www.foreignlaborcert.doleta.gov/.* The Department may also require *Applications for Temporary Employment Certification,* at a future date, to be filed electronically in addition to or instead of by mail, notice of which will be published in the FEDERAL REGISTER.

(d) *Original signature.* The *Application for Temporary Employment Certification* must bear the original signature of the employer (and that of the employer's authorized attorney or agent if the employer is represented by an attorney or agent). An association filing a master application as a joint employer may sign on behalf of its employer members. An association filing as an agent may not sign on behalf of its members but must obtain each member's signature on each *Application for Temporary Employment Certification* prior to filing.

(e) Information received in the course of processing *Applications for Temporary Employment Certification* and program integrity measures such as audits may be forwarded from OFLC to Wage and Hour Division (WHD) for enforcement purposes.

§ 655.131 Association filing requirements.

If an association files an *Application for Temporary Employment Certification,* in addition to complying with all the assurances, guarantees, and other requirements contained in this subpart and in part 653, subpart F, of this chapter, the following requirements also apply.

(a) *Individual applications.* Associations of agricultural employers may file an *Application for Temporary Employment Certification* for H–2A workers as a sole employer, a joint employer, or agent. The association must identify in the *Application for Temporary Employment Certification* in what capacity it is filing. The association must retain documentation substantiating the employer or agency status of the association and be prepared to submit such documentation in response to a Notice of Deficiency from the CO prior to issuing a Final Determination, or in the event of an audit.

(b) *Master applications.* An association may file a master application on behalf of its employer-members. The master application is available only when the association is filing as a joint employer. An association may submit a master application covering the same occupation or comparable work available with a number of its employer-members in multiple areas of intended employment, just as though all of the covered employers were in fact a single employer, as long as a single date of need is provided for all workers requested by the *Application for Temporary Employment Certification* and all employer-members are located in no more than two contiguous States. The association must identify on the *Application for Temporary Employment Certification* by name, address, total number of workers needed, and the crops and agricultural work to be performed, each employer that will employ H–2A workers. The association, as appropriate, will receive a certified *Application for Temporary Employment Certification* that can be copied and sent to the United States Citizenship and Immigration Services (USCIS) with each employer-member's petition.

§ 655.132 H–2A labor contractor (H–2ALC) filing requirements.

If an H–2ALC intends to file an *Application for Temporary Employment Certification*, the H–2ALC must meet all of the requirements of the definition of employer in § 655.103(b), and comply with all the assurances, guarantees, and other requirements contained in this part, including Assurances and Obligations of H–2A Employers, and in part 653, subpart F, of this chapter.

(a) *Scope of H–2ALC Applications*. An *Application for Temporary Employment Certification* filed by an H–2ALC must be limited to a single area of intended employment in which the fixed-site employer(s) to whom an H–2ALC is furnishing employees will be utilizing the employees.

(b) *Required information and submissions*. An H–2ALC must include in or with its *Application for Temporary Employment Certification* the following:

(1) The name and location of each fixed-site agricultural business to which the H–2ALC expects to provide H–2A workers, the expected beginning and ending dates when the H–2ALC will be providing the workers to each fixed site, and a description of the crops and activities the workers are expected to perform at such fixed site.

(2) A copy of the Migrant and Seasonal Agricultural Worker Protection Act (MSPA) Farm Labor Contractor (FLC) Certificate of Registration, if required under MSPA at 29 U.S.C. 1801 *et seq.*, identifying the specific farm labor contracting activities the H–2ALC is authorized to perform as an FLC.

(3) Proof of its ability to discharge financial obligations under the H–2A program by including with the *Application for Temporary Employment Certification* the original surety bond as required by 29 CFR 501.9. The bond document must clearly identify the issuer, the name, address, phone number, and contact person for the surety, and provide the amount of the bond (as calculated pursuant to 29 CFR 501.9) and any identifying designation used by the surety for the bond.

(4) Copies of the fully-executed work contracts with each fixed-site agricultural business identified under paragraph (b)(1) of this section.

(5) Where the fixed-site agricultural business will provide housing or transportation to the workers, proof that:

(i) All housing used by workers and owned, operated or secured by the fixed-site agricultural business complies with the applicable standards as set forth in § 655.122(d) and certified by the SWA; and

(ii) All transportation between the worksite and the workers' living quarters that is provided by the fixed-site agricultural business complies with all applicable Federal, State, or local laws and regulations and must provide, at a minimum, the same vehicle safety standards, driver licensure, and vehicle insurance as required under 29 U.S.C. 1841 and 29 CFR 500.105 and 500.120 to 500.128, except where workers' compensation is used to cover such transportation as described in § 655.125(h).

§ 655.133 Requirements for agents.

(a) An agent filing an *Application for Temporary Employment Certification* on behalf of an employer must provide a copy of the agent agreement or other document demonstrating the agent's authority to represent the employer.

(b) In addition the agent must provide a copy of the MSPA FLC Certificate of Registration, if required under MSPA at 29 U.S.C. 1801 *et seq.*, identifying the specific farm labor contracting activities the agent is authorized to perform.

§ 655.134 Emergency situations.

(a) *Waiver of time period*. The CO may waive the time period for filing for employers who did not make use of temporary alien agricultural workers during the prior year's agricultural season or for any employer that has other good and substantial cause (which may include unforeseen changes in market conditions), provided that the CO has sufficient time to test the domestic labor market on an expedited basis to make the determinations required by § 655.100.

(b) *Employer requirements.* The employer requesting a waiver of the required time period must concurrently submit to the NPC and to the SWA serving the area of intended employment a completed *Application for Temporary Employment Certification,* a completed job order on the Form ETA–790, and a statement justifying the request for a waiver of the time period requirement. The statement must indicate whether the waiver request is due to the fact that the employer did not use H–2A workers during the prior agricultural season or whether the request is for good and substantial cause. If the waiver is requested for good and substantial cause, the employer's statement must also include detailed information describing the good and substantial cause which has necessitated the waiver request. Good and substantial cause may include, but is not limited to, the substantial loss of U.S. workers due to weather-related activities or other reasons, unforeseen events affecting the work activities to be performed, pandemic health issues, or similar conditions.

(c) *Processing of emergency applications.* The CO will process emergency *Applications for Temporary Employment Certification* in a manner consistent with the provisions set forth in §§ 655.140 through 655.145 and make a determination on the *Application for Temporary Employment Certification* in accordance with §§ 655.160 through 655.167. The CO may advise the employer in writing that the certification cannot be granted because, pursuant to paragraph (a) of this section, the request for emergency filing was not justified and/or there is not sufficient time to test the availability of U.S. workers such that the CO can make a determination on the *Application for Temporary Employment Certification* in accordance with § 655.161. Such notification will so inform the employer using the procedures applicable to a denial of certification set forth in § 655.164.

§ 655.135 Assurances and obligations of H–2A employers.

An employer seeking to employ H–2A workers must agree as part of the *Application for Temporary Employment Certification* and job offer that it will abide by the requirements of this subpart and make each of the following additional assurances:

(a) *Non-discriminatory hiring practices.* The job opportunity is, and through the period set forth in paragraph (d) of this section must continue to be, open to any qualified U.S. worker regardless of race, color, national origin, age, sex, religion, handicap, or citizenship. Rejections of any U.S. workers who applied or apply for the job must be only for lawful, job-related reasons, and those not rejected on this basis have been or will be hired. In addition, the employer has and will continue to retain records of all hires and rejections as required by § 655.167.

(b) *No strike or lockout.* The worksite for which the employer is requesting H–2A certification does not currently have workers on strike or being locked out in the course of a labor dispute.

(c) *Recruitment requirements.* The employer has and will continue to cooperate with the SWA by accepting referrals of all eligible U.S. workers who apply (or on whose behalf an *Application for Temporary Employment Certification* is made) for the job opportunity until the end of the period as specified in paragraph (d) of this section and must independently conduct the positive recruitment activities, as specified in § 655.154, until the date on which the H–2A workers depart for the place of work. Unless the SWA is informed in writing of a different date, the date that is the third day preceding the employer's first date of need will be determined to be the date the H–2A workers departed for the employer's place of business.

(d) *Fifty percent rule.* From the time the foreign workers depart for the employer's place of employment, the employer must provide employment to any qualified, eligible U.S. worker who applies to the employer until 50 percent of the period of the work contract has elapsed. Start of the work contract timeline is calculated from the first date of need stated on the *Application for Temporary Employment Certification*, under which the foreign worker who is in the job was hired. This provision will not apply to any employer who certifies to the CO in the *Application for Temporary Employment Certification* that the employer:

(1) Did not, during any calendar quarter during the preceding calendar year, use more than 500 man-days of agricultural labor, as defined in sec. 203(u) of Title 29;

(2) Is not a member of an association which has petitioned for certification under this subpart for its members; and

(3) Has not otherwise associated with other employers who are petitioning for temporary foreign workers under this subpart.

(e) *Compliance with applicable laws.* During the period of employment that is the subject of the *Application for Temporary Employment Certification*, the employer must comply with all applicable Federal, State and local laws and regulations, including health and safety laws. In compliance with such laws, including the William Wilberforce Trafficking Victims Protection Reauthorization Act of 2008, Pub. L. 110–457, 18 U.S.C. 1592(a), the employer may not hold or confiscate workers' passports, visas, or other immigration documents. H–2A employers may also be subject to the FLSA. The FLSA operates independently of the H–2A program and has specific requirements that address payment of wages, including deductions from wages, the payment of Federal minimum wage and payment of overtime.

(f) *Job opportunity is full-time.* The job opportunity is a full-time temporary position, calculated to be at least 35 hours per work week.

(g) *No recent or future layoffs.* The employer has not laid off and will not lay off any similarly employed U.S. worker in the occupation that is the subject of the *Application for Temporary Employment Certification* in the area of intended employment except for lawful, job-related reasons within 60 days of the date of need, or if the employer has laid off such workers, it has offered the job opportunity that is the subject of the *Application for Temporary Employment Certification* to those laid-off U.S. worker(s) and the U.S. worker(s) refused the job opportunity, was rejected for the job opportunity for lawful, job-related reasons, or was hired. A layoff for lawful, job-related reasons such as lack of work or the end of the growing season is permissible if all H–2A workers are laid off before any U.S. worker in corresponding employment.

(h) *No unfair treatment.* The employer has not and will not intimidate, threaten, restrain, coerce, blacklist, discharge or in any manner discriminate against, and has not and will not cause any person to intimidate, threaten, restrain, coerce, blacklist, or in any manner discriminate against, any person who has:

(1) Filed a complaint under or related to 8 U.S.C. 1188, or this subpart or any other Department regulation promulgated thereunder;

(2) Instituted or caused to be instituted any proceeding under or related to 8 U.S.C. 1188 or this subpart or any other Department regulation promulgated thereunder;

(3) Testified or is about to testify in any proceeding under or related to 8 U.S.C. 1188 or this subpart or any other Department regulation promulgated thereunder;

(4) Consulted with an employee of a legal assistance program or an attorney on matters related to 8 U.S.C. 1188 or this subpart or any other Department regulation promulgated thereunder; or

(5) Exercised or asserted on behalf of himself/herself or others any right or protection afforded by 8 U.S.C. 1188 or this subpart or any other Department regulation promulgated thereunder.

(i) *Notify workers of duty to leave United States.* (1) The employer must inform H–2A workers of the requirement that they leave the U.S. at the end of the period certified by the Department or separation from the employer, whichever is earlier, as required under paragraph (i)(2) of this section, unless the H–2A worker is being sponsored by another subsequent H–2A employer.

(2) As defined further in DHS regulations, a temporary labor certification limits the validity period of an H–2A petition, and therefore, the authorized period of stay for an H–2A worker. See 8 CFR 214.2(h)(5)(vii) A foreign worker

may not remain beyond his or her authorized period of stay, as determined by DHS, nor beyond separation from employment prior to completion of the H–2A contract, absent an extension or change of such worker's status under DHS regulations. See 8 CFR 214.2(h)(5)(viii)(B).

(j) *Comply with the prohibition against employees paying fees.* The employer and its agents have not sought or received payment of any kind from any employee subject to 8 U.S.C. 1188 for any activity related to obtaining H–2A labor certification, including payment of the employer's attorneys' fees, application fees, or recruitment costs. For purposes of this paragraph, payment includes, but is not limited to, monetary payments, wage concessions (including deductions from wages, salary, or benefits), kickbacks, bribes, tributes, in kind payments, and free labor. This provision does not prohibit employers or their agents from receiving reimbursement for costs that are the responsibility and primarily for the benefit of the worker, such as government-required passport fees.

(k) *Contracts with third parties comply with prohibitions.* The employer has contractually forbidden any foreign labor contractor or recruiter (or any agent of such foreign labor contractor or recruiter) whom the employer engages, either directly or indirectly, in international recruitment of H–2A workers to seek or receive payments or other compensation from prospective employees. This documentation is to be made available upon request by the CO or another Federal party.

(l) *Notice of worker rights.* The employer must post and maintain in a conspicuous location at the place of employment, a poster provided by the Secretary in English, and, to the extent necessary, any language common to a significant portion of the workers if they are not fluent in English, which sets out the rights and protections for workers employed pursuant to 8 U.S.C. 1188.

PROCESSING OF APPLICATIONS FOR TEMPORARY EMPLOYMENT CERTIFICATION

§ 655.140 Review of applications.

(a) *NPC review.* The CO will promptly review the *Application for Temporary Employment Certification* and job order for compliance with all applicable program requirements, including compliance with the requirements set forth in this subpart.

(b) *Mailing and postmark requirements.* Any notice or request sent by the CO(s) to an employer requiring a response will be sent using the provided address via traditional methods to assure next day delivery. The employer's response to such a notice or request must be filed using traditional methods to assure next day delivery and be sent by the date due or the next business day if the due date falls on a Sunday or Federal Holiday.

§ 655.141 Notice of deficiency.

(a) *Notification timeline.* If the CO determines the *Application for Temporary Employment Certification* or job order are incomplete, contain errors or inaccuracies, or do not meet the requirements set forth in this subpart, the CO will notify the employer within 7 calendar days of the CO's receipt of the *Application for Temporary Employment Certification.* A copy of this notification will be sent to the SWA serving the area of intended employment.

(b) *Notice content.* The notice will:

(1) State the reason(s) why the *Application for Temporary Employment Certification* or job order fails to meet the criteria for acceptance;

(2) Offer the employer an opportunity to submit a modified *Application for Temporary Employment Certification* or job order within 5 business days from date of receipt stating the modification that is needed for the CO to issue the Notice of Acceptance;

(3) Except as provided for under the expedited review or de novo administrative hearing provisions of this section, state that the CO's determination on whether to grant or deny the *Application for Temporary Employment Certification* will be made no later than 30 calendar days before the date of need, provided that the employer submits the

requested modification to the *Application for Temporary Employment Certification* within 5 business days and in a manner specified by the CO;

(4) Offer the employer an opportunity to request an expedited administrative review or a de novo administrative hearing before an ALJ of the Notice of Deficiency. The notice will state that in order to obtain such a review or hearing, the employer, within 5 business days of the receipt of the notice, must file by facsimile or other means normally assuring next day delivery a written request to the Chief ALJ of DOL and simultaneously serve a copy on the CO. The notice will also state that the employer may submit any legal arguments that the employer believes will rebut the basis of the CO's action; and

(5) State that if the employer does not comply with the requirements of § 655.142 or request an expedited administrative review or a de novo hearing before an ALJ within 5 business days the CO will deny the *Application for Temporary Employment Certification*. That denial is final cannot be appealed and the Department will not further consider that *Application for Temporary Employment Certification*.

(c) *Appeal from Notice of Deficiency*. The employer may timely request an expedited administrative review or de novo hearing before an ALJ by following the procedures set forth in § 655.171.

§ 655.142 Submission of modified applications.

(a) *Submission requirements and certification delays*. If the employer chooses to submit a modified *Application for Temporary Employment Certification*, the CO's Final Determination will be postponed by 1 calendar day for each day that passes beyond the 5 business-day period allowed under § 655.141(b) to submit a modified *Application for Temporary Employment Certification*, up to maximum of 5 days. The *Application for Temporary Employment Certification* will be deemed abandoned if the employer does not submit a modified *Application for Temporary Employment Certification* within 12 calendar days after the notice of deficiency was issued.

(b) *Provisions for denial of modified Application for Temporary Employment Certification*. If the modified *Application for Temporary Employment Certification* is not approved, the CO will deny the *Application for Temporary Employment Certification* in accordance with the labor certification determination provisions in § 655.164.

(c) *Appeal from denial of modified Application for Temporary Employment Certification*. The procedures for appealing a denial of a modified *Application for Temporary Employment Certification* are the same as for a non-modified *Application for Temporary Employment Certification* as long as the employer timely requests an expedited administrative review or de novo hearing before an ALJ by following the procedures set forth in § 655.171.

§ 655.143 Notice of acceptance.

(a) *Notification timeline*. When the CO determines the *Application for Temporary Employment Certification* and job order are complete and meet the requirements set forth in this subpart, the CO will notify the employer within 7 calendar days of the CO's receipt of the *Application for Temporary Employment Certification*. A copy will be sent to the SWA serving the area of intended employment.

(b) *Notice content*. The notice must:

(1) Authorize conditional access to the interstate clearance system and direct the SWA to circulate a copy of the job order to other such States the CO determines to be potential sources of U.S. workers;

(2) Direct the employer to engage in positive recruitment of U.S. workers in a manner consistent with § 655.154 and to submit a report of its positive recruitment efforts as specified in § 655.156;

(3) State that positive recruitment is in addition to and will occur during the period of time that the job order is being circulated by the SWA(s) for interstate clearance under § 655.150 of this subpart and will terminate on the actual date on which the H–2A workers depart for the place of work, or 3 calendar days prior to the first date the employer requires the services of the H–2A workers, whichever occurs first; and

(4) State that the CO will make a determination either to grant or deny the *Application for Temporary Employment Certification* no later than 30 calendar days before the date of need, except as provided for under § 655.144 for modified *Applications for Temporary Employment Certification.*

§ 655.144 Electronic job registry.

(a) *Location of and placement in the electronic job registry.* Upon acceptance of the *Application for Temporary Employment Certification* under § 655.143, the CO will promptly place for public examination a copy of the job order on an electronic job registry maintained by the Department, including any required modifications approved by the CO, as specified in § 655.142. This procedure will be implemented once the Department initiates operation of the registry.

(b) *Length of posting on electronic job registry.* Unless otherwise provided, the Department will keep the job order posted on the Electronic Job Registry until the end of 50 percent of the contract period as set forth in § 655.135(d).

§ 655.145 Amendments to applications for temporary employment certification.

(a) *Increases in number of workers.* The *Application for Temporary Employment Certification* may be amended at any time before the CO's certification determination to increase the number of workers requested in the initial *Application for Temporary Employment Certification* by not more than 20 percent (50 percent for employers requesting less than 10 workers) without requiring an additional recruitment period for U.S. workers. Requests for increases above the percent prescribed, without additional recruitment, may be approved by the CO only when the employer demonstrates that the need for additional workers could not have been foreseen, and the crops or commodities will be in jeopardy prior to the expiration of an additional recruitment period. All requests for increasing the number of workers must be made in writing.

(b) *Minor changes to the period of employment.* The *Application for Temporary Employment Certification* may be amended to make minor changes in the total period of employment. Changes will not be effective until submitted in writing and approved by the CO. In considering whether to approve the request, the CO will review the reason(s) for the request, determine whether the reason(s) are on the whole justified, and take into account the effect any change(s) would have on the adequacy of the underlying test of the domestic labor market for the job opportunity. An employer must demonstrate that the change to the period of employment could not have been foreseen, and the crops or commodities will be in jeopardy prior to the expiration of an additional recruitment period. If the request is for a delay in the start date and is made after workers have departed for the employer's place of work, the CO may only approve the change if the employer includes with the request a written assurance signed and dated by the employer that all workers who are already traveling to the job site will be provided housing and subsistence, without cost to the workers, until work commences. Upon acceptance of an amendment, the CO will submit to the SWA any necessary modification to the job order.

Post-Acceptance Requirements

§ 655.150 Interstate clearance of job order.

(a) *SWA posts in interstate clearance system.* The SWA must promptly place the job order in interstate clearance to all States designated by the CO. At a minimum, the CO will instruct the SWA to transmit a copy of its active job order to all States listed in the job order as anticipated worksites covering the area of intended employment.

(b) *Duration of posting.* Each of the SWAs to which the job order was transmitted must keep the job order on its active file until 50 percent of the contract term has elapsed, and must refer each qualified U.S. worker who applies (or on whose behalf an application is made) for the job opportunity.

§ 655.151 Newspaper advertisements.

(a) The employer must place an advertisement (in a language other than

English, where the CO determines appropriate) on 2 separate days, which may be consecutive, one of which must be a Sunday (except as provided in paragraph (b) of this section), in a newspaper of general circulation serving the area of intended employment and is appropriate to the occupation and the workers likely to apply for the job opportunity. Newspaper advertisements must satisfy the requirements set forth in §655.152.

(b) If the job opportunity is located in a rural area that does not have a newspaper with a Sunday edition, the CO may direct the employer, in place of a Sunday edition, to advertise in the regularly published daily edition with the widest circulation in the area of intended employment.

§655.152 Advertising requirements.

All advertising conducted to satisfy the required recruitment activities under §655.151 must meet the requirements set forth in this section and must contain terms and conditions of employment which are not less favorable than those offered to the H–2A workers. All advertising must contain the following information:

(a) The employer's name, or in the event that a master application will be filed by an association, a statement indicating that the name and location of each member of the association can be obtained from the SWA of the State in which the advertisement is run;

(b) The geographic area of intended employment with enough specificity to apprise applicants of any travel requirements and where applicants will likely have to reside to perform the services or labor;

(c) A description of the job opportunity for which certification is sought with sufficient information to apprise U.S. workers of services or labor to be performed and the anticipated start and end dates of employment of the job opportunity;

(d) The wage offer, or in the event that there are multiple wage offers (such as where a master application will be filed by an association and/or where there are multiple crop activities for a single employer), the range of applicable wage offers and, where a master application will be filed by an association, a statement indicating that the rate(s) applicable to each employer can be obtained from the SWA of the State in which the advertisement is run;

(e) The three-fourths guarantee specified in §655.122(i);

(f) If applicable, a statement that work tools, supplies, and equipment will be provided at no cost to the worker;

(g) A statement that housing will be made available at no cost to workers, including U.S. workers who cannot reasonably return to their permanent residence at the end of each working day;

(h) A statement that transportation and subsistence expenses to the worksite will be provided by the employer or paid by the employer upon completion of 50 percent of the work contract, or earlier, if appropriate;

(i) A statement that the position is temporary and a specification of the total number of job openings the employer intends to fill;

(j) A statement directing applicants to apply for the job opportunity at the nearest office of the SWA in the State in which the advertisement appeared. Employers who wish to require interviews must conduct those interviews by phone or provide a procedure for the interviews to be conducted in the location where the worker is being recruited at little or no cost to the worker. Employers cannot provide potential H–2A workers more favorable treatment with respect to the requirement and conduct of interviews; and

(k) Contact information for the applicable SWA and, if available, the job order number.

§655.153 Contact with former U.S. employees.

The employer must contact, by mail or other effective means, its former U.S. workers (except those who were dismissed for cause or who abandoned the worksite) employed by the employer in the occupation at the place of employment during the previous year and solicit their return to the job. This contact must occur during the period of time that the job order is being circulated by the SWA(s) for interstate clearance and documentation sufficient to prove contact must be maintained in the event of an audit.

§ 655.154 Additional positive recruitment.

(a) *Where to conduct additional positive recruitment.* The employer must conduct positive recruitment within a multistate region of traditional or expected labor supply where the CO finds that there are a significant number of qualified U.S. workers who, if recruited, would be willing to make themselves available for work at the time and place needed.

(b) *Additional requirements should be comparable to non-H–2A employers in the area.* The CO will ensure that the effort, including the location(s) and method(s) of the positive recruitment required of the potential H–2A employer must be no less than the normal recruitment efforts of non-H–2A agricultural employers of comparable or smaller size in the area of intended employment, and the kind and degree of recruitment efforts which the potential H–2A employer made to obtain foreign workers.

(c) *Nature of the additional positive recruitment.* The CO will describe the precise nature of the additional positive recruitment but the employer will not be required to conduct positive recruitment in more than three States for each area of intended employment listed on the employer's application.

(d) *Proof of recruitment.* The CO will specify the documentation or other supporting evidence that must be maintained by the employer as proof that the positive recruitment requirements were met.

§ 655.155 Referrals of U.S. workers.

SWAs may only refer for employment individuals who have been apprised of all the material terms and conditions of employment and have indicated, by accepting referral to the job opportunity, that he or she is qualified, able, willing, and available for employment.

§ 655.156 Recruitment report.

(a) *Requirements of a recruitment report.* The employer must prepare, sign, and date a written recruitment report. The recruitment report must be submitted on a date specified by the CO in the Notice of Acceptance set forth in § 655.141 and contain the following information:

(1) Identify the name of each recruitment source;

(2) State the name and contact information of each U.S. worker who applied or was referred to the job opportunity up to the date of the preparation of the recruitment report, and the disposition of each worker;

(3) Confirm that former U.S. employees were contacted and by what means; and

(4) If applicable, for each U.S. worker who applied for the position but was not hired, explain the lawful job-related reason(s) for not hiring the U.S. worker.

(b) *Duty to update recruitment report.* The employer must continue to maintain the recruitment report throughout the recruitment period including the 50 percent period. The updated report is not to be automatically submitted to the Department, but must be made available in the event of a post-certification audit or upon request by authorized representatives of the Secretary.

§ 655.157 Withholding of U.S. workers prohibited.

(a) *Filing a complaint.* Any employer who has reason to believe that a person or entity has willfully and knowingly withheld U.S. workers prior to the arrival at the worksite of H–2A workers in order to force the hiring of U.S. workers during the recruitment period, as set forth in § 655.135(d), may submit a written complaint to the CO. The complaint must clearly identify the person or entity who the employer believes has withheld the U.S. workers, and must specify sufficient facts to support the allegation (e.g., dates, places, numbers and names of U.S. workers) which will permit an investigation to be conducted by the CO.

(b) *Duty to investigate.* Upon receipt, the CO must immediately investigate the complaint. The investigation must include interviews with the employer who has submitted the complaint, the person or entity named as responsible for withholding the U.S. workers, and the individual U.S. workers whose availability has purportedly been withheld.

(c) *Duty to suspend the recruitment period.* Where the CO determines, after conducting the interviews required by paragraph (b) of this section, that the employer's complaint is valid and justified, the CO will immediately suspend the application of the 50 percent rule of the recruitment period, as set forth in § 655.135(d), to the employer. The CO's determination is the final decision of the Secretary.

§ 655.158 Duration of positive recruitment.

Except as otherwise noted, the obligation to engage in positive recruitment described in §§ 655.150 through 655.154 shall terminate on the date H–2A workers depart for the employer's place of work. Unless the SWA is informed in writing of a different date, the date that is the third day preceding the employer's first date of need will be determined to be the date the H–2A workers departed for the employer's place of business.

LABOR CERTIFICATION DETERMINATIONS

§ 655.160 Determinations.

Except as otherwise noted in this section, the CO will make a determination either to grant or deny the *Application for Temporary Employment Certification* no later than 30 calendar days before the date of need identified in the *Application for Temporary Employment Certification.* An *Application for Temporary Employment Certification* that is modified under § 655.142 or that otherwise does not meet the requirements for certification in this subpart is not subject to the 30-day timeframe for certification.

§ 655.161 Criteria for certification.

(a) The criteria for certification include whether the employer has established the need for the agricultural services or labor to be performed on a temporary or seasonal basis; complied with the requirements of parts 653 and 654 of this chapter; complied with all of this subpart, including but not limited to the timeliness requirements in § 655.130(b); complied with the offered wage rate criteria in § 655.120; made all the assurances in § 655.135; and met all the recruitment obligations required by § 655.121 and § 655.152.

(b) In making a determination as to whether there are insufficient U.S. workers to fill the employer's job opportunity, the CO will count as available any U.S. worker referred by the SWA or any U.S. worker who applied (or on whose behalf an application is made) directly to the employer, but who was rejected by the employer for other than a lawful job-related reason or who has not been provided with a lawful job-related reason for rejection by the employer.

§ 655.162 Approved certification.

If temporary labor certification is granted, the CO will send the certified *Application for Temporary Employment Certification* and a Final Determination letter to the employer by means normally assuring next-day delivery and a copy, if appropriate, to the employer's agent or attorney.

§ 655.163 Certification fee.

A determination by the CO to grant an *Application for Temporary Employment Certification* in whole or in part will include a bill for the required certification fees. Each employer of H–2A workers under the *Application for Temporary Employment Certification* (except joint employer associations, which may not be assessed a fee in addition to the fees assessed to the members of the association) must pay in a timely manner a non-refundable fee upon issuance of the certification granting the *Application for Temporary Employment Certification* (in whole or in part), as follows:

(a) *Amount.* The *Application for Temporary Employment Certification* fee for each employer receiving a temporary agricultural labor certification is $100 plus $10 for each H–2A worker certified under the *Application for Temporary Employment Certification,* provided that the fee to an employer for each temporary agricultural labor certification received will be no greater than $1,000. There is no additional fee to the association filing the *Application for Temporary Employment Certification.* The fees must be paid by check or money order made payable to United States Department of Labor. In the case of an agricultural association acting as a joint employer applying on behalf of its H–2A employer members, the aggregate fees for all employers of H–2A workers under the *Application for Temporary Employment Certification* must be paid by one check or money order.

(b) *Timeliness.* Fees must be received by the CO no more than 30 days after the date of the certification. Non-payment or untimely payment may be considered a substantial violation subject to the procedures in § 655.182.

§ 655.164 Denied certification.

If temporary labor certification is denied, the Final Determination letter will be sent to the employer by means normally assuring next-day delivery and a copy, if appropriate, to the employer's agent or attorney. The Final Determination Letter will:

(a) State the reason(s) certification is denied;

(b) Offer the applicant an opportunity to request an expedited administrative review, or a de novo administrative hearing before an ALJ, of the denial. The notice must state that in order to obtain such a review or hearing, the employer, within 7 calendar days of the date of the notice, must file by facsimile (fax), or other means normally assuring next day delivery, a written request to the Chief ALJ of DOL (giving the address) and simultaneously serve a copy on the CO. The notice will also state that the employer may submit any legal arguments which the employer believes will rebut the basis of the CO's action; and

(c) State that if the employer does not request an expedited administrative judicial review or a de novo hearing before an ALJ within the 7 calendar days, the denial is final and the Department will not further consider that *Application for Temporary Employment Certification.*

§ 655.165 Partial certification.

The CO may issue a partial certification, reducing either the period of need or the number of H–2A workers being requested or both for certification, based upon information the CO receives during the course of processing the *Application for Temporary Employment Certification*, an audit, or otherwise. The number of workers certified will be reduced by one for each referred U.S. worker who is able, willing, and qualified, and who will be available at the time and place needed and has not been rejected for lawful job-related reasons, to perform the services or labor. If a partial labor certification is issued, the Final Determination letter will:

(a) State the reason(s) why either the period of need and/or the number of H–2A workers requested has been reduced;

(b) Offer the applicant an opportunity to request an expedited administrative review, or a de novo administrative hearing before an ALJ, of the decision. The notice will state that in order to obtain such a review or hearing, the employer, within 7 calendar days of the date of the notice, will file by facsimile or other means normally assuring next day delivery a written request to the Chief ALJ of DOL (giving the address) and simultaneously serve a copy on the CO. The notice will also state that the employer may submit any legal arguments which the employer believes will rebut the basis of the CO's action; and

(c) State that if the employer does not request an expedited administrative judicial review or a de novo hearing before an ALJ within the 7 calendar days, the partial certification is final and the Department will not further consider that *Application for Temporary Employment Certification.*

§ 655.166 Requests for determinations based on nonavailability of U.S. workers.

(a) *Standards for requests.* If a temporary labor certification has been partially granted or denied based on the CO's determination that able, willing, available, eligible, and qualified U.S. workers are available, and, on or after 30 calendar days before the date of need, some or all of those U.S. workers are, in fact, no longer able, willing, eligible, qualified, or available, the employer may request a new temporary labor certification determination from the CO. Prior to making a new determination the CO will promptly ascertain (which may be through the SWA or other sources of information on U.S. worker availability) whether specific able, willing, eligible and qualified replacement U.S. workers are available or can be reasonably expected to be present at the employer's establishment within 72 hours from the date the employer's request was received. The CO will expeditiously, but in no case later than 72 hours after the time a complete request (including the signed statement included in paragraph (b) of this section) is received, make a determination on the request. An employer may appeal a denial of such a determination in accordance with the procedures contained in §655.171.

(b) *Unavailability of U.S. workers.* The employer's request for a new determination must be made directly to the CO by telephone or electronic mail, and must be confirmed by the employer in writing as required by this paragraph. If the employer telephonically or via electronic mail requests the new determination by asserting solely that U.S. workers have become unavailable, the employer must submit to the CO a signed statement confirming such assertion. If such signed statement is not received by the CO within 72 hours of the CO's receipt of the request for a new determination, the CO will deny the request.

(c) *Notification of determination.* If the CO determines that U.S. workers have become unavailable and cannot identify sufficient available U.S. workers who are able, willing, eligible, and qualified or who are likely to become available, the CO will grant the employer's request for a new determination. However, this does not preclude an employer from submitting subsequent requests for new determinations, if warranted, based on subsequent facts concerning purported nonavailability of U.S. workers or referred workers not being eligible workers or not able, willing, or qualified because of lawful job-related reasons.

§655.167 Document retention requirements.

(a) *Entities required to retain documents.* All employers filing an *Application for Temporary Employment Certification* requesting H–2A agricultural workers under this subpart are required to retain the documents and records proving compliance with this subpart.

(b) *Period of required retention.* Records and documents must be retained for a period of 3 years from the date of certification of the *Application for Temporary Employment Certification* or from the date of determination if the *Application for Temporary Employment Certification* is denied or withdrawn.

(c) *Documents and records to be retained by all applicants.* (1) Proof of recruitment efforts, including:

(i) Job order placement as specified in §655.121;

(ii) Advertising as specified in §655.152, or, if used, professional, trade, or ethnic publications;

(iii) Contact with former U.S. workers as specified in §655.153; or

(iv) Additional positive recruitment efforts (as specified in §655.154).

(2) Substantiation of information submitted in the recruitment report prepared in accordance with §655.156, such as evidence of nonapplicability of contact of former employees as specified in §655.153.

(3) The final recruitment report and any supporting resumes and contact information as specified in §655.156(b).

(4) Proof of workers' compensation insurance or State law coverage as specified in §655.122(e).

(5) Records of each worker's earnings as specified in §655.122(j).

(6) The work contract or a copy of the *Application for Temporary Employment Certification* as defined in 29 CFR 501.10 and specified in §655.122(q).

(d) *Additional retention requirement for associations filing Application for Temporary Employment Certification.* In addition to the documents specified in paragraph (c) above, Associations must retain documentation substantiating their status as an employer or agent, as specified in §655.131.

Post Certification

§655.170 Extensions.

An employer may apply for extensions of the period of employment in the following circumstances.

(a) *Short-term extension.* Employers seeking extensions of 2 weeks or less of the certified *Application for Temporary*

Employment Certification must apply directly to DHS for approval. If granted, the *Application for Temporary Employment Certification* will be deemed extended for such period as is approved by DHS.

(b) *Long-term extension.* Employers seeking extensions of more than 2 weeks may apply to the CO. Such requests must be related to weather conditions or other factors beyond the control of the employer (which may include unforeseen changes in market conditions). Such requests must be supported in writing, with documentation showing that the extension is needed and that the need could not have been reasonably foreseen by the employer. The CO will notify the employer of the decision in writing if time allows, or will otherwise notify the employer of the decision. The CO will not grant an extension where the total work contract period under that *Application for Temporary Employment Certification* and extensions would be 12 months or more, except in extraordinary circumstances. The employer may appeal a denial of a request for an extension by following the procedures in § 655.171.

(c) *Disclosure.* The employer must provide to the workers a copy of any approved extension in accordance with § 655.122(q), as soon as practicable.

§ 655.171 Appeals.

Where authorized in this subpart, employers may request an administrative review or de novo hearing before an ALJ of a decision by the CO. In such cases, the CO will send a copy of the OFLC administrative file to the Chief ALJ by means normally assuring next-day delivery. The Chief ALJ will immediately assign an ALJ (which may be a panel of such persons designated by the Chief ALJ from the Board of Alien Labor Certification Appeals (BALCA)).

(a) *Administrative review.* Where the employer has requested administrative review, within 5 business days after receipt of the ETA administrative file the ALJ will, on the basis of the written record and after due consideration of any written submissions (which may not include new evidence) from the parties involved or amici curiae, either affirm, reverse, or modify the CO's decision, or remand to the CO for further action. The decision of the ALJ must specify the reasons for the action taken and must be immediately provided to the employer, the CO, the OFLC Administrator and DHS by means normally assuring next-day delivery. The ALJ's decision is the final decision of the Secretary.

(b) *De novo hearing*—(1) *Conduct of hearing.* Where the employer has requested a de novo hearing the procedures in 29 CFR part 18 apply to such hearings, except that:

(i) The appeal will not be considered to be a complaint to which an answer is required;

(ii) The ALJ will ensure that the hearing is scheduled to take place within 5 business days after the ALJ's receipt of the OFLC administrative file, if the employer so requests, and will allow for the introduction of new evidence; and

(iii) The ALJ's decision must be rendered within 10 calendar days after the hearing.

(2) *Decision.* After a de novo hearing, the ALJ must affirm, reverse, or modify the CO's determination, or remand to the CO for further action. The decision of the ALJ must specify the reasons for the action taken and must be immediately provided to the employer, CO, OFLC Administrator and DHS by means normally assuring next-day delivery. The ALJ's decision is the final decision of the Secretary.

§ 655.172 Withdrawal of job order and application for temporary employment certification.

(a) Employers may withdraw a job order from intrastate posting if the employer no longer plans to file an *Application for Temporary Employment Certification.* However, a withdrawal of a job order does not nullify existing obligations to those workers recruited in connection with the placement of a job order pursuant to this subpart or the filing of an *Application for Temporary Employment Certification.*

(b) Employers may withdraw an *Application for Temporary Employment Certification* once it has been formally accepted by the NPC. However, the employer is still obligated to comply with the terms and conditions of employment contained in the *Application for*

Temporary Employment Certification with respect to workers recruited in connection with that application.

§ 655.173 Setting meal charges; petition for higher meal charges.

(a) *Meal charges.* Until a new amount is set under this paragraph, an employer may charge workers up to $10.64 for providing them with three meals per day. The maximum charge allowed by this paragraph (a) will be changed annually by the same percentage as the 12 month percentage change for the Consumer Price Index for all Urban Consumers for Food between December of the year just concluded and December of the year prior to that. The annual adjustments will be effective on the date of their publication by the OFLC Administrator as a Notice in the FEDERAL REGISTER. When a charge or deduction for the cost of meals would bring the employee's wage below the minimum wage set by the FLSA at 29 U.S.C. 206 the charge or deduction must meet the requirements of 29 U.S.C. 203(m) of the FLSA, including the recordkeeping requirements found at 29 CFR 516.27.

(b) *Filing petitions for higher meal charges.* The employer may file a petition with the CO to charge more than the applicable amount for meal charges if the employer justifies the charges and submits to the CO the documentation required by paragraph (b)(1) of this section.

(1) Documentation submitted must include the cost of goods and services directly related to the preparation and serving of meals, the number of workers fed, the number of meals served and the number of days meals were provided. The cost of the following items may be included: Food; kitchen supplies other than food, such as lunch bags and soap; labor costs that have a direct relation to food service operations, such as wages of cooks and dining hall supervisors; fuel, water, electricity, and other utilities used for the food service operation; and other costs directly related to the food service operation. Charges for transportation, depreciation, overhead and similar charges may not be included. Receipts and other cost records for a representative pay period must be retained and must be available for inspection by the CO for a period of 1 year.

(2) The employer may begin charging the higher rate upon receipt of a favorable decision from the CO unless the CO sets a later effective date in the decision.

(c) *Appeal rights.* In the event the employer's petition for a higher meal charge is denied in whole or in part, the employer may appeal the denial. Appeals will be filed with the Chief ALJ, pursuant to § 655.171.

§ 655.174 Public disclosure.

The Department will maintain an electronic file accessible to the public with information on all employers applying for temporary agricultural labor certifications. The database will include such information as the number of workers requested, the date filed, the date decided, and the final disposition.

INTEGRITY MEASURES

§ 655.180 Audit.

The CO may conduct audits of applications for which certifications have been granted.

(a) *Discretion.* The applications selected for audit will be chosen within the sole discretion of the CO.

(b) *Audit letter.* Where an application is selected for audit, the CO will issue an audit letter to the employer and a copy, if appropriate, to the employer's agent or attorney. The audit letter will:

(1) State the documentation that must be submitted by the employer;

(2) Specify a date no more than 30 days from the date of the audit letter by which the required documentation must be received by the CO; and

(3) Advise that failure to comply with the audit process may result in the revocation of the certification or program debarment.

(c) *Supplemental information request.* During the course of the audit examination, the CO may request supplemental information and/or documentation from the employer in order to complete the audit.

(d) *Potential referrals.* In addition to steps in this subpart, the CO may determine to provide the audit findings and underlying documentation to DHS or another appropriate enforcement agency. The CO will refer any findings that an employer discouraged an eligible U.S. worker from applying, or failed to hire, discharged, or otherwise discriminated against an eligible U.S. worker, to the Department of Justice, Civil Rights Division, Office of Special Counsel for Unfair Immigration Related Employment Practices.

§ 655.181 Revocation.

(a) *Basis for DOL revocation.* The OFLC Administrator may revoke a temporary agricultural labor certification approved under this subpart, if the OFLC Administrator finds:

(1) The issuance of the temporary agricultural labor certification was not justified due to fraud or misrepresentation in the application process;

(2) The employer substantially violated a material term or condition of the approved temporary agricultural labor certification, as defined in § 655.182;

(3) The employer failed to cooperate with a DOL investigation or with a DOL official performing an investigation, inspection, audit (as discussed in § 655.180), or law enforcement function under 8 U.S.C. 1188, 29 CFR part 501, or this subpart; or

(4) The employer failed to comply with one or more sanctions or remedies imposed by the WHD, or with one or more decisions or orders of the Secretary or a court order secured by the Secretary under 8 U.S.C. 1188, 29 CFR part 501, or this subpart.

(b) *DOL procedures for revocation.* (1) Notice of Revocation. If the OFLC Administrator makes a determination to revoke an employer's temporary labor certification, the OFLC Administrator will send to the employer (and its attorney or agent) a Notice of Revocation. The Notice will contain a detailed statement of the grounds for the revocation, and it will inform the employer of its right to submit rebuttal evidence or to appeal. If the employer does not file rebuttal evidence or an appeal within 14 days of the date of the Notice of Revocation, the Notice is the final agency action and will take effect immediately at the end of the 14-day period.

(2) *Rebuttal.* The employer may submit evidence to rebut the grounds stated in the Notice of Revocation within 14 calendar days of the date the Notice is issued. If rebuttal evidence is timely filed by the employer, the OFLC Administrator will inform the employer of the OFLC Administrator's final determination on the revocation within 14 calendar days of receiving the rebuttal evidence. If the OFLC Administrator determines that the certification should be revoked, the OFLC Administrator will inform the employer of its right to appeal according to the procedures of § 655.171. The employer must file the appeal within 10 calendar days after the OFLC Administrator's final determination, or the OFLC Administrator's determination is the final agency action and will take effect immediately at the end of the 10-day period.

(3) *Appeal.* An employer may appeal a Notice of Revocation, or a final determination of the OFLC Administrator after the review of rebuttal evidence, according to the appeal procedures of § 655.171. The ALJ's decision is the final agency action.

(4) *Stay.* The timely filing of rebuttal evidence or an administrative appeal will stay the revocation pending the outcome of those proceedings.

(5) *Decision.* If the temporary agricultural labor certification is revoked, the OFLC Administrator will send a copy of the final agency action of the Secretary to DHS and the Department of State (DOS).

(c) *Employer's obligations in the event of revocation.* If an employer's temporary agricultural labor certification is revoked pursuant to this section, the employer is responsible for:

(1) Reimbursement of actual inbound transportation and subsistence expenses, as if the worker meets the requirements for payment under § 655.122(h)(1);

(2) The worker's outbound transportation expenses, as if the worker meets the requirements for payment under § 655.122(h)(2);

(3) Payment to the worker of the amount due under the three-fourths guarantee as required by § 655.122(i); and

(4) Any other wages, benefits, and working conditions due or owing to the worker under this subpart.

§ 655.182 Debarment.

(a) *Debarment of an employer.* The OFLC Administrator may debar an employer or any successor in interest to that employer from receiving future labor certifications under this subpart, subject to the time limits set forth in paragraph (c) of this section, if the OFLC Administrator finds that the employer substantially violated a material term or condition of its temporary labor certification, with respect to H–2A workers, workers in corresponding employment, or U.S. workers improperly rejected for employment, or improperly laid off or displaced.

(b) *Debarment of an agent or attorney.* The OFLC Administrator may debar an agent or attorney from participating in any action under 8 U.S.C. 1188, this subpart, or 29 CFR part 501, if the OFLC Administrator finds that the agent or attorney participated in an employer's substantial violation. The OFLC Administrator may not issue future labor certifications under this subpart to any employer represented by a debarred agent or attorney, subject to the time limits set forth in paragraph (c) of this section.

(c) *Statute of limitations and period of debarment.* (1) The OFLC Administrator must issue any Notice of Debarment no later than 2 years after the occurrence of the violation.

(2) No employer, attorney, or agent may be debarred under this subpart for more than 3 years from the date of the final agency decision.

(d) *Definition of violation.* For the purposes of this section, a violation includes:

(1) One or more acts of commission or omission on the part of the employer or the employer's agent which involve:

(i) Failure to pay or provide the required wages, benefits or working conditions to the employer's H–2A workers and/or workers in corresponding employment;

(ii) Failure, except for lawful, job-related reasons, to offer employment to qualified U.S. workers who applied for the job opportunity for which certification was sought;

(iii) Failure to comply with the employer's obligations to recruit U.S. workers;

(iv) Improper layoff or displacement of U.S. workers or workers in corresponding employment;

(v) Failure to comply with one or more sanctions or remedies imposed by the WHD Administrator for violation(s) of contractual or other H–2A obligations, or with one or more decisions or orders of the Secretary or a court under 8 U.S.C. 1188, 29 CFR part 501, or this subpart;

(vi) Impeding an investigation of an employer under 8 U.S.C. 1188 or 29 CFR part 501, or an audit under § 655.180 of this subpart;

(vii) Employing an H–2A worker outside the area of intended employment, in an activity/activities not listed in the job order or outside the validity period of employment of the job order, including any approved extension thereof;

(viii) A violation of the requirements of § 655.135(j) or (k);

(ix) A violation of any of the provisions listed in 29 CFR 501.4(a); or

(x) A single heinous act showing such flagrant disregard for the law that future compliance with program requirements cannot reasonably be expected;

(2) The employer's failure to pay a necessary certification fee in a timely manner;

(3) Fraud involving the *Application for Temporary Employment Certification;* or

(4) A material misrepresentation of fact during the application process.

(e) *Determining whether a violation is substantial.* In determining whether a violation is so substantial so as to merit debarment, the factors the OFLC Administrator may consider include, but are not limited to, the following:

(1) Previous history of violation(s) of 8 U.S.C. 1188, 29 CFR part 501, or this subpart;

(2) The number of H–2A workers, workers in corresponding employment, or U.S. workers who were and/or are affected by the violation(s);

(3) The gravity of the violation(s);

(4) Efforts made in good faith to comply with 8 U.S.C. 1188, 29 CFR part 501, and this subpart;

(5) Explanation from the person charged with the violation(s);

(6) Commitment to future compliance, taking into account the public health, interest, or safety, and whether the person has previously violated 8 U.S.C. 1188;

(7) The extent to which the violator achieved a financial gain due to the violation(s), or the potential financial loss or potential injury to the worker(s).

(f) *Debarment procedure*—(1) *Notice of Debarment*. If the OFLC Administrator makes a determination to debar an employer, attorney, or agent, the OFLC Administrator will send the party a Notice of Debarment. The Notice will state the reason for the debarment finding, including a detailed explanation of the grounds for and the duration of the debarment, and it will inform the party subject to the Notice of its right to submit rebuttal evidence or to request a debarment hearing. If the party does not file rebuttal evidence or request a hearing within 30 calendar days of the date of the Notice of Debarment, the Notice will be the final agency action and the debarment will take effect at the end of the 30-day period.

(2) *Rebuttal*. The party who received the Notice of Debarment may choose to submit evidence to rebut the grounds stated in the Notice within 30 calendar days of the date the Notice is issued. If rebuttal evidence is timely filed, the OFLC Administrator will issue a final determination on the debarment within 30 days of receiving the rebuttal evidence. If the OFLC Administrator determines that the party should be debarred, the OFLC Administrator will inform the party of its right to request a debarment hearing according to the procedures of § 655.182(f)(3). The party must request a hearing within 30 calendar days after the date of the OFLC Administrator's final determination, or the OFLC Administrator's determination will be the final agency order and the debarment will take effect at the end of the 30-day period.

(3) *Hearing*. The recipient of a Notice of Debarment may request a debarment hearing within 30 calendar days of the date of a Notice of Debarment or the date of a final determination of the OFLC Administrator after review of rebuttal evidence submitted pursuant to § 655.182(f)(2). To obtain a debarment hearing, the debarred party must, within 30 days of the date of the Notice or the final determination, file a written request to the Chief Administrative Law Judge, United States Department of Labor, 800 K Street, NW., Suite 400–N, Washington, DC 20001–8002, and simultaneously serve a copy to the OFLC Administrator. The debarment will take effect 30 days from the date the Notice of Debarment or final determination is issued, unless a request for review is properly filed within 30 days from the issuance of the Notice of Debarment or final determination. The timely filing of a request for a hearing stays the debarment pending the outcome of the hearing. Within 10 days of receipt of the request for a hearing, the OFLC Administrator will send a certified copy of the ETA case file to the Chief ALJ by means normally assuring next-day delivery. The Chief ALJ will immediately assign an ALJ to conduct the hearing. The procedures in 29 CFR part 18 apply to such hearings, except that the request for a hearing will not be considered to be a complaint to which an answer is required.

(4) *Decision*. After the hearing, the ALJ must affirm, reverse, or modify the OFLC Administrator's determination. The ALJ will prepare the decision within 60 days after completion of the hearing and closing of the record. The ALJ's decision will be provided immediately to the parties to the debarment hearing by means normally assuring next-day delivery. The ALJ's decision is the final agency action, unless either party, within 30 calendar days of the ALJ's decision, seeks review of the decision with the Administrative Review Board (ARB).

(5) *Review by the ARB*. (i) Any party wishing review of the decision of an ALJ must, within 30 days of the decision of the ALJ, petition the ARB to review the decision. Copies of the petition must be served on all parties and on the ALJ. The ARB will decide whether to accept the petition within 30 days of receipt. If the ARB declines to accept the petition, or if the ARB does not issue a notice accepting a petition within 30 days after the receipt of a timely filing of the petition, the decision of the ALJ will be deemed the

final agency action. If a petition for review is accepted, the decision of the ALJ will be stayed unless and until the ARB issues an order affirming the decision. The ARB must serve notice of its decision to accept or not to accept the petition upon the ALJ and upon all parties to the proceeding.

(ii) Upon receipt of the ARB's notice to accept the petition, the Office of Administrative Law Judges will promptly forward a copy of the complete hearing record to the ARB.

(iii) Where the ARB has determined to review such decision and order, the ARB will notify each party of the issue(s) raised, the form in which submissions must be made (e.g., briefs or oral argument), and the time within which such presentation must be submitted.

(6) *ARB decision.* The ARB's final decision must be issued within 90 days from the notice granting the petition and served upon all parties and the ALJ. If the ARB fails to provide a decision within 90 days from the notice granting the petition, the ALJ's decision will be the final agency decision.

(g) *Concurrent debarment jurisdiction.* OFLC and the WHD have concurrent jurisdiction to impose a debarment remedy under this section or under 29 CFR 501.20. When considering debarment, OFLC and the WHD may inform one another and may coordinate their activities. A specific violation for which debarment is imposed will be cited in a single debarment proceeding. Copies of final debarment decisions will be forwarded to DHS promptly.

(h) *Debarment involving members of associations.* If the OFLC Administrator determines that an individual employer-member of a joint employer association has committed a substantial violation, the debarment determination will apply only to that member unless the OFLC Administrator determines that the association or another association member participated in the violation, in which case the debarment will be invoked against the association or other complicit association member(s) as well.

(i) *Debarment involving associations acting as joint employers.* If the OFLC Administrator determines that an association acting as a joint employer with its members has committed a substantial violation, the debarment determination will apply only to the association, and will not be applied to any individual employer-member of the association. However, if the OFLC Administrator determines that the member participated in, had knowledge of, or had reason to know of the violation, the debarment may be invoked against the complicit association member as well. An association debarred from the H–2A temporary labor certification program will not be permitted to continue to file as a joint employer with its members during the period of the debarment.

(j) *Debarment involving associations acting as sole employers.* If the OFLC Administrator determines that an association acting as a sole employer has committed a substantial violation, the debarment determination will apply only to the association and any successor in interest to the debarred association.

§655.183 Less than substantial violations.

(a) *Requirement of special procedures.* If the OFLC Administrator determines that a less than substantial violation has occurred, but the OFLC Administrator has reason to believe that past actions on the part of the employer (or agent or attorney) may have had and may continue to have a chilling or otherwise negative effect on the recruitment, employment, and retention of U.S. workers, the OFLC Administrator may require the employer to conform to special procedures before and after the temporary labor certification determination. These special procedures may include special on-site positive recruitment and streamlined interviewing and referral techniques. The special procedures are designed to enhance U.S. worker recruitment and retention in the next year as a condition for receiving a temporary agricultural labor certification. Such requirements will be reasonable; will not require the employer to offer better wages, working conditions, and benefits than those specified in §655.122; and will be no more than deemed necessary to assure employer compliance with the test of

U.S. worker availability and adverse effect criteria of this subpart.

(b) *Notification of required special procedures.* The OFLC Administrator will notify the employer (or agent or attorney) in writing of the special procedures that will be required in the coming year. The notification will state the reasons for the imposition of the requirements, state that the employer's agreement to accept the conditions will constitute inclusion of them as bona fide conditions and terms of a temporary agricultural labor certification, and will offer the employer an opportunity to request an administrative review or a de novo hearing before an ALJ. If an administrative review or de novo hearing is requested, the procedures prescribed in § 655.171 will apply.

(c) *Failure to comply with special procedures.* If the OFLC Administrator determines that the employer has failed to comply with special procedures required pursuant to paragraph (a) of this section, the OFLC Administrator will send a written notice to the employer, stating that the employer's otherwise affirmative H–2A certification determination will be reduced by 25 percent of the total number of H–2A workers requested (which cannot be more than those requested in the previous year) for a period of 1 year. Notice of such a reduction in the number of workers requested will be conveyed to the employer by the OFLC Administrator in the OFLC Administrator's written certification determination. The notice will offer the employer an opportunity to request administrative review or a de novo hearing before an ALJ. If administrative review or a de novo hearing is requested, the procedures prescribed in § 655.171 will apply, provided that if the ALJ affirms the OFLC Administrator's determination that the employer has failed to comply with special procedures required by paragraph (a) of this section, the reduction in the number of workers requested will be 25 percent of the total number of H–2A workers requested (which cannot be more than those requested in the previous year) for a period of 1 year.

§ 655.184 Applications involving fraud or willful misrepresentation.

(a) *Referral for investigation.* If the CO discovers possible fraud or willful misrepresentation involving an *Application for Temporary Employment Certification*, the CO may refer the matter to the DHS and the Department's Office of the Inspector General for investigation.

(b) *Sanctions.* If the WHD, a court or the DHS determines that there was fraud or willful misrepresentation involving an *Application for Temporary Employment Certification* and certification has been granted, a finding under this paragraph will be cause to revoke the certification. The finding of fraud or willful misrepresentation may also constitute a debarrable violation under § 655.182.

§ 655.185 Job service complaint system; enforcement of work contracts.

(a) *Filing with DOL.* Complaints arising under this subpart must be filed through the Job Service Complaint System, as described in 20 CFR part 658, subpart E. Complaints involving allegations of fraud or misrepresentation must be referred by the SWA to the CO for appropriate handling and resolution. Complaints that involve worker contracts must be referred by the SWA to the WHD for appropriate handling and resolution, as described in 29 CFR part 501. As part of this process, the WHD may report the results of its investigation to the OFLC Administrator for consideration of employer penalties or such other action as may be appropriate.

(b) *Filing with the Department of Justice.* Complaints alleging that an employer discouraged an eligible U.S. worker from applying, failed to hire, discharged, or otherwise discriminated against an eligible U.S. worker, or discovered violations involving the same, will be referred to the U.S. Department of Justice, Civil Rights Division, Office of Special Counsel for Unfair Immigration Related Employment Practices (OSC), in addition to any activity, investigation, and/or enforcement action taken by ETA or a SWA. Likewise, if OSC becomes aware of a violation of the regulations in this subpart, it may provide such information to the appropriate SWA and the CO.

LABOR CERTIFICATION PROCESS FOR TEMPORARY AGRICULTURAL EMPLOYMENT IN RANGE SHEEP HERDING, GOAT HERDING, AND PRODUCTION OF LIVESTOCK OCCUPATIONS

SOURCE: 80 FR 63066, Oct. 16, 2015, unless otherwise noted.

§ 655.200 Scope and purpose of herding and range livestock regulations.

(a) *Purpose.* The purpose of §§ 655.200–655.235 is to establish certain procedures for employers who apply to the Department of Labor to obtain labor certifications to hire temporary agricultural foreign workers to perform herding or production of livestock on the range, as defined in § 655.201. Unless otherwise specified in §§ 655.200–655.235, employers whose job opportunities meet the qualifying criteria under §§ 655.200–655.235 must fully comply with all of the requirements of §§ 655.100–655.185; part 653, subparts B and F; and part 654 of this chapter.

(b) *Jobs subject to §§ 655.200–655.235.* These procedures apply to job opportunities with the following unique characteristics:

(1) The work activities involve the herding or production of livestock (which includes work that is closely and directly related to herding and/or the production of livestock), as defined under § 655.201;

(2) The work is performed on the range for the majority (meaning more than 50 percent) of the workdays in the work contract period. Any additional work performed at a place other than the range must constitute the production of livestock (which includes work that is closely and directly related to herding and/or the production of livestock); and

(3) The work activities generally require the workers to be on call 24 hours per day, 7 days a week.

§ 655.201 Definition of herding and range livestock terms.

The following are terms that are not defined in §§ 655.100–655.185 and are specific to applications for labor certifications involving the herding or production of livestock on the range.

Herding. Activities associated with the caring, controlling, feeding, gathering, moving, tending, and sorting of livestock on the range.

Livestock. An animal species or species group such as sheep, cattle, goats, horses, or other domestic hooved animals. In the context of §§ 655.200–655.235, livestock refers to those species raised on the range.

Production of livestock. The care or husbandry of livestock throughout one or more seasons during the year, including guarding and protecting livestock from predatory animals and poisonous plants; feeding, fattening, and watering livestock; examining livestock to detect diseases, illnesses, or other injuries; administering medical care to sick or injured livestock; applying vaccinations and spraying insecticides on the range; and assisting with the breeding, birthing, raising, weaning, castration, branding, and general care of livestock. This term also includes duties performed off the range that are closely and directly related to herding and/or the production of livestock. The following are non-exclusive examples of ranch work that is closely and directly related: repairing fences used to contain the herd; assembling lambing jugs; cleaning out lambing jugs; feeding and caring for the dogs that the workers use on the range to assist with herding or guarding the flock; feeding and caring for the horses that the workers use on the range to help with herding or to move the sheep camps and supplies; and loading animals into livestock trucks for movement to the range or to market. The following are examples of ranch work that is not closely and directly related: working at feedlots; planting, irrigating and harvesting crops; operating or repairing heavy equipment; constructing wells or dams; digging irrigation ditches; applying weed control; cutting trees or chopping wood; constructing or repairing the bunkhouse or other ranch buildings; and delivering supplies from the ranch to the herders on the range.

Range. The range is any area located away from the ranch headquarters used by the employer. The following factors are indicative of the range: it involves land that is uncultivated; it involves wide expanses of land, such as thousands of acres; it is located in a remote, isolated area; and typically range housing is required so that the herder can be in constant attendance to the herd. No one factor is controlling and the totality of the circumstances is considered in determining what should be considered range. The range does not include feedlots, corrals, or any area where the stock involved would be near ranch headquarters. Ranch headquarters, which is a place where the business of the ranch occurs and is often where the owner resides, is limited and does not embrace large acreage; it only includes the ranchhouse, barns, sheds, pen, bunkhouse, cookhouse, and other buildings in the vicinity. The range also does not include any area where a herder is not required to be available constantly to attend to the livestock and to perform tasks, including but not limited to, ensuring the livestock do not stray, protecting them from predators, and monitoring their health.

Range housing. Range housing is housing located on the range that meets the standards articulated under § 655.235.

§ 655.205 Herding and range livestock job orders.

The employer whose job opportunity has been determined to qualify for these procedures, whether individual, association, or H–2ALC, is not required to comply with the job order filing requirements in § 655.121(a) through (d). Rather, the employer must submit Form ETA–790, directly to the National Processing Center (NPC) designated by the Office of Foreign Labor Certification (OFLC Administrator) along with a completed *H–2A Application for Temporary Employment Certification*, Form ETA–9142A, as required in § 655.215.

§ 655.210 Contents of herding and range livestock job orders.

(a) *Content of job offers.* Unless otherwise specified in §§ 655.200–655.235, the employer, whether individual, association, or H–2ALC, must satisfy the requirements for job orders established under § 655.121(e) and for the content of job offers established under part 653, subpart F of this chapter and § 655.122.

(b) *Job qualifications and requirements.* The job offer must include a statement that the workers are on call for up to 24 hours per day, 7 days per week and that the workers spend the majority (meaning more than 50 percent) of the workdays during the contract period in the herding or production of livestock on the range. Duties may include activities performed off the range only if such duties constitute the production of livestock (which includes work that is closely and directly related to herding and/or the production of livestock). All such duties must be specifically disclosed on the job order. The job offer may also specify that applicants must possess up to 6 months of experience in similar occupations involving the herding or production of livestock on the range and require reference(s) for the employer to verify applicant experience. An employer may specify other appropriate job qualifications and requirements for its job opportunity. Job offers may not impose on U.S. workers any restrictions or obligations that will not be imposed on the employer's H–2A workers engaged in herding or the production of livestock on the range. Any such requirements must be applied equally to both U.S. and foreign workers. Each job qualification and requirement listed in the job offer must be bona fide, and the Certifying Officer (CO) may require the employer to submit documentation to substantiate the appropriateness of any other job qualifications and requirements specified in the job offer.

(c) *Range housing.* The employer must specify in the job order that range housing will be provided. The range housing must meet the requirements set forth in § 655.235.

(d) *Employer-provided items.* (1) The employer must provide to the worker, without charge or deposit charge, all tools, supplies, and equipment required by law, by the employer, or by the nature of the work to perform the duties assigned in the job offer safely and effectively. The employer must specify in the job order which items it will provide to the worker.

(2) Because of the unique nature of the herding or production of livestock on the range, this equipment must include effective means of communicating with persons capable of responding to the worker's needs in case of an emergency including, but not limited to, satellite phones, cell phones, wireless devices, radio transmitters, or other types of electronic communication systems. The employer must specify in the job order:

(i) The type(s) of electronic communication device(s) and that such device(s) will be provided without charge or deposit charge to the worker during the entire period of employment; and

(ii) If there are periods of time when the workers are stationed in locations where electronic communication devices may not operate effectively, the employer must specify in the job order, the means and frequency with which the employer plans to make contact with the workers to monitor the worker's well-being. This contact must include either arrangements for the workers to be located, on a regular basis, in geographic areas where the electronic communication devices operate effectively, or arrangements for regular, pre-scheduled, in-person visits between the workers and the employer, which may include visits between the workers and other persons designated by the employer to resupply the workers' camp.

(e) *Meals.* The employer must specify in the job offer and provide to the worker, without charge or deposit charge:

(1) Either three sufficient meals a day, or free and convenient cooking facilities and adequate provision of food to enable the worker to prepare his own meals. To be sufficient or adequate, the meals or food provided must include a daily source of protein, vitamins, and minerals; and

(2) Adequate potable water, or water that can be easily rendered potable and the means to do so. Standards governing the provision of water to range workers are also addressed in § 655.235(e).

(f) *Hours and earnings statements.* (1) The employer must keep accurate and adequate records with respect to the worker's earnings and furnish to the worker on or before each payday a statement of earnings. The employer is exempt from recording the hours actually worked each day, the time the worker begins and ends each workday, as well as the nature and amount of work performed, but all other regulatory requirements in § 655.122(j) and (k) apply.

(2) The employer must keep daily records indicating whether the site of the employee's work was on the range or off the range. If the employer prorates a worker's wage pursuant to paragraph (g)(2) of this section because of the worker's voluntary absence for personal reasons, it must also keep a record of the reason for the worker's absence.

(g) *Rates of pay.* The employer must pay the worker at least the monthly AEWR, as specified in § 655.211, the agreed-upon collective bargaining wage, or the applicable minimum wage imposed by Federal or State law or judicial action, in effect at the time work is performed, whichever is highest, for every month of the job order period or portion thereof.

(1) The offered wage shall not be based on commissions, bonuses, or other incentives, unless the employer guarantees a wage that equals or exceeds the monthly AEWR, the agreed-upon collective bargaining wage, or the applicable minimum wage imposed by Federal or State law or judicial action, or any agreed-upon collective bargaining rate, whichever is highest, and must be paid to each worker free and clear without any unauthorized deductions.

(2) The employer may prorate the wage for the initial and final pay periods of the job order period if its pay period does not match the beginning or ending dates of the job order. The employer also may prorate the wage if an employee is voluntarily unavailable to work for personal reasons.

(h) *Frequency of pay.* The employer must state in the job offer the frequency with which the worker will be paid, which must be at least twice monthly. Employers must pay wages when due.

§ 655.211 Herding and range livestock wage rate.

(a) *Compliance with rates of pay.* (1) To comply with its obligation under § 655.210(g), an employer must offer, advertise in its recruitment and pay each worker employed under §§ 655.200–655.235 a wage that is the highest of the monthly AEWR established under this section, the agreed-upon collective bargaining wage, or the applicable minimum wage imposed by Federal or State law or judicial action.

(2) If the monthly AEWR established under this section is adjusted during a work contract, and is higher than both the agreed-upon collective bargaining wage and the applicable minimum wage imposed by Federal or State law or judicial action in effect at the time the work is performed, the employer must pay that adjusted monthly AEWR upon publication by the Department in the FEDERAL REGISTER.

(b) *Publication of the monthly AEWR.* The OFLC Administrator will publish a notice in the FEDERAL REGISTER, at least once in each calendar year, on a date to be determined by the OFLC Administrator, establishing the monthly AEWR.

(c) *Monthly AEWR Rate.* (1) The monthly AEWR shall be $7.25 multiplied by 48 hours, and then multiplied by 4.333 weeks per month; and

(2) Beginning for calendar year 2017, the monthly AEWR shall be adjusted annually based on the Employment Cost Index for wages and salaries published by the Bureau of Labor Statistics (ECI) for the preceding October—October period.

(d) *Transition Rates.* (1) For the period from the effective date of this rule through calendar year 2016, the Department shall set the monthly AEWR at 80% of the result of the formula in paragraph (c) of this section.

(2) For calendar year 2017, the Department shall set the monthly AEWR at 90% of the result of the formula in paragraph (c) of this section.

(3) For calendar year 2018 and beyond, the Department shall set the monthly AEWR at 100% of the result of the formula in paragraph (c) of this section.

§ 655.215 Procedures for filing herding and range livestock applications for temporary employment certification.

(a) *Compliance with §§ 655.130–655.132.* Unless otherwise specified in §§ 655.200–655.235, the employer must satisfy the requirements for filing an *H–2A Application for Temporary Employment Certification* with the NPC designated by the OFLC Administrator as required under §§ 655.130–655.132.

(b) *What to file.* An employer must file a completed *H–2A Application for Temporary Employment Certification* (Form ETA–9142A), *Agricultural and Food Processing Clearance Order* (Form ETA–790), and an attachment identifying, with as much geographic specificity as possible for each farmer/rancher, the names, physical locations and estimated start and end dates of need where work will be performed under the job order.

(1) The *H–2A Application for Temporary Employment Certification* and Form ETA–790 may be filed by an individual employer, association, or an H–2ALC, covering multiple areas of intended employment and more than two contiguous States.

(2) The period of need identified on the *H–2A Application for Temporary Employment Certification* and job order for range sheep or goat herding or production occupations must be no more than 364 calendar days. The period of need identified on the *H–2A Application for Temporary Employment Certification* and job order for range herding or production of cattle, horses, or other domestic hooved livestock, except sheep and goats, must be for no more than 10 months.

(3) An association of agricultural employers filing as a joint employer may submit a single Form ETA–790 and master *H–2A Application for Temporary Employment Certification* on behalf of its employer-members located in more than two contiguous States with different start dates of need. Unless modifications to a sheep or goat herding or production of livestock job order are required by the CO or requested by the employer, pursuant to § 655.121(e), the association is not required to re-submit the Form ETA–790 during the calendar

year with its H–2A Application for Temporary Employment Certification.

§ 655.220 Processing herding and range livestock applications for temporary employment certification.

(a) *NPC Review.* Unless otherwise specified in §§ 655.200–655.235, the CO will review and process the *H–2A Application for Temporary Employment Certification* and the Form ETA–790 in accordance with the requirements outlined in §§ 655.140–655.145, and will work with the employer to address any deficiencies in the job order in a manner consistent with §§ 655.140–655.141.

(b) *Notice of acceptance.* Once the job order is determined to meet all regulatory requirements, the NPC will issue a Notice of Acceptance consistent with § 655.143(b)(1). The CO will provide notice to the employer authorizing conditional access to the interstate clearance system; identify and transmit a copy of the Form ETA–790 to any one of the SWAs having jurisdiction over the anticipated worksites, and direct the SWA to place the job order promptly in intrastate and interstate clearance (including all States where the work will take place); and commence recruitment of U.S. workers. Where an association of agricultural employers files as a joint employer and submits a single Form ETA–790 on behalf of its employer-members, the CO will transmit a copy of the Form ETA–790 to the SWA having jurisdiction over the location of the association, again directing that SWA to place the job order in intrastate and interstate clearance, including to those other States where the work will take place, and commence recruitment of U.S. workers.

(c) *Electronic job registry.* Under § 655.144(b), where a single job order is approved for an association of agricultural employers filing as a joint employer on behalf of its employer-members with different start dates of need, the Department will keep the job order posted on the OFLC electronic job registry until 50 percent of the period of the work contract has elapsed for all employer-members identified on the job order.

§ 655.225 Post-acceptance requirements for herding and range livestock.

(a) Unless otherwise specified in this section, the requirements for recruiting U.S. workers by the employer and SWA must be satisfied, as specified in §§ 655.150–655.158.

(b) *Interstate clearance of job order.* Pursuant to § 655.150(b), where a single job order is approved for an association of agricultural employers filing as a joint employer on behalf of its employer-members with different start dates of need, each of the SWAs to which the Form ETA–790 was transmitted by the CO or the SWA having jurisdiction over the location of the association must keep the job order on its active file until 50 percent of the period of the work contract has elapsed for all employer-members identified on the job order, and must refer to the association each qualified U.S. worker who applies (or on whose behalf an application is made) for the job opportunity.

(c) Any eligible U.S. worker who applies (or on whose behalf an application is made) for the job opportunity and is hired will be placed at the location nearest to him/her absent a request for a different location by the U.S. worker. Employers must make reasonable efforts to accommodate such placement requests by the U.S. worker.

(d) The employer will not be required to place an advertisement in a newspaper of general circulation serving the area of intended employment, as required in § 655.151.

(e) An association that fulfills the recruitment requirements for its members is required to maintain a written recruitment report containing the information required by § 655.156 for each individual employer-member identified in the application or job order, including any approved modifications.

§ 655.230 Range housing.

(a) Housing for work performed on the range must meet the minimum standards contained in § 655.235 and § 655.122(d)(2).

(b) The SWA with jurisdiction over the location of the range housing must inspect and certify that such housing used on the range is sufficient to accommodate the number of certified workers and meets all applicable standards contained in § 655.235. The SWA must conduct a housing inspection no less frequently than once every three calendar years after the initial inspection and provide documentation to the employer certifying the housing for a period lasting no more than 36 months. If the SWA determines that an employer's housing cannot be inspected within a 3-year timeframe or, when it is inspected, the housing does not meet all the applicable standards, the CO may deny the H–2A application in full or in part or require additional inspections, to be carried out by the SWA, in order to satisfy the regulatory requirement.

(c)(1) The employer may self-certify its compliance with the standards contained in § 655.235 only when the employer has received a certification from the SWA for the range housing it seeks to use within the past 36 months.

(2) To self-certify the range housing, the employer must submit a copy of the valid SWA housing certification and a written statement, signed and dated by the employer, to the SWA and the CO assuring that the housing is available, sufficient to accommodate the number of workers being requested for temporary labor certification, and meets all the applicable standards for range housing contained in § 655.235.

(d) The use of range housing at a location other than the range, where fixed site employer-provided housing would otherwise be required, is permissible only when the worker occupying the housing is performing work that constitutes the production of livestock (which includes work that is closely and directly related to herding and/or the production of livestock). In such a situation, workers must be granted access to facilities, including but not limited to toilets and showers with hot and cold water under pressure, as well as cooking and cleaning facilities, that would satisfy the requirements contained in § 655.122(d)(1)(i). When such work does not constitute the production of livestock, workers must be housed in housing that meets all the requirements of § 655.122(d).

§ 655.235 Standards for range housing.

An employer employing workers under §§ 655.200–655.235 may use a mobile unit, camper, or other similar mobile housing vehicle, tents, and remotely located stationary structures along herding trails, which meet the following standards:

(a) *Housing site.* Range housing sites must be well drained and free from depressions where water may stagnate.

(b) *Water supply.* (1) An adequate and convenient supply of water that meets the standards of the state or local health authority must be provided.

(2) The employer must provide each worker at least 4.5 gallons of potable water, per day, for drinking and cooking, delivered on a regular basis, so that the workers will have at least this amount available for their use until this supply is next replenished. Employers must also provide an additional amount of water sufficient to meet the laundry and bathing needs of each worker. This additional water may be non-potable, and an employer may require a worker to rely on natural sources of water for laundry and bathing needs if these sources are available and contain water that is clean and safe for these purposes. If an employer relies on alternate water sources to meet any of the workers' needs, it must take precautionary measures to protect the worker's health where these sources are also used to water the herd, dogs, or horses, to prevent contamination of the sources if they collect runoff from areas where these animals excrete.

(3) The water provided for use by the workers may not be used to water dogs, horses, or the herd.

(4) In situations where workers are located in areas that are not accessible by motorized vehicle, an employer may request a variance from the requirement that it deliver potable water to workers, provided the following conditions are satisfied:

(i) It seeks the variance at the time it submits its *H–2A Application for Temporary Employment Certification*, Form ETA–9142A;

(ii) It attests that it has identified natural sources of water that are potable or may be easily rendered potable in the area in which the housing will be located, and that these sources will remain available during the period the worker is at that location;

(iii) It attests that it shall provide each worker an effective means to test whether the water is potable and, if not potable, the means to easily render it potable; and

(iv) The CO approves the variance.

(5) Individual drinking cups must be provided; and

(6) Containers appropriate for storing and using potable water must be provided and, in locations subject to freezing temperatures, containers must be small enough to allow storage in the housing unit to prevent freezing.

(c) *Excreta and liquid waste disposal.* (1) Facilities, including shovels, must be provided and maintained for effective disposal of excreta and liquid waste in accordance with the requirements of the state health authority or involved Federal agency; and

(2) If pits are used for disposal by burying of excreta and liquid waste, they must be kept fly-tight when not filled in completely after each use. The maintenance of disposal pits must be in accordance with state and local health and sanitation requirements.

(d) *Housing structure.* (1) Housing must be structurally sound, in good repair, in a sanitary condition and must provide shelter against the elements to occupants;

(2) Housing, other than tents, must have flooring constructed of rigid materials easy to clean and so located as to prevent ground and surface water from entering;

(3) Each housing unit must have at least one window that can be opened or skylight opening directly to the outdoors; and

(4) Tents appropriate to weather conditions may be used only where the terrain and/or land use regulations do not permit the use of other more substantial housing.

(e) *Heating.* (1) Where the climate in which the housing will be used is such that the safety and health of a worker requires heated living quarters, all such quarters must have properly installed operable heating equipment that supplies adequate heat. Where the climate in which the housing will be used is mild and the low temperature for any day in which the housing will be used is not reasonably expected to drop below 50 degrees Fahrenheit, no separate heating equipment is required as long as proper protective clothing and bedding are made available, free of charge or deposit charge, to the workers.

(2) Any stoves or other sources of heat using combustible fuel must be installed and vented in such a manner as to prevent fire hazards and a dangerous concentration of gases. If a solid or liquid fuel stove is used in a room with wooden or other combustible flooring, there must be a concrete slab, insulated metal sheet, or other fireproof material on the floor under each stove, extending at least 18 inches beyond the perimeter of the base of the stove.

(3) Any wall or ceiling within 18 inches of a solid or liquid fuel stove or stove pipe must be made of fireproof material. A vented metal collar must be installed around a stovepipe or vent passing through a wall, ceiling, floor or roof.

(4) When a heating system has automatic controls, the controls must be of the type that cuts off the fuel supply when the flame fails or is interrupted or whenever a predetermined safe temperature or pressure is exceeded.

(5) A heater may be used in a tent if the heater is approved by a testing service and if the tent is fireproof.

(f) *Lighting.* (1) In areas where it is not feasible to provide electrical service to range housing units, including tents, lanterns must be provided (kerosene wick lights meet the definition of lantern); and

(2) Lanterns, where used, must be provided in a minimum ratio of one per occupant of each unit, including tents.

(g) *Bathing, laundry, and hand washing.* Bathing, laundry and hand washing facilities must be provided when it is not feasible to provide hot and cold water under pressure.

(h) *Food storage.* When mechanical refrigeration of food is not feasible, the worker must be provided with another means of keeping food fresh and preventing spoilage, such as a butane or propane gas refrigerator. Other proven methods of safeguarding fresh foods, such as dehydrating or salting, are acceptable.

(i) *Cooking and eating facilities.* (1) When workers or their families are permitted or required to cook in their individual unit, a space must be provided with adequate lighting and ventilation; and

(2) Wall surfaces next to all food preparation and cooking areas must be of nonabsorbent, easy to clean material. Wall surfaces next to cooking areas must be made of fire-resistant material.

(j) *Garbage and other refuse.* (1) Durable, fly-tight, clean containers must be provided to each housing unit, including tents, for storing garbage and other refuse; and

(2) Provision must be made for collecting or burying refuse, which includes garbage, at least twice a week or more often if necessary, except where the terrain in which the housing is located cannot be accessed by motor vehicle and the refuse cannot be buried, in which case the employer must provide appropriate receptacles for storing the refuse and for removing the trash when the employer next transports supplies to the location.

(k) *Insect and rodent control.* Appropriate materials, including sprays, and sealed containers for storing food, must be provided to aid housing occupants in combating insects, rodents and other vermin.

(l) *Sleeping facilities.* A separate comfortable and clean bed, cot, or bunk, with a clean mattress, must be provided for each person, except in a family arrangement, unless a variance is requested from and granted by the CO. When filing an application for certification and only where it is demonstrated to the CO that it is impractical to provide a comfortable and clean bed, cot, or bunk, with a clean mattress, for each range worker, the employer may request a variance from this requirement to allow for a second worker to join the range operation. Such a variance must be used infrequently, and the period of the variance will be temporary, *i.e.*, the variance shall be for no more than 3 consecutive days. Should the CO grant the variance, the employer must supply a sleeping bag or bed roll for the second occupant free of charge or deposit charge.

(m) *Fire, safety, and first aid.* (1) All units in which people sleep or eat must be constructed and maintained according to applicable state or local fire and safety law.

(2) No flammable or volatile liquid or materials may be stored in or next to rooms used for living purposes, except for those needed for current household use.

(3) Housing units for range use must have a second means of escape through which the worker can exit the unit without difficulty.

(4) Tents are not required to have a second means of escape, except when large tents with walls of rigid material are used.

(5) Adequate, accessible fire extinguishers in good working condition and first aid kits must be provided in the range housing.

Subparts C–D [Reserved]

Subpart E—Labor Certification Process for Temporary Employment in the Commonwealth of the Northern Mariana Islands (CW–1 Workers)

SOURCE: 84 FR 12431, Apr. 1, 2019, unless otherwise noted.

EFFECTIVE DATE NOTE: At 84 FR 12431, Apr. 1, 2019, Subpart E, consisting of §§ 655.400 through 655.499 was added, effective Apr. 4, 2019.

§ 655.400 Scope and purpose of this subpart.

(a) *Purpose.* (1) A temporary labor certification (TLC) issued under this subpart reflects a determination by the Secretary of Labor (Secretary), pursuant to 48 U.S.C. 1806(d)(2)(A), that:

(i) There are not sufficient U.S. workers in the Commonwealth who are able, willing, and qualified and who will be available at the time and place needed to perform the services or labor for which an employer desires to hire foreign workers; and

(ii) The employment of the CNMI-Only Transitional Worker visa program (CW–1) nonimmigrant worker(s) will not adversely affect the wages and working conditions of U.S. workers similarly employed.

(2) This subpart describes the process by which the Department of Labor (Department or DOL) makes such a determination and certifies its determination to the Department of Homeland Security (DHS).

(b) *Scope.* This subpart sets forth the procedures governing the labor certification process for the employment of foreign workers in the CW–1 nonimmigrant classification, as defined in 48 U.S.C. 1806(d). It also establishes standards and obligations with respect to the terms and conditions of the temporary labor certification (TLC) with which CW–1 employers must comply, as well as the rights and obligations of CW–1 workers and workers in corresponding employment. Additionally, this subpart sets forth integrity measures for ensuring employers' continued compliance with the terms and conditions of the TLC.

§ 655.401 Authority of the agencies, offices, and divisions in the Department of Labor.

The Secretary has delegated authority to the Assistant Secretary for the Employment and Training Administration (ETA), who in turn has delegated that authority to the Office of Foreign Labor Certification (OFLC), to issue certifications and carry out other statutory responsibilities as required by 48 U.S.C. 1806. Determinations on a *CW–1 Application for Temporary Employment Certification* are made by the OFLC Administrator who, in turn, may delegate this responsibility to designated staff members, e.g., a Certifying Officer (CO).

§ 655.402 Definition of terms.

For purposes of this subpart:

Administrative Law Judge (ALJ) means a person within the Department's Office of Administrative Law Judges appointed under 5 U.S.C. 3105.

Agent means a person or a legal entity, such as an association or other organization of employers, or an attorney for an association or other organization of employers, that:

(1) Is authorized to act on behalf of the employer for Temporary Labor Certification (TLC) purposes;

(2) Is not itself an employer, or a joint employer, as defined in this subpart with respect to the specific application; and

(3) Is not under suspension, debarment, expulsion, disbarment, or otherwise restricted from practice before any court, the Department, the Executive Office for Immigration Review or DHS under 8 CFR 292.3 or 1003.101.

Applicant (or U.S. applicant) means a U.S. worker who is applying for a job opportunity for which an employer has filed a *CW–1 Application for Temporary Employment Certification.*

Application for Prevailing Wage Determination means the Office of Management and Budget (OMB)-approved Form ETA–9141C (or successor form) and the appropriate appendices, submitted by an employer to secure a prevailing wage determination (PWD) from the National Prevailing Wage Center (NPWC).

CW–1 Application for Temporary Employment Certification means the OMB-approved Form ETA–9142C (or successor form) and the appropriate appendices, a valid wage determination, as required by § 655.410, and all supporting documentation submitted by an employer to secure a TLC determination from the OFLC Administrator.

Attorney means any person who is a member in good standing of the bar of the highest court of any State, possession, territory, or commonwealth of the United States, or the District of Columbia. Such a person is also permitted to act as an agent under this subpart. No attorney who is under suspension, debarment, expulsion, or disbarment from practice before any court, the Department, the Executive Office for Immigration Review, or DHS under 8 CFR 1003.101 or 292.3, may represent an employer under this subpart.

Board of Alien Labor Certification Appeals (BALCA or Board) means the permanent Board established by part 656 of this chapter, chaired by the Chief Administrative Law Judge (Chief ALJ), and consisting of ALJs appointed pursuant to 5 U.S.C. 3105 and designated by the Chief ALJ to be members of BALCA.

Certifying Officer or CO means the person who makes determination on a *CW–1 Application for Temporary Employment Certification* filed under the CW–1 program. The OFLC Administrator is the national CO. Other COs may also be designated by the OFLC Administrator to make the determinations required under this subpart, including making PWDs.

Chief Administrative Law Judge or Chief ALJ means the chief official of the Department's Office of Administrative Law Judges or the Chief ALJ's designee.

CNMI Department of Labor means the executive Department of the Commonwealth Government that administers employment and job training activities for employers and U.S. workers in the Commonwealth.

Commonwealth or CNMI means the Commonwealth of the Northern Mariana Islands.

Corresponding employment means the employment of U.S. workers who are not CW–1 workers by an employer who has an approved *CW–1 Application for Temporary Employment Certification* in any work included in the approved job offer, or in any work performed by the CW–1 workers. To qualify as corresponding employment the work must be performed during the validity period of the *CW–1 Application for Temporary Employment Certification* and approved job offer, including any approved extension thereof.

CW–1 Petition means the U.S. Citizenship and Immigration Services (USCIS) Form I–129CW, *Petition for a CNMI–Only Nonimmigrant Transitional Worker*, a successor form, other form, or electronic equivalent, any supplemental information requested by USCIS, and additional evidence as may be prescribed or requested by USCIS.

CW–1 worker means any foreign worker who is lawfully present in the Commonwealth and authorized by DHS to perform temporary labor or services under 48 U.S.C. 1806(d).

Date of need means the first date the employer requires services of the CW–1 workers as indicated on the *CW–1 Application for Temporary Employment Certification.*

Department of Homeland Security or DHS means the Federal Department having jurisdiction over certain immigration-related functions, acting through its component agencies, including USCIS.

Employee means a person who is engaged to perform work for an employer, as defined under the general common law of agency. Some of the factors relevant to the determination of employee status include: The hiring party's right to control the manner and means by which the work is accomplished; the skill required to perform the work; the source of the instrumentalities and tools for accomplishing the work; the location of the work; the hiring party's discretion over when and how long to work; and whether the work is part of the regular business of the hiring party. Other applicable factors may be considered and no one factor is dispositive. The terms employee and worker are used interchangeably in this subpart.

Employer means a person (including any individual, partnership, association, corporation, cooperative, firm, joint stock company, trust, or other organization with legal rights and duties) that:

(1) Has a place of business (physical location) in the Commonwealth and a means by which it may be contacted for employment;

(2) Has an employer relationship (such as the ability to hire, pay, fire, supervise or otherwise control the work of employees) with respect to a CW–1 worker or a worker in corresponding employment, as defined under the common law of agency; and

(3) Possesses, for purposes of filing a *CW–1 Application for Temporary Employment Certification*, a valid Federal Employer Identification Number (FEIN).

Employer-client means an employer that has entered into an agreement with a job contractor and that is not an affiliate, branch, or subsidiary of the job contractor, under which the job contractor provides services or labor to the employer-client on a temporary basis and will not exercise substantial, direct day-to-day supervision and control in the performance of the services or labor to be performed other than hiring, paying, and firing the workers.

Employment and Training Administration or ETA means the agency within the Department that includes OFLC and has been delegated authority by the Secretary to fulfill the Secretary's mandate under for the administration and adjudication of a *CW–1 Application for Temporary Employment Certification* and related functions.

Federal holiday means a legal public holiday as defined at 5 U.S.C. 6103.

Full-time means 35 or more hours of work per week.

Governor means the Governor of the Commonwealth of the Northern Mariana Islands.

Job contractor means a person, association, firm, or a corporation that meets the definition of an employer and that contracts services or labor on a temporary basis to one or more employers that are not an affiliate, branch, or subsidiary of the job contractor and where the job contractor will not exercise substantial, direct day-to-day supervision and control in the performance of the services or labor to be performed other than hiring, paying, and releasing the workers.

Job offer means the offer made by an employer or potential employer of CW–1 workers to both U.S. and CW–1 workers describing all the material terms and conditions of employment, including those relating to wages, working conditions, and other benefits.

Job opportunity means full-time employment at a place in the Commonwealth to which U.S. workers can be referred.

Joint employment means that where two or more employers each have sufficient definitional indicia of being a joint employer of a worker under the common law of agency, they are, at all times, joint employers of that worker.

Layoff means any involuntary separation of one or more U.S. employees other than for cause.

Long-term worker means an alien who was admitted to the CNMI as a CW–1 nonimmigrant during fiscal year (FY) 2015, and who was granted CW–1 nonimmigrant status during each of FYs 2016 through 2018, as defined by DHS.

National Prevailing Wage Center or NPWC means that office within OFLC from which employers, agents, or attorneys who wish to file a *CW–1 Application for Temporary Employment Certification* receive a PWD.

NPWC Director means the OFLC official to whom the OFLC Administrator has delegated authority to carry out certain NPWC operations and functions.

National Processing Center (NPC) means the office within OFLC in which the COs operate, and which are charged with the adjudication of *CW–1 Applications for Temporary Employment Certification.*

NPC Director means the OFLC official to whom the OFLC Administrator has delegated authority for purposes of certain NPC operations and functions.

Occupational employment statistics (OES) survey means the program under the jurisdiction of the Bureau of Labor Statistics (BLS) that reports annual wage estimates, including those for Guam, based on standard occupational classifications (SOCs).

Offered wage means the wage offered by an employer in the *CW–1 Application for Temporary Employment Certification* and job offer. The offered wage must equal or exceed the highest of the prevailing wage, or the Federal minimum wage, or the Commonwealth minimum wage.

Office of Foreign Labor Certification or OFLC means the organizational component of the ETA that provides national leadership and policy guidance and develops regulations to carry out the Secretary's responsibilities, including determinations related to an employer's request for an *Application for Prevailing Wage Determination* or *CW–1 Application for Temporary Employment Certification.*

Place of employment means the worksite (or physical location) where work under the *CW–1 Application for Temporary Employment Certification* and job offer actually is performed by the CW–1 workers and workers in corresponding employment.

Prevailing wage (PW) means the official wage issued by the NPWC on the Form ETA 9141C, *Application for Prevailing Wage Determination for the CW–1 Program,* or successor form. At least that amount must be paid to all CW–1 workers and U.S. workers in corresponding employment.

Prevailing wage determination (PWD) means the prevailing wage issued by the OFLC NPWC on the Form ETA-9141C, *Application for Prevailing Wage Determination for the CW–1 Program,* or successor form. The PWD is used in support of the *CW–1 Application for Temporary Employment Certification*.

Secretary of Labor or Secretary means the chief official of the U.S. DOL, or the Secretary's designee.

Secretary of Homeland Security means the chief official of DHS or the Secretary of Homeland Security's designee.

Secretary of State means the chief official of the U.S. Department of State or the Secretary of State's designee.

Strike means a concerted stoppage of work by employees as a result of a labor dispute, or any concerted slowdown or other concerted interruption of operation (including stoppage by reason of the expiration of a collective bargaining agreement).

Successor in interest means an employer, agent, or attorney that is controlling and carrying on the business of a previous employer.

(1) Where an employer, agent, or attorney has violated 48 U.S.C. 1806 or the regulations in this subpart and has ceased doing business or cannot be located for purposes of enforcement, a successor in interest to that employer, agent, or attorney may be held liable for the duties and obligations of the violating employer in certain circumstances. The following factors, as used under Title VII of the Civil Rights Act and the Vietnam Era Veterans' Readjustment Assistance Act, may be considered in determining whether an employer, agent, or attorney is a successor in interest; no one factor is dispositive, and all the circumstances will be considered as a whole:

(i) Substantial continuity of the same business operations;

(ii) Use of the same facilities;

(iii) Continuity of the work force;

(iv) Similarity of jobs and working conditions;

(v) Similarity of supervisory personnel;

(vi) Whether the former management or owner retains a direct or indirect interest in the new enterprise;

(vii) Similarity in machinery, equipment, and production methods;

(viii) Similarity of products and services; and

(ix) The ability of the predecessor to provide relief.

(2) For purposes of debarment only, the primary consideration will be the personal involvement of the firm's ownership, management, supervisors, and others associated with the firm in the violation(s) at issue.

Temporary labor certification or TLC means the certification made by the OFLC Administrator, based on the *CW–1 Application for Temporary Employment Certification*, job offer, and all supporting documentation, with respect to an employer seeking to file with DHS a visa petition to employ one or more foreign nationals as a CW–1 worker.

United States means the continental United States, Alaska, Hawaii, the Commonwealth of Puerto Rico, Guam, the U.S. Virgin Islands, and the Commonwealth.

United States worker (U.S. worker) means a worker who is:

(1) A citizen or national of the United States;

(2) An alien lawfully admitted for permanent residence; or

(3) A citizen of the Federated States of Micronesia, the Republic of the Marshall Islands, or the Republic of Palau, who is eligible for nonimmigrant admission and is employment-authorized under the Compacts of Free Association between the United States and those nations.

U.S. Citizenship and Immigration Services or USCIS means the Federal agency within DHS that makes the determination whether to grant petitions filed by employers seeking CW–1 workers to perform temporary work in the Commonwealth.

Wages mean all forms of cash remuneration to a worker by an employer in payment for labor or services.

Work contract means the document containing all the material terms and conditions of employment relating to wages, hours, working conditions, places of employment, and other benefits, including all assurances and obligations required to be included under this subpart. The contract between the employer and the worker may be in the form of a separate written document containing the advertised terms and conditions of the job offer. In the absence of a separate, written work contract incorporating the required terms and conditions of employment, agreed to by both the employer and the worker, the required terms of the certified *CW–1 Application for Temporary Employment Certification* will be the work contract.

§ 655.403 Persons and entities authorized to file.

(a) *Persons authorized to file.* In addition to the employer, a request for a PWD or TLC under this subpart may be filed by an attorney or agent, as defined in § 655.402.

(b) *Employer's signature required.* Regardless of whether the employer is represented by an attorney or agent, the employer is required to sign the *CW–1 Application for Temporary Employment Certification* and all documentation submitted to the Department.

§ 655.404 Requirements for agents.

An agent filing a *CW–1 Application for Temporary Employment Certification* on behalf of an employer must provide a copy of the agent agreement or other document demonstrating the agent's authority to represent the employer to the NPC at the time of filing the application.

§§ 655.405–655.409 [Reserved]

PREFILING PROCEDURES

§ 655.410 Offered wage rate and determination of prevailing wage.

(a) *Offered wage.* (1) The employer must advertise the position to all potential workers at a wage that is at least the highest of the following:

(i) The prevailing wage for the job opportunity obtained from the NPWC;

(ii) The Federal minimum wage; or

(iii) The Commonwealth minimum wage.

(2) The employer must offer and pay at least the wage provided in paragraph (a)(1) of this section to both its CW–1 workers and its workers in corresponding employment. The issuance of a PWD under this section does not permit an employer to pay a wage lower than the highest wage required by any applicable Federal or Commonwealth law.

(b) *Determinations*—(1) *Methods.* The OFLC Administrator will determine prevailing wages in the Commonwealth and occupational classification as follows:

(i) If the mean hourly wage for the occupational classification in the Commonwealth is reported by the Governor, annually, and meets the requirements set forth in paragraph (e) of this section, as determined by the OFLC Administrator, that wage must be the prevailing wage for the occupational classification;

(ii) If the OFLC Administrator has not approved a survey, as reported by the Governor, for the occupational classification under paragraph (b)(1)(i) of this section, and the BLS OES survey reports a mean wage paid to workers in the SOC in Guam, the prevailing wage must be the mean wage paid to workers in the SOC in Guam from the BLS OES survey; and

(iii) If the OFLC Administrator has not approved a survey, as reported by the Governor, for the occupational classification under paragraph (b)(1)(i) of this section and the BLS OES survey does not report the mean wage paid to workers in the SOC in Guam under paragraph (b)(1)(ii) of this section, the prevailing wage must be the mean wage paid to workers in the SOC in the United States from the BLS OES Survey, adjusted based on the ratio of the mean wage paid to workers in all SOCs in Guam compared to the mean wage paid to workers in all SOCs in the United States from the BLS OES survey.

(2) *Multiple occupations.* If the job duties on the *Application for Prevailing Wage Determination* do not fall within a single occupational classification, the NPC will determine the applicable prevailing wage based on the highest prevailing wage for all applicable occupational classifications.

(c) *Request for PWD*—(1) *Filing requirement.* An employer must electronically request and receive a PWD from the NPWC then electronically file the *CW–1 Application for Temporary Employment Certification* with the NPC.

(2) *Location and methods of filing*—(i) *Electronic filing.* The employer must file the *Application for Prevailing Wage Determination* and all required supporting documentation with the NPWC using the electronic method(s) designated by the OFLC Administrator. The NPWC

will return without review any application submitted using a method other than the designated electronic method(s), unless the employer submits with the application a statement of the need to file by mail.

(ii) *Filing by mail.* Employers that are unable to file electronically, either due to lack of internet access or physical disability precluding electronic filing, may file the application by mail. The mailed application must include a statement indicating the need to file by mail. The NPWC will return, without review, mailed applications that do not contain such a statement. OFLC will publish the address for mailed applications in the instructions to Form ETA–9141C.

(d) *NPWC action.* The NPWC will provide the PWD, indicate the source of the PWD, and return the *Application for Prevailing Wage Determination* with its endorsement to the employer.

(e) *Wage survey reported by the Governor.* The OFLC Administrator will issue a prevailing wage for the occupational classification in the Commonwealth based on a wage survey reported by the Governor if all of the following requirements are met:

(1) The survey was independently conducted and issued by the Governor of the Commonwealth, including through any Commonwealth agency, Commonwealth college, or Commonwealth university;

(2) The survey provides the arithmetic mean of the wages of workers in the occupational classification in the Commonwealth;

(3) The surveyor either made a reasonable, good faith attempt to contact all employers in the Commonwealth employing workers in the occupation or conducted a randomized sampling of such employers;

(4) The survey includes the wages of at least 30 workers in the Commonwealth;

(5) The survey includes the wages of workers in the Commonwealth employed by at least three employers;

(6) The survey was conducted across industries that employ workers in the occupational classification;

(7) The wage reported in the survey includes all types of pay;

(8) The survey is based on wages paid to workers in the occupational classification not more than 12 months before the date the survey is submitted to the OFLC Administrator for consideration; and

(9) The Governor submits the survey to the OFLC Administrator, with specific information about the survey methodology, including such items as sample size and source, sample selection procedures, and survey job descriptions, to allow a determination of the adequacy of the data provided and validity of the statistical methodology used in conducting the survey.

(f) *Review of wage survey reported by the Governor.* (1) If the OFLC Administrator finds the wage reported for any occupational classification not to be acceptable, the OFLC Administrator must inform the Governor in writing of the reasons the wage reported in the survey was not accepted.

(2) The Governor, after receiving notification from the OFLC Administrator that the wage reported in the survey it provided for consideration is not acceptable, may submit corrected wage data or conduct a new wage survey and submit revised wage data to the OFLC Administrator for consideration under this section.

(g) *Validity period.* The NPWC will specify the validity period of the prevailing wage, which in no event may be more than 365 days or fewer than 90 days from the date that the determination is issued.

(h) *Retention of documentation.* The employer must retain the PWD for 3 years from the date of issuance if not used in support of a TLC application or if it is used in support of a TLC application that is denied, and 3 years from the date on which the certification of the *CW–1 Application for Temporary Employment Certification* expires, whichever is later. The employer must submit the PWD to a CO if requested by a Notice of Deficiency (NOD), described in §655.431, or audit, as described in §655.470, or to any Federal Government Official performing an investigation, inspection, audit, or law enforcement function.

§ 655.411 Review of prevailing wage determinations.

(a) *Request for review of PWDs.* Any employer desiring review of a PWD must make a written request for such review to the NPWC Director. The written request must be received by the NPWC Director within 7 business days from the date the PWD was issued. The request for review must clearly identify the PWD for which review is sought; set forth the particular grounds for the request; and include any materials submitted to the NPWC for purposes of securing the PWD.

(b) *NPWC review.* Upon the receipt of the written request for review, the NPWC Director will review the employer's request and accompanying documentation, including any supplementary material submitted by the employer, and after review must issue a Final Determination letter; that letter may:

(1) Affirm the PWD issued by the NPWC; or

(2) Modify the PWD.

(c) *Request for review by BALCA.* Any employer desiring review of the NPWC Director's decision on a PWD must make a written request to BALCA for review of the determination, with a copy simultaneously sent to the NPWC Director who issued the final determination. The written request must be received by BALCA within 10 business days from the date the Final Determination letter was issued.

(1) Upon receipt of a request for BALCA review, the NPWC will prepare an Appeal File and submit it to BALCA.

(2) The request for review, statements, briefs, and other submissions of the parties must contain only legal arguments and may refer to only the evidence that was within the record upon which the decision on the PWD by the NPWC Director was based.

(3) BALCA will handle appeals in accordance with § 655.461.

§§ 655.412–655.419 [Reserved]

CW–1 APPLICATION FOR TEMPORARY EMPLOYMENT CERTIFICATION FILING PROCEDURES

§ 655.420 Application filing requirements.

An employer seeking to hire CW–1 workers must electronically file a *CW–1 Application for Temporary Employment Certification* with the NPC designated by the OFLC Administrator. This section provides the procedures an employer must follow when filing.

(a) *What to file.* An employer seeking a TLC must file a completed *CW–1 Application for Temporary Employment Certification* (Form ETA–9142C and the appropriate appendices and valid PWD), and all supporting documentation and information required at the time of filing under this subpart. Applications that are incomplete at the time of submission will be returned to the employer without review.

(b) *Timeliness.* (1) Except as provided in paragraph (b)(2) of this section, a completed *CW–1 Application for Temporary Employment Certification* must be filed no more than 120 calendar days before the employer's date of need.

(2) If the employer is seeking a TLC to extend the employment of a CW–1 worker, a completed *CW–1 Application for Temporary Employment Certification* must be filed no more than 180 calendar days before the date on which the CW–1 status expires.

(c) *Location and methods of filing*—(1) *Electronic filing.* The employer must file the *CW–1 Application for Temporary Employment Certification* and all required supporting documentation with the NPC using the electronic method(s) designated by the OFLC Administrator. The NPC will return, without review, any application submitted using a method other than the designated electronic method(s), unless the employer submits with the application a statement of the need to file by mail or indicates that it already submitted such a statement to NPWC during the same fiscal year.

(2) *Filing by mail.* Employers that are unable to file electronically, either due to lack of internet access or physical disability precluding electronic filing,

may file the application by mail. The mailed application must include a statement indicating the need to file by mail as indicated above. The NPC will return, without review, mailed applications that do not contain such a statement. OFLC will publish the address for mailed applications in the instructions to Form ETA–9142C.

(d) *Original signature and acceptance of electronic signatures.* An electronically filed *CW–1 Application for Temporary Employment Certification* must contain an electronic (scanned) copy of the original signature of the employer (and that of the employer's authorized attorney or agent, if the employer is represented by an attorney or agent) or, in the alternative, use a verifiable electronic signature method, as directed by the OFLC Administrator. If submitted by mail, the *CW–1 Application for Temporary Employment Certification* must bear the original signature of the employer and, if applicable, the employer's authorized attorney or agent.

(e) *Requests for multiple positions.* An employer may request certification of more than one position on its *CW–1 Application for Temporary Employment Certification* as long as all CW–1 workers will perform the same services or labor under the same terms and conditions, in the same occupation, during the same period of employment, and at a location (or locations) covered by the application.

(f) *Scope of application.* (1) A *CW–1 Application for Temporary Employment Certification* must be limited to places of employment within the Commonwealth.

(2) In a single application filing, an association or other organization of employers is not permitted to file a *CW–1 Application for Temporary Employment Certification* on behalf of more than one employer-member under the CW–1 program.

(g) *Period of employment.* (1) Except as provided in paragraph (g)(2) of this section, the period of need identified in the *CW–1 Application for Temporary Employment Certification* must not exceed 1 year.

(2) If the employer is seeking TLC to employ a long-term CW–1 worker, the period of need identified in the *CW–1 Application for Temporary Employment Certification* must not exceed 3 years.

(h) *Return of applications based on USCIS CW–1 cap notice.* (1) Except as provided in paragraph (h)(3) of this section, if USCIS issues a public notice stating that it has received a sufficient number of CW–1 petitions to meet the statutory numerical limit on the total number of foreign nationals who may be issued a CW–1 permit or otherwise granted CW–1 status for the fiscal year, the OFLC Administrator must return without review any *CW–1 Applications for Temporary Employment Certification* with dates of need in that fiscal year received on or after the date that the OFLC Administrator provides the notice in paragraph (h)(2) of this section.

(2) The OFLC Administrator will announce the return of future *CW–1 Applications for Temporary Employment Certification* with dates of need in the fiscal year for which the cap is met with a notice on the OFLC's website. This notice will be effective on the date of its publication on the OFLC's website and will remain valid for the fiscal year unless:

(i) USCIS issues a public notice stating additional CW–1 permits are available for the fiscal year; and

(ii) The OFLC Administrator publishes a new notice announcing that additional TLCs may be granted in the fiscal year.

(3) After the notice that OFLC will return future *CW–1 Applications for Temporary Employment Certification*, the OFLC Administrator will continue to process *CW–1 Applications for Temporary Employment Certification* filed before the effective date of the suspension notice and will continue to permit the filing of *CW–1 Applications for Temporary Employment Certification* by employers who identify in the *CW–1 Application for Temporary Employment Certification* that the employment of all CW–1 workers employed under the *CW–1 Application for Temporary Employment Certification* will be exempt from the statutory numerical limit on the total number of foreign nationals who may be issued a CW–1 permit or otherwise granted CW–1 status.

§ 655.421 Job contractor filing requirements.

(a) A job contractor may submit a *CW–1 Application for Temporary Employment Certification* on behalf of itself and that employer-client. By doing so, the Department deems the job contractor a joint employer.

(b) A job contractor must have separate contracts with each different employer-client. A single contract or agreement may support only one *CW–1 Application for Temporary Employment Certification* for each employer-client job opportunity in the Commonwealth.

(c) Either the job contractor or its employer-client may submit an *Application for Prevailing Wage Determination* describing the job opportunity to the NPWC. However, each of the joint employers is separately responsible for ensuring that the wage offer(s) listed in the *CW–1 Application for Temporary Employment Certification* and related recruitment at least equals the prevailing wage obtained from the NPWC, or the Federal or Commonwealth minimum wage, whichever is highest, and that all other wage obligations are met.

(d)(1) A job contractor that is filing as a joint employer with its employer-client must submit to the NPC a completed *CW–1 Application for Temporary Employment Certification* that clearly identifies the joint employers (the job contractor and its employer-client) and the employment relationship (including the places of employment), in accordance with instructions provided by the OFLC Administrator. The *CW–1 Application for Temporary Employment Certification* must bear the original signature of the job contractor and the employer-client or use a verifiable electronic signature method, consistent with the requirements set forth at § 655.420(d), and be accompanied by the contract or agreement establishing the employers' relationships related to the workers sought.

(2) By signing the *CW–1 Application for Temporary Employment Certification*, each employer independently attests to the conditions of employment required of an employer participating in the CW–1 program and assumes full responsibility for the accuracy of the representations made in the application and for all of the responsibilities of an employer in the CW–1 program.

(e)(1) Either the job contractor or its employer-client may place the required advertisements and conduct recruitment as described in §§ 655.442 through 655.445. Also, either one of the joint employers may assume responsibility for interviewing applicants. However, both of the joint employers must sign the recruitment report that is submitted to the NPC meeting the requirement set forth in § 655.446.

(2) All recruitment conducted by the joint employers must satisfy the job offer assurance and advertising content requirements identified in § 655.441. Additionally, in order to fully inform applicants of the job opportunity and avoid potential confusion inherent in a job opportunity involving two employers, joint employer recruitment must clearly identify both employers (the job contractor and its employer-client) by name and must clearly identify the place(s) of employment where workers will perform labor or services.

(3)(i) Provided that all of the employer-clients' job opportunities are in the same occupation located in the Commonwealth and have the same requirements and terms and conditions of employment, including dates of employment, a job contractor may combine more than one of its joint employer employer-clients' job opportunities in a single advertisement. Each advertisement must fully inform potential workers of the job opportunity available with each employer-client and otherwise satisfy the job offer assurances and advertising content requirements identified in § 655.441. Such a shared advertisement must clearly identify the job contractor by name, the joint employment relationship, and the number of workers sought for each job opportunity, identified by employer-client names and locations (e.g., five openings with Employer-Client A (place of employment location), three openings with Employer-Client B (place of employment location)).

(ii) In addition, the advertisement must contain the following statement: "Applicants may apply for any or all of the jobs listed. When applying, please identify the job(s) (by company and work location) you are applying to for the entire period of employment specified.'' If an applicant fails to identify one or more specific work location(s), that applicant is presumed to have applied to all work locations listed in the advertisement.

(f) If a TLC for the joint employers is granted, the Final Determination certifying the *CW–1 Application for Temporary Employment Certification* will be sent to both the job contractor and employer-client.

§ 655.422 Emergency situations.

(a) *Waiver of PWD requirement prior to application filing.* The CO may waive the requirement to obtain a PWD, as required under § 655.410(c), prior to filing a *CW–1 Application for Temporary Employment Certification* for employers that have good and substantial cause, provided that the CO has sufficient time to thoroughly test the labor market and to make a final determination as required by § 655.450. The requirement to obtain a PWD prior to filing the *CW–1 Application for Temporary Employment Certification*, under § 655.410(c), is the only provision of this subpart which will be waived under these emergency situation procedures.

(b) *Employer requirements.* The employer requesting a waiver of the requirement to obtain a PWD must submit to the NPC a completed *Application for Prevailing Wage Determination*, a completed *CW–1 Application for Temporary Employment Certification*, and a statement justifying the waiver request. The employer's waiver request must include detailed information describing the good and substantial cause that has necessitated the waiver request. Good and substantial cause may include, but is not limited to, the substantial loss of U.S. workers due to an Act of God, or similar unforeseeable man-made catastrophic events (such as a hazardous materials emergency or government-controlled flooding), unforeseeable changes in market conditions, pandemic health issues, or similar conditions that are wholly outside of the employer's control. Issues related to the CW–1 visa cap are not good and substantial cause for a waiver of the filing requirements. Further, a denial of a previously submitted *CW–1 Application for Temporary Employment Certification* or CW–1 petition with USCIS does not constitute good and substantial cause necessitating a waiver under this section.

(c) *Processing of emergency applications.* The CO will process the emergency *CW–1 Application for Temporary Employment Certification*, including the *Application for Prevailing Wage Determination for the CW–1 Program*, in a manner consistent with the provisions of this subpart and make a determination in accordance with § 655.450. The CO will notify the employer, if the application cannot be processed because, pursuant to paragraph (a) of this section, the request for emergency filing was not justified and/or the filing does not meet the requirements set forth in this subpart.

§ 655.423 Assurances and obligations of CW–1 employers.

An employer employing CW–1 workers and/or workers in corresponding employment under a *CW–1 Application for Temporary Employment Certification* has agreed as part of the *CW–1 Application for Temporary Employment Certification* that it will abide by the following conditions with respect to its CW–1 workers and any workers in corresponding employment:

(a) *Rate of pay.* (1) The offered wage in the work contract equals or exceeds the highest of the prevailing wage, Federal minimum wage, or Commonwealth minimum wage. The employer must pay at least the offered wage, free and clear, during the entire period of the *CW–1 Application for Temporary Employment Certification* granted by OFLC.

(2) The offered wage is not based on commissions, bonuses, or other incentives, including paying on a piece-rate basis, unless the employer guarantees a wage earned every workweek that equals or exceeds the offered wage.

(3) If the employer requires one or more minimum productivity standards of workers as a condition of job retention, the standards must be specified in the work contract and the employer must demonstrate that they are normal and usual for non-CW–1 employers for the same occupation in the Commonwealth.

(4) An employer that pays on a piece-rate basis must demonstrate that the

piece-rate is no less than the normal rate paid by non-CW–1 employers to workers performing the same activity in the Commonwealth. The average hourly piece-rate earnings must result in an amount at least equal to the offered wage. If the worker is paid on a piece-rate basis and at the end of the workweek the piece-rate does not result in average hourly piece-rate earnings during the workweek at least equal to the amount the worker would have earned had the worker been paid at the offered hourly wage, then the employer must supplement the worker's pay at that time so that the worker's earnings are at least as much as the worker would have earned during the workweek if the worker had instead been paid at the offered hourly wage for each hour worked.

(b) *Wages free and clear.* The payment requirements for wages in this section will be satisfied by the timely payment of such wages to the worker either in cash or in negotiable instrument payable at par. The payment must be made finally and unconditionally and "free and clear." The principles applied in determining whether deductions are reasonable and payments are received free and clear, and the permissibility of deductions for payments to third persons are explained in more detail in 29 CFR part 531.

(c) *Deductions.* The employer must make all deductions from the worker's paycheck required by law. The work contract must specify all deductions not required by law that the employer will make from the worker's pay; any such deductions not disclosed in the work contract are prohibited. The wage payment requirements of paragraph (b) of this section are not met where unauthorized deductions, rebates, or refunds reduce the wage payment made to the worker below the minimum amounts required by the offered wage or where the worker fails to receive such amounts free and clear because the worker "kick backs" directly or indirectly to the employer or to another person for the employer's benefit the whole or part of the wages delivered to the worker. Authorized deductions are limited to: Those required by law, such as taxes payable by workers that are required to be withheld by the employer and amounts due workers which the employer is required by court order to pay to another; deductions for the reasonable cost or fair value of board, lodging, and facilities furnished; and deductions of amounts which are authorized to be paid to third persons for the worker's account and benefit through his or her voluntary assignment or order or which are authorized by a collective bargaining agreement with bona fide representatives of workers which covers the employer. Deductions for amounts paid to third persons for the worker's account and benefit which are not so authorized or are contrary to law or from which the employer, agent, or recruiter, including any agents or employees of these entities or any affiliated person, derives any payment, rebate, commission, profit, or benefit directly or indirectly, may not be made if they reduce the actual wage paid to the worker below the offered wage indicated on the *CW–1 Application for Temporary Employment Certification.*

(d) *Job opportunity is full time.* The job opportunity is a full-time position, consistent with § 655.402, and the employer must use a single workweek as its standard for computing wages due. An employee's workweek must be a fixed and regularly recurring period of 168 hours—7 consecutive 24-hour periods. It need not coincide with the calendar week but may begin on any day and at any hour of the day.

(e) *Job qualifications and requirements.* Each job qualification and requirement must be listed in the work contract and must be bona fide and consistent with the normal and accepted qualifications and requirements imposed by non-CW–1 employers in the same occupation and in the Commonwealth. The employer's job qualifications and requirements imposed on U.S. workers must not be less favorable than the qualifications and requirements that the employer is imposing or will impose on CW–1 workers. A qualification means a characteristic that is necessary to the individual's ability to perform the job in question. A requirement means a term or condition of employment that a worker is required to accept in order to obtain the job opportunity. The CO may require the employer to submit documentation to substantiate the appropriateness of any job qualification and/or requirement.

(f) *Three-fourths guarantee*—(1) *Offer to worker.* The employer must guarantee to offer the worker employment for a total number of work hours equal to at least three-fourths of the workdays of the total period of employment specified in the work contract, beginning with the first workday after the arrival of the worker at the place of employment or the advertised contractual first date of need, whichever is later, and ending on the expiration date specified in the work contract or in its extensions, if any. See the exception in paragraph (f)(1)(iv) of this section.

(i) For purposes of this paragraph (f), a workday means the number of hours in a workday as stated in the work contract. The employer must offer a total number of hours to ensure the provision of sufficient work to reach the three-fourths guarantee. The work hours must be offered during the work period specified in the work contract, or during any modified work contract period to which the worker and employer have mutually agreed and that has been approved by the CO.

(ii) In the event the worker begins working later than the start date of need specified in the application, the guarantee period begins with the first workday after the arrival of the worker at the place of employment and continues until the last day during which the work contract and all extensions thereof are in effect.

(iii) Therefore, if, for example, a work contract is for a 10-week period, during which a normal workweek is specified as 6 days a week, 8 hours per day, the worker would have to be guaranteed employment for at least 360 hours (10 weeks × 48 hours/week = 480 hours × 75 percent = 360). If a Federal holiday occurred during the 10-week period, the 8 hours would be deducted from the total hours for the work contract, before the guarantee is calculated. Continuing with the above example, the worker would have to be guaranteed employment for 354 hours (10 weeks × 48 hours/week = 480 hours − 8 hours (Federal holiday) = 472 hours × 75 percent = 354 hours).

(iv) A worker may be offered more than the specified hours of work on a single workday. For purposes of meeting the guarantee, the worker will not be required to work more than the number of hours specified in the work contract for a workday but all hours of work actually performed may be counted by the employer in calculating whether the period of guaranteed employment has been met. If during the total work contract period the employer affords the U.S. or CW–1 worker less employment than that required under this paragraph (f)(1)(iv), the employer must pay such worker the amount the worker would have earned had the worker, in fact, worked for the guaranteed number of days. An employer will not be considered to have met the work guarantee if the employer has merely offered work on three-fourths of the workdays of the work contract period if each workday did not consist of a full number of hours of work time as specified in the work contract.

(2) *Guarantee for piece-rate paid worker.* If the worker is paid on a piece-rate basis, the employer must use the worker's average hourly piece-rate earnings or the offered wage, whichever is higher, to calculate the amount due under the guarantee in accordance with paragraph (f)(1) of this section.

(3) *Failure to work.* Any hours the worker fails to work, up to a maximum of the number of hours specified in the work contract for a workday, when the worker has been offered an opportunity to work in accordance with paragraph (f)(1) of this section, and all hours of work actually performed (including voluntary work over 8 hours in a workday), may be counted by the employer in calculating whether the period of guaranteed employment has been met. An employer seeking to calculate whether the guaranteed number of hours has been met must maintain the payroll records in accordance with this subpart.

(g) *Impossibility of fulfillment.* If before the expiration date specified in the work contract, the services of the worker are no longer required for reasons beyond the control of the employer due to fire, weather, or other Act of God, or similar unforeseeable man-made catastrophic event (such as an oil spill or controlled flooding) that is wholly outside the employer's control that makes the fulfillment of the work contract impossible, the employer may terminate the work contract with the approval of the CO. In the event of such termination, the employer must fulfill a three-fourths guarantee, as described in paragraph (f) of this section, for the time that has elapsed from the start date listed in the work contract or the first workday after the arrival of the worker at the place of employment, whichever is later, to the time of its termination. The employer must make efforts to transfer the CW–1 worker or worker in corresponding employment to other comparable employment acceptable to the worker and consistent with immigration laws, as applicable. If a transfer is not affected, the employer must return the worker, at the employer's expense, to the place from which the worker (disregarding intervening employment) came to work for the employer, or transport the worker to the worker's next certified CW–1 employer, whichever the worker prefers.

(h) *Frequency of pay.* The employer must state in the work contract the frequency with which the worker will be paid, which must be at least every 2 weeks. Employers must pay wages when due.

(i) *Earnings statements.* (1) The employer must keep accurate and adequate records with respect to the workers' earnings, including but not limited to: Records showing the nature, amount, and location(s) of the work performed; the number of hours of work offered each day by the employer (broken out by hours offered both in accordance with and over and above the three-fourths guarantee in paragraph (f) of this section); the hours actually worked each day by the worker; if the number of hours worked by the worker is less than the number of hours offered, the reason(s) the worker did not work; the time the worker began and ended each workday; the rate of pay (both piece-rate and hourly, if applicable); the worker's earnings per pay period; the worker's home address; and the amount of and reasons for any and all deductions taken from or additions made to the worker's wages.

(2) The employer must furnish to the worker on or before each payday in one or more written statements the following information:

(i) The worker's total earnings for each workweek in the pay period;

(ii) The worker's hourly rate or piece-rate of pay;

(iii) For each workweek in the pay period the hours of employment offered to the worker (showing offers in accordance with the three-fourths guarantee as determined in paragraph (f) of this section, separate from any hours offered over and above the guarantee);

(iv) For each workweek in the pay period the hours actually worked by the worker;

(v) An itemization of all deductions made from or additions made to the worker's wages;

(vi) If piece-rates are used, the units produced daily;

(vii) The beginning and ending dates of the pay period; and

(viii) The employer's name, address, and FEIN.

(j) *Transportation and visa fees*—(1)(i) *Transportation to the place of employment.* The employer must provide or reimburse the worker for transportation and subsistence from the place from which the worker has come to work for the employer, whether in the United States, including another part of the Commonwealth, or abroad, to the place of employment if the worker completes 50 percent of the period of employment covered by the work contract (not counting any extensions). The employer may arrange and pay for the transportation and subsistence directly, advance at a minimum the most economical and reasonable common carrier cost of the transportation and subsistence to the worker before the worker's departure, or pay the worker for the reasonable costs incurred by the worker. When it is the prevailing practice of non-CW–1 employers in the occupation and in the Commonwealth to do so or when the employer extends such benefits to similarly situated CW–

1 workers, the employer must advance the required transportation and subsistence costs (or otherwise provide them) to workers in corresponding employment who are traveling to the employer's place of employment from such a distance that the worker is not reasonably able to return to their residence each day. The amount of the transportation payment must be no less (and is not required to be more) than the most economical and reasonable common carrier transportation charges for the distances involved. The amount of the daily subsistence must be at least the amount permitted in § 655.173. Where the employer will reimburse the reasonable costs incurred by the worker, it must keep accurate and adequate records of: The costs of transportation and subsistence incurred by the worker; the amount reimbursed; and the date(s) of reimbursement. Note that the Fair Labor Standards Act applies independently of the CW–1 requirements and imposes obligations on employers regarding payment of wages.

(ii) *Transportation from the place of employment.* If the worker completes the period of employment covered by the work contract (not counting any extensions), or if the worker is dismissed from employment for any reason by the employer before the end of the period, and the worker has no immediate subsequent CW–1 employment, the employer must provide or pay at the time of departure for the worker's cost of return transportation and daily subsistence from the place of employment to the place from which the worker, disregarding intervening employment, departed to work for the employer. If the worker has contracted with a subsequent employer that has not agreed in the work contract to provide or pay for the worker's transportation from the former employer's place of employment to such subsequent employer's place of employment, the former employer must provide or pay for that transportation and subsistence. If the worker has contracted with a subsequent employer that has agreed in the work contract to provide or pay for the worker's transportation from the former employer's place of employment to such subsequent employer's place of employment, the subsequent employer must provide or pay for such expenses.

(iii) *Employer-provided transportation.* All employer-provided transportation must comply with all applicable Federal and Commonwealth laws and regulations including, but not limited to, vehicle safety standards, driver licensure requirements, and vehicle insurance coverage.

(2) The employer must pay or reimburse the worker in the first workweek for all visa, visa processing, border crossing, and other related fees (including those mandated by the government) incurred by the CW–1 worker, but not for passport expenses or other charges primarily for the benefit of the worker.

(k) *Employer-provided items.* The employer must provide to the worker, without charge or deposit charge, all tools, supplies, and equipment required to perform the duties assigned.

(l) *Disclosure of work contract.* The employer must provide to a CW–1 worker outside of the United States no later than the time at which the worker applies for the visa, or to a worker in corresponding employment no later than on the day work commences, a copy of the work contract including any subsequent approved modifications. For a CW–1 worker changing employment from a CW–1 employer to a subsequent CW–1 employer, the copy must be provided no later than the time an offer of employment is made by the subsequent CW–1 employer. The disclosure of all documents required by this paragraph (l) must be provided in a language understood by the worker. At a minimum, the work contract must contain all of the provisions required to be included by this section. In the absence of a separate, written work contract entered into between the employer and the worker, the required terms of the certified *CW–1 Application for Temporary Employment Certification* will be the work contract.

(m) *No unfair treatment.* The employer has not and will not intimidate, threaten, restrain, coerce, blacklist, discharge, or in any manner discriminate against, and has not and will not cause any person to intimidate, threaten, restrain, coerce, blacklist, discharge, or in any manner discriminate against, any person who has, related to the CW-1 program:

(1) Filed a complaint under or related to any applicable Federal or Commonwealth laws and regulations;

(2) Instituted or caused to be instituted any proceeding under or related to any applicable Federal or Commonwealth laws and regulations;

(3) Testified or is about to testify in any proceeding under or related to any applicable Federal or Commonwealth laws and regulations;

(4) Consulted with a workers' center, community organization, labor union, legal assistance program, or an attorney on matters related to any applicable Federal or Commonwealth laws and regulations; or

(5) Exercised or asserted on behalf of himself/herself or others any right or protection afforded by any applicable Federal or Commonwealth laws and regulations.

(n) *Comply with the prohibitions against employees paying fees.* The employer and its attorney, agents, or employees have not sought or received payment of any kind from the worker for any activity related to obtaining CW–1 labor certification or employment, including payment of the employer's attorney or agent fees, application and *CW–1 Petition* fees, recruitment costs, or any fees attributed to obtaining the approved *CW–1 Application for Temporary Employment Certification.* For purposes of this paragraph (n), payment includes, but is not limited to, monetary payments, wage concessions (including deductions from wages, salary, or benefits), kickbacks, bribes, tributes, in-kind payments, and free labor. All wages must be paid free and clear. This paragraph (n) does not prohibit employers or their agents from receiving reimbursement for costs that are the responsibility and primarily for the benefit of the worker, such as government-required passport fees.

(o) *Contracts with third parties to comply with prohibitions.* The employer must contractually prohibit in writing any agent or recruiter (or any agent or employee of such agent or recruiter) whom the employer engages, either directly or indirectly, in recruitment of CW–1 workers to seek or receive payments or other compensation from prospective workers. The contract must include the following statement: "Under this agreement, [name of agent, recruiter] and any agent of or employee of [name of agent or recruiter] are prohibited from seeking or receiving payments from any prospective employee of [employer name] at any time, including before or after the worker obtains employment. Payments include but are not limited to, any direct or indirect fees paid by such employees for recruitment, job placement, processing, maintenance, attorneys' fees, agent fees, application fees, or petition fees."

(p) *Prohibition against preferential treatment of foreign workers.* The employer's job offer must offer to U.S. workers no less than the same benefits, wages, and working conditions that the employer is offering, intends to offer, or will provide to CW–1 workers. Job offers may not impose on U.S. workers any restrictions or obligations that will not be imposed on the employer's CW–1 workers. This does not relieve the employer from providing to CW–1 workers at least the minimum benefits, wages, and working conditions which must be offered to U.S. workers consistent with this section.

(q) *Nondiscriminatory hiring practices.* The job opportunity is open to any qualified U.S. worker as defined in § 655.402, regardless of race, color, national origin, age, sex, religion, disability, or citizenship. Rejections of any U.S. workers who applied or apply for the job must only be for lawful, job-related reasons, and those not rejected on this basis have been or will be hired. In addition, the employer has and will continue to retain records of all hired workers and rejected applicants as required by § 655.456.

(r) *Recruitment requirements.* The employer must conduct all required recruitment activities, including any additional employer-conducted recruitment activities as directed by the CO, and as specified in §§ 655.442 through 655.445.

(s) *No strike or lockout.* There is no strike or lockout at any of the employer's place(s) of employment within the Commonwealth for which the employer is requesting CW–1 certification at the time the *CW–1 Application for Temporary Employment Certification* is filed.

(t) *No recent or future layoffs.* The employer has not laid off and will not lay off any similarly employed U.S. worker in the occupation that is the subject of the *CW–1 Application for Temporary Employment Certification* in the Commonwealth within the period beginning 270 calendar days before the date of need and through the end of the TLC's period of certification. A layoff for lawful, job-related reasons such as lack of work or the end of a season is permissible if all CW–1 workers are laid off before any U.S. worker in corresponding employment.

(u) *No work performed outside the Commonwealth and job opportunity.* The employer must not place any CW–1 workers employed under the approved *CW–1 Application for Temporary Employment Certification* outside the Commonwealth or in a job opportunity not listed on the approved *CW–1 Application for Temporary Employment Certification.*

(v) *Abandonment/termination of employment.* Upon the separation from employment of any worker employed under the *CW–1 Application for Temporary Employment Certification* or workers in corresponding employment, if such separation occurs before the end date of the employment period specified in the *CW–1 Application for Temporary Employment Certification*, the employer must notify OFLC in writing of the separation from employment not later than 2 working days after such separation is discovered by the employer. An abandonment or abscondment is deemed to begin after a worker fails to report for work at the regularly scheduled time for 5 consecutive working days without the consent of the employer. If the separation is due to the voluntary abandonment of employment by the CW–1 worker or worker in corresponding employment or is terminated for cause, and the employer provides appropriate notification specified under this paragraph (v), the employer will not be responsible for providing or paying for the subsequent transportation and subsistence costs of that worker under this section, and that worker is not entitled to the three-fourths guarantee described in paragraph (f) of this section.

(w) *Compliance with applicable laws.* During the period of employment specified on the *CW–1 Application for Temporary Employment Certification*, the employer must comply with all applicable Federal and Commonwealth employment-related laws and regulations, including health and safety laws. This includes compliance with 18 U.S.C. 1592(a), with respect to prohibitions against employers, the employer's agents, or their attorneys knowingly holding, destroying or confiscating workers' passports, visas, or other immigration documents.

§§ 655.424–655.429 [Reserved]

PROCESSING OF AN CW–1 APPLICATION FOR TEMPORARY EMPLOYMENT CERTIFICATION

§ 655.430 Review of applications.

(a) *NPC review.* The CO will review the *CW–1 Application for Temporary Employment Certification* for compliance with all applicable program requirements, including compliance with the requirements set forth in this subpart, and make a decision as to whether to issue a NOD under § 655.431 or a Notice of Acceptance (NOA) under § 655.433.

(b) *Mailing and postmark requirements.* Any notice or request sent by the CO to an employer requiring a response will be sent electronically or via first class mail using the address, including electronic mail address, provided on the *CW–1 Application for Temporary Employment Certification.* The employer's response to such a notice or request must be filed electronically or via first class mail. The employer's response must be filed electronically or postmarked by the date due or the next business day if the due date falls on a Saturday, Sunday, or Federal Holiday.

(c) *Information dissemination.* OFLC may forward, to DHS or any other Federal Government Official performing an investigation, inspection, audit, or law enforcement function, information OFLC receives in the course of processing a request for a *CW–1 Application for Temporary Employment Certification* or of administering program integrity measures such as audits.

§ 655.431 Notice of Deficiency.

(a) *Notification*. If the CO determines the *CW–1 Application for Temporary Employment Certification* contains errors or inaccuracies, or does not meet the requirements set forth in this subpart, the CO will issue a NOD to the employer and, if applicable, the employer's attorney or agent.

(b) *Notice content*. The NOD will:

(1) State the reason(s) the *CW–1 Application for Temporary Employment Certification* fails to meet the criteria for acceptance;

(2) Offer the employer an opportunity to submit a modified *CW–1 Application for Temporary Employment Certification* within 10 business days from the date of the NOD, and state the modification that is required for the CO to issue a NOA; and

(3) State that if the employer does not comply with the requirements of § 655.432 for submitting a modified application, the CO will deny the *CW–1 Application for Temporary Employment Certification*.

§ 655.432 Submission of modified applications.

(a) *Review of a modified CW–1 Application for Temporary Employment Certification*. Upon receipt of a response to a NOD, including any modifications, the CO will review the response. The CO may issue one or more additional NODs before issuing a decision. The employer's failure to comply with a NOD, including not responding in a timely manner or not providing all required documentation, will result in a denial of the *CW–1 Application for Temporary Employment Certification*.

(b) *Acceptance of a modified CW–1 Application for Temporary Employment Certification*. If the CO accepts the modification(s) to the *CW–1 Application for Temporary Employment Certification*, the CO will issue a NOA to the employer and, if applicable, the employer's attorney or agent.

(c) *Denial of modified CW–1 Application for Temporary Employment Certification*. If the modified *CW–1 Application for Temporary Employment Certification* does not cure the deficiencies cited in the NOD(s) or otherwise fails to satisfy the criteria required for certification, the CO will, at its discretion, either send a second NOD or deny the *CW–1 Application for Temporary Employment Certification* in accordance with the labor certification determination provisions in § 655.453.

(d) *Appeal from denial of modified CW–1 Application for Temporary Employment Certification*. The procedures for appealing a denial of a modified *CW–1 Application for Temporary Employment Certification* are the same as for appealing the denial of a nonmodified *CW–1 Application for Temporary Employment Certification*, outlined in § 655.461.

(e) *Post acceptance modifications*. Notwithstanding the decision to accept the *CW–1 Application for Temporary Employment Certification*, the CO may require modifications to the *CW–1 Application for Temporary Employment Certification* at any time before the final determination to grant or deny the *CW–1 Application for Temporary Employment Certification* if the CO determines that the job offer does not contain the minimum benefits, wages, and working conditions set forth in § 655.441. The employer must make such modifications, or the application will be denied under § 655.453. The employer must provide all workers recruited in connection with the job opportunity in the *CW–1 Application for Temporary Employment Certification* with a copy of the modified *CW–1 Application for Temporary Employment Certification*, as approved by the CO, no later than the date work commences.

§ 655.433 Notice of Acceptance.

(a) *Notification*. When the CO determines the *CW–1 Application for Temporary Employment Certification* contains no errors or inaccuracies, and meets the requirements set forth in this subpart, the CO will issue a NOA to the employer and, if applicable, the employer's attorney or agent.

(b) *Notice content*. The NOA must:

(1) Direct the employer to engage in recruitment of U.S. workers as provided in §§ 655.442 through 655.444, including any additional recruitment ordered by the CO under § 655.445;

(2) State that such employer-conducted recruitment must begin within 14 calendar days from the date the NOA is issued, consistent with § 655.440(b);

(3) Require the employer to submit a report of its recruitment efforts, by the

date required by the CO in the NOA, as specified in § 655.446; and

(4) Advise the employer that failure to submit a complete recruitment report by the deadline will lead to denial of the application.

§ 655.434 Amendments to an application.

(a) *Increases in number of workers.* The *CW–1 Application for Temporary Employment Certification* may be amended at any time before the CO's certification determination to increase the number of workers requested in the initial *CW–1 Application for Temporary Employment Certification* by not more than 20 percent (50 percent for employers requesting less than 10 workers) without requiring an additional recruitment period for U.S. workers. Requests for increases above the percent prescribed, without additional recruitment, may be approved by the CO only when the employer demonstrates that the need for additional workers could not have been foreseen and is wholly outside of the employer's control. All requests to increase the number of workers must be made in writing and will not be effective until approved by the CO. Upon acceptance of an amendment, the employer must promptly provide copies of any approved amendments to all U.S. workers recruited and hired under the original job offer.

(b) *Minor changes to the period of employment.* The *CW–1 Application for Temporary Employment Certification* may be amended at any time before the CO's certification determination to make minor changes (meaning a change of up to 14 calendar days) in the total period of employment, without requiring an additional recruitment period for U.S. workers. Changes will not be effective until submitted in writing and approved by the CO. In considering whether to approve the request, the CO will review the reason(s) for the request, determine whether the reason(s) are on the whole justified, and take into account the effect any change(s) would have on the adequacy of the underlying test of the domestic labor market for the job opportunity. An employer must demonstrate that the change to the period of employment could not have been foreseen and is wholly outside of the employer's control. The CO will deny any request to change the period of employment where the total amended period of employment will exceed the maximum applicable duration permitted under § 655.420(g). Upon acceptance of an amendment, the employer must promptly provide copies of any approved amendments to all U.S. workers recruited and hired under the original job offer.

(c) *Other minor amendments to the CW–1 Application for Temporary Employment Certification.* The employer may request other minor amendments to the *CW–1 Application for Temporary Employment Certification* at any time before the CO's certification determination is issued. In considering whether to approve the request, the CO will determine whether the proposed amendment(s) are sufficiently justified and must take into account the effect of the changes on the underlying labor market test for the job opportunity. All requests for minor changes must be made in writing and will not be effective until approved by the CO. Upon acceptance of an amendment, the employer must promptly provide copies of any approved amendments to all U.S. workers recruited and hired under the original job offer.

(d) *Amendments after certification are not permitted.* After the CO has made a determination to certify the *CW–1 Application for Temporary Employment Certification*, the employer may no longer request amendments.

§§ 655.435–655.439 [Reserved]

POST ACCEPTANCE REQUIREMENTS

§ 655.440 Employer-conducted recruitment.

(a) *Employer obligations.* Employers must conduct recruitment of U.S. workers to ensure that there are not qualified U.S. workers who will be available for the positions listed in the *CW–1 Application for Temporary Employment Certification.*

(b) *Period to begin employer-conducted recruitment.* Unless otherwise instructed by the CO, the employer must begin the recruitment required in §§ 655.442 through 655.445 within 14 calendar days from the date the NOA is issued. All employer-conducted recruitment must be completed before the employer submits the recruitment report as required in § 655.446.

(c) *Interviewing U.S. workers.* Employers that wish to require interviews must conduct those interviews by phone or provide a procedure for the interviews to be conducted in the location where the worker is being recruited so that the worker incurs little or no cost. Employers cannot provide potential CW–1 workers with more favorable treatment with respect to the requirement for, and conduct of, interviews.

(d) *Qualified and available U.S. workers.* The employer must consider all U.S. applicants for the job opportunity and must hire all U.S. applicants who are qualified and who will be available for the job opportunity. U.S. applicants may be rejected only for lawful, job-related reasons, and those not rejected on this basis will be hired.

(e) *Recruitment report.* The employer must prepare a recruitment report meeting the requirements of § 655.446, by the date specified by the CO in the NOA.

§ 655.441 Job offer assurances and advertising contents.

(a) *General.* All recruitment conducted under §§ 655.442 through 655.445 in connection with an *CW–1 Application for Temporary Employment Certification* must contain terms and conditions of employment that are not less favorable than those offered to the CW–1 workers and must comply with the assurances applicable to job offers as set forth in § 655.423.

(b) *Contents.* All advertising must contain the following information:

(1) The employer's name and contact information;

(2) A statement that the job opportunity is a temporary, full-time position and identify the job title and total number of job openings the employer intends to fill;

(3) A description of the job opportunity with sufficient information to apprise applicants of the services or labor to be performed, including the job duties, the minimum education and experience requirements, the work hours and days, and the anticipated start and end dates of the job opportunity;

(4) The place(s) of employment with enough specificity to apprise applicants of any travel requirements and where applicants will likely have to reside to perform the services or labor;

(5) The wage that the employer is offering, intends to offer or will provide to the CW–1 workers or, in the event that there are multiple wage offers, the range of applicable wage offers, each of which must equal or exceed the highest of the prevailing wage or the Federal or Commonwealth minimum wage;

(6) If applicable, a statement that overtime will be available to the worker and specify the wage offer(s) for working any overtime hours;

(7) The frequency with which the worker will be paid as required by § 655.423(h);

(8) A statement that the employer will make all deductions from the worker's paycheck required by law, and must specify any deductions the employer intends to make from the worker's paycheck which are not required by law, including, if applicable, any deductions for the reasonable cost of board, lodging, or other facilities;

(9) A statement summarizing the three-fourths guarantee as required by § 655.423(f);

(10) A statement that transportation and subsistence will be provided to the worker while traveling from the worker's origin to the place of employment as will the return transportation and subsistence at the conclusion of the job opportunity, as required by § 655.423(j)(1);

(11) If applicable, a statement that daily transportation to and from the place(s) of employment will be provided by the employer;

(12) If applicable, a statement that the employer will provide to the worker, without charge or deposit charge, all tools, supplies, and equipment required to perform the duties assigned, in accordance with § 655.423(k);

(13) If applicable, any board, lodging, or other facilities the employer will offer to workers or intends to assist workers in securing;

(14) If applicable, a statement indicating that on-the-job training will be provided to the worker; and

(15) A statement that directs applicants to apply for the job opportunity directly with the employer, and that indicates at least two verifiable methods by which applicants may apply for the job opportunity, one of which must be via electronic means, and that provides the days and hours during which applicants may be interviewed for the job opportunity.

§ 655.442 Place advertisement with CNMI Department of Labor.

(a) The employer must place an advertisement with the CNMI Department of Labor for a period of 21 consecutive calendar days satisfying the requirements set forth in § 655.441.

(b) Documentation of this step must include:

(1) Either printouts of web pages in which the advertisement appeared on the CNMI Department of Labor job listing system, or other verifiable evidence from the CNMI Department of Labor containing the text of the advertisement; and

(2) The dates of publication demonstrating compliance with the requirement of this section.

§ 655.443 Contact with former U.S. workers.

The employer must contact (by mail or other effective means) its former U.S. workers, including those who have been laid off within 270 calendar days before the date of need, employed by the employer in the occupation at the place(s) of employment during the previous year (except those who were dismissed for cause or who abandoned the place(s) of employment), provide a copy of the *CW–1 Application for Temporary Employment Certification*, and solicit their return to the job. This contact must occur during the period of time that the job offer is being advertised on the CNMI Department of Labor's job listing system under § 655.442. The employer must retain documentation sufficient to prove such contact in accordance with § 655.456. An employer has no obligation to contact U.S. workers it terminated for cause or who abandoned employment at any time during the previous year, if the employer provided timely notice to the NPC of the termination or abandonment in the manner described in § 655.423(v).

§ 655.444 Notice of posting requirement.

The employer must post a copy of the *CW–1 Application for Temporary Employment Certification* in at least two conspicuous locations at the place(s) of employment or in some other manner that provides reasonable notification to all employees in the job classification and area in which the work will be performed by the CW–1 workers. Electronic posting, such as displaying an electronic copy of the *CW–1 Application for Temporary Employment Certification* prominently on any internal or external website that is maintained by the employer and customarily used for notices to employees about terms and conditions of employment, is sufficient to meet this posting requirement as long as it otherwise meets the requirements of this section. The notice must be posted for a period of 21 consecutive calendar days. The employer must maintain proof the *CW–1 Application for Temporary Employment Certification* was posted and identify where and during what period of time it was posted in accordance with § 655.456.

§ 655.445 Additional employer-conducted recruitment.

(a) *Requirement to conduct additional recruitment.* The employer may be instructed by the CO to conduct additional reasonable recruitment. Such recruitment may be required at the discretion of the CO where the CO has determined that there is a likelihood that U.S. workers who are qualified will be available for the work.

(b) *Nature of the additional employer-conducted recruitment.* The CO will describe the precise number and nature of the additional recruitment efforts. Additional recruitment may include, but is not limited to, advertising the job offer on the employer's website or another electronic job search website; advertising with community-based organizations, local unions, or trade unions; or other advertising using a professional, trade, or other publication where such a publication is appropriate for the workers likely to apply for the job opportunity. When assessing the appropriateness of a particular recruitment method, the CO will consider the cost of the additional recruitment and the likelihood that the additional recruitment method(s) will identify qualified and available U.S. workers.

(c) *Proof of the additional employer-conducted recruitment.* The CO will specify the documentation or other supporting evidence that must be retained by the employer as proof that the additional recruitment requirements were met. Documentation must be retained as required in §655.456.

§655.446 Recruitment report.

(a) *Requirements of the recruitment report.* No fewer than 2 calendar days after the last date on which the last advertisement appeared, as required by the NOA issued under §655.433, the employer must prepare, sign, and date a recruitment report. Where recruitment was conducted by a job contractor or its employer-client, both joint employers must sign the recruitment report in accordance with §655.421(e)(1). The recruitment report must be submitted to the NPC, by the date specified in the NOA, and contain the following information:

(1) The name of each recruitment activity or source;

(2) The name and contact information of each U.S. worker who applied or was referred to the job opportunity up to the date of the preparation of the recruitment report, and the disposition of each worker's application. The employer must clearly indicate whether the job opportunity was offered to the U.S. worker and whether the U.S. worker accepted or declined;

(3) Confirmation that the advertisement was posted on the CNMI Department of Labor's job listing system and the dates of advertising;

(4) Confirmation that former U.S. employees were contacted, if applicable, and by what means and the date(s) of contact;

(5) Confirmation the employer posted the availability of the job opportunity to all employees in the job classification and area in which the work will be performed by the CW–1 workers and the dates of advertising;

(6) If applicable, confirmation that additional recruitment was conducted as directed by the CO and the date(s) of advertising; and

(7) If applicable, for each U.S. worker who applied for the position but was not hired, the lawful job-related reason(s) for not hiring the U.S. worker.

(b) *Duty to update and retain the recruitment report.* The employer must update the recruitment report throughout the recruitment period. In a joint employment situation, either the job contractor or the employer-client may update the recruitment report throughout the recruitment period. The employer must retain the recruitment report as required in §655.456.

§§655.447–655.449 [Reserved]

LABOR CERTIFICATION DETERMINATIONS

§655.450 Determinations.

Except as otherwise noted in this section, the OFLC Administrator and CO(s), by virtue of delegation from the OFLC Administrator, have the authority to certify or deny *CW–1 Applications for Temporary Employment Certification.* The CO will certify the application only if the employer has met all the requirements of this subpart, including the criteria for certification in §655.451, thus demonstrating that there is an insufficient number of U.S. workers in the Commonwealth who are able, willing, qualified and who will be available at the time and place of the job opportunity for which certification is sought and that the employment of the CW–1 workers will not adversely affect the wages and working conditions of similarly employed U.S. workers.

§655.451 Criteria for temporary labor certification.

(a) The criteria for TLC include whether the employer has complied with all of the requirements of this subpart, which are required to grant the labor certification.

(b) In determining whether there are insufficient U.S. workers in the Commonwealth to fill the employer's job opportunity, the CO will count as available any U.S. worker who applied (or on whose behalf an application is made) directly to the employer, but who was rejected by the employer for other than a lawful job-related reason. In making this determination, the CO will also consider the employer's contacts with its former U.S. workers, including workers that have been laid off within 270 calendar days before the date of need.

§ 655.452 Approved certification.

If the TLC is granted, the CO will send a Final Determination notice and a copy of the certified *CW–1 Application for Temporary Employment Certification* to the employer and a copy, if applicable, to the employer's agent or attorney using an electronic method(s) designated by the OFLC Administrator. For employers permitted to file by mail as set forth in § 655.420(c), the CO will send the Final Determination notice and a copy of the certified *CW–1 Application for Temporary Employment Certification* by first class mail. The CO will send the certified *CW–1 Application for Temporary Employment Certification*, including approved modifications, on behalf of the employer, directly to USCIS using an electronic method(s) designated by the OFLC Administrator. The employer must retain a copy of the certified *CW–1 Application for Temporary Employment Certification*, including the original signed Appendix C, as required by § 655.456.

§ 655.453 Denied certification.

If an electronically filed TLC is denied, the CO will send the Final Determination notice to the employer and a copy, if applicable, to the employer's agent or attorney using an electronic method(s) designated by the OFLC Administrator. For employers permitted to file by mail as set forth in § 655.420(c), the CO will send the Final Determination notice by first class mail. The Final Determination notice will:

(a) State the reason(s) certification is denied, citing the relevant regulatory standards;

(b) Offer the employer an opportunity to request administrative review of the denial under § 655.461; and

(c) State that if the employer does not request administrative review in accordance with § 655.461, the denial is final, and the Department will not accept any appeal on that *CW–1 Application for Temporary Employment Certification*.

§ 655.454 Partial certification.

The CO may issue a partial certification, reducing either the period of need or the number of CW–1 workers or both, based upon information the CO receives during the course of processing the *CW–1 Application for Temporary Employment Certification*, an audit, or otherwise. The number of workers certified will be reduced by one for each U.S. worker who is able, willing, and qualified, and who will be available at the time and place needed and who has not been rejected for lawful, job-related reasons, to perform the labor or services. If a partial labor certification is issued, the CO will send the Final Determination notice approving partial certification using the procedures at § 655.452.

The Final Determination notice will:

(a) State the reason(s) the period of employment or the number of CW–1 workers requested has been reduced, citing the relevant regulatory standards;

(b) Offer the employer an opportunity to request administrative review of the partial certification under § 655.461; and

(c) State that if the employer does not request administrative judicial review in accordance with § 655.461, the partial certification is final, and the Department will not accept any appeal on that *CW–1 Application for Temporary Employment Certification*.

§ 655.455 Validity of temporary labor certification.

(a) *Validity period*. A TLC is valid only for the period of employment as approved on the *CW–1 Application for Temporary Employment Certification*. The certification expires after the last day of authorized employment, including any approved extensions thereof.

(b) *Scope of validity*. A TLC is valid only for the number of CW–1 positions, the places of employment located in the Commonwealth, the job classification and specific services or labor to be performed, and the employer(s) specified on the approved *CW–1 Application for Temporary Employment Certification*, including any approved modifications. The TLC may not be transferred from one employer to another unless the employer to which it is transferred is a successor in interest to the employer to which it was issued.

§ 655.456 Document retention requirements for CW–1 employers.

(a) *Entities required to retain documents.* All CW–1 employers filing a *CW–1 Application for Temporary Employment Certification* are required to retain the documents and records establishing compliance with this subpart, including but not limited to those specified in paragraph (c) of this section.

(b) *Period of record retention.* The employer must retain records and documents for 3 years from the date on which the certification of the *CW–1 Application for Temporary Employment Certification* expires, or 3 years from the date of the final determination if the *CW–1 Application for Temporary Employment Certification* is denied, or 3 years from the date the Department receives the request for withdrawal of a *CW–1 Application for Temporary Employment Certification* under § 655.462.

(c) *Documents and records to be retained by all employers.* All employers filing a *CW–1 Application for Temporary Employment Certification* must retain the following documents and records and must provide the documents and records to the Department and any other Federal Government Official in the event of an audit or investigation:

(1) Proof of recruitment efforts, including:

(i) Placement of the job offer with the CNMI Department of Labor as specified in § 655.442;

(ii) Contact with former U.S. employees as specified in § 655.443, including documents demonstrating that each such U.S. worker had been offered the job opportunity listed in the *CW–1 Application for Temporary Employment Certification*, and that the U.S. worker either refused the job opportunity or was rejected only for lawful, job-related reasons;

(iii) Posting notice of the job opportunity to all employees in the job classification and area in which the work will be performed by the CW–1 workers as specified in § 655.444; and

(iv) All additional employer-conducted recruitment required by the CO as specified in § 655.445.

(2) Documentation supporting the information submitted in the recruitment report prepared in accordance with § 655.446, such as evidence of nonapplicability of contact with former workers as specified in § 655.443 and any supporting resumes and contact information as specified in § 655.446.

(3) Records of each worker's earnings, hours offered and worked, location(s) where work is performed, and other information as specified in § 655.423(i).

(4) If applicable, records of reimbursement of transportation and subsistence costs incurred by the workers, as specified in § 655.423(j).

(5) Copies of written contracts with third parties demonstrating compliance with the prohibition of seeking or receiving payments or other compensation of any kind from prospective workers as specified in § 655.423(o).

(6) Evidence of the employer's contact with U.S. workers who applied for the job opportunity in the *CW–1 Application for Temporary Employment Certification*, including, but not limited to, documents demonstrating that any rejections of U.S. workers were for lawful, job-related reasons, as specified in § 655.423(q).

(7) Written notice provided to and informing OFLC that a CW–1 worker or worker in corresponding employment has separated from employment before the end date of employment specified in the *CW–1 Application for Temporary Employment Certification*, as specified in § 655.423(v).

(8) A copy of the *CW–1 Application for Temporary Employment Certification* and all accompanying appendices, including any modifications, amendments, or extensions, signed by the employer as directed by the CO.

(d) *Availability of documents and records for enforcement purposes.* The employer must make available to the Department, DHS or to any Federal Government Official performing an investigation, inspection, audit, or law enforcement function all documents and records required to be retained under this subpart for purposes of copying, transcribing, or inspecting them.

§§ 655.457–655.459 [Reserved]

POST CERTIFICATION ACTIVITIES

§ 655.460 Extensions.

(a) *Basis for extension.* Under certain circumstances an employer may apply for extensions of the period of employment. A request for extension must be related to weather conditions or other factors beyond the control of the employer (which may include unforeseen changes in market conditions). Such requests must be supported in writing, with documentation showing that the extension is needed and that the need could not have been reasonably foreseen by the employer. The CO will not grant an extension where the total period of employment under that *CW–1 Application for Temporary Employment Certification* and the authorized extension would exceed the maximum applicable duration permitted under § 655.420(g).

(b) *Decision by the CO.* The CO will notify the employer of the decision in writing. The employer may appeal a denial of a request for an extension by following the appeal procedures in § 655.461.

(c) *Obligations during period of extension.* The CW–1 employer's assurances and obligations under the TLC will continue to apply during the extended period of employment. The employer must immediately provide to its CW–1 workers and workers in corresponding employment a copy of any approved extension.

§ 655.461 Administrative review.

(a) *Request for review.* Where authorized in this subpart, an employer wishing review of a determination by the CO must request an administrative review before BALCA of that determination to exhaust its administrative remedies. In such cases, the request for review:

(1) Must be received by BALCA, and the CO who issued the determination, within 10 business days from the date of the determination;

(2) Must clearly identify the particular determination for which review is sought;

(3) Must include a copy of the CO's determination;

(4) Must set forth the particular grounds for the request, including the specific factual issues the requesting party alleges needs to be examined in connection with the CO's determination;

(5) May contain any legal argument that the employer believes will rebut the basis for the CO's determination, including any briefing the employer wishes to submit; and

(6) May contain only such evidence as was actually before the CO at the time of the CO's determination.

(b) *Appeal File.* After the receipt of a request for review, the CO will send a copy of the Appeal File, as soon as practicable by means normally assuring next-day delivery, to BALCA, the employer, the employer's attorney or agent (if applicable), and the Associate Solicitor for Employment and Training Legal Services, Office of the Solicitor, U.S. Department of Labor (counsel).

(c) *Assignment.* The Chief ALJ will immediately, upon receipt of the appeal file from the CO, assign either a single member or a three-member panel of BALCA to consider a particular case.

(d) *Administrative review*—(1) *Briefing schedule.* If the employer wishes to submit a brief on appeal, it must do so as part of its request for review. Within 7 business days of receipt of the Appeal File, the counsel for the CO may submit a brief in support of the CO's decision and, if applicable, in response to the employer's brief.

(2) *Standard of review.* The ALJ must uphold the CO's decision unless shown by the employer to be arbitrary, capricious, an abuse of discretion, or otherwise not in accordance with the law.

(e) *Scope of review.* BALCA will affirm, reverse, or modify the CO's determination, or remand to the CO for further action. BALCA will reach this decision after due consideration of the documents in the Appeal File that were before the CO at the time of the CO's determination, the request for review, and any legal briefs submitted. BALCA may not consider evidence not before the CO at the time of the CO's determination, even if such evidence is in the Appeal File, request for review, or legal briefs.

(f) *Decision.* The decision of BALCA must specify the reasons for the action taken and must be provided to the employer, the CO, and counsel for the CO within 7 business days of the submission of the CO's brief or 10 business days after receipt of the Appeal File, whichever is later, using means normally assuring expedited delivery.

§ 655.462 Withdrawal of a CW–1 Application for Temporary Employment Certification.

(a) The employer may withdraw a *CW–1 Application for Temporary Employment Certification* after it has been submitted to the NPC for processing, including after the CO grants certification under § 655.450. However, the employer is still obligated to comply with the terms and conditions of employment contained in the *CW–1 Application for Temporary Employment Certification* and work contract with respect to all workers recruited and hired in connection with that application.

(b) To request withdrawal, the employer must submit a request in writing to the NPC identifying the *CW–1 Application for Temporary Employment Certification* and stating the reason(s) for the withdrawal.

§ 655.463 Public disclosure.

The Department will maintain an electronic file accessible to the public with information on all employers applying for TLCs. The database will include such information as the number of workers requested, the date filed, the date decided, and the final disposition.

§§ 655.464–655.469 [Reserved]

INTEGRITY MEASURES

§ 655.470 Audits.

The CO may conduct audits of certified *CW–1 Applications for Temporary Employment Certification.*

(a) *Discretion.* The CO has the sole discretion to choose the certified applications selected for audit.

(b) *Audit letter.* Where an application is selected for audit, the CO will issue an audit letter to the employer and a copy, if appropriate, to the employer's attorney or agent. The audit letter will:

(1) Specify the documentation that must be submitted by the employer;

(2) Specify a date, no more than 30 calendar days from the date the audit letter is issued, by which the required documentation must be sent to the CO; and

(3) Advise that failure to comply fully with the audit process may result:

(i) In the requirement that the employer undergo the assisted recruitment procedures in § 655.471 in future filings of *CW–1 Applications for Temporary Employment Certification* for a period of up to 2 years; or

(ii) In a revocation of the certification or debarment from the CW–1 program and any other foreign labor certification program administered by the Department.

(c) *Supplemental information request.* During the course of the audit examination, the CO may request supplemental information or documentation from the employer in order to complete the audit. If circumstances warrant, the CO can issue one or more requests for supplemental information.

(d) *Potential referrals.* In addition to measures in this subpart, the CO may decide to provide the audit findings and underlying documentation to DHS or other appropriate enforcement agencies. The CO may refer any findings that an employer discouraged a qualified U.S. worker from applying, or failed to hire, discharged, or otherwise discriminated against a qualified U.S. worker, to the Department of Justice, Civil Rights Division, Immigrant and Employee Rights Section.

§ 655.471 Assisted recruitment.

(a) *Requirement of assisted recruitment.* If, as a result of audit or otherwise, the CO determines that a violation has occurred that does not warrant debarment, the CO may require the employer to engage in assisted recruitment for a defined period of time for any future *CW–1 Application for Temporary Employment Certification.*

(b) *Notification of assisted recruitment.* The CO will notify the employer (and its attorney or agent, if applicable) in writing of the assisted recruitment that will be required of the employer for a period of up to 2 years from the date the notice is issued. The notification will state the reasons for the imposition of the additional requirements, state that the employer's agreement to accept the conditions will constitute their inclusion as bona fide conditions and terms of a *CW–1 Application for Temporary Employment Certification*, and offer the employer an opportunity to request an administrative review. If administrative review is requested, the procedures in § 655.461 apply.

(c) *Assisted recruitment*. The assisted recruitment process will be in addition to any recruitment required of the employer by §§ 655.442 through 655.445 and may consist of, but is not limited to, one or more of the following:

(1) Requiring the employer to submit a draft advertisement to the CO for review and approval at the time of filing the *CW–1 Application for Temporary Employment Certification*;

(2) Designating the sources where the employer must recruit for U.S. workers in the Commonwealth and directing the employer to place the advertisement(s) in such sources;

(3) Extending the length of the placement of the advertisements;

(4) Requiring the employer to notify the CO in writing when the advertisement(s) are placed;

(5) Requiring an employer to perform any additional assisted recruitment directed by the CO;

(6) Requiring the employer to provide proof of the publication of all advertisements as directed by the CO;

(7) Requiring the employer to provide proof of all U.S. workers who applied (or on whose behalf an application is made) in response to the employer's recruitment efforts;

(8) Requiring the employer to submit any proof of contact with all referrals and former U.S. workers; or

(9) Requiring the employer to provide any additional documentation verifying it conducted the assisted recruitment as directed by the CO.

(d) *Failure to comply*. If an employer materially fails to comply with requirements ordered by the CO under this section, the certification will be denied and the employer and its attorney or agent may be debarred under § 655.473.

§ 655.472 Revocation.

(a) *Basis for revocation*. The OFLC Administrator may revoke a TLC approved under this subpart, if the OFLC Administrator finds:

(1) The issuance of the TLC was not justified due to fraud or misrepresentation of a material fact in the application process;

(2) The employer substantially failed to comply with any of the terms or conditions of the approved TLC. A substantial failure is a failure to comply that constitutes a significant deviation from the terms and conditions of the approved certification and is further defined in § 655.473(d); or

(3) The employer impeded the audit process, as set forth in § 655.470, or impeded any Federal Government Official performing an investigation, inspection, audit, or law enforcement function.

(b) *DOL procedures for revocation*—(1) *Notice of Revocation*. If the OFLC Administrator makes a determination to revoke an employer's TLC, the OFLC Administrator will issue a Notice of Revocation to the employer (and its attorney or agent, if applicable). The notice will contain a detailed statement of the grounds for the revocation and inform the employer of its right to submit rebuttal evidence to the OFLC Administrator or to request administrative review of the Notice of Revocation by BALCA. If the employer does not submit rebuttal evidence or request administrative review within 10 business days from the date the Notice of Revocation is issued, the notice will become the final agency action and will take effect immediately at the end of the 10 business days.

(2) *Rebuttal*. If the employer timely submits rebuttal evidence, the OFLC Administrator will inform the employer of the final determination on the revocation within 10 business days of receiving the rebuttal evidence. If the OFLC Administrator determines that the certification must be revoked, the OFLC Administrator will inform the employer of its right to appeal the final determination to BALCA according to the procedures of § 655.461. If the employer does not appeal the final determination, it will become the final agency action.

(3) *Request for review.* An employer may appeal a Notice of Revocation or a final determination of the OFLC Administrator after the review of rebuttal evidence to BALCA, according to the appeal procedures of §655.461. The ALJ's decision is the final agency action.

(4) *Stay.* The timely submission of rebuttal evidence or a request for administrative review will stay the revocation pending the outcome of the proceeding.

(5) *Decision.* If the TLC is revoked, the OFLC Administrator will provide copies of final revocation decisions to DHS and DOS promptly.

(c) *Employer's obligations in the event of revocation.* If an employer's TLC is revoked, the employer is responsible for:

(1) Reimbursement of actual inbound transportation and other required expenses;

(2) The workers' outbound transportation and other required expenses;

(3) Payment to the workers of the amount due under the three-fourths guarantee; and

(4) Any other wages, benefits, and working conditions due or owing to the workers under this subpart.

§655.473 Debarment.

(a) *Debarment of an employer, agent, or attorney.* The OFLC Administrator may debar an employer, agent, attorney, or any successor in interest to that employer, agent, or attorney, from participating in any action under this subpart, subject to the time limits set forth in paragraph (c) of this section, if the OFLC Administrator finds that the employer, agent, or attorney substantially violated a material term or condition of the *Application for Prevailing Wage Determination* or *CW–1 Application for Temporary Employment Certification,* as defined in paragraph (d) of this section. The OFLC Administrator will provide copies of final debarment decisions to DHS and DOS promptly.

(b) *Effect on future applications in all foreign labor programs.* The debarred employer, or a debarred agent or attorney, or any successor in interest to any debarred employer, agent, or attorney, will be disqualified from filing any labor certification applications or labor condition applications with the Department subject to the term limits set forth in paragraph (c) of this section. If such an application is filed, it will be denied without review.

(c) *Period of debarment.* No employer, agent, or attorney may be debarred under this subpart for more than 5 years for a single violation.

(d) *Definition of violation.* For the purposes of this section, a violation of a material term or condition of the *Application for Prevailing Wage Determination* or *CW–1 Application for Temporary Employment Certification* includes:

(1) One or more acts of commission or omission on the part of the employer or the employer's agent or attorney that involve:

(i) Failure to pay or provide the required wages, benefits, or working conditions to the employer's CW–1 workers or workers in corresponding employment;

(ii) Failure, except for lawful, job-related reasons, to offer employment to qualified U.S. workers who applied for the job opportunity for which certification was sought;

(iii) Failure to comply with the employer's obligations to recruit U.S. workers;

(iv) Improper layoff or displacement of U.S. workers or workers in corresponding employment;

(v) Failure to comply with the NOD process, as set forth in §655.431, or the assisted recruitment process, as set forth in §655.471;

(vi) Impeding the audit process, as set forth in §655.470, or impeding any Federal Government Official performing an investigation, inspection, audit, or law enforcement function;

(vii) Employing a CW–1 worker outside of the Commonwealth, in an activity not listed in the work contract, or outside the validity period of employment of the work contract, including any approved extension thereof;

(viii) A violation of the requirements of §655.423(n) or (o);

(ix) A violation of any of the provisions listed in §655.423(q); or

(x) Any other act showing such flagrant disregard for the law that future compliance with program requirements cannot reasonably be expected;

(2) Fraud involving the *Application for Prevailing Wage Determination* or the *CW–1 Application for Temporary Employment Certification* under this subpart; or

(3) A material misrepresentation of fact during the course of processing the *CW–1 Application for Temporary Employment Certification.*

(e) *Determining whether a violation is substantial.* In determining whether a violation is substantial as to merit debarment, the factors the OFLC Administrator may consider include, but are not limited to, the following:

(1) Previous history of violation(s) under the CW–1 program;

(2) The number of CW–1 workers, workers in corresponding employment, or U.S. workers who were or are affected by the violation(s);

(3) The gravity of the violation(s); or

(4) The extent to which the violator achieved a financial gain due to the violation(s), or the potential financial loss or potential injury to the worker(s).

(f) *Debarment procedure*—(1) *Notice of Debarment.* If the OFLC Administrator makes a determination to debar an employer, agent, attorney, or any successor in interest to that employer, agent, or attorney, the OFLC Administrator will issue the party a Notice of Debarment. The notice will state the reason(s) for the debarment finding, including a detailed explanation of the grounds for and the duration of the debarment, and it will inform the party subject to the notice of its right to submit rebuttal evidence to the OFLC Administrator, or to request administrative review of the decision by BALCA. If the party does not file rebuttal evidence or a request for review within 30 calendar days of the date of the Notice of Debarment, the notice is the final agency action and the debarment will take effect on the date specified in the notice or if no date is specified, at the end of 30 calendar days The timely filing of rebuttal evidence or a request for review stays the debarment pending the outcome of the appeal as provided in paragraphs (f)(2) through (6) of this section.

(2) *Rebuttal.* The party who received the Notice of Debarment may choose to submit evidence to rebut the grounds stated in the notice within 30 calendar days of the date the notice is issued. If rebuttal evidence is timely filed, the OFLC Administrator will issue a Final Determination on the debarment within 30 calendar days of receiving the rebuttal evidence. If the OFLC Administrator determines that the party must be debarred, the OFLC Administrator will issue a Final Determination and inform the party of its right to request administrative review of the debarment by BALCA according to the procedures in this section. The party must request review within 30 calendar days after the date of the Final Determination, or the Final Determination will be the final agency order and the debarment will take effect on the date specified in the Final Determination or if no date is specified, at the end of 30 calendar days.

(3) *Request for review.* (i) The recipient of a Notice of Debarment or Final Determination seeking to challenge the debarment must request review of the debarment within 30 calendar days of the date of the Notice of Debarment or the date of the Final Determination by the OFLC Administrator after review of rebuttal evidence submitted under paragraph (f)(2) of this section. A request for review of debarment must be sent in writing to the Chief ALJ, United States Department of Labor, with a simultaneous copy served on the OFLC Administrator; the request must clearly identify the particular debarment determination for which review is sought; and must set forth the particular grounds for the request. If no timely request for review is filed, the debarment will take effect on the date specified in the Notice of Debarment or Final Determination, or if no date is specified, 30 calendar days from the date the Notice of Debarment or Final Determination is issued.

(ii) Upon receipt of a request for review, the OFLC Administrator will promptly send a certified copy of the ETA case file to the Chief ALJ by means normally assuring expedited delivery. The Chief ALJ will immediately assign an ALJ to conduct the review.

(iii) Statements, briefs, and other submissions of the parties must contain only legal argument and only such evidence that was within the record upon which the debarment was based, including any rebuttal evidence submitted pursuant to paragraph (f)(2) of this section.

(4) *Review by the ALJ.* (i) In considering requests for review, the ALJ must afford all parties 30 days to submit or decline to submit any appropriate Statement of Position or legal brief. The ALJ must review the debarment determination on the basis of the record upon which the decision was made, the request for review, and any Statements of Position or legal briefs submitted.

(ii) The ALJ's final decision must affirm, reverse, or modify the OFLC Administrator's determination. The ALJ's decision will be provided to the parties by expedited mail. The ALJ's decision is the final agency action, unless either party, within 30 calendar days of the ALJ's decision, seeks review of the decision with the Administrative Review Board (ARB).

(5) *Review by the ARB.* (i) Any party wishing review of the decision of an ALJ must, within 30 calendar days of the decision of the ALJ, petition the ARB to review the decision. Copies of the petition must be served on all parties and on the ALJ. The ARB will decide whether to accept the petition within 30 calendar days of receipt. If the ARB declines to accept the petition, or if the ARB does not issue a notice accepting a petition within 30 calendar days after the receipt of a timely filing of the petition, the decision of the ALJ is the final agency action. If a petition for review is accepted, the decision of the ALJ will be stayed unless and until the ARB issues an order affirming the decision. The ARB must serve notice of its decision to accept or not to accept the petition upon the ALJ and upon all parties to the proceeding.

(ii) Upon receipt of the ARB's notice to accept the petition, the Office of Administrative Law Judges will promptly forward a copy of the complete appeal record to the ARB.

(iii) Where the ARB has determined to review the decision and order, the ARB will notify each party of the issue(s) raised, the form in which submissions must be made (e.g., briefs or oral argument), and the time within which the presentation must be submitted.

(6) *ARB Decision.* The ARB's final decision must be issued within 90 calendar days from the notice granting the petition and served upon all parties and the ALJ.

§§655.474–655.499 [Reserved]

Subpart F—Attestations by Employers Using Alien Crewmembers for Longshore Activities in U.S. Ports

SOURCE: 60 FR 3956, 3976, Jan. 19, 1995, unless otherwise noted.

GENERAL PROVISIONS

§655.500 Purpose, procedure and applicability of subparts F and G of this part.

(a) *Purpose.* (1) Section 258 of the Immigration and Nationality Act ("Act") prohibits nonimmigrant alien crewmembers admitted to the United States on D-visas from performing longshore work at U.S. ports except in five specific instances:

(i) Where the vessel's country of registration does not prohibit U.S. crewmembers from performing longshore work in that country's ports and nationals of a country (or countries) which does not prohibit U.S. crewmembers from performing longshore work in that country's ports hold a majority of the ownership interest in the vessel, as determined by the Secretary of State (henceforth referred to as the "reciprocity exception");

(ii) Where there is in effect in a local port one or more collective bargaining agreement(s), each covering at least thirty percent of the longshore workers, and each permitting the activity to be performed under the terms of such agreement(s);

(iii) Where there is no collective bargaining agreement covering at least thirty percent of the longshore workers at the particular port and an attestation with accompanying documentation has been filed with the Department of Labor attesting that, among other things, the use of alien crewmembers to perform a particular activity of longshore work is permitted under the prevailing practice of the particular port (henceforth referred to as the "prevailing practice exception");

(iv) Where the longshore work is to be performed at a particular location in the State of Alaska and an attestation with accompanying documentation has been filed with the Department of Labor attesting that, among other things, before using alien crewmembers to perform the activity specified in the attestation, the employer will make a bona fide request for and employ United States longshore workers who are qualified and available in sufficient numbers from contract stevedoring companies, labor organizations recognized as exclusive bargaining representatives of United States longshore workers, and private dock operators (henceforth referred to as the "Alaska exception"); or

(v) Where the longshore work involves an automated self-unloading conveyor belt or vacuum-actuated system on a vessel and the Administrator has not previously determined that an attestation must be filed pursuant to this part as a basis for performing those functions (henceforth referred to as the "automated vessel exception").

(2) The term "longshore work" does not include the loading or unloading of hazardous cargo, as determined by the Secretary of Transportation, for safety and environmental protection. The Department of Homeland Security (DHS) through the United States Citizenship and Immigration Services (USCIS), determines whether an employer may use alien crewmembers for longshore work at U.S. ports. In those cases where an employer must file an attestation in order to perform such work, the Department of Labor shall be responsible for accepting the filing of such attestations. Subpart F of this part sets forth the procedure for filing attestations with the Department of Labor for employers proposing to use alien crewmembers for longshore work at U.S. ports under the prevailing practice exception, the Alaska exception, and where it has been determined that an attestation is required under the automated vessel exception listed in paragraph (a)(1)(iv) of this section. Subpart G of this part sets forth complaint, investigation, and penalty provisions with respect to such attestations.

(b) *Procedure.* (1) Under the prevailing practice exception in sec. 258(c) of the Act, and in those cases where it has been determined that an attestation is required under the automated vessel exception for longshore work to be performed at locations other than in the State of Alaska, the procedure involves filing an attestation with the Department of Labor attesting that:

(i) The use of alien crewmembers for a particular activity of longshore work is the prevailing practice at the particular port;

(ii) The use of alien crewmembers is not during a strike or lockout nor designed to influence the election of a collective bargaining representative; and

(iii) Notice of the attestation has been provided to the bargaining representative of longshore workers in the local port, or, where there is none, notice has been provided to longshore workers employed at the local port.

(2) Under the automated vessel exception in sec. 258(c) of the Act, no attestation is required in cases where longshore activity consists of the use of an automated self-unloading conveyor belt or vacuum-actuated system on a vessel. The legislation creates a rebuttable presumption that the use of alien crewmembers for the operation of such automated systems is the prevailing practice. In order to overcome such presumption, it must be shown by the preponderance of the evidence submitted by any interested party, that the use of alien crewmembers for such activity is not the prevailing practice at the particular port, that it is during a strike or lockout, or that it is intended or designed to influence an election of a bargaining representative for workers in the local port.

(3) Under the Alaska exception in sec. 258(d) of the Act, and in those cases where it has been determined that an attestation is required under the automated vessel exception consisting of the use of such equipment for longshore work to be performed in the State of Alaska, the procedure involves filing an attestation with the Department of Labor attesting that:

(i) The employer will make a bona fide request for United States longshore workers who are qualified and available in sufficient numbers to perform the activity at the particular time and location from the parties to whom notice has been provided under paragraph (b)(3)(iv) (B) and (C) of this section, except that:

(A) Wherever two or more contract stevedoring companies which meet the requirements of section 32 of the Longshore and Harbor Workers' Compensation Act (33 U.S.C. 932) have signed a joint collective bargaining agreement with a single labor organization recognized as an exclusive bargaining representative of United States longshore workers within the meaning of the National Labor Relations Act (29 U.S.C. 141 *et seq.*), the employer may request longshore workers from only one such contract stevedoring company, and

(B) A request for longshore workers to an operator of a private dock may be made only for longshore work to be performed at that dock and only if the operator meets the requirements of section 32 of the Longshore and Harbor Workers' Compensation Act (33 U.S.C. 932);

(ii) The employer will employ all United States longshore workers made available in response to the request made pursuant to paragraph (b)(3)(i) of this section who are qualified and available in sufficient numbers and who are needed to perform the longshore activity at the particular time and location attested to;

(iii) The use of alien crewmembers for such activity is not intended or designed to influence and election of a bargaining representative for workers in the State of Alaska; and

(iv) Notice of the attestation has been provided to:

(A) Labor organizations which have been recognized as exclusive bargaining representatives of United States longshore workers within the meaning of the National Labor Relations Act (29 U.S.C. 141 *et seq.*) and which make available or intend to make available workers to the particular location where the longshore work is to be performed;

(B) Contract stevedoring companies which employ or intend to employ United States longshore workers at that location; and

(C) Operators of private docks at which the employer will use longshore workers.

(c) *Applicability.* Subparts F and G of this part apply to all employers who seek to employ alien crewmembers for longshore work at U.S. ports under the prevailing practice exception, to all employers who seek to employ alien crewmembers for longshore work at locations in the State of Alaska under the Alaska exception, to all employers claiming the automated vessel exception, and to those cases where it has been determined that an attestation is required under the automated vessel exception.

[60 FR 3956, 3976, Jan. 19, 1995, as amended at 71 FR 35520, June 21, 2006]

§ 655.501 Overview of responsibilities.

This section provides a context for the attestation process, to facilitate understanding by employers that may seek to employ alien crewmembers for longshore work under the prevailing practice exception, under the Alaska exception, and in those cases where an attestation is necessary under the automated vessel exception.

(a) *Department of Labor's responsibilities.* The United States Department of Labor (DOL) administers the attestation process. Within DOL, the Employment and Training Administration (ETA) shall have responsibility for setting up and operating the attestation process; the Employment Standards Administration's Wage and Hour Division shall be responsible for investigating and resolving any complaints filed concerning such attestations.

(b) *Employer attestation responsibilities.* (1) Each employer seeking to use alien crewmembers for longshore work at a local U.S. port pursuant to the prevailing practice exception or where an attestation is required under the automated vessel exception for longshore work to be performed at locations other than in the State of Alaska shall, as the first step, submit an attestation on Form ETA 9033, as described in § 655.510 of this part, to ETA at the address set forth at § 655.510(b) of this part. If ETA accepts the attestation for filing, pursuant to § 655.510 of this part, ETA shall return the cover form of the accepted attestation to the employer, and, at the same time, shall provide notice of the filing to the United States Citizenship and Immigration Services of the Department of Homeland Security (DHS) office having jurisdiction over the port where longshore work will be performed.

(2) Each employer seeking to use alien crewmembers for longshore work at a particular location in the State of Alaska pursuant to the Alaska exception or where an attestation is required under the automated vessel exception for longshore work to be performed at a particular location in Alaska shall submit, as a first step, an attestation on Form ETA 9033–A, as described in § 655.533 of this part, to ETA at the address of the Seattle regional office as set forth at § 655.532 of this part. The address appears in the instructions to Form ETA 9033–A. ETA shall return the cover form of the accepted attestation to the employer, and, at the same time, shall provide notice of the filing to the DHS office having jurisdiction over the location where longshore work will be performed.

(c) *Complaints.* Complaints concerning misrepresentation in the attestation, failure of the employer to carry out the terms of the attestation, or complaints that an employer is required to file an attestation under the automated vessel exception, may be filed with the Wage and Hour Division, according to the procedures set forth in subpart G of this part. Complaints of "misrepresentation" may include assertions that an employer has attested to the use of alien crewmembers only for a particular activity of longshore work and has thereafter used such alien crewmembers for another activity of longshore work. If the Division determines that the complaint presents reasonable cause to warrant an investigation, the Division shall then investigate, and, where appropriate, after an opportunity for a hearing, assess sanctions and penalties. Subpart G of this part further provides that interested parties may obtain an administrative law judge hearing on the Division's determination after an investigation and may seek the Secretary's review of the administrative law judge's decision. Subpart G of this part also provides that a complainant may request that the Wage and Hour Administrator issue a cease and desist order in the case of either alleged violation(s) of an attestation or longshore work by alien crewmember(s) employed by an employer allegedly not qualified for the claimed automated vessel exception. Upon the receipt of such a request, the Division shall notify the employer, provide an opportunity for a response and an informal meeting, and then rule on the request, which shall be granted if the preponderance of the evidence submitted supports the complainant's position.

[60 FR 3956, 3976, Jan. 19, 1995, as amended at 71 FR 35521, June 21, 2006]

§ 655.502 Definitions.

For the purposes of subparts F and G of this part:

Accepted for filing means that a properly completed attestation on Form ETA 9033, including accompanying documentation for each of the requirements in § 655.510 (d) through (f) of this part, or a properly completed attestation on Form ETA 9033–A, including accompanying documentation for the requirement in § 655.537 of this part in the case of an attestation under the Alaska exception, submitted by the employer or its designated agent or representative has been received and filed by the Employment and Training Administration of the Department of Labor (DOL). (Unacceptable attestations under the prevailing practice exception are described at § 655.510(g)(2) of this part. Unacceptable attestations under the Alaska exception are described at § 655.538(b) of this part.)

Act and *INA* mean the Immigration and Nationality Act, as amended, 8 U.S.C. 1101 *et seq.*

Activity means any activity relating to loading cargo; unloading cargo; operation of cargo-related equipment; or handling of mooring lines on the dock when a vessel is made fast or let go.

Administrative law judge means an official appointed pursuant to 5 U.S.C. 3105.

Administrator means the Administrator of the Wage and Hour Division,

Employment Standards Administration, Department of Labor, or such authorized representatives as may be designated to perform any of the functions of the Administrator under subparts F and G of this part.

Administrator, Office of Foreign Labor Certification (OFLC Administrator) means the primary official of the Office of Foreign Labor Certification (OFLC Administrator), or the OFLC Administrator's designee.

Attestation means documents submitted by an employer attesting to and providing accompanying documentation to show that, under the prevailing practice exception, the use of alien crewmembers for a particular activity of longshore work at a particular U.S. port is the prevailing practice, and is not during a strike or lockout nor intended to influence an election of a bargaining representative for workers; and that notice of the attestation has been provided to the bargaining representative, or, where there is none, to the longshore workers at the local port. Under the Alaska exception, such documents shall show that, before using alien crewmen to perform longshore work, the employer will make bona fide requests for dispatch of United States longshore workers who are qualified and available in sufficient numbers and that the employer will employ all such United States longshore workers in response to such a request for dispatch; that the use of alien crewmembers is not intended or designed to influence an election of a bargaining representative for workers in the State of Alaska; and that notice of the attestation has been provided to labor organizations recognized as exclusive bargaining representatives of United States longshore workers, contract stevedoring companies, and operators of private docks at which the employer will use longshore workers.

Attesting employer means an employer who has filed an attestation.

Attorney General means the chief official of the U.S. Department of Justice or the Attorney General's designee.

Automated vessel means a vessel equipped with an automated self-unloading conveyor belt or vacuum-actuated system which is utilized for loading or unloading cargo between the vessel and the dock.

Certifying Officer (CO) means a Department of Labor official, or the CO's designee, who makes determinations about whether or not to grant applications for labor certification. The National Certifying Officer, which is the OFLC Administrator, makes such determinations in the national office of the OFLC.

Chief Administrative Law Judge means the chief official of the Office of the Administrative Law Judges of the Department of Labor or the Chief Administrative Law Judge's designee.

Contract stevedoring company means a stevedoring company which is licensed to do business in the State of Alaska and which meets the requirements of section 32 of the Longshore and Harbor Workers' Compensation Act (33 U.S.C. 932).

Crewmember means any nonimmigrant alien admitted to the United States to perform services under sec. 101(a)(15)(D)(i) of the Act (8 U.S.C. 1101(a)(15)(D)(i)).

Date of filing means the date an attestation is *accepted for filing* by ETA.

Department and *DOL* mean the United States Department of Labor.

Department of Homeland Security (DHS) through the United States Citizenship and Immigration Services (USCIS) makes the determination under the Act on whether an employer of alien crewmembers may use such crewmembers for longshore work at a U.S. port.

Division means the Wage and Hour Division of the Employment Standards Administration, DOL.

Employer means a person, firm, corporation, or other association or organization, which suffers or permits, or proposes to suffer or permit, alien crewmembers to perform longshore work at a port within the U.S. For purposes of §§ 655.530 through 655.541, which govern the performance of longshore activities by alien crewmembers under the Alaska exception, "employer" includes any agent or representative designated by the employer.

Employment and Training Administration (ETA) means the agency within the

Department of Labor (DOL) which includes the Office of Foreign Labor (OFLC).

Employment Standards Administration (ESA) means the agency within the Department of Labor (DOL) which includes the Wage and Hour Division.

Lockout means a labor dispute involving a work stoppage, wherein an employer withholds work from its employees in order to gain a concession from them.

Longshore work means any activity (except safety and environmental protection work as described in sec. 258(b)(2) of the Act) relating to the loading or unloading of cargo, the operation of cargo related equipment (whether or not integral to the vessel), or the handling of mooring lines on the dock when the vessel is made fast or let go, in the United States or the coastal waters thereof.

Longshore worker means a U.S. worker who performs longshore work.

Office of Foreign Labor Certification (OFLC) means the organizational component within the ETA that provides national leadership and policy guidance and develops regulations and procedures to carry out the responsibilities of the Secretary of Labor under the INA concerning alien workers seeking admission to the United States in order to work under the Immigration and Nationality Act, as amended.

Port means a geographic area, either on a seacoast, lake, river or any other navigable body of water, which contains one or more publicly or privately owned terminals, piers, docks, or maritime facilities, which is commonly thought of as a port by other government maritime-related agencies, such as the Maritime Administration. U.S. ports include, but are not limited to, those listed in Appendix A to this subpart.

Qualified and available in sufficient numbers means the full complement of qualified longshore workers needed to perform the longshore activity, as determined by industry standards in the State of Alaska, including safety considerations.

Secretary means the Secretary of Labor or the Secretary's designee.

Strike means a labor dispute wherein employees engage in a concerted stoppage of work (including stoppage by reason of the expiration of a collective-bargaining agreement) or engage in any concerted slowdown or other concerted interruption of operations.

Unanticipated emergency means an unexpected and unavoidable situation, such as one involving severe weather conditions, natural disaster, or mechanical breakdown, where cargo must be immediately loaded on, or unloaded from, a vessel.

United States is defined at 8 U.S.C. 1101(a)(38).

United States (U.S.) worker means a worker who is a U.S. citizen, a U.S. national, a permanent resident alien, or any other worker legally permitted to work indefinitely in the United States.

[60 FR 3956, 3976, Jan. 19, 1995, as amended at 71 FR 35520, June 21, 2006]

§ 655.510 Employer attestations.

(a) *Who may submit attestations?* An employer (or the employer's designated U.S. agent or representative) seeking to employ alien crewmembers for a particular activity of longshore work under the prevailing practice exception shall submit an attestation, provided there is not in effect in the local port any collective bargaining agreement covering at least 30 percent of the longshore workers. An attestation is required for each port at which the employer intends to use alien crewmembers for longshore work. The attestation shall include: A completed Form ETA 9033, which shall be signed by the employer (or the employer's designated agent or representative); and facts and evidence prescribed in paragraphs (d) through (f) of this section. This § 655.510 shall not apply in the case of longshore work performed at a particular location in the State of Alaska. The procedures governing the filing of attestations under the Alaska exception are set forth at §§ 655.530 through 655.541.

(b) *Where and when should attestations be submitted?* (1) Attestations must be submitted, by U.S. mail, private carrier, or facsimile transmission to the U.S. Department of Labor office(s) which are designated by the OFLC Administrator. Attestations must be received and date-stamped by DOL at least 14 calendar days prior to the date of the first performance of the intended longshore activity, and shall be accepted for filing or returned by ETA in accordance with paragraph (g) of this section within 14 calendar days of the date received by ETA. An attestation which is accepted by ETA solely because it was not reviewed within 14 days is subject to subsequent invalidation pursuant to paragraph (i) of this section. Every employer filing an attestation shall have an agent or representative with a United States address. Such address shall be clearly indicated on the Form ETA 9033. In order to ensure that an attestation has been accepted for filing prior to the date of the performance of the longshore activity, employers are advised to take mailing time into account to make sure that ETA receives the attestation at least 14 days prior to the first performance of the longshore activity.

(2) *Unanticipated Emergencies.* ETA may accept for filing attestations received after the 14-day deadline when due to an unanticipated emergency, as defined in § 655.502 of this part. When an employer is claiming an unanticipated emergency, it shall submit documentation to support such a claim. ETA shall then make a determination on the validity of the claim, and shall accept the attestation for filing or return it in accordance with paragraph (g) of this section. ETA shall in no case accept an attestation received later than the date of the first performance of the activity.

(c) *What should be submitted?*—(1) *Form ETA 9033 with accompanying documentation.* For each port, a completed and dated original Form ETA 9033, or facsimile transmission thereof, containing the required attestation elements and the original signature of the employer (or the employer's designated agent or representative) shall be submitted, along with two copies of the completed, signed, and dated Form ETA 9033. (If the attestation is submitted by facsimile transmission, the attestation containing the original signature shall be maintained at the U.S. business address of the employer's designated agent or representative). Copies of Form ETA 9033 are available at the National Processing Centers and at the National Office. In addition, the employer shall submit two sets of all facts and evidence to show compliance with each of the attestation elements as prescribed by the regulatory standards in paragraphs (d) through (f) of this section. In the case of an investigation pursuant to subpart G of this part, the employer shall have the burden of proof to establish the validity of each attestation. The employer shall maintain in its records at the office of its U.S. agent, for a period of at least 3 years from the date of filing, sufficient documentation to meet its burden of proof, which shall at a minimum include the documentation described in this § 655.510, and shall make the documents available to Department of Labor officials upon request.

Whenever any document is submitted to a Federal agency or retained in the employer's records pursuant to this part, the document either shall be in the English language or shall be accompanied by a written translation into the English language certified by the translator as to the accuracy of the translation and his/her competency to translate.

(2) *Statutory precondition regarding collective bargaining agreements.* (i) The employer may file an attestation only when there is no collective bargaining agreement in effect in the port covering 30 percent or more of the longshore workers in the port. The employer shall attest on the Form ETA 9033 that no such collective bargaining agreement exists at the port at the time that the attestation is filed.

(ii) The employer is not required to submit with the Form ETA 9033 documentation substantiating that there is no collective bargaining agreement in effect in the port covering 30 percent or more of the longshore workers. If a complaint is filed which presents reasonable cause to believe that such an agreement exists, the Department shall conduct an investigation. In such an investigation, the employer shall have the burden of proving that no such collective bargaining agreement exists.

(3) *Ports for which attestations may be filed.* Employers may file an attestation for a port which is listed in appendix A (U.S. Seaports) to this subpart. Employers may also file an attestation for a particular location not in appendix A to this subpart if additional facts

and evidence are submitted with the attestation to demonstrate that the location is a port, meeting all of the criteria as defined by § 655.502 of this part.

(4) *Attestation elements*. The attestation elements referenced in paragraph (c)(1) of this section are mandated by sec. 258(c)(1)(B) of the Act (8 U.S.C. 1288(c)(1)(B)). Section 258(c)(1)(B) of the Act requires employers who seek to have alien crewmembers engage in a longshore activity to attest as follows:

(i) The performance of the activity by alien crewmembers is permitted under the prevailing practice of the particular port as of the date of filing of the attestation;

(ii) The use of the alien crewmembers for such activity is not during a strike or lockout in the course of a labor dispute, and is not intended or designed to influence an election of a bargaining representative for workers in the local port; and

(iii) Notice of the attestation has been provided by the owner, agent, consignee, master, or commanding officer to the bargaining representative of longshore workers in the local port, or, where there is no such bargaining representative, notice has been provided to longshore workers employed at the local port.

(d) *The first attestation element: prevailing practice*. For an employer to be in compliance with the first attestation element, it is required to have been the prevailing practice during the 12-month period preceding the filing of the attestation, for a particular activity of longshore work at the particular port to be performed by alien crewmembers. For each port, a prevailing practice can exist for any of four different types of longshore work: loading of cargo, unloading of cargo, operation of cargo-related equipment, or handling of mooring lines. It is thus possible that at a particular port it is the prevailing practice for alien crewmembers to unload vessels but not the prevailing practice to load them. An employer shall indicate on the attestation form which of the four longshore activities it is claiming is the prevailing practice for such work to be performed by alien crewmembers.

(1) *Establishing a prevailing practice*. (i) In establishing that a particular activity of longshore work is the prevailing practice at a particular port, an employer shall submit facts and evidence to show that in the 12-month period preceding the filing of the attestation, one of the following conditions existed:

(A) Over fifty percent of vessels docking at the port used alien crewmembers for the activity; or

(B) Alien crewmembers made up over fifty percent of the workers in the port who engaged in the activity.

(ii) *Prevailing practice after Secretary of State determination of non-reciprocity*. Section 258(d) of the Act provides a reciprocity exception (separate from the prevailing practice exception) to the prohibition on performance of longshore work by alien crewmembers in U.S. ports. However, this reciprocity exception becomes nonapplicable where the Secretary of State determines that, for a particular activity of longshore work, a particular country (by law, regulation, or practice) prohibits such activity by U.S. crewmembers in its ports. When the Secretary of State places a country on the non-reciprocity list (which means, for the purposes of this section, *Prohibitions on longshore work by U.S. nationals; listing by country* at 22 CFR 89.1), crewmembers on vessels from that country (that is, vessels that are registered in that country or vessels whose majority ownership interest is held by nationals of that country) are not permitted to perform longshore work in U.S. waters, absent applicability of some exception other than the reciprocity exception. The Secretary of State's determination has the following effects in the establishment of a prevailing practice for a particular longshore activity at a particular U.S. port for purposes of the prevailing practice exception.

(A) An employer from any country, other than the country which is placed on the non-reciprocity list, may include the longshore activities performed by alien crewmembers on all vessels in establishing the prevailing practice for a particular longshore activity in a particular port.

(B) An employer from a country which is placed on the non-reciprocity list may file an attestation for the prevailing practice exception under the standards and requirements established in this subpart F (except as provided in paragraph (d)(1)(ii)(C) of this section), provided that the attestation is filed at least 12 months after the date on which the employer's country is placed on the list.

(C) An employer from a country which is placed on the non-reciprocity list may file an attestation pursuant to the prevailing practice exception earlier than 12 months from the date on which the employer's country is placed on the list, except that the following restrictions shall apply to such attestation:

(*1*) The employer shall submit facts and evidence to show that, for the 12-month period preceding the date of the attestation, the use of alien crewmembers to perform a particular activity of longshore work was permitted by the prevailing practice in the port (as defined in paragraph (d)(1)(i) of this section) without considering or including such activity by crewmembers on vessels from the employer's country; or

(*2*) The employer shall submit facts and evidence (including data on activities performed by crewmembers on vessels from the employer's country) to show that the use of alien crewmembers to perform a particular activity of longshore work was permitted by the prevailing practice in the port (as defined in paragraph (d)(1)(i) of this section) for one of two periods—

(*i*) For the employer whose country has not previously been on the non-reciprocity list, the period is the continuous 12-month period prior to May 28, 1991 (the effective date of section 258 of the Act); or

(*ii*) For the employer whose country was at some time on the non-reciprocity list, but was subsequently removed from the non-reciprocity list and then restored to the non-reciprocity list (on one or more occasions), the period is the last continuous 12-month period during which the employer's country was not under the reciprocity exception (that is, was listed on the non-reciprocity list).

(*iii*) For purposes of this paragraph (d)(1):

(A) "Workers in the port engaged in the activity" means any person who performed the activity in any calendar day;

(B) Vessels shall be counted each time they dock at the particular port):

(C) Vessels exempt from section 258 of the INA for safety and environmental protection shall not be included in counting the number of vessels which dock at the port (see Department of Transportation Regulations); and

(D) Automated vessels shall not be included in counting the number of vessels which dock at the port. For establishing a prevailing practice under the automated vessel exception see § 655.520 of this part.

(2) *Documentation.* In assembling the facts and evidence required by paragraph (d)(1) of this section, the employer may consult with the port authority which has jurisdiction over the local port, the collective bargaining representative(s) of longshore workers at the local port, other employers, or any other entity which is familiar with the practices at the port. Such documentation shall include a written summary of a survey of the experience of shipmasters who entered the local port in the previous year; or a letter, affidavit, or other written statement from an appropriate local port authority regarding the use of alien crewmembers to perform the longshore activity at the port in the previous year; or other documentation of comparable weight. Written statements from collective bargaining representatives and/or shipping agents with direct knowledge of practices regarding the use of alien crewmembers in the local port may also be pertinent. Such documentation shall accompany the Form ETA 9033, and any underlying documentation which supports the employer's burden of proof shall be maintained in the employer's records at the office of the U.S. agent as required by paragraph (c)(1) of this section.

(e) *The second attestation element: no strike or lockout; no intention or design to influence bargaining representative election.* (1) The employer shall attest that, at the time of submitting the attestation, there is not a strike or lockout in the course of a labor dispute covering the employer's activity, and that it will not use alien crewmembers during a strike or lockout after filing the attestation. The employer shall also attest that the employment of such aliens is not intended or designed to influence an election for a bargaining representative for workers in the local port. Labor disputes for purposes of this attestation element relate only to those involving longshore workers at the port of intended employment. This attestation element applies to strikes and lockouts and elections of bargaining representatives at the local port where the use of alien crewmembers for longshore work is intended.

(2) *Documentation.* As documentation to substantiate the requirement in paragraph (e)(1) of this section, an employer may submit a statement of the good faith efforts made to determine whether there is a strike or lockout at the particular port, as, for example, by contacting the port authority or the collective bargaining representative for longshore workers at the particular port.

(f) *The third attestation element: notice of filing.* The employer of alien crewmembers shall attest that at the time of filing the attestation, notice of filing has been provided to the bargaining representative of the longshore workers in the local port, or, where there is no such bargaining representative, notice of the filing has been provided to longshore workers employed at the local port through posting in conspicuous locations and through other appropriate means.

(1) *Notification of bargaining representative.* No later than the date the attestation is received by DOL to be considered for filing, the employer of alien crewmembers shall notify the bargaining representative (if any) of longshore workers at the local port that the attestation is being submitted to DOL. The notice shall include a copy of the Form ETA 9033, shall state the activity(ies) for which the attestation is submitted, and shall state in that notice that the attestation and accompanying documentation are available at the national office of ETA for review by interested parties. The employer may have its owner, agent, consignee, master, or commanding officer provide such notice. Notices under this paragraph (f)(1) shall include the following statement: "Complaints alleging misrepresentation of material facts in the attestation and/or failure to comply with the terms of the attestation may be filed with any office of the Wage and Hour Division of the United States Department of Labor."

(2) *Posting notice where there is no bargaining representative.* If there is no bargaining representative of longshore workers at the local port when the employer submits an attestation to ETA, the employer shall provide written notice to the port authority for distribution to the public on request. In addition, the employer shall post one or more written notices at the local port, stating that the attestation with accompanying documentation has been submitted, the activity(ies) for which the attestation has been submitted, and that the attestation and accompanying documentation are available at the national office of ETA for review by interested parties. Such posted notice shall be clearly visible and unobstructed, and shall be posted in conspicuous places where the longshore workers readily can read the posted notice on the way to or from their duties. Appropriate locations for posting such notices include locations in the immediate proximity of mandatory Fair Labor Standards Act wage and hour notices and Occupational Safety and Health Act occupational safety and health notices. The notice shall include a copy of the Form ETA 9033 filed with DOL, shall provide information concerning the availability of supporting documents for examination at the national office of ETA, and shall include the following statement: "Complaints alleging misrepresentation of material facts in the attestation and/or failure to comply with the terms of the attestation may be filed with any office of the Wage and Hour Division of the United States Department of Labor."

(3) *Documentation.* The employer shall provide a statement setting forth the name and address of the person to whom the notice was provided and where and when the notice was posted and shall attach a copy of the notice.

(g) *Actions on attestations submitted for filing.* Once an attestation has been received from an employer, a determination shall be made by the Certifying Officer whether to accept the attestation for filing or return it. The Certifying Officer may request additional explanation and/or documentation from the employer in making this determination. An attestation which is properly filled out and which includes accompanying documentation for each of the requirements set forth at § 655.510(d) through (f) shall be accepted for filing by ETA on the date it is signed by the Certifying Officer unless it falls within one of the categories set forth in paragraph (g)(2) of this section. Once an attestation is accepted for filing, ETA shall then follow the procedures set forth in paragraph (g)(1) of this section. Upon acceptance of the employer's attestation by ETA, the attestation and accompanying documentation will be forwarded and shall be available in a timely manner for public examination at the ETA national office. ETA shall not consider information contesting an attestation received by ETA prior to the determination to accept or return the attestation for filing. Such information shall not be made part of ETA's administrative record on the attestation, but shall be referred to ESA to be processed as a complaint pursuant to subpart G of this part if the attestation is accepted by ETA for filing.

(1) *Acceptance.* (i) If the attestation is properly filled out and includes accompanying documentation for each of the requirements at § 655.510(d) through (f), and does not fall within one of the categories set forth at paragraph (g)(2) of this section, ETA shall accept the attestation for filing, provide notification to the DHS office having jurisdiction over the port where longshore work will be performed, and return to the employer, or the employer's agent or representative at a U.S. address, one copy of the attestation form submitted by the employer, with ETA's acceptance indicated thereon. The employer may then use alien crewmembers for the particular activity of longshore work at the U.S. port cited in the attestation in accordance with DHS regulations.

(ii) DOL is not the guarantor of the accuracy, truthfulness or adequacy of an attestation accepted for filing.

(2) *Unacceptable attestations.* ETA shall not accept an attestation for filing and shall return such attestation to the employer, or the employer's agent or representative at a U.S. address, when one of the following conditions exists:

(i) When the Form ETA 9033 is not properly filled out. Examples of improperly filled out Form ETA 9033's include instances where the employer has neglected to check all the necessary boxes, or where the employer has failed to include the name of the port where it intends to use the alien crewmembers for longshore work, or where the employer has named a port that is not listed in appendix A and has failed to submit facts and evidence to support a showing that the location is a port as defined by § 655.502, or when the employer has failed to sign the attestation or to designate an agent in the United States;

(ii) When the Form ETA 9033 with accompanying documentation is not received by ETA at least 14 days prior to the date of performance of the first activity indicated on the Form ETA 9033; unless the employer is claiming an unanticipated emergency, has included documentation which supports such claim, and ETA has found the claim to be valid;

(iii) When the Form ETA 9033 does not include accompanying documentation for each of the requirements set forth at § 655.510 (d) through (f);

(iv) When the accompanying documentation required by paragraph (c) of this section submitted by the employer, on its face, is inconsistent with the requirements set forth at § 655.510 (d) through (f). Examples of such a situation include instances where the Form ETA 9033 pertains to one port and the accompanying documentation to another; where the Form ETA 9033 pertains to one activity of longshore work and the accompanying documentation obviously refers to another; or where the documentation clearly indicates that only thirty percent, instead of the required fifty percent, of the activity attested to is performed by alien crewmembers;

(v) When the Administrator, Wage and Hour Division, has notified ETA, in writing, after an investigation pursuant to subpart G of this part, that the particular activity of longshore work which the employer has attested is the prevailing practice at a particular port, is not, in fact, the prevailing practice at the particular port;

(vi) When the Administrator, Wage and Hour Division, has notified ETA, in writing, that a cease and desist order has been issued pursuant to subpart G of this part, with respect to the attesting employer's performance of the particular activity and port, in violation of a previously accepted attestation;

(vii) When the Administrator, Wage and Hour Division, has notified ETA, in writing, after an investigation pursuant to subpart G of this part, that the particular employer has misrepresented or failed to comply with an attestation previously submitted and accepted for filing, but in no case for a period of more than one year after the date of the Administrator's notice and provided that DHS has not advised ETA that the prohibition is in effect for a lesser period; or

(viii) When the Administrator, Wage and Hour Division, has notified ETA, in writing, that the employer has failed to comply with any penalty, sanction, or other remedy assessed in a final agency action following an investigation by the Wage and Hour Division pursuant to subpart G of this part.

(3) *Resubmission.* If the attestation is not accepted for filing pursuant to the categories set forth in paragraph (g)(2) of this section, ETA shall return to the employer, or the employer's agent or representative, at a U.S. address, the attestation form and accompanying documentation submitted by the employer. ETA shall notify the employer, in writing, of the reason(s) that the attestation is unacceptable. When an attestation is found to be unacceptable pursuant to paragraphs (g)(2) (i) through (iv) of this section, the employer may resubmit the attestation with the proper documentation. When an attestation is found to be unacceptable pursuant to paragraphs (g)(2) (v) through (viii) of this section and returned, such action shall be the final decision of the Secretary of Labor.

(h) *Effective date and validity of filed attestations.* An attestation is filed and effective as of the date it is accepted and signed by the Certifying Officer. Such attestation is valid for the 12-month period beginning on the date of acceptance for filing, unless suspended or invalidated pursuant to subpart G of this part or paragraph (i) of this section. The filed attestation expires at the end of the 12-month period of validity.

(i) *Suspension or invalidation of filed attestations.* Suspension or invalidation of an attestation may result from enforcement action(s) under subpart G of this part (*i.e.*, investigation(s) conducted by the Administrator or cease and desist order(s) issued by the Administrator regarding the employer's misrepresentation in or failure to carry out its attestation); or from a discovery by ETA that it made an error in accepting the attestation because such attestation falls within one of the categories set forth in paragraph (g)(2) of this section.

(1) *Result of Wage and Hour Division action.* Upon the determination of a violation under subpart G of this part, the Administrator shall, pursuant to § 655.660(b), notify the DHS of the violation and of the Administrator's notice to ETA.

(2) *Result of ETA action.* If, after accepting an attestation for filing, ETA finds that the attestation is unacceptable because it falls within one of the categories set forth at paragraph (g)(2) of this section, and as a result, ETA suspends or invalidates the attestation, ETA shall notify the DHS of such suspension or invalidation and shall return a copy of the attestation form to the employer, or the employer's agent or representative, at a U.S. address. ETA shall notify the employer, in writing, of the reason(s) that the attestation is suspended or invalidated. When an attestation is found to be suspended or invalidated pursuant to paragraphs (g)(2) (i) through (iv) of this section, the employer may resubmit the attestation with the proper documentation. When an attestation is suspended or invalidated because it falls within one of the categories in paragraphs (g)(2) (v) through (viii) of this section, such action shall be the final decision of the

Secretary of Labor, except as set forth in subpart G of this part.

(j) *Withdrawal of accepted attestations.* (1) An employer who has submitted an attestation which has been accepted for filing may withdraw such attestation at any time before the 12-month period of its validity terminates, unless the Administrator has found reasonable cause under subpart G to commence an investigation of the particular attestation. Such withdrawal may be advisable, for example, when the employer learns that the particular activity(ies) of longshore work which it has attested is the prevailing practice to perform with alien crewmembers may not, in fact, have been the prevailing practice at the particular port at the time of filing. Requests for such withdrawals shall be in writing and shall be directed to the Certifying Officer.

(2) Withdrawal of an attestation shall not affect an employer's liability with respect to any failure to meet the conditions attested to which took place before the withdrawal, or for misrepresentations in an attestation. However, if an employer has not yet performed the particular longshore activity(ies) at the port in question, the Administrator will not find reasonable cause to investigate unless it is alleged, and there is reasonable cause to believe, that the employer has made misrepresentations in the attestation or documentation thereof, or that the employer has not in fact given the notice attested to.

(Approved by the Office of Management and Budget under Control No. 1205–0309)

[60 FR 3956, 3976, Jan. 19, 1995, as amended at 71 FR 35520, June 21, 2006]

§ 655.520 Special provisions regarding automated vessels.

In general, an attestation is not required in the case of a particular activity of longshore work consisting of the use of automated self-unloading conveyor belt or vacuum-actuated systems on a vessel. The legislation creates a rebuttable presumption that the use of alien crewmembers for the operation of such automated systems is the prevailing practice. In order to overcome such presumption, it must be shown by the preponderance of the evidence submitted by any interested party, that the use of alien crewmembers for such activity is not the prevailing practice. Longshore work involving the use of such equipment shall be exempt from the attestation requirement only if the activity consists of using that equipment. If the automated equipment is not used in the particular activity of longshore work, an attestation is required as described under § 655.510 of this part if it is the prevailing practice in the port to use alien crewmembers for this work, except that in all cases, where an attestation is required for longshore work to be performed at a particular location in the State of Alaska, an employer shall file such attestation under the Alaska exception pursuant to §§ 655.530 through 655.541 on Form ETA 9033–A. When automated equipment is used in the particular activity of longshore work, an attestation is required only if the Administrator finds, based on a preponderance of the evidence which may be submitted by any interested party, that the performance of the particular activity of longshore work is not the prevailing practice at the port, or was during a strike or lockout or intended to influence an election of a bargaining representative for workers in the local port, or if the Administrator issues a cease and desist order against use of the automated equipment without such attestation.

(a) *Procedure when attestation is required.* If it is determined pursuant to subpart G of this part that an attestation is required for longshore work consisting of the use of automated equipment at a location other than in the State of Alaska, the employer shall comply with all the requirements set forth at § 655.510 of this part except paragraph (d) of § 655.510. In lieu of complying with § 655.510(d) of this part, the employer shall comply with paragraph (b) of this section. If it is determined pursuant to subpart G of this part that an attestation is required for longshore work consisting of the use of automated equipment at a particular location in the State of Alaska, the employer shall comply with all the requirements set forth at §§ 655.530 through 655.541 of this part.

(b) *The first attestation element: prevailing practice for automated vessels.* For an employer to be in compliance with the first attestation element, it is required to have been the prevailing practice that over fifty percent (as described in paragraph (b)(1) of this section) of a particular activity of longshore work which was performed through the use of automated self-unloading conveyor belt or vacuum-actuated equipment at the particular port during the 12-month period preceding the filing of the attestation, was performed by alien crewmembers. For purposes of this paragraph (b), only automated vessels shall be included in counting the number of vessels which dock at the port.

(1) *Establishing a prevailing practice.* (i) In establishing that the use of alien crewmembers to perform a particular activity of longshore work consisting of the use of self-unloading conveyor belt or vacuum-actuated systems on a vessel is the prevailing practice at a particular port, an employer shall submit facts and evidence to show that in the 12-month period preceding the filing of the attestation, one of the following conditions existed:

(A) Over fifty percent of the automated vessels docking at the port used alien crewmembers for the activity (for purposes of this paragraph (b)(1), a vessel shall be counted each time it docks at the particular port); or

(B) Alien crewmembers made up over fifty percent of the workers who performed the activity with respect to such automated vessels.

(ii) *Prevailing practice after Secretary of State determination of non-reciprocity.* Section 258(d) of the Act provides a reciprocity exception (separate from the prevailing practice exception) to the prohibition on performance of longshore work by alien crewmembers in U.S. ports. However, this reciprocity exception becomes nonapplicable where the Secretary of State determines that, for a particular activity of longshore work, a particular country (by law, regulation, or practice) prohibits such activity by U.S. crewmembers in its ports. When the Secretary of State places a country on the non-reciprocity list (which means, for the purposes of this section, *Prohibitions on longshore work by U.S. nationals; listing by country* at 22 CFR 89.1), crewmembers on vessels from that country (that is, vessels that are registered in that country or vessels whose majority ownership interest is held by nationals of that country) are not permitted to perform longshore work in U.S. waters, absent applicability of some exception other than the reciprocity exception. The Secretary of State's determination has the following effects in the establishment of a prevailing practice for a particular longshore activity at a particular U.S. port for purposes of the prevailing practice exception.

(A) An employer from any country, other than the country which is placed on the non-reciprocity list, may include the longshore activities performed by alien crewmembers on all vessels in establishing the prevailing practice for a particular longshore activity in a particular port.

(B) An employer from a country which is placed on the non-reciprocity list may file an attestation for the prevailing practice exception under the standards and requirements established in this subpart F (except as provided in paragraph (b)(1)(ii)(C) of this section), provided that the attestation is filed at least 12 months after the date on which the employer's country is placed on the list.

(C) An employer from a country which is placed on the non-reciprocity list may file an attestation pursuant to the prevailing practice exception earlier than 12 months from the date on which the employer's country is placed on the list, except that the following restrictions shall apply to such attestation:

(*1*) The employer shall submit facts and evidence to show that, for the 12-month period preceding the date of the attestation, the use of alien crewmembers to perform a particular activity of longshore work was permitted by the prevailing practice in the port (as defined in paragraph (d)(1)(i) of this section) without considering or including such activity by crewmembers on vessels from the employer's country; or

(*2*) The employer shall submit facts and evidence (including data on activities performed by crewmembers on vessels from the employer's country) to show that the use of alien crewmembers to perform a particular activity of longshore work was permitted by the prevailing practice in the port (as defined in paragraph (b)(1)(i) of this section) for one of two periods—

(*i*) For the employer whose country has not previously been on the non-reciprocity list, the period is the continuous 12-month period prior to May 28, 1991 (the effective date of section 258 of the Act); or

(*ii*) For the employer whose country was at some time on the non-reciprocity list, but was subsequently removed from the non-reciprocity list and then restored to the non-reciprocity list (on one or more occasions), the period is the last continuous 12-month period during which the employer's country was not under the reciprocity exception (that is, was listed on the non-reciprocity list).

(2) *Documentation*. In assembling the documentation described in paragraph (b)(1) of this section, the employer may consult with the port authority which has jurisdiction over the local port, the collective bargaining representative(s) of longshore workers at the local port, other employers, or any other entity which is familiar with the practices at the port. The documentation shall include a written summary of a survey of the experience of shipmasters who entered the local port in the previous year; or a letter, affidavit, or other written statement from an appropriate local port authority regarding the use of alien crewmembers to perform the longshore activity at the port in the previous year; or other documentation of comparable weight. Written statements from collective bargaining representatives and/or shipping agents with direct knowledge of practices regarding the use of alien crewmembers may also be pertinent. Such documentation shall accompany the Form ETA 9033, and any underlying documentation which supports the employer's burden of proof shall be maintained in the employer's records at the office of the U.S. agent as required under § 655.510(c)(1) of this part.

(Approved by the Office of Management and Budget under Control No. 1205–0309)

ALASKA EXCEPTION

§ 655.530 Special provisions regarding the performance of longshore activities at locations in the State of Alaska.

Applicability. Section § 655.510 of this part shall not apply to longshore work performed at locations in the State of Alaska. The performance of longshore work by alien crewmembers at locations in the State of Alaska shall instead be governed by §§ 655.530 through 655.541. The use of alien crewmembers to perform longshore work in Alaska consisting of the use of an automated self-unloading conveyor belt or vacuum-actuated system on a vessel shall continue to be governed by the provisions of § 655.520 of this part, except that, if the Administrator finds, based on a preponderance of the evidence which may be submitted by any interested party, that an attestation is required because the performance of the particular activity of longshore work is not the prevailing practice at the location in the State of Alaska, or was during a strike or lockout or intended to influence an election of a bargaining representative for workers at that location, or if the Administrator issues a cease and desist order against use of the automated equipment without such an attestation, the required attestation shall be filed pursuant to the Alaska exception at §§ 655.530 through 655.541 and not the prevailing practice exception at § 655.510.

§ 655.531 Who may submit attestations for locations in Alaska?

In order to use alien crewmembers to perform longshore activities at a particular location in the State of Alaska an employer shall submit an attestation on Form ETA 9033–A. As noted at § 655.502, "Definitions," for purposes of §§ 655.530 through 655.541, which govern the performance of longshore activities by alien crewmembers under the Alaska exception, "employer" includes any agent or representative designated by the employer. An employer may file a single attestation for multiple locations in the State of Alaska.

§ 655.532 Where and when should attestations be submitted for locations in Alaska?

(a) Attestations shall be submitted, by U.S. mail, private carrier, or facsimile transmission to the U.S. Department of Labor regional office of the Employment and Training Administration in Seattle, Washington. Except as provided in paragraph (b) of this section, attestations shall be received and date-stamped by the Department at least 30 calendar days prior to the date of the first performance of the longshore activity. The attestation shall be accepted for filing or returned by ETA in accordance with § 655.538 within 14 calendar days of the date received by ETA. An attestation which is accepted by ETA solely because it was not reviewed within 14 days is subject to subsequent invalidation pursuant to § 655.540 of this part. An employer filing an attestation shall have an agent or representative with a United States address. Such address shall be clearly indicated on the Form ETA 9033–A. In order to ensure that an attestation has been accepted for filing prior to the date of the first performance of the longshore activity, employers are advised to take mailing time into account to make sure that ETA receives the attestation at least 30 days prior to the first performance of the longshore activity.

(b) *Late filings.* ETA may accept for filing attestations received after the 30-day deadline where the employer could not have reasonably anticipated the need to file an attestation for the particular location at that time. When an employer states that it could not have reasonably anticipated the need to file the attestation at that time, it shall submit documentation to ETA to support such a claim. ETA shall then make a determination on the validity of the claim and shall accept the attestation for filing or return it in accordance with § 655.538 of this part. ETA in no case shall accept an attestation received less than 24 hours prior to the first performance of the activity.

§ 655.533 What should be submitted for locations in Alaska?

(a) *Form ETA 9033–A with accompanying documentation.* A completed and dated original Form ETA 9033–A, or facsimile transmission thereof, containing the required attestation elements and the original signature of the employer or the employer's agent or designated representative, along with two copies of the completed, signed, and dated Form ETA 9033–A shall be submitted to ETA. (If the attestation is submitted by facsimile transmission, the attestation containing the original signature shall be maintained at the U.S. business address of the employer's designated agent or representative). Copies of Form ETA 9033–A are available at the National Processing Centers and at the National office. In addition, the employer shall submit two sets of facts and evidence to show compliance with the fourth attestation element at § 655.537 of this part. In the case of an investigation pursuant to subpart G of this part, the employer has the burden of proof to establish the validity of each attestation. The employer shall maintain in its records at the office of its U.S. agent, for a period of at least 3 years from the date of filing, sufficient documentation to meet its burden of proof, which shall at a minimum include the documentation described in §§ 655.530 through 655.541, and shall make the documents available to Department of Labor officials upon request. Whenever any document is submitted to a Federal agency or retained in the employer's records pursuant to this part, the document shall either be in the English language or shall be accompanied by a written translation into the English language certified by the translator as to the accuracy of the translation and his/her competency to translate.

(b) *Attestation elements.* The attestation elements referenced in §§ 655.534 through 655.537 of this part are mandated by Sec. 258(d)(1) of the Act (8 U.S.C. 1288(d)(1)). Section 258(d)(1) of the Act requires employers who seek to have alien crewmembers engage in longshore activity at locations in the State of Alaska to attest as follows:

(1) The employer will make a bona fide request for United States longshore workers who are qualified and available in sufficient numbers to perform the activity at the particular time and location from the parties to

whom notice has been provided under § 655.537(a)(1) (ii) and (iii), except that:

(i) Wherever two or more contract stevedoring companies have signed a joint collective bargaining agreement with a single labor organization recognized as an exclusive bargaining representative of United States longshore workers within the meaning of the National Labor Relations Act (29 U.S.C. 141 *et seq.*), the employer may request longshore workers from only one such contract stevedoring company, and

(ii) A request for longshore workers to an operator of a private dock may be made only for longshore work to be performed at that dock and only if the operator meets the requirements of section 32 of the Longshore and Harbor Workers' Compensation Act (33 U.S.C. 932);

(2) The employer will employ all United States longshore workers made available in response to the request made pursuant to § 655.534(a)(1) who are qualified and available in sufficient numbers and who are needed to perform the longshore activity at the particular time and location to which the employer has attested;

(3) The use of alien crewmembers for such activity is not intended or designed to influence an election of a bargaining representative for workers in the State of Alaska; and

(4) Notice of the attestation has been provided to:

(i) Labor organizations which have been recognized as exclusive bargaining representatives of United States longshore workers within the meaning of the National Labor Relations Act (29 U.S.C. 141 *et seq.*) and which make available or intend to make available workers to the particular location where the longshore work is to be performed;

(ii) Contract stevedoring companies which employ or intend to employ United States longshore workers at that location; and

(iii) Operators of private docks at which the employer will use longshore workers.

[60 FR 3956, 3976, Jan. 19, 1995, as amended at 71 FR 35520, June 21, 2006]

§ 655.534 The first attestation element for locations in Alaska: Bona fide request for dispatch of United States longshore workers.

(a) The first attestation element shall be satisfied when the employer signs Form ETA 9033–A, attesting that, before using alien crewmembers to perform longshore work during the validity period of the attestation, the employer will make a bona fide request for United States longshore workers who are qualified and available in sufficient numbers to perform the specified longshore activity from the parties to whom notice is provided under § 655.537(a)(1) (ii) and (iii). Although an employer is required to provide notification of filing to labor organizations recognized as exclusive bargaining representatives of United States longshore workers pursuant to § 655.537(a)(1)(i) of this part, an employer need not request dispatch of United States longshore workers directly from such parties. The requests for dispatch of United States longshore workers pursuant to this section shall be directed to contract stevedoring companies which employ or intend to employ United States longshore workers at that location, and to operators of private docks at which the employer will use longshore workers. An employer is not required to request dispatch of United States longshore workers from private dock operators or contract stevedoring companies which do not meet the requirements of section 32 of the Longshore and Harbor Workers' Compensation Act (33 U.S.C. 932) or, in the case of contract stevedoring companies, which are not licensed to do business in the State of Alaska.

(1) Wherever two or more contract stevedoring companies have signed a joint collective bargaining agreement with a single qualified labor organization, the employer may request longshore workers from only one of such contract stevedoring companies. A qualified labor organization is one which has been recognized as an exclusive bargaining representative of United States longshore workers within the meaning of the National Labor Relations Act (29 U.S.C. 141 *et seq.*) and which makes available or intends to

make available workers to the particular location where the longshore work is to be performed.

(2) A request for longshore workers to an operator of a private dock may be made only for longshore work to be performed at that dock.

(3) An employer shall not be required to request longshore workers from a party if that party has notified the employer in writing that it does not intend to make available United States longshore workers who are qualified and available in sufficient numbers to the time and location at which the longshore work is to be performed.

(4) A party that has provided such written notice to the employer under paragraph (a)(3) of this section may subsequently notify the employer in writing that it is prepared to make available United States longshore workers who are qualified and available in sufficient numbers to perform the longshore activity at the time and location where the longshore work is to be performed. In that event, the employer's obligations to that party under §§ 655.534 and 655.535 of this part shall recommence 60 days after its receipt of such notice.

(5) When a party has provided written notice to the employer under paragraph (a)(3) of this section that it does not intend to dispatch United States longshore workers to perform the longshore work attested to by the employer, such notice shall expire upon the earliest of the following events:

(i) When the terms of such notice specify an expiration date at which time the employer's obligation to that party under §§ 655.534 and 655.535 of this part shall recommence;

(ii) When retracted pursuant to paragraph (a)(4) of this section; or

(iii) Upon the expiration of the validity of the attestation.

(b) *Documentation.* To substantiate the requirement in paragraph (a) of this section, an employer shall develop and maintain documentation to meet the employer's burden of proof under the first attestation element. The employer shall retain records of all requests for dispatch of United States longshore workers to perform the longshore work attested to. Such documentation shall consist of letters, telephone logs, facsimiles or other memoranda to show that, before using alien crewmembers to perform longshore work, the employer made a bona fide request for United States longshore workers who are qualified and available in sufficient numbers to perform the longshore activity. At a minimum, such documentation shall include the date the request was made, the name and telephone number of the particular individual(s) to whom the request for dispatch was directed, and the number and composition of full work units requested. Further, whenever any party has provided written notice to the employer under paragraph (a)(3) of this section, the employer shall retain the notice for the period of time specified in § 655.533 of this part, and, if appropriate, any subsequent notice by that party that it is prepared to make available United States longshore workers at the times and locations attested to.

§ 655.535 The second attestation element for locations in Alaska: Employment of United States longshore workers.

(a) The second attestation element shall be satisfied when the employer signs Form ETA 9033–A, attesting that during the validity period of the attestation, the employer will employ all United States longshore workers made available in response to the request for dispatch who, in compliance with applicable industry standards in the State of Alaska, including safety considerations, are qualified and available in sufficient numbers and are needed to perform the longshore activity at the particular time and location attested to.

(1) In no case shall an employer filing an attestation be required to hire less than a full work unit of United States longshore workers needed to perform the longshore activity nor be required to provide overnight accommodations for the longshore workers while employed. For purposes of this section, "full work unit" means the full complement of longshore workers needed to perform the longshore activity, as determined by industry standards in the State of Alaska, including safety considerations. Where the makeup of a full work unit is covered by one or

more collective bargaining agreements in effect at the time and location where longshore work is to be performed, the provisions of such agreement(s) shall be deemed to be in conformance with industry standards in the State of Alaska.

(2) In no case shall an employer be required to provide transportation to the vessel where the longshore work is to be performed, except where:

(i) Surface transportation is available; for purposes of this section, "surface transportation" means a tugboat or other vessel which is appropriately insured, operated by licensed personnel, and capable of safely transporting U.S. longshore workers from shore to a vessel on which longshore work is to be performed;

(ii) Such transportation may be safely accomplished; and

(iii)(A) Travel time to the vessel does not exceed one-half hour each way; and

(B) Travel distance to the vessel from the point of embarkation does not exceed 5 miles; for purposes of this section, "point of embarkation" means a dock or landing at which U.S. longshore workers may be safely boarded for transport from shore to a vessel on which longshore work is to be performed; or

(C) In the cases of Wide Bay, Alaska, and Klawock/Craig, Alaska, travel time does not exceed 45 minutes each way and travel distance to the vessel from the point of embarkation does not exceed 7.5 miles, unless the party responding to the request for dispatch agrees to lesser time and distance specifications.

(3) If a United States longshore worker is capable of getting to and from the vessel where longshore work is to be performed when the vessel is beyond the time and distance limitations specified in paragraph (a)(2)(iii) of this section, and where all of the other criteria governing the employment of United States longshore workers under this subpart are met (e.g., "qualified and available in sufficient numbers"), the employer is still obligated to employ the worker to perform the longshore activity. In such instance, however, the employer shall not be required to provide such transportation nor to reimburse the longshore worker for the cost incurred in transport to and from the vessel.

(4) Where an employer is required to provide transportation to the vessel because it is within the time and distance limitations specified in (a)(2)(iii) of this section, the employer also shall be required to provide return transportation to the point of embarkation.

(b) *Documentation.* To substantiate the requirement in paragraph (a) of this section, an employer shall develop and maintain documentation to meet the employer's burden of proof. Such documentation shall include records of payments to contract stevedoring companies or private dock operators, payroll records for United States longshore workers employed, or other documentation to show clearly that the employer has met its obligation to employ all United States longshore workers made available in response to a request for dispatch who are qualified and available in sufficient numbers. The documentation shall specify the number of full work units employed pursuant to this section, the composition of such full work units (*i.e.*, number of workers by job title), and the date(s) and location(s) where the longshore work was performed. The employer also shall develop and maintain documentation concerning the provision of transportation from the point of embarkation to the vessel on which longshore work is to be performed. Each time one or more United States longshore workers are dispatched in response to the request under § 655.534, the employer shall retain a written record of whether transportation to the vessel was provided and the time and distance from the point of embarkation to the vessel.

§ 655.536 The third attestation element for locations in Alaska: No intention or design to influence bargaining representative election.

(a) The employer shall attest that use of alien crewmembers to perform the longshore activity specified on the Form ETA 9033–A is not intended or designed to influence an election of a bargaining representative for workers in the State of Alaska.

(b) *Documentation.* The employer need not develop nor maintain documentation to substantiate the statement referenced in paragraph (a) of this section. In the case of an investigation, however, the employer has the burden of proof to show that the use of alien crewmembers to perform the longshore activity specified on the Form ETA 9033–A was not intended nor designed to influence an election of a bargaining representative for workers in the State of Alaska.

§ 655.537 The fourth attestation element for locations in Alaska: Notice of filing.

(a)(1) The employer shall attest that at the time of filing the attestation, notice of filing has been provided to:

(i) Labor organizations which have been recognized as exclusive bargaining representatives of United States longshore workers within the meaning of the National Labor Relations Act (29 U.S.C. 141 *et seq.*) and which make available or intend to make available workers to the particular location where the longshore work is to be performed;

(ii) Contract stevedoring companies which employ or intend to employ United States longshore workers at the location where the longshore work is to be performed; and

(iii) Operators of private docks at which the employer will use longshore workers.

(2) The notices provided under paragraph (a)(1) of this section shall include a copy of the Form ETA 9033–A to be submitted to ETA, shall provide information concerning the availability of supporting documents for public examination at the national office of ETA, and shall include the following statement: "Complaints alleging a misrepresentation of material facts in the attestation and/or failure to comply with the terms of the attestation may be filed with any office of the Wage and Hour Division of the United States Department of Labor."

(b) The employer shall request a copy of the Certificate of Compliance issued by the district director of the Office of Workers' Compensation Programs under section 37 of the Longshore and Harbor Workers' Compensation Act (33 U.S.C. 932) from the parties to whom notice is provided pursuant to paragraphs (a)(1) (ii) and (iii) of this section. An employer's obligation to make a bona fide request for dispatch of U.S. longshore workers under § 655.534 of this part before using alien crewmembers to perform the longshore work attested to shall commence upon receipt of the copy of the Certificate of Compliance.

(c) *Documentation.* The employer shall develop and maintain documentation sufficient to meet its burden of proving the validity of the statement referenced in paragraphs (a) and (b) of this section and attested to on the Form ETA 9033–A. Such documentation shall include a copy of the notices provided, as required by paragraph (a)(1) of this section, and shall be submitted to ETA along with the Form ETA 9033–A.

§ 655.538 Actions on attestations submitted for filing for locations in Alaska.

Once an attestation has been received from an employer, a determination shall be made by the Certifying Officer whether to accept the attestation for filing or return it. The Certifying Officer may request additional explanation and/or documentation from the employer in making this determination. An attestation which is properly filled out and which includes accompanying documentation for the requirement set forth at § 655.537 of this part shall be accepted for filing by ETA on the date it is signed by the Certifying Officer unless it falls within one of the categories set forth in paragraph (b) of this section. Once an attestation is accepted for filing, ETA shall then follow the procedures set forth in paragraph (a)(1) of this section. Upon acceptance of the employer's attestation by ETA, the attestation and accompanying documentation shall be forwarded to and be available for public examination at the ETA national office in a timely manner. ETA shall not consider information contesting an attestation received by ETA prior to the determination to accept or return the attestation for filing. Such information shall not be made a part of ETA's administrative record on the attestation, but shall be referred to ESA to be processed as a complaint pursuant to subpart G of this part if the attestation is accepted by ETA for filing.

(a) *Acceptance.* (1) If the attestation is properly filled out and includes accompanying documentation for the requirement set forth at § 655.537, and does not fall within one of the categories set forth at paragraph (b) of this section, ETA shall accept the attestation for filing, provide notification to the DHS office having jurisdiction over the location where longshore work will be performed, and return to the employer, or the employer's agent or representative at a U.S. address, one copy of the attestation form submitted by the employer, with ETA's acceptance indicated thereon. Before using alien crewmembers to perform the longshore work attested to on Form ETA 9033–A, the employer shall make a bona fide request for and employ United States longshore workers who are qualified and available in sufficient numbers pursuant to §§ 655.534 and 655.535. Where such a request for dispatch of United States longshore workers is unsuccessful, either in whole or in part, any use of alien crewmembers to perform longshore activity shall be in accordance with DHS regulations.

(2) DOL is not the guarantor of the accuracy, truthfulness or adequacy of an attestation accepted for filing.

(b) *Unacceptable attestations.* ETA shall not accept an attestation for filing and shall return such attestation to the employer, or the employer's agent or representative at a U.S. address, when any one of the following conditions exists:

(1) When the Form ETA 9033–A is not properly filled out. Examples of improperly filled out Form ETA 9033–A's include instances where the employer has neglected to check all the necessary boxes, where the employer has failed to include the name of any port, city, or other geographical reference point where longshore work is to be performed, or where the employer has failed to sign the attestation or to designate an agent in the United States.

(2) When the Form ETA 9033–A with accompanying documentation is not received by ETA at least 30 days prior to the first performance of the longshore activity, unless the employer is claiming that it could not have reasonably anticipated the need to file the attestation for that location at that time, and has included documentation which supports this contention, and ETA has found the claim to be valid.

(3) When the Form ETA 9033–A does not include accompanying documentation for the requirement set forth at § 655.537.

(4) When the accompanying documentation submitted by the employer and required by § 655.537, on its face, is inconsistent with that section. Examples of such a situation include an instance where the Form ETA 9033–A indicates that the longshore work will be performed at a particular private dock and the documentation required under the notice attestation element indicates that notice was provided to an operator of a different private dock, or where the longshore work is to be performed at a particular time and location in the State of Alaska and the notice of filing provided to qualified labor organizations and contract stevedoring companies indicates that the longshore work is to be performed at a different time and/or location.

(5) When the Administrator, Wage and Hour Division, has notified ETA, in writing, after an investigation pursuant to subpart G of this part, that a cease and desist order has been issued pursuant to subpart G of this part, with respect to the attesting employer's performance of longshore work at a particular location in the State of Alaska, in violation of a previously accepted attestation.

(6) When the Administrator, Wage and Hour Division, has notified ETA, in writing, after an investigation pursuant to subpart G of this part, that the particular employer has misrepresented or failed to comply with an attestation previously submitted and accepted for filing, but in no case for a period of more than one year after the date of the Administrator's notice and provided that DHS has not advised ETA that the prohibition is in effect for a lesser period.

(7) When the Administrator, Wage and Hour Division, has notified ETA, in writing, that the employer has failed to comply with any penalty, sanction,

or other remedy assessed in a final agency action following an investigation by the Wage and Hour Division pursuant to subpart G of this part.

(c) *Resubmission.* If the attestation is not accepted for filing pursuant to paragraph (b) of this section, ETA shall return to the employer, or the employer's agent or representative, at a U.S. address, the attestation form and accompanying documentation submitted by the employer. ETA shall notify the employer, in writing, of the reason(s) that the attestation is unacceptable. When an attestation is found to be unacceptable pursuant to paragraph (b) (1), (2), (3), or (4) of this section, the employer may resubmit the corrected attestation with the proper documentation. When an attestation is found to be unacceptable pursuant to paragraph (b) (5), (6), or (7) of this section and returned, such action shall be the final decision of the Secretary of Labor.

§ 655.539 Effective date and validity of filed attestations for locations in Alaska.

An attestation is filed and effective as of the date it is accepted and signed by the Certifying Officer. Such attestation is valid for the 12-month period beginning on the date of acceptance for filing, unless suspended or invalidated pursuant to § 655.540 of this part. The filed attestation expires at the end of the 12-month period of validity.

§ 655.540 Suspension or invalidation of filed attestations for locations in Alaska.

Suspension or invalidation of an attestation may result from enforcement action(s) under subpart G of this part (*i.e.*, investigation(s) conducted by the Administrator or cease and desist order(s) issued by the Administrator regarding the employer's misrepresentation in or failure to carry out its attestation); or from a discovery by ETA that it made an error in accepting the attestation because such attestation falls within one of the categories set forth in § 655.538(b).

(a) *Result of Wage and Hour Division action.* Upon the determination of a violation under subpart G of this part, the Administrator shall, pursuant to § 655.665(b), notify the DHS of the violation and of the Administrator's notice to ETA.

(b) *Result of ETA action.* If, after accepting an attestation for filing, ETA finds that the attestation is unacceptable because it falls within one of the categories set forth at § 655.538(b) and, as a result, ETA suspends or invalidates the attestation, ETA shall notify the DHS of such suspension or invalidation and shall return a copy of the attestation form to the employer, or the employer's agent or representative at a U.S. address. ETA shall notify the employer, in writing, of the reason(s) that the attestation is suspended or invalidated.

§ 655.541 Withdrawal of accepted attestations for locations in Alaska.

(a) An employer who has submitted an attestation which has been accepted for filing may withdraw such attestation at any time before the 12-month period of its validity terminates, unless the Administrator has found reasonable cause under subpart G to commence an investigation of the particular attestation. Such withdrawal may be advisable, for example, when the employer learns that the country in which the vessel is registered and of which nationals of such country hold a majority of the ownership interest in the vessel has been removed from the non-reciprocity list (which means, for purposes of this section, *Prohibitions on longshore work by U.S. nationals; listing by country* at 22 CFR 89.1). In that event, an attestation would no longer be required under subpart F of this part, since upon being removed from the non-reciprocity list the performance of longshore work by alien crewmembers would be permitted under the reciprocity exception at sec. 258(e) of the Act (8 U.S.C. 1288(e)). Requests for withdrawals shall be in writing and shall be directed to the Certifying Officer.

(b) Withdrawal of an attestation shall not affect an employer's liability with respect to any failure to meet the conditions attested to which took place before the withdrawal, or for misrepresentations in an attestation. However, if an employer has not yet performed the longshore activities at the location(s) in question, the Administrator shall not find reasonable cause to investigate unless it is alleged, and there is reasonable cause to believe, that the employer has made misrepresentations in the attestation or documentation thereof, or that the employer has not in fact given the notice attested to.

PUBLIC ACCESS

§ 655.550 Public access.

(a) *Public examination at ETA.* ETA shall make available for public examination in Washington, DC, a list of employers which have filed attestations under this subpart, and for each such employer, a copy of the employer's attestation and accompanying documentation it has received.

(b) *Notice to public.* ETA periodically shall publish a list in the FEDERAL REGISTER identifying under this subpart employers which have submitted attestations; employers which have attestations on file; and employers which have submitted attestations which have been found unacceptable for filing.

(Approved by the Office of Management and Budget under Control No. 1205–0309)

APPENDIX A TO SUBPART F OF PART 655—U.S. SEAPORTS

The list of 224 seaports includes all major and most smaller ports serving ocean and Great Lakes commerce.

NORTH ATLANTIC RANGE

Bucksport, ME
Eastport, ME
Portland, ME
Searsport, ME
Portsmouth, NH
Boston, MA
Fall River, MA
New Bedford, MA
Providence, RI
Bridgeport, CT
New Haven, CT
New London, CT
Albany, NY
New York, NY/NJ
Camden, NJ
Gloucester City, NJ
Paulsboro, NJ
Chester, PA
Marcus Hook, PA
Philadelphia, PA
Delaware City, DE
Wilmington, DE
Baltimore, MD
Cambridge, MD
Alexandria, VA
Chesapeake, VA
Hopewell, VA
Newport News, VA
Norfolk, VA
Portsmouth, VA
Richmond, VA

SOUTH ATLANTIC RANGE

Morehead City, NC
Southport, NC
Wilmington, NC
Charleston, SC
Georgetown, SC
Port Royal, SC
Brunswick, GA
Savannah, GA
St. Mary, GA
Cocoa, FL
Fernandina Beach, FL
Fort Lauderdale, FL
Fort Pierce, FL
Jacksonville, FL
Miami, FL
Palm Beach, FL
Port Canaveral, FL
Port Everglades, FL
Riviera, FL
Aguadilla, PR
Ceiba, PR
Guanica, PR
Guayanilla, PR
Humacao, PR
Jobos, PR
Mayaguez, PR
Ponce, PR
San Juan, PR
Vieques, PR
Yabucoa, PR
Alucroix, VI
Charlotte Amalie, VI
Christiansted, VI
Frederiksted, VI
Limetree Bay, VI

NORTH PACIFIC RANGE

Astoria, OR
Bandon, OR
Columbia City, OR
Coos Bay, OR
Mapleton, OR
Newport, OR
Portland, OR
Rainier, OR
Reedsport, OR
St. Helens, OR
Toledo, OR
Anacortes, WA
Bellingham, WA
Edmonds (Edwards Point), WA
Everett, WA
Ferndale, WA
Friday Harbor, WA
Grays Harbor, WA
Kalama, WA
Longview, WA
Olympia, WA
Point Wells, WA
Portage, WA
Port Angeles, WA
Port Gamble, WA
Port Townsend, WA
Raymond, WA
Seattle, WA
Tacoma, WA
Vancouver, WA
Willapa Harbor, WA
Winslow, WA

GREAT LAKES RANGE

Duluth, MN
Silver Bay, MN
Green Bay, WI
Kenosha, WI
Manitowoc, WI
Milwaukee, WI
Sheboygan, WI
Superior, WI
Alpena, MI
Bay City, MI
Detroit, MI
De Tour Village, MI
Essexville, MI
Ferrysburg, MI
Grand Haven, MI
Marine City, MI
Muskegon, MI
Port Huron, MI
Presque Isle, MI
Rogers City, MI
Saginaw, MI
Sault Ste Marie, MI
Chicago, IL
Ashtabula, OH
Cincinnati, OH
Cleveland, OH
Conneaut, OH
Fairport, OH
Huron, OH
Lorain, OH
Sandusky, OH
Toledo, OH
Erie, PA
Buffalo, NY
Odgensburg, NY
Oswego, NY
Rochester, NY
Burns Harbor, IN
E. Chicago, IN
Gary, IN

GULF COAST RANGE

Panama City, FL
Pensacola, FL
Port Manatee, FL
Port St. Joe, FL
Tampa, FL
Mobile, AL
Gulfport, MS
Pascagoula, MS
Baton Rouge, LA
Gretna, LA
Lake Charles, LA

Louisiana Offshore Oil Port, LA	Houston, TX
New Orleans, LA	Orange, TX
Beaumont, TX	Port Arthur, TX
Brownsville, TX	Port Isabel, TX
Corpus Christi, TX	Port Lavaca, TX
Freeport, TX	Port Neches, TX
Galveston, TX	Sabine, TX
Harbor Island, TX	Texas City, TX

SOUTH PACIFIC RANGE

Alameda, CA	Port Hueneme, CA
Antioch, CA	Port San Luis, CA
Benicia, CA	Redwood City, CA
Carlsbad, CA	Richmond, CA
Carpinteria, CA	Sacramento, CA
Crockett, CA	San Diego, CA
El Segundo, CA	San Francisco, CA
Eureka, CA	Selby, CA
Estero Bay, CA	Stockton, CA
Gaviota, CA	Vallejo, CA
Huntington Beach, CA	Ventura, CA
Long Beach, CA	Barbers Point, HI
Los Angeles, CA	Hilo, HI
Mandalay Beach, CA	Honolulu, HI
Martinez, CA	Kahului, HI
Moss Landing, CA	Kaunakakai, HI
Oakland, CA	Kawaihae, HI
Pittsburg, CA	Nawiliwili, HI
Port Costa, CA	Port Allen, HI

Subpart G—Enforcement of the Limitations Imposed on Employers Using Alien Crewmembers for Longshore Activities in U.S. Ports

SOURCE: 60 FR 3969, 3977, Jan. 19, 1995, unless otherwise noted.

§ 655.600 Enforcement authority of Administrator, Wage and Hour Division.

(a) The Administrator shall perform all the Secretary's investigative and enforcement functions under section 258 of the INA (8 U.S.C. 1288) and subparts F and G of this part.

(b) The Administrator, pursuant to a complaint, shall conduct such investigations as may be appropriate and, in connection therewith, enter and inspect such places and such records (and make transcriptions or copies thereof), question such persons and gather such information as deemed necessary by the Administrator to determine compliance regarding the matters which are the subject of the investigation.

(c) An employer being investigated shall make available to the Administrator such records, information, persons, and places as the Administrator deems appropriate to copy, transcribe, question, or inspect. No employer subject to the provisions of section 258 of the INA (8 U.S.C. 1288) and subparts F and G of this part shall interfere with any official of the Department of Labor performing an investigation, inspection or law enforcement function pursuant to 8 U.S.C. 1288 or subpart F or G of this part. Any such interference shall be a violation of the attestation and subparts F and G of this part, and the Administrator may take such further actions as the Administrator considers appropriate. (NOTE: Federal criminal statutes prohibit certain interference with a Federal officer in the performance of official duties. 18 U.S.C. 111 and 18 U.S.C. 1114.)

(d)(1) An employer subject to subparts F and G of this part shall at all times cooperate in administrative and enforcement proceedings. No employer shall intimidate, threaten, restrain, coerce, blacklist, discharge, retaliate, or in any manner discriminate against any person because such person has:

(i) Filed a complaint or appeal under or related to section 258 of the INA (8 U.S.C. 1288) or subpart F or G of this part;

(ii) Testified or is about to testify in any proceeding under or related to section 258 of the INA (8 U.S.C. 1288) or subpart F or G of this part;

(iii) Exercised or asserted on behalf of himself or herself or others any right or protection afforded by section 258 of the INA (8 U.S.C. 1288) or subpart F or G of this part.

(iv) Consulted with an employee of a legal assistance program or an attorney on matters related to section 258 of the Act or to subpart F or G of this part or any other DOL regulation promulgated pursuant to 8 U.S.C. 1288.

(2) In the event of such intimidation or restraint as are described in paragraph (d)(1) of this section, the conduct shall be a violation of the attestation and subparts F and G of this part, and the Administrator may take such further actions as the Administrator considers appropriate.

(e) The Administrator shall, to the extent possible under existing law, protect the confidentiality of any person who provides information to the Department in confidence in the course of an investigation or otherwise under subpart F or G of this part. However, confidentiality will not be afforded to the complainant or to information provided by the complainant.

§ 655.605 Complaints and investigative procedures.

(a) The Administrator, through an investigation, shall determine whether a basis exists to make a finding that:

(1) An attesting employer has—

(i) Failed to meet conditions attested to; or

(ii) Misrepresented a material fact in an attestation.

(NOTE: Federal criminal statutes provide penalties of up to $10,000 and/or imprisonment of up to 5 years for knowing and willful submission of false statements to the Federal Government. 18 U.S.C. 1001; see also 18 U.S.C. 1546.); or

(2) In the case of an employer operating under the automated vessel exception to the prohibition on utilizing alien crewmembers to perform longshore activity(ies) at a U.S. port, the employer—

(i) Is utilizing alien crewmember(s) to perform longshore activity(ies) at a port where the prevailing practice has not been to use such workers for such activity(ies); or

(ii) Is utilizing alien crewmember(s) to perform longshore activities:

(A) During a strike or lockout in the course of a labor dispute at the U.S. port; and/or

(B) With intent or design to influence an election of a bargaining representative for workers at the U.S. port; or

(3) An employer failed to comply in any other manner with the provisions of subpart F or G of this part.

(b) Any aggrieved person or organization may file a complaint of a violation of the provisions of subpart F or G of this part.

(1) No particular form of complaint is required, except that the complaint shall be written or, if oral, shall be reduced to writing by the Wage and Hour Division official who receives the complaint.

(2) The complaint shall set forth sufficient facts for the Administrator to determine—

(i) Whether, in the case of an attesting employer, there is reasonable cause to believe that particular part or parts of the attestation or regulations have been violated; or

(ii) Whether, in the case of an employer claiming the automated vessel exception, the preponderance of the evidence submitted by any interested party shows that conditions exist that would require the employer to file an attestation.

(3) The complaint may be submitted to any local Wage and Hour Division office; the addresses of such offices are found in local telephone directories. The office or person receiving such a complaint shall refer it to the office of the Wage and Hour Division administering the area in which the reported violation is alleged to have occurred.

(c) The Administrator shall determine whether there is reasonable cause to believe that the complaint warrants investigation. If the Administrator determines that the complaint fails to present reasonable cause for an investigation, the Administrator shall so notify the complainant, who may submit a new complaint, with such additional information as may be necessary. There shall be no hearing pursuant to § 655.625 for the Administrator's determination not to conduct an investigation. If the Administrator determines that an investigation on the complaint is warranted, the investigation shall be conducted and a determination issued within 180 calendar days of the Administrator's receipt of the complaint, or later for good cause shown.

(d) In conducting an investigation, the Administrator may consider and make part of the investigation file any evidence or materials that have been compiled in any previous investigation regarding the same or a closely related matter.

(e) In conducting an investigation under an attestation, the Administrator shall take into consideration the employer's burden to provide facts and evidence to establish the matters asserted. In conducting an investigation regarding an employer's eligibility for the automated vessel exception, the Administrator shall not impose the burden of proof on the employer, but shall consider all evidence from any interested party in determining whether the employer is not eligible for the exception.

(f) In an investigation regarding the use of alien crewmembers to perform longshore activity(ies) in a U.S. port (whether by an attesting employer or by an employer claiming the automated vessel exception), the Administrator shall accept as conclusive proof a previous Departmental determination, published in the FEDERAL REGISTER pursuant to § 655.670, establishing that such use of alien crewmembers is not the prevailing practice for the activity(ies) and U.S. port at issue. The Administrator shall give appropriate weight to a previous Departmental determination published in the FEDERAL REGISTER pursuant to § 655.670, establishing that at the time of such determination, such use of alien crewmembers was the prevailing practice for the activity(ies) and U.S. port at issue.

(g) When an investigation has been conducted, the Administrator shall, within the time period specified in paragraph (c) of this section, issue a written determination as to whether a basis exists to make a finding stated in paragraph (a) of this section. The determination shall be issued and an opportunity for a hearing shall be afforded in accordance with the procedures specified in § 655.625(d) of this part.

§ 655.610 Automated vessel exception to prohibition on utilization of alien crewmember(s) to perform longshore activity(ies) at a U.S. port.

(a) The Act establishes a rebuttable presumption that the prevailing practice in U.S. ports is for automated vessels (*i.e.*, vessels equipped with automated self- unloading conveyor belts or vacuum-actuated systems) to use alien crewmembers to perform longshore activity(ies) through the use of the self-unloading equipment. An employer claiming the automated vessel exception does not have the burden of establishing eligibility for the exception.

(b) In the event of a complaint asserting that an employer claiming the automated vessel exception is not eligible for such exception, the Administrator shall determine whether the preponderance of the evidence submitted by any interested party shows that:

(1) It is not the prevailing practice at the U.S. port to use alien crewmember(s) to perform the longshore activity(ies) through the use of the self-unloading equipment; or

(2) The employer is using alien crewmembers to perform longshore activity(ies)—

(i) During a strike or lockout in the course of a labor dispute at the U.S. port; and/or

(ii) With intent or design to influence an election of a bargaining representative for workers at the U.S. port.

(c) In making the prevailing practice determination required by paragraph (b)(1) of this section, the Administrator shall determine whether, in the 12-month period preceding the date of the Administrator's receipt of the complaint, one of the following conditions existed:

(1) Over fifty percent of the automated vessels docking at the port used alien crewmembers for the activity (for purposes of this paragraph (c)(1) of this section, a vessel shall be counted each time it docks at the particular port); or

(2) Alien crewmembers made up over fifty percent of the workers who performed the activity with respect to such automated vessels.

(d) An interested party, complaining that the automated vessel exception is not applicable to a particular employer, shall provide to the Administrator evidence such as:

(1) A written summary of a survey of the experience of masters of automated vessels which entered the local port in the previous year, describing the practice in the port as to the use of alien crewmembers;

(2) A letter, affidavit, or other written statement from an appropriate local port authority regarding the use of alien crewmembers to perform the longshore activity at the port in the previous year;

(3) Written statements from collective bargaining representatives and/or shipping agents with direct knowledge

of practices regarding the use of alien crewmembers at the port in the previous year.

§655.615 Cease and desist order.

(a) If the Administrator determines that reasonable cause exists to conduct an investigation with respect to an attestation, the complainant may request that the Administrator enter a cease and desist order against the employer against whom the complaint is lodged.

(1) The request for a cease and desist order may be filed along with the complaint, or may be filed subsequently. The request, including all accompanying documents, shall be filed in duplicate with the same Wage and Hour Division office that received the complaint.

(2) No particular form is prescribed for a request for a cease and desist order pursuant to this paragraph (a). However, any such request shall:

(i) Be dated;

(ii) Be typewritten or legibly written;

(iii) Specify the attestation provision(s) with respect to which the employer allegedly failed to comply and/or submitted misrepresentation(s) of material fact(s);

(iv) Be accompanied by evidence to substantiate the allegation(s) of noncompliance and/or misrepresentation;

(v) Be signed by the complaining party making the request or by the authorized representative of such party;

(vi) Include the address at which such complaining party or authorized representative desires to receive further communications relating thereto.

(3) Upon receipt of a request for a cease and desist order, the Administrator shall promptly notify the employer of the request. The Administrator's notice shall:

(i) Inform the employer that it may respond to the request and meet with a Wage and Hour Division official within 14 calendar days of the date of the notice;

(ii) Be served upon the employer by facsimile transmission, in person, or by certified or regular mail, at the address of the U.S. agent stated on the employer's attestation;

(iii) Be accompanied by copies of the complaint, the request for a cease and desist order, the evidence submitted by the complainant, and any evidence from other investigation(s) of the same or a closely related matter which the Administrator may incorporate into the record. (Any such evidence from other investigation(s) shall also be made available for examination by the complaining party at the Wage and Hour Division office which issued the notice.)

(4) No particular form is prescribed for the employer's response to the complaining party's request for a cease and desist order under this paragraph (a), however, any such response shall:

(i) Be dated;

(ii) Be submitted by facsimile transmission, in person, by certified or regular mail, or by courier service to the Wage and Hour Division office which issued the notice of the request;

(iii) Be received by the appropriate Wage and Hour Division office no later than 14 calendar days from the date of the notice of the request;

(iv) Be typewritten or legibly written;

(v) Explain, in any detail desired by the employer, the employer's grounds or reasons as to why the Administrator should deny the requested cease and desist order;

(vi) Be accompanied by evidence to substantiate the employer's grounds or reasons as to why the Administrator should deny the requested cease and desist order;

(vii) Specify whether the employer desires an informal meeting with a Wage and Hour Division official;

(viii) Be signed by the employer or its authorized representative; and

(ix) Include the address at which the employer or its authorized representative desires to receive further communications relating thereto, if such address is different from the address of the U.S. agent stated on the attestation.

(5) In the event the employer requests a meeting with a Wage and Hour Division official, the Administrator shall provide the employer and the complaining party, or their authorized representatives, an opportunity for such a meeting to present their views regarding the evidence and arguments submitted by the parties. This shall be

an informal meeting, not subject to any procedural rules. The meeting shall be held within the 14 calendar days permitted for the employer's response to the request for the cease and desist order, and shall be held at a time and place set by the Wage and Hour Division official, who shall notify the parties.

(6) After receipt of the employer's timely response and after any informal meeting which may have been held with the parties, the Administrator shall promptly issue a written determination, either denying the request or issuing a cease and desist order. In making the determination, the Administrator shall consider all the evidence submitted, including any evidence from the same or a closely related matter which the Administrator has incorporated into the record and provided to the employer. If the Administrator determines that the complaining party's position is supported by a preponderance of the evidence submitted, the Administrator shall order that the employer cease the activities specified in the determination, until the completion of the Administrator's investigation and any subsequent proceedings pursuant to § 655.625 of this part, unless the prohibition is lifted by subsequent order of the Administrator because it is later determined that the employer's position was correct. While the cease and desist order is in effect, ETA shall suspend the subject attestation, either in whole or in part, and shall not accept any subsequent attestation from the employer for the activity(ies) and U.S. port or location in the State of Alaska at issue.

(7) The Administrator's cease and desist order shall be served on the employer at the address of its designated U.S. based representative or at the address specified in the employer's response, by facsimile transmission, personal service, or certified mail.

(b) If the Administrator determines that reasonable cause exists to conduct an investigation with respect to a complaint that a non-attesting employer is not entitled to the automated vessel exception to the requirement for the filing of an attestation, a complaining party may request that the Administrator enter a cease and desist order against the employer against whom the complaint is lodged.

(1) The request for a cease and desist order may be filed along with the complaint, or may be filed subsequently. The request, including all accompanying documents, shall be filed in duplicate with the same Wage and Hour Division office that received the complaint.

(2) No particular form is prescribed for a request for a cease and desist order pursuant to this paragraph. However, any such request shall:

(i) Be dated;

(ii) Be typewritten or legibly written;

(iii) Specify the circumstances which allegedly require that the employer be denied the use of the automated vessel exception;

(iv) Be accompanied by evidence to substantiate the allegation(s);

(v) Be signed by the complaining party making the request or by the authorized representative of such party; and

(vi) Include the address at which such complaining party or authorized representative desires to receive further communications relating thereto.

(3) Upon receipt of a request for a cease and desist order, the Administrator shall notify the employer of the request. The Administrator's notice shall:

(i) Inform the employer that it may respond to the request and meet with a Wage and Hour Division official within 14 calendar days of the date of the notice;

(ii) Be served upon the employer by facsimile transmission, in person, or by certified or regular mail, at the employer's last known address; and

(iii) Be accompanied by copies of the complaint, the request for a cease and desist order, the evidence submitted by the complainant, and any evidence from other investigation(s) of the same or a closely related matter which the Administrator may incorporate into the record. (Any such evidence from other investigation(s) shall also be made available for examination by the complaining party at the Wage and Hour Division office which issued the notice.)

(4) No particular form is prescribed for the employer's response to the complaining party's request for a cease and desist order under this paragraph (b). However, any such response shall:

(i) Be dated;

(ii) Be submitted by facsimile transmission, in person, by certified or regular mail, or by courier service to the Wage and Hour Division office which issued the notice of the request;

(iii) Be received by the appropriate Wage and Hour Division office no later than 14 calendar days from the date of the notice of the request;

(iv) Be typewritten or legibly written;

(v) Explain, in any detail desired by the employer, the employer's grounds or reasons as to why the Administrator should deny the requested cease and desist order;

(vi) Be accompanied by evidence to substantiate the employer's grounds or reasons as to why the Administrator should deny the requested cease and desist order;

(vii) Specify whether the employer desires an informal meeting with a Wage and Hour Division official;

(viii) Be signed by the employer or its authorized representative; and

(ix) Include the address at which the employer or its authorized representative desires to receive further communications relating thereto.

(5) In the event the employer requests a meeting with a Wage and Hour Division official, the Administrator shall provide the employer and the complaining party, or their authorized representatives, an opportunity for such a meeting to present their views regarding the evidence and arguments submitted by the parties. This shall be an informal meeting, not subject to any procedural rules. The meeting shall be held within the 14 calendar days permitted for the employer's response to the request for the cease and desist order, and shall be held at a time and place set by the Wage and Hour Division official, who shall notify the parties.

(6) After receipt of the employer's timely response and after any informal meeting which may have been held with the parties, the Administrator shall promptly issue a written determination, either denying the request or issuing a cease and desist order. If the Administrator determines that the complaining party's position is supported by a preponderance of the evidence submitted, the Administrator shall order that the employer cease the use of alien crewmembers to perform the longshore activity(ies) specified in the order. In making the determination, the Administrator shall consider all the evidence submitted, including any evidence from the same or a closely related matter which the Administrator has incorporated into the record and provided to the employer. The order shall remain in effect until the completion of the investigation and any subsequent hearing proceedings pursuant to § 655.625 of this part, unless the employer files and maintains on file with ETA an attestation pursuant to § 655.520 of this part or unless the prohibition is lifted by subsequent order of the Administrator because it is later determined that the employer's position was correct.

(7) The Administrator's cease and desist order shall be served on the employer or its designated representative by facsimile transmission, personal service, or by certified mail at the address specified in the employer's response or, if no such address was specified, at the employer's last known address.

§ 655.620 Civil money penalties and other remedies.

(a) The Administrator may assess a civil money penalty not to exceed $9,472 for each alien crewmember with respect to whom there has been a violation of the attestation or subpart F or G of this part. The Administrator may also impose appropriate remedy(ies).

(b) In determining the amount of civil money penalty to be assessed, the Administrator shall consider the type of violation committed and other relevant factors. The factors which may be considered include, but are not limited to, the following:

(1) Previous history of violation, or violations, by the employer under the Act and subpart F or G of this part;

(2) The number of workers affected by the violation or violations;

(3) The gravity of the violation or violations;

(4) Efforts made by the violator in good faith to comply with the provisions of 8 U.S.C. 1288(c) and subparts F and G of this part;

(5) The violator's explanation of the violation or violations;

(6) The violator's commitment to future compliance; and/or

(7) The extent to which the violator achieved a financial gain due to the violation, or the potential financial loss, potential injury or adverse effect with respect to other parties.

(c) The civil money penalty, and any other remedy determined by the Administrator to be appropriate, are immediately due for payment or performance upon the assessment by the Administrator, or the decision by an administrative law judge where a hearing is requested, or the decision by the Secretary where review is granted. The employer shall remit the amount of the civil money penalty, by certified check or money order made payable to the order of "Wage and Hour Division, Labor." The remittance shall be delivered or mailed to the Wage and Hour Division office for the area in which the violations occurred. The performance of any other remedy prescribed by the Administrator shall follow procedures established by the Administrator. The employer's failure to pay the civil money penalty, or to perform any other remedy prescribed by the Administrator, shall result in the rejection by ETA of any future attestation submitted by the employer, until such payment or performance is accomplished.

[60 FR 3969, 3977, Jan. 19, 1995, as amended at 81 FR 43448, July 1, 2016; 82 FR 5380, Jan. 18, 2017; 83 FR 11, Jan. 2, 2018; 84 FR 217, Jan. 23, 2019]

§ 655.625 Written notice, service and Federal Register publication of Administrator's determination.

(a) The Administrator's determination, issued pursuant to § 655.605 of this part, shall be served on the complainant, the employer, and other known interested parties by personal service or by certified mail at the parties' last known addresses. Where service by certified mail is not accepted by the party, the Administrator may exercise discretion to serve the determination by regular mail.

(b) Where the Administrator determines the prevailing practice regarding the use of alien crewmember(s) to perform longshore activity(ies) in a U.S. port (whether the Administrator's investigation involves an employer operating under an attestation, or under the automated vessel exception), the Administrator shall, simultaneously with issuance of the determination, publish in the FEDERAL REGISTER a notice of the determination. The notice shall identify the activity(ies), the U.S. port, and the prevailing practice regarding the use of alien crewmembers. The notice shall also inform interested parties that they may request a hearing pursuant to § 655.630 of this part, within 15 days of the date of the determination.

(c) The Administrator shall file with the Chief Administrative Law Judge, U.S. Department of Labor, a copy of the complaint and the Administrator's determination.

(d) The Administrator's written determination required by § 655.605 of this part shall:

(1) Set forth the determination of the Administrator and the reason or reasons therefor, and in the case of a finding of violation(s) by an attesting employer, prescribe any remedies, including the amount of any civil money penalties assessed and the reason therefor, and/or any other remedies required for compliance with the employer's attestation.

(2) Inform the interested parties that they may request a hearing pursuant to § 655.625 of this part.

(3) Inform the interested parties that in the absence of a timely request for a hearing, received by the Chief Administrative Law Judge within 15 calendar days of the date of the determination, the determination of the Administrator shall become final and not appealable.

(4) Set forth the procedure for requesting a hearing, and give the address of the Chief Administrative Law Judge (with whom the request must be filed) and the representative(s) of the Solicitor of Labor (upon whom copies of the request must be served).

(5) Inform the parties that, pursuant to § 655.665, the Administrator shall notify ETA and the DHS of the occurrence of a violation by the attesting employer or of the non-attesting employer's ineligibility for the automated vessel exception.

§ 655.630 Request for hearing.

(a) Any interested party desiring to request an administrative hearing on a determination issued pursuant to §§ 655.605 and 655.625 of this part shall make such request in writing to the Chief Administrative Law Judge at the address stated in the notice of determination.

(b) Interested parties may request a hearing in the following circumstances:

(1) The complainant or any other interested party may request a hearing where the Administrator determines, after investigation, that there is no basis for a finding that an attesting employer has committed violation(s) or that the employer is eligible for the automated vessel exception. In such a proceeding, the requesting party and the employer shall be parties; the Administrator may intervene as a party or appear as *amicus curiae* at any time in the proceeding, at the Administrator's discretion.

(2) The employer or any other interested party may request a hearing where the Administrator determines, after investigation, that there is a basis for a finding that an attesting employer has committed violation(s) or that a non- attesting employer is not eligible for the automated vessel exception. In such a proceeding, the Administrator and the employer shall be parties.

(c) No particular form is prescribed for any request for hearing permitted by this section. However, any such request shall:

(1) Be dated;

(2) Be typewritten or legibly written;

(3) Specify the issue or issues stated in the notice of determination giving rise to such request;

(4) State the specific reason or reasons why the party requesting the hearing believes such determination is in error;

(5) Be signed by the party making the request or by an authorized representative of such party; and

(6) Include the address at which such party or authorized representative desires to receive further communications relating thereto.

(d) The request for such hearing must be received by the Chief Administrative Law Judge, at the address stated in the Administrator's notice of determination, no later than 15 calendar days after the date of the determination. An interested party that fails to meet this 15-day deadline for requesting a hearing may thereafter participate in the proceedings only by consent of the administrative law judge, either through intervention as a party pursuant to 29 CFR 18.10 (b) through (d) or through participation as an amicus curiae pursuant to 18 CFR 18.12.

(e) The request may be filed in person, by facsimile transmission, by certified or regular mail, or by courier service. For the requesting party's protection, if the request is filed by mail, it should be by certified mail. If the request is filed by facsimile transmission, the original of the request, signed by the requestor or authorized representative, shall be filed within ten days.

(f) Copies of the request for a hearing shall be sent by the requestor to the Wage and Hour Division official who issued the Administrator's notice of determination, to the representative(s) of the Solicitor of Labor identified in the notice of determination, and to all known interested parties.

§ 655.635 Rules of practice for administrative law judge proceedings.

(a) Except as specifically provided in this subpart, and to the extent they do not conflict with the provisions of this subpart, the "Rules of Practice and Procedure for Administrative Hearings Before the Office of Administrative Law Judges" established by the Secretary at 29 CFR part 18 shall apply to administrative proceedings under this subpart.

(b) As provided in the Administrative Procedure Act, 5 U.S.C. 556, any oral or documentary evidence may be received in proceedings under this part. The Federal Rules of Evidence and subpart

B of the Rules of Practice and Procedure for Administrative Hearings Before the Office of Administrative Law Judges (29 CFR part 18, subpart B) shall not apply, but principles designed to ensure production of relevant and probative evidence shall guide the admission of evidence. The administrative law judge may exclude evidence which is immaterial, irrelevant, or unduly repetitive.

§ 655.640 Service and computation of time.

(a) Under this subpart, a party may serve any pleading or document by regular mail. Service on a party is complete upon mailing to the last known address or, in the case of the attesting employer, to the employer's designated representative in the U.S. No additional time for filing or response is authorized where service is by mail. In the interest of expeditious proceedings, the administrative law judge may direct the parties to serve pleadings or documents by a method other than regular mail.

(b) Two (2) copies of all pleadings and other documents in any administrative law judge proceeding shall be served on the attorneys for the Administrator. One copy shall be served on the Associate Solicitor, Division of Fair Labor Standards, Office of the Solicitor, U.S. Department of Labor, 200 Constitution Avenue NW., Washington, DC 20210, and one copy on the attorney representing the Administrator in the proceeding.

(c) Time will be computed beginning with the day following the action and includes the last day of the period unless it is a Saturday, Sunday, or federally-observed holiday, in which case the time period includes the next business day.

§ 655.645 Administrative law judge proceedings.

(a) Upon receipt of a timely request for a hearing filed pursuant to and in accordance with § 655.630 of this part, the Chief Administrative Law Judge shall promptly appoint an administrative law judge to hear the case.

(b) Within seven calendar days following the assignment of the case, the administrative law judge shall notify all interested parties of the date, time and place of the hearing. All parties shall be given at least fourteen calendar days' notice of such hearing.

(c) The date of the hearing shall be not more than 60 calendar days from the date of the Administrator's determination. Because of the time constraints imposed by the Act, no requests for postponement shall be granted except for compelling reasons. Even if such reasons are shown, no extension of the hearing date beyond 60 days from the date of the Administrator's determination shall be granted except by consent of all the parties to the proceeding.

(d) The administrative law judge may prescribe a schedule by which the parties are permitted to file a prehearing brief or other written statement of fact or law. Any such brief or statement shall be served upon each other party in accordance with § 655.640 of this part. Posthearing briefs will not be permitted except at the request of the administrative law judge. When permitted, any such brief shall be limited to the issue or issues specified by the administrative law judge, shall be due within the time prescribed by the administrative law judge, and shall be served on each other party in accordance with § 655.640 of this part.

(e) In reaching a decision, the administrative law judge shall, in accordance with the Act, impose the following burden of proof—

(1) The attesting employer shall have the burden of producing facts and evidence to establish the matters required by the attestation at issue;

(2) The burden of proof as to the applicability of the automated vessel exception shall be on the party to the hearing who is asserting that the employer is not eligible for the exception.

(f) The administrative law judge proceeding shall not be an appeal or review of the Administrator's ruling on a request for a cease and desist order pursuant to § 655.615.

§ 655.650 Decision and order of administrative law judge.

(a) Within 90 calendar days after receipt of the transcript of the hearing, the administrative law judge shall issue a decision. If any party desires review of the decision, including judicial review, a petition for Secretary's review thereof shall be filed as provided in § 655.655 of this subpart. If a petition for review is filed, the decision of the administrative law judge shall be inoperative unless and until the Secretary issues an order affirming the decision, or, unless and until 30 calendar days have passed after the Secretary's receipt of the petition for review and the Secretary has not issued notice to the parties that the Secretary will review the administrative law judge's decision.

(b) The decision of the administrative law judge shall include a statement of findings and conclusions, with reasons and basis therefor, upon each material issue presented on the record. The decision shall also include an appropriate order which may affirm, deny, reverse, or modify, in whole or in part, the determination of the Administrator; the reason or reasons for such order shall be stated in the decision. The administrative law judge shall not render determinations as to the legality of a regulatory provision or the constitutionality of a statutory provision.

(c) The decision shall be served on all parties in person or by certified or regular mail.

§ 655.655 Secretary's review of administrative law judge's decision.

(a) The Administrator or any interested party desiring review of the decision and order of an administrative law judge shall petition the Secretary to review the decision and order. To be effective, such petition shall be received by the Secretary within 30 calendar days of the date of the decision and order. Copies of the petition shall be served on all parties and on the administrative law judge.

(b) No particular form is prescribed for any petition for Secretary's review permitted by this subpart. However, any such petition shall:

(1) Be dated;

(2) Be typewritten or legibly written;

(3) Specify the issue or issues stated in the administrative law judge decision and order giving rise to such petition;

(4) State the specific reason or reasons why the party petitioning for review believes such decision and order are in error;

(5) Be signed by the party filing the petition or by an authorized representative of such party;

(6) Include the address at which such party or authorized representative desires to receive further communications relating thereto; and

(7) Attach copies of the administrative law judge's decision and order, and any other record documents which would assist the Secretary in determining whether review is warranted.

(c) Whenever the Secretary determines to review the decision and order of an administrative law judge, a notice of the Secretary's determination shall be served upon the administrative law judge and upon all parties to the proceeding within 30 calendar days after the Secretary's receipt of the petition for review.

(d) Upon receipt of the Secretary's notice, the Office of Administrative Law Judges shall within fifteen calendar days forward the complete hearing record to the Secretary.

(e) The Secretary's notice may specify:

(1) The issue or issues to be reviewed;

(2) The form in which submissions shall be made by the parties (e.g., briefs); and

(3) The time within which such submissions shall be made.

(f) All documents submitted to the Secretary shall be filed with the Secretary of Labor, U.S. Department of Labor, Washington, DC 20210, Attention: Executive Director, Office of Administrative Appeals, room S-4309. An original and two copies of all documents shall be filed. Documents are not deemed filed with the Secretary until actually received by the Secretary. All documents, including documents filed by mail, shall be received by the Secretary either on or before the due date.

(g) Copies of all documents filed with the Secretary shall be served upon all other parties involved in the proceeding. Service upon the Administrator shall be in accordance with § 655.640(b) of this part.

(h) The Secretary's final decision shall be issued within 180 calendar days from the date of the notice of intent to review. The Secretary's decision shall be served upon all parties and the administrative law judge.

(i) Upon issuance of the Secretary's decision, the Secretary shall transmit the entire record to the Chief Administrative Law Judge for custody pursuant to § 655.660 of this part.

§ 655.660 Administrative record.

The official record of every completed administrative hearing procedure provided by subparts F and G of this part shall be maintained and filed under the custody and control of the Chief Administrative Law Judge. Upon receipt of a complaint seeking review of the final agency action in a United States District Court, the Chief Administrative Law Judge shall certify the official record and shall transmit such record to the clerk of the court.

§ 655.665 Notice to the Department of Homeland Security and the Employment and Training Administration.

(a) The Administrator shall promptly notify the DHS and ETA of the entry of a cease and desist order pursuant to § 655.615 of this part. The order shall remain in effect until the completion of the Administrator's investigation and any subsequent proceedings pursuant to § 655.630 of this part, unless the Administrator notifies the DHS and ETA of the entry of a subsequent order lifting the prohibition.

(1) The DHS, upon receipt of notification from the Administrator that a cease and desist order has been entered against an employer:

(i) Shall not permit the vessels owned or chartered by the attesting employer to use alien crewmembers to perform the longshore activity(ies) at the port or location in the State of Alaska specified in the cease and desist order; and

(ii) Shall, in the case of an employer seeking to utilize the automated vessel exception, require that such employer not use alien crewmembers to perform the longshore activity(ies) at the port or location in the State of Alaska specified in the cease and desist order, without having on file with ETA an attestation pursuant to § 655.520 of this part.

(2) ETA, upon receipt of the Administrator's notice shall, in the case of an attesting employer, suspend the employer's attestation, either in whole or in part, for the activity(ies) and port or location in the State of Alaska specified in the cease and desist order.

(b) The Administrator shall notify the DHS and ETA of the final determination of a violation by an attesting employer or of the ineligibility of an employer for the automated vessel exception, upon the earliest of the following events:

(1) Where the Administrator determines that there is a basis for a finding of violation by an attesting employer or a finding of nonapplicability of the automated vessel exception, and no timely request for hearing is made pursuant to § 655.630 of this part;

(2) Where, after a hearing, the administrative law judge issues a decision and order finding a violation by an attesting employer or finding inapplicable the automated vessel exception, and no timely petition for review to the Secretary is made pursuant to § 655.655 of this part; or

(3) Where a petition for review is taken from an administrative law judge's decision finding a violation or finding inapplicable the automated vessel exception, and the Secretary either declines within thirty days to entertain the appeal, pursuant to § 655.655(c) of this part, or the Secretary affirms the administrative law judge's determination; or

(4) Where the administrative law judge finds that there was no violation by an attesting employer or that the automated vessel exception does apply, and the Secretary, upon review, issues a decision pursuant to § 655.655 of this part, holding that a violation was committed by an attesting employer or holding that the automated vessel exception does not apply.

(c) The DHS, upon receipt of notification from the Administrator pursuant to paragraph (b) of this section:

(1) Shall not permit the vessels owned or chartered by the attesting employer to enter any port of the U.S. for a period of up to one year;

(2) Shall, in the case of an employer determined to be ineligible for the automated vessel exception, thereafter

require that such employer not use alien crewmembers(s) to perform the longshore activity(ies) at the specified port or location in the State of Alaska without having on file with ETA an attestation pursuant to § 655.520 of this part; and

(3) Shall, in the event that the Administrator's notice constitutes a conclusive determination (pursuant to § 655.670) that the prevailing practice at a particular U.S. port does not permit the use of nonimmigrant alien crewmembers for particular longshore activity(ies), thereafter permit no employer to use alien crewmembers for the particular longshore activity(ies) at that port.

(d) ETA, upon receipt of the Administrator's notice pursuant to paragraph (b) of this section:

(1) Shall, in the case of an attesting employer, suspend the employer's attestation, either in whole or in part, for the port or location at issue and for any other U.S. port, and shall not accept for filing any attestation submitted by the employer for a period of 12 months or for a shorter period if such is specified for that employer by the DHS; and

(2) Shall, if the Administrator's notice constitutes a conclusive determination (pursuant to § 655.670) that the prevailing practice at a particular U.S. port does not permit the use of alien crewmembers for the longshore activity(ies), thereafter accept no attestation under the prevailing practice exception on Form ETA 9033 from any employer for the performance of the activity(ies) at that port, and shall invalidate any current attestation under the prevailing practice exception on Form ETA 9033 for any employer for the performance of the activity(ies) at that port.

[60 FR 3969, 3977, Jan. 19, 1995, as amended at 71 FR 35520, June 21, 2006]

§ 655.670 Federal Register notice of determination of prevailing practice.

(a) Pursuant to § 655.625(b), the Administrator shall publish in the FEDERAL REGISTER a notice of the Administrator's determination of any investigation regarding the prevailing practice for the use of alien crewmembers for particular longshore activity(ies) in a particular U.S. port (whether under an attestation or under the automated vessel exception). Where the Administrator has determined that the prevailing practice in that U.S. port does not permit such use of alien crewmembers, and no timely request for a hearing is filed pursuant to § 655.630, the Administrator's determination shall be the conclusive determination for purposes of the Act and subparts F and G of this part; the DHS and ETA shall, upon notice from the Administrator, take the actions specified in § 655.665. Where the Administrator has determined that the prevailing practice in that U.S. port at the time of the investigation permits such use of alien crewmembers, the Administrator shall, in any subsequent investigation, give that determination appropriate weight, unless the determination is reversed in proceedings under § 655.630 or § 655.655.

(b) Where an interested party, pursuant to § 655.630, requests a hearing on the Administrator's determination, the Administrator shall, upon the issuance of the decision of the administrative law judge, publish in the FEDERAL REGISTER a notice of the judge's decision as to the prevailing practice for the longshore activity(ies) and U.S. port at issue, if the administrative law judge:

(1) Reversed the determination of the Administrator published in the FEDERAL REGISTER pursuant to paragraph (a) of this section; or

(2) Determines that the prevailing practice for the particular activity in the port does not permit the use of alien crewmembers.

(c) If the administrative law judge determines that the prevailing practice in that port does not permit such use of alien crewmembers, the judge's decision shall be the conclusive determination for purposes of the Act and subparts F and G of this part (unless and until reversed by the Secretary on discretionary review pursuant to § 655.655). The DHS and ETA shall upon notice from the Administrator, take the actions specified in § 655.665.

(d) In the event that the Secretary, upon discretionary review pursuant to § 655.655, issues a decision that reverses the administrative law judge on a matter on which the Administrator has published notices in the FEDERAL REGISTER pursuant to paragraphs (a) and (b) of this section, the Administrator shall publish in the FEDERAL REGISTER a notice of the Secretary's decision and shall notify the DHS and ETA.

(1) Where the Secretary reverses the administrative law judge and determines that, contrary to the judge's decision, the prevailing practice for the longshore activity(ies) in the U.S. port at issue does not permit the use of alien crewmembers, the Secretary's decision shall be the conclusive determination for purposes of the Act and subparts F and G of this part. Upon notice from the Administrator, the DHS and ETA shall take the actions specified in § 655.665.

(2) Where the Secretary reverses the administrative law judge and determines that, contrary to the judge's decision, the use of alien crewmembers is permitted by the prevailing practice for the longshore activity(ies) in the U.S. port at issue, the judge's decision shall no longer have the conclusive effect specified in paragraph (b) of this section. Upon notice from the Administrator, the DHS and ETA shall cease the actions specified in § 655.665.

§ 655.675 Non-applicability of the Equal Access to Justice Act.

A proceeding under subpart G of this part is not subject to the Equal Access to Justice Act, as amended, 5 U.S.C. 504. In such a proceeding, the administrative law judge shall have no authority to award attorney fees and/or other litigation expenses pursuant to the provisions of the Equal Access to Justice Act.

Subpart H—Labor Condition Applications and Requirements for Employers Seeking To Employ Nonimmigrants on H–1b Visas in Specialty Occupations and as Fashion Models, and Requirements for Employers Seeking To Employ Nonimmigrants on H–1b1 and E–3 Visas in Specialty Occupations

SOURCE: 59 FR 65659, 65676, Dec. 20, 1994, unless otherwise noted.

§ 655.700 What statutory provisions govern the employment of H–1B, H–1B1, and E–3 nonimmigrants and how do employers apply for H–1B, H–1B1, and E–3 visas?

Under the E–3 visa program, the Immigration and Nationality Act (INA), as amended, permits certain nonimmigrant treaty aliens to be admitted to the United States solely to perform services in a specialty occupation (INA section 101(a)(15)(E)(iii)). Under the H–1B1 visa program, the INA permits nonimmigrant professionals in specialty occupations from countries with which the United States has entered into certain agreements that are identified in section 214(g)(8)(A) of the INA to temporarily enter the United States for employment in a specialty occupation. Employers seeking to employ nonimmigrant workers in specialty occupations under H–1B, H–1B1, or E–3 visas must file a labor condition application with the Department of Labor as described in § 655.730(c) and (d). Certain procedures described in this subpart H for obtaining a visa and entering the U.S. after the Department of Labor attestation process, including procedures in § 655.705, apply only to H–1B nonimmigrants. The procedures for receiving an E–3 or H–1B1 visa and entering the U.S. on an E–3 or H–1B1 visa after the attestation process is certified by the Department of Labor are identified in the regulations and procedures of the Department of State and the United States Citizenship and Immigration Services (USCIS) of the Department of Homeland Security. Consult the Department of State (*http://www.state.gov/*) and USCIS (*http://www.uscis.gov/*) Web sites and regulations for specific instructions regarding the E–3 and H–1B1 visas.

(a) *Statutory provisions regarding H–1B visas.* With respect to nonimmigrant workers entering the U.S. on H–1B visas, which are available to nonimmigrant aliens in specialty occupations or certain fashion models from any country, the INA, as amended, provides as follows:

(1) Establishes an annual ceiling (exclusive of spouses and children) on the number of foreign workers who may be issued H–1B visas—

(i) 195,000 in fiscal year 2001;

(ii) 195,000 in fiscal year 2002;

(iii) 195,000 in fiscal year 2003; and

(iv) 65,000 in each succeeding fiscal year;

(2) Defines the scope of eligible occupations for which nonimmigrants may be issued H–1B visas and specifies the qualifications that are required for entry as an H–1B nonimmigrant ;

(3) Requires an employer seeking to employ H–1B nonimmigrants to file a labor condition application (LCA) agreeing to various attestation requirements and have it certified by the Department of Labor (DOL) before a nonimmigrant may be provided H–1B status by the United States Citizenship and Immigration Services of the Department of Homeland Security (DHS); and

(4) Establishes an enforcement system under which DOL is authorized to determine whether an employer has engaged in misrepresentation or failed to meet a condition of the LCA, and is authorized to impose fines and penalties.

(b) *Procedure for obtaining an H–1B visa classification.* Before a nonimmigrant may be admitted to work in a "specialty occupation" or as a fashion model of distinguished merit and ability in the United States under the H–1B visa classification, there are certain steps which must be followed:

(1) First, an employer shall submit to the Department of Labor (DOL), and obtain DOL certification of, a labor condition application (LCA). The requirements for obtaining a certified LCA are provided in this subpart. The electronic LCA (Form ETA 9035E) is available at *http://www.lca.doleta.gov.* The paper-version LCA (Form ETA 9035) and the LCA cover pages (Form ETA 9035CP), which contain the full attestation statements incorporated by reference into Form ETA 9035 and Form ETA 9035E, may be obtained from *http://ows.doleta.gov* and from the Employment and Training Administration (ETA) National Office. Employers must file LCAs in the manner prescribed in § 655.720.

(2) After obtaining DOL certification of an LCA, the employer may submit a nonimmigrant visa petition (DHS Form I–129), together with the certified LCA, to DHS, requesting H–1B classification for the foreign worker. The requirements concerning the submission of a petition to, and its processing by, DHS are set forth in DHS regulations. The DHS petition (Form I–129) may be obtained from an DHS district or area office.

(3) If DHS approves the H–1B classification, the nonimmigrant then may apply for an H–1B visa abroad at a consular office of the Department of State. If the nonimmigrant is already in the United States in a status other than H–1B, he/she may apply to the DHS for a change of visa status.

(c) *Applicability.* (1) This subpart H and subpart I of this part apply to all employers seeking to employ foreign workers under the H–1B visa classification in specialty occupations or as fashion models of distinguished merit and ability.

(2) During the period that the provisions of Appendix 1603.D.4 of Annex 1603 of the North American Free Trade Agreement (NAFTA) apply, this subpart H and subpart I of this part shall apply (except for the provisions relating to the recruitment and displacement of U.S. workers (see §§ 655.738 and 655.739)) to the entry and employment of a nonimmigrant who is a citizen of Mexico under and pursuant to the provisions of section D or Annex 1603 of NAFTA in the case of all professions set out in Appendix 1603.D.1 of Annex 1603 of NAFTA other than registered nurses. Therefore, the references in this part to "H–1B nonimmigrant" apply to any Mexican citizen nonimmigrant who is classified by DHS as "TN." In the case of a registered nurse, the following provisions shall apply: subparts D and E of this part or the Nursing Relief for Disadvantaged Areas Act of 1999 (Public Law 106–95) and the regulations issued thereunder, 20 CFR part 655, subparts L and M.

(3) *E–3 visas:* Except as provided in paragraph (d) of this section, this subpart H and subpart I of this part apply to all employers seeking to employ foreign workers under the E–3 visa classification in specialty occupations under INA section 101(a)(15)(E)(iii) (8 U.S.C. 1101(a)(15)(E)(iii)). This paragraph (c)(3) applies to labor condition applications filed on or after April 11, 2008. E–3 labor condition applications filed prior to that date but on or after May 11, 2005

(*i.e.*, the effective date of the statute), will be processed according to the E–3 statutory terms and the E–3 processing procedures published on July 19, 2005 in the FEDERAL REGISTER at 74 FR 41434.

(4) *H–1B1 visas:* Except as provided in paragraph (d) of this section, subparts H and I of this part apply to all employers seeking to employ foreign workers under the H–1B1 visa classification in specialty occupations described in INA section 101(a)(15)(H)(i)(b1) (8 U.S.C. 1101(a)(15)(H)(i)(b1)), under the U.S.-Chile and U.S.-Singapore Free Trade Agreements as long as the Agreements are in effect. (INA section 214(g)(8)(A) (8 U.S.C. 1184(g)(8)(A)). This paragraph (c)(4) applies to H–1B1 labor condition applications filed on or after November 23, 2004. Further, H–1B1 labor condition applications filed prior to that date but on or after January 1, 2004, the effective date of the H–1B1 program, will be handled according to the H–1B1 statutory terms and the H–1B1 processing procedures as described in paragraph (d)(3) of this section.

(d) *Nonimmigrants on E–3 or H–1B1 visas*—(1) *Exclusions.* The following sections in this subpart and in subpart I of this part do not apply to E–3 and H–1B1 nonimmigrants, but apply only to H–1B nonimmigrants: §§ 655.700(a), (b), (c)(1) and (2); 655.710(b); 655.730(d)(5) and (e); 655.735; 655.736; 655.737; 655.738; 655.739; 655.760(a)(7), (8), (9), and (10); and 655.805(a)(7), (8), and (9). Further, the following references in subparts H or I of this part, whether in the excluded sections listed above or elsewhere, do not apply to E–3 and H–1B1 nonimmigrants, but apply only to H–1B nonimmigrants: references to fashion models of distinguished merit and ability (H–1B visas, but not H–1B1 and E–3 visas, are available to such fashion models); references to a petition process before USCIS (the petition process applies only to H–1B, but not to initial H–1B1 and E–3 visas unless it is a petition to accord a change of status); references to additional attestation obligations of H–1B-dependent employers and employers found to have willfully violated the H–1B program requirements (these provisions do not apply to the H–1B1 and E–3 programs); and references in § 655.750(a) or elsewhere in this part to the provision in INA section 214(n) (formerly INA section 214(m)) (8 U.S.C. 1184(n)) regarding increased portability of H–1B status (by the statutory terms, the portability provision is inapplicable to H–1B1 and E–3 nonimmigrants).

(2) *Terminology.* For purposes of subparts H and I of this part, except in those sections identified in paragraph (d)(1) of this section as inapplicable to E–3 and H–1B1 nonimmigrants and as otherwise excluded:

(i) The term "H–1B" includes "E–3" and "H–1B1" (INA section 101(a)(15)(E)(iii) and (a)(15)(H)(i)(b1)) (8 U.S.C. 1101(a)(15)(E)(iii) and (a)(15)(H)(i)(b1)); and

(ii) The term "labor condition application" or "LCA" includes a labor attestation made under section 212(t)(1) of the INA for an E–3 or H–1B1 nonimmigrant professional classified under INA section 101(a)(15)(E)(iii) and (a)(15)(H)(i)(b1) (8 U.S.C. 1101(a)(15)(E)(iii) and (a)(15)(H)(i)(b1)).

(3) *Filing procedures for E–3 and H–1B1 labor attestations.* Employers seeking to employ an E–3 or H–1B1 nonimmigrant must submit a completed ETA Form 9035 or ETA Form 9035E (electronic) to DOL in the manner prescribed in §§ 655.720 and 655.730. Employers must indicate on the form whether the labor condition application is for an "E–3 Australia," "H–1B1 Chile," or "H–1B1 Singapore" nonimmigrant. Any changes in the procedures and instructions for submitting labor condition applications will be provided in a notice published in the FEDERAL REGISTER and posted on the ETA Web site at *http://www.foreignlaborcert.doleta.gov/*.

(4) *Employer's responsibilities regarding E–3 and H–1B1 labor attestation.* Each employer seeking an E–3 or H–1B1 nonimmigrant in a specialty occupation has several responsibilities, as described more fully in subparts H and I of this part, including the following:

(i) By submitting a signed and completed LCA, the employer makes certain representations and agrees to several attestations regarding the employer's responsibilities, including the wages, working conditions, and benefits to be provided to the E–3 or H–1B1 nonimmigrant. These attestations are specifically identified and incorporated in the LCA, and are fully described on Form ETA 9035CP (cover pages).

(ii) The employer reaffirms its acceptance of all of the attestation obligations by transmitting the certified labor attestation to the nonimmigrant, the Department of State, and/or the USCIS according to the procedures of those agencies.

(iii) The employer shall maintain the original signed and certified LCA in its files, and shall make a copy of the filed LCA, as well as necessary supporting documentation (as identified under this subpart), available for public examination in a public access file at the employer's principal place of business in the U.S. or at the place of employment within one working day after the date on which the LCA is filed with ETA.

(iv) The employer shall develop sufficient documentation to meet its burden of proof, in the event that such statement or information is challenged, with respect to the validity of the statements made in its LCA and the accuracy of information provided. The employer shall also maintain such documentation at its principal place of business in the U.S. and shall make such documentation available to DOL for inspection and copying upon request.

(5) *Application to Chile.* During the period that the provisions of Chapter 14 and Section D of Annex 14.3 of the United States-Chile Free Trade Agreement (Chile FTA) are in effect, this subpart H and subpart I of this part shall apply (except for the provisions excluded under paragraph (d)(1) of this section) to the temporary entry and employment of a nonimmigrant who is a national of Chile under the provisions of Article 14.9 and Annex 2.1 of the Chile FTA and who is a professional under the provisions of Annex 14.3(D) of the Chile FTA.

(6) *Application to Singapore.* During the period that the provisions of Section IV of Annex 11A of the United States-Singapore Free Trade Agreement (Singapore FTA) are in effect, this subpart H and subpart I of this part shall apply (except for the provisions excluded under paragraph (d)(1) of this section) to the temporary entry and employment of a nonimmigrant who is a national of Singapore under the provisions of Chapter 11 and Section IV of Annex 11A of the Singapore FTA and who is a professional under the provisions of Annex 11A(IV) of the Singapore FTA.

[65 FR 80209, Dec. 20, 2000, as amended at 66 FR 63300, Dec. 5, 2001; 69 FR 68226, Nov. 23, 2004; 70 FR 72560, Dec. 5, 2005; 71 FR 35520, 35521, June 21, 2006; 71 FR 37804, June 30, 2006; 73 FR 19947, Apr. 11, 2008]

§655.705 What Federal agencies are involved in the H–1B and H–1B1 programs, and what are the responsibilities of those agencies and of employers?

Four federal agencies (Department of Labor, Department of State, Department of Justice, and Department of Homeland Security) are involved in the process relating to H–1B nonimmigrant classification and employment. The employer also has continuing responsibilities under the process. This section briefly describes the responsibilities of each of these entities.

(a) *Department of Labor (DOL) responsibilities.* DOL administers the labor condition application process and enforcement provisions (exclusive of complaints regarding non-selection of U.S. workers, as described in 8 U.S.C. 1182(n)(1)(G)(i)(II) and 1182(n)(5)). Two DOL agencies have responsibilities:

(1) The Employment and Training Administration (ETA) is responsible for receiving and certifying labor condition applications (LCAs) in accordance with this subpart H. ETA is also responsible for compiling and maintaining a list of LCAs and makes such list available for public examination at the Department of Labor, 200 Constitution Avenue, NW., Room C–4312, Washington, DC 20210.

(2) The Wage and Hour Division of the Employment Standards Administration (ESA) is responsible, in accordance with subpart I of this part, for investigating and determining an employer's misrepresentation in or failure to comply with LCAs in the employment of H–1B nonimmigrants.

(b) *Department of Justice (DOJ), Department of Homeland Security (DHS) and Department of State (DOS) responsibilities.* The Department of State, through U.S. Embassies and Consulates, is responsible for issuing H–1B,

H–1B1, and E–3 visas. For H–1B visas, the following agencies are involved: DHS accepts the employer's petition (DHS Form I–129) with the DOL-certified LCA attached. In doing so, the DHS determines whether the petition is supported by an LCA which corresponds with the petition, whether the occupation named in the labor condition application is a specialty occupation or whether the individual is a fashion model of distinguished merit and ability, and whether the qualifications of the nonimmigrant meet the statutory requirements for H–1B visa classification. If the petition is approved, DHS will notify the U.S. Consulate where the nonimmigrant intends to apply for the visa unless the nonimmigrant is in the U.S. and eligible to adjust status without leaving this country. See 8 U.S.C. 1255(h)(2)(B)(i). The Department of Justice administers the system for the enforcement and disposition of complaints regarding an H–1B-dependent employer's or willful violator employer's failure to offer a position filled by an H–1B nonimmigrant to an equally or better qualified United States worker (8 U.S.C. 1182(n)(1)(E), 1182(n)(5)), or such employer's willful misrepresentation of material facts relating to this obligation. DHS, is responsible for disapproving H–1B and other petitions filed by an employer found to have engaged in misrepresentation or failed to meet certain conditions of the labor condition application (8 U.S.C. 1182(n)(2)(C)(i)–(iii); 1182(n)(5)(E)). DOL and DOS are involved in the process relating to the initial issuance of H–1B1 and E–3 visas. DHS is involved in change of status and extension of stays for the H–1B1 and E–3 category.

(c) *Employer's responsibilities*. This paragraph applies only to the H–1B program; employer's responsibilities under the H–1B1 and E–3 programs are found at § 655.700(d)(4). Each employer seeking an H–1B nonimmigrant in a specialty occupation or as a fashion model of distinguished merit and ability has several responsibilities, as described more fully in this subpart and subpart I of this part, including:

(1) The employer shall submit a completed labor condition application (LCA) on Form ETA 9035E or Form ETA 9035 in the manner prescribed in § 655.720. By completing and submitting the LCA, and by signing the LCA, the employer makes certain representations and agrees to several attestations regarding its responsibilities, including the wages, working conditions, and benefits to be provided to the H–1B nonimmigrants (8 U.S.C. 1182(n)(1)); these attestations are specifically identified and incorporated by reference in the LCA, as well as being set forth in full on Form ETA 9035CP. The LCA contains additional attestations for certain H–1B-dependent employers and employers found to have willfully violated the H–1B program requirements; these attestations impose certain obligations to recruit U.S. workers, to offer the job to U.S. applicants who are equally or better qualified than the H–1B nonimmigrant(s) sought for the job, and to avoid the displacement of U.S. workers (either in the employer's workforce, or in the workforce of a second employer with whom the H–1B nonimmigrant(s) is placed, where there are indicia of employment with a second employer (8 U.S.C. 1182(n)(1)(E)–(G)). These additional attestations are specifically identified and incorporated by reference in the LCA, as well as being set forth in full on Form ETA 9035CP. If ETA certifies the LCA, notice of the certification will be sent to the employer by the same means the employer used to submit the LCA (that is, electronically where the Form ETA 9035E was submitted electronically, and by U.S. Mail where the Form ETA 9035 was submitted by U.S. Mail). The employer reaffirms its acceptance of all of the attestation obligations by submitting the LCA to the U.S. Citizenship and Immigration Services (formerly the Immigration and Naturalization Service or INS) in support of the Petition for Nonimmigrant Worker, Form I–129, for an H–1B nonimmigrant. See 8 CFR 214.2(h)(4)(iii)(B)(2), which specifies the employer will comply with the terms of the LCA for the duration of the H–1B nonimmigrant's authorized period of stay.

(2) The employer shall maintain the original signed and certified LCA in its files, and shall make a copy of the LCA, as well as necessary supporting documentation (as identified under this

subpart), available for public examination in a public access file at the employer's principal place of business in the U.S. or at the place of employment within one working day after the date on which the LCA is filed with ETA.

(3) The employer then may submit a copy of the certified, signed LCA to DHS with a completed petition (Form I-129) requesting H-1B classification.

(4) The employer shall not allow the nonimmigrant worker to begin work until DHS grants the alien authorization to work in the United States for that employer or, in the case of a nonimmigrant previously afforded H-1B status who is undertaking employment with a new H-1B employer, until the new employer files a nonfrivolous petition (Form I-129) in accordance with DHS requirements.

(5) The employer shall develop sufficient documentation to meet its burden of proof with respect to the validity of the statements made in its LCA and the accuracy of information provided, in the event that such statement or information is challenged. The employer shall also maintain such documentation at its principal place of business in the U.S. and shall make such documentation available to DOL for inspection and copying upon request.

[65 FR 80210, Dec. 20, 2000, as amended at 66 FR 63300, Dec. 5, 2001; 70 FR 72560, Dec. 5, 2005; 71 FR 35520, June 21, 2006; 73 FR 19948, Apr. 11, 2008]

§655.710 What is the procedure for filing a complaint?

(a) Except as provided in paragraph (b) of this section, complaints concerning misrepresentation in the labor condition application or failure of the employer to meet a condition specified in the application shall be filed with the Administrator, Wage and Hour Division (Administrator), ESA, according to the procedures set forth in subpart I of this part. The Administrator shall investigate where appropriate, and after an opportunity for a hearing, assess appropriate sanctions and penalties, as described in subpart I of this part.

(b) Complaints arising under section 212(n)(1)(G)(i)(II) of the INA, 8 U.S.C. 1182(n)(1)(G)(i)(II), alleging failure of the employer to offer employment to an equally or better qualified U.S. applicant, or an employer's misrepresentation regarding such offer(s) of employment, may be filed with the Department of Justice, Civil Rights Division, Office of Special Counsel for Immigration-Related Unfair Employment Practices, 950 Pennsylvania Avenue, NW., Washington, DC 20530, Telephone: 1-800-255-8155 (employers), 1-800-255-7688 (employees); Web address: *http://www.usdoj.gov/crt/osc*. The Department of Justice shall investigate where appropriate, and take action as appropriate under that Department's regulations and procedures.

[65 FR 80210, Dec. 20, 2000, as amended at 70 FR 72561, Dec. 5, 2005]

§655.715 Definitions.

For the purposes of subparts H and I of this part:

Actual wage means the wage rate paid by the employer to all individuals with experience and qualifications similar to the H-1B nonimmigant's experience and qualifications for the specific employment in question at the place of employment. The actual wage established by the employer is *not* an average of the wage rates paid to all workers employed in the occupation.

Administrative Law Judge (ALJ) means an official appointed pursuant to 5 U.S.C. 3105.

Administrator means the Administrator of the Wage and Hour Division, Employment Standards Administration, Department of Labor, and such authorized representatives as may be designated to perform any of the functions of the Administrator under subpart H or I of this part.

Aggrieved party means a person or entity whose operations or interests are adversely affected by the employer's alleged non-compliance with the labor condition application and includes, but is not limited to:

(1) A worker whose job, wages, or working conditions are adversely affected by the employer's alleged non-compliance with the labor condition application;

(2) A bargaining representative for workers whose jobs, wages, or working conditions are adversely affected by

the employer's alleged non-compliance with the labor condition application;

(3) A competitor adversely affected by the employer's alleged non-compliance with the labor condition application; and

(4) A government agency which has a program that is impacted by the employer's alleged non-compliance with the labor condition application.

Area of intended employment means the area within normal commuting distance of the place (address) of employment where the H–1B nonimmigrant is or will be employed. There is no rigid measure of distance which constitutes a normal commuting distance or normal commuting area, because there may be widely varying factual circumstances among different areas (e.g., normal commuting distances might be 20, 30, or 50 miles). If the place of employment is within a Metropolitan Statistical Area (MSA) or a Primary Metropolitan Statistical Area (PMSA), any place within the MSA or PMSA is deemed to be within normal commuting distance of the place of employment; however, all locations within a Consolidated Metropolitan Statistical Area (CMSA) will not automatically be deemed to be within normal commuting distance. The borders of MSAs and PMSAs are not controlling with regard to the identification of the normal commuting area; a location outside of an MSA or PMSA (or a CMSA) may be within normal commuting distance of a location that is inside (e.g., near the border of) the MSA or PMSA (or CMSA).

Attorney General means the chief official of the U.S. Department of Justice or the Attorney General's designee.

Authorized agent and *authorized representative* mean an official of the employer who has the legal authority to commit the employer to the statements in the labor condition application.

Center Director means the Department official to whom the Administrator has delegated his authority for purposes of NPC operations and functions.

Certification means the determination by a certifying officer that a labor condition application is not incomplete and does not contain obvious inaccuracies.

Certify means the act of making a certification.

Certifying Officer means a Department of Labor official, or such official's designee, who makes determinations about whether or not to certify labor condition applications.

Chief Administrative Law Judge (Chief ALJ) means the chief official of the Office of the Administrative Law Judges of the Department of Labor or the Chief Administrative Law Judge's designee.

Department and *DOL* mean the United States Department of Labor.

Department of Homeland Security (DHS) through the United States Citizenship and Immigration Services (USCIS) makes the determination under the INA on whether to grant visa petitions of employers seeking the admission of non-immigrants under H–1B visa for the purpose of employment.

Division means the Wage and Hour Division of the Employment Standards Administration, DOL.

Employed, employed by the employer, or employment relationship means the employment relationship as determined under the common law, under which the key determinant is the putative employer's right to control the means and manner in which the work is performed. Under the common law, "no shorthand formula or magic phrase * * * can be applied to find the answer * * *. [A]ll of the incidents of the relationship must be assessed and weighed with no one factor being decisive." *NLRB* v. *United Ins. Co. of America*, 390 U.S. 254, 258 (1968).

Employer means a person, firm, corporation, contractor, or other association or organization in the United States that has an employment relationship with H–1B, H–1B1, or E–3 nonimmigrants and/or U.S. worker(s). In the case of an H–1B nonimmigrant (not including E–3 and H–1B1 nonimmigrants), the person, firm, contractor, or other association or organization in the United States that files a petition with the United States Citizenship and Immigration Services (USCIS) of the Department of Homeland Security (DHS) on behalf of the nonimmigrant is deemed to be the employer of that nonimmigrant. In the case of an E–3 and H–1B1 nonimmigrant, the person, firm, contractor, or other association or organization in the United States that files an LCA with the Department of Labor on behalf of the nonimmigrant is deemed to be the employer of that nonimmigrant.

Employment and Training Administration (ETA) means the agency within the Department which includes the Office of Foreign Labor Certification (OFLC).

Employment Standards Administration (ESA) means the agency within the Department which includes the Wage and Hour Division.

INA means the Immigration and Nationality Act, as amended, 8 U.S.C. 1101 *et seq.*

Independent authoritative source means a professional, business, trade, educational or governmental association, organization, or other similar entity, not owned or controlled by the employer, which has recognized expertise in an occupational field.

Independent authoritative source survey means a survey of wages conducted by an independent authoritative source and published in a book, newspaper, periodical, loose-leaf service, newsletter, or other similar medium, within the 24-month period immediately preceding the filing of the employer's application. Such survey shall:

(1) Reflect the average wage paid to workers similarly employed in the area of intended employment;

(2) Be based upon recently collected data—e.g., within the 24-month period immediately preceding the date of publication of the survey; and

(3) Represent the latest published prevailing wage finding by the authoritative source for the occupation in the area of intended employment.

Interested party means a person or entity who or which may be affected by the actions of an H–1B employer or by the outcome of a particular investigation and includes any person, organization, or entity who or which has notified the Department of his/her/its interest or concern in the Administrator's determination.

Lockout means a labor dispute involving a work stoppage, wherein an employer withholds work from its employees in order to gain a concession from them.

Occupation means the occupational or job classification in which the H–1B nonimmigrant is to be employed.

Office of Foreign Labor Certification (OFLC) means the organizational component within the ETA that provides national leadership and policy guidance and develops regulations and procedures to carry out the responsibilities of the Secretary of Labor under the INA concerning alien workers seeking admission to the United States in order to work under the Immigration and Nationality Act, as amended.

Period of intended employment means the time period between the starting and ending dates inclusive of the H–1B nonimmigrant's intended period of employment in the occupational classification at the place of employment as set forth in the labor condition application.

Place of employment means the worksite or physical location where the work actually is performed by the H–1B, H–1B1, or E–3 nonimmigrant.

(1) The term does not include any location where either of the following criteria—paragraph (1)(i) or (ii)—is satisfied:

(i) *Employee developmental activity.* An H–1B worker who is stationed and regularly works at one location may temporarily be at another location for a particular individual or employer-required developmental activity such as a management conference, a staff seminar, or a formal training course (other than "on-the-job-training" at a location where the employee is stationed and regularly works). For the H–1B worker participating in such activities, the location of the activity would not be considered a "place of employment" or "worksite," and that worker's presence at such location—whether owned or controlled by the employer or by a third party—would not invoke H–1B program requirements with regard to that employee at that location. However, if the employer uses H–1B nonimmigrants as instructors or resource or support staff who continuously or regularly perform their duties at such locations, the locations would be "places of employment" or "worksites" for any such employees and, thus, would be subject to H–1B program requirements with regard to those employees.

(ii) *Particular worker's job functions.* The nature and duration of an H–1B nonimmigrant's job functions may necessitate frequent changes of location with little time spent at any one location. For such a worker, a location would not be considered a "place of employment" or "worksite" if the following three requirements (*i.e.*, paragraphs (1)(ii)(A) through (C)) are all met—

(A) The nature and duration of the H–1B worker's job functions mandates his/her short-time presence at the location. For this purpose, either:

(*1*) The H–1B nonimmigrant's job must be peripatetic in nature, in that the normal duties of the worker's occupation (rather than the nature of the employer's business) requires frequent travel (local or non-local) from location to location; or

(*2*) The H–1B worker's duties must require that he/she spend most work time at one location but occasionally travel for short periods to work at other locations; and

(B) The H–1B worker's presence at the locations to which he/she travels from the "home" worksite is on a casual, short-term basis, which can be recurring but not excessive (*i.e.*, not exceeding five consecutive workdays for any one visit by a peripatetic worker, or 10 consecutive workdays for any one visit by a worker who spends most work time at one location and travels occasionally to other locations); and

(C) The H–1B nonimmigrant is not at the location as a "strikebreaker" (*i.e.*, the H–1B nonimmigrant is not performing work in an occupation in which workers are on strike or lockout).

(2) Examples of "non-worksite" locations based on worker's job functions: A computer engineer sent out to customer locations to "troubleshoot" complaints regarding software malfunctions; a sales representative making calls on prospective customers or established customers within a "home office" sales territory; a manager monitoring the performance of out-stationed employees; an auditor providing advice or conducting reviews at customer facilities; a physical therapist providing services to patients in their homes within an area of employment; an individual making a court appearance; an individual lunching with a customer representative at a restaurant; or an individual conducting research at a library.

(3) Examples of "worksite" locations based on worker's job functions: A computer engineer who works on projects or accounts at different locations for weeks or months at a time; a sales representative assigned on a continuing basis in an area away from his/her "home office;" an auditor who works for extended periods at the customer's offices; a physical therapist who "fills in" for full-time employees of health care facilities for extended periods; or a physical therapist who works for a contractor whose business is to provide staffing on an "as needed" basis at hospitals, nursing homes, or clinics.

(4) Whenever an H–1B worker performs work at a location which is not a "worksite" (under the criterion in paragraph (1)(i) or (1)(ii) of this definition), that worker's "place of employment" or "worksite" for purposes of H–1B obligations is the worker's home station or regular work location. The employer's obligations regarding notice, prevailing wage and working conditions are focused on the home station "place of employment" rather than on the above-described location(s) which do not constitute worksite(s) for these purposes. However, whether or not a location is considered to be a "worksite"/"place of employment" for an H–1B nonimmigrant, the employer is required to provide reimbursement to the H–1B nonimmigrant for expenses incurred in traveling to that location on the employer's business, since such expenses are considered to be ordinary business expenses of employers (§§ 655.731(c)(7)(iii)(C); 655.731(c)(9)). In determining the worker's "place of employment" or "worksite," the Department will look carefully at situations which appear to be contrived or abusive; the Department would seriously question any situation where the H–1B nonimmigrant's purported "place of

employment" is a location other than where the worker spends most of his/her work time, or where the purported "area of employment" does not include the location(s) where the worker spends most of his/her work time.

Required wage rate means the rate of pay which is the higher of:

(1) The actual wage for the specific employment in question; or

(2) The prevailing wage rate (determined as of the time of filing the LCA application) for the occupation in which the H–1B, H–1B1, or E–3 nonimmigrant is to be employed in the geographic area of intended employment. The prevailing wage rate must be no less than the minimum wage required by Federal, State, or local law.

Secretary means the Secretary of Labor or the Secretary's designee.

Specialty occupation:

(1) For purposes of the E–3 and H–1B programs (but not the H–1B1 program), *specialty occupation* means an occupation that requires theoretical and practical application of a body of specialized knowledge, and attainment of a bachelor's or higher degree (or its equivalent) in the specific specialty as a minimum for entry into the occupation in the United States. The nonimmigrant in a specialty occupation shall possess the following qualifications:

(i) Full state licensure to practice in the occupation, if licensure is required for the occupation;

(ii) Completion of the required degree; or

(iii) Experience in the specialty equivalent to the completion of such degree and recognition of expertise in the specialty through progressively responsible positions relating to the specialty. INA, 8 U.S.C. 1184(i)(1) and (2).

(2) For purposes of the H–1B1 program, *specialty occupation* means an occupation that requires theoretical and practical application of a body of specialized knowledge, and attainment of a bachelor's or higher degree (or its equivalent) in the specific specialty as a minimum for entry into the occupation in the United States. INA, 8 U.S.C. 1184(i)(3). For H–1B1 nonimmigrants from Chile, additional occupations that qualify as specialty occupations are Disaster Relief Claims Adjuster, Management Consultant, Agricultural Manager, and Physical Therapist, as defined in Appendix 14.3(D)(2) of the United States-Chile Free Trade Agreement. For H–1B1 nonimmigrants from Singapore, additional occupations that qualify as specialty occupations are Disaster Relief Claims Adjuster and Management Consultant, as defined in Appendix 11A.2 of the United States-Singapore Free Trade Agreement.

(3) Determinations of specialty occupation and of nonimmigrant qualifications for the H–1B and H–1B1 programs are not made by the Department of Labor, but by the Department of State and/or United States Citizenship and Immigration Services (USCIS) of the Department of Homeland Security in accordance with the procedures of those agencies for processing visas, petitions, extensions of stay, or requests for change of nonimmigrant status for H–1B or H–1B1 nonimmigrants.

Specific employment in question means the set of duties and responsibilities performed or to be performed by the H–1B nonimmigrant at the place of employment.

State means one of the 50 States, the District of Columbia, Guam, Puerto Rico, and the U.S. Virgin Islands.

State Workforce Agency, formerly State Employment Security Agency or SESA means the State agency which, under the State Administrator, is designated by the Governor to administer Wagner-Peyser Act funded employment and workforce information services (State agency) and the State unemployment compensation program.

Strike means a labor dispute wherein employees engage in a concerted stoppage of work (including stoppage by reason of the expiration of a collective-bargaining agreement) or engage in any concerted slowdown or other concerted interruption of operation.

United States worker ("U.S. worker") means an employee who is either

(1) A citizen or national of the United States, or

(2) An alien who is lawfully admitted for permanent residence in the United States, is admitted as a refugee under section 207 of the INA, is granted asylum under section 208 of the INA, or is an immigrant otherwise authorized (by

the INA or by DHS) to be employed in the United States.

Wage rate means the remuneration (exclusive of fringe benefits) to be paid, stated in terms of amount per hour, day, month or year (see definition of "Required Wage Rate").

[59 FR 65659, 65676, Dec. 20, 1994, as amended at 65 FR 80211, Dec. 20, 2000; 69 FR 68228, Nov. 23, 2004; 70 FR 72561, Dec. 5, 2005; 71 FR 35520, June 21, 2006; 73 FR 19948, Apr. 11, 2008; 73 FR 78067, Dec. 19, 2008]

§ 655.720 Where are labor condition applications (LCAs) to be filed and processed?

(a) Employers must file all LCAs regarding H–1B, H–1B1, and E–3 nonimmigrants through the electronic submission procedure identified in paragraph (b) of this section except as provided in the next sentence. If a physical disability or lack of access to the Internet prevents an employer from using the electronic filing system, an LCA may be filed by U.S. Mail in accordance with paragraphs (c) and (d) of this section. Requirements for signing, providing public access to, and use of certified LCAs are identified in § 655.730(c). If the LCA is certified by DOL, notice of the certification will be sent to the employer by the same means that the employer used to submit the LCA, that is, electronically where the Form ETA 9035E was submitted electronically, and by U.S. Mail where the Form ETA 9035 was submitted by U.S. Mail.

(b) *Electronic submission.* Employers must file the electronic LCA, Form ETA 9035E, through the Department of Labor's Web site at *http://www.lca.doleta.gov.* The employer must follow instructions for electronic submission posted on the Web site. In the event ETA implements the Government Paperwork Elimination Act (44 U.S.C.A. 3504 n.) and/or the Electronic Records and Signatures in Global and National Commerce Act (E–SIGN) (15 U.S.C. 7001–7006) for the submission and certification of the Form ETA 9035E, instructions will be provided (by public notice(s) and by instructions on the Department's Web site) to employers as to how the requirements of these statutes will be met in the Form ETA 9035E procedures.

(c) *Approval to file LCAs by U.S. Mail.* (1) Employers with physical disabilities or lacking Internet access and wishing to file LCAs by U.S. Mail may submit a written request to the Chief, Division of Foreign Labor Certification in accordance with paragraphs (c)(2) through (c)(4) of this section. The ETA shall identify the address to which such written request shall be mailed in a Notice in the FEDERAL REGISTER and on the Department's Web site at *http://www.lca.doleta.gov.*

(2) The written request must establish the employer's need to file by U.S. Mail, including providing an explanation of how physical disability or lack of access to the Internet prevents the employer from using the electronic filing system. No particular form or format is required for this request.

(3) ETA will review the submitted justification, and may require the employer to submit supporting documentation. In the case of employers asserting a lack of Internet access, supporting documentation could, for example, consist of documentation that the Internet cannot be accessed from the employer's worksite or physical location (for example because no Internet service provider serves the site), and there is no publicly available Internet access, at public libraries or elsewhere, within a reasonable distance of the employer. In the case of employers with physical disabilities supporting documentation could, for example, consist of physicians' statements or invoices for medical devices or aids relevant to the employer's disability.

(4) ETA may approve or deny employers' requests to submit LCAs by U.S. Mail. Approvals shall be valid for 1 year from the date of approval.

(d) *U.S. Mail.* If an employer has a valid approval to file by U.S. Mail in accordance with paragraph (c) of this section, the employer may use Form ETA 9035 and send it by U.S. Mail to ETA. ETA shall publish a Notice in the FEDERAL REGISTER identifying the address, and any future address changes, to which paper LCAs must be mailed, and shall also post these addresses on the DOL Internet Web site at *http://www.lca.doleta.gov.* When Form ETA 9035 is submitted by U.S. Mail, the form must bear the original signature of the employer (or that of the employer's authorized agent or representative) at the time it is submitted to ETA.

(e) The ETA National Office is responsible for policy questions and other issues regarding LCAs. Prevailing wage challenges are handled in accordance with the procedures identified in § 655.731(a)(2).

[70 FR 72561, Dec. 5, 2005, as amended at 73 FR 19949, Apr. 11, 2008]

§ 655.721 [Reserved]

§ 655.730 What is the process for filing a labor condition application?

This section applies to the filing of labor condition applications for H–1B, H–1B1, and E–3 nonimmigrants. The term H–1B is meant to apply to all three categories unless exceptions are specifically noted.

(a) *Who must submit labor condition applications?* An employer, or the employer's authorized agent or representative, which meets the definition of "employer" set forth in § 655.715 and intends to employ an H–1B nonimmigrant in a specialty occupation or as a fashion model of distinguished merit and ability shall submit an LCA to the Department.

(b) *Where and when is an LCA to be submitted?* An LCA shall be submitted by the employer to ETA in accordance with the procedure prescribed in § 655.720 no earlier than six months before the beginning date of the period of intended employment shown on the LCA. It is the employer's responsibility to ensure ETA receives a complete and accurate LCA. Incomplete or obviously inaccurate LCAs will not be certified by ETA. ETA will process all LCAs sequentially and will usually make a determination to certify or not certify an LCA within seven working days of the date ETA receives the LCA. LCAs filed by U.S. Mail may not be processed as quickly as those filed electronically.

(c) *What is to be submitted and what are its contents?* Form ETA 9035 or ETA 9035E.

(1) *General.* The employer (or the employer's authorized agent or representative) must submit to ETA one completed and dated LCA as prescribed in § 655.720. The electronic LCA, Form ETA 9035E, is found on the DOL Web site where the electronic submission is made, at *http://www.lca.doleta.gov.* Copies of the paper form, Form ETA 9035, and cover pages Form ETA 9035CP are available on the DOL Web site at *http://www.ows.doleta.gov* and from the ETA National Office, and may be used by employers with approval under § 655.720 to file by U.S. Mail during the approval's validity period.

(2) *Undertaking of the Employer.* In submitting the LCA, and by affixing the signature of the employer or its authorized agent or representative on Form ETA 9035E or Form ETA 9035, the employer (or its authorized agent or representative on behalf of the employer) attests the statements in the LCA are true and promises to comply with the labor condition statements (attestations) specifically identified in Forms ETA 9035E and ETA 9035, as well as set forth in full in the Form ETA 9035CP. The labor condition statements (attestations) are described in detail in §§ 655.731 through 655.734, and the additional attestations for LCAs filed by certain H–1B-dependent employers and employers found to have willfully violated the H–1B program requirements are described in §§ 655.736 through 655.739.

(3) *Signed Originals, Public Access, and Use of Certified LCAs.* In accordance with § 655.760(a) and (a)(1), the employer must maintain in its files and make available for public examination the LCA as submitted to ETA and as certified by ETA. When Form ETA 9035E is submitted electronically, a signed original is created by the employer (or by the employer's authorized agent or representative) printing out and signing the form immediately upon certification by ETA. When Form ETA 9035 is submitted by U.S. Mail as permitted by § 655.720(a), the form must bear the original signature of the employer (or of the employer's authorized agent or representative) when submitted to ETA. For H–1B visas only, the employer must submit a copy of the signed, certified Form ETA 9035 or ETA 9035E to the U.S. Citizenship and Immigration Services (USCIS, formerly INS) in support of the Form I–129 petition,

thereby reaffirming the employer's acceptance of all of the attestation obligations in accordance with 8 CFR 214.2(h)(4)(iii)(B)(2).

(4) *Contents of LCA.* Each LCA shall identify the occupational classification for which the LCA is being submitted and shall state:

(i) The occupation, by Dictionary of Occupational Titles (DOT) Three-Digit Occupational Groups code and by the employer's own title for the job;

(ii) The number of nonimmigrants sought;

(iii) The gross wage rate to be paid to each nonimmigrant, expressed on an hourly, weekly, biweekly, monthly, or annual basis;

(iv) The starting and ending dates of the nonimmigrants' employment;

(v) The place(s) of intended employment;

(vi) The prevailing wage for the occupation in the area of intended employment and the specific source (e.g., name of published survey) relied upon by the employer to determine the wage. If the wage is obtained from a SESA, now known as a State Workforce Agency (SWA), the appropriate box must be checked and the wage must be stated; the source for a wage obtained from a source other than a SWA must be identified along with the wage; and

(vii) For applications filed regarding H–1B nonimmigrants only (and not applications regarding H–1B1 and E–3 nonimmigrants), the employer's status as to whether or not the employer is H–1B-dependent and/or a willful violator, and, if the employer is H–1B-dependent and/or a willful violator, whether the employer will use the application only in support of petitions for exempt H–1B nonimmigrants.

(5) *Multiple positions and/or places of employment.* The employer shall file a separate LCA for each occupation in which the employer intends to employ one or more nonimmigrants, but the LCA may cover more than one intended position (employment opportunity) within that occupation. All intended places of employment shall be identified on the LCA; the employer may file one or more additional LCAs to identify additional places of employment. Separate LCAs must be filed for H–1B, H–1B1, and E–3 nonimmigrants.

(6) *Full-time and part-time jobs.* The position(s) covered by the LCA may be either full-time or part-time; full-time and part-time positions can not be combined on a single LCA.

(d) *What attestations does the LCA contain?* An employer's LCA shall contain the labor condition statements referenced in §§ 655.731 through 655.734, and § 655.736 through 655.739 (if applicable), which provide that no individual may be admitted or provided status as an H–1B nonimmigrant in an occupational classification unless the employer has filed with the Secretary an application stating that:

(1) The employer is offering and will offer during the period of authorized employment to H–1B nonimmigrants no less than the greater of the following wages (such offer to include benefits and eligibility for benefits provided as compensation for services, which are to be offered to the nonimmigrants on the same basis and in accordance with the same criteria as the employer offers such benefits to U.S. workers):

(i) The actual wage paid to the employer's other employees at the worksite with similar experience and qualifications for the specific employment in question; or

(ii) The prevailing wage level for the occupational classification in the area of intended employment;

(2) The employer will provide working conditions for such nonimmigrants that will not adversely affect the working conditions of workers similarly employed (including benefits in the nature of working conditions, which are to be offered to the nonimmigrants on the same basis and in accordance with the same criteria as the employer offers such benefits to U.S. workers);

(3) There is not a strike or lockout in the course of a labor dispute in the occupational classification at the place of employment;

(4) The employer has provided and will provide notice of the filing of the labor condition application to:

(i)(A) The bargaining representative of the employer's employees in the occupational classification in the area of intended employment for which the H–

1B nonimmigrants are sought, in the manner described in § 655.734(a)(1)(i); or

(B) If there is no such bargaining representative, affected workers by providing electronic notice of the filing of the LCA or by posting notice in conspicuous locations at the place(s) of employment, in the manner described in § 655.734(a)(1)(ii); and

(ii) H–1B nonimmigrants by providing a copy of the LCA to each H–1B nonimmigrant at the time that such nonimmigrant actually reports to work, in the manner described in § 655.734(a)(2).

(5) For applications filed regarding H–1B nonimmigrants only (and not applications regarding H–1B1 or E–3 nonimmigrants), the employer has determined its status concerning H–1B-dependency and/or willful violator (as described in § 655.736), has indicated such status, and if either such status is applicable to the employer, has indicated whether the LCA will be used only for exempt H–1B nonimmigrant(s), as described in § 655.737.

(6) The employer has provided the information about the occupation required in paragraph (c) of this section.

(e) *Change in employer's corporate structure or identity.* (1) Where an employer corporation changes its corporate structure as the result of an acquisition, merger, "spin-off," or other such action, the new employing entity is not required to file new LCAs and H–1B petitions with respect to the H–1B nonimmigrants transferred to the employ of the new employing entity (regardless of whether there is a change in the Federal Employer Identification Number (FEIN)), *provided that* the new employing entity maintains in its records a list of the H–1B nonimmigrants transferred to the employ of the new employing entity, and maintains in the public access file(s) (see § 655.760) a document containing all of the following:

(i) Each affected LCA number and its date of certification;

(ii) A description of the new employing entity's actual wage system applicable to H–1B nonimmigrant(s) who become employees of the new employing entity;

(iii) The Federal Employer Identification Number (FEIN) of the new employing entity (whether or not different from that of the predecessor entity); and

(iv) A sworn statement by an authorized representative of the new employing entity expressly acknowledging such entity's assumption of all obligations, liabilities and undertakings arising from or under attestations made in each certified and still effective LCA filed by the predecessor entity. Unless such statement is executed and made available in accordance with this paragraph, the new employing entity shall not employ any of the predecessor entity's H–1B nonimmigrants without filing new LCAs and petitions for such nonimmigrants. The new employing entity's statement shall include such entity's explicit agreement to:

(A) Abide by the DOL's H–1B regulations applicable to the LCAs;

(B) Maintain a copy of the statement in the public access file (see § 655.760); and

(C) Make the document available to any member of the public or the Department upon request.

(2) Notwithstanding the provisions of paragraph (e)(1) of this section, the new employing entity must file new LCA(s) and H–1B petition(s) when it hires any new H–1B nonimmigrant(s) or seeks extension(s) of H–1B status for existing H–1B nonimmigrant(s). In other words, the new employing entity may not utilize the predecessor entity's LCA(s) to support the hiring or extension of any H–1B nonimmigrant after the change in corporate structure.

(3) A change in an employer's H–1B-dependency status which results from the change in the corporate structure has no effect on the employer's obligations with respect to its current H–1B nonimmigrant employees. However, the new employing entity shall comply with § 655.736 concerning H–1B-dependency and/or willful-violator status and § 655.737 concerning exempt H–1B nonimmigrants, in the event that such entity seeks to hire new H–1B nonimmigrant(s) or to extend the H–1B status of existing H–1B nonimmigrants. (See § 655.736(d)(6).)

[65 FR 80212, Dec. 20, 2000, as amended at 66 FR 63301, Dec. 5, 2001; 69 FR 68228, Nov. 23, 2004; 70 FR 72562, Dec. 5, 2005; 71 FR 35521, June 21, 2006; 73 FR 19949, Apr. 11, 2008]

§ 655.731 What is the first LCA requirement, regarding wages?

An employer seeking to employ H–1B nonimmigrants in a specialty occupation or as a fashion model of distinguished merit and ability shall state on Form ETA 9035 or 9035E that it will pay the H–1B nonimmigrant the required wage rate. For the purposes of this section, "H–1B" includes "E–3 and H–1B1" as well.

(a) *Establishing the wage requirement.* The first LCA requirement shall be satisfied when the employer signs Form ETA 9035 or 9035E attesting that, for the entire period of authorized employment, the required wage rate will be paid to the H–1B nonimmigrant(s); that is, that the wage shall be the greater of the actual wage rate (as specified in paragraph (a)(1) of this section) or the prevailing wage (as specified in paragraph (a)(2) of this section). The wage requirement includes the employer's obligation to offer benefits and eligibility for benefits provided as compensation for services to H–1B nonimmigrants on the same basis, and in accordance with the same criteria, as the employer offers to U.S. workers.

(1) The *actual wage* is the wage rate paid by the employer to all other individuals with similar experience and qualifications for the specific employment in question. In determining such wage level, the following factors may be considered: Experience, qualifications, education, job responsibility and function, specialized knowledge, and other legitimate business factors. "Legitimate business factors," for purposes of this section, means those that it is reasonable to conclude are necessary because they conform to recognized principles or can be demonstrated by accepted rules and standards. Where there are other employees with substantially similar experience and qualifications in the specific employment in question—*i.e.*, they have substantially the same duties and responsibilities as the H–1B nonimmigrant—the actual wage shall be the amount paid to these other employees. Where no such other employees exist at the place of employment, the actual wage shall be the wage paid to the H–1B nonimmigrant by the employer. Where the employer's pay system or scale provides for adjustments during the period of the LCA—e.g., cost of living increases or other periodic adjustments, or the employee moves to a more advanced level in the same occupation—such adjustments shall be provided to similarly employed H–1B nonimmigrants (unless the prevailing wage is higher than the actual wage).

(2) The prevailing wage for the occupational classification in the area of intended employment must be determined as of the time of filing the application. The employer shall base the prevailing wage on the best information available as of the time of filing the application. Except as provided in this section, the employer is not required to use any specific methodology to determine the prevailing wage and may utilize a wage obtained from an OFLC NPC (OES), an independent authoritative source, or other legitimate sources of wage data. One of the following sources shall be used to establish the prevailing wage:

(i) A collective bargaining agreement which was negotiated at arms-length between a union and the employer which contains a wage rate applicable to the occupation;

(ii) If the job opportunity is in an occupation which is not covered by paragraph (a)(2)(i) of this section, the prevailing wage shall be the arithmetic mean of the wages of workers similarly employed, except that the prevailing wage shall be the median when provided by paragraphs (a)(2)(ii)(A), (b)(3)(iii)(B)(2), and (b)(3)(iii)(C)(2) of this section. The prevailing wage rate shall be based on the best information available. The following prevailing wage sources may be used:

(A) *OFLC National Processing Center (NPC) determination.* Prior to January 1, 2010, the SWA having jurisdiction over the area of intended employment shall continue to receive and process prevailing wage determination requests, but shall do so in accordance with these regulatory provisions and Department guidance. On or after January 1, 2010, the NPC shall receive and process prevailing wage determination requests in accordance with these regulations and with Department guidance. Upon receipt of a written request for a PWD on or after January 1, 2010, the

NPC will determine whether the occupation is covered by a collective bargaining agreement which was negotiated at arms length, and, if not, determine the arithmetic mean of wages of workers similarly employed in the area of intended employment. The wage component of the Bureau of Labor Statistics Occupational Employment Statistics survey shall be used to determine the arithmetic mean, unless the employer provides an acceptable survey. The NPC shall determine the wage in accordance with secs. 212(n) and 212(t) of the INA. If an acceptable employer-provided wage survey provides a median and does not provide an arithmetic mean, the median shall be the prevailing wage applicable to the employer's job opportunity. In making a PWD, the Chicago NPC will follow 20 CFR 656.40 and other administrative guidelines or regulations issued by ETA. The Chicago NPC shall specify the validity period of the PWD, which in no event shall be for less than 90 days or more than 1 year from the date of the determination.

(*1*) An employer who chooses to utilize an NPC PWD shall file the labor condition application within the validity period of the prevailing wage as specified in the PWD. Any employer desiring review of an NPC PWD, including judicial review, shall follow the appeal procedures at 20 CFR 656.41. Employers which challenge an NPC PWD under 20 CFR 656.41 must obtain a ruling prior to filing an LCA. In any challenge, the Department and the NPC shall not divulge any employer wage data collected under the promise of confidentiality. Once an employer obtains a PWD from the NPC and files an LCA supported by that PWD, the employer is deemed to have accepted the PWD (as to the amount of the wage) and thereafter may not contest the legitimacy of the PWD by filing an appeal with the CO (see 20 CFR 656.41) or in an investigation or enforcement action.

(*2*) If the employer is unable to wait for the NPC to produce the requested prevailing wage for the occupation in question, or for the CO and/or the BALCA to issue a decision, the employer may rely on other legitimate sources of available wage information as set forth in paragraphs (a)(2)(ii)(B) and (C) of this section. If the employer later discovers, upon receipt of the PWD from the NPC, that the information relied upon produced a wage below the final PWD and the employer was paying the NPC-determined wage, no wage violation will be found if the employer retroactively compensates the H–2B nonimmigrant(s) for the difference between wage paid and the prevailing wage, within 30 days of the employer's receipt of the PWD.

(*3*) In all situations where the employer obtains the PWD from the NPC, the Department will deem that PWD as correct as to the amount of the wage. Nevertheless, the employer must maintain a copy of the NPC PWD. A complaint alleging inaccuracy of an NPC PWD, in such cases, will not be investigated.

(B) *An independent authoritative source.* The employer may use an independent authoritative wage source in lieu of an NPC PWD. The independent authoritative source survey must meet all the criteria set forth in paragraph (b)(3)(iii)(B) of this section.

(C) *Another legitimate source of wage information.* The employer may rely on other legitimate sources of wage data to obtain the prevailing wage. The other legitimate source survey must meet all the criteria set forth in paragraph (b)(3)(iii)(C) of this section. The employer will be required to demonstrate the legitimacy of the wage in the event of an investigation.

(iii) For purposes of this section, "similarly employed" means "having substantially comparable jobs in the occupational classification in the area of intended employment," except that if a representative sample of workers in the occupational category can not be obtained in the area of intended employment, "similarly employed" means:

(A) Having jobs requiring a substantially similar level of skills within the area of intended employment; or

(B) If there are no substantially comparable jobs in the area of intended employment, having substantially comparable jobs with employers outside of the area of intended employment.

(iv) A prevailing wage determination for LCA purposes made pursuant to this section shall not permit an employer to pay a wage lower than required under any other applicable Federal, state or local law.

(v) Where a range of wages is paid by the employer to individuals in an occupational classification or among individuals with similar experience and qualifications for the specific employment in question, a range is considered to meet the prevailing wage requirement so long as the bottom of the wage range is at least the prevailing wage rate.

(vi) The employer shall enter the prevailing wage on the LCA in the form in which the employer will pay the wage (e.g., an annual salary or an hourly rate), except that in all cases the prevailing wage must be expressed as an hourly wage if the H–1B nonimmigrant will be employed part-time. Where an employer obtains a prevailing wage determination (from any of the sources identified in paragraphs (a)(2)(i) and (ii) of this section) that is expressed as an hourly rate, the employer may convert this determination to a yearly salary by multiplying the hourly rate by 2080. Conversely, where an employer obtains a prevailing wage (from any of these sources) that is expressed as a yearly salary, the employer may convert this determination to an hourly rate by dividing the salary by 2080.

(vii) In computing the prevailing wage for a job opportunity in an occupational classification in an area of intended employment in the case of an employee of an institution of higher education or an affiliated or related nonprofit entity, a nonprofit research organization, or a Governmental research organization as these terms are defined in 20 CFR 656.40(e), the prevailing wage level shall only take into account employees at such institutions and organizations in the area of intended employment.

(viii) An employer may file more than one LCA for the same occupational classification in the same area of employment and, in such circumstances, the employer could have H–1B employees in the same occupational classification in the same area of employment, brought into the U.S. (or accorded H–1B status) based on petitions approved pursuant to different LCAs (filed at different times) with different prevailing wage determinations. Employers are advised that the prevailing wage rate as to any particular H–1B nonimmigrant is prescribed by the LCA which supports that nonimmigrant's H–1B petition. The employer is required to obtain the prevailing wage at the time that the LCA is filed (see paragraph (a)(2) of this section). The LCA is valid for the period certified by ETA, and the employer must satisfy all the LCA's requirements (including the required wage which encompasses both prevailing and actual wage rates) for as long as any H–1B nonimmigrants are employed pursuant to that LCA (§ 655.750). Where new nonimmigrants are employed pursuant to a new LCA, that new LCA prescribes the employer's obligations as to those new nonimmigrants. The prevailing wage determination on the later/subsequent LCA does not "relate back" to operate as an "update" of the prevailing wage for the previously-filed LCA for the same occupational classification in the same area of employment. However, employers are cautioned that the actual wage component to the required wage may, as a practical matter, eliminate any wage-payment differentiation among H–1B employees based on different prevailing wage rates stated in applicable LCAs. Every H–1B nonimmigrant is to be paid in accordance with the employer's actual wage system, and thus is to receive any pay increases which that system provides.

(3) Once the prevailing wage rate is established, the H–1B employer then shall compare this wage with the actual wage rate for the specific employment in question at the place of employment and must pay the H–1B nonimmigrant at least the higher of the two wages.

(b) *Documentation of the wage statement.* (1) The employer shall develop and maintain documentation sufficient to meet its burden of proving the validity of the wage statement required in paragraph (a) of this section and attested to on Form ETA 9035 or 9035E. The documentation shall be made available to DOL upon request. Documentation shall also be made available for public examination to the extent required by § 655.760. The employer shall also document that the wage rate(s) paid to H–1B nonimmigrant(s) is(are) no less than the required wage rate(s). The documentation shall include information about the employer's wage rate(s) for all other employees for the specific employment in question at the place of employment, beginning with the date the labor condition application was submitted and continuing throughout the period of employment. The records shall be retained for the period of time specified in § 655.760. The payroll records for each such employee shall include:

(i) Employee's full name;

(ii) Employee's home address;

(iii) Employee's occupation;

(iv) Employee's rate of pay;

(v) Hours worked each day and each week by the employee if:

(A) The employee is paid on other than a salary basis (e.g., hourly, piece-rate; commission); or

(B) With respect only to H–1B nonimmigrants, the worker is a part-time employee (whether paid a salary or an hourly rate).

(vi) Total additions to or deductions from pay each pay period, by employee; and

(vii) Total wages paid each pay period, date of pay and pay period covered by the payment, by employee.

(viii) Documentation of offer of benefits and eligibility for benefits provided as compensation for services on the same basis, and in accordance with the same criteria, as the employer offers to U.S. workers (see paragraph (c)(3) of this section):

(A) A copy of any document(s) provided to employees describing the benefits that are offered to employees, the eligibility and participation rules, how costs are shared, etc. (e.g., summary plan descriptions, employee handbooks, any special or employee-specific notices that might be sent);

(B) A copy of all benefit plans or other documentation describing benefit plans and any rules the employer may have for differentiating benefits among groups of workers;

(C) Evidence as to what benefits are actually provided to U.S. workers and H–1B nonimmigrants, including evidence of the benefits selected or declined by employees where employees are given a choice of benefits;

(D) For multinational employers who choose to provide H–1B nonimmigrants with "home country" benefits, evidence of the benefits provided to the nonimmigrant before and after he/she went to the United States. See paragraph (c)(3)(iii)(C) of this section.

(2) *Actual wage*. In addition to payroll data required by paragraph (b)(1) of this section (and also by the Fair Labor Standards Act), the employer shall retain documentation specifying the basis it used to establish the actual wage. The employer shall show how the wage set for the H–1B nonimmigrant relates to the wages paid by the employer to all other individuals with similar experience and qualifications for the specific employment in question at the place of employment. Where adjustments are made in the employer's pay system or scale during the validity period of the LCA, the employer shall retain documentation explaining the change and clearly showing that, after such adjustments, the wages paid to the H–1B nonimmigrant are at least the greater of the adjusted actual wage or the prevailing wage for the occupation and area of intended employment.

(3) *Prevailing wage*. The employer also shall retain documentation regarding its determination of the prevailing wage. This source documentation shall not be submitted to ETA with the labor condition application, but shall be retained at the employer's place of business for the length of time required in § 655.760(c). Such documentation shall consist of the documentation described in paragraph (b)(3)(i), (ii), or (iii) of this section and the documentation described in paragraph (b)(1) of this section.

(i) If the employer used a wage determination issued pursuant to the provisions of the Davis-Bacon Act, 40 U.S.C. 276a *et seq.* (*see* 29 CFR part 1), or the McNamara-O'Hara Service Contract Act, 41 U.S.C. 351 *et seq.* (*see* 29 CFR part 4), the documentation shall include a copy of the determination showing the wage rate for the occupation in the area of intended employment.

(ii) If the employer used an applicable wage rate from a union contract which was negotiated at arms-length between a union and the employer, the documentation shall include an excerpt from the union contract showing the wage rate(s) for the occupation.

(iii) If the employer did not use a wage covered by the provisions of paragraph (b)(3)(i) or (b)(3)(ii) of this section, the employer's documentation shall consist of:

(A) A copy of the prevailing wage finding from the NPC for the occupation within the area of intended employment.

(B) A copy of the prevailing wage survey for the occupation within the area of intended employment published by an independent authoritative source. For purposes of this paragraph (b)(3)(iii)(B), a prevailing wage survey for the occupation in the area of intended employment published by an independent authoritative source shall mean a survey of wages published in a book, newspaper, periodical, loose-leaf service, newsletter, or other similar medium, within the 24-month period immediately preceding the filing of the employer's application. Such survey shall:

(*1*) Reflect the weighted average wage paid to workers similarly employed in the area of intended employment;

(*2*) Reflect the median wage of workers similarly employed in the area of intended employment if the survey provides such a median and does not provide a weighted average wage of workers similarly employed in the area of intended employment;

(*3*) Be based upon recently collected data—e.g., within the 24-month period immediately preceding the date of publication of the survey; and

(*4*) Represent the latest published prevailing wage finding by the independent authoritative source for the occupation in the area of intended employment; or

(C) A copy of the prevailing wage survey or other source data acquired from another legitimate source of wage information that was used to make the prevailing wage determination. For purposes of this paragraph (b)(3)(iii)(C), a prevailing wage provided by another legitimate source of such wage information shall be one which:

(*1*) Reflects the weighted average wage paid to workers similarly employed in the area of intended employment;

(*2*) Reflect the median wage of workers similarly employed in the area of intended employment if the survey provides such a median and does not provide a weighted average wage of workers similarly employed in the area of intended employment;

(*3*) Is based on the most recent and accurate information available; and

(*4*) Is reasonable and consistent with recognized standards and principles in producing a prevailing wage.

(c) *Satisfaction of required wage obligation.* (1) The required wage must be paid to the employee, cash in hand, free and clear, when due, *except that* deductions made in accordance with paragraph (c)(9) of this section may reduce the cash wage below the level of the required wage. Benefits and eligibility for benefits provided as compensation for services must be offered in accordance with paragraph (c)(3) of this section.

(2) "Cash wages paid," for purposes of satisfying the H–1B required wage, shall consist only of those payments that meet all the following criteria:

(i) Payments shown in the employer's payroll records as earnings for the employee, and disbursed to the employee, cash in hand, free and clear, when due, except for deductions authorized by paragraph (c)(9) of this section;

(ii) Payments reported to the Internal Revenue Service (IRS) as the employee's earnings, with appropriate withholding for the employee's tax paid to the IRS (in accordance with the Internal Revenue Code of 1986, 26 U.S.C. 1, *et seq.*);

(iii) Payments of the tax reported and paid to the IRS as required by the Federal Insurance Contributions Act, 26 U.S.C. 3101, *et seq.* (FICA). The employer must be able to document that the payments have been so reported to the IRS and that both the employer's and employee's taxes have been paid *except that* when the H–1B nonimmigrant is a citizen of a foreign country with which the President of the United States has entered into an agreement as authorized by section 233 of the Social Security Act, 42 U.S.C. 433 (*i.e.*, an agreement establishing a totalization arrangement between the social security system of the United States and that of the foreign country), the employer's documentation shall show that all appropriate reports have been filed and taxes have been paid in the employee's home country.

(iv) Payments reported, and so documented by the employer, as the employee's earnings, with appropriate employer and employee taxes paid to all other appropriate Federal, State, and local governments in accordance with any other applicable law.

(v) Future bonuses and similar compensation (*i.e.*, unpaid but to-be-paid) may be credited toward satisfaction of the required wage obligation if their payment is assured (*i.e.*, they are not conditional or contingent on some event such as the employer's annual profits). Once the bonuses or similar compensation are paid to the employee, they must meet the requirements of paragraphs (c)(2)(i) through (iv) of this section (*i.e.*, recorded and reported as "earnings" with appropriate taxes and FICA contributions withheld and paid).

(3) *Benefits and eligibility for benefits* provided as compensation for services (e.g., cash bonuses; stock options; paid vacations and holidays; health, life, disability and other insurance plans; retirement and savings plans) shall be offered to the H–1B nonimmigrant(s) on the same basis, and in accordance with the same criteria, as the employer offers to U.S. workers.

(i) For purposes of this section, the offer of benefits "on the same basis, and in accordance with the same criteria" means that the employer shall offer H–1B nonimmigrants the same benefit package as it offers to U.S. workers, and may not provide more strict eligibility or participation requirements for the H–1B nonimmigrant(s) than for similarly employed U.S. workers(s) (e.g., full-time workers compared to full-time workers; professional staff compared to professional staff). H–1B nonimmigrants are not to be denied benefits on the basis that they are "temporary employees" by virtue of their nonimmigrant status. An employer may offer greater or additional benefits to the H–1B nonimmigrant(s) than are offered to similarly employed U.S. worker(s), *provided* that such differing treatment is consistent with the requirements of all applicable nondiscrimination laws (e.g., Title VII of the 1964 Civil Rights Act, 42 U.S.C. 2000e–2000e17). Offers of benefits by employers shall be made in good faith and shall result in the H–1B nonimmigrant(s)'s actual receipt of the benefits that are offered by the employer and elected by the H–1B nonimmigrant(s).

(ii) The benefits received by the H–1B nonimmigrant(s) need not be identical to the benefits received by similarly employed U.S. workers(s), *provided that* the H–1B nonimmigrant is offered the same benefits package as those workers but voluntarily chooses to receive different benefits (e.g., elects to receive cash payment rather than stock option, elects not to receive health insurance because of required employee contributions, or elects to receive different benefits among an array of benefits) or, in those instances where the employer is part of a multinational corporate operation, the benefits received by the H–1B nonimmigrant are provided in accordance with an employer's practice that satisfies the requirements of paragraph (c)(3)(iii)(B) or (C) of this section. In all cases, however, an employer's practice must comply with the requirements of any applicable nondiscrimination laws (e.g., Title VII of the 1964 Civil Rights Act, 42 U.S.C. 2000e–2000e17).

(iii) If the employer is part of a multinational corporate operation (*i.e.*, operates in affiliation with business entities in other countries, whether as subsidiaries or in some other arrangement), the following three options (*i.e.*, (A), (B) or (C)) are available to the employer with respect to H–1B nonimmigrants who remain on the "home country" payroll.

(A) The employer may offer the H–1B nonimmigrant(s) benefits in accordance with paragraphs (c)(3)(i) and (ii) of this section.

(B) Where an H–1B nonimmigrant is in the U.S. for no more than 90 consecutive calendar days, the employer during that period may maintain the

H–1B nonimmigrant on the benefits provided to the nonimmigrant in his/her permanent work station (ordinarily the home country), and not offer the nonimmigrant the benefits that are offered to similarly employed U.S. workers, *provided that* the employer affords reciprocal benefits treatment for any U.S. workers (*i.e.*, allows its U.S. employees, while working out of the country on a temporary basis away from their permanent work stations in the United States, or while working in the United States on a temporary basis away from their permanent work stations in another country, to continue to receive the benefits provided them at their permanent work stations). Employers are cautioned that this provision is available only if the employer's practices do not constitute an evasion of the benefit requirements, such as where the H–1B nonimmigrant remains in the United States for most of the year, but briefly returns to the "home country" before any 90-day period would expire.

(C) Where an H–1B nonimmigrant is in the U.S. for more than 90 consecutive calendar days (or from the point where the worker is transferred to the U.S. or it is anticipated that the worker will likely remain in the U.S. more than 90 consecutive days), the employer may maintain the H–1B nonimmigrant on the benefits provided in his/her home country (*i.e.*, "home country benefits") (and not offer the nonimmigrant the benefits that are offered to similarly employed U.S. workers) *provided that* all of the following criteria are satisfied:

(*1*) The H–1B nonimmigrant continues to be employed in his/her home country (either with the H–1B employer or with a corporate affiliate of the employer);

(*2*) The H–1B nonimmigrant is enrolled in benefits in his/her home country (in accordance with any applicable eligibility standards for such benefits);

(*3*) The benefits provided in his/her home country are equivalent to, or equitably comparable to, the benefits offered to similarly employed U.S. workers (*i.e.*, are no less advantageous to the nonimmigrant);

(*4*) The employer affords reciprocal benefits treatment for any U.S. workers while they are working out of the country, away from their permanent work stations (whether in the United States or abroad), on a temporary basis (*i.e.*, maintains such U.S. workers on the benefits they received at their permanent work stations);

(*5*) If the employer offers health benefits to its U.S. workers, the employer offers the same plan on the same basis to its H–1B nonimmigrants in the United States where the employer does not provide the H–1B nonimmigrant with health benefits in the home country, or the employer's home-country health plan does not provide full coverage (*i.e.*, coverage comparable to what he/she would receive at the home work station) for medical treatment in the United States; and

(*6*) The employer offers H–1B nonimmigrants who are in the United States more than 90 continuous days those U.S. benefits which are paid directly to the worker (e.g., paid vacation, paid holidays, and bonuses).

(iv) Benefits provided as compensation for services may be credited toward the satisfaction of the employer's required wage obligation only if the requirements of paragraph (c)(2) of this section are met (e.g., recorded and reported as "earnings" with appropriate taxes and FICA contributions withheld and paid).

(4) For *salaried employees*, wages will be due in prorated installments (e.g., annual salary divided into 26 bi-weekly pay periods, where employer pays bi-weekly) paid no less often than monthly *except that*, in the event that the employer intends to use some other form of nondiscretionary payment to supplement the employee's regular/pro-rata pay in order to meet the required wage obligation (e.g., a quarterly production bonus), the employer's documentation of wage payments (including such supplemental payments) must show the employer's commitment to make such payment and the method of determining the amount thereof, and must show unequivocally that the required wage obligation was met for prior pay periods and, upon payment and distribution of such other payments that are pending, will be met for each current or future pay period. An employer that is a school or other educational

institution may apply an established salary practice under which the employer pays to H–1B nonimmigrants and U.S. workers in the same occupational classification an annual salary in disbursements over fewer than 12 months, *provided that* the nonimmigrant agrees to the compressed annual salary payments prior to the commencement of the employment and the application of the salary practice to the nonimmigrant does not otherwise cause him/her to violate any condition of his/her authorization under the INA to remain in the U.S.

(5) For *hourly-wage employees,* the required wages will be due for all hours worked and/or for any nonproductive time (as specified in paragraph (c)(7) of this section) at the end of the employee's ordinary pay period (e.g., weekly) but in no event less frequently than monthly.

(6) Subject to the standards specified in paragraph (c)(7) of this section (regarding nonproductive status), an H–1B nonimmigrant shall receive the required pay beginning on the date when the nonimmigrant "enters into employment" with the employer.

(i) For purposes of this paragraph (c)(6), the H–1B nonimmigrant is considered to "enter into employment" when he/she first makes him/herself available for work or otherwise comes under the control of the employer, such as by waiting for an assignment, reporting for orientation or training, going to an interview or meeting with a customer, or studying for a licensing examination, and includes all activities thereafter.

(ii) Even if the H–1B nonimmigrant has not yet "entered into employment" with the employer (as described in paragraph (c)(6)(i) of this section), the employer that has had an LCA certified and an H–1B petition approved for the H–1B nonimmigrant shall pay the nonimmigrant the required wage beginning 30 days after the date the nonimmigrant first is admitted into the U.S. pursuant to the petition, or, if the nonimmigrant is present in the United States on the date of the approval of the petition, beginning 60 days after the date the nonimmigrant becomes eligible to work for the employer. For purposes of this latter requirement, the H–1B nonimmigrant is considered to be eligible to work for the employer upon the date of need set forth on the approved H–1B petition filed by the employer, or the date of adjustment of the nonimmigrant's status by DHS, whichever is later. Matters such as the worker's obtaining a State license would not be relevant to this determination.

(7) *Wage obligation(s) for H–1B nonimmigrant in nonproductive status*—(i) *Circumstances where wages must be paid.* If the H–1B nonimmigrant is not performing work and is in a nonproductive status due to a decision by the employer (e.g., because of lack of assigned work), lack of a permit or license, or any other reason except as specified in paragraph (c)(7)(ii) of this section, the employer is required to pay the salaried employee the full pro-rata amount due, or to pay the hourly-wage employee for a full-time week (40 hours or such other number of hours as the employer can demonstrate to be full-time employment for hourly employees, or the full amount of the weekly salary for salaried employees) at the required wage for the occupation listed on the LCA. If the employer's LCA carries a designation of "part-time employment," the employer is required to pay the nonproductive employee for at least the number of hours indicated on the I–129 petition filed by the employer with the DHS and incorporated by reference on the LCA. If the I–129 indicates a range of hours for part-time employment, the employer is required to pay the nonproductive employee for at least the average number of hours normally worked by the H–1B nonimmigrant, provided that such average is within the range indicated; in no event shall the employee be paid for fewer than the minimum number of hours indicated for the range of part-time employment. In all cases the H–1B nonimmigrant must be paid the required wage for all hours performing work within the meaning of the Fair Labor Standards Act, 29 U.S.C. 201 *et seq.*

(ii) *Circumstances where wages need not be paid.* If an H–1B nonimmigrant experiences a period of nonproductive status due to conditions unrelated to employment which take the nonimmigrant away from his/her duties at his/her voluntary request and convenience (e.g., touring the U.S., caring for ill relative) or render the nonimmigrant unable to work (e.g., maternity leave, automobile accident which temporarily incapacitates the nonimmigrant), then the employer shall not be obligated to pay the required wage rate during that period, *provided that* such period is not subject to payment under the employer's benefit plan or other statutes such as the Family and Medical Leave Act (29 U.S.C. 2601 *et seq.*) or the Americans with Disabilities Act (42 U.S.C. 12101 *et seq.*). Payment need not be made if there has been a *bona fide* termination of the employment relationship. DHS regulations require the employer to notify the DHS that the employment relationship has been terminated so that the petition is canceled (8 CFR 214.2(h)(11)), and require the employer to provide the employee with payment for transportation home under certain circumstances (8 CFR 214.2(h)(4)(iii)(E)).

(8) If the employee works in an occupation other than that identified on the employer's LCA, the employer's required wage obligation is based on the occupation identified on the LCA, and not on whatever wage standards may be applicable in the occupation in which the employee may be working.

(9) "Authorized deductions," for purposes of the employer's satisfaction of the H–1B required wage obligation, means a deduction from wages in complete compliance with one of the following three sets of criteria (*i.e.*, paragraph (c)(9)(i), (ii), or (iii))—

(i) Deduction which is required by law (e.g., income tax; FICA); or

(ii) Deduction which is authorized by a collective bargaining agreement, or is reasonable and customary in the occupation and/or area of employment (e.g., union dues; contribution to premium for health insurance policy covering all employees; savings or retirement fund contribution for plan(s) in compliance with the Employee Retirement Income Security Act, 29 U.S.C. 1001, *et seq.*), *except that* the deduction may not recoup a business expense(s) of the employer (including attorney fees and other costs connected to the performance of H–1B program functions which are required to be performed by the employer, e.g., preparation and filing of LCA and H–1B petition); the deduction must have been revealed to the worker prior to the commencement of employment and, if the deduction was a condition of employment, had been clearly identified as such; and the deduction must be made against wages of U.S. workers as well as H–1B nonimmigrants (where there are U.S. workers); or

(iii) Deduction which meets the following requirements:

(A) Is made in accordance with a voluntary, written authorization by the employee (Note to paragraph (c)(9)(iii)(A): an employee's mere acceptance of a job which carries a deduction as a condition of employment does not constitute voluntary authorization, even if such condition were stated in writing);

(B) Is for a matter principally for the benefit of the employee (Note to paragraph (c)(9)(iii)(B): housing and food allowances would be considered to meet this "benefit of employee" standard, unless the employee is in travel status, or unless the circumstances indicate that the arrangements for the employee's housing or food are principally for the convenience or benefit of the employer (e.g., employee living at worksite in "on call" status));

(C) Is not a recoupment of the employer's business expense (e.g., tools and equipment; transportation costs where such transportation is an incident of, and necessary to, the employment; living expenses when the employee is traveling on the employer's business; attorney fees and other costs connected to the performance of H–1B program functions which are required to be performed by the employer (e.g., preparation and filing of LCA and H–1B petition)). (For purposes of this section, initial transportation from, and end-of-employment travel, to the worker's home country shall not be considered a business expense.);

(D) Is an amount that does not exceed the fair market value or the actual cost (whichever is lower) of the matter covered (Note to paragraph (c)(9)(iii)(D): The employer must document the cost and value); and

(E) Is an amount that does not exceed the limits set for garnishment of wages in the Consumer Credit Protection Act, 15 U.S.C. 1673, and the regulations of the Secretary pursuant to that Act, 29 CFR part 870, under which garnishment(s) may not exceed 25 percent of an employee's disposable earnings for a workweek.

(10) A deduction from or reduction in the payment of the required wage is not authorized (and is therefore prohibited) for the following purposes (*i.e.*, paragraphs (c)(10) (i) and (ii)):

(i) A penalty paid by the H–1B nonimmigrant for ceasing employment with the employer prior to a date agreed to by the nonimmigrant and the employer.

(A) The employer is not permitted to require (directly or indirectly) that the nonimmigrant pay a penalty for ceasing employment with the employer prior to an agreed date. Therefore, the employer shall not make any deduction from or reduction in the payment of the required wage to collect such a penalty.

(B) The employer is permitted to receive *bona fide* liquidated damages from the H–1B nonimmigrant who ceases employment with the employer prior to an agreed date. However, the requirements of paragraph (c)(9)(iii) of this section must be fully satisfied, if such damages are to be received by the employer via deduction from or reduction in the payment of the required wage.

(C) The distinction between liquidated damages (which are permissible) and a penalty (which is prohibited) is to be made on the basis of the applicable State law. In general, the laws of the various States recognize that *liquidated damages* are amounts which are fixed or stipulated by the parties at the inception of the contract, and which are reasonable approximations or estimates of the anticipated or actual damage caused to one party by the other party's breach of the contract. On the other hand, the laws of the various States, in general, consider that penalties are amounts which (although fixed or stipulated in the contract by the parties) are not reasonable approximations or estimates of such damage. The laws of the various States, in general, require that the relation or circumstances of the parties, and the purpose(s) of the agreement, are to be taken into account, so that, for example, an agreement to a payment would be considered to be a prohibited penalty where it is the result of fraud or where it cloaks oppression. Furthermore, as a general matter, the sum stipulated must take into account whether the contract breach is total or partial (*i.e.*, the percentage of the employment contract completed). (*See*, e.g., *Vanderbilt University* v. *DiNardo*, 174 F.3d 751 (6th Cir. 1999) (applying Tennessee law); *Overholt Crop Insurance Service Co.* v. *Travis*, 941 F.2d 1361 (8th Cir. 1991) (applying Minnesota and South Dakota law); *BDO Seidman* v. *Hirshberg*, 712 N.E.2d 1220 (N.Y. 1999); *Guiliano* v. *Cleo, Inc.*, 995 S.W.2d 88 (Tenn. 1999); *Wojtowicz* v. *Greeley Anesthesia Services, P.C.*, 961 P.2d 520 (Colo.Ct.App. 1998); *see generally*, Restatement (Second) Contracts § 356 (comment b); 22 Am.Jur.2d Damages §§ 683, 686, 690, 693, 703). In an enforcement proceeding under subpart I of this part, the Administrator shall determine, applying relevant State law (including consideration where appropriate to actions by the employer, if any, contributing to the early cessation, such as the employer's constructive discharge of the nonimmigrant or non-compliance with its obligations under the INA and its regulations) whether the payment in question constitutes liquidated damages or a penalty. (Note to paragraph (c)(10)(i)(C): The $500/$1,000 filing fee, if any, under section 214(c) of the INA can never be included in any liquidated damages received by the employer. *See* paragraph (c)(10)(ii), which follows.)

(ii) *A rebate of the $500/$1,000 filing fee paid by the employer, if any, under section 214(c) of the INA.* The employer may not receive, and the H–1B nonimmigrant may not pay, any part of the $500 additional filing fee (for a petition filed prior to December 18, 2000) or $1,000 additional filing fee (for a petition filed on or subsequent to December 18, 2000), whether directly or indirectly, voluntarily or involuntarily. Thus, no deduction from or reduction in wages for purposes of a rebate of any part of this fee is permitted. Further, if liquidated damages are received by the employer from the H–1B nonimmigrant upon the nonimmigrant's ceasing employment with the employer prior to a date agreed to by the nonimmigrant and the employer, such liquidated damages shall not include any part of the $500/$1,000 filing fee (*see* paragraph (c)(10)(i) of this section). If the filing fee is paid by a third party and the H–1B nonimmigrant reimburses all or part of the fee to such third party, the employer shall be considered to be in violation of this prohibition since the employer would in such circumstances have been spared the expense of the fee which the H–1B nonimmigrant paid.

(11) Any unauthorized deduction taken from wages is considered by the Department to be non-payment of that amount of wages, and in the event of an investigation, will result in back wage assessment (plus civil money penalties and/or disqualification from H–1B and other immigration programs, if willful).

(12) Where the employer depresses the employee's wages below the required wage by imposing on the employee any of the employer's business expenses(s), the Department will consider the amount to be an unauthorized deduction from wages even if the matter is not shown in the employer's payroll records as a deduction.

(13) Where the employer makes deduction(s) for repayment of loan(s) or wage advance(s) made to the employee, the Department, in the event of an investigation, will require the employer to establish the legitimacy and purpose(s) of the loan(s) or wage advance(s), with reference to the standards set out in paragraph (c)(9)(iii) of this section.

(d) *Enforcement actions.* (1) In the event that a complaint is filed pursuant to subpart I of this part, alleging a failure to meet the "prevailing wage" condition or a material misrepresentation by the employer regarding the payment of the required wage, or pursuant to such other basis for investigation as the Administrator may find, the Administrator shall determine whether the employer has the documentation required in paragraph (b)(3)of this section, and whether the documentation supports the employer's wage attestation. Where the documentation is either nonexistent or is insufficient to determine the prevailing wage (e.g., does not meet the criteria specified in this section, in which case the Administrator may find a violation of paragraph (b)(1), (2), or (3), of this section); or where, based on significant evidence regarding wages paid for the occupation in the area of intended employment, the Administrator has reason to believe that the prevailing wage finding obtained from an independent authoritative source or another legitimate source varies substantially from the wage prevailing for the occupation in the area of intended employment; or where the employer has been unable to demonstrate that the prevailing wage determined by another legitimate source is in accordance with the regulatory criteria, the Administrator may contact ETA, which shall provide the Administrator with a prevailing wage determination, which the Administrator shall use as the basis for determining violations and for computing back wages, if such wages are found to be owed. The 30-day investigatory period shall be suspended while ETA makes the prevailing wage determination and, in the event that the employer timely challenges the determination (see § 655.731(d)(2)), shall be suspended until the challenge process is completed and the Administrator's investigation can be resumed.

(2) In the event the Administrator obtains a prevailing wage from ETA pursuant to paragraph (d)(1) of this section, and the employer desires review, including judicial review, the employer shall challenge the ETA prevailing wage only by filing a request for review under § 656.41 of this chapter within 30 days of the employer's receipt of the PWD from the Administrator. If the request is timely filed, the decision of OFLC is suspended until the Center Director issues a determination on the employer's appeal. If the employer desires review, including judicial review, of the decision of the NPC Center Director, the employer shall make a request for review of the determination by the Board of Alien Labor Certification Appeals (BALCA) under § 656.41(e) of this chapter within 30 days of the receipt of the decision of the

Center Director. If a request for review is timely filed with the BALCA, the determination by the Center Director is suspended until the BALCA issues a determination on the employer's appeal. In any challenge to the wage determination, neither ETA nor the NPC shall divulge any employer wage data collected under the promise of confidentiality.

(i) Where an employer timely challenges an OFLC PWD obtained by the Administrator, the 30-day investigative period shall be suspended until the employer obtains a final ruling. Upon such a final ruling, the investigation and any subsequent enforcement proceeding shall continue, with the PWD as determined by the BALCA serving as the conclusive determination for all purposes.

(ii) [Reserved]

(3) For purposes of this paragraph (d), OFLC may consult with the NPC to ascertain the prevailing wage applicable under the circumstances of the particular complaint.

[65 FR 80214, Dec. 20, 2000, as amended at 66 FR 63302, Dec. 5, 2001; 69 FR 68228, Nov. 23, 2004; 69 FR 77384, Dec. 27, 2004; 71 FR 35521, June 21, 2006; 73 FR 19949, Apr. 11, 2008; 73 FR 78067, Dec. 19, 2008; 74 FR 45561, Sept. 3, 2009]

§ 655.732 What is the second LCA requirement, regarding working conditions?

An employer seeking to employ H–1B nonimmigrants in specialty occupations or as fashion models of distinguished merit and ability shall state on Form ETA 9035 or 9035E that the employment of H–1B nonimmigrants will not adversely affect the working conditions of workers similarly employed in the area of intended employment. For the purposes of this section, "H–1B" includes "E–3 and H–1B1" as well.

(a) *Establishing the working conditions requirement.* The second LCA requirement shall be satisfied when the employer affords working conditions to its H–1B nonimmigrant employees on the same basis and in accordance with the same criteria as it affords to its U.S. worker employees who are similarly employed, and without adverse effect upon the working conditions of such U.S. worker employees. Working conditions include matters such as hours, shifts, vacation periods, and benefits such as seniority-based preferences for training programs and work schedules. The employer's obligation regarding working conditions shall extend for the longer of two periods: the validity period of the certified LCA, or the period during which the H–1B nonimmigrant(s) is(are) employed by the employer.

(b) *Documentation of the working condition statement.* In the event of an enforcement action pursuant to subpart I of this part, the employer shall produce documentation to show that it has afforded its H–1B nonimmigrant employees working conditions on the same basis and in accordance with the same criteria as it affords its U.S. worker employees who are similarly employed.

[65 FR 80221, Dec. 20, 2000, as amended at 66 FR 63302, Dec. 5, 2001; 73 FR 19949, Apr. 11, 2008]

§ 655.733 What is the third LCA requirement, regarding strikes and lockouts?

An employer seeking to employ H–1B nonimmigrants shall state on Form ETA 9035 or 9035E that there is not at that time a strike or lockout in the course of a labor dispute in the occupational classification at the place of employment. A strike or lockout which occurs after the labor condition application is filed by the employer with DOL is covered by DHS regulations at 8 CFR 214.2(h)(17). For the purposes of this section, "H–1B" includes "E–3 and H–1B1" as well.

(a) *Establishing the no strike or lockout requirement.* The third labor condition application requirement shall be satisfied when the employer signs the labor condition application attesting that, as of the date the application is filed, the employer is not involved in a strike, lockout, or work stoppage in the course of a labor dispute in the occupational classification in the area of intended employment. Labor disputes for the purpose of this section relate only to those disputes involving employees of the employer working at the place of employment in the occupational classification named in the labor condition application. See also DHS regulations at 8 CFR 214.2(h)(17) for effects of strikes or lockouts in general on the H–1B nonimmigrant's employment.

(1) *Strike or lockout subsequent to certification of labor condition application.* In order to remain in compliance with the no strike or lockout labor condition statement, if a strike or lockout of workers in the same occupational classification as the H–1B nonimmigrant occurs at the place of employment during the validity of the labor condition application, the employer, within three days of the occurrence of the strike or lockout, shall submit to ETA, by U.S. mail, facsimile (FAX), or private carrier, written notice of the strike or lockout. Further, the employer shall not place, assign, lease, or otherwise contract out an H–1B nonimmigrant, during the entire period of the labor condition application's validity, to any place of employment where there is a strike or lockout in the course of a labor dispute in the same occupational classification as the H–1B nonimmigrant. Finally, the employer shall not use the labor condition application in support of any petition filings for H–1B nonimmigrants to work in such occupational classification at such place of employment until ETA determines that the strike or lockout has ended.

(2) *ETA notice to DHS.* Upon receiving from an employer a notice described in paragraph (a)(1) of this section, ETA shall examine the documentation, and may consult with the union at the employer's place of business or other appropriate entities. If ETA determines that the strike or lockout is covered under DHS's "*Effect of strike*" regulation for "H" visa holders, ETA shall certify to DHS, in the manner set forth in that regulation, that a strike or other labor dispute involving a work stoppage of workers in the same occupational classification as the H–1B nonimmigrant is in progress at the place of employment. See 8 CFR 214.2(h)(17).

(b) *Documentation of the third labor condition statement.* The employer need not develop nor maintain documentation to substantiate the statement referenced in paragraph (a) of this section. In the case of an investigation, however, the employer has the burden of proof to show that there was no strike or lockout in the course of a labor dispute for the occupational classification in which an H–1B nonimmigrant is employed, either at the time the application was filed or during the validity period of the LCA.

[59 FR 65659, 65676, Dec. 20, 1994, as amended at 66 FR 63302, Dec. 5, 2001; 73 FR 19949, Apr. 11, 2008]

§ 655.734 What is the fourth LCA requirement, regarding notice?

An employer seeking to employ H–1B nonimmigrants shall state on Form ETA 9035 or 9035E that the employer has provided notice of the filing of the labor condition application to the bargaining representative of the employer's employees in the occupational classification in which the H–1B nonimmigrants will be employed or are intended to be employed in the area of intended employment, or, if there is no such bargaining representative, has posted notice of filing in conspicuous locations in the employer's establishment(s) in the area of intended employment, in the manner described in this section. For the purposes of this section, "H–1B" includes "E–3 and H–1B1" as well.

(a) *Establishing the notice requirement.* The fourth labor condition application requirement shall be established when the conditions of paragraphs (a)(1) and (a)(2) of this section are met.

(1)(i) Where there is a collective bargaining representative for the occupational classification in which the H–1B nonimmigrants will be employed, on or within 30 days before the date the labor condition application is filed with ETA, the employer shall provide notice to the bargaining representative that a labor condition application is being, or will be, filed with ETA. The notice shall identify the number of H–1B nonimmigrants the employer is seeking to employ; the occupational classification in which the H–1B nonimmigrants will be employed; the wages offered; the period of employment; and the location(s) at which the H–1B nonimmigrants will be employed. Notice under this paragraph (a)(1)(i) shall include the following statement: "Complaints alleging misrepresentation of material facts in the labor condition application and/or failure to comply with the terms of the labor condition application may be filed with any office of the Wage and Hour Division of the United States Department of Labor."

(ii) Where there is no collective bargaining representative, the employer shall, on or within 30 days before the date the LCA is filed with ETA, provide a notice of the filing of the LCA. The notice shall indicate that H–1B nonimmigrants are sought; the number of such nonimmigrants the employer is seeking; the occupational classification; the wages offered; the period of employment; the location(s) at which the H–1B nonimmigrants will be employed; and that the LCA is available for public inspection at the H–1B employer's principal place of business in the U.S. or at the worksite. The notice shall also include the statement: "Complaints alleging misrepresentation of material facts in the labor condition application and/or failure to comply with the terms of the labor condition application may be filed with any office of the Wage and Hour Division of the United States Department of Labor." If the employer is an H–1B-dependent employer or a willful violator, and the LCA is not being used only for exempt H–1B nonimmigrants, the notice shall also set forth the nondisplacement and recruitment obligations to which the employer has attested, and shall include the following additional statement: "Complaints alleging failure to offer employment to an equally or better qualified U.S. applicant or an employer's misrepresentation regarding such offers of employment may be filed with the Department of Justice, Civil Rights Division, Office of Special Counsel for Immigration-Related Unfair Employment Practices, 950 Pennsylvania Avenue, NW., Washington, DC 20530, Telephone: 1 (800) 255–8155 (employers), 1 (800) 255–7688 (employees); Web address: *http://www.usdoj.gov/crt/osc*." The notice shall be provided in one of the two following manners:

(A) *Hard copy notice*, by posting a notice in at least two conspicuous locations at each place of employment where any H–1B nonimmigrant will be employed (whether such place of employment is owned or operated by the employer or by some other person or entity).

(*1*) The notice shall be of sufficient size and visibility, and shall be posted in two or more conspicuous places so that workers in the occupational classification at the place(s) of employment can easily see and read the posted notice(s).

(*2*) Appropriate locations for posting the notices include, but are not limited to, locations in the immediate proximity of wage and hour notices required by 29 CFR 516.4 or occupational safety and health notices required by 29 CFR 1903.2(a).

(*3*) The notices shall be posted on or within 30 days before the date the labor condition application is filed and shall remain posted for a total of 10 days.

(B) *Electronic notice*, by providing electronic notification to employees in the occupational classification (including both employees of the H–1B employer and employees of another person or entity which owns or operates the place of employment) for which H–1B nonimmigrants are sought, at each place of employment where any H–1B nonimmigrant will be employed. Such notification shall be given on or within 30 days before the date the labor condition application is filed, and shall be available to the affected employees for a total of 10 days, except that if employees are provided individual, direct notice (as by e-mail), notification only need be given once during the required time period. Notification shall be readily available to the affected employees. An employer may accomplish this by any means it ordinarily uses to communicate with its workers about job vacancies or promotion opportunities, including through its "home page" or "electronic bulletin board" to employees who have, as a practical matter, direct access to these resources; or through e-mail or an actively circulated electronic message such as the employer's newsletter. Where affected employees at the place of employment are not on the "intranet" which provides direct access to the home page or other electronic site but do have computer access readily available, the employer may provide notice to such workers by direct electronic communication such as e-mail (*i.e.*, a single, personal e-mail message to each such employee) or by arranging to have the notice appear for 10 days on an intranet which includes the affected employees (e.g., contractor arranges to have notice on customer's intranet accessible to affected employees). Where employees lack practical computer access, a hard copy must be posted in accordance with paragraph (a)(1)(ii)(A) of this section, or the employer may provide employees individual copies of the notice.

(2) Where the employer places any H–1B nonimmigrant(s) at one or more worksites not contemplated at the time of filing the application, but which are within the area of intended employment listed on the LCA, the employer is required to post electronic or hard-copy notice(s) at such worksite(s), in the manner described in paragraph (a)(1) of this section, on or before the date any H–1B nonimmigrant begins work.

(3) The employer shall, no later than the date the H–1B nonimmigrant reports to work at the place of employment, provide the H–1B nonimmigrant with a copy of the LCA (Form ETA 9035, or Form ETA 9035E) certified by ETA and signed by the employer (or by the employer's authorized agent or representative). Upon request, the employer shall provide the H–1B nonimmigrant with a copy of the cover pages, Form ETA 9035CP.

(b) *Documentation of the fourth labor condition statement.* The employer shall develop and maintain documentation sufficient to meet its burden of proving the validity of the statement referenced in paragraph (a) of this section and attested to on Form ETA 9035 or 9035E. Such documentation shall include a copy of the dated notice and the name and address of the collective bargaining representative to whom the notice was provided. Where there is no collective bargaining representative, the employer shall note and retain the dates when, and locations where, the notice was posted and shall retain a copy of the posted notice.

(c) *Records retention; records availability.* The employer's documentation shall not be submitted to ETA with the labor condition application, but shall be retained for the period of time specified in § 655.760(c) of this part. The documentation shall be made available for public examination as required in § 655.760(a) of this part, and shall be made available to DOL upon request.

[65 FR 65659, 65676, Dec. 20, 1994, as amended at 65 FR 80221, Dec. 20, 2000; 66 FR 63302, Dec. 5, 2001; 70 FR 72563, Dec. 5, 2005; 73 FR 19949, Apr. 11, 2008]

§ 655.735 What are the special provisions for short-term placement of H–1B nonimmigrants at place(s) of employment outside the area(s) of intended employment listed on the LCA?

This section does not apply to E–3 and H–1B1 nonimmigrants.

(a) Subject to the conditions specified in this section, an employer may make short-term placements or assignments of H–1B nonimmigrant(s) at worksite(s) (place(s) of employment) in areas not listed on the employer's approved LCA(s) without filing new labor condition application(s) for such area(s).

(b) The following conditions must be fully satisfied by an employer during all short-term placement(s) or assignment(s) of H–1B nonimmigrant(s) at worksite(s) (place(s) of employment) in areas not listed on the employer's approved LCA(s):

(1) The employer has fully satisfied the requirements of §§ 655.730 through 655.734 with regard to worksite(s) located within the area(s) of intended employment listed on the employer's LCA(s).

(2) The employer shall not place, assign, lease, or otherwise contract out any H–1B nonimmigrant(s) to any worksite where there is a strike or lockout in the course of a labor dispute in the same occupational classification(s) as that of the H–1B nonimmigrant(s).

(3) For every day the H–1B nonimmigrant(s) is placed or assigned outside the area(s) of employment listed on the approved LCA(s) for such worker(s), the employer shall:

(i) Continue to pay such worker(s) the required wage (based on the prevailing wage at such worker's(s') permanent worksite, or the employer's actual wage, whichever is higher);

(ii) Pay such worker(s) the actual cost of lodging (for both workdays and non-workdays); and

(iii) Pay such worker(s) the actual cost of travel, meals and incidental or miscellaneous expenses (for both workdays and non-workdays).

(c) An employer's short-term placement(s) or assignment(s) of H–1B nonimmigrant(s) at any worksite(s) in an area of employment not listed on the employer's approved LCA(s) shall not exceed a total of 30 workdays in a one-year period for any H–1B nonimmigrant at any worksite or combination of worksites in the area, *except that* such placement or assignment of an H–1B nonimmigrant may be for longer than 30 workdays but for no more than a total of 60 workdays in a one-year period where the employer is able to show the following:

(1) The H–1B nonimmigrant continues to maintain an office or work station at his/her permanent worksite (e.g., the worker has a dedicated workstation and telephone line(s) at the permanent worksite);

(2) The H–1B nonimmigrant spends a substantial amount of time at the permanent worksite in a one-year period; and

(3) The H–1B nonimmigrant's U.S. residence or place of abode is located in the area of the permanent worksite and not in the area of the short-term worksite(s) (e.g., the worker's personal mailing address; the worker's lease for an apartment or other home; the worker's bank accounts; the worker's automobile driver's license; the residence of the worker's dependents).

(d) For purposes of this section, the term *workday* shall mean any day on which an H–1B nonimmigrant performs any work at any worksite(s) within the area of short-term placement or assignment. For example, three workdays would be counted where a nonimmigrant works three non-consecutive days at three different worksites (whether or not the employer owns or controls such worksite(s)), within the same area of employment. Further, for purposes of this section, the term *one-year period* shall mean the calendar year (*i.e.*, January 1 through December 31) or the employer's fiscal year, whichever the employer chooses.

(e) The employer may not make short-term placement(s) or assignment(s) of H–1B nonimmigrant(s) under this section at worksite(s) in any area of employment for which the employer has a certified LCA for the occupational classification. Further, an H–1B nonimmigrant entering the U.S. is required to be placed at a worksite in accordance with the approved petition and supporting LCA; thus, the nonimmigrant's initial placement or assignment cannot be a short-term placement under this section. In addition, the employer may not continuously rotate H–1B nonimmigrants on short-term placement or assignment to an area of employment in a manner that would defeat the purpose of the short-term placement option, which is to provide the employer with flexibility in assignments to afford enough time to obtain an approved LCA for an area where it intends to have a continuing presence (e.g., an employer may not rotate H–1B nonimmigrants to an area of employment for 20-day periods, with the result that nonimmigrants are continuously or virtually continuously employed in the area of employment, in order to avoid filing an LCA; such an employer would violate the short-term placement provisions).

(f) Once any H–1B nonimmigrant's short-term placement or assignment has reached the workday limit specified in paragraph (c) of this section in an area of employment, the employer shall take one of the following actions:

(1) File an LCA and obtain ETA certification, and thereafter place any H–1B nonimmigrant(s) in that occupational classification at worksite(s) in that area pursuant to the LCA (*i.e.*, the employer shall perform all actions required in connection with such LCA, including determination of the prevailing wage and notice to workers); or

(2) Immediately terminate the placement of any H–1B nonimmigrant(s) who reaches the workday limit in an area of employment. No worker may exceed the workday limit within the one-year period specified in paragraph (d) of this section, unless the employer first files an LCA for the occupational classification for the area of employment. Employers are cautioned that if any worker exceeds the workday limit

within the one-year period, then the employer has violated the terms of its LCA(s) and the regulations in the subpart, and thereafter the short-term placement option cannot be used by the employer for H–1B nonimmigrants in that occupational classification in that area of employment.

(g) An employer is not required to use the short-term placement option provided by this section, but may choose to make each placement or assignment of an H–1B nonimmigrant at worksite(s) in a new area of employment pursuant to a new LCA for such area. Further, an employer which uses the short-term placement option is not required to continue to use the option. Such an employer may, at any time during the period identified in paragraphs (c) and (d) of this section, file an LCA for the new area of employment (performing all actions required in connection with such LCA); upon certification of such LCA, the employer's obligation to comply with this section concerning short-term placement shall terminate. (However, see § 655.731(c)(9)(iii)(C) regarding payment of business expenses for employee's travel on employer's business.)

[65 FR 80222, Dec. 20, 2000, as amended at 73 FR 19949, Apr. 11, 2008]

§ 655.736 What are H–1B-dependent employers and willful violators?

Two attestation obligations apply only to two types of employers: H–1B-dependent employers (as described in paragraphs (a) through (e) of this section) and employers found to have willfully violated their H–1B obligations within a certain five-year period (as described in paragraph (f) of this section). These obligations apply only to certain labor condition applications filed by such employers (as described in paragraph (g) of this section), and do not apply to LCAs filed by such employers solely for the employment of "exempt" H–1B nonimmigrants (as described in paragraph (g) of this section and § 655.737). These obligations require that such employers not displace U.S. workers from jobs (as described in § 655.738) and that such employers recruit U.S. workers before hiring H–1B nonimmigrants (as described in § 655.739).

(a) *What constitutes an "H–1B-dependent" employer?* (1) "H–1B-dependent employer," for purposes of THIS subpart H and subpart I of this part, means an employer that meets one of the three following standards, which are based on the ratio between the employer's total work force employed in the U.S. (including both U.S. workers and H–1B nonimmigrants, and measured according to full-time equivalent employees) and the employer's H–1B nonimmigrant employees (a "head count" including both full-time and part-time H–1B employees)—

(i)(A) The employer has 25 or fewer full-time equivalent employees who are employed in the U.S.; and

(B) Employs more than seven H–1B nonimmigrants;

(ii)(A) The employer has at least 26 but not more than 50 full-time equivalent employees who are employed in the U.S.; and

(B) Employs more than 12 H–1B nonimmigrant; or

(iii)(A) The employer has at least 51 full-time equivalent employees who are employed in the U.S.; and

(B) Employs H–1B nonimmigrants in a number that is equal to at least 15 percent of the number of such full-time equivalent employees.

(2) *"Full-time equivalent employees" (FTEs)*, for purposes of paragraph (a) of this section are to be determined according to the following standards:

(i) The determination of FTEs is to include only persons employed by the employer (as defined in § 655.715), and does not include *bona fide* consultants and independent contractors. For purposes of this section, the Department will accept the employer's designation of persons as "employees," provided that such persons are consistently treated as "employees" for all purposes including FICA, FLSA, etc.

(ii) The determination of FTEs is to be based on the following records:

(A) To determine the number of employees, the employer's quarterly tax statement (or similar document) is to be used (assuming there is no issue as to whether all employees are listed on the tax statement); and

(B) To determine the number of hours of work by part-time employees, for purposes of aggregating such employees to FTEs, the last payroll (or the payrolls over the previous quarter, if the last payroll is not representative) is to be used, or where hours of work records are not maintained, other available information is to be used to make a reasonable approximation of hours of work (such as a standard work schedule). (But see paragraph (a)(2)(iii)(B)(*1*) of this section regarding the determination of FTEs for part-time employees without a computation of the hours worked by such employees.)

(iii) *The FTEs employed by the employer* means the total of the two numbers yielded by paragraphs (a)(2)(iii)(A) and (B), which follow:

(A) The number of full-time employees. A full-time employee is one who works 40 or more hours per week, unless the employer can show that less than 40 hours per week is full-time employment in its regular course of business (however, in no event would less than 35 hours per week be considered to be full-time employment). Each full-time employee equals one FTE (e.g., 50 full-time employees would yield 50 FTEs). (Note to paragraph (a)(2)(iii)(A): An employee who commonly works more than the number of hours constituting full-time employment cannot be counted as more than one FTE.); plus

(B) The part-time employees aggregated to a number of full-time equivalents, if the employer has part-time employees. For purposes of this determination, a part-time employee is one who regularly works fewer than the number of hours per week which constitutes full-time employment (e.g., employee regularly works 20 hours, where full-time employment is 35 hours per week). The aggregation of part-time employees to FTEs may be performed by either of the following methods (*i.e.*, paragraphs (a)(2)(iii)(B)(*1*) or (*2*)):

(*1*) Each employee working fewer than full-time hours counted as one-half of an FTE, with the total rounded to the next higher whole number (e.g., three employees working fewer than 35 hours per week, where full-time employment is 35 hours, would yield two FTEs (*i.e.*, 1.5 rounded to 2)); or

(*2*) The total number of hours worked by all part-time employees in the representative pay period, divided by the number of hours per week that constitute full-time employment, with the quotient rounded to the nearest whole number (e.g., 72 total hours of work by three part-time employees, divided by 40 (hours per week constituting full-time employment), would yield two FTEs (*i.e.*, 1.8 rounded to 2)).

(iv) *Examples of determinations of FTEs:* Employer A has 100 employees, 70 of whom are full-time (with full-time employment shown to be 44 hours of work per week) and 30 of whom are part-time (with a total of 1004 hours of work by all 30 part-time employees during the representative pay period). Utilizing the method in paragraph (a)(2)(iii)(B)(*1*) of this section, this employer would have 85 FTEs: 70 FTEs for full-time employees, plus 15 FTEs for part-time employees (*i.e.*, each of the 30 part-time employees counted as one-half of a full-time employee, as described in paragraph (a)(2)(iii)(B)(*1*) of this section). (This employer would have 23 FTEs for part-time employees, if these FTEs were computed as described in paragraph (a)(2)(iii)(B)(*2*) of this section: 1004 total hours of work by part-time employees, divided by 44 (full-time employment), yielding 22.8, rounded to 23)). Employer B has 100 employees, 80 of whom are full-time (with full-time employment shown to be 40 hours of work per week) and 20 of whom are part-time (with a total of 630 hours of work by all 30 part-time employees during the representative pay period). This employer would have 90 FTEs: 80 FTEs for full-time employees, plus 10 FTEs for part-time employees (*i.e.*, each of the 20 part-time employees counted as one-half of a full-time employee, as described in paragraph (a)(2)(iii)(B)(*1*) of this section) (This employer would have 16 FTEs for part-time employees, if these FTEs were computed as described in paragraph (a)(2)(iii)(B)(*2*) of this section: 630 total hours of work by part-time employees, divided by 40 (full-time employment), yielding 15.7, rounded to 16)).

(b) *What constitutes an "employer" for purposes of determining H–1B-dependency status?* Any group treated as a single employer under the Internal Revenue

Code (IRC) at 26 U.S.C. 414(b), (c), (m) or (o) shall be treated as a single employer for purposes of the determination of H–1B-dependency. Therefore, if an employer satisfies the requirements of the IRC and relevant regulations with respect to the following groups of employees, those employees will be treated as employees of a single employer for purposes of determining whether that employer is an H–1B-dependent employer.

(1) Pursuant to section 414(b) of the IRC and related regulations, all employees "within a controlled group of corporations" (within the meaning of section 1563(a) of the IRC, determined without regard to section 1563(a)(4) and (e)(3)(C)), will be treated as employees of a single employer. A *controlled group of corporations* is a parent-subsidiary-controlled group, a brother-sister-controlled group, or a combined group. 26 U.S.C. 1563(a), 26 CFR 1.414(b)–1(a).

(i) A *parent-subsidiary-controlled group* is one or more chains of corporations connected through stock ownership with a common parent corporation where at least 80 percent of the stock (by voting rights or value) of each subsidiary corporation is owned by one or more of the other corporations (either another subsidiary or the parent corporation), and the common parent corporation owns at least 80 percent of the stock of at least one subsidiary.

(ii) A *brother-sister-controlled group* is a group of corporations in which five or fewer persons (individuals, estates, or trusts) own 80 percent or more of the stock of the corporations and certain other ownership criteria are satisfied.

(iii) A *combined group* is a group of three or more corporations, each of which is a member of a parent-subsidiary controlled group or a brother-sister-controlled group and one of which is a common parent corporation of a parent-subsidiary-controlled group and is also included in a brother-sister-controlled group.

(2) Pursuant to section 414(c) of the IRC and related regulations, all employees of trades or businesses (whether or not incorporated) that are under common control are treated as employees of a single employer. 26 U.S.C. 414(c), 26 CFR 1.414(c)–2.

(i) Trades or businesses are under common control if they are included in:

(A) A parent-subsidiary group of trades or businesses;

(B) A brother-sister group of trades or businesses; or

(C) A combined group of trades or businesses.

(ii) Trades or businesses include sole proprietorships, partnerships, estates, trusts or corporations.

(iii) The standards for determining whether trades or businesses are under common control are similar to standards that apply to controlled groups of corporations. However, pursuant to 26 CFR 1.414(c)–2(b)(2), ownership of at least an 80 percent interest in the profits or capital interest of a partnership or the actuarial value of a trust or estate constitutes a controlling interest in a trade or business.

(3) Pursuant to section 414(m) of the IRC and related regulations, all employees of the members of an affiliated service group are treated as employees of a single employer. 26 U.S.C. 414(m).

(i) An *affiliated service group* is, generally, a group consisting of a service organization (the "first organization"), such as a health care organization, a law firm or an accounting firm, and one or more of the following:

(A) A second service organization that is a shareholder or partner in the first organization and that regularly performs services for the first organization (or is regularly associated with the first organization in performing services for third persons); or

(B) Any other organization if:

(*1*) A significant portion of the second organization's business is the performance of services for the first organization (or an organization described in paragraph (b)(3)(i) of this section or for both) of a type historically performed in such service field by employees, and

(*2*) Ten percent or more of the interest in the second organization is held by persons who are highly compensated employees of the first organization (or an organization described in paragraph (b)(3)(i) of this section).

(ii) [Reserved]

(4) Section 414(o) of the IRC provides that the Department of the Treasury may issue regulations addressing other

business arrangements, including employee leasing, in which a group of employees are treated as employed by the same employer. However, the Department of the Treasury has not issued any regulations under this provision. Therefore, that section of the IRC will not be taken into account in determining what groups of employees are considered employees of a single employer for purposes of H–1B dependency determinations, unless regulations are issued by the Treasury Department during the period the dependency provisions of the ACWIA are effective.

(5) The definitions of "single employer" set forth in paragraphs (b)(1) through (b)(3) of this section are established by the Internal Revenue Service (IRS) in regulations located at 26 CFR 1.414(b)–1(a), (c)–2 and (m)–5. Guidance on these definitions should be sought from those regulations or from the IRS.

(c) *Which employers are required to make determinations of H–1B-dependency status?* Every employer that intends to file an LCA regarding H–1B nonimmigrants or to file H–1B petition(s) or request(s) for extension(s) of H–1B status from January 19, 2001 through September 30, 2003, and after March 7, 2005, is required to determine whether it is an H–1B-dependent employer or a willful violator which, except as provided in § 655.737, will be subject to the additional obligations for H–1B-dependent employers (see paragraph (g) of this section). No H–1B-dependent employer or willful violator may use an LCA filed before January 19, 2001, and during the period of October 1, 2003 through March 7, 2005, to support a new H–1B petition or request for an extension of status. Furthermore, on all H–1B LCAs filed from January 19, 2001 through September 30, 2003, and on or after March 8, 2005, an employer will be required to attest whether it is an H–1B-dependent employer or willful violator. An employer that attests it is non-H–1B-dependent but does not meet the "snap shot" test set forth in paragraph (c)(2) of this section shall make and document a full calculation of its status. However, as explained in paragraphs (c)(1) and (2) of this section, which follow, most employers would not be required to make any calculations or to create any documentation as to the determination of their H–1B status.

(1) *Employers with readily apparent status concerning H–1B-dependency need not calculate that status.* For most employers, regardless of their size, H–1B-dependency status (*i.e.*, H–1B-dependent or non-H–1B-dependent) is readily apparent and would require no calculations, in that the ratio of H–1B employees to the total workforce is obvious and can easily be compared to the definition of "H–1B-dependency" (see definition set out in paragraph (a)(1) of this section).

For example: Employer A with 20 employees, only one of whom is an H–1B nonimmigrant, would obviously not be H–1B-dependent and would not need to make calculations to confirm that status. Employer B with 45 employees, 30 of whom are H–1B nonimmigrants, would obviously be H–1B-dependent and would not need to make calculations. Employer C with 500 employees, only 30 of whom are H–1B nonimmigrants, would obviously not be H–1B-dependent and would not need to make calculations. Employer D with 1,000 employees, 850 of whom are H–1B nonimmigrants, would obviously be H–1B-dependent and would not have to make calculations.

(2) *Employers with borderline H–1B-dependency status may use a "snap-shot" test to determine whether calculation of that status is necessary.* Where an employer's H–1B-dependency status (*i.e.*, H–1B-dependent or non-H–1B-dependent) is not readily apparent, the employer may use one of the following tests to determine whether a full calculation of the status is needed:

(i) *Small employer* (50 or fewer employees). If the employer has 50 or fewer employees (both full-time and part-time, including H–1B nonimmigrants and U.S. workers), then the employer may compare the number of its H–1B nonimmigrant employees (both full-time and part-time) to the numbers specified in the definition set out in paragraph (a)(1) of this section, and shall fully calculate its H–1B-dependency status (*i.e.*, calculate FTEs) where the number of its H–1B nonimmigrant employees is above the number specified in the definition. In other words, if the employer has 25 or fewer employees, and more than seven of them are

H–1B nonimmigrants, then the employer shall fully calculate its status; if the employer has at least 26 but no more than 50 employees, and more than 12 of them are H–1B nonimmigrants, then the employer shall fully calculate its status.

(ii) *Large employer* (51 or more employees). If the number of H–1B nonimmigrant employees (both full-time and part-time), divided by the number of full-time employees (including H–1B nonimmigrants and U.S. workers), is 0.15 or more, then an employer which believes itself to be non-H–1B-dependent shall fully calculate its H–1B-dependency status (including the calculation of FTEs). In other words, if the number of full-time employees (including H–1B nonimmigrants and U.S. workers) multiplied by 0.15 yields a number that is equal to or less than the number of H–1B nonimmigrant employees (both full-time and part-time), then the employer shall attest that it is H–1B-dependent or shall fully calculate its H–1B dependency status (including the calculation of FTEs).

(d) *What documentation is the employer required to make or maintain, concerning its determination of H–1B-dependency status?* All employers are required to retain copies of H–1B petitions and requests for extensions of H–1B status filed with the DHS, as well as the payroll records described in §655.731(b)(1). The nature of any additional documentation would depend upon the general characteristics of the employer's workforce, as described in paragraphs (d)(1) through (4), which follow.

(1) *Employer with readily apparent status concerning H–1B-dependency.* If an employer's H–1B-dependency status (*i.e.*, H–1B-dependent or non-H–1B-dependent) is readily apparent (as described in paragraph (c)(1) of this section), then that status must be reflected on the employer's LCA but the employer is not required to make or maintain any particular documentation. The public access file maintained in accordance with §655.760 would show the H–1B-dependency status, by means of copy(ies) of the LCA(s). In the event of an enforcement action pursuant to subpart I of this part, the employer's readily apparent status could be verified through records to be made available to the Administrator (e.g., copies of H–1B petitions; payroll records described in §655.731(b)(1)).

(2) *Employer with borderline H–1B-dependency status.* An employer which uses a "snap-shot" test to determine whether it should undertake a calculation of its H–1B-dependency status (as described in paragraph (c)(2) of this section) is not required to make or maintain any documentation of that "snap-shot" test. The employer's status must be reflected on the LCA(s), which would be available in the public access file. In the event of an enforcement action pursuant to subpart I of this part, the employer's records to be made available to the Administrator would enable the employer to show and the Administrator to verify the "snap-shot" test (e.g., copies of H–1B petitions; payroll records described in §655.731(b)(1)) .

(3) *Employer with H–1B-dependent status.* An employer which attests that it is H–1B-dependent—whether that status is readily apparent or is determined through calculations—is not required to make or maintain any documentation of the calculation. The employer's status must be reflected on the LCA(s), which would be available in the public access file. In the event of an enforcement action pursuant to subpart I of this part, the employer's designation of H–1B-dependent status on the LCA(s) would be conclusive and sufficient documentation of that status (except where the employer's status had altered to non-H–1B-dependent and had been appropriately documented, as described in paragraph (d)(5)(ii) of this section).

(4) *Employer with non-H–1B-dependent status who is required to perform full calculation.* An employer which attests that it is non-H–1B-dependent and does not meet the "snap shot" test set forth in paragraph (c)(2) of this section shall retain in its records a dated copy of its calculation that it is not H–1B-dependent. In the event of an enforcement action pursuant to subpart I of this part, the employer's records to be made available to the Administrator would enable the employer to show and the Administrator to verify the employer's

determination (e.g., copies of H–1B petitions; payroll records described in § 655.731(b)(1)).

(5) *Employer which changes its H–1B-dependency status due to changes in workforce.* An employer may experience a change in its H–1B-dependency status, due to changes in the ratio of H–1B nonimmigrant to U.S. workers in its workforce. Thus it is important that employers who wish to file a new LCA or a new H–1B petition or request for extension of status remain cognizant of their dependency status and do a re-check of such status if the make-up of their workforce changes sufficiently that their dependency status might possibly change. In the event of such a change of status, the following standards will apply:

(i) Change from non-H–1B-dependent to H–1B-dependent. An employer which experiences this change in its workforce is not required to make or maintain any record of its determination of the change of its H–1B-dependency status. The employer is not required to file new LCA(s) (which would accurately state its H–1B-dependent status), unless it seeks to hire new H–1B nonimmigrants or extend the status of existing H–1B nonimmigrants (see paragraph (g) of this section).

(ii) Change from H–1B-dependent to non-H–1B-dependent. An employer which experiences this change in its workforce is required to perform a full calculation of its status (as described in paragraph (c) of this section) and to retain a copy of such calculation in its records. If the employer seeks to hire new H–1B nonimmigrants or extend the status of existing H–1B nonimmigrants (see paragraph (g) of this section), the employer shall either file new LCAs reflecting its non-H–1B-dependent status or use its existing certified LCAs reflecting an H–1B-dependency status, in which case it shall continue to be bound by the dependent-employer attestations on such LCAs. In the event of an enforcement action pursuant to subpart I of this part, the employer's records to be made available to the Administrator would enable the employer to show and the Administrator to verify the employer's determination (e.g., copies of H–1B petitions; payroll records described in § 655.731(b)(1)).

(6) *Change in corporate structure or identity of employer.* If an employer which experiences a change in its corporate structure as the result of an acquisition, merger, "spin-off," or other such action wishes to file a new LCA or a new H–1B petition or request for extension of status, the new employing entity shall redetermine its H–1B-dependency status in accordance with paragraphs (a) and (c) of this section (see paragraph (g) of this section). (See § 655.730(e), regarding change in corporate structure or identity of employer.) In the event of an enforcement action pursuant to subpart I of this part, the employer's calculations where required under paragraph (c) of this section and its records to be made available to the Administrator would enable the employer to show and the Administrator to verify the employer's determination (e.g., copies of H–1B petitions; payroll records described in § 655.731(b)(1)).

(7) *"Single employer" under IRC test.* If an employer utilizes the IRC single-employer definition and concludes that it is non-H–1B-dependent, the employer shall perform the "snap-shot" test set forth in paragraph (c)(2) of this section, and if it fails to meet that test, shall attest that it is H–1B-dependent or shall perform the full calculation of dependency status in accordance with paragraph (a) of this section. The employer shall place a list of the entities included as a "single employer" in the public access file maintained in accordance with § 766.760. In addition, the employer shall retain in its records the "snap-shot" or full calculation of its status, as appropriate (showing the number of employees of each entity who are included in the numerator and denominator of the equation, whether the employer utilizes the "snap shot" test or a complete calculation as described in paragraph (c) of this section). In the event of an enforcement action pursuant to subpart I of this part, the employer's records to be made available to the Administrator would enable the employer to show and the Administrator to verify the employer's determination (e.g., copies of H–1B petitions; payroll records described in § 655.731(b)(1)).

(e) *How is an employer's H–1B-dependency status to be shown on the LCA?* The employer is required to designate its status by marking the appropriate box on the Form ETA–9035 or 9035E (*i.e.*, either H–1B-dependent or non-H–1B-dependent). An employer which marks the designation of "H–1B-dependent" may also mark the designation of its intention to seek only "exempt" H–1B nonimmigrants on the LCA (see paragraph (g) of this section, and § 655.737). In the event that an employer has filed an LCA designating its H–1B-dependency status (either H–1B-dependent or non-H–1B-dependent) and thereafter experiences a change of status, the employer cannot use that LCA to support H–1B petitions for new nonimmigrants or requests for extension of H–1B status for existing nonimmigrants. Similarly, an employer that is or becomes H–1B-dependent cannot continue to use an LCA filed before January 19, 2001 to support new H–1B petitions or requests for extension of status. In such circumstances, the employer shall file a new LCA accurately designating its status and shall use that new LCA to support new petitions or requests for extensions of status.

(f) *What constitutes a "willful violator" employer and what are its special obligations?* (1) "*Willful violator*" or "*willful violator employer,*" for purposes of this subpart H and subpart I of this part means an employer that meets all of the following standards (*i.e.*, paragraphs (f)(1)(i) through (iii))—

(i) A finding of violation by the employer (as described in paragraph (f)(1)(ii)) is entered in either of the following two types of enforcement proceeding:

(A) A Department of Labor proceeding under section 212(n)(2) of the Act (8 U.S.C. 1182(n)(2)(C) and subpart I of this part; or

(B) A Department of Justice proceeding under section 212(n)(5) of the Act (8 U.S.C. 1182(n)(5).

(ii) The agency finds that the employer has committed either a willful failure or a misrepresentation of a material fact during the five-year period preceding the filing of the LCA; and

(iii) The agency's finding is entered on or after October 21, 1998.

(2) For purposes of this paragraph, "willful failure" means a violation which is a "willful failure" as defined in § 655.805(c).

(g) *What LCAs are subject to the additional attestation obligations?* (1) An employer that is "H–1B-dependent" (under the standards described in paragraphs (a) through (e) of this section) or is a "willful violator" (under the standards described in paragraph (f) of this section) is subject to the attestation obligations regarding displacement of U.S. workers and recruitment of U.S. workers (under the standards described in §§ 655.738 and 655.739, respectively) for all LCAs that are filed during the time period specified in paragraph (g)(2) of this section, to be used to support any petitions for new H–1B nonimmigrants or any requests for extensions of status for existing H–1B nonimmigrants. An LCA which does not accurately indicate the employer's H–1B-dependency status or willful violator status shall not be used to support H–1B petitions or requests for extensions. Further, an employer which falsely attests to non-H–1B-dependency status, or which experiences a change of status to H–1B-dependency but continues to use the LCA to support new H–1B petitions or requests for extension of status shall—despite the LCA designation of non-H–1B-dependency—be held to its obligations to comply with the attestation requirements concerning nondisplacement of U.S. workers and recruitment of U.S. workers (as described in §§ 655.738 and 655.739, respectively), as explicitly acknowledged and agreed on the LCA.

(2) During the period between January 19, 2001 through September 30, 2003, and on or after March 8, 2005, any employer that is "H–1B-dependent" (under the standards described in paragraphs (a) through (e) of this section) or is a "willful violator" (under the standards described in paragraph (f) of this section) shall file a new LCA accurately indicating that status in order to be able to file petition(s) for new H–1B nonimmigrant(s) or request(s) for extension(s) of status for existing H–1B nonimmigrant(s). An LCA filed during a period when the special attestation

obligations for H–1B dependent employers and willful violators were not in effect (that is before January 19, 2001, and from October 1, 2003 through March 7, 2005) may not be used by an H–1B dependent employer or willful violator to support petition(s) for new H–1B nonimmigrant(s) or request(s) for extension(s) of status for existing H–1B nonimmigrants.

(3) An employer that files an LCA indicating "H–1B-dependent" and/or "willful violator" status may also indicate on the LCA that all the H–1B nonimmigrants to be employed pursuant to that LCA will be "exempt H–1B nonimmigrants" as described in § 655.737. Such an LCA is not subject to the additional LCA attestation obligations, *provided that* all H–1B nonimmigrants employed under it are, in fact, exempt. An LCA which indicates that it will be used only for exempt H–1B nonimmigrants shall not be used to support H–1B petitions or requests for extensions of status for H–1B nonimmigrants who are not, in fact, exempt. Further, an employer which attests that the LCA will be used only for exempt H–1B nonimmigrants but uses the LCA to employ non-exempt H–1B nonimmigrants (through petitions and/or extensions of status) shall—despite the LCA designation of exempt H–1B nonimmigrants—be held to its obligations to comply with the attestation requirements concerning nondisplacement of U.S. workers and recruitment of U.S. workers (as described in §§ 655.738 and 655.739, respectively), as explicitly acknowledged and agreed on the LCA.

(4) The special provisions for H–1B-dependent employers and willful violator employers do not apply to LCAs filed from October 1, 2003 through March 7, 2005, or before January 19, 2001. However, all LCAs filed before October 1, 2003, and containing the additional attestation obligations described in this section and §§ 655.737 through 655.739, will remain in effect with regard to those obligations, for so long as any H–1B nonimmigrant(s) employed pursuant to the LCA(s) remain employed by the employer.

[65 FR 80223, Dec. 20, 2000; 66 FR 1375, Jan. 8, 2001, as amended at 66 FR 63302, Dec. 5, 2001; 70 FR 72563, Dec. 5, 2005]

§ 655.737 What are "exempt" H–1B nonimmigrants, and how does their employment affect the additional attestation obligations of H–1B-dependent employers and willful violator employers?

(a) An employer that is H–1B-dependent or a willful violator of the H-1B program requirements (as described in § 655.736) is subject to the attestation obligations regarding displacement of U.S. workers and recruitment of U.S. workers (as described in §§ 655.738 and 655.739, respectively) for all LCAs that are filed during the time period specified in § 655.736(g). However, these additional obligations do not apply to an LCA filed by such an employer if the LCA is used only for the employment of "exempt" H–1B nonimmigrants (through petitions and/or extensions of status) as described in this section.

(b) *What is the test or standard for determining an H–1B nonimmigrant's "exempt" status?* An H–1B nonimmigrant is "exempt" for purposes of this section if the nonimmigrant meets either of the two following criteria:

(1) Receives wages (including cash bonuses and similar compensation) at an annual rate equal to at least $60,000; or

(2) Has attained a master's or higher degree (or its equivalent) in a specialty related to the intended employment.

(c) *How is the $60,000 annual wage to be determined?* The H–1B nonimmigrant can be considered to be an "exempt" worker, for purposes of this section, if the nonimmigrant actually receives hourly wages or annual salary totaling at least $60,000 in the calendar year. The standards applicable to the employer's satisfaction of the required wage obligation are applicable to the determination of whether the $60,000 wages or salary are received (see § 655.731(c)(2) and (3)). Thus, employer contributions or costs for benefits such as health insurance, life insurance, and pension plans cannot be counted toward this $60,000. The compensation to be counted or credited for these purposes could include cash bonuses and similar payments, *provided that* such compensation is paid to the worker "cash in hand, free and clear, when due" (§ 655.731(c)(1)), meaning that the compensation has readily determinable market value, is readily convertible to cash tender, and is actually received by the employee when due (which must be within the year for which the employer seeks to count or credit the compensation toward the employee's $60,000 earnings to qualify for exempt status). Cash bonuses and similar compensation can be counted or credited toward the $60,000 for "exempt" status only if payment is assured (*i.e.*, if the payment is contingent or conditional on some event such as the employer's annual profits, the employer must guarantee payment even if the contingency is not met). The full $60,000 annual wages or salary must be received by the employee in order for the employee to have "exempt" status. The wages or salary required for "exempt" status cannot be decreased or *pro rated* based on the employee's part-time work schedule; an H–1B nonimmigrant working part-time, whose actual annual compensation is less than $60,000, would not qualify as exempt on the basis of wages, even if the worker's earnings, if projected to a full-time work schedule, would theoretically exceed $60,000 in a year. Where an employee works for less than a full year, the employee must receive at least the appropriate *pro rata* share of the $60,000 in order to be "exempt" (e.g., an employee who resigns after three months must be paid at least $15,000). In the event of an investigation pursuant to subpart I of this part, the Administrator will determine whether the employee has received the required $60,000 per year, using the employee's anniversary date to determine the one-year period; for an employee who had worked for less than a full year (either at the beginning of employment, or after his/her last anniversary date), the determination as to the $60,000 annual wages will be on a *pro rata* basis (*i.e.*, whether the employee had been paid at a rate of $60,000 per year (or $5,000 per month) including any unpaid, guaranteed bonuses or similar compensation).

(d) *How is the "master's or higher degree (or its equivalent) in a specialty related to the intended employment" to be determined?* (1) "Master's or higher degree (or its equivalent)," for purposes of this section means a foreign academic degree from an institution which is accredited or recognized under the law of the country where the degree was obtained, and which is equivalent to a master's or higher degree issued by a U.S. academic institution. The equivalence to a U.S. academic degree cannot be established through experience or through demonstration of expertise in the academic specialty (*i.e.*, no "time equivalency" or "performance equivalency" will be recognized as substituting for a degree issued by an academic institution). The DHS and the Department will consult appropriate sources of expertise in making the determination of equivalency between foreign and U.S. academic degrees. Upon the request of the DHS or the Department, the employer shall provide evidence to establish that the H–1B nonimmigrant has received the degree, that the degree was earned in the asserted field of study, including an academic transcript of courses, and that the institution from which the degree was obtained was accredited or recognized.

(2) "Specialty related to the intended employment," for purposes of this section, means that the academic degree is in a specialty which is generally accepted in the industry or occupation as an appropriate or necessary credential or skill for the person who undertakes the employment in question. A "specialty" which is not generally accepted as appropriate or necessary to the employment would not be considered to be sufficiently "related' to afford the H–1B nonimmigrant status as an "exempt H–1B nonimmigrant."

(e) *When and how is the determination of the H–1B nonimmigrant's "exempt" status to be made?* An employer that is H–1B-dependent or a willful violator (as described in § 655.736) may designate on the LCA that the LCA will be used only to support H–1B petition(s) and/or request(s) for extension of status for "exempt" H–1B nonimmigrants.

(1) If the employer makes the designation of "exempt" H–1B nonimmigrant(s) on the LCA, then the DHS—as part of the adjudication of the H–1B petition or request for extension of status—will determine the worker's

"exempt" status, since an H–1B petition must be supported by an LCA consistent with the petition (*i.e.*, occupation, area of intended employment, exempt status). The employer shall maintain, in the public access file maintained in accordance with §755.760, a list of the H–1B nonimmigrant(s) whose petition(s) and/or request(s) are supported by LCA(s) which the employer has attested will be used only for exempt H–1B nonimmigrants. In the event of an investigation under subpart I of this part, the Administrator will give conclusive effect to an DHS determination of "exempt" status based on the nonimmigrant's educational attainments (*i.e.*, master's or higher degree (or its equivalent) in a specialty related to the intended employment) unless the determination was based on false information. If the DHS determination of "exempt" status was based on the assertion that the nonimmigrant would receive wages (including cash bonuses and similar compensation) at an annual rate equal to at least $60,000, the employer shall provide evidence to show that such wages actually were received by the nonimmigrant (consistent with paragraph (c) of this section and the regulatory standards for satisfaction or payment of the required wages as described in §655.731(c)(3)).

(2) If the employer makes the designation of "exempt" H–1B nonimmigrants on the LCA, but is found in an enforcement action under subpart I of this part to have used the LCA to employ nonimmigrants who are, in fact, not exempt, then the employer will be subject to a finding that it failed to comply with the nondisplacement and recruitment obligations (as described in §§655.738 and 655.739, respectively) and may be assessed appropriate penalties and remedies.

(3) If the employer does not make the designation of "exempt" H–1B nonimmigrants on the LCA, then the employer has waived the option of not being subject to the additional LCA attestation obligations on the basis of employing only exempt H–1B nonimmigrants under the LCA. In the event of an investigation under subpart I of this part, the Administrator will not consider the question of the nonimmigrant(s)'s "exempt" status in determining whether an H–1B-dependent employer or willful violator employer has complied with such additional LCA attestation obligations.

[65 FR 80227, Dec. 20, 2000]

§655.738 What are the "non-displacement of U.S. workers" obligations that apply to H–1B-dependent employers and willful violators, and how do they operate?

An employer that is subject to these additional attestation obligations (under the standards described in §655.736) is prohibited from displacement of any U.S. worker(s)—whether directly (in its own workforce) or secondarily (at a worksite of a second employer)—under the standards set out in this section.

(a) *United States worker* (*U.S. worker*) is defined in §655.715.

(b) *Displacement*, for purposes of this section, has two components: "lay off" of U.S. worker(s), and "essentially equivalent jobs" held by U.S. worker(s) and H–1B nonimmigrant(s).

(1) *Lay off* of a U.S. worker means that the employer has caused the worker's loss of employment, other than through—

(i) Discharge of a U.S. worker for inadequate performance, violation of workplace rules, or other cause related to the worker's performance or behavior on the job;

(ii) A U.S. worker's voluntary departure or voluntary retirement (to be assessed in light of the totality of the circumstances, under established principles concerning "constructive discharge" of workers who are pressured to leave employment);

(iii) Expiration of a grant or contract under which a U.S. worker is employed, other than a temporary employment contract entered into in order to evade the employer's non-displacement obligation. The question is whether the loss of the contract or grant has caused the worker's loss of employment. It would not be a layoff where the job loss results from the expiration of a grant or contract without which there is no alternative funding or need for the U.S. worker's position on that or any other grant or contract (e.g., the expiration of a research grant that funded a project on which the worker was employed at an academic or research institution; the expiration of a staffing firm's contract with a customer where the U.S. worker was hired expressly to work pursuant to that contract and the employer has no practice of moving workers to other customers or projects upon the expiration of contract(s)). On the other hand, it would be a layoff where the employer's normal practice is to move the U.S. worker from one contract to another when a contract expires, and work on another contract for which the worker is qualified is available (e.g., staffing firm's contract with one customer ends and another contract with a different customer begins); or

(iv) A U.S. worker who loses employment is offered, as an alternative to such loss, a similar employment opportunity with the same employer (or, in the case of secondary displacement at a worksite of a second employer, as described in paragraph (d) of this section, a similar employment opportunity with either employer) at equivalent or higher compensation and benefits than the position from which the U.S. worker was discharged, regardless of whether or not the U.S. worker accepts the offer. The validity of the offer of a similar employment opportunity will be assessed in light of the following factors:

(A) The offer is a *bona fide* offer, rather than an offer designed to induce the U.S. worker to refuse or an offer made with the expectation that the worker will refuse;

(B) The offered job provides the U.S. worker an opportunity similar to that provided in the job from which he/she is discharged, in terms such as a similar level of authority, discretion, and responsibility, a similar opportunity for advancement within the organization, and similar tenure and work scheduling;

(C) The offered job provides the U.S. worker equivalent or higher compensation and benefits to those provided in the job from which he/she is discharged. The comparison of compensation and benefits includes all forms of remuneration for employment, whether or not called wages and irrespective of the time of payment (e.g., salary or hourly wage rate; profit sharing; retirement plan; expense account; use of company car). The comparison also includes such matters as cost of living differentials and relocation expenses (e.g., a New York City "opportunity" at equivalent or higher compensation and benefits offered to a worker discharged from a job in Kansas City would provide a wage adjustment from the Kansas City pay scale and would include relocation costs).

(2) *Essentially equivalent jobs.* For purposes of the displacement prohibition, the job from which the U.S. worker is laid off must be essentially equivalent to the job for which an H–1B nonimmigrant is sought. To determine whether the jobs of the laid off U.S. worker(s) and the H–1B nonimmigrant(s) are essentially equivalent, the comparison(s) shall be on a one-to-one basis where appropriate (*i.e.*, one U.S. worker left employment and one H–1B nonimmigrant joined the workforce) but shall be broader in focus where appropriate (e.g., an employer, through reorganization, eliminates an entire department with several U.S. workers and then staffs this department's function(s) with H–1B nonimmigrants). The following comparisons are to be made:

(i) *Job responsibilities.* The job of the H–1B nonimmigrant must involve essentially the same duties and responsibilities as the job from which the U.S. worker was laid off. The comparison focuses on the core elements of and competencies for the job, such as supervisory duties, or design and engineering functions, or budget and financial accountability. Peripheral, non-essential duties that could be tailored to the particular abilities of the individual workers would not be determinative in this comparison. The job responsibilities must be similar and both workers capable of performing those duties.

(ii) *Qualifications and experience of the workers.* The qualifications of the laid off U.S. worker must be substantially equivalent to the qualifications of the H–1B nonimmigrant. The comparison is to be confined to the experience and qualifications (e.g., training, education, ability) of the workers which are directly relevant to the actual performance requirements of the job, including the experience and qualifications that would materially affect a worker's relative ability to perform the job better or more efficiently. While it would be appropriate to compare whether the workers in question have "substantially equivalent" qualifications and experience, the workers need not have identical qualifications and experience (e.g., a bachelor's degree from one accredited university would be considered to be substantially equivalent to a bachelor's degree from another accredited university; 15 years experience in an occupation would be substantially equivalent to 10 years experience in that occupation). It would not be appropriate to compare the workers' relative ages, their sexes, or their ethnic or religious identities.

(iii) *Area of employment.* The job of the H–1B nonimmigrant must be located in the same area of employment as the job from which the U.S. worker was laid off. The comparison of the locations of the jobs is confined to the area within normal commuting distance of the worksite or physical location where the work of the H–1B nonimmigrant is or will be performed. For purposes of this comparison, if both such worksites or locations are within a Metropolitan Statistical Area or a Primary Metropolitan Statistical Area, they will be deemed to be within the same area of employment.

(3) The worker's rights under a collective bargaining agreement or other employment contract are not affected by the employer's LCA obligations as to non-displacement of such worker.

(c) *Direct displacement.* An H–1B-dependent or willful-violator employer (as described in § 655.736) is prohibited from displacing a U.S. worker in its own workforce (*i.e.*, a U.S. worker "employed by the employer") within the period beginning 90 days before and ending 90 days after the filing date of an H–1B petition supported by an LCA described in § 655.736(g). The following standards and guidance apply under the direct displacement prohibition:

(1) *Which U.S. workers are protected against "direct displacement"?* This prohibition covers the H–1B employer's own workforce—U.S. workers "employed by the employer"—who are employed in jobs that are essentially equivalent to the jobs for which the H–1B nonimmigrant(s) are sought (as described in paragraph (b)(2) of this section). The term "employed by the employer" is defined in § 655.715.

(2) *When does the "direct displacement" prohibition apply?* The H–1B employer is prohibited from displacing a U.S. worker during a specific period of time before and after the date on which the employer files any H-1B petition supported by the LCA which is subject to the non-displacement obligation (as described in § 655.736(g)). This protected period is from 90 days before until 90 days after the petition filing date.

(3) *What constitutes displacement of a U.S. worker?* The H–1B employer is prohibited from laying off a U.S. worker from a job that is essentially the equivalent of the job for which an H–1B nonimmigrant is sought (as described in paragraph (b)(1) of this section).

(d) *Secondary displacement.* An H–1B-dependent or willful-violator employer (as described in § 655.736) is prohibited from placing certain H–1B nonimmigrant(s) with another employer where there are indicia of an employment relationship between the nonimmigrant and that other employer (thus possibly affecting the jobs of U.S. workers employed by that other employer), unless and until the H–1B employer makes certain inquiries and/or has certain information concerning that other employer's displacement of similarly employed U.S. workers in its workforce. Employers are cautioned that even if the required inquiry of the secondary employer is made, the H–1B-dependent or willful violator employer shall be subject to a finding of a violation of the secondary displacement prohibition if the secondary employer, in fact, displaces any U.S. worker(s) during the applicable time period (see § 655.810(d)). The following standards and guidance apply under the secondary displacement prohibition:

(1) *Which U.S. workers are protected against "secondary displacement"?* This provision applies to U.S. workers employed by the other or "secondary" employer (not those employed by the H–1B employer) in jobs that are essentially equivalent to the jobs for which

certain H–1B nonimmigrants are placed with the other/secondary employer (as described in paragraph (b)(2) of this section). The term "employed by the employer" is defined in § 655.715.

(2) *Which H–1B nonimmigrants activate the secondary displacement prohibition?* Not every placement of an H–1B nonimmigrant with another employer will activate the prohibition and—depending upon the particular facts—an H–1B employer (such as a service provider) may be able to place H–1B nonimmigrant(s) at a client or customer's worksite without being subject to the prohibition. The prohibition applies to the placement of an H–1B nonimmigrant whose H–1B petition is supported by an LCA described in § 655.736(g) and whose placement with the other/secondary employer meets both of the following criteria:

(i) The nonimmigrant performs duties in whole or in part at one or more worksites owned, operated, or controlled by the other/secondary employer; and

(ii) There are indicia of an employment relationship between the nonimmigrant and the other/secondary employer. The relationship between the H–1B-nonimmigrant and the other/secondary need not constitute an "employment" relationship (as defined in § 655.715), and the applicability of the secondary displacement provision does not establish such a relationship. Relevant indicia of an employment relationship include:

(A) The other/secondary employer has the right to control when, where, and how the nonimmigrant performs the job (the presence of this indicia would suggest that the relationship between the nonimmigrant and the other/secondary employer approaches the relationship which triggers the secondary displacement provision);

(B) The other/secondary employer furnishes the tools, materials, and equipment;

(C) The work is performed on the premises of the other/secondary employer (this indicia alone would not trigger the secondary displacement provision);

(D) There is a continuing relationship between the nonimmigrant and the other/secondary employer;

(E) The other/secondary employer has the right to assign additional projects to the nonimmigrant;

(F) The other/secondary employer sets the hours of work and the duration of the job;

(G) The work performed by the nonimmigrant is part of the regular business (including governmental, educational, and non-profit operations) of the other/secondary employer;

(H) The other/secondary employer is itself in business; and

(I) The other/secondary employer can discharge the nonimmigrant from providing services.

(3) *What other/secondary employers are included in the prohibition on secondary displacement of U.S. workers by the H–1B employer?* The other/secondary employer who accepts the placement and/or services of the H–1B employer's nonimmigrant employee(s) need not be an H–1B employer. The other/secondary employer would often be (but is not limited to) the client or customer of an H–1B employer that is a staffing firm or a service provider which offers the services of H–1B nonimmigrants under a contract (e.g., a medical staffing firm under contract with a nursing home provides H–1B nonimmigrant physical therapists; an information technology staffing firm under contract with a bank provides H–1B nonimmigrant computer engineers). Only the H–1B employer placing the nonimmigrant with the secondary employer is subject to the non-displacement obligation on the LCA, and only that employer is liable in an enforcement action pursuant to subpart I of this part if the other/secondary employer, in fact, displaces any of its U.S. worker(s) during the applicable time period. The other/secondary employer will not be subject to sanctions in an enforcement action pursuant to subpart I of this part (except in circumstances where such other/secondary employer is, in fact, an H–1B employer and is found to have failed to comply with its own obligations). (Note to paragraph (d)(3): Where the other/secondary employer's relationship to the H–1B nonimmigrant constitutes "employment" for purposes of a statute other than the H–1B provision of the INA, such as the Fair Labor Standards Act (29 U.S.C. 201 *et seq.*), the

other/secondary employer would be subject to all obligations of an employer of the nonimmigrant under such other statute.)

(4) *When does the "secondary displacement" prohibition apply?* The H–1B employer's obligation of inquiry concerns the actions of the other/secondary employer during the specific period beginning 90 days before and ending 90 days after the date of the placement of the H–1B nonimmigrant(s) with such other/secondary employer.

(5) *What are the H–1B employer's obligations concerning inquiry and/or information as to the other/secondary employer's displacement of U.S. workers?* The H–1B employer is prohibited from placing the H–1B nonimmigrant with another employer, unless the H–1B employer has inquired of the other/secondary employer as to whether, and has no knowledge that, within the period beginning 90 days before and ending 90 days after the date of such placement, the other/secondary employer has displaced or intends to displace a similarly-employed U.S. worker employed by such other/secondary employer. The following standards and guidance apply to the H–1B employer's obligation:

(i) The H–1B employer is required to exercise due diligence and to make a reasonable effort to enquire about potential secondary displacement, through methods which may include (but are not limited to)—

(A) Securing and retaining a written assurance from the other/secondary employer that it has not and does not intend to displace a similarly-employed U.S. worker within the prescribed period;

(B) Preparing and retaining a memorandum to the file, prepared at the same time or promptly after receiving the other/secondary employer's oral statement that it has not and does not intend to displace a similarly-employed U.S. worker within the prescribed period (such memorandum shall include the substance of the conversation, the date of the communication, and the names of the individuals who participated in the conversation, including the person(s) who made the inquiry on behalf of the H–1B employer and made the statement on behalf of the other/secondary employer); or

(C) including a secondary displacement clause in the contract between the H–1B employer and the other/secondary employer, whereby the other/secondary employer would agree that it has not and will not displace similarly-employed U.S. workers within the prescribed period.

(ii) The employer's exercise of due diligence may require further, more particularized inquiry of the other/secondary employer in circumstances where there is information which indicates that U.S. worker(s) have been or will be displaced (e.g., where the H–1B nonimmigrants will be performing functions that the other/secondary employer performed with its own workforce in the past). The employer is not permitted to disregard information which would provide knowledge about potential secondary displacement (e.g., newspaper reports of relevant lay-offs by the other/secondary employer) if such information becomes available before the H–1B employer's placement of H–1B nonimmigrants with such employer. Under such circumstances, the H–1B employer would be expected to recontact the other/secondary employer and receive credible assurances that no lay-offs of similarly-employed U.S. workers are planned or have occurred within the prescribed period.

(e) *What documentation is required of H–1B employers concerning the non-displacement obligation?* The H–1B employer is responsible for demonstrating its compliance with the non-displacement obligation (whether direct or indirect), if applicable.

(1) Concerning *direct displacement* (as described in paragraph (c) of this section), the employer is required to retain all records the employer creates or receives concerning the circumstances under which each U.S. worker, in the same locality and same occupation as any H–1B nonimmigrant(s) hired, left its employ in the period from 90 days before to 90 days after the filing date of the employer's petition for the H–1B nonimmigrant(s), and for any such U.S. worker(s) for whom the employer has taken any action during the period from 90 days before to 90 days after the filing date of the H–1B petition to cause the U.S. worker's termination (e.g., a notice of future termination of

the employee's job). For all such employees, the H–1B employer shall retain at least the following documents: the employee's name, last-known mailing address, occupational title and job description; any documentation concerning the employee's experience and qualifications, and principal assignments; all documents concerning the departure of such employees, such as notification by the employer of termination of employment prepared by the employer or the employee and any responses thereto, and evaluations of the employee's job performance. Finally, the employer is required to maintain a record of the terms of any offers of similar employment to such U.S. workers and the employee's response thereto.

(2) Concerning *secondary displacement* (as described in paragraph (d) of this section), the H–1B employer is required to maintain documentation to show the manner in which it satisfied its obligation to make inquiries as to the displacement of U.S. workers by the other/secondary employer with which the H–1B employer places any H–1B nonimmigrants (as described in paragraph (d)(5) of this section).

[65 FR 80228, Dec. 20, 2000]

§ 655.739 What is the "recruitment of U.S. workers" obligation that applies to H–1B-dependent employers and willful violators, and how does it operate?

An employer that is subject to this additional attestation obligation (under the standards described in § 655.736) is required—prior to filing the LCA or any petition or request for extension of status supported by the LCA—to take good faith steps to recruit U. S. workers in the United States for the job(s) in the United States for which the H–1B nonimmigrant(s) is/are sought. The recruitment shall use procedures that meet industry-wide standards and offer compensation that is at least as great as the required wage to be paid to H–1B nonimmigrants pursuant to § 655.731(a) (*i.e.*, the higher of the local prevailing wage or the employer's actual wage). The employer may use legitimate selection criteria relevant to the job that are normal or customary to the type of job involved, so long as such criteria are not applied in a discriminatory manner. This section provides guidance for the employer's compliance with the recruitment obligation.

(a) "*United States worker*" ("U.S. worker") is defined in § 655.715.

(b) "*Industry,*" for purposes of this section, means the set of employers which primarily compete for the same types of workers as those who are the subjects of the H–1B petitions to be filed pursuant to the LCA. Thus, a hospital, university, or computer software development firm is to use the recruitment standards utilized by the health care, academic, or information technology industries, respectively, in hiring workers in the occupations in question. Similarly, a staffing firm, which places its workers at job sites of other employers, is to use the recruitment standards of the industry which primarily employs such workers (e.g., the health care industry, if the staffing firm is placing physical therapists (whether in hospitals, nursing homes, or private homes); the information technology industry, if the staffing firm is placing computer programmers, software engineers, or other such workers).

(c) "*Recruitment,*" for purposes of this section, means the process by which an employer seeks to contact or to attract the attention of person(s) who may apply for employment, solicits applications from person(s) for employment, receives applications, and reviews and considers applications so as to present the appropriate candidates to the official(s) who make(s) the hiring decision(s) (*i.e.*, pre-selection treatment of applications and applicants).

(d) "*Solicitation methods,*" for purposes of this section, means the techniques by which an employer seeks to contact or to attract the attention of potential applicants for employment, and to solicit applications from person(s) for employment.

(1) Solicitation methods may be either external or internal to the employer's workforce (with internal solicitation to include current and former employees).

(2) Solicitation methods may be either active (where an employer takes

positive, proactive steps to identify potential applicants and to get information about its job openings into the hands of such person(s)) or passive (where potential applicants find their way to an employer's job announcements).

(i) Active solicitation methods include direct communication to incumbent workers in the employer's operation and to workers previously employed in the employer's operation and elsewhere in the industry; providing training to incumbent workers in the employer's organization; contact and outreach through collective bargaining organizations, trade associations and professional associations; participation in job fairs (including at minority-serving institutions, community/junior colleges, and vocational/technical colleges); use of placement services of colleges, universities, community/junior colleges, and business/trade schools; use of public and/or private employment agencies, referral agencies, or recruitment agencies ("headhunters").

(ii) Passive solicitation methods include advertising in general distribution publications, trade or professional journals, or special interest publications (e.g., student-oriented; targeted to underrepresented groups, including minorities, persons with disabilities, and residents of rural areas); America's Job Bank or other Internet sites advertising job vacancies; notices at the employer's worksite(s) and/or on the employer's Internet "home page."

(e) *How are "industry-wide standards for recruitment" to be identified?* An employer is not required to utilize any particular number or type of recruitment methods, and may make a determination of the standards for the industry through methods such as trade organization surveys, studies by consultative groups, or reports/statements from trade organizations. An employer which makes such a determination should be prepared to demonstrate the industry-wide standards in the event of an enforcement action pursuant to subpart I of this part. An employer's recruitment shall be at a level and through methods and media which are normal, common or prevailing in the industry, including those strategies that have been shown to be successfully used by employers in the industry to recruit U.S. workers. An employer may not utilize only the lowest common denominator of recruitment methods used in the industry, or only methods which could reasonably be expected to be likely to yield few or no U.S. worker applicants, even if such unsuccessful recruitment methods are commonly used by employers in the industry. An employer's recruitment methods shall include, at a minimum, the following:

(1) Both internal and external recruitment (*i.e.*, both within the employer's workforce (former as well as current workers) and among U.S. workers elsewhere in the economy); and

(2) At least some active recruitment, whether internal (e.g., training the employer's U.S. worker(s) for the position(s)) or external (e.g., use of recruitment agencies or college placement services).

(f) *How are "legitimate selection criteria relevant to the job that are normal or customary to the type of job involved" to be identified?* In conducting recruitment of U.S. workers (*i.e.*, in soliciting applications and in pre-selection screening or considering of applicants), an employer shall apply selection criteria which satisfy all of the following three standards (*i.e.*, paragraph (b) (1) through (3)). Under these standards, an employer would not apply spurious criteria that discriminate against U.S. worker applicants in favor of H–1B nonimmigrants. An employer that uses criteria which fail to meet these standards would be considered to have failed to conduct its recruitment of U.S. workers in good faith.

(1) *Legitimate criteria*, meaning criteria which are legally cognizable and not violative of any applicable laws (e.g., employer may not use age, sex, race or national origin as selection criteria);.

(2) *Relevant to the job*, meaning criteria which have a nexus to the job's duties and responsibilities; and

(3) *Normal and customary to the type of job involved*, meaning criteria which would be necessary or appropriate based on the practices and expectations of the industry, rather than on the preferences of the particular employer.

(g) *What actions would constitute a prohibited "discriminatory manner" of recruitment?* The employer shall not apply otherwise-legitimate screening criteria in a manner which would skew the recruitment process in favor of H–1B nonimmigrants. In other words, the employer's application of its screening criteria shall provide full and fair solicitation and consideration of U.S. applicants. The recruitment would be considered to be conducted in a discriminatory manner if the employer applied its screening criteria in a disparate manner (whether between H–1B and U.S. workers, or between jobs where H–1B nonimmigrants are involved and jobs where such workers are not involved). The employer would also be considered to be recruiting in a discriminatory manner if it used screening criteria that are prohibited by any applicable discrimination law (e.g., sex, race, age, national origin). The employer that conducts recruitment in a discriminatory manner would be considered to have failed to conduct its recruitment of U.S. workers in good faith.

(h) *What constitute "good faith steps" in recruitment of U.S. workers?* The employer shall perform its recruitment, as described in paragraphs (d) through (g) of this section, so as to offer fair opportunities for employment to U.S. workers, without skewing the recruitment process against U.S. workers or in favor of H–1B nonimmigrants. No specific regimen is required for solicitation methods seeking applicants or for pre-selection treatment screening applicants. The employer's recruitment process, including pre-selection treatment, must assure that U.S. workers are given a fair chance for consideration for a job, rather than being ignored or rejected through a process that serves the employer's preferences with respect to the make up of its workforce (e.g., the Department would look with disfavor on a practice of interviewing H–1B applicants but not U.S. applicants, or a practice of screening the applications of H–1B nonimmigrants differently from the applications of U.S. workers). The employer shall not exercise a preference for its incumbent nonimmigrant workers who do not yet have H–1B status (e.g., workers on student visas). The employer shall recruit in the United States, seeking U.S. worker(s), for the job(s) in the United States for which H–1B nonimmigrant(s) are or will be sought.

(i) What documentation is the employer required to make or maintain, concerning its recruitment of U.S. workers?

(1) The employer shall maintain documentation of the recruiting methods used, including the places and dates of the advertisements and postings or other recruitment methods used, the content of the advertisements and postings, and the compensation terms (if such are not included in the content of the advertisements and postings). The documentation may be in any form, including copies of advertisements or proofs from the publisher, the order or confirmation from the publisher, an electronic or printed copy of the Internet posting, or a memorandum to the file.

(2) The employer shall retain any documentation it has received or prepared concerning the treatment of applicants, such as copies of applications and/or related documents, test papers, rating forms, records regarding interviews, and records of job offers and applicants' responses. To comply with this requirement, the employer is not required to create any documentation it would not otherwise create.

(3) The documentation maintained by the employer shall be made available to the Administrator in the event of an enforcement action pursuant to subpart I of this part. The documentation shall be maintained for the period of time specified in § 655.760.

(4) The employer's public access file maintained in accordance with § 655.760 shall contain information summarizing the principal recruitment methods used and the time frame(s) in which such recruitment methods were used. This may be accomplished either through a memorandum or through copies of pertinent documents.

(j) In addition to conducting good faith recruitment of U.S. workers (as described in paragraphs (a) through (h) of this section), the employer is required to have offered the job to any U.S. worker who applies and is equally or better qualified for the job than the H–1B nonimmigrant (see 8 U.S.C. 1182(n)(1)(G)(i)(II)); this requirement is enforced by the Department of Justice (see 8 U.S.C. 1182(n)(5); 20 CFR 655.705(c)).

[65 FR 80231, Dec. 20, 2000]

§ 655.740 What actions are taken on labor condition applications?

(a) *Actions on labor condition applications submitted for filing.* Once a labor condition application has been received from an employer, a determination shall be made by the ETA Certifying Officer whether to certify the labor condition application or return it to the employer not certified.

(1) *Certification of labor condition application.* Where all items on Form ETA 9035 or Form ETA 9035E have been completed, the form is not obviously inaccurate, and in the case of Form ETA 9035, it contains the signature of the employer or its authorized agent or representative, the Certifying Officer shall certify the labor condition application unless it falls within one of the categories set forth in paragraph (a)(2) of this section. The Certifying Officer shall make a determination to certify or not certify the labor condition application within 7 working days of the date the application is received and date-stamped by the Department. If the labor condition application is certified, the Certifying Officer shall return a certified copy of the labor condition application to the employer or the employer's authorized agent or representative. The employer shall file the certified labor condition application with the appropriate DHS office in the manner prescribed by DHS. The DHS shall determine whether each occupational classification named in the certified labor condition application is a specialty occupation or is a fashion model of distinguished merit and ability.

(2) *Determinations not to certify labor condition applications.* ETA shall not certify a labor condition application and shall return such application to the employer or the employer's authorized agent or representative, when either or both of the following two conditions exists:

(i) *When the Form ETA 9035 or 9035E is not properly completed.* Examples of a Form ETA 9035 or 9035E which is not properly completed include instances where the employer has failed to check all the necessary boxes; or where the employer has failed to state the occupational classification, number of nonimmigrants sought, wage rate, period of intended employment, place of intended employment, or prevailing wage and its source; or, in the case of Form ETA 9035, where the application does not contain the signature of the employer or the employer's authorized representative.

(ii) *When the Form ETA 9035 or ETA 9035E contains obvious inaccuracies.* An obvious inaccuracy will be found if the employer files an application in error—e.g., where the Administrator, Wage and Hour Division, after notice and opportunity for a hearing pursuant to subpart I of this part, has notified ETA in writing that the employer has been disqualified from employing H–1B nonimmigrants under section 212(n)(2) of the INA (8 U.S.C. 1182(n)(2)) or from employing H–1B1 or E–3 nonimmigrants under section 212(t)(3) of the INA (8 U.S.C. 1182(t)(3)). Examples of other obvious inaccuracies include stating a wage rate below the FLSA minimum wage, submitting an LCA earlier than six months before the beginning date of the period of intended employment, identifying multiple occupations on a single LCA, identifying a wage which is below the prevailing wage listed on the LCA, or identifying a wage range where the bottom of such wage range is lower than the prevailing wage listed on the LCA.

(3) *Correction and resubmission of labor condition application.* If the labor condition application is not certified pursuant to paragraph (a)(2) (i) or (ii) of this section, ETA shall return it to the employer, or the employer's authorized agent or representative, explaining the reasons for such return without certification. The employer may immediately submit a corrected application to ETA. A "resubmitted" or "corrected" labor condition application shall be treated as a new application by ETA (*i.e.*, on a "first come, first served" basis) *except that* if the labor condition application is not certified pursuant to paragraph

(a)(2)(ii) of this section because of notification by the Administrator of the employer's disqualification, such action shall be the final decision of the Secretary and no application shall be resubmitted by the employer.

(b) *Challenges to labor condition applications.* ETA shall not consider information contesting a labor condition application received by ETA prior to the determination on the application. Such information shall not be made part of ETA's administrative record on the application, but shall be referred to ESA to be processed as a complaint pursuant to subpart I of this part, and, if such application is certified by ETA, the complaint will be handled by ESA under subpart I of this part.

(c) *Truthfulness and adequacy of information.* DOL is not the guarantor of the accuracy, truthfulness or adequacy of a certified labor condition application. The burden of proof is on the employer to establish the truthfulness of the information contained on the labor condition application.

[59 FR 65659, 65676, Dec. 20, 1994, as amended at 65 FR 80232, Dec. 20, 2000; 66 FR 63302, Dec. 5, 2001; 69 FR 68228, Nov. 23, 2004; 70 FR 72563, Dec. 5, 2005; 73 FR 19949, Apr. 11, 2008]

§ 655.750 What is the validity period of the labor condition application?

(a) *Validity of certified labor condition applications.* A labor condition application (LCA) certified under § 655.740 is valid for the period of employment indicated by the authorized DOL official on Form ETA 9035E or ETA 9035. The validity period of an LCA will not begin before the application is certified. If the approved LCA is the initial LCA issued for the nonimmigrant, the period of authorized employment must not exceed 3 years for an LCA issued on behalf of an H–1B or H–1B1 nonimmigrant and must not exceed 2 years for an LCA issued on behalf of an E–3 nonimmigrant. If the approved LCA is for an extension of an H–1B1 it must not exceed two years. The period of authorized employment in the aggregate is based on the first date of employment and ends:

(1) In the case of an H–1B or initial H–1B1 LCA, on the latest date indicated or three years after the employment start date under the LCA, whichever comes first; or

(2) In the case of an E–3 or an H–1B1 extension LCA, on the latest date indicated or two years after the employment start date under the LCA, whichever comes first.

(b) *Withdrawal of certified labor condition applications.* (1) An employer who has filed a labor condition application which has been certified pursuant to § 655.740 of this part may withdraw such labor condition application at any time before the expiration of the validity period of the application, provided that:

(i) H–1B, H–1B1, and E–3 nonimmigrants are not employed at the place of employment pursuant to the LCA; and

(ii) The Administrator has not commenced an investigation of the particular application. Any such request for withdrawal shall be null and void; and the employer shall remain bound by the labor condition application until the enforcement proceeding is completed, at which time the application may be withdrawn.

(2) Requests for withdrawals must be in writing and must be sent to ETA, Office of Foreign Labor Certification. ETA will publish the mailing address, and any future mailing address changes, in the FEDERAL REGISTER, and will also post the address on the DOL Web site at *http://www.foreignlaborcert.doleta.gov/*.

(3) An employer shall comply with the "required wage rate" and "prevailing working conditions" statements of its labor condition application required under §§ 655.731 and 655.732 of this part, respectively, even if such application is withdrawn, at any time H–1B nonimmigrants are employed pursuant to the application, unless the application is superseded by a subsequent application which is certified by ETA.

(4) An employer's obligation to comply with the "no strike or lockout" and "notice" statements of its labor condition application (required under §§ 655.733 and 655.734 of this part, respectively), shall remain in effect and the employer shall remain subject to investigation and sanctions for misrepresentation on these statements even if such application is withdrawn, regardless of

whether H–1B nonimmigrants are actually employed, unless the application is superseded by a subsequent application which is certified by ETA.

(5) Only for the purpose of assuring the labor standards protections afforded under the H–1B program, where an employer files a petition with DHS under the H–1B classification pursuant to a certified LCA that had been withdrawn by the employer, such petition filing binds the employer to all obligations under the withdrawn LCA immediately upon receipt of such petition by DHS.

(c) *Invalidation or suspension of a labor condition application.* (1) Invalidation of a labor condition application shall result from enforcement action(s) by the Administrator, Wage and Hour Division, under subpart I of this part—e.g., a final determination finding the employer's failure to meet the application's condition regarding strike or lockout; or the employer's willful failure to meet the wage and working conditions provisions of the application; or the employer's substantial failure to meet the notice of specification requirements of the application; see §§ 655.734 and 655.760 of this part; or the misrepresentation of a material fact in an application. Upon notice by the Administrator of the employer's disqualification, ETA shall invalidate the application and notify the employer, or the employer's authorized agent or representative. ETA shall notify the employer in writing of the reason(s) that the application is invalidated. When a labor condition application is invalidated, such action shall be the final decision of the Secretary.

(2) Suspension of a labor condition application may result from a discovery by ETA that it made an error in certifying the application because such application is incomplete, contains one or more obvious inaccuracies, or has not been signed. In such event, ETA shall immediately notify DHS and the employer. When an application is suspended, the employer may immediately submit to the certifying officer a corrected or completed application. If ETA does not receive a corrected application within 30 days of the suspension, or if the employer was disqualified by the Administrator, the application shall be immediately invalidated as described in paragraph (c) of this section.

(3) An employer shall comply with the "required wages rate" and "prevailing working conditions" statements of its labor condition application required under §§ 655.731 and 655.732 of this part, respectively, even if such application is suspended or invalidated, at any time H–1B nonimmigrants are employed pursuant to the application, unless the application is superseded by a subsequent application which is certified by ETA.

(4) An employer's obligation to comply with the "no strike or lockout" and "notice" statements of its labor condition application (required under §§ 655.733 and 655.734 of this part, respectively), shall remain in effect and the employer shall remain subject to investigation and sanctions for misrepresentation on these statements even if such application is suspended or invalidated, regardless of whether H–1B nonimmigrants are actually employed, unless the application is superseded by a subsequent application which is certified by ETA.

(d) *Employers subject to disqualification.* No labor condition application shall be certified for an employer which has been found to be disqualified from participation, in the H–1B program as determined in a final agency action following an investigation by the Wage and Hour Division pursuant to subpart I of this part.

[59 FR 65659, 65676, Dec. 20, 1994, as amended at 65 FR 80232, Dec. 20, 2000; 66 FR 63302, Dec. 5, 2001; 70 FR 72563, Dec. 5, 2005; 73 FR 19949, Apr. 11, 2008]

§ 655.760 What records are to be made available to the public, and what records are to be retained?

Paragraphs (a)(1) thru (a)(6) and paragraphs (b) and (c) of this section also apply to the H–1B1 and E–3 visa categories.

(a) *Public examination.* The employer shall make a filed labor condition application and necessary supporting documentation available for public examination at the employer's principal place of business in the U.S. or at the place of employment within one working day after the date on which the labor condition application is filed with DOL. The following documentation shall be necessary:

(1) A copy of the certified labor condition application (Form ETA 9035E or Form ETA 9035) and cover pages (Form ETA 9035CP). If the Form ETA 9035E is submitted electronically, a printout of the certified application shall be signed by the employer and maintained in its files and included in the public examination file.

(2) Documentation which provides the wage rate to be paid the H–1B nonimmigrant;

(3) A full, clear explanation of the system that the employer used to set the "actual wage" the employer has paid or will pay workers in the occupation for which the H–1B nonimmigrant is sought, including any periodic increases which the system may provide—e.g., memorandum summarizing the system or a copy of the employer's pay system or scale (payroll records are not required, although they shall be made available to the Department in an enforcement action).

(4) A copy of the documentation the employer used to establish the "prevailing wage" for the occupation for which the H–1B nonimmigrant is sought (a general description of the source and methodology is all that is required to be made available for public examination; the underlying individual wage data relied upon to determine the prevailing wage is not a public record, although it shall be made available to the Department in an enforcement action); and

(5) A copy of the document(s) with which the employer has satisfied the union/employee notification requirements of § 655.734 of this part.

(6) A summary of the benefits offered to U.S. workers in the same occupational classifications as H–1B nonimmigrants, a statement as to how any differentiation in benefits is made where not all employees are offered or receive the same benefits (such summary need not include proprietary information such as the costs of the benefits to the employer, or the details of stock options or incentive distributions), and/or, where applicable, a statement that some/all H–1B nonimmigrants are receiving "home country" benefits (*see* § 655.731(c)(3));

(7) Where the employer undergoes a change in corporate structure, a sworn statement by a responsible official of the new employing entity that it accepts all obligations, liabilities and undertakings under the LCAs filed by the predecessor employing entity, together with a list of each affected LCA and its date of certification, and a description of the actual wage system and FEIN of the new employing entity (*see* § 655.730(e)(1)).

(8) Where the employer utilizes the definition of "single employer"in the IRC, a list of any entities included as part of the single employer in making the determination as to its H–1B-dependency status (*see* § 655.736(d)(7));

(9) Where the employer is H–1B-dependent and/or a willful violator, and indicates on the LCA(s) that only "exempt" H–1B nonimmigrants will be employed, a list of such "exempt" H–1B nonimmigrants (*see* § 655.737(e)(1));

(10) Where the employer is H–1B-dependent or a willful violator, a summary of the recruitment methods used and the time frames of recruitment of U.S. workers (or copies of pertinent documents showing this information) (*see* § 655.739(i)(4).

(b) *National lists of applications and attestations.* ETA shall compile and maintain on a current basis a list of the labor condition applications filed under INA section 212(n) regarding H–1B nonimmigrants and a list of labor attestations filed under INA section 212(t) regarding H–1B1 nonimmigrants. Each list shall be by employer, showing the occupational classification, wage rate(s), number of nonimmigrants sought, period(s) of intended employment, and date(s) of need for each employer's application. The list shall be available for public examination at the Office of Foreign Labor Certification, Department of Labor, 200 Constitution Avenue, NW., Room C–4312, Washington, DC 20210.

(c) *Retention of records.* Either at the employer's principal place of business in the U.S. or at the place of employment, the employer shall retain copies of the records required by this subpart for a period of one year beyond the last date on which any H–1B nonimmigrant is employed under the labor condition application or, if no nonimmigrants were employed under the labor condition application, one year from the date the labor condition application expired or was withdrawn. Required payroll records for the H–1B employees and other employees in the occupational classification shall be retained at the employer's principal place of business in the U.S. or at the place of employment for a period of three years from the date(s) of the creation of the record(s), except that if an enforcement action is commenced, all payroll records shall be retained until the enforcement proceeding is completed through the procedures set forth in subpart I of this part.

(Approved by the Office of Management and Budget under control number 1205–0310)

[59 FR 65659, 65676, Dec. 20, 1994, as amended at 60 FR 4029, Jan. 19, 1995; 65 FR 80232, Dec. 20, 2000; 66 FR 63302, Dec. 5, 2001; 69 FR 68228, Nov. 23, 2004; 70 FR 72563, Dec. 5, 2005; 71 FR 35521, June 21, 2006; 73 FR 19950, Apr. 11, 2008]

Subpart I—Enforcement of H–1B Labor Condition Applications and H–1B1 and E–3 Labor Attestations

SOURCE: 59 FR 65672, 65676, Dec. 20, 1994, unless otherwise noted.

§655.800 Who will enforce the LCAs and how will they be enforced?

(a) *Authority of Administrator*. Except as provided in §655.807, the Administrator shall perform all the Secretary's investigative and enforcement functions under sections 212(n) and (t) of the INA (8 U.S.C. 1182(n) and (t)) and this subpart I and subpart H of this part.

(b) *Conduct of investigations*. The Administrator, either pursuant to a complaint or otherwise, shall conduct such investigations as may be appropriate and, in connection therewith, enter and inspect such places and such records (and make transcriptions or copies thereof), question such persons and gather such information as deemed necessary by the Administrator to determine compliance regarding the matters which are the subject of the investigation.

(c) *Employer cooperation/availability of records*. An employer shall at all times cooperate in administrative and enforcement proceedings. An employer being investigated shall make available to the Administrator such records, information, persons, and places as the Administrator deems appropriate to copy, transcribe, question, or inspect. No employer subject to the provisions of sections 212(n) or (t) of the INA and/or this subpart I or subpart H of this part shall interfere with any official of the Department of Labor performing an investigation, inspection or law enforcement function pursuant to 8 U.S.C. 1182(n) or (t) or this subpart I or subpart H of this part. Any such interference shall be a violation of the labor condition application and this subpart I and subpart H of this part, and the Administrator may take such further actions as the Administrator considers appropriate. (Federal criminal statutes prohibit certain interference with a Federal officer in the performance of official duties. 18 U.S.C. 111 and 18 U.S.C. 1114.)

(d) *Confidentiality*. The Administrator shall, to the extent possible under existing law, protect the confidentiality of any person who provides information to the Department in confidence in the course of an investigation or otherwise under this subpart I or subpart H of this part.

[65 FR 80233, Dec. 20, 2000, as amended at 69 FR 68228, Nov. 23, 2004]

§655.801 What protection do employees have from retaliation?

(a) No employer subject to this subpart I or subpart H of this part shall intimidate, threaten, restrain, coerce, blacklist, discharge or in any other manner discriminate against an employee (which term includes a former employee or an applicant for employment) because the employee has—

(1) Disclosed information to the employer, or to any other person, that the employee reasonably believes evidences a violation of sections 212(n) or (t) of the INA or any regulation relating to sections 212(n) or (t), including this subpart I and subpart H of this part and any pertinent regulations of DHS or the Department of Justice; or

(2) Cooperated or sought to cooperate in an investigation or other proceeding concerning the employer's compliance

with the requirements of sections 212(n) or (t) of the INA or any regulation relating to sections 212(n) or (t).

(b) It shall be a violation of this section for any employer to engage in the conduct described in paragraph (a) of this section. Such conduct shall be subject to the penalties prescribed by sections 212(n)(2)(C)(ii) or (t)(3)(C)(ii) of the INA and § 655.810(b)(2), *i.e.*, a fine of up to $7,710, disqualification from filing petitions under section 204 or section 214(c) of the INA for at least two years, and such further administrative remedies as the Administrator considers appropriate.

(c) Pursuant to sections 212(n)(2)(C)(v) and (t)(3)(C)(v) of the INA, an H–1B nonimmigrant who has filed a complaint alleging that an employer has discriminated against the employee in violation of paragraph (a)(1) of this section may be allowed to seek other appropriate employment in the United States, provided the employee is otherwise eligible to remain and work in the United States. Such employment may not exceed the maximum period of stay authorized for a nonimmigrant classified under sections 212(n) or (t) of the INA, as applicable. Further information concerning this provision should be sought from the United States Citizenship and Immigration Services of the Department of Homeland Security.

[65 FR 80233, Dec. 20, 2000, as amended at 69 FR 68229, Nov. 23, 2004; 71 FR 35521, June 21, 2006; 81 FR 43448, July 1, 2016; 82 FR 5380, Jan. 18, 2017; 83 FR 11, Jan. 2, 2018; 84 FR 217, Jan. 23, 2019]

§ 655.805 What violations may the Administrator investigate?

(a) The Administrator, through investigation, shall determine whether an H–1B employer has—

(1) Filed a labor condition application with ETA which misrepresents a material fact (Note to paragraph (a)(1): Federal criminal statutes provide penalties of up to $10,000 and/or imprisonment of up to five years for knowing and willful submission of false statements to the Federal Government. 18 U.S.C. 1001; see also 18 U.S.C. 1546);

(2) Failed to pay wages (including benefits provided as compensation for services), as required under § 655.731 (including payment of wages for certain nonproductive time);

(3) Failed to provide working conditions as required under § 655.732;

(4) Filed a labor condition application for H–1B nonimmigrants during a strike or lockout in the course of a labor dispute in the occupational classification at the place of employment, as prohibited by § 655.733;

(5) Failed to provide notice of the filing of the labor condition application, as required in § 655.734;

(6) Failed to specify accurately on the labor condition application the number of workers sought, the occupational classification in which the H–1B nonimmigrant(s) will be employed, or the wage rate and conditions under which the H–1B nonimmigrant(s) will be employed;

(7) Displaced a U.S. worker (including displacement of a U.S. worker employed by a secondary employer at the worksite where an H–1B worker is placed), as prohibited by § 655.738 (if applicable);

(8) Failed to make the required displacement inquiry of another employer at a worksite where H–1B nonimmigrant(s) were placed, as set forth in § 655.738 (if applicable);

(9) Failed to recruit in good faith, as required by § 655.739 (if applicable);

(10) Displaced a U.S. worker in the course of committing a willful violation of any of the conditions in paragraphs (a)(2) through (9) of this section, or willful misrepresentation of a material fact on a labor condition application;

(11) Required or accepted from an H–1B nonimmigrant payment or remittance of the additional $500/$1,000 fee incurred in filing an H–1B petition with the DHS, as prohibited by § 655.731(c)(10)(ii);

(12) Required or attempted to require an H–1B nonimmigrant to pay a penalty for ceasing employment prior to an agreed upon date, as prohibited by § 655.731(c)(10)(i);

(13) Discriminated against an employee for protected conduct, as prohibited by § 655.801;

(14) Failed to make available for public examination the application and

necessary document(s) at the employer's principal place of business or worksite, as required by § 655.760(a);

(15) Failed to maintain documentation, as required by this part; and

(16) Failed otherwise to comply in any other manner with the provisions of this subpart I or subpart H of this part.

(b) The determination letter setting forth the investigation findings (see § 655.815) shall specify if the violations were found to be substantial or willful. Penalties may be assessed and disqualification ordered for violation of the provisions in paragraphs (a)(5), (6), or (9) of this section only if the violation was found to be substantial or willful. The penalties may be assessed and disqualification ordered for violation of the provisions in paragraphs (a)(2) or (3) of this section only if the violation was found to be willful, but the Secretary may order payment of back wages (including benefits) due for such violation whether or not the violation was willful.

(c) For purposes of this part, *"willful failure"* means a knowing failure or a reckless disregard with respect to whether the conduct was contrary to sections 212(n)(1)(A)(i) or (ii), or 212(t)(1)(A)(i) or (ii) of the INA, or §§ 655.731 or 655.732. See *McLaughlin* v. *Richland Shoe Co.*, 486 U.S. 128 (1988); see also *Trans World Airlines* v. *Thurston*, 469 U.S. 111 (1985).

(d) The provisions of this part become applicable upon the date that the employer's LCA is certified pursuant to §§ 655.740 and 655.750, or upon the date employment commences pursuant to section 214(m) of the INA, whichever is earlier. The employer's submission and signature on the LCA (whether Form ETA 9035 or Form ETA 9035E) each constitutes the employer's representation that the statements on the LCA are accurate and its acknowledgment and acceptance of the obligations of the program. The employer's acceptance of these obligations is re-affirmed by the employer's submission of the petition (Form I–129) to the DHS, supported by the LCA. See 8 CFR 214.2(h)(4)(iii)(B)(*2*), which specifies that the employer will comply with the terms of the LCA for the duration of the H–1B nonimmigrant's authorized period of stay. If the period of employment specified in the LCA expires or the employer withdraws the application in accordance with § 655.750(b), the provisions of this part will no longer apply with respect to such application, except as provided in § 655.750(b)(3) and (4).

[65 FR 80233, Dec. 20, 2000, as amended at 66 FR 63302, Dec. 5, 2001; 69 FR 68229, Nov. 23, 2004]

§ 655.806 Who may file a complaint and how is it processed?

(a) Any aggrieved party, as defined in § 655.715, may file a complaint alleging a violation described in § 655.805(a). The procedures for filing a complaint by an aggrieved party and its processing by the Administrator are set forth in this section. The procedures for filing and processing information alleging violations from persons or organizations that are not aggrieved parties are set forth in § 655.807. With regard to complaints filed by any aggrieved person or organization—

(1) No particular form of complaint is required, except that the complaint shall be written or, if oral, shall be reduced to writing by the Wage and Hour Division official who receives the complaint.

(2) The complaint shall set forth sufficient facts for the Administrator to determine whether there is reasonable cause to believe that a violation as described in § 655.805 has been committed, and therefore that an investigation is warranted. This determination shall be made within 10 days of the date that the complaint is received by a Wage and Hour Division official. If the Administrator determines that the complaint fails to present reasonable cause for an investigation, the Administrator shall so notify the complainant, who may submit a new complaint, with such additional information as may be necessary. No hearing or appeal pursuant to this subpart shall be available where the Administrator determines that an investigation on a complaint is not warranted.

(3) If the Administrator determines that an investigation on a complaint is warranted, the complaint shall be accepted for filing; an investigation shall be conducted and a determination

issued within 30 calendar days of the date of filing. The time for the investigation may be increased with the consent of the employer and the complainant, or if, for reasons outside of the control of the Administrator, the Administrator needs additional time to obtain information needed from the employer or other sources to determine whether a violation has occurred. No hearing or appeal pursuant to this subpart shall be available regarding the Administrator's determination that an investigation on a complaint is warranted.

(4) In the event that the Administrator seeks a prevailing wage determination from ETA pursuant to § 655.731(d), or advice as to prevailing working conditions from ETA pursuant to § 655.732(c)(2), the 30-day investigation period shall be suspended from the date of the Administrator's request to the date of the Administrator's receipt of the wage determination (or, in the event that the employer challenges the wage determination through the Employment Service complaint system, to the date of the completion of such complaint process).

(5) A complaint must be filed not later than 12 months after the latest date on which the alleged violation(s) were committed, which would be the date on which the employer allegedly failed to perform an action or fulfill a condition specified in the LCA, or the date on which the employer, through its action or inaction, allegedly demonstrated a misrepresentation of a material fact in the LCA. This jurisdictional bar does not affect the scope of the remedies which may be assessed by the Administrator. Where, for example, a complaint is timely filed, back wages may be assessed for a period prior to one year before the filing of a complaint.

(6) A complaint may be submitted to any local Wage and Hour Division office. The addresses of such offices are found in local telephone directories, and on the Department's informational site on the Internet at *http://www.dol.gov/dol/esa/public/contacts/whd/america2.htm*. The office or person receiving such a complaint shall refer it to the office of the Wage and Hour Division administering the area in which the reported violation is alleged to have occurred.

(b) When an investigation has been conducted, the Administrator shall, pursuant to § 655.815, issue a written determination as described in § 655.805(a).

[65 FR 80234, Dec. 20, 2000]

§ 655.807 How may someone who is not an "aggrieved party" allege violations, and how will those allegations be processed?

(a) Persons who are not aggrieved parties may submit information concerning possible violations of the provisions described in § 655.805(a)(1) through (4) and (a)(7) through (9). No particular form is required to submit the information, except that the information shall be submitted in writing or, if oral, shall be reduced to writing by the Wage and Hour Division official who receives the information. An optional form shall be available to be used in setting forth the information. The information provided shall include:

(1) The identity of the person submitting the information and the person's relationship, if any, to the employer or other information concerning the person's basis for having knowledge of the employer's employment practices or its compliance with the requirements of this subpart I and subpart H of this part; and

(2) A description of the possible violation, including a description of the facts known to the person submitting the information, in sufficient detail for the Secretary to determine if there is reasonable cause to believe that the employer has committed a willful violation of the provisions described in § 655.805(a)(1), (2), (3), (4), (7), (8), or (9).

(b) The Administrator may interview the person submitting the information as appropriate to obtain further information to determine whether the requirements of this section are met. In addition, the person submitting information under this section shall be informed that his or her identity will not be disclosed to the employer without his or her permission.

(c) Information concerning possible violations must be submitted not later than 12 months after the latest date on which the alleged violation(s) were committed. The 12-month period shall be applied in the manner described in § 655.806(a)(5).

(d) Upon receipt of the information, the Administrator shall promptly review the information submitted and determine:

(1) Does the source likely possess knowledge of the employer's practices or employment conditions or the employer's compliance with the requirements of subpart H of this part?

(2) Has the source provided specific credible information alleging a violation of the requirements of the conditions described in § 655.805(a)(1), (2), (3), (4), (7), (8), or (9)?

(3) Does the information in support of the allegations appear to provide reasonable cause to believe that the employer has committed a violation of the provisions described in § 655.805(a)(1), (2), (3), (4), (7), (8), or (9), and that

(i) The alleged violation is willful?

(ii) The employer has engaged in a pattern or practice of violations? or

(iii) The employer has committed substantial violations, affecting multiple employees?

(e) "Information" within the meaning of this section does not include information from an officer or employee of the Department of Labor unless it was obtained in the course of a lawful investigation, and does not include information submitted by the employer to the DHS or the Secretary in securing the employment of an H–1B nonimmigrant.

(f)(1) Except as provided in paragraph (f)(2) of this section, where the Administrator has received information from a source other than an aggrieved party which satisfies all of the requirements of paragraphs (a) through (d) of this section, or where the Administrator or another agency of the Department obtains such information in a lawful investigation under this or any other section of the INA or any other Act, the Administrator (by mail or facsimile transmission) shall promptly notify the employer that the information has been received, describe the nature of the allegation in sufficient detail to permit the employer to respond, and request that the employer respond to the allegation within 10 days of its receipt of the notification. The Administrator shall not identify the source or information which would reveal the identity of the source without his or her permission.

(2) The Administrator may dispense with notification to the employer of the alleged violations if the Administrator determines that such notification might interfere with an effort to secure the employer's compliance. This determination shall not be subject to review in any administrative proceeding and shall not be subject to judicial review.

(g) After receipt of any response to the allegations provided by the employer, the Administrator will promptly review all of the information received and determine whether the allegations should be referred to the Secretary for a determination whether an investigation should be commenced by the Administrator.

(h) If the Administrator refers the allegations to the Secretary, the Secretary shall make a determination as to whether to authorize an investigation under this section.

(1) No investigation shall be commenced unless the Secretary (or the Deputy Secretary or other Acting Secretary in the absence or disability) personally authorizes the investigation and certifies—

(i) That the information provided under paragraph (a) of this section or obtained pursuant to a lawful investigation by the Department of Labor provides reasonable cause to believe that the employer has committed a violation of the provisions described in § 655.805(a)(1), (2), (3), (4), (7), (8), or (9);

(ii) That there is reasonable cause to believe the alleged violations are willful, that the employer has engaged in a pattern or practice of such violations, or that the employer has committed substantial violations, affecting multiple employees; and

(iii) That the other requirements of paragraphs (a) through (d) of this section have been met.

(2) No hearing shall be available from a decision by the Administrator declining to refer allegations addressed by this section to the Secretary, and none shall be available from a decision by the Secretary certifying or declining to

certify that an investigation is warranted.

(i) If the Secretary issues a certification, an investigation shall be conducted and a determination issued within 30 days after the certification is received by the local Wage and Hour office undertaking the investigation. The time for the investigation may be increased upon the agreement of the employer and the Administrator or, if for reasons outside of the control of the Administrator, additional time is necessary to obtain information needed from the employer or other sources to determine whether a violation has occurred.

(j) In the event that the Administrator seeks a prevailing wage determination from ETA pursuant to § 655.731(d), or advice as to prevailing working conditions from ETA pursuant to § 655.732(c)(2), the 30-day investigation period shall be suspended from the date of the Administrator's request to the date of the Administrator's receipt of the wage determination (or, in the event that the employer challenges the wage determination through the Employment Service complaint system, to the date of the completion of such complaint process).

(k) Following the investigation, the Administrator shall issue a determination in accordance with to § 655.815.

(l) This section shall expire on September 30, 2003 unless section 212(n)(2)(G) of the INA is extended by future legislative action. Absent such extension, no investigation shall be certified by the Secretary under this section after that date; however, any investigation certified on or before September 30, 2003 may be completed.

[65 FR 80234, Dec. 20, 2000]

§ 655.808 Under what circumstances may random investigations be conducted?

(a) The Administrator may conduct random investigations of an employer during a five-year period beginning with the date of any of the following findings, provided such date is on or after October 21, 1998:

(1) A finding by the Secretary that the employer willfully violated any of the provisions described in § 655.805(a)(1) through (9);

(2) A finding by the Secretary that the employer willfully misrepresented material fact(s) in a labor condition application filed pursuant to § 655.730; or

(3) A finding by the Attorney General that the employer willfully failed to meet the condition of section 212(n)(1)(G)(i)(II) of the INA (pertaining to an offer of employment to an equally or better qualified U.S. worker).

(b) A finding within the meaning of this section is a final, unappealed decision of the agency. See §§ 655.520(a), 655.845(c), and 655.855(b).

(c) An investigation pursuant to this section may be made at any time the Administrator, in the exercise of discretion, considers appropriate, without regard to whether the Administrator has reason to believe a violation of the provisions of this subpart I and subpart H of this part has been committed. Following an investigation, the Administrator shall issue a determination in accordance with § 655.815.

[65 FR 80236, Dec. 20, 2000]

§ 655.810 What remedies may be ordered if violations are found?

(a) Upon determining that an employer has failed to pay wages or provide fringe benefits as required by § 655.731 and § 655.732, the Administrator shall assess and oversee the payment of back wages or fringe benefits to any H–1B nonimmigrant who has not been paid or provided fringe benefits as required. The back wages or fringe benefits shall be equal to the difference between the amount that should have been paid and the amount that actually was paid to (or with respect to) such nonimmigrant(s).

(b) *Civil money penalties.* The Administrator may assess civil money penalties for violations as follows:

(1) An amount not to exceed $1,895 per violation for:

(i) A violation pertaining to strike/lockout (§ 655.733) or displacement of U.S. workers (§ 655.738);

(ii) A substantial violation pertaining to notification (§ 655.734), labor condition application specificity (§ 655.730), or recruitment of U.S. workers (§ 655.739);

(iii) A misrepresentation of material fact on the labor condition application;

(iv) An early-termination penalty paid by the employee (§ 655.731(c)(10)(i));

(v) Payment by the employee of the additional $500/$1,000 filing fee (§ 655.731(c)(10)(ii)); or

(vi) Violation of the requirements of the regulations in this subpart I and subpart H of this part or the provisions regarding public access (§ 655.760) where the violation impedes the ability of the Administrator to determine whether a violation of sections 212(n) or (t) of the INA has occurred or the ability of members of the public to have information needed to file a complaint or information regarding alleged violations of sections 212(n) or (t) of the INA;

(2) An amount not to exceed $7,710 per violation for:

(i) A willful failure pertaining to wages/working conditions (§§ 655.731, 655.732), strike/lockout, notification, labor condition application specificity, displacement (including placement of an H–1B nonimmigrant at a worksite where the other/secondary employer displaces a U.S. worker), or recruitment;

(ii) A willful misrepresentation of a material fact on the labor condition application; or

(iii) Discrimination against an employee (§ 655.801(a)); or

(3) An amount not to exceed $53,969 per violation where an employer (whether or not the employer is an H–1B-dependent employer or willful violator) displaced a U.S. worker employed by the employer in the period beginning 90 days before and ending 90 days after the filing of an H–1B petition in conjunction with any of the following violations:

(i) A willful violation of any of the provisions described in § 655.805(a)(2) through (9) pertaining to wages/working condition, strike/lockout, notification, labor condition application specificity, displacement, or recruitment; or

(ii) A willful misrepresentation of a material fact on the labor condition application (§ 655.805(a)(1)).

(c) In determining the amount of the civil money penalty to be assessed, the Administrator shall consider the type of violation committed and other relevant factors. The factors which may be considered include, but are not limited to, the following:

(1) Previous history of violation, or violations, by the employer under the INA and this subpart I or subpart H of this part;

(2) The number of workers affected by the violation or violations;

(3) The gravity of the violation or violations;

(4) Efforts made by the employer in good faith to comply with the provisions of 8 U.S.C. 1182(n) or (t) and this subparts H and I of this part;

(5) The employer's explanation of the violation or violations;

(6) The employer's commitment to future compliance; and

(7) The extent to which the employer achieved a financial gain due to the violation, or the potential financial loss, potential injury or adverse effect with respect to other parties.

(d) *Disqualification from approval of petitions.* The Administrator shall notify the DHS pursuant to § 655.855 that the employer shall be disqualified from approval of any petitions filed by, or on behalf of, the employer pursuant to section 204 or section 214(c) of the INA for the following periods:

(1) At least one year for violation(s) of any of the provisions specified in paragraph (b)(1)(i) through (iii) of this section;

(2) At least two years for violation(s) of any of the provisions specified in paragraph (b)(2) of this section; or

(3) At least three years, for violation(s) specified in paragraph (b)(3) of this section.

(e) *Other administrative remedies.* (1) If the Administrator finds a violation of the provisions specified in paragraph (b)(1)(iv) or (v) of this section, the Administrator may issue an order requiring the employer to return to the employee (or pay to the U.S. Treasury if the employee cannot be located) any money paid by the employee in violation of those provisions.

(2) If the Administrator finds a violation of the provisions specified in paragraph (b)(1)(i) through (iii), (b)(2), or (b)(3) of this section, the Administrator may impose such other administrative remedies as the Administrator determines to be appropriate, including but not limited to reinstatement of workers who were discriminated against in violation of § 655.805(a), reinstatement

of displaced U.S. workers, back wages to workers who have been displaced or whose employment has been terminated in violation of these provisions, or other appropriate legal or equitable remedies.

(f) The civil money penalties, back wages, and/or any other remedy(ies) determined by the Administrator to be appropriate are immediately due for payment or performance upon the assessment by the Administrator, or upon the decision by an administrative law judge where a hearing is timely requested, or upon the decision by the Secretary where review is granted. The employer shall remit the amount of the civil money penalty by certified check or money order made payable to the order of "Wage and Hour Division, Labor." The remittance shall be delivered or mailed to the Wage and Hour Division office in the manner directed in the Administrator's notice of determination. The payment or performance of any other remedy prescribed by the Administrator shall follow procedures established by the Administrator. Distribution of back wages shall be administered in accordance with existing procedures established by the Administrator.

(g) The Federal Civil Penalties Inflation Adjustment Act of 1990, as amended (28 U.S.C. 2461 note), requires that inflationary adjustments to civil money penalties in accordance with a specified cost-of-living formula be made, by regulation, at least every four years. The adjustments are to be based on changes in the Consumer Price Index for all Urban Consumers (CPI-U) for the U.S. City Average for All Items. The adjusted amounts will be published in the FEDERAL REGISTER. The amount of the penalty in a particular case will be based on the amount of the penalty in effect at the time the violation occurs.

[65 FR 80236, Dec. 20, 2000, as amended at 69 FR 68229, Nov. 23, 2004; 81 FR 43448, July 1, 2016; 82 FR 5380, Jan. 18, 2017; 83 FR 11, Jan. 2, 2018; 84 FR 217, Jan. 23, 2019]

§ 655.815 What are the requirements for the Administrator's determination?

(a) The Administrator's determination, issued pursuant to § 655.806, 655.807, or 655.808, shall be served on the complainant, the employer, and other known interested parties by personal service or by certified mail at the parties' last known addresses. Where service by certified mail is not accepted by the party, the Administrator may exercise discretion to serve the determination by regular mail.

(b) The Administrator shall file with the Chief Administrative Law Judge, U.S. Department of Labor, a copy of the complaint and the Administrator's determination.

(c) The Administrator's written determination required by § 655.805 of this part shall:

(1) Set forth the determination of the Administrator and the reason or reasons therefor, and in the case of a finding of violation(s) by an employer, prescribe any remedies, including the amount of any back wages assessed, the amount of any civil money penalties assessed and the reason therefor, and/or any other remedies assessed.

(2) Inform the interested parties that they may request a hearing pursuant to § 655.820 of this part.

(3) Inform the interested parties that in the absence of a timely request for a hearing, received by the Chief Administrative Law Judge within 15 calendar days of the date of the determination, the determination of the Administrator shall become final and not appealable.

(4) Set forth the procedure for requesting a hearing, give the addresses of the Chief Administrative Law Judge (with whom the request must be filed) and the representative(s) of the Solicitor of labor (upon whom copies of the request must be served).

(5) Where appropriate, inform the parties that, pursuant to § 655.855, the Administrator shall notify ETA and the DHS of the occurrence of a violation by the employer.

[59 FR 65672, 65676, Dec. 20, 1994, as amended at 65 FR 80237, Dec. 20, 2000]

§ 655.820 How is a hearing requested?

(a) Any interested party desiring review of a determination issued under §§ 655.805 and 655.815, including judicial review, shall make a request for such an administrative hearing in writing to the Chief Administrative Law Judge at the address stated in the notice of determination. If such a request for an administrative hearing is timely filed, the Administrator's determination shall be inoperative unless and until the case is dismissed or the Administrative Law Judge issues an order affirming the decision.

(b) Interested parties may request a hearing in the following circumstances:

(1) The complainant or any other interested party may request a hearing where the Administrator determines, after investigation, that there is no basis for a finding that an employer has committed violation(s). In such a proceeding, the party requesting the hearing shall be the prosecuting party and the employer shall be the respondent; the Administrator may intervene as a party or appear as *amicus curiae* at any time in the proceeding, at the Administrator's discretion.

(2) The employer or any other interested party may request a hearing where the Administrator determines, after investigation, that the employer has committed violation(s). In such a proceeding, the Administrator shall be the prosecuting party and the employer shall be the respondent.

(c) No particular form is prescribed for any request for hearing permitted by this section. However, any such request shall:

(1) Be dated;

(2) Be typewritten or legibly written;

(3) Specify the issue or issues stated in the notice of determination giving rise to such request;

(4) State the specific reason or reasons why the party requesting the hearing believes such determination is in error;

(5) Be signed by the party making the request or by an authorized representative of such party; and

(6) Include the address at which such party or authorized representative desires to receive further communications relating thereto.

(d) The request for such hearing shall be received by the Chief Administrative Law Judge, at the address stated in the Administrator's notice of determination, no later than 15 calendar days after the date of the determination. An interested party which fails to meet this 15-day deadline for requesting a hearing may thereafter participate in the proceedings only by consent of the administrative law judge, either through intervention as a party pursuant to 29 CFR 18.10 (b) through (d) or through participation as an *amicus curiae* pursuant to 29 CFR 18.12.

(e) The request may be filed in person, by facsimile transmission, by certified or regular mail, or by courier service. For the requesting party's protection, if the request is by mail, it should be by certified mail. If the request is by facsimile transmission, the original of the request, signed by the requestor or authorized representative, shall be filed within ten days.

(f) Copies of the request for a hearing shall be sent by the requestor to the Wage and Hour Division official who issued the Administrator's notice of determination, to the representative(s) of the Solicitor of Labor identified in the notice of determination, and to all known interested parties.

[59 FR 65672, 65676, Dec. 20, 1994, as amended at 65 FR 80237, Dec. 20, 2000]

§ 655.825 What rules of practice apply to the hearing?

(a) Except as specifically provided in this subpart, and to the extent they do not conflict with the provisions of this subpart, the "Rules of Practice and Procedure for Administrative Hearings Before the Office of Administrative Law Judges" established by the Secretary at 29 CFR part 18 shall apply to administrative proceedings under this subpart.

(b) As provided in the Administrative Procedure Act, 5 U.S.C. 556, any oral or documentary evidence may be received in proceedings under this part. The Federal Rules of Evidence and subpart B of the Rules of Practice and Procedure for Administrative Hearings Before the Office of Administrative Law Judges (29 CFR part 18, subpart B) shall not apply, but principles designed to ensure production of relevant and probative evidence shall guide the admission of evidence. The administrative law judge may exclude evidence which is immaterial, irrelevant, or unduly repetitive.

§ 655.830 What rules apply to service of pleadings?

(a) Under this subpart, a party may serve any pleading or document by regular mail. Service on a party is complete upon mailing to the last known address. No additional time for filing or response is authorized where service is by mail. In the interest of expeditious proceedings, the administrative law judge may direct the parties to serve pleadings or documents by a method other than regular mail.

(b) Two (2) copies of all pleadings and other documents in any administrative law judge proceeding shall be served on the attorneys for the Administrator. One copy shall be served on the Associate Solicitor, Division of Fair Labor Standards, Office of the Solicitor, U.S. Department of Labor, 200 Constitution Avenue NW., Room N–2716, Washington, DC 20210, and one copy shall be served on the attorney representing the Administrator in the proceeding.

(c) Time will be computed beginning with the day following the action and includes the last day of the period unless it is a Saturday, Sunday, or federally-observed holiday, in which case the time period includes the next business day.

§ 655.835 How will the administrative law judge conduct the proceeding?

(a) Upon receipt of a timely request for a hearing filed pursuant to and in accordance with § 655.820 of this part, the Chief Administrative Law Judge shall promptly appoint an administrative law judge to hear the case.

(b) Within 7 calendar days following the assignment of the case, the administrative law judge shall notify all interested parties of the date, time and place of the hearing. All parties shall be given at least fourteen calendar days notice of such hearing.

(c) The date of the hearing shall be not more than 60 calendar days from the date of the Administrator's determination. Because of the time constraints imposed by the INA, no request for postponement shall be granted except for compelling reasons. Even where such reasons are shown, no request for postponement of the hearing beyond the 60-day deadline shall be granted except by consent of all the parties to the proceeding.

(d) The administrative law judge may prescribe a schedule by which the parties are permitted to file a prehearing brief or other written statement of fact or law. Any such brief or statement shall be served upon each other party in accordance with § 655.830 of this part. Posthearing briefs will not be permitted except at the request of the administrative law judge. When permitted, any such brief shall be limited to the issue or issues specified by the administrative law judge, shall be due within the time prescribed by the administrative law judge, and shall be served on each other party in accordance with § 655.830 of this part.

§ 655.840 What are the requirements for a decision and order of the administrative law judge?

(a) Within 60 calendar days after the date of the hearing, the administrative law judge shall issue a decision. If any party desires review of the decision, including judicial review, a petition for Secretary's review thereof shall be filed as provided in § 655.845 of this subpart. If a petition for review is filed, the decision of the administrative law judge shall be inoperative unless and until the Secretary issues an order affirming the decision, or, unless and until 30 calendar days have passed after the Secretary's receipt of the petition for review and the Secretary has not issued notice to the parties that the Secretary will review the administrative law judge's decision.

(b) The decision of the administrative law judge shall include a statement of findings and conclusions, with reasons and basis therefor, upon each material issue presented on the record. The decision shall also include an appropriate order which may affirm, deny, reverse, or modify, in whole or in part, the determination of the Administrator; the reason or reasons for such order shall be stated in the decision.

(c) In the event that the Administrator's determination of wage violation(s) and computation of back wages are based upon a wage determination obtained by the Administrator from

ETA during the investigation (pursuant to § 655.731(d)) and the administrative law judge determines that the Administrator's request was not warranted (under the standards in § 655.731(d)), the administrative law judge shall remand the matter to the Administrator for further proceedings on the existence of wage violations and/or the amount(s) of back wages owed. If there is no such determination and remand by the administrative law judge, the administrative law judge shall accept as final and accurate the wage determination obtained from ETA or, in the event either the employer or another interested party filed a timely complaint through the Employment Service complaint system, the final wage determination resulting from that process. See § 655.731; see also 20 CFR 658.420 through 658.426. Under no circumstances shall the administrative law judge determine the validity of the wage determination or require submission into evidence or disclosure of source data or the names of establishments contacted in developing the survey which is the basis for the prevailing wage determination.

(d) The administrative law judge shall not render determinations as to the legality of a regulatory provision or the constitutionality of a statutory provision.

(e) The decision shall be served on all parties in person or by certified or regular mail.

[59 FR 65672, 65676, Dec. 20, 1994, as amended at 65 FR 80237, Dec. 20, 2000]

§ 655.845 What rules apply to appeal of the decision of the administrative law judge?

(a) The Administrator or any interested party desiring review of the decision and order of an administrative law judge, including judicial review, shall petition the Department's Administrative Review Board (Board) to review the decision and order. To be effective, such petition shall be received by the Board within 30 calendar days of the date of the decision and order. Copies of the petition shall be served on all parties and on the administrative law judge.

(b) No particular form is prescribed for any petition for the Board's review permitted by this subpart. However, any such petition shall:

(1) Be dated;

(2) Be typewritten or legibly written;

(3) Specify the issue or issues stated in the administrative law judge decision and order giving rise to such petition;

(4) State the specific reason or reasons why the party petitioning for review believes such decision and order are in error;

(5) Be signed by the party filing the petition or by an authorized representative of such party;

(6) Include the address at which such party or authorized representative desires to receive further communications relating thereto; and

(7) Attach copies of the administrative law judge's's decision and order, and any other record documents which would assist the Board in determining whether review is warranted.

(c) Whenever the Board determines to review the decision and order of an administrative law judge, a notice of the Board's determination shall be served upon the administrative law judge, upon the Office of Administrative Law Judges, and upon all parties to the proceeding within 30 calendar days after the Board's receipt of the petition for review. If the Board determines that it will review the decision and order, the order shall be inoperative unless and until the Board issues an order affirming the decision and order.

(d) Upon receipt of the Board's notice, the Office of Administrative Law Judges shall within 15 calendar days forward the complete hearing record to the Board.

(e) The Board's notice shall specify:

(1) The issue or issues to be reviewed;

(2) The form in which submissions shall be made by the parties (e.g., briefs);

(3) The time within which such submissions shall be made.

(f) All documents submitted to the Board shall be filed with the Administrative Review Board, Room S–4309, U.S. Department of Labor, Washington, DC 20210. An original and two copies of all documents shall be filed. Documents are not deemed filed with the Board until actually received by the

Board. All documents, including documents filed by mail, shall be received by the Board either on or before the due date.

(g) Copies of all documents filed with the Board shall be served upon all other parties involved in the proceeding. Service upon the Administrator shall be in accordance with § 655.830(b).

(h) The Board's final decision shall be issued within 180 calendar days from the date of the notice of intent to review. The Board's decision shall be served upon all parties and the administrative law judge.

(i) Upon issuance of the Board's decision, the Board shall transmit the entire record to the Chief Administrative Law Judge for custody pursuant to § 655.850.

[65 FR 80237, Dec. 20, 2000]

§ 655.850 Who has custody of the administrative record?

The official record of every completed administrative hearing procedure provided by subparts H and I of this part shall be maintained and filed under the custody and control of the Chief Administrative Law Judge. Upon receipt of a complaint seeking review of the final agency action in a United States District Court, the Chief Administrative Law Judge shall certify the official record and shall transmit such record to the clerk of the court.

§ 655.855 What notice shall be given to the Employment and Training Administration and the DHS of the decision regarding violations?

(a) The Administrator shall notify the DHS and ETA of the final determination of any violation requiring that the DHS not approve petitions filed by an employer. The Administrator's notification will address the type of violation committed by the employer and the appropriate statutory period for disqualification of the employer from approval of petitions. Violations requiring notification to the DHS are identified in § 655.810(f).

(b) The Administrator shall notify the DHS and ETA upon the earliest of the following events:

(1) Where the Administrator determines that there is a basis for a finding of violation by an employer, and no timely request for hearing is made pursuant to § 655.820; or

(2) Where, after a hearing, the administrative law judge issues a decision and order finding a violation by an employer, and no timely petition for review is filed with the Department's Administrative Review Board (Board) pursuant to § 655.845; or

(3) Where a timely petition for review is filed from an administrative law judge's decision finding a violation and the Board either declines within 30 days to entertain the appeal, pursuant to § 655.845(c), or the Board reviews and affirms the administrative law judge's determination; or

(4) Where the administrative law judge finds that there was no violation by an employer, and the Board, upon review, issues a decision pursuant to § 655.845, holding that a violation was committed by an employer.

(c) The DHS, upon receipt of notification from the Administrator pursuant to paragraph (a) of this section, shall not approve petitions filed with respect to that employer under sections 204 or 214(c) of the INA (8 U.S.C. 1154 and 1184(c)) for nonimmigrants to be employed by the employer, for the period of time provided by the Act and described in § 655.810(f).

(d) ETA, upon receipt of the Administrator's notice pursuant to paragraph (a) of this section, shall invalidate the employer's labor condition application(s) under this subpart I and subpart H of this part, and shall not accept for filing any application or attestation submitted by the employer under 20 CFR part 656 or subparts A, B, C, D, E, H, or I of this part, for the same calendar period as specified by the DHS.

[65 FR 80238, Dec. 20, 2000]

Subparts J–K [Reserved]

Subpart L—What Requirements Must a Facility Meet to Employ H–1C Nonimmigrant Workers as Registered Nurses?

SOURCE: 65 FR 51149, Aug. 22, 2000, unless otherwise noted.

EDITORIAL NOTE: Nomenclature changes to subpart L of part 655 appear at 75 FR 10403, Mar. 5, 2010.

§ 655.1100 What are the purposes, procedures and applicability of these regulations in subparts L and M of this part?

(a) *Purpose.* The Immigration and Nationality Act (INA), as amended by the Nursing Relief for Disadvantaged Areas Act of 1999, establishes the H–1C nonimmigrant visa program to provide qualified nursing professionals for narrowly defined health professional shortage areas. Subpart L of this part sets forth the procedure by which facilities seeking to use nonimmigrant registered nurses must submit attestations to the Department of Labor demonstrating their eligibility to participate as facilities, their wages and working conditions for nurses, their efforts to recruit and retain United States workers as registered nurses, the absence of a strike/lockout or layoff, notification of nurses, and the numbers of and worksites where H–1C nurses will be employed. Subpart M of this part sets forth complaint, investigation, and penalty provisions with respect to such attestations.

(b) *Procedure.* The INA establishes a procedure for facilities to follow in seeking admission to the United States for, or use of, nonimmigrant nurses under H–1C visas. The procedure is designed to reduce reliance on nonimmigrant nurses in the future, and calls for the facility to attest, and be able to demonstrate in the course of an investigation, that it is taking timely and significant steps to develop, recruit, and retain U.S. nurses. Subparts L and M of this part set forth the specific requirements of those procedures.

(c) *Applicability.* (1) Subparts L and M of this part apply to all facilities that seek the temporary admission or use of H–1C nonimmigrants as registered nurses.

(2) During the period that the provisions of Appendix 1603.D.4 of Annex 1603 of the North American Free Trade Agreement (NAFTA) apply, subparts L and M of this part shall apply to the entry of a nonimmigrant who is a citizen of Mexico under the provisions of section D of Annex 1603 of NAFTA. Therefore, the references in this part to "H–1C nurse" apply to such nonimmigrants who are classified by USCIS as "TN."

§ 655.1101 What are the responsibilities of the government agencies and the facilities that participate in the H–1C program?

(a) *Federal agencies' responsibilities.* The Department of Labor (DOL), Department of Homeland Security, and Department of State are involved in the H–1C visa process. Within DOL, the Employment and Training Administration (ETA) and the Wage and Hour Division have responsibility for different aspects of the process.

(b) *Facility's attestation responsibilities.* Each facility seeking one or more H–1C nurse(s) must, as the first step, submit an attestation on Form ETA 9081, as described in § 655.1110 of this part, to the U.S. Department of Labor, Employment and Training Administration, Office of Foreign Labor Certification, Chicago National Processing Center, 536 South Clark Street, Chicago, IL 60605–1509. If the attestation satisfies the criteria stated in § 655.1130 and includes the supporting information required by § 655.1110 and by § 655.1114, ETA shall accept the attestation form for filing, and return the accepted attestation to the facility.

(c) *H–1C petitions.* Upon ETA's acceptance of the attestation, the facility may then file petitions with U.S. Citizenship and Immigration Services (USCIS) for the admission of, change to, or extension of status of H–1C nurses. The facility must attach a copy of the accepted attestation (Form ETA 9081) to the petition or the request for adjustment or extension of status, filed with USCIS. At the same time that the facility files an H–1C petition with USCIS, it must also send a copy of the petition to the Employment and Training Administration, Administrator, Office of Foreign Labor Certification, 200 Constitution Avenue, NW., Room C–4312, Washington, DC 20210. The facility must also send to this same ETA address a copy of the USCIS petition approval notice within 5 days after it is received from USCIS.

(d) *Visa issuance.* USCIS makes determinations, in adjudicating an H–1C petition, whether the foreign worker possesses the required qualifications and credentials to be employed as an H–1C nurse. The Department of State is subsequently responsible for determining visa eligibility.

(e) *Board of Alien Labor Certification Appeals (BALCA) review of Attestations accepted and not accepted for filing.* Any interested party may seek review by the BALCA of an Attestation accepted or not accepted for filing by ETA. However, such appeals are limited to ETA actions on the three Attestation matters on which ETA conducts a substantive review (*i.e.*, the employer's eligibility as a facility; the facility's attestation to alternative timely and significant steps; and the facility's assertion that taking a second timely and significant step would not be reasonable).

(f) *Complaints.* Complaints concerning misrepresentation of material fact(s) in the Attestation or failure of the facility to carry out the terms of the Attestation may be filed with the Wage and Hour Division of DOL, according to the procedures set forth in subpart M of this part. The Wage and Hour Administrator shall investigate and, where appropriate, after an opportunity for a hearing, assess remedies and penalties. Subpart M of this part also provides that interested parties may obtain an administrative law judge hearing and may seek review of the administrative law judge's decision at the Department's Administrative Review Board.

[75 FR 10403, Mar. 5, 2010]

§ 655.1102 What are the definitions of terms that are used in these regulations?

For the purposes of subparts L and M of this part:

Accepted for filing means that the Attestation and any supporting documentation submitted by the facility have been received by the Employment and Training Administration of the Department of Labor and have been found to be complete and acceptable for purposes of Attestation requirements in §§ 655.1110 through 655.1118.

Administrative Law Judge means an official appointed under 5 U.S.C. 3105.

Administrator means the Administrator of the Wage and Hour Division, Employment Standards Administration, Department of Labor, and such authorized representatives as may be designated to perform any of the functions of the Administrator under subparts L and M of this part.

Administrator, Office of Foreign Labor Certification (OFLC) means the primary official of the Office of Foreign Labor Certification (OFLC Administrator), or the OFLC Administrator's designee.

Aggrieved party means a person or entity whose operations or interests are adversely affected by the employer's alleged misrepresentation of material fact(s) or non-compliance with the Attestation and includes, but is not limited to:

(1) A worker whose job, wages, or working conditions are adversely affected by the facility's alleged misrepresentation of material fact(s) or non-compliance with the attestation;

(2) A bargaining representative for workers whose jobs, wages, or working conditions are adversely affected by the facility's alleged misrepresentation of material fact(s) or non-compliance with the attestation;

(3) A competitor adversely affected by the facility's alleged misrepresentation of material fact(s) or non-compliance with the attestation; and

(4) A government agency which has a program that is impacted by the facility's alleged misrepresentation of material fact(s) or non-compliance with the attestation.

Attorney General means the chief official of the U.S. Department of Justice or the Attorney General's designee.

Board of Alien Labor Certification Appeals (BALCA) means a panel of one or more administrative law judges who serve on the permanent Board of Alien Labor Certification Appeals established by 20 CFR part 656. BALCA consists of administrative law judges assigned to the Department of Labor and designated by the Chief Administrative Law Judge to be members of the Board of Alien Labor Certification Appeals.

Certifying Officer means a Department of Labor official, or such official's designee, who makes determinations about whether or not H–1C attestations are acceptable for certification.

Chief Administrative Law Judge means the chief official of the Office of the Administrative Law Judges of the Department of Labor or the Chief Administrative Law Judge's designee.

Date of filing means the date an Attestation is "accepted for filing" by ETA.

Department and *DOL* mean the United States Department of Labor.

Division means the Wage and Hour Division of the Employment

Standards Administration, DOL.

Employed or *employment* means the employment relationship as determined under the common law, except that a facility which files a petition on behalf of an H–1C nonimmigrant is deemed to be the employer of that H–1C nonimmigrant without the necessity of the application of the common law test. Under the common law, the key determinant is the putative employer's right to control the means and manner in which the work is performed. Under the common law, "no shorthand formula or magic phrase * * * can be applied to find the answer * * *. [A]ll of the incidents of the relationship must be assessed and weighed with no one factor being decisive." *NLRB* v. *United Ins. Co. of America*, 390 U.S. 254, 258 (1968). The determination should consider the following factors and any other relevant factors that would indicate the existence of an employment relationship:

(1) The firm has the right to control when, where, and how the worker performs the job;

(2) The work does not require a high level of skill or expertise;

(3) The firm rather than the worker furnishes the tools, materials, and equipment;

(4) The work is performed on the premises of the firm or the client;

(5) There is a continuing relationship between the worker and the firm;

(6) The firm has the right to assign additional projects to the worker;

(7) The firm sets the hours of work and the duration of the job;

(8) The worker is paid by the hour, week, month or an annual salary, rather than for the agreed cost of performing a particular job;

(9) The worker does not hire or pay assistants;

(10) The work performed by the worker is part of the regular business (including governmental, educational and nonprofit operations) of the firm;

(11) The firm is itself in business;

(12) The worker is not engaged in his or her own distinct occupation or business;

(13) The firm provides the worker with benefits such as insurance, leave, or workers' compensation;

(14) The worker is considered an employee of the firm for tax purposes (*i.e.*, the entity withholds federal, state, and Social Security taxes);

(15) The firm can discharge the worker; and

(16) The worker and the firm believe that they are creating an employer-employee relationship.

Employment and Training Administration (ETA) means the agency within the Department of Labor (DOL) which includes the Office of Foreign Labor Certification (OFLC).

Facility means a "subsection (d) hospital" (as defined in section 1886(d)(1)(B) of the Social Security Act (42 U.S.C. 1395ww(d)(1)(B)) that meets the following requirements:

(1) As of March 31, 1997, the hospital was located in a health professional shortage area (as defined in section 332 of the Public Health Service Act (42 U.S.C. 245e)); and

(2) Based on its settled cost report filed under Title XVIII of the Social Security Act (42 U.S.C. 1395 *et seq.*) for its cost reporting period beginning during fiscal year 1994—

(i) The hospital has not less than 190 licensed acute care beds;

(ii) The number of the hospital's inpatient days for such period which were made up of patients who (for such days) were entitled to benefits under part A of such title is not less than 35 percent of the total number of such hospital's acute care inpatient days for such period; and

(iii) The number of the hospital's inpatient days for such period which were made up of patients who (for such days) were eligible for medical assistance under a State plan approved under Title XIX of the Social Security Act, is not less than 28 percent of the total number of such hospital's acute care inpatient days for such period.

(3) The requirements of paragraph (2) of this definition shall not apply to a facility in Guam, the Commonwealth of the Northern Mariana Islands, or the Virgin Islands.

Full-time employment means work where the nurse is regularly scheduled to work 40 hours or more per week, unless the facility documents that it is common practice for the occupation at the facility or for the occupation in the geographic area for full-time nurses to work fewer hours per week.

Geographic area means the area within normal commuting distance of the place (address) of the intended worksite. If the geographic area does not include a sufficient number of facilities to make a prevailing wage determination, the term "geographic area" shall be expanded with respect to the attesting facility to include a sufficient number of facilities to permit a prevailing wage determination to be made. If the place of the intended worksite is within a Metropolitan Statistical Area (MSA) or Primary Metropolitan Statistical Area (PMSA), any place within the MSA or PMSA will be deemed to be within normal commuting distance of the place of intended employment.

H–1C nurse means any nonimmigrant alien admitted to the United States to perform services as a nurse under section 101(a)(15)(H)(i)(c) of the Act (8 U.S.C. 1101(a)(15)(H)(i)(c)).

INA means the Immigration and Nationality Act, as amended, 8 U.S.C. 1101 *et seq.*

Lockout means a labor dispute involving a work stoppage in which an employer withholds work from its employees in order to gain a concession from them.

Nurse means a person who is or will be authorized by a State Board of Nursing to engage in registered nursing practice in a State or U.S. territory or possession at a facility which provides health care services. A staff nurse means a nurse who provides nursing care directly to patients. In order to qualify under this definition of "nurse" the alien must:

(1) Have obtained a full and unrestricted license to practice nursing in the country where the alien obtained nursing education, or have received nursing education in the United States;

(2) Have passed the examination given by the Commission on Graduates for Foreign Nursing Schools (CGFNS), or have obtained a full and unrestricted (permanent) license to practice as a registered nurse in the state of intended employment, or have obtained a full and unrestricted (permanent) license in any state or territory of the United States and received temporary authorization to practice as a registered nurse in the state of intended employment; and,

(3) Be fully qualified and eligible under the laws (including such temporary or interim licensing requirements which authorize the nurse to be employed) governing the place of intended employment to practice as a registered nurse immediately upon admission to the United States, and be authorized under such laws to be employed by the employer. For purposes of this paragraph, the temporary or interim licensing may be obtained immediately after the alien enters the United States and registers to take the first available examination for permanent licensure.

Office of Foreign Labor Certification (OFLC) means the organizational component within the ETA that provides national leadership and policy guidance and develops regulations and procedures to carry out the responsibilities of the Secretary of Labor under the INA concerning foreign workers seeking admission to the United States.

Prevailing wage means the weighted average wage paid to similarly employed registered nurses within the geographic area.

Secretary means the Secretary of Labor or the Secretary's designee.

Similarly employed means employed by the same type of facility (acute care or long-term care) and working under like conditions, such as the same shift, on the same days of the week, and in the same specialty area.

State means one of the 50 States, the District of Columbia, Puerto Rico, the U.S. Virgin Islands, and Guam.

Strike means a labor dispute in which employees engage in a concerted stoppage of work (including stoppage by reason of the expiration of a collective-bargaining agreement) or engage in any concerted slowdown or other concerted interruption of operations.

United States (U.S.) means the continental U.S., Alaska, Hawaii, the Commonwealth of Puerto Rico, and the territories of Guam, the Virgin Islands, and the Commonwealth of the Northern Mariana Islands.

U.S. Citizenship and Immigration Services (USCIS) means the bureau within the Department of Homeland Security that makes determinations under the INA on whether to approve petitions seeking classification and/or admission of nonimmigrant nurses under the H–1C program.

United States (U.S.) nurse means any nurse who: is a U.S. citizen; is a U.S. national; is lawfully admitted for permanent residence; is admitted as a refugee under 8 U.S.C. 1157; or is granted asylum under 8 U.S.C. 1158.

Worksite means the location where the nurse is involved in the practice of nursing.

[65 FR 51149, Aug. 22, 2000, as amended at 73 FR 78068, Dec. 19, 2008; 75 FR 10404, Mar. 5, 2010]

§ 655.1110 What requirements are imposed in the filing of an attestation?

(a) *Who may file Attestations?* (1) Any hospital which meets the definition of facility in §§ 655.1102 and 655.1111 may file an Attestation.

(2) ETA shall determine the hospital's eligibility as a facility through a review of this attestation element on the first Attestation filed by the hospital. ETA's determination on this point is subject to a hearing before the BALCA upon the request of any interested party. The BALCA proceeding shall be limited to the point.

(3) Upon the hospital's filing of a second or subsequent Attestation, its eligibility as a facility shall be controlled by the determination made on this point in the ETA review (and BALCA proceeding, if any) of the hospital's first Attestation.

(b) *Where and when should attestations be submitted?* (1) Attestations shall be submitted, by U.S. mail or private carrier, to ETA at the following address: U.S. Department of Labor, Employment and Training Administration, Office of Foreign Labor Certification, Chicago National Processing Center, 536 South Clark Street, Chicago, IL 60605–1509.

(2) Attestations shall be reviewed and accepted for filing or rejected by ETA within 30 calendar days of the date they are received by ETA. Therefore, it is recommended that attestations be submitted to ETA at least 35 calendar days prior to the planned date for filing an H–1C visa petition with USCIS.

(c) *What shall be submitted?* (1) Form ETA 9081 and required supporting documentation, as described in paragraphs (c)(1)(i) through (iv) of this section.

(i) A completed and dated original Form ETA 9081, containing the required attestation elements and the original signature of the chief executive officer of the facility, shall be submitted, along with one copy of the completed, signed, and dated Form ETA 9081. Copies of the form and instructions are available at the address listed in paragraph (b) of this section.

(ii) If the Attestation is the first filed by the hospital, it shall be accompanied by copies of pages from the hospital's Form HCFA 2552 filed with the Department of Health and Human Services (pursuant to title XVIII of the Social Security Act) for its 1994 cost reporting period, showing the number of its acute care beds and the percentages of Medicaid and Medicare reimbursed acute care inpatient days (*i.e.*, Form HCFA–2552–92, Worksheet S–3, Part I; Worksheet S, Parts I and II).

(iii) If the facility attests that it will take one or more timely and significant steps other than the steps identified on Form ETA 9081, then the facility must submit (in duplicate) an explanation of the proposed step(s) and an explanation of how the proposed step(s) is/are of comparable significance to those set forth on the Form and in § 655.1114. (*See* § 655.1114(b)(2)(v).)

(iv) If the facility attests that taking more than one timely and significant step is unreasonable, then the facility must submit (in duplicate) an explanation of this attestation. (*See* § 655.1114(c).)

(2) Filing fee of $250 per Attestation. Payment must be in the form of a check or money order, payable to the "U.S. Department of Labor." Remittances must be drawn on a bank or other financial institution located in the U.S. and be payable in U.S. currency.

(3) Copies of H–1C petitions and USCIS approval notices. After ETA has approved the attestation used by the facility to support any H–1C petition, the facility must send copies of each H–1C petition and USCIS approval notice on such petition to Employment and Training Administration, Administrator, Office of Foreign Labor Certification, 200 Constitution Avenue, NW., Room C–4312, Washington, DC 20210.

(d) *Attestation elements*. The attestation elements referenced in paragraph (c)(1) of this section are mandated by section 212(m)(2)(A) of the INA (8 U.S.C. 1182(m)(2)(A)). Section 212(m)(2)(A) requires a prospective employer of H–1C nurses to attest to the following:

(1) That it qualifies as a facility (*See* § 655.1111);

(2) That employment of H–1C nurses will not adversely affect the wages or working conditions of similarly employed nurses (*See* § 655.1112);

(3) That the facility will pay the H–1C nurse the facility wage rate (*See* § 655.1113);

(4) That the facility has taken, and is taking, timely and significant steps to recruit and retain U.S. nurses (*See* § 655.1114);

(5) That there is not a strike or lockout at the facility, that the employment of H–1C nurses is not intended or designed to influence an election for a bargaining representative for RNs at the facility, and that the facility did not lay off and will not lay off a registered nurse employed by the facility 90 days before and after the date of filing a visa petition (*See* § 655.1115);

(6) That the facility will notify its workers and give a copy of the Attestation to every nurse employed at the facility (*See* § 655.1116);

(7) That no more than 33 percent of nurses employed by the facility will be H–1C nonimmigrants (*See* § 655.1117); and

(8) That the facility will not authorize H–1C nonimmigrants to work at a worksite not under its control, and will not transfer an H–1C nonimmigrant from one worksite to another (*See* § 655.1118).

[75 FR 10404, Mar. 5, 2010]

§ 655.1111 Element I—What hospitals are eligible to participate in the H–1C program?

(a) The first attestation element requires that the employer be a "facility" for purposes of the H–1C program, as defined in INA Section 212(m)(6), 8 U.S.C. 1182 (2)(m)(6).

(b) A qualifying facility under that section is a "subpart (d) hospital," as defined in Section 1886(d)(1)(B) of the Social Security Act, 42 U.S.C. 1395ww(d)(1)(B), which:

(1) Was located in a health professional shortage area (HPSA), as determined by the Department of Health and Human Services, on March 31, 1997. A list of HPSAs, as of March 31, 1997, was published in the FEDERAL REGISTER on May 30, 1997 (62 FR 29395);

(2) Had at least 190 acute care beds, as determined by its settled cost report, filed under Title XVIII of the Social Security Act, (42 U.S.C. 1395 *et seq.*), for its fiscal year 1994 cost reporting period (*i.e.*, Form HCFA–2552–92, Worksheet S–3, Part I, column 1, line 8);

(3) Had at least 35% of its acute care inpatient days reimbursed by Medicare, as determined by its settled cost report, filed under Title XVIII of the Social Security Act, for its fiscal year 1994 cost reporting period (*i.e.*, Form HCFA–2552–92, Worksheet S–3, Part I, column 4, line 8 as a percentage of column 6, line 8); and

(4) Had at least 28% of its acute care inpatient days reimbursed by Medicaid, as determined by its settled cost report, filed under Title XVIII of the Social Security Act, for its fiscal year 1994 cost reporting period (*i.e.*, Form HCFA–2552–92, Worksheet S–3, Part I, column 5, line 8 as a percentage of column 6, line 8).

(c) The FEDERAL REGISTER notice containing the controlling list of HPSAs (62 FR 29395), can be found in federal depository libraries and on the Government Printing Office Internet website at *http://www.access.gpo.gov*.

(d) To make a determination about information in the settled cost report, the employer shall examine its own Worksheet S–3, Part I, Hospital and Hospital Health Care Complex Statistical Data, in the Hospital and Hospital Health Care Complex Cost Report, Form HCFA 2552, filed for the fiscal year 1994 cost reporting period.

(e) The facility must maintain a copy of the portions of Worksheet S–3, Part I and Worksheet S, Parts I and II of HCFA Form 2552 which substantiate the attestation of eligibility as a "facility." One set of copies of this document must be kept in the facility's public access file. The full Form 2552 for fiscal year 1994 must be made available to the Department upon request.

§ 655.1112 Element II—What does "no adverse effect on wages and working conditions" mean?

(a) The second attestation element requires that the facility attest that "the employment of the alien will not adversely affect the wages and working conditions of registered nurses similarly employed."

(b) For purposes of this program, "employment" is full-time employment as defined in § 655.1102; part-time employment of H–1C nurses is not authorized.

(c) *Wages*. To meet the requirement of no adverse effect on wages, the facility must attest that it will pay each nurse employed by the facility at least the prevailing wage for the occupation in the geographic area. The facility must pay the higher of the wage required under this paragraph or the wage required under § 655.1113 (*i.e.*, the third attestation element: facility wage).

(1) *Collectively bargained wage rates*. Where wage rates for nurses at a facility are the result of arms-length collective bargaining, those rates shall be considered "prevailing" for that facility for the purposes of this subpart.

(2) Determination of prevailing wage for H–1C purposes. In the absence of collectively bargained wage rates, the National Processing Center (NPC) having jurisdiction as determined by OFLC shall determine the prevailing wage for similarly employed nurses in the geographic area in accordance with administrative guidelines issued by ETA for prevailing wage determination requests submitted on or after the effective date of these regulations.

(i) Prior to the effective date of these regulations, the SWA having jurisdiction over the area of intended employment shall continue to receive and process prevailing wage determination requests in accordance with the regulatory provisions and Department guidance in effect prior to January 1, 2009. On or after the effective date of these regulations, the NPC shall receive and process prevailing wage determination requests in accordance with these regulations and with Department guidance. A facility seeking to determine the prevailing wage must request a prevailing wage determination from the NPC having jurisdiction for providing the prevailing wage over the proposed area of intended employment not more than 90 days prior to the date the attestation is submitted to the Department. The NPC must enter its wage determination on the form it uses and return the form with its endorsement to the employer. Once a facility obtains a prevailing wage determination from the NPC and files an attestation supported by that prevailing wage determination, the facility shall be deemed to have accepted the prevailing wage determination as accurate and appropriate (as to both the occupational classification and the wage rate) and thereafter shall not contest the legitimacy of that prevailing wage determination in an investigation or enforcement action pursuant to subpart M of this part.

(ii) A facility may challenge the prevailing wage determination with the NPC having provided such determination according to administrative guidelines issued by ETA, but must obtain a final ruling prior to filing an attestation.

(3) *Total compensation package*. The prevailing wage under this paragraph relates to wages only. Employers are cautioned that each item in the total compensation package for U.S. nurses, H–1C, and other nurses employed by the facility must be the same within a

given facility, including such items as housing assistance and fringe benefits.

(4) *Documentation of pay and total compensation.* The facility must maintain in its public access file a copy of the prevailing wage, which shall be either the collective bargaining agreement or the determination that was obtained from the NPC. The facility must maintain payroll records, as specified in § 655.1113, and make such records available to the Administrator in the event of an enforcement action pursuant to subpart M.

(d) *Working conditions.* To meet the requirement of no adverse effect on working conditions, the facility must attest that it will afford equal treatment to U.S. and H–1C nurses with the same seniority, with respect to such working conditions as the number and scheduling of hours worked (including shifts, straight days, weekends); vacations; wards and clinical rotations; and overall staffing-patient patterns. In the event of an enforcement action pursuant to subpart M, the facility must provide evidence substantiating compliance with this attestation.

[65 FR 51149, Aug. 22, 2000, as amended at 73 FR 78068, Dec. 19, 2008]

§ 655.1113 Element III—What does "facility wage rate" mean?

(a) The third attestation element requires that the facility employing or seeking to employ the alien must attest that "the alien employed by the facility will be paid the wage rate for registered nurses similarly employed by the facility."

(b) The facility must pay the higher of the wage required in this section (*i.e.* facility wage), or the wage required in § 655.1112 (*i.e.*, prevailing wage).

(c) *Wage obligations for H–1C nurses in nonproductive status*—(1) *Circumstances where wages must be paid.* If the H–1C nurse is not performing work and is in a nonproductive status due to a decision by the facility (e.g., because of lack of assigned work), because the nurse has not yet received a license to work as a registered nurse, or any other reason except as specified in paragraph (c)(2) of this section, the facility is required to pay the salaried H–1C nurse the full amount of the weekly salary, or to pay the hourly-wage H–1C nurse for a full-time week (40 hours or such other number of hours as the facility can demonstrate to be full-time employment) at the applicable wage rate.

(2) *Circumstances where wages need not be paid.* If an H–1C nurse experiences a period of nonproductive status due to conditions unrelated to employment which take the nurse away from his/her duties at his/her voluntary request and convenience (e.g., touring the U.S., caring for ill relative) or render the nonimmigrant unable to work (e.g., maternity leave, automobile accident which temporarily incapacitates the nonimmigrant), then the facility is not obligated to pay the required wage rate during that period, *provided that* such period is not subject to payment under the facility's benefit plan. Payment need not be made if there has been a *bona fide* termination of the employment relationship, as demonstrated by notification to USCIS that the employment relationship has been terminated and the petition should be canceled.

(d) *Documentation.* The facility must maintain documentation substantiating compliance with this attestation element. The public access file shall contain the facility pay schedule for nurses or a description of the factors taken into consideration by the facility in making compensation decisions for nurses, if either of these documents exists. Categories of nursing positions not covered by the public access file documentation shall not be covered by the Attestation, and, therefore, such positions shall not be filled or held by H–1C nurses. The facility must maintain the payroll records, as required under the Fair Labor Standards Act at 29 CFR part 516, and make such records available to the Administrator in the event of an enforcement action pursuant to subpart M of this part.

§ 655.1114 Element IV—What are the timely and significant steps an H–1C employer must take to recruit and retain U.S. nurses?

(a) The fourth attestation element requires that the facility attest that it "has taken and is taking timely and significant steps designed to recruit and retain sufficient registered nurses who are United States citizens or immigrants who are authorized to perform nursing services, in order to remove as quickly as reasonably possible the dependence of the facility on nonimmigrant registered nurses." The facility must take at least two such steps, unless it demonstrates that taking a second step is not reasonable. The steps described in this section shall not be considered to be an exclusive list of the significant steps that may be taken to meet the conditions of this section. Nothing in this subpart or subpart M of this part shall require a facility to take more than one step, if the facility can demonstrate that taking a second step is not reasonable. A facility choosing to take timely and significant steps other than those specifically described in this section must submit with its Attestation a description of the step(s) it is proposing to take and an explanation of how the proposed step(s) are of comparable timeliness and significance to those described in this section (*See* § 655.1110(c)(1)(iii)). A facility claiming that a second step is unreasonable must submit an explanation of why such second step would be unreasonable (*See* § 655.1110(c)(1)(iv)).

(b) *Descriptions of steps.* Each of the actions described in this section shall be considered a significant step reasonably designed to recruit and retain U.S. nurses. A facility choosing any of these steps shall designate such step on Form ETA 9081, thereby attesting that its program(s) meets the regulatory requirements set forth for such step. Section 212(m)(2)(E)(ii) of the INA provides that a violation shall be found if a facility fails to meet a condition attested to. Thus, a facility shall be held responsible for all timely and significant steps to which it attests.

(1) *Statutory steps*—(i) *Operating a training program for registered nurses at the facility or financing (or providing participation in) a training program for registered nurses elsewhere.* Training programs may include either courses leading to a higher degree (*i.e.*, beyond an associate or a baccalaureate degree), or continuing education courses. If the program includes courses leading to a higher degree, they must be courses which are part of a program accepted for degree credit by a college or university and accredited by a State Board of Nursing or a State Board of Higher Education (or its equivalent), as appropriate. If the program includes continuing education courses, they must be courses which meet criteria established to qualify the nurses taking the courses to earn continuing education units accepted by a State Board of Nursing (or its equivalent). In either type of program, financing by the facility (either directly or arranged through a third party) shall cover the total costs of such training. The number of U.S. nurses for whom such training actually is provided shall be no less than half of the number of nurses who left the facility during the 12-month period prior to submission of the Attestation. U.S. nurses to whom such training was offered, but who rejected such training, may be counted towards those provided training.

(ii) *Providing career development programs and other methods of facilitating health care workers to become registered nurses.* This may include programs leading directly to a degree in nursing, or career ladder/career path programs which could ultimately lead to a degree in nursing. Any such degree program shall be, at a minimum, through an accredited community college (leading to an associate's degree), 4-year college (a bachelor's degree), or diploma school, and the course of study must be one accredited by a State Board of Nursing (or its equivalent). The facility (either directly or arranged through a third party) must cover the total costs of such programs. U.S. workers participating in such programs must be working or have worked in health care occupations or facilities. The number of U.S. workers for whom such training is provided must be equal to no less than half the average number of vacancies for nurses during the 12-month period prior to the submission of the Attestation. U.S. nurses to whom such training was offered, but who rejected such training, may be counted towards those provided training.

(iii) *Paying registered nurses wages at a rate higher than currently being paid to registered nurses similarly employed in the geographic area.* The facility's entire schedule of wages for nurses shall be at least 5 percent higher than the prevailing wage as determined by the NPC, and such differentials shall be maintained throughout the period of the Attestation's effectiveness.

(iv) *Providing reasonable opportunities for meaningful salary advancement by registered nurses.* This may include salary advancement based on factors such as merit, education, and specialty, and/or salary advancement based on length of service, with other bases for wage differentials remaining constant.

(A) *Merit, education, and specialty.* Salary advancement may be based on factors such as merit, education, and specialty, or the facility may provide opportunities for professional development of its nurses which lead to salary advancement (e.g., participation in continuing education or in-house educational instruction; service on special committees, task forces, or projects considered of a professional development nature; participation in professional organizations; and writing for professional publications). Such opportunities must be available to all the facility's nurses.

(B) *Length of service.* Salary advancement may be based on length of service using clinical ladders which provide, annually, salary increases of 3 percent or more for a period of no less than 10 years, over and above the costs of living and merit, education, and specialty increases and differentials.

(2) *Other possible steps.* The Act indicates that the four steps described in the statute (and set out in paragraph (b)(1) of this section) are not an exclusive list of timely and significant steps which might qualify. The actions described in paragraphs (b)(2)(i) through (iv) of this section, are also deemed to be qualified; in paragraph (b)(2)(v) of this section, the facility is afforded the opportunity to identify a timely and significant step of its own devising.

(i) *Monetary incentives.* The facility provides monetary incentives to nurses, through bonuses and merit pay plans not included in the base compensation package, for additional education, and for efforts by the nurses leading to increased recruitment and retention of U.S. nurses. Such monetary incentives may be based on actions by nurses such as: Instituting innovations to achieve better patient care, increased productivity, reduced waste, and/or improved workplace safety; obtaining additional certification in a nursing specialty; accruing unused sick leave; recruiting other U.S. nurses; staying with the facility for a given number of years; taking less desirable assignments (other than shift differential); participating in professional organizations; serving on task forces and on special committees; or contributing to professional publications.

(ii) *Special perquisites.* The facility provides nurses with special perquisites for dependent care or housing assistance of a nature and/or extent that constitute a "significant" factor in inducing employment and retention of U.S. nurses.

(iii) *Work schedule options.* The facility provides nurses with non-mandatory work schedule options for part-time work, job-sharing, compressed work week or non-rotating shifts (provided, however, that H–1C nurses are employed only in full-time work) of a nature and/or extent that constitute a "significant" factor in inducing employment and retention of U.S. nurses.

(iv) *Other training options.* The facility provides training opportunities to U.S. workers not currently in health care occupations to become registered nurses by means of financial assistance (e.g., scholarship, loan or pay-back programs) to such persons.

(v) *Alternative but significant steps.* Facilities are encouraged to be innovative in devising timely and significant steps other than those described in paragraphs (b)(1) and (b)(2)(i) through (iv) of this section. To qualify, an alternative step must be of a timeliness and significance comparable to those in this section. A facility may designate on Form ETA 9081 that it has taken and is taking such alternate step(s), thereby attesting that the step(s) meet the statutory test of timeliness and significance comparable to those described in paragraphs (b)(1) and (b)(2)(i) through (iv) in promoting the development, recruitment, and retention of U.S. nurses. If such a designation is made on Form ETA 9081, the submission of the Attestation to ETA must include an explanation and appropriate documentation of the alternate step(s), and of the manner in which they satisfy the statutory test in comparison to the steps described in paragraphs (b)(1) and (b)(2)(i) through (iv). ETA will review the explanation and documentation and determine whether the alternate step(s) qualify under this subsection. The ETA determination is subject to review by the BALCA, upon the request of an interested party; such review shall be limited to this matter.

(c) *Unreasonableness of second step.* Nothing in this subpart or subpart M of this part requires a facility to take more than one step, if the facility can demonstrate that taking a second step is not reasonable. However, a facility shall make every effort to take at least two steps. The taking of a second step may be considered unreasonable if it would result in the facility's financial inability to continue providing the same quality and quantity of health care or if the provision of nursing services would otherwise be jeopardized by the taking of such a step.

(1) A facility may designate on Form ETA 9081 that the taking of a second step is not reasonable. If such a designation is made on Form ETA 9081, the submission of the Attestation to ETA shall include an explanation and appropriate documentation with respect to each of the steps described in paragraph (b) of this section (other than the step designated as being taken by the facility), showing why it would be unreasonable for the facility to take each such step and why it would be unreasonable for the facility to take any other step designed to recruit, develop and retain sufficient U.S. nurses to meet its staffing needs.

(2) ETA will review the explanation and documentation, and will determine whether the taking of a second step would not be reasonable. The ETA determination is subject to review by the BALCA, upon the request of an interested party; such review shall be limited to this matter.

(d) *Performance-based alternative to criteria for specific steps.* Instead of complying with the specific criteria for one or more of the steps in the second and/or succeeding years of participation in the H–1C program, a facility may include in its *prior* year's Attestation, in addition to the actions taken under specifically attested steps, that it will reduce the number of H–1C nurses it utilizes within one year from the date of the Attestation by at least 10 percent, without reducing the quality or quantity of services provided. If this goal is achieved, the facility shall so indicate on its subsequent year's Attestation. Further, the facility need not attest to any "timely and significant step" on that subsequent attestation, if it again indicates that it shall again reduce the number of H–1C nurses it utilizes within one year from the date of the Attestation by at least 10 percent. This performance-based alternative is designed to permit a facility to achieve the objectives of the Act, without subjecting the facility to detailed requirements and criteria as to the specific means of achieving that objective.

(e) *Documentation.* The facility must include in the public access file a description of the activities which constitute its compliance with each timely and significant step which is attested on Form ETA 9081 (e.g., summary of a training program for registered nurses; description of a career ladder showing meaningful opportunities for pay advancements for nurses). If the facility has attested that it will take an alternative step or that taking a second step is unreasonable, then the public access file must include the documentation which was submitted to ETA under paragraph (c) of this section. The facility must maintain in its non-public files, and must make available to the Administrator in the event of an enforcement action pursuant to subpart M of this part, documentation which provides a complete description of the nature and operation of its program(s) sufficient to substantiate its full compliance with the requirements of each timely and significant step which is attested to on Form ETA 9081. This documentation should include information relating to all of the requirements for the step in question.

§655.1115 Element V—What does "no strike/lockout or layoff" mean?

(a) The fifth attestation element requires that the facility attest that "there is not a strike or lockout in the course of a labor dispute, the facility did not lay off and will not lay off a registered nurse employed by the facility within the period beginning 90 days before and ending 90 days after the date of filing of any visa petition, and the employment of such an alien is not intended or designated to influence an election for a bargaining representative for registered nurses of the facility." Labor disputes for purposes of this attestation element relate only to those involving nurses providing nursing services; other health service occupations are not included. A facility which has filed a petition for H–1C nurses is also prohibited from interfering with the right of the nonimmigrant to join or organize a union.

(b) *Notice of strike or lockout.* In order to remain in compliance with the no strike or lockout portion of this attestation element, the facility must notify ETA if a strike or lockout of nurses at the facility occurs during the 1 year validity period of the attestation. Within 3 days of the occurrence of such strike or lockout, the facility must submit to the Administrator, Office of Foreign Labor Certification, Employment and Training Administration, Department of Labor, 200 Constitution Avenue, NW., Room C–4312, Washington, DC 20210, by U.S. mail or private carrier, written notice of the strike or lockout. Upon receiving a notice described in this section from a facility, ETA will examine the documentation, and may consult with the union at the facility or other appropriate entities. If ETA determines that the strike or lockout is covered under USCIS regulation 8 CFR 214.2(h)(17), *Effect of a strike,* for "H" nonimmigrants, ETA must certify to USCIS, in the manner set forth in that regulation, that a strike or other labor dispute involving a work stoppage of nurses is in progress at the facility.

(c) *Lay off* of a U.S. nurse means that the employer has caused the nurse's loss of employment in circumstances *other than* where—

(1) A U.S. nurse has been discharged for inadequate performance, violation of workplace rules, or other reasonable work-related cause;

(2) A U.S. nurse's departure or retirement is voluntary (to be assessed in light of the totality of the circumstances, under established principles concerning "constructive discharge" of workers who are pressured to leave employment);

(3) The grant or contract under which the work performed by the U.S. nurse is required and funded has expired, and without such grant or contract the nurse would not continue to be employed because there is no alternative funding or need for the position; or

(4) A U.S. nurse who loses employment is offered, as an alternative to such loss, a similar employment opportunity with the same employer. The validity of the offer of a similar employment opportunity will be assessed in light of the following factors:

(i) The offer is a *bona fide* offer, rather than an offer designed to induce the U.S. nurse to refuse or an offer made with the expectation that the worker will refuse;

(ii) The offered job provides the U.S. nurse an opportunity similar to that provided in the job from which he/she is discharged, in terms such as a similar level of authority, discretion, and responsibility, a similar opportunity for advancement within the organization, and similar tenure and work scheduling;

(iii) The offered job provides the U.S. nurse equivalent or higher compensation and benefits to those provided in the job from which he/she is discharged.

(d) *Documentation.* The facility must include in its public access file, copies of all notices of strikes or other labor disputes involving a work stoppage of nurses at the facility (submitted to ETA under paragraph (b) of this section). The facility must retain in its non-public files, and make available in the event of an enforcement action pursuant to subpart M of this part, any existing documentation with respect to the departure of each U.S. nurse who left his/her employment with the facility in the period from 90 days before until 90 days after the facility's petition for H–1C nurse(s). The facility is also required to have a record of the terms of any offer of alternative employment to such a U.S. nurse and the nurse's response to the offer (which may be a note to the file or other record of the nurse's response), and to make such record available in the event of an enforcement action pursuant to subpart M.

[65 FR 51149, Aug. 22, 2000, as amended at 75 FR 10405, Mar. 5, 2010]

§655.1116 Element VI—What notification must facilities provide to registered nurses?

(a) The sixth attestation element requires the facility to attest that at the time of filing of the petition for registered nurses under section 101(a)(15)(H)(i)(c) of the INA, notice of filing has been provided by the facility to the bargaining representative of the registered nurses at the facility or, where there is no such bargaining representative, notice of the filing has been provided to registered nurses at the facility through posting in conspicuous locations, and individual copies of the Attestation have been provided to registered nurses employed at the facility.

(b) *Notification of bargaining representative.* (1) At a time no later than the date the attestation is transmitted to ETA, on ETA Form 9081, Attestation for H–1C Nonimmigrant Nurses, the facility must notify the bargaining representative (if any) for nurses at the facility that the attestation is being submitted. This notice may be either a copy of the attestation (ETA Form 9081) or a document stating that the attestations are available for review by interested parties at the facility (explaining how they can be inspected or obtained) and at the Office of Foreign Labor Certification, Employment and Training Administration, Department of Labor, 200 Constitution Avenue, NW., Room C–4312, Washington, DC 20210. The notice must include the following statement: "Complaints alleging misrepresentation of material facts in the attestation or failure to comply with the terms of the attestation may be filed with any office of the Wage and Hour Division, United States Department of Labor."

(2) No later than the date the facility transmits a petition for H–1C nurses to USCIS, the facility must notify the bargaining representative (if any) for nurses at the facility that the H–1C petition is being submitted. This notice may be either a copy of petition, or a document stating that the attestations and H–1C petition are available for review by interested parties at the facility (explaining how they can be inspected or obtained) and at the Office of Foreign Labor Certification, Employment and Training Administration, Department of Labor, 200 Constitution Avenue, NW., Room C–4312, Washington, DC 20210. The notice must include the following statement: "Complaints alleging misrepresentation of material facts in the attestation or failure to comply with the terms of the attestation may be filed with any office of the Wage and Hour Division, United States Department of Labor."

(c) *Posting notice.* If there is no bargaining representative for nurses at the facility, the facility must post a written notice in two or more conspicuous locations at the facility. Such notices shall be clearly visible and unobstructed while posted, and shall be posted in conspicuous places where nurses can easily read the notices on their way to or from their duties. Appropriate locations for posting hard copy notices include locations in the immediate proximity of mandatory Fair Labor Standards Act wage and hour notices and Occupational Safety and Health Act occupational safety and health notices. In the alternative, the facility may use electronic means it ordinarily uses to communicate with its nurses about job vacancies or promotion opportunities, including through its "home page" or "electronic bulletin board," provided that the nurses have, as a practical matter, direct access to those sites; or, where the nurses have individual e-mail accounts, the facility may use e-mail. This must be accomplished no later than the date when the facility transmits an Attestation to ETA and the date when the facility transmits an H–1C petition to the USCIS. The notice may be either a copy of the Attestation or petition, or a document stating that the Attestation or petition has been filed and is available for review by interested parties at the facility (explaining how these documents can be inspected or obtained) and at the national office of

ETA. The notice shall include the following statement: "Complaints alleging misrepresentation of material facts in the Attestation or failure to comply with the terms of the Attestation may be filed with any office of the Wage and Hour Division of the United States Department of Labor." Unless it is sent to an individual e-mail address, the Attestation notice shall remain posted during the validity period of the Attestation; the petition notice shall remain posted for ten days. Copies of all notices shall be available for examination in the facility's public access file.

(d) *Individual notice to RNs.* In addition to notifying the bargaining representative or posting notice as described in paragraphs (b) and (c) of this section, the facility must provide a copy of the Attestation, within 30 days of the date of filing, to every registered nurse employed at the facility. This requirement may be satisfied by electronic means if an individual e-mail message, with the Attestation as an attachment, is sent to every RN at the facility. This notification includes not only the RNs employed by the facility, but also includes any RN who is providing service at the facility as an employee of another entity, such as a nursing contractor.

(e) Where RNs lack practical computer access, a hard copy must be posted in accordance with paragraph (c) of this section and a hard copy of the Attestation delivered, within 30 days of the date of filing, to every RN employed at the facility in accordance with paragraph (d) of this section.

(f) The facility must maintain, in its public access file, copies of the notices required by this section. The facility must make such documentation available to the Administrator in the event of an enforcement action pursuant to subpart M of this part.

[65 FR 51149, Aug. 22, 2000, as amended at 75 FR 10405, Mar. 5, 2010]

§ 655.1117 Element VII—What are the limitations as to the number of H–1C nonimmigrants that a facility may employ?

(a) The seventh attestation element requires that the facility attest that it will not, at any time, employ a number of H–1C nurses that exceeds 33% of the total number of registered nurses employed by the facility. The calculation of the population of nurses for purposes of this attestation includes only nurses who have an employer-employee relationship with the facility (as defined in § 655.1102).

(b) The facility must maintain documentation (e.g., payroll records, copies of H–1C petitions) that demonstrates its compliance with this attestation. The facility must make such documentation available to the Administrator in the event of an enforcement action pursuant to subpart M of this part.

§ 655.1118 Element VIII—What are the limitations as to where the H–1C nonimmigrant may be employed?

The eighth attestation element requires that the facility attest that it will not authorize any H–1C nurse to perform services at any worksite not controlled by the facility or transfer any H–1C nurse from one worksite to another worksite, even if all of the worksites are controlled by the facility.

§ 655.1130 What criteria does the Department use to determine whether or not to certify an Attestation?

(a) An Attestation form which is complete and has no obvious inaccuracies will be accepted for filing by ETA without substantive review, *except that* ETA will conduct a substantive review on particular attestation elements in the following limited circumstances:

(1) Determination of whether the hospital submitting the Attestation is a qualifying "facility" (*see* § 655.1110(c)(ii), regarding the documentation required, and the process for review);

(2) Where the facility attests that it is taking or will take a "timely and significant step" other than those identified on the Form ETA 9081 (*see* § 655.1114(b)(2)(v), regarding the documentation required, and the process for review);

(3) Where the facility asserts that taking a second "timely and significant step" is unreasonable (*see* § 655.1114(c), regarding the documentation required, and the process for review).

(b) The certifying officer will act on the Attestation in a timely manner. If the officer does not contact the facility for information or make any determination within 30 days of receiving the Attestation, the Attestation shall be accepted for filing. If ETA receives information contesting the truth of the statements attested to or compliance with an Attestation prior to the determination to accept or reject the Attestation for filing, such information shall not be made part of ETA's administrative record on the Attestation but shall be referred to the Administrator to be processed as a complaint pursuant to subpart M of this part if such Attestation is accepted by ETA for filing.

(c) When the facility submits the attestation to ETA and provides the notice required by §655.1116, the attestation must be made available for public examination at the facility. When ETA accepts the attestation for filing, the attestation will be made available, upon request, for public examination in the Office of Foreign Labor Certification, Employment Training Administration, U.S. Department of Labor, Room C–4312, 200 Constitution Avenue, NW., Washington, DC 20210.

(d) *Standards for acceptance of Attestation.* ETA will accept the Attestation for filing under the following standards:

(1) The Attestation is complete and contains no obvious inaccuracies.

(2) The facility's explanation and documentation are sufficient to satisfy the requirements for the Attestation elements on which substantive review is conducted (as described in paragraph (a) of this section).

(3) The facility has no outstanding "insufficient funds" check(s) in connection with filing fee(s) for prior Attestation(s).

(4) The facility has no outstanding civil money penalties and/or has not failed to satisfy a remedy assessed by the Wage and Hour Administrator, under subpart M of this part, where that penalty or remedy assessment has become the final agency action.

(5) The facility has not been disqualified from approval of any petitions filed by, or on behalf of, the facility under section 204 or section 212(m) of the INA.

(e) *DOL not the guarantor.* DOL is not the guarantor of the accuracy, truthfulness or adequacy of an Attestation accepted for filing.

(f) *Attestation Effective and Expiration Dates.* An Attestation becomes filed and effective as of the date it is accepted and signed by the ETA certifying officer. Such Attestation is valid until the date that is the later of the end of the 12-month period beginning on the date of acceptance for filing with the Secretary, or the end of the period of admission (under INA section 101(a)(15)(H)(i)(c)) of the last alien with respect to whose admission the Attestation was applied, unless the Attestation is suspended or invalidated earlier than such date pursuant to §655.1132.

[65 FR 51149, Aug. 22, 2000, as amended at 75 FR 10406, Mar. 5, 2010]

§655.1132 When will the Department suspend or invalidate an approved Attestation?

(a) Suspension or invalidation of an Attestation may result where: the facility's check for the filing fee is not honored by a financial institution; a Board of Alien Labor Certification Appeals (BALCA) decision reverses an ETA certification of the Attestation; ETA finds that it made an error in its review and certification of the Attestation; an enforcement proceeding has finally determined that the facility failed to meet a condition attested to, or that there was a misrepresentation of material fact in an Attestation; the facility has failed to pay civil money penalties and/or failed to satisfy a remedy assessed by the Wage and Hour Administrator, where that penalty or remedy assessment has become the final agency action. If an Attestation is suspended or invalidated, ETA will notify USCIS.

(b) *BALCA decision or final agency action in an enforcement proceeding.* If an Attestation is suspended or invalidated as a result of a BALCA decision overruling an ETA acceptance of the Attestation for filing, or is suspended or invalidated as a result of an enforcement action by the Administrator under subpart M of this part, such suspension or invalidation may not be separately appealed, but shall be merged with appeals on the underlying matter.

(c) *ETA action.* If, after accepting an Attestation for filing, ETA discovers that it erroneously accepted that Attestation for filing and, as a result, ETA suspends or invalidates that acceptance, the facility may appeal such suspension or invalidation under § 655.1135 as if that suspension or invalidation were a decision to reject the Attestation for filing.

(d) A facility must comply with the terms of its Attestation, even if such Attestation is suspended, invalidated or expired, as long as any H–1C nurse is at the facility, unless the Attestation is superseded by a subsequent Attestation accepted for filing by ETA.

§ 655.1135 What appeals procedures are available concerning ETA's actions on a facility's Attestation?

(a) *Appeals of acceptances or rejections.* Any interested party may appeal ETA's acceptance or rejection of an Attestation submitted by a facility for filing. However, such an appeal shall be limited to ETA's determination on one or more of the attestation elements for which ETA conducts a substantive review (as described in § 655.1130(a)). Such appeal must be filed no later than 30 days after the date of the acceptance or rejection, and will be considered under the procedures set forth at paragraphs (d) and (f) of this section.

(b) *Appeal of invalidation or suspension.* An interested party may appeal ETA's invalidation or suspension of a filed Attestation due to a discovery by ETA that it made an error in its review of the Attestation, as described in § 655.1132.

(c) *Parties to the appeal.* In the case of an appeal of an acceptance, the facility will be a party to the appeal; in the case of the appeal of a rejection, invalidation, or suspension, the collective bargaining representative (if any) representing nurses at the facility shall be a party to the appeal. Appeals shall be in writing; shall set forth the grounds for the appeal; shall state if *de novo* consideration by BALCA is requested; and shall be mailed by certified mail within 30 calendar days of the date of the action from which the appeal is taken (*i.e.*, the acceptance, rejection, suspension or invalidation of the Attestation).

(d) *Where to file appeals.* Appeals made under this section must be in writing and must be mailed by certified mail to: U.S. Department of Labor, Employment and Training Administration, Office of Foreign Labor Certification, Chicago National Processing Center, 536 South Clark Street, Chicago, IL 60605–1509.

(e) *Transmittal of the case file to BALCA.* Upon receipt of an appeal under this section, the Certifying Office shall send to BALCA a certified copy of the ETA case file, containing the Attestation and supporting documentation and any other information or data considered by ETA in taking the action being appealed. The administrative law judge chairing BALCA shall assign a panel of one or more administrative law judges who serve on BALCA to review the record for legal sufficiency and to consider and rule on the appeal.

(f) *Consideration on the record; de novo hearings.* BALCA may not remand, dismiss, or stay the case, except as provided in paragraph (h) of this section, but may otherwise consider the appeal on the record or in a *de novo* hearing (on its own motion or on a party's request). Interested parties and *amici curiae* may submit briefs in accordance with a schedule set by BALCA. The ETA official who made the determination which was appealed will be represented by the Associate Solicitor for Employment and Training Legal Services, Office of the Solicitor, Department of Labor, or the Associate Solicitor's designee. If BALCA determines to hear the appeal on the record without a *de novo* hearing, BALCA shall render a decision within 30 calendar days after BALCA's receipt of the case file. If BALCA determines to hear the appeal through a *de novo* hearing, the procedures contained in 29 CFR part 18 will apply to such hearings, except that:

(1) The appeal will not be considered to be a complaint to which an answer is required.

(2) BALCA shall ensure that, at the request of the appellant, the hearing is scheduled to take place within a reasonable period after BALCA's receipt of the case file (see also the time period described in paragraph (f)(4) of this section).

(3) Technical rules of evidence, such as the Federal Rules of Evidence and subpart B of the Rules of Practice and Procedure for Administrative Hearings Before the Office of Administrative Law Judges (29 CFR part 18, subpart B), will not apply to any hearing conducted pursuant to this subpart, but rules or principles designed to assure production of the most credible evidence available, and to subject testimony to test by cross-examination, shall be applied where reasonably necessary by BALCA in conducting the hearing. BALCA may exclude irrelevant, immaterial, or unduly repetitious evidence. The certified copy of the case file transmitted to BALCA by the Certifying Officer must be made part of the evidentiary record of the case and need not be moved into evidence.

(4) BALCA's decision shall be rendered within 120 calendar days after BALCA's receipt of the case file.

(g) *Dismissals and stays.* If BALCA determines that the appeal is solely a question of misrepresentation by the facility or is solely a complaint of the facility's nonperformance of the Attestation, BALCA shall dismiss the case and refer the matter to the Administrator, Wage and Hour Division, for action under subpart M. If BALCA determines that the appeal is partially a question of misrepresentation by the facility, or is partially a complaint of the facility's nonperformance of the Attestation, BALCA shall refer the matter to the Administrator, Wage and Hour Division, for action under subpart M of this part and shall stay BALCA consideration of the case pending final agency action on such referral. During such stay, the 120-day period described in paragraph (f)(1)(iv) of this section shall be suspended.

(h) *BALCA's decision.* After consideration on the record or a *de novo* hearing, BALCA shall either affirm or reverse ETA's decision, and shall so notify the appellant; and any other parties.

(i) *Decisions on Attestations.* With respect to an appeal of the acceptance, rejection, suspension or invalidation of an Attestation, the decision of BALCA shall be the final decision of the Secretary, and no further review shall be given to the matter by any DOL official.

[65 FR 51149, Aug. 22, 2000, as amended at 75 FR 10406, Mar. 5, 2010]

§ 655.1150 What materials must be available to the public?

(a) *Public examination at ETA.* ETA will make available, upon request, for public examination at the Office of Foreign Labor Certification, Employment Training Administration, U.S. Department of Labor, Room C–4312, 200 Constitution Avenue, NW., Washington, DC 20210, a list of facilities which have filed attestations; a copy of the facility's attestation(s) and any supporting documentation; and a copy of each of the facility's H–1C petitions (if any) to USCIS along with the USCIS approval notices (if any).

(b) *Public examination at facility.* For the duration of the Attestation's validity and thereafter for so long as the facility employs any H–1C nurse under the Attestation, the facility must maintain a separate file containing a copy of the Attestation, a copy of the prevailing wage determination, a description of the facility pay system or a copy of the facility's pay schedule if either document exists, copies of the notices provided under § 655.1115 and § 655.1116, a description of the "timely and significant steps" as described in § 655.1114, and any other documentation required by this part to be contained in the public access file. The facility must make this file available to any interested parties within 72 hours upon written or oral request. If a party requests a copy of the file, the facility shall provide it and any charge for such copy shall not exceed the cost of reproduction.

(c) *ETA Notice to public.* ETA will periodically publish a notice in the FEDERAL REGISTER announcing the names and addresses of facilities which have submitted Attestations; facilities which have Attestations on file; facilities which have submitted Attestations which have been rejected for filing; and facilities which have had Attestations suspended.

[65 FR 51149, Aug. 22, 2000, as amended at 75 FR 10406, Mar. 5, 2010]

Subpart M—What are the Department's enforcement obligations with respect to H–1C Attestations?

SOURCE: 65 FR 51149, Aug. 22, 2000, unless otherwise noted.

EDITORIAL NOTE: Nomenclature changes to subpart M of part 655 appear at 75 FR 10403, Mar. 5, 2010.

§ 655.1200 What enforcement authority does the Department have with respect to a facility's H–1C Attestations?

(a) The Administrator shall perform all the Secretary's investigative and enforcement functions under 8 U.S.C. 1182(m) and subparts L and M of this part.

(b) The Administrator, either because of a complaint or otherwise, shall conduct such investigations as may be appropriate and, in connection therewith, enter and inspect such places and such records (and make transcriptions thereof), question such persons and gather such information as deemed necessary by the Administrator to determine compliance with the matters to which a facility has attested under section 212(m) of the INA (8 U.S.C. 1182(m)) and subparts L and M of this part.

(c) A facility being investigated must make available to the Administrator such records, information, persons, and places as the Administrator deems appropriate to copy, transcribe, question, or inspect. A facility must fully cooperate with any official of the Department of Labor performing an investigation, inspection, or law enforcement function under 8 U.S.C. 1182(m) or subparts L or M of this part. Such cooperation shall include producing documentation upon request. The Administrator may deem the failure to cooperate to be a violation, and take such further actions as the Administrator considers appropriate.

(NOTE: Federal criminal statutes prohibit certain interference with a Federal officer in the performance of official duties. 18 U.S.C. 111 and 1114.)

(d) No facility may intimidate, threaten, restrain, coerce, blacklist, discharge, or in any manner discriminate against any person because such person has:

(1) Filed a complaint or appeal under or related to section 212(m) of the INA (8 U.S.C. 1182(m)) or subpart L or M of this part;

(2) Testified or is about to testify in any proceeding under or related to section 212(m) of the INA (8 U.S.C. 1182(m)) or subpart L or M of this part.

(3) Exercised or asserted on behalf of himself/herself or others any right or protection afforded by section 212(m) of the INA (8 U.S.C. 1182(m)) or subpart L or M of this part.

(4) Consulted with an employee of a legal assistance program or an attorney on matters related to the Act or to subparts L or M of this part or any other DOL regulation promulgated under 8 U.S.C. 1182(m).

(5) In the event of such intimidation or restraint as are described in this paragraph, the Administrator may deem the conduct to be a violation and take such further actions as the Administrator considers appropriate.

(e) A facility subject to subparts L and M of this part must maintain a separate file containing its Attestation and required documentation, and must make that file or copies thereof available to interested parties, as required by § 655.1150. In the event of a facility's failure to maintain the file, to provide access, or to provide copies, the Administrator may deem the conduct to be a violation and take such further actions as the Administrator considers appropriate.

(f) No facility may seek to have an H–1C nurse, or any other nurse similarly employed by the employer, or any other employee waive rights conferred under the Act or under subpart L or M of this part. In the event of such waiver, the Administrator may deem the conduct to be a violation and take such further actions as the Administrator considers appropriate. This prohibition of waivers does not prevent agreements to settle litigation among private parties, and a waiver or modification of rights or obligations in favor of the Secretary shall be valid for purposes of enforcement of the provisions of the Act or subpart L and M of this part.

(g) The Administrator shall, to the extent possible under existing law, protect the confidentiality of any complainant or other person who provides information to the Department.

§ 655.1205 What is the Administrator's responsibility with respect to complaints and investigations?

(a) The Administrator, through investigation, shall determine whether a facility has failed to perform any attested conditions, misrepresented any material facts in an Attestation (including misrepresentation as to compliance with regulatory standards), or otherwise violated the Act or subpart L or M of this part. The Administrator's authority applies whether an Attestation is expired or unexpired at the time a complaint is filed. (Note: Federal criminal statutes provide for fines and/or imprisonment for knowing and willful submission of false statements to the Federal Government. 18 U.S.C. 1001; *see also* 18 U.S.C. 1546.)

(b) Any aggrieved person or organization may file a complaint of a violation of the provisions of section 212(m) of the INA (8 U.S.C. 1182(m)) or subpart L or M of this part. No particular form of complaint is required, except that the complaint shall be written or, if oral, shall be reduced to writing by the Wage and Hour Division official who receives the complaint. The complaint must set forth sufficient facts for the Administrator to determine what part or parts of the Attestation or regulations have allegedly been violated. Upon the request of the complainant, the Administrator shall, to the extent possible under existing law, maintain confidentiality about the complainant's identity; if the complainant wishes to be a party to the administrative hearing proceedings under this subpart, the complainant shall then waive confidentiality. The complaint may be submitted to any local Wage and Hour Division office; the addresses of such offices are found in local telephone directories. Inquiries concerning the enforcement program and requests for technical assistance regarding compliance may also be submitted to the local Wage and Hour Division office.

(c) The Administrator shall determine whether there is reasonable cause to believe that the complaint warrants investigation and, if so, shall conduct an investigation, within 180 days of the receipt of a complaint. If the Administrator determines that the complaint fails to present reasonable cause for an investigation, the Administrator shall so notify the complainant, who may submit a new complaint, with such additional information as may be necessary.

(d) When an investigation has been conducted, the Administrator shall, within 180 days of the receipt of a complaint, issue a written determination, stating whether a basis exists to make a finding that the facility failed to meet a condition of its Attestation, made a misrepresentation of a material fact therein, or otherwise violated the Act or subpart L or M. The determination shall specify any sanctions imposed due to violations. The Administrator shall provide a notice of such determination to the interested parties and shall inform them of the opportunity for a hearing pursuant to § 655.1220.

§ 655.1210 What penalties and other remedies may the Administrator impose?

(a) The Administrator may assess a civil money penalty not to exceed $1,000 per nurse per violation, with the total penalty not to exceed $10,000 per violation. The Administrator also may impose appropriate remedies, including the payment of back wages, the performance of attested obligations such as providing training, and reinstatement and/or wages for laid off U.S. nurses.

(b) In determining the amount of civil money penalty to be assessed for any violation, the Administrator will consider the type of violation committed and other relevant factors. The matters which may be considered include, but are not limited to, the following:

(1) Previous history of violation, or violations, by the facility under the Act and subpart L or M of this part;

(2) The number of workers affected by the violation or violations;

(3) The gravity of the violation or violations;

(4) Efforts made by the violator in good faith to comply with the Attestation as provided in the Act and subparts L and M of this part;

(5) The violator's explanation of the violation or violations;

(6) The violator's commitment to future compliance, taking into account the public health, interest, or safety; and

(7) The extent to which the violator achieved a financial gain due to the violation, or the potential financial loss or potential injury or adverse effect upon the workers.

(c) The civil money penalty, back wages, and any other remedy determined by the Administrator to be appropriate, are immediately due for payment or performance upon the assessment by the Administrator, or the decision by an administrative law judge where a hearing is requested, or the decision by the Secretary where review is granted. The facility must remit the amount of the civil money penalty, by certified check or money order made payable to the order of "Wage and Hour Division, Labor." The remittance must be delivered or mailed to the Wage and Hour Division Regional Office for the area in which the violation(s) occurred. The payment of back wages, monetary relief, and/or the performance or any other remedy prescribed by the Administrator will follow procedures established by the Administrator. The facility's failure to pay the civil money penalty, back wages, or other monetary relief, or to perform any other assessed remedy, will result in the rejection by ETA of any future Attestation submitted by the facility until such payment or performance is accomplished.

(d) The Federal Civil Penalties Inflation Adjustment Act of 1990, as amended (28 U.S.C. 2461 note), requires that inflationary adjustments to civil money penalties in accordance with a specified cost-of-living formula be made, by regulation, at least every four years. The adjustments are to be based on changes in the Consumer Price Index for all Urban Consumers (CPI-U) for the U.S. City Average for All Items. The adjusted amounts will be published in the FEDERAL REGISTER. The amount of the penalty in a particular case will be based on the amount of the penalty in effect at the time the violation occurs.

§ 655.1215 How are the Administrator's investigation findings issued?

(a) The Administrator's determination, issued under § 655.1205(d), shall be served on the complainant, the facility, and other interested parties by personal service or by certified mail at the parties' last known addresses. Where service by certified mail is not accepted by the party, the Administrator may exercise discretion to serve the determination by regular mail. Where the complainant has requested confidentiality, the Administrator shall serve the determination in a manner which will not breach that confidentiality.

(b) The Administrator's written determination required by § 655.1205(c) shall:

(1) Set forth the determination of the Administrator and the reason or reasons therefore; prescribe any remedies or penalties including the amount of any unpaid wages due, the actions required for compliance with the facility Attestation, and the amount of any civil money penalty assessment and the reason or reasons therefore.

(2) Inform the interested parties that they may request a hearing under § 655.1220.

(3) Inform the interested parties that if a request for a hearing is not received by the Chief Administrative Law Judge within 15 days of the date of the determination, the determination of the Administrator shall become final and not appealable.

(4) Set forth the procedure for requesting a hearing, and give the address of the Chief Administrative Law Judge.

(5) Inform the parties that, under § 655.1255, the Administrator shall notify the Department of Homeland Security and ETA of the occurrence of a violation by the employer.

[75 FR 10406, Mar. 5, 2010]

§ 655.1220 Who can appeal the Administrator's findings and what is the process?

(a) Any interested party desiring review of a determination issued under

§ 655.1205(d), including judicial review, must make a request for an administrative hearing in writing to the Chief Administrative Law Judge at the address stated in the notice of determination. If such a request for an administrative hearing is timely filed, the Administrator's determination shall be inoperative unless and until the case is dismissed or the Administrative Law Judge issues an order affirming the decision.

(b) An interested party may request a hearing in the following circumstances:

(1) Where the Administrator determines that there is no basis for a finding of violation, the complainant or other interested party may request a hearing. In such a proceeding, the party requesting the hearing shall be the prosecuting party and the facility shall be the respondent; the Administrator may intervene as a party or appear as *amicus curiae* at any time in the proceeding, at the Administrator's discretion.

(2) Where the Administrator determines that there is a basis for a finding of violation, the facility or other interested party may request a hearing. In such a proceeding, the Administrator shall be the prosecuting party and the facility shall be the respondent.

(c) No particular form is prescribed for any request for hearing permitted by this part. However, any such request shall:

(1) Be dated;

(2) Be typewritten or legibly written;

(3) Specify the issue or issues stated in the notice of determination giving rise to such request;

(4) State the specific reason or reasons why the party requesting the hearing believes such determination is in error;

(5) Be signed by the party making the request or by an authorized representative of such party; and

(6) Include the address at which such party or authorized representative desires to receive further communications relating thereto.

(d) The request for such hearing must be received by the Chief Administrative Law Judge, at the address stated in the Administrator's notice of determination, no later than 10 days after the date of the determination. An interested party which fails to meet this 10-day deadline for requesting a hearing may thereafter participate in the proceedings only by consent of the administrative law judge, either through intervention as a party under 29 CFR 18.10 (b) through (d) or through participation as an *amicus curiae* under 29 CFR 18.12.

(e) The request may be filed in person, by facsimile transmission, by certified or regular mail, or by courier service. For the requesting party's protection, if the request is filed by mail, it should be certified mail. If the request is filed by facsimile transmission, the original of the request, signed by the requestor or authorized representative, must be filed within 10 days of the date of the Administrator's notice of determination.

(f) Copies of the request for a hearing must be sent by the requestor to the Wage and Hour Division official who issued the Administrator's notice of determination, to the representative(s) of the Solicitor of Labor identified in the notice of determination, and to all known interested parties.

§ 655.1225 What are the rules of practice before an ALJ?

(a) Except as specifically provided in this subpart, and to the extent they do not conflict with the provisions of this subpart, the "Rules of Practice and Procedure for Administrative Hearings Before the Office of Administrative Law Judges" established by the Secretary at 29 CFR part 18 shall apply to administrative proceedings under this subpart.

(b) As provided in the Administrative Procedure Act, 5 U.S.C. 556, any oral or documentary evidence may be received in proceedings under this part. The Federal Rules of Evidence and subpart B of the Rules of Practice and Procedure for Administrative Hearings Before the Office of Administrative Law Judges (29 CFR part 18, subpart B) do not apply, but principles designed to ensure production of relevant and probative evidence shall guide the admission of evidence. The administrative law judge may exclude evidence which is immaterial, irrelevant, or unduly repetitive.

§ 655.1230 What time limits are imposed in ALJ proceedings?

(a) Under this subpart, a party may serve any pleading or document by regular mail. Service is complete upon mailing to the last known address. No additional time for filing or response is authorized where service is by mail. In the interest of expeditious proceedings, the administrative law judge may direct the parties to serve pleadings or documents by a method other than regular mail.

(b) Two (2) copies of all pleadings and other documents in any administrative law judge proceeding shall be served on the attorneys for the Administrator. One copy must be served on the Associate Solicitor, Division of Fair Labor Standards, Office of the Solicitor, U.S. Department of Labor, 200 Constitution Avenue N.W., Washington, D.C. 20210, and one copy on the attorney representing the Administrator in the proceeding.

(c) Time will be computed beginning with the day following the action and includes the last day of the period unless it is a Saturday, Sunday, or Federally-observed holiday, in which case the time period includes the next business day.

§ 655.1235 What are the ALJ proceedings?

(a) Upon receipt of a timely request for a hearing filed in accordance with § 655.1220, the Chief Administrative Law Judge shall appoint an administrative law judge to hear the case.

(b) Within seven (7) days following the assignment of the case, the administrative law judge shall notify all interested parties of the date, time, and place of the hearing. All parties shall be given at least five (5) days notice of such hearing.

(c) The date of the hearing shall be not more than 60 days from the date of the Administrator's determination. Because of the time constraints imposed by the Act, no requests for postponement shall be granted except for compelling reasons and by consent of all the parties to the proceeding.

(d) The administrative law judge may prescribe a schedule by which the parties are permitted to file a pre-hearing brief or other written statement of fact or law. Any such brief or statement shall be served upon each other party in accordance with § 655.1230. Posthearing briefs will not be permitted except at the request of the administrative law judge. When permitted, any such brief shall be limited to the issue or issues specified by the administrative law judge, shall be due within the time prescribed by the administrative law judge, and shall be served on each other party in accordance with § 655.1230.

§ 655.1240 When and how does an ALJ issue a decision?

(a) Within 90 days after receipt of the transcript of the hearing, the administrative law judge shall issue a decision.

(b) The decision of the administrative law judge shall include a statement of findings and conclusions, with reasons and basis therefore, upon each material issue presented on the record. The decision shall also include an appropriate order which may affirm, deny, reverse, or modify, in whole or in part, the determination of the Administrator; the reason or reasons for such order shall be stated in the decision. The administrative law judge shall not render determinations as to the legality of a regulatory provision or the constitutionality of a statutory provision.

(c) The decision shall be served on all parties in person or by certified or regular mail.

§ 655.1245 Who can appeal the ALJ's decision and what is the process?

(a) The Administrator or any interested party desiring review of the decision and order of an administrative law judge, including judicial review, must petition the Department's Administrative Review Board (Board) to review the ALJ's decision and order. To be effective, such petition must be received by the Board within 30 days of the date of the decision and order. Copies of the petition must be served on all parties and on the administrative law judge.

(b) No particular form is prescribed for any petition for the Board's review permitted by this subpart. However, any such petition must:

(1) Be dated;

(2) Be typewritten or legibly written;

(3) Specify the issue or issues stated in the administrative law judge's decision and order giving rise to such petition;

(4) State the specific reason or reasons why the party petitioning for review believes such decision and order are in error;

(5) Be signed by the party filing the petition or by an authorized representative of such party;

(6) Include the address at which such party or authorized representative desires to receive further communications relating thereto; and

(7) Attach copies of the administrative law judge's decision and order, and any other record documents which would assist the Board in determining whether review is warranted.

(c) Whenever the Board determines to review the decision and order of an administrative law judge, a notice of the Board's determination must be served upon the administrative law judge and upon all parties to the proceeding within 30 days after the Board's receipt of the petition for review. If the Board determines that it will review the decision and order, the order shall be inoperative unless and until the Board issues an order affirming the decision and order.

(d) Within 15 days of receipt of the Board's notice, the Office of Administrative Law Judges shall forward the complete hearing record to the Board.

(e) The Board's notice shall specify:

(1) The issue or issues to be reviewed;

(2) The form in which submissions must be made by the parties (e.g., briefs, oral argument);

(3) The time within which such submissions must be made.

(f) All documents submitted to the Board must be filed with the Administrative Review Board, Room S–4309, U.S. Department of Labor, Washington, D.C. 20210. An original and two copies of all documents must be filed. Documents are not deemed filed with the Board until actually received by the Board. All documents, including documents filed by mail, must be received by the Board either on or before the due date.

(g) Copies of all documents filed with the Board must be served upon all other parties involved in the proceeding. Service upon the Administrator must be in accordance with §655.1230(b).

(h) The Board's final decision shall be issued within 180 days from the date of the notice of intent to review. The Board's decision shall be served upon all parties and the administrative law judge.

(i) Upon issuance of the Board's decision, the Board shall transmit the entire record to the Chief Administrative Law Judge for custody in accordance with §655.1250.

§655.1250 Who is the official record keeper for these administrative appeals?

The official record of every completed administrative hearing procedure provided by subparts L and M of this part shall be maintained and filed under the custody and control of the Chief Administrative Law Judge. Upon receipt of a complaint seeking review of the final agency action in a United States District Court, the Chief Administrative Law Judge shall certify the official record and shall transmit such record to the clerk of the court.

§655.1255 What are the procedures for debarment of a facility based on a finding of violation?

(a) The Administrator shall notify the Department of Homeland Security and ETA of the final determination of a violation by a facility upon the earliest of the following events:

(1) Where the Administrator determines that there is a basis for a finding of violation by a facility, and no timely request for hearing is made under §655.1220; or

(2) Where, after a hearing, the administrative law judge issues a decision and order finding a violation by a facility, and no timely petition for review to the Board is made under §655.1245; or

(3) Where a petition for review is taken from an administrative law judge's decision and the Board either declines within 30 days to entertain the appeal, under §655.1245(c), or the Board affirms the administrative law judge's determination; or

(4) Where the administrative law judge finds that there was no violation

by a facility, and the Board, upon review, issues a decision under § 655.1245(h), holding that a violation was committed by a facility.

(b) U.S. Citizenship and Immigration Services, upon receipt of the Administrator's notice under paragraph (a) of this section, shall not approve petitions filed with respect to that employer under section 212(m) of the INA (8 U.S.C. 1182(m)) during a period of at least 12 months from the date of receipt of the Administrator's notification. The Administrator must provide USCIS with a recommendation as to the length of the debarment.

(c) ETA, upon receipt of the Administrator's notice under paragraph (a) of this section, shall suspend the employer's attestation(s) under subparts L and M of this part, and shall not accept for filing any attestation submitted by the employer under subparts L and M of this part, for a period of 12 months from the date of receipt of the Administrator's notification or for a longer period if one is specified by the Department of Homeland Security for visa petitions filed by that employer under section 212(m) of the INA.

[75 FR 10406, Mar. 5, 2010]

§ 655.1260 Can Equal Access to Justice Act attorney fees be awarded?

A proceeding under subpart L or M of this part is not subject to the Equal Access to Justice Act, as amended, 5 U.S.C. 504. In such a proceeding, the administrative law judge shall have no authority to award attorney fees and/or other litigation expenses under the provisions of the Equal Access to Justice Act.

Subpart N—Labor Certification Process for Temporary Agricultural Employment in the United States (H–2A Workers)

SOURCE: 73 FR 77207, Dec. 18, 2008, unless otherwise noted. Redesignated at 74 FR 25985, May 29, 2009.

EFFECTIVE DATE NOTE: At 74 FR 25985, May 29, 2009, subpart B, consisting of §§ 655.90, 655.92, 655.93, and 655.100 through 655.119, was redesignated as subpart N, consisting of §§ 655.1290, 655.1292, 655.1293, and 655.1300 through 655.1319, and newly designated subpart N was suspended, effective June 29, 2009.

§ 655.1290 Purpose and scope of subpart B.

This subpart sets out the procedures established by the Secretary of the United States Department of Labor (the Secretary) to acquire information sufficient to make factual determinations of:

(a) Whether there are sufficient able, willing, and qualified U.S. workers available to perform the temporary and seasonal agricultural employment for which an employer desires to import nonimmigrant foreign workers (H–2A workers); and

(b) Whether the employment of H–2A workers will adversely affect the wages and working conditions of workers in the U.S. similarly employed.

§ 655.1292 Authority of ETA–OFLC.

Temporary agricultural labor certification determinations are made by the Administrator, Office of Foreign Labor Certification (OFLC) in the Department of Labor's (the Department or DOL) Employment & Training Administration (ETA), who, in turn, may delegate this responsibility to a designated staff member; e.g., a Certifying Officer (CO).

§ 655.1293 Special procedures.

(a) *Systematic process.* This subpart provides procedures for the processing of applications from agricultural employers and associations of employers for the certification of employment of nonimmigrant workers in agricultural employment.

(b) *Establishment of special procedures.* To provide for a limited degree of flexibility in carrying out the Secretary's responsibilities under the Immigration and Nationality Act (INA), while not deviating from statutory requirements, the Administrator, OFLC has the authority to establish or to devise, continue, revise, or revoke special procedures in the form of variances for processing certain H–2A applications when employers can demonstrate upon written application to the Administrator, OFLC that special procedures are necessary. These include special procedures in effect for the handling of applications for sheepherders in the Western States (and adaptation of such procedures to occupations in the range production of other livestock), and for custom combine crews. In a like manner, for work in occupations characterized by other than a reasonably regular workday or workweek, such as the range production of sheep or other livestock, the Administrator, OFLC has the authority to establish monthly, weekly, or bi-weekly adverse effect wage rates (AEWR) for those occupations for a statewide or other geographical area. Prior to making determinations under this section, the Administrator, OFLC will consult with employer and worker representatives.

§ 655.1300 Overview of subpart B and definition of terms.

(a) *Overview*—(1) *Application filing process.* (i) This subpart provides guidance to employers desiring to apply for a labor certification for the employment of H–2A workers to perform agricultural employment of a temporary or seasonal nature. The regulations in this subpart provide that such employers must file with the Administrator, OFLC an H–2A application on forms prescribed by the ETA that describe the material terms and conditions of employment to be offered and afforded to U.S. and H–2A workers. The application must be filed with the Administrator, OFLC at least 45 calendar days before the first date the employer requires the services of the H–2A workers. The application must contain attestations of the employer's compliance or promise to comply with program requirements regarding recruitment of eligible U.S. workers, the payment of an appropriate wage, and terms and conditions of employment.

(ii) No more than 75 and no fewer than 60 calendar days before the first date the employer requires the services of the H–2A workers, and as a precursor to the filing of an *Application for Temporary Employment Certification*, the employer must initiate positive recruitment of eligible U.S. workers and cooperate with the local office of the State Workforce Agency (SWA) which serves the area of intended employment to place a job order into intrastate and interstate recruitment. Prior to commencing recruitment an employer must obtain the appropriate wage for the position directly from the ETA National Processing Center (NPC). The employer must then place a job order with the SWA; place print advertisements meeting the requirements of this regulation; contact former U.S. employees; and, when so designated by the Secretary, recruit in other States of traditional or expected labor supply with a significant number of U.S. workers who, if recruited, would be willing to make themselves available at the time and place needed. The SWA will post the job order locally, as well as in all States listed in the application as anticipated work sites, and in any additional States designated by the Secretary as States of traditional or expected labor supply. The SWA will keep the job order open until the end of the designated recruitment period. No more than 50 days prior to the first date the employer requires the services of the H–2A workers, the employer will prepare and sign an initial written recruitment report that it must submit with its *Application for Temporary Employment Certification* (*www.foreignlaborcert.doleta.gov*). The recruitment report must contain information regarding the original number of openings for which the employer recruited. The employer's obligation to engage in positive recruitment will end on the actual date on which the H–2A workers depart for the place of work, or 3 days prior to the first date the employer requires the services of the H–2A workers, whichever occurs first.

(iii) The *Application for Temporary Employment Certification* must be filed by mail unless the Department publishes a Notice in the FEDERAL REGISTER requiring that applications be filed electronically. Applications that meet threshold requirements for completeness and accuracy will be processed by NPC staff, who will review each application for compliance with the criteria for certification. Each application must meet requirements for timeliness and temporary need and must provide assurances and other safeguards against adverse impact on the wages and working conditions of U.S. workers. Employers receiving a labor certification must continue to cooperate with the SWA by accepting referrals—and have the obligation to hire qualified and eligible U.S. workers who apply—until the end of the designated recruitment period.

(2) *Deficient applications.* The CO will promptly review the application and notify the applicant in writing if there are deficiencies that render the application not acceptable for certification, and afford the applicant a 5 calendar day period (from date of the employer's receipt) to resubmit a modified application or to file an appeal of the CO's decision not to approve the application as acceptable for consideration. Modified applications that fail to cure deficiencies will be denied.

(3) *Amendment of applications.* This subpart provides for the amendment of applications. Where the recruitment is not materially affected by such amendments, additional positive recruitment will not be required.

(4) *Determinations*—(i) *Determinations.* If the employer has complied with the criteria for certification, including recruitment of eligible U.S. workers, the CO must make a determination on the application by 30 days before the first date the employer requires the services of the H–2A workers. An employer's failure to comply with any of the certification criteria or to cure deficiencies identified by the CO may lengthen the time required for processing, resulting in a final determination less than 30 days prior to the stated date of need.

(ii) *Certified applications.* This subpart provides that an application for temporary agricultural labor certification will be certified if the CO finds that the employer has not offered and does not intend to offer foreign workers higher wages, better working conditions, or fewer restrictions than those offered and afforded to U.S. workers; that sufficient U.S. workers who are able, willing, qualified, and eligible will not be available at the time and place needed to perform the work for which H–2A workers are being requested; and that the employment of such nonimmigrants will not adversely affect the wages and working conditions of similarly employed U.S. workers.

(iii) *Fees*—(A) *Amount.* This subpart provides that each employer (except joint employer associations) of H–2A workers will pay the appropriate fees to the Department for each temporary agricultural labor certification received.

(B) *Timeliness of payment.* The fee must be received by the CO no later than 30 calendar days after the granting of each temporary agricultural labor certification. Fees received any later are untimely. A persistent or prolonged failure to pay fees in a timely manner is a substantial program violation which may result in the denial of future temporary agricultural labor certifications and/or program debarment.

(iv) *Denied applications.* This subpart provides that if the application for temporary agricultural labor certification is denied, in whole or in part, the employer may seek expedited review of the denial, or a de novo hearing, by an administrative law judge as provided in this subpart.

(b) *Transition of filing procedures from current regulations*—(1) *Compliance with these regulations.* Employers with a date of need for H–2A workers for temporary or seasonal agricultural services on or after January 1, 2010 must comply with all of the obligations and assurances required in this subpart.

(2) *Transition from former regulations.* Employers with a date of need for H–2A workers for temporary or seasonal agricultural services prior to January 1, 2010 will file applications in the following manner:

(i) *Obtaining required wage rate.* An employer will not obtain an offered wage rate through the NPC prior to filing an application, but will complete and submit Form ETA–9142, *Application for Temporary Employment Certification* no less than 45 days prior to their date of need. The employer will simultaneously submit Form ETA–790 *Agricultural and Food Processing Clearance Order*, along with the *Application for Temporary Employment Certification*, directly to the NPC having jurisdiction over H–2A applications.

(ii) *Pre-filing activities.* Activities required to be conducted prior to filing under the final rule will be conducted post-filing during this transition period. The employer will be expected to make attestations in its application applicable to its future activities concerning recruitment, payment of the offered wage rate, etc. Employers will not be required to complete an initial recruitment report for submission with the application, but will be required to complete a recruitment report for submission to the NPC prior to certification, and will also be required to complete a final recruitment report covering the entire recruitment period.

(iii) *Acceptance of application.* Upon receipt, the NPC will provide the employer with the wage rate to be offered, at a minimum, by the employer, and will process the application in a manner consistent with new § 655.107, issuing a notification of deficiencies for any curable deficiencies within 7 calendar days.

(iv) *Processing of application.* Once the application and job order have been accepted, the NPC will transmit a copy of the job order to the SWA(s) serving the area of intended employment to initiate intrastate and interstate clearance, request that the SWA(s) schedule an inspection of the housing, and provide instructions to the employer to commence positive recruitment in a manner consistent with § 655.102(d)(2) through (4). The NPC will designate labor supply States during this period on a case-by-case basis. Such designations must be based on information provided by State agencies or by other sources, and will to the extent information is available take into account the success of recent efforts by out-of-State employers to recruit in that State.

(c) *Definitions of terms used in this subpart.* For the purposes of this subpart:

Administrative Law Judge (ALJ) means a person within the DOL's Office of Administrative Law Judges appointed pursuant to 5 U.S.C. 3105, or a panel of such persons designated by the Chief Administrative Law Judge from the Board of Alien Labor Certification Appeals (BALCA) established by part 656 of this chapter, which will hear and decide appeals as set forth in § 655.115.

Administrator, OFLC means the primary official of the Office of Foreign Labor Certification (*OFLC*), or the Administrator, OFLC 's designee.

Adverse effect wage rate (AEWR) means the minimum wage rate that the Administrator, OFLC has determined must be offered and paid to every H–2A worker employed under the DOL-approved *Application for Temporary Employment Certification* in a particular occupation and/or area, as well as to U.S. workers hired by employers into corresponding employment during the H–2A recruitment period, to ensure that the wages of similarly employed U.S. workers will not be adversely affected.

Agent means a legal entity or person, such as an association of agricultural employers, or an attorney for an association, that:

(1) Is authorized to act on behalf of the employer for temporary agricultural labor certification purposes;

(2) Is not itself an employer, or a joint employer, as defined in this paragraph (c) of this section with respect to a specific application; and

(3) Is not under suspension, debarment, expulsion, or disbarment from practice before any court or the Department, the Board of Immigration Appeals, the immigration judges, or the Department of Homeland Security (DHS) under 8 CFR 292.3 or 1003.101.

Agricultural association means any nonprofit or cooperative association of farmers, growers, or ranchers (including but not limited to processing establishments, canneries, gins, packing sheds, nurseries, or other fixed-site agricultural employers), incorporated or qualified under applicable State law, that recruits, solicits, hires, employs, furnishes, houses or transports any worker that is subject to sec. 218 of the INA. An agricultural association may act as the agent of an employer for purposes of filing an *Application for Temporary Employment Certification*, and may also act as the sole or joint employer of H–2A workers.

Application for Temporary Employment Certification means the Office of Management and Budget (OMB)-approved form submitted by an employer to secure a temporary agricultural labor certification determination from DOL. A complete submission of the *Application for Temporary Employment Certification* includes both the form and the employer's initial recruitment report.

Area of intended employment means the geographic area within normal commuting distance of the place (worksite address) of the job opportunity for which the certification is sought. There is no rigid measure of distance which constitutes a normal commuting distance or normal commuting area, because there may be widely varying factual circumstances among different areas (e.g., average commuting times, barriers to reaching the worksite, quality of the regional transportation network, etc.). If the place of intended employment is within a Metropolitan Statistical Area (MSA), including a multistate MSA, any place within the MSA is deemed to be within normal commuting distance of the place of intended employment. The borders of MSAs are not controlling in the identification of the normal commuting area; a location outside of an MSA may be within normal commuting distance of a location that is inside (e.g., near the border of) the MSA.

Attorney means any person who is a member in good standing of the bar of the highest court of any State, possession, territory, or commonwealth of the U.S., or the District of Columbia, and who is not under suspension, debarment, expulsion, or disbarment from practice before any court or the Department, the Board of Immigration Appeals, the immigration judges, or DHS under 8 CFR. 292.3 or 1003.101. Such a person is permitted to act as an agent or attorney for an employer and/or foreign worker under this subpart.

Certifying Officer (CO) means the person designated by the Administrator, OFLC to make determinations on applications filed under the H–2A program.

Chief Administrative Law Judge means the chief official of the DOL Office of Administrative Law Judges or the Chief Administrative Law Judge's designee.

Date of need means the first date the employer requires the services of H–2A worker as indicated in the employer's *Application for Temporary Employment Certification.*

Department of Homeland Security (DHS) means the Federal agency having control over certain immigration functions that, through its sub-agency, *United States Citizenship and Immigration Services* (USCIS), makes the determination under the INA on whether to grant visa petitions filed by employers seeking H–2A workers to perform temporary agricultural work in the U.S.

DOL or Department means the United States Department of Labor.

Eligible worker means an individual who is not an unauthorized alien (as defined in sec. 274A(h)(3) of the INA, 8 U.S.C. 1324a(h)(3)) with respect to the employment in which the worker is engaging.

Employee means employee as defined under the general common law of agency. Some of the factors relevant to the determination of employee status include: the hiring party's right to control the manner and means by which the work is accomplished; the skill required to perform the work; the source of the instrumentalities and tools for accomplishing the work; the location of the work; the hiring party's discretion over when and how long to work; and whether the work is part of the regular business of the hiring party. Other applicable factors may be considered and no one factor is dispositive.

Employer means a person, firm, corporation or other association or organization that:

(1) Has a place of business (physical location) in the U.S. and a means by which it may be contacted for employment;

(2) Has an employer relationship with respect to H–2A employees or related U.S. workers under this subpart; and

(3) Possesses, for purposes of filing an *Application for Temporary Employment Certification,* a valid Federal Employer Identification Number (FEIN).

Employment Standards Administration (ESA) means the agency within DOL that includes the Wage and Hour Division (WHD), and which is charged with carrying out certain investigative and enforcement functions of the Secretary under the INA.

Employment Service (ES) refers to the system of Federal and State entities responsible for administration of the labor certification process for temporary and seasonal agricultural employment of nonimmigrant foreign workers. This includes the SWAs and the OFLC, including the NPCs.

Employment and Training Administration (ETA) means the agency within the DOL that includes OFLC.

Federal holiday means a legal public holiday as defined at 5 U.S.C. 6103.

Fixed-site employer means any person engaged in agriculture who meets the definition of an employer as those terms are defined in this subpart who owns or operates a farm, ranch, processing establishment, cannery, gin, packing shed, nursery, or other similar fixed-site location where agricultural activities are performed and who recruits, solicits, hires, employs, houses, or transports any worker subject to sec. 218 of the INA or these regulations as incident to or in conjunction with the owner's or operator's own agricultural operation. For purposes of this subpart, *person* includes any individual, partnership, association, corporation, cooperative, joint stock company, trust, or other organization with legal rights and duties.

H–2A Labor Contractor (H–2ALC) means any person who meets the definition of employer under this paragraph (c) of this section and is not a fixed-site employer, an agricultural association, or an employee of a fixed-site employer or agricultural association, as those terms are used in this part, who recruits, solicits, hires, employs, furnishes, houses, or transports any worker subject to sec. 218 of the INA or these regulations.

H–2A worker means any temporary foreign worker who is lawfully present in the U.S. to perform agricultural labor or services of a temporary or seasonal nature pursuant to sec. 101(a)(15)(H)(ii)(a) of the INA, as amended.

INA means the Immigration and Nationality Act, as amended, 8 U.S.C. 1101 *et seq.*

Job offer means the offer made by an employer or potential employer of H–2A workers to eligible workers describing all the material terms and conditions of employment, including those relating to wages, working conditions, and other benefits.

Job opportunity means a job opening for temporary, full-time employment at a place in the U.S. to which a U.S. worker can be referred.

Joint employment means that where two or more employers each have sufficient definitional indicia of employment to be considered the employer of an employee, those employers will be considered to jointly employ that employee. Each employer in a joint employment relationship to an employee is considered a joint employer of that employee.

Occupational Safety and Health Administration (OSHA) means the organizational component of the Department that assures the safety and health of America's workers by setting and enforcing standards; providing training, outreach, and education; establishing partnerships; and encouraging continual improvement in workplace safety and health under the Occupational Safety and Health Act, as amended.

Office of Foreign Labor Certification (OFLC) means the organizational component of the ETA that provides national leadership and policy guidance and develops regulations and procedures to carry out the responsibilities of the Secretary under the INA concerning the admission of foreign workers to the U.S. to perform work described in sec. 101(a)(15)(H)(ii)(a) of the INA, as amended.

Positive recruitment means the active participation of an employer or its authorized hiring agent in recruiting and interviewing qualified and eligible individuals in the area where the employer's job opportunity is located and any other State designated by the Secretary as an area of traditional or expected labor supply with respect to the area where the employer's job opportunity is located, in an effort to fill specific job openings with U.S. workers.

Prevailing means, with respect to practices engaged in by employers and benefits other than wages provided by employers, that:

(1) Fifty percent or more of employers in an area and for an occupation engage in the practice or offer the benefit; but only if

(2) This 50 percent or more of employers also employs in aggregate 50 percent or more of U.S. workers in the occupation and area (including H–2A and non-H–2A employers for purposes of determinations concerning the provision of family housing, frequency of wage payments, and workers supplying their own bedding, but non-H–2A employers

only for determinations concerning the provision of advance transportation).

Prevailing piece rate means that amount that is typically paid to an agricultural worker per piece (which includes, but is not limited to, a load, bin, pallet, bag, bushel, etc.), to be determined by the SWA according to a methodology published by the Department. As is currently the case, the unit of production will be required to be clearly described; e.g., a field box of oranges (1½ bushels), a bushel of potatoes, and Eastern apple box (1½ metric bushels), a flat of strawberries (twelve quarts), etc.

Prevailing hourly wage means the hourly wage determined by the SWA to be prevailing in the area in accordance with State-based wage surveys.

Representative means a person or entity employed by, or duly authorized to act on behalf of, the employer with respect to activities entered into for, and/or attestations made with respect to, the *Application for Temporary Employment Certification.*

Secretary means the Secretary of the United States Department of Labor, or the Secretary's designee.

Secretary of Homeland Security means the chief official of the United States Department of Homeland Security (DHS) or the Secretary of Homeland Security's designee.

Secretary of State means the chief official of the United States Department of State (DOS) or the Secretary of State's designee.

State Workforce Agency (SWA) means the State government agency that receives funds pursuant to the Wagner-Peyser Act to administer the public labor exchange delivered through the State's One-Stop delivery system in accordance with the Wagner-Peyser Act at 29 U.S.C. 49 *et seq*. Separately, SWAs receive ETA grants, administered by OFLC, to assist them in performing certain activities related to foreign labor certification, including conducting housing inspections.

Strike means a labor dispute wherein employees engage in a concerted stoppage of work (including stoppage by reason of the expiration of a collective-bargaining agreement) or engage in any concerted slowdown or other concerted interruption of operation. Whether a job opportunity is vacant by reason of a strike or lock out will be determined by evaluating for each position identified as vacant in the *Application for Temporary Employment Certification* whether the specific vacancy has been caused by the strike or lock out.

Successor in interest means that, in determining whether an employer is a successor in interest, the factors used under Title VII of the Civil Rights Act and the Vietnam Era Veterans' Readjustment Assistance Act will be considered. When considering whether an employer is a successor for purposes of § 655.118, the primary consideration will be the personal involvement of the firm's ownership, management, supervisors, and others associated with the firm in the violations resulting in a debarment recommendation. Normally, wholly new management or ownership of the same business operation, one in which the former management or owner does not retain a direct or indirect interest, will not be deemed to be a successor in interest for purposes of debarment. A determination of whether or not a successor in interest exists is based on the entire circumstances viewed in their totality. The factors to be considered include:

(1) Substantial continuity of the same business operations;

(2) Use of the same facilities;

(3) Continuity of the work force;

(4) Similarity of jobs and working conditions;

(5) Similarity of supervisory personnel;

(6) Similarity in machinery, equipment, and production methods;

(7) Similarity of products and services; and

(8) The ability of the predecessor to provide relief.

Temporary agricultural labor certification means the certification made by the Secretary with respect to an employer seeking to file with DHS a visa petition to employ one or more foreign nationals as an H–2A worker, pursuant to secs. 101(a)(15)(H)(ii)(a), 214(a) and (c), and 218 of the INA that:

(1) There are not sufficient workers who are able, willing, and qualified, and who will be available at the time

and place needed, to perform the agricultural labor or services involved in the petition, and

(2) The employment of the foreign worker in such agricultural labor or services will not adversely affect the wages and working conditions of workers in the U.S. similarly employed (8 U.S.C. 1101(a)(15)(H)(ii)(a), 1184(a) and (c), and 1188).

United States (U.S.), when used in a geographic sense, means the continental United States, Alaska, Hawaii, the Commonwealth of Puerto Rico, and the territories of Guam, the Virgin Islands, and, as of the transition program effective date, as defined in the Consolidated Natural Resources Act of 2008, Public Law 110–229, Title VII, the Commonwealth of the Northern Mariana Islands.

United States Citizenship and Immigration Services (USCIS) means the Federal agency making the determination under the INA whether to grant petitions filed by employers seeking H–2A workers to perform temporary agricultural work in the U.S.

United States worker (U.S. worker) means a worker who is

(1) A citizen or national of the U.S., or

(2) An alien who is lawfully admitted for permanent residence in the U.S., is admitted as a refugee under sec. 207 of the INA, is granted asylum under sec. 208 of the INA, or is an immigrant otherwise authorized (by the INA or by DHS) to be employed in the U.S.

Wages means all forms of cash remuneration to a worker by an employer in payment for personal services.

Within [number and type] days means, for purposes of determining an employer's compliance with the timing requirements for appeals and requests for review, a period that begins to run on the first business day after the Department sends a notice to the employer by means normally assuring next-day delivery, and will end on the day that the employer sends whatever communication is required by these rules back to the Department, as evidenced by a postal mark or other similar receipt.

Work contract means all the material terms and conditions of employment relating to wages, hours, working conditions, and other benefits, required by the applicable regulations in Subpart B of 20 CFR part 655, *Labor Certification for Temporary Agricultural Employment of H–2A Aliens in the U.S. (H–2A Workers)*, or these regulations, including those terms and conditions attested to by the H–2A employer, which contract between the employer and the worker may be in the form of a separate written document. In the absence of a separate written work contract incorporating the required terms and conditions of employment, agreed to by both the employer and the worker, the work contract at a minimum shall be the terms of the job order, as provided in 20 CFR part 653, Subpart F, and covered provisions of the work contract shall be enforced in accordance with these regulations.

(d) *Definition of agricultural labor or services of a temporary or seasonal nature.* For the purposes of this subpart means the following:

(1) *Agricultural labor or services*, pursuant to sec. 101(a)(15)(H)(ii)(a) of the INA at 8 U.S.C. 1101(a)(15)(H)(ii)(a), is defined as:

(i) Agricultural labor as defined and applied in sec. 3121(g) of the Internal Revenue Code of 1954 at 26 U.S.C. 3121(g);

(ii) Agriculture as defined and applied in sec. 3(f) of the Fair Labor Standards Act of 1938 (FLSA) at 29 U.S.C. 203(f). Work performed by H–2A workers, or workers in corresponding employment, that is not defined as agriculture in sec. 3(f) is subject to the provisions of the FLSA as provided therein, including the overtime provisions in sec. 7(a) 29 U.S.C. 207(a);

(iii) The pressing of apples for cider on a farm;

(iv) Logging employment; or

(v) Handling, planting, drying, packing, packaging, processing, freezing, grading, storing, or delivering to storage or to market or to a carrier for transportation to market, in its unmanufactured state, any agricultural or horticultural commodity while in the employ of the operator of a farm where no H–2B workers are employed to perform the same work at the same establishment; or

(vi) Other work typically performed on a farm that is not specifically listed on the *Application for Temporary Employment Certification* and is minor (*i.e.*, less than 20 percent of the total time worked on the job duties and activities that are listed on the *Application for Temporary Employment Certification*) and incidental to the agricultural labor or services for which the H–2A worker was sought.

(2) An occupation included in either of the statutory definitions cited in paragraphs (d)(1)(i) and (ii) of this section is *agricultural labor or services*, notwithstanding the exclusion of that occupation from the other statutory definition.

(i) *Agricultural labor.* For purposes of paragraph (d)(1)(i) of this section means all services performed:

(A) On a farm, in the employ of any person, in connection with cultivating the soil, or in connection with raising or harvesting any agricultural or horticultural commodity, including the raising, shearing, feeding, caring for, training, and management of livestock, bees, poultry, and furbearing animals and wildlife;

(B) In the employ of the owner or tenant or other operator of a farm, in connection with the operation or maintenance of such farm and its tools and equipment, or in salvaging timber or clearing land of brush and other debris left by a hurricane, if the major part of such service is performed on a farm;

(C) In connection with the production or harvesting of any commodity defined as an agricultural commodity in sec. 15(g) of the Agricultural Marketing Act, as amended at 12 U.S.C. 1141j, or in connection with the ginning of cotton, or in connection with the operation or maintenance of ditches, canals, reservoirs, or waterways, not owned or operated for profit, used exclusively for supplying and storing water for farming purposes;

(D)(*1*) In the employ of the operator of a farm in handling, planting, drying, packing, packaging, processing, freezing, grading, storing, or delivering to storage or to market or to a carrier for transportation to market, in its unmanufactured state, any agricultural or horticultural commodity, but only if such operator produced more than one-half of the commodity with respect to which such service is performed;

(*2*) In the employ of a group of operators of farms (other than a cooperative organization) in the performance of service described in paragraph (d)(2)(i)(D)(*1*) of this section, but only if such operators produced all of the commodity with respect to which such service is performed. For purposes of this paragraph, any unincorporated group of operators will be deemed a cooperative organization if the number of operators comprising such group is more than 20 at any time during the calendar quarter in which such service is performed;

(*3*) The provisions of paragraphs (d)(2)(i)(D)(*1*) and (*2*) of this section do not apply to services performed in connection with commercial canning or commercial freezing or in connection with any agricultural or horticultural commodity after its delivery to a terminal market for distribution for consumption; or

(*4*) On a farm operated for profit if such service is not in the course of the employer's trade or business and is not domestic service in a private home of the employer.

(E) For purposes of (d)(2)(i) of this section, the term farm includes stock, dairy, poultry, fruit, fur-bearing animal, and truck farms, plantations, ranches, nurseries, ranges, greenhouses or other similar structures used primarily for the raising of agricultural or horticultural commodities, and orchards. See sec. 3121(g) of the Internal Revenue Code of 1986 at 26 U.S.C. 3121(g).

(ii) *Agriculture.* For purposes of paragraph (d)(1)(ii) of this section agriculture means farming in all its branches and among other things includes the cultivation and tillage of the soil, dairying, the production, cultivation, growing, and harvesting of any agricultural or horticultural commodities (including commodities as defined as agricultural commodities in 12 U.S.C. 1141j(g)), the raising of livestock, bees, fur-bearing animals, or poultry, and any practices (including any forestry or lumbering operations) performed by a farmer or on a farm as an incident to or in conjunction with such farming operations, including preparation for market, delivery to storage or to market or to carriers for transportation to market. See 29 U.S.C. 203(f), as amended.

(iii) *Agricultural commodity.* For purposes of paragraph (d)(2)(ii) of this section agricultural commodity includes, in addition to other agricultural commodities, crude gum (oleoresin) from a living tree, and gum spirits of turpentine and gum rosin as processed by the original producer of the crude gum (oleoresin) from which derived. *Gum spirits of turpentine* means spirits of turpentine made from gum (oleoresin) from a living tree and *gum rosin* means rosin remaining after the distillation of gum spirits of turpentine. See 12 U.S.C. 1141j(g), sec. 15(g) of the Agricultural Marketing Act, as amended, and 7 U.S.C. 92.

(3) *Of a temporary or seasonal nature*—(i) *On a seasonal or other temporary basis.* For the purposes of this subpart, of a temporary or seasonal nature means on a seasonal or other temporary basis, as defined in the WHD's regulation at 29 CFR 500.20 under the Migrant and Seasonal Agricultural Worker Protection Act (MSPA).

(ii) *MSPA definition.* The definition of *on a seasonal or other temporary basis* found in MSPA is summarized as follows:

(A) Labor is performed on a seasonal basis where, ordinarily, the employment pertains to or is of the kind exclusively performed at certain seasons or periods of the year and which, from its nature, may not be continuous or carried on throughout the year. A worker who moves from one seasonal activity to another, while employed in agriculture or performing agricultural labor, is employed on a seasonal basis even though the worker may continue to be employed during a major portion of the year.

(B) A worker is employed on other temporary basis where he or she is employed for a limited time only or the worker's performance is contemplated for a particular piece of work, usually of short duration. Generally, employment which is contemplated to continue indefinitely is not temporary.

(C) On a seasonal or other temporary basis does not include (i) the employment of any foreman or other supervisory employee who is employed by a specific agricultural employer or agricultural association essentially on a year round basis; or (ii) the employment of any worker who is living at his or her permanent place of residence, when that worker is employed by a specific agricultural employer or agricultural association on essentially a year round basis to perform a variety of tasks for his or her employer and is not primarily employed to do field work.

(iii) *Temporary.* For the purposes of this subpart, the definition of "temporary" in paragraph (d)(3) of this section refers to any job opportunity covered by this subpart where the employer needs a worker for a position for a limited period of time, including, but not limited to, a peakload need, which is generally less than 1 year, unless the original temporary agricultural labor certification is extended pursuant to § 655.110.

[73 FR 77207, Dec. 18, 2008, as amended at 74 FR 17601, Apr. 16, 2009]

§ 655.1301 Applications for temporary employment certification in agriculture.

(a) *Application filing requirements.* (1) An employer that desires to apply for temporary employment certification of one or more nonimmigrant foreign workers must file a completed DOL *Application for Temporary Employment Certification* form and, unless a specific exemption applies, the initial recruitment report. If an association of agricultural producers files the application, the association must identify whether it is the sole employer, a joint employer with its employer-member employers, or the agent of its employer-members. The association must retain documentation substantiating the employer or agency status of the association and be prepared to submit such documentation to the CO in the event of an audit.

(2) If an H–2ALC intends to file an application, the H–2ALC must meet all of the requirements of the definition of employer in § 655.100(b), and comply with all the assurances, guarantees, and other requirements contained in this part and in part 653, subpart F, of this chapter. The H–2ALC must have a place of business (physical location) in the U.S. and a means by which it may be contacted for employment. H–2A

workers employed by an H–2ALC may not perform services for a fixed-site employer unless the H–2ALC is itself providing the housing and transportation required by § 655.104(d) and (h), or has filed a statement confirming that the fixed-site employer will provide compliant housing and/or transportation, as required by § 655.106, with the OFLC, for each fixed-site employer listed on the application. The H–2ALC must retain a copy of the statement of compliance required by § 655.106(b)(6).

(3) An association of agricultural producers may submit a master application covering a variety of job opportunities available with a number of employers in multiple areas of intended employment, just as though all of the covered employers were in fact a single employer, as long as a single date of need is provided for all workers requested by the application and the combination of job opportunities is supported by an explanation demonstrating a business reason for the combination. The association must identify on the *Application for Temporary Employment Certification,* by name and address, each employer that will employ H–2A workers. If the association is acting solely as an agent, each employer will receive a separate labor certification.

(b) *Filing.* The employer may send the *Application for Temporary Employment Certification* and all supporting documentation by U.S. Mail or private mail courier to the NPC. The Department will publish a Notice in the FEDERAL REGISTER identifying the address(es), and any future address changes, to which applications must be mailed, and will also post these addresses on the DOL Internet Web site at *http://www.foreignlaborcert.doleta.gov/.* The form must bear the original signature of the employer (and that of the employer's authorized attorney or agent if the employer is represented by an attorney or agent). An association filing a master application as a joint employer may sign on behalf of its employer members. The Department may also require applications to be filed electronically in addition to or instead of by mail.

(c) *Timeliness.* A completed *Application for Temporary Employment Certification* must be filed no less than 45 calendar days before date of need.

(d) *Emergency situations*—(1) *Waiver of time period and required pre-filing activity.* The CO may waive the time period for filing and pre-filing wage and recruitment requirements set forth in § 655.102, along with their associated attestations, for employers who did not make use of temporary alien agricultural workers during the prior year's agricultural season or for any employer that has other good and substantial cause (which may include unforeseen changes in market conditions), provided that the CO can timely make the determinations required by § 655.109(b).

(2) *Employer requirements.* The employer requesting a waiver of the required time period and pre-filing wage and recruitment requirements must submit to the NPC a completed *Application for Temporary Employment Certification,* a completed job offer on the ETA Form 790 *Agricultural and Food Processing Clearance Order,* and a statement justifying the request for a waiver of the time period requirement. The statement must indicate whether the waiver request is due to the fact that the employer did not use H–2A workers during the prior agricultural season or whether the request is for other good and substantial cause. If the waiver is requested for good and substantial cause, the employer's statement must also include detailed information describing the good and substantial cause which has necessitated the waiver request. Good and substantial cause may include, but is not limited to, such things as the substantial loss of U.S. workers due to weather-related activities or other reasons, unforeseen events affecting the work activities to be performed, pandemic health issues, or similar conditions.

(3) *Processing of applications.* The CO shall promptly transmit the job order, on behalf of the employer, to the SWA serving the area of intended employment and request an expedited review of the job order in accordance with § 655.102(e) and an inspection of housing in accordance with § 655.104(d)(6)(iii). The CO shall process the application and job order in accordance with § 655.107, issue a wage determination in

accordance with §655.108 and, upon acceptance, require the employer to engage in positive recruitment consistent with §655.102(d)(2), (3), and (4). The CO shall require the SWA to transmit the job order for interstate clearance consistent with §655.102(f). The CO shall specify a date on which the employer will be required to submit a recruitment report in accordance with §655.102(k). The CO will make a determination on the application in accordance with §655.109.

§655.1302 Required pre-filing activity.

(a) *Time of filing of application.* An employer may not file an *Application for Temporary Employment Certification* before all of the pre-filing recruitment steps set forth in this section have been fully satisfied, except where specifically exempted from some or all of those requirements by these regulations. Modifications to these requirements for H–2ALCs are set forth in §655.106.

(b) *General attestation obligation.* An employer must attest on the *Application for Temporary Employment Certification* that it will comply with all of the assurances and obligations of this subpart and to performing all necessary steps of the recruitment process as specified in this section.

(c) *Retention of documentation.* An employer filing an *Application for Temporary Employment Certification* must maintain documentation of its advertising and recruitment efforts as required in this subpart and be prepared to submit this documentation in response to a Notice of Deficiency from the CO prior to the CO rendering a Final Determination, or in the event of an audit. The documentation required in this subpart must be retained for a period of no less than 3 years from the date of the certification. There is no record retention requirement for any application (and supporting documentation) after the Secretary has made a final decision to deny the application.

(d) *Positive recruitment steps.* An employer filing an application must:

(1) Submit a job order to the SWA serving the area of intended employment;

(2) Run two print advertisements (one of which must be on a Sunday, except as provided in paragraph (g) of this section);

(3) Contact former U.S. employees who were employed within the last year as described in paragraph (h) of this section; and

(4) Based on an annual determination made by the Secretary, as described in paragraph (i) of this section, recruit in all States currently designated as a State of traditional or expected labor supply with respect to each area of intended employment in which the employer's work is to be performed as required in paragraph (i)(2) of this section.

(e) *Job order.* (1) The employer must submit a job order to the SWA serving the area of intended employment no more than 75 calendar days and no fewer than 60 calendar days before the date of need for intrastate and interstate clearance, identifying it as a job order to be placed in connection with a future application for H–2A workers. If the job opportunity is located in more than one State, the employer may submit a job order to any one of the SWAs having jurisdiction over the anticipated worksites. Where a future master application will be filed by an association of agricultural employers, the SWA will prepare a single job order in the name of the association on behalf of all employers that will be duly named on the *Application for Temporary Employment Certification.* Documentation of this step by the applicant is satisfied by maintaining proof of posting from the SWA identifying the job order number(s) with the start and end dates of the posting of the job order.

(2) The job order submitted to the SWA must satisfy all the requirements for newspaper advertisements contained in §655.103 and comply with the requirements for agricultural clearance orders in 20 CFR part 653 Subpart F and the requirements set forth in §655.104.

(3) The SWA will review the contents of the job order as provided in 20 CFR part 653 Subpart F and will work with the employer to address any deficiencies, except that the order may be placed prior to completion of the housing inspection required by 20 CFR

653.501(d)(6) where necessary to meet the timeframes required by statute and regulation. However, the SWA must ensure that housing within its jurisdiction is inspected as expeditiously as possible thereafter. Any issue with regard to whether a job order may properly be placed in the job service system that cannot be resolved with the applicable SWA may be brought to the attention of the NPC, which may direct that the job order be placed in the system where the NPC determines that the applicable program requirements have been met. If the NPC concludes that the job order is not acceptable, it shall so inform the employer using the procedures applicable to a denial of certification set forth in § 655.109(e).

(f) *Intrastate/Interstate recruitment.* (1) Upon receipt and acceptance of the job order, the SWA must promptly place the job order in intrastate clearance on its active file and begin recruitment of eligible U.S. workers. The SWA receiving the job order under paragraph (e) of this section will promptly transmit, on behalf of the employer, a copy of its active job order to all States listed in the job order as anticipated worksites. The SWA must also transmit a copy of all active job orders to no fewer than three States, which must include those States, if any, designated by the Secretary as traditional or expected labor supply States ("out-of-State recruitment States") for the area of intended employment in which the employer's work is to be performed as defined in paragraph (i) of this section.

(2) Unless otherwise directed by the CO, the SWA must keep the job order open for interstate clearance until the end of the recruitment period, as set forth in § 655.102(f)(3). Each of the SWAs to which the job order was referred must keep the job order open for that same period of time and must refer each eligible U.S. worker who applies (or on whose behalf an application is made) for the job opportunity.

(3)(i) For the first 5 years after the effective date of this rule, the recruitment period shall end 30 days after the first date the employer requires the services of the H–2A workers, or on the last day the employer requires the services of H–2A workers in the applicable area of intended employment, whichever is sooner (the 30-day rule). During that 5-year period, the Department will endeavor to study the costs and benefits of providing for continuing recruitment of U.S. workers after the H–2A workers have already entered the country. Unless prior to the expiration of the 5-year period the Department conducts a study and publishes a notice determining that the economic benefits of such extended recruitment period outweigh its costs, the recruitment period will, after the expiration of the 5-year period, end on the first date the employer requires the services of the H–2A worker.

(ii) *Withholding of U.S. workers prohibited.* The provisions of this paragraph shall apply so as long as the 30-day rule is in place.

(A) *Complaints.* Any employer who has reason to believe that a person or entity has willfully and knowingly withheld U.S. workers prior to the arrival at the job site of H–2A workers in order to force the hiring of U.S. workers during the 30-day rule under paragraph (f)(3)(i) of this section may submit a written complaint to the CO. The complaint must clearly identify the person or entity who the employer believes has withheld the U.S. workers, and must specify sufficient facts to support the allegation (e.g., dates, places, numbers and names of U.S. workers) which will permit an investigation to be conducted by the CO.

(B) *Investigations.* The CO must immediately investigate the complaint. The investigation must include interviews with the employer who has submitted the complaint, the person or entity named as responsible for withholding the U.S. workers, and the individual U.S. workers whose availability has purportedly been withheld.

(C) *Written findings.* Where the CO determines, after conducting the interviews required by this paragraph, that the employer's complaint is valid and justified, the CO shall immediately suspend the application of the 30-day rule under paragraph (f)(3)(i) of this section to the employer. The CO's determination shall be the final decision of the Secretary.

(g) *Newspaper advertisements.* (1) During the period of time that the job order is being circulated by the SWA(s) for interstate clearance under paragraph (f) of this section, the employer must place an advertisement on 2 separate days, which may be consecutive, one of which must be a Sunday (except as provided in paragraph (g)(2) of this section), in a newspaper of general circulation serving the area of intended employment that has a reasonable distribution and is appropriate to the occupation and the workers likely to apply for the job opportunity. Both newspaper advertisements must be published only after the job order is accepted by the SWA for intrastate/interstate clearance.

(2) If the job opportunity is located in a rural area that does not have a newspaper with a Sunday edition, the employer must, in place of a Sunday edition, advertise in the regularly published daily edition with the widest circulation in the area of intended employment.

(3) The newspaper advertisements must satisfy the requirements of §§ 655.103 and 655.104. The employer must maintain copies of newspaper pages (with date of publication and full copy of ad), or tear sheets of the pages of the publication in which the advertisements appeared, or other proof of publication containing the text of the printed advertisements and the dates of publication furnished by the newspaper.

(4) If a professional, trade or ethnic publication is more appropriate for the occupation and the workers likely to apply for the job opportunity than a general circulation newspaper, and is the most likely source to bring responses from able, willing, qualified, and available U.S. workers, the employer may use a professional, trade or ethnic publication in place of one of the newspaper advertisements, but may not replace the Sunday advertisement (or the substitute required by paragraph (g)(2) of this section).

(h) *Contact with former U.S. employees.* The employer must contact by mail or other effective means its former U.S. employees (except those who were dismissed for cause, abandoned the worksite, or were provided documentation at the end of their previous period of employment explaining the lawful, job-related reasons they would not be recontacted) employed by the employer in the occupation at the place of employment during the previous year and solicit their return to the job. The employer must maintain copies of correspondence signed and dated by the employer or, if other means are used, maintain dated logs demonstrating that each worker was contacted, including the phone number, e-mail address, or other means that was used to make contact. The employer must list in the recruitment report any workers who did not return to the employ of the employer because they were either unable or unwilling to return to the job or did not respond to the employer's request, and must retain documentation, if provided by the worker, showing evidence of their inability, unwillingness, or non-responsiveness.

(i) *Additional positive recruitment.* (1) Each year, the Secretary will make a determination with respect to each State whether there are other States ("traditional or expected labor supply States") in which there are a significant number of able and qualified workers who, if recruited, would be willing to make themselves available for work in that State, as well as which newspapers in each traditional or expected labor supply State that the employer may use to fulfill its obligation to run a newspaper advertisement in that State. Such determination must be based on information provided by State agencies or by other sources within the 120 days preceding the determination (which will be solicited by notice in the FEDERAL REGISTER), and will to the extent information is available take into account the success of recent efforts by out-of-State employers to recruit in that State. The Secretary will not designate a State as a traditional or expected labor supply State if the State has a significant number of employers that are recruiting for U.S. workers for the same types of occupations and comparable work. The Secretary's annual determination as to traditional or expected labor supply States, if any, from which applicants from each State must recruit will be published in the FEDERAL REGISTER and made available through the ETA Web site.

(2) Each employer must engage in positive recruitment in those States designated in accordance with paragraph (i)(1) with respect to the State in which the employer's work is to be performed. Such recruitment will consist of one newspaper advertisement in each State in one of the newspapers designated by the Secretary, published within the same period of time as the newspaper advertisements required under paragraph (g) of this section. An employer will not be required to conduct positive recruitment in more than three States designated in accordance with paragraph (i)(1) for each area of intended employment listed on the employer's application. The advertisement must refer applicants to the SWA nearest the area in which the advertisement was placed.

(j) *Referrals of U.S. workers.* SWAs may only refer for employment individuals for whom they have verified identity and employment authorization through the process for employment verification of all workers that is established by INA sec. 274A(b). SWAs must provide documentation certifying the employment verification that satisfies the standards of INA sec. 274A(a)(5) and its implementing regulations at 8 CFR 274a.6.

(k) *Recruitment report.* (1) No more than 50 days before the date of need the employer must prepare, sign, and date a written recruitment report. The recruitment report must be submitted with the *Application for Temporary Employment Certification.* The recruitment report must:

(i) List the original number of openings for which the employer recruited;

(ii) Identify each recruitment source by name;

(iii) State the name and contact information of each U.S. worker who applied or was referred to the job opportunity up to the date of the preparation of the recruitment report, and the disposition of each worker;

(iv) Confirm that former employees were contacted and by what means; and

(v) If applicable, explain the lawful job-related reason(s) for not hiring any U.S. workers who applied for the position.

(2) The employer must update the recruitment report within 48 hours of the date that is the end of the recruitment period as specified in § 655.102(f)(3). This supplement to the recruitment report must meet the requirements of paragraph (k)(1) of this section. The employer must sign and date this supplement to the recruitment report and retain it for a period of no less than 3 years. The supplement to the recruitment report must be provided in the event of an audit.

(3) The employer must retain resumes (if provided) of, and evidence of contact with (which may be in the form of an attestation), each U.S. worker who applied or was referred to the job opportunity. Such resumes and evidence of contact must be retained along with the recruitment report and the supplemental recruitment report for a period of no less than 3 years, and must be provided in response to a Notice of Deficiency or in the event of an audit.

§ 655.1303 Advertising requirements.

All advertising conducted to satisfy the required recruitment steps under § 655.102 before filing the *Application for Temporary Employment Certification* must meet the requirements set forth in this section and at § 655.104 and must contain terms and conditions of employment which are not less favorable than those that will be offered to the H–2A workers. All advertising must contain the following information:

(a) The employer's name and location(s) of work, or in the event that a master application will be filed by an association, a statement indicating that the name and location of each member of the association can be obtained from the SWA of the State in which the advertisement is run;

(b) The geographic area(s) of employment with enough specificity to apprise applicants of any travel requirements and where applicants will likely have to reside to perform the services or labor;

(c) A description of the job opportunity for which certification is sought with sufficient information to apprise U.S. workers of services or labor to be performed and the anticipated period of employment of the job opportunity;

(d) The wage offer, or in the event that there are multiple wage offers (such as where a master application will be filed by an association and/or where there are multiple crop activities for a single employer), the range of applicable wage offers and, where a master application will be filed by an association, a statement indicating that the rate(s) applicable to each employer can be obtained from the SWA;

(e) The three-fourths guarantee specified in §655.104(i);

(f) If applicable, a statement that work tools, supplies, and equipment will be provided at no cost to the worker;

(g) A statement that housing will be made available at no cost to workers, including U.S. workers, who cannot reasonably return to their permanent residence at the end of each working day;

(h) If applicable, a statement that transportation and subsistence expenses to the worksite will be provided by the employer;

(i) A statement that the position is temporary and a specification of the total number of job openings the employer intends to fill;

(j) A statement directing applicants to report or send resumes to the SWA of the State in which the advertisement is run for referral to the employer;

(k) Contact information for the applicable SWA and the job order number.

§655.1304 Contents of job offers.

(a) *Preferential treatment of aliens prohibited.* The employer's job offer must offer to U.S. workers no less than the same benefits, wages, and working conditions that the employer is offering, intends to offer, or will provide to H–2A workers. Except where otherwise permitted under this section, no job offer may impose on U.S. workers any restrictions or obligations that will not be imposed on the employer's H–2A workers.

(b) *Job qualifications.* Each job qualification listed in the job offer must not substantially deviate from the normal and accepted qualifications required by employers that do not use H–2A workers in the same or comparable occupations and crops.

(c) *Minimum benefits, wages, and working conditions.* Every job offer accompanying an H–2A application must include each of the minimum benefit, wage, and working condition provisions listed in paragraphs (d) through (q) of this section.

(d) *Housing*—(1) *Obligation to provide housing.* The employer must provide housing at no cost to the worker, except for those U.S. workers who are reasonably able to return to their permanent residence at the end of the work day. Housing must be provided through one of the following means:

(i) *Employer-provided housing.* Employer-provided housing that meets the full set of DOL OSHA standards set forth at 29 CFR 1910.142, or the full set of standards at §§654.404 through 654.417 of this chapter, whichever are applicable under §654.401; or

(ii) *Rental and/or public accommodations.* Rental or public accommodations or other substantially similar class of habitation that meets applicable local standards for such housing. In the absence of applicable local standards, State standards will apply. In the absence of applicable local or State standards, DOL OSHA standards at 29 CFR 1910.142 will apply. Any charges for rental housing must be paid directly by the employer to the owner or operator of the housing. The employer must document that the housing complies with the local, State, or Federal housing standards. Such documentation may include but is not limited to a certificate from a State Department of Health or other State or local agency or a statement from the manager or owner of the housing.

(2) *Standards for range housing.* Housing for workers principally engaged in the range production of livestock shall meet standards of DOL OSHA for such housing. In the absence of such standards, range housing for sheepherders and other workers engaged in the range production of livestock must meet guidelines issued by ETA.

(3) *Deposit charges.* Charges in the form of deposits for bedding or other similar incidentals related to housing must not be levied upon workers. However, employers may require workers

to reimburse them for damage caused to housing, bedding, or other property by the individual workers found to have been responsible for damage which is not the result of normal wear and tear related to habitation.

(4) *Charges for public housing.* If public housing provided for migrant agricultural workers under the auspices of a local, county, or State government is secured by the employer, the employer must pay any charges normally required for use of the public housing units (but need not pay for optional, extra services) directly to the housing's management.

(5) *Family housing.* When it is the prevailing practice in the area of intended employment and the occupation to provide family housing, family housing must be provided to workers with families who request it.

(6) *Housing inspection.* In order to ensure that the housing provided by an employer under this section meets the relevant standard:

(i) An employer must make the required attestation, which may include an attestation that the employer is complying with the procedures set forth in § 654.403, at the time of filing the *Application for Temporary Employment Certification* pursuant to § 655.105(e)(2).

(ii) The employer must make a request to the SWA for a housing inspection no less than 60 days before the date of need, except where otherwise provided under this part.

(iii) The SWA must make its determination that the housing meets the statutory criteria applicable to the type of housing provided prior to the date on which the Secretary is required to make a certification determination under INA sec. 218(c)(3)(A), which is 30 days before the employer's date of need. SWAs must not adopt rules or restrictions on housing inspections that unreasonably prevent inspections from being completed in the required time frame, such as rules that no inspections will be conducted where the housing is already occupied or is not yet leased. If the employer has attested to and met all other criteria for certification, and the employer has made a timely request for a housing inspection under this paragraph, and the SWA has failed to complete a housing inspection by the statutory deadline of 30 days prior to date of need, the certification will not be withheld on account of the SWA's failure to meet the statutory deadline. The SWA must in such cases inspect the housing prior to or during occupation to ensure it meets applicable housing standards. If, upon inspection, the SWA determines the supplied housing does not meet the applicable housing standards, the SWA must promptly provide written notification to the employer and the CO. The CO will take appropriate action, including notice to the employer to cure deficiencies. An employer's failure to cure substantial violations can result in revocation of the temporary labor certification.

(7) *Certified housing that becomes unavailable.* If after a request to certify housing (but before certification), or after certification of housing, such housing becomes unavailable for reasons outside the employer's control, the employer may substitute other rental or public accommodation housing that is in compliance with the local, State, or Federal housing standards applicable under paragraph (d)(1)(ii) of this section and for which the employer is able to submit evidence of such compliance. The employer must notify the SWA in writing of the change in accommodations and the reason(s) for such change and provide the SWA evidence of compliance with the applicable local, State or Federal safety and health standards, in accordance with the requirements of paragraph (d)(1)(ii) of this section. The SWA must notify the CO of all housing changes and of any noncompliance with the standards set forth in paragraph (d)(1)(ii) of this section. Substantial noncompliance can result in revocation of the temporary labor certification under § 655.117.

(e) *Workers' compensation.* The employer must provide workers' compensation insurance coverage in compliance with State law covering injury and disease arising out of and in the course of the worker's employment. If the type of employment for which the certification is sought is not covered by or is exempt from the State's workers' compensation law, the employer must provide, at no cost to the worker, insurance covering injury and disease arising out of and in the course of the worker's employment that will provide benefits at least equal to those provided under the State workers' compensation law for other comparable employment. The employer must retain for 3 years from the date of certification of the application, the name of the insurance carrier, the insurance policy number, and proof of insurance for the dates of need, or, if appropriate, proof of State law coverage.

(f) *Employer-provided items.* Except as provided in this paragraph, the employer must provide to the worker, without charge or deposit charge, all tools, supplies, and equipment required to perform the duties assigned. The employer may charge the worker for reasonable costs related to the worker's refusal or negligent failure to return any property furnished by the employer or due to such worker's willful damage or destruction of such property. Where it is a common practice in the particular area, crop activity and occupation for workers to provide tools and equipment, with or without the employer reimbursing the workers for the cost of providing them, such an arrangement will be permitted, provided that the requirements of sec. 3(m) of the FLSA at 29 U.S.C. 203(m) are met. Section 3(m) does not permit deductions for tools or equipment primarily for the benefit of the employer that reduce an employee's wage below the wage required under the minimum wage, or, where applicable, the overtime provisions of the FLSA.

(g) *Meals.* The employer either must provide each worker with three meals a day or must furnish free and convenient cooking and kitchen facilities to the workers that will enable the workers to prepare their own meals. Where the employer provides the meals, the job offer must state the charge, if any, to the worker for such meals. The amount of meal charges is governed by § 655.114.

(h) *Transportation; daily subsistence*—(1) *Transportation to place of employment.* If the employer has not previously advanced such transportation and subsistence costs to the worker or otherwise provided such transportation or subsistence directly to the worker by other means and if the worker completes 50 percent of the work contract period, the employer must pay the worker for reasonable costs incurred by the worker for transportation and daily subsistence from the place from which the worker has departed to the employer's place of employment. For an H–2A worker coming from outside of the U.S., the place from which the worker has departed is the place of recruitment, which the Department interprets to mean the appropriate U.S. consulate or port of entry. When it is the prevailing practice of non-H–2A agricultural employers in the occupation in the area to do so, or when the employer extends such benefits to similarly situated H–2A workers, the employer must advance the required transportation and subsistence costs (or otherwise provide them) to U.S. workers. The amount of the transportation payment must be no less (and is not required to be more) than the most economical and reasonable common carrier transportation charges for the distances involved. The amount of the daily subsistence payment must be at least as much as the employer would charge the worker for providing the worker with three meals a day during employment (if applicable), but in no event less than the amount permitted under paragraph (g) of this section.

(2) *Transportation from last place of employment to home country.* If the worker completes the work contract period, and the worker has no immediately subsequent H–2A employment, the employer must provide or pay for the worker's transportation and daily subsistence from the place of employment to the place from which the worker, disregarding intervening employment, departed to work for the employer. For an H–2A worker coming from outside of the U.S., the place from which the worker has departed will be considered to be the appropriate U.S. consulate or port of entry.

(3) *Transportation between living quarters and worksite.* The employer must provide transportation between the worker's living quarters (*i.e.*, housing provided or secured by the employer pursuant to paragraph (d) of this section) and the employer's worksite at no

cost to the worker, and such transportation must comply with all applicable Federal, State or local laws and regulations, and must provide, at a minimum, the same vehicle safety standards, driver licensure, and vehicle insurance as required under 29 U.S.C. 1841 and 29 CFR part 500, subpart D. If workers' compensation is used to cover such transportation, in lieu of vehicle insurance, the employer must either ensure that the workers' compensation covers all travel or that vehicle insurance exists to provide coverage for travel not covered by workers' compensation.

(i) *Three-fourths guarantee*—(1) *Offer to worker.* The employer must guarantee to offer the worker employment for a total number of work hours equal to at least three-fourths of the workdays of the total period beginning with the first workday after the arrival of the worker at the place of employment or the advertised contractual first date of need, whichever is later, and ending on the expiration date specified in the work contract or in its extensions, if any. For purposes of this paragraph a workday means the number of hours in a workday as stated in the job order and excludes the worker's Sabbath and Federal holidays. The employer must offer a total number of hours to ensure the provision of sufficient work to reach the three-fourths guarantee. The work hours must be offered during the work period specified in the work contract, or during any modified work contract period to which the worker and employer have mutually agreed and has been approved by the CO. The work contract period can be shortened by agreement of the parties only with the approval of the CO. In the event the worker begins working later than the specified beginning date of the contract, the guarantee period begins with the first workday after the arrival of the worker at the place of employment, and continues until the last day during which the work contract and all extensions thereof are in effect. Therefore, if, for example, a work contract is for a 10-week period, during which a normal workweek is specified as 6 days a week, 8 hours per day, the worker would have to be guaranteed employment for at least 360 hours (e.g., 10 weeks × 48 hours/week = 480-hours × 75 percent = 360). If a Federal holiday occurred during the 10-week span, the 8 hours would be deducted from the total guaranteed. A worker may be offered more than the specified hours of work on a single workday. For purposes of meeting the guarantee, however, the worker will not be required to work for more than the number of hours specified in the job order for a workday, or on the worker's Sabbath or Federal holidays. However, all hours of work actually performed may be counted by the employer in calculating whether the period of guaranteed employment has been met. If the employer affords the U.S. or H–2A worker during the total work contract period less employment than that required under this paragraph, the employer must pay such worker the amount the worker would have earned had the worker, in fact, worked for the guaranteed number of days.

(2) *Guarantee for piece rate paid worker.* If the worker will be paid on a piece rate basis, the employer must use the worker's average hourly piece rate earnings or the AEWR, whichever is higher, to calculate the amount due under the guarantee.

(3) *Failure to work.* Any hours the worker fails to work, up to a maximum of the number of hours specified in the job order for a workday, when the worker has been offered an opportunity to do so in accordance with paragraph (i)(1) of this section, and all hours of work actually performed (including voluntary work over 8 hours in a workday or on the worker's Sabbath or Federal holidays), may be counted by the employer in calculating whether the period of guaranteed employment has been met. An employer seeking to calculate whether the number of hours has been met must maintain the payroll records in accordance with paragraph (j)(2) of this section.

(4) *Displaced H–2A worker.* The employer is not liable for payment under paragraph (i)(1) of this section to an H–2A worker whom the CO certifies is displaced because of the employer's compliance with § 655.105(d) with respect to referrals made after the employer's date of need. The employer is, however, liable for return transportation for any

such displaced worker in accordance with paragraph (h)(2) of this section.

(5) *Obligation to provide housing and meals.* Notwithstanding the three-fourths guarantee contained in this section, employers are obligated to provide housing and subsistence for each day of the contract period up until the day the workers depart for other H–2A employment, depart to the place outside of the U.S. from which the worker came, or, if the worker voluntarily abandons employment or is terminated for cause, the day of such abandonment or termination.

(j) *Earnings records.* (1) The employer must keep accurate and adequate records with respect to the workers' earnings, including but not limited to field tally records, supporting summary payroll records, and records showing the nature and amount of the work performed; the number of hours of work offered each day by the employer (broken out by hours offered both in accordance with and over and above the three-fourths guarantee at paragraph (i)(3) of this section); the hours actually worked each day by the worker; the time the worker began and ended each workday; the rate of pay (both piece rate and hourly, if applicable); the worker's earnings per pay period; the worker's home address; and the amount of and reasons for any and all deductions taken from the worker's wages.

(2) Each employer must keep the records required by this part, including field tally records and supporting summary payroll records, safe and accessible at the place or places of employment, or at one or more established central recordkeeping offices where such records are customarily maintained. All records must be available for inspection and transcription by the Secretary or a duly authorized and designated representative, and by the worker and representatives designated by the worker as evidenced by appropriate documentation (an Entry of Appearance as Attorney or Representative, Form G–28, signed by the worker, or an affidavit signed by the worker confirming such representation). Where the records are maintained at a central recordkeeping office, other than in the place or places of employment, such records must be made available for inspection and copying within 72 hours following notice from the Secretary, or a duly authorized and designated representative, and by the worker and designated representatives as described in this paragraph.

(3) To assist in determining whether the three-fourths guarantee in paragraph (i) of this section has been met, if the number of hours worked by the worker on a day during the work contract period is less than the number of hours offered, as specified in the job offer, the records must state the reason or reasons therefore.

(4) The employer must retain the records for not less than 3 years after the completion of the work contract.

(k) *Hours and earnings statements.* The employer must furnish to the worker on or before each payday in one or more written statements the following information:

(1) The worker's total earnings for the pay period;

(2) The worker's hourly rate and/or piece rate of pay;

(3) The hours of employment offered to the worker (broken out by offers in accordance with, and over and above, the guarantee);

(4) The hours actually worked by the worker;

(5) An itemization of all deductions made from the worker's wages; and

(6) If piece rates are used, the units produced daily.

(l) *Rates of pay.* (1) If the worker is paid by the hour, the employer must pay the worker at least the AEWR in effect at the time recruitment for the position was begun, the prevailing hourly wage rate, the prevailing piece rate, or the Federal or State minimum wage rate, whichever is highest, for every hour or portion thereof worked during a pay period; or

(2)(i) If the worker is paid on a piece rate basis and the piece rate does not result at the end of the pay period in average hourly piece rate earnings during the pay period at least equal to the amount the worker would have earned had the worker been paid at the appropriate hourly rate, the worker's pay must be supplemented at that time so that the worker's earnings are at least as much as the worker would have earned during the pay period if the worker had instead been paid at the appropriate hourly wage rate for each hour worked;

(ii) The piece rate must be no less than the piece rate prevailing for the activity in the area of intended employment; and

(iii) If the employer who pays by the piece rate requires one or more minimum productivity standards of workers as a condition of job retention, such standards must be specified in the job offer and must be normal, meaning that they may not be unusual for workers performing the same activity in the area of intended employment.

(m) *Frequency of pay.* The employer must state in the job offer the frequency with which the worker will be paid, which must be at least twice monthly.

(n) *Abandonment of employment or termination for cause.* If the worker voluntarily abandons employment before the end of the contract period, fails to report for employment at the beginning of the contract period, or is terminated for cause, and the employer notifies the Department and DHS in writing or by any other method specified by the Department or DHS in a manner specified in a notice published in the FEDERAL REGISTER not later than 2 working days after such abandonment or abscondment occurs, the employer will not be responsible for providing or paying for the subsequent transportation and subsistence expenses of that worker under paragraph (h) of this section, and that worker is not entitled to the three-fourths guarantee described in paragraph (i) of this section. An abandonment or abscondment shall be deemed to begin after a worker fails to report for work at the regularly scheduled time for 5 consecutive working days without the consent of the employer. Employees may be terminated for cause, however, for shorter unexcused periods of time that shall not be considered abandonment or abscondment.

(o) *Contract impossibility.* If, before the expiration date specified in the work contract, the services of the worker are no longer required for reasons beyond the control of the employer due to fire, weather, or other Act of God that makes the fulfillment of the contract impossible, the employer may terminate the work contract. Whether such an event constitutes a contract impossibility will be determined by the CO. In the event of such termination of a contract, the employer must fulfill a three-fourths guarantee for the time that has elapsed from the start of the work contract to the time of its termination as described in paragraph (i)(1) of this section. The employer must:

(1) Return the worker, at the employer's expense, to the place from which the worker (disregarding intervening employment) came to work for the employer, or transport the worker to the worker's next certified H–2A employer (but only if the worker can provide documentation supporting such employment), whichever the worker prefers. For an H–2A worker coming from outside of the U.S., the place from which the worker (disregarding intervening employment) came to work for the employer is the appropriate U.S. consulate or port of entry;

(2) Reimburse the worker the full amount of any deductions made from the worker's pay by the employer for transportation and subsistence expenses to the place of employment; and

(3) Pay the worker for any costs incurred by the worker for transportation and daily subsistence to that employer's place of employment. Daily subsistence will be computed as set forth in paragraph (h) of this section. The amount of the transportation payment will be no less (and is not required to be more) than the most economical and reasonable common carrier transportation charges for the distances involved.

(p) *Deductions.* The employer must make all deductions from the worker's paycheck that are required by law. The job offer must specify all deductions not required by law which the employer will make from the worker's paycheck. All deductions must be reasonable. However, an employer subject to the FLSA may not make deductions that would violate the FLSA.

(q) *Copy of work contract.* The employer must provide to the worker, no later than on the day the work commences, a copy of the work contract between the employer and the worker.

The work contract must contain all of the provisions required by paragraphs (a) through (p) of this section. In the absence of a separate, written work contract entered into between the employer and the worker, the job order, as provided in 20 CFR part 653, Subpart F, will be the work contract.

§ 655.1305 Assurances and obligations of H–2A employers.

An employer seeking to employ H–2A workers must attest as part of the *Application for Temporary Employment Certification* that it will abide by the following conditions of this subpart:

(a) The job opportunity is and will continue through the recruitment period to be open to any qualified U.S. worker regardless of race, color, national origin, age, sex, religion, handicap, or citizenship, and the employer has conducted and will continue to conduct the required recruitment, in accordance with regulations, and has been unsuccessful in locating sufficient numbers of qualified U.S. applicants for the job opportunity for which certification is sought. Any U.S. workers who applied or apply for the job were or will be rejected only for lawful, job-related reasons, and those not rejected on this basis have been or will be hired. In addition, the employer attests that it will retain records of all rejections as required by § 655.119.

(b) The employer is offering terms and working conditions which are not less favorable than those offered to the H–2A worker(s) and are not less than the minimum terms and conditions required by this subpart.

(c) The specific job opportunity for which the employer is requesting H–2A certification is not vacant because the former occupant is on strike or being locked out in the course of a labor dispute.

(d) The employer will continue to cooperate with the SWA by accepting referrals of all eligible U.S. workers who apply (or on whose behalf an application is made) for the job opportunity until the end of the recruitment period as specified in § 655.102(f)(3).

(e) During the period of employment that is the subject of the labor certification application, the employer will:

(1) Comply with applicable Federal, State and local employment-related laws and regulations, including employment-related health and safety laws;

(2) Provide for or secure housing for those workers who are not reasonably able to return to their permanent residence at the end of the work day, without charge to the worker, that complies with the applicable standards as set forth in § 655.104(d);

(3) Where required, has timely requested a preoccupancy inspection of the housing and, if one has been conducted, received certification;

(4) Provide insurance, without charge to the worker, under a State workers' compensation law or otherwise, that meets the requirements of § 655.104(e); and

(5) Provide transportation in compliance with all applicable Federal, State or local laws and regulations between the worker's living quarters (*i.e.*, housing provided by the employer under § 655.104(d)) and the employer's worksite without cost to the worker.

(f) Upon the separation from employment of H–2A worker(s) employed under the labor certification application, if such separation occurs prior to the end date of the employment specified in the application, the employer will notify the Department and DHS in writing (or any other method specified by the Department or DHS) of the separation from employment not later than 2 work days after such separation is discovered by the employer. The procedures for reporting abandonments and abscondments are outlined in § 655.104(n) of this subpart.

(g) The offered wage rate is the highest of the AEWR in effect at the time recruitment is initiated, the prevailing hourly wage or piece rate, or the Federal or State minimum wage, and the employer will pay the offered wage during the entire period of the approved labor certification.

(h) The offered wage is not based on commission, bonuses, or other incentives, unless the employer guarantees a wage paid on a weekly, bi-weekly, or monthly basis that equals or exceeds the AEWR, prevailing hourly wage or piece rate, or the legal Federal or

State minimum wage, whichever is highest.

(i) The job opportunity is a full-time temporary position, calculated to be at least 30 hours per work week, the qualifications for which do not substantially deviate from the normal and accepted qualifications required by employers that do not use H–2A workers in the same or comparable occupations or crops.

(j) The employer has not laid off and will not lay off any similarly employed U.S. worker in the occupation that is the subject of the *Application for Temporary Employment Certification* in the area of intended employment except for lawful, job related reasons within 60 days of the date of need, or if the employer has laid off such workers, it has offered the job opportunity that is the subject of the application to those laid-off U.S. worker(s) and the U.S. worker(s) either refused the job opportunity or was rejected for the job opportunity for lawful, job-related reasons.

(k) The employer has not and will not intimidate, threaten, restrain, coerce, blacklist, or in any manner discriminate against, and has not and will not cause any person to intimidate, threaten, restrain, coerce, blacklist, or in any manner discriminate against, any person who has with just cause:

(1) Filed a complaint under or related to sec. 218 of the INA at 8 U.S.C. 1188, or this subpart or any other Department regulation promulgated under sec. 218 of the INA;

(2) Instituted or caused to be instituted any proceeding under or related to sec. 218 of the INA, or this subpart or any other Department regulation promulgated under sec. 218 of the INA;

(3) Testified or is about to testify in any proceeding under or related to sec. 218 of the INA or this subpart or any other Department regulation promulgated under sec. 218 of the INA;

(4) Consulted with an employee of a legal assistance program or an attorney on matters related to sec. 218 of the INA or this subpart or any other Department regulation promulgated under sec. 218 of the INA; or

(5) Exercised or asserted on behalf of himself/herself or others any right or protection afforded by sec. 218 of the INA, or this subpart or any other Department regulation promulgated under sec. 218 of the INA.

(l) The employer shall not discharge any person because of that person's taking any action listed in paragraphs (k)(1) through (k)(5) of this section.

(m) All fees associated with processing the temporary labor certification will be paid in a timely manner.

(n) The employer will inform H–2A workers of the requirement that they leave the U.S. at the end of the period certified by the Department or separation from the employer, whichever is earlier, as required under § 655.111, unless the H–2A worker is being sponsored by another subsequent employer.

(o) The employer and its agents have not sought or received payment of any kind from the employee for any activity related to obtaining labor certification, including payment of the employer's attorneys' fees, application fees, or recruitment costs. For purposes of this paragraph, payment includes, but is not limited to, monetary payments, wage concessions (including deductions from wages, salary, or benefits), kickbacks, bribes, tributes, in kind payments, and free labor. This provision does not prohibit employers or their agents from receiving reimbursement for costs that are the responsibility of the worker, such as government required passport or visa fees.

(p) The employer has contractually forbidden any foreign labor contractor or recruiter whom the employer engages in international recruitment of H–2A workers to seek or receive payments from prospective employees, except as provided for in DHS regulations at 8 CFR 214.2(h)(5)(xi)(A).

(q) The applicant is either a fixed-site employer, an agent or recruiter, an H–2ALC (as defined in these regulations), or an association.

§ 655.1306 Assurances and obligations of H–2A Labor Contractors.

(a) The pre-filing activity requirements set forth in § 655.102 are modified as follows for H–2ALCs:

(1) The job order for an H–2ALC may contain work locations in multiple areas of intended employment, and may be submitted to any one of the

SWAs having jurisdiction over the anticipated work areas. The SWA receiving the job order shall promptly transmit, on behalf of the employer, a copy of its active job order to all States listed in the application as anticipated worksites, as well as those States, if any, designated by the Secretary as traditional or expected labor supply States for each area in which the employer's work is to be performed. Each SWA shall keep the H–2ALC's job order posted until the end of the recruitment period, as set forth in § 655.102(f)(3), for the area of intended employment that is covered by the SWA. SWAs in States that have been designated as traditional or expected labor supply States for more than one area of intended of employment that are listed on an application shall keep the H–2ALC's job order posted until the end of the applicable recruitment period that is last in time, and may make referrals for job opportunities in any area of intended employment that is still in an active recruitment period, as defined by § 655.102(f)(3).

(2) The H–2ALC must conduct separate positive recruitment under § 655.102(g) through (i) for each area of intended employment in which the H–2ALC intends to perform work, but need not conduct separate recruitment for each work location within a single area of intended employment. The positive recruitment for each area of intended employment must list the name and location of each fixed-site agricultural business to which the H–2ALC expects to provide H–2A workers, the expected beginning and ending dates when the H–2ALC will be providing the workers to each fixed site, and a description of the crops and activities the workers are expected to perform at such fixed site. Such positive recruitment must be conducted pre-filing for the first area of intended employment, but must be started no more than 75 and no fewer than 60 days before the listed arrival date (or the amended date, if applicable) for each subsequent area of intended employment. For each area of intended employment, the advertising that must be placed in any applicable States designated as traditional or expected labor supply States must be placed at the same time as the placement of other positive recruitment for the area of intended employment in accordance with § 655.102(i)(2).

(3) The job order and the positive recruitment in each area of intended employment may require that workers complete the remainder of the H–2ALC's itinerary.

(4) An H–2ALC who hires U.S. workers during the course of its itinerary, and accordingly releases one or more of its H–2A workers, is eligible for the release from the three-quarters guarantee with respect to the released H–2A workers that is provided for in § 655.104(i)(4).

(5) An H–2ALC may amend its application subsequent to submission in accordance with § 655.107(d)(3) to account for new or changed worksites or areas of intended employment during the course of the itinerary in the following manner:

(i) If the additional worksite(s) are in the same area(s) of intended employment as represented on the *Application for Temporary Employment Certification*, the H–2ALC is not required to re-recruit in those areas of intended employment if that recruitment has been completed and if the job duties at the new work sites are similar to those already covered by the application.

(ii) If the additional worksite(s) are outside the area(s) of intended employment represented on the *Application for Temporary Employment Certification*, the H–2ALC must submit in writing the new area(s) of intended employment and explain the reasons for the amendment of the labor certification itinerary. The CO will order additional recruitment in accordance with § 655.102(d).

(iii) For any additional worksite not included on the original application that necessitates a change in housing of H–2A workers, the H–2ALC must secure the statement of housing as described in paragraph (b)(6) of this section and obtain an inspection of such housing from the SWA in the area of intended employment.

(iv) Where additional recruitment is required under paragraphs (a)(5)(i) or (a)(5)(ii) of this section, the CO shall allow it to take place on an expedited basis, where possible, so as to allow the amended dates of need to be met.

(6) Consistent with paragraph (a)(5) of this section, no later than 30 days prior to the commencement of employment in each area of intended employment in the itinerary of an H–2ALC, the SWA having jurisdiction over that area of intended employment must complete the housing inspections for any employer-provided housing to be used by the employees of the H–2ALC.

(7) To satisfy the requirements of § 655.102(h), the H–2ALC must contact all U.S employees that worked for the H–2ALC during the previous season, except those excluded by that section, before filing its application, and must advise those workers that a separate job opportunity exists for each area of intended employment that is covered by the application. The employer may advise contacted employees that for any given job opportunity, workers may be required to complete the remainder of the H–2ALC's itinerary.

(b) In addition to the assurances and obligations listed in § 655.105, H–2ALC applicants are also required to:

(1) Provide the MSPA Farm Labor Contractor (FLC) certificate of registration number and expiration date if required under MSPA at 29 U.S.C. 1801 *et seq.*, to have such a certificate;

(2) Identify the farm labor contracting activities the H–2ALC is authorized to perform as an FLC under MSPA as shown on the FLC certificate of registration, if required under MSPA at 29 U.S.C. 1801 *et seq.*, to have such a certificate of registration;

(3) List the name and location of each fixed-site agricultural business to which the H–2A Labor Contractor expects to provide H–2A workers, the expected beginning and ending dates when the H–2ALC will be providing the workers to each fixed site, and a description of the crops and activities the workers are expected to perform at such fixed site;

(4) Provide proof of its ability to discharge financial obligations under the H–2A program by attesting that it has obtained a surety bond as required by 29 CFR 501.8, stating on the application the name, address, phone number, and contact person for the surety, and providing the amount of the bond (as calculated pursuant to 29 CFR 501.8) and any identifying designation utilized by the surety for the bond;

(5) Attest that it has engaged in, or will engage in within the timeframes required by § 655.102 as modified by § 655.106(a), recruitment efforts in each area of intended employment in which it has listed a fixed-site agricultural business; and

(6) Attest that it will be providing housing and transportation that complies with the applicable housing standards in § 655.104(d) or that it has obtained from each fixed-site agricultural business that will provide housing or transportation to the workers a written statement stating that:

(i) All housing used by workers and owned, operated or secured by the fixed-site agricultural business complies with the applicable housing standards in § 655.104(d); and

(ii) All transportation between the worksite and the workers' living quarters that is provided by the fixed-site agricultural business complies with all applicable Federal, State, or local laws and regulations and will provide, at a minimum, the same vehicle safety standards, driver licensure, and vehicle insurance as required under 29 U.S.C. 1841 and 29 CFR part 500, subpart D, except where workers' compensation is used to cover such transportation as described in § 655.104(h)(3).

§ 655.1307 Processing of applications.

(a) *Processing.* (1) Upon receipt of the application, the CO will promptly review the application for completeness and an absence of errors that would prevent certification, and for compliance with the criteria for certification. The CO will make a determination to certify, deny, or issue a Notice of Deficiency prior to making a Final Determination on the application. Applications requesting that zero job opportunities be certified for H–2A employment because the employer has been able to recruit a sufficient number of U.S. workers must comply with other requirements for H–2A applications and must be supported by a recruitment report, in which case the application will be accepted but will then be denied. Criteria for certification, as used in this subpart, include, but are not limited to, whether the employer has established the need for the agricultural services or labor to be performed on a temporary or seasonal basis; made all the assurances and met all the obligations required by § 655.105, and/or, if an H–2ALC, by § 655.106; complied with the timeliness requirements in § 655.102; and complied with the recruitment obligations required by §§ 655.102 and 655.103.

(2) Unless otherwise noted, any notice or request sent by the CO or OFLC to an applicant requiring a response shall be sent by means normally assuring next-day delivery, to afford the applicant sufficient time to respond. The employer's response shall be considered filed with the Department when sent (by mail, certified mail, or any other means indicated to be acceptable by the CO) to the Department, which may be demonstrated, for example, by a postmark.

(b) *Notice of deficiencies.* (1) If the CO determines that the employer has made all necessary attestations and assurances, but the application fails to comply with one or more of the criteria for certification in paragraph (a) of this section, the CO will promptly notify the employer within 7 calendar days of the CO's receipt of the application.

(2) The notice will:

(i) State the reason(s) why the application fails to meet the criteria for temporary labor certification, citing the relevant regulatory standard(s);

(ii) Offer the employer an opportunity to submit a modified application within 5 business days from date of receipt, stating the modification that is needed for the CO to accept the application for consideration;

(iii) Except as provided for under paragraph (b)(2)(iv) of this section, state that the CO's determination on whether to grant or deny the *Application for Temporary Employment Certification* will be made no later than 30 calendar days before the date of need, provided that the employer submits the requested modification to the application within 5 business days and in a manner specified by the CO;

(iv) Where the CO determines the employer failed to comply with the recruitment obligations required by §§ 655.102 and 655.103, offer the employer an opportunity to correct its recruitment and conduct it on an expedited schedule. The CO shall specify the positive recruitment requirements, request the employer submit proof of corrected advertisement and an initial recruitment report meeting the requirements of § 655.102(k) no earlier than 48 hours after the last corrected advertisement is printed, and state that the CO's determination on whether to grant or deny the *Application for Temporary Employment Certification* will be made within 5 business days of receiving the required documentation, which may be a date later than 30 days before the date of need:

(v) Offer the employer an opportunity to request an expedited administrative review or a de novo administrative hearing before an ALJ, of the *Notice of Deficiency*. The notice will state that in order to obtain such a review or hearing, the employer, within 5 business days of the receipt of the notice, must file by facsimile or other means normally assuring next day delivery, a written request to the Chief Administrative Law Judge of DOL and simultaneously serve a copy on the CO. The notice will also state that the employer may submit any legal arguments that the employer believes will rebut the basis of the CO's action; and

(vi) State that if the employer does not comply with the requirements under paragraphs (b)(2)(ii) and (iv) of this section or request an expedited administrative judicial review or a de novo hearing before an ALJ within the 5 business days the CO will deny the application in accordance with the labor certification determination provisions in § 655.109.

(c) *Submission of modified applications.* (1) If the CO notifies the employer of any deficiencies within the 7 calendar day timeframe set forth in paragraph (b)(1) of this section, the date by which the CO's Final Determination is required by statute to be made will be postponed by 1 day for each day that passes beyond the 5 business-day period allowed under paragraph (b)(2)(ii) of this section to submit a modified application.

(2) Where the employer submits a modified application as required by the CO, and the CO approves the modified application, the CO will not deny the application based solely on the fact that it now does not meet the timeliness requirements for filing applications.

(3) If the modified application is not approved, the CO will deny the application in accordance with the labor certification determination provisions in § 655.109.

(d) *Amendments to applications.* (1) Applications may be amended at any time before the CO's certification determination to increase the number of workers requested in the initial application by not more than 20 percent (50 percent for employers requesting less than 10 workers) without requiring an additional recruitment period for U.S. workers. Requests for increases above the percent prescribed, without additional recruitment, may be approved by the CO only when the request is submitted in writing, the need for additional workers could not have been foreseen, and the crops or commodities will be in jeopardy prior to the expiration of an additional recruitment period.

(2) Applications may be amended to make minor changes in the total period of employment, but only if a written request is submitted to the CO and approved in advance. In considering whether to approve the request, the CO will review the reason(s) for the request, determine whether the reason(s) are on the whole justified, and take into account the effect(s) of a decision to approve on the adequacy of the underlying test of the domestic labor market for the job opportunity. If a request for a change in the start date of the total period of employment is made after workers have departed for the employer's place of work, the CO may only approve the change if the request is accompanied by a written assurance signed and dated by the employer that all such workers will be provided housing and subsistence, without cost to the workers, until work commences. Upon acceptance of an amendment, the CO will submit to the SWA any necessary modification to the job order.

(3) Other amendments to the application, including elements of the job offer and the place of work, may be approved by the CO if the CO determines the proposed amendment(s) are justified by a business reason and will not prevent the CO from making the labor certification determination required under § 655.109. Requested amendments will be reviewed as quickly as possible, taking into account revised dates of need for work locations associated with the amendment.

(e) *Appeal procedures.* With respect to either a Notice of Deficiency issued under paragraph (b) of this section, the denial of a requested amendment under paragraph (d) of this section, or a notice of denial issued under § 655.109(e), if the employer timely requests an expedited administrative review or *de novo* hearing before an ALJ, the procedures set forth in § 655.115 will be followed.

§ 655.1308 Offered wage rate.

(a) *Highest wage.* To comply with its obligation under § 655.105(g), an employer must offer a wage rate that is the highest of the AEWR in effect at the time recruitment for a position is begun, the prevailing hourly wage or piece rate, or the Federal or State minimum wage.

(b) *Wage rate request.* The employer must request and obtain a wage rate determination from the NPC, on a form prescribed by ETA, before commencing any recruitment under this subpart, except where specifically exempted from this requirement by these regulations.

(c) *Validity of wage rate.* The recruitment must begin within the validity period of the wage determination obtained from the NPC. Recruitment for this purpose begins when the job order is accepted by the SWA for posting.

(d) *Wage offer.* The employer must offer and advertise in its recruitment a wage at least equal to the wage rate required by paragraph (a) of this section.

(e) *Adverse effect wage rate.* The AEWR will be based on published wage data for the occupation, skill level, and geographical area from the Bureau of Labor Statistics (BLS), Occupational Employment Statistics (OES) survey. The NPC will obtain wage information on the AEWR using the On-line Wage

Library (OWL) found on the Foreign Labor Certification Data Center Web site (*http://www.flcdatacenter.com/*). This wage shall not be less than the July 24, 2009 Federal minimum wage of $7.25.

(f) *Wage determination.* The NPC must enter the wage rate determination on a form it uses, indicate the source, and return the form with its endorsement to the employer.

(g) *Skill level.* (1) Level I wage rates are assigned to job offers for beginning level employees who have a basic understanding of the occupation. These employees perform routine tasks that require limited, if any, exercise of judgment. The tasks provide experience and familiarization with the employer's methods, practices, and programs. The employees may perform higher level work for training and developmental purposes. These employees work under close supervision and receive specific instructions on required tasks and results expected. Their work is closely monitored and reviewed for accuracy.

(2) Level II wage rates are assigned to job offers for employees who have attained, through education or experience, a good understanding of the occupation. These employees perform moderately complex tasks that require limited judgment. An indicator that the job request warrants a wage determination at Level II would be a requirement for years of education and/or experience that are generally required as described in the O*NET Job Zones.

(3) Level III wage rates are assigned to job offers for employees who have a sound understanding of the occupation and have attained, either through education or experience, special skills or knowledge. These employees perform tasks that require exercising judgment and may coordinate the activities of other staff. They may have supervisory authority over those staff. A requirement for years of experience or educational degrees that are at the higher ranges indicated in the O*NET Job Zones would be an indicator that a Level III wage should be considered. Frequently, key words in the job title can be used as indicators that an employer's job offer is for an experienced worker. Words such as lead, senior, crew chief, or journeyman would be indicators that a Level III wage should be considered.

(4) Level IV wage rates are assigned to job offers for employees who have sufficient experience in the occupation to plan and conduct work requiring judgment and the independent evaluation, selection, modification, and application of standard procedures and techniques. Such employees receive only minimal guidance and their work is reviewed only for application of sound judgment and effectiveness in meeting the establishment's procedures and expectations. They generally have management and/or supervisory responsibilities.

(h) *Retention of documentation.* An employer filing an *Application for Temporary Employment Certification* must maintain documentation of its wage determination from the NPC as required in this subpart and be prepared to submit this documentation with the filing of its application. The documentation required in this subpart must be retained for a period of no less than 3 years from the date of the certification. There is no record retention requirement for applications (and supporting documentation) that are denied.

§ 655.1309 Labor certification determinations.

(a) *COs.* The Administrator, OFLC is the Department's National CO. The Administrator, OFLC, and the CO(s) in the NPC(s) (by virtue of delegation from the Administrator, OFLC), have the authority to certify or deny applications for temporary employment certification under the H–2A nonimmigrant classification. If the Administrator, OFLC has directed that certain types of temporary labor certification applications or specific applications under the H–2A nonimmigrant classification be handled by the National OFLC, the Director(s) of the NPC(s) will refer such applications to the Administrator, OFLC.

(b) *Determination.* No later than 30 calendar days before the date of need, as identified in the *Application for Temporary Employment Certification*, except as provided for under § 655.107(c) for modified applications, or applications not otherwise meeting certification criteria by that date, the CO will make a determination either to grant or deny the *Application for Temporary Employment Certification*. The CO will grant the application if and only if: the employer has met the requirements of this subpart, including the criteria for certification set forth in § 655.107(a), and thus the employment of the H–2A workers will not adversely affect the wages and working conditions of similarly employed U.S. workers.

(c) *Notification*. The CO will notify the employer in writing (either electronically or by mail) of the labor certification determination.

(d) *Approved certification*. If temporary labor certification is granted, the CO must send the certified *Application for Temporary Employment Certification* and a Final Determination letter to the employer, or, if appropriate, to the employer's agent or attorney. The Final Determination letter will notify the employer to file the certified application and any other documentation required by USCIS with the appropriate USCIS office and to continue to cooperate with the SWA by accepting all referrals of eligible U.S. workers who apply (or on whose behalf an application is made) for the job opportunity until the end of the recruitment period as set forth in § 655.102(f)(3). However, the employer will not be required to accept referrals of eligible U.S. workers once it has hired or extended employment offers to eligible U.S. workers equal to the number of H–2A workers sought.

(e) *Denied certification*. If temporary labor certification is denied, the Final Determination letter will be sent to the employer by means normally assuring next-day delivery. The Final Determination Letter will:

(1) State the reasons certification is denied, citing the relevant regulatory standards and/or special procedures;

(2) If applicable, address the availability of U.S. workers in the occupation as well as the prevailing benefits, wages, and working conditions of similarly employed U.S. workers in the occupation and/or any applicable special procedures;

(3) Offer the applicant an opportunity to request an expedited administrative review, or a *de novo* administrative hearing before an ALJ, of the denial. The notice must state that in order to obtain such a review or hearing, the employer, within 7 calendar days of the date of the notice, must file by facsimile (fax), telegram, or other means normally assuring next day delivery, a written request to the Chief Administrative Law Judge of DOL (giving the address) and simultaneously serve a copy on the CO. The notice will also state that the employer may submit any legal arguments which the employer believes will rebut the basis of the CO's action; and

(4) State that if the employer does not request an expedited administrative judicial review or a *de novo* hearing before an ALJ within the 7 calendar days, the denial is final and the Department will not further consider that application for temporary alien agricultural labor certification.

(f) *Partial certification*. The CO may, to ensure compliance with all regulatory requirements, issue a partial certification, reducing either the period of need or the number of H–2A workers being requested or both for certification, based upon information the CO receives in the course of processing the temporary labor certification application, an audit, or otherwise. The number of workers certified shall be reduced by one for each referred U.S. worker who is qualified, able, available and willing. If a partial labor certification is issued, the Final Determination letter will:

(1) State the reasons for which either the period of need and/or the number of H–2A workers requested has been reduced, citing the relevant regulatory standards and/or special procedures;

(2) If applicable, address the availability of U.S. workers in the occupation;

(3) Offer the applicant an opportunity to request an expedited administrative review, or a *de novo* administrative hearing before an ALJ, of the decision. The notice will state that in order to obtain such a review or hearing, the employer, within 7 calendar days of the date of the notice, will file by facsimile or other means normally assuring next day delivery a written request to the Chief Administrative Law Judge of

DOL (giving the address) and simultaneously serve a copy on the CO. The notice will also state that the employer may submit any legal arguments which the employer believes will rebut the basis of the CO's action; and

(4) State that if the employer does not request an expedited administrative judicial review or a *de novo* hearing before an ALJ within the 7 calendar days, the denial is final and the Department will not further consider that application for temporary alien agricultural labor certification.

(g) *Appeal procedures.* If the employer timely requests an expedited administrative review or *de novo* hearing before an ALJ under paragraph (e)(3) or (f)(3) of this section, the procedures at §655.115 will be followed.

(h) *Payment of processing fees.* A determination by the CO to grant an *Application for Temporary Employment Certification* in whole or in part under paragraph (d) or (f) of this section will include a bill for the required fees. Each employer of H–2A workers under the *Application for Temporary Employment Certification* (except joint employer associations, which shall not be assessed a fee in addition to the fees assessed to the members of the association) must pay in a timely manner a non-refundable fee upon issuance of the certification granting the application (in whole or in part), as follows:

(1) *Amount.* The application fee for each employer receiving a temporary agricultural labor certification is $100 plus $10 for each H–2A worker certified under the *Application for Temporary Employment Certification*, provided that the fee to an employer for each temporary agricultural labor certification received will be no greater than $1,000. There is no additional fee to the association filing the application. The fees must be paid by check or money order made payable to "United States Department of Labor." In the case of H–2A employers that are members of an agricultural association acting as a joint employer applying on their behalf, the aggregate fees for all employers of H–2A workers under the application must be paid by one check or money order.

(2) *Timeliness.* Fees received by the CO no more than 30 days after the date the temporary labor certification is granted will be considered timely. Non-payment of fees by the date that is 30 days after the issuance of the certification will be considered a substantial program violation and subject to the procedures in §655.115.

§655.1310 Validity and scope of temporary labor certifications.

(a) *Validity period.* A temporary labor certification is valid for the duration of the job opportunity for which certification is granted to the employer. Except as provided in paragraph and (d) of this section, the validity period is that time between the beginning and ending dates of certified employment, as listed on the *Application for Temporary Employment Certification.* The certification expires on the last day of authorized employment.

(b) *Scope of validity.* Except as provided in paragraphs (c) and (d) of this section, a temporary labor certification is valid only for the number of H–2A workers, the area of intended employment, the specific occupation and duties, and the employer(s) specified on the certified *Application for Temporary Employment Certification* (as originally filed or as amended) and may not be transferred from one employer to another.

(c) *Scope of validity—associations*—(1) *Certified applications.* If an association is requesting temporary labor certification as a joint employer, the certified *Application for Temporary Employment Certification* will be granted jointly to the association and to each of the association's employer members named on the application. Workers authorized by the temporary labor certification may be transferred among its certified employer members to perform work for which the temporary labor certification was granted, provided the association controls the assignment of such workers and maintains a record of such assignments. All temporary agricultural labor certifications to associations may be used for the certified job opportunities of any of its employer members named on the application. If an association is requesting temporary labor certification as a sole employer, the certified *Application for Temporary*

Employment Certification is granted to the association only.

(2) *Ineligible employer-members.* Workers may not be transferred or referred to an association's employer member if that employer member has been debarred from participation in the H–2A program.

(d) *Extensions on period of employment*—(1) *Short-term extension.* An employer who seeks an extension of 2 weeks or less of the certified *Application for Temporary Employment Certification* must apply for such extension to DHS. If DHS grants the extension, the corresponding *Application for Temporary Employment Certification* will be deemed extended for such period as is approved by DHS.

(2) *Long-term extension.* For extensions beyond 2 weeks, an employer may apply to the CO at any time for an extension of the period of employment on the certified *Application for Temporary Employment Certification* for reasons related to weather conditions or other factors beyond the control of the employer (which may include unforeseen changes in market conditions), provided that the employer's need for an extension is supported in writing, with documentation showing that the extension is needed and that the need could not have been reasonably foreseen by the employer. The CO will grant or deny the request for extension of the period of employment on the *Application for Temporary Employment Certification* based on the available information, and will notify the employer of the decision in writing. The employer may appeal a denial for a request of an extension in accordance with the procedures contained in § 655.115. The CO will not grant an extension where the total work contract period under that application and extensions would be 12 months or more, except in extraordinary circumstances.

(e) *Requests for determinations based on nonavailability of able, willing, available, eligible, and qualified U.S. workers*—(1) *Standards for requests.* If a temporary labor certification has been partially granted or denied based on the CO's determination that able, willing, available, eligible, and qualified U.S. workers are available, and, on or after 30 calendar days before the date of need, some or all of those U.S. workers are, in fact, no longer able, willing, eligible, qualified, or available, the employer may request a new temporary labor certification determination from the CO. Prior to making a new determination the CO will promptly ascertain (which may be through the SWA or other sources of information on U.S. worker availability) whether specific able, willing, eligible and qualified replacement U.S. workers are available or can be reasonably expected to be present at the employer's establishment within 72 hours from the date the employer's request was received. The CO will expeditiously, but in no case later than 72 hours after the time a complete request (including the signed statement included in paragraph (e)(2) of this section) is received, make a determination on the request. An employer may appeal a denial of such a determination in accordance with the procedures contained in § 655.115.

(2) *Unavailability of U.S. workers.* The employer's request for a new determination must be made directly to the CO by telephone or electronic mail, and must be confirmed by the employer in writing as required by this paragraph. If the employer telephonically or via electronic mail requests the new determination by asserting solely that U.S. workers have become unavailable, the employer must submit to the CO a signed statement confirming such assertion. If such signed statement is not received by the CO within 72 hours of the CO's receipt of the request for a new determination, the CO will deny the request.

(3) *Notification of determination.* If the CO determines that U.S. workers have become unavailable and cannot identify sufficient specific able, willing, eligible, and qualified U.S. workers who are or who are likely to be available, the CO will grant the employer's request for a new determination. However, this does not preclude an employer from submitting subsequent requests for new determinations, if warranted, based on subsequent facts concerning purported nonavailability of U.S. workers or referred workers not being eligible workers or not able, willing, or qualified because of lawful job-related reasons.

§ 655.1311 Required departure.

(a) *Limit to worker's stay.* As defined further in DHS regulations, a temporary labor certification limits the authorized period of stay for an H–2A worker. *See* 8 CFR 214.2(h). A foreign worker may not remain beyond his or her authorized period of stay, as established by DHS, which is based upon the validity period of the labor certification under which the H–2A worker is employed, nor beyond separation from employment prior to completion of the H–2A contract, absent an extension or change of such worker's status under DHS regulations.

(b) *Notice to worker.* Upon establishment of a program by DHS for registration of departure, an employer must notify any H–2A worker that when the worker departs the U.S. by land at the conclusion of employment as provided in paragraph (a) of this section, the worker must register such departure at the place and in the manner prescribed by DHS.

§ 655.1312 Audits.

(a) *Discretion.* The Department will conduct audits of temporary labor certification applications for which certification has been granted. The applications selected for audit will be chosen within the sole discretion of the Department.

(b) *Audit letter.* Where an application is selected for audit, the CO will issue an audit letter to the employer/applicant. The audit letter will:

(1) State the documentation that must be submitted by the employer;

(2) Specify a date, no fewer than 14 days and no more than 30 days from the date of the audit letter, by which the required documentation must be received by the CO; and

(3) Advise that failure to comply with the audit process may result in a finding by the CO to:

(i) Revoke the labor certification as provided in § 655.117 and/or

(ii) Debar the employer from future filings of H–2A temporary labor certification applications as provided in § 655.118.

(c) *Supplemental information request.* During the course of the audit examination, the CO may request supplemental information and/or documentation from the employer in order to complete the audit.

(d) *Audit violations.* If, as a result of the audit, the CO determines the employer failed to produce required documentation, or determines that the employer violated the standards set forth in § 655.117(a) with respect to the application, the employer's labor certification may be revoked under § 655.117 and/or the employer may be referred for debarment under § 655.118. The CO may determine to provide the audit findings and underlying documentation to DHS or another appropriate enforcement agency. The CO shall refer any findings that an employer discouraged an eligible U.S. worker from applying, or failed to hire, discharged, or otherwise discriminated against an eligible U.S. worker, to the Department of Justice, Civil Rights Division, Office of Special Counsel for Unfair Immigration Related Employment Practices.

§ 655.1313 H–2A applications involving fraud or willful misrepresentation.

(a) *Referral for investigation.* If the CO discovers possible fraud or willful misrepresentation involving an *Application for Temporary Employment Certification* the CO may refer the matter to the DHS and the Department's Office of the Inspector General for investigation.

(b) *Terminated processing.* If a court or the DHS determines that there was fraud or willful misrepresentation involving an *Application for Temporary Employment Certification*, the application will be deemed invalid. The determination is not appealable. If a certification has been granted, a finding under this paragraph will be cause to revoke the certification.

§ 655.1314 Setting meal charges; petition for higher meal charges.

(a) *Meal charges.* Until a new amount is set under this paragraph an employer may charge workers up to $9.90 for providing them with three meals per day. The maximum charge allowed by this paragraph (a) will be changed annually by the same percentage as the 12 month percentage change for the Consumer Price Index for all Urban Consumers for Food between December of the year just concluded and December of the year prior to that. The annual adjustments will be effective on the date of their publication by the Administrator, OFLC, as a Notice in the FEDERAL REGISTER. When a charge or deduction for the cost of meals would bring the employee's wage below the minimum wage set by the FLSA at 29 U.S.C. 206 (FLSA), the charge or deduction must meet the requirements of 29 U.S.C. 203(m) of the FLSA, including the recordkeeping requirements found at 29 CFR 516.27.

(b) *Filing petitions for higher meal charges.* The employer may file a petition with the CO to charge more than the applicable amount for meal charges if the employer justifies the charges and submits to the CO the documentation required by paragraph (b)(1) of this section.

(1) *Required documentation.* Documentation submitted must include the cost of goods and services directly related to the preparation and serving of meals, the number of workers fed, the number of meals served and the number of days meals were provided. The cost of the following items may be included: Food; kitchen supplies other than food, such as lunch bags and soap; labor costs that have a direct relation to food service operations, such as wages of cooks and dining hall supervisors; fuel, water, electricity, and other utilities used for the food service operation; and other costs directly related to the food service operation. Charges for transportation, depreciation, overhead and similar charges may not be included. Receipts and other cost records for a representative pay period must be retained and must be available for inspection by the CO for a period of 1 year.

(2) *Effective date for higher charge.* The employer may begin charging the higher rate upon receipt of a favorable decision from the CO unless the CO sets a later effective date in the decision.

(c) *Appeal.* In the event the employer's petition for a higher meal charge is denied in whole or in part, the employer may appeal the denial. Appeals will be filed with the Chief Administrative Law Judge. ALJ's will hear such appeals according to the procedures in 29 CFR part 18, except that the appeal will not be considered as a complaint to which an answer is required. The decision of the ALJ is the final decision of the Secretary.

§ 655.1315 Administrative review and de novo hearing before an administrative law judge.

(a) *Administrative review*—(1) *Consideration.* Whenever an employer has requested an administrative review before an ALJ of a decision by the CO: Not to accept for consideration an *Application for Temporary Employment Certification;* to deny an *Application for Temporary Employment Certification;* to deny an amendment of an *Application for Temporary Employment Certification;* or to deny an extension of an *Application for Temporary Employment Certification,* the CO will send a certified copy of the ETA case file to the Chief Administrative Law Judge by means normally assuring next-day delivery. The Chief Administrative Law Judge will immediately assign an ALJ (which may be a panel of such persons designated by the Chief Administrative Law Judge from BALCA established by 20 CFR part 656, which will hear and decide the appeal as set forth in this section) to review the record for legal sufficiency. The ALJ may not remand the case and may not receive evidence in addition to what the CO used to make the determination.

(2) *Decision.* Within 5 business days after receipt of the ETA case file the ALJ will, on the basis of the written record and after due consideration of any written submissions (which may not include new evidence) from the parties involved or amici curiae, either affirm, reverse, or modify the CO's decision by written decision. The decision of the ALJ must specify the reasons for the action taken and must be immediately provided to the employer, the CO, the Administrator, OFLC, and DHS by means normally assuring next-day delivery. The ALJ's decision is the final decision of the Secretary.

(b) *De novo hearing.* (1) *Request for hearing; conduct of hearing.* Whenever an employer has requested a de novo hearing before an ALJ of a decision by the CO: Not to accept for consideration an *Application for Temporary Employment Certification;* to deny an *Application for Temporary Employment Certification;* to deny an amendment of an *Application for Temporary Employment Certification;* or to deny an extension of an *Application for Temporary Employment Certification,* the CO will send a certified copy of the ETA case file to the Chief Administrative Law Judge by means normally assuring next-day delivery. The Chief Administrative Law Judge will immediately assign an ALJ (which may be a panel of such persons designated by the Chief Administrative Law Judge from BALCA established by 20 CFR part 656 of this chapter, but which will hear and decide the appeal as provided in this section) to conduct the *de novo* hearing. The procedures in 29 CFR part 18 apply to such hearings, except that:

(i) The appeal will not be considered to be a complaint to which an answer is required;

(ii) The ALJ will ensure that the hearing is scheduled to take place within 5 calendar days after the ALJ's receipt of the ETA case file, if the employer so requests, and will allow for the introduction of new evidence; and

(iii) The ALJ's decision must be rendered within 10 calendar days after the hearing.

(2) *Decision.* After a *de novo* hearing, the ALJ must affirm, reverse, or modify the CO's determination, and the ALJ's decision must be provided immediately to the employer, CO, Administrator, OFLC, and DHS by means normally assuring next-day delivery. The ALJ's decision is the final decision of the Secretary.

§ 655.1316 Job Service Complaint System; enforcement of work contracts.

(a) Complaints arising under this subpart may be filed through the Job Service Complaint System, as described in 20 CFR part 658, Subpart E. Complaints which involve worker contracts must be referred by the SWA to ESA for appropriate handling and resolution, as described in 29 CFR part 501. As part of this process, ESA may report the results of its investigation to the Administrator, OFLC for consideration of employer penalties or such other action as may be appropriate.

(b) Complaints alleging that an employer discouraged an eligible U.S. worker from applying, failed to hire, discharged, or otherwise discriminated against an eligible U.S. worker, or discovered violations involving the same, may be referred to the U.S. Department of Justice, Civil Rights Division, Office of Special Counsel for Unfair Immigration Related Employment Practices (OSC), in addition to any activity, investigation, and/or enforcement action taken by ETA or an SWA. Likewise, if OSC becomes aware of a violation of these regulations, it may provide such information to the appropriate SWA and the CO.

§ 655.1317 Revocation of approved labor certifications.

(a) *Basis for DOL revocation.* The CO, in consultation with the Administrator, OFLC, may revoke a temporary agricultural labor certification approved under this subpart, if, after notice and opportunity for a hearing (or failure to file rebuttal evidence), it is found that any of the following violations were committed with respect to that temporary agricultural labor certification:

(1) The CO finds that issuance of the temporary agricultural labor certification was not justified due to a willful misrepresentation on the application;

(2) The CO finds that the employer:

(i) Willfully violated a material term or condition of the approved temporary agricultural labor certification or the H–2A regulations, unless otherwise provided under paragraphs (a)(2)(ii) through (iv) of this section; or

(ii) Failed, after notification, to cure a substantial violation of the applicable housing standards set out in 20 CFR 655.104(d); or

(iii) Significantly failed to cooperate with a DOL investigation or with a DOL official performing an investigation, inspection, or law enforcement function under sec. 218 of the INA at 8 U.S.C. 1188, this subpart, or 29 CFR part 501 (ESA enforcement of contractual obligations); or

(iv) Failed to comply with one or more sanctions or remedies imposed by the ESA for violation(s) of obligations found by that agency, or with one or more decisions or orders of the Secretary or a court order secured by the Secretary under sec. 218 of the INA at 8 U.S.C. 1188, this subpart, or 29 CFR part 501 (ESA enforcement of contractual obligations).

(3) The CO determines after a recommendation is made by the WHD ESA in accordance with 29 CFR 501.20, which governs when a recommendation of revocation may be made to ETA, that the conduct complained of upon examination meets the standards of paragraph (a)(1) or (2) of this section; or

(4) If a court or the DHS, or, as a result of an audit, the CO, determines that there was fraud or willful misrepresentation involving the *Application for Temporary Employment Certification*.

(b) *DOL procedures for revocation.* (1) The CO will send to the employer (and his attorney or agent) a *Notice of Intent to Revoke* by means normally ensuring next-day delivery, which will contain a detailed statement of the grounds for the proposed revocation and the time period allowed for the employer's rebuttal. The employer may submit evidence in rebuttal within 14 calendar days of the date the notice is issued. The CO must consider all relevant evidence presented in deciding whether to revoke the temporary agricultural labor certification.

(2) If rebuttal evidence is not timely filed by the employer, the *Notice of Intent to Revoke* will become the final decision of the Secretary and take effect immediately at the end of the 14-day period.

(3) If, after reviewing the employer's timely filed rebuttal evidence, the CO finds that the employer more likely than not meets one or more of the bases for revocation under § 655.117(a), the CO will notify the employer, by means normally ensuring next-day delivery, within 14 calendar days after receiving such timely filed rebuttal evidence, of his/her final determination that the temporary agricultural labor certification should be revoked. The CO's notice will contain a detailed statement of the bases for the decision, and must offer the employer an opportunity to request a hearing. The notice must state that, to obtain such a hearing, the employer must, within 10 calendar days of the date of the notice file a written request to the Chief Administrative Law Judge, United States Department of Labor, 800 K Street, NW., Suite 400–N, Washington, DC 20001–8002, and simultaneously serve a copy to the Administrator, OFLC. The timely filing of a request for a hearing will stay the revocation pending the outcome of the hearing.

(c) *Hearing.* (1) Within 5 business days of receipt of the request for a hearing, the CO will send a certified copy of the ETA case file to the Chief Administrative Law Judge by means normally assuring next-day delivery. The Chief Administrative Law Judge will immediately assign an ALJ to conduct the hearing. The procedures in 29 CFR part 18 apply to such hearings, except that:

(i) The request for a hearing will not be considered to be a complaint to which an answer is required;

(ii) The ALJ will ensure that the hearing is scheduled to take place within 15 calendar days after the ALJ's receipt of the ETA case file, if the employer so requests, and will allow for the introduction of new evidence; and

(iii) The ALJ's decision must be rendered within 20 calendar days after the hearing.

(2) *Decision.* After the hearing, the ALJ must affirm, reverse, or modify the CO's determination. The ALJ's decision must be provided immediately to the employer, CO, Administrator, OFLC, DHS, and DOS by means normally assuring next-day delivery. The ALJ's decision is the final decision of the Secretary.

(d) *Employer's obligations in the event of revocation.* If an employer's temporary agricultural labor certification is revoked under this section, and the workers have departed the place of recruitment, the employer will be responsible for:

(1) Reimbursement of actual inbound transportation and subsistence expenses, as if the worker meets the requirements for payment under § 655.104(h)(1);

(2) The worker's outbound transportation expenses, as if the worker meets the requirements for payment under § 655.104(h)(2);

(3) Payment to the worker of the amount due under the three-fourths

guarantee as required by § 655.104(i); and

(4) Any other wages, benefits, and working conditions due or owing to the worker under these regulations.

§ 655.1318 Debarment.

(a) The Administrator, OFLC may not issue future labor certifications under this subpart to an employer and any successor in interest to the debarred employer, subject to the time limits set forth in paragraph (c) of this section, if:

(1) The Administrator, OFLC finds that the employer substantially violated a material term or condition of its temporary labor certification with respect to the employment of domestic or nonimmigrant workers; and

(2) The Administrator, OFLC issues a *Notice of Intent to Debar* no later than 2 years after the occurrence of the violation.

(b) The Administrator, OFLC may not issue future labor certifications under this subpart to an employer represented by an agent or attorney, subject to the time limits set forth in paragraph (c) of this section, if:

(1) The Administrator, OFLC finds that the agent or attorney participated in, had knowledge of, or had reason to know of, an employer's substantial violation; and

(2) The Administrator, OFLC issues the agent or attorney a *Notice of Intent to Debar* no later than 2 years after the occurrence of the violation.

(c) No employer, attorney, or agent may be debarred under this subpart for more than 3 years.

(d) For the purposes of this section, a substantial violation includes:

(1) A pattern or practice of acts of commission or omission on the part of the employer or the employer's agent which:

(i) Are significantly injurious to the wages or benefits required to be offered under the H–2A program, or working conditions of a significant number of the employer's U.S. or H–2A workers; or

(ii) Reflect a significant failure to offer employment to all qualified domestic workers who applied for the job opportunity for which certification was being sought, except for lawful job-related reasons; or

(iii) Reflect a willful failure to comply with the employer's obligations to recruit U.S. workers as set forth in this subpart; or

(iv) Reflect a significant failure to comply with the audit process in violation of § 655.112; or

(v) Reflect the employment of an H–2A worker outside the area of intended employment, or in an activity/activities, not listed in the job order (other than an activity minor and incidental to the activity/activities listed in the job order), or after the period of employment specified in the job order and any approved extension;

(2) The employer's persistent or prolonged failure to pay the necessary fee in a timely manner, following the issuance of a deficiency notice to the applicant and allowing for a reasonable period for response;

(3) Fraud involving the *Application for Temporary Employment Certification* or a response to an audit;

(4) A significant failure to cooperate with a DOL investigation or with a DOL official performing an investigation, inspection, or law enforcement function under sec. 218 of the INA at 8 U.S.C. 1188, this subpart, or 29 CFR part 501 (ESA enforcement of contractual obligations); or

(5) A significant failure to comply with one or more sanctions or remedies imposed by the ESA for violation(s) of obligations found by that agency (if applicable), or with one or more decisions or orders of the Secretary or a court order secured by the Secretary under sec. 218 of the INA at 8 U.S.C. 1188, this subpart, or 29 CFR part 501 (ESA enforcement of contractual obligations); or

(6) A single heinous act showing such flagrant disregard for the law that future compliance with program requirements cannot reasonably be expected.

(e) DOL procedures for debarment under this section will be as follows:

(1) The Administrator, OFLC will send to the employer, attorney, or agent a *Notice of Intent to Debar* by means normally ensuring next-day delivery, which will contain a detailed

statement of the grounds for the proposed debarment. The employer, attorney or agent may submit evidence in rebuttal within 14 calendar days of the date the notice is issued. The Administrator, OFLC must consider all relevant evidence presented in deciding whether to debar the employer, attorney, or agent.

(2) If rebuttal evidence is not timely filed by the employer, attorney, or agent, the *Notice of Intent to Debar* will become the final decision of the Secretary and take effect immediately at the end of the 14-day period.

(3) If, after reviewing the employer's timely filed rebuttal evidence, the Administrator, OFLC determines that the employer, attorney, or agent more likely than not meets one or more of the bases for debarment under § 655.118(d), the Administrator, OFLC will notify the employer, by means normally ensuring next-day delivery, within 14 calendar days after receiving such timely filed rebuttal evidence, of his/her final determination of debarment and of the employer, attorney, or agent's right to appeal.

(4) The *Notice of Debarment* must be in writing, must state the reason for the debarment finding, including a detailed explanation of the grounds for and the duration of the debarment, and must offer the employer, attorney, or agent an opportunity to request a hearing. The notice must state that, to obtain such a hearing, the debarred party must, within 30 calendar days of the date of the notice, file a written request to the Chief Administrative Law Judge, United States Department of Labor, 800 K Street, NW., Suite 400–N, Washington, DC 20001–8002, and simultaneously serve a copy to the Administrator, OFLC. The debarment will take effect 30 days from the date the *Notice of Debarment* is issued unless a request for a hearing is properly filed within 30 days from the date the *Notice of Debarment* is issued. The timely filing of the request for a hearing stays the debarment pending the outcome of the hearing.

(5)(i) *Hearing*. Within 10 days of receipt of the request for a hearing, the Administrator, OFLC will send a certified copy of the ETA case file to the Chief Administrative Law Judge by means normally assuring next-day delivery. The Chief Administrative Law Judge will immediately assign an ALJ to conduct the hearing. The procedures in 29 CFR part 18 apply to such hearings, except that the request for a hearing will not be considered to be a complaint to which an answer is required;

(ii) *Decision*. After the hearing, the ALJ must affirm, reverse, or modify the Administrator, OFLC 's determination. The ALJ's decision must be provided immediately to the employer, Administrator, OFLC, DHS, and DOS by means normally assuring next-day delivery. The ALJ's decision is the final decision of the Secretary, unless either party, within 30 calendar days of the ALJ's decision, seeks review of the decision with the Administrative Review Board (ARB).

(iii) Review by the ARB.

(A) Any party wishing review of the decision of an ALJ must, within 30 days of the decision of the ALJ, petition the ARB to review the decision. Copies of the petition must be served on all parties and on the ALJ. The ARB must decide whether to accept the petition within 30 days of receipt. If the ARB declines to accept the petition or if the ARB does not issue a notice accepting a petition within 30 days after the receipt of a timely filing of the petition, the decision of the ALJ shall be deemed the final agency action. If a petition for review is accepted, the decision of the ALJ shall be stayed unless and until the ARB issues an order affirming the decision. The ARB must serve notice of its decision to accept or not to accept the petition upon the ALJ and upon all parties to the proceeding in person or by certified mail.

(B) Upon receipt of the ARB's notice to accept the petition, the Office of Administrative Law Judges shall promptly forward a copy of the complete hearing record to the ARB.

(C) Where the ARB has determined to review such decision and order, the ARB shall notify each party of:

(*1*) The issue or issues raised;

(*2*) The form in which submissions shall be made (*i.e.*, briefs, oral argument, etc.); and

(*3*) The time within which such presentation shall be submitted.

(D) The ARB's final decision must be issued within 90 days from the notice granting the petition and served upon all parties and the ALJ, in person or by certified mail. If the ARB fails to provide a decision within 90 days from the notice granting the petition, the ALJ's decision will be the final decision of the Secretary.

(f) *Debarment involving members of associations.* If the Administrator, OFLC determines a substantial violation has occurred, and if an individual employer-member of an agricultural association acting as a joint employer is determined to have committed the violation, the debarment determination will apply only to that member of the association unless the Administrator, OFLC determines that the association or other association members participated in the violation, in which case the debarment will be invoked against the complicit association or other association members.

(g) *Debarment involving agricultural associations acting as joint employers.* If the Administrator, OFLC determines a substantial violation has occurred, and if an agricultural association acting as a joint employer with its members is found to have committed the violation, the debarment determination will apply only to the association, and will not be applied to any individual employer-member of the association unless the Administrator, OFLC determines that the member participated in the violation, in which case the debarment will be invoked against any complicit association members as well. An association debarred from the H–2A temporary labor certification program will not be permitted to continue to file as a joint employer with its members during the period of the debarment.

(h) *Debarment involving agricultural associations acting as sole employers.* If the Administrator, OFLC determines a substantial violation has occurred, and if an agricultural association acting as a sole employer is determined to have committed the violation, the debarment determination will apply only to the association and any successor in interest to the debarred association.

§ 655.1319 Document retention requirements.

(a) *Entities required to retain documents.* All employers receiving a certification of the *Application for Temporary Employment Certification* for agricultural workers under this subpart are required to retain the documents and records as provided in the regulations cited in paragraph (c) of this section.

(b) *Period of required retention.* Records and documents must be retained for a period of 3 years from the date of certification of the *Application for Temporary Employment Certification.*

(c) *Documents and records to be retained.* (1) All applicants must retain the following documentation:

(i) Proof of recruitment efforts including:

(A) Job order placement as specified in § 655.102(e)(1);

(B) Advertising as specified in § 655.102(g)(3), or, if used, professional, trade, or ethnic publications;

(C) Contact with former U.S. workers as specified in § 655.102(h);

(D) Multi-state recruitment efforts (if required under § 655.102(i)) as specified in § 655.102(g)(3);

(ii) Substantiation of information submitted in the recruitment report prepared in accordance with § 655.102(k)(2), such as evidence of nonapplicability of contact of former employees as specified in § 655.102(h);

(iii) The supplemental recruitment report as specified in § 655.102(k) and any supporting resumes and contact information as specified in § 655.102(k)(3);

(iv) Proof of workers' compensation insurance or State law coverage as specified in § 655.104(e);

(v) Records of each worker's earnings as specified in § 655.104(j);

(vi) The work contract or a copy of the *Application for Temporary Employment Certification* as defined in 29 CFR 501.10 and specified in § 655.104(q);

(vii) The wage determination provided by the NPC as specified in § 655.108;

(viii) Copy of the request for housing inspection submitted to the SWA as specified in § 655.104(d); and

(2) In addition to the documentation specified in paragraph (c)(1) of this section, H–2ALCs must also retain:

(i) Statements of compliance with the housing and transportation obligations for each fixed-site employer which provided housing or transportation and to which the H–2ALC provided workers during the validity period of the certification, unless such housing and transportation obligations were met by the H–2ALC itself, in which case proof of compliance by the H–2ALC must be retained, as specified in § 655.101(a)(5);

(ii) Proof of surety bond coverage which includes the name, address, and phone number of the surety, the bond number of other identifying designation, the amount of coverage, and the payee, as specified in 29 CFR 501.8; and

(3) Associations filing must retain documentation substantiating their status as an employer or agent, as specified in § 655.101(a)(1).

EFFECTIVE DATE NOTE: At 84 FR 12431, Apr. 1, 2019, the authority citation for part 655 was revised and subpart E was added, effective Apr. 4, 2019. For the convenience of the user, the added and revised text is set forth as follows:

AUTHORITY: Section 655.0 issued under 8 U.S.C. 1101(a)(15)(E)(iii), 1101(a)(15)(H)(i) and (ii), 8 U.S.C. 1103(a)(6), 1182(m), (n), and (t), 1184(c), (g), and (j), 1188, and 1288(c) and (d); sec. 3(c)(1), Pub. L. 101–238, 103 Stat. 2099, 2102 (8 U.S.C. 1182 note); sec. 221(a), Pub. L. 101–649, 104 Stat. 4978, 5027 (8 U.S.C. 1184 note); sec. 303(a)(8), Pub. L. 102–232, 105 Stat. 1733, 1748 (8 U.S.C. 1101 note); sec. 323(c), Pub. L. 103–206, 107 Stat. 2428; sec. 412(e), Pub. L. 105–277, 112 Stat. 2681 (8 U.S.C. 1182 note); sec. 2(d), Pub. L. 106–95, 113 Stat. 1312, 1316 (8 U.S.C. 1182 note); 29 U.S.C. 49k; Pub. L. 107–296, 116 Stat. 2135, as amended; Pub. L. 109–423, 120 Stat. 2900; 8 CFR 214.2(h)(4)(i); 8 CFR 214.2(h)(6)(iii); and sec. 6, Pub. L. 115–218, 132 Stat. 1547 (48 U.S.C. 1806).

Subpart A issued under 8 CFR 214.2(h).

Subpart B issued under 8 U.S.C. 1101(a)(15)(H)(ii)(a), 1184(c), and 1188; and 8 CFR 214.2(h).

Subpart E issued under 48 U.S.C. 1806.

Subparts F and G issued under 8 U.S.C. 1288(c) and (d); sec. 323(c), Pub. L. 103–206, 107 Stat. 2428; and 28 U.S.C. 2461 note, Pub. L. 114–74 at section 701.

Subparts H and I issued under 8 U.S.C. 1101(a)(15)(H)(i)(b) and (b)(1), 1182(n) and (t), and 1184(g) and (j); sec. 303(a)(8), Pub. L. 102–232, 105 Stat. 1733, 1748 (8 U.S.C. 1101 note); sec. 412(e), Pub. L. 105–277, 112 Stat. 2681; 8 CFR 214.2(h); and 28 U.S.C. 2461 note, Pub. L. 114–74 at section 701.

Subparts L and M issued under 8 U.S.C. 1101(a)(15)(H)(i)(c) and 1182(m); sec. 2(d), Pub. L. 106–95, 113 Stat. 1312, 1316 (8 U.S.C. 1182 note); Pub. L. 109–423, 120 Stat. 2900; and 8 CFR 214.2(h)* * * * *

Subpart E—Labor Certification Process for Temporary Employment in the Commonwealth of the Northern Mariana Islands (CW–1 Workers)

Subpart E—Labor Certification Process for Temporary Employment in the Commonwealth of the Northern Mariana Islands (CW–1 Workers)

§655.400 Scope and purpose of this subpart.

(a) *Purpose.* (1) A temporary labor certification (TLC) issued under this subpart reflects a determination by the Secretary of Labor (Secretary), pursuant to 48 U.S.C. 1806(d)(2)(A), that:

(i) There are not sufficient U.S. workers in the Commonwealth who are able, willing, and qualified and who will be available at the time and place needed to perform the services or labor for which an employer desires to hire foreign workers; and

(ii) The employment of the CNMI-Only Transitional Worker visa program (CW–1) nonimmigrant worker(s) will not adversely affect the wages and working conditions of U.S. workers similarly employed.

(2) This subpart describes the process by which the Department of Labor (Department or DOL) makes such a determination and certifies its determination to the Department of Homeland Security (DHS).

(b) *Scope.* This subpart sets forth the procedures governing the labor certification process for the employment of foreign workers in the CW–1 nonimmigrant classification, as defined in 48 U.S.C. 1806(d). It also establishes standards and obligations with respect to the terms and conditions of the temporary labor certification (TLC) with which CW–1 employers must comply, as well as the rights and obligations of CW–1 workers and workers in corresponding employment. Additionally, this subpart sets forth integrity measures for ensuring employers' continued compliance with the terms and conditions of the TLC.

§655.401 Authority of the agencies, offices, and divisions in the Department of Labor.

The Secretary has delegated authority to the Assistant Secretary for the Employment and Training Administration (ETA), who in turn has delegated that authority to the Office of Foreign Labor Certification (OFLC), to issue certifications and carry out other statutory responsibilities as required by 48 U.S.C. 1806. Determinations on a *CW–1 Application for Temporary Employment Certification* are made by the OFLC Administrator who, in turn, may delegate this responsibility to designated staff members, e.g., a Certifying Officer (CO).

§655.402 Definition of terms.

For purposes of this subpart:

Administrative Law Judge (ALJ) means a person within the Department's Office of Administrative Law Judges appointed under 5 U.S.C. 3105.

Agent means a person or a legal entity, such as an association or other organization of employers, or an attorney for an association or other organization of employers, that:

(1) Is authorized to act on behalf of the employer for Temporary Labor Certification (TLC) purposes;

(2) Is not itself an employer, or a joint employer, as defined in this subpart with respect to the specific application; and

(3) Is not under suspension, debarment, expulsion, disbarment, or otherwise restricted from practice before any court, the Department, the Executive Office for Immigration Review or DHS under 8 CFR 292.3 or 1003.101.

Applicant (or U.S. applicant) means a U.S. worker who is applying for a job opportunity for which an employer has filed a *CW–1 Application for Temporary Employment Certification.*

Application for Prevailing Wage Determination means the Office of Management and Budget (OMB)-approved Form ETA–9141C (or successor form) and the appropriate appendices, submitted by an employer to secure a prevailing wage determination (PWD) from the National Prevailing Wage Center (NPWC).

CW–1 Application for Temporary Employment Certification means the OMB-approved Form ETA–9142C (or successor form) and the appropriate appendices, a valid wage determination, as required by § 655.410, and all supporting documentation submitted by an employer to secure a TLC determination from the OFLC Administrator.

Attorney means any person who is a member in good standing of the bar of the highest court of any State, possession, territory, or commonwealth of the United States, or the District of Columbia. Such a person is also permitted to act as an agent under this subpart. No attorney who is under suspension, debarment, expulsion, or disbarment from practice before any court, the Department, the Executive Office for Immigration Review, or DHS under 8 CFR 1003.101 or 292.3, may represent an employer under this subpart.

Board of Alien Labor Certification Appeals (BALCA or Board) means the permanent Board established by part 656 of this chapter, chaired by the Chief Administrative Law Judge (Chief ALJ), and consisting of ALJs appointed pursuant to 5 U.S.C. 3105 and designated by the Chief ALJ to be members of BALCA.

Certifying Officer or CO means the person who makes determination on a *CW–1 Application for Temporary Employment Certification* filed under the CW–1 program. The OFLC Administrator is the national CO. Other COs may also be designated by the OFLC Administrator to make the determinations required under this subpart, including making PWDs.

Chief Administrative Law Judge or Chief ALJ means the chief official of the Department's Office of Administrative Law Judges or the Chief ALJ's designee.

CNMI Department of Labor means the executive Department of the Commonwealth Government that administers employment and job training activities for employers and U.S. workers in the Commonwealth.

Commonwealth or CNMI means the Commonwealth of the Northern Mariana Islands.

Corresponding employment means the employment of U.S. workers who are not CW–1 workers by an employer who has an approved *CW–1 Application for Temporary Employment Certification* in any work included in the approved job offer, or in any work performed by the CW–1 workers. To qualify as corresponding employment the work must be performed during the validity period of the *CW–1 Application for Temporary Employment Certification* and approved job offer, including any approved extension thereof.

CW–1 Petition means the U.S. Citizenship and Immigration Services (USCIS) Form I–129CW, *Petition for a CNMI-Only Nonimmigrant Transitional Worker,* a successor form, other form, or electronic equivalent, any supplemental information requested by USCIS, and additional evidence as may be prescribed or requested by USCIS.

CW–1 worker means any foreign worker who is lawfully present in the Commonwealth and authorized by DHS to perform temporary labor or services under 48 U.S.C. 1806(d).

Date of need means the first date the employer requires services of the CW–1 workers as indicated on the *CW–1 Application for Temporary Employment Certification.*

Department of Homeland Security or DHS means the Federal Department having jurisdiction over certain immigration-related functions, acting through its component agencies, including USCIS.

Employee means a person who is engaged to perform work for an employer, as defined under the general common law of agency. Some of the factors relevant to the determination of employee status include: The hiring party's right to control the manner and means by which the work is accomplished; the skill required to perform the work; the source of the instrumentalities and tools for accomplishing the work; the location of the work; the hiring party's discretion over when and how long to work; and whether the work is part of the regular business of the hiring party. Other applicable factors may be considered and no one factor is dispositive. The terms employee and worker are used interchangeably in this subpart.

Employer means a person (including any individual, partnership, association, corporation, cooperative, firm, joint stock company, trust, or other organization with legal rights and duties) that:

(1) Has a place of business (physical location) in the Commonwealth and a means by which it may be contacted for employment;

(2) Has an employer relationship (such as the ability to hire, pay, fire, supervise or otherwise control the work of employees) with respect to a CW–1 worker or a worker in corresponding employment, as defined under the common law of agency; and

(3) Possesses, for purposes of filing a *CW–1 Application for Temporary Employment Certification*, a valid Federal Employer Identification Number (FEIN).

Employer-client means an employer that has entered into an agreement with a job contractor and that is not an affiliate, branch, or subsidiary of the job contractor, under which the job contractor provides services or labor to the employer-client on a temporary basis and will not exercise substantial, direct day-to-day supervision and control in the performance of the services or labor to be performed other than hiring, paying, and firing the workers.

Employment and Training Administration or ETA means the agency within the Department that includes OFLC and has been delegated authority by the Secretary to fulfill the Secretary's mandate under for the administration and adjudication of a *CW–1 Application for Temporary Employment Certification* and related functions.

Federal holiday means a legal public holiday as defined at 5 U.S.C. 6103.

Full-time means 35 or more hours of work per week.

Governor means the Governor of the Commonwealth of the Northern Mariana Islands.

Job contractor means a person, association, firm, or a corporation that meets the definition of an employer and that contracts services or labor on a temporary basis to one or more employers that are not an affiliate, branch, or subsidiary of the job contractor and where the job contractor will not exercise substantial, direct day-to-day supervision and control in the performance of the services or labor to be performed other than hiring, paying, and releasing the workers.

Job offer means the offer made by an employer or potential employer of CW–1 workers to both U.S. and CW–1 workers describing all the material terms and conditions of employment, including those relating to wages, working conditions, and other benefits.

Job opportunity means full-time employment at a place in the Commonwealth to which U.S. workers can be referred.

Joint employment means that where two or more employers each have sufficient definitional indicia of being a joint employer of a worker under the common law of agency, they are, at all times, joint employers of that worker.

Layoff means any involuntary separation of one or more U.S. employees other than for cause.

Long-term worker means an alien who was admitted to the CNMI as a CW–1 nonimmigrant during fiscal year (FY) 2015, and who was granted CW–1 nonimmigrant status during each of FYs 2016 through 2018, as defined by DHS.

National Prevailing Wage Center or NPWC means that office within OFLC from which employers, agents, or attorneys who wish to file a *CW–1 Application for Temporary Employment Certification* receive a PWD.

NPWC Director means the OFLC official to whom the OFLC Administrator has delegated authority to carry out certain NPWC operations and functions.

National Processing Center (NPC) means the office within OFLC in which the COs operate, and which are charged with the adjudication of *CW–1 Applications for Temporary Employment Certification*.

NPC Director means the OFLC official to whom the OFLC Administrator has delegated authority for purposes of certain NPC operations and functions.

Occupational employment statistics (OES) survey means the program under the jurisdiction of the Bureau of Labor Statistics (BLS) that reports annual wage estimates, including those for Guam, based on standard occupational classifications (SOCs).

Offered wage means the wage offered by an employer in the *CW–1 Application for Temporary Employment Certification* and job offer. The offered wage must equal or exceed the highest of the prevailing wage, or the Federal minimum wage, or the Commonwealth minimum wage.

Office of Foreign Labor Certification or OFLC means the organizational component of the ETA that provides national leadership and policy guidance and develops regulations to carry out the Secretary's responsibilities, including determinations related to an employer's request for an *Application for Prevailing Wage Determination* or *CW–1 Application for Temporary Employment Certification.*

Place of employment means the worksite (or physical location) where work under the *CW–1 Application for Temporary Employment Certification* and job offer actually is performed by the CW–1 workers and workers in corresponding employment.

Prevailing wage (PW) means the official wage issued by the NPWC on the Form ETA 9141C, *Application for Prevailing Wage Determination for the CW–1 Program,* or successor form. At least that amount must be paid to all CW–1 workers and U.S. workers in corresponding employment.

Prevailing wage determination (PWD) means the prevailing wage issued by the OFLC NPWC on the Form ETA-9141C, *Application for Prevailing Wage Determination for the CW–1 Program,* or successor form. The PWD is used in support of the *CW–1 Application for Temporary Employment Certification.*

Secretary of Labor or Secretary means the chief official of the U.S. DOL, or the Secretary's designee.

Secretary of Homeland Security means the chief official of DHS or the Secretary of Homeland Security's designee.

Secretary of State means the chief official of the U.S. Department of State or the Secretary of State's designee.

Strike means a concerted stoppage of work by employees as a result of a labor dispute, or any concerted slowdown or other concerted interruption of operation (including stoppage by reason of the expiration of a collective bargaining agreement).

Successor in interest means an employer, agent, or attorney that is controlling and carrying on the business of a previous employer.

(1) Where an employer, agent, or attorney has violated 48 U.S.C. 1806 or the regulations in this subpart and has ceased doing business or cannot be located for purposes of enforcement, a successor in interest to that employer, agent, or attorney may be held liable for the duties and obligations of the violating employer in certain circumstances. The following factors, as used under Title VII of the Civil Rights Act and the Vietnam Era Veterans' Readjustment Assistance Act, may be considered in determining whether an employer, agent, or attorney is a successor in interest; no one factor is dispositive, and all the circumstances will be considered as a whole:

(i) Substantial continuity of the same business operations;

(ii) Use of the same facilities;

(iii) Continuity of the work force;

(iv) Similarity of jobs and working conditions;

(v) Similarity of supervisory personnel;

(vi) Whether the former management or owner retains a direct or indirect interest in the new enterprise;

(vii) Similarity in machinery, equipment, and production methods;

(viii) Similarity of products and services; and

(ix) The ability of the predecessor to provide relief.

(2) For purposes of debarment only, the primary consideration will be the personal involvement of the firm's ownership, management, supervisors, and others associated with the firm in the violation(s) at issue.

Temporary labor certification or TLC means the certification made by the

OFLC Administrator, based on the *CW–1 Application for Temporary Employment Certification*, job offer, and all supporting documentation, with respect to an employer seeking to file with DHS a visa petition to employ one or more foreign nationals as a CW–1 worker.

United States means the continental United States, Alaska, Hawaii, the Commonwealth of Puerto Rico, Guam, the U.S. Virgin Islands, and the Commonwealth.

United States worker (U.S. worker) means a worker who is:

(1) A citizen or national of the United States;

(2) An alien lawfully admitted for permanent residence; or

(3) A citizen of the Federated States of Micronesia, the Republic of the Marshall Islands, or the Republic of Palau, who is eligible for nonimmigrant admission and is employment-authorized under the Compacts of Free Association between the United States and those nations.

U.S. Citizenship and Immigration Services or USCIS means the Federal agency within DHS that makes the determination whether to grant petitions filed by employers seeking CW–1 workers to perform temporary work in the Commonwealth.

Wages mean all forms of cash remuneration to a worker by an employer in payment for labor or services.

Work contract means the document containing all the material terms and conditions of employment relating to wages, hours, working conditions, places of employment, and other benefits, including all assurances and obligations required to be included under this subpart. The contract between the employer and the worker may be in the form of a separate written document containing the advertised terms and conditions of the job offer. In the absence of a separate, written work contract incorporating the required terms and conditions of employment, agreed to by both the employer and the worker, the required terms of the certified *CW–1 Application for Temporary Employment Certification* will be the work contract.

§ 655.403 Persons and entities authorized to file.

(a) *Persons authorized to file.* In addition to the employer, a request for a PWD or TLC under this subpart may be filed by an attorney or agent, as defined in § 655.402.

(b) *Employer's signature required.* Regardless of whether the employer is represented by an attorney or agent, the employer is required to sign the *CW–1 Application for Temporary Employment Certification* and all documentation submitted to the Department.

§ 655.404 Requirements for agents.

An agent filing a *CW–1 Application for Temporary Employment Certification* on behalf of an employer must provide a copy of the agent agreement or other document demonstrating the agent's authority to represent the employer to the NPC at the time of filing the application.

§§ 655.405–655.409 [Reserved]

PREFILING PROCEDURES

§ 655.410 Offered wage rate and determination of prevailing wage.

(a) *Offered wage.* (1) The employer must advertise the position to all potential workers at a wage that is at least the highest of the following:

(i) The prevailing wage for the job opportunity obtained from the NPWC;

(ii) The Federal minimum wage; or

(iii) The Commonwealth minimum wage.

(2) The employer must offer and pay at least the wage provided in paragraph (a)(1) of this section to both its CW–1 workers and its workers in corresponding employment. The issuance of a PWD under this section does not permit an employer to pay a wage lower than the highest wage required by any applicable Federal or Commonwealth law.

(b) *Determinations*—(1) *Methods.* The OFLC Administrator will determine prevailing wages in the Commonwealth and occupational classification as follows:

(i) If the mean hourly wage for the occupational classification in the Commonwealth is reported by the Governor, annually, and meets the requirements set forth in paragraph (e) of this section, as determined by the OFLC Administrator, that wage must be the prevailing wage for the occupational classification;

(ii) If the OFLC Administrator has not approved a survey, as reported by the Governor, for the occupational classification under paragraph (b)(1)(i) of this section, and the BLS OES survey reports a mean wage paid to workers in the SOC in Guam, the prevailing wage must be the mean wage paid to workers in the SOC in Guam from the BLS OES survey; and

(iii) If the OFLC Administrator has not approved a survey, as reported by the Governor, for the occupational classification under paragraph (b)(1)(i) of this section and the BLS OES survey does not report the mean wage paid to workers in the SOC in Guam under paragraph (b)(1)(ii) of this section, the prevailing wage must be the mean wage paid to workers in the SOC in the United States from the BLS OES Survey, adjusted based on the ratio of the mean wage paid to workers in all SOCs in Guam compared to the mean wage paid to workers in all SOCs in the United States from the BLS OES survey.

(2) *Multiple occupations.* If the job duties on the *Application for Prevailing Wage Determination* do not fall within a single occupational classification, the NPC will determine the applicable prevailing wage based on the highest prevailing wage for all applicable occupational classifications.

(c) *Request for PWD*—(1) *Filing requirement.* An employer must electronically request and receive a PWD from the NPWC then electronically file the *CW-1 Application for Temporary Employment Certification* with the NPC.

(2) *Location and methods of filing*—(i) *Electronic filing.* The employer must file the *Application for Prevailing Wage Determination* and all required supporting documentation with the NPWC using the electronic method(s) designated by the OFLC Administrator. The NPWC will return without review any application submitted using a method other than the designated electronic method(s), unless the employer submits with the application a statement of the need to file by mail.

(ii) *Filing by mail.* Employers that are unable to file electronically, either due to lack of internet access or physical disability precluding electronic filing, may file the application by mail. The mailed application must include a statement indicating the need to file by mail. The NPWC will return, without review, mailed applications that do not contain such a statement. OFLC will publish the address for mailed applications in the instructions to Form ETA–9141C.

(d) *NPWC action.* The NPWC will provide the PWD, indicate the source of the PWD, and return the *Application for Prevailing Wage Determination* with its endorsement to the employer.

(e) *Wage survey reported by the Governor.* The OFLC Administrator will issue a prevailing wage for the occupational classification in the Commonwealth based on a wage survey reported by the Governor if all of the following requirements are met:

(1) The survey was independently conducted and issued by the Governor of the Commonwealth, including through any Commonwealth agency, Commonwealth college, or Commonwealth university;

(2) The survey provides the arithmetic mean of the wages of workers in the occupational classification in the Commonwealth;

(3) The surveyor either made a reasonable, good faith attempt to contact all employers in the Commonwealth employing workers in the occupation or conducted a randomized sampling of such employers;

(4) The survey includes the wages of at least 30 workers in the Commonwealth;

(5) The survey includes the wages of workers in the Commonwealth employed by at least three employers;

(6) The survey was conducted across industries that employ workers in the occupational classification;

(7) The wage reported in the survey includes all types of pay;

(8) The survey is based on wages paid to workers in the occupational classification not more than 12 months before the date the survey is submitted to the OFLC Administrator for consideration; and

(9) The Governor submits the survey to the OFLC Administrator, with specific information about the survey methodology, including such items as sample size and source, sample selection procedures, and survey job descriptions, to allow a determination of the adequacy of the data provided and validity of the statistical methodology used in conducting the survey.

(f) *Review of wage survey reported by the Governor.* (1) If the OFLC Administrator finds the wage reported for any occupational classification not to be acceptable, the OFLC Administrator must inform the Governor in writing of the reasons the wage reported in the survey was not accepted.

(2) The Governor, after receiving notification from the OFLC Administrator that the wage reported in the survey it provided for consideration is not acceptable, may submit corrected wage data or conduct a new wage survey and submit revised wage data to the OFLC Administrator for consideration under this section.

(g) *Validity period.* The NPWC will specify the validity period of the prevailing wage, which in no event may be more than 365 days or fewer than 90 days from the date that the determination is issued.

(h) *Retention of documentation.* The employer must retain the PWD for 3 years from the date of issuance if not used in support of a TLC application or if it is used in support of a TLC application that is denied, and 3 years from the date on which the certification of the *CW–1 Application for Temporary Employment Certification* expires, whichever is later. The employer must submit the PWD to a CO if requested by a Notice of Deficiency (NOD), described in §655.431, or audit, as described in §655.470, or to any Federal Government Official performing an investigation, inspection, audit, or law enforcement function.

§655.411 Review of prevailing wage determinations.

(a) *Request for review of PWDs.* Any employer desiring review of a PWD must make a written request for such review to the NPWC Director. The written request must be received by the NPWC Director within 7 business days from the date the PWD was issued. The request for review must clearly identify the PWD for which review is sought; set forth the particular grounds for the request; and include any materials submitted to the NPWC for purposes of securing the PWD.

(b) *NPWC review.* Upon the receipt of the written request for review, the NPWC Director will review the employer's request and accompanying documentation, including any supplementary material submitted by the employer, and after review must issue a Final Determination letter; that letter may:

(1) Affirm the PWD issued by the NPWC; or

(2) Modify the PWD.

(c) *Request for review by BALCA.* Any employer desiring review of the NPWC Director's decision on a PWD must make a written request to BALCA for review of the determination, with a copy simultaneously sent to the NPWC Director who issued the final determination. The written request must be received by BALCA within 10 business days from the date the Final Determination letter was issued.

(1) Upon receipt of a request for BALCA review, the NPWC will prepare an Appeal File and submit it to BALCA.

(2) The request for review, statements, briefs, and other submissions of the parties must contain only legal arguments and may refer to only the evidence that was within the record upon which the decision on the PWD by the NPWC Director was based.

(3) BALCA will handle appeals in accordance with §655.461.

§§ 655.412–655.419 [Reserved]

CW–1 APPLICATION FOR TEMPORARY EMPLOYMENT CERTIFICATION FILING PROCEDURES

§ 655.420 Application filing requirements.

An employer seeking to hire CW–1 workers must electronically file a *CW–1 Application for Temporary Employment Certification* with the NPC designated by the OFLC Administrator. This section provides the procedures an employer must follow when filing.

(a) *What to file.* An employer seeking a TLC must file a completed *CW–1 Application for Temporary Employment Certification* (Form ETA–9142C and the appropriate appendices and valid PWD), and all supporting documentation and information required at the time of filing under this subpart. Applications that are incomplete at the time of submission will be returned to the employer without review.

(b) *Timeliness.* (1) Except as provided in paragraph (b)(2) of this section, a completed *CW–1 Application for Temporary Employment Certification* must be filed no more than 120 calendar days before the employer's date of need.

(2) If the employer is seeking a TLC to extend the employment of a CW–1 worker, a completed *CW–1 Application for Temporary Employment Certification* must be filed no more than 180 calendar days before the date on which the CW–1 status expires.

(c) *Location and methods of filing*—(1) *Electronic filing.* The employer must file the *CW–1 Application for Temporary Employment Certification* and all required supporting documentation with the NPC using the electronic method(s) designated by the OFLC Administrator. The NPC will return, without review, any application submitted using a method other than the designated electronic method(s), unless the employer submits with the application a statement of the need to file by mail or indicates that it already submitted such a statement to NPWC during the same fiscal year.

(2) *Filing by mail.* Employers that are unable to file electronically, either due to lack of internet access or physical disability precluding electronic filing, may file the application by mail. The mailed application must include a statement indicating the need to file by mail as indicated above. The NPC will return, without review, mailed applications that do not contain such a statement. OFLC will publish the address for mailed applications in the instructions to Form ETA–9142C.

(d) *Original signature and acceptance of electronic signatures.* An electronically filed *CW–1 Application for Temporary Employment Certification* must contain an electronic (scanned) copy of the original signature of the employer (and that of the employer's authorized attorney or agent, if the employer is represented by an attorney or agent) or, in the alternative, use a verifiable electronic signature method, as directed by the OFLC Administrator. If submitted by mail, the *CW–1 Application for Temporary Employment Certification* must bear the original signature of the employer and, if applicable, the employer's authorized attorney or agent.

(e) *Requests for multiple positions.* An employer may request certification of more than one position on its *CW–1 Application for Temporary Employment Certification* as long as all CW–1 workers will perform the same services or labor under the same terms and conditions, in the same occupation, during the same period of employment, and at a location (or locations) covered by the application.

(f) *Scope of application.* (1) A *CW–1 Application for Temporary Employment Certification* must be limited to places of employment within the Commonwealth.

(2) In a single application filing, an association or other organization of employers is not permitted to file a *CW–1 Application for Temporary Employment Certification* on behalf of more than one employer-member under the CW–1 program.

(g) *Period of employment.* (1) Except as provided in paragraph (g)(2) of this section, the period of need identified in the *CW–1 Application for Temporary Employment Certification* must not exceed 1 year.

(2) If the employer is seeking TLC to employ a long-term CW–1 worker, the period of need identified in the *CW–1*

Application for Temporary Employment Certification must not exceed 3 years.

(h) *Return of applications based on USCIS CW–1 cap notice.* (1) Except as provided in paragraph (h)(3) of this section, if USCIS issues a public notice stating that it has received a sufficient number of CW–1 petitions to meet the statutory numerical limit on the total number of foreign nationals who may be issued a CW–1 permit or otherwise granted CW–1 status for the fiscal year, the OFLC Administrator must return without review any *CW–1 Applications for Temporary Employment Certification* with dates of need in that fiscal year received on or after the date that the OFLC Administrator provides the notice in paragraph (h)(2) of this section.

(2) The OFLC Administrator will announce the return of future *CW–1 Applications for Temporary Employment Certification* with dates of need in the fiscal year for which the cap is met with a notice on the OFLC's website. This notice will be effective on the date of its publication on the OFLC's website and will remain valid for the fiscal year unless:

(i) USCIS issues a public notice stating additional CW–1 permits are available for the fiscal year; and

(ii) The OFLC Administrator publishes a new notice announcing that additional TLCs may be granted in the fiscal year.

(3) After the notice that OFLC will return future *CW–1 Applications for Temporary Employment Certification*, the OFLC Administrator will continue to process *CW–1 Applications for Temporary Employment Certification* filed before the effective date of the suspension notice and will continue to permit the filing of *CW–1 Applications for Temporary Employment Certification* by employers who identify in the *CW–1 Application for Temporary Employment Certification* that the employment of all CW–1 workers employed under the *CW–1 Application for Temporary Employment Certification* will be exempt from the statutory numerical limit on the total number of foreign nationals who may be issued a CW–1 permit or otherwise granted CW–1 status.

§ 655.421 Job contractor filing requirements.

(a) A job contractor may submit a *CW–1 Application for Temporary Employment Certification* on behalf of itself and that employer-client. By doing so, the Department deems the job contractor a joint employer.

(b) A job contractor must have separate contracts with each different employer-client. A single contract or agreement may support only one *CW–1 Application for Temporary Employment Certification* for each employer-client job opportunity in the Commonwealth.

(c) Either the job contractor or its employer-client may submit an *Application for Prevailing Wage Determination* describing the job opportunity to the NPWC. However, each of the joint employers is separately responsible for ensuring that the wage offer(s) listed in the *CW–1 Application for Temporary Employment Certification* and related recruitment at least equals the prevailing wage obtained from the NPWC, or the Federal or Commonwealth minimum wage, whichever is highest, and that all other wage obligations are met.

(d)(1) A job contractor that is filing as a joint employer with its employer-client must submit to the NPC a completed *CW–1 Application for Temporary Employment Certification* that clearly identifies the joint employers (the job contractor and its employer-client) and the employment relationship (including the places of employment), in accordance with instructions provided by the OFLC Administrator. The *CW–1 Application for Temporary Employment Certification* must bear the original signature of the job contractor and the employer-client or use a verifiable electronic signature method, consistent with the requirements set forth at § 655.420(d), and be accompanied by the contract or agreement establishing the employers' relationships related to the workers sought.

(2) By signing the *CW–1 Application for Temporary Employment Certification*, each employer independently attests to the conditions of employment required of an employer participating in the CW–1 program and assumes full responsibility for the accuracy of the representations made in the application

and for all of the responsibilities of an employer in the CW–1 program.

(e)(1) Either the job contractor or its employer-client may place the required advertisements and conduct recruitment as described in §§ 655.442 through 655.445. Also, either one of the joint employers may assume responsibility for interviewing applicants. However, both of the joint employers must sign the recruitment report that is submitted to the NPC meeting the requirement set forth in § 655.446.

(2) All recruitment conducted by the joint employers must satisfy the job offer assurance and advertising content requirements identified in § 655.441. Additionally, in order to fully inform applicants of the job opportunity and avoid potential confusion inherent in a job opportunity involving two employers, joint employer recruitment must clearly identify both employers (the job contractor and its employer-client) by name and must clearly identify the place(s) of employment where workers will perform labor or services.

(3)(i) Provided that all of the employer-clients' job opportunities are in the same occupation located in the Commonwealth and have the same requirements and terms and conditions of employment, including dates of employment, a job contractor may combine more than one of its joint employer employer-clients' job opportunities in a single advertisement. Each advertisement must fully inform potential workers of the job opportunity available with each employer-client and otherwise satisfy the job offer assurances and advertising content requirements identified in § 655.441. Such a shared advertisement must clearly identify the job contractor by name, the joint employment relationship, and the number of workers sought for each job opportunity, identified by employer-client names and locations (e.g., five openings with Employer-Client A (place of employment location), three openings with Employer-Client B (place of employment location)).

(ii) In addition, the advertisement must contain the following statement: "Applicants may apply for any or all of the jobs listed. When applying, please identify the job(s) (by company and work location) you are applying to for the entire period of employment specified." If an applicant fails to identify one or more specific work location(s), that applicant is presumed to have applied to all work locations listed in the advertisement.

(f) If a TLC for the joint employers is granted, the Final Determination certifying the *CW–1 Application for Temporary Employment Certification* will be sent to both the job contractor and employer-client.

§ 655.422 Emergency situations.

(a) *Waiver of PWD requirement prior to application filing.* The CO may waive the requirement to obtain a PWD, as required under § 655.410(c), prior to filing a *CW–1 Application for Temporary Employment Certification* for employers that have good and substantial cause, provided that the CO has sufficient time to thoroughly test the labor market and to make a final determination as required by § 655.450. The requirement to obtain a PWD prior to filing the *CW–1 Application for Temporary Employment Certification*, under § 655.410(c), is the only provision of this subpart which will be waived under these emergency situation procedures.

(b) *Employer requirements.* The employer requesting a waiver of the requirement to obtain a PWD must submit to the NPC a completed *Application for Prevailing Wage Determination*, a completed *CW–1 Application for Temporary Employment Certification*, and a statement justifying the waiver request. The employer's waiver request must include detailed information describing the good and substantial cause that has necessitated the waiver request. Good and substantial cause may include, but is not limited to, the substantial loss of U.S. workers due to an Act of God, or similar unforeseeable man-made catastrophic events (such as a hazardous materials emergency or government-controlled flooding), unforeseeable changes in market conditions, pandemic health issues, or similar conditions that are wholly outside of the employer's control. Issues related to the CW–1 visa cap are not good and substantial cause for a waiver of the filing requirements. Further, a denial of a previously submitted *CW–1 Application for Temporary Employment*

Certification or CW–1 petition with USCIS does not constitute good and substantial cause necessitating a waiver under this section.

(c) *Processing of emergency applications.* The CO will process the emergency *CW–1 Application for Temporary Employment Certification*, including the *Application for Prevailing Wage Determination for the CW–1 Program*, in a manner consistent with the provisions of this subpart and make a determination in accordance with §655.450. The CO will notify the employer, if the application cannot be processed because, pursuant to paragraph (a) of this section, the request for emergency filing was not justified and/or the filing does not meet the requirements set forth in this subpart.

§655.423 Assurances and obligations of CW–1 employers.

An employer employing CW–1 workers and/or workers in corresponding employment under a *CW–1 Application for Temporary Employment Certification* has agreed as part of the *CW–1 Application for Temporary Employment Certification* that it will abide by the following conditions with respect to its CW–1 workers and any workers in corresponding employment:

(a) *Rate of pay.* (1) The offered wage in the work contract equals or exceeds the highest of the prevailing wage, Federal minimum wage, or Commonwealth minimum wage. The employer must pay at least the offered wage, free and clear, during the entire period of the *CW–1 Application for Temporary Employment Certification* granted by OFLC.

(2) The offered wage is not based on commissions, bonuses, or other incentives, including paying on a piece-rate basis, unless the employer guarantees a wage earned every workweek that equals or exceeds the offered wage.

(3) If the employer requires one or more minimum productivity standards of workers as a condition of job retention, the standards must be specified in the work contract and the employer must demonstrate that they are normal and usual for non-CW–1 employers for the same occupation in the Commonwealth.

(4) An employer that pays on a piece-rate basis must demonstrate that the piece-rate is no less than the normal rate paid by non-CW–1 employers to workers performing the same activity in the Commonwealth. The average hourly piece-rate earnings must result in an amount at least equal to the offered wage. If the worker is paid on a piece-rate basis and at the end of the workweek the piece-rate does not result in average hourly piece-rate earnings during the workweek at least equal to the amount the worker would have earned had the worker been paid at the offered hourly wage, then the employer must supplement the worker's pay at that time so that the worker's earnings are at least as much as the worker would have earned during the workweek if the worker had instead been paid at the offered hourly wage for each hour worked.

(b) *Wages free and clear.* The payment requirements for wages in this section will be satisfied by the timely payment of such wages to the worker either in cash or in negotiable instrument payable at par. The payment must be made finally and unconditionally and "free and clear." The principles applied in determining whether deductions are reasonable and payments are received free and clear, and the permissibility of deductions for payments to third persons are explained in more detail in 29 CFR part 531.

(c) *Deductions.* The employer must make all deductions from the worker's paycheck required by law. The work contract must specify all deductions not required by law that the employer will make from the worker's pay; any such deductions not disclosed in the work contract are prohibited. The wage payment requirements of paragraph (b) of this section are not met where unauthorized deductions, rebates, or refunds reduce the wage payment made to the worker below the minimum amounts required by the offered wage or where the worker fails to receive such amounts free and clear because the worker "kick backs" directly or indirectly to the employer or to another person for the employer's benefit the whole or part of the wages delivered to the worker. Authorized deductions are limited to: Those required by law, such as taxes payable by workers that are required to be withheld by the employer and amounts due workers which the employer is required by court order to pay to another; deductions for the reasonable cost or fair value of board, lodging, and facilities furnished; and deductions of amounts which are authorized to be paid to third persons for the worker's account and benefit through his or her voluntary assignment or order or which are authorized by a collective bargaining agreement with bona fide representatives of workers which covers the employer. Deductions for amounts paid to third persons for the worker's account and benefit which are not so authorized or are contrary to law or from which the employer, agent, or recruiter, including any agents or employees of these entities or any affiliated person, derives any payment, rebate, commission, profit, or benefit directly or indirectly, may not be made if they reduce the actual wage paid to the worker below the offered wage indicated on the *CW–1 Application for Temporary Employment Certification.*

(d) *Job opportunity is full time.* The job opportunity is a full-time position, consistent with § 655.402, and the employer must use a single workweek as its standard for computing wages due. An employee's workweek must be a fixed and regularly recurring period of 168 hours—7 consecutive 24-hour periods. It need not coincide with the calendar week but may begin on any day and at any hour of the day.

(e) *Job qualifications and requirements.* Each job qualification and requirement must be listed in the work contract and must be bona fide and consistent with the normal and accepted qualifications and requirements imposed by non-CW–1 employers in the same occupation and in the Commonwealth. The employer's job qualifications and requirements imposed on U.S. workers must not be less favorable than the qualifications and requirements that the employer is imposing or will impose on CW–1 workers. A qualification means a characteristic that is necessary to the individual's ability to perform the job in question. A requirement means a term or condition of employment that a worker is required to accept in order to obtain the job opportunity. The CO may require the employer to submit documentation to substantiate the appropriateness of any job qualification and/or requirement.

(f) *Three-fourths guarantee*—(1) *Offer to worker.* The employer must guarantee to offer the worker employment for a total number of work hours equal to at least three-fourths of the workdays of the total period of employment specified in the work contract, beginning with the first workday after the arrival of the worker at the place of employment or the advertised contractual first date of need, whichever is later, and ending on the expiration date specified in the work contract or in its extensions, if any. See the exception in paragraph (f)(1)(iv) of this section.

(i) For purposes of this paragraph (f), a workday means the number of hours in a workday as stated in the work contract. The employer must offer a total number of hours to ensure the provision of sufficient work to reach the three-fourths guarantee. The work hours must be offered during the work period specified in the work contract, or during any modified work contract period to which the worker and employer have mutually agreed and that has been approved by the CO.

(ii) In the event the worker begins working later than the start date of need specified in the application, the guarantee period begins with the first workday after the arrival of the worker at the place of employment and continues until the last day during which the work contract and all extensions thereof are in effect.

(iii) Therefore, if, for example, a work contract is for a 10-week period, during which a normal workweek is specified as 6 days a week, 8 hours per day, the worker would have to be guaranteed employment for at least 360 hours (10 weeks × 48 hours/week = 480 hours × 75 percent = 360). If a Federal holiday occurred during the 10-week period, the 8 hours would be deducted from the total hours for the work contract, before the guarantee is calculated. Continuing with the above example, the worker would have to be guaranteed employment for 354 hours (10 weeks × 48 hours/week = 480 hours − 8 hours (Federal holiday) = 472 hours × 75 percent = 354 hours).

(iv) A worker may be offered more than the specified hours of work on a single workday. For purposes of meeting the guarantee, the worker will not be required to work more than the number of hours specified in the work contract for a workday but all hours of work actually performed may be counted by the employer in calculating whether the period of guaranteed employment has been met. If during the total work contract period the employer affords the U.S. or CW–1 worker less employment than that required under this paragraph (f)(1)(iv), the employer must pay such worker the amount the worker would have earned had the worker, in fact, worked for the guaranteed number of days. An employer will not be considered to have met the work guarantee if the employer has merely offered work on three-fourths of the workdays of the work contract period if each workday did not consist of a full number of hours of work time as specified in the work contract.

(2) *Guarantee for piece-rate paid worker.* If the worker is paid on a piece-rate basis, the employer must use the worker's average hourly piece-rate earnings or the offered wage, whichever is higher, to calculate the amount due under the guarantee in accordance with paragraph (f)(1) of this section.

(3) *Failure to work.* Any hours the worker fails to work, up to a maximum of the number of hours specified in the work contract for a workday, when the worker has been offered an opportunity to work in accordance with paragraph (f)(1) of this section, and all hours of work actually performed (including voluntary work over 8 hours in a workday), may be counted by the employer in calculating whether the period of guaranteed employment has been met. An employer seeking to calculate whether the guaranteed number of hours has been met must maintain the payroll records in accordance with this subpart.

(g) *Impossibility of fulfillment.* If before the expiration date specified in the work contract, the services of the worker are no longer required for reasons beyond the control of the employer due to fire, weather, or other Act of God, or similar unforeseeable man-made catastrophic event (such as an oil spill or controlled flooding) that is wholly outside the employer's control that makes the fulfillment of the work contract impossible, the employer may terminate the work contract with the approval of the CO. In the event of such termination, the employer must fulfill a three-fourths guarantee, as described in paragraph (f) of this section, for the time that has elapsed from the start date listed in the work contract or the first workday after the arrival of the worker at the place of employment, whichever is later, to the time of its termination. The employer must make efforts to transfer the CW–1 worker or worker in corresponding employment to other comparable employment acceptable to the worker and consistent with immigration laws, as applicable. If a transfer is not affected, the employer must return the worker, at the employer's expense, to the place from which the worker (disregarding intervening employment) came to work for the employer, or transport the worker to the worker's next certified CW–1 employer, whichever the worker prefers.

(h) *Frequency of pay.* The employer must state in the work contract the frequency with which the worker will be paid, which must be at least every 2 weeks. Employers must pay wages when due.

(i) *Earnings statements.* (1) The employer must keep accurate and adequate records with respect to the workers' earnings, including but not limited to: Records showing the nature, amount, and location(s) of the work performed; the number of hours of work offered each day by the employer (broken out by hours offered both in accordance with and over and above the three-fourths guarantee in paragraph (f) of this section); the hours actually worked each day by the worker; if the number of hours worked by the worker is less than the number of hours offered, the reason(s) the worker did not work; the time the worker began and ended each workday; the rate of pay (both piece-rate and hourly, if applicable); the worker's earnings per pay period; the worker's home address; and the amount of and reasons for any and all deductions taken from or additions made to the worker's wages.

(2) The employer must furnish to the worker on or before each payday in one or more written statements the following information:

(i) The worker's total earnings for each workweek in the pay period;

(ii) The worker's hourly rate or piece-rate of pay;

(iii) For each workweek in the pay period the hours of employment offered to the worker (showing offers in accordance with the three-fourths guarantee as determined in paragraph (f) of this section, separate from any hours offered over and above the guarantee);

(iv) For each workweek in the pay period the hours actually worked by the worker;

(v) An itemization of all deductions made from or additions made to the worker's wages;

(vi) If piece-rates are used, the units produced daily;

(vii) The beginning and ending dates of the pay period; and

(viii) The employer's name, address, and FEIN.

(j) *Transportation and visa fees*—(1)(i) *Transportation to the place of employment.* The employer must provide or reimburse the worker for transportation and subsistence from the place from which the worker has come to work for the employer, whether in the United States, including another part of the Commonwealth, or abroad, to the place of employment if the worker completes 50 percent of the period of employment covered by the work contract (not counting any extensions). The employer may arrange and pay for the transportation and subsistence directly, advance at a minimum the most economical and reasonable common carrier cost of the transportation and subsistence to the worker before the worker's departure, or pay the worker for the reasonable costs incurred by the worker. When it is the prevailing practice of non-CW–1 employers in the occupation and in the Commonwealth to do so or when the employer extends such benefits to similarly situated CW–1 workers, the employer must advance the required transportation and subsistence costs (or otherwise provide them) to workers in corresponding employment who are traveling to the employer's place of employment from such a distance that the worker is not reasonably able to return to their residence each day. The amount of the transportation payment must be no less (and is not required to be more) than the most economical and reasonable common carrier transportation charges for the distances involved. The amount of the daily subsistence must be at least the amount permitted in §655.173. Where the employer will reimburse the reasonable costs incurred by the worker, it must keep accurate and adequate records of: The costs of transportation and subsistence incurred by the worker; the amount reimbursed; and the date(s) of reimbursement. Note that the Fair Labor Standards Act applies independently of the CW–1 requirements and imposes obligations on employers regarding payment of wages.

(ii) *Transportation from the place of employment.* If the worker completes the period of employment covered by the work contract (not counting any extensions), or if the worker is dismissed from employment for any reason by the employer before the end of the period, and the worker has no immediate subsequent CW–1 employment, the employer must provide or pay at the time of departure for the worker's cost of return transportation and daily subsistence from the place of employment to the place from which the worker, disregarding intervening employment, departed to work for the employer. If the worker has contracted with a subsequent employer that has not agreed in the work contract to provide or pay for the worker's transportation from the former employer's place of employment to such subsequent employer's place of employment, the former employer must provide or pay for that transportation and subsistence. If the worker has contracted with a subsequent employer that has agreed in the work contract to provide or pay for the worker's transportation from the former employer's place of employment to such subsequent employer's place of employment, the subsequent employer must provide or pay for such expenses.

(iii) *Employer-provided transportation.* All employer-provided transportation must comply with all applicable Federal and Commonwealth laws and regulations including, but not limited to, vehicle safety standards, driver licensure requirements, and vehicle insurance coverage.

(2) The employer must pay or reimburse the worker in the first workweek for all visa, visa processing, border crossing, and other related fees (including those mandated by the government) incurred by the CW–1 worker, but not for passport expenses or other charges primarily for the benefit of the worker.

(k) *Employer-provided items.* The employer must provide to the worker, without charge or deposit charge, all tools, supplies, and equipment required to perform the duties assigned.

(l) *Disclosure of work contract.* The employer must provide to a CW–1 worker outside of the United States no later than the time at which the worker applies for the visa, or to a worker in corresponding employment no later than on the day work commences, a copy of the work contract including any subsequent approved modifications. For a CW–1 worker changing employment from a CW–1 employer to a subsequent CW–1 employer, the copy must be provided no later than the time an offer of employment is made by the subsequent CW–1 employer. The disclosure of all documents required by this paragraph (l) must be provided in a language understood by the worker. At a minimum, the work contract must contain all of the provisions required to be included by this section. In the absence of a separate, written work contract entered into between the employer and the worker, the required terms of the certified *CW–1 Application for Temporary Employment Certification* will be the work contract.

(m) *No unfair treatment.* The employer has not and will not intimidate, threaten, restrain, coerce, blacklist, discharge, or in any manner discriminate against, and has not and will not cause any person to intimidate, threaten, restrain, coerce, blacklist, discharge, or in any manner discriminate against, any person who has, related to the CW–1 program:

(1) Filed a complaint under or related to any applicable Federal or Commonwealth laws and regulations;

(2) Instituted or caused to be instituted any proceeding under or related to any applicable Federal or Commonwealth laws and regulations;

(3) Testified or is about to testify in any proceeding under or related to any applicable Federal or Commonwealth laws and regulations;

(4) Consulted with a workers' center, community organization, labor union, legal assistance program, or an attorney on matters related to any applicable Federal or Commonwealth laws and regulations; or

(5) Exercised or asserted on behalf of himself/herself or others any right or protection afforded by any applicable Federal or Commonwealth laws and regulations.

(n) *Comply with the prohibitions against employees paying fees.* The employer and its attorney, agents, or employees have not sought or received payment of any kind from the worker for any activity related to obtaining CW–1 labor certification or employment, including payment of the employer's attorney or agent fees, application and *CW–1 Petition* fees, recruitment costs, or any fees attributed to obtaining the approved *CW–1 Application for Temporary Employment Certification.* For purposes of this paragraph (n), payment includes, but is not limited to, monetary payments, wage concessions (including deductions from wages, salary, or benefits), kickbacks, bribes, tributes, in-kind payments, and free labor. All wages must be paid free and clear. This paragraph (n) does not prohibit employers or their agents from receiving reimbursement for costs that are the responsibility and primarily for the benefit of the worker, such as government-required passport fees.

(o) *Contracts with third parties to comply with prohibitions.* The employer must contractually prohibit in writing any agent or recruiter (or any agent or employee of such agent or recruiter) whom the employer engages, either directly or indirectly, in recruitment of CW–1 workers to seek or receive payments or other compensation from prospective workers. The contract must include the following statement: "Under this agreement, [name of agent, recruiter] and any agent of or employee of [name of agent or recruiter] are prohibited from seeking or receiving payments from any prospective employee of [employer name] at any time, including before or after the worker obtains employment. Payments include but are not limited to, any direct or indirect fees paid by such employees for recruitment, job placement, processing, maintenance, attorneys' fees, agent fees, application fees, or petition fees."

(p) *Prohibition against preferential treatment of foreign workers.* The employer's job offer must offer to U.S. workers no less than the same benefits, wages, and working conditions that the employer is offering, intends to offer, or will provide to CW–1 workers. Job offers may not impose on U.S. workers any restrictions or obligations that will not be imposed on the employer's CW–1 workers. This does not relieve the employer from providing to CW–1 workers at least the minimum benefits, wages, and working conditions which must be offered to U.S. workers consistent with this section.

(q) *Nondiscriminatory hiring practices.* The job opportunity is open to any qualified U.S. worker as defined in § 655.402, regardless of race, color, national origin, age, sex, religion, disability, or citizenship. Rejections of any U.S. workers who applied or apply for the job must only be for lawful, job-related reasons, and those not rejected on this basis have been or will be hired. In addition, the employer has and will continue to retain records of all hired workers and rejected applicants as required by § 655.456.

(r) *Recruitment requirements.* The employer must conduct all required recruitment activities, including any additional employer-conducted recruitment activities as directed by the CO, and as specified in §§ 655.442 through 655.445.

(s) *No strike or lockout.* There is no strike or lockout at any of the employer's place(s) of employment within the Commonwealth for which the employer is requesting CW–1 certification at the time the *CW–1 Application for Temporary Employment Certification* is filed.

(t) *No recent or future layoffs.* The employer has not laid off and will not lay off any similarly employed U.S. worker in the occupation that is the subject of the *CW–1 Application for Temporary Employment Certification* in the Commonwealth within the period beginning 270 calendar days before the date of need and through the end of the TLC's period of certification. A layoff for lawful, job-related reasons such as lack of work or the end of a season is permissible if all CW–1 workers are laid off before any U.S. worker in corresponding employment.

(u) *No work performed outside the Commonwealth and job opportunity.* The employer must not place any CW–1 workers employed under the approved *CW–1 Application for Temporary Employment Certification* outside the Commonwealth or in a job opportunity not listed on the approved *CW–1 Application for Temporary Employment Certification.*

(v) *Abandonment/termination of employment.* Upon the separation from employment of any worker employed under the *CW–1 Application for Temporary Employment Certification* or workers in corresponding employment, if such separation occurs before the end date of the employment period specified in the *CW–1 Application for Temporary Employment Certification,* the employer must notify OFLC in writing of the separation from employment not later than 2 working days after such separation is discovered by the employer. An abandonment or abscondment is deemed to begin after a worker fails to report for work at the regularly scheduled time for 5 consecutive working days without the consent of the employer. If the separation is due to the voluntary abandonment of employment by the CW–1 worker or worker in corresponding employment or is terminated for cause, and the employer provides appropriate notification specified under this paragraph (v), the employer will not be responsible for providing or paying for the subsequent transportation and subsistence costs of that worker under this section, and that worker is not entitled to the three-fourths guarantee described in paragraph (f) of this section.

(w) *Compliance with applicable laws.* During the period of employment specified on the *CW–1 Application for Temporary Employment Certification,* the employer must comply with all applicable Federal and Commonwealth employment-related laws and regulations, including health and safety laws. This includes compliance with 18 U.S.C. 1592(a), with respect to prohibitions against employers, the employer's agents, or their attorneys knowingly holding, destroying or confiscating workers' passports, visas, or other immigration documents.

§§ 655.424–655.429 [Reserved]

PROCESSING OF AN CW–1 APPLICATION FOR TEMPORARY EMPLOYMENT CERTIFICATION

§ 655.430 Review of applications.

(a) *NPC review.* The CO will review the *CW–1 Application for Temporary Employment Certification* for compliance with all applicable program requirements, including compliance with the requirements set forth in this subpart, and make a decision as to whether to issue a NOD under § 655.431 or a Notice of Acceptance (NOA) under § 655.433.

(b) *Mailing and postmark requirements.* Any notice or request sent by the CO to an employer requiring a response will be sent electronically or via first class mail using the address, including electronic mail address, provided on the *CW–1 Application for Temporary Employment Certification.* The employer's response to such a notice or request must be filed electronically or via first class mail. The employer's response must be filed electronically or postmarked by the date due or the next business day if the due date falls on a Saturday, Sunday, or Federal Holiday.

(c) *Information dissemination.* OFLC may forward, to DHS or any other Federal Government Official performing an investigation, inspection, audit, or law enforcement function, information OFLC receives in the course of processing a request for a *CW–1 Application for Temporary Employment Certification* or of administering program integrity measures such as audits.

§ 655.431 Notice of Deficiency.

(a) *Notification.* If the CO determines the *CW–1 Application for Temporary Employment Certification* contains errors or inaccuracies, or does not meet the requirements set forth in this subpart, the CO will issue a NOD to the employer and, if applicable, the employer's attorney or agent.

(b) *Notice content.* The NOD will:

(1) State the reason(s) the *CW–1 Application for Temporary Employment Certification* fails to meet the criteria for acceptance;

(2) Offer the employer an opportunity to submit a modified *CW–1 Application for Temporary Employment Certification* within 10 business days from the date of the NOD, and state the modification that is required for the CO to issue a NOA; and

(3) State that if the employer does not comply with the requirements of § 655.432 for submitting a modified application, the CO will deny the *CW–1 Application for Temporary Employment Certification.*

§ 655.432 Submission of modified applications.

(a) *Review of a modified CW–1 Application for Temporary Employment Certification.* Upon receipt of a response to a NOD, including any modifications, the CO will review the response. The CO may issue one or more additional NODs before issuing a decision. The employer's failure to comply with a NOD, including not responding in a timely manner or not providing all required documentation, will result in a denial of the *CW–1 Application for Temporary Employment Certification.*

(b) *Acceptance of a modified CW–1 Application for Temporary Employment Certification.* If the CO accepts the modification(s) to the *CW–1 Application for Temporary Employment Certification,* the CO will issue a NOA to the employer and, if applicable, the employer's attorney or agent.

(c) *Denial of modified CW–1 Application for Temporary Employment Certification.* If the modified *CW–1 Application for Temporary Employment Certification* does not cure the deficiencies cited in the NOD(s) or otherwise fails to satisfy the criteria required for certification, the CO will, at its discretion, either send a second NOD or deny the *CW–1 Application for Temporary Employment Certification* in accordance with the labor certification determination provisions in § 655.453.

(d) *Appeal from denial of modified CW–1 Application for Temporary Employment Certification.* The procedures for appealing a denial of a modified *CW–1 Application for Temporary Employment Certification* are the same as for appealing the denial of a nonmodified *CW–1 Application for Temporary Employment Certification*, outlined in § 655.461.

(e) *Post acceptance modifications.* Notwithstanding the decision to accept the *CW–1 Application for Temporary Employment Certification*, the CO may require modifications to the *CW–1 Application for Temporary Employment Certification* at any time before the final determination to grant or deny the *CW–1 Application for Temporary Employment Certification* if the CO determines that the job offer does not contain the minimum benefits, wages, and working conditions set forth in § 655.441. The employer must make such modifications, or the application will be denied under § 655.453. The employer must provide all workers recruited in connection with the job opportunity in the *CW–1 Application for Temporary Employment Certification* with a copy of the modified *CW–1 Application for Temporary Employment Certification*, as approved by the CO, no later than the date work commences.

§ 655.433 Notice of Acceptance.

(a) *Notification.* When the CO determines the *CW–1 Application for Temporary Employment Certification* contains no errors or inaccuracies, and meets the requirements set forth in this subpart, the CO will issue a NOA to the employer and, if applicable, the employer's attorney or agent.

(b) *Notice content.* The NOA must:

(1) Direct the employer to engage in recruitment of U.S. workers as provided in §§ 655.442 through 655.444, including any additional recruitment ordered by the CO under § 655.445;

(2) State that such employer-conducted recruitment must begin within 14 calendar days from the date the NOA is issued, consistent with § 655.440(b);

(3) Require the employer to submit a report of its recruitment efforts, by the date required by the CO in the NOA, as specified in § 655.446; and

(4) Advise the employer that failure to submit a complete recruitment report by the deadline will lead to denial of the application.

§ 655.434 Amendments to an application.

(a) *Increases in number of workers.* The *CW–1 Application for Temporary Employment Certification* may be amended at any time before the CO's certification determination to increase the number of workers requested in the initial *CW–1 Application for Temporary Employment Certification* by not more than 20 percent (50 percent for employers requesting less than 10 workers) without requiring an additional recruitment period for U.S. workers. Requests for increases above the percent prescribed, without additional recruitment, may be approved by the CO only when the employer demonstrates that the need for additional workers could not have been foreseen and is wholly outside of the employer's control. All requests to increase the number of workers must be made in writing and will not be effective until approved by the CO. Upon acceptance of an amendment, the employer must promptly provide copies of any approved amendments to all U.S. workers recruited and hired under the original job offer.

(b) *Minor changes to the period of employment.* The *CW–1 Application for Temporary Employment Certification* may be amended at any time before the CO's certification determination to make minor changes (meaning a change of up to 14 calendar days) in the total period of employment, without requiring an additional recruitment period for U.S. workers. Changes will not be effective until submitted in writing and approved by the CO. In considering whether to approve the request, the CO will review the reason(s) for the request, determine whether the reason(s) are on the whole justified, and take into account the effect any change(s) would have on the adequacy of the underlying test of the domestic labor market for the job opportunity. An employer must demonstrate that the change to the period of employment could not have been foreseen and is wholly outside of the employer's control. The CO will deny any request to change the period of employment where the total amended period of employment will exceed the maximum applicable duration permitted under § 655.420(g). Upon acceptance of an amendment, the employer must promptly provide copies of any approved amendments to all U.S. workers recruited and hired under the original job offer.

(c) *Other minor amendments to the CW-1 Application for Temporary Employment Certification.* The employer may request other minor amendments to the *CW-1 Application for Temporary Employment Certification* at any time before the CO's certification determination is issued. In considering whether to approve the request, the CO will determine whether the proposed amendment(s) are sufficiently justified and must take into account the effect of the changes on the underlying labor market test for the job opportunity. All requests for minor changes must be made in writing and will not be effective until approved by the CO. Upon acceptance of an amendment, the employer must promptly provide copies of any approved amendments to all U.S. workers recruited and hired under the original job offer.

(d) *Amendments after certification are not permitted.* After the CO has made a determination to certify the *CW-1 Application for Temporary Employment Certification*, the employer may no longer request amendments.

§§ 655.435–655.439 [Reserved]

POST ACCEPTANCE REQUIREMENTS

§ 655.440 Employer-conducted recruitment.

(a) *Employer obligations.* Employers must conduct recruitment of U.S. workers to ensure that there are not qualified U.S. workers who will be available for the positions listed in the *CW-1 Application for Temporary Employment Certification.*

(b) *Period to begin employer-conducted recruitment.* Unless otherwise instructed by the CO, the employer must begin the recruitment required in §§ 655.442 through 655.445 within 14 calendar days from the date the NOA is issued. All employer-conducted recruitment must be completed before the employer submits the recruitment report as required in § 655.446.

(c) *Interviewing U.S. workers.* Employers that wish to require interviews must conduct those interviews by phone or provide a procedure for the interviews to be conducted in the location where the worker is being recruited so that the worker incurs little or no cost. Employers cannot provide potential CW-1 workers with more favorable treatment with respect to the requirement for, and conduct of, interviews.

(d) *Qualified and available U.S. workers.* The employer must consider all U.S. applicants for the job opportunity and must hire all U.S. applicants who are qualified and who will be available for the job opportunity. U.S. applicants may be rejected only for lawful, job-related reasons, and those not rejected on this basis will be hired.

(e) *Recruitment report.* The employer must prepare a recruitment report meeting the requirements of § 655.446, by the date specified by the CO in the NOA.

§ 655.441 Job offer assurances and advertising contents.

(a) *General.* All recruitment conducted under §§ 655.442 through 655.445 in connection with an *CW-1 Application for Temporary Employment Certification* must contain terms and conditions of employment that are not less favorable than those offered to the CW-1 workers and must comply with the assurances applicable to job offers as set forth in § 655.423.

(b) *Contents.* All advertising must contain the following information:

(1) The employer's name and contact information;

(2) A statement that the job opportunity is a temporary, full-time position and identify the job title and total number of job openings the employer intends to fill;

(3) A description of the job opportunity with sufficient information to apprise applicants of the services or labor to be performed, including the job duties, the minimum education and experience requirements, the work hours and days, and the anticipated

start and end dates of the job opportunity;

(4) The place(s) of employment with enough specificity to apprise applicants of any travel requirements and where applicants will likely have to reside to perform the services or labor;

(5) The wage that the employer is offering, intends to offer or will provide to the CW–1 workers or, in the event that there are multiple wage offers, the range of applicable wage offers, each of which must equal or exceed the highest of the prevailing wage or the Federal or Commonwealth minimum wage;

(6) If applicable, a statement that overtime will be available to the worker and specify the wage offer(s) for working any overtime hours;

(7) The frequency with which the worker will be paid as required by § 655.423(h);

(8) A statement that the employer will make all deductions from the worker's paycheck required by law, and must specify any deductions the employer intends to make from the worker's paycheck which are not required by law, including, if applicable, any deductions for the reasonable cost of board, lodging, or other facilities;

(9) A statement summarizing the three-fourths guarantee as required by § 655.423(f);

(10) A statement that transportation and subsistence will be provided to the worker while traveling from the worker's origin to the place of employment as will the return transportation and subsistence at the conclusion of the job opportunity, as required by § 655.423(j)(1);

(11) If applicable, a statement that daily transportation to and from the place(s) of employment will be provided by the employer;

(12) If applicable, a statement that the employer will provide to the worker, without charge or deposit charge, all tools, supplies, and equipment required to perform the duties assigned, in accordance with § 655.423(k);

(13) If applicable, any board, lodging, or other facilities the employer will offer to workers or intends to assist workers in securing;

(14) If applicable, a statement indicating that on-the-job training will be provided to the worker; and

(15) A statement that directs applicants to apply for the job opportunity directly with the employer, and that indicates at least two verifiable methods by which applicants may apply for the job opportunity, one of which must be via electronic means, and that provides the days and hours during which applicants may be interviewed for the job opportunity.

§ 655.442 Place advertisement with CNMI Department of Labor.

(a) The employer must place an advertisement with the CNMI Department of Labor for a period of 21 consecutive calendar days satisfying the requirements set forth in § 655.441.

(b) Documentation of this step must include:

(1) Either printouts of web pages in which the advertisement appeared on the CNMI Department of Labor job listing system, or other verifiable evidence from the CNMI Department of Labor containing the text of the advertisement; and

(2) The dates of publication demonstrating compliance with the requirement of this section.

§ 655.443 Contact with former U.S. workers.

The employer must contact (by mail or other effective means) its former U.S. workers, including those who have been laid off within 270 calendar days before the date of need, employed by the employer in the occupation at the place(s) of employment during the previous year (except those who were dismissed for cause or who abandoned the place(s) of employment), provide a copy of the *CW–1 Application for Temporary Employment Certification*, and solicit their return to the job. This contact must occur during the period of time that the job offer is being advertised on the CNMI Department of Labor's job listing system under § 655.442. The employer must retain documentation sufficient to prove such contact in accordance with § 655.456. An employer has no obligation to contact U.S. workers it terminated for cause or who abandoned employment at any time during the previous year, if the employer provided timely notice to the

NPC of the termination or abandonment in the manner described in §655.423(v).

§655.444 Notice of posting requirement.

The employer must post a copy of the *CW–1 Application for Temporary Employment Certification* in at least two conspicuous locations at the place(s) of employment or in some other manner that provides reasonable notification to all employees in the job classification and area in which the work will be performed by the CW–1 workers. Electronic posting, such as displaying an electronic copy of the *CW–1 Application for Temporary Employment Certification* prominently on any internal or external website that is maintained by the employer and customarily used for notices to employees about terms and conditions of employment, is sufficient to meet this posting requirement as long as it otherwise meets the requirements of this section. The notice must be posted for a period of 21 consecutive calendar days. The employer must maintain proof the *CW–1 Application for Temporary Employment Certification* was posted and identify where and during what period of time it was posted in accordance with §655.456.

§655.445 Additional employer-conducted recruitment.

(a) *Requirement to conduct additional recruitment.* The employer may be instructed by the CO to conduct additional reasonable recruitment. Such recruitment may be required at the discretion of the CO where the CO has determined that there is a likelihood that U.S. workers who are qualified will be available for the work.

(b) *Nature of the additional employer-conducted recruitment.* The CO will describe the precise number and nature of the additional recruitment efforts. Additional recruitment may include, but is not limited to, advertising the job offer on the employer's website or another electronic job search website; advertising with community-based organizations, local unions, or trade unions; or other advertising using a professional, trade, or other publication where such a publication is appropriate for the workers likely to apply for the job opportunity. When assessing the appropriateness of a particular recruitment method, the CO will consider the cost of the additional recruitment and the likelihood that the additional recruitment method(s) will identify qualified and available U.S. workers.

(c) *Proof of the additional employer-conducted recruitment.* The CO will specify the documentation or other supporting evidence that must be retained by the employer as proof that the additional recruitment requirements were met. Documentation must be retained as required in §655.456.

§655.446 Recruitment report.

(a) *Requirements of the recruitment report.* No fewer than 2 calendar days after the last date on which the last advertisement appeared, as required by the NOA issued under §655.433, the employer must prepare, sign, and date a recruitment report. Where recruitment was conducted by a job contractor or its employer-client, both joint employers must sign the recruitment report in accordance with §655.421(e)(1). The recruitment report must be submitted to the NPC, by the date specified in the NOA, and contain the following information:

(1) The name of each recruitment activity or source;

(2) The name and contact information of each U.S. worker who applied or was referred to the job opportunity up to the date of the preparation of the recruitment report, and the disposition of each worker's application. The employer must clearly indicate whether the job opportunity was offered to the U.S. worker and whether the U.S. worker accepted or declined;

(3) Confirmation that the advertisement was posted on the CNMI Department of Labor's job listing system and the dates of advertising;

(4) Confirmation that former U.S. employees were contacted, if applicable, and by what means and the date(s) of contact;

(5) Confirmation the employer posted the availability of the job opportunity to all employees in the job classification and area in which the work will be performed by the CW–1 workers and the dates of advertising;

(6) If applicable, confirmation that additional recruitment was conducted as directed by the CO and the date(s) of advertising; and

(7) If applicable, for each U.S. worker who applied for the position but was not hired, the lawful job-related reason(s) for not hiring the U.S. worker.

(b) *Duty to update and retain the recruitment report.* The employer must update the recruitment report throughout the recruitment period. In a joint employment situation, either the job contractor or the employer-client may update the recruitment report throughout the recruitment period. The employer must retain the recruitment report as required in § 655.456.

§§ 655.447–655.449 [Reserved]

LABOR CERTIFICATION DETERMINATIONS

§ 655.450 Determinations.

Except as otherwise noted in this section, the OFLC Administrator and CO(s), by virtue of delegation from the OFLC Administrator, have the authority to certify or deny *CW–1 Applications for Temporary Employment Certification.* The CO will certify the application only if the employer has met all the requirements of this subpart, including the criteria for certification in § 655.451, thus demonstrating that there is an insufficient number of U.S. workers in the Commonwealth who are able, willing, qualified and who will be available at the time and place of the job opportunity for which certification is sought and that the employment of the CW–1 workers will not adversely affect the wages and working conditions of similarly employed U.S. workers.

§ 655.451 Criteria for temporary labor certification.

(a) The criteria for TLC include whether the employer has complied with all of the requirements of this subpart, which are required to grant the labor certification.

(b) In determining whether there are insufficient U.S. workers in the Commonwealth to fill the employer's job opportunity, the CO will count as available any U.S. worker who applied (or on whose behalf an application is made) directly to the employer, but who was rejected by the employer for other than a lawful job-related reason. In making this determination, the CO will also consider the employer's contacts with its former U.S. workers, including workers that have been laid off within 270 calendar days before the date of need.

§ 655.452 Approved certification.

If the TLC is granted, the CO will send a Final Determination notice and a copy of the certified *CW–1 Application for Temporary Employment Certification* to the employer and a copy, if applicable, to the employer's agent or attorney using an electronic method(s) designated by the OFLC Administrator. For employers permitted to file by mail as set forth in § 655.420(c), the CO will send the Final Determination notice and a copy of the certified *CW–1 Application for Temporary Employment Certification* by first class mail. The CO will send the certified *CW–1 Application for Temporary Employment Certification,* including approved modifications, on behalf of the employer, directly to USCIS using an electronic method(s) designated by the OFLC Administrator. The employer must retain a copy of the certified *CW–1 Application for Temporary Employment Certification,* including the original signed Appendix C, as required by § 655.456.

§ 655.453 Denied certification.

If an electronically filed TLC is denied, the CO will send the Final Determination notice to the employer and a copy, if applicable, to the employer's agent or attorney using an electronic method(s) designated by the OFLC Administrator. For employers permitted to file by mail as set forth in § 655.420(c), the CO will send the Final Determination notice by first class mail. The Final Determination notice will:

(a) State the reason(s) certification is denied, citing the relevant regulatory standards;

(b) Offer the employer an opportunity to request administrative review of the denial under § 655.461; and

(c) State that if the employer does not request administrative review in accordance with § 655.461, the denial is final, and the Department will not accept any appeal on that *CW–1 Application for Temporary Employment Certification.*

§ 655.454 Partial certification.

The CO may issue a partial certification, reducing either the period of need or the number of CW–1 workers or both, based upon information the CO receives during the course of processing the *CW–1 Application for Temporary Employment Certification,* an audit, or otherwise. The number of workers certified will be reduced by one for each U.S. worker who is able, willing, and qualified, and who will be available at the time and place needed and who has not been rejected for lawful, job-related reasons, to perform the labor or services. If a partial labor certification is issued, the CO will send the Final Determination notice approving partial certification using the procedures at § 655.452.

The Final Determination notice will:

(a) State the reason(s) the period of employment or the number of CW–1 workers requested has been reduced, citing the relevant regulatory standards;

(b) Offer the employer an opportunity to request administrative review of the partial certification under § 655.461; and

(c) State that if the employer does not request administrative judicial review in accordance with § 655.461, the partial certification is final, and the Department will not accept any appeal on that *CW–1 Application for Temporary Employment Certification.*

§ 655.455 Validity of temporary labor certification.

(a) *Validity period.* A TLC is valid only for the period of employment as approved on the *CW–1 Application for Temporary Employment Certification.* The certification expires after the last day of authorized employment, including any approved extensions thereof.

(b) *Scope of validity.* A TLC is valid only for the number of CW–1 positions, the places of employment located in the Commonwealth, the job classification and specific services or labor to be performed, and the employer(s) specified on the approved *CW–1 Application for Temporary Employment Certification,* including any approved modifications. The TLC may not be transferred from one employer to another unless the employer to which it is transferred is a successor in interest to the employer to which it was issued.

§ 655.456 Document retention requirements for CW–1 employers.

(a) *Entities required to retain documents.* All CW–1 employers filing a *CW–1 Application for Temporary Employment Certification* are required to retain the documents and records establishing compliance with this subpart, including but not limited to those specified in paragraph (c) of this section.

(b) *Period of record retention.* The employer must retain records and documents for 3 years from the date on which the certification of the *CW–1 Application for Temporary Employment Certification* expires, or 3 years from the date of the final determination if the *CW–1 Application for Temporary Employment Certification* is denied, or 3 years from the date the Department receives the request for withdrawal of a *CW–1 Application for Temporary Employment Certification* under § 655.462.

(c) *Documents and records to be retained by all employers.* All employers filing a *CW–1 Application for Temporary Employment Certification* must retain the following documents and records and must provide the documents and records to the Department and any other Federal Government Official in the event of an audit or investigation:

(1) Proof of recruitment efforts, including:

(i) Placement of the job offer with the CNMI Department of Labor as specified in § 655.442;

(ii) Contact with former U.S. employees as specified in § 655.443, including documents demonstrating that each such U.S. worker had been offered the job opportunity listed in the *CW–1 Application for Temporary Employment Certification,* and that the U.S. worker either refused the job opportunity or was rejected only for lawful, job-related reasons;

(iii) Posting notice of the job opportunity to all employees in the job classification and area in which the work will be performed by the CW–1 workers as specified in § 655.444; and

(iv) All additional employer-conducted recruitment required by the CO as specified in § 655.445.

(2) Documentation supporting the information submitted in the recruitment report prepared in accordance with § 655.446, such as evidence of nonapplicability of contact with former workers as specified in § 655.443 and any supporting resumes and contact information as specified in § 655.446.

(3) Records of each worker's earnings, hours offered and worked, location(s) where work is performed, and other information as specified in § 655.423(i).

(4) If applicable, records of reimbursement of transportation and subsistence costs incurred by the workers, as specified in § 655.423(j).

(5) Copies of written contracts with third parties demonstrating compliance with the prohibition of seeking or receiving payments or other compensation of any kind from prospective workers as specified in § 655.423(o).

(6) Evidence of the employer's contact with U.S. workers who applied for the job opportunity in the *CW–1 Application for Temporary Employment Certification*, including, but not limited to, documents demonstrating that any rejections of U.S. workers were for lawful, job-related reasons, as specified in § 655.423(q).

(7) Written notice provided to and informing OFLC that a CW–1 worker or worker in corresponding employment has separated from employment before the end date of employment specified in the *CW–1 Application for Temporary Employment Certification*, as specified in § 655.423(v).

(8) A copy of the *CW–1 Application for Temporary Employment Certification* and all accompanying appendices, including any modifications, amendments, or extensions, signed by the employer as directed by the CO.

(d) *Availability of documents and records for enforcement purposes.* The employer must make available to the Department, DHS or to any Federal Government Official performing an investigation, inspection, audit, or law enforcement function all documents and records required to be retained under this subpart for purposes of copying, transcribing, or inspecting them.

§§ 655.457–655.459 [Reserved]

Post Certification Activities

§ 655.460 Extensions.

(a) *Basis for extension.* Under certain circumstances an employer may apply for extensions of the period of employment. A request for extension must be related to weather conditions or other factors beyond the control of the employer (which may include unforeseen changes in market conditions). Such requests must be supported in writing, with documentation showing that the extension is needed and that the need could not have been reasonably foreseen by the employer. The CO will not grant an extension where the total period of employment under that *CW–1 Application for Temporary Employment Certification* and the authorized extension would exceed the maximum applicable duration permitted under § 655.420(g).

(b) *Decision by the CO.* The CO will notify the employer of the decision in writing. The employer may appeal a denial of a request for an extension by following the appeal procedures in § 655.461.

(c) *Obligations during period of extension.* The CW–1 employer's assurances and obligations under the TLC will continue to apply during the extended period of employment. The employer must immediately provide to its CW–1 workers and workers in corresponding employment a copy of any approved extension.

§ 655.461 Administrative review.

(a) *Request for review.* Where authorized in this subpart, an employer wishing review of a determination by the CO must request an administrative review before BALCA of that determination to exhaust its administrative remedies. In such cases, the request for review:

(1) Must be received by BALCA, and the CO who issued the determination, within 10 business days from the date of the determination;

(2) Must clearly identify the particular determination for which review is sought;

(3) Must include a copy of the CO's determination;

(4) Must set forth the particular grounds for the request, including the specific factual issues the requesting party alleges needs to be examined in connection with the CO's determination;

(5) May contain any legal argument that the employer believes will rebut the basis for the CO's determination, including any briefing the employer wishes to submit; and

(6) May contain only such evidence as was actually before the CO at the time of the CO's determination.

(b) *Appeal File.* After the receipt of a request for review, the CO will send a copy of the Appeal File, as soon as practicable by means normally assuring next-day delivery, to BALCA, the employer, the employer's attorney or agent (if applicable), and the Associate Solicitor for Employment and Training Legal Services, Office of the Solicitor, U.S. Department of Labor (counsel).

(c) *Assignment.* The Chief ALJ will immediately, upon receipt of the appeal file from the CO, assign either a single member or a three-member panel of BALCA to consider a particular case.

(d) *Administrative review*—(1) *Briefing schedule.* If the employer wishes to submit a brief on appeal, it must do so as part of its request for review. Within 7 business days of receipt of the Appeal File, the counsel for the CO may submit a brief in support of the CO's decision and, if applicable, in response to the employer's brief.

(2) *Standard of review.* The ALJ must uphold the CO's decision unless shown by the employer to be arbitrary, capricious, an abuse of discretion, or otherwise not in accordance with the law.

(e) *Scope of review.* BALCA will affirm, reverse, or modify the CO's determination, or remand to the CO for further action. BALCA will reach this decision after due consideration of the documents in the Appeal File that were before the CO at the time of the CO's determination, the request for review, and any legal briefs submitted. BALCA may not consider evidence not before the CO at the time of the CO's determination, even if such evidence is in the Appeal File, request for review, or legal briefs.

(f) *Decision.* The decision of BALCA must specify the reasons for the action taken and must be provided to the employer, the CO, and counsel for the CO within 7 business days of the submission of the CO's brief or 10 business days after receipt of the Appeal File, whichever is later, using means normally assuring expedited delivery.

§ 655.462 Withdrawal of a CW–1 Application for Temporary Employment Certification.

(a) The employer may withdraw a *CW–1 Application for Temporary Employment Certification* after it has been submitted to the NPC for processing, including after the CO grants certification under § 655.450. However, the employer is still obligated to comply with the terms and conditions of employment contained in the *CW–1 Application for Temporary Employment Certification* and work contract with respect to all workers recruited and hired in connection with that application.

(b) To request withdrawal, the employer must submit a request in writing to the NPC identifying the *CW–1 Application for Temporary Employment Certification* and stating the reason(s) for the withdrawal.

§ 655.463 Public disclosure.

The Department will maintain an electronic file accessible to the public with information on all employers applying for TLCs. The database will include such information as the number of workers requested, the date filed, the date decided, and the final disposition.

§§ 655.464–655.469 [Reserved]

INTEGRITY MEASURES

§ 655.470 Audits.

The CO may conduct audits of certified *CW–1 Applications for Temporary Employment Certification.*

(a) *Discretion.* The CO has the sole discretion to choose the certified applications selected for audit.

(b) *Audit letter.* Where an application is selected for audit, the CO will issue an audit letter to the employer and a copy, if appropriate, to the employer's attorney or agent. The audit letter will:

(1) Specify the documentation that must be submitted by the employer;

(2) Specify a date, no more than 30 calendar days from the date the audit letter is issued, by which the required documentation must be sent to the CO; and

(3) Advise that failure to comply fully with the audit process may result:

(i) In the requirement that the employer undergo the assisted recruitment procedures in § 655.471 in future filings of *CW–1 Applications for Temporary Employment Certification* for a period of up to 2 years; or

(ii) In a revocation of the certification or debarment from the CW–1 program and any other foreign labor certification program administered by the Department.

(c) *Supplemental information request.* During the course of the audit examination, the CO may request supplemental information or documentation from the employer in order to complete the audit. If circumstances warrant, the CO can issue one or more requests for supplemental information.

(d) *Potential referrals.* In addition to measures in this subpart, the CO may decide to provide the audit findings and underlying documentation to DHS or other appropriate enforcement agencies. The CO may refer any findings that an employer discouraged a qualified U.S. worker from applying, or failed to hire, discharged, or otherwise discriminated against a qualified U.S. worker, to the Department of Justice, Civil Rights Division, Immigrant and Employee Rights Section.

§ 655.471 Assisted recruitment.

(a) *Requirement of assisted recruitment.* If, as a result of audit or otherwise, the CO determines that a violation has occurred that does not warrant debarment, the CO may require the employer to engage in assisted recruitment for a defined period of time for any future *CW–1 Application for Temporary Employment Certification.*

(b) *Notification of assisted recruitment.* The CO will notify the employer (and its attorney or agent, if applicable) in writing of the assisted recruitment that will be required of the employer for a period of up to 2 years from the date the notice is issued. The notification will state the reasons for the imposition of the additional requirements, state that the employer's agreement to accept the conditions will constitute their inclusion as bona fide conditions and terms of a *CW–1 Application for Temporary Employment Certification,* and offer the employer an opportunity to request an administrative review. If administrative review is requested, the procedures in § 655.461 apply.

(c) *Assisted recruitment.* The assisted recruitment process will be in addition to any recruitment required of the employer by §§ 655.442 through 655.445 and may consist of, but is not limited to, one or more of the following:

(1) Requiring the employer to submit a draft advertisement to the CO for review and approval at the time of filing the *CW–1 Application for Temporary Employment Certification;*

(2) Designating the sources where the employer must recruit for U.S. workers in the Commonwealth and directing the employer to place the advertisement(s) in such sources;

(3) Extending the length of the placement of the advertisements;

(4) Requiring the employer to notify the CO in writing when the advertisement(s) are placed;

(5) Requiring an employer to perform any additional assisted recruitment directed by the CO;

(6) Requiring the employer to provide proof of the publication of all advertisements as directed by the CO;

(7) Requiring the employer to provide proof of all U.S. workers who applied (or on whose behalf an application is made) in response to the employer's recruitment efforts;

(8) Requiring the employer to submit any proof of contact with all referrals and former U.S. workers; or

(9) Requiring the employer to provide any additional documentation verifying it conducted the assisted recruitment as directed by the CO.

(d) *Failure to comply.* If an employer materially fails to comply with requirements ordered by the CO under this section, the certification will be denied and the employer and its attorney or agent may be debarred under § 655.473.

§ 655.472 Revocation.

(a) *Basis for revocation*. The OFLC Administrator may revoke a TLC approved under this subpart, if the OFLC Administrator finds:

(1) The issuance of the TLC was not justified due to fraud or misrepresentation of a material fact in the application process;

(2) The employer substantially failed to comply with any of the terms or conditions of the approved TLC. A substantial failure is a failure to comply that constitutes a significant deviation from the terms and conditions of the approved certification and is further defined in § 655.473(d); or

(3) The employer impeded the audit process, as set forth in § 655.470, or impeded any Federal Government Official performing an investigation, inspection, audit, or law enforcement function.

(b) *DOL procedures for revocation*—(1) *Notice of Revocation*. If the OFLC Administrator makes a determination to revoke an employer's TLC, the OFLC Administrator will issue a Notice of Revocation to the employer (and its attorney or agent, if applicable). The notice will contain a detailed statement of the grounds for the revocation and inform the employer of its right to submit rebuttal evidence to the OFLC Administrator or to request administrative review of the Notice of Revocation by BALCA. If the employer does not submit rebuttal evidence or request administrative review within 10 business days from the date the Notice of Revocation is issued, the notice will become the final agency action and will take effect immediately at the end of the 10 business days.

(2) *Rebuttal*. If the employer timely submits rebuttal evidence, the OFLC Administrator will inform the employer of the final determination on the revocation within 10 business days of receiving the rebuttal evidence. If the OFLC Administrator determines that the certification must be revoked, the OFLC Administrator will inform the employer of its right to appeal the final determination to BALCA according to the procedures of § 655.461. If the employer does not appeal the final determination, it will become the final agency action.

(3) *Request for review*. An employer may appeal a Notice of Revocation or a final determination of the OFLC Administrator after the review of rebuttal evidence to BALCA, according to the appeal procedures of § 655.461. The ALJ's decision is the final agency action.

(4) *Stay*. The timely submission of rebuttal evidence or a request for administrative review will stay the revocation pending the outcome of the proceeding.

(5) *Decision*. If the TLC is revoked, the OFLC Administrator will provide copies of final revocation decisions to DHS and DOS promptly.

(c) *Employer's obligations in the event of revocation*. If an employer's TLC is revoked, the employer is responsible for:

(1) Reimbursement of actual inbound transportation and other required expenses;

(2) The workers' outbound transportation and other required expenses;

(3) Payment to the workers of the amount due under the three-fourths guarantee; and

(4) Any other wages, benefits, and working conditions due or owing to the workers under this subpart.

§ 655.473 Debarment.

(a) *Debarment of an employer, agent, or attorney*. The OFLC Administrator may debar an employer, agent, attorney, or any successor in interest to that employer, agent, or attorney, from participating in any action under this subpart, subject to the time limits set forth in paragraph (c) of this section, if the OFLC Administrator finds that the employer, agent, or attorney substantially violated a material term or condition of the *Application for Prevailing Wage Determination* or *CW–1 Application for Temporary Employment Certification*, as defined in paragraph (d) of this section. The OFLC Administrator will provide copies of final debarment decisions to DHS and DOS promptly.

(b) *Effect on future applications in all foreign labor programs*. The debarred employer, or a debarred agent or attorney, or any successor in interest to any debarred employer, agent, or attorney, will be disqualified from filing any labor certification applications or labor condition applications with the Department subject to the term limits set forth in paragraph (c) of this section. If such an application is filed, it will be denied without review.

(c) *Period of debarment.* No employer, agent, or attorney may be debarred under this subpart for more than 5 years for a single violation.

(d) *Definition of violation.* For the purposes of this section, a violation of a material term or condition of the *Application for Prevailing Wage Determination* or *CW–1 Application for Temporary Employment Certification* includes:

(1) One or more acts of commission or omission on the part of the employer or the employer's agent or attorney that involve:

(i) Failure to pay or provide the required wages, benefits, or working conditions to the employer's CW–1 workers or workers in corresponding employment;

(ii) Failure, except for lawful, job-related reasons, to offer employment to qualified U.S. workers who applied for the job opportunity for which certification was sought;

(iii) Failure to comply with the employer's obligations to recruit U.S. workers;

(iv) Improper layoff or displacement of U.S. workers or workers in corresponding employment;

(v) Failure to comply with the NOD process, as set forth in § 655.431, or the assisted recruitment process, as set forth in § 655.471;

(vi) Impeding the audit process, as set forth in § 655.470, or impeding any Federal Government Official performing an investigation, inspection, audit, or law enforcement function;

(vii) Employing a CW–1 worker outside of the Commonwealth, in an activity not listed in the work contract, or outside the validity period of employment of the work contract, including any approved extension thereof;

(viii) A violation of the requirements of § 655.423(n) or (o);

(ix) A violation of any of the provisions listed in § 655.423(q); or

(x) Any other act showing such flagrant disregard for the law that future compliance with program requirements cannot reasonably be expected;

(2) Fraud involving the *Application for Prevailing Wage Determination* or the *CW–1 Application for Temporary Employment Certification* under this subpart; or

(3) A material misrepresentation of fact during the course of processing the *CW–1 Application for Temporary Employment Certification.*

(e) *Determining whether a violation is substantial.* In determining whether a violation is substantial as to merit debarment, the factors the OFLC Administrator may consider include, but are not limited to, the following:

(1) Previous history of violation(s) under the CW–1 program;

(2) The number of CW–1 workers, workers in corresponding employment, or U.S. workers who were or are affected by the violation(s);

(3) The gravity of the violation(s); or

(4) The extent to which the violator achieved a financial gain due to the violation(s), or the potential financial loss or potential injury to the worker(s).

(f) *Debarment procedure*—(1) *Notice of Debarment.* If the OFLC Administrator makes a determination to debar an employer, agent, attorney, or any successor in interest to that employer, agent, or attorney, the OFLC Administrator will issue the party a Notice of Debarment. The notice will state the reason(s) for the debarment finding, including a detailed explanation of the grounds for and the duration of the debarment, and it will inform the party subject to the notice of its right to submit rebuttal evidence to the OFLC Administrator, or to request administrative review of the decision by BALCA. If the party does not file rebuttal evidence or a request for review within 30 calendar days of the date of the Notice of Debarment, the notice is the final agency action and the debarment will take effect on the date specified in the notice or if no date is specified, at the end of 30 calendar days The timely filing of rebuttal evidence or a request for review stays the debarment pending the outcome of the appeal as provided in paragraphs (f)(2) through (6) of this section.

(2) *Rebuttal.* The party who received the Notice of Debarment may choose to submit evidence to rebut the grounds stated in the notice within 30 calendar

days of the date the notice is issued. If rebuttal evidence is timely filed, the OFLC Administrator will issue a Final Determination on the debarment within 30 calendar days of receiving the rebuttal evidence. If the OFLC Administrator determines that the party must be debarred, the OFLC Administrator will issue a Final Determination and inform the party of its right to request administrative review of the debarment by BALCA according to the procedures in this section. The party must request review within 30 calendar days after the date of the Final Determination, or the Final Determination will be the final agency order and the debarment will take effect on the date specified in the Final Determination or if no date is specified, at the end of 30 calendar days.

(3) *Request for review.* (i) The recipient of a Notice of Debarment or Final Determination seeking to challenge the debarment must request review of the debarment within 30 calendar days of the date of the Notice of Debarment or the date of the Final Determination by the OFLC Administrator after review of rebuttal evidence submitted under paragraph (f)(2) of this section. A request for review of debarment must be sent in writing to the Chief ALJ, United States Department of Labor, with a simultaneous copy served on the OFLC Administrator; the request must clearly identify the particular debarment determination for which review is sought; and must set forth the particular grounds for the request. If no timely request for review is filed, the debarment will take effect on the date specified in the Notice of Debarment or Final Determination, or if no date is specified, 30 calendar days from the date the Notice of Debarment or Final Determination is issued.

(ii) Upon receipt of a request for review, the OFLC Administrator will promptly send a certified copy of the ETA case file to the Chief ALJ by means normally assuring expedited delivery. The Chief ALJ will immediately assign an ALJ to conduct the review.

(iii) Statements, briefs, and other submissions of the parties must contain only legal argument and only such evidence that was within the record upon which the debarment was based, including any rebuttal evidence submitted pursuant to paragraph (f)(2) of this section.

(4) *Review by the ALJ.* (i) In considering requests for review, the ALJ must afford all parties 30 days to submit or decline to submit any appropriate Statement of Position or legal brief. The ALJ must review the debarment determination on the basis of the record upon which the decision was made, the request for review, and any Statements of Position or legal briefs submitted.

(ii) The ALJ's final decision must affirm, reverse, or modify the OFLC Administrator's determination. The ALJ's decision will be provided to the parties by expedited mail. The ALJ's decision is the final agency action, unless either party, within 30 calendar days of the ALJ's decision, seeks review of the decision with the Administrative Review Board (ARB).

(5) *Review by the ARB.* (i) Any party wishing review of the decision of an ALJ must, within 30 calendar days of the decision of the ALJ, petition the ARB to review the decision. Copies of the petition must be served on all parties and on the ALJ. The ARB will decide whether to accept the petition within 30 calendar days of receipt. If the ARB declines to accept the petition, or if the ARB does not issue a notice accepting a petition within 30 calendar days after the receipt of a timely filing of the petition, the decision of the ALJ is the final agency action. If a petition for review is accepted, the decision of the ALJ will be stayed unless and until the ARB issues an order affirming the decision. The ARB must serve notice of its decision to accept or not to accept the petition upon the ALJ and upon all parties to the proceeding.

(ii) Upon receipt of the ARB's notice to accept the petition, the Office of Administrative Law Judges will promptly forward a copy of the complete appeal record to the ARB.

(iii) Where the ARB has determined to review the decision and order, the ARB will notify each party of the issue(s) raised, the form in which submissions must be made (e.g., briefs or oral argument), and the time within which the presentation must be submitted.

(6) *ARB Decision.* The ARB's final decision must be issued within 90 calendar days from the notice granting the petition and served upon all parties and the ALJ.

§§ 655.474–655.499 [Reserved]

PART 656—LABOR CERTIFICATION PROCESS FOR PERMANENT EMPLOYMENT OF ALIENS IN THE UNITED STATES

AUTHORITY: 8 U.S.C. 1182(a)(5)(A), 1182(p)(1); sec.122, Public Law 101–649, 109 Stat. 4978; and Title IV, Public Law 105–277, 112 Stat. 2681.

SOURCE: 69 FR 77386, Dec. 27, 2004, unless otherwise noted.

Subpart A—Purpose and Scope of Part 656

§ 656.1 Purpose and scope of part 656.

(a) Under section 212(a)(5)(A) of the Immigration and Nationality Act (INA or Act) (8 U.S.C. 1182(a)(5)(A)), certain aliens may not obtain immigrant visas for entrance into the United States in order to engage in permanent employment unless the Secretary of Labor has first certified to the Secretary of State and to the Secretary of Homeland Security that:

(1) There are not sufficient United States workers who are able, willing, qualified and available at the time of application for a visa and admission into the United States and at the place where the alien is to perform the work; and

(2) The employment of the alien will not adversely affect the wages and working conditions of United States workers similarly employed.

(b) The regulations under this part set forth the procedures through which such immigrant labor certifications may be applied for, and granted or denied.

(c) Correspondence and questions about the regulations in this part should be addressed to: Office of Foreign Labor Certification, Employment and Training Administration, 200 Constitution Avenue, NW., Room C–4312, Washington, DC 20210.

[69 FR 77386, Dec. 27, 2004, as amended at 71 FR 35522, June 21, 2006]

§656.2 Description of the Immigration and Nationality Act and of the Department of Labor's role thereunder.

(a) *Description of the Act.* The Act (8 U.S.C. 1101 *et seq.*) regulates the admission of aliens into the United States. The Act designates the Secretary of Homeland Security and the Secretary of State as the principal administrators of its provisions.

(b) *Burden of proof under the Act.* Section 291 of the Act (8 U.S.C. 1361) provides, in pertinent part, that:

> Whenever any person makes application for a visa or any other documentation required for entry, or makes application for admission, or otherwise attempts to enter the United States, the burden of proof shall be upon such person to establish that he is eligible to receive such visa or such document, or is not subject to exclusion under any provision of this Act * * *.

(c)(1) *Role of the Department of Labor.* The permanent labor certification role of the Department of Labor under the Act derives from section 212(a)(5)(A) (8 U.S.C. 1182(a)(5)(A)), which provides that any alien who seeks admission or status as an immigrant for the purpose of employment under paragraph (2) or (3) of section 203(b) of the Act may not be admitted unless the Secretary of Labor has first certified to the Secretary of State and to the Secretary of Homeland Security that:

(i) There are not sufficient United States workers who are able, willing, qualified, and available at the time of application for a visa and admission to the United States and at the place where the alien is to perform such skilled or unskilled labor; and

(ii) The employment of such alien will not adversely affect the wages and working conditions of workers in the United States similarly employed.

(2) This certification is referred to in this part 656 as a "labor certification."

(3) We certify the employment of aliens in several instances: For the permanent employment of aliens under this part; and for temporary employment of aliens for agricultural and nonagricultural employment in the United States classified under 8 U.S.C. 1101(a)(15)(H)(ii), under the DHS regulation at 8 CFR 214.2(h)(5) and (6) and sections 101(a)(15)(H)(ii), 214, and 218 of the Act. See 8 U.S.C. 1101(a)(15)(H)(ii), 1184, and 1188. We also administer labor attestation and labor condition application programs for the admission and/or work authorization of the following nonimmigrants: Specialty occupations and fashion models (H–1B visas), specialty occupations from countries with which the U.S. has entered agreements listed in the INA (H–1B1 visas), registered nurses (H–1C visas), and crewmembers performing longshore work (D visas), classified under 8 U.S.C. 1101(a)(15)(H)(i)(b), 1101(a)(15)(H)(i)(b1), 1101(a)(15)(H)(i)(c), and 1101(a)(15)(D), respectively. See also 8 U.S.C. 1184(c), (m), and (n), and 1288.

§656.3 Definitions, for purposes of this part, of terms used in this part.

Act means the Immigration and Nationality Act, as amended, 8 U.S.C. 1101 *et seq.*

Agent means a person who is not an employee of an employer, and who has been designated in writing to act on behalf of an alien or employer in connection with an application for labor certification.

Applicant means a U.S. worker (see definition of U.S. worker below) who is applying for a job opportunity for which an employer has filed an *Application for Permanent Employment Certification* (ETA Form 9089).

Application means an *Application for Permanent Employment Certification* submitted by an employer (or its agent or attorney) in applying for a labor certification under this part.

Area of intended employment means the area within normal commuting distance of the place (address) of intended employment. There is no rigid measure of distance which constitutes a normal commuting distance or normal commuting area, because there may be widely varying factual circumstances among different areas (e.g., normal commuting distances might be 20, 30, or 50 miles). If the place of intended employment is within a Metropolitan Statistical Area (MSA) or a Primary Metropolitan Statistical Area (PMSA), any place within the MSA or PMSA is deemed to be within normal commuting distance of the place of intended employment; however, not all locations within a Consolidated Metropolitan Statistical Area (CMSA) will be deemed automatically to be within normal commuting distance. The borders of MSA's and PMSA's are not controlling in the identification of the normal commuting area; a location outside of an MSA or PMSA (or a CMSA) may be within normal commuting distance of a location that is inside (e.g., near the border of) the MSA or PMSA (or CMSA). The terminology CMSAs and PMSAs are being replaced by the Office of Management and Budget (OMB). However, ETA will continue to recognize the use of these area concepts as well as their replacements.

Attorney means any person who is a member in good standing of the bar of the highest court of any state, possession, territory, or commonwealth of the United States, or the District of Columbia, and who is not under suspension or disbarment from practice before any court or before DHS or the United States Department of Justice's Executive Office for Immigration Review. Such a person is permitted to act as an agent, representative, or attorney for an employer and/or alien under this part.

Barter, for purposes of an Application for Permanent Employment Certification (Form ETA 9089) or an Application for Alien Labor Certification (Form ETA 750), means the transfer of ownership of a labor certification application or certification from one person to another by voluntary act or agreement in exchange for a commodity, service, property or other valuable consideration.

Board of Alien Labor Certification Appeals (BALCA or Board) means the permanent Board established by this part, chaired by the Chief Administrative Law Judge, and consisting of Administrative Law Judges assigned to the Department of Labor and designated by the Chief Administrative Law Judge to be members of the Board of Alien Labor Certification Appeals. The Board of Alien Labor Certification Appeals is located in Washington, DC, and reviews and decides appeals in Washington, DC.

Certifying Officer (CO) means a Department of Labor official who makes determinations about whether or not to grant applications for labor certifications.

Closely-held Corporation means a corporation that typically has relatively few shareholders and whose shares are not generally traded in the securities market.

Employer means:

(1) A person, association, firm, or a corporation that currently has a location within the United States to which U.S. workers may be referred for employment and that proposes to employ a full-time employee at a place within the United States, or the authorized representative of such a person, association, firm, or corporation. An employer must possess a valid Federal Employer Identification Number (FEIN). For purposes of this definition, an "authorized representative" means an employee of the employer whose position or legal status authorizes the employee to act for the employer in labor certification matters. A labor certification can not be granted for an *Application for Permanent Employment Certification* filed on behalf of an independent contractor.

(2) Persons who are temporarily in the United States, including but not limited to, foreign diplomats, intracompany transferees, students, and exchange visitors, visitors for business or pleasure, and representatives of foreign information media can not be employers for the purpose of obtaining a labor certification for permanent employment.

Employment means:

(1) Permanent, full-time work by an employee for an employer other than oneself. For purposes of this definition, an investor is not an employee. In the event of an audit, the employer must be prepared to document the permanent and full-time nature of the position by furnishing position descriptions and payroll records for the job opportunity involved in the *Application for Permanent Employment Certification.*

(2) Job opportunities consisting solely of job duties that will be performed totally outside the United States, its territories, possessions, or commonwealths can not be the subject of an *Application for Permanent Employment Certification.*

Employment and Training Administration (ETA) means the agency within the Department of Labor (DOL) that includes the Office of Foreign Labor Certification (OFLC).

Immigration Officer means an official of the Department of Homeland Security, United States Citizenship and Immigration Services (USCIS) who handles applications for labor certifications under this part.

Job opportunity means a job opening for employment at a place in the United States to which U.S. workers can be referred.

Nonprofessional occupation means any occupation for which the attainment of a bachelor's or higher degree is not a usual requirement for the occupation.

Non-profit or tax-exempt organization for the purposes of § 656.40 means an organization that:

(1) Is defined as a tax exempt organization under the Internal Revenue Code of 1986, section 501(c)(3), (c)(4), or (c)(6) (26 U.S.C. 501(c)(3), (c)(4) or (c)(6)); and

(2) Has been approved as a tax-exempt organization for research or educational purposes by the Internal Revenue Service.

Office of Foreign Labor Certification means the organizational component within the Employment and Training Administration that provides national leadership and policy guidance and develops regulations and procedures to carry out the responsibilities of the Secretary of Labor under the Immigration and Nationality Act, as amended, concerning alien workers seeking admission to the United States in order to work under section 212(a)(5)(A) of the Immigration and Nationality Act, as amended.

*O*NET* means the system developed by the Department of Labor, Employment and Training Administration, to provide to the general public information on skills, abilities, knowledge, work activities, interests and specific vocational preparation levels associated with occupations. O*NET is based on the Standard Occupational Classification system. Further information about O*NET can be found at *http://www.onetcenter.org*.

Prevailing wage determination (PWD) means the prevailing wage provided or approved by an OFLC National Processing Center (NPC), in accordance with OFLC guidance governing foreign labor certification programs. This includes PWD requests processed for purposes of employer petitions filed with DHS under Schedule A or for sheepherders.

Professional occupation means an occupation for which the attainment of a bachelor's or higher degree is a usual education requirement. A beneficiary of an application for permanent alien employment certification involving a professional occupation need not have a bachelor's or higher degree to qualify for the professional occupation. However, if the employer is willing to accept work experience in lieu of a baccalaureate or higher degree, such work experience must be attainable in the U.S. labor market and must be stated on the application form. If the employer is willing to accept an equivalent foreign degree, it must be clearly stated on the *Application for Permanent Employment Certification form.*

Purchase, for purposes of an Application for Permanent Employment Certification (Form ETA 9089) or an Application for Alien Labor Certification (Form ETA 750), means the transfer of ownership of a labor certification application or certification from one person to another by voluntary act and agreement, based on a valuable consideration.

Sale, for purposes of an Application for Permanent Employment Certification (Form ETA 9089) or an Application for Alien Labor Certification (Form ETA 750), means an agreement between two parties, called, respectively, the seller (or vendor) and the buyer (or purchaser) by which the seller, in consideration of the payment or promise of payment of a certain price in money terms, transfers ownership of a labor certification application or certification to the buyer.

Secretary means the Secretary of Labor, the chief official of the U.S. Department of Labor, or the Secretary's designee.

Secretary of Homeland Security means the chief official of the U.S. Department of Homeland Security or the Secretary of Homeland Security's designee.

Secretary of State means the chief official of the U.S. Department of State or the Secretary of State's designee.

Specific vocational preparation (SVP) means the amount of lapsed time required by a typical worker to learn the techniques, acquire the information, and develop the facility needed for average performance in a specific job-worker situation. Lapsed time is not the same as work time. For example, 30 days is approximately 1 month of lapsed time and not six 5-day work weeks, and 3 months refers to 3 calendar months and not 90 work days. The various levels of specific vocational preparation are provided below.

Level	Time
1	Short demonstration.
2	Anything beyond short demonstration up to and including 30 days.
3	Over 30 days up to and including 3 months.
4	Over 3 months up to and including 6 months.
5	Over 6 months up to and including 1 year.
6	Over 1 year up to and including 2 years.
7	Over 2 years up to and including 4 years.
8	Over 4 years up to and including 10 years.
9	Over 10 years.

State Workforce Agency (SWA), formerly known as State Employment Security Agency (SESA), means the state agency that receives funds under the Wagner-Peyser Act to provide employment-related services to U.S. workers and employers and/or administers the public labor exchange delivered through the state's one-stop delivery system in accordance with the Wagner-Peyser Act.

United States, when used in a geographic sense, means the 50 states, the District of Columbia, Puerto Rico, the U.S. Virgin Islands, and Guam.

United States worker means any worker who is:

(1) A U.S. citizen;

(2) A U.S. national;

(3) Lawfully admitted for permanent residence;

(4) Granted the status of an alien lawfully admitted for temporary residence under 8 U.S.C. 1160(a), 1161(a), or 1255a(a)(1);

(5) Admitted as a refugee under 8 U.S.C. 1157; or

(6) Granted asylum under 8 U.S.C. 1158.

[69 FR 77386, Dec. 27, 2004, as amended at 71 FR 35522, June 21, 2006; 72 FR 27944, May 17, 2007; 73 FR 78068, Dec. 19, 2008]

Subpart B—Occupational Labor Certification Determinations

§ 656.5 Schedule A.

We have determined there are not sufficient United States workers who are able, willing, qualified, and available for the occupations listed below on *Schedule A* and the wages and working conditions of United States workers similarly employed will not be adversely affected by the employment of aliens in *Schedule A* occupations. An employer seeking a labor certification for an occupation listed on *Schedule A* may apply for that labor certification under § 656.15.

SCHEDULE A

(a) Group I:

(1) Persons who will be employed as physical therapists, and who possess all the qualifications necessary to take the physical therapist licensing examination in the state in which they propose to practice physical therapy.

(2) Aliens who will be employed as professional nurses; and

(i) Who have received a Certificate from the Commission on Graduates of Foreign Nursing Schools (CGFNS);

(ii) Who hold a permanent, full and unrestricted license to practice professional nursing in the state of intended employment; or

(iii) Who have passed the National Council Licensure Examination for Registered Nurses (NCLEX–RN), administered by the National Council of State Boards of Nursing.

(3) Definitions of Group I occupations:

(i) *Physical therapist* means a person who applies the art and science of physical therapy to the treatment of patients with disabilities, disorders and injuries to relieve pain, develop or restore function, and maintain performance, using physical means, such as exercise, massage, heat, water, light, and electricity, as prescribed by a physician (or a surgeon).

(ii) *Professional nurse* means a person who applies the art and science of nursing which reflects comprehension of principles derived from the physical, biological and behavioral sciences. Professional nursing generally includes making clinical judgments involving the observation, care and counsel of persons requiring nursing care; administering of medicines and treatments prescribed by the physician or dentist; and participation in the activities for the promotion of health and prevention of illness in others. A program of study for professional nurses generally includes theory and practice in clinical areas such as obstetrics, surgery, pediatrics, psychiatry, and medicine.

(b) Group II:

(1) *Sciences or arts (except performing arts).* Aliens (except for aliens in the performing arts) of exceptional ability in the sciences or arts including college and university teachers of exceptional ability who have been practicing their science or art during the year prior to application and who intend to practice the same science or art in the United States. For purposes of this group, the term "science or art" means any field of knowledge and/or skill with respect to which colleges and universities commonly offer specialized courses leading to a degree in the knowledge and/or skill. An alien, however, need not have studied at a college or university in order to qualify for the Group II occupation.

(2) *Performing arts.* Aliens of exceptional ability in the performing arts whose work during the past 12 months did require, and whose intended work in the United States will require, exceptional ability.

Subpart C—Labor Certification Process

§ 656.10 General instructions.

(a) *Filing of applications.* A request for a labor certification on behalf of any alien who is required by the Act to be a beneficiary of a labor certification in order to obtain permanent resident status in the United States may be filed as follows:

(1) Except as provided in paragraphs (a)(2), (3), and (4) of this section, an employer seeking a labor certification must file under this section and § 656.17.

(2) An employer seeking a labor certification for a college or university teacher must apply for a labor certification under this section and must also file under either § 656.17 or § 656.18.

(3) An employer seeking labor certification for an occupation listed on *Schedule A* must apply for a labor certification under this section and § 656.15.

(4) An employer seeking labor certification for a sheepherder must apply for a labor certification under this section and must also choose to file under either § 656.16 or § 656.17.

(b) *Representation.* (1) Employers may have agents or attorneys represent them throughout the labor certification process. If an employer intends to be represented by an agent or attorney, the employer must sign the statement set forth on the *Application for Permanent Employment Certification* form: That the attorney or agent is representing the employer and the employer takes full responsibility for the accuracy of any representations made by the attorney or agent. Whenever, under this part, any notice or other document is required to be sent to the employer, the document will be sent to the attorney or agent who has been authorized to represent the employer on the *Application for Permanent Employment Certification* form.

(2)(i) It is contrary to the best interests of U.S. workers to have the alien and/or agents or attorneys for either the employer or the alien participate in interviewing or considering U.S. workers for the job offered the alien. As the beneficiary of a labor certification application, the alien can not represent the best interests of U.S. workers in the job opportunity. The alien's agent and/or attorney can not represent the alien effectively and at the same time truly be seeking U.S. workers for the job opportunity. Therefore, the alien and/or the alien's agent and/or attorney may not interview or consider U.S. workers for the job offered to the alien, unless the agent and/or attorney is the employer's representative, as described in paragraph (b)(2)(ii) of this section.

(ii) The employer's representative who interviews or considers U.S. workers for the job offered to the alien must be the person who normally interviews or considers, on behalf of the employer, applicants for job opportunities such as that offered the alien, but which do not involve labor certifications.

(3) No person under suspension or disbarment from practice before any court or before the DHS or the United States Department of Justice's Executive Office for Immigration Review is permitted to act as an agent, representative, or attorney for an employer and/or alien under this part.

(c) *Attestations.* The employer must certify to the conditions of employment listed below on the *Application for Permanent Employment Certification* under penalty of perjury under 18 U.S.C. 1621 (2). Failure to attest to any of the conditions listed below results in a denial of the application.

(1) The offered wage equals or exceeds the prevailing wage determined pursuant to § 656.40 and § 656.41, and the wage the employer will pay to the alien to begin work will equal or exceed the prevailing wage that is applicable at the time the alien begins work or from the time the alien is admitted to take up the certified employment;

(2) The wage offered is not based on commissions, bonuses or other incentives, unless the employer guarantees a prevailing wage paid on a weekly, bi-weekly, or monthly basis that equals or exceeds the prevailing wage;

(3) The employer has enough funds available to pay the wage or salary offered the alien;

(4) The employer will be able to place the alien on the payroll on or before the date of the alien's proposed entrance into the United States;

(5) The job opportunity does not involve unlawful discrimination by race, creed, color, national origin, age, sex, religion, handicap, or citizenship;

(6) The employer's job opportunity is not:

(i) Vacant because the former occupant is on strike or locked out in the course of a labor dispute involving a work stoppage;

(ii) At issue in a labor dispute involving a work stoppage.

(7) The job opportunity's terms, conditions and occupational environment are not contrary to Federal, state or local law;

(8) The job opportunity has been and is clearly open to any U.S. worker;

(9) The U.S. workers who applied for the job opportunity were rejected for lawful job-related reasons;

(10) The job opportunity is for full-time, permanent employment for an employer other than the alien.

(d) *Notice.* (1) In applications filed under §§ 656.15 (*Schedule A*), 656.16 (Sheepherders), 656.17 (Basic Process), 656.18 (College and University Teachers), and 656.21 (Supervised Recruitment), the employer must give notice of the filing of the *Application for Permanent Employment Certification* and be able to document that notice was provided, if requested by the Certifying Officer, as follows:

(i) To the bargaining representative(s) (if any) of the employer's employees in the occupational classification for which certification of the job opportunity is sought in the employer's location(s) in the area of intended employment. Documentation may consist of a copy of the letter and a copy of the *Application for Permanent Employment Certification* form that was sent to the bargaining representative.

(ii) If there is no such bargaining representative, by posted notice to the employer's employees at the facility or location of the employment. The notice must be posted for at least 10 consecutive business days. The notice must be clearly visible and unobstructed while posted and must be posted in conspicuous places where the employer's U.S. workers can readily read the posted notice on their way to or from their place of employment. Appropriate locations for posting notices of the job opportunity include locations in the immediate vicinity of the wage and hour notices required by 29 CFR 516.4 or occupational safety and health notices required by 29 CFR 1903.2(a). In addition, the employer must publish the notice in any and all in-house media, whether electronic or printed, in accordance with the normal procedures used for the recruitment of similar positions in the employer's organization. The documentation requirement may be satisfied by providing a copy of the posted notice and stating where it was posted, and by providing copies of all the in-house media, whether electronic or print, that were used to distribute notice of the application in accordance with the procedures used for similar positions within the employer's organization.

(2) In the case of a private household, notice is required under this paragraph (d) only if the household employs one or more U.S. workers at the time the application for labor certification is filed. The documentation requirement may be satisfied by providing a copy of the posted notice to the Certifying Officer.

(3) The notice of the filing of an *Application for Permanent Employment Certification* must:

(i) State the notice is being provided as a result of the filing of an application for permanent alien labor certification for the relevant job opportunity;

(ii) State any person may provide documentary evidence bearing on the application to the Certifying Officer of the Department of Labor;

(iii) Provide the address of the appropriate Certifying Officer; and

(iv) Be provided between 30 and 180 days before filing the application.

(4) If an application is filed under § 656.17, the notice must contain the information required for advertisements by § 656.17(f), must state the rate of pay (which must equal or exceed the prevailing wage entered by the SWA on the prevailing wage request form), and must contain the information required by paragraph (d)(3) of this section.

(5) If an application is filed on behalf of a college and university teacher selected in a competitive selection and recruitment process, as provided by § 656.18, the notice must include the information required for advertisements by § 656.18(b)(3), and must include the information required by paragraph (d)(3) of this section.

(6) If an application is filed under the *Schedule A* procedures at § 656.15, or the procedures for sheepherders at § 656.16, the notice must contain a description of the job and rate of pay, and must meet the requirements of this section.

(e)(1)(i) *Submission of evidence.* Any person may submit to the Certifying Officer documentary evidence bearing on an application for permanent alien labor certification filed under the basic labor certification process at § 656.17 or an application involving a college and university teacher selected in a competitive recruitment and selection process under § 656.18.

(ii) Documentary evidence submitted under paragraph (e)(1)(i) of this section may include information on available workers, information on wages and working conditions, and information on the employer's failure to meet the terms and conditions for the employment of alien workers and co-workers. The Certifying Officer must consider this information in making his or her determination.

(2)(i) Any person may submit to the appropriate DHS office documentary evidence of fraud or willful misrepresentation in a *Schedule A* application filed under § 656.15 or a sheepherder application filed under § 656.16.

(ii) Documentary evidence submitted under paragraph (e)(2) of this section is limited to information relating to possible fraud or willful misrepresentation. The DHS may consider this information under § 656.31.

(f) *Retention of documents.* Copies of applications for permanent employment certification filed with the Department of Labor and all supporting documentation must be retained by the employer for 5 years from the date of filing the *Application for Permanent Employment Certification.*

[69 FR 77386, Dec. 27, 2004, as amended at 71 FR 35523, June 21, 2006]

§ 656.11 Substitutions and modifications to applications.

(a) Substitution or change to the identity of an alien beneficiary on any application for permanent labor certification, whether filed under this part or 20 CFR part 656 in effect prior to March 28, 2005, and on any resulting certification, is prohibited for any request to substitute submitted after July 16, 2007.

(b) Requests for modifications to an application will not be accepted for applications submitted after July 16, 2007.

[72 FR 27944, May 17, 2007]

§ 656.12 Improper commerce and payment.

The following provision applies to applications filed under both this part and 20 CFR part 656 in effect prior to March 28, 2005, and to any certification resulting from those applications:

(a) Applications for permanent labor certification and approved labor certifications are not articles of commerce. They shall not be offered for sale, barter or purchase by individuals or entities. Any evidence that an application for permanent labor certification or an approved labor certification has been sold, bartered, or purchased shall be grounds for investigation under this part and may be grounds for denial under § 656.24, revocation under § 656.32, debarment under § 656.31(f), or any combination thereof.

(b) An employer must not seek or receive payment of any kind for any activity related to obtaining permanent labor certification, including payment of the employer's attorneys' fees, whether as an incentive or inducement to filing, or as a reimbursement for costs incurred in preparing or filing a permanent labor certification application, except when work to be performed by the alien in connection with the job opportunity would benefit or accrue to the person or entity making the payment, based on that person's or entity's established business relationship with the employer. An alien may pay his or her own costs in connection with a labor certification, including attorneys' fees for representation of the alien, except that where the same attorney represents both the alien and the employer, such costs shall be borne by the employer. For purposes of this paragraph (b), payment includes, but is not limited to, monetary payments; wage concessions, including deductions from wages, salary, or benefits; kickbacks, bribes, or tributes; in kind payments; and free labor.

(c) Evidence that an employer has sought or received payment from any source in connection with an application for permanent labor certification or an approved labor certification, except for a third party to whose benefit work to be performed in connection with the job opportunity would accrue, based on that person's or entity's established business relationship with the employer, shall be grounds for investigation under this part or any appropriate Government agency's procedures, and may be grounds for denial under § 656.32, revocation under § 656.32, debarment under § 656.31(f), or any combination thereof.

[72 FR 27945, May 17, 2007]

§ 656.15 Applications for labor certification for *Schedule A* occupations.

(a) *Filing application.* An employer must apply for a labor certification for a *Schedule A* occupation by filing an application with the appropriate DHS office, and not with an ETA application processing center.

(b) *General documentation requirements.* A *Schedule A* application must include:

(1) An *Application for Permanent Employment Certification* form, which includes a prevailing wage determination in accordance with §§ 656.40 and 656.41.

(2) Evidence that notice of filing the *Application for Permanent Employment Certification* was provided to the bargaining representative or the employer's employees as prescribed in § 656.10(d).

(c) *Group I documentation.* An employer seeking labor certification under Group I of *Schedule A* must file with DHS, as part of its labor certification application, documentary evidence of the following:

(1) An employer seeking *Schedule A* labor certification for an alien to be employed as a physical therapist (§ 656.5(a)(1)) must file as part of its labor certification application a letter or statement, signed by an authorized state physical therapy licensing official in the state of intended employment, stating the alien is qualified to take that state's written licensing examination for physical therapists. Application for certification of permanent employment as a physical therapist may be made only under this § 656.15 and not under § 656.17.

(2) An employer seeking a *Schedule A* labor certification for an alien to be

employed as a professional nurse (§ 656.5(a)(2)) must file as part of its labor certification application documentation that the alien has received a Certificate from the Commission on Graduates of Foreign Nursing Schools (CGFNS); that the alien holds a full and unrestricted (permanent) license to practice nursing in the state of intended employment; or that the alien has passed the National Council Licensure Examination for Registered Nurses (NCLEX–RN). Application for certification of employment as a professional nurse may be made only under this § 656.15(c) and not under § 656.17.

(d) *Group II documentation.* An employer seeking a *Schedule A* labor certification under Group II of *Schedule A* must file with DHS, as part of its labor certification application, documentary evidence of the following:

(1) An employer seeking labor certification on behalf of an alien to be employed as an alien of exceptional ability in the sciences or arts (excluding those in the performing arts) must file documentary evidence showing the widespread acclaim and international recognition accorded the alien by recognized experts in the alien's field; and documentation showing the alien's work in that field during the past year did, and the alien's intended work in the United States will, require exceptional ability. In addition, the employer must file documentation about the alien from at least two of the following seven groups:

(i) Documentation of the alien's receipt of internationally recognized prizes or awards for excellence in the field for which certification is sought;

(ii) Documentation of the alien's membership in international associations, in the field for which certification is sought, which require outstanding achievement of their members, as judged by recognized international experts in their disciplines or fields;

(iii) Published material in professional publications about the alien, about the alien's work in the field for which certification is sought, which shall include the title, date, and author of such published material;

(iv) Evidence of the alien's participation on a panel, or individually, as a judge of the work of others in the same or in an allied field of specialization to that for which certification is sought;

(v) Evidence of the alien's original scientific or scholarly research contributions of major significance in the field for which certification is sought;

(vi) Evidence of the alien's authorship of published scientific or scholarly articles in the field for which certification is sought, in international professional journals or professional journals with an international circulation;

(vii) Evidence of the display of the alien's work, in the field for which certification is sought, at artistic exhibitions in more than one country.

(2) An employer seeking labor certification on behalf of an alien of exceptional ability in the performing arts must file documentary evidence that the alien's work experience during the past twelve months did require, and the alien's intended work in the United States will require, exceptional ability; and must submit documentation to show this exceptional ability, such as:

(i) Documentation attesting to the current widespread acclaim and international recognition accorded to the alien, and receipt of internationally recognized prizes or awards for excellence;

(ii) Published material by or about the alien, such as critical reviews or articles in major newspapers, periodicals, and/or trade journals (the title, date, and author of such material shall be indicated);

(iii) Documentary evidence of earnings commensurate with the claimed level of ability;

(iv) Playbills and star billings;

(v) Documents attesting to the outstanding reputation of theaters, concert halls, night clubs, and other establishments in which the alien has appeared or is scheduled to appear; and/or

(vi) Documents attesting to the outstanding reputation of theaters or repertory companies, ballet troupes, orchestras, or other organizations in which or with which the alien has performed during the past year in a leading or starring capacity.

(e) *Determination.* An Immigration Officer determines whether the employer and alien have met the applicable requirements of § 656.10 and of *Schedule A* (§ 656.5); reviews the application; and determines whether or not the alien is qualified for and intends to pursue the *Schedule A* occupation. The *Schedule A* determination of DHS is conclusive and final. The employer, therefore, may not appeal from any such determination under the review procedures at § 656.26.

(f) *Refiling after denial.* If an application for a *Schedule A* occupation is denied, the employer, except where the occupation is as a physical therapist or a professional nurse, may at any time file for a labor certification on the alien beneficiary's behalf under § 656.17. Labor certifications for professional nurses and for physical therapists shall not be considered under § 656.17.

[69 FR 77386, Dec. 27, 2004, as amended at 73 FR 78068, Dec. 19, 2008]

§ 656.16 Labor certification applications for sheepherders.

(a) *Filing requirements and required documentation.* (1) An employer may apply for a labor certification to employ an alien (who has been employed legally as a nonimmigrant sheepherder in the United States for at least 33 of the preceding 36 months) as a sheepherder by filing an *Application for Permanent Employment Certification* form directly with DHS, not with an office of DOL.

(2) A signed letter or letters from each U.S. employer who has employed the alien as a sheepherder during the immediately preceding 36 months, attesting the alien has been employed in the United States lawfully and continuously as a sheepherder for at least 33 of the immediately preceding 36 months, must be filed with the application.

(b) *Determination.* An Immigration Officer reviews the application and the letters attesting to the alien's previous employment as a sheepherder in the United States, and determines whether or not the alien and the employer(s) have met the requirements of this section.

(1) The determination of the Immigration Officer under this paragraph (b) is conclusive and final. The employer(s) and the alien, therefore, may not make use of the review procedures set forth at §§ 656.26 and 656.27 to appeal such a determination.

(2) If the alien and the employer(s) have met the requirements of this section, the Immigration Officer must indicate on the *Application for Permanent Employment Certification* form the occupation, the immigration office that made the determination, and the date of the determination (see § 656.30 for the significance of this date). The Immigration Officer must then promptly forward a copy of the *Application for Permanent Employment Certification* form, without attachments, to the Office of Foreign Labor Certification (OFLC) Administrator.

(c) *Alternative filing.* If an application for a sheepherder does not meet the requirements of this section, the application may be filed under § 656.17.

[69 FR 77386, Dec. 27, 2004, as amended at 71 FR 35523, June 21, 2006]

§ 656.17 Basic labor certification process.

(a) *Filing applications.* (1) Except as otherwise provided by §§ 656.15, 656.16, and 656.18, an employer who desires to apply for a labor certification on behalf of an alien must file a completed Department of Labor *Application for Permanent Employment Certification* form (ETA Form 9089). The application must be filed with an ETA application processing center. Incomplete applications will be denied. Applications filed and certified electronically must, upon receipt of the labor certification, be signed immediately by the employer in order to be valid. Applications submitted by mail must contain the original signature of the employer, alien, attorney, and/or agent when they are received by the application processing center. DHS will not process petitions unless they are supported by an original certified ETA Form 9089 that has been signed by the employer, alien, attorney and/or agent.

(2) The Department of Labor may issue or require the use of certain identifying information, including user identifiers, passwords, or personal identification numbers (PINS). The purpose of these personal identifiers is to allow the Department of Labor to associate a

given electronic submission with a single, specific individual. Personal identifiers can not be issued to a company or business. Rather, a personal identifier can only be issued to specific individual. Any personal identifiers must be used solely by the individual to whom they are assigned and can not be used or transferred to any other individual. An individual assigned a personal identifier must take all reasonable steps to ensure that his or her personal identifier can not be compromised. If an individual assigned a personal identifier suspects, or becomes aware, that his or her personal identifier has been compromised or is being used by someone else, then the individual must notify the Department of Labor immediately of the incident and cease the electronic transmission of any further submissions under that personal identifier until such time as a new personal identifier is provided. Any electronic transmissions submitted with a personal identifier will be presumed to be a submission by the individual assigned that personal identifier. The Department of Labor's system will notify those making submissions of these requirements at the time of each submission.

(3) Documentation supporting the application for labor certification should not be filed with the application, however in the event the Certifying Officer notifies the employer that its application is to be audited, the employer must furnish required supporting documentation prior to a final determination.

(b) *Processing.* (1) Applications are screened and are certified, are denied, or are selected for audit.

(2) Employers will be notified if their applications have been selected for audit by the issuance of an audit letter under § 656.20.

(3) Applications may be selected for audit in accordance with selection criteria or may be randomly selected.

(c) *Filing date.* Non-electronically filed applications accepted for processing shall be date stamped. Electronically filed applications will be considered filed when submitted.

(d) *Refiling procedures.* (1) Employers that filed applications under the regulations in effect prior to March 28, 2005, may, if a job order has not been placed pursuant to those regulations, refile such applications under this part without loss of the original filing date by:

(i) Submitting an application for an identical job opportunity after complying with all of the filing and recruiting requirements of this part 656; and

(ii) Withdrawing the original application in accordance with ETA procedures. Filing an application under this part stating the employer's desire to use the original filing date will be deemed to be a withdrawal of the original application. The original application will be deemed withdrawn regardless of whether the employer's request to use the original filing date is approved.

(2) Refilings under this paragraph must be made within 210 days of the withdrawal of the prior application.

(3) A copy of the original application, including amendments, must be sent to the appropriate ETA application processing center when requested by the CO under § 656.20.

(4) For purposes of paragraph (d)(1)(i) of this section, a job opportunity shall be considered identical if the employer, alien, job title, job location, job requirements, and job description are the same as those stated in the original application filed under the regulations in effect prior to March 28, 2005. For purposes of determining identical job opportunity, the original application includes all accepted amendments up to the time the application was withdrawn, including amendments in response to an assessment notice from a SWA pursuant to § 656.21(h) of the regulations in effect prior to March 28, 2005.

(e) *Required pre-filing recruitment.* Except for labor certification applications involving college or university teachers selected pursuant to a competitive recruitment and selection process (§ 656.18), *Schedule A* occupations (§§ 656.5 and 656.15), and sheepherders (§ 656.16), an employer must attest to having conducted the following recruitment prior to filing the application:

(1) *Professional occupations.* If the application is for a professional occupation, the employer must conduct the recruitment steps within 6 months of

filing the application for alien employment certification. The employer must maintain documentation of the recruitment and be prepared to submit this documentation in the event of an audit or in response to a request from the Certifying Officer prior to rendering a final determination.

(i) *Mandatory steps.* Two of the steps, a job order and two print advertisements, are mandatory for all applications involving professional occupations, except applications for college or university teachers selected in a competitive selection and recruitment process as provided in § 656.18. The mandatory recruitment steps must be conducted at least 30 days, but no more than 180 days, before the filing of the application.

(A) *Job order.* Placement of a job order with the SWA serving the area of intended employment for a period of 30 days. The start and end dates of the job order entered on the application shall serve as documentation of this step.

(B) *Advertisements in newspaper or professional journals.* (*1*) Placing an advertisement on two different Sundays in the newspaper of general circulation in the area of intended employment most appropriate to the occupation and the workers likely to apply for the job opportunity and most likely to bring responses from able, willing, qualified, and available U.S. workers.

(*2*) If the job opportunity is located in a rural area of intended employment that does not have a newspaper with a Sunday edition, the employer may use the edition with the widest circulation in the area of intended employment.

(*3*) The advertisements must satisfy the requirements of paragraph (f) of this section. Documentation of this step can be satisfied by furnishing copies of the newspaper pages in which the advertisements appeared or proof of publication furnished by the newspaper.

(*4*) If the job involved in the application requires experience and an advanced degree, and a professional journal normally would be used to advertise the job opportunity, the employer may, in lieu of one of the Sunday advertisements, place an advertisement in the professional journal most likely to bring responses from able, willing, qualified, and available U.S. workers. Documentation of this step can be satisfied by providing a copy of the page in which the advertisement appeared.

(ii) *Additional recruitment steps.* The employer must select three additional recruitment steps from the alternatives listed in paragraphs (e)(1)(ii)(A)–(J) of this section. Only one of the additional steps may consist solely of activity that took place within 30 days of the filing of the application. None of the steps may have taken place more than 180 days prior to filing the application.

(A) *Job fairs.* Recruitment at job fairs for the occupation involved in the application, which can be documented by brochures advertising the fair and newspaper advertisements in which the employer is named as a participant in the job fair.

(B) *Employer's Web site.* The use of the employer's Web site as a recruitment medium can be documented by providing dated copies of pages from the site that advertise the occupation involved in the application.

(C) *Job search Web site other than the employer's.* The use of a job search Web site other than the employer's can be documented by providing dated copies of pages from one or more website(s) that advertise the occupation involved in the application. Copies of web pages generated in conjunction with the newspaper advertisements required by paragraph (e)(1)(i)(B) of this section can serve as documentation of the use of a Web site other than the employer's.

(D) *On-campus recruiting.* The employer's on-campus recruiting can be documented by providing copies of the notification issued or posted by the college's or university's placement office naming the employer and the date it conducted interviews for employment in the occupation.

(E) *Trade or professional organizations.* The use of professional or trade organizations as a recruitment source can be documented by providing copies of pages of newsletters or trade journals containing advertisements for the occupation involved in the application for alien employment certification.

(F) *Private employment firms.* The use of private employment firms or placement agencies can be documented by providing documentation sufficient to demonstrate that recruitment has been conducted by a private firm for the occupation for which certification is sought. For example, documentation might consist of copies of contracts between the employer and the private employment firm and copies of advertisements placed by the private employment firm for the occupation involved in the application.

(G) *Employee referral program with incentives.* The use of an employee referral program with incentives can be documented by providing dated copies of employer notices or memoranda advertising the program and specifying the incentives offered.

(H) *Campus placement offices.* The use of a campus placement office can be documented by providing a copy of the employer's notice of the job opportunity provided to the campus placement office.

(I) *Local and ethnic newspapers.* The use of local and ethnic newspapers can be documented by providing a copy of the page in the newspaper that contains the employer's advertisement.

(J) *Radio and television advertisements.* The use of radio and television advertisements can be documented by providing a copy of the employer's text of the employer's advertisement along with a written confirmation from the radio or television station stating when the advertisement was aired.

(2) *Nonprofessional occupations.* If the application is for a nonprofessional occupation, the employer must at a minimum, place a job order and two newspaper advertisements within 6 months of filing the application. The steps must be conducted at least 30 days but no more that 180 days before the filing of the application.

(i) *Job order.* Placing a job order with the SWA serving the area of intended employment for a period of 30 days. The start and end dates of the job order entered on the application serve as documentation of this step.

(ii) *Newspaper advertisements.* (A) Placing an advertisement on two different Sundays in the newspaper of general circulation in the area of intended employment most appropriate to the occupation and the workers likely to apply for the job opportunity.

(B) If the job opportunity is located in a rural area of intended employment that does not have a newspaper that publishes a Sunday edition, the employer may use the newspaper edition with the widest circulation in the area of intended employment.

(C) Placement of the newspaper advertisements can be documented in the same way as provided in paragraph (e)(1)(i)(B)(*3*) of this section for professional occupations.

(D) The advertisements must satisfy the requirements of paragraph (f) of this section.

(f) *Advertising requirements.* Advertisements placed in newspapers of general circulation or in professional journals before filing the *Application for Permanent Employment Certification* must:

(1) Name the employer;

(2) Direct applicants to report or send resumes, as appropriate for the occupation, to the employer;

(3) Provide a description of the vacancy specific enough to apprise the U.S. workers of the job opportunity for which certification is sought;

(4) Indicate the geographic area of employment with enough specificity to apprise applicants of any travel requirements and where applicants will likely have to reside to perform the job opportunity;

(5) Not contain a wage rate lower than the prevailing wage rate;

(6) Not contain any job requirements or duties which exceed the job requirements or duties listed on the ETA Form 9089; and

(7) Not contain wages or terms and conditions of employment that are less favorable than those offered to the alien.

(g) *Recruitment report.* (1) The employer must prepare a recruitment report signed by the employer or the employer's representative noted in § 656.10(b)(2)(ii) describing the recruitment steps undertaken and the results achieved, the number of hires, and, if applicable, the number of U.S. workers rejected, categorized by the lawful job related reasons for such rejections. The Certifying Officer, after reviewing the employer's recruitment report, may request the U.S. workers' resumes or applications, sorted by the reasons the workers were rejected.

(2) A U.S. worker is able and qualified for the job opportunity if the worker can acquire the skills necessary to perform the duties involved in the occupation during a reasonable period of on-the-job training. Rejecting U.S. workers for lacking skills necessary to perform the duties involved in the occupation, where the U.S. workers are capable of acquiring the skills during a reasonable period of on-the-job training is not a lawful job-related reason for rejection of the U.S. workers.

(h) *Job duties and requirements.* (1) The job opportunity's requirements, unless adequately documented as arising from business necessity, must be those normally required for the occupation and must not exceed the Specific Vocational Preparation level assigned to the occupation as shown in the O*NET Job Zones. To establish a business necessity, an employer must demonstrate the job duties and requirements bear a reasonable relationship to the occupation in the context of the employer's business and are essential to perform the job in a reasonable manner.

(2) A foreign language requirement can not be included, unless it is justified by business necessity. Demonstrating business necessity for a foreign language requirement may be based upon the following:

(i) The nature of the occupation, e.g., translator; or

(ii) The need to communicate with a large majority of the employer's customers, contractors, or employees who can not communicate effectively in English, as documented by:

(A) The employer furnishing the number and proportion of its clients, contractors, or employees who can not communicate in English, and/or a detailed plan to market products or services in a foreign country; and

(B) A detailed explanation of why the duties of the position for which certification is sought requires frequent contact and communication with customers, employees or contractors who can not communicate in English and why it is reasonable to believe the allegedly foreign-language-speaking customers, employees, and contractors can not communicate in English.

(3) If the job opportunity involves a combination of occupations, the employer must document that it has normally employed persons for that combination of occupations, and/or workers customarily perform the combination of occupations in the area of intended employment, and/or the combination job opportunity is based on a business necessity. Combination occupations can be documented by position descriptions and relevant payroll records, and/or letters from other employers stating their workers normally perform the combination of occupations in the area of intended employment, and/or documentation that the combination occupation arises from a business necessity.

(4)(i) Alternative experience requirements must be substantially equivalent to the primary requirements of the job opportunity for which certification is sought; and

(ii) If the alien beneficiary already is employed by the employer, and the alien does not meet the primary job requirements and only potentially qualifies for the job by virtue of the employer's alternative requirements, certification will be denied unless the application states that any suitable combination of education, training, or experience is acceptable.

(i) *Actual minimum requirements.* DOL will evaluate the employer's actual minimum requirements in accordance with this paragraph (i).

(1) The job requirements, as described, must represent the employer's actual minimum requirements for the job opportunity.

(2) The employer must not have hired workers with less training or experience for jobs substantially comparable to that involved in the job opportunity.

(3) If the alien beneficiary already is employed by the employer, in considering whether the job requirements represent the employer's actual minimums, DOL will review the training and experience possessed by the alien beneficiary at the time of hiring by the employer, including as a contract employee. The employer can not require domestic worker applicants to possess training and/or experience beyond what

the alien possessed at the time of hire unless:

(i) The alien gained the experience while working for the employer, including as a contract employee, in a position not substantially comparable to the position for which certification is being sought, or

(ii) The employer can demonstrate that it is no longer feasible to train a worker to qualify for the position.

(4) In evaluating whether the alien beneficiary satisfies the employer's actual minimum requirements, DOL will not consider any education or training obtained by the alien beneficiary at the employer's expense unless the employer offers similar training to domestic worker applicants.

(5) For purposes of this paragraph (i):

(i) The term "employer" means an entity with the same Federal Employer Identification Number (FEIN), provided it meets the definition of an employer at §656.3.

(ii) A "substantially comparable" job or position means a job or position requiring performance of the same job duties more than 50 percent of the time. This requirement can be documented by furnishing position descriptions, the percentage of time spent on the various duties, organization charts, and payroll records.

(j) *Conditions of employment.* (1) Working conditions must be normal to the occupation in the area and industry.

(2) Live-in requirements are acceptable for household domestic service workers only if the employer can demonstrate the requirement is essential to perform, in a reasonable manner, the job duties as described by the employer and there are not cost-effective alternatives to a live-in household requirement. Mere employer assertions do not constitute acceptable documentation. For example, a live-in requirement could be supported by documenting two working parents and young children in the household, and/or the existence of erratic work schedules requiring frequent travel and a need to entertain business associates and clients on short notice. Depending upon the situation, acceptable documentation could consist of travel vouchers, written estimates of costs of alternatives such as babysitters, or a detailed listing of the frequency and length of absences of the employer from the home.

(k) *Layoffs.* (1) If there has been a layoff by the employer applicant in the area of intended employment within 6 months of filing an application involving the occupation for which certification is sought or in a related occupation, the employer must document it has notified and considered all potentially qualified laid off (employer applicant) U.S. workers of the job opportunity involved in the application and the results of the notification and consideration. A layoff shall be considered any involuntary separation of one or more employees without cause or prejudice.

(2) For the purposes of paragraph (k)(1) of this section, a related occupation is any occupation that requires workers to perform a majority of the essential duties involved in the occupation for which certification is sought.

(l) *Alien influence and control over job opportunity.* If the employer is a closely held corporation or partnership in which the alien has an ownership interest, or if there is a familial relationship between the stockholders, corporate officers, incorporators, or partners, and the alien, or if the alien is one of a small number of employees, the employer in the event of an audit must be able to demonstrate the existence of a bona fide job opportunity, *i.e.*, the job is available to all U.S. workers, and must provide to the Certifying Officer, the following supporting documentation:

(1) A copy of the articles of incorporation, partnership agreement, business license or similar documents that establish the business entity;

(2) A list of all corporate/company officers and shareholders/partners of the corporation/firm/business, their titles and positions in the business' structure, and a description of the relationships to each other and to the alien beneficiary;

(3) The financial history of the corporation/company/partnership, including the total investment in the business entity and the amount of investment of each officer, incorporator/partner and the alien beneficiary; and

(4) The name of the business' official with primary responsibility for interviewing and hiring applicants for positions within the organization and the name(s) of the business' official(s) having control or influence over hiring decisions involving the position for which labor certification is sought.

(5) If the alien is one of 10 or fewer employees, the employer must document any family relationship between the employees and the alien.

§ 656.18 Optional special recruitment and documentation procedures for college and university teachers.

(a) *Filing requirements.* Applications for certification of employment of college and university teachers must be filed by submitting a completed *Application for Permanent Employment Certification* form to the appropriate ETA application processing center.

(b) *Recruitment.* The employer may recruit for college and university teachers under § 656.17 or must be able to document the alien was selected for the job opportunity in a competitive recruitment and selection process through which the alien was found to be more qualified than any of the United States workers who applied for the job. For purposes of this paragraph (b), documentation of the "competitive recruitment and selection process" must include:

(1) A statement, signed by an official who has actual hiring authority from the employer outlining in detail the complete recruitment procedures undertaken; and which must set forth:

(i) The total number of applicants for the job opportunity;

(ii) The specific lawful job-related reasons why the alien is more qualified than each U.S. worker who applied for the job; and

(2) A final report of the faculty, student, and/or administrative body making the recommendation or selection of the alien, at the completion of the competitive recruitment and selection process;

(3) A copy of at least one advertisement for the job opportunity placed in a national professional journal, giving the name and the date(s) of publication; and which states the job title, duties, and requirements;

(4) Evidence of all other recruitment sources utilized; and

(5) A written statement attesting to the degree of the alien's educational or professional qualifications and academic achievements.

(c) *Time limit for filing.* Applications for permanent alien labor certification for job opportunities as college and university teachers must be filed within 18 months after a selection is made pursuant to a competitive recruitment and selection process.

(d) *Alternative procedure.* An employer that can not or does not choose to satisfy the special recruitment procedures for a college or university teacher under this section may avail itself of the basic process at § 656.17. An employer that files for certification of employment of college and university teachers under § 656.17 or this section must be able to document, if requested by the Certifying Officer, in accordance with § 656.24(a)(2)(ii), the alien was found to be more qualified than each U.S. worker who applied for the job opportunity.

§ 656.19 Live-in household domestic service workers.

(a) *Processing.* Applications on behalf of live-in household domestic service occupations are processed pursuant to the requirements of the basic process at § 656.17.

(b) *Required documentation.* Employers filing applications on behalf of live-in household domestic service workers must provide, in event of an audit, the following documentation:

(1) A statement describing the household living accommodations, including the following:

(i) Whether the residence is a house or apartment;

(ii) The number of rooms in the residence;

(iii) The number of adults and children, and ages of the children, residing in the household; and

(iv) That free board and a private room not shared with any other person will be provided to the alien.

(2) Two copies of the employment contract, each signed and dated prior to the filing of the application by both the employer and the alien (not by

their attorneys or agents). The contract must clearly state:

(i) The wages to be paid on an hourly and weekly basis;

(ii) Total hours of employment per week, and exact hours of daily employment;

(iii) That the alien is free to leave the employer's premises during all non-work hours except the alien may work overtime if paid for the overtime at no less than the legally required hourly rate;

(iv) That the alien will reside on the employer's premises;

(v) Complete details of the duties to be performed by the alien;

(vi) The total amount of any money to be advanced by the employer with details of specific items, and the terms of repayment by the alien of any such advance by the employer;

(vii) That in no event may the alien be required to give more than two weeks' notice of intent to leave the employment contracted for and the employer must give the alien at least two weeks' notice before terminating employment;

(viii) That a duplicate contract has been furnished to the alien;

(ix) That a private room and board will be provided at no cost to the worker; and

(x) Any other agreement or conditions not specified on the *Application for Permanent Employment Certification* form.

(3) Documentation of the alien's paid experience in the form of statements from past or present employers setting forth the dates (month and year) employment started and ended, hours of work per day, number of days worked per week, place where the alien worked, detailed statement of duties performed on the job, equipment and appliances used, and the amount of wages paid per week or month. The total paid experience must be equal to one full year's employment on a full-time basis. For example, two year's experience working half-days is the equivalent of one year's full time experience. Time spent in a household domestic service training course can not be included in the required one year of paid experience. Each statement must contain the name and address of the person who signed it and show the date on which the statement was signed. A statement not in English shall be accompanied by a written translation into English certified by the translator as to the accuracy of the translation, and as to the translator's competency to translate.

§ 656.20 Audit procedures.

(a) Review of the labor certification application may lead to an audit of the application. Additionally, certain applications may be selected randomly for audit and quality control purposes. If an application is selected for audit, the Certifying Officer shall issue an audit letter. The audit letter will:

(1) State the documentation that must be submitted by the employer;

(2) Specify a date, 30 days from the date of the audit letter, by which the required documentation must be submitted; and

(3) Advise that if the required documentation has not been sent by the date specified the application will be denied.

(i) Failure to provide documentation in a timely manner constitutes a refusal to exhaust available administrative remedies; and

(ii) The administrative-judicial review procedure provided in § 656.26 is not available.

(b) A substantial failure by the employer to provide required documentation will result in that application being denied under § 656.24 and may result in a determination by the Certifying Officer pursuant to § 656.24 to require the employer to conduct supervised recruitment under § 656.21 in future filings of labor certification applications for up to 2 years.

(c) The Certifying Officer may in his or her discretion provide one extension, of up to 30 days, to the 30 days specified in paragraph (a)(2) of this section.

(d) Before making a final determination in accordance with the standards in § 656.24, whether in course of an audit or otherwise, the Certifying Officer may:

(1) Request supplemental information and/or documentation; or

(2) Require the employer to conduct supervised recruitment under §656.21.

[69 FR 77386, Dec. 27, 2004, as amended at 71 FR 35523, June 21, 2006]

§656.21 Supervised recruitment.

(a) *Supervised recruitment.* Where the Certifying Officer determines it appropriate, post-filing supervised recruitment may be required of the employer for the pending application or future applications pursuant to §656.20(b).

(b) *Requirements.* Supervised recruitment shall consist of advertising for the job opportunity by placing an advertisement in a newspaper of general circulation or in a professional, trade, or ethnic publication, and any other measures required by the CO. If placed in a newspaper of general circulation, the advertisement must be published for 3 consecutive days, one of which must be a Sunday; or, if placed in a professional, trade, or ethnic publication, the advertisement must be published in the next available published edition. The advertisement must be approved by the Certifying Officer before publication, and the CO will direct where the advertisement is to be placed.

(1) The employer must supply a draft advertisement to the CO for review and approval within 30 days of being notified that supervised recruitment is required.

(2) The advertisement must:

(i) Direct applicants to send resumes or applications for the job opportunity to the CO for referral to the employer;

(ii) Include an identification number and an address designated by the Certifying Officer;

(iii) Describe the job opportunity;

(iv) Not contain a wage rate lower than the prevailing wage rate;

(v) Summarize the employer's minimum job requirements, which can not exceed any of the requirements entered on the application form by the employer;

(vi) Offer training if the job opportunity is the type for which employers normally provide training; and

(vii) Offer wages, terms and conditions of employment no less favorable than those offered to the alien.

(c) *Timing of advertisement.* (1) The advertisement shall be placed in accordance with the guidance provided by the CO.

(2) The employer will notify the CO when the advertisement will be placed.

(d) *Additional or substitute recruitment.* The Certifying Officer may designate other appropriate sources of workers from which the employer must recruit for U.S. workers in addition to the advertising described in paragraph (b) of this section.

(e) *Recruitment report.* The employer must provide to the Certifying Officer a signed, detailed written report of the employer's supervised recruitment, signed by the employer or the employer's representative described in §656.10(b)(2)(ii), within 30 days of the Certifying Officer's request for such a report. The recruitment report must:

(1) Identify each recruitment source by name and document that each recruitment source named was contacted. This can include, for example, copies of letters to recruitment sources such as unions, trade associations, colleges and universities and any responses received to the employer's inquiries. Advertisements placed in newspapers, professional, trade, or ethnic publications can be documented by furnishing copies of the tear sheets of the pages of the publication in which the advertisements appeared, proof of publication furnished by the publication, or dated copies of the web pages if the advertisement appeared on the web as well as in the publication in which the advertisement appeared.

(2) State the number of U.S. workers who responded to the employer's recruitment.

(3) State the names, addresses, and provide resumes (other than those sent to the employer by the CO) of the U.S. workers who applied for the job opportunity, the number of workers interviewed, and the job title of the person who interviewed the workers.

(4) Explain, with specificity, the lawful job-related reason(s) for not hiring each U.S. worker who applied. Rejection of one or more U.S. workers for lacking skills necessary to perform the duties involved in the occupation, where the U.S. workers are capable of acquiring the skills during a reasonable period of on-the-job training, is

not a lawful job-related reason for rejecting the U.S. workers. For the purpose of this paragraph (e)(4), a U.S. worker is able and qualified for the job opportunity if the worker can acquire the skills necessary to perform the duties involved in the occupation during a reasonable period of on-the-job training.

(f) The employer shall supply the CO with the required documentation or information within 30 days of the date of the request. If the employer does not do so, the CO shall deny the application.

(g) The Certifying Officer in his or her discretion, for good cause shown, may provide one extension to any request for documentation or information.

§656.24 Labor certification determinations.

(a)(1) The Office of Foreign Labor Certification Administrator (OFLC Administrator) is the National Certifying Officer. The OFLC Administrator and the certifying officers in the ETA application processing centers have the authority to certify or deny labor certification applications.

(2) If the labor certification presents a special or unique problem, the Director of an ETA application processing center may refer the matter to the Office of Foreign Labor Certification Administrator (OFLC Administrator). If the OFLC Administrator has directed that certain types of applications or specific applications be handled in the ETA national office, the Directors of the ETA application processing centers shall refer such applications to the OFLC Administrator.

(b) The Certifying Officer makes a determination either to grant or deny the labor certification on the basis of whether or not:

(1) The employer has met the requirements of this part.

(2) There is in the United States a worker who is able, willing, qualified, and available for and at the place of the job opportunity.

(i) The Certifying Officer must consider a U.S. worker able and qualified for the job opportunity if the worker, by education, training, experience, or a combination thereof, is able to perform in the normally accepted manner the duties involved in the occupation as customarily performed by other U.S. workers similarly employed. For the purposes of this paragraph (b)(2)(i), a U.S. worker is able and qualified for the job opportunity if the worker can acquire the skills necessary to perform the duties involved in the occupation during a reasonable period of on-the-job training.

(ii) If the job involves a job opportunity as a college or university teacher, the U.S. worker must be at least as qualified as the alien.

(3) The employment of the alien will not have an adverse effect upon the wages and working conditions of U.S. workers similarly employed. In making this determination, the Certifying Officer considers such things as: labor market information, the special circumstances of the industry, organization, and/or occupation, the prevailing wage in the area of intended employment, and prevailing working conditions, such as hours, in the occupation.

(c) The Certifying Officer shall notify the employer in writing (either electronically or by mail) of the labor certification determination.

(d) If a labor certification is granted, except for a labor certification for an occupation on *Schedule A* (§656.5) or for employment as a sheepherder under §656.16, the Certifying Officer must send the certified application and complete Final Determination form to the employer, or, if appropriate, to the employer's agent or attorney, indicating the employer may file all the documents with the appropriate DHS office.

(e) If the labor certification is denied, the Final Determination form will:

(1) State the reasons for the determination;

(2) Quote the request for review procedures at §656.26 (a) and (b);

(3) Advise that failure to request review within 30 days of the date of the determination, as specified in §656.26(a), constitutes a failure to exhaust administrative remedies;

(4) Advise that, if a request for review is not made within 30 days of the date of the determination, the denial shall become the final determination of the Secretary;

(5) Advise that if an application for a labor certification is denied, and a request for review is not made in accordance with the procedures at § 656.26(a) and (b), a new application may be filed at any time; and

(6) Advise that a new application in the same occupation for the same alien can not be filed while a request for review is pending with the Board of Alien Labor Certification Appeals.

(f) If the Certifying Officer determines the employer substantially failed to produce required documentation, or the documentation was inadequate, or determines a material misrepresentation was made with respect to the application, or if the Certifying Officer determines it is appropriate for other reasons, the employer may be required to conduct supervised recruitment pursuant to § 656.21 in future filings of labor certification applications for up to two years from the date of the Final Determination.

(g)(1) The employer may request reconsideration within 30 days from the date of issuance of the denial.

(2) For applications submitted after July 16, 2007, a request for reconsideration may include only:

(i) Documentation that the Department actually received from the employer in response to a request from the Certifying Officer to the employer; or

(ii) Documentation that the employer did not have an opportunity to present previously to the Certifying Officer, but that existed at the time the Application for Permanent Labor Certification was filed, and was maintained by the employer to support the application for permanent labor certification in compliance with the requirements of § 656.10(f).

(3) Paragraphs (g)(1) and (2) of this section notwithstanding, the Certifying Officer will not grant any request for reconsideration where the deficiency that caused denial resulted from the applicant's disregard of a system prompt or other direct instruction.

(4) The Certifying Officer may, in his or her discretion, reconsider the determination or treat it as a request for review under § 656.26(a).

[69 FR 77386, Dec. 27, 2004, as amended at 71 FR 35523, June 21, 2006; 72 FR 27945, May 17, 2007]

§ 656.26 Board of Alien Labor Certification Appeals review of denials of labor certification.

(a) *Request for review.* (1) If a labor certification is denied, if a labor certification is revoked pursuant to § 656.32, or if a debarment is issued under § 656.31(f), a request for review of the denial, revocation, or debarment may be made to the Board of Alien Labor Certification Appeals by the employer or debarred person or entity by making a request for such an administrative review in accordance with the procedures provided in paragraph (a) of this section. In the case of a finding of debarment, receipt by the Department of a request for review, if made in accordance with this section, shall stay the debarment until such time as the review has been completed and a decision rendered thereon.

(2) A request for review of a denial or revocation:

(i) Must be sent within 30 days of the date of the determination to the Certifying Officer who denied the application or revoked the certification;

(ii) Must clearly identify the particular labor certification determination for which review is sought;

(iii) Must set forth the particular grounds for the request; and

(iv) Must include a copy of the Final Determination.

(3) A request for review of debarment:

(i) Must be sent to the Administrator, Office of Foreign Labor Certification, within 30 days of the date of the debarment determination;

(ii) Must clearly identify the particular debarment determination for which review is sought;

(iii) Must set forth the particular grounds for the request; and

(iv) Must include a copy of the Notice of Debarment.

(4)(i) With respect to a denial of the request for review, statements, briefs, and other submissions of the parties and amicus curiae must contain only legal argument and only such evidence that was within the record upon which the denial of labor certification was based.

(ii) With respect to a revocation or a debarment determination, the BALCA proceeding may be de novo.

(b) Upon the receipt of a request for review, the Certifying Officer immediately must assemble an indexed Appeal File:

(1) The Appeal File must be in chronological order, must have the index on top followed by the most recent document, and must have consecutively numbered pages. The Appeal File must contain the request for review, the complete application file, and copies of all the written material, such as pertinent parts and pages of surveys and/or reports upon which the denial was based.

(2) The Certifying Officer must send the Appeal File to the Board of Alien Labor Certification Appeals, Office of Administrative Law Judges, 800 K Street, NW., Suite 400–N, Washington, DC 20001–8002.

(3) The Certifying Officer must send a copy of the Appeal File to the employer. The employer may furnish or suggest directly to the Board of Alien Labor Certification Appeals the addition of any documentation that is not in the Appeal File, but that was submitted to DOL before the issuance of the Final Determination. The employer must submit such documentation in writing, and must send a copy to the Associate Solicitor for Employment and Training Legal Services, Office of the Solicitor, U.S. Department of Labor, Washington, DC 20210.

(c) *Debarment Appeal File.* Upon the receipt of a request for review of debarment, the Administrator, Office of Foreign Labor Certification, immediately must assemble an indexed Appeal File:

(1) The Appeal File must be in chronological order, must have the index on top followed by the most recent document, and must have consecutively numbered pages. The Appeal File must contain the request for review, the complete application file(s), and copies of all written materials, such as pertinent parts and pages of surveys and/or reports or documents received from any court, DHS, or the Department of State, upon which the debarment was based.

(2) The Administrator, Office of Foreign Labor Certification, must send the Appeal File to the Board of Alien Labor Certification Appeals, Office of Administrative Law Judges, 800 K St., NW., Suite 400–N, Washington, DC 20001–8002.

(3) The Administrator, Office of Foreign Labor Certification, must send a copy of the Appeal File to the debarred person or entity. The debarred person or entity may furnish or suggest directly to the Board of Alien Labor Certification Appeals the addition of any documentation that is not in the Appeal File. The debarred person or entity must submit such documentation in writing, and must send a copy to the Associate Solicitor for Employment and Training Legal Services, Office of the Solicitor, U.S. Department of Labor, 200 Constitution Ave., NW., Washington, DC 20210.

[69 FR 77386, Dec. 27, 2004, as amended at 72 FR 27945, May 17, 2007]

§ 656.27 Consideration by and decisions of the Board of Alien Labor Certification Appeals.

(a) *Panel designations.* In considering requests for review before it, the Board of Alien Labor Certification Appeals may sit in panels of three members. The Chief Administrative Law Judge may designate any Board of Alien Labor Certification Appeals member to submit proposed findings and recommendations to the Board of Alien Labor Certification Appeals or to any duly designated panel thereof to consider a particular case.

(b) *Briefs and Statements of Position.* In considering the requests for review before it, the Board of Alien Labor Certification Appeals must afford all parties 30 days to submit or decline to submit any appropriate Statement of Position or legal brief. The Certifying Officer is to be represented solely by the Solicitor of Labor or the Solicitor's designated representative.

(c) *Review on the record.* The Board of Alien Labor Certification Appeals must review a denial of labor certification under § 656.24, a revocation of a certification under § 656.32, or an affirmation of a prevailing wage determination under § 656.41 on the basis of the record upon which the decision was made, the request for review, and any Statements of Position or legal briefs submitted and must:

(1) Affirm the denial of the labor certification, the revocation of certification, or the affirmation of the PWD; or

(2) Direct the Certifying Officer to grant the certification, overrule the revocation of certification, or overrule the affirmation of the PWD; or

(3) Direct that a hearing on the case be held under paragraph (e) of this section.

(d) *Notifications of decisions.* The Board of Alien Labor Certification Appeals must notify the employer, the Certifying Officer, and the Solicitor of Labor of its decision, and must return the record to the Certifying Officer unless the case has been set for hearing under paragraph (e) of this section.

(e) *Hearings*—(1) *Notification of hearing.* If the case has been set for a hearing, the Board of Alien Labor Certification Appeals must notify the employer, the alien, the Certifying Officer, and the Solicitor of Labor of the date, time, and place of the hearing, and that the hearing may be rescheduled upon written request and for good cause shown.

(2) *Hearing procedure.* (i) The "Rules of Practice and Procedure For Administrative Hearings Before the Office of Administrative Law Judges," at 29 CFR part 18, apply to hearings under this paragraph (e).

(ii) For the purposes of this paragraph (e)(2), references in 29 CFR part 18 to: "administrative law judge" mean the Board of Alien Labor Certification Appeals member or the Board of Alien Labor Certification Appeals panel duly designated under § 656.27(a); "Office of Administrative Law Judges" means the Board of Alien Labor Certification Appeals; and "Chief Administrative Law Judge" means the Chief Administrative Law Judge in that official's function of chairing the Board of Alien Labor Certification Appeals.

§ 656.30 Validity of and invalidation of labor certifications.

(a) *Priority date.* (1) The filing date for a Schedule A occupation or sheepherders is the date the application was dated by the Immigration Officer.

(2) The filing date, established under § 656.17(c), of an approved labor certification may be used as a priority date by the Department of Homeland Security and the Department of State, as appropriate.

(b) *Expiration of labor certifications.* For certifications resulting from applications filed under this part and 20 CFR part 656 in effect prior to March 28, 2005, the following applies:

(1) An approved permanent labor certification granted on or after July 16, 2007 expires if not filed in support of a Form I–140 petition with the Department of Homeland Security within 180 calendar days of the date the Department of Labor granted the certification.

(2) An approved permanent labor certification granted before July 16, 2007 expires if not filed in support of a Form I–140 petition with the Department of Homeland Security within 180 calendar days of July 16, 2007.

(c) *Scope of validity.* For certifications resulting from applications filed under this part or 20 CFR part 656 in effect prior to March 28, 2005, the following applies:

(1) A permanent labor certification for a Schedule A occupation or sheepherders is valid only for the occupation set forth on the *Application for Alien Employment Certification* (Form ETA 750) or the *Application for Permanent Employment Certification* (Form ETA 9089) and only for the alien named on the original application, unless a substitution was approved prior to July 16, 2007. The certification is valid throughout the United States unless the certification contains a geographic limitation.

(2) A permanent labor certification involving a specific job offer is valid only for the particular job opportunity, the alien named on the original application (unless a substitution was approved prior to July 16, 2007), and the area of intended employment stated on the *Application for Alien Employment Certification* (Form ETA 750) or the *Application for Permanent Employment Certification* (Form ETA 9089).

(d) *Invalidation of labor certifications.* After issuance, a labor certification may be revoked by ETA using the procedures described in §656.32. Additionally, after issuance, a labor certification is subject to invalidation by the DHS or by a Consul of the Department of State upon a determination, made in accordance with those agencies' procedures or by a court, of fraud or willful misrepresentation of a material fact involving the labor certification application. If evidence of such fraud or willful misrepresentation becomes known to the CO or to the Chief, Division of Foreign Labor Certification, the CO, or the Chief of the Division of Foreign Labor Certification, as appropriate, shall notify in writing the DHS or Department of State, as appropriate. A copy of the notification must be sent to the regional or national office, as appropriate, of the Department of Labor's Office of Inspector General.

(e) *Duplicate labor certifications.* (1) The Certifying Officer shall issue a duplicate labor certification at the written request of a Consular or Immigration Officer. The Certifying Officer shall issue such duplicate labor certifications only to the Consular or Immigration Officer who initiated the request.

(2) The Certifying Officer shall issue a duplicate labor certification to a Consular or Immigration Officer at the written request of an alien, employer, or an alien's or employer's attorney/agent. Such request for a duplicate labor certification must be addressed to the Certifying Officer who issued the labor certification; must include documentary evidence from a Consular or Immigration Officer that a visa application or visa petition, as appropriate, has been filed; and must include a Consular Office or DHS tracking number.

(3) A duplicate labor certification shall be issued by the Certifying Officer with the same filing and expiration dates, as described in paragraphs (a) and (b) of this section, as the original approved labor certification.

[69 FR 77386, Dec. 27, 2004, as amended at 72 FR 27946, May 17, 2007]

§656.31 Labor certification applications involving fraud, willful misrepresentation, or violations of this part.

The following provisions apply to applications filed under both this part and 20 CFR part 656 in effect prior to March 28, 2005, and to any certifications resulting from those applications.

(a) *Denial.* A Certifying Officer may deny any application for permanent labor certification if the officer finds the application contains false statements, is fraudulent, or was otherwise submitted in violation of the Department's permanent labor certification regulations.

(b) *Possible fraud or willful misrepresentation.* (1) If the Department learns an employer, attorney, or agent is involved in possible fraud or willful misrepresentation in connection with the permanent labor certification program, the Department will refer the matter to the Department of Justice, Department of Homeland Security, or other government entity, as appropriate, for investigation, and send a copy of the referral to the Department of Labor's Office of Inspector General (OIG). In these cases, or if the Department learns an employer, attorney, or agent is under investigation by the Department of Justice, Department of Homeland Security, or other government entity for possible fraud or willful misrepresentation in connection with the permanent labor certification program, the Department may suspend processing of any permanent labor certification application involving such employer, attorney, or agent until completion of any investigation and/or judicial proceedings. Unless the investigatory agency, in writing, requests the Department to do otherwise, the Department shall provide written notification to the employer of the suspension in processing.

(2) A suspension pursuant to paragraph (b)(1) of this section may last initially for up to 180 days. No later than 180 days after the suspension began, if no criminal indictment or information has been issued, or judicial proceedings have not been concluded,

the National Certifying Officer may resume processing some or all of the applications, or may extend the suspension in processing until completion of any investigation and/or judicial proceedings.

(c) *Criminal indictment or information.* If the Department learns that an employer, attorney, or agent is named in a criminal indictment or information in connection with the permanent labor certification program, the processing of applications related to that employer, attorney, or agent may be suspended until the judicial process is completed. Unless the investigatory or prosecutorial agency, in writing, requests the Department to do otherwise, the Department shall provide written notification to the employer of the suspension in processing.

(d) *No finding of fraud or willful misrepresentation.* If an employer, attorney, or agent is acquitted of fraud or willful misrepresentation charges, or if such criminal charges are withdrawn or otherwise fail to result in a finding of fraud or willful misrepresentation, the Certifying Officer shall decide each pending permanent labor certification application related to that employer, attorney, or agent on the merits of the application.

(e) *Finding of fraud or willful misrepresentation.* If an employer, attorney, or agent is found to have committed fraud or willful misrepresentation involving the permanent labor certification program, whether by a court, the Department of State or DHS, as referenced in § 656.30(d), or through other proceedings:

(1) Any suspension of processing of pending applications related to that employer, attorney, or agent will terminate.

(2) The Certifying Officer will decide each such application on its merits, and may deny any such application as provided in § 656.24 and in paragraph (a) of this section.

(3) In the case of a pending application involving an attorney or agent found to have committed fraud or willful misrepresentation, DOL will notify the employer associated with that application of the finding and require the employer to notify DOL in writing, within 30 days of the notification, whether the employer will withdraw the application, designate a new attorney or agent, or continue the application without representation. Failure of the employer to respond within 30 days of the notification will result in a denial. If the employer elects to continue representation by the attorney or agent, DOL will suspend processing of affected applications while debarment proceedings are conducted under paragraph (f) of this section.

(f) *Debarment.* (1) No later than six years after the date of filing of the labor certification application that is the basis for the finding, or, if such basis requires a pattern or practice as provided in paragraphs (f)(1)(iii), (iv), and (v) of this section, no later than six years after the date of filing of the last labor certification application which constitutes a part of the pattern or practice, the Administrator, Office of Foreign Labor Certification, may issue to an employer, attorney, agent, or any combination thereof a Notice of Debarment from the permanent labor certification program for a reasonable period of no more than three years, based upon any action that was prohibited at the time the action occurred, upon determining the employer, attorney, or agent has participated in or facilitated one or more of the following:

(i) The sale, barter, or purchase of permanent labor applications or certifications, or any other action prohibited under § 656.12;

(ii) The willful provision or willful assistance in the provision of false or inaccurate information in applying for permanent labor certification;

(iii) A pattern or practice of a failure to comply with the terms of the Form ETA 9089 or Form ETA 750;

(iv) A pattern or practice of failure to comply in the audit process pursuant to § 656.20;

(v) A pattern or practice of failure to comply in the supervised recruitment process pursuant to § 656.21; or

(vi) Conduct resulting in a determination by a court, DHS or the Department of State of fraud or willful misrepresentation involving a permanent labor certification application, as referenced in § 656.31(e).

(2) The Notice of Debarment shall be in writing; shall state the reason for

the debarment finding, including a detailed explanation of how the employer, attorney or agent has participated in or facilitated one or more of the actions listed in paragraphs (f)(1)(i) through (v) of this section; shall state the start date and term of the debarment; and shall identify appeal opportunities under § 656.26. The debarment shall take effect on the start date identified in the Notice of Debarment unless a request for review is filed within the time permitted by § 656.26. DOL will notify DHS and the Department of State regarding any Notice of Debarment.

(g) *False statements.* To knowingly and willfully furnish any false information in the preparation of the *Application for Permanent Employment Certification* (Form ETA 9089) or the *Application for Alien Employment Certification* (Form ETA 750) and any supporting documentation, or to aid, abet, or counsel another to do so is a Federal offense, punishable by fine or imprisonment up to five years, or both under 18 U.S.C. 2 and 1001. Other penalties apply as well to fraud or misuse of ETA immigration documents and to perjury with respect to such documents under 18 U.S.C. 1546 and 1621.

[72 FR 27946, May 17, 2007]

§ 656.32 Revocation of approved labor certifications.

(a) *Basis for DOL revocation.* The Certifying Officer in consultation with the Chief, Division of Foreign Labor Certification may take steps to revoke an approved labor certification, if he/she finds the certification was not justified. A labor certification may also be invalidated by DHS or the Department of State as set forth in § 656.30(d).

(b) *Department of Labor procedures for revocation.* (1) The Certifying Officer sends to the employer a *Notice of Intent to Revoke* an approved labor certification which contains a detailed statement of the grounds for the revocation and the time period allowed for the employer's rebuttal. The employer may submit evidence in rebuttal within 30 days of receipt of the notice. The Certifying Officer must consider all relevant evidence presented in deciding whether to revoke the labor certification.

(2) If rebuttal evidence is not filed by the employer, the *Notice of Intent to Revoke* becomes the final decision of the Secretary.

(3) If the employer files rebuttal evidence and the Certifying Officer determines the certification should be revoked, the employer may file an appeal under § 656.26.

(4) The Certifying Officer will inform the employer within 30 days of receiving any rebuttal evidence whether or not the labor certification will be revoked.

(5) If the labor certification is revoked, the Certifying Officer will also send a copy of the notification to the DHS and the Department of State.

Subpart D—Determination of Prevailing Wage

§ 656.40 Determination of prevailing wage for labor certification purposes.

(a) *Application process.* The employer must request a PWD from the NPC, on a form or in a manner prescribed by OFLC. Prior to January 1, 2010, the SWA having jurisdiction over the area of intended employment shall continue to receive and process prevailing wage determination requests in accordance with the regulatory provisions and Department guidance in effect prior to January 1, 2009. On or after January 1, 2010, the NPC shall receive and process prevailing wage determination requests in accordance with these regulations and with Department guidance. The NPC will provide the employer with an appropriate prevailing wage rate. The NPC shall determine the wage in accordance with sec. 212(t) of the INA. Unless the employer chooses to appeal the center's PWD under § 656.41(a) of this part, it files the Application for Permanent Employment Certification either electronically or by mail with the processing center of jurisdiction and maintains the PWD in its files. The determination shall be submitted to the CO, if requested.

(b) *Determinations.* The National Processing Center will determine the appropriate prevailing wage as follows:

(1) Except as provided in paragraphs (e) and (f) of this section, if the job opportunity is covered by a collective

bargaining agreement (CBA) that was negotiated at arms-length between the union and the employer, the wage rate set forth in the CBA agreement is considered as not adversely affecting the wages of U.S. workers similarly employed, that is, it is considered the "prevailing wage" for labor certification purposes.

(2) If the job opportunity is not covered by a CBA, the prevailing wage for labor certification purposes shall be the arithmetic mean, except as provided in paragraph (b)(3) of this section, of the wages of workers similarly employed in the area of intended employment. The wage component of the DOL Occupational Employment Statistics Survey shall be used to determine the arithmetic mean, unless the employer provides an acceptable survey under paragraph (g) of this section.

(3) If the employer provides a survey acceptable under paragraph (g) of this section that provides a median and does not provide an arithmetic mean, the prevailing wage applicable to the employer's job opportunity shall be the median of the wages of workers similarly employed in the area of intended employment.

(4) The employer may utilize a current wage determination in the area under the Davis-Bacon Act, 40 U.S.C. 276a *et seq.*, 29 CFR part 1, or the McNamara-O'Hara Service Contract Act, 41 U.S.C. 351 *et seq.*

(c) *Validity period.* The National Processing Center must specify the validity period of the prevailing wage, which in no event may be less than 90 days or more than 1 year from the determination date. To use a prevailing wage rate provided by the NPC, employers must file their applications or begin the recruitment period required by §§ 656.17(e) or 656.21 of this part within the validity period specified by the NPC.

(d) *Similarly employed.* For purposes of this section, similarly employed means having substantially comparable jobs in the occupational category in the area of intended employment, except that, if a representative sample of workers in the occupational category can not be obtained in the area of intended employment, similarly employed means:

(1) Having jobs requiring a substantially similar level of skills within the area of intended employment; or

(2) If there are no substantially comparable jobs in the area of intended employment, having substantially comparable jobs with employers outside of the area of intended employment.

(e) *Institutions of higher education and research entities.* In computing the prevailing wage for a job opportunity in an occupational classification in an area of intended employment for an employee of an institution of higher education, or an affiliated or related nonprofit entity, a nonprofit research organization, or a Governmental research organization, the prevailing wage level takes into account the wage levels of employees only at such institutions and organizations in the area of intended employment.

(1) The organizations listed in this paragraph (e) are defined as follows:

(i) *Institution of higher education* means an institution of higher education as defined in section 101(a) of the Higher Education Act of 1965. Section 101(a) of that Act, 20 U.S.C. 1001(a)(2000), provides an institution of higher education is an educational institution in any state that:

(A) Admits as regular students only persons having a certificate of graduation from a school providing secondary education, or the recognized equivalent of such a certificate;

(B) Is legally authorized within such state to provide a program of education beyond secondary education;

(C) Provides an educational program for which the institution awards a bachelor's degree or provides not less than a two-year program that is acceptable for full credit toward such a degree;

(D) Is a public or other nonprofit institution; and

(E) Is accredited by a nationally recognized accrediting agency or association or, if not so accredited, is an institution that has been granted preaccreditation status by such an agency or association that has been recognized by the Secretary of Education for the granting of preaccreditation status, and the Secretary of Education has determined there is satisfactory assurance the institution will meet the accreditation standards of such an agency or association within a reasonable time.

(ii) *Affiliated or related nonprofit entity* means a nonprofit entity (including but not limited to a hospital and a medical or research institution) connected or associated with an institution of higher education, through shared ownership or control by the same board or federation, operated by an institution of higher education, or attached to an institution of higher education as a member, branch, cooperative, or subsidiary.

(iii) *Nonprofit research organization or Governmental research organization* means a research organization that is either a nonprofit organization or entity primarily engaged in basic research and/or applied research, or a United States Government entity whose primary mission is the performance or promotion of basic research and/or applied research. Basic research is general research to gain more comprehensive knowledge or understanding of the subject under study, without specific applications in mind. Basic research is also research that advances scientific knowledge, but does not have specific immediate commercial objectives although it may be in fields of present or commercial interest. It may include research and investigation in the sciences, social sciences, or humanities. Applied research is research to gain knowledge or understanding to determine the means by which a specific, recognized need may be met. Applied research includes investigations oriented to discovering new scientific knowledge that has specific commercial objectives with respect to products, processes, or services. It may include research and investigation in the sciences, social sciences, or humanities.

(2) *Nonprofit organization or entity*, for the purpose of this paragraph (e), means an organization qualified as a tax exempt organization under the Internal Revenue Code of 1986, section 501(c)(3), (c)(4), or (c)(6) (26 U.S.C. 501(c)(3), (c)(4) or (c)(6)), and which has received approval as a tax exempt organization from the Internal Revenue Service, as it relates to research or educational purposes.

(f) *Professional athletes*. In computing the prevailing wage for a professional athlete (defined in Section 212(a)(5)(A)(iii)(II) of the Act) when the job opportunity is covered by professional sports league rules or regulations, the wage set forth in those rules or regulations is considered the prevailing wage (see Section 212(p)(2) of the Act). INA Section 212(a)(5)(A)(iii)(II), 8 U.S.C. 1182(a)(5)(A)(iii)(II) (1999), defines "professional athlete" as an individual who is employed as an athlete by—

(1) A team that is a member of an association of six or more professional sports teams whose total combined revenues exceed $10,000,000 per year, if the association governs the conduct of its members and regulates the contests and exhibitions in which its member teams regularly engage; or

(2) Any minor league team that is affiliated with such an association.

(g) *Employer-provided wage information*. (1) If the job opportunity is not covered by a CBA, or by a professional sports league's rules or regulations, the NPC will consider wage information provided by the employer in making a PWD. An employer survey can be submitted either initially or after NPC issuance of a PWD derived from the OES survey. In the latter situation, the new employer survey submission will be deemed a new PWD request.

(2) In each case where the employer submits a survey or other wage data for which it seeks acceptance, the employer must provide the NPC with enough information about the survey methodology, including such items as sample size and source, sample selection procedures, and survey job descriptions, to allow the NPC to make a determination about the adequacy of the data provided and validity of the statistical methodology used in conducting the survey in accordance with guidance issued by the OFLC national office.

(3) The survey submitted to the NPC must be based upon recently collected data.

(i) A published survey must have been published within 24 months of the date of submission to the NPC, must be the most current edition of the survey, and the data upon which the survey is based must have been collected within 24 months of the publication date of the survey.

(ii) A survey conducted by the employer must be based on data collected within 24 months of the date it is submitted to the NPC.

(4) If the employer-provided survey is found not to be acceptable, the NPC will inform the employer in writing of the reasons the survey was not accepted.

(5) The employer, after receiving notification that the survey it provided for NPC consideration is not acceptable, may file supplemental information as provided by paragraph (h) of this section, file a new request for a PWD, or appeal under § 656.41.

(h) *Submittal of supplemental information by employer.* (1) If the employer disagrees with the skill level assigned to its job opportunity, or if the NPC informs the employer its survey is not acceptable, or if there are other legitimate bases for such a review, the employer may submit supplemental information to the NPC.

(2) The NPC will consider one supplemental submission about the employer's survey or the skill level the NPC assigned to the job opportunity or any other legitimate basis for the employer to request such a review. If the NPC does not accept the employer's survey after considering the supplemental information, or affirms its determination concerning the skill level, it will inform the employer of the reasons for its decision.

(3) The employer may then apply for a new wage determination or appeal under § 656.41 of this part.

(i) *Frequent users.* The Secretary will issue guidance regarding the process by which employers may obtain a wage determination to apply to a subsequent application, when the wage is for the same occupation, skill level, and area of intended employment. In no case may the wage rate the employer provides the NPC be lower than the highest wage required by any applicable Federal, State, or local law.

(j) *Fees prohibited.* No SWA or SWA employee may charge a fee in connection with the filing of a request for a PWD, responding to such a request, or responding to a request for a review of a SWA prevailing wage determination under § 656.41.

[69 FR 77386, Dec. 27, 2004, as amended at 73 FR 78068, Dec. 19, 2008]

§ 656.41 Review of prevailing wage determinations.

(a) *Review of NPC PWD.* Any employer desiring review of a PWD made by a CO must make a request for such review within 30 days of the date from when the PWD was issued. The request for review must be sent to the director of the NPC that issued the PWD within 30 days of the date of the PWD; clearly identify the PWD from which review is sought; set forth the particular grounds for the request; and include all the materials pertaining to the PWD submitted to the NPC up to the date of the PWD received from the NPC.

(b) *Processing of request by NPC.* Upon the receipt of a request for review, the NPC will review the employer's request and accompanying documentation, and add any material that may have been omitted by the employer, including any material the NPC sent the employer up to the date of the PWD.

(c) *Review on the record.* The director will review the PWD solely on the basis upon which the PWD was made and, upon the request for review, may either affirm or modify the PWD.

(d) *Request for review by BALCA.* Any employer desiring review of the director's determination must make a request for review by the BALCA within 30 days of the date of the Director's decision.

(1) The request for review, statements, briefs, and other submissions of the parties and amicus curiae must contain only legal arguments and only such evidence that was within the record upon which the director made his/her affirmation of the PWD.

(2) The request for review must be in writing and addressed to the director of the NPC making the determination. Upon receipt of a request for a review, the director will assemble an indexed appeal file in reverse chronological order, with the index on top followed by the most recent document.

(3) The director will send the Appeal File to the Office of Administrative

Law Judges, BALCA. The BALCA handles the appeals in accordance with §§ 656.26 and 656.27.

[73 FR 78069, Dec. 19, 2008]

FINDING AIDS

A list of CFR titles, subtitles, chapters, subchapters and parts and an alphabetical list of agencies publishing in the CFR are included in the CFR Index and Finding Aids volume to the Code of Federal Regulations which is published separately and revised annually.

Table of CFR Titles and Chapters

(Revised as of April 1, 2019)

Title 1—General Provisions

Title 2—Grants and Agreements

Title 2—Grants and Agreements—Continued

Title 3—The President

Title 4—Accounts

Title 5—Administrative Personnel

Title 5—Administrative Personnel—Continued

Chap.	
XXVIII	Department of Justice (Parts 3800—3899)
XXIX	Federal Communications Commission (Parts 3900—3999)
XXX	Farm Credit System Insurance Corporation (Parts 4000—4099)
XXXI	Farm Credit Administration (Parts 4100—4199)
XXXIII	Overseas Private Investment Corporation (Parts 4300—4399)
XXXIV	Securities and Exchange Commission (Parts 4400—4499)
XXXV	Office of Personnel Management (Parts 4500—4599)
XXXVI	Department of Homeland Security (Parts 4600—4699)
XXXVII	Federal Election Commission (Parts 4700—4799)
XL	Interstate Commerce Commission (Parts 5000—5099)
XLI	Commodity Futures Trading Commission (Parts 5100—5199)
XLII	Department of Labor (Parts 5200—5299)
XLIII	National Science Foundation (Parts 5300—5399)
XLV	Department of Health and Human Services (Parts 5500—5599)
XLVI	Postal Rate Commission (Parts 5600—5699)
XLVII	Federal Trade Commission (Parts 5700—5799)
XLVIII	Nuclear Regulatory Commission (Parts 5800—5899)
XLIX	Federal Labor Relations Authority (Parts 5900—5999)
L	Department of Transportation (Parts 6000—6099)
LII	Export-Import Bank of the United States (Parts 6200—6299)
LIII	Department of Education (Parts 6300—6399)
LIV	Environmental Protection Agency (Parts 6400—6499)
LV	National Endowment for the Arts (Parts 6500—6599)
LVI	National Endowment for the Humanities (Parts 6600—6699)
LVII	General Services Administration (Parts 6700—6799)
LVIII	Board of Governors of the Federal Reserve System (Parts 6800—6899)
LIX	National Aeronautics and Space Administration (Parts 6900—6999)
LX	United States Postal Service (Parts 7000—7099)
LXI	National Labor Relations Board (Parts 7100—7199)
LXII	Equal Employment Opportunity Commission (Parts 7200—7299)
LXIII	Inter-American Foundation (Parts 7300—7399)
LXIV	Merit Systems Protection Board (Parts 7400—7499)
LXV	Department of Housing and Urban Development (Parts 7500—7599)
LXVI	National Archives and Records Administration (Parts 7600—7699)
LXVII	Institute of Museum and Library Services (Parts 7700—7799)
LXVIII	Commission on Civil Rights (Parts 7800—7899)
LXIX	Tennessee Valley Authority (Parts 7900—7999)
LXX	Court Services and Offender Supervision Agency for the District of Columbia (Parts 8000—8099)
LXXI	Consumer Product Safety Commission (Parts 8100—8199)
LXXIII	Department of Agriculture (Parts 8300—8399)

Title 5—Administrative Personnel—Continued

Title 6—Domestic Security

Title 7—Agriculture

Title 8—Aliens and Nationality

Chap.	
I	Department of Homeland Security (Immigration and Naturalization) (Parts 1—499)
V	Executive Office for Immigration Review, Department of Justice (Parts 1000—1399)

Title 9—Animals and Animal Products

I	Animal and Plant Health Inspection Service, Department of Agriculture (Parts 1—199)
II	Grain Inspection, Packers and Stockyards Administration (Packers and Stockyards Programs), Department of Agriculture (Parts 200—299)
III	Food Safety and Inspection Service, Department of Agriculture (Parts 300—599)

Title 10—Energy

I	Nuclear Regulatory Commission (Parts 0—199)
II	Department of Energy (Parts 200—699)
III	Department of Energy (Parts 700—999)
X	Department of Energy (General Provisions) (Parts 1000—1099)
XIII	Nuclear Waste Technical Review Board (Parts 1300—1399)
XVII	Defense Nuclear Facilities Safety Board (Parts 1700—1799)
XVIII	Northeast Interstate Low-Level Radioactive Waste Commission (Parts 1800—1899)

Title 11—Federal Elections

I	Federal Election Commission (Parts 1—9099)
II	Election Assistance Commission (Parts 9400—9499)

Title 12—Banks and Banking

I	Comptroller of the Currency, Department of the Treasury (Parts 1—199)
II	Federal Reserve System (Parts 200—299)
III	Federal Deposit Insurance Corporation (Parts 300—399)
IV	Export-Import Bank of the United States (Parts 400—499)
V	(Parts 500—599) [Reserved]
VI	Farm Credit Administration (Parts 600—699)
VII	National Credit Union Administration (Parts 700—799)
VIII	Federal Financing Bank (Parts 800—899)
IX	Federal Housing Finance Board (Parts 900—999)
X	Bureau of Consumer Financial Protection (Parts 1000—1099)
XI	Federal Financial Institutions Examination Council (Parts 1100—1199)
XII	Federal Housing Finance Agency (Parts 1200—1299)
XIII	Financial Stability Oversight Council (Parts 1300—1399)

Title 12—Banks and Banking—Continued

Title 13—Business Credit and Assistance

Title 14—Aeronautics and Space

Title 15—Commerce and Foreign Trade

Title 15—Commerce and Foreign Trade—Continued

Title 16—Commercial Practices

Title 17—Commodity and Securities Exchanges

Title 18—Conservation of Power and Water Resources

Title 19—Customs Duties

Title 20—Employees' Benefits

Title 20—Employees' Benefits—Continued

Title 21—Food and Drugs

Title 22—Foreign Relations

Title 23—Highways

Title 23—Highways—Continued

Chap.

II National Highway Traffic Safety Administration and Federal Highway Administration, Department of Transportation (Parts 1200—1299)

III National Highway Traffic Safety Administration, Department of Transportation (Parts 1300—1399)

Title 24—Housing and Urban Development

SUBTITLE A—OFFICE OF THE SECRETARY, DEPARTMENT OF HOUSING AND URBAN DEVELOPMENT (PARTS 0—99)

SUBTITLE B—REGULATIONS RELATING TO HOUSING AND URBAN DEVELOPMENT

I Office of Assistant Secretary for Equal Opportunity, Department of Housing and Urban Development (Parts 100—199)

II Office of Assistant Secretary for Housing-Federal Housing Commissioner, Department of Housing and Urban Development (Parts 200—299)

III Government National Mortgage Association, Department of Housing and Urban Development (Parts 300—399)

IV Office of Housing and Office of Multifamily Housing Assistance Restructuring, Department of Housing and Urban Development (Parts 400—499)

V Office of Assistant Secretary for Community Planning and Development, Department of Housing and Urban Development (Parts 500—599)

VI Office of Assistant Secretary for Community Planning and Development, Department of Housing and Urban Development (Parts 600—699) [Reserved]

VII Office of the Secretary, Department of Housing and Urban Development (Housing Assistance Programs and Public and Indian Housing Programs) (Parts 700—799)

VIII Office of the Assistant Secretary for Housing—Federal Housing Commissioner, Department of Housing and Urban Development (Section 8 Housing Assistance Programs, Section 202 Direct Loan Program, Section 202 Supportive Housing for the Elderly Program and Section 811 Supportive Housing for Persons With Disabilities Program) (Parts 800—899)

IX Office of Assistant Secretary for Public and Indian Housing, Department of Housing and Urban Development (Parts 900—1699)

XII Office of Inspector General, Department of Housing and Urban Development (Parts 2000—2099)

XV Emergency Mortgage Insurance and Loan Programs, Department of Housing and Urban Development (Parts 2700—2799) [Reserved]

XX Office of Assistant Secretary for Housing—Federal Housing Commissioner, Department of Housing and Urban Development (Parts 3200—3899)

XXIV Board of Directors of the HOPE for Homeowners Program (Parts 4000—4099) [Reserved]

XXV Neighborhood Reinvestment Corporation (Parts 4100—4199)

Title 25—Indians

Title 26—Internal Revenue

Title 27—Alcohol, Tobacco Products and Firearms

Title 28—Judicial Administration

Title 29—Labor

Title 30—Mineral Resources

Title 31—Money and Finance: Treasury

Title 31—Money and Finance: Treasury—Continued

Title 32—National Defense

Title 33—Navigation and Navigable Waters

Title 34—Education

Title 34—Education—Continued

Title 35 [Reserved]

Title 36—Parks, Forests, and Public Property

Title 37—Patents, Trademarks, and Copyrights

Title 38—Pensions, Bonuses, and Veterans' Relief

Title 39—Postal Service

Chap.

I United States Postal Service (Parts 1—999)

III Postal Regulatory Commission (Parts 3000—3099)

Title 40—Protection of Environment

I Environmental Protection Agency (Parts 1—1099)

IV Environmental Protection Agency and Department of Justice (Parts 1400—1499)

V Council on Environmental Quality (Parts 1500—1599)

VI Chemical Safety and Hazard Investigation Board (Parts 1600—1699)

VII Environmental Protection Agency and Department of Defense; Uniform National Discharge Standards for Vessels of the Armed Forces (Parts 1700—1799)

VIII Gulf Coast Ecosystem Restoration Council (Parts 1800—1899)

Title 41—Public Contracts and Property Management

SUBTITLE A—FEDERAL PROCUREMENT REGULATIONS SYSTEM [NOTE]

SUBTITLE B—OTHER PROVISIONS RELATING TO PUBLIC CONTRACTS

50 Public Contracts, Department of Labor (Parts 50–1—50–999)

51 Committee for Purchase From People Who Are Blind or Severely Disabled (Parts 51–1—51–99)

60 Office of Federal Contract Compliance Programs, Equal Employment Opportunity, Department of Labor (Parts 60–1—60–999)

61 Office of the Assistant Secretary for Veterans' Employment and Training Service, Department of Labor (Parts 61–1—61–999)

62—100 [Reserved]

SUBTITLE C—FEDERAL PROPERTY MANAGEMENT REGULATIONS SYSTEM

101 Federal Property Management Regulations (Parts 101–1—101–99)

102 Federal Management Regulation (Parts 102–1—102–299)

103—104 [Reserved]

105 General Services Administration (Parts 105–1—105–999)

109 Department of Energy Property Management Regulations (Parts 109–1—109–99)

114 Department of the Interior (Parts 114–1—114–99)

115 Environmental Protection Agency (Parts 115–1—115–99)

128 Department of Justice (Parts 128–1—128–99)

129—200 [Reserved]

SUBTITLE D—OTHER PROVISIONS RELATING TO PROPERTY MANAGEMENT [RESERVED]

SUBTITLE E—FEDERAL INFORMATION RESOURCES MANAGEMENT REGULATIONS SYSTEM [RESERVED]

SUBTITLE F—FEDERAL TRAVEL REGULATION SYSTEM

300 General (Parts 300–1—300–99)

301 Temporary Duty (TDY) Travel Allowances (Parts 301–1—301–99)

Title 41—Public Contracts and Property Management—Continued

Title 42—Public Health

Title 43—Public Lands: Interior

Title 44—Emergency Management and Assistance

Title 45—Public Welfare

Title 45—Public Welfare—Continued

Chap.

Chap.	
V	Foreign Claims Settlement Commission of the United States, Department of Justice (Parts 500—599)
VI	National Science Foundation (Parts 600—699)
VII	Commission on Civil Rights (Parts 700—799)
VIII	Office of Personnel Management (Parts 800—899)
IX	Denali Commission (Parts 900—999)
X	Office of Community Services, Administration for Children and Families, Department of Health and Human Services (Parts 1000—1099)
XI	National Foundation on the Arts and the Humanities (Parts 1100—1199)
XII	Corporation for National and Community Service (Parts 1200—1299)
XIII	Administration for Children and Families, Department of Health and Human Services (Parts 1300—1399)
XVI	Legal Services Corporation (Parts 1600—1699)
XVII	National Commission on Libraries and Information Science (Parts 1700—1799)
XVIII	Harry S. Truman Scholarship Foundation (Parts 1800—1899)
XXI	Commission of Fine Arts (Parts 2100—2199)
XXIII	Arctic Research Commission (Parts 2300—2399)
XXIV	James Madison Memorial Fellowship Foundation (Parts 2400—2499)
XXV	Corporation for National and Community Service (Parts 2500—2599)

Title 46—Shipping

I	Coast Guard, Department of Homeland Security (Parts 1—199)
II	Maritime Administration, Department of Transportation (Parts 200—399)
III	Coast Guard (Great Lakes Pilotage), Department of Homeland Security (Parts 400—499)
IV	Federal Maritime Commission (Parts 500—599)

Title 47—Telecommunication

I	Federal Communications Commission (Parts 0—199)
II	Office of Science and Technology Policy and National Security Council (Parts 200—299)
III	National Telecommunications and Information Administration, Department of Commerce (Parts 300—399)
IV	National Telecommunications and Information Administration, Department of Commerce, and National Highway Traffic Safety Administration, Department of Transportation (Parts 400—499)
V	The First Responder Network Authority (Parts 500—599)

Title 48—Federal Acquisition Regulations System

Chap.	
1	Federal Acquisition Regulation (Parts 1—99)
2	Defense Acquisition Regulations System, Department of Defense (Parts 200—299)
3	Department of Health and Human Services (Parts 300—399)
4	Department of Agriculture (Parts 400—499)
5	General Services Administration (Parts 500—599)
6	Department of State (Parts 600—699)
7	Agency for International Development (Parts 700—799)
8	Department of Veterans Affairs (Parts 800—899)
9	Department of Energy (Parts 900—999)
10	Department of the Treasury (Parts 1000—1099)
12	Department of Transportation (Parts 1200—1299)
13	Department of Commerce (Parts 1300—1399)
14	Department of the Interior (Parts 1400—1499)
15	Environmental Protection Agency (Parts 1500—1599)
16	Office of Personnel Management, Federal Employees Health Benefits Acquisition Regulation (Parts 1600—1699)
17	Office of Personnel Management (Parts 1700—1799)
18	National Aeronautics and Space Administration (Parts 1800—1899)
19	Broadcasting Board of Governors (Parts 1900—1999)
20	Nuclear Regulatory Commission (Parts 2000—2099)
21	Office of Personnel Management, Federal Employees Group Life Insurance Federal Acquisition Regulation (Parts 2100—2199)
23	Social Security Administration (Parts 2300—2399)
24	Department of Housing and Urban Development (Parts 2400—2499)
25	National Science Foundation (Parts 2500—2599)
28	Department of Justice (Parts 2800—2899)
29	Department of Labor (Parts 2900—2999)
30	Department of Homeland Security, Homeland Security Acquisition Regulation (HSAR) (Parts 3000—3099)
34	Department of Education Acquisition Regulation (Parts 3400—3499)
51	Department of the Army Acquisition Regulations (Parts 5100—5199)
52	Department of the Navy Acquisition Regulations (Parts 5200—5299)
53	Department of the Air Force Federal Acquisition Regulation Supplement (Parts 5300—5399) [Reserved]
54	Defense Logistics Agency, Department of Defense (Parts 5400—5499)
57	African Development Foundation (Parts 5700—5799)
61	Civilian Board of Contract Appeals, General Services Administration (Parts 6100—6199)
99	Cost Accounting Standards Board, Office of Federal Procurement Policy, Office of Management and Budget (Parts 9900—9999)

Title 49—Transportation

Chap.

SUBTITLE A—OFFICE OF THE SECRETARY OF TRANSPORTATION (PARTS 1—99)

SUBTITLE B—OTHER REGULATIONS RELATING TO TRANSPORTATION

I Pipeline and Hazardous Materials Safety Administration, Department of Transportation (Parts 100—199)

II Federal Railroad Administration, Department of Transportation (Parts 200—299)

III Federal Motor Carrier Safety Administration, Department of Transportation (Parts 300—399)

IV Coast Guard, Department of Homeland Security (Parts 400—499)

V National Highway Traffic Safety Administration, Department of Transportation (Parts 500—599)

VI Federal Transit Administration, Department of Transportation (Parts 600—699)

VII National Railroad Passenger Corporation (AMTRAK) (Parts 700—799)

VIII National Transportation Safety Board (Parts 800—999)

X Surface Transportation Board (Parts 1000—1399)

XI Research and Innovative Technology Administration, Department of Transportation (Parts 1400—1499) [Reserved]

XII Transportation Security Administration, Department of Homeland Security (Parts 1500—1699)

Title 50—Wildlife and Fisheries

I United States Fish and Wildlife Service, Department of the Interior (Parts 1—199)

II National Marine Fisheries Service, National Oceanic and Atmospheric Administration, Department of Commerce (Parts 200—299)

III International Fishing and Related Activities (Parts 300—399)

IV Joint Regulations (United States Fish and Wildlife Service, Department of the Interior and National Marine Fisheries Service, National Oceanic and Atmospheric Administration, Department of Commerce); Endangered Species Committee Regulations (Parts 400—499)

V Marine Mammal Commission (Parts 500—599)

VI Fishery Conservation and Management, National Oceanic and Atmospheric Administration, Department of Commerce (Parts 600—699)

Alphabetical List of Agencies Appearing in the CFR

(Revised as of April 1, 2019)

Agency	CFR Title, Subtitle or Chapter
Administrative Conference of the United States	1, III
Advisory Council on Historic Preservation	36, VIII
Advocacy and Outreach, Office of	7, XXV
Afghanistan Reconstruction, Special Inspector General for	5, LXXXIII
African Development Foundation	22, XV
Federal Acquisition Regulation	48, 57
Agency for International Development	2, VII; 22, II
Federal Acquisition Regulation	48, 7
Agricultural Marketing Service	7, I, IX, X, XI
Agricultural Research Service	7, V
Agriculture, Department of	2, IV; 5, LXXIII
Advocacy and Outreach, Office of	7, XXV
Agricultural Marketing Service	7, I, IX, X, XI
Agricultural Research Service	7, V
Animal and Plant Health Inspection Service	7, III; 9, I
Chief Financial Officer, Office of	7, XXX
Commodity Credit Corporation	7, XIV
Economic Research Service	7, XXXVII
Energy Policy and New Uses, Office of	2, IX; 7, XXIX
Environmental Quality, Office of	7, XXXI
Farm Service Agency	7, VII, XVIII
Federal Acquisition Regulation	48, 4
Federal Crop Insurance Corporation	7, IV
Food and Nutrition Service	7, II
Food Safety and Inspection Service	9, III
Foreign Agricultural Service	7, XV
Forest Service	36, II
Grain Inspection, Packers and Stockyards Administration	7, VIII; 9, II
Information Resources Management, Office of	7, XXVII
Inspector General, Office of	7, XXVI
National Agricultural Library	7, XLI
National Agricultural Statistics Service	7, XXXVI
National Institute of Food and Agriculture	7, XXXIV
Natural Resources Conservation Service	7, VI
Operations, Office of	7, XXVIII
Procurement and Property Management, Office of	7, XXXII
Rural Business-Cooperative Service	7, XVIII, XLII
Rural Development Administration	7, XLII
Rural Housing Service	7, XVIII, XXXV
Rural Telephone Bank	7, XVI
Rural Utilities Service	7, XVII, XVIII, XLII
Secretary of Agriculture, Office of	7, Subtitle A
Transportation, Office of	7, XXXIII
World Agricultural Outlook Board	7, XXXVIII
Air Force, Department of	32, VII
Federal Acquisition Regulation Supplement	48, 53
Air Transportation Stabilization Board	14, VI
Alcohol and Tobacco Tax and Trade Bureau	27, I
Alcohol, Tobacco, Firearms, and Explosives, Bureau of	27, II
AMTRAK	49, VII
American Battle Monuments Commission	36, IV
American Indians, Office of the Special Trustee	25, VII
Animal and Plant Health Inspection Service	7, III; 9, I

Agency	CFR Title, Subtitle or Chapter
Army Department	32, V; 33, II; 36, III; 48, 51
Defense Acquisition Regulations System	48, 2
Defense Intelligence Agency	32, I
Defense Logistics Agency	32, I, XII; 48, 54
Engineers, Corps of	33, II; 36, III
National Imagery and Mapping Agency	32, I
Navy Department	32, VI; 48, 52
Secretary of Defense, Office of	2, XI; 32, I
Defense Contract Audit Agency	32, I
Defense Intelligence Agency	32, I
Defense Logistics Agency	32, XII; 48, 54
Defense Nuclear Facilities Safety Board	10, XVII
Delaware River Basin Commission	18, III
Denali Commission	45, IX
Disability, National Council on	5, C; 34, XII
District of Columbia, Court Services and Offender Supervision Agency for the	5, LXX; 28, VIII
Drug Enforcement Administration	21, II
East-West Foreign Trade Board	15, XIII
Economic Analysis, Bureau of	15, VIII
Economic Development Administration	13, III
Economic Research Service	7, XXXVII
Education, Department of	2, XXXIV; 5, LIII
Bilingual Education and Minority Languages Affairs, Office of	34, V
Career, Technical, and Adult Education, Office of	34, IV
Civil Rights, Office for	34, I
Educational Research and Improvement, Office of	34, VII
Elementary and Secondary Education, Office of	34, II
Federal Acquisition Regulation	48, 34
Postsecondary Education, Office of	34, VI
Secretary of Education, Office of	34, Subtitle A
Special Education and Rehabilitative Services, Office of	34, III
Educational Research and Improvement, Office of	34, VII
Election Assistance Commission	2, LVIII; 11, II
Elementary and Secondary Education, Office of	34, II
Emergency Oil and Gas Guaranteed Loan Board	13, V
Emergency Steel Guarantee Loan Board	13, IV
Employee Benefits Security Administration	29, XXV
Employees' Compensation Appeals Board	20, IV
Employees Loyalty Board	5, V
Employment and Training Administration	20, V
Employment Policy, National Commission for	1, IV
Employment Standards Administration	20, VI
Endangered Species Committee	50, IV
Energy, Department of	2, IX; 5, XXIII; 10, II, III, X
Federal Acquisition Regulation	48, 9
Federal Energy Regulatory Commission	5, XXIV; 18, I
Property Management Regulations	41, 109
Energy, Office of	7, XXIX
Engineers, Corps of	33, II; 36, III
Engraving and Printing, Bureau of	31, VI
Environmental Protection Agency	2, XV; 5, LIV; 40, I, IV, VII
Federal Acquisition Regulation	48, 15
Property Management Regulations	41, 115
Environmental Quality, Office of	7, XXXI
Equal Employment Opportunity Commission	5, LXII; 29, XIV
Equal Opportunity, Office of Assistant Secretary for	24, I
Executive Office of the President	3, I
Environmental Quality, Council on	40, V
Management and Budget, Office of	2, Subtitle A; 5, III, LXXVII; 14, VI; 48, 99
National Drug Control Policy, Office of	2, XXXVI; 21, III
National Security Council	32, XXI; 47, 2

Agency	CFR Title, Subtitle or Chapter
Contract Appeals, Board of	48, 61
Federal Acquisition Regulation	48, 5
Federal Management Regulation	41, 102
Federal Property Management Regulations	41, 101
Federal Travel Regulation System	41, Subtitle F
General	41, 300
Payment From a Non-Federal Source for Travel Expenses	41, 304
Payment of Expenses Connected With the Death of Certain Employees	41, 303
Relocation Allowances	41, 302
Temporary Duty (TDY) Travel Allowances	41, 301
Geological Survey	30, IV
Government Accountability Office	4, I
Government Ethics, Office of	5, XVI
Government National Mortgage Association	24, III
Grain Inspection, Packers and Stockyards Administration	7, VIII; 9, II
Gulf Coast Ecosystem Restoration Council	2, LIX; 40, VIII
Harry S. Truman Scholarship Foundation	45, XVIII
Health and Human Services, Department of	2, III; 5, XLV; 45, Subtitle A
Centers for Medicare & Medicaid Services	42, IV
Child Support Enforcement, Office of	45, III
Children and Families, Administration for	45, II, III, IV, X, XIII
Community Services, Office of	45, X
Family Assistance, Office of	45, II
Federal Acquisition Regulation	48, 3
Food and Drug Administration	21, I
Indian Health Service	25, V
Inspector General (Health Care), Office of	42, V
Public Health Service	42, I
Refugee Resettlement, Office of	45, IV
Homeland Security, Department of	2, XXX; 5, XXXVI; 6, I; 8, I
Coast Guard	33, I; 46, I; 49, IV
Coast Guard (Great Lakes Pilotage)	46, III
Customs and Border Protection	19, I
Federal Emergency Management Agency	44, I
Human Resources Management and Labor Relations Systems	5, XCVII
Immigration and Customs Enforcement Bureau	19, IV
Transportation Security Administration	49, XII
HOPE for Homeowners Program, Board of Directors of	24, XXIV
Housing and Urban Development, Department of	2, XXIV; 5, LXV; 24, Subtitle B
Community Planning and Development, Office of Assistant Secretary for	24, V, VI
Equal Opportunity, Office of Assistant Secretary for	24, I
Federal Acquisition Regulation	48, 24
Federal Housing Enterprise Oversight, Office of	12, XVII
Government National Mortgage Association	24, III
Housing—Federal Housing Commissioner, Office of Assistant Secretary for	24, II, VIII, X, XX
Housing, Office of, and Multifamily Housing Assistance Restructuring, Office of	24, IV
Inspector General, Office of	24, XII
Public and Indian Housing, Office of Assistant Secretary for	24, IX
Secretary, Office of	24, Subtitle A, VII
Housing—Federal Housing Commissioner, Office of Assistant Secretary for	24, II, VIII, X, XX
Housing, Office of, and Multifamily Housing Assistance Restructuring, Office of	24, IV
Immigration and Customs Enforcement Bureau	19, IV
Immigration Review, Executive Office for	8, V
Independent Counsel, Office of	28, VII
Independent Counsel, Offices of	28, VI
Indian Affairs, Bureau of	25, I, V
Indian Affairs, Office of the Assistant Secretary	25, VI

Agency	CFR Title, Subtitle or Chapter
Federal Procurement Regulations System	41, 50
Labor-Management Standards, Office of	29, II, IV
Mine Safety and Health Administration	30, I
Occupational Safety and Health Administration	29, XVII
Public Contracts	41, 50
Secretary of Labor, Office of	29, Subtitle A
Veterans' Employment and Training Service, Office of the Assistant Secretary for	41, 61; 20, IX
Wage and Hour Division	29, V
Workers' Compensation Programs, Office of	20, I, VII
Labor-Management Standards, Office of	29, II, IV
Land Management, Bureau of	43, II
Legal Services Corporation	45, XVI
Libraries and Information Science, National Commission on	45, XVII
Library of Congress	36, VII
Copyright Royalty Board	37, III
U.S. Copyright Office	37, II
Local Television Loan Guarantee Board	7, XX
Management and Budget, Office of	5, III, LXXVII; 14, VI; 48, 99
Marine Mammal Commission	50, V
Maritime Administration	46, II
Merit Systems Protection Board	5, II, LXIV
Micronesian Status Negotiations, Office for	32, XXVII
Military Compensation and Retirement Modernization Commission	5, XCIX
Millennium Challenge Corporation	22, XIII
Mine Safety and Health Administration	30, I
Minority Business Development Agency	15, XIV
Miscellaneous Agencies	1, IV
Monetary Offices	31, I
Morris K. Udall Scholarship and Excellence in National Environmental Policy Foundation	36, XVI
Museum and Library Services, Institute of	2, XXXI
National Aeronautics and Space Administration	2, XVIII; 5, LIX; 14, V
Federal Acquisition Regulation	48, 18
National Agricultural Library	7, XLI
National Agricultural Statistics Service	7, XXXVI
National and Community Service, Corporation for	2, XXII; 45, XII, XXV
National Archives and Records Administration	2, XXVI; 5, LXVI; 36, XII
Information Security Oversight Office	32, XX
National Capital Planning Commission	1, IV, VI
National Counterintelligence Center	32, XVIII
National Credit Union Administration	5, LXXXVI; 12, VII
National Crime Prevention and Privacy Compact Council	28, IX
National Drug Control Policy, Office of	2, XXXVI; 21, III
National Endowment for the Arts	2, XXXII
National Endowment for the Humanities	2, XXXIII
National Foundation on the Arts and the Humanities	45, XI
National Geospatial-Intelligence Agency	32, I
National Highway Traffic Safety Administration	23, II, III; 47, VI; 49, V
National Imagery and Mapping Agency	32, I
National Indian Gaming Commission	25, III
National Institute of Food and Agriculture	7, XXXIV
National Institute of Standards and Technology	15, II; 37, IV
National Intelligence, Office of Director of	5, IV; 32, XVII
National Labor Relations Board	5, LXI; 29, I
National Marine Fisheries Service	50, II, IV
National Mediation Board	5, CI; 29, X
National Oceanic and Atmospheric Administration	15, IX; 50, II, III, IV, VI
National Park Service	36, I
National Railroad Adjustment Board	29, III
National Railroad Passenger Corporation (AMTRAK)	49, VII
National Science Foundation	2, XXV; 5, XLIII; 45, VI
Federal Acquisition Regulation	48, 25
National Security Council	32, XXI

List of CFR Sections Affected

All changes in this volume of the Code of Federal Regulations (CFR) that were made by documents published in the FEDERAL REGISTER since January 1, 2014 are enumerated in the following list. Entries indicate the nature of the changes effected. Page numbers refer to FEDERAL REGISTER pages. The user should consult the entries for chapters, parts and subparts as well as sections for revisions.

For changes to this volume of the CFR prior to this listing, consult the annual edition of the monthly List of CFR Sections Affected (LSA). The LSA is available at *www.govinfo.gov*. For changes to this volume of the CFR prior to 2001, see the "List of CFR Sections Affected, 1949–1963, 1964–1972, 1973–1985, and 1986–2000" published in 11 separate volumes. The "List of CFR Sections Affected 1986–2000" is available at *www.govinfo.gov*.

2014

20 CFR

79 FR Page

Chapter V

619 Added 9411

2015

20 CFR

80 FR Page

Chapter V

655 Authority citation revised 24108
Authority citation amended 63066

655.1—655.99 (Subpart A) Revised; interim 24108

655.10 Second (h) and second (i) removed; CFR correction 23443
(b) and (f) added 24184

655.200 Undesignated center heading and section added 63066

655.201 Added 63066

655.205 Added 63066

655.210 Added 63066

655.211 Added 63066

655.215 Added 63066

655.220 Added 63066

655.225 Added 63066

655.230 Added 63066

655.235 Added 63066

2016

20 CFR

81 FR Page

Chapter V

603 Authority citation revised 56333

603.2 (d) revised 56333

603.5 (e) revised 56333

603.6 (b)(8) added 56333

615 Authority citation revised 57778

615.1 Revised 57778

615.2 Revised 57778

615.3 Amended 57778, 57781

615.4 (a) and (b) introductory text amended 57778

615.7 (b)(3) added; (d) introductory text revised 57781

615.8 (a) introductory text, (c) introductory text, (2), (d) introductory text, (3), (4), (e) introductory text, (8), (f)(1) introductory text, (ii), (4), (g)(1) and (5) amended 57778
(e)(5)(iii), (f)(2)(i), (iii), (h)(3) and (4) amended 57781

615.9 (d) amended 57778

615.11 Revised 57781

615.12 (e) redesignated as (f); (d)(1), (2) and new (f) revised; (d)(3) and new (e) added 57782

615.13 Revised 57783

20 CFR—Continued

81 FR Page

Chapter V—Continued

615.14 (a)(1) through (4), (b) introductory text, (c)(1), (2), (3) introductory text, (5), (6), (7)(i), (ii), (iii), (d)(1), (2), (3) and (6) amended....57778

(c)(4) revised....57783

615.15 Revised....57783

620 Added....50302

651 Revised....56333

652 Revised....56337

653 Revised....56341

654 Authority citation revised....56349

654.400—654.417 (Subpart E) Revised....56349

655 Authority citation revised....43448

Authority citation corrected....48700

655.620 (a) revised....43448

655.801 (b) revised....43448

655.810 (b)(1) introductory text, (2) introductory text and (3) introductory text revised....43448

2017

20 CFR

82 FR Page

Chapter V

620 Removed....21916

641 Authority citation revised; interim....56880

641.100 Introductory text and (b) revised; interim....56880

641.140 Amended....56880

641.200—641.240 (Subpart B) Revised; interim....56881

641.300 Revised; interim....56882

641.302 (f) and (g) revised; interim....56882

641.315 (a)(2) revised; interim....56882

641.320 (b) revised; interim....56882

641.325 (c) through (f) revised; interim....56882

641.335 Revised; interim....56882

641.365 (a) revised; interim....56883

641.370 Added; interim....56883

641.410 (c) revised; interim....56883

641.500 Revised; interim....56883

641.512 Revised; interim....56883

641.535 (a)(2)(ii), (3)(i), and (7) revised; interim....56883

641.540 (c) revised; interim....56883

641.545 (a) revised; interim....56883

641.565 (a)(1)(ii) revised; interim....56883

641.630 Heading and (b)(2) revised; interim....56884

20 CFR—Continued

82 FR Page

Chapter V—Continued

641.700—641.750 (Subpart G) Revised; interim....56884

641.827 (b) revised; interim....56885

641.833 (a) revised; interim....56886

641.850 (d) revised; interim....56886

641.910 (d) revised; interim....56886

641.920 (b) revised; interim....56886

655.64 Added (temporary)....32999

655.65 Added (temporary)....32999

655.620 (a) amended....5380

655.801 (b) amended....5380

655.810 (b)(1) introductory text, (2) introductory text and (3) introductory text amended....5380

2018

20 CFR

83 FR Page

Chapter V

641.100 Regulation at 82 FR 56880 confirmed....36417

641.140 Regulation at 82 FR 56880 confirmed....36417

641.200—641.240 (Subpart B) Regulation at 82 FR 56881 confirmed....36417

641.300 Regulation at 82 FR 56882 confirmed....36417

641.302 Regulation at 82 FR 56882 confirmed....36417

641.315 Regulation at 82 FR 56882 confirmed....36417

641.320 Regulation at 82 FR 56882 confirmed....36417

641.325 Regulation at 82 FR 56882 confirmed....36417

641.335 Regulation at 82 FR 56882 confirmed....36417

641.365 Regulation at 82 FR 56883 confirmed....36417

641.370 Regulation at 82 FR 56883 confirmed....36417

641.410 Regulation at 82 FR 56883 confirmed....36417

641.500 Regulation at 82 FR 56883 confirmed....36417

641.512 Regulation at 82 FR 56883 confirmed....36417

641.535 Regulation at 82 FR 56883 confirmed....36417

641.540 Regulation at 82 FR 56883 confirmed....36417

641.545 Regulation at 82 FR 56883 confirmed....36417

641.565 Regulation at 82 FR 56883 confirmed....36417

20 CFR—Continued

83 FR Page

Chapter V—Continued

641.630 Regulation at 82 FR 56884 confirmed....36417

641.700—641.750 (Subpart G) Regulation at 82 FR 56884 confirmed....36417

641.827 Regulation at 82 FR 56885 confirmed....36417

641.833 Regulation at 82 FR 56886 confirmed....36417

641.850 Regulation at 82 FR 56886 confirmed....36417

641.910 Regulation at 82 FR 56886 confirmed....36417

641.920 Regulation at 82 FR 56886 confirmed....36417

655.64 Added (temporary)....24918

655.66 Added (temporary)....24918

655.620 (a) amended....11

655.801 (b) amended....11

20 CFR—Continued

83 FR Page

Chapter V—Continued

655.810 (b)(1) introductory text, (2) introductory text and (3) introductory text amended....11

2019

(Regulations published from January 1, 2019, through April 1, 2019)

20 CFR

84 FR Page

Chapter V

655 Authority citation revised; eff. 4-4-19....12431

655.400–655.499 (Subpart E) added; eff. 4-4-19....12431

655.620 (a) amended....217

655.801 (b) amended....217

655.810 (b)(1) introductory text, (2) introductory text, and (3) introductory text amended....217

www.ingramcontent.com/pod-product-compliance
Lightning Source LLC
LaVergne TN
LVHW052206200926
848481LV00001B/43
* 9 7 8 1 6 4 0 2 4 5 5 1 8 *